Strategy
Process, Content, Context
An International Perspective

To Pam and Monique

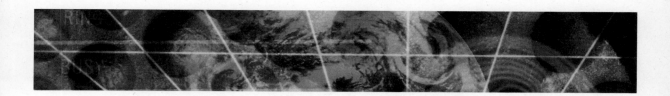

Strategy
Process, Content, Context

An International Perspective

Second edition

■ **Bob de Wit**

Maastricht School of Management
The Netherlands

■ **Ron Meyer**

Rotterdam School of Management
Erasmus University
The Netherlands

with the assistance of
Pursey Heugens

INTERNATIONAL THOMSON BUSINESS PRESS
I(T)P® An International Thomson Publishing Company

London • Bonn • Johannesburg • Madrid • Melbourne • Mexico City • New York • Paris
Singapore • Tokyo • Toronto • Albany, NY • Belmont, CA • Cincinnati, OH • Detroit, MI

Strategy: Process, Content, Context

Copyright © 1998 Bob de Wit and Ron Meyer

A division of International Thomson Publishing Inc.
I(T)P® The ITP logo is a trademark under licence

British Library Cataloguing-in-Publication Data
A catalogue record for this book is available from the British Library

First edition published by West Publishing Company
Second edition published 1998 by International Thomson Business Press
Reprinted 1998

Typeset by J&L Composition Ltd, Filey, North Yorkshire
Printed in Italy by Legoprint S.r.l., Lavis (TN)

ISBN 1–86152–139–1

International Thomson Business Press
Berkshire House
168–173 High Holborn
London WC1V 7AA
UK

http://www.itbp.com

General Table of Contents

Section I   STRATEGY   Chapter 1   Introduction

Section II STRATEGY PROCESS   Chapter 2   Strategic Thinking

                                      Chapter 3   Strategy Formation

                                      Chapter 4   Strategic Change

Section III STRATEGY CONTENT   Chapter 5   Business Level Strategy

                                      Chapter 6   Corporate Level Strategy

                                      Chapter 7   Network Level Strategy

Section IV STRATEGY CONTEXT   Chapter 8   The Industry Context

                                      Chapter 9   The Organizational Context

                                      Chapter 10   The International Context

Section V   PURPOSE   Chapter 11   Organizational Purpose

Section VI CASES

Contents

Acknowledgements   xvii

Preface   xix

SECTION I
Strategy   1

1   Introduction   3

The Nature of Strategy   3

Identifying the Strategy Issues   4

Structuring the Strategy Debates   13

Developing an International Perspective   18

Exhibit 1.1   MTV Networks: Between Rock and a Hard Place?   20

The Readings   22

Reading 1.1   The First Strategists   *by Stephen Cummings*   25

Reading 1.2   Defining the Concept of Strategy
  by Arnoldo Hax   28

Reading 1.3   The Evaluation of Business Strategy
  by Richard Rumelt   33

Reading 1.4   Complexity: The Nature of Real World Problems
  by Richard Mason & Ian Mitroff   41

Reading 1.5   Cultural Constraints in Management Theories
  by Geert Hofstede   51

Further Readings   63

References   64

SECTION II

Strategy Process   67

_____

2   Strategic Thinking   69

The Paradox of Logic and Creativity   69

Defining the Issues: Cognition and Reasoning   75

Exhibit 2.1   Mercedes-Benz and Swatch: A Smart Move?   81

The Debate and the Readings   83

Reading 2.1   The Concept of Corporate Strategy
by Kenneth Andrews   86

Reading 2.2   The Mind of the Strategist   by Kenichi Ohmae   93

Reading 2.3   Game Theory and Strategic Thinking
by Teck Hua Ho & Keith Weigelt   103

Reading 2.4   Conceptual Mapping   by Michael McCaskey   120

Reading 2.5 Strategic Management in an Enacted World
by Linda Smircich & Charles Stubbart   131

Strategic Thinking in International Perspective   142

Further Readings   145

References   146

3   Strategy Formation   150

The Paradox of Deliberateness and Emergentness   150

Defining the Issues: Plans and Planning   157

Exhibit 3.1   Ceteco: A Durable Conquistador?   162

The Debate and the Readings   164

Reading 3.1   Managing the Strategy Process
by Balaji Chakravarthy & Peter Lorange   167

Reading 3.2   Logical Incrementalism by James Quinn   173

Reading 3.3   Conceptual Models and Decision-Making
   by Graham Allison   185
Reading 3.4   Removing the Obstacles to Strategic Planning
   by Thomas Marx   204
Reading 3.5   The Fall and Rise of Strategic Planning
   by Henry Mintzberg   217
Strategy Formation in International Perspective   226
Further Readings   231
References   232

4   Strategic Change   237

The Paradox of Revolution and Evolution   237
Defining the Issues: Magnitude and Pace   242
Exhibit 4.1   Morgan Motor Company: (W)reckless Driving?   246
The Debate and the Readings   248
Reading 4.1   Reengineering Work: Don't Automate, Obliterate
   by Michael Hammer   250
Reading 4.2   Kaizen by Masaaki Imai   261
Reading 4.3   Convergence and Upheaval by Michael Tushman,
   William Newman & Elaine Romanelli   275
Reading 4.4   Building Learning Organizations by Peter Senge   285
Reading 4.5   Choosing the Right Change Path by Paul Strebel   297
Strategic Change in International Perspective   318
Further Readings   322
References   323

SECTION III
Strategy Content   327

5   Business Level Strategy   329

The Paradox of Markets and Resources   329
Defining the Issues: Adaptation and Advantage   332

Exhibit 5.1   Avon: Keeping Those Doorbells Ringing?   339

The Debate and the Readings   341

Reading 5.1   Competitive Strategy *by Michael Porter*   344

Reading 5.2   Competing on Capabilities *by George Stalk,*
Phillip Evans & Lawrence Shulman   358

Reading 5.3   PIMS: Market Position and Profitability
by Robert Buzzell & Bradley Gale   367

Reading 5.4   Firm Resources and Sustained Competitive
Advantage   *by Jay Barney*   383

Reading 5.5   The Capabilities of Market-Driven Organizations
by George Day   395

Business Level Strategy in International Perspective   406

Further Readings   408

References   409

6   Corporate Level Strategy   412

The Paradox of Responsiveness and Synergy   412

Defining the Issues: Composition and Coordination   416

Exhibit 6.1   Philips: Rewire or Shortcircuit?   420

The Debate and the Readings   423

Reading 6.1   Strategy and the Business Portfolio
by Barry Hedley   426

Reading 6.2   The Core Competence of the Corporation
by C.K. Prahalad & Gary Hamel   436

Reading 6.3   The Synergy Trap *by Mark Sirower*   449

Reading 6.4   The Value of the Parent Company
by Andrew Campbell, Michael Goold & Marcus Alexander   468

Reading 6.5   Adding Value from Corporate Headquarters
by Andrew Campbell & Michael Goold   484

Corporate Level Strategy in International Perspective   501

Further Readings   504

References   505

7 Network Level Strategy   508

The Paradox of Competition and Cooperation   508

Defining the Issues: Boundaries and Relationships   513

Exhibit 7.1   Merck: A Medicine Against Anorexia?   520

The Debate and the Readings   522

Reading 7.1   Collaborate with Your Competitors – and Win
  by Gary Hamel, Yves Doz & C.K. Prahalad   525

Reading 7.2   On Strategic Networks by Carlos Jarillo   533

Reading 7.3   Incorporating International Strategic Alliances into
  Overall Firm Strategy by Stephen Preece   543

Reading 7.4   Creating a Strategic Center to Manage a Web of Partners
  by Gianni Lorenzoni & Charles Baden-Fuller   552

Reading 7.5   The Bamboo Network by Murray Weidenbaum &
  Samuel Hughes   566

Network Level Strategy in International Perspective   578

Further Readings   583

References   584

SECTION IV
Strategy Context   589

8 The Industry Context   591

The Paradox of Compliance and Choice   591

Defining the Issues: Rules and Recipes   595

Exhibit 8.1   CarMax: To the Max?   596

The Debate and the Readings   598

Reading 8.1   Industry Evolution by Michael Porter   601

Reading 8.2   The Firm Matters, Not the Industry
  by Charles Baden-Fuller & John Stopford   610

Reading 8.3   The Population Ecology of Organizations
  by Michael Hannan & John Freeman   617

Reading 8.4   Competing for the Future *by Gary Hamel &*
C.K. Prahalad   624
Reading 8.5   Increasing Returns and the New World of Business
by Brian Arthur   632
The Industry Context in International Perspective   643
Further Readings   653
References   654

9   The Organizational Context   657

The Paradox of Control and Chaos   657
Defining the Issues: Inheritance and Initiative   661
Exhibit 9.1   Kodak: Manual or Autofocus?   663
The Debate and the Readings   665
Reading 9.1   The CEO: Leadership in Organizations
by Roland Christensen et al.   668
Reading 9.2   Strategy as Order Emerging from Chaos
by Ralph Stacey   673
Reading 9.3   Linking Planning and Implementation
by L.J. Bourgeois & David Brodwin   682
Reading 9.4   Rethinking Incrementalism *by Gerry Johnson*   691
Reading 9.5   Inertia and Transformation *by Richard Rumelt*   701
The Organizational Context in International Perspective   711
Further Readings   713
References   714

10   The International Context   719

The Paradox of Globalization and Localization   719
Defining the Issues: Dimensions and Subjects   724
Exhibit 10.1   Ikea: Globalization By Design?   728
The Debate and the Readings   730
Reading 10.1   The Globalization of Markets
by Theodore Levitt   733
Reading 10.2   The Myth of Globalization *by Susan Douglas &*
Yoram Wind   741

Reading 10.3   The Dynamics of Global Competition
   by C.K. Prahalad & Yves Doz   753

Reading 10.4   The Competitive Advantage of Nations
   by Michael Porter   773

Reading 10.5   Managing across Borders *by Christopher Bartlett &*
   Sumantra Ghoshal   785

The International Context in International Perspective   797

Further Readings   799

References   800

SECTION V

Purpose   803

11 Organizational Purpose   805

The Paradox of Profitability and Responsibility   805

Defining the Issues: Governance and Mission   811

Exhibit 11.1   Daimler Benz: Burnt at the Stake?   814

The Debate and the Readings   817

Reading 11.1   Shareholder Value and Corporate Purpose
   by Alfred Rappaport   820

Reading 11.2   Stockholders and Stakeholders *by Edward Freeman*
   & David Reed   829

Reading 11.3   Whose Company Is It? *by Masaru Yoshimori*   838

Reading 11.4   Corporate Governance: Lifespace and
   Accountability   *by Ada Demb & Friedrich Neubauer*   852

Reading 11.5   Creating a Sense of Mission *by Andrew Campbell*
   & Sally Yeung   874

Further Readings   883

References   885

SECTION VI

Cases

891

Case 1 Honda *Andrew Mair* 893

Case 2 Swatch *Arieh Ullmann* 912

Case 3 Virgin *Manfred Kets de Vries & Robert Dick* 930

Case 4 Stantret *Igor Touline, Abby Hansen & Derek Abell* 948

Case 5 Oldelft *Ron Meyer* 963

Case 6 Kao Corporation *Sumantra Ghoshal & Charlotte Butler* 976

Case 7 Carl Zeiss Jena *Manfred Kets de Vries & Marc Cannizzo* 995

Case 8 Encyclopaedia Britannica *Jeffrey Rayport & Thomas Gerace* 1015

Case 9 Southwest Airlines *Don Parks & Ivan Noer* 1028

Case 10 Canon *Sumantra Ghoshal & Mary Ackenhusen* 1038

Case 11 Shell & Billiton *Bob de Wit & Richard Renner* 1054

Case 12 Grand Metropolitan *David Sadtler & Andrew Campbell* 1074

Case 13 KLM and the Alcazar Alliance *Ron Meyer, Bob de Wit & Howard Kwok* 1091

Case 14 The Salim Group *Hellmut Schütte, Lizabeth Froman & Marc Canizzo* 1112

Case 15 The Champagne Industry *Karel Cool, James Howe & James Henderson* 1120

Case 16 National Bicycle Industry *Suresh Kotha & Andrew Fried* 1141

Case 17 Teléfonos de Mexico *Robert E. Hoskisson, Jennifer Alexander, Tom Blackley, Linda Chen, Dru Ubben, John Economou, Sewardi Luis & Richard Martinez* 1156

Case 18 Cartier *Sumantra Ghoshal, Francois-Xavier Huard & Charlotte Butler* 1173

Case 19 Saatchi & Saatchi *Ron Meyer* 1188

Case 20A Cap Gemini Sogeti *Tom Elfring* 1200

Case 20B Cap Gemini Sogeti *Tom Elfring, Ron Meyer &*
            Herve Amoussou   1210
Case 21   Burroughs Wellcome and AZT *Ram Subramanian*   1219
Case 22   The Body Shop International *Andrew Campbell*   1224

Acknowledgements

This book is not the product of our labors alone – we are merely its architects. As architects we have been responsible for the underlying philosophy and general design of this book. We have determined the necessary structure and the building materials needed. However, for the realization of our ideas we have been dependent on the skills, support and input of a very large number of other people.

Foremost, this book would not have been possible without the high quality building blocks supplied by external authors. We are much indebted to these writers, and to their publishers, and greatly appreciate their goodwill and cooperative spirit. Without their collaboration we would not have been able to create the structure of the book as we had envisioned.

Furthermore, we wish to thank the many people who have provided feedback on the first edition and commented on our 'blue prints' for the second edition. Without the valuable inputs from many book users and colleagues, this book would never be as it is today. The same is true with regard to the very useful comments and ideas brought forward by our students and workshop participants. In the four years since the publishing of the first edition, we have had the opportunity to present our ideas to universities and companies in dozens of countries around the world, and this has led to major changes in the second edition. In this context, we would specifically like to thank the Maastricht School of Management and director El-Namaki for supporting this international learning experience.

Once the blue prints are ready and the building blocks are assembled, someone must start turning plans into reality. In this case, International Thomson Publishing has played the important role of helping us to realize our intentions. For the first edition we were lucky to be teamed up with David Godden, whose enthusiasm, creativity and professionalism greatly expedited the process of transforming our manuscript into a marketable book. For this second edition we have again been fortunate, with Steven Reed as our editor, who has been supportive, open-minded and patient during the entire project.

Last, but not least, we would like to express our appreciation to a number of individuals who closely helped us during the designing process.

First, we would like to thank Marc Huygens, who was our assistant for two years during the development of the first edition, and was again, now as a colleague, of great help. Furthermore, thanks are due to Melbert Visscher for keeping us, and the growing mountain of files, organized, and to Marja Manders, who we regularly sent on safari into the darkest reaches of the library to find cases and articles, and always came through with the right material. But most of all, we would like to thank our assistant of the past two years, Pursey Heugens. His ability to combine flexibility with perseverance, and humor with studiousness, have proven to be very valuable in getting this second edition out of its scaffolding.

Preface

Not only is there an art in knowing a
thing, but also a certain art in teaching it.

(Cicero 106–43 BC; Roman orator and statesman)

What is a good strategy for teaching the topic of strategy? Judging by the similarity of the strategic management textbooks currently available, there seems to be a general consensus among business professors on the best approach to teaching strategy. It is not an exaggeration to say that strategic management education is dominated by a strong *industry recipe* (Spender, 1989). Almost all textbooks share the following characteristics:

- The presentation of a *limited number of perspectives and theories* as accepted knowledge, from which prescriptions can easily be derived.

- The use of a simple *step-by-step strategic planning approach* as the books' basic structure.

- The reworking of original material into the textbook authors' own words to create *consistent and easily digestable pieces of text*.

- The choice of perspectives, theories, examples and cases that are heavily biased towards the textbook authors' own *domestic context*.

It is interesting to speculate on the causes of this isomorphism in the 'strategic management education' industry. Institutionalists would probably point to the need for legitimacy, which leads textbook authors to conform to widely accepted practices and to avoid major innovations (e.g. Abrahamson, 1996; Powell and DiMaggio, 1991). Social psychologists would likely suggest that over the years shared cognitive structures have developed within the strategic management community, which makes the prevailing educational paradigm difficult to challenge (e.g. McCaskey, 1982, reading 2.4 in this book; Smircich and Stubbart, 1985, reading 2.5). Theorists taking a new institutional economics perspective would probably interpret the uniformity of strategic management textbooks as a form of lock-in, caused by the large investments already made by publishers and business professors based on a shared educational 'standard' (e.g. Arthur, 1996, reading 8.5; David, 1994). Whatever the reason, it is striking that the character of strategic management textbooks has not significantly changed since the founding of the field.

But what would strategy education look like if educational orthodoxy was actively challenged and the industry rules were broken? How might strategy be taught if the current constraints were thrown aside and the teaching process was boldly reengineered? In short, what would happen if some strategic thinking were applied to the teaching of strategy?

During the last 10 years, we have continuously asked ourselves these questions. Our conclusion is that all four of the above features of current strategic management textbooks greatly inhibit the development of independent strategic thinkers and therefore urgently need to be changed. It is for this reason that we decided to create a book ourselves, with the following characteristics:

- A *broad representation of differing, and often conflicting, perspectives and theories*, reflecting the richness of current debate among academics and practitioners in the field of strategic management.

- An *issue-based book structure*, focusing on 10 key strategy questions, that are discussed from a variety of angles, leaving readers to draw their own conclusions.

- The presentation of *original articles and book chapters*, to offer readers a first-hand account of the ideas and theories of influential strategy thinkers.

- A strong *international orientation*, as reflected in the choice of topics, theories, readings, examples and cases.

In the following paragraphs the rationale behind the choice for these characteristics will be explained. Following this discussion, the structure of the book and the ways in which it can be employed will be further clarified.

Using Multiple Strategy Perspectives

> Some people are so good at learning the tricks of the trade that they never get to learn the trade.
> (Sam Levenson 1911–1980; American teacher and comedian)

What do we actually want students in a strategic management or business policy course to learn? It seems an obvious question to start with, especially for professors who teach about objective setting. Yet, in practice, the large majority of strategic management textbooks on the market do not make their teaching objectives explicit. These books implicitly assume that the type of teaching objectives and teaching methods needed for a strategic management course do not radically differ from any other subject – basically, strategy can be taught in the same way as accounting or baking cookies. Their approach is based on the following teaching objectives:

1   *Knowledge*. To get the student to clearly understand and memorize all of the major 'ingredients'.

2   *Skills*. To develop the student's ability to follow the detailed 'recipes'.

3   *Attitude*. To instill a disciplined frame of mind, whereby the student automatically attempts to approach all issues by following established procedures.

This is an important way of teaching – it is how all of us were taught to read and write, do arithmetic and drive a car. This type of teaching can be referred to as *instructional*, because students are *told* what to know and do. The instructor is the authority who has all of the necessary knowledge and skills, and it is the instructor's role to *transfer* these to the students. Thus the educational emphasis is on communicating know how and ensuring that students are able to repeat what they have heard. Students are not encouraged to question the knowledge they receive – on the contrary, it is the intention of instructional teaching to get students to absorb an accepted body of knowledge and to follow established recipes. The student should *accept, absorb and apply*.

However, while instructing students on a subject and programming their behavior might be useful in such areas as mathematics, cooking and karate, we believe it is not a very good way of teaching strategy. In our opinion, a strategic management professor should have a different set of teaching objectives:

1   *Knowledge*. To encourage the understanding of the many, often conflicting, schools of thought and to facilitate the gaining of insight into the assumptions, possibilities and limitations of each set of theories.

2   *Skills*. To develop the student's ability to define strategic issues, to critically reflect on existing theories, to creatively combine or develop conceptual models where necessary and to flexibly employ theories where useful.

3   *Attitude*. To instill a critical, analytical, flexible and creative mindset, which challenges organizational, industry and national paradigms and problem-solving recipes.

In other words, strategy professors should want to achieve the opposite of instructors – not to instill recipes, but rather to encourage students to dissect and challenge recipes. Strategic thinking is in its very essence questioning, challenging, unconventional and innovative. These aspects of strategic thinking cannot be transferred through instruction. A critical, analytical, flexible and creative state of mind must be developed by practicing these very qualities. Hence, a learning situation must encourage students to be critical, must challenge them to be analytical, must force them to be mentally flexible and must demand creativity and unconventional thinking. In short, students cannot be instructed, but must learn the art of strategy by thinking and acting themselves – they must *discuss, deliberate and do*. The role of the professor is to create the circumstances for this learning. We therefore refer to this type of teaching as *facilitative*.

This teaching philosophy has led to a radical departure from traditional textbooks that focus on knowledge transfer and application skills, and that have often been written from the perspective of just one paradigm. In this book the fundamental differences of opinion within strategic management are not ignored or smoothed over. On the contrary, it is the mission of this book to expose students to the many, often conflicting, perspectives in the field of strategy (for classifications see Bailey and Johnson, 1992; Mahoney and Pandian, 1992; Mintzberg, 1990; Schoemaker, 1993; Whittington, 1993). It is our experience that the challenge of comparing and reconciling rivalling strategy perspectives sharpens the mind of the 'apprentice' strategists. Throwing students into the midst of the central strategy debates, while simultaneously demanding that they apply their thinking to practical strategic problems, is the most likely way to enhance the qualities of creativity, flexibility, independence and analytical depth that students will need to become true strategic thinkers.

Focusing on Strategy Debates

Education, n. That which discloses to the wise and disguises from the foolish their lack of understanding.
(*The Devil's Dictionary*, Ambrose Bierce 1842–1914; American columnist)

While it is the objective of this book to increase students' strategic thinking abilities by exposing them to a wide range of theories and perspectives, it is not the intention to confuse and disorient. Yet in a subject area like strategic management, in which there is a broad spectrum of different views, there is a realistic threat that students might go deaf listening to the cacophony of different opinions. The variety of ideas can easily become overwhelming and difficult to integrate.

For this reason, the many theories, models, approaches and perspectives have been clustered around 10 central strategy issues, each of which is discussed in a separate chapter. These 10 strategy issues represent the key questions with which strategists must deal in practice. Only the theorists whose ideas have a direct bearing on the issue at hand are discussed in each chapter.

To stimulate students' interest and to avoid a dry summary of the various theories, each chapter has been structured as a *debate*. Students are introduced to each new topic by witnessing a 'virtual debate' between theorists with radically different points of view. From the outset of each chapter, the conflicting perspectives are contrasted with one another, to encourage students' engagement and to provoke critical thinking.

To further structure the 10 debates, each chapter opens by comparing two important perspectives that are largely each others' opposite. By introducing the two opposite poles in the debate, students quickly acquire an overview of the range of ideas on the issue and gain insight into the major points of contention. As such, this way of staging a debate, by starting with two opposite positions, has many of the advantages of *dialectical inquiry*

(Hampden-Turner, 1990; Mason and Mitroff, 1981; Schwenk, 1988). By providing students with a *thesis* and an *antithesis*, they are challenged to search for some type of *synthesis* themselves. It should be noted, however, that the debates only begin with this simplified bipolar world, but that additional points of view are brought in as each chapter progresses.

Using Original Readings

> You must learn from the mistakes of others. You can't possibly live long enough to make them all yourself.
> (Sam Levenson 1911–1980; American teacher and comedian)

There are no better and more lively debates than when rivals put forward their own ideas as forcefully as they can. For this reason, we have chosen to structure the strategy debates by letting influential theorists speak for themselves. Instead of translating the important ideas of key writers into our own words, each chapter contains five original readings in which the theorists state their own case. These five readings can be viewed as the discussants in the debate, while our role is that of chairmen. At the beginning of each chapter we set the stage for the debate and introduce the various perspectives and 'speakers', but as conscientious chairmen we avoid taking a position in the debate ourselves.

The five readings in each chapter have been selected with a number of criteria in mind. As a starting point, we were looking for the articles or books that are widely judged to be classics in the field of strategy. However, to ensure the broad representation of different perspectives, we occasionally looked beyond established classics to find a challenging minority point of view. Finally, discussants are only as good as their ability to communicate to the non-initiated, and therefore we have sometimes excluded certain classics as too technical.

To keep the size of the book within acceptable limits, most readings have had to be reduced in length, while extensive footnotes and references have had to be dropped. At all times this editing has been guided by the principle that the author's key ideas and arguments must be preserved intact. To compensate for the loss of references in each article, a combined list of the most important references has been added to the end of each chapter.

Taking an International Perspective

> He who knows only his side of the case, knows little of that.
> (John Stuart Mill 1806–1873; English philosopher)

While almost all strategic management textbooks have been mainly produced for their author's domestic market and are later exported overseas, this book has been explicitly developed with an international audience in mind. For students the international orientation of this book has a number of distinct advantages:

- *Cross-cultural differences*. Although there has been relatively little cross-cultural research in the field of strategy, results so far indicate that there are significant differences in strategy styles between companies from different countries. This calls into question the habit among strategy researchers to present universal theories, without indicating the cultural assumptions on which their ideas have been based. It is not unlikely that strategy theories have a strong cultural bias and therefore can not be simply transferred from one national setting to another. Much of the debate going on between strategy theorists might actually be based on such divergent cultural assumptions. In this book the issue of cross-cultural differences in strategy style is raised in each chapter, to debate whether strategists need to adapt their theories, perspectives and approaches to the country in which they are operating.

- *International context*. Besides adapting to a specific country, many companies are operating in a variety of countries at the same time. In this international arena they are confronted with a distinct set of issues, ranging from global integration and coordination, to localization and transnationalization. This set of issues presented by the international context is debated in depth in Chapter 10.

- *International cases*. To explore how the various strategy perspectives can be applied to different national contexts, it is imperative to have cases from a wide variety of countries, spread around the world. In this book the 33 cases (22 long and 11 short cases) cover more than 20 countries and most of the cases have an international orientation.

Changes to the Second Edition

> Change is not made without inconvenience, even from worse to better.
> (Samuel Johnson 1709–1784; English lexicographer)

The second edition contains significant changes compared to the first edition. While the basic approach and structure have remained largely the same, major revisions have been implemented. These alterations are partially due to new advancements in the field of strategic management, but also reflect the continual learning that has taken place as this new teaching format has developed emergently. Furthermore, additional changes were necessary as the first edition was oriented towards European readers, while this second edition directs itself to a world-wide audience. Professors using the first edition will recognize the following improvements:

- *New chapters*. The second edition contains three new chapters. The most significant changes have been in the strategy process section, where the old chapters 2 (strategy process paradigms) and 3 (strategy process organization) have been merged into a new Chapter 3, entitled 'Strategy Formation'. The old Chapter 4 on strategy process tools, which as an exception did not revolve around a debate, but merely contained a set of strategic management techniques, has been dropped. To the strategy process section we have now added a new Chapter 2 on 'Strategic Thinking' and a new Chapter 4 on 'Strategic Change'. The other major change has been the deletion of the old Chapter 11, which dealt with the European context. In its place we have introduced a new Chapter 11 on the topic of 'Organizational Purpose'. The total number of chapters has therefore remained constant, while the total amount of material has increased only slightly.

- *New introductions*. Another important change is that all chapter introductions have been rewritten and expanded. In the first edition the chapter introductions were short and the readings made up the bulk of the text. This made the book difficult for students to comprehend without assistance and left professors with the task of tying the readings together. The new chapter introductions are longer and do a more thorough job of structuring the debates and setting the stage for the readings that follow.

- *New readings*. About half of the readings (28) are new. Of course, most of the readings in the new chapters were not represented in the first edition. Furthermore, some new 'classics-to-be' have been recently published and have made their way into the book. A few other changes were made to ensure a balanced coverage of the most important perspectives on strategic management.

- *In international perspective*. A new feature in the second edition is that each chapter is concluded by a discussion on whether there are international differences in approach to the topic being debated. At the end of each chapter the question is raised whether some views on strategy are more predominant, and possibly more appropriate, in one country than in another. These pieces have been inserted to enhance the cross-cultural aspect in the strategy debates.

- *New cases*. To remain up to date and to create a better geographic spread, approximately half of the cases have been replaced by new ones. What remains unchanged is that there are two cases per chapter that provide an excellent fit. A new feature is that each chapter now also contains a short, two-page case, which provides a good illustration of the debate at hand, and can also be used if there is insufficient time to prepare one of the longer cases. These short cases are particularly useful in executive programs and in-company courses, where managers can read and discuss them on the spot.

We are aware that these changes might bring inconvenience, even though they are 'from worse to better'. As every strategist knows, 'software upgrades' require users to invest time and energy to acquaint themselves with the new version. However, we trust that previous 'users' will find the 2.0 version of our book well worth the additional investment.

References

Abrahamson, E. (1996) Management Fashion, *Academy of Management Review*, Vol. 21, pp. 254–85.

Bailey, A., and Johnson, G. (1992) How Strategies Develop in Organisations, in Faulkner, D., and Johnson, G. (eds), *The Challenge of Strategic Management*, Kogan Page, London.

David, P.A. (1994) Why are Institutions the 'Carriers of History'?: Path Dependence and the Evolution of Conventions, Organizations and Institutions, *Structural Change and Economic Dynamics*, pp. 205–20.

Hampden-Turner, C. (1990) *Charting the Corporate Mind: From Dilemma to Strategy*, Basil Blackwell, Oxford.

Mahoney, J.T., and Pandian, J.R. (1992) The Resource-based View within the Conversation of Strategic Management, *Strategic Management Journal*, Vol. 13, pp. 363–80.

Mason, R.O., and Mitroff, I.I. (1981) *Challenging Strategic Planning Assumptions*, John Wiley, New York.

Mintzberg, H. (1990) Strategy Formation: Schools of Thought, in Frederickson, J.W., (ed.), *Perspectives on Strategic Management*, Harper, New York, pp. 105–235.

Powell, W.W., and DiMaggio, P.J. (eds) (1991) *The New Institutionalism in Organization Analysis*, University of Chicago Press, Chicago.

Schoemaker, P.J.H. (1993) Strategic Decisions in Organizations: Rational and Behavioural Views, *Journal of Management Studies*, Vol. 30, January, pp. 107–29.

Schwenk, C.R. (1988) *The Essence of Strategic Decision Making*, Lexington Books, Lexington, MA.

Spender, J.-C. (1989) *Industry Recipes: The Nature and Sources of Managerial Judgement*, Basil Blackwell, Oxford.

Whittington, R. (1993) *What is Strategy and Does It Matter?*, Routledge, London.

Strategy

❏   **1 Introduction**

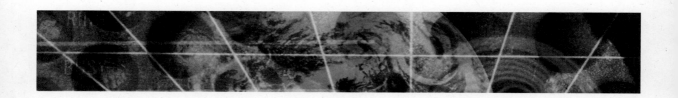

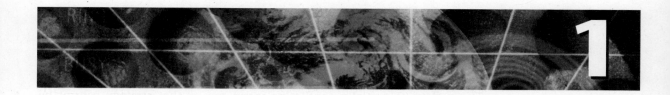

Introduction

*Men like the opinions to which they have
become accustomed from youth; this
prevents them from finding the truth, for
they cling to the opinions of habit.*

(Moses Maimonides 1135–1204; Egyptian physician and philosopher)

*Where there is much desire to learn, there
of necessity will be much arguing, much
writing, many opinions; for opinion in
good men is but knowledge in the making.*

(John Milton 1608–1674; English poet)

The Nature of Strategy

In a book entitled *Strategy*, it would seem reasonable to expect Chapter 1 to begin with a clear definition of strategy, that would be employed with consistence in all subsequent chapters. An early and precise definition of the topic under study would help to avoid conflicting interpretations of what should be considered strategy and, by extension, what should be understood by the term 'strategic management'. However, any such sharp definition of strategy here would actually be misleading. It would suggest that there is widespread agreement among practitioners, researchers and theorists as to what strategy exactly is. The impression would be given that the fundamental concepts in the area of strategy are generally accepted and hardly questioned. Yet, even a quick glance through current literature on the topic indicates otherwise. There are strongly differing opinions on most of the key issues within the field and the disagreements run so deep that even a common definition of the term strategy is illusive.

This is bad news for those who prefer simplicity and certainty. It means that the topic of strategy cannot be explained as a set of straightforward definitions and rules, fit for simple memorization and application. The variety of partially conflicting views means that strategy cannot be reduced to a number of matrices or flow diagrams that one must learn to fill in. If the fundamental differences of opinion are not swept under the carpet, the consequence is that a book on strategy cannot be like an instruction manual that takes you through the steps of how something should be done. On the contrary, a strategy book should acknowledge the disagreements and encourage thinking about the value of each of the different points of view. That is the intention of this book.

The philosophy embraced here is that an understanding of the topic of strategy can only be gained by grappling with the diversity of insights presented by so many prominent thinkers and by coming to terms with the fact that there is no simple answer to the question of what strategy is. Readers who prefer the certainty of reading only one opinion, as opposed to the intellectual stimulation of being confronted with a wide variety, should read no further – there are plenty of alternatives available. Those who wish to proceed should lay aside their 'opinions of habit,' and open their minds to the many other opinions presented, for in these pages there is 'knowledge in the making.'

Identifying the Strategy Issues

> If the only tool you have is a hammer, you treat everything like a nail.
> (Abraham Maslow 1908–1970; American psychologist)

As should be clear by now, the approach taken in this book is in line with the moral of Maslow's remark. To avoid hammering strategy issues with only one theory, a variety of ways of viewing strategic questions will be presented. But there are two different ways of presenting a broad spectrum of theoretical lenses. This point can be made clear by extending Maslow's hammer-and-nail analogy. To become a good carpenter, who wisely uses a variety of tools depending on what is being crafted, an apprentice carpenter will need to learn about these different instruments. One way is for the apprentice to study the characteristics and functioning of all tools individually, and only then to apply each where appropriate. However, another possibility is for the apprentice to first learn about what must be crafted, getting a feel for the materials and the problems that must be solved, and only then to turn to the study of the necessary tools. The first approach to learning can be called *tools-oriented* – understanding each tool comes first, while combining them to solve real problems comes later. The second approach can be labelled *problem-oriented* – understanding problems comes first, while searching for the appropriate tools is based on the type of problem.

Both options can also be used for the apprentice strategist. In a tools-oriented approach to learning about strategy, all major theories can first be understood separately, to be compared or combined later when using them in practice. A logical structure for a book aiming at this mode of learning would be to allot one chapter to each of the major theories or schools of thought. The advantage of such a *theory-based* book structure would be that each chapter would focus on giving the reader a clear and cohesive overview of one major theory within the field of strategy. For readers with an interest in grasping the essence of each theory individually, this would probably be the ideal book format. However, the principle disadvantage of a theory-by-theory summary of the field of strategy would be that the reader would not have a clear picture of how the various theories relate to one another. The apprentice strategist would be left with important questions such as: Where do the theories agree and where do they differ? Which strategy phenomena does each theory claim to explain and which phenomena are left unaccounted for? Can various theories be successfully combined or are they based on mutually exclusive assumptions? And which strategy is right, or at least most appropriate under particular circumstances? Not knowing the answers to these questions, how could the apprentice strategist try to apply these new theoretical tools to practice?

This book is based on the assumption that the reader wants to be able to actively solve strategic problems. Understanding the broad spectrum of theories is not an end in itself, but a means for more effective strategizing. Therefore, the problem-oriented approach to learning about strategy has been adopted. In this approach, key strategy issues are first identified and then each looked at from the perspective of the most appropriate theories. This has resulted in an *issue-based* book structure, in which each chapter deals with a particular set of strategy issues. In each chapter, only the theories that shed some light on the issues under discussion are brought forward and compared to one another. Of course, some theories are relevant to more than one set of issues and therefore appear in various chapters.

In total, ten sets of strategy issues have been identified, that together largely cover the entire field of strategic management. These ten will be the subjects of the remaining ten chapters of this book. How the various strategy issues have been divided into these ten sets will be explained in the following paragraphs.

Strategy Dimensions: Process, Content, and Context

The most fundamental distinction made in this book is between strategy process, strategy content and strategy context (see Figure 1.1). These are the three *dimensions of strategy* that can be recognized in every real-life strategic problem situation. They can be generally defined as follows:

- *Strategy Process*. The manner in which strategies come about is referred to as the strategy process. Stated in terms of a number of questions, strategy process is concerned with the *how*, *who* and *when* of strategy – how is, and should, strategy be made, analyzed, dreamt-up, formulated, implemented, changed and controlled; who is involved; and when do the necessary activities take place?

■ *Strategy Content*. The product of a strategy process is referred to as the strategy content. Stated in terms of a question, strategy content is concerned with the *what* of strategy – what is, and should be, the strategy for the company and each of its constituent units?

■ *Strategy Context*. The set of circumstances under which both the strategy process and the strategy content are determined is referred to as the strategy context. Stated in terms of a question, strategy context is concerned with the *where* of strategy – where, that is in which firm and which environment, are the strategy process and strategy content embedded.

It cannot be emphasized enough that strategy process, content and context are not different parts of strategy, but are distinguishable *dimensions*. Just as it is silly to speak of the length, width and height parts of a box, one cannot speak of the three parts of strategy either. Each strategic problem situation is by its nature three dimensional, possessing process, content and context characteristics, and only the understanding of all three dimensions will give the strategist real *depth* of comprehension. In particular, it must be acknowledged that the three dimensions interact (Pettigrew and Whipp, 1991; Ketchen, Thomas and McDaniel, 1996). For instance, the manner in which the strategy process is organized will have a significant impact on the resulting strategy content, while, likewise, the content of the current strategy will strongly influence the way in which the strategy process will be conducted in future. If these linkages are ignored, the strategist will have but a *flat*, instead of a *three-dimensional*, view of strategy. A useful analytical distinction for temporarily unravelling a strategic problem situation will have turned into permanent means for fragmenting reality.

However, it is possible to concentrate on one of the strategy dimensions, if the other two are kept in mind. In fact, to have a focused discussion, it is even necessary to look at one dimension at a time. The alternative is a debate in which all topics on all three dimensions would be discussed

FIGURE 1.1
Dimensions of strategy

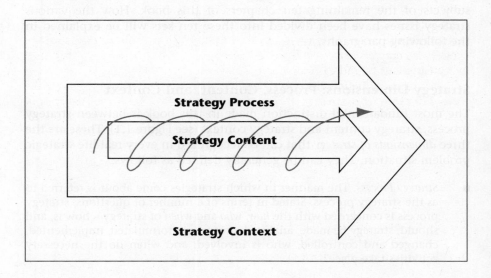

simultaneously – such a cacophony of opinions would be lively, but most likely less than fruitful. Therefore, the process-content-context distinction will cautiously be used as the main structuring principle of this book, splitting the text into three major sections.

This structure also fits closely with the situation within the academic field of strategic management. To a large extent, strategy literature is divided along these lines. Most strategy research, by its very nature, is more analytic than synthetic – focusing on just a few variables at once. Consequently, most writings on strategy, including most of theories discussed in this book, tend to favor just one, or at most two, strategy dimensions, which is usually complex enough, given the need to remain comprehensible. Especially the divide between strategy process and strategy content has been quite pronounced – to the extent of worrying some scholars about whether the connections between the two are being sufficiently recognized (Pettigrew, 1992). Although sharing this concern, use of the process-content-context distinction here reflects the reality of the current state of debate within the field of strategic management.

Strategy Process: Thinking, Forming, and Changing

Section II of this book will deal with the strategy process. Traditionally, most text books have portrayed the strategy process as a basically linear progression through a number of distinct steps. Usually a split is made between the *strategy analysis* stage, the *strategy formulation* stage and the *strategy implementation* stage. In the analysis stage, strategists identify the opportunities and threats in the environment, as well as the strengths and weaknesses of the organization. Next, in the formulation stage, strategists determine which strategic options are available to them, evaluate each and choose one. Finally, in the implementation stage the selected strategic option is translated into a number of concrete activities that are then carried out. It is commonly presumed that this process is not only *linear*, but also largely *rational* – strategists identify, determine, evaluate, choose, translate and carry out based on rigorous logic and extensive knowledge of all important factors. Furthermore, the assumption is frequently made that the strategy process is *comprehensive* – strategy is made for the entire organization and everything can be radically changed all at once.

All of these beliefs have been challenged. For instance, many authors have criticized the strong emphasis on rationality in these traditional views of the strategy process. Some writers have even argued that the true nature of strategic thinking is more intuitive and creative than rational. In their opinion, strategizing is about perceiving strengths and weaknesses, envisioning opportunities and threats, and creating the future, for which imagination and judgement are more important than analysis and logic. This constitutes quite a fundamental disagreement about the cognitive processes of the strategist. These issues surrounding the nature of *strategic thinking* will be discussed in Chapter 2.

The division of the strategy process into a number of sequential phases has also drawn heavy criticism from authors who believe that in reality no such identifiable stages exist. They dismiss the linear analysis-formulation-implementation distinction as an unwarranted simplification, arguing that the strategy process is more messy, with analysis, formulation and implementation activities going on all the time, thoroughly intertwined with one another. In their view, organizations do not first make strategic plans and then execute them as intended. Rather, strategies are usually formed incrementally, as organizations think and act in small iterative steps, letting strategies emerge as they go along. This represents quite a difference of opinion on how strategies are conceived within organizations. These issues surrounding the nature of *strategy formation* will be discussed in Chapter 3.

The third major assumption of the traditional view, comprehensiveness, has also been challenged. Many authors have pointed out that it is unrealistic to suppose that a company can be boldly redesigned. They argue that it is terribly difficult to orchestrate an overarching strategy for the entire organization, that is a significant departure from the current course of action. It is virtually impossible to get various aspects of an organization all lined up to go through a change at the same time, certainly if a radical change is intended. In practice, different aspects of an organization will be under different pressures, on different timetables and have different abilities to change, leading to a differentiated approach to change. Moreover, the rate and direction of change will be seriously limited by the cultural, political and cognitive inheritance of the firm. Hence, it is argued, strategic change is usually more gradual and fragmented, than radical and co-ordinated. The issues surrounding this difference of opinion on the nature of *strategic change* will be discussed in Chapter 4.

These three chapter topics – strategic thinking, strategy formation, and strategic change – do not constitute entirely separate subjects. Let it be clear that they are not phases, stages or elements of the strategy process, that can be understood in isolation. Strategic thinking, strategy formation and strategic change are different aspects of the strategy process, that are strongly linked and partially overlapping. They have been selected because they are sets of issues on which there is significant debate within the field of strategy. As will become clear, having a particular opinion on one of these aspects will have a consequence for views held on all others aspects as well.

Strategy Content: Business, Corporate and Network Levels

Section III of this book will deal with the strategy content. Strategies come in all shapes and sizes, and almost all strategy writers, researchers and practitioners agree that each strategy is essentially unique. There is widespread disagreement, however, about the principles to which strategies should adhere. The debates are numerous, but there are three fundamental sets of issues around which most conflicts generally center. These three topics can be clarified by distinguishing the *level of strategy* at which each is most relevant.

Strategies can be made for different groups of people and/or activities within an organization. The lowest level of aggregation is one person or task, while the highest level of aggregation encompasses all people and/or activities within an organization. The most common distinction between aggregation levels made in strategic management literature is between the functional, business and corporate levels (see Figure 1.2). Strategy issues at the *functional level* refer to questions regarding specific functional aspects of a company (operations strategy, marketing strategy, financial strategy, etc.). Strategy at the *business level* requires the integration of functional level strategies for a distinct set of products and/or services, that are intended for a specific group of customers. Often companies only operate in one such business, so that this is the highest level of aggregation within the firm.

FIGURE 1.2
Levels of Strategy

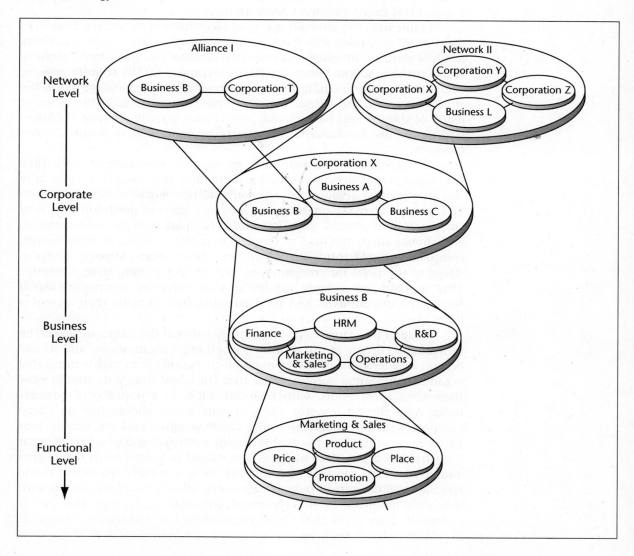

However, there are also many companies that are in two or more businesses. In such companies, a multibusiness or *corporate level* strategy is required, that aligns the various business level strategies.

A logical extension of the functional-business-corporate distinction is to explicitly recognize the level of aggregation higher than the individual organization. Firms often cluster together into groups of two or more organizations. This level is referred to as the multi-company or network level. Most multi-company groups consist of only a few parties, as is the case in strategic alliances, joint ventures and value-adding partnerships. However, networks can also have dozens, even hundreds, of participants. In some circumstances, the corporation as a whole might be a member of a group, while in other situations only a part of the firm joins forces with other organizations. In all cases, when a strategy is developed for a group of firms, this is called a network level strategy.

In line with the generally accepted boundaries of the strategic management field, this book will focus on the business, corporate and network levels of strategy, although this will often demand consideration of strategy issues at the functional level as well. In Section II, on the strategy process, this level distinction will not be emphasized yet, but in Section III, on the strategy content, the different strategy issues encountered at the different levels of strategy will be explored. And at each level of strategy, the focus will be on the fundamental differences of opinion that divide strategy theorists.

Chapter 5 will deal with strategy issues at the business level. Here the fundamental debate is whether firms are, and should be, primarily market-driven or resource-driven. Some authors argue that firms should be strongly externally-oriented, engaged in a game of positioning *vis-à-vis* customers, competitors, suppliers and other parties in the environment, and should adopt the firm to the demands of the game. In other words, companies should think outside-in. Yet, other authors strongly disagree, stressing the need for companies to exploit and expand their strengths. They recommend a more inside-out view, whereby companies search for those environments and positions that best fit with their resource-base.

Chapter 6 is concerned with strategy issues at the corporate level. The fundamental debate in this chapter is whether corporations are, and should be, run as federations of autonomous business units or as highly integrated organizations. Some authors argue that corporate strategists should view themselves as investors, with financial stakes in a portfolio of business units. As a shrewd investor, the corporate center should buy up cheap companies, divest underperforming business units, and put money into its business units with the highest profit potential, independent of what industry they are in. Each business unit should be judged on its own merits and given a large measure of autonomy, to be optimally responsive to the specific conditions in its industry. However, other authors are at odds with this view, pointing to the enormous potential for synergy that is left untapped. They argue that corporations should be tightly-knit groupings of closely-related business units, that share resources and align their strategies with one another. The ensuing synergies, it is forecast, will provide an important source of competitive advantage.

Chapter 7 focuses on the strategy issues at the network level. The fundamental debate in this chapter revolves around the question whether firms should develop long-term collaborative relationships with other firms or should remain essentially independent. Some authors believe that competition between organizations is sometimes more destructive than beneficial, and argue that building up durable partnerships with other organizations can often be mutually advantageous. Participation in joint ventures, alliances and broader networks requires a higher level of inter-organizational trust and interdependence, but can pay off handsomely. It is therefore recommended to selectively engage in joint – that is, multi-company – strategy development. Other authors, however, are thoroughly sceptical about the virtues of interdependence. They prefer independence, pointing to the dangers of opportunistic partners and creeping dependence on the other. Therefore, it is recommended to avoid multi-company level strategy development and only to use alliances as a temporary measure.

Again, it must be emphasized that the analytical distinction employed here should not be interpreted as an absolute means for isolating issues. In reality, these three levels of strategy do not exist as tidy categories, but are strongly interrelated and partially overlapping. As a consequence, the three sets of strategy issues identified above are also linked to one another. In Section III, it will become clear that taking a stand in one debate, will affect the position that one can take in others as well.

Strategy Context: Organizational, Industry, International

Section IV in this book is devoted to the strategy context. While Sections II and III discuss strategy process and strategy content issues in general, Section IV explicitly acknowledges that process and content are embedded in a particular strategy context. Strategy researchers, writers and practitioners largely agree that every strategy context is unique. Moreover, they are almost unanimous that it is usually wise for strategists to adapt the strategy process and strategy content to the specific circumstances prevalent in the strategy context. However, disagreement arises as soon as the discussion turns to the actual level of influence that the strategy context has. Some people argue or assume that the strategy context fully determines the strategy process and the strategy content. These *determinists* believe that strategists do not really have much liberty to make their own choices. Rather, process and content are largely the result of circumstances that strategists do not control. On the other hand, people with a *voluntarist* perspective believe that strategists are not driven by the context, but have a large measure of freedom to set their own course of action. Frequently it is argued that strategists can, and should, create their own circumstances, instead of being enslaved by the circumstances they find. In short, the strategy context can be determined, instead of letting it determine.

In Section IV, the same difference of opinion on the power of the context to determine strategy surfaces when discussing the various aspects of the strategy context. The section has been split into three chapters, each focusing on a different aspect of the strategy context. Two distinctions have been used to arrive at the division into three chapters. The first dichotomy employed is that between the organization and its industry environment. The *industry context* will be the subject of Chapter 8. In this chapter, the strategic issues revolve around the question whether the industry circumstances set the rules to which companies must comply, or companies have the freedom to choose their own strategy and even change the industry conditions. The *organizational context* will be dealt with in Chapter 9. Here, the key strategic issues have to do with the question of whether the organizational circumstances largely determine the strategy process and strategy content followed, or whether the strategist has a significant amount of control over the course of action adopted.

The second dichotomy employed is that between the domestic and the international strategy context. The domestic context does not raise any additional strategic issues, but the international context clearly does. Strategists must deal with the question whether adaptation to the diversity of the international context is strictly required or companies have considerable freedom to choose their strategy process and content irrespective of the international context. The difference of opinion between writers on the international context actually goes even one step further. Some authors predict that the diversity of the international context will decline over time and that companies can encourage this process. If global convergence takes place, it is argued, adaptation to the international context will become a non-issue. Other authors, however, disagree that international diversity is declining and therefore argue that the international context will remain an issue that strategists must attempt to deal with. This debate on the future of the international context is conducted in Chapter 10.

Organizational Purpose

While there are many different opinions about what strategy is, it is clear to all that strategies are used to achieve something. Making strategy is not an end in itself, but a means for reaching particular objectives. Organizations exist to fulfil a purpose and strategies are employed to ensure that the organizational purpose is realized.

Oddly enough, most authors write about strategy without any reference to the organizational purpose being pursued. It is generally assumed that all organizations exist for the same basic reasons, and that this is widely accepted. However, in reality, there is extensive disagreement about what the current purposes of organizations are, and especially about what their purpose should be. Some people argue that it is the business of business to make money. In their view, firms are owned by shareholders and therefore should pursue shareholders' interests. And it is the primary interest of shareholders to see the value of their stocks increase. On the other hand, many other people believe that companies exist to serve the interests of multiple stakeholders. In their opinion, having a financial stake in a firm should not give shareholders a dominant position *vis-à-vis* other groups that also have an interest in what the organization does. Other stakeholders usually include the employees, customers, suppliers and bankers, but could also include the local community, the industry and even the natural environment.

This is a very fundamental debate, with broader societal implications than any of the other strategy issues. Given the important role played by business organizations in modern times, the purposes they attempt to fulfil will have a significant impact on the functioning of society. It is not surprising, therefore, to see that organizational purpose is also discussed by others than strategy theorists and practitioners. The role of firms and the interests they should pursue are widely debated by members of political parties, unions, political action groups, environmental conservation groups, the media, and the general public.

Arguably, in a book on strategy, organizational purpose should be discussed before moving on to the subject of strategy itself. In principle this is true, but the 'issue of existence' is not an easy topic with which to begin a book – it would be quite a hefty appetizer to start a strategy meal. Therefore, to avoid intellectual indigestion, the topic of purpose will be saved for dessert. The last text part of the book, Chapter 11, will be devoted to the issues surrounding purpose.

Structuring the Strategy Debates

> For every complex problem there is a simple solution that is wrong.
> (George Bernard Shaw 1856–1950; Irish playwright and critic)

Every real-life strategic problem is complex. Most of the strategic issues outlined above will be present in every strategic problem, making the prospect of a simple solution an illusion. Yet, even if each set of strategy issues is looked at independently, it seems that strategy theorists cannot agree on the right way to approach them. On each of the topics, there is widespread disagreement, indicating that no simple solution can be expected here either.

Why is it that theorists cannot agree on how to solve strategic problems? Might it be that some theorists are right, while others are just plain wrong? In that case, it would be wise for problem-solvers to select the valid theory and discard the false ones. While this might be true in some cases, it seems unlikely that false theories would stay around long enough to keep a lively debate going. Eventually, the right (i.e. unfalsified) theory would prevail and disagreements would disappear. Yet, this does not seem to be happening in the field of strategic management.

Could it be that each theorist only emphasizes one aspect of an issue – only takes one cut of a multifaceted reality? In that case, it would be wise for problem-solvers to combine the various theories that each look at the problem from a different angle. However, if this were true, one would expect the different theories to be largely complementary. Each theory would simply be a piece in the bigger puzzle of strategic management. Yet, this does not explain why there is so much disagreement, and even contradiction, within the field of strategy.

It could also be that strategy theorists start from divergent assumptions about the nature of each strategy issue and therefore logically arrive at a different perspective on how to solve strategic problems. In that case, it would be wise for problem-solvers to uncover the assumptions on which each theory is built and to decide which assumptions seem most appropriate.

All three possibilities for explaining the existing theoretical disagreements should be kept open. However, entertaining the thought that divergent positions are rooted in fundamentally different assumptions about strategy issues is by far the most fruitful to the strategist confronted with complex problems. It is too simple to hope that one can deal with the contradictory opinions within the field of strategy by discovering which strategy theories are right and which are wrong. But it is also not particularly practical to accept all divergent theories as valid depictions of different aspects of reality – if two theories suggest a different approach to the same problem, the strategist will have to sort out this contradiction. Therefore, in this book the emphasis will be on surfacing the basic assumptions underlying the major theoretical perspectives on strategy, and to debate whether, or under which circumstances, these assumptions are appropriate.

Assumptions about Strategy Tensions

At the heart of every set of strategic issues, a fundamental tension between apparent opposites can be identified. For instance, in Chapter 7 on network level strategy, the issues revolve around the fundamental tension between competition and cooperation. In Chapter 8 on the industry context, the fundamental tension between the opposites of compliance and choice lies at the center of the subject (see Table 1.1). Each pair of opposites creates a tension, as they seem to be inconsistent, or even incompatible, with one another – it seems as if both elements cannot be fully true at the same time. If firms are competing, they are not cooperating. If firms must comply to the industry context, they have no choice. Yet, although these opposites confront strategists with conflicting pressures, strategists must somehow deal with them simultaneously. Strategists are caught in a bind, trying to cope with contradictory forces at the same time.

The challenge of strategic management is to wrestle with these tricky strategy tensions. Consequently, all strategy theories make assumptions, explicitly or implicitly, about the nature of these tensions and the way in which to deal with them. However, their assumptions differ significantly, giving rise to a wide variety of positions. In fact, many of the major disagreements within the field of strategic management are rooted in the different assumptions made about coping with strategy tensions. For this reason, the theoretical debate in each chapter will be centered around the different perspectives on dealing with a particular strategy tension.

TABLE 1.1
The 10 strategy tensions

Chapter	Strategy Tension	Strategy Perspectives
2. Strategic Thinking	Logic vs. Creativity	Rational Thinking vs. Generative Thinking
3. Strategy Formation	Deliberateness vs. Emergentness	Planning vs. Incrementalism
4. Strategic Change	Revolution vs. Evolution	Discontinuous Change vs. Continuous Change
5. Business Level Strategy	Markets vs. Resources	Outside-in vs. Inside-out
6. Corporate Level Strategy	Responsiveness vs. Synergy	Portfolio vs. Core Competence
7. Network Level Strategy	Competition vs. Cooperation	Discrete Organization vs. Embedded Organization
8. The Industry Context	Compliance vs. Choice	Industry Evolution vs. Industry Creation
9. The Organizational Context	Control vs. Chaos	Organizational Leadership vs. Organizational Dynamics
10. The International Context	Globalization vs. Localization	Global Convergence vs. International Diversity
11. Organizational Purpose	Profitability vs. Responsibility	Shareholder Value vs. Stakeholder Values

Identifying Strategy Perspectives

The strategy issues in each chapter can be viewed from many perspectives. On each topic there are many different theories and hundreds of books and articles. While very interesting, a comparison or debate between all of these would probably be very chaotic, unfocused and incomprehensible. Therefore, in each chapter the debate has been condensed into its most powerful form – two diametrically opposed perspectives are confronted with one another. These two poles of each debate are not always the most widely held perspectives on the particular set of strategy issues, but they do expose the major points of contention within the topic area.

In every chapter, the two strategy perspectives selected for the debate each emphasize one side of a strategy tension over the other. For instance, in Chapter 7 the discrete organization perspective stresses competition over cooperation, while the embedded organization perspective does the opposite. In Chapter 8, the industry evolution perspective accentuates compliance over choice, while the industry creation perspective does the opposite (see Table 1.1). In other words, the two perspectives represent the two extreme ways of dealing with a strategy tension – emphasizing one side or emphasizing the other.

In the first pages of each chapter, the strategic issues and the underlying strategy tension will be explained. Also, the two strategy perspectives will be outlined and compared. However, such a measured overview of the perspectives lacks color, depth and vigor. Reading the summary of a debate does not do it justice. Therefore, to give readers a first hand impression of the debate, theorists representing both sides will be given an opportunity to state their own case by means of a reading. Readers will be part of a virtual debate, in which the authors of five readings will participate. The first two contributions in each chapter will speak on behalf of the two perspectives. The third and fourth contributions are intended to bring in additional issues and arguments, that are not fully covered in the two leaders. Finally, the fifth reading is generally more demanding, with the intention of giving the debate even further depth. All of the contributions will receive a short introduction, to assist readers in understanding their pertinence to the debate at hand. The only thing that will not be done – and cannot be done – is give readers the outcome of the debate. This readers will have to decide for themselves.

Viewing Strategy Tensions as Strategy Paradoxes

So, what should readers be getting out of each debate? With both strategy perspectives emphasizing the importance of one side of a strategy tension over the other, how should readers deal with these opposites? Of course, after hearing the arguments, it is up to readers to judge for themselves how the strategy tensions should be handled. However, there are four general ways of approaching them:

■   *As a puzzle*. A puzzle is a challenging problem with an *optimal solution*. Think of a crossword puzzle as an example. Puzzles can be quite complex and extremely difficult to analyze, but there is a best way of solving them. Some of the most devious puzzles are those with seemingly contradictory premises. Strategy tensions can also be viewed as puzzles. While the pair of opposites seem to be incompatible with one another, this is only because the puzzle is not yet well understood. In reality, there is one best way of relieving the tension, but the strategist must unravel the problem first. Some writers seem to suggest that there are optimal ways of dealing with strategy tensions under all circumstances, but others argue that the optimal solution is situation dependent.

■   *As a dilemma*. A dilemma is a vexing problem with *two possible solutions*, neither of which is logically the best. Think of the famous prisoner's dilemma as an example. Dilemmas confront problem-solvers with difficult *either-or* choices, each with its own advantages and disadvantages, but neither clearly superior to the other. The uneasy feeling this gives the decision-maker is reflected in the often used expression 'horns of a dilemma' – neither choice is particularly comfortable. Strategy tensions can also be viewed as dilemmas. If this approach is taken, the incompatibility of the opposites is accepted, and the strategist is forced to make a choice for either one or the other. For instance, the strategist must choose to either compete or cooperate. Which of the two the strategist judges to be most appropriate will usually depend on the specific circumstances.

- *As a trade-off*. A trade-off is a problem situation in which there are *many possible solutions*, each striking a different balance between two conflicting pressures. Think of the trade-off between work and leisure time as an example – more of one will necessarily mean less of the other. In a trade-off, many different combinations between the two opposites can be found, each with its own pros and cons, but none of the many solutions is inherently superior to the others. Strategy tensions can also be viewed as trade-offs. If this approach is taken, the conflict between the two opposites is accepted, and the strategist will constantly strive to find the most appropriate balance between them. For instance, the strategist will attempt to balance the pressures for competition and co-operation, depending on the circumstances encountered.

- *As a paradox*. A paradox is a situation in which two seeming contradictory, or even mutually exclusive, factors appear to be true at the same time (Poole and Van de Ven, 1989; Quinn and Cameron, 1988). A problem that is a paradox has *no real solution*, as there is no way to logically integrate the two opposites into an internally consistent understanding of the problem. As opposed to the either-or nature of the dilemma, the paradox can be characterized as a *both-and* problem – one factor is true and a contradictory factor is simultaneously true (e.g. Collins and Porras, 1994; Quinn, 1988). Hence, a paradox presents the problem-solver with the difficult task of wrestling with the problem, without ever arriving at a definitive solution. At best, the problem-solver can find a workable compromise to temporarily cope with the unsolvable paradox. Strategy tensions can also be viewed as paradoxes. If this approach is taken, the conflict between the two opposites is accepted, but the strategist will strive to accommodate both factors at the same time. The strategist will search for new ways of reconciling the opposites as best as possible. To take the same example as above, the strategist faced with the tension between competition and cooperation will attempt to do both as much as possible at the same time, reaping the benefits of both.

Most people are used to solving puzzles, resolving dilemmas and making trade-offs. These ways of understanding and solving problems are common in daily life. They are based on the assumption that, by analysis, one or a number of logical solutions can be identified. It might require a sharp mind and considerable effort, but the answers can be found.

However, most people are not used to, or inclined to, think of a problem as a paradox. A paradox has no answer or set of answers – it can only be coped with as best as possible. Faced with a paradox, one can try to find novel ways of combining opposites, but will know that none of these creative reconciliations will ever be *the* answer. Paradoxes will always remain surrounded by uncertainty and disagreements on how best to cope.

So, should strategy tensions be seen as puzzles, dilemmas, trade-offs or paradoxes? Arguments can be made for all, but viewing strategy tensions as strategy paradoxes is the ultimate intellectual challenge. Looking at the tensions as paradoxes will help readers to avoid 'jumping to solutions' and will encourage readers to use their creativity to find ways of benefiting from both sides of a tension at the same time. Hence, throughout the book, the strategy tensions will be presented as strategy paradoxes, and readers will be invited to view them as such.

Developing an International Perspective

> Every man takes the limits of his own field of vision for the limits of the world.
>
> (Arthur Schopenhauer 1788–1860; German Philosopher)

In a highly integrated world economy, in which many firms operate across national boundaries, strategy is by nature an international affair. Some theorists ignore the international arena as irrelevant, uninteresting or too complex, but most theorists, particularly those interested in strategy content, acknowledge the importance of the international context and write extensively on international competition and global strategy. In this book, there has been a strong preference to include those authors who explicitly place their arguments within an international setting. Gaining an international perspective is greatly enhanced by reading works that do not take a domestic arena as their default assumption.

To further accentuate the international angle in this book, the international context has been singled out for a closer look in Chapter 10. In this chapter, the conflicting views about the developments in the international context will be debated. This, too, should challenge readers to take an international perspective.

However, despite all this attention paid to the international competitive arena, internationalizing companies, cross-border strategies, and global products, few authors explicitly question whether their own strategy theories can be globally standardized. Most fail to wonder whether their theories are equally applicable in a variety of national settings. It is seldom asked whether they base themselves on universally valid assumptions, or they have been severely limited by their domestic 'field of vision'. Yet, there is a very real danger that theories are based on local assumptions that are not true or appropriate in other nations – a threat that could be called 'think local, generalize global.'

Developing an international perspective requires that strategists guard against the indiscriminate export of domestically-generated strategy theories across international borders. For international strategists it is important to question whether theories 'travel' as well as the companies they describe. Unfortunately, at the moment, strategists have little to base themselves on. There has been only a modest amount of international comparative research done in the field of strategy. National differences in strategic management practices and preferences have occasionally been identified, but in general the topic has received little attention. In practice, the international validity of locally-formulated strategy theories has gone largely unquestioned in international journals and fora.

Although there is still so little published material to go on, in this book readers will be encouraged to question the international limitations of strategy theories. Furthermore, readers will be challenged to question whether certain strategy perspectives are more popular and/or appropriate in some countries than in others. To point readers in the right direction, at the end of each chapter a paragraph will be presented that places the strategy topic being debated in an international perspective. In these paragraphs, it will be argued that the strategy paradoxes identified in this book are fundamentally the same around the world, but that there might be international differences in how each paradox is coped with. Strategy perspectives and theories might be more predominant in particular countries because they are based on certain assumptions about dealing with the strategy paradoxes that are more suitable to the national context. In each 'international perspective' paragraph, a number of factors will be discussed that might cause national differences in strategy styles.

Using the Cases

An additional way of gaining an international perspective is by trying to employ the strategy perspectives in a variety of national settings. It is especially when trying to deal with concrete strategic problems on an international stage, that the limitations of each theory will become more apparent. For this reason, 33 cases have been included in this book, from a large number of different countries. In each case, readers are encouraged to evaluate the specific national circumstances in which the problem situation is embedded, and to question whether the national context will have an influence on the validity or appropriateness of the various strategy theories and perspectives.

The cases have been selected to cover a wide variety of countries and industries. Furthermore, they have been chosen for their fit with a particular chapter. Each of the following ten chapters in this book has three corresponding cases, in which the paradox under discussion is prominently present. Two of the three cases per chapter are relatively lengthy, and have been grouped together in Section VI of this book. The short case for each chapter is only two pages long and has been inserted as an exhibit into the main text. In each case readers will encounter that grappling with strategy paradoxes in 'practice' is just as difficult as dealing with them in 'theory'.

EXHIBIT 1.1
MTV Short Case

MTV NETWORKS: BETWEEN ROCK AND A HARD PLACE?

Back in the 1980s, Mark Knopfler of Dire Straits sang 'I want my MTV,' and since then 280 million households in 76 countries have been granted this request. Launched in the United States in 1981, MTV was the first 24-hour music television network in the world, and has been leading internationally ever since. It was the first network with a presence on all five continents and currently broadcasts a number of geographically customized versions of the American original around the globe. For instance, MTV Latino is the Spanish-language affiliate broadcasting two region-specific versions of MTV for the Latin American market, while MTV Europe produces three English-language variations for different parts of Europe. Back home, MTV reaches more than 62 million households across the United States, either via cable or by satellite.

MTV is part of MTV Networks, that also operates a number of other TV channels, including VH-1 (music), Nickelodeon (children), Nick at Nite (classic sitcoms), Showtime (films) and Showtime Event Television. Of these, only VH-1 has followed MTV abroad, recently starting in Germany and the UK. Just like MTV, VH-1 is a 24-hour a day music channel, but while MTV is directed at the age group 15–35, VH-1 aims at the 25–40 year-olds. MTV Networks is in turn owned by media giant Viacom, which also owns Paramount Pictures, various television and radio stations and a number of cable systems.

A large part of MTV's success is attributable to the network's ability to understand, follow and even shape the volatile audience of teens and twenty-somethings in a way that suit-and-tie wearing executives at stodgier networks have found difficult to imitate. In many countries young people have been a poorly served segment, opening the door for MTV's entrance into the market. However, in broadcasting much more is needed to be successful than only a good channel format and a receptive target audience. Success depends on a network's ability to manage relationships with a number of key external stakeholders. First, a channel needs suppliers – someone must provide MTV with videos. At this moment, the record companies produce these highly expensive videos as promotional devices to sell their CDs and supply them free of cost to music channels. But while both sides benefit from this relationship, it places the record companies in a relatively dependent position. If MTV decides not to broadcast a new video, the record company has few alternatives. Unsurprisingly, the record companies would be happy if MTV had more competitors. Writing on the wall for MTV is that its leading challenger in Germany, VIVA, was initiated by the record companies PolyGram, EMI Music, Sony and Time Warner.

Second, to survive as a TV channel, advertisers are essential. Most commercial broadcasters do not rely on viewers to pay for the programs watched (either by subscription or pay-per-view), but largely finance operations out of advertising revenues. This is also true for MTV, which is heavily dependent on attracting enough advertisers interested in the 15–35 year old age segment. Some advertisers have become whole-hearted partners of MTV. For instance, PepsiCo has a long-term relationship with MTV, with the intention of co-promoting both brands and reinforcing each others' positions world-wide. However, there are not very many companies that want the internationally standardized advertising that MTV is so good at offering outside of the US. Furthermore, many advertisers in the US wouldn't mind a bit of competition for MTV, to keep advertising prices down.

A third success factor for TV channels is distribution – programs need to reach viewers' TV sets, either by satellite or by cable. Transmitting via satellite is relatively simple. Satellite 'slots' can be rented from third parties and viewers can receive transmissions with a dish. However, in most countries the number of households with a dish is quite low, given the high initial cost, varying from $1000 to $3000. Therefore, most commercial channels prefer distribution via cable systems, which have a high level of penetration in most developed economies. Yet getting cable operators to carry a channel often proves to be an arduous task. Most cable operators have small regional monopolies and need to be convinced of the need to make extra costs to carry an additional channel. Many cable systems are technically limited to a fixed number of channels and therefore need to drop an existing broadcaster before a new channel can be accommodated. This gives cable companies quite a bit of power, leading operators in some countries to demand that commercial channels pay for a slot on the cable.

Although MTV has been at the top of the charts for more than 15 years, other channels have been steadily rising in the ratings, challenging MTV's virtual ownership of the youth market. In the US, real competition has only recently emerged. The Canadian network MuchMusic launched a channel in the US in 1994 and by 1997 was also present in Mexico, Argentina and Finland. The Box, a channel that allows viewers to call in and select the videos to be played, has been doing moderately well, expanding from the US to the UK, the Netherlands, Argentina, Peru and Chile. MOR Music Television is a music shopping network that combines videos with merchandising breaks. Besides these general music channels, MTV is facing a number of competitors focusing on only one type of music. BET on Jazz, Black Entertainment Television, The Nashville Network, Country Music Television, The Gospel Network and Z Music (Christian) may all draw viewers away from MTV.

Outside its home base, competition varies per country, but is becoming fierce in a number of mature markets. For instance, in Germany MTV's position is under siege by VIVA, which employs German-speaking VJs and mixes international and local music. The same is true in the Netherlands, where MTV is being battered by the local player TMF, and in the UK, where Kiss TV and BBC Radio One channel have launched an assault. In all these cases the competitive advantage of MTV's new rivals is their ability to tailor programming to the demands of the local market. The success of the local upstarts has lead many commentators to question whether 'the new generation' is really as globally similar as once thought.

Taken together, these developments form a rather wicked strategic problem for MTV. Its competitive formula as the globally standardized youth channel is being attacked from a variety of angles, which seems to demand some type of response. Yet, any move by MTV will need to acknowledge the web of interdependency relationships with the record companies, advertisers and cable operators, in which the company is embedded.

Until now, MTV has not initiated any radical strategic changes, but is actively searching for ways to gradually adapt to the new competitive circumstances. One idea that emerged and was implemented within a few months, was the launch of M2 in the US market in August 1996. M2 is an all-video channel that closely resembles the early free-form MTV, before it began running more long-form non-music programs. Industry analysts remark that even if M2 does not break even, it might block the way for new competitors and should satisfy record companies' complaints that MTV does not offer enough airtime to new acts.

Outside the US, MTV is expanding to new markets, such as India, largely according to plan. However, MTV's head of international activities, Bill Roedy, seems to have seriously altered his views on the international context. Instead of sticking to a globally standardized product, based on a belief in global convergence, Roedy has acknowledged the need to go local – he wants to adapt MTV's programming to meet national tastes. Roedy is contemplating partially autonomous regional channels in the local language, to counter MTV's crumbling marketshare. Yet, reaping the advantages of localization, while not losing too many of the benefits of globalization, is proving to be an interesting paradox.

But there are many more strategy paradoxes confronting MTV. As a former rule-breaker within the broadcasting industry, MTV must ask to what extent it can still set, or must follow, the industry rules – a paradox of compliance and choice. Should they primarily be driven by market considerations or should they focus more on perfecting and leveraging their unique resources – a paradox of markets and resources. Should their relationships with advertisers, cable operators and record companies be arm's length and tough, or close and collaborative – a paradox of competition and cooperation. MTV must also work out whether there is added value to working with other parts of its parent, Viacom, or whether MTV should remain largely autonomous – a paradox of responsiveness and synergy. In answering all of these questions, MTV can adopt a strategic thinking style that is either more analytical or more imaginative – a paradox of logic and creativity. It can develop strategic plans or let strategies form more incrementally over time – a paradox of deliberateness and emergentness. And the strategic changes realized can come about more gradually or more radically – a paradox of evolution and revolution. In short, MTV has some difficult nuts to crack – which is not exactly getting 'your money for nothing and your chicks for free.'

Sources: *Financial Times*, February 20 1997; *Broadcasting & Cable*, September 2 1996; *The Economist*, February 25 1995.

The Readings

Unless a variety of opinions are laid before us, we have no opportunity of selection, but are bound of necessity to adopt the particular view which may have been brought forward. The purity of gold cannot be ascertained by a single specimen; but when we have carefully compared it with others, we are able to fix upon the finest ore.

(Herodotus Fifth century BC; Greek historian)

In the following ten chapters the readings will represent the different points of view in the debate and will lay the variety of opinions before us. However, in this chapter there is no central debate. Therefore, five contributions have been selected that provide an interesting introduction to the topic of strategy, or reinforce some of the arguments made in the preceding pages. Here, each of the articles will be shortly introduced and the relevance for the discussion at hand will be underlined.

The opening reading, 'The First Strategists' by Stephen Cummings, places the central question of this book – What is strategy? – in a historical perspective. Cummings takes the reader back to the ancient Greeks, to whom we owe the term strategy, in a quest to uncover some fundamental characteristics of military strategy and strategists, which he believes are still important for business strategists today. The charm of this contribution lies not only in its clear and concise rendition of Hellenic thought, but also in its ability to place the current state of the art of strategic thinking in the humbling context of history. This reading convincingly points out that many seemingly modern strategy issues are actually millennia old. The development of the business strategy field may be a recent academic trend, stretching no further back than the 1960s, but outside commerce many of the great minds throughout history have occupied themselves with the topic of strategy, especially in the fields of war (see, for instance, the famous Chinese theorist Sun Tzu's *The Art of War* and Karl von Clausewitz's *On War*) and politics (for example, Niccolo Machiavelli's *The Prince and the Discourses*). The debate, which Cummings opens with this contribution, is to what extent the principles of military strategy can be applied to the business context. Can business strategists learn from military strategists, and vice versa? Stated even more broadly, to what measure are there parallels between strategy in such diverse fields as war, politics, sports, biology and business? Are there universal principles of strategy? The extent to which the strategy principles of one area are valid in another is a recurrent theme in strategy literature.

The second reading, 'Defining the Concept of Strategy,' does exactly what its title promises to do, not by giving a five-line dictionary definition, but by trying to identify a number of fundamental characteristics of strategy in the business context. The author, Arnoldo Hax, skilfully seeks the common ground between the major schools of thought within the field of strategy, attempting to put forward a number of key features of strategy on which most strategists would probably agree. This contribution has been selected because it makes strategy just a bit more tangible for readers who prefer to start with a temporary definition of strategy and revise it as they go along.

In the same vein, the third reading, 'The Evaluation of Business Strategy' by Richard Rumelt, has been selected because it uncovers a number of basic strategy characteristics, on which an initial understanding of the subject can be based. Rumelt describes the difficulties of evaluating whether strategies will lead to survival and success. He argues that it is impossible to judge beforehand whether an intended strategy will work, but that it can be tested for flaws. He concludes that there are four broad criteria which strategies should meet to be deemed potentially viable. Strategies should possess the characteristics of consistency, consonance, advantage and feasibility. As will be seen in the following chapters, these features of a sound strategy are generally accepted – but still open for considerable differences of interpretation.

The fourth reading, 'Complexity: The Nature of Real World Problems,' is the first chapter of Richard Mason and Ian Mitroff's classic book, *Challenging Strategic Planning Assumptions*. In this thought-provoking contribution, Mason and Mitroff argue that most strategic problems facing organizations are not *tame* – that is, they are not simple problems that can be separated and reduced to a few variables and relationships, and then quickly solved. Strategic problems are usually *wicked*. Strategists are faced with a situation of organized complexity in which problems are complicated and interconnected, there is much uncertainty and ambiguity, and they must deal with conflicting views and interests. Therefore, strategic problems have no clearly identifiable correct solutions, but must be tackled by debating the alternatives and selecting the most promising option. Mason and Mitroff call on strategists to systematically doubt the value of all available solutions and to employ *dialectics* – a method of argumentation that contrasts two diametrically opposed positions, the thesis and the antithesis, to arrive at a better understanding of the subject. This is in fact the approach adopted in this book. The presentation of two diametrically opposed positions in each chapter is used as a means for gaining a richer understanding of the complex strategy issues under discussion.

The fifth reading, 'Cultural Constraints in Management Theories' by Geert Hofstede, has been selected to sow further doubt about the universal validity of strategic management theories. Hofstede is one of the most prominent cross-cultural researchers in the field of management and is known, in particular, for his five dimensions for measuring cultural traits. In this article he briefly describes the major characteristics of management in Germany, Japan, France, Holland, South-East Asia, Africa, Russia and China, contrasting them all to the US, to drive home his point that management practices differ from country to country, depending on the local culture. Each national style is based on cultural characteristics, that differ sharply around the world. Hofstede argues that theories are formulated within these national cultural contexts, and thus reflect the local demands and predispositions. Therefore, he concludes that universal management theories do not exist – each theory is culturally constrained. If Hofstede is right, this reemphasizes the necessity to view strategic management and strategy theories from an international perspective. Readers must judge which strategy approach is best suited to the national circumstances with which they are confronted.

1.1   The First Strategists

By Stephen Cummings[1]

Origin of Strategy

The word *strategy* derives from the ancient Athenian position of *strategos*. The title was coined in conjunction with the democratic reforms of Kleisthenes (508–7 BC), who developed a new sociopolitical structure in Athens after leading a popular revolution against a Spartan-supported oligarchy. Kleisthenes instituted 10 new tribal divisions, which acted as both military and political subunits of the district of Athens. At the head of each tribe was elected a strategos. Collectively, the 10 incumbent *strategoi* formed the Athenian war council. This council and its individual members, by virtue of the kudos granted them, also largely controlled nonmilitary politics.

Strategos was a compound of *stratos*; which meant 'army,' or more properly an encamped army *spread out* over ground (in this way *stratos* is also allied to *stratum*) and *agein*, 'to lead.' The emergence of the term paralleled increasing military decision-making complexity. Warfare had evolved to a point where winning sides no longer relied on the deeds of heroic individuals, but on the coordination of many units of men each fighting in close formation. Also, the increasing significance of naval forces in this period multiplied the variables a commander must consider in planning action. Consequently, questions of coordination and synergy among the various emergent units of their organizations became imperative considerations for successful commanders.

Of what interest are the origins of strategy to those engaging in strategic activities and decision making in organizations today? In the words of Adlai Stevenson, we can see our future clearly and wisely only when we know the path that leads to the present. Most involved in corporate strategy have little knowledge of where that path began. A great deal of insight into strategy can be gained from examining those from whom we inherit the term. The first strategists, the Greek strategoi, perhaps practiced strategy in its purest sense.

Strategy and Strategist as Defined by Ancient Theorists

Aineias the Tactician, who wrote the earliest surviving Western volume on military strategy, *How to Survive under Siege*, in the mid fourth century BC,

---

[1] Source: Reprinted with permission from *Long Range Planning*, 'Brief Case: The First Strategists', June 1993, Pergamon Press Ltd, Oxford, England.

was primarily concerned with how to deploy available manpower and other resources to best advantage. The term strategy is defined in more detail by Frontinus in the first century AD, as 'everything achieved by a commander, be it characterized by foresight, advantage, enterprise, or resolution.'

Ancient Athenian theorists also had clear ideas about the characteristics that were necessary in an effective strategos. According to Xenophon, a commander 'must be ingenious, energetic, careful, full of stamina and presence of mind, loving and tough, straightforward and crafty, alert and deceptive, ready to gamble everything and wishing to have everything, generous and greedy, trusting and suspicious.' These criteria for identifying an excellent strategist still ring true.

Xenophon goes on to describe the most important attribute for an aspiring strategos/statement as 'knowing the business which you propose to carry out.' The Athenians in this period were very concerned that their leaders had an awareness of how things worked at the 'coal-face.' Strategoi were publicly elected by their fellow members of the Athenian organization; and to be considered a credible candidate, one had to have worked one's way into this position by demonstrating prowess at both individual combat and hands-on military leadership. Wisdom was considered to be a citizen's ability to combine political acumen and practical intelligence, and strategoi should be the wisest of citizens. The organization's future lay in the hands of these men and, ipso facto, the strategic leadership of the Athenian organization was not to consider itself immune from hardship when times were tough: 'No man was fitted to give fair and honest advice in council if he has not, like his fellows, a family at stake in the hour of the city's danger.'

To the ancient Athenians strategy was very much a line of function. The formulation of strategy was a leadership task. The Athenian organization developed by Kleisthenes was extremely recursive. The new tribes, and the local communities that these tribes comprised, formed the units and subunits of the army, and were, in their sociopolitical structures, tantamount to the city-state in microcosm. Decision makers at all levels of the corporation were expected to think strategically, in accordance with the behavior exhibited by those in leadership roles at higher levels of the Athenian system. Strategoi were expected both to direct and take part in the thick of battle, leading their troops into action. For a strategos not to play an active combat role would have resulted in a significant diminution in the morale of those fighting for his tribe.

Practical Lessons from the Strategoi

If military practice is identified as a metaphor for business competition, the strategic principles of the great strategoi still provide useful guides for those in the business of strategy formulation today. For Pericles, perhaps the greatest of the Athenian strategoi, the goal of military strategies was 'to limit risk while holding fast to essential points and principles.' His often quoted maxims of 'Opportunity waits for no man' and 'Do not make any new conquests during the war' are still applicable advice in a modern business environment.

Epaminondas of Thebes was said to have brought the two arms of his military corporation, infantry and cavalry, together in a 'fruitful organizational blend.' The Theban's strategic principles included economy of force coupled with overwhelming strength at the decisive point; close coordination between units and meticulous staff planning combined with speed of attack; and as the quickest and most economical way of winning a decision, defeat of the competition not at his weakest point but at his strongest. Epaminondas was Philip of Macedon's mentor, and it was largely due to the application of the Theban's innovations that the Macedonian army grew to an extent where it was able to realize Alexander the Great's (Philip's son) vast ambitions. The close integration of all its individual units became the major strength of the Macedonian army organization.

Alexander himself is perhaps the most famous ancient exponent of a contingency approach to strategy. It is often told that as a young man he was asked by his tutor Aristotle what he would do in a given situation. Alexander replied that his answer would depend on the circumstances. Aristotle described a hypothetical set of circumstances and asked his original question again. To this the student answered, 'I cannot tell until the circumstances arise.' In practice Alexander was not often caught without a 'plan B.' An example is related by Frontinus: 'At Arbela, Alexander, fearing the numbers of the enemy, yet confident in the valour of his own troops, drew up a line of battle facing in all directions, in order that the men, if surrounded, might be able to fight from any side.'

Ancient Approaches to the Learning of Strategy

The ancient Greeks took great interest in both the practical and theoretical aspects of strategic leadership. They favored the case method as the best means of passing this knowledge from one generation of strategists to the next. Frontinus argued that 'in this way commanders will be furnished with specimens of wisdom and foresight, which will serve to foster their own power of conceiving and executing like deeds.' Aineias and Xenophon also used and championed such methods in ways that would please any Harvardophile. The best-crafted exposition of the case method, however, belongs to Plutarch, biographer to the ancient world's greatest leaders:

> It is true, of course, that our outward sense cannot avoid apprehending the various objects it encounters, merely by virtue of their impact and regardless of whether they are useful or not: but a man's conscious intellect is something which he may bring to bear or avert as he chooses, and can very easily transfer . . . to another object as he sees fit. For this reason, we ought to seek out virtue not merely to contemplate it, but to derive benefit from doing so. A colour, for example, is well suited to the eye if its bright and agreeable tones stimulate and refresh the vision, and in the same way we ought to apply our intellectual vision to those models which can

inspire it to attain its own proper virtue through the sense of delight they arouse . . . [Such a model is] no sooner seen than it rouses the spectator into action, and yet it does not form his character by mere imitation, but by promoting the understanding of virtuous deeds it provides him with a dominating purpose.

Now, as then, our strategic vision can be refreshed and stimulated through studying the character and deeds of the great strategic leaders of the past.

1.2   Defining the Concept of Strategy

By Arnoldo Hax[1]

What is strategy? Once upon a time strategy could be defined as a rendition of the CEO's personal mission statement, rationalized by the corporate planner, and bought into by the executive committee and chief stock-holders. But even this simplistic and somewhat cynical answer begs the question of how the strategy was really formed. Did it flash through a CEO's mind while at his or her morning ablutions, or was it a logical model for growing the business, developed after years of studying the industry and the capabilities of the firm? Now that more and more line managers are becoming responsible for planning and strategies, and the sum of their increasingly fast-paced decisions may affect a firm's strategy almost over-night or create a new implicit aspect of it, it's time for a fresh look at what strategy is and how it may come about.

But providing a simple definition is not easy. There are some elements of strategy that have universal validity and can be applied to any institution. However, other elements are heavily dependent on the nature of the firm, its constituencies, its structure, and its culture.

Six Dimensions of Strategy

To clarify the definition process, it is useful to consider the concept of strategy separately from the process of strategy formation. Let's start by assuming that strategy actually embraces all the critical activities of a firm. Let's also hypothesize that strategy provides a sense of unity, direction

---

[1] Source: This article is reprinted from 'Redefining the Concept of Strategy', *Planning Review*, (May/June 1990), with permission from The Planning Forum, The International Society for Strategic Management and Planning.

and purpose, as well as facilitating the necessary changes induced by a firm's environment. The following six critical dimensions must therefore be included in any unified definition of the concept of strategy.

Strategy as a Coherent, Unifying, and Integrative Pattern of Decisions

Many business people would accept the definition that strategy is the major force that provides a comprehensive and integrative blueprint for an organization as a whole. As such, strategy gives rise to the plans that assure that the basic objectives of the total enterprise are fulfilled. This assumes that strategy is conscious, explicit, and proactive.

But skeptics can offer many examples of firms where strategy is implicit, murkily communicated, and practiced covertly. By expanding our definition we can include even firms that practice strategy as a black art. So, broadly defined, strategy is the pattern of decisions a firm makes.

This definition has historical validity. Strategy is a matter of record – it emerges from what the firm does. To examine strategy as an evolutionary process, we can study the nature of an organization's decision making and its resulting performance. Strategic patterns can be discerned by examining major changes or discontinuities in a firm's direction. These may be caused by changes in its top management or changes triggered by important external events that call for strategic repositioning.

Analyzing a firm in terms of these historical eras usually provides a more or less coherent strategic pattern. Significant strategies emerge. They are discovered by following the footprints of the major steps a firm has taken in the past. Often this path of strategic footprints – like a woodland trail that heads toward a mountain peak on the horizon – indicates the organization's future destination.

Strategy as a Means of Establishing an Organization's Purpose in Terms of its Long-Term Objectives

This classical view looks at strategy as a way of explicitly shaping the long-term goals and objectives of an organization; of defining the major action programs needed to achieve those objectives; and of deploying the necessary resources.

To make this concept useful, we first need to define a firm's long-term objectives. If these change constantly, the value of this approach decreases. There should be little change in this area unless external conditions or internal shifts call for a reexamination of the long-term commitments. Nothing could be more debilitating to a firm than an erratic reorientation of its objectives without substantive reasons. Continuous strategic redirections simply end up confusing all of a firm's stakeholders – but most importantly, its customers, employees, and stockholders.

The desirable stability of long-term objectives does not, however, preclude frequent refining of a firm's programs. This is accomplished by continually reexamining the short-term strategic action programs that are congruent with long-term objectives.

This approach makes it clear that resource allocation is a firm's most critical step in strategic implementation. The alignment between strategic objectives and programs on the one hand, and the allocation of a firm's overall resources – human, financial, technological, and physical – on the other, is required to achieve strategic effectiveness.

Strategy as a Definition of a Firm's Competitive Domain

It has long been recognized that one of the central concerns of strategy is defining the businesses a firm is in or intends to be in. The process of definition requires strategy makers to address issues of growth, diversification, and investment.

A key step in defining a formal strategic planning process is effective business segmentation. Segmentation is a crucial step in business analysis, strategic positioning, resource allocation, and portfolio management. Segmentation explicitly identifies a firm's domain: Where is it going to be engaged in competitive actions, and how is it going to compete?

The basic questions to be addressed are 'What businesses are we in?' and 'What businesses should we be in?' If a firm operating in a complex and dynamic business environment has never attempted to respond seriously to these questions, it may at first find them trivial. Yet, extracting a clear-cut answer from an experienced group of managers when these questions are addressed for the first time is often a surprisingly difficult procedure. Consensus is hard to come by.

The issues are further complicated because business segmentation ultimately has an enormous impact on defining the organizational structure of the firm. Consciously or unconsciously, issues of turf and executive responsibilities tend to have a major influence on the way these questions are addressed.

Strategy as a Response to External Opportunities and Threats and to Internal Strengths and Weaknesses as a Means of Achieving Competitive Advantage

According to this perspective, the central thrust of strategy is to achieve a long-term sustainable advantage over a firm's key competitors in every business in which it participates. This view of strategy is what underlies most of the modern analytical approaches used to support the search for a favorable competitive position. It recognizes that:

- The ultimate objective is for a firm to achieve a long-term competitive advantage over its key competitors in all of its businesses.

- This competitive advantage is the result of a thorough understanding of the external and internal forces that strongly affect an organization. Externally, a firm must recognize its relative industry attractiveness and trends, and the characteristics of the major competitors. This helps generate the discovery of the opportunities and threats that must be reckoned with. Internally, a firm must identify its competitive capabilities. This leads to the defining of its strengths and weaknesses.

■ Strategy allows organizations to achieve a viable match between their external environment and their internal capabilities. The role of strategy is not viewed simply as a passive response to the opportunities and threats presented by the external environment, but rather as a process of continuously and actively adapting the organization to meet the demands of a changing environment.

Given this perspective, it is now easy to see that the fundamental framework of business strategy encompasses three primary focal points:

1   The business unit, which is the central subject of analysis.

2   The industry structure, which determines the key environmental trends.

3   The internal competencies, which define the ways to compete.

Thus, the long-term objectives, strategic action programs, and resource allocation priorities adapt to the role the business unit intends to play within the total portfolio of the firm's businesses. They also adapt to the favorable or unfavorable trends of the industry structure, as well as to the internal capabilities a firm needs to deploy in order to achieve the desired competitive position.

Strategy as a Logical System for Differentiating Managerial Tasks at Corporate, Business, and Functional Levels

The various hierarchical levels in the organization have quite different managerial responsibilities in terms of their contribution to defining the strategy of the firm. The corporate level is responsible for tasks that need the fullest scope in order to be addressed properly. Primarily, this means defining a firm's overall mission; validating proposals emerging from business and functional levels; identifying and exploiting linkages between distinct but related business units; and allocating resources with a sense of strategic priorities.

The business level is the proper place for all of the activities needed to enhance the competitive position of each individual business unit.

The key assignment of the functional level is to develop the necessary competencies – in finance, administrative infrastructure, human resources, technology, procurement, logistics, manufacturing, distribution, marketing, sales, and services – needed to sustain competitive advantage. Recognizing the differences in these managerial roles, and integrating them harmoniously, is another key dimension of strategy.

Regardless of the structure adopted by a firm, three highly differentiated strategic concerns still remain: The first addresses the organization as a whole (corporate strategy); the second is intrinsic to the business unit (business strategy); and the third involves the development of functional capabilities (functional strategy).

Strategy as a Definition of the Economic and Noneconomic Contribution the Firm Intends to Make to Its Stakeholders

The notion of stakeholders has gained importance as an element of strategic concern in the past few years. The term *stakeholders* refers to everyone who directly or indirectly receives the benefits or sustains the costs that result from a firm's actions. Stakeholders include shareholders, employees, managers, customers, suppliers, debt holders, communities, government, and others.

'Taking care of the stakeholders' is an extremely useful way of looking at a firm's concerns. In a profit-making organization, the proverbial bottom line becomes an important objective; but it can also become a dangerous trap. Managers must guard against looking at short-term profitability as the ultimate driving force. Sustained profitability is the legitimate and deserved reward of a job well done – one that emanates from being responsible to a firm's remaining stakeholders.

Toward a Unified Concept of Strategy

The concept of strategy embraces the overall purpose of an organization. It is not surprising, therefore, that defining it properly means examining the many facets that make up the whole. By combining them, we arrive at a more comprehensive definition of strategy.

From this unifying point of view, strategy becomes a fundamenatal framework through which an organization can assert its vital continuity, while at the same time purposefully managing its adaptation to the changing environment to gain competitive advantage. Strategy includes the formal recognition that the recipients of the results of a firm's actions are the wide constituency of its stakeholders. Therefore, the ultimate objective of strategy is to address stakeholders' benefits – to provide a base for establishing the host of transactions and social contracts that link a firm to its stakeholders.

1.3   The Evaluation of Business Strategy

By Richard Rumelt[1]

Strategy can neither be formulated nor adjusted to changing circumstances without a process of strategy evaluation. Whether performed by an individual or as part of an organizational review procedure, strategy evaluation forms an essential step in the process of guiding an enterprise.

For many executives strategy evaluation is simply an appraisal of how well a business performs. Has it grown? Is the profit rate normal or better? If the answers to these questions are affirmative, it is argued that the firm's strategy must be sound. Despite its unassailable simplicity, this line of reasoning misses the whole point of strategy – that the critical factors determining the quality of current results are often not directly observable or simply measured, and that by the time strategic opportunities or threats do directly affect operating results, it may well be too late for an effective response. Thus, strategy evaluation is an attempt to look beyond the obvious facts regarding the short-term health of a business and appraise instead those more fundamental factors and trends that govern success in the chosen field of endeavor.

The Challenge of Evaluation

However it is accomplished, the products of a business strategy evaluation are answers to these three questions:

1   Are the objectives of the business appropriate?

2   Are the major policies and plans appropriate?

3   Do the results obtained to date confirm or refute critical assumptions on which the strategy rests?

Devising adequate answers to these questions is neither simple nor straightforward. It requires a reasonable store of situation-based knowledge and more than the usual degree of insight. In particular, the major issues that make evaluation difficult and with which the analyst must come to grips are these:

■   Each business strategy is unique. For example, one paper manufacturer might rely on its vast timber holdings to weather almost any storm while another might place primary reliance in modern machinery and an

---

[1] Source: This article was originally published in *Business Policy and Strategic Management*, edited by W.F. Glueck (McGraw-Hill, 1980). Reproduced with permission.

extensive distribution system. Neither strategy is wrong or right in any absolute sense; both may be right or wrong for the firms in question. Strategy evaluation must, then, rest on a type of situational logic that does not focus on one best way that can be tailored to each problem as it is faced.

■ Strategy is centrally concerned with the selection of goals and objectives. Many people, including seasoned executives, find it much easier to set or try to achieve goals than to evaluate them. In part this is a consequence of training in problem structuring. It also arises out of a tendency to confuse *values*, which are fundamental expressions of human personality, with objectives, which are *devices* for lending coherence to action.

■ Formal systems of strategic review, while appealing in principle, can create explosive conflict situations. Not only are there serious questions as to who is qualified to give an objective evaluation, the whole idea of strategy evaluation implies management by 'much more than results' and runs counter to much of currently popular management philosophy.

The Principles of Strategy Evaluation

For our purposes a strategy is a set of objectives, policies, and plans that taken together define the scope of the enterprise and its approach to survival and success. Alternatively, we could say that the particular policies, plans, and objectives of a business express its strategy for coping with a complex competitive environment.

One of the fundamental tenets of science is that a theory can never be proven to be absolutely true. A theory can, however, be declared absolutely false if it fails to stand up to testing. Similarly, it is impossible to demonstrate conclusively that a particular business strategy is optimal or even to guarantee that it will work. One can, nevertheless, test it for critical flaws. Of the many tests that could justifiably be applied to a business strategy, most will fit within one of these broad criteria:

■ *Consistency*. The strategy must not present mutually inconsistent goals and policies.

■ *Consonance*. The strategy must represent an adaptive response to the external environment and to the critical changes occurring within it.

■ *Advantage*. The strategy must provide for the creation and/or maintenance of a competitive advantage in the selected area of activity.

■ *Feasibility*. The strategy must neither overtax available resources nor create unsolvable subproblems.

A strategy that fails to meet one or more of these criteria is strongly suspect. It fails to perform at least one of the key functions that are necessary for the survival of the business. Experience within a particular industry or other setting will permit the analyst to sharpen these criteria and add others that are appropriate to the situation at hand.

Consistency

Gross inconsistency within a strategy seems unlikely until it is realized that many strategies have not been explicitly formulated but have evolved over time in an *ad hoc* fashion. Even strategies that are the result of formal procedures may easily contain compromise arrangements between opposing power groups.

Inconsistency in strategy is not simply a flaw in logic. A key function of strategy is to provide coherence to organizational action. A clear and explicit concept of strategy can foster a climate of tacit coordination that is more efficient than most administrative mechanisms. Many high-technology firms, for example, face a basic strategic choice between offering high-cost products with high custom-engineering content and lower-cost products that are more standardized and sold at higher volume. If senior management does not enunciate a clear, consistent sense of where the corporation stands on these issues, there will be continuing conflict between sales, design, engineering, and manufacturing people. A clear, consistent strategy, by contrast, allows a sales engineer to negotiate a contract with a minimum of coordination – the trade-offs are an explicit part of the firm's posture.

Organizational conflict and interdepartmental bickering are often symptoms of a managerial disorder but may also indicate problems of strategic inconsistency. Here are some indicators that can help sort out these two different problems:

- If problems in coordination and planning continue despite changes in personnel and tend to be issue rather than people based, they are probably due to inconsistencies in strategy.

- If success for one organizational department means, or is interpreted to mean, failure for another department, the basic objective structure is inconsistent.

- If, despite attempts to delegate authority, operating problems continue to be brought to the top for the resolution of *policy* issues, the basic strategy is probably inconsistent.

A final type of consistency that must be sought in strategy is between organizational objectives and the values of the management group. Inconsistency in this area is more of a problem in strategy formulation than in the evaluation of a strategy that has already been implemented. It can still arise, however, if the future direction of the business requires changes that conflict with managerial values. The most frequent source of such conflict is growth. As a business expands beyond the scale that allows an easy informal method of operation, many executives experience a sharp sense of loss. While growth can of course be curtailed, it often will require special attention to a firm's competitive position if survival without growth is desired. The same basic issues arise when other types of personal or social values come into conflict with existing or apparently necessary policies: the resolution of the conflict will normally require an adjustment in the competitive strategy.

Consonance

The way in which a business relates to its environment has two aspects: the business must both match and be adapted to its environment and it must at the same time compete with other firms that are also trying to adapt. This dual character of the relationship between the firm and its evironment has its analog in two different aspects of strategic choice and two different methods of strategy evaluation.

The first aspect of fit deals with the basic mission or scope of the business and the second with its special competitive position or 'edge.' Analysis of the first is normally done by looking at changing economic and social conditions over time. Analysis of the second, by contrast, typically focuses on the differences across firms at a given time. We call the first the generic aspect of strategy and the second, competitive strategy. Table 1.3.1 summarizes the differences between these concepts.

The notion of consonance, or matching, therefore, invites a focus on generic strategy. The role of the evaluator in this case is to examine the basic pattern of economic relationships that characterize the business and determine whether or not sufficient value is being created to sustain the strategy. Most macroanalysis of changing economic conditions is oriented toward the formulation or evaluation of generic strategies. For example, a planning department forecasts that within 10 years home appliances will no longer use mechanical timers or logic. Instead, microprocessors will do the job more reliably and less expensively. The basic message here for the makers of mechanical timers is that their generic strategies are becoming obsolete, especially if they specialize in major home appliances. Note that the threat in this case is not to a particular firm, competitive position, or individual approach to the marketplace but to the basic generic mission.

TABLE 1.3.1
Generic versus competitive strategy

	Generic	Competitive
Measure of success	Sales growth	Market Share
Return to the firm	Value added	Return on investment
Function	Provision of value to the customer	Maintaining or obtaining a defensible position
Basic strategic tasks	Adapting to change and innovation	Creating barriers and deterring rivals
Method of expressing strategy	Product/market terms, functional terms	Policies leading to defensible position
Basic approach to analysis	Study of group of businesses over time	Comparison across rivals at a given time

One major difficulty in evaluating consonance is that most of the critical threats to a business are those that come from without, threatening an entire group of firms. Management, however, is often so engrossed in competitive thinking that such threats are only recognized after the damage has reached considerable proportions.

The key to evaluating consonance is an understanding of why the business, as it currently stands, exists at all and how it assumed its current pattern. Once the analyst obtains a good grasp of the basic economic foundation that supports and defines the business, it is possible to study the consequences of key trends and changes. Without such an understanding, there is no good way of deciding what kinds of changes are most crucial, and the analyst can quickly be overwhelmed with data.

Advantage

It is no exaggeration to say that competitive strategy is the art of creating or exploiting those advantages that are most telling, enduring, and most difficult to duplicate.

Competitive strategy, in contrast to generic strategy, focuses on the differences among firms rather than their common missions. The problem it addresses is not so much, 'How can this function be performed?' but 'How can *we* perform it either better than, or at least instead of our rivals?' The chain supermarket, for example, represents a successful generic strategy. As a way of doing business, of organizing economic transactions, it has replaced almost all the smaller owner-managed food shops of an earlier era. Yet a potential or actual participant in the retail food business must go beyond this generic strategy and find a way of competing in the business. As another illustration, American Motors' early success in compact cars was generic – other firms soon copied the basic product concept. Once this happened, AMC had to try to either forge a strong competitive strategy in this area or seek a different type of competitive arena. Competitive advantages can normally be traced to one of three roots:

- superior resources;

- superior skills;

- superior position.

The advantages produced by the first two are obvious. They represent the ability of a business to do more and/or do it better than its rivals. The critical analytical issue here is the question of which skills and resources represent advantages in which competitive arenas. The skills that make for success in the aerospace electronics industry, for instance, do not seem to have much to do with those needed in consumer electronics. Similarly, what makes for success in the early phases of an industry life cycle may be quite different from what ensures top performance in the later phases.

The idea that certain arrangements of one's resources can enhance their combined effectiveness, and perhaps even put rival forces in a state of disarray, is at the heart of the traditional notion of strategy. This kind of 'positional' advantage is familiar to military theorists, chess players, and diplomats. Position plays a crucial role in business strategy as well.

Positional advantage can be gained by foresight, superior skill and/or resources, or just plain luck. Once gained, a good position is defensible. This means that it (a) returns enough value to warrant its continued maintenance and (b) would be so costly to capture that rivals are deterred from full-scale attacks on the core of the business. Position, it must be noted, tends to be self-sustaining as long as the basic environmental factors that underlie it remain stable. Thus entrenched firms can be almost impossible to unseat even if their raw skill levels are only average. And when a shifting environment allows position to be gained by a new entrant or innovator, the results can be spectacular.

The types of positional advantage that are most well known are those associated with size or scale. As the scale of operations increases, most firms are able to reduce both the marginal and the total cost of each additional unit produced. Marginal costs fall due to the effects of learning and more efficient processes, and total costs per unit fall even faster as fixed overheads are spread over a larger volume of activity. The larger firm can simply take these gains in terms of increased profitability or it can invest some of the extra returns in position-maintaining activities. By engaging in more research and development, being first to go abroad, having the largest advertising budget, and absorbing the costs involved with acting as an industry spokesman, the dominant business is rechanneling the gains obtained from its advantages into activities designed to maintain those advantages. This kind of positive feedback is the source of the power of position-based advantages – the policies that act to enhance position do not require unusual skills; they simply work most effectively for those who are already in the position in the first place.

While it is not true that larger businesses always have the advantages, it is true that larger businesses will tend to operate in markets and use procedures that turn their size to advantage. Large national consumer-products firms, for example, will normally have an advantage over smaller regional firms in the efficient use of mass advertising, especially network TV. The larger firm will, then, tend to deal in those products where the marginal effect of advertising is most potent, while the smaller firms will seek product-market positions that exploit other types of advantage.

Not all positional advantages are associated with size, although some type of uniqueness is a virtual prerequisite. The principal characteristic of good position is that it permits the firm to obtain advantage from policies that would not similarly benefit rivals without the position. For example, Volkswagen in 1966 had a strong, well-defined position as the preeminent maker of inexpensive, well-engineered, functional automobiles. This position allowed it to follow a policy of not changing its body styling. The policy both enhanced VW's position and reduced costs. Rivals could not similarly benefit from such a policy unless they could also duplicate the other aspects of VW's position. At the other end of the spectrum, Rolls-Royce employed a policy of deliberately limiting its output, a policy that enhanced its unique position and that could do so only because of its position in the first place. Mintzberg calls strongly defensible positions and the associated policies 'gestalt strategies,' recognizing that they are difficult either to analyze or attack in a piecemeal fashion.

Another type of positional advantage derives from successful trade names. These brands, especially when advertised, place retailers in the position of having to stock them, which in turn reinforces the position and raises the barrier to entry still further. Such famous names as Sara Lee, Johnson & Johnson, and Kraft greatly reduce, for their holders, both the problems of gaining wide distribution for new products and obtaining trial use of new products by the buying public.

Other position-based advantages follow from such factors as:

- Owning special raw material sources or long-term supply contracts.

- Being geographically located near key customers in a business involving significant fixed investment and high transport costs.

- Being a leader in a service field that permits or requires the building of a unique experience base while serving clients.

- Being a full-line producer in a market with heavy trade-up phenomena.

- Having a wide reputation for providing a needed product or service reliably and dependably.

In each case, the position permits competitive policies to be adopted that can serve to reinforce the position. Whenever this type of positive-feedback phenomena is encountered, the particular policy mix that creates it will be found to be a defensible business position. The key factors that sparked industrial success stories such as IBM and Eastman Kodak were the early and rapid domination of strong positions opened up by new technologies.

Feasibility

The final broad test of strategy is its feasibility. Can the strategy be attempted within the physical, human, and financial resources available? The financial resources of a business are the easiest to quantify and are normally the first limitation against which strategy is tested. It is sometimes forgotten, however, that innovative approaches to financing expansion can both stretch the ultimate limitations and provide a competitive advantage, even if it is only temporary. Devices such as captive finance subsidiaries, sale-leaseback arrangements, and tying plant mortgages to long-term contracts have all been used effectively to help win key positions in suddenly expanding industries.

The less quantifiable but actually more rigid limitation on strategic choice is that imposed by the individual and organizational capabilities available.

In assessing the organization's ability to carry out a strategy, it is helpful to ask three separate questions.

1   Has the organization demonstrated that it possesses the problem-solving abilities and/or special competences required by the strategy? A strategy, as

such, does not and cannot specify in detail each action that must be carried out. Its purpose is to provide structure to the general issue of the business's goals and approaches to coping with its environment. It is up to the members and departments of the organization to carry out the tasks defined by strategy. A strategy that requires tasks to be accomplished that fall outside the realm of available or easily obtainable skill and knowledge cannot be accepted. It is either infeasible or incomplete.

2   Has the organization demonstrated the degree of coordinative and integrative skill necessary to carry out the strategy? The key tasks required of a strategy not only require specialized skill, but often make considerable demands on the organization's ability to integrate disparate activities.

3   Does the strategy challenge and motivate key personnel, and is it acceptable to those who must lend their support? The purpose of strategy is to effectively deploy the unique and distinctive resources of an enterprise. If key managers are unmoved by a strategy, not excited by its goals or methods, or strongly support an alternative, it fails in a major way.

Conclusions

In most medium- to large-size firms, strategy evaluation is not a purely intellectual task. The issues involved are too important and too closely associated with the distribution of power and authority for either strategy formulation or evaluation to take place in an ivory tower environment. In fact, most firms rarely engage in explicit formal strategy evaluation. Rather, the evaluation of current strategy is a continuing process and one that is difficult to separate from the normal planning, reporting, control, and reward systems of the firm. From this point of view, strategy evaluation is not so much an intellectual task as it is an organizational process.

As process, strategy evaluation is the outcome of activities and events that are strongly shaped by the firm's control and reward systems, its information and planning systems, its structure, and its history and particular culture. Thus its performance is, in practice, tied more directly to the quality of the firm's strategic management than to any particular analytical scheme. In particular, organizing major units around the primary strategic tasks and making the extra effort required to incorporate measures of strategic success in the control system may play vital roles in facilitating strategy evaluation within the firm.

Ultimately, a firm's ability to maintain its competitive position in a world of rivalry and change may be best served by managers who can maintain a dual view of strategy and strategy evaluation – they must be willing and able to perceive the strategy within the welter of daily activity *and* to build and maintain structures and systems that make strategic factors the object of current activity.

1.4 Complexity: The Nature of Real World Problems

By Richard Mason and Ian Mitroff[1]

Try a little experiment. Make a short list of the major problems or issues facing policymakers in the world today. Now take your list and arrange it as a matrix like the one in Figure 1.4.1. For each element in the matrix ask yourself the following question: Is the solution to one problem (the row problem) in any way related to the solution of the other problem (the column problem)? If the answer is yes, place a check mark at the point where the row and column intersect; otherwise leave it blank. When you have completed the process, review the matrix and count the number of blanks. Are there any?

'No fair!' you may say. 'There were a lot of check marks in my matrix because many of these world problems are linked together.' World problems involve all nations. One would not expect to get the same result if the focus was, say, on one's company, city, family, or personal life. Really? Try it and

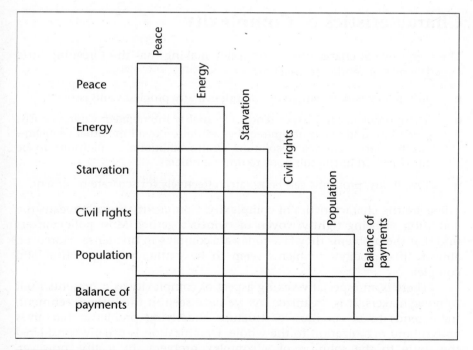

FIGURE 1.4.1
Problem interaction matrix

[1] Source: This article was adapted with permission from chapter 1 of *Challenging Strategic Planning Assumptions*, Wiley, New York, 1981.

see. Recently, several managers at a major corporation tried this little experiment as part of a strategic planning effort. Among the issues and problem areas they identified were the following:

- Satisfy stockholder dividend and risk requirements.
- Acquire adequate funds for expansion from the capital markets.
- Insure a stable supply of energy at reasonable prices.
- Train a corps of middle managers to assume more responsibility.
- Develop a marketing force capable of handling new product lines.

The managers found that all of these problems and issues were related to each other. Some were only related weakly, but most were related quite strongly. Repeated attempts in other contexts give the same result: *basically, every real world policy problem is related to every other real world problem*. This is an important finding. It means that every time a policymaker attempts to solve a particular policy problem he or she must consider its potential relationship with all other problems. To do this one must have both a comprehensive set of concepts for dealing with any policy and a rich set of tools for acquiring the holistic information needed to guide policy making.

Characteristics of Complexity

There are several characteristics of policy making that the foregoing little experiment is intended to illustrate:

- Any policy-making situation comprises many problems and issues.
- These problems and issues tend to be highly interrelated. Consequently, the solution to one problem requires a solution to all the other problems. At the same time, each solution creates additional dimensions to be incorporated in the solutions to other problems.
- Few, if any, problems can be isolated effectively for separate treatment.

These are the characteristics of complexity. Complexity literally means the condition of being tightly woven or twined together. Most policymakers find that the problems they face today are complex in this sense. Moreover, almost all of today's problems seem to be getting more plentiful and complex.

There is an especially vexing aspect of complexity as it presents itself to policymakers. It is organized. As we have seen in the little experiment, there tends to be an illusive structure underlying problems that gives pattern and organization to the whole. Organization is usually considered the route to the solution of a complex problem. In reality, however, organization in complexity can become an insurmountable barrier to the solution of a problem. This is the major challenge to real world problem solving because we have very few intellectual tools for coping with 'organized complexity.'

The tools we have available seem to work best on simple problems, those that can be separated and reduced to relatively few variables and relationships. These problems of simplicity usually have a one-dimensional value system or goal structure that guides the solution. Three factors – separability, reducibility, and one-dimensional goal structure – mean that simple problems can be bounded, managed, and, as Horst Rittel (1972) puts it, 'tamed.'

Ironically, problems of the utmost complexity can also be tamed as long as the complexity is 'disorganized.' That is, whenever the number of variables is very large and the variables are relatively disconnected, the problem can be tamed with the elegant simplicity of statistical mechanics. For example, there is no known way of predicting how a given individual will vote on a political candidate. However, using polling procedures and statistical techniques it is possible to predict with a fair degree of confidence how an entire population of voters will vote. Similarly, it is difficult to predict whether a given customer will purchase a new product or not. However, using market research methods, a fairly good estimate can be made of a new product's potential market share.

Perhaps one of the greatest insights of the twentieth century is the discovery that when a problem situation meets the condition for random sampling – many individual elements exhibiting independent, probabilistic behavior – there is a potential statistical solution to the problem. In short, disorganized complexity can generally be tamed by statistical means.

One place where the assumption of disorganized complexity has proven invaluable in the past is in the actuarial sciences. Today, however, the insurance industry is discovering that many of the risks once assumed to be reasonably independent and hence analyzable according to standard actuarial methods are no longer so. People, organizations, and facilities have become more tightly woven together over wider geographical areas. Consequently, the probabilities of death, accident, fire, or disaster on which the risks and premiums are based are no longer as straightforward as they once were. The result is that the statistical methods that applied under conditions of disorganized complexity have become less reliable as the system has become more organized.

The great difficulty with connected systems of organized complexity is that deviations in one element can be transmitted to other elements. In turn, these deviations can be magnified, modified, and reverberated so that the system takes on a kind of unpredictable life of its own. Emery and Trist (1965) refer to this condition as 'environmental connectedness' and have labeled this type of environment the 'turbulent' environment.

Emery and Trist cite an interesting case to illustrate the nature of environmental connectedness and the great difficulties it presents to policy makers. In Great Britain after World War II, a large food canning company began to expand. Its main product was a canned vegetable – a staple in the English diet. As part of the expansion plan, the company decided to build a new, automated factory, requiring an investment of several million pounds sterling. For over a decade the company had enjoyed a 65 percent market share for their product line and saw no reason for this strong market position to deteriorate. Given this large volume, the new plant offered the 'experience curve' advantages of economies to scale and made possible the long production runs required to meet the demand from the traditional market.

After ground was broken, but well before the factory was completed, a series of seemingly detached and isolated socioeconomic events occurred. These relatively insignificant events were to change the destiny of the company. Taken collectively, they rendered the factory economically obsolete and threw the corporate board of directors into a state of turmoil. The scenario of events went something like this. Due to the release of wartime controls on steel strip and tin, a number of new small firms that could economically can imported fruit sprang up. Initially, they in no way competed directly with the large vegetable canner. However, since their business was seasonal, they began to look for ways to keep their machinery and labor employed during the winter. Their answer came from a surprising source – the US quick-frozen food industry. The quick-freezing process requires a substantial degree of consistency in the crop. This consistency is very difficult to achieve. However, it turned out that large crops of the vegetable were grown in the United States and a substantial portion of US crops was unsuitable for quick freezing (a big industry in the United States) but quite suitable for canning. Furthermore, American farmers had been selling this surplus crop at a very low price for animal feed and were only too happy to make it available at an attractive price to the small canners in the United Kingdom. The canners jumped at the opportunity and imported the crop. Using off-season production capacity they began to offer a low-cost product in the large canner's market. The small canners' position was further strengthened as underdeveloped countries began to vie with the United States in an effort to become the cheapest source of supply for the crop.

These untimely events in the large canner's supply market were compounded by events in its product market. Prior to the introduction of quick-freezing, the company featured a high quality, higher price premier brand that dominated the market. This market advantage, however, was diminished by the cascading effect of several more unpredictable events. As the scenario unfolded the quick-frozen product captured the high quality strata of the market, a growing dimension due to increased affluence. The smaller canners stripped off the lower price layers of the market, aided in part by another seemingly unrelated development in retailing – the advent of supermarkets. As supermarkets and large grocery chains developed, they sought to improve their position by establishing their own in-house brand names and by buying in bulk. The small canner filled this need for the supermarket chains. Small canners could undercut the price of the manufacturer's brand product because they had low production costs and almost no marketing expenses. Soon supermarket house brands (which had accounted for less than 1 percent of the market prior to the war) became the source of 50 percent of the market sales. The smaller canners were the benefactors of almost all of this growth.

As a result, the company's fancy new automated factory was totally inappropriate for the current market situation. The company's management had failed to appreciate that a number of outside events were becoming connected with each other in a way that was leading up to an inevitable general change. They tried desperately to defend their traditional product lines, but, in the end, this was to no avail. After a series of financial setbacks, the company had to change its mission. It reemerged several years later with a new product mix and a new identity. Management had learned the hard way that their strategy problems were neither problems of simplicity nor problems of disorganized complexity. They were problems of organized complexity.

Many corporate policy planning and strategy issues exhibit this property of organized complexity. The vegetable canning company's automated plant decision clearly was made under conditions of organized complexity. Pricing problems also frequently display this characteristic. Recently, a large pharmaceutical firm addressed the seemingly simple problem of setting a price for its primary drug line. The company's management soon learned, however, that there was an intricate web of corporate relationships woven around this one decision. Below the surface there was a structure of complex relationships between the firm's drug pricing policy and physicians, pharmacists, patients, competitors, suppliers, the FDA, and other parties. These relationships organized the complexity of the firm's pricing decision problem. Purely analytical or statistical methods were rendered inappropriate.

'Wicked' Problems

Today, few of the pressing problems are truly problems of simplicity or of disorganized complexity. They are more like the problems described in the illustrative cases above and the ones we uncovered in our little experiment – problems of organized complexity. These problems simply cannot be tamed in the same way that other problems can. For this reason Rittle refers to these problems of organized complexity as 'wicked' problems. Wicked problems are not necessarily wicked in the perverse sense of being evil. Rather, they are wicked like the head of a hydra. They are an ensnarled web of tentacles. The more you attempt to tame them, the more complicated they become.

Rittel (1972) has identified several characteristic properties of wicked problems that distinguish them from tame problems. These properties are:

1   *Ability to formulate the problem*

   (a) Tame problems can be exhaustively formulated and written down on a piece of paper.

   (b) Wicked problems have no definitive formulation.

2   *Relationship between problem and solution*

    (a) Tame problems can be formulated separately from any notion of what their solution might be.

    (b) Every formulation of a wicked problem corresponds to a statement of solution and vice versa. Understanding the problem is synonymous with solving it.

3   *Testability*

    (a) The solution to a tame problem can be tested. Either it is correct or it is false. Mistakes and errors can be pinpointed.

    (b) There is no single criteria system or rule that determines whether the solution to a wicked problem is correct or false. Solutions can only be good or bad relative to one another.

4   *Finality*

    (a) Tame problems have closure – a clear solution and ending point. The end can be determined by means of a test.

    (b) There is no stopping rule for wicked problems. Like a Faustian bargain, they require eternal vigilance. There is always room for improvement. Moreover, since there is neither an immediate or ultimate test for the solution to the problem, one never knows when one's work is done. As a result, the potential consequences of the problem are played out indefinitely.

5   *Tractability*

    (a) There is an exhaustive list of permissible operations that can be used to solve a tame problem.

    (b) There is no exhaustive, enumerable list of permissible operations to be used for solving a wicked problem.

6   *Explanatory characteristics*

    (a) A tame problem may be stated as a 'gap' between what 'is' and what 'ought' to be and there is a clear explanation for every gap.

    (b) Wicked problems have many possible explanations for the same discrepancy. Depending on which explanation one chooses, the solution takes on a different form.

7   *Level of analysis*

    (a) Every tame problem has an identifiable, certain, natural form; there is no need to argue about the level of the problem. The proper level of generality can be found for bounding the problem and identifying its root cause.

    (b) Every wicked problem can be considered as a symptom of another problem. It has no identifiable root cause; since curing symptoms does not cure problems, one is never sure the problem is being attacked at the proper level.

8   *Reproducibility*

    (a) A tame problem can be abstracted from the real world, and attempts can be made to solve it over and over again until the correct solution is found.

    (b) Each wicked problem is a one-shot operation. Once a solution is attempted, you can never undo what you have already done. There is no trial and error.

9   *Replicability*

    (a) The same tame problem may repeat itself many times.

    (b) Every wicked problem is essentially unique.

10   *Responsibility*

    (a) No one can be blamed for failing to solve a tame problem, although solving a tame problem may bring someone acclaim.

    (b) The wicked problem solver has 'no right to be wrong.' He is morally responsible for what he is doing and must share the blame when things go wrong. However, since there is no way of knowing when a wicked problem is solved, very few people are praised for grappling with them.

Characteristics of wicked problems   Most policy planning and strategy problems are wicked problems of organized complexity. These complex wicked problems also exhibit the following characteristics:

1   *Interconnectedness.* Strong connections link each problem to other problems. As a result, these connections sometimes circle back to form feedback loops. 'Solutions' aimed at the problem seem inevitably to have important opportunity costs and side effects. How they work out depends on events beyond the scope of any one problem.

2   *Complicatedness.* Wicked problems have numerous important elements with relationships among them, including important 'feedback loops' through which a change tends to multiply itself or perhaps even cancel itself out. Generally, there are various leverage points where analysis and ideas for intervention might focus, as well as many possible approaches and plausible programs of action. There is also a likelihood that different programs should be combined to deal with a given problem.

3   *Uncertainty.* Wicked problems exist in a dynamic and largely uncertain environment, which creates a need to accept risk, perhaps incalculable risk. Contingency planning and also the flexibility to respond to un-imagined and perhaps unimaginable contingencies are both necessary.

4   *Ambiguity.* The problem can be seen in quite different ways, depending on the viewer's personal characteristics, loyalties, past experiences, and even on accidental circumstances of involvement. There is no single 'correct view' of the problem.

5   *Conflict.* Because of competing claims, there is often a need to trade off

'goods' against 'bads' within the same value system. Conflicts of interest among persons or organizations with different or even antagonistic value systems are to be expected. How things will work out may depend on interaction among powerful interests that are unlikely to enter into fully cooperative arrangements.

6   *Societal Constraints.* Social, organizational, and political constraints and capabilities, as well as technological ones, are central both to the feasibility and the desirability of solutions.

These characteristics spell difficulty for the policymaker who seeks to serve a social system by changing it for the better. Policymakers must choose the means for securing improvement for the people they serve. They must design, steer, and maintain a stable social system in the context of a complex environment. To do this, they require new methods of real world problem solving to guide their policy-making activities. Otherwise, they run the risk of setting their social systems adrift.

Implications for policy making   The wicked problems of organized complexity have two major implications for designing processes for making policy:

1   There must be a broader participation of affected parties, directly and indirectly, in the policy-making process.

2   Policy making must be based on a wider spectrum of information gathered from a larger number of diverse sources.

Let us consider each of these implications in turn. The first implication indicates that policy making is increasingly becoming a political process, political in the sense that it involves individuals forming into groups to pursue common interests. Turn again to the results of the little experiment conducted at the outset of this chapter. You will find that in almost every case there are a variety of individual interests at stake in each problem area cited. Furthermore, one of the major factors creating the linkages between problem areas – organizing their complexity – is the number of diverse individual interests that cut across problem areas. Individuals are part of the problem and hence must be part of the solution.

This means that the raw material for forging solutions to wicked problems is not concentrated in a single head, but rather is widely dispersed among the various parties at stake. For any given wicked problem there is a variety of classes of expertise. Every affected party is an expert on some aspect of the problem and its solution. Furthermore, the disparate parties are bound together in a common venture. Thus some form of collective risk sharing is needed in order to deal effectively with the consequences of wicked problems. This suggests the need for a substantial degree of involvement in the policy-making process by those potentially affected by a policy in its formulation process. Effective policy is made *with*, or if adequate representation is present, *for*, but *not at* people. At least those involved should be able to voice their opinion on the relative goodness or badness of proposed solutions.

The diversity of parties at stake is related to the second implication. Since much of the necessary information for coping with wicked problems resides in the heads of several individuals, methods are needed to obtain this information from them and to communicate it to others. This means that as many of the different sources of information as possible must be identified. The relevant information must be obtained from each and stated in an explicit manner.

Contained in the minds of each participant in a wicked problem are powerful notions as to what is, what ought to be, why things are the way they are, how they can be changed, and how to think about their complexity. This represents a much broader class of information than is commonly used to solve problems of simplicity or of disorganized complexity. Also, this participant-based information is less likely to have been stated and recorded in a communicable form. Consequently, this information must be 'objectified' – explicitly, articulated – so that the basis for each party's judgments may be exchanged with others. Objectification has the advantages of being explicit, providing a memory, controlling the delegation of judgments, and raising pertinent issues that might have been ignored otherwise. It also stimulates *doubt*.

To be in doubt about a piece of information is to withhold assent to it. Given the range of diverse information that characterizes a wicked problem, participants in the policy-making process are well advised to develop a healthy respect for the method of doubt. In dealing with problems of organized complexity one should start with Descartes' rule: 'The first precept was never to accept a thing as true until I knew it was such without a single doubt.' This does not mean that one should be a 'nay sayer' or a permanent skeptic. To do so would impede responsible action that must be taken. What it does imply is that one should withhold judgment on things until they have been tested.

All problem-solving methods presuppose some form of guarantor for the correctness of their solutions. Problems of simplicity can be tested and solutions guaranteed by means of repeated solving, just as a theorem is proven in mathematics. This is because simple problems can be stated in closed form. The solutions to problems of disorganized complexity can be guaranteed within some stated confidence interval or degree of risk because the problems are statistical in nature. However, since there are no clearly identifiable correct solutions to problems of organized complexity, neither analytic nor statistical proofs can guarantee results. For solutions to wicked problems, the method of doubt is the best guarantor available.

Dialectics and argumentation are methods of *systematizing* doubt. They entail the processes of

1   making information and its underlying assumptions explicit;

2   raising questions and issues toward which different positions can be taken;

3   gathering evidence and building arguments for and against each position;

4   attempting to arrive at some final conclusion.

Being fundamentally an argumentative process, these four processes are inherent to policy making. For every policy decision there are always at least two alternative choices that can be made. There is an argument for and against each alternative. It is by weighing the pros and cons of each argument that an informed decision can be reached. In policy making these processes of dialectics and argumentation are inescapable.

In addition to the need for participation by a variety of parties and the existence of diverse information sources, two other characteristics of wicked problems should be noted. One is that they must be dealt with in a holistic or synthetic way as well as in an analytic way. Two processes are necessary: to subdivide a complex problem into its elements and to determine the nature of the linkages that give organization to its complexity – the task of analysis; and to understand the problem as a *whole* – the task of synthesis. A critical dimension of wicked problems of organized complexity is that they must ultimately be dealt with in their totality. This calls for holistic thinking. Analysis is only an aid toward reaching a synthesis.

A second characteristic of these problems is that there is some form of latent structure within them. They are organized to some extent. Organization is not an all or nothing phenomenon. Consequently, systems thinking and methods can be used to gain better insight into the structural aspects of wicked problems.

Quest for new methods   The nature and implications of organized complexity suggest some new criteria for the design of real world problem-solving methods. These criteria are:

1   *Participative*. Since the relevant knowledge necessary to solve a complex problem and also the relevant resources necessary to implement the solution are distributed among many individuals, the methods must incorporate the active involvement of groups of people.

2   *Adversarial*. We believe that the best judgment on the assumptions in a complex problem is rendered in the context of opposition. Doubt is the guarantor.

3   *Integrative*. A unified set of assumptions and a coherent plan of action are needed to guide effective policy planning and strategy making. Participation and the adversarial process tend to differentiate and expand the knowledge base. Something else is needed to bring this diverse but relevant knowledge together in the form of a total picture.

4   *Managerial Mind Supporting*. Most problem-solving methods and computer aids focus on 'decision support systems,' that is, on systems that provide guidance for choosing a particular course of action to solve a particular decision problem. Problems of organized complexity, as we have seen, are ongoing, ill structured, and generally 'wicked.' The choice of individual courses of action is only a part of the manager's or policymaker's need. More important is the need to achieve insight into the nature of the complexity and to formulate concepts and world views for coping with it. It is the policymaker's thinking process and his or her mind that needs to be supported.

1.5 Cultural Constraints in Management Theories

By Geert Hofstede[1]

Lewis Carroll's *Alice in Wonderland* contains the famous story of Alice's croquet game with the Queen of Hearts. Alice thought she had never seen such a curious croquet-ground in all her life; it was all ridges and furrows; the balls were live hedgehogs, the mallets live flamingoes, and the soldiers had to double themselves up and to stand on their hands and feet to make the arches. You probably know how the story goes: Alice's flamingo mallet turns its head whenever she wants to strike with it; her hedgehog ball runs away; and the doubled-up soldier arches walk around all the time. The only rule seems to be that the Queen of Hearts always wins.

Alice's croquet playing problems are good analogies to attempts to build culture-free theories of management. Concepts available for this purpose are themselves alive with culture, having been developed within a particular cultural context. They have a tendency to guide our thinking toward our desired conclusion. As the same reasoning may also be applied to the arguments in this reading, I better tell you my conclusion before I continue – so that the rules of my game are understood. In this reading we take a trip around the world to demonstrate that there are no such things as universal management theories.

Diversity in management *practices* as we go around the world has been recognized in US management literature for more than 30 years. The term 'comparative management' has been used since the 1960s. However, it has taken much longer for the US academic community to accept that not only practices but also the validity of theories may stop at national borders, and I wonder whether even today everybody would agree with this statement.

The idea that the validity of a theory is constrained by national borders is more obvious in Europe, with all its borders, than in a huge borderless country like the US. Already in the sixteenth century Michel de Montaigne, a Frenchman, wrote a statement which was made famous by Blaise Pascal about a century later; '*Vérite en-deça des Pyrenées, erreur au-delà*' – 'There are truths on this side of the Pyrenées which are falsehoods on the other.'

---

[1] Source: This article was adapted with permission from Cultural Constraints in Management Theories, *Academy of Management Executive*, vol. 7 No. 1, 1993.

From Don Armado's Love to Taylor's Science

According to the comprehensive ten-volume Oxford English Dictionary, the words 'manage,' 'management,' and 'manager' appeared in the English language in the 16th century. The oldest recorded use of the word 'manager' is in Shakespeare's *Love's Labour's Lost*, dating from 1588, in which Don Adriano de Armado, 'a fantastical Spaniard,' exclaims (Act I scene ii. 188): 'Adieu, valour! rust, rapier! be still, drum! for your manager is in love; yea, he loveth'.

The linguistic origin of the word is from Latin *manus*, hand, via the Italian *maneggiare*, which is the training of horses in the manege; subsequently its meaning was extended to skillful handling in general, like of arms and musical instruments, as Don Armado illustrates. However, the word also became associated with the French *menage*, household, as an equivalent of 'husbandry' in its sense of the art of running a household. The theater of present-day management contains elements of both *manege* and *menage* and different managers and cultures may use different accents.

The founder of the science of economics, the Scot Adam Smith, in his 1776 book *The Wealth of Nations*, used 'manage,' 'management' (even 'bad management') and 'manager' when dealing with the process and the persons involved in operating joint stock companies. British economist John Stuart Mill (1806–1873) followed Smith in this use and clearly expressed his distrust of such hired people who were not driven by ownership. Since the 1880s the word 'management' appeared occasionally in writings by American engineers, until it was canonized as a modern science by Frederick W. Taylor in *Shop Management* in 1903 and in *The Principles of Scientific Management* in 1911.

While Smith and Mill used 'management' to describe a process and 'managers' for the persons involved, 'management' in the American sense – which has since been taken back by the British – refers not only to the process but also to the managers as a class of people. This class (1) does not own a business but sells its skills to act on behalf of the owners and (2) does not produce personally but is indispensable for making others produce, through motivation. Members of this class carry a high status and many American boys and girls aspire to the role. In the US, the manager is a cultural hero.

Let us now turn to other parts of the world. We will look at management in its context in other successful modern economies: Germany, Japan, France, Holland, and among the Overseas Chinese. Then we will examine management in the much larger part of the world that is still poor, especially South-East Asia and Africa, and in the new political configurations of Eastern Europe, and Russia in particular. We will then return to the US via mainland China.

Germany

The manager is not a cultural hero in Germany. If anybody, it is the engineer who fills the hero role. Frederick Taylor's scientific management was conceived in a society of immigrants – where a large number of workers with diverse backgrounds and skills had to work together. In Germany this heterogeneity never existed.

Elements of the mediaeval guild system have survived in historical continuity in Germany until the present day. In particular, a very effective apprenticeship system exists both on the shop floor and in the office, which alternates practical work and classroom courses. At the end of the apprenticeship the worker receives a certificate, the *Facharbeiterbrief*, which is recognized throughout the country. About two thirds of the German worker population holds such a certificate and a corresponding occupational pride. In fact, quite a few German company presidents have worked their way up from the ranks through an apprenticeship. In comparison, two thirds of the worker population in Britain have no occupational qualification at all.

The highly skilled and responsible German workers do not necessarily need a manager, American-style, to 'motivate' them. They expect their boss or Meister to assign their tasks and to be the expert in resolving technical problems. Comparisons of similar German, British, and French organizations show the Germans as having the highest rate of personnel in productive roles and the lowest both in leadership and staff roles.

Japan

The American type of manager is also missing in Japan. In the United States, the core of the enterprise is the managerial class. The core of the Japanese enterprise is the permanent worker group; workers who for all practical purposes are tenured and who aspire at life-long employment. They are distinct from the non-permanent employees – most women and sub-contracted teams led by gang bosses, to be laid off in slack periods. University graduates in Japan first join the permanent worker group and subsequently fill various positions, moving from line to staff as the need occurs while paid according to seniority rather than position. They take part in Japanese-style group consultation sessions for important decisions, which extend the decision-making period but guarantee fast implementation afterwards. Japanese are to a large extent controlled by their peer group rather than by their manager.

American theories of leadership are ill-suited for the Japanese group-controlled situation. During the past two decades, the Japanese have developed their own 'PM' theory of leadership, in which P stands for performance and M for maintenance. The latter is less a concern for individual employees than for maintaining social stability. In view of the amazing success of the Japanese economy in the past 30 years, many Americans have sought for the secrets of Japanese management hoping to copy them.

France

The manager, US style, does not exist in France either. The French researcher Philippe d'Iribarne (1990) identifies three kinds of basic principles (*logiques*) of management. In the USA, the principle is the *fair contract* between employer and employee, which gives the manager considerable prerogatives, but within its limits. This is really a labor market in which the worker sells his or her labor for a price. In France, the principle is the *honor* of each class in a society which has always been and remains extremely stratified, in which superiors behave as superior beings and subordinates accept and expect this, conscious of their own lower level in the national hierarchy but also of the honor of their own class. The French do not think in terms of managers versus nonmanagers but in terms of *cadres* versus *non-cadres*; one becomes cadre by attending the proper schools and one remains it forever; regardless of their actual task, cadres have the privileges of a higher social class, and it is very rare for a non-cadre to cross the ranks.

The conflict between French and American theories of management became apparent in the beginning of the twentieth century, in a criticism by the great French management pioneer Henri Fayol (1841–1925) on his US colleague and contemporary Frederick W. Taylor (1856–1915). Fayol was a French engineer whose career as a cadre supérieur culminated in the position of *Président-Directeur-Général* of a mining company. After his retirement he formulated his experiences in a pathbreaking text on organization: *Administration industrielle et générale*, in which he focused on the sources of authority. Taylor was an American engineer who started his career in industry as a worker and attained his academic qualifications through evening studies. From chief engineer in a steel company he became one of the first management consultants. Taylor was not really concerned with the issue of authority at all; his focus was on efficiency. He proposed to split the task of the first-line boss into eight specialisms, each exercised by a different person; an idea which eventually led to the idea of a matrix organization.

Taylor's work appeared in a French translation in 1913, and Fayol read it and showed himself generally impressed but shocked by Taylor's 'denial of the principle of the Unity of Command' in the case of the eight-boss-system. Seventy years later André Laurent, another of Fayol's compatriots, found that French managers in a survey reacted very strongly against a suggestion that one employee could report to two different bosses, while US managers in the same survey showed fewer misgivings. Matrix organization has never become popular in France as it has in the United States.

Holland

In my own country, Holland or as it is officially called, the Netherlands, the study by Philippe d'Iribarne found the management principle to be a need for consensus among all parties, neither predetermined by a contractual relationship nor by class distinctions, but based on an open-ended exchange of views and a balancing of interests. In terms of the different origins of the word 'manager,' the organization in Holland is more menage (household) while in the United States it is more manege (horse drill).

At my university, the University of Limburg at Maastricht, we asked both the Americans and a matched group of Dutch students to describe their ideal job after graduation, using a list of 22 job characteristics. The Americans attached significantly more importance than the Dutch to earnings, advancement, benefits, a good working relationship with their boss, and security of employment. The Dutch attached more importance to freedom to adopt their own approach to the job, being consulted by their boss in his or her decisions, training opportunities, contributing to the success of their organization, fully using their skills and abilities, and helping others. This list confirms d'Iribarne's findings of a contractual employment relationship in the United States, based on earnings and career opportunities, against a consensual relationship in Holland. The latter has centuries-old roots, the Netherlands were the first republic in Western Europe (1609–1810), and a model for the American republic. The country has been and still is governed by a careful balancing of interests in a multi-party system.

In terms of management theories, both motivation and leadership in Holland are different from what they are in the United States. Leadership in Holland presupposes modesty, as opposed to assertiveness in the United States. No US leadership theory has room for that. Working in Holland is not a constant feast, however. There is a built-in premium on mediocrity and jealousy, as well as time-consuming ritual consultations to maintain the appearance of consensus and the pretense of modesty. There is unfortunately another side to every coin.

The Overseas Chinese

Among the champions of economic development in the past 30 years we find three countries mainly populated by Chinese living outside the Chinese mainland: Taiwan, Hong Kong and Singapore. Moreover, overseas Chinese play a very important role in the economies of Indonesia, Malaysia, the Philippines and Thailand, where they form an ethnic minority. If anything, the little dragons – Taiwan, Hong Kong and Singapore – have been more economically successful than Japan, moving from rags to riches and now counted among the world's wealthy industrial countries. Yet very little attention has been paid to the way in which their enterprises have been managed.

Overseas Chinese enterprises lack almost all characteristics of modern management. They tend to be small, cooperating for essential functions with other small organizations through networks based on personal relations. They are family-owned, without the separation between ownership and management typical in the West, or even in Japan and Korea. They normally focus on one product or market, with growth by opportunistic diversification; in this, they are extremely flexible. Decision making is centralized in the hands of one dominant family member, but other family members may be given new ventures to try their skills on. They are low-profile and extremely cost-conscious, applying Confucian virtues of thrift and persistence. Their size is kept small by the assumed lack of loyalty of non-family employees, who, if they are any good, will just wait and save until they can start their own family business.

Overseas Chinese prefer economic activities in which great gains can be made with little manpower, like commodity trading and real estate. They employ few professional managers, except their sons and sometimes daughters who have been sent to prestigious business schools abroad, but who upon return continue to run the family business the Chinese way.

The origin of this system, or – in the Western view – this lack of system, is found in the history of Chinese society, in which there were no formal laws, only formal networks of powerful people guided by general principles of Confucian virtue. The favors of the authorities could change daily, so nobody could be trusted except one's kinfolk – of whom, fortunately, there used to be many, in an extended family structure. The overseas Chinese way of doing business is also very well adapted to their position in the countries in which they form ethnic minorities, often envied and threatened by ethnic violence.

Overseas Chinese businesses following this unprofessional approach command a collective gross national product of some 200 to 300 billion US dollars, exceeding the GNP of Australia. There is no denying that it works.

Management Transfer to Poor Countries

Four-fifths of the world population live in countries that are not rich but poor. After World War II and decolonization, the stated purpose of the United Nations and the World Bank has been to promote the development of all the world's countries in a war on poverty. After 40 years it looks very much like we are losing this war. If one thing has become clear, it is that the export of Western – mostly American – management practices and theories to poor countries has contributed little to nothing to their development. There has been no lack of effort and money spent for this purpose: students from poor countries have been trained in this country, and teachers and Peace Corps workers have been sent to the poor countries. If nothing else, the general lack of success in economic development of other countries should be sufficient argument to doubt the validity of Western management theories in non-Western environments.

If we examine different parts of the world, the development picture is not equally bleak, and history is often a better predictor than economic factors for what happens today. There is a broad regional pecking order with East Asia leading. The little dragons have passed into the camp of the wealthy: then follow South-East Asia (with its overseas Chinese minorities), Latin America (in spite of the debt crisis), South Asia, and Africa always trails behind. Several African countries have only become poorer since decolonization.

Russia and China

The crumbling of the former Eastern bloc has left us with a scattering of states and would-be states of which the political and economic future is extremely uncertain. The best predictions are those based on a knowledge of history, because historical trends have taken revenge on the arrogance of the Soviet rulers who believed they could turn them around by brute power. One obvious fact is that the former bloc is extremely heterogeneous, including countries traditionally closely linked with the West by trade and travel, like Czechia, Hungary, Slovenia, and the Baltic states, as well as others with a Byzantine or Turkish past: some having been prosperous, others always extremely poor.

Let me limit myself to the Russian republic, a huge territory with some 140 million inhabitants, mainly Russians. We know quite a bit about the Russians as their country was a world power for several hundreds of years before communism, and in the nineteenth century it has produced some of the greatest writers in world literature. If I want to understand the Russians – including how they could so long support the Soviet regime – I tend to re-read Lev Nikolayevich Tolstoy. In his most famous novel *Anna Karenina* one of the main characters is a landowner, Levin, whom Tolstoy uses to express his own views and convictions about his people. Russian peasants used to be serfs; serfdom had been abolished in 1861, but the peasants, now tenants, remained as passive as before. Levin wanted to break this passivity by dividing the land among his peasants in exchange for a share of the crops; but the peasants only let the land deteriorate further. Here follows a quote:

> [Levin] read political economy and socialistic works . . . but, as he had expected, found nothing in them related to his undertaking. In the political economy books – in [John Stuart] Mill, for instance, whom he studied first and with great ardour, hoping every minute to find an answer to the questions that were engrossing him – he found only certain laws deduced from the state of agriculture in Europe; but he could not for the life of him see why these laws, which did not apply to Russia, should be considered universal. . . . Political economy told him that the laws by which Europe had developed and was developing her wealth were universal and absolute. Socialist teaching told him that development along those lines leads to ruin. And neither of them offered the smallest enlightenment as to what he, Levin, and all the Russian peasants and landowners were to do with their millions of hands and millions of acres, to make them as productive as possible for the common good.

In the summer of 1991, the Russian lands yielded a record harvest, but a large share of it rotted in the fields because no people were to be found for harvesting. The passivity is still there, and not only among the peasants. And the heirs of John Stuart Mill (whom we met before as one of the early analysts of 'management') again present their universal recipes which simply do not apply.

Citing Tolstoy, I implicitly suggest that management theorists cannot neglect the great literature of the countries they went their ideas to apply to. The greatest novel in the Chinese literature is considered Cao Xueqin's *The*

Story of the Stone, also known as *The Dream of the Red Chamber* which appeared around 1760. It describes the rise and fall of two branches of an aristocratic family in Beijing, who live in adjacent plots in the capital. Their plots are joined by a magnificent garden with several pavilions in it, and the young, mostly female members of both families are allowed to live in them. One day the management of the garden is taken over by a young woman, Tan-Chun, who states:

> I think we ought to pick out a few experienced trust-worthy old women from among the ones who work in the Garden – women who know something about gardening already – and put the upkeep of the Garden into their hands. We needn't ask them to pay us rent; all we need ask them for is an annual share of the produce. There would be four advantages in this arrangement, In the first place, if we have people whose sole occupation is to look after trees and flowers and so on, the condition of the Garden will improve gradually year after year and there will be no more of those long periods of neglect followed by bursts of feverish activity when things have been allowed to get out of hand. Secondly there won't be the spoiling and wastage we get at present. Thirdly the women themselves will gain a little extra to add to their incomes which will compensate them for the hard work they put in throughout the year. And fourthly, there's no reason why we shouldn't use the money we should otherwise have spent on nurserymen, rockery specialists, horticultural cleaners and so on for other purposes.

As the story goes on, the capitalist privatization – because that is what it is – of the Garden is carried through, and it works. When in the 1980s Deng Xiaoping allowed privatization in the Chinese villages, it also worked. If we remember what Chinese entrepreneurs are able to do once they have become Overseas Chinese, we shouldn't be too surprised. But what works in China – and worked two centuries ago – does not have to work in Russia, not in Tolstoy's days and not today. I am not offering a solution: I only protest against a naive universalism that knows only one recipe for development, the one supposed to have worked in the United States.

A Theory of Culture in Management

There is something in all countries called 'management,' but its meaning differs to a larger or smaller extent from one country to the other, and it takes considerable historical and cultural insight into local conditions to understand its processes, philosophies, and problems. If already the word may mean so many different things, how can we expect one country's theories of management to apply abroad? One should be extremely careful in making this assumption, and test it before considering it proven. Management is not a phenomenon that can be isolated from other processes taking place in a society. It interacts with what happens in the family, at school, in politics, and government. It is obviously also related to religion and to beliefs about science. Theories of management always had to be interdisciplinary, but if we cross national borders they should become more interdisciplinary than ever.

As the word culture plays such an important role in my theory, let me give you my definition, which differs from some other very respectable definitions. Culture to me is *the collective programming of the mind which distinguishes one group or category of people from another.* In the part of my work I am referring to now, the category of people is the nation.

Cultural differences between nations can be, to some extent, described using five bipolar dimensions. The position of a country on these dimensions allows us to make some predictions on the way their society operates, including their management processes and the kind of theories applicable to their management.

The first dimension is labeled *power distance,* and it can be defined as the degree of inequality among people which the population of a country considers as normal: from relatively equal (that is, small power distance) to extremely unequal (large power distance). All societies are unequal, but some are more unequal than others.

The second dimension is labeled *individualism,* and it is the degree to which people in a country prefer to act as individuals rather than as members of groups. The opposite of individualism can be called *collectivism,* so collectivism is low individualism. The way I use the word it has no political connotations. In collectivist societies a child learns to respect the group to which it belongs, usually the family, and to differentiate between in-group members and out-group members (that is, all other people). When children grow up they remain members of their group, and they expect the group to protect them when they are in trouble, In return, they have to remain loyal to their group throughout life. In individualist societies, a child learns very early to think of itself as 'I' instead of a part of 'we'. It expects one day to have to stand on its own feet and not to get protection from its group any more; and therefore it also does not feel a need for strong loyalty.

The third dimension is called *masculinity* and its opposite pole *femininity.* It is the degree to which tough values like assertiveness, performance, success and competition, which in nearly all societies are associated with the role of men, prevail over tender values like the quality of life, maintaining warm personal relationships, service, care for the weak, and solidarity, which in nearly all societies are more associated with women's roles. Women's roles differ from men's roles in all countries; but in tough societies, the differences are larger than in tender ones.

The fourth dimension is labeled *uncertainty avoidance,* and it can be defined as the degree to which people in a country prefer structured over unstructured situations. Structured situations are those in which there are clear rules as to how one should behave. These rules can be written down, but they can also be unwritten and imposed by tradition. In countries that score high on uncertainty avoidance, people tend to show more nervous energy, while in countries that score low, people are more easy-going. A (national) society with strong uncertainty avoidance can be called rigid; one with weak uncertainty avoidance, flexible. In countries where uncertainty avoidance is strong a feeling prevails of 'what is different, is dangerous.' In weak uncertainty avoidance societies, the feeling would rather be 'what is different, is curious.'

The fifth dimension is labeled *long-term versus short-term orientation*. On the long-term side one finds values oriented towards the future, like thrift (saving) and persistence. On the short-term side one finds values rather oriented towards the past and present, like respect for tradition and fulfilling social obligations.

Table 1.5.1 lists the scores on all five dimensions for the United States and for the other countries we just discussed. The table shows that each country has its own configuration on the four dimensions. Some of the values in the table have been estimated based on imperfect replications or personal impressions. The different dimension scores do not 'explain' all the differences in management I described earlier. To understand management in a country, one should have both knowledge of and empathy with the entire local scene. However, the scores should make us aware that people in other countries may think, feel, and act very differently from us when confronted with basic problems of society.

Idiosyncrasies of American Management Theories

In comparison to other countries, the US culture profile presents itself as below average on power distance and uncertainty avoidance, highly individualistic, fairly masculine, and short-term oriented. The Germans show a stronger uncertainty avoidance and less extreme individualism; the Japanese are different on all dimensions, least on power distance; the French show larger power distance and uncertainty avoidance, but are less

TABLE 1.5.1
Culture dimension scores for 10 countries

	PD	ID	MA	UA	LT
USA	40 L	91 H	62 H	46 L	29 L
Germany	35 L	67 H	66 H	65 M	31 M
Japan	54 M	46 M	95 H	92 H	80 H
France	68 H	71 H	43 M	86 H	30*L
Netherlands	38 L	80 H	14 L	53 M	44 M
Hong Kong	68 H	25 L	57 H	29 L	96 H
Indonesia	78 H	14 L	46 M	48 L	25*L
West Africa	77 H	20 L	46 M	54 M	16 L
Russia	95*H	50*M	40*L	90*H	10*L
China	80*H	20*L	50*M	60*M	118 H

* estimated
Key: PD = Power Distance; ID = Individualism; MA = Masculinity; UA = Uncertainty
Avoidance; LT = Long Term Orientation
H = top third, M = medium third, L = bottom third (among 53 countries and
regions for the first four dimensions; among 23 countries for the fifth)

individualistic and somewhat feminine, the Dutch resemble the Americans on the first three dimensions, but score extremely feminine and relatively long-term oriented; Hong Kong Chinese combine large power distance with weak uncertainty avoidance, collectivism, and are very long-term oriented; and so on.

The American culture profile is reflected in American management theories. I will just mention three elements not necessarily present in other countries: the stress on market processes, the stress on the individual, and the focus on managers rather than on workers.

The Stress on Market Processes

During the 1970s and 1980s it has become fashionable in the United States to look at organizations from a 'transaction costs' viewpoint. Economist Oliver Williamson has opposed 'hierarchies' to 'markets.' The reasoning is that human social life consists of economic transactions between individuals. We found the same in d'Iribarne's description of the US principle of the contract between employer and employee, the labor market in which the worker sells his or her labor for a price. These individuals will form hierarchical organizations when the cost of the economic transactions (such as getting information, finding out whom to trust etc.) is lower in a hierarchy than when all transactions would take place on a free market.

From a cultural perspective the important point is that the 'market' is the point of departure or base model, and the organization is explained from market failure. A culture that produces such a theory is likely to prefer organizations that internally resemble markets to organizations that internally resemble more structured models, like those in Germany of France. The ideal principle of control in organizations in the market philosophy is competition between individuals. This philosophy fits a society that combines a not-too-large power distance with a not-too-strong uncertainty avoidance and individualism; besides the USA, it will fit all other Anglo countries.

The Stress on the Individual

I find this constantly in the design of research projects and hypotheses; also in the fact that in the US psychology is clearly a more respectable discipline in management circles than sociology. Culture however is a collective phenomenon. Although we may get our information about culture from individuals, we have to interpret it at the level of collectivities. There are snags here known as the 'ecological fallacy' and the 'reverse ecological fallacy.' None of the US college textbooks on methodology I know deals sufficiently with the problem of multilevel analysis.

A striking example is found in the otherwise excellent book *Organizational Culture and Leadership* by Edgar H. Schein (1985). On the basis of his consulting experience he compares two large companies, nicknamed 'Action' and 'Multi.' He explains the difference in cultures between these companies by the group dynamics in their respective boardrooms. Nowhere in the book are any conclusions drawn from the fact that the first company is an American-based computer firm, and the second a Swiss-based pharmaceutics firm. This information is not even mentioned. A stress on interactions among individuals obviously fits a culture identified as the most individualistic in the world, but it will not be so well understood by the four-fifths of the world population for whom the group prevails over the individual.

One of the conclusions of my own multilevel research has been that culture at the national level and culture at the organizational level – corporate culture – are two very different phenomena and that the use of a common term for both is confusing. If we do use the common term, we should also pay attention to the occupational and the gender level of culture. National cultures differ primarily in the fundamental, invisible values held by a majority of their members, acquired in early childhood, whereas organization cultures are a much more superficial phenomenon residing mainly in the visible practices of the organization, acquired by socialization of the new members who join as young adults. National cultures change only very slowly if at all; organizational cultures may be consciously changed, although this isn't necessarily easy. This difference between the two types of culture is the secret of the existence of multinational corporations that employ employees with extremely different national cultural values. What keeps them together is a corporate culture based on common practices.

The Stress on Managers rather than Workers

The core element of a work organization around the world is the people who do the work. All the rest is superstructure, and I hope to have demonstrated to you that it may take many different shapes. In the US literature on work organization, however, the core element, if not explicitly than implicitly, is considered the manager. This may well be the result of the combination of extreme individualism with fairly strong masculinity, which has turned the manager into a cultural hero of almost mythical proportions. For example, he – not really she – is supposed to make decisions all the time. Those of you who are or have been managers must know that this is a fable. Very few management decisions are just 'made' as the myth suggests it. Managers are much more involved in maintaining networks; if anything, it is the rank-and-file worker who can really make decisions on his or her own, albeit on a relatively simple level.

Conclusion

This article started with Alice in Wonderland. In fact, the management theorist who ventures outside his or her own country into other parts of the world is like Alice in Wonderland. He or she will meet strange beings, customs, ways of organizing or disorganizing and theories that are dearly stupid, old-fashioned or even immoral – yet they may work, or at least they may not fail more frequently than corresponding theories do at home. Then, after the first culture shock, the traveler to Wonderland will feel enlightened, and may be able to take his or her experiences home and use them advantageously. All great ideas in science, politics and management have traveled from one country to another, and been enriched by foreign influences. The roots of American management theories are mainly in Europe: with Adam Smith, John Stuart Mill, Lev Tolstoy, Max Weber, Henri Fayol, Sigmund Freud, Kurt Lewin and many others. These theories were re-planted here and they developed and bore fruit. The same may happen again. The last thing we need is a Monroe doctrine for management.

Further Readings

> Woe be to him who reads but one book.
> (George Herbert 1593–1632; English poet)

At the end of each chapter, a number of follow up books and articles will be suggested for readers who wish to delve deeper into a particular topic and avoid the dangers of reading only one book. These lists of recommended readings will be selective, instead of exhaustive, to assist readers in finding a few key works that can provide a stimulating introduction to the subject and a good starting point for further exploration.

As a follow up to this chapter, readers seeking a general survey of the fragmented field of strategic management might want to look at Henry Mintzberg's article 'Strategy Formation: Schools of Thought'. In this article, Mintzberg gives a broad overview of the strategy process literature and identifies ten schools of thought. Unfortunately, the same type of overview for the strategy content literature is lacking. However, Kathleen Conner's article 'A Historical Comparison of Resource Based Theory and Five Schools of Thought within Industrial Economics: Do We Have a New Theory of the Firm?' gives a useful summary of the predominant economics-based theoretical approaches in the strategy content area. For a good discussion on the pluriformity of strategy theories, Richard Whitley's article 'The Fragmented State of Management Studies: Reasons and Consequences' is recommended.

If readers are interested in tensions, paradoxes and the dialectical method, Richard Mason and Ian Mitroff's book *Challenging Strategic Planning Assumptions* is truly challenging. Charles Hampden-Turner's *Charting the Corporate Mind: From Dilemma to Strategy* is also a thought-provoking account of how dialectics can be employed as a problem-solving approach. For a more detailed account of wicked problems, readers should actually go back to Horst Rittel, who coined the term. His article, together with Melvin Webber, titled 'Dilemmas in a General Theory of Planning,' is a particularly readable essay.

On the topic of international cultural differences, Geert Hofstede's original book, *Culture's Consequences*, and its more popular follow up, *Cultures and Organizations: Software of the Mind*, are highly recommended. For a broader discussion of international differences in management and business systems, readers are advised to turn to *The Seven Cultures of Capitalism*, by Charles Hampden-Turner and Fons Trompenaars, *European Management Systems*, by Ronnie Lessem and Fred Neubauer, and *A European Management Model: Beyond Diversity*, by Roland Calori and Philippe de Woot.

References

Calori, R., and Ph. de Woot (eds.) (1994) *A European Management Model: Beyond Diversity*, Prentice Hall, London.

Collins, J.C., and Porras, J.I. (1994) *Built to Last: Succesful Habits of Visionary Companies*, Harper Business, New York.

Conner, K.R. (1992) A Historical Comparison of Resource Based Theory and Five Schools of Thought within Industrial Economics: Do we have a new Theory of the Firm?', *Journal of Management*, Vol. 17, pp. 121–54.

Cummings, S. (1993) Brief Case: The First Strategists, *Long Range Planning*, June, pp. 133–5.

D'Iribarne, P. (1990) *La logique d'honneur*, Editions du Seuil, Paris.

Emery, F.E., and Trist, E.L. (1965) The Causual Texture of Organizational Environments, *Human Relations*, vol. 18, pp. 21–32.

Hampden-Turner, C. (1990) *Charting the Corporate Mind: From Dilemma to Strategy*, Basil Blackwell, Oxford.

Hampden-Turner, C., and Trompenaars, F. (1993) *The Seven Cultures of Capitalism*, Doubleday, New York.

Hax, A.C. (1990) Redefining the Concept of Strategy and the Strategy Formation Process, *Planning Review*, May/June, pp. 34–40.

Hinterhuber, H.H., and Popp, W. (1992) Are You a Strategist or Just a Manager? *Harvard Business Review*, January/February, pp. 105–113.

Hofstede, G. (1980) *Culture's Consequences*, Sage, London.

Hofstede, G. (1991) *Cultures and Organizations: Software of the Mind*, McGraw-Hill, London.

Hofstede, G. (1993) Cultural Constraints in Management Theories, *Academy of Management Executive*, vol. 7 No. 1.

Ketchen, D.J., Thomas, J.B. and McDaniel, R.R. (1996) Process, Content and Context: Synergistic Effects on Organizational Performance, *Journal of Management*, Vol. 22, pp. 231–57.

Lessem, R., and Neubauer, F.F. (1994) *European Management Systems*, McGraw-Hill, London.

Machiavelli, N. (1950) *The Prince and the Discourses*, Modern Library, New York.

Mason, R.O., and Mitroff, I.I. (1981) *Challenging Strategic Planning Assumptions*, Wiley, New York.

Mintzberg, H. (1987) The Strategy Concept I: Five P's for Strategy, *California Management Review*, Fall, pp. 11–24.

Mintzberg, H. (1990) Strategy Formation: Schools of Thought, in Frederickson, J.W., (Ed.), *Perspectives on Strategic Management*, Harper & Row, New York.

Pettigrew, A. (1992) The Character and Significance of Strategy Process Research, *Strategic Management Journal*, Vol. 13, pp. 5–16.

Pettigrew, A., and Whipp, R. (1991) *Managing Change for Competitive Success*, Basil Blackwell, Oxford.

Poole, M.S., and Van de Ven, A.H. (1989) Using Paradox to Build Management and Organizational Theories, *Academy of Management Review*, Vol. 14, pp. 562–578.

Quinn, R.E. (1988) *Beyond Rational Management: Mastering the Paradoxes and Competing Demands of High Performance*, Jossey-Bass, San Francisco.

Quinn, R.E., and Cameron, K.S. (1988) *Paradox and Transformation: Toward a Theory of Change in Organization and Management*, Ballinger Publishing, Cambridge, Mass.

Rittel, H. (1972) On the Planning Crisis: Systems Analysis of the 'First and Second Generations', Bedriftsokonomen nr 8, pp. 390–6.

Rittel, H., and Webber, M. (1973) Dilemmas in a General Theory of Planning, *Policy Sciences*, 4, pp. 155–69.

Rumelt, R.P. (1980) The Evaluation of Business Strategy, in Glueck, W.F., *Business Policy and Strategic Management*, Third Edition, McGraw-Hill, New York.

Schein, E.H. (1985) *Organizational Culture and Leadership*, Jossey-Bass, San Francisco.

Sun Tzu (1983) *The Art of War*, Delacorte Press, New York.

Von Clausewitz, K. (1982) *On War*, Penguin, Harmondsworth.

Wing, R.L. (1988) *The Art of Strategy: A New Translation of Sun Tzu's Classic 'The Art of War'*, Doubleday, New York.

Whitley, R. (1984) The Fragmented State of Management Studies: Reasons and Consequences, *Journal of Management Studies*, Autumn.

Whittington, R. (1993) *What Is Strategy and Does It Matter?* Routledge, London.

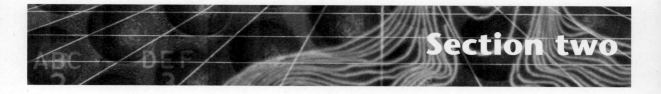

Strategy Process

❑   2 Strategic Thinking
❑   3 Strategy Formation
❑   4 Strategic Change

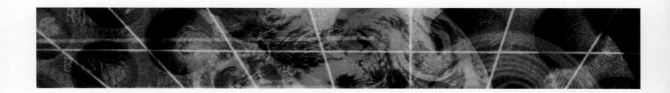

Strategic Thinking

When you have eliminated the impossible,
whatever remains, however improbable,
must be the truth.

(*Sherlock Holmes*, Arthur Conan Doyle 1859–1930; English novelist)

Imagination is more important
than knowledge.

(Albert Einstein 1879–1955; German-American physicist)

The Paradox of Logic and Creativity

At the beginning of Chapter 1 a concise definition of strategy was intentionally avoided. However, as the chapter progressed, it surfaced that strategy can be broadly conceived as a course of action for achieving an organization's purpose. It was argued that managers need strategies to solve the complicated, often wicked, problems with which they are confronted.

While the term *strategic problem* might have a negative connotation to some, it is not intended to denote only troublesome situations. It is a more general term, that refers to any challenging situation encountered by an organization that demands a reconsideration of the current course of action, either to profit from observed opportunities or to respond to perceived threats. The term *problem-solving* also has a connotation to many, namely, finding the optimal answer to a puzzle. However, what was said of strategy tensions in Chapter 1 can be extended to strategic problems in general – there might not be one best solution. Therefore, problem-solving should not be interpreted as the activity of finding *the* solution to a problem, but as the activity of finding *a* solution.

This chapter deals with the mode of thinking employed by people when confronted with strategic problems. Two issues will be central to this discussion on strategic thinking. First, how do people *define* strategic problems – how are problems identified and conceptualized? Second, how do people actually *solve* strategic problems – how are potential solutions generated, evaluated, and decided on? On both issues it is of interest to know what people really do (descriptive) and to know what people should do to be successful (prescriptive). Both an understanding of what is commonly done, and what leads to the best results, is of importance.

So, what is the fundamental nature of strategic thought processes? How does the mind of the strategist work and how should readers themselves think strategically? Opinions on this matter differ considerably, both among practitioners and theorists (who will jointly be referred to as *strategists* throughout this book). A whole spectrum of views exists, without any coherent clusters or schools of thought identifiable. However, two diametrically opposed positions can be observed at the extremes of the spectrum. On the one hand, there are strategists who argue that strategic thinking is one of the most advanced forms of analytical reasoning, requiring the consistent and rigorous use of logic. We shall refer to this point of view as the *rational thinking* perspective. On the other hand, there are strategists who argue that the essence of strategic thinking is the ability to break through orthodox beliefs, requiring the use of creativity. This point of view will be referred to as the *generative thinking* perspective.

Based on these two extremes, it seems that the disagreement between strategists revolves around the question whether strategic thinking is primarily logical or creative. These two factors are opposites and might be (partially) contradictory. To explore this paradox of logic and creativity, this chapter will proceed by means of *dialectical inquiry* – that is, a debate will be staged between the two opposite perspectives, with the intention of gaining a better understanding of the issues under discussion. In the next few pages, the rational and generative thinking perspectives will be further explained, and finally summarized in Table 2.1.

The Rational Thinking Perspective

Strategists employing the rational thinking perspective argue that strategic thinking is predominantly a 'logical activity' (Andrews, 1987; reading 2.1 in this book). To deal with strategic problems the strategist must first consciously and thoroughly analyse the problem situation. Data must be gathered on all developments external to the organization, and this data must be processed to pinpoint the opportunities and threats in the organization's environment. Furthermore, the organization itself must be appraised, to uncover its strengths and weaknesses and to establish which resources are available. Once the problem has been defined, a number of alternative strategies can be identified by matching external opportunities to internal strengths. Then, the strategic options must be extensively screened, by evaluating them on a number of criteria, such as consistency, consonance, advantage, feasibility, potential return and risks. The best strategy can be selected by comparing the scores of all options and determining the level of risk the strategist is willing to take. The chosen strategy can subsequently be implemented.

This type of intellectual effort requires well-developed analytical skills. Strategists must be able to rigorously, consistently and objectively comb through huge amounts of data, interpreting and combining findings to arrive at a complete picture of the current problem situation. Possible solutions require critical appraisal and all possible contingencies must be logically thought through. Advocates of the rational perspective argue that such thinking strongly resembles the problem-solving approach of chess grand masters. They also thoroughly assess their competitive position, sift through a variety of options and calculate which course of action brings the best chances of success. Therefore, the thought processes of chess grand masters can be used as an analogy for what goes on in the mind of the strategist.

While depicted here as a purely linear process of analysis, evaluation and choice, proponents of the rational thinking perspective note that in reality strategists often have to backtrack and redo some of these steps, as new information becomes available or chosen strategies do not work out. Strategists attempt to be as comprehensive, consistent and rigorous as possible in their analyses and calculations, but of course they cannot know everything and their conclusions are not always perfect. Even with the most advanced forecasting techniques, not all developments can be foreseen. Even with state of the art market research, some trends can be missed. Even with cutting edge test marketing, scenario analyses, competitive simulations and net present value calculations, some selected strategies can turn out to be failures. Strategists are not all-knowing, and do make mistakes – their rationality is limited by incomplete information and imperfect cognitive facilities. Yet, strategists try to be as rational as possible. Simon (1957) refers to this as *bounded rationality* – 'people act intentionally rational, but only limitedly so.' This coincides with Ambrose Bierce's famous sarcastic definition of logic as 'the art of thinking and reasoning in strict accordance with the limitations and incapacities of the human misunderstanding.'

The (boundedly) rational strategist must sometimes improvise to make up for a lack of information, but will try to do this as logically as possible. Inferences and speculation will always be based on the facts as known. By articulating assumptions and explicitly stating the facts and arguments on which conclusions have been based, problem definitions and solutions can be debated within the firm, to confirm that they have been arrived at using sound reasoning.

The alternative to a rational approach, it is often pointed out, is to be irrational and illogical, which surely can not be a desirable alternative for the strategist. Non-rational thinking comes in a variety of forms. For instance, people's thinking can be guided by their *emotions*. Feelings such as love, hate, guilt, regret, pride, anxiety, frustration, and embarrassment, can all cloud the strategist's understanding of a problem situation and the possible solutions. Adherents of the rational thinking perspective do not dispute the importance of emotions – the purpose of an organization is often based on 'personal values, aspirations and ideals,' while the motivation to implement strategies is also rooted in human emotions. However, the actual determination of the optimal strategy is a 'rational undertaking' *par excellence* (Andrews, 1987; reading 2.1).

Another form of non-rationality is to let conscious thinking be largely superseded by *routine* and *habit*. Routines are programmed courses of action that originally were deliberately conceived, but are subsequently internalized and used automatically (March and Simon, 1993). Habits are programmed courses of action that have developed unconsciously. Humans approach many everyday problems by reverting to routine and habit, which is a good thing, because conscious deliberation would cost too much time and effort. There is always a danger that routines can become outdated and that habits are totally nonsense, but there is a value to programmed behavior in some realms of human activity. However, strategic management is not one of these.

Intuition is sometimes also seen as a form of non-rational reasoning. Intuition has been defined in many ways (Behling and Eckel, 1991), but in general it can be understood as the opposite of formal analysis (Von Winterfeldt and Edwards, 1986). Intuition is informal and synthetic. Informal means that the reasoning is largely unconscious and based on assumptions, variables and causal relationships not explicitly identifiable by those doing the thinking. Synthetic means that the thinker does not aim at unravelling phenomena into their constituent parts, but rather maintains a more holistic view of reality. Many management theorists have noted that the opposites of analysis and intuition pose a paradox in themselves – when should managers use analysis and when intuition, or can both be combined (e.g. Langley, 1989, 1995; Pondy, 1983; Schoemaker and Russo, 1993)? However, in this discussion on strategic thinking it is important to point out that intuition is not necessarily irrational. If intuition is viewed as a set of unconscious and uncodified decision rules largely derived from experience (Simon, 1987), intuitive judgements can be quite logical. Decision rules based on extensive experience are often correct, even if they have been arrived at unconsciously. For example, Simon argues that even chess grand masters make many decisions intuitively, based on tacit (that is, unarticulated) rules of thumb, formulated through years of experience. Unconscious does not mean illogical and therefore most proponents of the rational perspective do not dismiss intuition out of hand.

However, intuitive judgements are viewed with great suspicion, as they are difficult to verify and infamously unreliable (Hogarth, 1980; Schwenk, 1984). Where possible, intuitive reasoning should be made explicit – the *cognitive map* in the strategist's head (McCaskey, 1982; reading 2.4 in this book) should be captured on paper (Eden, 1989), so that the reasoning of the strategist can be checked for logical inconsistencies.

In short, advocates of the rational thinking perspective argue that strategic thinking should not be based on emotions, routines, habit or pure intuition, but on explicit logical reasoning, just like a science. Scientific methods of research, analysis, theorizing and falsification are all directly applicable to developing strategy. Consequently, the best preparation for strategic thinking is to be trained in the scientific tradition.

The Generative Thinking Perspective

Strategists taking a generative thinking perspective are strongly at odds with the unassailable position given to logic in the rational perspective. They agree that logic is important, but stress that logical reasoning is often more a hindrance than a help. The heavy emphasis placed on rationality can actually stifle creativity, while creativity is essential for generating novel insights, new ways of defining problems and innovative solutions (e.g. Baden-Fuller and Stopford, 1992; reading 8.2; Senge 1990; reading 4.4). Therefore, proponents of the generative perspective argue that strategists should not get too caught up in rational approaches to strategic thinking, but should nurture creativity as their primary cognitive asset.

The generative thinking perspective is based on the assumption that strategic problems are *wicked* (Rittel, 1972; Mason and Mitroff, 1981; reading 1.4). It is believed that strategic problems cannot be easily and objectively defined, but that they are open to interpretation from a limitless variety of angles. The same is true for the possible solutions – there is no fixed set of problem solutions from which the strategist must select the best one. Defining and solving strategic problems, it is believed, is fundamentally a creative activity. As such, strategic thinking has very little in common with the thought processes of the aforementioned chess grand master, as was presumed by the rationalists. Playing chess is a *tame* problem. The problem definition is clear and all options are known. In the average game of chess, consisting of 40 moves, 10^{120} possibilities have to be considered (Simon, 1972). This makes it a difficult game for humans to play, because of their limited computational capacities. Chess grand masters are better at making these calculations than other people and are particularly good at computational short-cuts – recognizing which things to figure out and which not. However, even the best chess grand masters have been beaten at the game by highly logical computers with a superior number crunching capability. For the poor chess grand master, the rules of the game are fixed and there is little room for redefining the problem or introducing innovative approaches.

Engaging in business strategy is an entirely different matter. Strategic problems are wicked. Problem definitions are highly subjective and there are no fixed solution sets. It is therefore impossible to 'identify' the problem and 'calculate' an optimal solution. Opportunities and threats do not exist, waiting for the analyst to discover them. A strategist believes that a situation can be viewed as an opportunity and sees that certain factors can be threatening if not approached properly. Neither can strengths and weaknesses be objectively determined – a strategist can employ a company characteristic as a strength, but can also turn a unique company quality into a weakness by a lack of vision. Hence, doing a SWOT analysis (Strengths, Weaknesses, Opportunities and Threats) actually has little to do with logical analysis, but in reality is nothing less than a creative interpretation of a problem situation. Which factors in the environment and the organization are seen to be important and how they should be evaluated depends on the idiosyncratic views held by strategists.

Likewise, it is a fallacy to believe that strategic options follow more or less logically from the characteristics of the firm and its environment. Strategic options are not 'identified' or selected from a 2×2 matrix, but are dreamt up. Strategists must be able to use their imaginations to generate previously unknown solutions. If more than one strategic option emerges from the mind of the strategist, these can also not be simply scored and ranked to chose the optimal one. Some analyses can be done, but ultimately the strategist will have to intuitively judge which vision for the future has the best chance of being created in reality.

Hence, the major limitation of logic, according to adherents of the generative thinking perspective, is that it entraps strategists in the current orthodoxy. Logical reasoning can be an intellectual straight-jacket. 'Being logical' means engaging in consistent reasoning based on a number of accepted theories, ideas and assumptions about reality. When a group of people share such premises that shape how they view specific situations or problems, it is said that they have a common *paradigm* (e.g. Kuhn, 1970; Johnson, 1988; reading 9.4 in this book). Prahalad and Bettis (1986) speak of the *dominant logic* within a group, while others speak of a shared *cognitive map* (e.g. McCaskey, 1982; reading 2.4; Weick and Bougnon, 1986) or *belief system* (e.g. Noorderhaven, 1995; Smircich and Stubbart, 1985; reading 2.5). Rational thinking, then, is nothing other than interpreting problems and selecting solutions in accordance with the prevailing paradigm. Breaking out of the status quo requires that strategists question and contradict established wisdom. To find innovative ways of defining and solving problems, it is imperative that strategists think creatively – they must make leaps of imagination, that are not logical from the perspective of the current paradigm. Strategists must be willing to leave the intellectual safety of generally-accepted concepts to explore new ideas, guided by little else than their intuition. De Bono (1970) refers to such generative, frame-breaking reasoning as *lateral thinking*, as opposed to vertical thinking, which remains neatly within the existing paradigm.

To proponents of the generative thinking perspective, it is essential for strategists to have a slightly contrarian (Hurst, Rush and White, 1989), revolutionary predisposition (Hamel, 1996). Strategists must enjoy the challenge of thinking 'out of the box', even when this is disruptive of the status quo and not much appreciated by those with their two feet (stuck) on the ground. As Picasso once remarked, 'every act of creation is first of all an act of destruction' – strategists must enjoy the task of demolishing old paradigms and confronting the defenders of these beliefs.

In short, advocates of the generative perspective argue that the essence of strategic thinking is the ability to creatively challenge 'the tyranny of the given' (Kao, 1996) and to generate new and unique ways of understanding and doing things. As such, strategic thinking closely resembles the frame-breaking behavior common in the arts. In fields such as painting, music, motion pictures, dancing and architecture, artists are propelled by the drive to challenge convention and to seek out innovative approaches. Many of their methods, such as brainstorming, experimentation, openness to intuition, and the use of metaphors, contradictions and paradoxes, are directly applicable to developing strategy. Consequently, the best preparation for strategic thinking is to be trained in the artistic tradition of creativity and mental flexibility.

The question within the field of strategic management is, therefore, whether strategic thinking is primarily a rational activity or has more to do with ingenuity and imagination. Should strategists train themselves to follow *procedural rationality* – rigorously analyzing problems using scientific methods and calculating the optimal course of action? Or should strategists boldly think *out of the box* – inventing entirely new courses of action? Not all strategists give the same answers to these questions. This places readers in the position that they themselves must think about the nature of strategic thinking. Together, logic and creativity present a paradox that strategists, and prospective strategists, must come to terms with.

Defining the Issues: Cognition and Reasoning

Before proceeding with the 'debate' between proponents of the rational and generative thinking perspectives, it is useful to clarify the key topics under discussion. As will be seen, the disagreements between the two extreme points of view revolve around two major issues: the nature of *cognition* and the nature of *reasoning*. In the next paragraphs these two issues will be further explored, to set the stage for the debates that follow.

TABLE 2.1
The rational thinking versus generative thinking perspective

	Rational Thinking Perspective	Generative Thinking Perspective
Emphasis on	Logic over creativity	Creativity over logic
Cognitive style	Analytical	Intuitive
Reasoning follows	Formal, fixed rules	Informal, variable rules
Nature of reasoning	Computational	Imaginative
Direction of reasoning	Vertical	Lateral
Value placed on	Consistency and rigor	Unorthodoxy and vision
Reasoning hindered by	Incomplete information	Adherence to current ideas
Assumption about reality	Objective, (partially) knowable	Subjective, (partially) createable
Decisions based on	Calculation	Judgement
Metaphor	Strategy as science	Strategy as art

The Nature of Cognition

The mind of the strategist is a complex and fascinating apparatus, that never fails to astonish and dazzle on the one hand, and disappoint and frustrate on the other. We are often surprised by the power of the human mind, but equally often stunned by its limitations. For the discussion at hand it is not necessary to unravel all of the mysteries surrounding the functioning of the human brain, but a short overview of the capabilities and limitations of the human mind will greatly help to focus the debate.

The human ability to know is referred to as *cognition*. Knowledge that people have is stored in their minds in the form of *cognitive maps*, also referred to as *cognitive schemata* (e.g. Anderson, 1983; Schwenk, 1988). These cognitive maps are representations in the mind of an individual of how the world works. A cognitive map of a certain situation reflects a person's beliefs about the importance of the issues and about the cause and effect relationships between them. Cognitive maps are formed over time through education, experience and interaction with others.

It is clear that people are not omniscient – they do not have infinite knowledge. The cognitive abilities of humans are limited. These *cognitive limitations* are largely due to three factors:

- *Limited information processing capacity.* As was clear in the chess example cited earlier, humans do not have unlimited data processing abilities. Thinking through problems with many variables and huge amounts of data is a task that people find extremely difficult to perform. Approaching every activity in this way would totally overload a person's brain. For this reason, humans hardly ever think through a problem with full use of all available data, but make extensive use of mental shortcuts, referred to as *cognitive heuristics* (Janis, 1989). Cognitive heuristics are mental 'rules of thumb' that simplify a problem, so that it can be more quickly understood and solved. Cognitive heuristics focus a person's attention on a number of key variables that are believed to be most important, and present a number of simple decision rules to rapidly resolve an issue. The set of possible solutions to be considered is also limited in advance. The specific cognitive heuristics used by individuals are rooted in their cognitive maps.

- *Limited information sensing ability.* Human cognition is also severely handicapped by the limitations of people's senses. While the senses – touch, smell, taste, hearing and seeing – are bombarded with stimuli, much of reality remains unobservable to humans. This is partially due to the physical inability to be everywhere, all the time, noticing everything. However, people's limited ability to register the structure of reality is also due to the inherent superficiality of the senses and the complexity of reality. The human senses cannot directly identify the way the world works and the underlying causal relationships. Only the physical consequences of the complex interactions between elements in reality can be picked up by a person's sensory system. Therefore, the mental representations of the world that individuals build up in their minds are based on circumstantial evidence. Cognitive maps are formed by inferring causal relationships, making guesses about unobservable factors and resolving inconsistencies between the bits of information received. Hence, the models of reality constructed in the minds of individuals are highly subjective. In turn, people's cognitive maps steer their senses – while cognitive maps are built on past sensory data, they will consequently direct which new information will be sought and perceived. A person's cognitive map will focus attention on particular phenomena, while blocking out other data as noise, and will quickly explain how a situation should be perceived. In this way, a cognitive map provides an *interpretive filter*, aiding the senses in selecting and understanding external stimuli (Johnson and Scholes, 1993).

■ *Limited information storage capacity.* Another human cognitive shortcoming is poor memory. People have only a limited capacity for storing information. Remembering all individuals, events, dates, places and circumstances is beyond the ability of the human brain. Therefore, people must store information very selectively and organize this information in a way that it can be easily retrieved when necessary. Here, again, cognitive heuristics are at play – 'rules of thumb' make the memorization process manageable in the face of severe capacity limitations. Such heuristics help to simplify complex clusters of data into manageable chunks and help to categorize, label and store this information so that it can be recalled at a later moment.

With these drawbacks, humans can never be as perfectly rational as computers. Even when people try to be as rational as possible – that is, they avoid emotional, routine and intuitive behavior – they will still be hindered by these cognitive limitations. Two types of problems, in particular, confront the boundedly rational thinker:

■ *Cognitive biases.* As was stated earlier, cognitive heuristics are mental shortcuts, needed to cope with limited information processing and storage capacity. Everyone uses them for a large part of their thinking. Yet, these shortcuts are 'quick and dirty' – efficient, but imprecise. They help people to intuitively jump to conclusions without thorough analysis, which increases speed, but also increases the risk of drawing faulty conclusions. The main danger of cognitive heuristics is that they are inherently biased, as they focus attention on only a few variables and interpret them in a particular way, even when this is not appropriate (e.g. Tversky and Kahneman, 1986; Bazerman, 1990). For this reason, many academicians urge practitioners to bolster their intuitive judgements with more explicit rational analysis. Especially in the case of strategic decisions, time and energy should be made available to avoid falling prey to common cognitive biases (e.g. Isenberg, 1984; Schoemaker and Russo, 1993). Others are quick to point out that without extensive use of cognitive heuristics, and all the dangers involved, strategists would grind to a halt, overloaded by the sheer complexity of the analyses that would need to be carried out – a situation of rationality gone rampant, usually referred to as *paralysis by analysis* (Lenz and Lyles, 1985; Langley, 1995). This has led to an on-going debate on how to balance rational analysis and intuitive judgement.

■ *Cognitive rigidities.* A second problem is that people are generally not inclined to change their minds – cognitive maps exhibit a high level of rigidity. Once people's cognitive maps have formed, and they have a grip on reality, they become resistant to signals that challenge their conceptions. As McCaskey remarks in reading 2.4, the mind 'strives mightily to bring order, simplicity, consistency, and stability to the world it encounters,' and is therefore reluctant to welcome the ambiguity presented by contradicting data. People tend to significantly overestimate the value of information that confirms their cognitive map, underestimate disconfirming information, and they actively seek out evidence that supports their current beliefs (Schwenk, 1984). Once an interpretive filter is in place, seeing is not believing, but believing is seeing. Cognitive rigidity is particularly strong when an individual's cognitive map is supported by similar beliefs shared within a social group or organization. How rigid cognitive maps actually are and how open people can be to evidence and new ideas is, however, an on-going debate within the fields of (strategic) management and (social) psychology.

The main question in this chapter is whether cognitive rigidities present a major problem to strategists. Do strategists need to 'change their minds' in significant ways or is it sufficient for strategists to build on their current understanding, with occasional minor adaptations? Must strategists consistently try to break through cognitive rigidities, by creatively generating other ways of understanding the world, or should they progress rationally, by logically extending their existing cognitive maps? Is it necessary for strategists to be intellectual revolutionaries, overthrowing the established order, or should they respect accepted knowledge and build on these foundations?

The issue, therefore, is how realistic or constraining strategists' cognitive maps actually are. If the cognitive maps employed by strategists are faithful representations of the world and strategists are relatively open to any dissonant signals indicating that their maps are incorrect, then they will have *objective knowledge* of reality. All thinking should then take this objective knowledge as a starting point and rationally build on these premises. New insights, new ideas, and new strategies should be arrived at by analytical reasoning, making them logically consistent with what is known to be objectively true.

However, if in fact the cognitive maps used by strategists are highly colored representations of the world and strategists are often immune to dissonant signals that do not fit in with their beliefs, then their knowledge of the world will be *subjective*. Their understanding of reality will be slanted. As people do not develop their cognitive maps in isolation, but in interaction with other individuals, their subjective understanding of the world will be largely *socially constructed* (Weick, 1979; Smircich and Stubbart, 1985; reading 2.5 in this book). When people within a social group construct a common worldview, based on shared assumptions about reality, this is referred to as a *paradigm*. Thinking within the boundaries of a paradigm is usually very 'logical'. Once the subjective assumptions and the reasoning rules have been accepted, people proceed to think rationally – that is, they try to avoid logical inconsistencies. Challenging a paradigm's fundamental assumptions, however, cannot be done in a way that is logically consistent with the paradigm. Contradicting a paradigm is illogical from the point of view of those who accept the paradigm. Therefore, changing a rigid and subjective cognitive map, rooted in a shared paradigm, would require strategists to imagine new ways of understanding the world, that do not logically follow from past beliefs. Strategists would have to be willing and able to break with orthodoxy and make leaps of imagination, that are not logically justified, but needed to generate novel ways of looking at old problems. Strategic thinking would require a large dose of creativity – that is, the ability to understand problems and formulate solutions in a way that contradicts conventional wisdom. Strategists with a strong preference to remain rational would, in practice, become prisoners of their own rigid cognitive maps.

Which portrayal of cognition is right? As unanimity is lacking, readers will have to form an opinion of their own. Which position in this debate each reader takes will ultimately depend on their view on the nature of reality (which philosophers refer to as the issue of *ontology*) and the nature of knowledge (the issue of *epistemology*).

The Nature of Reasoning

Reasoning and cognition are intimately related – reasoning is the thought process leading to knowing. As a process, reasoning involves a number of mental activities taking place over time. In the context of strategy, reasoning is the thought process used to define and solve strategic problems.

Most strategists, whether of rational or generative inclination, agree that reasoning about strategic problems can be decomposed into four broad categories of mental activities (see Figure 2.1). These four elements of strategic reasoning are:

1   *Identifying.* Before strategists can move to benefit from opportunities or to counter threats, they must be aware of these challenges and acknowledge their importance. This part of the thought process is variably referred to as identifying, recognizing or sense-making.

2   *Diagnosing.* To come to grips with a problem, strategists must try to understand the structure of the problem and its underlying causes. This part of the thought process is variably referred to as diagnosing, analyzing or reflecting.

3   *Conceiving.* To deal with a strategic problem, strategists must come up with a potential solution. If more than one solution is available, the strategist must select the most promising one. This part of the thought process is variably referred to as conceiving, formulating, or envisioning.

4   *Realizing.* A strategic problem is only really solved once concrete actions are undertaken that achieve results. Strategists must therefore carry out problem-solving activities and evaluate whether the consequences are positive. This part of the thought process is variably referred to as realizing, implementing, or acting.

What strategists do not agree on, is how each activity is carried out and in what order. From the rational thinking perspective, it is logical to start by identifying problems and then to move from diagnosing to conceiving solutions and realizing them (clockwise movement in Figure 2.1). In

FIGURE 2.1
Elements of strategic
thought process

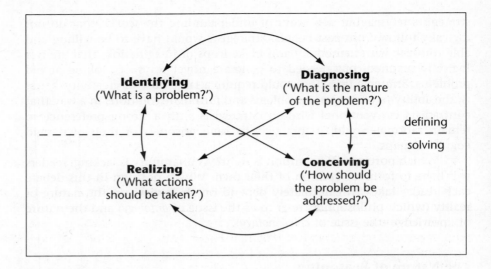

general, adherents of the rational thinking perspective believe that identifying strategic problems requires extensive external and internal scanning, thorough sifting of incoming information, and the selecting of priority issues. In the next mental phase, the major strategic problems that have been recognized are diagnosed by gathering more detailed data, and further analyzing and refining this information. Once the problem has been properly defined, a strategy can be formulated by evaluating the available options and deciding which solution is the best. In the final phase of realization, the strategist must ensure execution of the proposed solution by consciously planning and controlling implementation activities. Therefore, in the vocabulary of rational thinking perspective the four elements of the strategic thought process are usually referred to as *recognizing, analyzing, formulating* and *implementing*.

Proponents of the generative thinking perspective do not believe that strategists reason in this linear (or actually circular) fashion. They do not accept that the four categories of mental activities are phases. In their view, reasoning is usually far more messy, with identifying, diagnosing, conceiving and realizing intermingled with one another and often going on at the same time. The more creative, the less linear are the thought processes (clockwise movement in Figure 2.1 is literally far too mechanical for the creative thinker). Nor do the advocates of the generative thinking perspective agree with the rationalist's characterization of the four groups of mental activities. In the generative view, identifying strategic problems is not about recognizing, but interpreting – by looking at the world from a particular angle, strategists see and value particular strengths, weaknesses, opportunities and threats. Such sense-making activities (Weick, 1979) lead to attention being paid to some issues, while others do not make the *strategic agenda* (Dutton, 1988). Likewise, diagnosing strategic problems is not a straightforward analytical process. Reflecting on strategic problems may involve explicit analysis, but also intuition – understanding problems through unconscious and synthetic reasoning.

Conceiving strategic solutions is equally messy and creative, according to supporters of the generative perspective. Solutions are not lying around, waiting to be discovered, but are envisioned – strategists imagine how things could be done. Such idea generation may involve reasoning by analogy or metaphor, brainstorming, or pure fantasizing. New solutions may come to the strategist in a flash (eureka!) or emerge over time, but usually require a period of incubation beforehand, and a period of nurturing afterwards. Which new idea will be the best solution is, however, not something that can be objectively evaluated and decided. Therefore judgement, not calculation, will determine which idea will win the upper hand.

Finally, it is emphasized that realization-oriented thinking does not come last, as straightforward implementation. Acting does not wait for a problem to be precisely defined and for a solution to be fully conceived. Often, to really understand a problem, people must first act – they must have experience with a problem and know that the current strategy will not be able to overcome the problem. To generate a solution it is often also necessary to test certain assumptions in practice and to experiment. In short, in the generative thinking perspective the four elements of the strategic thought process are thoroughly intertwined, and best understood as *sense-making*, *reflecting*, *envisioning* and *acting*.

EXHIBIT 2.1
Mercedes-Benz and
Swatch Short Case

MERCEDES-BENZ AND SWATCH: A SMART MOVE?

Among the flurry of strategic alliances initiated during the last few years, the collaboration between the luxury car manufacturer Mercedes-Benz, and the Swiss watch producer SMH (known for its brands Swatch and Omega) has stood out as exceptionally eye-catching. At a press conference in May 1995, it was announced to surprised business journalists that the two companies had embarked on a major joint venture, with the intention of developing and manufacturing a revolutionary new automobile. The new firm, Micro Compact Car (MCC), would be 51 percent owned by Mercedes Benz, and would be endowed with DM 1.5bn ($1bn) of equity from the parent companies. The car would be called 'Smart,' which according to Hans Jürgen Schör, head of the MCC joint venture, combines the first letters of the two collaborating companies, Swatch (S) and Mercedes-Benz (M), with the way they are working together.

It is not very likely that anyone is going to spot Jürgen Hubbert, the chief executive of Mercedes-Benz, and Nicolas Hayek, chairman of SMH, taking long drives together in the Smart car. Not necessarily due to their relationship, but because of the dimensions of this micro car. With a length of 2.5 metres (8'4") and a width of 1.4 metres (4'8"), the Smart is going to be the world's smallest production vehicle, hardly sufficient to lure Mr. Hubbert out of his chauffeur-driven Mercedes. Yet, size may not even be the most unconventional characteristic of this tiny two seater urban vehicle. The original concept involves changeable car body panels, to match the color of the car with your favorite wardrobe items. On top of that, the little giant will have the right green credentials. The eco turbo diesel engines will offer unprecedented fuel economy and there will even be a battery-powered version, together with a diesel/electric hybrid, allowing the car to operate in zero-emission areas such as downtown LA.

The background of this venture is equally surprising. In 1990, Nicolas Hayek came up with the idea of diversifying SMH into the automobile industry, driven by an urgent desire to make driving fashionable, more in line with environmental constraints and, most of all, more fun. Yet, for a watchmaker it is not an easy job to build an automobile plant on its own, so SMH had to search for a reliable and sincere partner. Originally, Hayek tried to strike up a relationship with Volkswagen, the German manufacturer of medium-sized cars, for whom a micro compact might be a logical range extension. However, both parties had differing ideas and Volkswagen was financially restrained, so the brief flirt was quickly ended. Unexpectedly, Mercedes-Benz, which only produces high quality, top of the range cars, was particularly interested in Hayek's concept and willing to team up with this industry outsider.

To intrigued industry analysts, the motives of both companies are not entirely clear. Swatch seems to be propelled by the vision of its CEO, Nicolas Hayek. He feels that it is his personal responsibility to 'prevent the world from being out of oxygen in ten years,' and therefore he is determined to build a cleaner, more fuel-efficient car, which implies a significant decrease in size compared to regular vehicles. Of course, Hayek also believes that Swatch has many of the critical capabilities needed to make Smart a success, especially in the area of design, miniaturization, sensing the wishes of young people and marketing. Smart is an excellent opportunity for SMH to leverage these capabilities and to become less dependent on the watch-making business. Critics, however, point out that the Smart project might also have been intended to appease SMH shareholders, who have recently been confronted with declining profits and falling dividends.

Industry analysts are even more curious about the cooperative rationale of Mercedes-Benz. Why would a prestigious, conservative and highly rational firm like Mercedes-Benz collaborate with a fashion-driven, progressive and highly creative Swiss watchmaker? It seems clear that the company is currently locked into a narrow product range, resulting in a very limited target audience and few opportunities for growth. As Mr. Hubbert admits, demand is stagnant in the big luxury car segment, which includes Mercedes-Benz' flagship S Class saloon. In his view, significant growth will be limited to smaller, cheaper models. As a company that wants to expand, Mercedes-Benz needed to find a way to break into these segments. For such a move its image could be both an asset and a liability. The Smart project fits the needs of Mercedes-Benz exactly, because it can leverage its quality image, without suffering from its conservative connotations. At the same time, it is hoped, the company's traditional and loyal customer base will not be upset by a dilution of the Mercedes-Benz brand name.

However, it is not only a matter of piggy-backing on Swatch's fashionable image. The top management of Mercedes-Benz seems to recognize that its production skills and engineering excellence are not the only capabilities needed to successfully enter the small market segment. The company's rationalist culture is ill-suited to the development of other needed capabilities, such as the radical rethinking of the automobile concept, imaginative design, and creative marketing. These are exactly the qualities that Swatch can also bring in to the joint venture.

It is from this perspective that the decision must be understood to establish the Smart production location in France, instead of near Mercedes-Benz' main manufacturing hub in Stuttgart, Germany. Production will be located at Hambach, near Sarreguimes in north-eastern France, where a start has been made to build a plant with a capacity of 200,000 vehicles. This location, just across the French-German border, should be physically close enough to keep the Smart factory connected to the core company, to ensure quality, financial control and just-in-time delivery by Mercedes suppliers. However, it should also be far enough to allow a new culture to evolve combining the best of both worlds – Mercedes-Benz' analytical rigor on the one hand, and Swatch's creative capabilities on the other. Significant additional benefits are the lower French wages and energy prices, and the weaker French currency.

Yet, some market analysts have expressed their reservations about the success potential of the new-born joint venture. They question whether a car manufacturer and a watch maker could ever make a compatible couple, even under the best of circumstances. Their doubts are even larger given the enormous cultural gap between the rationally-inclined managers at Mercedes-Benz and the creatively-inclined people at Swatch. Isn't it likely that their relationship will crack under the first real strains, as the Smart cars reach the market? Managers from both companies have had experience in cooperative ventures, Hayek as a coordinator within the network of Swiss companies producing watches, and Mercedes-Benz managers in joint new product development projects with suppliers (such as Bosch, with whom they developed an advanced Anti-Blocking System (ABS) for brakes). However, this collaborative venture is of a more structural nature and the partners are more strongly divergent. Many analysts wondered whether the companies' differences would be complementary or contradictory – whether the tensions created would be constructive or destructive.

Ultimately, the question which Mercedes-Benz and Swatch will have to ask themselves is whether logic and creativity can be, and need to be, combined in MCC's culture and strategy process. And, if so, which of the two should, or will dominate? The answers to these questions will determine whether we will see Mercedes-Benz and Swatch racing ahead together, or one partner towing the other, or even the joint venture crashing before completing its first lap.

Sources: *Financial Times*, various issues 1996.

The Debate and the Readings

As stated at the outset of this chapter, few authors make a point of explaining their rational thinking perspective. The position of logical reasoning is so strong in much of the literature, that many strategists adopt the rational perspective without making this choice explicit. It is, therefore, not possible to present a vocal defender of this perspective to get a nicely polarized debate going. Instead, as the first debate contribution to this chapter, a classic work has been selected that is a good example of the rational perspective on strategic thinking. This reading, 'The Concept of Corporate Strategy,' by Kenneth Andrews, has been drawn from one of the most influential textbooks in the field of strategy, *Business Policy: Text and Cases* (Christensen, Andrews, *et al.*, 1987). Andrews is arguably one of the god-fathers of strategic management and this chapter from his book has had considerable impact on theorists and practitioners alike. True to the rational thinking perspective, Andrews argues that strategy analysis and formulation should be conducted consciously, explicitly and rationally. In his view, strategic thinking is a 'logical activity,' while subsequent strategy implemen-tation 'comprises a series of subactivities that are primarily administrative.' It should be noted that in this reading Andrews is positioning himself in opposition to incrementalists (see Chapter 3), not *vis-à-vis* proponents of the generative thinking perspective. Therefore, he does not counter any of the major arguments raised by advocates of this perspective.

The second reading in this chapter, highlighting the views of the generative thinking perspective, is 'The Mind of the Strategist,' by Kenichi Ohmae. Ohmae, formerly head of McKinsey's Tokyo office, is one of Japan's most well-known strategy authors. In this contribution, taken from the book of the same name, Ohmae argues that the mind of the strategist is not dominated by linear, logical thinking. On the contrary, a strategist's thought processes are 'basically creative and intuitive rather than rational.' In his view, 'great strategies . . . originate in insights that are beyond the reach of conscious analysis.' He does not dismiss logic as unnecessary, but notes that it is insufficient for arriving at innovative strategies. Yet, he observes that in most large companies creative strategists 'are being pushed to the sidelines in favor of rational, by-the-numbers strategic and financial planners,' leading to a withering of strategic thinking ability.

The third reading, 'Game Theory and Strategic Thinking,' by Teck Hua Ho and Keith Weigelt, adds an extra dimension to the debate, not yet covered by the initial two discussants. For many people, strategy is about behavior in situations of competitive interaction. Generals develop strategies to outmaneuver their military opponents, sports coaches adopt strategic moves to outwit other teams and politicians use strategic ploys to outfox their rivals. In other words, strategy is about playing interactive games. Strategists are engaged in understanding the rules of a game and developing game strategies better than their opponents. This is where game theorists come in, who generally argue that strategic thinking should focus on the rational analysis of complex game situations and the selection of the most promising strategy. Games confront strategists with a competitive logic they can not escape and therefore game theorists propose that strategists rationally figure out their optimal moves and countermoves. Much of the work on game theory is actually strongly mathematically-oriented, supporting strategists in their calculations of the best courses of action. In their contribution, Hua Ho and Weigelt give a stimulating overview of game theoretical thinking, including the strong emphasis on logical reasoning and calculative decision-making. They, too, conclude that playing games well requires rigorous analysis and a rational perspective. In the context of this debate, their input is to raise the question whether the 'logic of competitive interactions' forces strategists to be rational.

While the first three contributions discuss different forms of reasoning, they only pay indirect attention to the issue of human cognition. Therefore, the fourth reading, 'Conceptual Mapping,' by Michael McCaskey, has been added to the debate, to further emphasize the role of cognitive biases and rigidities in strategic thinking. In this extract from his book, *The Executive Challenge*, McCaskey vividly describes how cognitive (or conceptual) maps are formed and maintained. He argues that once cognitive maps are in place, challenging them is extremely difficult. People fight to retain their cognitive maps, effectively making themselves captives of their own experiences. McCaskey compares the forced relinquishing of a cognitive map to the mourning process – first denial and anger, followed by bargaining, depression and only finally acceptance. In the context of this debate, the question McCaskey raises is how strategists can proactively change their cognitive maps. Is altering one's worldview a logical or a creative process?

Finally, the fifth contribution, 'Strategic Management in an Enacted World,' by Linda Smircich and Charles Stubbart, takes the debate yet a step further by discussing how cognitive maps are constructed through social interaction. Smircich and Stubbart challenge readers to abandon the notion that there is an objective reality out there, that strategists should try to discover. They do not doubt the existence of a physical reality, but argue that the 'reality' that is important to strategists – e.g. organizations, environments, competition, markets, strengths, opportunities – is not material. The world of the strategist is enacted – that is, created – by the interaction between people, who each have their own interpretation of what is going on. As people who interact with one another will come to share their interpretations of the world, their common understanding of 'reality' is said to be socially constructed. Their cognitive maps will develop in a similar direction. According to Smircich and Stubbart, the social construction of reality makes the strategist's task 'an imaginative one, a creative one, an art.' Strategists must reinterpret the chaos of activities taking place around them, and challenge existing views. Ultimately, strategists must manage 'the subjective process of reality-building,' without creating new cognitive rigidities that may burden the organization in the future. In the context of this debate, Smircich and Stubbart's discussion on the nature of reality strongly supports the generative thinking approach. The question is, however, whether reality truly is as subjective as they claim.

2.1 The Concept of Corporate Strategy

By Kenneth Andrews[1]

What Strategy Is

Corporate strategy is the pattern of decisions in a company that determines and reveals its objectives, purposes, or goals, produces the principal policies and plans for achieving those goals, and defines the range of business the company is to pursue, the kind of economic and human organization it is or intends to be, and the nature of the economic and noneconomic contribution it intends to make to its shareholders, employees, customers, and communities. In an organization of any size or diversity, *corporate strategy* usually applies to the whole enterprise, while *business strategy*, less comprehensive, defines the choice of product or service and market of individual businesses within the firm. Business strategy, that is, is the determination of how a company will compete in a given business and position itself among its competitors. Corporate strategy defines the businesses in which a company will compete, preferably in a way that focuses resources to convert distinctive competence into competitive advantage. Both are outcomes of a continuous process of strategic management that we will later analyze in detail.

The strategic decision contributing to this pattern is one that is effective over long periods of time, affects the company in many different ways, and focuses and commits a significant portion of its resources to the expected outcomes. The pattern resulting from a series of such decisions will probably define the central character and image of a company, the individuality it has for its members and various publics, and the position it will occupy in its industry and markets. It will permit the specification of particular objectives to be attained through a timed sequence of investment and implementation decisions and will govern directly the deployment or redeployment of resources to make these decisions effective.

Some aspects of such a pattern of decisions may be in an established corporation unchanging over long periods of time, like a commitment to quality, or high technology, or certain raw materials, or good labor relations. Other aspects of a strategy must change as or before the world changes, such as a product line, manufacturing process, or merchandising and styling practices. The basic determinants of company character, if purposefully institutionalized, are likely to persist through and shape the nature of substantial changes in product-market choices and allocation of resources.

---

[1] Source: This article was adapted with permission from chapter 2 of *The Concept of Corporate Strategy*, Irwin, Homewood, 1987.

It would be possible to extend the definition of strategy for a given company to separate a central character and the core of its special accomplishment from the manifestations of such characteristics in changing product lines, markets, and policies designed to make activities profitable from year to year. *The New York Times*, for example, after many years of being shaped by the values of its owners and staff, is now so self-conscious and respected an institution that its nature is likely to remain unchanged, even if the services it offers are altered drastically in the direction of other outlets for its news-processing capacity.

It is important, however, not to take the idea apart in another way, that is, to separate goals from the policies designed to achieve those goals. The essence of the definition of strategy I have just recorded is pattern. The interdependence of purposes, policies, and organized action is crucial to the particularity of an individual strategy and its opportunity to identify competitive advantage. It is the unity, coherence, and internal consistency of a company's strategic decisions that position the company in its environment and give the firm its identity, its power to mobilize its strengths, and its likelihood of success in the marketplace. It is the interrelationship of a set of goals and policies that crystallizes from the formless reality of a company's environment a set of problems an organization can seize upon and solve.

What you are doing, in short, is never meaningful unless you can say or imply what you are doing it for: the quality of administrative action and the motivation lending it power cannot be appraised without knowing its relationship to purpose. Breaking up the system of corporate goals and the character-determining major policies for attainment leads to narrow and mechanical conceptions of strategic management and endless logic chopping.

We should get on to understanding the need for strategic decisions and for determining the most satisfactory pattern of goals in concrete instances. Refinement of definition can wait, for you will wish to develop definition in practice in directions useful to you.

Summary Statements of Strategy

Before we proceed to clarification of this concept by application, we should specify the terms in which strategy is usually expressed. A summary statement of strategy will characterize the product line and services offered or planned by the company, the markets and market segments for which products and services are now or will be designed, and the channels through which these markets will be reached. The means by which the operation is to be financed will be specified, as will the profit objectives and the emphasis to be placed on the safety of capital versus level of return. Major policy in central functions such as marketing, manufacturing, procurement, research and development, labor relations, and personnel, will be stated where they distinguish the company from others, and usually the intended size, form, and climate of the organization will be included.

Each company, if it were to construct a summary strategy from what it understands itself to be aiming at, would have a different statement with different categories of decision emphasized to indicate what it wanted to be or do.

Reasons for Not Articulating Strategy

For a number of reasons companies seldom formulate and publish a complete strategy statement. Conscious planning of the long-term development of companies has been until recently less common than individual executive responses to environmental pressure, competitive threat, or entrepreneurial opportunity. In the latter mode of development, the unity or coherence of corporate effort is unplanned, natural, intuitive, or even nonexistent. Incrementalism in practice sometimes gives the appearance of consciously formulated strategy, but may be the natural result of compromise among coalitions backing contrary policy proposals or skillful improvisatory adaptation to external forces. Practicing managers who prefer muddling through to the strategic process would never commit themselves to an articulate strategy.

Other reasons for the scarcity of concrete statements of strategy include the desirability of keeping strategic plans confidential for security reasons and ambiguous to avoid internal conflict or even final decision. Skillful incrementalists may have plans in their heads that they do not reveal, to avoid resistance and other trouble in their own organization. A company with a large division in an obsolescent business that it intends to drain of cash until operations are discontinued could not expect high morale and cooperation to follow publication of this intent. In a dynamic company, moreover, where strategy is continually evolving, the official statement of strategy, unless couched in very general terms, would be as hard to keep up to date as an organization chart. Finally, a firm that has internalized its strategy does not feel the need to keep saying what it is, valuable as that information might be to new members.

Deducing Strategy from Behavior

In your own company you can do what most managements have not done. In the absence of explicit statements and on the basis of your experience, you may deduce from decisions observed what the pattern is and what the company's goals and policies are, on the assumption that some perhaps unspoken consensus lies behind them. Careful examination of the behavior of competitors will reveal what their strategy must be. At the same time none of us should mistake apparent strategy visible in a pattern of past incremental decisions for conscious planning for the future. What will pass as the current strategy of a company may almost always be deduced from its behavior, but a strategy for a future of changed circumstances may not always be distinguishable from performance in the present. Strategists who do not look beyond present behavior to the future are vulnerable to surprise.

Formulation of Strategy

Corporate strategy is an organization process, in many ways inseparable from the structure, behavior, and culture of the company in which it takes place. Nevertheless, we may abstract from the process two important aspects, interrelated in real life but separable for the purposes of analysis. The first of these we may call formulation, the second implementation. Deciding what strategy should be may be approached as a rational under-taking, even if, as in life, emotional attachments (to metal skis or investi-gative reporting) may complicate choice among future alternatives (for ski manufacturers or alternative newspapers). The principle subactivities of strategy formulation as a logical activity include indentifying opportunities and threats in the company's environment and attaching some estimate or risk to the discernible alternatives. Before a choice can be made, the company's strengths and weaknesses should be appraised together with the resources on hand and available. Its actual or potential capacity to take advantage of perceived market needs or to cope with attendant risks should be estimated as objectively as possible. The strategic alternative that results from matching opportunity and corporate capability at an acceptable level of risk is what we may call an *economic strategy*.

The process described thus far assumes that strategists are analytically objective in estimating the relative capacity of their company and the opportunity they see or anticipate in developing markets. The extent to which they wish to undertake low or high risk presumably depends on their profit objectives. The higher they set the latter, the more willing they must be to assume a correspondingly high risk that the market opportunity they see will not develop or that the corporate competence required to excel competition will not be forthcoming.

So far we have described the intellectual processes of ascertaining what a company *might do* in terms of environmental opportunity, of deciding what it *can do* in terms of ability and power, and of bringing these two considerations together in optimal equilibrium. The determination of strategy also requires consideration of what alternatives are preferred by the chief executive and perhaps by his or her immediate associates as well, quite apart from economic considerations. Personal values, aspirations and ideals do, and in our judgment quite properly should, influence the final choice of purposes. Thus what the executives of a company *want to do* must be brought into the strategic decision.

Finally strategic choice has an ethical aspect – a fact much more dramatically illustrated in some industries than in others. Just as alternatives may be ordered in terms of the degree of risk they entail, so may they be examined against the standards of responsiveness to the expectations of society the strategist elects. Some alternatives may seem to the executive considering them more attractive than others when the public good or service to society is considered. What a company *should do* thus appears as a fourth element of the strategic decision.

The ability to identify the four components of strategy – (a) market opportunity, (b) corporate competence and resources, (c) personal values and aspirations, and (d) acknowledged obligations to segments of society other than stockholders – is easier to exercise than the art of reconciling their implications in a final choice of purpose. Taken by itself each consideration might lead in a different direction.

If you put the various aspirations of individuals in your own organization against this statement you will see what I mean. Even in a single mind contradictory aspirations can survive a long time before the need to calculate trade-offs and integrate divergent inclinations becomes clear. Growth opportunity attracted many companies to the computer business after World War II. The decision to diversify out of typewriters and calculators was encouraged by growth opportunity and excitement that captivated the managements of RCA, General Electric, and Xerox, among others. But the financial, technical, and marketing requirements of this business exceeded the capacity of most of the competitors of IBM. The magnet of opportunity and the incentive of desire obscured the calculations of what resources and competence were required to succeed. Most crucially, where corporate capability leads, executives do not always want to go. Of all the components of strategic choice, the combination of resources and competence is most crucial to success.

The Implementation of Strategy

Since effective implementation can make a sound strategic decision ineffective or a debatable choice successful, it is as important to examine the processes of implementation as to weigh the advantages of available strategic alternatives. The implementation of strategy comprises a series of subactivities that are primarily administrative. If purpose is determined, then the resources of a company can be mobilized to accomplish it. An organizational structure appropriate for the efficient performance of the required tasks must be made effective by information systems and relationships permitting coordination of subdivided activities. The organizational processes of performance measurement, compensation, management development – all of them enmeshed in systems of incentives and controls – must be directed toward the kind of behavior required by organizational purpose. The role of personal leadership is important and sometimes decisive in the accomplishment of strategy. Although we know that organizational structure and processes of compensation, incentives, control, and management development influence and constrain the formulation of strategy, we should look first at the logical proposition that structure should follow strategy in order to cope later with the organizational reality that strategy also follows structure. When we have examined both tendencies, we will understand and to some extent be prepared to deal with the interdependence of the formulation and implementation of corporate purpose. Figure 2.1.1 may be useful in understanding the analysis of strategy as a pattern of interrelated decisions.

Criteria for Evaluation

How is the actual or proposed strategy to be judged? How are we to know that one strategy is better than another? A number of important questions can regularly be asked. As is already evident, no infallible indicators are available. With practice they will lead to reliable intuitive discriminations.

■   *Is the strategy indentifiable and has it been made clear either in words or in practice?* The degree to which attention has been given to the strategic

FIGURE 2.1.1
The strategy process

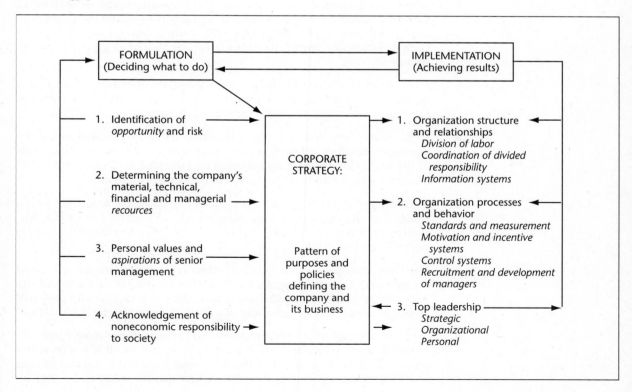

alternatives available to a company is likely to be basic to the soundness of its strategic decision. To cover in empty phrases ('Our policy is planned profitable growth in any market we can serve well') an absence of analysis of opportunity or actual determination of corporate strength is worse than to remain silent, for it conveys the illusion of a commitment when none has been made. The unstated strategy cannot be tested or contested and is likely therefore to be weak. If it is implicit in the intuition of a strong leader, the organization is likely to be weak and the demands the strategy makes upon it are likely to remain unmet. A strategy must be explicit to be effective and specific enough to require some actions and exclude others.

- *Does the strategy exploit fully domestic and international environmental opportunity?* The relation between market opportunity and organizational development is a critical one in the design of future plans. Unless growth is incompatible with the resources of an organization or the aspirations of its management, it is likely that a strategy that does not purport to make full use of market opportunity will be weak also in other aspects. Vulnerability to competition is increased by lack of interest in market share.

- *Is the strategy consistent with corporate competence and resources, both present and projected?* Although additional resources, both financial and managerial, are available to companies with genuine opportunity, the availability of each must be finally determined and programmed along a practicable time scale. This may be the most difficult question in this series.

- *Are the major provisions of the strategy and the program of major policies of which it is comprised internally consistent?* One advantage of making as specific a statement of strategy as is practicable is the resultant availability of a careful check on fit, unity, coherence, compatibility, and synergy – the state in which the whole of anything can be viewed as greater than the sum of its parts.

- *Is the chosen level of risk feasible in economic and personal terms?* The riskiness of any future plan should be compatible with the economic resources of the organization and the temperament of the managers concerned.

- *Is the strategy appropriate to the personal values and aspirations of the key managers?* Conflict between personal preferences, aspirations, and goals of the key members of an organization and the plan for its future is a sign of danger and a harbinger of mediocre performance or failure.

- *Is the strategy appropriate to the desired level of contribution to society?* To the extent that the chosen economic opportunity of the firm has social costs, such as air or water pollution, a statement of intention to deal with these is desirable and prudent.

- *Does the strategy constitute a clear stimulus to organizational effort and commitment?* Generally speaking, the bolder the choice of goals and the wider range of human needs they reflect, the more successfully they will appeal to the capable membership of a healthy and energetic organization.

- *Are there early indications of the responsiveness of markets and market segments to the strategy?* A strategy may pass with flying colors all the tests so far proposed, and may be in internal consistency and uniqueness an admirable work of art. But if within a time period made reasonable by the company's resources and the original plan the strategy does not work, then it must be weak in some way that has escaped attention.

A business enterprise guided by a clear sense of purpose rationally arrived at and emotionally ratified by commitment is more likely to have a successful outcome, in terms of profit and social good, than a company whose future is left to guesswork and chance. Conscious strategy does not preclude brilliance of improvisation or the welcome consequences of good fortune. Its cost is principally thought and work for which it is hard but not impossible to find time.

2.2   The Mind of the Strategist

By Kenichi Ohmae[1]

As a consultant I have had the opportunity to work with many large Japanese companies. Among them are many companies whose success you would say must be the result of superb strategies. But when you look more closely, you discover a paradox. They have no big planning staffs, no elaborate, gold-plated strategic planning processes. Some of them are painfully handicapped by lack of the resources – people, money, and technology – that seemingly would be needed to implement an ambitious strategy. Yet despite all these handicaps, they are outstanding performers in the marketplace. Year after year, they manage to build share and create wealth.

How do they do it? The answer is easy. They may not have a strategic planning staff, but they do have a strategist of great natural talent: usually the founder or chief executive. Often – especially in Japan, where there is no business school – these outstanding strategists have had little or no formal business education, at least at the college level. They may never have taken a course or read a book on strategy. But they have an intuitive grasp of the basic elements of strategy. They have an idiosyncratic mode of thinking in which company, customers, and competition merge in a dynamic interaction out of which a comprehensive set of objectives and plans for action eventually crystallizes.

Insight is the key to this process. Because it is creative, partly intuitive, and often disruptive of the status quo, the resulting plans might not even hold water from the analyst's point of view. It is the creative element in these plans and the drive and will of the mind that conceived them that give these strategies their extraordinary competitive impact.

---

[1] Source: This article was adapted with permission from chapter 1 and 17, and the introduction to *The Mind of the Strategist: The Art of Japanese Business*, McGraw-Hill, New York, 1982.

Both in Japan and in the West, this breed of natural or instinctive strategist is dying out or at least being pushed to the sidelines in favor of rational, by-the-numbers strategic and financial planners. Today's giant institutions, both public and private, are by and large not organized for innovation. Their systems and processes are all oriented toward incremental improvement – doing better what they are doing already. In the United States, the pressure of innumerable social and governmental constraints on corporate activities – most notably, perhaps, the proliferation of government regulations during the 1960s and 1970s – has put a premium on the talent for adaptation and reduced still further the incentive to innovate. Advocates of bold and ambitious strategies too often find themselves on the sidelines, labeled as losers, while the rewards go to those more skilled at working within the system. This is especially true in mature industries, where actions and ideas often move in narrow grooves, forcing out innovators. Conversely, venture capital groups tend to attract the flexible, adaptive minds.

In all times and places, large institutions develop cultures of their own, and success is often closely tied to the ability to conform. In our day, the culture of most business corporations exalts logic and rationality; hence, it is analysts rather than innovators who tend to get ahead. It is not unreasonable to say that many large US corporations today are run like the Soviet economy. In order to survive, they must plan ahead comprehensively, controlling an array of critical functions in every detail. They specify policies and procedures in meticulous detail, spelling out for practically everyone what can and what cannot be done in particular circumstances. They establish hurdle rates, analyze risks, and anticipate contingencies. As strategic planning processes have burgeoned in these companies, strategic thinking has gradually withered away.

My message, as you will have guessed by now, is that successful business strategies result not from rigorous analysis but from a particular state of mind. In what I call the mind of the strategist, insight and a consequent drive for achievement, often amounting to a sense of mission, fuel a thought process which is basically creative and intuitive rather than rational. Strategists do not reject analysis. Indeed they can hardly do without it. But they use it only to stimulate the creative process, to test the ideas that emerge, to work out their strategic implications, or to ensure successful execution of high potential 'wild' ideas that might otherwise never be implemented properly. Great strategies, like great works of art or great scientific discoveries, call for technical mastery in the working out but originate in insights that are beyond the reach of conscious analysis.

If this is so – if the mind of the strategist is so deeply at odds with the culture of the corporation – how can an already institutionalized company recover the capacity to conceive and execute creative business strategies? In a book entitled The Corporate Strategist that was published in Japan in 1975, I attempted to answer that question in a specifically Japanese context.

In Japan, a different set of conditions from those in the West inhibits the creation of bold and innovative strategies. In the large Japanese company, promotion is based on tenure; there is no fast track for brilliant performers. No one reaches a senior management post before the mid-fifties, and chief executives are typically over 60 – well past the age when they are likely to be able to generate dynamic strategic ideas. At the same time, the inventive, often aggressive younger people have no means of contributing in a significant way to the strategy of the corporation. The result: strategic stagnation or the strong probability of it.

How, I asked myself, could the mind of the strategist, with its inventive élan, be reproduced in this kind of corporate culture? What were the ingredients of an excellent strategist, and how could they be reproduced in the Japanese context? These were the questions I addressed in my book. The answer I came up with involved the formation within the corporation of a group of young 'samurais' who would play a dual role. On the one hand they would function as real strategists, giving free rein to their imagination and entrepreneurial flair in order to come up with bold and innovative strategic ideas. On the other hand they would serve as staff analysts, testing out, digesting, and assigning priorities to the ideas, and providing staff assistance to line managers in implementin the approved strategies. This 'samurai' concept has since been adopted in several Japanese firms with great success.

Such a solution would not fit the circumstances of the typical American or European company. Yet it seems to me that the central notion of my book and of a sequel published in Japan 18 months later is relevant to the problem of strategic stagnation in any organization. There are ways in which the mind of the strategist can be reproduced, or simulated, by people who may lack a natural talent for strategy. Putting it another way, although there is no secret formula for inventing a successful strategy, there are some specific concepts and approaches that can help anyone develop the kind of mentality that comes up with superior strategic ideas. Thus the reader will find in this reading no formulas for successful business strategy. What I will try to supply in their place is a series of hints that may help him or her develop the capacity for and the habit of strategic thinking.

Analysis: The Starting Point

Analysis is the critical starting point of strategic thinking. Faced with problems, trends, events, or situations that appear to constitute a harmonious whole or come packaged as a whole by the common sense of the day, the strategic thinker dissects them into their constituent parts. Then, having discovered the significance of these constituents, he reassembles them in a way calculated to maximize his advantage.

In business as on the battlefield, the object of strategy is to bring about the conditions most favorable to one's own side, judging precisely the right moment to attack or withdraw and always assessing the limits of compromise correctly. Besides the habit of analysis, what marks the mind of the strategist is an intellectual elasticity or flexibility that enables him to come up with realistic responses to changing situations, not simply to discriminate with great precision among different shades of gray.

In strategic thinking, one first seeks a clear understanding of the particular character of each element of a situation and then makes the fullest possible use of human brainpower to restructure the elements in the most advantageous way. Phenomena and events in the real world do not always fit a linear model. Hence the most reliable means of dissecting a situation into its constituent parts and reassembling them in the desired pattern is not a step-by-step methodology such as systems analysis. Rather, it is that ultimate nonlinear thinking tool, the human brain. True strategic thinking thus contrasts sharply with the conventional mechanical systems approach based on linear thinking. But it also contrasts with the approach that stakes everything on intuition, reaching conclusions without any real breakdown or analysis (Figure 2.2.1).

No matter how difficult or unprecedented the problem, a breakthrough to the best possible solution can come only from a combination of rational analysis, based on the real nature of things, and imaginative reintegration of all the different items into a new pattern, using nonlinear brainpower. This is always the most effective approach to devising strategies for dealing successfully with challenges and opportunities, in the market arena as on the battlefield.

Determining the Critical Issue

The first stage in strategic thinking is to pinpoint the critical issue in the situation. Everyone facing a problem naturally tries in his or her own way to penetrate to the key issue. Some may think that one way is as good as another and that whether their efforts hit the mark is largely a matter of luck. I believe it is not a question of luck at all but of attitude and method. In problem solving, it is vital at the start to formulate the question in a way that will facilitate the discovery of a solution.

Suppose, for example, that overtime work has become chronic in a company, dragging down profitability. If we frame the question as: What should be done to reduce overtime? Many answers will suggest themselves:

- work harder during the regular working hours;

- shorten the lunch period and coffee breaks;

- forbid long private telephone conversations.

Such questioning is often employed by companies trying to lower costs and improve product quality by using zero defect campaigns and quality control (QC) circles that involve the participation of all employees. Ideas are gathered, screened, and later incorporated in the improvement program. But this approach has an intrinsic limitation. *The questions are not framed to point toward a solution; rather, they are directed toward finding remedies to symptoms.*

FIGURE 2.2.1
Three kinds of thinking
process

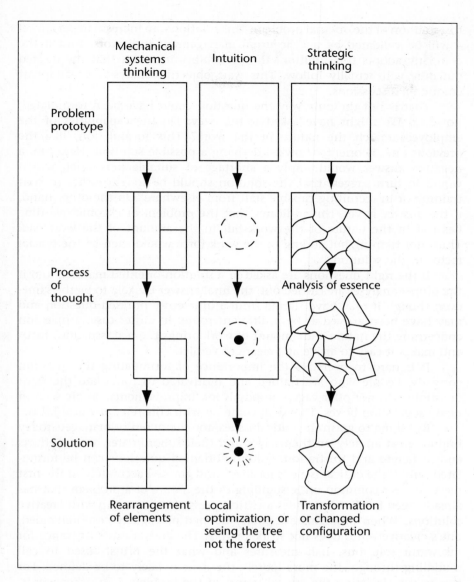

Returning to our overtime problem, suppose we frame the question in a more solution-oriented way: Is this company's work force large enough to do all the work required? To this question there can be only one of two answers – yes or no. To arrive at the answer yes, a great deal of analysis would be needed, probably including a comparison with other companies in the same industries, the historical trend of workload per employee, and the degree of automation and computerization and their economic effectiveness. On the other hand, if – after careful perusal of the sales record, profit per employee, ratio between direct and indirect labor, comparison with other companies, and so on – the answer should turn out to be no (i.e. the company is currently understaffed), this in itself would be tantamount to a solution of the original problem. This solution – an increase in personnel – will be validated by all the usual management indicators. And if the company adopts this solution, the probability increases that the desired outcome will actually follow. This way, objective analysis can supplant emotional discussions.

That is not the only way the question could have been formulated, however. We might have asked it this way: Do the capabilities of the employees match the nature of the work? This formulation, like the previous one, is oriented toward deriving a possible solution. Here too, a negative answer would imply a shortage of suitable personnel, which would in turn suggest that the solution should be sought either in staff training or in recruiting capable staff from elsewhere. On the other hand, if the answer is yes, this indicates that the problem of chronic overtime lies not in the nature of the work but in the amount of the workload. Thus, not training but adding to the work force would then be the crucial factor in the solution.

If the right questions are asked in a solution-oriented manner, and if the proper analyses are carried out, the final answer is likely to be the same, even though it may have started from a differently phrased question and may have been arrived at by a different route. In either case, a question concerning the nature and amount of work brings the real issue into focus and makes it easy to arrive at a clear-cut verdict.

It is hard to overstate the importance of formulating the question correctly. People who are trained and motivated to formulate the right questions will not offer vague proposals for 'improvements,' as are seen in many suggestion boxes. They will come up with concrete, practical ideas.

By failing to grasp the critical issues, too many senior managers today impose great anxiety on themselves and their subordinates, whose efforts end in failure and frustration. Solution-oriented questions can be formulated only if the critical issue is localized and grasped accurately in the first place. A clear common understanding of the nature of a problem that has already been localized provides a critical pressure to come up with creative solutions. When problems are poorly defined or vaguely comprehended, one's creative mind does not work sharply. The greater one's tolerance for lukewarm solutions, half measures and what the British used to call muddling through, the more loosely the issue is likely to be defined. For this reason, isolating the crucial points of the problem – in other words, determining the critical issue – is most important to the discovery of a solution. The key at this initial stage is to *narrow down the issue by studying the observed phenomena closely.*

Figure 2.2.2 illustrates one method often used by strategists in the process of abstraction, showing how it might work in the case of a large, established company faced with the problem of declining competitive vigor.

The first step in the abstraction process is to use such means as brainstorming and opinion polls to assemble and itemize the respects in which the company is at a disadvantage *vis-à-vis* its competitors. These points can then be classified under a smaller number of headings (shown in Figure 2.2.2 as Concrete Phenomena) according to their common factors.

FIGURE 2.2.2
Narrowing down the issue

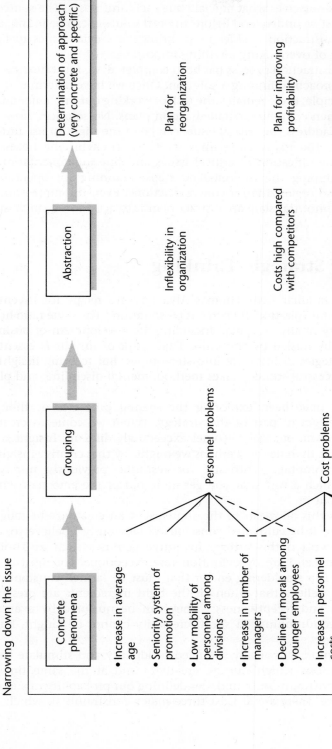

Next, phenomena sharing some common denominator are themselves combined into groups. Having done this, we look once again at each group as a unit and ask ourselves what crucial issue each unit poses. The source of the problem must be understood before any real solution can be found, and the process of abstraction enables us to bring the crucial issues to light without the risk of overlooking anything important.

Once the abstraction process has been completed, we must next decide on the right approach to finding a solution. Once we have determined the solution in principle, there remains the task of working out implementation programs and then compiling detailed action plans. No solution, however perfectly it may address the critical issue, can be of the slightest use until it is implemented. Too many companies try to short-circuit the necessary steps between identification of critical issues and line implementation of solutions by skipping the intermediate steps: planning for operational improvement and organizing for concrete actions. Even the most brilliant line manager cannot translate an abstract plan into action in a single step.

The Art of Strategic Thinking

Most of us are familiar with Thomas Alva Edison's recipe for inventive genius: '1 percent inspiration, 99 percent perspiration.' The same ratio holds true for creativity in any endeavor, including the development of business strategy. Don't be misled by the ratio. That spark of insight *is* essential. Without it, strategies disintegrate into stereotypes. But to bring insight to fruition as a successful strategy takes method, mental discipline, and plain hard work.

So far we have been exploring the mental processes or thought patterns for the 'grunt' part of the strategy. When we come to creative inspiration, however, our task becomes exceedingly difficult. Insight is far easier to recognize than define. Perhaps we might say that creative insight is the ability to combine, synthesize, or reshuffle previously unrelated phenomena in such a way that you get more out of the emergent whole than you have put in.

What does this all mean to the strategist? Can creativity be taught? Perhaps not. Can it be cultivated consciously? Obviously I believe so, or I wouldn't have written this article. Inventive geniuses such as Thomas Edison or Edwin Land are by definition rare exceptions. For most of us, creative insight is a smoldering ember that must be fanned constantly to glow. I strongly believe that when all the right ingredients are present – sensitivity, will, and receptiveness – they can be nurtured by example, direction, and conditioning. In short, creativity cannot be taught, but it can be learned.

Putting it more prosaically, we need to identify and stimulate those habits or conditions which nurture creativity and at the same time to crystallize the constraints or boundaries defining our probability of success. In my experience, there are at least three major constraints to which the business strategist needs to be sensitive. I think of them as the essential Rs: reality, ripeness, and resources.

Let's begin with *reality*. Unlike scientific conceptualizers or creative artists, business strategists must always be aware of the customer, the competition, and the company's field of competence. *Ripeness*, or timing, is the second key consideration that the business strategist must address. Unless the time is ripe for the proposed strategy, it is virtually certain to fail. *Resources*, my third R, constitute such an obvious constraint that it is amazing that they should be ignored or neglected by strategists. Yet examples abound of strategies that failed because their authors were not sensitive to their own resource limitations. Take diversification as a case in point. Few food companies trying to move into pharmaceuticals, chemical companies moving into foods, or electronic component manufacturers moving into final assembly have succeeded. The basic reason in most cases has been that the companies involved were not sensitive to the limitations of their own internal resources and skills.

Conditions of Creativity

Being attuned to the three Rs is a necessary precondition of creative insight, but in itself it will not fan the spark of creative power within us. For that, other elements are needed. Obviously, there is no single approach that will dependably turn anyone into a superstrategist, but there are certain things we can consciously do to stretch or stimulate our creative prowess. Most important, I believe, we need to cultivate three interrelated conditions an initial charge, directional antennae, and a capacity to tolerate static.

Call it what you will – vision, focus, inner drive – the initial charge must be there. It is the mainspring of intuitive creativity. We have seen how Yamaha, originally a wood-based furniture company, was transformed into a major force in the leisure industry by just such a vision, born of one man's desire to bring positive enrichment into the lives of the work-oriented Japanese. From this vision he developed a totally new thrust for Yamaha.

An entire family of musical instruments and accessories – organs, trumpets, cornets, trombones, guitars, and so on – was developed to complement Yamaha's pianos. These were followed by stereo equipment, sporting goods, motorcycles and pleasure boats. Music schools were established. Then came the Yamaha Music Camp, complete with a resort lodge complex, a game reserve, an archery range, and other leisure-oriented pursuits. Today, Yamaha plans concerts and is involved with concert hall management as well, reaping profits while enriching the lives of millions of Japanese.

If the initial charge provides the creative impetus, directional antennae are required to recognize phenomena which, as the saying goes, are in the air. These antennae are the component in the creative process that uncovers and selects, among a welter of facts and existing conditions, potentially profitable ideas that were always there but were visible only to eyes not blinded by habit.

Consider how these directional antennae work for Dr Kazuma Tateishi, founder and chairman of Omron Tateishi Electronics. Tateishi has an uncanny flair for sensing phenomena to which the concept of flow can be applied. He perceived the banking business as a flow of cash, traffic jams and congested train stations as blocked flows of cars and people, and production lines as a physical flow of parts. From these perceptions evolved the development of Japan's first automated banking system, the introduction of sequence controllers that automatically regulate traffic according to road conditions and volume, and the evolution of the world's first unmanned railroad station based on a completely automatic system that can exchange bills for coins, issue tickets and season passes, and adjust fares and operate turnstiles. Today, Omron's automated systems are used in many industrial operations from production to distribution. Dr Tateishi is a remarkable example of a man whose directional antennae have enabled him to implement his youthful creed: 'Man should do only what only man can do.'

Creative concepts often have a disruptive as well as a constructive aspect. They can shatter set patterns of thinking, threaten the status quo, or at the very least stir up people's anxieties. Often when people set out to sell or implement a creative idea, they are taking a big risk of failing, losing money, or simply making fools of themselves. That is why the will to cope with criticism, hostility, and even derision, while not necessarily a condition of creative thinking, does seem to be an important characteristic of successful innovative strategists. To squeeze the last drop out of my original metaphor, I call this the static-tolerance component of creativity.

Witness the static that Soichiro Honda had to tolerate in order to bring his clean-engine car to market. Only corporate insiders can tell how much intracompany interference he had to cope with. That the government vainly brought severe pressure on him to stay out of the auto market is no secret, however. Neither is the public ridicule he bore when industry experts scoffed at his concept.

Dr Koji Kobayashi of NEC tolerated static of a rather different kind. Despite prevailing industry trends, he clung fast to his intuitive belief (some 20 years ahead of its time) that computers and telecommunications would one day be linked. To do so, he had to bear heavy financial burdens, internal dissension, and scorn. All this leads me to a final observation. Strategic success cannot be reduced to a formula, nor can anyone become a strategic thinker merely by reading a book. Nevertheless, there are habits of mind and modes of thinking that can be acquired through practice to help you free the creative power of your subconscious and improve your odds of coming up with winning strategic concepts.

The main purpose of this contribution is to encourage you to do so and to point out the directions you should pursue. The use of Japanese examples to illustrate points and reinforce assertions may at times have given it an exotic flavor, but that is ultimately of no importance. Creativity, mental productivity and the power of strategic insight know no national boundaries. Fortunately for all of us, they are universal.

2.3   Game Theory and Strategic Thinking

By Teck Hua Ho and Keith Weigelt[1]

In his seminal strategic treatise, The Art of War, Sun Tzu writes

> Thus, it is said that one who knows the enemy and knows himself will not
> be endangered in a hundred engagements. One who does not know the
> enemy but knows himself will sometimes be victorious, sometimes meet
> with defeat. One who knows neither the enemy nor himself will invariably
> be defeated in every engagement.

Game theory provides a formal methodology for knowing oneself and
one's competitors. It helps analyze and anticipate the strategic moves of
rivals. It also shows how a firm's actions and those of its competitors are
interrelated, linked by a strategic umbilical cord. This article introduces
basic concepts of game theory and then uses them to examine key strategic
principles. In exploring these principles, we show how game theory can be
applied to issues such as interpreting signals, sequential market entry,
setting production quantities, and reputation.

Game Theory's 2,500–Year March into the Boardroom

The principles of game theory were applied by Chinese military planners
2,500 years ago. Modern economists expanded and formalized these
principles. Game theorists recently celebrated their first half-century by
winning the 1994 Nobel prize in economics. While this award illustrates
game theory's maturing as an economic discipline, the usefulness of game
theory in business strategy has only recently begun to be recognized. We
show how managers can use game theory to:

1   Create a common language for modeling strategic situations.

2   Classify situations and transfer strategic insights across contexts (e.g.
markets, products, organizations).

3   Channel resources only to assets that significantly improve the firm's
competitive market position.

---

[1] Source: This article was adapted with permission from 'Game Theory and Strategic Thinking',
in: Day G., and D.J. Reibstein (Eds.), *Wharton on Dynamic Competitive Strategy*, Wiley, New York,
1997.

4   Generate specific prescriptions if enough relevant information is available. For example, game theory has been used in bidding an optimal price for bandwidth channels in the recent FCC auction; deciding whether to enter a new product market and choosing whether to issue an affinity credit card.

Even if parameters are not known exactly, game theory can help classify strategic situations, which is often a critical step in strategic planning. This classification may either offer new insights or simply confirm those already known. Game theorists have studied extensively many categories or classes of games, and have developed strategic insights about game parameters. A celebrated example is the Prisoner's Dilemma game, whose key insight is that individually rational action can hurt the group as a whole. This insight has been applied, but not restricted to, strategic situations such as price wars, intrafirm cooperation and international trade.

Because game theory is a model with restrictive assumptions, some managers question its relevance to real competitive situations. All formal models require some simplification of reality to be used. Even for skeptics, however, game theory generates core strategic principles and insights that belong in the toolbox of all managers. Further, game theory provides a method of formal analysis of these principles.

This article provides an introductory review of game theory for the layperson. After a brief discussion of key concepts of game theory, we examine several strategic principles through the lens of game theory. These principles can help analyze many recurrent issues in competitive analysis, including cooperative and non-cooperative behavior, trade-offs between individual and group goals, short- and long-term payoffs, and altruistic and self-interested behaviors.

Key Concepts of Game Theory

Any strategic analysis should create a common mental model of the underlying strategic situation. It is difficult to communicate ideas among managers if they do not share the same mental model. Because of the exactness of its language, game theory is useful in precisely describing strategic situations. The theory uses visual representations and a unique set of terms to describe situations; this enforces the creation of a common mental model among managers. Thus, game theory provides a consistent framework for structuring competitive decision problems. This structuring process, in turn, focuses managerial attention on relevant competitive factors and helps configure a firm's resource base for strategic advantage.

Game visually represent strategic situations in one of two related ways. Figure 2.3.1 shows a situation where two firms (A and B) are introducing a product and must decide whether to advertise. This representation is called a *normal* or *matrix* form game. Consider it a summary of the strategic situation. It identifies all players (Firms A and B), their available strategies (advertise or not), and payoffs associated with all consequences (if Firm A advertises, and B doesn't, then A receives a payoff of 9, and B a payoff of 7).

Figure 2.3.2 shows the same strategic situation in an extensive form game. Extensive form games illustrate all the information of normal form games (players, available strategies, consequences, and associated pay-offs), but add a time dimension. Specifically, they show whether the game is a simultaneous or sequential move game (any normal form game is one of simultaneous moves).

The game in Figure 2.3.2a, is a simultaneous move game: Decision nodes are represented by squares, and random shocks by circles. The dotted line linking Firm B's decision nodes represent an *information set* – managers at Firm B do not know whether they are at the left (Firm A advertises) or right (Firm A does not advertise) decision node. So they must select their action without knowing Firm A's choice. Thus their moves are simultaneous. Even if both players do not move at the same time, they act 'as if' they do because they do not know the choices of the others.

Figure 2.3.2b shows a sequential move game. Note that the only difference is the absence of a dotted line linking B's decision nodes in Figure 2.3.2b. This indicates that B's managers know A's decision before choosing their strategy. Thus, their moves are sequential.

As indicated in Figures 2.3.1 and 2.3.2, strategic situations are characterized by interactive payoffs – one player's actions affect the payoffs of others. For example, in Figure 2.3.1, if managers at Firm A choose to advertise, they realize either a payoff of 6 or 9, depending on whether B's managers advertise. This interdependency is prevalent across strategic situations. Game theory's capacity to analyze strategic situations lies in its explicit recognition of the mutual interdependence of players (because of interactive payoffs). So, in strategic situations, managers must consider themselves connected by a strategic umbilical cord: no independent optimal strategic choice exists; optimality is conditional on the actions of

FIGURE 2.3.1
An advertising game

		Firm A	
		Advertise	Don't advertise
Firm B	Advertise	11.6	16.1
	Don't advertise	7.9	21.3

FIGURE 2.3.2
Extensive form game

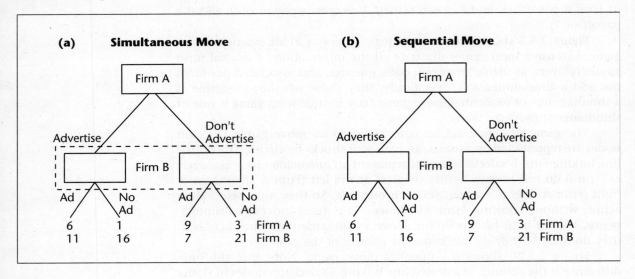

others. One player's actions can cause others to change their actions, and vice versa. Hence, managers need to understand the strategic perception of others; that is, what characteristics do others ascribe to the situation, and how do these characteristics affect their strategy choices?

For managers, a key implication of game theory's focus on interactive payoffs is that strategic planning is a process-based function. Because the strategic umbilical cord ties you to others, as you move, you move others, and vice versa. Strategic situations are never static; they continually evolve. If managers recognize the relevant strategic variables, then any disadvantage is an opportunity; any success, a potential failure. Within the sphere of strategic interdependence, you shape the future.

Equilibrium Strategies

A distinct feature of game theory is its prescriptive power: it identifies which strategies players should choose by designating equilibrium strategies. Equilibrium strategies are characterized by three traits: stability, optimality, and rationality. First, no player has an incentive to unilaterally shift from its equilibrium strategy. Second, it is a strategy of mutual best response: my action choice is optimal if given others choose their optimal choices. Third, all players are rational and believe others are rational. The most commonly used equilibrium concept is the Nash equilibrium, an array of strategies (or action choices) such that each player believes he or she is doing the best he or she possibly can, given the actions of others.

In Figure 2.3.1 the Nash equilibrium is that both firms advertise. One can interpret this as a prediction regarding the future strategies of each firm, assuming that each firm will try to maximize its payoff. If both firms advertise, then Firm B has no incentive to shift to another strategy. If B shifts to 'Don't advertise,' it would earn a payoff of 7 instead of 11. The same reasoning holds true for Firm A. If Firm A shifts to 'Don't advertise,' its payoff is 1 instead of 6. So by advertising, each firm is doing the best it can, given that the other is doing the best it can.

Equilibrium strategies depend on the configurations of players' strategic states. We define a strategic state along four dimensions:

1   *The feasible strategy set.* The set of possible strategies for the player. Managers may shift equilibria by enlarging their feasible strategy set. That is, they may play strategies that were previously assigned a zero probability. For example, before Frank Perdue differentiated his chicken via a brand name, managers in that industry had assigned a zero probability to a differentiation strategy. Or, when John D. Rockefeller entered the oil industry, it was regarded as a commodity business with low-profit margins. Using a strategy of vertical integration, Rockefeller shifted the equilibrium and was handsomely rewarded for it.

2   *Information flows.* The flow of information also affects the structure of the game. First, is information perfect or imperfect? This relates to our earlier discussion of sequential or simultaneous moves. If information is perfect, then managers recognize previous moves of others (i.e. a sequential move game); if information is imperfect, managers do not completely know the previous actions of others (i.e. a simultaneous move game). Obviously, this type of uncertainty can affect strategic choice. Is information complete or not? In a complete information setting, players know (with certainty) all strategic configuration dimensions (e.g. payoffs, feasible strategy sets, identities of players, and so on). Information is incomplete if some uncertainty exists among players about relevant strategic variables. When this occurs, players may have different mental models regarding the strategic situation. Any information gathering that helps reduce this uncertainty may help managers in choosing a strategy.

3   *Payoffs.* Payoffs are the level of rewards that players receive from a given outcome. For example, in Figure 2.3.1, if both firms advertise, Firm A receives a payoff of 6 and B a payoff of 11. A player's payoff depends on its underlying preference function, so different players can realize different reward levels from identical consequences. Because the reward level depends on the subjective preferences of the manager, managers can shift equilibria (i.e. change the strategy choice of others) by changing the reward level associated with an action. For example, preemptive entry into a market can change the payoff associated with the subsequent market entry of others. Payoff structures can define strategic situations; for example, zero-sum game versus non-zero-sum games. In a zero-sum game, the total payoff space shared by players remains constant. So any gain by one player must result in a loss to another player. This is typical of many bargaining situations. In non-zero-sum games, the payoff space

varies. When the payoff space is increasing (as in high-growth markets), all players can increase their payoffs.

4   *Players*. Both the number of players and their identities are important. As the number of players change, payoffs to individual players may also change. For example, in forming strategic alliances, identities are important because of the subjective nature of payoffs. A payoff not highly valued by one player may be highly valued by others.

A situation's strategic configuration can significantly affect the underlying nature of the interaction. Game theorists have developed a classification scheme of games that can be used to identify important types of strategic situations. We describe some classes of these in the following discussion of several strategic principles.

Strategic Principles

Although game theory has much more depth and complexity than presented in the preceding brief overview, perhaps its greatest power is in presenting very simple, but crucial, strategic principles. The importance of strategic principles, which we illustrate with game theoretic models, were recognized by Chinese philosophers 2,500 years ago and are contained in the seven military classics. Principles expounded in the military classics were considered so valuable that the unauthorized possession of a classic was punishable by death. At the time these books were written, China consisted of a collection of individual states, each striving to survive in a very competitive environment. Alliances between states were perpetually changing, and there was a constant threat of war. The Chinese belief that there is no distinction between theory and application meant strategic principles were well tested.

So, while the techniques available to strategists have certainly improved, both in the sophistication of modeling (e.g. game theory, decision analysis) and analytic power (computers versus Chinese 'counting sticks'), the importance of these principles remains constant. Given this consistency, we use insights of classic Chinese philosophy to help explain their more formal game theoretic interpretations.

Principle 1: Use Strategic Foresight

Unlike Westerners, the Chinese did not define knowledge as a mapping from theory to objective reality; their knowledge was the ability to trace out or unravel a strategic situation. Today we might characterize this as strategic foresight; game theory can be used to analyze future competitive actions. It is the ability to analyze a strategic situation, anticipate where it is going, and then make decisions today that will favorably affect future payoffs (since strategy is a process). Thus knowledge corresponds to controlling the dynamics of the strategic situation – we shape the future by manipulating strategic variables. The Chinese refer to this ability as 'taking care of the great, while the great is small.' Game theorists call this ability *backward induction*.

Example: Credible and noncredible signals When managers of a firm state their intention to do something, should they be believed? Backward induction can help determine whether the signal is truly in line with the payoffs of the action. For example, when a firm acquires another firm, managers at the acquiring firm (Firm 1) may fear that managers at the acquired firm (Firm 2) will fight relentlessly if their autonomy is threatened. So managers at Firm 1 publicly promise to adopt a hands-off policy and give managers at Firm 2 autonomy. If managers at Firm 2 believe this promise, they acquiesce to a friendly takeover. However, the promise is not credible, as shown in Figure 2.3.3.

The acquisition scenario is the following: managers at Firm 2 must decide whether to agree to a friendly takeover, or fight it. If they fight (R) they realize a payoff of 1 (because they keep their independence), and managers at Firm 1 realize a payoff of 1 (because they don't incur the costs of a hostile takeover). If they agree to a takeover (L), then managers at Firm 1 must choose their strategy. They can keep their promise and give autonomy to Firm 2 (L). Then managers at Firm 1 realize a payoff of −1 because even though they paid for Firm 2, they cannot impose their preferences, control and monitoring systems, and more on it. However, managers at Firm 2 realize a payoff of 2 since they both have their freedom and the use of Firm 1's resources. Or, managers at Firm 1 can renege on their promise (R), and not give managers at Firm 2 their autonomy. Now managers at Firm 1 realize a payoff of 2, since they induced Firm 1's managers to agree to a friendly takeover, and now they can impose their monitoring, control, and incentive systems on them. Conversely, managers at Firm 2 realize a payoff

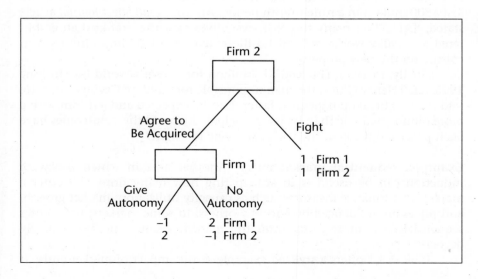

FIGURE 2.3.3
Acquisition game

of −1, since they forgo their managerial freedom. If you were a manager at Firm 1, which payoff would you choose?

Game theorists suggest managers use backward induction to solve this game. That is, a manager should go to the game's end and trace out what each player should do along the 'choice path.' For example, if managers at Firm 1 reach their decision node, what will they do? They could either give autonomy and realize a payoff of −1, or not give it and realize a payoff of 2. Clearly, they prefer a payoff of 2 over −1, so they will not give autonomy.

But, from Figure 2.3.3 we clearly see that managers at Firm 2 would agree to a takeover (move left) only if they thought they would receive a payoff of 2 (managers at Firm 1 give them autonomy). If they did not believe the promise, they are clearly better off retaining their freedom (a payoff of 1 versus −1).

So if they use strategic foresight (i.e. backward induction), they should not believe the promise by Firm 1's managers (since it is not credible). Good strategic players should always anticipate the future actions of others – they must consider future moves in choosing today's strategy. Managers who are myopic do not anticipate the future, because they fail to realize the process like nature of strategy. Such managers may make good short-run decisions, but may not be as successful in the long run, because they lack strategic foresight.

This dynamic can be seen in many actual examples of corporate acquisitions. For example, just 99 days after IBM spent $3.5 billion to acquire Lotus, Jim Manzi, the CEO of Lotus quit because of differences about managerial control. *The Wall Street Journal* noted that '. . . IBMers grumbled that Mr. Manzi campaigned in the press to win broader powers inside the company,' and that IBM could be hurt by '. . . disarray and disruption in Mr. Manzi's wake – more executive departures, delays in development . . .'

Lotus was not alone. AT&T spent $7.48 billion in 1990 to acquire NCR. Five years later, it took a $1.2 billion charge, laid off 10,000 employees, and lost $500 million in a nine-month period. Another *Wall Street Journal* article stated, '[AT&T] let many top NCR executives exit, then rankled an embittered and balky workforce and hostile management by imposing its own culture on the new property.'

Finally, in 1995, ITT paid $1.7 billion for Caesar's World Inc. In June 1995, CEO Henry Gluck, the man responsible for building Caesar's, quit. He said the '. . . breakup happened faster than he expected and left him with a more diminished role than he had anticipated.' Could these outcomes have been predicted through the use of strategic foresight?

Example: sequential market entry Another area in which backward induction can be useful is in anticipating how many firms will enter a market. Performance measures such as capacity utilization, market growth, and prices are influenced by entry by others. In some markets, firms enter sequentially. As more firms enter the market, per-firm profits generally decrease.

Table 2.3.1 offers a stylized example of the impact of market entry. It

Number of Firms	Profits per Firm ($ millions)
1	20
2	16
3	7.5
4	–

TABLE 2.3.1
Sequential entry game

shows the profits per firm (think of these as the present value of the future earning stream) for one firm and for all players if other firms enter. When there is only one firm in the market, it earns $520 million. If two firms enter the market, then competition drives per-firm profits to $16 million.

Entrants enter sequentially. Customers exhibit brand loyalty, so incumbents can use advertising to deter entry. To enter, an entrant must spend twice the total spent on advertising by an individual incumbent firm. Assume all incumbent firms provide the same level of advertising. For example, if two firms are in the market, and they each spend $5 million on advertising, an entrant must spend $10 million on advertising to successfully enter the market.

How many firms will enter the market and how much should Firm 1 spend to keep others out? The profits in Table 2.3.1 are gross before any spending on advertising. To act as a deterrent, advertising must be directed against a specific entrant. Hence, if Firm 1 tries to keep out Firm 2 and fails, its advertising cost is considered sunk and non-salvageable. If you are the manager of the incumbent firm (Firm 1), how many firms should you expect to enter the market, and what is the net per-firm profit?

Most individuals respond that two firms will enter the market, and their net profits will be $12.25 million. They reason that if two firms enter the market, each must spend $3.75 million (one-half of $7.5 million) to keep out the third entrant. Their net profits will thus be $12.25 million ($16 − 3.75$). If the first firm wants to keep out the second firm, the first firm must spend $8 million (one-half of $16 million). Its net profit would equal $12 million. So it is better for the first firm ($12.25 million versus $12 million) to let the second firm enter the market and share the cost of keeping out the third firm. Unfortunately, this reasoning is wrong, because it doesn't use backward induction.

The correct way to view the situation is if the first firm lets the second enter the market, then the per-firm profit is $12.25 million. But if the first firm wants to prevent the second firm from entering the market, it only has to spend $6.125 million, not $8 million. For if the second firm enters the market, it is looking at a payoff of $12.25 million, not $16 million (see Table 2.3.1). Managers at the second firm should realize if they enter the market, they will have to spend $3.75 million to keep out the third entrant ($16 − 3.75 = 12.25 million). So Firm 1 is better off spending the money on advertising to keep out the second firm ($20 − 6.125 = $13.88 million). Hence, using strategic foresight, only one firm should enter this market, not two.

Both the acquisition and advertising examples illustrate the importance of strategic foresight. Managers have to realize they must think about the future when making today's decisions: In both examples, strategic actions taken early in the game affect later behavior. Because of the interdependence between players, managers can control the strategic situation, and help determine its future path.

Given the importance of this principle, it is imperative that managers be taught to think about the long-term implications of decisions. Simple game theoretic examples like these may encourage managers to think more about these long-term implications.

Principle 2: Know Yourself as Well as Others

As noted in the preceding examples, many strategic decisions depend on understanding the structure of the game and the payoffs from the view of the competitor. In other words, it is important 'to be sure you are playing the right game.' Managers who successfully use game theory create models that mirror reality-their models capture the essential elements of the actual strategic situation.

Many managers underestimate the difficulty of this task, and fail to carefully construct models. Most managers learn game theory through examples like those in the preceding figures, where payoffs are given and feasible strategy sets and players are specified. In real strategic situations, determining these payoffs, players, strategy sets, and other factors is half the battle. Information is not perfect and complete as it is in most examples.

Most individuals are trained to solve game theory models, but receive scant formal training in constructing them. This is unfortunate, for much of game theory's strategic value is derived from forcing managers to correctly model the strategic situation. Given the evidence of the poor decision-making abilities of individuals managers should engage in a disciplined process of constructing a game model of their strategic situation. To construct these models, managers must specify the number and identity of players, feasible strategy sets, and underlying preference functions. And, most important, they must specify both their beliefs and those of others regarding these strategic dimensions. This is why Principle 2 is so important.

Many times it is said that game theory forces you to view the situation from the viewpoint of others. This is a half-truth, and like many half-truths its use will produce suboptimal results. What game theory suggests you do is to view the situation as others do. In *The Book of Five Rings*, the famous samurai warrior Musashi states: 'Small men must know thoroughly what it is like to be big men, and big men must know what it is like to be small men.'

If you are to think like others, you must adopt their mind-set. Musashi was discussing sword fighting, where small men use different strategies (e.g. quickness, maneuverability) relative to big men (e.g. strength, reach) because each relies on different resources. So if a big man anticipates the moves of a smaller opponent without adopting his mind-set, he will likely be wrong (with fatal consequences), because he will anticipate the moves of a big man.

Similarly, in today's business world, many entrepreneurs have different mental models from managers at Fortune 500 firms. Managers at large firms have different resource bundles, incentive plans, decision-making procedures, and so on. When the large firms treat their opponents like large firms, they are often surprised when these nimble entrepreneurs outmaneuver them. Even managers at firms that diversify into new markets often have initial difficulties because they haven't grasped an understanding of their rivals' mind-sets.

Because of the strategic umbilical cord of interactive payoffs connecting a firm to other players, a manager cannot know him- or herself well unless he or she knows others well. One's strengths and weaknesses are defined relative to those of others. Some managers have difficulty 'knowing themselves' because they must recognize both their strengths and weaknesses (and those of their organizations). Managers often overlook weak points and focus on strengths. Those who ignore weaknesses find it difficult to be successful strategists. Since managers should pit strengths against others' weaknesses, weaknesses must be recognized to identify vulnerable areas.

Example: Production quantity game   Figure 2.3.4 is a game-theoretic example of why Principle 2 is important. It illustrates a simple quantity-type (i.e. Cournot) game. You and a rival share the market. While you know your cost function with certainty, you are unsure about your rival's costs. Figure 2.3.4a shows the situation where your cost function is higher, relative to that of your rival. Figure 2.3.4b shows the opposite situation.

Game theory suggests if your strategic situation is that represented in Figure 2.3.4a, you should produce low quantities of the good (and your rival, high quantities). If the strategic situation more closely resembles that in Figure 2.3.4b, you should produce high quantities of the good (and your rival, low quantities). So the predicted optimal strategy conditional on the characteristics of you and your rival, namely who has the higher cost function. The absolute level of the cost function is of less strategic importance than the function's relative level.

This example again illustrates the strategic value of constructing payoff matrices (even for simplified situations). Once you know whether your cost function is relatively higher or lower, choosing the optimal strategy is straightforward. The difficulty is in deciding your cost level, relative to that of rivals. Many times, this requires a lot of thought about the strategic situation, including rational reasons (or evidence) about why you think your cost function is lower (or higher) than those of rivals.

Benchmarking studies are one way managers heed the advice of Principle 2. These studies provide a measure of a firm's performance relative to that of others. For example, Motorola initiated the six-sigma program as a result of benchmarking *vis-à-vis* Japanese companies. Benchmarking studies help motivate organizations to move to new goals and to 'convince' agents

FIGURE 2.3.4
A production quality
game

(a) High-Cost

		You	
		Produces High Quantities	Produces Low Quantities
Your Rival	Produces High Quantities	4.1	8.4
	Produces Low Quantities	1.5	3.3

(b) Low-Cost

		You	
		Produces High Quantities	Produces Low Quantities
Your Rival	Produces High Quantities	2.2	5.1
	Produces Low Quantities	4.8	3.3

of the feasibility of such goals. In this sense, through benchmarking studies, managers use the principle of knowing others and themselves to motivate organizational improvements. However, managers must also recognize the principle's value in formulating strategy. It is this use that creates the most strategic value.

Sometimes it is impossible to determine all the attributes of a competitive game. Uncertainty about others' characteristics is the norm for most business-related strategic situations. Although this uncertainty does complicate modeling, game theory can help managers think about its implications. When managers are uncertain about attributes of others, they can use incomplete information game models. These models assume managers hold different information sets about game parameters (e.g. payoffs, player attributes, and so on). Because managerial beliefs are dependent on information sets, and beliefs affect strategic choice, managers must consider the beliefs of others. As previously shown, if I think my costs are lower than my rival's, I will choose a different strategy than if I think they are higher. If one player has lower relative costs, but its managers believe it has higher costs, they will act accordingly.

Principle 3: Differentiate Between One-Time and Repeated Interactions

Many times, game theory prescribes different behaviors for identical strategic situations depending on whether the game is played once or repeatedly. Repeated interaction increases the strategy space and allows today's strategy to depend on past history. The Chinese recognized this and summarized it in the following principle: 'When there is trust in verbal agreements, the trust is there before the words.'

For instance, in repeated play, a penalty for past uncooperative behaviors can be built into the current strategy. Because of this strategy space expansion, prescriptions for optimal behavior can change. For example, in a single-shot Prisoner's Dilemma game, the optimal response is to 'defect.' If players were to play the same game repeatedly, then it could be optimal to exhibit cooperative behavior – if players care about future payoffs, since any defective behavior could be penalized in the future.

Repeated interaction also can change the ways firms behave in incomplete information games. Next we show how managers can use corporate reputations to generate future rents.

Example: Reputation Firm B is the dominant player in a growing market it developed. Your firm, Firm A, is one of several thinking about entering B's market. Imagine you are a manager at Firm A, and you must decide whether to enter B's market. You are unsure about some characteristics of managers at Firm B. These managers may be 'weak types' who would rather share their market with you than start a price war. Or they may be 'tough types' who do not want to share, and are willing to start a price war to keep you out. These two scenarios are shown in Figure 2.3.5. Looking at the figure, your decision is straightforward – if you know the incumbent's true type. If the incumbent is a weak type, you enter the market; if it is tough, you don't enter.

This is an example of why Principles 2 and 3 are so important. The more you know about rivals, the better you can anticipate their next move and use this information in choosing your action. In this example, if the rival is weak, enter: if tough, stay out.

However, when uncertain about characteristics of others, managers form beliefs about them. Managers at Firm B should exploit the uncertainty. If they are smart (though weak), they recognize the incentive to mimic the behavior of tough types. If they do (i.e. start a price war), they may convince other entrants they are actually tough and not enter. And why is this convincing? Because when uncertain, we seek information to resolve the uncertainty. We infer a player's type from available information; that is, we look for 'signals' about types. One signal is past behavior – we infer future behavior by examining past behavior. This behavioral history is what game theorists call *reputation*.

FIGURE 2.3.5
Type of incumbent

(a) Weak

		You (Entrant)	
		Enter Market	Do Not Enter
Incumbent	Share Market	2.2	6.1
	Start Price War	0.0	5.1

(b) Tough

		You (Entrant)	
		Enter Market	Do Not Enter
Incumbent	Share Market	−1.2	3.1
	Start Price War	1.0	7.1

By acting tough against early entrants, managers at Firm B establish a reputation for being tough. This reputation then generates future rents because it causes later entrants not to enter. Although costly in the short run, the mimicry of tough types by weak ones is profitable in the long run (given reasonable assumptions about discount rates and time horizons).

There are many examples of reputation-building behavior in markets, usually by firms that are admired for their management skills. Procter & Gamble has clearly cultivated the image of being a tough competitor, by forcefully responding to any entry into its markets. Intel is currently establishing a 'tough type' reputation in the chip market. It seems determined to hold its leadership position at all costs. Between 1990 and 1995, Frito-Lay expanded its market share in salty snacks from 43 percent to 52 percent. *The Wall Street Journal* noted: '[Frito-Lay] continues to expand its realm. I'd tell anyone else trying to get into the business, don't try to expand, don't try to impinge on Frito's territory or you'll get crushed.'

Reputation models help explain many aspects of strategic planning. Besides entry deterrence, they can explain why producers use non-informative advertising to signal the quality of their products, the widespread use of consulting and accounting firms, and even corporate culture. Repeated interactions thus change the competitive game because managers change their perceptions after each round. Also, payoffs for a single round of play may be very different from those of multiple-round games, so it is important to understand at the outset whether the game is one-time or repeated.

Principle 4: Managers Must Unify Minds to Promote Cooperation

We have focused on competitive strategic situations. In business, these are commonly represented by interfirm interactions. However, game theory is also useful in analyzing cooperative behaviors – either within firms or within alliances among different firms. In these situations, the emphasis is on promoting cooperative behavior.

All the Chinese classics discuss how important, yet difficult, the 'planning' of cooperation is. As one classic notes, 'As for the Tao of the military, nothing surpasses unity.' Or, as Napoleon more recently remarked, 'In war, morale is to materials as 3 is to 1.' Unfortunately, many managers underestimate the significant difficulty of building co-operation within groups. Simple game theory models pinpoint the source of difficulty.

The Chinese model of unity is based on mutual trust. Individuals sacrifice personal goals for group goals when they 'commit' to a group goal. Individually, though, the question is, 'Yes, I'll sacrifice as much as you, but how do I know you are sacrificing the same as I?' Unless everyone trusts others to be as committed as they to group goals, support for group commitment is incomplete. Mutual trust is not.

Figure 2.3.6 shows why. Group members choose an 'effort contribution' toward group goals represented by seven numbered levels. Your payoff depends on your contribution and those of others. Contribute significantly less than others, you free-ride off them; significantly more, they off you. Individuals want to coordinate their effort with that of others.

All players should select the maximum effort level of 7, since everyone realizes the highest possible payoff ($5.00). No player can possibly receive a higher payoff by choosing any other effort level. So if players want to coordinate their effort with that of others, then everyone should want to coordinate on 7.

The key caveat to this thinking is that you must trust others to provide their maximum effort, for if they don't and you do, your payoff is negative: They simply free-ride off your effort. So if you don't trust others to give maximum effort, you hesitate to give yours. And if group members think this way, they choose a suboptimal effort level. This line of thinking results in organizations where members give effort levels of say 3 or 4. This results in mediocre performing organizations or alliances; mediocrity sets in because of a lack of mutual trust.

Substantial empirical evidence shows the modal response to this game is 4. One question research has addressed is: How does one

FIGURE 2.3.6
The median effort game

FIGURE 2.3.6
The median effort game

		\multicolumn{7}{c}{**Group**}					
		7	6	5	4	3	2	1
	7	$5.00	–$2.00	–$2.50	–$3.00	–$3.50	–$4.00	–$4.50
	6	$4.75	$4.50	–$2.00	–$2.50	–$3.00	–$3.50	–$4.00
	5	$4.50	$4.25	$4.00	–$2.00	–$2.50	–$3.00	–$3.50
You	4	$4.25	$4.00	$3.75	$3.50	–$2.00	–$2.50	–$3.00
	3	$4.00	$3.75	$3.50	$3.25	$3.00	–$2.00	–$2.50
	2	$3.75	$3.50	$3.25	$3.00	$2.75	$2.50	–$2.00
	1	$3.50	$3.25	$3.00	$2.75	$2.50	$2.25	$2.00

measure group effort? Some studies use the median effort of players: If there are seven group members, group effort is equal to the group's median choice. Using this measure of group effort, the modal choice across studies is 4.

However, some believe corporations are better represented by minimum effort games. This is the view that the chain is only as strong as its weakest link, so group effort is equal to the lowest level selected by any member. Getting a product to the final consumer involves several functional areas: purchasing, manufacturing, design, engineering, manufacturing, distribution, service, and more. If only one person performs poorly, then the entire organization is blamed. So if you receive poor service, you tend to blame the organization, not the individual service-person.

When minimum effort games are played, the modal response is lower than 4. Trust is even more important in these games because if only one group member chooses low effort, the entire group is punished. And, while many managers recognize the importance of trust-building, most organizations have a difficult time building trust among agents. And this trust-building can be even more difficult across organizations.

Our example illustrates that game theory's strategic value is not limited to competitive strategic situations. It is also useful in modeling strategic situations where cooperation and coordination are optimal strategies. In addition to formal modeling, game theory can be used as a powerful training device to show group members the consequences of not building mutual trust.

Conclusion

As shown in the preceding examples, game theory provides a variety of insights to competitive strategy. It helps managers understand and apply key strategic principles such as those discussed. Further, game theory can be used for more detailed modeling and analysis of these principles and the competitive situation.

Our overview of principles and applications of game theory for strategic analysis emphasized the situational dependency of any strategy. Understanding and anticipating the moves of rivals – the payoffs and players and their perceptions – determines the structure of the game, and, ultimately, its outcome. The rightness or wrongness of a strategy depends on the situation. There is no optimal strategy across all strategic situations. Because of this situational dependency, strategic planning is an evolving process. If you don't like your current situation, you have the power to change it.

By changing in a strategic situation, you change others. There is a strategic umbilical cord connecting you to others. As they move, you move, and vice versa. Game theory explicitly models this dependency via interactive payoffs. And it identifies strategies that help managers anticipate the moves of rivals and improve their payoffs.

The four strategic principles we discussed are important in shaping strategy, whether or not formal game theoretic models are used to analyze the strategic situation. The first principle is that managers must possess strategic foresight and be able to look ahead. Only by doing so can they configure their resource base in the most advantageous position for the future. Next, we stressed managers must know themselves and their competitors. This principle follows since a manager's payoff in any strategic situation depends on the company's strategic state relative to that of others. The third principle highlights the importance of recognizing the difference between one-time and repeated interaction in strategic situations. Finally, we stressed the importance of coordination in an organization. Only when managers unify their minds can their organization be an effective competitor.

These examples show that game theory, when used correctly, can be a very powerful modeling tool. Like any planning tool, game theory has its limitations, but these limitations are not as great as generally perceived. We believe game theory's use in the future will grow as managers become familiar with models, and computer programs help managers configure strategic situations. However, lest managers forget, analytic models are always replaced by newer more sophisticated ones. It is the underlying strategic principles that remain unchanged.

2.4   Conceptual Mapping

By Michael McCaskey[1]

We live in conceptual worlds composed of our ideas, images, memories, plans, and knowledge, which inform the way we talk and think about the physical world. Our conceptualizations, or representations, of the parts of reality we have learned to see as meaningful, interesting, and important guide our actions and our work with others. Many researchers have found the idea of a 'conceptual map' a helpful metaphor for these conceptual systems that are usually taken for granted and assumed to be reality.

At any moment we have only a limited, tangible physical reality around us – the office, the hallway and the elevator, for example. We see chairs, walls, lights, color and other people. We have names for, and knowledge about, all of these familiar objects. Most of this knowledge lies in the background of our attention, to be called to the foreground as needed. Our sense of reality, however, is not limited to the world immediately before us. We can visualize buildings, spaces, people and events beyond our eyes. We can picture current and historical events around the world and use tools to extend our senses. These images, our names, our knowledge of how things fit together and what causes what to happen, constitute our 'map.' A map is an interconnected set of understandings, formed by frequently implicit views of what one's interests and concerns are, what is important, and what demands action and what does not. It is a cognitive representation of the world and ourselves in it.

Each of us has unique maps that have grown out of our experiences and needs. Of course, we also share some maps more or less closely with family, office colleagues, neighbors, members of a political party, and with other groups of which we feel a part.

As we consider how managers cope with ambiguity, mapping represents a useful tool for understanding and exploring our mental representations and their connection to act on. Maps come in many sizes, shapes, and degrees of accuracy. Think of a car's glove compartment, filled with road maps of different areas and of the same area drawn to different scales. Another kind of map can be as simple as the sketch a friend draws to show us the way to his house. Maps of the New World drawn during the age of discovery show large unknown areas and coastlines that gradually became more accurate. Maps can also include pictorial representations that uncover new relationships by depicting the known in an unfamiliar way. Like many of these physical maps, mental maps are guides that are not always correct and are subject to revision.

---

[1] Source: This article was adapted with permission from chapter 2 of *The Executive Challenge: Managing Change and Ambiguity*, Pitman, Boston, 1982.

The metaphor of mapping embraces both product and process. Since we are talking about managers operating in poorly mapped terrain, we will emphasize the process of creating new knowledge and extending old knowledge through exploration, study, and action. Horace Freeland Judson, examining the role of physical maps in the history of ideas, likens maps to models. The maps of early explorers reduced the complexity of the world to a model that people could conveniently study. Figure 2.4.1 shows the new world as mapped by a French priest in 1546. By that time detailed knowledge of the coastline was available, but little was reliably known about the American interior. Maps as models, Judson says, 'are ships in which explorers journey into the unknown. They embody what we know and carry us toward what we don't know.'

FIGURE 2.4.1
Desceliers's Map of the Coastline of the New World, 1546. (Reproduced courtesy of the Research Libraries, The New York Public Library.)

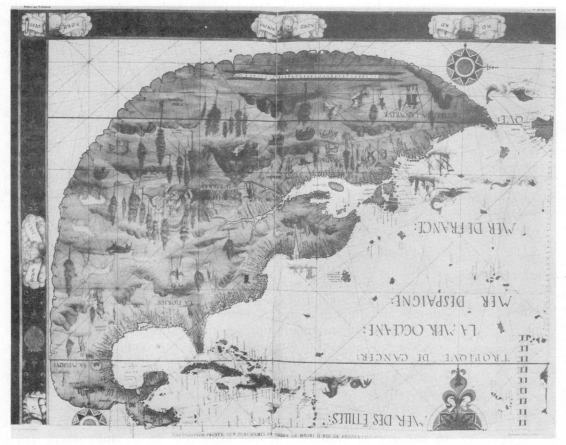

'Desceliers's map was 9 feet by 3 feet, so large that it was designed to be laid out on a table and read from both top and bottom, which is why the lettering in this detail is upside down. Most of the land mass of North America is a blur of speculation inhabited by confident aborigines and nervous Europeans.'

The manager who realizes he is following a conceptual map has taken an important first step toward being able to manage ambiguity. Our maps can be priceless guides, but they can also limit our perceptions, sometimes becoming rigid and confining. Understanding a map as a revisable model generally induces a healthy skepticism as to its infallibility, and engenders more flexible thinking. Mapping and remapping is a fundamental process that a manager facing ambiguity and change must master.

How Are Maps Created And Maintained?

Ordinarily people think of reality as objective, factual, and as undeniable as the physical world within our reach. What we experience as real are the events that we notice and can make sense of, those that have some significance for our lives and well-being. Reality is what we have become familiar with, and have learned to attend to, through our experience. Yet the recognized and named 'world' is complex and ever-changing, and so we need to organize what is important and what is trivial, what is safe and what is dangerous, what is associated with what, and what causes what. The mental process and the product of this *organizing of reality*, this creating and maintaining a frame of reference, is what we call 'conceptual mapping.'

Imagine, for example, that you are coming out of a building in a foreign country and find the street unexpectedly jammed with people. What is going on? This is *real*, but it doesn't make any sense yet. You haven't related it to anything else. The event needs to be interpreted. Is it a disaster or a celebration? Are people panicky or cheerful? If the crowds are gathering on either side of the street, that usually means a parade and not a riot. If you recall mention of a festival, you have a plausible reason for a parade. You begin to map the reality of the crowd in the street. You search your experience and try to find a name for what is happening which will tell you how to act.

People have maps for different domains and for different purposes. Perhaps it helps to think of your mind as a chart room full of maps – maps for your personal life, history, work, particular problem areas, routine procedures, and so on. Maps are pulled out according to occasion and purpose, and differ in degree of clarity, reliability and completeness.

Because our information processing abilities are limited, mapping is selective. On the basis of our values and past experience, we perceive some events as noteworthy, while most features of the world around us are relegated to the background. Otherwise we would be overwhelmed by complexity and change. Out of what is noticed, people build a picture that makes sense to themselves and provides a common base of understanding with others. Although necessary, the selectivity of mapping has its dangers, as illustrated by the experience of US automakers. These manufacturers ignored or downplayed the early signals that their business was undergoing fundamental change, since those signals conflicted with the main tenets of their map. While we can never grasp all of reality, what we defend against knowing can hurt us.

Mapping is a dialectic between events and our ideas about those events. Our conceptual maps determine what elements in the turbulence of daily events we focus on and how we interpret them; our experience of events in turn can refine and enlarge our maps. This means that ambiguity resides in the situation, in the mind of the manager, and in the interaction of the two. Like the paradox of Escher's two hands drawing each other, it is both the situation that is perplexing and the manager who is perplexed.

A map becomes increasingly 'objective' as more people come to share its view of reality. While one person holds a unique map it is a fragile construction. The map is strengthened as it is transmitted and accepted by more people. Because the coherence of a social group depends upon developing a common map, mapping is heavily influenced by the social setting in which it occurs.

Mapping by a social group is not always a straightforward or an easy process. Two sociologists who have studied the process of clashing views point out that, 'He who has the bigger stick has the better chance of imposing his definitions of reality.'

In a managerial group the social process of constructing reality this way involves the interaction, perhaps the collision, of several subjective readings (or personal maps) of the surrounding world. The work of a group in its early stages includes forming a publicly held map that is generally agreed to by all members. Once formed, this version of reality is treated as real; it *is* real for group members and is slow to change. The map guides a member's daily decisions about what to notice, what to do, and how to interact with others.

When a map is more completely drawn and begins to make the surrounding landscape of events intelligible, group members often pressure each other to conform to using the group's map. The group has a range of punishments and inducements which few can withstand and still remain a group member in good standing. During a recent strike by Chicago fire-fighters, for example, most men refused a federal court order to return to work. A television news report captured the dynamics of the situation by focusing on one fireman who had been working, but then decided to rejoin his fellows amidst much cheering and backslapping. The firefighters' map of what was fair and what was legal obviously differed from the maps held by the mayor and the courts, and the firefighters were able to enforce the norms implied by their map on most of their fellows.

Groups and individuals use maps in such a way that the existing maps tend to be reconfirmed. Argyris and Schon have called this the 'self-sealing' quality of some systems or models. Since a map points out what is to be noticed and valued among the plethora of events in each day, those events that do not jibe with the map tend to be ignored, or called aberrations, and thus forgotten. Discrepant events can create anxiety or, more rarely, wonder. If the discrepancy is too great, the map holder is likely to defend against seeing or appreciating the event. If the discrepancy is not too great, and individuals vary widely on this, the event provides an opportunity to redefine one's understanding of reality.

The same territory can be mapped in different ways. The map of the Roman empire presented in Figure 2.4.2, for example, reflects the needs, strengths, and worries of its inhabitants. The land masses where Roman armies operated are given proportionately more space than are the seas on which the enemy, Carthage, operated her superior navy. And just as the territory can be depicted politically, topographically, or geographically, organizations or groups will map their worlds in distinctive ways. The more the maps of groups diverge, the more problematic communication becomes.

Finally, mapping is so natural a dimension of our everyday lives that large parts of our own maps are created outside our awareness. Mapping organizes what is put in the foreground and is often itself unnoticed.

FIGURE 2.4.2
Map of Ancient Rome and Italy. (Reproduced courtesy of The Research Libraries, The New York Public Library.)

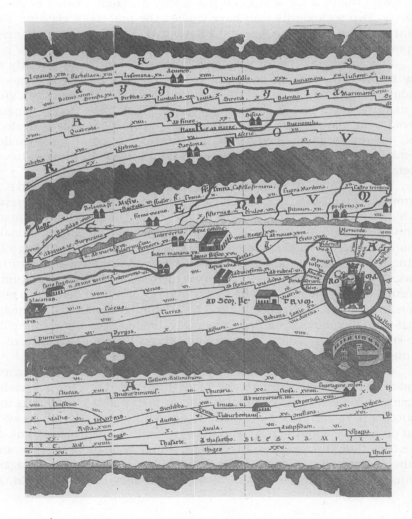

'Roman road maps distorted sea and land masses in order to fit the imperial road system into a confined space . . . The center strip is Italy; the Adriatic and Mediterranean are attenuated into mere rivers. Across from Rome and her harbor lies Carthage.'

Frequently, a map and its embedded assumptions only become visible when they fail to provide a suitable basis for action. Managers must search for ways to make maps visible before they break down. Some specific suggestions on what to do when maps are weak are presented later in this article.

Maps And Ambiguity: Imposing Order On Chaos

One way of defining an ambiguous situation is to say it is one in which none of your maps works well. Events are puzzling, confusing, and don't fit with what you know. The world seems baffling when events outpace ideas. Remember how frightening the initial outbreak of Legionnaire's Disease was? Many of those attending a Philadelphia convention mysteriously fell ill, no one knew why, and several died. People were deeply shaken by an occurrence that seemed to expose the limits of modern medicine.

Crisis situations like this expose the transient quality of any map. A messy problem disrupts the map's ability to explain the everyday activities of members of a group. Members may have differing ways of stating what the problem is, but no one way appears adequate to solve the problem or compels widespread agreement. Since the ambiguous problem cannot be adequately defined, people do not respond to it in predictable, dependable ways. Because familiar routines and patterns are disrupted, group members feel increased stress. As the consensus about what is real breaks down, individuals are thrown upon more subjective and idiosyncratic interpretations and tend to want to withdraw from the situation. Without an adequate and commonly shared way to define the problem, communication and coordination become problematic.

Half a century ago John Dewey clearly pointed out how ill at ease we tend to be when nature is indeterminate. We greatly dislike confusion, disorder, obscurity, and indeterminateness, but 'nature is characterized by a constant mixture of the precarious and stable.' Our reaction sometimes is to think and take intelligent action, but more often we settle for a feeling or an illusion of order. People want 'to do something at once; there is impatience with suspense, and lust for immediate action.' We invent theories, rituals, or superstitions to make what was uncertain and confused into something clear and stable.

Dewey's observations on human nature are strongly supported by a review of work in cognitive psychology during the last several decades. Steinbruner found that, while researchers might disagree at the frontiers of knowledge about how the mind works, there was general agreement on five basic principles. Researchers found:

1   The mind is an inference machine that actively imposes order on highly ambiguous situations.

2   The mind works to keep internal core beliefs consistent and unchallenged. (The stress literature also shows that the mind will deny, distort, or ignore signals that contradict core beliefs.)

3   The mind prefers simplicity.

4   The mind is constrained by reality (here the objective side of reality) in important ways.

5   The mind prefers stable and enduring relationships among its core beliefs.

These five principles are all of interest to managers facing ambiguity but the first is perhaps the most important; the others can all be gathered into it. *The mind is an inference machine that strives mightily to bring order, simplicity, consistency, and stability to the world it encounters. In other words, where nature is ambiguous, people develop strong beliefs and act upon them.* People tend to simplify complexity and make the inconsistent seem consistent. These tendencies are heightened when we perceive a threat to our identity, safety, security, or status. Generally speaking, we dislike disorder especially in areas where we are invested.

Mapping is affected by the mind's very active, interpretive quality. Our cognitive faculties operate ahead of conscious awareness, sorting through a wealth of potential information. Our mental processes make rapid estimates of what is valuable to notice and what can be treated as background. The mind takes fragments and makes something that fits existing organizing schemes. In the felicitous apothegm of Norwood Russell Hanson, 'There is more to seeing than meets the eyeball.' Everywhere we look, we see with theory-laden vision.

Holding On To Maps And 'Little Dying'

Perhaps because maps are so hard-won and so necessary for orderly interaction with others, people are very reluctant to change them. In fact, people fight to retain their maps. They want to hold on to that order, and suffer a little death if they have to relinquish it. 'Little dying' is Keleman's term for the painful letting-go of any of the major anchors of our life: separation from a loved one, moving from the home town, leaving a successful position in a company. 'Big dying' is biological death.

Little deaths compel the acknowledgment of our finiteness; we see that we cannot do or be everything we value, and that forces exist outside of us that have their own power. Acknowledgment of such hard facts is difficult and often avoided. Little dying involves giving up something central and important in our map.

In a thought-provoking paper, Robert Tannenbaum has urged that more attention be paid to the process of little dying and holding on in organizational change. Organization development specialists and managers often underestimate the need for people in a system to maintain continuity and to hold on to what they know has worked in the past. Tannenbaum argues for a balance in attending to the yin of stability and the yang of change. An organizational unit may have to die in order to clear the ground for something new to grow or for the unit, phoenix-like, to be reborn into new vitality. Each person undergoing such change faces the prospect of a little death and can be expected to try to maintain the existing map.

Other researchers have seen parallels to something like little dying on the organizational level. Fink, Beak, and Taddeo (1971) have identified four phases in an organization's response to a crisis:

1   *Shock.* Organizational members become aware of a threat to existing structures.

2   *Defensive retreat.* Holding on to the old map.

3   *Acknowledgment.* Giving up the old map.

4   *Adaptation and change.* Establishing a new structure and a sense of worth.

The process resembles that seen by psychiatrist Elisabeth Kubler-Ross in her studies of the terminally ill. She finds that patients pass through the following stages in coming to terms with their own deaths:

1   *Denial and isolation.* The patient is shocked and disbelieves, puts off, or forgets.

2   *Anger.* Also rage, resentment, and envy – 'Why me?'

3   *Bargaining.* An extension of time is sought to complete unfinished business.

4   *Depression and grief.* Two phases: mourning what has already been lost and then mourning losses that lie in the future.

5   *Acceptance.* Accompanied by an inner and outer peace.

These two models trace through the responses of an organization and an individual to a threatening disruption. When the disruption is perceived to be life-threatening, human systems at both levels feel shocked, deny the disruption, and strenuously attempt to hold on to old maps. This phase gives way to feelings of anger and resentment and eventually to a period of mourning that looks backward and then toward the future. Only after grieving can the past be relinquished. Leaving one safe spot becomes easier when the next is in sight. Individuals create new meanings and definitions – a new or revised map – for what is happening. We have seen that our perceived reality is at least partly a social construct, and the transition to the acceptance phase of the sequence can be greatly facilitated by the help of friends and others who have undergone the pain of mourning and renewal.

Maintaining Order By Dynamic Conservatism

How powerful the need is to hold on to familiar ways of knowing can be seen in Elting Morison's history of the adoption of continuous aim firing in the United States Navy. First devised by an English officer in 1898, this system allowed a ship's gun to be continuously aimed and readjusted as it was being fired. (Technically, this was achieved by altering the gear ratio in a battery's elevating gear so that the gun could adjust to the inertial roll of the ship and mounting a telescopic sight away from the recoil of the gun barrel.) A US Navy lieutenant stationed in China, William Sims, learned about the system from its originator, Percy Scott of the British Royal Navy.

With Scott's assistance, Sims had the system installed on an American ship and trained a crew to use it. After a few months, the American crew showed the same remarkable improvement in accuracy as British crews had. Sims wrote 13 official reports, complete with great masses of data, to naval officers in Washington arguing the merits of the new system.

At first Washington officials made no response. According to their conceptual maps of naval gunnery, Sims's claims simply were not credible. As Sims became deliberately challenging and shocking in his reports, officials began to rebut the claims. They argued that existing American equipment was as good as British equipment and that any deficiencies must lie in the training of the men. They also conducted gunnery practice on dry land where, deprived of the benefits of the inertial movement, their results proved that the new system could not work as Sims claimed. They called Sims a 'crack-brain egoist' and accused him of deliberately falsifying evidence. Not to be denied, Sims, who had the combative personality of a bantam rooster, circulated news of the new gunnery system among his fellow officers in the fleet. Finally in 1902, he took the bold step of writing directly to President Theodore Roosevelt. Roosevelt brought Sims back from China and forced change upon the Navy by installing Sims as Inspector of Target Practice.

In his analysis of the events, Morison points out that the Navy had its own reasons for resisting the technological innovation. The officers in Washington identified strongly with the existing equipment and their instinctive desire was to protect the established pecking order of the Navy. Intuitively they realized that the Navy's social system was organized around its major weapons systems and that a change would significantly disrupt the existing hierarchy of status. Indeed, the chaos of subsequent events proved this fear justified. In the terms of our discussion, the Washington officers sought to protect their map and the culture in which it was embedded. They held onto the map as long as possible and only let go when forced to do so by greater, outside authority.

Commenting on the same case, Donald Schon (1971) uses the term 'dynamic conservatism' to describe the tendency to fight to remain the same. He goes on to depict a social system as a set of concentric rings. Change is more readily accommodated in the outer rings – that is, in the more superficially held elements of the system. But toward the center are core values and ideas whose change would necessarily induce a large-scale restructuring of the whole system. Here human systems fight hardest to conserve their sense of identity and reality. Maintaining a map becomes a fight to protect what is familiar and known – and to maintain identity, status, income, and standing.

What To Do When Maps Are Weak

When the terrain is poorly mapped, what can managers do? Researchers of business and public administration have made several suggestions. In such situations managers often shift from optimizing to 'satisficing.' Instead of trying to perform a complete analysis that will identify the best course of action, they settle for taking the first satisfactory alternative that comes along. This represents an important shift in outlook and captures an attitude of mind more likely to be effective in moving through uncharted territory. However, it is not, and is not meant to be, a detailed method for dealing with a particular problem.

Lindblom (1979) comes closer to describing a method. Government administrators, he observes, regularly muddle through poorly mapped problems. They make limited comparisons with the recent past and take circumscribed steps into the future that conform to past trends. Administrators, he says, should accept their limited ability to foresee or plan for the long term and should advance by small, often uncoordinated steps. There is no room for revolutions here, and thus such an approach will not work well in a crisis that demands a complete shift in paradigm.

Christensen (1972) argues that when the terrain is poorly mapped managers should turn to 'negative thinking.' Negative thinking proceeds more by refuting errors than by positively and conclusively proving a case. According to this view, managers confronting a poorly defined problem should not seek conclusive evidence and argument. They should instead treat contradictions as opportunities and aspire only to reasoning in terms of sufficient rather than necessary causes. Learning to recognize errors and avoid an associated course of action is the more important logical operation for advancing into unknown territory.

Barnard (1938) would, I think, agree with Christensen. As decision materials become more speculative, Barnard argues, the balance of a manager's mental operations should move toward nonlogical processes, thoughts that cannot be expressed in words, and which derive from judgment, intuition, and the grasp of an overall pattern. Barnard is uncertain, however, about how to enhance these qualities in managers, or how to judge them except after the fact, on the basis of performance.

I suggest an alternative to goal setting, one that employs a more holistic sensing of the situation. When goals cannot be specified with confidence, as when the terrain is poorly mapped, you can shift your focus away from goals and toward influencing the domain in which you are working and the direction in which you are heading. March and Olsen (1976) has also argued that managers should not always wait to act until goals are clear; rather, in some situations they should act in order to discover what their goals are. Among other provocative recommendations, he urges that we treat memory as an enemy that preserves too many past answers that no longer work, and that we view a plan more as a summary of past decisions than as a program for future use.

Mason and Mitroff (1981; reading 1.4 in this book) describe

how to attack ill-structured organizational problems through a dialectical process. Central to this method, the assumptions made in framing the problem must be brought to the surface. Two groups are put to work, one using the original assumptions, the other using directly opposite assumptions. Both groups go through a cycle of searching out relevant data and building a strategy. Since what one sees depends on one's theory, the second group should uncover new facts unnoticed by the first group. Under conditions designed to prevent premature compromise, the two groups meet and argue their positions. Out of this dialectic a new pool of assumptions is created from which a strategy is drawn.

In closing let us look at one final example of how a different way of mapping can reveal new features in what might seem familiar. Figure 2.4.3 shows a map of the world constructed under new rules, with countries sized in proportion to their gross national product. This particular way of representing the territory highlights relationships that perhaps not everyone has recognized before.

Figure 2.4.3
Map of the world with countries sized in proportion to their gross national product

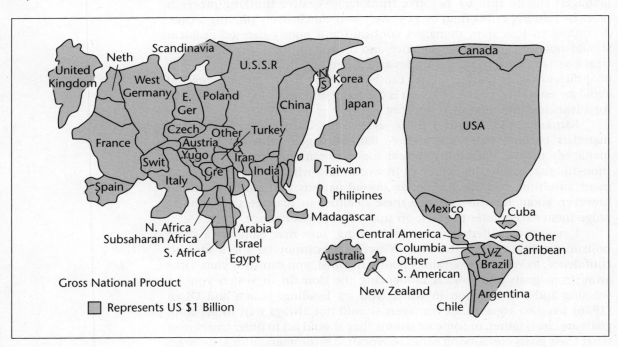

2.5   Strategic Management in an Enacted World

by Linda Smircich and Charles Stubbart[1]

A major debate within organization theory and strategic management concerns whether environments are objective or perceptual phenomena. This article develops a third view – that environments are enacted through the social construction and interaction processes of organized actors.

For any single 'organization,' the 'environmental' field contains an infinite number of situations and events, each of which could provide some material for environmental scanning. Obviously, to consider every situation, event, condition, and so on, and furthermore, to evaluate the vast combinations of environmental relationships is far beyond the capacity of any imaginable method of environmental analysis. Yet, this is what seems to be required for effective strategic management. Somehow, the tidal wave of environmental data must be funneled down to a small pipeline of information. It is like analyzing the world's oceans using a glass of water. How can strategic managers accomplish this feat? Three different models that represent ideal types for explaining how organized participants know their environments are offered here.

An Objective Environment

The words 'organization' and 'environment' create a dichotomy that profoundly shapes thinking about strategic management. This dichotomy clearly underlies the objective environment model which assumes that an 'organization' is embedded within an 'environment' that has an external and independent existence. 'Environments' constitute some thing or some set of forces to be adapted to, coaligned with, controlled, or controlled by. Terms that seem to capture this sense of 'environment' include concrete, objective, independent, given, imminent, out there.

The open system analogy provides a common way of thinking about the relationship between an 'organization' and its objective 'environment.' The open system idea was originally derived from, and applied to, plant and animal communities, but the image of an organization-as-organism is now strongly entrenched in organizational studies. Much of the biologist's theory and language has been borrowed by organization theorists and strategic management theorists (e.g. adaptation, population ecology, the life cycle approach).

---

[1] Source: This article was adapted with permission from Strategic Management in an Enacted World, *Academy of Management Review*, vol. 10 No. 4, 1985.

Nearly all strategic management research and writing incorporates the assumption that 'organization' and 'environment' are real, material and separate – just as they appear to be in the biological world. Strategists search for opportunities or threats in the 'environment.' Strategists search for strengths and weaknesses inside an 'organization.' In the figures theorists draw, an 'organization' and its 'environment' occupy opposite ends of the arrows. This view emphasizes recognition of what already exists. Environmental analysis thus entails discovery, or finding things that are already somewhere waiting to be found. Strategy, naturally, is defined as the fit between an 'organization' and its 'environment.' Given this set of concepts, research proceeds directly to find the successful combinations of organization-strategy-environment.

Within the strategic management literature there is some disagreement about the nature of the relationship between 'organizations' and their 'environments.' Child (1972) emphasizes the importance of strategic choice – the powerful-organization theory. Child argues that organizations can select their environmental domains, that environmental forces are not so confining that they cannot be outflanked or sometimes even safely ignored. On the contrary, Aldrich (1979) maintains that most organizations flounder helplessly in the grip of environmental forces-the weak-organization theory. Aldrich believes that 'environments' are relentlessly efficient in weeding out any organization that does not closely align itself with environmental demands. He doubts that many organizations self-consciously change themselves very much or very often, or that the conscious initiatives by organizations are likely to succeed. Most researchers seem to place themselves somewhere between these polar views. *Despite the heated discussion, however, neither the strategic choicers, nor the environmental determinists, nor those in between, question the pivotal notion of environments as independent, external, and tangible entities.*

Therefore, a strategist must look out into the world to see what is there. Strategists function (in theory) like perfect information processors – able to access, organize, and evaluate data without mistakes. Strategists overcome the problem of deciding what information is worth bothering about by using frameworks or lists. Within an objective 'environment,' a strategist faces an intellectual challenge to delineate a strategy that will meet the real demands and real constraints that exist 'out there.'

The Perceived Environment

The difference between objective 'environments' and perceived 'environments' is not attributable to a change in the conception of environment (which remains real, material, and external). Instead, the difference between objective and perceived environments involves a distinction about strategists. Strategists are permanently trapped by bounded rationality (Simon, 1957) and by their incomplete and imperfect perceptions of the 'environment.'

The idea of a perceived environment raises new problems. For now, research has to encompass the real external 'environment' and the partly mistaken beliefs of organizational strategists. Acrimonious debates have cropped up around questions about how accurate perceivers are (or can be) and whether organization behavior is more responsive to the environmental perceptions of strategists or to the real, material, environment.

From a practical standpoint, the challenge for strategists, who must labor within the confines of flawed perceptions, is minimizing the gap between these flawed perceptions and the reality of their 'environment.'

The Enacted Environment

Recently, under the influence of interpretive sociology, the sociology of knowledge, and cognitive social psychology, another perspective vies for attention. The assumption is that organization and environment are created together (enacted) through the social interaction processes of key organizational participants. From an interpretive worldview, separate objective 'environments' simply do not exist. Instead, organizations and environments are convenient labels for patterns of activity. What people refer to as their environment is generated by human actions and accompanying intellectual efforts to make sense out of these actions. The character of this produced environment depends on the particular theories and frameworks, patterns of attention, and affective dispositions supplied by the actor-observers.

In an enacted environment model the world is essentially an ambiguous field of experience. There are no threats or opportunties out there in an environment, just material and symbolic records of action. But a strategist – determined to find meaning – makes relationships by bringing connections and patterns to the action.

The timeless practice of scanning the heavens in search of constellations provides an analogy. There is really no Big Dipper in the sky, although people find it useful to imagine that there is. People see the Big Dipper when they furnish imaginary lines to cluster and make sense of the stars. In finding constellations astronomers organize material reality (the stars) using their own imaginations to produce a symbolic reality (Orion, the Lion, etc.). The same is true for strategists. Physical phenomena (like stars) in a strategist's world are real and have an independent existence. The automobiles that roll off the production line in a day, the oil well that was either dry or a gusher, the number of missiles stockpiled by the enemy – these are surely material elements in the material world. By themselves, however, automobiles, oil wells, and missiles are meaningless, and they appear as random as the stars appear to an untrained eye. Strategists create imaginary lines between events, objects, and situations so that events, objects, and situations become meaningful for the members of an organizational world. The majority of many excellent top managers' time and effort goes into this interpretive process – drawing some imaginary lines so that the world of

IBM, Hewlett-Packard, or 3M, for example, makes sense to employees and clientele.

Enactment implies a combination of attention and action on the part of organizational members. Processes of action and attention differentiate the organization from not-the-organization (the environment). The action component often is poorly appreciated by theorists who discuss sense-making processes. An enactment model implies that an environment of which strategists can make sense has been put there by strategists' patterns of action – not by a process of perceiving the environment, but by a process of making the environment. Consequently, the analogy of finding the constellations is partly an inadequate one for capturing the full scope of enactment. The analogy does not allow an emphasis on how the material records of action (e.g. automobile production, oil wells, missiles) have actually been put there by activities of organizational participants who subsequently interpret them. In other words, managers and other organization members create not only their organization, but also their environment.

In summary, theories involving objective or perceived 'environments' envision concrete, material 'organizations' that are within, but separate from, real material 'environments.' The relationships between the two are expressed in terms of cause and effect. On the other hand, enactment theory abandons the idea of concrete, material 'organizations/environments' in favor of a largely socially-created symbolic world.

Organization and Environment from an Interpretive Perspective

If one accepts the notion that people understand the world through bracketing and chunking experience into meaningful units, it then follows that 'organizations'and 'environments' provide convenient, but also arbitrary, labels for some portions of experience. But no inherent rationale compels researchers to employ the everyday language and common-sense understanding of these terms – in their analyses. In fact, doing so misdirects one's attention. Misdirection occurs because analysts investigate concepts such as strategy, organization structure, standardization, and technology as if the concepts correspond to freestanding material entities. Researchers often ignore the metaphoric and symbolic bases of organized life that create and sustain these organizational ideas. An interpretive perspective places these processes and symbolic entities at the center of analysis.

To illustrate the differences in approach, consider an interpretive definition of organization. Organization is defined as the degree to which a set of people share many beliefs, values, and assumptions that encourage them to make mutually-reinforcing interpretations of their own acts and the acts of others. Organization exists in this pattern of on-going action-reaction ('interacts,' Weick, 1979) among social actors. For instance, the organization of the music industry rests in particular patterns of beliefs, values and assumptions that support the ongoing creation, distribution, and enjoyment of the various forms of music. Thus, from an interpretive perspective, such organization is different from the everyday conceptualization of legally constituted 'organization,' and refers instead to a quality of interaction. Organization can extend across 'organizations.' Some 'organizations' are disorganized. From an interpretive perspective the interesting questions concern *how patterns of organization are achieved, sustained, and changed.*

Similarly, environment takes on a different meaning, and different questions are important. From an interpretive view the term environment refers only to a specific set of events and relationships noticed and made meaningful by a specific set of strategists. An interpretive perspective does not treat environment as separate objective forces that impinge on an organization. Instead, environment refers to the ecological context of thought and action, which is not independent of the observer-actor's theories, experiences, and tastes. Multiple groups of people enact the ecological context; neither historical necessity nor the operation of inexorable social laws imposes it on them. From the standpoint of strategic management, strategists' social knowledge constitutes their environment. An interpretive perspective on strategic management and the environment asks questions about the *processes of knowing* – those social processes that produce the rules by which an 'organization' is managed and judged.

Implications of an Interpretive Perspective

'Organization' and 'environment' are key concepts in the vocabulary of strategic management. The reconceptualization of these building block concepts that flows from an interpretive approach changes perspectives as well as words. The language through which people understand actions powerfully shapes future actions as well as the questions they are likely to ask about those actions. The logic of the interpretive perspective on organization and environment leads to three major implications for strategic management.

Abandoning the prescription that organizations should adapt to their environments   The conventional wisdom of strategic management urges organizations to adapt to their environments. This taken-for-granted maxim is more problematic than it appears. It obscures a good deal of the complexity, ambiguity, and abstractness in the strategic management process.

A brief example drawn from the American steel industry illustrates this point. By 1980, American steel producers lagged behind the Soviet Union, Japan, and Europe. The United States had become the world's largest importer of steel. American integrated steel producers increasingly suffer from outdated technology, inefficient plants, declining productivity, labor unrest, and inadequate cash flow for facility investment needs. The integrated companies vigorously called for import quotas or trigger-pricing levels that would choke off the flood of imports, imports said to be dumped at unfair prices by companies subsidized by foreign governments.

To the casual observer, the integrated steel companies seem to be having difficulties in adjusting to a hostile environment. The managers of the Big Eight steel companies feel that their problems have been caused by foreign competitors and government intervention. Big Steel claims help-lessness in the face of forces beyond their control and invites sympathy for their plight. Industry analysts, on the other hand, reproach steel executives for their conservatism and resistance to creative thinking.

Regardless of which explanations one accepts, important questions remain: what should the managers of Big Steel do now? Should the steel companies build new facilities? Should they diversify? Merge? Should they sell plants to the workers? Should they import semifinished steel? Which actions are the adaptive ones?

When one theorizes from the present into the past as strategic analysts often do, one finds what seems to be a powerful argument about adaptation to an objective 'environment.' But the power of this explanation ends in the present. Although the argument about environmental adaptation may initially seem appealing, it does not provide much help for strategists in the here and now. The advice from much strategic management literature that stresses fit, congruence, and alignment is not sufficient for dealing with issues in day-to-day management. The executives in an industry cannot simply stand outside the action and adjust themselves to trends; their actions make the trends. Thus, if every firm rushes to take advantage of an opportunity, the opportunity vanishes. Trends are complex functions of multilateral behavior, making future outcomes problematic. The nature of what constitutes adaptation can be stated only retrospectively, never prospectively. Accordingly, the admonition to adapt to trends and forces is not very helpful.

An interpretive perspective argues that strategic managers can manage their organizations only on the basis of their knowledge of events and situations. But events and situations are always open to multiple interpreta-tions. The facts never speak for themselves. If facts seem to 'go without saying,' it is only because observers happen to be saying very similar things.

For example, many commentators and participants in steel convey the impression that the industry is a scene of unrelieved devastation, using imagery reminiscent of The Alamo, Custer's last stand, or The Apocalypse, but other views can be brought to bear. To foreign steel producers the US domestic market is a fragile opportunity. US minimills are doing fine. The President of the United States views the situation as a painful, but necessary, evolutionary step into the golden age of techno-information, an era when former steelworkers will repair home computers, when kindly foreign governments will subsidize the cost of US domestic steel. None of these views is dictated by the 'environment.' Each view flows from applying certain preconceived, limited frameworks to available contexts. Many other guiding images or views are possible. It is in terms of these multiple views that expectations and strategic action will congeal and shape the future. Old visions of what the industry is, how it works, who the participants are, and which strategic avenues are open, are becoming unglued. Out of this turmoil, new visions may emerge. Will the future bring a rapprochement with labor? Does the turmoil foreshadow the reawakening of a sleeping giant? Can one hear the death knell of steel? Whatever is possible depends on which visions people believe in and act on – not on environmental fiat.

Analysis of a firm's environment cannot aspire to the status of a science, because there are no independent, authoritative observers. Instead, the choice of frameworks and interpretations becomes a creative and political art. Strategists need to concentrate on their choices *vis-à-vis* frameworks and interpretations. Novel and interesting frameworks may stimulate novel and interesting environments that could in turn preface novel and interesting strategic initiatives.

Rethinking constraints, threats, opportunities Managers face a tidal wave of situations, events, pressures, and uncertainties, and they naturally resort to collective discussion (in the broadest sense) to negotiate an acceptable set of relationships that provide satisfactory explanations of their social worlds. The scope and meaning of events are funneled down to manageable dimensions by formal and informal processes leading to industry wisdom. Huff (1982) points out that industry groups and other industry forums provide organized sense-making mechanisms.

A corresponding problem occurs, however, when strategic managers, by holding untested assumptions, unwittingly collude to restrict their knowledge. They may suffer from 'collective ignorance' (Weick, 1979).

Evidence of the fragile nature of industry wisdom often draws attention. What everyone knows about an industry translates into an opportunity for those who do not know. Many, if not most, really novel and exciting new strategies that invade an industry are perpetrated by outsiders who do not know the rules. Consider the introduction of Lite beer by the Miller Brewing unit of Philip Morris. Traditional companies knew that a diet beer could not be sold, but a foolish interloper tested the assumption and thereby enacted the most significant product innovation in beer industry history.

These observations about the way social reality is formed in organizational settings suggest a powerful prescription for strategic managers. They must look first to themselves and their actions and inactions, and not to 'the environment' for explanations of their situations. Indeed, recent research on organizational crises reveals that in many cases top managers' thinking patterns, not external environments, cause crises. As Karl Weick advises:

> If people want to change their environment, they need to change themselves and their actions – not someone else. . . . Problems that never get solved, never get solved because managers keep tinkering with everything but what they do.
>
> (Weick, 1979: 152).

Because of the temptation to assign convenient blame, the contributions of strategic management research should help managers reflect on the ways in which managers' actions create and sustain their particular organizational realities. With the development of a greater capacity for self-reflection, corporate officials, governmental policy makers, and all organization members can examine and critique their own enactment processes. By maintaining a dual focus of attention – an ability to transcend the momentary situation in which they are entangled and to see and under-stand their actions within a system of meanings that is continually open to reflection and reassessment – strategic managers can challenge the apparent limits and test the possibilities for organizational existence.

Thinking differently about the role of strategic managers   The enact-ment model places strategy makers in an entirely different role from that envisaged by the objective or perceived models. Environmental scanning in those models sends managers 'out' to collect facts and to amass an inventory of information. A strategic manager is portrayed as a decision-formulator, an implementer of structure, and a controller of events who derives ideas from information.

The interpretive perspective, on the other hand, defines a strategist's task as an imaginative one, a creative one, an art. In the chaotic world, a continuous stream of ecological changes and discontinuities must be sifted through and interpreted. Relevant and irrelevant categories of experience must be defined. People make sense of their situation by engaging in an interpretive process that forms the basis for their organized behavior. This interpretive process spans both intellectual and emotional realms. Managers can strategically influence this process. They can provide a vision to account for the streams of events and actions that occur – a universe within which organizational events and experiences take on meaning. The best work of strategic managers inspires splendid meanings.

The juxtaposition of events and context, figure and ground, is one mechanism for the management of meaning. Through this process, strategists work in the background to construct the basis on which other people will interpret their own specific experiences. The interpretive back-ground makes a difference because people use it to decide what is happening and to judge whether they are engaged in worthwhile activities or nonsense.

How can strategic managers generate the context for meaning in organizational life? The management-of-meaning can be accomplished through values and their symbolic expression, dramas, and language. Although researchers are aware of the powerful effects of some value/ symbol systems (e.g. advertising), research has only just begun to explore how these processes occur in organizations, how symbolic realities change, and how symbolic realities may be manageable. Nevertheless, many strategic managers probably can sharpen their strategic impact by gaining awareness of the less than obvious values/symbols that pervade their organizations.

For example, dramas include the standard ceremonies and rituals of an organization (regular meetings, socialization and training, the Christmas party, etc.) as well as unique happenings ('campaigns,' 'challenges,' 'struggles to the top,' 'takeovers,' 'the New XYZ Co.'). The standard ceremonies provide continuity and reaffirmation of values, status, individual and collective achievements. The 'big meetings' are occasions for heightened awareness, reawakening, and sometimes for exciting changes. Strategic managers should be aware of the impact these dramas can have and realize that they (the managers) exercise wide discretion in defining what the dramas are and when and how they will occur.

Powerful language and metaphors set a tone, provide direction, and gain commitment. Wise strategic managers take advantage of language, metaphors, and stories to convey their messages. They also pay attention to language, metaphors, and stories that originate elsewhere.

Values, dramas, and language comprise the symbolic foundations that support the everyday prosaic realities of management information systems, hierarchy, incentive systems, and so on – the surface architecture of organizations. Until now, strategic managers have been taught to consider organizational design problems exclusively in terms of surface architecture. These conventional approaches to designing organized activity have been further restricted by focusing nearly all attention on intellectual (rather than emotional) issues and on massive, unremittant control (rather than imagination).

An interpretive approach, probing the subjective process of reality-building, redirects the strategic manager's attention toward deep images of organizational life. Strategic managers can improve their efforts – make them *more* strategic – by recognizing the powerful nature of those deep images and by consciously approaching this deeper level. The challenge to management research is to understand that world and to make such knowledge useful.

Following this advice would lead to a major reorientation of some strategic managers' thinking and behavior. Rather than concentrating on issues of product-market strategies, for example, a strategic manager would concentrate on process issues. Rather than concentrating on decisions or design of decision making structures, a strategic manager would concentrate on the values, symbols, language, and dramas that form the backdrop for decision making structures. Rather than confining themselves to the technical/intellectual aspects of organizational structures, many strategic managers would learn to express and to elaborate on the social/emotional basis for organizational life.

Managing in an Enacted World

Given a world increasingly characterized by organized, rather than individual action, what guidelines can be derived from an interpretive perspective to aid those responsible for managing human affairs?

Managerial Analysis

The idea of enactment underscores a view that one's own actions and the actions of others make an 'organization' and its 'environment.' Because of this sequence, environmental analysis is much less critical than managerial analysis. Managerial analysis means challenging the assumptions on which managers act and improving managers' capacity for self-reflection – seeing themselves as enactors of their world. This dual (active-reflective) posture toward action is difficult for managers to maintain. In fact, consultants often are called in to help organization members get a different perspective on what members are doing. Consultants state the obvious, ask foolish questions, and doubt – all of which helps organization members get outside of themselves. Management groups can institutionalize the role of 'wise fool' in order to provoke the capacity for critical self-examination.

Creation of Context

The answers to such questions as 'Who are we? What is important to us? What do we do? and What don't we do?' set the stage for strategy formulation. These questions elicit the values framework within which activity becomes meaningful.

The creation of context is different from setting objectives. Setting objectives implies that an organization falls short in some way, needing to move from point A to point B. This sort of striving characterizes many strategic management models, suggesting that organizations have a place at which to arrive. Objectives present a management orientation of going-to-be instead of already-is. An interpretive perspective promotes managerial deliberations about the present-especially about management values and actions.

Encouraging Multiple Realities

An interpretive perspective urges the consideration of multiple interpretations. But, in strategic management, multiple interpretations often are viewed as communication problems to be overcome by more information, rather than as a natural state of affairs.

Successful strategists have often contemplated the same facts that everyone knew, and they have invented startling insights (e.g. Ray Kroc and the hamburger restaurant chain). Interesting enactments blossom when strategists draw out novel interpretations from prosaic facts. Quite often, novel interpretations occur when companies enter an industry for which they have no specific experience. They try out novel strategies that run counter to conventional assumptions.

Companies might be able to enlarge their capacities for novel interpretations by systematically varying metaphors, by hiring in-house experts from distant industries, and by encouraging novel and conflicting viewpoints (e.g. a coal company hires an environmentalist; Caterpillar hires a top executive from Komatsu, who remains outside the Caterpillar culture; or a company hires a philosopher). These efforts legitimate and expand the managerial capacity for tolerance of differences.

Testing and Experimenting

Every industry is saddled with a long list of dos and don'ts. These stipulated limits should be tested periodically. Enactment means action as well as thinking. Assumptions about what is related to what, what works (or doesn't), what we can do (or can't), should be tested periodically by acting as if counterassumptions are viable. Strategists should learn to act ambivalently about what they know, so that they do not become strait-jacketed by what they know. Learning compels forgetting. In fact, organizational wisdom may require continuous unlearning.

Managerial analysis, creation of context, encouraging multiple realities, and testing and experimenting are managerial principles derived from an interpretive worldview, recognizing that people enact their symbolic world. These principles of variety are largely ignored by approaches to strategic management that stress scanning of an objective/ perceived environment, setting objectives, and manipulating managerial controls.

Can any Reality be Enacted?

This argument may seem to imply that people can enact any symbolic reality that they choose. In a limited sense we are saying precisely that. Individual people occupy personal, subjective space – space in which intentions, meaning, and sensibility often are quite idiosyncratic – what the world means to them. And even those isolated lifeworlds can sometimes be transformed into social worlds (e.g. Hitler, Gandhi, Marx, Darwin). But in this contribution the special concern is with enactments in which numerous people collectively participate, in which people experience limits to what they can enact.

First, organized people often struggle within the confines of their own prior enactments. Patterns of enactment rooted in prior personal, organizational, and cultural experiences powerfully shape ongoing organizational and cultural options. Starbuck (1983) calls these patterns 'behavior programs' and emphasizes how past thinking gets concretized into standard operating procedures, job specifications, buildings, contracts, and so on that take on the aura of objective necessity. Behavior programs-institutionalized as unwritten rules and taken for granted assumptions-seem to dictate how things are and must be done. Changing these patterns requires people to intentionally forget some of what they know and to disbelieve some of what they believe. Depending on the weight of prior commitments, changing may seem risky, foolish, or taxing.

Second, enactment means thinking and *acting*. Enactments test one's physical, informational, imaginative, and emotional resources. Without sufficient resources (or without the ability to think imaginatively about what might constitute resources), one simply cannot support many conceivable enactments.

Finally, enactments may compete with each other. In an election, for example, the candidates struggle mightily to discredit an opposition candidacy. In a corporate context, various strategic initiatives compete in a similar fashion. For sizable organizational enactments to succeed, a critical mass of belief and acceptance must be reached. But reaching the critical mass depends on persuasion rather than objective factors.

For these reasons – prior enactments, problems with resources, and competing enactments – organizational enactment processes can be distinguished from fond hopes and castles in the air.

Strategic Thinking in International Perspective

Rational, adj. Devoid of all delusions
save those of observation, experience and
reflection.
(*The Devil's Dictionary*, Ambrose Bierce 1842–1914; American
columnist)

From the preceding contributions it has become clear that opinions differ sharply about what goes on, and should go on, in the mind of the strategist. There are strongly conflicting views on how managers deal with the paradox of logic and creativity. It is up to each reader to judge whether the rational or the generative perspective is more valuable for understanding strategic thinking. Yet, we hope that readers will feel challenged to consider the possibility that both perspectives may be useful at the same time. Although they are opposites, and partially contradictory, both perspectives might reveal crucial aspects of strategic thinking that need to be combined to achieve superior results. Blending logic and creativity in ingenious ways might allow strategists to get 'the best of both worlds.' What such mixes of logic and creativity in the mind of the strategist could be like, will remain a matter for debate – with strategists using their own logical and/or creative thinking to come up with answers.

Hence, this last part of the chapter is not intended to present a grand synthesis. Readers will have to grapple with the paradox of logic and creativity themselves, by contrasting the thesis (the rational thinking perspective) and the antithesis (the generative thinking perspective). In this final part of the chapter it is the intention to view the topic of strategic thinking from an international perspective. The explicit question that must be added to the debate on the mind of the strategist is whether there are discernible national differences in approaches to strategic thinking. Are there specific national preferences for the rational or the generative perspective, or are the differing views spread randomly across the globe? Are each of the perspectives rooted in a particular national context, making it difficult to extend them to other countries, or are they universally applicable? In short, are views on strategic thinking the same all around the world?

Unfortunately, this question is easier asked than answered. Little cross-cultural research has been done in the field of strategic management and hardly any on this specific topic. This may be partially due to the difficulty of international comparative research, but it probably also reflects the implicit assumption by most that theories on strategic thinking are universally applicable. Few of the authors cited in this chapter suggest that there are international differences or note that their theories might be culturally biased and of limited validity in other national settings.

Yet, the assumption that strategic thinking is viewed in the same way around the world should be questioned. The human inclination to suppose that all others are the same as ourselves, is well known – it is a common cognitive bias. In international affairs, however, such an assumption must always be challenged. Internationally-operating strategists can not afford the luxury of assuming that their views are universally accepted and applicable. Therefore, the thought must be entertained that strategists in some countries are more attracted to the rational perspective, while in other countries the generative perspective is more pervasive.

As a stimulus to the debate whether there are such national preferences in perspective on strategic thinking, we would like to bring forward a number of factors that might be of influence on how the paradox of logic and creativity is tackled in different countries. It goes almost without saying that more concrete international comparative research is needed to give this debate a firmer footing.

Position of Science

Science and the scientific method do not play the same role, and are not accorded the same value, in all societies. In some countries, science and scientists are held in high esteem, and scientific inquiry is believed to be the most fruitful way for obtaining new knowledge. Typical for these nations is that the scientific method has come to pervade almost all aspects of life. Objective knowledge and skill in analytical reasoning are widely believed to be the critical success factors in most professions – even to become a nurse, a journalist, a sports instructor, an actor or a musician requires a university education. Managers, too, are assumed to be scientifically trained, often specializing in management studies. Much of this education strongly promotes formal, explicit, analytical thinking, and pays little attention to creativity, imagination and intuition. In these nations a more pronounced preference for the rational thinking perspective might be expected.

In other countries, science holds a less predominant position (Redding, 1980). Scientific methods might shed some light on issues, both other ways of obtaining new insights – such as through experience, intuition, philosophizing, fantasizing, and drawing analogies – are also valued (Keegan, 1983; Kagono *et al.*, 1985). Socially acceptable reasoning is less constrictive than in more rationalist nations. Leaps of imagination and logical inconsistencies are tolerated, as normal aspects in the messy process of sense-making (Pascale, 1984). In general, thinking is viewed as an art and therefore science has not made deep inroads into most of the professions. Managers, in particular, do not require a specific scientific training, but need to be broadly-developed generalists with flexible minds (Nonaka and Johansson, 1985). In these countries, a stronger preference for the generative thinking perspective can be expected.

Level of Uncertainty Avoidance

National cultures also differ with regard to their tolerance for ambiguity. As Hofstede points out in Chapter 1, reading 1.5, some societies feel uncomfortable with uncertain situations and strive for security. Countries that score high on Hofstede's *uncertainty avoidance dimension* typically try to suppress deviant ideas and behaviors, and institute rules that everyone must follow. People in these countries exhibit a strong intellectual need to believe in absolute truths and they place great trust in experts (Schneider, 1989). They have a low tolerance for the ambiguity brought on by creative insights, novel interpretations and 'wild ideas' that are not analytically sound. Therefore, it can be expected that strategists in high uncertainty avoidance cultures will be more inclined towards the rational thinking perspective than in nations with a low score.

Level of Individualism

As stated at the beginning of this chapter, strategists with a generative inclination are slightly rebellious. They show little reverence for the status quo, by continuously questioning existing cognitive maps and launching creative reinterpretations. As the dissenting voice, they often stand alone, and are heavily criticized by the more orthodox. This lonely position is difficult to maintain under the best of circumstances, but is especially taxing in highly collectivist cultures. If strategists wish to be accepted within their group, organization and community, they cannot afford to stick out too much. There will be a strong pressure on the strategist to conform. In more individualist cultures, however, there is usually a higher tolerance for individual variety. People find it easier to have their own ideas, independent of their group, organization and community (see Hofstede's individualism dimension, reading 1.5). This gives strategists more intellectual and emotional freedom to be the 'odd man out.' Therefore, it can be expected that strategists in more individualist cultures will be more inclined towards the generative perspective than those in collectivist cultures.

Position of Strategists

Countries also differ sharply with regard to the hierarchical position of the managers engaged in strategy. In many countries strategic problems are largely defined and solved by the upper echelons of management. To reach this hierarchical position requires many years of hands on experience and climbing through the ranks. Therefore, by the time managers are in the position of being a strategist they are middle-aged and thoroughly familiar with their business – with the danger of being set in their ways. They will also have been promoted several times by senior managers who believe that they will function well within the organization. In general, the effect is that the competent and conformist managers are promoted to strategy positions, while innovative dissidents are selected out along the way. In such countries, creative strategic thinking often does not take place within large organizations, but within small start ups, to which the creatively-inclined flee.

In cultures that score lower on Hofstede's power distance dimension, managers throughout the organization are often involved in strategy discussions. The responsibility for strategy is spread more widely among the ranks. Younger, less experienced managers are expected to participate in strategy formation processes, together with their senior colleagues. In general, this leads to a more open, messy and lively debate about the organization's strategy and provokes more creative strategic thinking. Therefore, it can be expected that in less hierarchical cultures the generative thinking perspective will be more popular than in cultures with stronger hierarchical relations.

Further Readings

Anyone interested in the topic of strategic thinking will sooner or later run into the work of Herbert Simon. His concept of bounded rationality was originally explored in the book *Models of Man*, which is still interesting reading, but *Organizations*, written together with James March, is a more comprehensive and up-to-date source with which to start. Also a good introduction to (bounded) rationality is given by Niels Noorderhaven, in his book *Strategic Decision Making*, which additionally covers the topics of emotions, intuition and cognition in relationship to the strategy process.

On the topic of game theory, and its link to strategic thinking, readers are advised to start with John McMillan's very accessible book *Games, Strategies, and Managers*. Also highly recommended is *Thinking Strategically: The Competitive edge in Business, Politics, and Everyday Life*, by Avinash Dixit and Barry Nalebuff.

For a more in-depth discussion on the interplay between cognition and strategic decision-making, a stimulating book is R. Hogarth's *Judgement and Choice: The Psychology of Decision*. Also an excellent book is *The Essence of Strategic Decision Making*, by Charles Schwenk, in particular with regard to the discussion of cognitive biases. On the topic of the social construction of reality, Karl Weick's *The Social Psychology of Organizing* is still the classic that should be read.

Readers interested in the link between creativity and strategic thinking might want to start with *Creative Management*, an excellent reader edited by John Henry, which contains many classic articles on creativity from a variety of different disciplines. A second step would be to read Gareth Morgan's imaginative book *Imaginization: The Art of Creative Management*, or John Kao's *Jamming: The Art and Discipline of Business Creativity*, both of which make challenging proposals for improving an organization's creative thinking. Also stimulating is the book *Strategic Innovation*, by Charles Baden-Fuller and Martyn Pitt, which contains a large number of cases on companies exhibiting creative thinking. For a good follow-up article that strongly advocates the generative perspective, readers are advised to turn to the article 'Strategy as Revolution' by Gary Hamel.

References

Aldrich, H.E. (1979) *Organizations and Environments*, Prentice Hall, Englewood Cliffs, NJ.

Anderson, J.R. (1983) *The Architecture of Cognition*, Harvard University Press, Cambridge, MA.

Andrews, K. (1987) *The Concept of Corporate Strategy*, Irwin, Homewood.

Baden-Fuller, C.W.F., and Stopford, J.M. (1992) *Rejuvenating the Mature Business*, Routledge, London, pp.13–34.

Baden-Fuller, C., and Pitt, M. (1996) *Strategic Innovation*, Routledge, London.

Barnard, C.I. (1938) *The Functions of the Executive*, Harvard University Press, Cambridge, MA.

Bazerman, M.H. (1990) *Judgment in Managerial Decision Making*, 2nd edn, John Wiley, New York.

Behling, O., and Eckel, N.L. (1991) Making Sense out of Intuition, *Academy of Management Executive*, vol. 5, pp. 46–54.

Child, J. (1972) Organizational Structure, Environment, and Performance: The Role of Strategic Choice, *Sociology*, vol. 6, pp. 1–22.

Christensen, C. (1972) *The Power of Negative Thinking*, Working Paper, HBS 72–41, Graduate School of Business Admnistration, Boston, Harvard University, December.

Christensen, C.R., Andrews, K.R., Bower, J.L., Hamermesh, R.G., and Porter, M.E. (1982) (1987) *Business Policy: Text and Cases*, 5th and 6th edns, Irwin, Homewood, IL.

Cyert, R.M., and March, J.G. (1963) *A Behavioral Theory of the Firm*, Prentice Hall, Englewood Cliffs, NJ.

De Bono, E. (1970) *Lateral Thinking*, Harper and Rowe, New York.

Dixit, A.K., and Nalebuff, B.J. (1991) *Thinking Strategically: The Competitive edge in Business, Politics, and Everyday Life*, W.W. Norton, New York.

Dutton, J.E. (1988) Understanding Strategic Agenda Building and its Implications for Managing Change, in Pondy, L.R., R.J. Boland, Jr., and Thomas H. (eds), *Managing Ambiguity and Change*, Wiley, Chichester.

Eden, C. (1989) Using Cognitive Mapping for Strategic Options Development and Analysis (SODA), in Rosenhead, J., (ed.), *Rational Analysis in a Problematic World*, Wiley, London.

Fink, S.L., Beak, J., and Taddeo, K. (1971) Organizational Crisis and Change, *Journal of Applied Behavioral Science*, 7 (1), pp. 15–41.

Hamel, G. (1996) Strategy as Revolution, *Harvard Business Review*, July-August, pp. 69–82.

Hendry, J., Johnson, G. and Newton, J. (eds) (1993) *Strategic Thinking: Leadership and the Management of Change*, Wiley, Chichester.

Henry, J. (ed.) (1991) *Creative Management*, Sage in association with the Open University, London.

Hogarth, R.M. (1980) *Judgement and Choice: The Psychology of Decision*, Wiley, Chichester.

Huff, A.S. (1982) Industry Influences on Strategy Reformulation, *Strategic Management Journal*, vol. 3, pp. 119–31.

Huff, A.S. (ed.) (1990) *Mapping Strategic Thought*, Wiley, Chicester.

Hurst, D.K., Rush, J.C. and White, R.E. (1989) Top Management Teams and Organizational Renewal, *Strategic Management Journal*, Vol 10, pp. 87–105.

Isenberg, D.J. (1984) How Senior Managers Think, *Harvard Business Review*, November-December, pp. 81–90.

James, B.G. (1985) *Business Wargames*, Penguin, Harmondsworth.

Janis, I.L. (1985) Sources of Error in Strategic Decision Making, in: Pennings, J.M. (ed.), *Organizational Strategy and Change*, Jossey-Bass, San Francisco.

Janis, I.L. (1989) *Crucial Decisions: Leadership in Policymaking and Crisis Management*, Free Press, New York.

Johnson, G. (1988) Rethinking Incrementalism, *Strategic Management Journal*, January/February, pp. 75–91.

Johnson, G., and Scholes, K. (1993) *Exploring Corporate Strategy: Text and Cases*, 3rd edn, Prentice Hall, Hemel Hempstead.

Kagono, T.I., Nonaka, K., Sakakibira, K. and Okumara, A. (1985) *Strategic vs. Evolutionary Management*, North-Holland, Amsterdam.

Kao, J. (1996) *Jamming: The Art and Discipline of Business Creativity*, Harper-Business, New York.

Keegan, W.J. (1983) Strategic Market Planning: The Japanese Approach, *International Marketing Review*, Vol. I, pp.5–15.

Kuhn, T.S. (1970) *The Structure of Scientific Revolutions*, University of Chicago Press, Chicago.

Langley, A. (1989) In Search of Rationality: The Purposes behind the Use of Formal Analysis in Organizations, *Administrative Science Quarterly*, Vol. 34, pp. 598–631.

Langley, A. (1995) Between 'Paralysis by Analysis' and 'Extinction by Instinct', *Sloan Management Review*, Spring, pp. 63–76.

Lenz, R.T., and Lyles, M. (1985) Paralysis by Analysis: Is Your Planning System Becoming Too Rational?, *Long Range Planning*, Vol. 18, pp. 64–72.

Liddell-Hart, B.H. (1967) *Strategy*, 2nd edn, Praeger, New York.

Lindblom, C.E. (1959) The Science of Muddling Through, *Public Administration Review*, Spring, pp. 79–88.

Lindblom, C.E. (1979) Still Muddling, Not Yet Through, *Public Administration Review*, November/December, pp. 517–526.

Machiavelli, N. (1950) *The Prince, and the Discources*, Modern Library, New York.

March, J.G., and Olsen, J.P. (1976) *Ambiguity and Choice in Organizations*, Universitetsforlaget, Bergen, Norway, pp. 69–81.

March, J.G., and Simon, H.A. (1993) *Organizations*, 2nd edn, Blackwell, Cambridge, MA.

Mason, R.O., and Mitroff, I.I. (1981) *Challenging Strategic Planning Assumptions*, Wiley, New York.

McCaskey, M.B. (1982) *The Executive Challenge: Managing Change and Ambiguity*, Pitman, Boston.

McMillan, J. (1992) *Games, Strategies, and Managers*, Oxford University Press, Oxford.

Mintzberg, H., and Waters, J.A. (1983) The Mind of the Strategist(s), in Srivaste, S. (ed.), *The Executive Mind*, Jossey-Bass, San Francisco.

Morgan, G. (1993) *Imaginization: The Art of Creative Management*, Sage, Newbury Park, CA.

Nonaka, I., and Johansson, J.K. (1985) Japanese Management: What about 'Hard' Skills?, *Academy of Management Review*, Vol. 10, No. 2, pp. 181–91.

Noorderhaven, N.G. (1995) *Strategic Decision Making*, Addison-Wesley, Wokingham.

Ohmae, K. (1982) *The Mind of the Strategist*, McGraw-Hill.

Osborn, A. (1957) *Applied Imagination*, Scribner, New York.

Pascale, R.T. (1984) Perspectives on Strategy: The Real Story Behind Honda's Success, *California Management Review*, Vol. 26, No. 3, pp. 47–72.

Pondy, L.R. (1983) Union of Rationality and Intuition in Management Action, in Srivastva, S. (ed.), *The Executive Mind*, Jossey-Bass, San Francisco.

Prahalad, C.K. and Bettis, R.A. (1986) The Dominant Logic: A New Linkage Between Diversity and Performance, *Strategic Management Journal*, November/December, pp. 485–601.

Redding, S.G. (1980) Cognition as an Aspect of Culture and its Relationship to Management Processes: An Exploratory View of the Chinese Case, *Journal of Management Studies*, May, pp. 127–48.

Rittel, H. (1972) On the Planning Crisis: Systems Analysis of the 'First and Second Generations', *Bedriftsokonomen*, Nr. 8, pp. 390–96.

Schneider, S.C. (1989) Strategy Formulation: The Impact of National Culture, *Organization Studies*, Vol. 10, pp. 149–68.

Schoemaker, P.J.H. (1993) Strategic Decisions in Organizations: Rational and Behavioral Views, *Journal of Management Studies*, Vol. 30, pp. 107–129.

Schoemaker, P.J.H., and Russo, J.E. (1993) A Pyramid of Decision Approaches, *California Management Review*, Fall Vol. 36.

Schon, D.A. (1971) *Beyond the Stable State*, Random House, New York.

Schon, D.A. (1983) *The Reflective Practitioner: How Professionals Think in Action*, Temple Smith, London.

Schwenk, C.R. (1984) Cognitive Simplification Processes in Strategic Decision-Making, *Strategic Management Journal*, Vol. 5, pp. 111–28.

Schwenk, C.R. (1988) *The Essence of Strategic Decision Making*, Lexington Books, Lexington, MA.

Senge, P.M. (1990) The Leader's New Work: Building Learning Organizations, *Sloan Management Review*, Fall, pp. 7–23.

Simon, H.A. (1957) *Models of Man*, John Wiley, New York.

Simon, H.A. (1972) Theories of Bounded Rationality, in: McGuire, C., and Radner R. (eds), *Decision and Organization*, Amsterdam, pp. 161–76.

Simon, H.A. (1987) Making Management Decisions: The Role of Intuition and Emotion, *Academy of Management Executive*, Vol. 1, pp. 57–64.

Smircich, L., and Stubbart, C. (1985) Strategic Management in an Enacted World, *Academy of Management Review*, Vol. 10, pp. 724–36.

Spender, J-C. (1989) *Industry Recipes: The Nature and Sources of Managerial Judgement*, Basil Blackwell, Oxford.

Starbuck, W.H. (1983) Organizations as Action Generators, *American Sociological Review*, Vol. 48, pp. 91–102.

Teck Hua Ho and Weigelt, K. (1997) Game Theory and Strategic Thinking, in: Day, G., and Reibstein D.J. (eds.), *Wharton on Dynamic Competitive Strategy*, Wiley, New York.

Tversky, A., and Kahneman, D. (1986) Rational Choice and the Framing of Decisions, *Journal of Business*, Vol. 59, No.4, pp. 251–78.

Von Winterfeldt, D. and Edwards, W. (1986) *Decision Analysis and Behavioral Research*, Cambridge University Press, Cambridge.

Weick, K.E. (1979) *The Social Psychology of Organizing*, Random House, New York.

Weick, K.E., and Bougnon, M.G. (1986) Organizations as Cognitive Maps, in: Sims, H.P. Jr. and Gioia, D.A. (eds), *The Thinking Organization*, Jossey-Bass, San Francisco, pp. 102–35.

Weick, K.E. (1987) Substitutes for Corporate Strategy, in: Teece, D.J. (ed.), *The Competitive Challenge: Strategies for Industrial Innovation and Renewal*, Ballinger, Cambridge, MA.

3

Strategy Formation

Plans are nothing. Planning is everything.

(Dwight D. Eisenhower 1890–1969; American general and president)

It is a mistake to look too far ahead.
Only one link of the chain of destiny
can be handled at a time.

(Winston Churchill 1874–1965; British prime minister and writer)

The Paradox of Deliberateness and Emergentness

While the previous chapter dealt with the strategy processes going on in the minds of individuals, this chapter is concerned with the strategy processes going on in organizations. The central question here is how strategies are made in organizations – how the process of *strategy formation* takes place. It will be debated how organizations form their strategies in practice, as well as how the process of strategy formation can be made most effective.

Many conflicting opinions have been voiced about the best way of forming strategies. However, the debate between these rival points of view has not been very transparent. Much confusion has been caused by the fact that authors employ strongly differing definitions of what strategy actually is. Naturally, theorists starting with different implicit assumptions of what strategy is, will also disagree on how 'strategy' should be made. The most confusion has been between theorists who define strategy as a *pattern of decisions* and those who view strategy as a *pattern of actions*. Many authors speak of a strategy when an organization has decided on a consistent course of action, that it intends to pursue. Other authors speak of strategy when an organization has actually exhibited a consistent course of action in practice. To distinguish these two definitions of strategy, Mintzberg and Waters

(1985) have proposed to refer to the former as *intended strategy* and the latter as *realized strategy*. Intended strategies are the patterns of decisions that organizations plan to execute, while realized strategies are the patterns of action that have been accomplished.

In this chapter, both intended and realized strategy are important, as are the links between them. As Figure 3.1 indicates, one would expect that intended strategy would lead to realized strategy. Where realized strategies were fully intended, Mintzberg and Waters speak of *deliberate strategy*. However, they argue that realized strategies can also come about 'despite, or in the absence of, intentions,' which they label *emergent strategy*. Strategies can emerge unintentionally as strategists take one step at a time trying to piece together a viable course of action. Patterns of action unfold over time as strategists gradually learn and come to agree on a particular direction.

This distinction between deliberate and emergent strategy goes to the heart of the debate on the topic of strategy formation. While theorists disagree on many points, the crucial issue is whether strategy formation should be more deliberate or more emergent. A wide variety of opinions exists, each dealing with the tension between deliberateness and emergentness in a different way. At the extremes in this debate, two radically opposite positions can be identified. On the one hand, there are strategists who argue that organizations should strive to make strategy in a highly deliberate manner, by first explicitly formulating comprehensive plans, and only then implementing them. In accordance with common usage, we shall refer to this point of view as the *planning* perspective. On the other hand, there are strategists who argue that in reality most new strategies emerge over time and that organizations should facilitate this messy, fragmented, piecemeal formation process. This point of view shall be referred to as the *incrementalism* perspective.

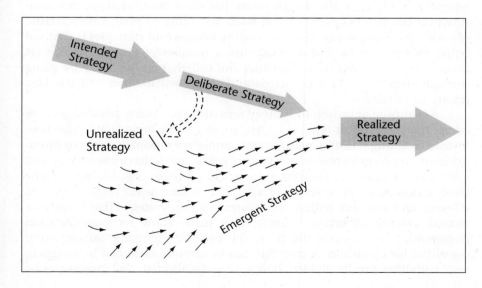

FIGURE 3.1
Forms of strategy (Mintzberg and Waters 1985)

Following the debate model introduced in Chapter 2, the inquiry into the nature of effective strategy formation in this chapter will also be structured by contrasting these two extremes. By comparing the two opposite ways of dealing with the paradox of deliberateness and emergentness, a better understanding of the issues under discussion should be gained. In the next few pages, the planning and incrementalism perspectives will be further explained, and finally summarized in Table 3.1.

The Planning Perspective

Advocates of the planning perspective argue that strategies should be deliberately planned and executed. In their view, anything that emerges unplanned is not really strategy. A successful pattern of action that was not intended cannot be called strategy, but should be seen for what it is – brilliant improvisation or just plain luck (Andrews, 1987; reading 2.1 in this book). However, strategists cannot afford to count on their good fortune or skill at muddling through. They must put time and effort into consciously formulating an explicit plan, making use of all available information and weighing all of the strategic alternatives. Tough decisions need to be made and priorities need to be set, before action is taken. 'Think before you act' is the planning perspective's motto. But once a strategic plan has been adopted, action should be swift, efficient and controlled. Implementation must be secured by detailing the activities to be undertaken, assigning responsibilities to managers and holding them accountable for achieving results.

Hence, in the planning perspective, strategies are intentionally designed, much as an engineer designs a bridge. Building a bridge requires a long formulation phase, including extensive analysis of the situation, the drawing up of a number of rough designs, evaluation of these alternatives, choice of a preferred design, and further detailing in the form of a blueprint. Only after the design phase has been completed, do the construction companies take over and build according to plan. Characteristic of such a planning approach to producing bridges and strategies is that the entire process can be disassembled into a number of distinct steps, that need to be carried out in a sequential and orderly manner. Only by going through these steps in a conscious and structured manner will the best results be obtained.

A planning approach to strategy formation has many advantages over *ad hoc* management, it is argued. First, plans give an organization *direction*, instead of letting it drift. Organizations cannot act rationally without intentions – if you do not know where you are going, any behavior is fine. By first setting a goal and then choosing a strategy to get there, organizations can be given a clear sense of direction. Managers can then select actions that are efficient and effective within the context of the strategy. This leads to a second, related advantage, namely, that plans allow for organizational *programming*. The clearer the plan, the better a company can get itself organized for execution. A structure can be chosen, tasks can be assigned, responsibilities can be divided, budgets can be allotted, and targets can be set. Not unimportantly, a control system can be created to measure results in comparison to the plan, so that corrective action can be taken.

A further advantage of planning is that it helps to achieve *optimization*. By explicitly considering all available options before making a decision, organizations can allocate their scarce resources to the most promising course of action. Not only can options be compared within a business area, but planning facilitates the corporate-wide comparison between strategic options in different businesses. Another related advantage is that planning also expedites *coordination* between all of the involved parties. By having to agree on a joint plan before action is taken, differences of opinion can be ironed out, activities can be mutually adjusted, and a consistent organization-wide strategy can be pursued.

A planning approach to strategy formation also allows for the *formalization* and *differentiation* of strategy tasks. Because of its highly structured and sequential nature, planning lends itself well to formalization. The steps of the planning approach can be captured in planning systems (Lorange and Vancil, 1977; Chakravarthy and Lorange, 1991; reading 3.1 in this book), and procedures can be developed to further enhance and organize the strategy formation process. In such planning systems, not all elements of strategy formation need to be carried out by one and the same person, but can be divided among a number of people. The most important division of labor is often between those formulating the plans and those implementing them. In many large companies the managers proposing the plans are also the one's implementing them, but deciding on the plans is passed up to a higher level. Often other tasks are also spun off or shared with others, such as analysis (staff department or external consultants), evaluation (corporate planner) and implementation (staff departments). Such task differentiation and specialization, it is argued, can lead to a better use of management talent, much as the division of labor has improved the field of production.

Last, but not least, an advantage of planning is that it encourages *long-term thinking* and *commitment*. *Ad hoc* management is short-term oriented, dealing with issues of strategic importance as they come up or as a crisis develops. Planning, on the other hand, directs attention to the future. Managers making strategic plans have to take a more long-term view and are stimulated to prepare for, or even create, the future (Ackoff, 1980). Instead of just muddling through, planning challenges strategists to define a desirable future and to work towards it. Instead of wavering and opportunism, planning commits the organization to a course of action and allows for investments to be made now that may only pay off in the long run.

One of the difficulties of planning, advocates of this perspective will readily admit, is that plans will always be based on assumptions about how future events will unfold. Plans require *forecasts*. And as the Danish physicist Niels Bohr once joked, 'prediction is very difficult, especially about the future.' Even enthusiastic planners acknowledge that forecasts will be inaccurate. As Makridakis, the most prolific writer on the topic of forecasting, writes (1990: 66), 'the future can be predicted only by extrapolating from the past, yet it is fairly certain that the future will be different from the past.' Consequently, it is clear that rigid long-range plans based on such unreliable forecasts would amount to nothing less than Russian roulette. Most proponents of the planning perspective therefore caution for overly deterministic plans. Some argue in favor of *contingency planning*, whereby a number of alternative plans are held in reserve in case key variables in the environment suddenly change. These contingency plans are commonly based on different future *scenarios* (Godet, 1987; Wack, 1985a and b). Others argue that organizations should stage regular reviews, and realign the strategic plans to match the altered circumstances. This is usually accomplished by going through the planning cycle every year, and adapting plans to fit with the new forecasts.

As the attentive reader may have already discerned, the planning perspective shares many of the assumptions underlying the rational perspective discussed in Chapter 2. Both perspectives value systematic, orderly, consistent, logical reasoning and assume that humans are capable of forming a fairly good understanding of reality. And both are based on a calculative and optimizing view of strategy making. It is, therefore, not surprising that many strategists who are rationally inclined also exhibit a distinct preference for the planning perspective in this debate.

The Incrementalism Perspective

To advocates of the incrementalism perspective, the planners' faith in deliberateness is misplaced and counterproductive. In reality, incrementalists argue, new strategies largely emerge over time, as managers proactively piece together a viable course of action or reactively adapt to unfolding circumstances. The formation process is not about comprehensively *figuring out* strategy in advance, but about actively *finding out* by doing and gradually blending together initiatives into a coherent pattern of actions. Making strategy involves sense-making, reflecting, learning, envisioning, experimenting and changing the organization, which cannot be neatly organized and programmed. Strategy formation is messy, fragmented, and piecemeal – much more like the unstructured and unpredictable processes of exploration and invention, than like the orderly processes of design and production.

Yet proponents of the planning perspective prefer to press strategy formation into an orderly, mechanistic straight-jacket. Strategies must be intentionally designed and executed. According to incrementalists, this excessive emphasis on deliberateness is due to planners' obsession with rationality and control (Wildavsky, 1979; Mintzberg, 1994a; reading 3.5 in this book). Planners are often compulsive in their desire for order, predictability and efficiency. It is the intention of planning to predict, analyse, optimize and program – to deliberately fine-tune and control the organization's future behavior. For them, 'to manage' is 'to control' and therefore only deliberate patterns of action constitute good strategic management (Stacey, 1993; reading 9.2).

Incrementalists do not question the value of planning and control as a means for managing some organizational processes, but point out that strategy formation is not one of them. In general, planning and control are valuable for routine activities that need to be efficiently organized (e.g. production or finance). But planning is less suitable for non-routine activities – that is, for doing new things. Planning is not appropriate for *innovation*. Just as R&D departments cannot plan the invention of new products, strategists cannot plan the development of new strategies. Innovation, whether in products or strategies, is not a process that can be neatly structured and controlled. Novel insights and creative ideas cannot be generated on demand, but surface at unexpected moments, often in unexpected places. Neither are new ideas born full grown, ready to be evaluated and implemented. In reality, innovation requires brooding, tinkering, experimentation, testing and patience, as new ideas grow and take shape. Throughout the innovation process it remains unclear which ideas might evolve into blockbuster strategies and which will turn out to be miserable disappointments. No one can objectively determine ahead of time which strategic initiatives will 'fly' and which will 'crash'. Therefore, strategists engaged in the formation of new strategies must move incrementally, letting novel ideas crystallize over time, and increase commitment as ideas gradually prove their viability in practice. This demands that strategists behave not as planners, but as *inventors* – searching, experimenting, learning, doubting, and avoiding premature closure and lock-in to one course of action.

Recognizing that strategy formation is essentially an innovation process has more consequences. Innovation is inherently subversive, rebelling against the status quo and challenging those who are emotionally, intellectually or politically wedded to the current state of affairs. Creating new strategies involves confronting people's cognitive maps, questioning the organizational culture, threatening individuals' current interests and disrupting the distribution of power within the organization (Johnson, 1988; reading 9.4). None of these processes can be conducted in an orderly fashion, let alone be incorporated into a planning system. Changing people's cognitive maps, as discussed in Chapter 2, requires complex processes of unlearning and learning. Cultural and political change, which will be discussed in Chapter 4, are also difficult processes to program. Even for the most powerful CEO, managing cognitive, cultural and political changes is not a matter of deliberate control, but of incremental shaping. Less powerful strategists will have even a weaker grip on the unfolding cognitive, cultural and political reality in their organization, and therefore will be even less able to plan. In short, strategists understanding that strategy formation is essentially a disruptive process of organizational change, will move incrementally, gradually molding the organization into a satisfactory form. This demands that strategists behave not as commanders, but as *organizational developers* – questioning assumptions, challenging ideas, getting points on the strategic agenda, encouraging learning, championing new initiatives, supporting change and building political support.

Incrementalists point out that planning is particularly inappropriate when dealing with *wicked problems*. While solving tame problems can often be planned and controlled, strategists rarely have the luxury of using generic solutions to fix clearly recognizable strategic problems. As Mason and Mitroff argued in reading 1.4, strategic problems are inherently wicked – they are essentially unique, highly complex, linked to other problems, can be defined and interpreted in many ways, have no correct answer, nor a delimited set of possible solutions. The planning approach of recognizing the problem, fully analyzing the situation, formulating a comprehensive plan and then implementing the solution, is sure to choke on a wicked problem. A number of weaknesses of planning show up when confronted with a wicked problem.

First, problems cannot be simply recognized and analyzed, but can be interpreted and defined in many ways, depending on how the strategist looks at it. Therefore, half the work of strategists is *making sense* out of complex problems. Or, as Rittel and Webber (1973) put it, the definition of a wicked problem *is* the problem! Strategists must search for new ways for understanding old problems and must be aware of how others are reinterpreting what they see (see Smircich and Stubbart, 1985; reading 2.5). This inhibits planning and encourages incrementalism.

Second, a full analysis of a wicked problem is impossible. Due to a wicked problem's complexity and links to other problems, a full analysis would take, literally, forever. And there would always be more ways of interpreting the problem, requiring more analysis. Planning based on the complete understanding of a problem in advance therefore necessarily leads to paralysis by analysis (Lenz and Lyles, 1985; Langley, 1995). In reality, however, strategists move proactively despite their incomplete understanding of a wicked problem, *learning* as they go along. By acting and thinking at the same time strategists can focus their analyses on what seems to be important and realistic in practice, gradually shaping their understanding along the way.

Third, developing a comprehensive plan to tackle a wicked problem is asking for trouble. Wicked problems are very complex, consisting of many subproblems. Formulating a master plan to solve all subproblems in one blow would require a very high level of planning sophistication and an organization with the ability to implement plans in a highly coordinated manner – much like the circus performers who can keep ten plates twirling at the ends of poles at the same time. Such organizations are rare at best, and the risk of a grand strategy failing is huge – once one plate falls, the rest usually comes crashing down. This is also known as Knagg's law: the more complex a plan, the larger the chance of failure. Incrementalists therefore argue that it is wiser to tackle *subproblems* individually, and gradually blend these solutions into a cohesive pattern of action.

Finally, planners who believe that formulation and implementation can be separated underestimate the extent to which wicked problems are interactive. As soon as an organization starts to implement a plan, its actions will induce counteractions. Customers will react, competitors will change behavior, suppliers will take a different stance, regulatory agencies might come into action, unions will respond, the stockmarkets will take notice and company employees will draw conclusions. Hence, action by the organization will change the nature of the problem. And since the many counterparties are intelligent players, capable of acting strategically, their responses will not be entirely predictable. Planners will not be able to forecast and incorporate other parties' reactions into the plans. Therefore, plans will be outdated as soon as implementation starts. For this reason, incrementalists argue that action must always be swiftly followed by redefinition of the problem and reconsideration of the course of action being pursued. Over time, this iterative process of *action-reaction-reconsideration* will lead to the emergence of a pattern of action, which is the best possible result given the interactive nature of wicked problems.

This last point, on the unpredictability of external and internal reactions to a plan, leads up to a weakness of planning that is possibly its most obvious one – strategy has to do with the future and the future is inherently unknown. Developments cannot be clearly forecast, future opportunities and threats can not predicted, nor can future strengths and weaknesses be accurately foreseen. In such unknown terrain, it is foolhardy to commit oneself to a preset course of action unless absolutely necessary. It makes much more sense in new and unpredictable circumstances to remain flexible and adaptive, postponing fixed commitments for as long as possible. An unknown future requires not the mentality of a train conductor, but of an *explorer* – curious, probing, venturesome, and entrepreneurial, yet moving cautiously, step-by-step, ready to shift course when needed.

To proponents of the incrementalism perspective, it is a caricature to call such behavior *ad hoc* or muddling through. Rather, it is behavior that acknowledges the fact that strategy formation is a process of innovation and organizational development in the face of wicked problems in an unknown future. Under these circumstances, strategies must be allowed to emerge and 'strategic planning' must be seen for what it is – a contradiction in terms.

The question within the field of strategic management is, therefore, whether strategy formation is primarily a deliberate process or more of an emergent one. Should strategists strive to formulate and implement strategic plans, supported by a formalized planning and control system? Or should strategists move incrementally, behaving as inventors, organizational developers and explorers? Not all strategists agree on the answers to these questions, leaving readers in the position of having to draw their own conclusions on the nature of strategy formation. Readers themselves will have to wrestle with the paradox of deliberateness and emergentness (see Table 3.1).

Defining the Issues: Plans and Planning

Before moving on to the 'debate readings,' the dispute between the proponents of the planning and the incrementalism perspectives can be greatly clarified by distinguishing between two major issues on which the parties disagree. First, the two sides are at odds about the need for explicit *plans*. Obviously, advocates of the planning perspective are in favor of articulating intended courses of action. Supporters of the incrementalism perspective doubt the value of plans and focus on the emergence of strategy in the

TABLE 3.1

Planning versus incrementalism perspective

	Planning Perspective	Incrementalism Perspective
Emphasis on	Deliberateness over emergentness	Emergentness over deliberateness
Nature of strategy	Intentionally designed	Gradually shaped
Nature of strategy formation	Figuring out	Finding out
Formation process	Formally structured and comprehensive	Unstructured and fragmented
Formation process steps	First think, then act	Thinking and acting intertwined
Focus on strategy as a	Pattern of decisions (plan)	Pattern of actions (behavior)
Decision-making	Hierarchical	Political
Decision-making focus	Optimal resource allocation & coordination	Experimentation and parallel initiatives
View of future developments	Forecast and anticipate	Partially unknown and unpredictable
Posture towards the future	Make commitments, prepare for the future	Postpone commitments, remain flexible
Implementation focused on	Programming (organizational efficiency)	Learning (organizational development)
Strategic change	Implemented top-down	Requires broad cultural and cognitive shifts

absence of explicit intentions. The second issue revolves around the need for formal *planning*. Here, proponents of the planning perspective champion the establishment of formal planning systems, while incrementalists dismiss such systems as counterproductive, favoring a less structured approach to strategy formation. In the next few paragraphs, these two issues will be further explored, to set the stage for the debate articles that follow.

The Need for Explicit Plans

A plan is an intended course of action. It stipulates which measures a person or organization deliberately proposes to take. In common usage, plans are assumed to be articulated (made explicit) and documented (written down), although strictly speaking this is not necessary to qualify as a plan.

As intended courses of action, plans are means towards an end. Plans detail which actions will be undertaken to reach a particular objective. In practice, however, plans can exist without explicit objectives. In such cases, the objectives are implicitly wrapped up in the plan – the plan incorporates both ends and means.

The first issue dividing planners and incrementalists is whether organizations need plans at all. More accurately, the question is which organizational activities benefit from plans and which do not. To clarify this issue, the aforementioned advantages of plans will be revisited and contrasted with corresponding advantages of not having plans. This leads to five sets of opposites that strategists must consider – five tensions, or we would say paradoxes, embedded within the paradox of deliberateness and emergentness.

- *Direction vs. Latitude.* Planners argue that plans are needed to give organizations direction. Without plans, incorporating objectives, organizations would be adrift. If organizations do not decide where they want to go, any direction and any activity is fine. People in organizations would not know what they were working towards and therefore would not be able to judge what constitutes effective managerial behavior. Incrementalists counter that direction-setting plans can lead to single-minded behavior. Plans, they argue, work as blinkers, blocking out peripheral vision, keeping organizations sharply, yet myopically, focused on one course of action (e.g. Pascale, 1984). Thus, plans limit organizations' ability to be open to new opportunities and threats as these unfold and to deviate from a set course as the organization interacts with its environment and learns. The absence of plans does give strategists this latitude for responsive action.

- *Commitment vs. Flexibility.* Planners argue that early commitment to a course of action is highly beneficial. By setting objectives and drawing up a plan to accomplish these, organizations can invest resources, train people, build up production capacity and take a clear position within their environment. Plans allow organizations to mobilize themselves and to dare to take actions that are difficult to reverse and have a long payback period (e.g. Ghemawat, 1991). Incrementalists, however, point out that commitment has a flip-side, inflexibility. Plans, they argue, indeed encourage strategists to take irreversible actions, locking the organization in to a preset course of action (e.g. Evans, 1991). Plans, therefore, inhibit organizations' ability to adapt to changing circumstances. The absence of plans does give strategists the flexibility to easily change course.

- *Coordination vs. Autonomy.* Plans also have the benefit of coordinating all strategic initiatives within an organization into a single cohesive pattern. An organization-wide master plan can ensure that differences of opinion are ironed out and one consistent course of action is followed throughout the entire organization, avoiding overlapping, conflicting and contradictory behavior. Yet, according to incrementalists, master plans usually lead to the squashing of initiative, either purposely or inadvertently. Coordination usually means centralization and unification, leaving little room for autonomous action by entrepreneurs within the organization (e.g. Burgelman, 1983, 1991). Bringing together all strategic action into one grand scheme, does not encourage an internal market for ideas, where managers pursue contrarian initiatives and try to sell these to the rest of the organization. The absence of a comprehensive plan does give strategists within an organization the autonomy to act as an intrapreneur (e.g. Pinchot, 1985; Quinn, 1985) and develop new courses of action. This issue will resurface in Chapter 6.

- *Optimization vs. Learning.* Planners point out that plans also facilitate optimal resource allocation. Drawing up a plan disciplines strategists to explicitly consider all available information and consciously evaluate all available options. This allows strategists to choose the optimal course of action, before committing resources. Documented plans also permit corporate-level strategists to compare the courses of action proposed by their various business units and to allocate scarce resources to the most promising initiatives. Incrementalists counter that plans place a disproportionate emphasis on thinking over action. Enormous amounts of time and effort are put into analyses, paperwork, meetings and presentations, trying to arrive at the optimal plan. Often the result is that producing a plan develops into an end in itself. Action is seen merely as operationalizing the plan, instead of as the primary input into further strategy formation. The absence of explicit plans, therefore, gives strategists the opportunity to merge thinking and acting, and to form strategies through learning.

■   *Programming vs. Self-organization.* Last, but not least, plans are a means for programming all organizational activities in advance. Having detailed plans allows organizations to be run with the clockwork precision, reliability and efficiency of a machine. Activities that might otherwise be plagued by poor organization, inconsistencies, redundant routines, random behavior, helter-skelter fire-fighting and chaos, can be programmed and controlled if plans are drawn up (e.g. Steiner, 1979). Incrementalists, however, frown on planners' worship of top-down control. According to incrementalists, using plans to pre-program all activities within an organization grossly overestimates the extent to which an organization can be run like a machine. For adaptation, experimentation and learning to take place and for new ideas to emerge from within the organization, a certain measure chaos might actually be beneficial (e.g. Stacey, 1993; reading 9.2 in this book). Top-down control by means of plans denies that 'implementers' can be anything more than cogs in the machine. The absence of detailed top-down plans encourages employees to be responsible, entrepreneurial and combine thinking and action. In this way, new strategic initiatives are not organized and controlled top-down, but emerge spontaneously through bottom-up processes of self-organization (e.g. Hedberg, Nystrom and Starbuck, 1976; Nonaka, 1988b). This issue will resurface in Chapter 9.

While for the sake of discussion these five paradoxes have been disentangled, in practice they are highly intertwined. A position taken in one debate will influence how the other pairs of opposites are dealt with.

The Need for Formal Planning

In the first pages of this chapter a sixth advantage of the planning approach was mentioned, namely that it facilitates process formalization and task differentiation. It was argued that strategy formation by means of planning lends itself well to formalization. By its very nature, planning is a very structured and sequential activity, and therefore can be readily organized by employing formal procedures. Extensive formalization can culminate in the establishment of a strategic planning system. In such a system, strategy formation steps can be scheduled, tasks can specified, responsibilities can be assigned, decision-making authority can be clarified, budgets can be allocated and control mechanisms can be installed. It was also argued that formalization goes hand in hand with a division of labor within the strategy process. By pulling the strategy formation process apart into a number of formal, sequential activities, strategy-making tasks can be divided among a larger group of people and specializations can develop.

Obviously, not everyone agrees that formal planning systems are worth instituting. Some incrementalists regard them as a mixed blessing (e.g. Quinn, 1980a; reading 3.2 in this book), while others are outright hostile (e.g. Mintzberg, 1994a; reading 3.5). Even some authors who value explicit plans, are not enthusiastic about formal planning (e.g. Andrews, 1987; reading 2.1). The debate between supporters and detractors of formal planning systems revolves around two major tensions. These two paradoxes are

- *Formal vs. Informal Process.* The advantage of formalization, according to advocates of the planning perspective, is that it structures and disciplines the strategy formation process (e.g. Hax and Majluf, 1984). Formalization facilitates tighter organization, unambiguous responsibilities, clearer accountability and stricter review of performance. A formal planning system forces managers to comply with a planned approach to strategy formation. It also gives top management more control over the organization, as all major activities must be in approved plans and the implementation of plans is checked. However, incrementalists challenge the value of such extensive procedures. In their view, formal planning systems are attempts to use bureaucratic means to make strategy. Formalization strongly overemphasizes those aspects which can be neatly organized such as meetings, writing reports, giving presentations, making decisions, allocating resources and reviewing progress, while marginalizing essential strategy-making activities that are difficult to capture in procedures. Important aspects such as creating new insights, learning, innovation, building political support and entrepreneurship are side-lined or crushed by the rote bureaucratic mechanisms used to produce strategy. Moreover, planning bureaucracies, once established, come to live a life of their own, creating rules, regulations, procedures, checks, paperwork, schedules, deadlines, and doublechecks, making the system inflexible, unresponsive, ineffective and demotivating.

- *Differentiated vs. Integrated Tasks.* Many advocates of the planning perspective also believe that a division of labor within strategy formation processes is an important advantage of formal planning systems. The most important split facilitated by planning systems is between those who formulate the plans and those who implement them (e.g. Jelinek, 1979). Formulation can also be divided into the task of developing plans and the task of deciding which plans should be implemented (e.g. Chakravarthy and Lorange, 1991; reading 3.1 in this book). Of course, other specialized functions can also be created such as strategic planner, competitive intelligence analyst, new business developer and controller. A major benefit of task differentiation is that the best managers are liberated from time-consuming operational matters, so that they can focus on strategic issues. Furthermore, a certain measure of isolation from day-to-day operations gives the manager formulating strategy the necessary distance to judge a business more objectively. Supporters of the incrementalism perspective, however, point out that such isolation of the cerebral strategy formulator from the reality of the business is the main reason why so few strategies are successfully implemented (Kiechel, 1984). According to incrementalists, separating formulation and implementation tasks seriously inhibits the formation of novel strategies. If strategists need to be explorers, inventors and organizational developers, they cannot afford to view formulation and implementation as distinct activities, but must approach them as tasks that should be integrated.

As noted, not all proponents of explicit plans are convinced of the need for formal planning systems. Writers, such as Andrews in Chapter 2, who believe that plans should be drawn up by the CEO or a small group of top managers, feel uneasy about rigid corporate-wide planning systems. In general, they argue that such extensive formalization creates bureaucracy and reduces top management's freedom to manoever. Their preference is to retain a certain level of organizational flexibility, despite the existence of plans, by keeping enough power in the hands of top management to push through a change of course on command. This position is variably been referred to as the entrepreneurial (Mintzberg, 1978), command (Hart, 1992), managerial autocracy (Shrivastava and Grant, 1985), and design (Mintzberg, 1990a) approach.

EXHIBIT 3.1
Ceteco Short Case

CETECO: A DURABLE CONQUISTADOR?

La Curacao, Tropigas, Ventura . . . To some, these might sound like tasty cocktails, but in fact these are names of large retailers of consumer durables in Latin America. La Curacao has about 200 stores selling white goods (e.g. stoves, refrigerators, washing machines and airconditioners), consumer electronics, household appliances and furniture throughout Central America and the Caribbean. Tropigas has 60 stores selling these items in Guatemala, El Salvador and Honduras, while Ventura has 12 stores in Argentina. What all three have in common is that they are part of Ceteco, one of the leading retailers in Latin America. Ceteco also owns about 100 stores in Venezuela (Imgeve and Lehaca), Ecuador (Orve Hogar) and Peru (Total Artefactos). In 1997, their turnover was approximately US$ 400 million and they employed over 7000 people.

Oddly enough, Ceteco is a Dutch company, headquartered in Utrecht, the Netherlands. Their history is equally curious. Ceteco was established in 1890 as the Curacao Trading Company, initially to profit from the lucrative trading opportunities between the Netherlands and its Caribbean colonies (the main island of the six being Curacao). After a period of trading simple goods, the company also became a local dealer for the Dutch firm Philips and branched out into Central America. Following the Second World War, the company added dealerships for the Japanese companies National and Sharp, and Korea's Samsung and Goldstar to its activities. Ceteco became involved in what Spanish-speakers call *meubleria*, everything needed to run a household. When in the 1960s many Latin American countries began to protect their own 'infant industries' behind high tariff walls, Ceteco started assembling its own electrical appliances. To this day, about a quarter of Ceteco's revenues are from its white goods production, assembly and wholesaling operations.

By the 1980s, Ceteco was a highly diversified trading company, importing all types of commodities such as milk, steel and paper into Latin America and acting as the local representative for larger scale projects by Dutch companies in Africa, the Middle East and South America. It had also become active in retailing through its La Curacao stores. To avoid a hostile takeover, Ceteco's management decided in 1987 to proactively merge with a strong parent company that would support it with good management and solid finances. The willing parent they found was the Dutch shipping and storage company Van Ommeren, which was seeking a related diversification opportunity. However, it soon turned out that the two were not at all 'related'. Ceteco's flexible, free-wheeling, deal-making, relationship-based approach to business collided head-on with Van Ommeren's solid, disciplined, investment-oriented culture. In 1992 Van Ommeren sold Ceteco to another Dutch trading company, Borsumij Wehry, for 50 million guilders (approximately US$ 25 million), taking a loss of 92 million guilders.

One advantage of the five-year Van Ommeren reign, according to Ceteco CEO Frits Eigenfeld, was that Van Ommeren demanded a more focused approach. Ceteco was forced to re-evaluate its highly scattered activities and pick out the most attractive ones. As a consequence, Ceteco withdrew from Africa and the Middle East, and sharply shifted its emphasis from trading to retailing. The company realized that it was a capable importer and wholesaler, but that its modest retailing activities were an unpolished gem. Through years of experience in the turbulent and idiosyncratic markets of Central America, Ceteco had gradually developed a durable goods retailing ability that no one could match. However, in its focused portfolio of activities, this unique capability had been buried under a mountain of other opportunities the company could pursue, and therefore received insufficient attention.

It became clear to Ceteco's management that it actually had a potential retailing formula on its hands that was well-suited to the entire Latin American market, and differed significantly from the approaches taken by American and European retailers. For instance, Ceteco had learned that low purchasing power does not mean that consumers in Latin America are willing to settle for inferior appliances. Most people prefer quality brands, but need to buy these products on credit. While local banks often do not lend money for consumption purposes, Ceteco is a willing banker, selling over 70 per cent of its products on credit. Only 3 per cent of all loans are not paid back – a percentage that would satisfy most commercial bankers. Furthermore, Ceteco has a nose for choosing the right locations, building smaller stores closer to less mobile consumers and adapting store designs to suit local tastes.

Retailing in Latin America was especially appealing to Ceteco because local competitors were not yet very strong, while the continent had been more or less shunned by other internationalizing retailers. As a Dutch company, Ceteco also had the benefit of not being perceived by local partners and acquisition candidates as a conquistador, but as a neutral party. Cross-border acquisitions are still very rare and delicate in Latin America, and therefore being from a far away country, without a bad reputation, is a significant advantage.

After the divorce from Van Ommeren in 1992, Ceteco was asked by its new owner, Borsumij Wehry, to indicate in which direction it wanted to develop. Eager to capitalize on the retailing formula it had just defined as its core business, Mr Eigenfeld and his top management team formulated a general course of action, which they labelled the Ceteco Turbo 2000 plan. In this plan, Ceteco articulated its ambitions to be Latin America's leading retailer in the year 2000. More specifically, Ceteco defined its objective as capturing a 10 per cent share of the US$ 5 billion spent annually on durable household goods in the Spanish-speaking countries of Latin America. In terms of concrete actions, the Turbo 2000 plan indicated that Ceteco would expand from its Central American base to Mexico, Venezuala, Equador, Peru, and Argentina, largely through acquisitions. Portugese-speaking Brazil, good for US$ 3 billion sales annually, was believed to be too big to consider yet. All acquired chains would be reorganized to fit with the evolving La Curacao concept, while retaining their own name and a certain measure of local autonomy to adapt to specific national demands.

Of course, making acquisitions is not something that can be easily scheduled. Candidates have to be available, and the price has to be right. Sometimes a courtship is short and intensive, while sometimes the acquiree is unwilling or plays 'hard-to-get'. In Mexico, the intention to expand locally had to be shelved for a few years, following the economic crisis there. According to Mr Eigenfeld, it's all in the game. 'The core of the Turbo plan was to articulate our desire to become the leading retailer in South America,' he remarks. 'We understand that not everything can be realized at once and we accept differences per country.'

By 1997, most of the Turbo 2000 objectives had been realized. Large-scale acquisitions had been made in Venezuela, Equador, and Peru, while first steps had been set in Mexico and Argentina. Ceteco's retail turnover had more than tripled in five years. Part of the company had been brought to the Amsterdam stock exchange to raise capital for the acquisitions and the stock price indicated that Ceteco was valued at approximately a billion guilders (US$ 500 million), twenty times higher than Van Ommeren's selling price in 1992. For Mr Eigenfeld the question was, what now? A broad Turbo 2005 plan, or something more specific? Until now, he had acted as a entrepreneur, piecing together an empire, but would his style need to change now the company had grown so large? Strategy formation was largely incremental and informal, based on frequent visits to the subsidiaries, personal contact and an exchange of ideas. There were regular events, where country managers met each other and compared best practices. In this way, rather than through top-down standardization, a common retail formula was gradually evolving. But, Mr Eigenfeld wondered, would this approach to strategy formation remain the most appropriate in future?

Sources: Company documents and interview with Mr Eigenfeld.

The Debate and the Readings

As the opening reading in this debate, 'Managing the Strategy Process,' by Balaji Chakravarthy and Peter Lorange, has been selected to represent the planning perspective. Lorange is one of the most well-known writers on the topic of formal planning systems (Lorange, 1980a; Lorange and Vancil, 1977) and this article is taken from the textbook he co-authored with Chakravarthy, entitled *Managing the Strategy Process: A Framework for a Multibusiness Firm*. As most proponents of the planning perspective, Chakravarthy and Lorange do not actively defend their assumption that explicit plans and formal planning are beneficial. Rather, basing themselves on this supposition, they concentrate on outlining a framework for effectively structuring strategic planning activities. Their ideal is an extensive strategic planning system, comprising a number of distinct steps, procedures, mechanisms and roles. However, they go further than only structuring strategic planning. In their view, a formal planning system will not lead to effective strategy formation if it is not linked to other organizational systems. In particular, the strategic planning system needs to interact with the monitoring, control, and learning system, the incentives system, and the staffing system. As such, Chakravarthy and Lorange champion a highly comprehensive and structured approach to strategic planning.

As spokesman for the incrementalism perspective, James Brian Quinn has been chosen. Together with Henry Mintzberg, Quinn has been one of the most influential pioneers on the topic of emergent strategy. Quinn's contribution, 'Logical Incrementalism,' that is reprinted here, and his subsequent book *Strategies for Change* (1980), are widely accepted as having been instrumental in developing the incrementalism perspective. In his reading, Quinn explains some of the key shortcomings of formal strategic planning and goes on to make a case for incrementalism. Important in his argument is that incrementalism is distinguished from muddling through. Incrementalism is a proactive approach to strategy formation – strategists can intentionally choose to let unintended strategies emerge. Muddling through is also incremental in nature, but reactive and *ad hoc* – opportunistic decisions are made to deal with unplanned and poorly controllable circumstances. To make this distinction more explicit, Quinn refers to the proactive strain of incremental behavior as *logical incrementalism*. By 'logical' he means 'reasonable and well-considered'. However, logic incrementalism is not always logical by the definition used in Chapter 2 – incremental behavior is not necessarily 'dictated by formal logic'. To avoid confusion, therefore, in this book we shall refer to reasonable and well-considered incrementalism simply as incrementalism.

To complement the initial arguments brought forward by the first discussants, three additional articles have been included in this chapter. Reading 3.3, 'Conceptual Models and Decision-Making,' is a classic study of strategy formation by Graham Allison. In this contribution and his famous book *Essence of Decision: Explaining the Cuban Missile Crisis*, Allison examines the organizational decision-making surrounding the Cuban Missile Crisis in 1962 and comes up with three opposing models for explaining the behavior of the parties involved. His base hypothesis is that people behave rationally and therefore that decision-making is focused on selecting the optimal course of action after a comprehensive analysis. This *rational actor model* largely fits with the rational and planning perspectives. He carries on to present two other models, that explain why suboptimal policies are often pursued. On the one hand, the *organizational process model* suggests that ingrained organizational routines often inhibit rational behavior. On the other hand, the *bureaucratic politics model* describes how conflicting interests and objectives can result in processes of political manoevering and positioning within an organization. In the context of this chapter, Allison's contribution is to highlight the importance of these behavioral dynamics on strategy formation. These are the sources of inertia and muddling through, with which strategists, both planners and incrementalists, have to struggle (see also Johnson, 1988; reading 9.4; Rumelt, 1994; reading 9.5).

Reading 3.4, 'Removing the Obstacles to Effective Strategic Planning,' by Thomas Marx, is an impassioned plea by a practitioner not to abandon ineffective strategic planning, but to improve it. Marx acknowledges that many formal planning systems have become overly bureaucratic, but he does not believe that this state of affairs is inherent to strategic planning. In fact, he argues that many of the characteristics normally associated with planning, such as 'formal presentations, large meetings, massive planning books and regularly scheduled, annual reviews,' are actually the obstacles to strategic planning that need to be, and can be, removed. The crux of Marx's argument is that excessive formalization is a developmental phase that most strategic planning systems go through. He, therefore, recommends that companies should not quit planning, but should progress beyond this bureaucratic phase and develop a more 'lean and mean' strategic planning system. As such, Marx's contribution to the debate is to support the planning perspective by arguing that planning systems and bureaucracy should not be equated – many planning systems may have failed in the past, but this does not rule out the establishment of more effective systems in the future.

In the final contribution, 'The Fall and Rise of Strategic Planning,' Henry Mintzberg is less optimistic than Marx about the future of strategic planning, although he stops short of calling for a complete abandonment of formal systems. In his view, conventional planning has been a failure at creating new and effective strategies because it is based on a number of fundamental fallacies. In line with the incrementalism perspective, Mintzberg argues that planning rests on the faulty assumptions that future events can be predicted, that thinking can be detached from doing, and that strategy making can be formalized. Mintzberg's criticisms are hard-hitting, although formulated more diplomatically than in his simultaneously published book, tellingly entitled *The Rise and Fall of Strategic Planning* (1994). Despite the detriments, however, he argues that organizations should not rid themselves of their planning or their planners, but should transform them. In particular, he believes there is a need for plans to communicate strategic intentions and to program and control operations. Strategic planners are also needed, although not to plan strategies, but to encourage strategic thinking within the organization. In the context of this chapter, it can be concluded that the reforms Mintzberg suggests are quite far-reaching. It remains to be debated whether his proposals go too far, or not far enough.

3.1   Managing the Strategy Process

By Balaji Chakravarthy and Peter Lorange[1]

Steps in the Strategy Process

There are five distinct steps in the strategy process (see Figure 3.1.1). The first three steps involve the strategic planning system; the final two steps cover the role of the monitoring, control, and learning system and the incentives and staffing systems, respectively.

FIGURE 3.1.1
The strategy process

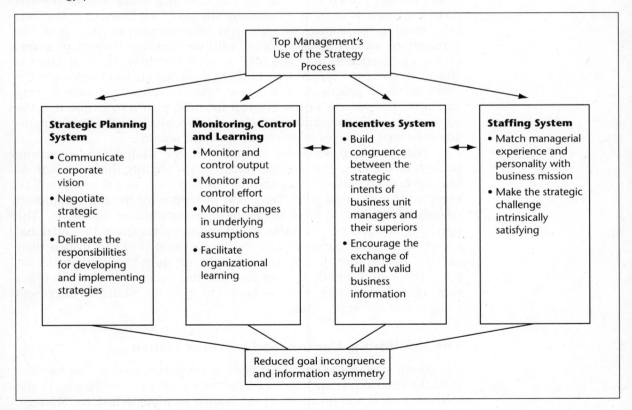

[1] Source: This article was adapted with permission from chapter 1 of *Managing the Strategy Process: A Framework for a Multibusiness Firm*, Prentice Hall, Englewood Cliffs, New Jersey, © 1991.

The Strategic Planning System

The purpose of the first step in the planning system, *objectives setting*, is to determine a strategic direction for the firm and each of its divisions and business units. Objectives setting calls for an open-ended reassessment of the firm's business environments and its strengths in dealing with these environments. At the conclusion of this step, there should be agreement at all levels of the organization on the goals that should be pursued and the strategies that will be needed to meet them. It is worth differentiating here between objectives and goals. Objectives refer to the strategic intent of the firm in the long run. Goals, on the other hand, are more specific statements of the achievements targeted for certain deadlines – goals can be accomplished, and when that happens the firm moves closer to meeting its objectives. Objectives represent a more enduring challenge.

The second step, *strategic programming*, develops the strategies identified in the first step and defines the cross-functional programs that will be needed to implement the chosen strategies. Cross-functional cooperation is essential to this step. At the end of the strategic programming step a long-term financial plan is drawn up for the firm as a whole and each of its divisions, business units, and functions. On top of the financial projections from existing operations, the long-term financial plan overlays both the expenditures and revenues associated with the approved strategic programs of an organizational unit. The time horizon for these financial plans is chosen to cover the typical lead times that are required to implement the firm's strategic programs. A five-year financial plan is, however, very common. The purpose of the five-year financial plan is to ensure that the approved strategic programs can be funded through either the firm's internally generated resources or externally financed resources.

The third step, *budgeting*, defines both the strategic and operating budgets of the firm. The strategic budget helps identify the contributions that the firm's functional departments, business units, and divisions will be expected to make in a given fiscal year in support of the firm's approved strategic programs. It incorporates new product/market initiatives. The operating budget, on the other hand, provides resources to functional departments, business units, and divisions so that they can sustain their existing momentum. It is based on projected short-term activity levels, given past trends. Failure to meet the operating budget will hurt the firm's short-term performance, whereas failure to meet the strategic budget will compromise the firm's future.

The Monitoring, Control, and Learning System

The fourth step in the strategy process is *monitoring, control, and learning*. Here the emphasis is not on output but on meeting key milestones in the strategic budget and on adhering to planned spending schedules. Strategic programs, like strategic budgets, are monitored for the milestones reached and for adherence to spending schedules. In addition, the key assumptions underlying these programs are validated periodically. As a natural extension to this validation process, even the agreed-on goals at various levels are reassessed in the light of changes to the resources of the firm and its business environment.

The Incentives and Staffing Systems

The fifth and final step in the strategy process is *incentives and staffing*. One part of this is the award of incentives as contracted to the firm's managers. If the incentives system is perceived to have failed in inducing the desired performance, redesigning the incentives system and reassessing the staffing of key managerial positions are considered at this step.

Linking Organizational Levels and Steps in Strategic Planning

An effective strategy process must allow for interactions between the organizational levels and iterations between the process steps. Figure 3.1.2 describes some of the interactions and iterations in the strategic planning steps. The formal interactions in the process are shown in the figure by the solid line that weaves up and down through the organizational levels and across the three steps. The informal interactions that complement the formal interactions are shown by dotted loops.

Objectives Setting

The first formal step of the strategy process commences soon after top management reaffirms or modifies the firm's objectives at the beginning of each fiscal year. Embedded in these objectives should be the vision of the chief executive officer (CEO) and his or her top management team. Top management's vision helps specify what will make the firm great. An elaboration of this vision can be done through a formal statement of objectives. However, it is not the formality of a firm's objectives but rather the excitement and challenge that top management's vision can bring to a firm's managers that is important to the strategy process.

Along with its communication of corporate objectives, top management must provide a forecast on key environmental factors. Assumptions on exchange rates, inflation, and other economic factors – as well as projections on the political risks associated with each country – are best compiled centrally so as to ensure objectivity and consistency. These objectives and forecasts are then discussed with a firm's divisional and business unit managers.

Once the corporate objectives are decided, top management negotiates, for each division and business unit in the firm, goals that are consistent with these objectives. The nature of these negotiations can vary. In some firms, top management may wish to set goals in a top-down

FIGURE 3.1.2
Steps in the strategy
process

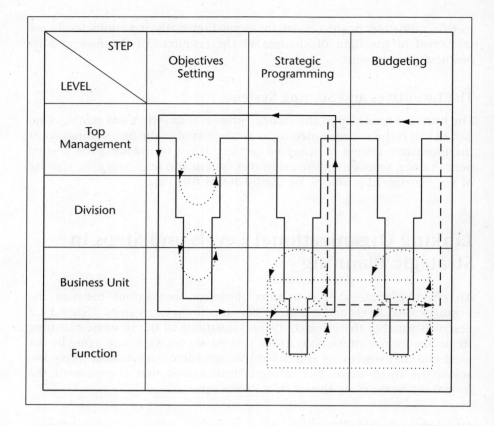

fashion; in others, it may invite subordinate managers to participate in the goal-setting process. Managers are encouraged to examine new strategies and modify existing ones in order to accomplish their goals. The proposed strategies are approved at each higher level in the organizational hierarchy, then eventually by top management. Top management tries to make certain that the strategies as proposed are consistent with the firm's objectives and can be supported with the resources available to the firm. Modifications, where necessary, are made to the objectives, goals, and strategies in order to bring them in alignment. Another important outcome of the objectives-setting step is to build a common understanding across the firm's managerial hierarchy of the goals and strategies that are intended for each organizational unit.

The objectives-setting step in Figure 3.1.2 does not include the functional departments. As we observed earlier, the primary role of these departments is a supporting one. They do not have a proifit or growth responsibility, and their goals cannot be decided until the second step, when strategic programs in support of approved business unit goals begin to be formed. It is not uncommon, however, for key functional managers to be invited to participate in the objectives-setting step either as experts in a corporate task force or, more informally, as participants in the deliberations that are held at the business unit level.

It is important that divisional proposals be evaluated on an overall basis as elements of a corporate portfolio and not reviewed in a sequential mode. In the latter case, the resulting overall balance in the corporate portfolio would be more or less incidental, representing the accumulated sum of individual approvals. It makes little sense to attempt to judge in isolation whether a particular business family or business strategy is attractive to the corporate portfolio. That will depend on a strategy's fit with the rest of the portfolio and on the competing investment opportunities available to the firm in its business portfolio.

Strategic Programming

The second step in the process has two purposes:

1   To forge an agreement between divisional, business unit, and functional managers on the strategic programs that have to be implemented over the next few years.

2   To deepen the involvement of functional managers in developing the strategies that were tentatively selected in the first step.

The strategic programming step begins with a communication from top management about the goals and strategies that were finally approved for the firm's divisions and business units. The divisonal manager then invites his or her business unit and functional managers to identify program alternatives in support of the approved goals and strategies. Examples of strategic programs include increasing market share for an existing product, introducing a new product, and launching a joint marketing campaign for a family of divisional products. As in these examples, a strategic program typically requires the cooperation of multiple functional departments.

However, the functional specialties within a firm often represent different professional cultures that do not necessarily blend easily. Further, day-to-day operating tasks can be so demanding that the functional managers may simply find it difficult to participate in the time-consuming cross-functional teamwork. A key challenge for both divisional and business managers is to bring about this interaction.

The proposed strategic programs travel up the hierarchy for approval at each level. At the division level, the programs are evaluated not only for how well they support the approved strategies but also for how they promote synergies within the firm. Synergies can come from two sources: through economies of scale and/or economies of scope. The creation of synergies based on economies of scale calls for a sharing of common functional activities – such as research and development (R&D), raw materials procurement, production, and distribution – so as to spread over a larger volume the overhead costs associated with these functions. The creation of economies of scope, on the other hand, requires a common approach to the market. Examples of such an approach include the development of a common trademark, the development of products/ services that have a complementary appeal to a customer group, and the ability to offer a common regional service organization for the firm's diverse businesses.

At the corporate level, the proposed strategic programs provide an estimate of the resources that will be required to support the divisional and business unit goals. These goals, as well as their supporting strategies, are once again reassessed; and where needed, modifications are sought in the proposed strategic programs. As noted earlier, a long-term financial plan is drawn at this stage for the firm as a whole and each of its organizational units. The approved strategic programs are communicated to the divisions, business units, and functional departments at the beginning of the budgeting cycle.

Budgeting

When top management decides on the strategic programs that the firm should pursue, it has de facto allocated all of the firm's human, technological, and financial resources that are available for internal development. This allocation influences the strategic budgets that may be requested at each level in the organizational hierarchy.

The strategic budgets, together with the operating budgets of the various organizational units, are consolidated and sent up for top management approval. When top management finally approves the budgets of the various organizational units, before the start of a new budget year, it brings to a close what can be a year-long journey through the three steps of the strategy-making subprocess. The strategy implementation subprocess is then set into motion. Even though the two subprocesses are described sequentially here, it is important to mention that even as the budget for a given year is being formed, the one for the prior year will be under implementation. Midcourse corrections to the prior year's budget can have an impact on the formulation of the current budget.

If the actual accomplishments fall short of the strategic budget, in particular, the negative variance may suggest that the firm's managers failed to implement its chosen strategy efficiently. But it can also suggest that the strategic programs that drive this budget may have been ill conceived or even that the goals underlying these programs may have been specified incorrectly. The monitoring, control, and learning system provides continuous information on both the appropriateness of a strategic budget and the efficiency with which the budget is implemented. This information, based on the implementation of the prior year's strategic budget, can trigger another set of iterations between the three strategy-making steps, calling into question the goals and strategies on which the current year's budget are based. These iterations are shown by the dotted rectangles in Figure 3.1.2.

3.2 Logical Incrementalism

By James Quinn[1]

> When I was younger I always conceived of a room where all these [strategic] concepts were worked out for the whole company. Later I didn't find any such room . . . . The strategy [of the company] may not even exist in the mind of one man. I certainly don't know where it is written down. It is simply transmitted in the series of decisions made.
>
> (Interview quote)

Introduction

When well-managed major organizations make significant changes in strategy, the approaches they use frequently bear little resemblance to the rational-analytical systems so often touted in the planning literature. The full strategy is rarely written down in any one place. The processes used to arrive at the total strategy are typically fragmented, evolutionary, and largely intuitive. Although one can usually find embedded in these fragments some very refined pieces of formal strategic analysis, the real strategy tends to evolve as internal decisions and external events flow together to create a new, widely shared consensus for action among key members of the top management team. Far from being an abrogation of good management practice, the rationale behind this kind of strategy formulation is so powerful that it perhaps provides the normative model for strategic decision making, rather than the step-by-step 'formal systems planning' approach so often espoused.

The Formal Systems Planning Approach

A strong normative literature states what factors should be included in a systematically planned strategy and how to analyze and relate these factors step-by-step. The main elements of this 'formal' planning approach include:

- analyzing one's own internal situation: strengths, weaknesses, competencies, problems;

- projecting current product lines, profits, sales, investment needs into the future;

---

[1] Source: This article was originally published as 'Strategic Change: "Logical Incrementalism,"' in *Sloan Management Review* (Fall 1978). Reproduced by permission of John Wiley and Sons Limited.

- analyzing selected external environments and opponents' actions for opportunities and threats;

- establishing broad goals as targets for subordinate groups' plans;

- identifying the gap between expected and desired results;

- communicating planning assumptions to the divisions;

- requesting proposed plans from subordinate groups with more specific target goals, resource needs, and supporting action plans;

- occasionally asking for special studies of alternatives, contingencies, or longer-term opportunities;

- reviewing and approving divisional plans and summing these for corporate needs;

- developing long-term budgets presumably related to plans;

- implementing plans;

- monitoring and evaluating performance (presumably against plans, but usually against budgets).

While this approach is excellent for some purposes, it tends to focus unduly on measurable quantitative factors and to underemphasize the vital qualitative, organizational, and power-behavioral factors that so often determine strategic success in one situation versus another. In practice, such planning is just one building block in a continuous stream of events that really determine corporate strategy.

The Power-Behavioral Approach

Other investigators have provided important insights on the crucial psychological, power, and behavioral relationships in strategy formulation. Among other things, these have enhanced understanding about: the multiple goal structures of organizations, the politics of strategic decisions, executive bargaining and negotiation processes, 'satisficing' (as opposed to maximizing) in decision making, the role of coalitions in strategic management, and the practice of 'muddling' in the public sphere. Unfortunately, however, many power-behavioral studies have been conducted in settings far removed from the realities of strategy formulation. Others have concentrated solely on human dynamics, power relationships, and organizational processes and ignored the ways in which systematic data analysis shapes and often dominates crucial aspects of strategic decisions. Finally, a few have offered much normative guidance for the strategist.

The Study

Recognizing the contributions and limitations of both approaches, I attempted to document the dynamics of actual strategic change processes in some 10 major companies as perceived by those most knowledgeably and intimately involved in them. Several important findings have begun to emerge from these investigations:

- Neither the power-behavioral nor the formal systems planning paradigm adequately characterizes the way successful strategic processes operate.

- Effective strategies tend to emerge from a series of 'strategic subsystems,' each of which attacks a specific class of strategic issue (e.g. acquisitions, divestitures, or major reorganizations) in a disciplined way, but which blends incrementally and opportunistically into a cohesive pattern that becomes the company's strategy.

- The logic behind each subsystem is so powerful that to some extent it may serve as a normative approach for formulating these key elements of strategy in large companies.

- Because of cognitive and process limits, almost all of these subsystems – and the formal planning activity itself – must be managed and linked together by an approach best described as logical incrementalism.

- Such incrementalism is not muddling. It is a purposeful, effective, pro-active management technique for improving and integrating both the analytical and behavioral aspects of strategy formulation.

This article will document these findings, suggest the logic behind several important subsystems for strategy formulation, and outline some of the management and thought processes executives in large organizations use to synthesize them into effective corporate strategies. Such strategies embrace those patterns of high-leverage decisions (on major goals, policies, and action sequences) that affect the viability and direction of the entire enterprise or determine its competitive posture for an extended time period.

Critical Strategic Issues

Although certain 'hard data' decisions (e.g. on product-market position or resource allocations) tend to dominate the analytical literature, executives identified other 'soft' changes that have at least as much importance in shaping their concern's strategic posture. Most often cited were changes in the company's

- overall organizational structure or its basic management style;

- relationships with the government or other external interest groups;

- acquisition, divestiture, or divisional control practices;

- international posture and relationships;

- innovative capabilities or personnel motivations as affected by growth;

- worker and professional relationships reflecting changed social expectations and values;

- past or anticipated technological environments.

When executives were asked to 'describe the processes through which their company arrived at its new posture' *vis-à-vis* each of these critical domains, several important points emerged. First, a few of these issues lent themselves to quantitative modeling techniques or perhaps even formal financial analyses. Second, successful companies used a different subsystem to formulate strategy for each major class of strategic issues, yet these sub-systems were quite similar among companies even in very different industries. Finally, no single formal analytical process could handle all strategic variables simultaneously on a planned basis. Why?

Precipitating Events

Often external or internal events over which managements had essentially no control would precipitate urgent, piecemeal, interim decisions that inexorably shaped the company's future strategic posture. One clearly observes this phenomenon in the decisions forced on General Motors by the 1973–74 oil crisis; the shift in posture pressed upon Exxon by sudden nationalizations; or the dramatic opportunities allowed for Haloid Corporation and Pilkingtom Brothers Ltd by the unexpected inventions of xerography and float glass.

In these cases, analyses from earlier formal planning cycles did contribute greatly, as long as the general nature of the contingency had been anticiapted. They broadened the information base available (as in Exxon's case), extended the options considered (Haloid-Xerox), created shared values to guide decisions about precipitating events in consistent directions (Pilkington), or built up resource bases, management flexibilities, or active search routines for opportunities whose specific nature could not be defined in advance (General Mills, Pillsbury). But no organization – no matter how brilliant, rational, or imaginative – could possibly foresee the timing, severity, or even the nature of all such precipitating events. Further, when these events did occur there might be neither time, resources, nor information enough to undertake a full formal strategic analysis of all possible options and their consequences. Yet early decisions made under stress conditions often meant new thrusts, precedents, or lost opportunities that were difficult to reverse later.

An Incremental Logic

Recognizing this, top executives usually consciously tried to deal with precipitating events in an incremental fashion. Early commitments were kept broadly formative, tentative, and subject to later review. In some cases neither the company nor the external players could understand the full implications of alternative actions. All parties wanted to test assumptions and have an opportunity to learn from and adapt to the others' responses. For example: Neither the potential producer nor user of a completely new product or process (like xerography or float glass) could fully conceptualize its ramifications without interactive testing. All parties benefited from procedures that purposely delayed decisions and allowed mutual feedback.

Some companies, like IBM or Xerox, have formalized this concept into 'phase program planning' systems. They make concrete decisions only on individual phases (or stages) of new product developments, establish interactive testing procedures with customers, and postpone final configuration commitments until the latest possible moment.

Similarly, even under pressure, most top executives were extremely sensitive to organizational and power relationships and consciously mananged decision processes to improve these dynamics. They often purposely delayed initial decisions, or kept such decisions vague, in order to encourage lower-level participation, to gain more information from specialists, or to build commitment to solutions. Even when a crisis atmosphere tended to shorten time horizons and make decisions more goal oriented than political, perceptive executives consciously tried to keep their options open until they understood how the crisis would affect the power bases and needs of their key constituents.

Incrementalism in Strategic Subsystems

One also finds that an incremental logic applies in attacking many of the critical subsystems of corporate strategy. Those subsystems for considering diversification moves, divestitures, major reorganizations, or government-external relations are typical and will be described here. In each case conscious incrementalism helps to

1   cope with both the cognitive and process limits on each major decision;

2   build the logical-analytical framework these decisions require;

3   create the personal and organizational awareness, understanding, acceptance, and commitment needed to implement the strategies effectively.

The Diversification Subsystem

Strategies for diversification, either through research and development (R&D) or acquisitions, provide excellent examples. The formal analytical steps needed for successful diversification are well documented. However, the precise directions that R&D may project the company can only be understood step-by-step as scientists uncover new phenomena, make and amplify discoveries, build prototypes, reduce concepts to practice, and interact with users during product introductions. Similarly, only as each acquisition is sequentially identified, investigated, negotiated for, and integrated into the organization can one predict its ultimate impact on the total enterprise.

A step-by-step approach is clearly necessary to guide and assess the strategic fit of each internal or external diversification candidate. Incremental processes are also required to manage the crucial psychological and power shifts that ultimately determine the program's overall direction and consequences. These processes help unify both the analytical and behavioral aspects of diversification decisions. They create the broad conceptual consensus, the risk-taking attitudes, the organizational and resource flexibilities, and the adaptive dynamism that determine both the timing and direction of diversification strategies. Most important among these processes are:

■ *Generating a genuine, top-level psychological commitment to diversification.* General Mills, Pillsbury, and Xerox all started their major diversification programs with broad analytical studies and goal-setting exercises designed both to build top-level consensus around the need to diversify and to establish the general directions for diversification. Without such action, top-level bargaining for resources would have continued to support only more familiar (and hence apparently less risky) old lines, and this could delay or undermine the entire diversification endeavor.

■ *Consciously preparing to move opportunistically.* Organizational and fiscal resources must be built up in advance to exploit candidates as they randomly appear. And a 'credible activist' for ventures must be developed and backed by someone with commitment power. All successful acquirers created the potential for profit centered divisions within their organizational structures, strengthened their financial-controllership capabilities, took action to create low-cost capital access, and maintained the shortest possible communication lines from the acquisitions activist to the resource-committing authority. All these actions integrally determined which diversifications actually could be made, the timing of their accession, and the pace at which they could be absorbed.

■ *Building a 'comfort factor' for risk taking.* Perceived risk is largely a function of one's knowledge about a field. Hence well-conceived diversification programs should anticipate a trial-and-error period during which top managers reject early proposed fields or opportunities until they have analyzed enough trial candidates to 'become comfortable' with an initial selection. Early successes tend to be 'sure things' close to the companies' past (real or supposed) expertise. After a few successful diversifications, managements tend to become more confident and accept other candidates – farther from traditional lines – at a faster rate. Again, the way this process is handled affects both the direction and pace of the actual program.

■ *Developing a new ethos.* If new divisions are more successful than the old – as they should be – they attract relatively more resources and their political power grows. Their most effective line managers move into corporate positions, and slowly the company's special competency and ethos change. Finally, the concepts and products that once dominated the company's culture may decline in importance or even disappear. Acknowledging these ultimate consequences to the organization at the beginning of a diversification program would clearly be impolitic, even if the manager both desired and could predict the probable new ethos. These factors must be handled adaptively, as opportunities present themselves and as individual leaders and power centers develop.

Each of the above processes interacts with all others (and with the random appearance of diversification candidates) to affect action sequences, elapsed time, and ultimate results in unexpected ways. Complexities are so great that few diversification programs end up as initially envisioned. Consequently, wise managers recognize the limits to systematic analysis in diversification, and use formal planning to build the 'comfort levels' executives need for risk taking and to guide the program's early directions and priorities. They then modify these flexibly, step-by-step, as new opportunities, power centers, and developed competencies merge to create new potentials.

The Divestiture Subsystem

Similar practices govern the handling of divestitures. Divisions often drag along in a less-than-desired condition for years before they can be strategically divested. In some cases, ailing divisions might have just enough yield or potential to offer hoped-for viability. In others, they might represent the company's vital core from earlier years, the creations of a powerful person nearing retirement, or the psychological touchstones of the company's past traditions.

Again, in designing divestiture strategies, top executives had to reinforce vaguely felt concerns with detailed data, build up managers' comfort levels about issues, achieve participation in and commitment to decisions, and move opportunistically to make actual changes. In many cases, the precise nature of the decision was not clear at the outset. Executives often made seemingly unrelated personnel shifts or appointments that changed the value set of critical groups, or started a series of staff studies that generated awareness or acceptance of a potential problem. They might then instigate goal assessment, business review, or 'planning' programs to provide broader forums for discussion and a wider consensus for action. Even then they might wait for a crisis, a crucial retirement, or an attractive sale opportunity to determine the timing and conditions of divestiture. In some cases, decisions could be direct and analytical. But when divestitures involved the psychological centers of the organization, the process had to be much more oblique and carefully orchestrated.

The Major Reorganization Subsystem

It is well recognized that major organizational changes are an integral part of strategy. Sometimes they constitute a strategy themselves, sometimes they precede and/or precipitate a new strategy, and sometimes they help to implement a strategy. However, like many other important strategic decisions, macro-organizational moves are typically handled incrementally and outside of formal planning processes. Their effects on personal or power relationships preclude discussion in open forums and reports of such processes.

In addition, major organizational changes have timing imperatives (or 'process limits') all their own. In making any significant shifts, executives must think through the new roles, capabilities, and probable individual reactions of the many principals affected. They may have to wait for the promotion or retirement of a valued colleague before consummating any change. They then frequently have to bring in, train, or test new people for substantial periods before they can staff key posts with confidence. During this testing period they may substantially modify their original concept of the reorganization, as they evaluate individuals' potentials, their performance in specific roles, their personal drives, and their relationships with other team members.

Because this chain of decisions affects the career development, power, affluence, and self-image of so many, executives tend to keep close counsel in their discussions, negotiate individually with key people, and make final commitments as late as possible in order to obtain the best matches between people's capabilities, personalities, and aspirations and their new roles. Typically, all these events do not come together at one convenient time, particularly the moment annual plans are due. Instead executives move opportunistically, step-by-step, selectively moving people toward a broadly conceived organizational goal, which is constantly modified and rarely articulated in detail until the last pieces fit together.

The Government-External Relations Subsystem

Almost all companies cited government and other external activist groups as among the most important forces causing significant changes in their strategic postures during the periods examined. However, when asked 'How did your company arrive at its own strategy *vis-à-vis* these forces?' it became clear that few companies had cohesive strategies (integrated sets of goals, policies, and programs) for government-external relations, other than lobbying for or against specific legislative actions. To the extent that other strategies did exist, they were piecemeal, *ad hoc* and had been derived in a very evolutionary manner. Yet there seemed to be very good reasons for such incrementalism. The following are two of the best short explanations of the way these practices develop:

> We are a very large company, and we understand that any massive overt action on our part could easily create more public antagonism than support for our viewpoint. It is also hard to say in advance exactly what public response any particular action might create. So we tend to test a number of different approaches on a small scale with only limited or local company identification. If one approach works, we'll test it further and amplify its use. If another bombs, we try to keep it from being used again. Slowly we find a series of advertising, public relations, community relations actions that seem to help. Then along comes another issue and we start all over again. Gradually the successful approaches merge into a pattern of actions that becomes our strategy.

> I [the president] start conversations with a number of knowledgeable people . . . . I collect articles and talk to people about how things get done in Washington in this particular field. I collect data from any reasonable source. I begin wide-ranging discussions with people inside and outside the corporation. From these a pattern eventually emerges. It's like fitting together a jigsaw puzzle. At first the vague outline of an approach

appears like the sail of a ship in a puzzle. Then suddenly the rest of the puzzle becomes quite clear. You wonder why you didn't see it all along. And once it's crystallized, it's not difficult to explain to others.

In this realm, uncontrollable forces dominate. Data are very soft, often can be only subjectively sensed, and may be costly to quantify. The possible responses of individuals and groups to different stimuli are difficult to determine in advance. The number of potential opponents with power is very high, and the diversity in their viewpoints and possible modes of attack is so substantial that it is physically impossible to lay out probabilistic decision diagrams that would have much meaning. Results are unpredictable and error costs extreme. Even the best intended and most rational-seeming strategies can be converted into disasters unless they are thoroughly and interactively tested.

Formal Planning in Corporate Strategy

What role do classical formal planning techniques play in strategy formulation? All companies in the sample do have formal planning procedures embedded in their management direction and control systems. These serve certain essential functions. In a process sense, they

- provide a discipline forcing managers to take a careful look ahead periodically;

- require rigorous communications about goals, strategic issues, and resource allocations;

- stimulate longer-term analyses than would otherwise be made;

- generate a basis for evaluating and integrating short-term plans;

- lengthen time horizons and protect long-term investments such as R&D;

- create a psychological backdrop and an information framework about the future against which managers can calibrate short-term or interim decisions.

In a decision-making sense, they

- fine-tune annual commitments;

- formalize cost-reduction programs;

- help implement strategic changes once decided on (for example, coordinating all elements of Exxon's decision to change its corporate name).

Formal Plans Also 'Increment'

Although individual staff planners were often effective in identifying potential problems and bringing them to top management's attention, the annual planning process itself was rarely (if ever) the initiating source of really new key issues or radical departures into new product/market realms. These almost always came from precipitating events, special studies, or conceptions implanted through the kinds of 'logical incremental' processes described above.

In fact, formal planning practices actually institutionalize incrementalism. There are two reasons for this. First, in order to utilize specialized expertise and to obtain executive involvement and commitment, most planning occurs from the bottom up in response to broadly defined assumptions or goals, many of which are longstanding or negotiated well in advance. Of necessity, lower-level groups have only a partial view of the corporation's total strategy, and command only a fragment of its resources. Their power bases, identity, expertise, and rewards also usually depend on their existing products or processes. Hence, these products or processes, rather than entirely new departures, should and do receive their primary attention. Second, most managements purposely design their plans to be 'living' or 'evergreen.' They are intended only as frameworks to guide and provide consistency for future decisions made incrementally. To act otherwise would be to deny that further information could have a value. Thus, properly formulated formal plans are also a part of an incremental logic.

Special Studies

Formal planning was most successful in stimulating significant change when it was set up as a special study on some important aspect of corporate strategy. For example, when it became apparent that Pilkington's new float glass process would work, the company formed a Directors' Float Glass Committee consisting of all internal directors associated with float glass 'to consider the broad issues of float glass [strategy] in both the present and the future.' The committee did not attempt detailed plans. Instead, it tried to deal in broad concepts, identify alternate routes, and think through the potential consequences of each route some 10 years ahead. Of some of the key strategic decisions it was later remarked, 'It would be difficult to identify an exact moment when the decision was made. . . . Nevertheless, over a period of time a consensus crystallized with great clarity.'

Such special strategic studies represent a subsystem of strategy formulation distinct from both annual planning activities and the other subsystems exemplified above. Each of these develops some important aspect of strategy, incrementally blending its conclusions with those of other subsystems, and it would be virtually impossible to force all these together to crystallize a completely articulated corporate strategy at any one instant.

Total Posture Planning

Occasionally, however, managements do attempt very broad assessments of their companies' total posture. Shortly after becoming CEO of General Mills, James McFarland decided that his job was 'to take a very good company and move it to greatness,' but that it was up to his management group, not himself alone, to decide what a great company was and how to get there. Consequently he took some 35 of the company's topmost managers away for a three-day management retreat. On the first day, after agreeing to broad financial goals, the group broke up into units of six to eight people. Each unit was to answer the question 'What is a great company?' from the viewpoints of stockholders, employees, suppliers, the public, and society. Each unit reported back at the end of the day, and the whole group tried to reach a consensus through discussion.

On the second day the groups, in the same format, assessed the company's strengths and weaknesses relative to the defined posture of 'greatness.' The third day focused on how to overcome the company's weaknesses and move it toward a great company. This broad consensus led, over the next several years, to the surveys of fields for acquisition, the building of management's initial comfort levels with certain fields, and the acquisition-divestiture strategy that characterized the McFarland era at General Mills.

Yet even such a major endeavor is only a portion of a total strategic process. Values that had been built up over decades stimulated or constrained alternatives. Precipitating events, acquisitions, divestitures, external relations, and organizational changes developed important segments of each strategy incrementally. Even the strategies articulated left key elements to be defined as new information became available, polities permitted, or particular opportunities appeared. Major product thrusts proved unsuccessful. Actual strategies therefore evolved as each company overextended, consolidated, made errors, and rebalanced various thrusts over time. And it was both logical and expected that this would be the case.

Logical Incrementalism

All of the above suggest that strategic decisions do not lend themselves to aggregation into a single massive decision matrix where all factors can be treated relatively simultaneously in order to arrive at a holistic optimum. Many have spoken of the cognitive limits that prevent this. Of equal importance are the process limits – that is, the timing and sequencing imperatives necessary to create awareness, build comfort levels, develop consensus, select and train people, and so forth – that constrain the system yet ultimately determine the decision itself. Unlike the preparation of a fine banquet, it is virtually impossible for the manager to orchestrate all internal decisions, external environmental events, behavioral and power relationships, technical and informational needs, and actions of intelligent opponents so that they come together at any precise moment.

Can the Process Be Managed?

Instead, executives usually deal with the logic of each subsystem of strategy formulation largely on its own merits and usually with a different subset of people. They try to develop or maintain in their own minds a consistent pattern among the decisions made in each subsystem. Knowing their own limitations and the unknowability of the events they face, they consciously try to tap the minds and psychic drives of others. They often purposely keep questions broad and decisions vague in early stages to avoid creating undue rigidities and to stimulate others' creativity. Logic, of course, dictates that they make final commitments *as late as possible* consistent with the information they have.

Consequently, many successful executives will initially set only broad goals and policies that can accommodate a variety of specific proposals from below, yet give a sense of guidance to the proposers. As they come forward the proposals automatically and beneficially attract the support and identity of their sponsors. Being only proposals, the executives can treat these at less politically charged levels, as specific projects rather than as larger goal or policy precedents. Therefore, they can encourage, discourage, or kill alternatives with considerably less political exposure. As events and opportunities emerge, they can incrementally guide the pattern of escalated or accepted proposals to suit their own purposes without getting prematurely committed to a rigid solution set that unpredictable events might prove wrong or that opponents find sufficiently threatening to coalesce against.

A Strategy Emerges

Successful executives link together and bring order to a series of strategic processes and decisions spanning years. At the beginning of the process it is literally impossible to predict all the events and forces that will shape the future of the company. The best executives can do is to forecast the forces most likely to impinge on the company's affairs and the ranges of their possible impact. They then attempt to build a resource base and a corporate posture so strong in selected areas that the enterprise can survive and prosper despite all but the most devastating events. They consciously select market/ technological/product segments the concern can dominate given its resource limits, and place some side bets in order to decrease the risk of catastrophic failure or to increase the company's flexibility for future options.

They then proceed incrementally to handle urgent matters, start longer-term sequences whose specific future branches and consequences are perhaps murky, respond to unforeseen events as they occur, build on successes, and brace up or cut losses on failures. They constantly reassess the future, find new congruencies as events unfurl, and blend the organization's skills and resources into new balances of dominance and risk aversion as various forces intersect to suggest better – but never perfect – alignments. The process is dynamic, with neither a real beginning nor end.

Strategy deals with the unknowable, not the uncertain. It involves forces of such great number, strength, and combinatory powers that one cannot predict events in a probabilistic sense. Hence logic dictates that one proceed flexibly and experimentally from broad concepts toward specific commitments, making the latter concrete as late as possible in order to narrow the bands of uncertainty and to benefit from the best available information. This is the process of logical incrementalism.

3.3   Conceptual Models and Decision-making

By Graham Allison[1]

This study proceeds from the premise that marked improvement in our understanding of such events depends critically on more self-consciousness about what observers bring to the analysis. What each analyst sees and judges to be important is a function not only of the evidence about what happened but also of the 'conceptual lenses' through which he looks at the evidence. The principal purpose of this paper is to explore some of the fundamental assumptions and categories employed by analysts in thinking about problems of governmental behavior, especially in foreign and military affairs. The general argument can be summarized in three propositions:

1   Analysts think about problems of foreign and military policy in terms of largely implicit conceptual models that have significant consequences for the content of their thought. Clusters of related assumptions constitute basic frames of reference or conceptual models in terms of which analysts both ask and answer the questions: What happened? Why did the event happen? What will happen? Such assumptions are central to the activities of explanation and prediction, for in attempting to explain a particular event, the analyst cannot simply describe the full state of the world leading up to that event. The logic explanation requires that he single out the relevant, important determinants of the occurrence. Moreover, as the logic of prediction underscores, the analyst must summarize the various determinants as they bear on the event in question. Conceptual models both fix the mesh of the nets that the analyst drags through the material in order to explain a particular action of decision and direct him to cast his net in select ponds, at certain depths, in order to catch the fish he is after.

2   Most analysts explain (and predict) the behavior of national governments in terms of various forms of one basic conceptual model, here entitled the Rational Policy Model (Model I). In terms of this conceptual model, analysts attempt to understand happenings as the more or less purposive acts of unified national governments. For these analysts, the point of an explanation is to show how the nation or government could have chosen the action in question, given the strategic problem that it faced.

3   Two 'alternative' conceptual models, here labeled an Organizational Process Model (Model II) and a Bureaucratic Politics Model (Model III) provide a base for improved explanation and prediction. Although the standard frame of reference has proved useful for many purposes, there is powerful evidence that it must be supplemented, if not supplanted, by

[1] Source: This article was adapted with permission from 'Conceptual Models and The Cuban Missile Crisis', *The American Political Science Review*, no. 3, September 1969, pp. 689–718.

frames of reference which focus upon the large organizations and political actors involved in the policy process. Model I's implication that important events have important causes, i.e. that monoliths perform large actions for big reasons, must be balanced by an appreciation of the facts (a) that monoliths are black boxes covering several gears and levers in a highly differentiated decision-making structure, and (b) that large acts are the consequences of innumerable and often conflicting smaller actions by individuals at various levels of bureaucratic organizations in the service of a variety of only partially compatible conceptions of national goals, organizational goals, and political objectives. Recent developments in the field of organization theory provide the foundation for the second model, what Model I categorizes as 'acts' and 'choices' are instead outputs of large organizations functioning according to certain regular patterns of behavior. The third model focuses on the internal politics of a government. Happenings in foreign affairs are understood, according to the bureaucratic politics model, neither as choices nor as outputs. Instead, what happens is categorized as outcomes of various overlapping bargaining games among players arranged hierarchically in the national government. A Model III analyst displays the perceptions, motivations, positions, power, and maneuvers of principal players from which the outcome emerged.

A central metaphor illuminates differences among these models. Foreign policy has often been compared to moves, sequences of moves, and games of chess. If one were limited to observations on a screen upon which moves in the chess game were projected without information as to how the pieces came to be moved, one would assume – as Model I does – that an individual chess player was moving the pieces with reference to plans and maneuvers toward the goal of winning the game. But a pattern of moves can be imagined that would lead the serious observer, after watching several games, to consider the hypothesis that the chess player was not a single individual but rather a loose alliance of semi-independent organizations, each of which moved its set of pieces according to standard operating procedures. For example, movement of separate sets of pieces might proceed in turn, each according to a routine, the king's rook, bishop, and their pawns repeatedly attacking the opponent according to a fixed plan. Furthermore, it is conceivable that the pattern of play would suggest to an observer that a number of distinct players, with distinct objectives but shared power over the pieces, were determining the moves as the resultant of collegial bargaining. For example, the black rook's move might contribute to the loss of a black knight with no comparable gain for the black team, but with the black rook becoming the principal guardian of the 'palace' on that side of the board.

The space available does not permit full development and support of such a general argument. Rather, the sections that follow simply sketch each conceptual model, articulate it as an analytic paradigm, and apply it to produce an explanation.

Model I: Rational Policy

How do analysts account for the coming of the First World War? According to Hans Morgenthau (1960), 'the first World War had its origin exclusively in the fear of a disturbance of the European balance of power.' In the period preceding World War I, the Triple Alliance precariously balanced the Triple Entente. If either power combination could gain a decisive advantage in the Balkans, it would achieve a decisive advantage in the balance of power. 'It was this fear,' Morgenthau asserts, 'that motivated Austria in July 1914 to settle its accounts with Serbia once and for all, and that induced Germany to support Austria unconditionally. It was the same fear that brought Russia to the support of Serbia, and France to the support of Russia.' How is Morgenthau able to resolve this problem so confidently? By imposing on the data a 'rational outline.' The value of this method, according to Morgenthau, is that 'it provides for rational discipline in action and creates astounding continuity in foreign policy which makes American, British, or Russian foreign policy appear as an intelligent, rational continuum . . . regardless of the different motives, preferences, and intellectual and moral qualities of successive statesmen.'

Deterrence is the cardinal problem of the contemporary strategic literature. Thomas Schelling's *Strategy of Conflict* (1960) formulates a number of propositions focused upon the dynamics of deterrence in the nuclear age. One of the major propositions concerns the stability of the balance of terror: in a situation of mutual deterrence, the probability of nuclear war is reduced not by the 'balance' (the sheer equality of the situation) but rather by the *stability* of the balance, i.e. the fact that neither opponent in striking first can destroy the other's ability to strike back. How does Schelling support this proposition? Confidence in the contention stems not from an inductive canvass of a large number of previous cases, but rather from two calculations. In a situation of 'balance' but vulnerability, there are values for which a rational opponent could choose to strike first, e.g. to destroy enemy capabilities to retaliate. In a 'stable balance' where no matter who strikes first, each has an assured capability to retaliate with unacceptable damage, no rational agent could choose such a course of action (since that choice is effectively equivalent to choosing mutual homicide). Whereas most contemporary strategic thinking is driven *implicitly* by the motor upon which this calculation depends, Schelling explicitly recognizes that strategic theory does assume a model. The foundation of a theory of strategy is, he asserts, 'the assumption of rational behavior – not just of intelligent behavior, but of behavior motivated by conscious calculation of advantages, calculation that in turn is based on an explicit and internally consistent value system.'

What is striking about these examples from the literature of foreign policy and international relations are the similarities among analysts of various styles when they are called upon to produce explanations. Each assumes that what must be explained is an action, i.e. the realization of some purpose or intention. Each assumes that the actor is the national government. Each assumes that the action is chosen as a calculated response to a strategic problem. For each, explanation consists of showing what goal the government was pursuing in committing the act and how this action was a reasonable choice, given the nation's objectives. This set of assumptions oharacterizes the rational policy model. The assertion that Model I is the standard frame of reference implies no denial of highly visible differences among the interests of Sovietologists, diplomatic historians, international relations theorists, and strategists. Indeed, in most respects, differences among the work of Hans Morgenthau and Thomas Schelling could not be more pointed. Appreciation of the extent to which each relies predominantly on Model I, however, reveals basic similarities among Morgenthau's method of 'rational reenactment,' and Schelling's 'vicarious problem solving;' family resemblances among Morgenthau's 'rational statesman' and Schelling's 'game theorist.'

Most contemporary analysts (as well as laymen) proceed predominantly – albeit most often implicitly – in terms of this model when attempting to explain happenings in foreign affairs. Indeed, that occurrences in foreign affairs are the *acts* of *nations* seems so fundamental to thinking about such problems that this underlying model has rarely been recognized: to explain an occurrence in foreign policy simply means to show how the government could have rationally chosen that action. To prove that most analysts think largely in terms of the rational policy model is not possible. In this limited space it is not even possible to illustrate the range of employment of the framework. Rather, my purpose is to convey to the reader a grasp of the model and a challenge: let the readers examine the literature with which they are most familiar and make their judgment.

The general characterization can be sharpened by articulating the rational policy model as an 'analytic paradigm.' Systematic statement of basic assumptions, concepts, and propositions employed by Model I analysts highlights the distinctive thrust of this style of analysis. To articulate a largely implicit framework is of necessity to caricature. But caricature can be instructive.

Model I: Basic Unit of Analysis: Policy as National Choice

Happenings in foreign affairs are conceived as actions chosen by the nation or national government. Governments select the action that will maximize strategic goals and objectives. These 'solutions' to strategic problems are the fundamental categories in terms of which the analyst perceives what is to be explained.

Model I: Organizing Concepts

National actor The nation or government, conceived as a rational, unitary decisionmaker, is the agent. This actor has one set of specified goals (the equivalent of a consistent utility function), one set of perceived options, and a single estimate of the consequences that follow from each alternative.

The problem   Action is chosen in response to the strategic problem which the nation faces. Threats and opportunities arising in the 'international strategic market place' move the nation to act.

Static selection   The sum of activity of representatives of the government relevant to a problem constitutes what the nation has chosen as its 'solution.' Thus the action is conceived as a steady-state choice among alternative outcomes (rather than, for example, a large number of partial choices in a dynamic stream).

Action as rational choice   The components include:

- *Goals and Objectives*. National security and national interests are the principal categories in which strategic goals are conceived. Nations seek security and a range of further objectives. (Analysts rarely translate strategic goals and objectives into an explicit utility function; nevertheless, analysts do focus on major goals and objectives and trade off side effects in an intuitive fashion.)

- *Options*. Various courses of action relevant to a strategic problem provide the spectrum of options.

- *Consequences*. Enactment of each alternative course of action will produce a series of consequences. The relevant consequences constitute benefits and costs in terms of strategic goals and objectives.

- *Choice*. Rational choice is value-maximizing. The rational agent selects the alternative whose consequences rank highest in terms of his goals and objectives.

Model I: Dominant Inference Pattern and General Propositions

This paradigm leads analysts to rely on the following pattern of inference: if a nation performed a particular action, that nation must have had ends towards which the action constituted an optimal means. The rational policy model's explanatory power stems from this inference pattern. Puzzlement is relieved by revealing the purposive pattern within which the occurrence can be located as a value-maximizing means.

The disgrace of political science is the infrequency with which propositions of any generality are formulated and tested. 'Paradigmatic analysis' argues for explicitness about the terms in which analysis proceeds, and seriousness about the logic of explanation. Simply to illustrate the kind of propositions on which analysts who employ this model rely, the formulation includes several.

The basic assumption of value-maximizing behavior produces propositions central to most explanations. The general principle can be formulated as follows: the likelihood of any particular action results from a combination of the nation's (1) relevant values and objectives, (2) perceived alternative courses of action, (3) estimates of various sets of consequences (which will follow from each alternative), and (4) net valuation of each set of consequences. This yields two propositions.

- An increase in the cost of an alternative, i.e. a reduction in the value of the set of consequences which will follow from that action, or a reduction in the probability of attaining fixed consequences, reduces the likelihood of that alternative being chosen.

- A decrease in the costs of an alternative, i.e. an increase in the value of the set of consequences which will follow from that alternative or an increase in the probability of attaining fixed consequences, increases the likelihood of that action being chosen.

Model II: Organizational Process

For some purposes, governmental behavior can be usefully summarized as action chosen by a unitary, rational decisionmaker: centrally controlled, completely informed, and value maximizing. But this simplification must not be allowed to conceal the fact that a 'government' consists of a conglomerate of semi-feudal, loosely allied organizations, each with a substantial life of its own. Government leaders do sit formally, and to some extent in fact, on top of this conglomerate. But governments perceive problems through organizational sensors. Governments define alternatives and estimate consequences as organizations process information. Governments act as these organizations enact routines. Government behavior can therefore be understood according to a second conceptual model, less as deliberate choices of leaders and more as *outputs* of large organizations functioning according to standard patterns of behavior.

To be responsive to a broad spectrum of problems, governments consist of large organizations among which primary responsibility for particular areas is divided. Each organization attends to a special set of problems and acts in quasi-independence on these problems. But few important problems fall exclusively within the domain of a single organization. Thus government behavior relevant to any important problem reflects the independent output of several organizations, partially coordinated by government leaders. Government leaders can substantially disturb, but not substantially control, the behavior of these organizations.

To perform complex routines, the behavior of large numbers of individuals must be coordinated. Coordination requires standard operating procedures: rules according to which things are done. Assured capability for reliable performance of action that depends upon the behavior of hundreds of persons requires established 'programs.' Indeed, if the 11 members of a football team are to perform adequately on any particular down, each player must not 'do what he thinks needs to be done' or 'do what the quarterback tells him to do.' Rather, each player must perform the maneuvers specified by a previously established play which the quarterback has simply called in this situation.

At any given time, a government consists of *existing* organizations, each with a *fixed* set of standard operating procedures and programs. The behavior of these organizations – and consequently of the government – relevant to an issue in any particular instance is therefore determined primarily by routines established in these organizations prior to that instance. But organizations do change. Learning occurs gradually, over time. Dramatic organizational change occurs in response to major crises. Both learning and change are influenced by existing organizational capabilities.

These loosely formulated propositions amount simply to *tendencies*. Each must be hedged by modifiers like 'other things being equal' and 'under certain conditions.' In particular instances, tendencies hold – more or less. In specific situations the relevant question is: more or less? But this is as it should be. For, on the one hand, 'organizations' are no more homogeneous a class than 'solids.' When scientists tried to generalize about 'solids,' they achieved similar results. Solids tend to expand when heated, but some do and some don't. More adequate categorization of the various elements now lumped under the rubric 'organizations' is thus required. On the other hand, the behavior of particular organizations seems considerably more complex than the behavior of solids. Additional information about a particular organization is required for further specification of the tendency statements. In spite of these two caveats, the characterization of government action as organizational output differs distinctly from Model I. Attempts to understand problems of foreign affairs in terms of this frame of reference should produce quite different explanations.

Model II: Basic Unit of Analysis: Policy as Organizational Output

The happenings of international politics are, in three critical senses, outputs of organizational processes. First, the actual occurences are organizational outputs. Government leaders' decisions trigger organizational routines. Government leaders can trim the edges of this output and exercise some choice in combining outputs. But the mass of behavior is determined by previously established procedures. Second, existing organizational routines for employing present physical capabilities constitute the effective options open to government leaders confronted with any problem. The fact that fixed programs (equipment, men, and routines which exist at the particular time) exhaust the range of buttons that leaders can push is not always perceived by these leaders. But in every case it is critical for an understanding of what is actually done. Third, organizational outputs structure the situation within the narrow constraints of which leaders must contribute their 'decision' concerning an issue. Outputs raise the problem, provide the information, and make the initial moves that color the face of the issue that is turned to the leaders. As Theodore Sorensen has observed: 'Presidents rarely, if ever, make decisions – particularly in foreign affairs – in the sense of writing their conclusions on a clean slate . . . The basic decisions, which confine their choices, have all too often been previously made.' If one understands the structure of the situation and the face of the issue – which are determined by the organizational outputs – the formal choice of the leaders is frequently anti-climatic.

Model II: Organizing Concepts

Organizational actors The actor is not a monolithic 'nation' or 'government' but rather a constellation of loosely allied organizations on top of which government leaders sit. This constellation acts only as component organizations perform routines.

Factored problems and fractionated power Surveillance of the multiple facets of foreign affairs requires that problems be cut up and parcelled out to various organizations. To avoid paralysis, primary power must accompany primary responsibility. But if organizations are permitted to do anything, a large part of what they do will be determined within the organization. Thus each organization perceives problems, processes information, and performs a range of actions in quasi-independence (within broad guidelines of national policy). Factored problems and fractionated power are two edges of the same sword. Factoring permits more specialized attention to particular facets of problems than would be possible if government leaders tried to cope with these problems by themselves. But this additional attention must be paid for in the coin of discretion for what an organization attends to, and how organizational responses are programmed.

Parochial priorities, perceptions, and issues Primary responsibility for a narrow set of problems encourages organizational parochialism. These tendencies are enhanced by a number of additional factors: (1) selective information available to the organization, (2) recruitment of personnel into the organization, (3) tenure of individuals in the organization, (4) small group pressures within the organization, and (5) distribution of rewards by the organization. Clients, government allies, and extra-national counterparts galvanize this parochialism. Thus organizations develop relatively stable propensities concerning operational priorities, perceptions, and issues.

Action as organizational output The pre-eminent feature of organizational activity is its programmed character: the extent to which behavior in any particular case is an enactment of preestablished routines. In producing outputs, the activity of each organization is characterized by:

- *Goals: constraints defining acceptable performance.* The operational goals of an organization are seldom revealed by formal mandates. Rather, each organization's operational goals emerge as a set of constraints defining acceptable performance. Central among these constraints is organizational health, defined usually in terms of bodies assigned and dollars appropriated. The set of constraints emerges from a mix of expectations and demands of other organizations in the government, statutory authority, demands from citizens and special interest groups, and bargaining within the organization. These constraints represent a quasi-resolution of conflict – the constraints are relatively stable, so there is some resolution. But conflict among alternative goals is always latent; hence, it is a quasi-resolution. Typically, the constraints are formulated as imperatives to avoid roughly specified discomforts and disasters.

- *Sequential attention to goals.* The existence of conflict among operational constraints is resolved by the device of sequential attention. As a problem arises, the subunits of the organization most concerned with that problem deal with it in terms of the constraints they take to be most important. When the next problem arises, another cluster of subunits deals with it, focusing on a different set of constraints.

- *Standard operating procedures.* Organizations perform their 'higher' functions, such as attending to problem areas, monitoring information, and preparing relevant responses for likely contingencies, by doing 'lower' tasks, for example, preparing budgets, producing reports, and developing hardware. Reliable performance of these tasks requires standard operating procedures (hereafter SOPs). Since procedures are 'standard' they do not change quickly or easily. Without these standard procedures, it would not be possible to perform certain concerted tasks. But because of standard procedures, organizational behavior in particular instances often appears unduly formalized, sluggish, or inappropriate.

- *Programs and repertoires.* Organizations must be capable of performing actions in which the behavior of large numbers of individuals is carefully coordinated. Assured performance requires clusters of rehearsed SOPs for producing specific actions, e.g. fighting enemy units or answering an embassy's cable. Each cluster comprises a 'program' (in the terms both of drama and computers) which the organization has available for dealing with a situation. The list of programs relevant to a type of activity, e.g. fighting, constitutes an organizational repertoire. The number of programs in a repertoire is always quite limited. When properly triggered, organizations execute programs; programs cannot be substantially changed in a particular situation. The more complex the action and the greater the number of individuals involved, the more important are programs and repertoires as determinants of organizational behavior.

- *Uncertainty avoidance.* Organizations do not attempt to estimate the probability distribution of future occurrences. Rather, organizations avoid uncertainty. By arranging a *negotiated environment*, organizations regularize the reactions of other actors with whom they have to deal. The primary environment, relations with other organizations that comprise the government, is stabilized by such arrangements as agreed budgetary splits, accepted areas of responsibility, and established conventional practices. The secondary environment, relations with the international world, is stabilized between allies by the establishment of contracts (alliances) and 'club relations' (US State and UK Foreign Office or US Treasury and UK Treasury). Between enemies, contracts and accepted conventional practices perform a similar function, for example, the rules of the 'precarious status quo' which President Kennedy referred to in the missile crisis. Where the international environment cannot be negotiated, organizations deal with remaining uncertainties by establishing a set of *standard scenarios* that constitute the contingencies for which they prepare.

■ *Problem-directed search*. Where situations cannot be construed as standard, organizations engage in search. The style of search and the solution are largely determined by existing routines. Organizational search for alternative courses of action is problem-oriented: it focuses on the atypical discomfort that must be avoided. It is simple-minded: the neighborhood of the symptom is searched first; then, the neighborhood of the current alternative. Patterns of search reveal biases which in turn reflect such factors as specialized training or experience and patterns of communication.

■ *Organizational learning and change*. The parameters of organizational behavior mostly persist. In response to non-standard problems, organizations search and routines evolve, assimilating new situations. Thus learning and change follow in large part from existing procedures. But marked changes in organizations do sometimes occur. Conditions in which dramatic changes are more likely include: (1) Periods of budgetary feast. Typically, organizations devour budgetary feasts by purchasing additional items on the existing shopping list. Nevertheless, if committed to change, leaders who control the budget can use extra funds to effect changes. (2) Periods of prolonged budgetary famine. Though a single year's famine typically results in few changes in organizational structure but a loss of effectiveness in performing some programs, prolonged famine forces major retrenchment. (3) Dramatic performance failures. Dramatic change occurs (mostly) in response to major disasters. Confronted with an undeniable failure of procedures and repertoires, authorities outside the organization demand change, existing personnel are less resistant to change, and critical members of the organization are replaced by individuals committed to change.

Central coordination and control Action requires decentralization of responsibility and power. But problems lap over the jurisdictions of several organizations. Thus the necessity for decentralization runs headlong into the requirement for coordination. Both the necessity for coordination and the centrality of foreign policy to national welfare guarantee the involvement of government leaders in the procedures of the organizations among which problems are divided and power shared. Each organization's propensities and routines can be disturbed by government leaders' intervention. Central direction and persistent control of organizational activity, however, is not possible. The relation among organizations, and between organizations and the government leaders depends critically on a number of structural variables including: (1) the nature of the job; (2) the measures and information available to government leaders; (3) the system of rewards and punishments for organizational members; and (4) the procedures by which human and material resources get committed. For example, to the extent that rewards and punishments for the members of an organization are distributed by higher authorities, these authorities can exercise some control by specifying criteria in terms of which organizational output is to be evaluated. These criteria become constraints within which organizational activity proceeds. But constraint is a crude instrument of control. Intervention by government leaders does sometimes change the activity of an organization in an intended direction. But instances are fewer than might be expected. As Franklin Roosevelt, the master manipulator of government organizations, remarked:

> The Treasury is so large and far-flung and ingrained in its practices that I find it is almost impossible to get the action and results I want . . . . But the Treasury is not to be compared with the State Department. You should go through the experience of trying to get any changes in the thinking, policy, and action of the career diplomats and then you'd know what a real problem was. But the Treasury and the State Department put together are nothing compared with the Na-a-vy . . . To change anything in the Na-a-vy is like punching a feather bed. You punch it with your right and you punch it with your left until you are finally exhausted, and then you find the damn bed just as it was before you started punching
>
> (Eccles, 1951: 336).

Decisions of Government leaders   Organizational persistence does not exclude shifts in governmental behavior. For government leaders sit atop the conglomerate of organizations. Many important issues of governmental action require that these leaders decide what organizations will play out which programs where. Thus stability in the parochialisms and SOPs of individual organizations is consistent with some important shifts in the behavior of governments. The range of these shifts is defined by existing organizational programs.

Model II: Dominant Inference Pattern and General Propositions

If a nation performs an action of this type today, its organizational components must yesterday have been performing (or have had established routines for performing) an action only marginally different from this action. At any specific point in time, a government consists of an established conglomerate of organizations, each with existing goals, programs, and repertoires. The characteristics of a government's action in any instance follows from those established routines, and from the choice of govermnent leaders -on the basis of information and estimates provided by existing routines – among existing programs. The best explanation of an organization's behavior at t is $t - 1$; the prediction of $t + 1$ is t. Model II's explanatory power is achieved by uncovering the organizational routines and repertoires that produced the outputs that comprise the puzzling occurrence.

A number of general propositions have been stated above. In order to illustrate clearly the type of proposition employed by model II analysts, this section formulates several more precisely.

Organizational action   Activity according to SOPs and programs does not constitute far-sighted, flexible adaptation to 'the issue' (as it is conceived by the analyst). Detail and nuance of actions by organizations are determined predominantly by organizational routines, not government leaders' directions.

■   SOPs constitute routines for dealing with standard situations. Routines allow large numbers of ordinary individuals to deal with numerous instances, day after day, without considerable thought, by responding to basic stimuli. But this regularized capability for adequate performance is purchased at the price of standardization. If the SOPs are appropriate, average performance, i.e. performance averaged over the range of cases, is better than it would be if each instance were approached individually (given fixed talent, timing, and resource constraints). But specific instances, particularly critical instances that typically do not have 'standard' characteristics, are often handled sluggishly or inappropriately.

■   A program, i.e. a complex action chosen from a short list of programs in a repertoire, is rarely tailored to the specific situation in which it is executed. Rather, the program is (at best) the most appropriate of the programs in a previously developed repertoire.

■   Since repertoires are developed by parochial organizations for standard scenarios defined by that organization, programs available for dealing with a particular situation are often ill-suited.

Limited flexibility and incremental change   Major lines of organizational action are straight, i.e. behavior at one time is marginally different from that behavior at $t - 1$. Simpleminded predictions work best: Behavior at $t + 1$ will be marginally different from behavior at the present time.

■   Organizational budgets change incrementally – both with respect to totals and with respect to intra-organizational splits. Though organizations could divide the money available each year by carving up the pie anew (in the light of changes in objectives or environment), in practice, organizations take last year's budget as a base and adjust incrementally. Predictions that require large budgetary shifts in a single year between organizations or between units within an organization should be hedged.

■   Once undertaken, an organizational investment is not dropped at the point where 'objective' costs outweigh benefits. Organizational stakes in adopted projects carry them quite beyond the loss point.

Administrative feasibility Adequate explanation, analysis, and prediction must include administrative feasibility as a major dimension. A considerable gap separates what leaders choose (or might rationally have chosen) and what organizations implement.

- Organizations are blunt instruments. Projects that require several organizations to act with high degrees of precision and coordination are not likely to succeed.

- Projects that demand that existing organizational units depart from their accustomed functions and perform previously unprogrammed tasks are rarely accomplished in their designed form.

- Government leaders can expect that each organization will do its 'part' in terms of what the organization knows how to do.

- Government leaders can expect incomplete and distorted information from each organization concerning its part of the problem.

- Where an assigned piece of a problem is contrary to the existing goals of an organization, resistance to implementation of that piece will be encountered.

Model III: Bureaucratic Politics

The leaders who sit on top of organizations are not a monolithic group. Rather, each is, in his own right, a player in a central, competitive game. The name of the game is bureaucratic politics: bargaining along regularized channels among players positioned hierarchically within the government. Government behavior can thus be understood according to a third conceptual model not as organizational outputs, but as outcomes of bargaining games. In contrast with Model I, the bureaucratic politics model sees no unitary actor but rather many actors as players, who focus not on a single strategic issue but on many diverse intra-national problems as well, in terms of no consistent set of strategic objectives but rather according to various conceptions of national, organizational, and personal goals, making government decisions not by rational choice but by the pulling and hauling that is politics.

The apparatus of each national government constitutes a complex arena for the intra-national game. Political leaders at the top of this apparatus plus the men who occupy positions on top of the critical organizations form the circle of central players. Ascendancy to this circle assures some independent standing. The necessary decentralization of decisions required for action on the broad range of foreign policy problems guarantees that each player has considerable discretion. Thus power is shared.

The nature of problems of foreign policy permits fundamental disagreement among reasonable men concerning what ought to be done. Analyses yield conflicting recommendations. Separate responsibilities laid on the shoulders of individual personalities encourage differences in perceptions and priorities. But the issues are of first order importance.

What the nation does really matters. A wrong choice could mean irreparable damage. Thus responsible men are obliged to fight for what they are convinced is right.

Men share power. Men differ concerning what must be done. The differences matter. This milieu necessitates that policy be resolved by politics. What the nation does is sometimes the result of the triumph of one group over others. More often, however, different groups pulling in different directions yield a resultant distinct from what anyone intended. What moves the chess pieces is not simply the reasons which support a course of action, nor the routines of organizations which enact an alternative, but the power and skill of proponents and opponents of the action in question.

This characterization captures the thrust of the bureaucratic politics orientation. If problems of foreign policy arose as discreet issues, and decisions were determined one game at a time, this account would suffice. But most 'issues' emerge piecemeal, over time, one lump in one context, a second in another. Hundreds of issues compete for players' attention every day. Each player is forced to fix upon his issues for that day, fight them on their own terms, and rush on to the next. Thus the character of emerging issues and the pace at which the game is played converge to yield government 'decisions' and 'actions' as collages. Choices by one player, outcomes of minor games, outcomes of central games, and 'foul-ups' – these pieces, when stuck to the same canvas, constitute government behavior relevant to an issue.

Model III: Basic Unit of Analysis: Policy as Political Outcome

The decisions and actions of governments are essentially intra-national political outcomes: outcomes in the sense that what happens is not chosen as a solution to a problem but rather results from compromise, coalition, competition, and confusion among government officials who see different faces of an issue; political in the sense that the activity from which the outcomes emerge is best characterized as bargaining. Following Wittgenstein's use of the concept of a 'game,' national behavior in international affairs can be conceived as outcomes of intricate and subtle, simultaneous, overlapping games among players located in positions, the hierarchical arrangement of which constitutes the government. These games proceed neither at random nor at leisure. Regular channels structure the game. Deadlines force issues to the attention of busy players. The moves in the chess game are thus to be explained in terms of the bargaining among players with separate and unequal power over particular pieces and with separable objectives in distinguishable subgames.

Model III: Organizing Concepts

Players in positions   The actor is neither a unitary nation, nor a conglomerate of organizations, but rather a number of individual players. Groups of these players constitute the agent for particular government decisions and actions. Players are men in jobs.

Individuals become players in the national security policy game by occupying a critical position in an administration. For example, in the US government the players include 'Chiefs': The President, Secretaries of State, Defense, and Treasury, Director of the CIA, Joint Chiefs of Staff and, since 1961, the Special Assistant for National Security Affairs; 'Staffers': the immediate staff of each Chief; 'Indians': the political appointees and permanent government officials within each of the departments and agencies; and 'Ad Hoc Players': actors in the wider government game (especially 'Congressional Influentials'), members of the press, spokesmen for important interest groups (especially the 'bipartisan foreign policy establishment' in and out of Congress), and surrogates for each of these groups. Other members of the Congress, press, interest groups, and public form concentric circles around the central arena – circles which demarcate the permissive limits within which the game is played.

Positions define what players both may and must do. The advantages and handicaps with which each player can enter and play in various games stems from his position. So does a cluster of obligations for the performance of certain tasks.

All of these obligations are his simultaneously. His performance in one affects his credit and power in the others. The perspective stemming from the daily work which he must oversee – the cable traffic by which his department maintains relations with other foreign offices – conflicts with the President's requirement that he serve as a generalist and coordinator of contrasting perspectives. The necessity that he be close to the President restricts the extent to which, and the force with which, he can front for his department. When he defers to the Secretary of Defense rather than fighting for his department's position – as he often must – he strains the loyalty of his officialdom. The Secretary's resolution of these conflicts depends not only upon the position but also upon the player who occupies the position.

For players are also people. Men's metabolisms differ. The core of the bureaucratic politics mix is personality. How each man manages to stand the heat in his kitchen, each player's basic operating style, and the complementarity or contradiction among personalities and styles in the inner circles are irreducible pieces of the policy blend. Moreover, each person comes to his position with baggage in tow, including sensitivities to certain issues, commitments to various programs, and personal standing and debts with groups in the society.

Parochial priorities, perceptions and issues   Answers to the questions: 'What is the issue?' and 'What must be done?' are colored by the position from which the questions are considered. For the factors which encourage organizational parochialism also influence the players who occupy positions on top of (or within) these organizations. To motivate members of his organization, a player must be sensitive to the organization's orientation. The games into which the player can enter and the advantages with which he plays enhance these pressures. Thus propensities of perception stemming from position permit reliable prediction about a player's stances in many cases. But these propensities are filtered through the baggage which players bring to positions. Sensitivity to both the pressures and the baggage is thus required for many predictions.

Interests, stakes, and power Games are played to determine outcomes. But outcomes advance and impede each player's conception of the national interest, specific programs to which he is committed, the welfare of his friends, and his personal interests. These overlapping interests constitute the stakes for which games are played. Each player's ability to play successfully depends upon his power. Power, i.e. effective influence on policy outcomes, is an elusive blend of at least three elements: bargaining advantages (drawn from formal authority and obligations, institutional backing, constituents, expertise, and status), skill and will in using bargaining advantages, and other players' perceptions of the first two ingredients. Power wisely invested yields an enhanced reputation for effectiveness. Unsuccessful investment depletes both the stock of capital and the reputation. Thus each player must pick the issues on which he can play with a reasonable probability of success. But no player's power is sufficient to guarantee satisfactory outcomes. Each player's needs and fears run to many other players. What ensues is the most intricate and subtle of games known to man.

The problem and the problems 'Solutions' to strategic problems are not derived by detached analysts focusing coolly on the problem. Instead, deadlines and events raise issues in games, and demand decisions of busy players in contexts that influence the face the issue wears. The problems for the players are both narrower and broader than the strategic problem For each player focuses not on the total strategic problem but rather on the decision that must be made now. But each decision has critical consequences not only for the strategic problem but for each player's organizational, reputational, and personal stakes. Thus the gap between the problems the player was solving and the problem upon which the analyst focuses is often very wide.

Action-channels Bargaining games do not proceed randomly. Action-channels, i.e. regularized ways of producing action concerning types of issues, structure the game by pre-selecting the major players, determining their points of entrance into the game, and distributing particular advantages and disadvantages for each game. Most critically, channels determine 'who's got the action,' that is, which department's Indians actually do whatever is chosen.

Action as politics Government decisions are made and government actions emerge neither as the calculated choice of a unified group, nor as a formal summary of leaders' preferences. Rather the context of shared power but separate judgments concerning important choices, determines that politics is the mechanism of choice. Note the environment in which the game is played: inordinate uncertainty about what must be done, the necessity that something be done, and crucial consequences of whatever is done. These features force responsible men to become active players. The *pace of the game* – hundreds of issues, numerous games, and multiple channels- compels players to fight to 'get other's attention,' to make them 'see the facts,' to assure that they 'take the time to think seriously about the broader issue.' The *structure of the game* – power shared by individuals with separate responsibilities – validates each player's feeling that 'others don't see my problem,' and 'others must be persuaded to look at the issue from a less parochial perspective.' The *rules of the game* – he who hesitates loses his chance to play at that point, and he who is uncertain about his recommendation is over-powered by others who are sure – pressures players to come down on one side of a 51–49 issue and play. The rewards of the game – effectiveness, i.e. impact on outcomes, as the immediate measure of performance – encourages hard play. Thus, most players come to fight to 'make the government do what is right.'

Streams of outcomes   Important government decisions or actions emerge as collages composed of individual acts, outcomes of minor and major games, and foul-ups. Outcomes which could never have been chosen by an actor and would never have emerged from bargaining in a single game over the issue are fabricated piece by piece. Understanding of the outcome requires that it be disaggregated.

Model III: Dominant Inference Pattern and General Propositions

If a nation performed an action, that action was the *outcome* of bargaining among individuals and groups within the government. That outcome included *results* achieved by groups committed to a decision or action, *resultants* which emerged from bargaining among groups with quite different positions and *foul-ups*. Model III's explanatory power is achieved by revealing the pulling and hauling of various players, with different perceptions and priorities, focusing on separate problems, which yielded the outcomes that constitute the action in question.

■   *Action and intention.* Action does not presuppose intention. The sum of behavior of representatives of a government relevant to an issue was rarely intendcd by any individual or group. Rather separate individuals with different intentions contributed pieces which compose an outcome distinct from what anyone would have chosen.

- *Where you stand depends on where you sit.* Horizontally, the diverse demands upon each player shape his priorities, perceptions, and issues. For large classes of issues, e.g. budgets and procurement decisions, the stance of a particular player can be predicted with high reliability from information concerning his seat.

- *Chiefs and Indians.* The aphorism 'where you stand depends on where you sit' has vertical as well as horizontal application. Vertically, the demands upon the President, Chiefs, Staffers, and Indians are quite distinct.

The foreign policy issues with which the President can deal are limited primarily by his crowded schedule: the necessity of dealing first with what comes next. His problem is to probe the special face worn by issues that come to his attention, to preserve his leeway until time has clarified the uncertainties, and to assess the relevant risks.

Foreign policy chiefs deal most often with the hottest issue *de jour*, though they can get the attention of the President and other members of the government for other issues which they judge important. What they cannot guarantee is that 'the President will pay the price' or that 'the others will get on board.' They must build a coalition of the relevant powers that be. They must 'give the President confidence' in the right course of action.

Most problems are framed, alternatives specified, and proposals pushed, however, by Indians. Indians fight with Indians of other departments; for example, struggles between International Security Affairs of the Department of Defense and Political-Military of the State Department are a microcosm of the action at higher levels. But the Indian's major problem is how to get the attention of chiefs, how to get an issue decided, how to get the government 'to do what is right.'

In policy making then, the issue looking down is options: how to preserve my leeway until time clarifies uncertainties. The issue looking *sideways* is commitment: how to get others committed to my coalition. The issue looking *upwards* is confidence: how to give the boss confidence in doing what must be done. To paraphrase one of Neustadt's assertions which can be applied down the length of the ladder, the essence of a responsible official's task is to induce others to see that what needs to be done is what their own appraisal of their own responsibilities requires them to do in their own interests.

Conclusion

At a minimum, the intended implications of the argument presented here are four. First, formulation of alternative frames of reference and demonstration that different analysts, relying predominantly on different models, produce quite different explanations should encourage the analyst's self-consciousness about the nets he employs. The effect of these 'spectacles' in sensitizing him to particular aspects of what is going on – framing the puzzle in one way rather than another, encouraging him to examine the problem in terms of certain categories rather than others, directing him to particular kinds of evidence, and relieving puzzlement by one procedure rather than another – must be recognized and explored.

Second, the argument implies a position on the problem of 'the state of the art.' While accepting the commonplace characterization of the present condition of foreign policy analysis – personalistic, non-cumulative, and sometimes insightful – this article rejects both the counsel of despair's justification of this condition as a consequence of the character of the enterprise, and the 'new frontiersmen's' demand for *a priori* theorizing on the frontiers and *ad hoc* appropriation of 'new techniques.' What is required as a first step is non-casual examination of the present product: inspection of existing explanations, articulation of the conceptual models employed in producing them, formulation of the propositions relied upon, specification of the logic of the various intellectual enterprises, and reflection on the questions being asked. Though it is difficult to overemphasize the need for more systematic processing of more data, these preliminary matters of formulating questions with clarity and sensitivity to categories and assumptions so that fruitful acquisition of large quantities of data is possible are still a major hurdle in considering most important problems.

Third, the preliminary, partial paradigms presented here provide a basis for serious reexamination of many problems of foreign and military policy. Model II and Model III cuts at problems typically treated in Model I terms can permit significant improvements in explanation and prediction. Full Model II and III analyses require large amounts of information. But even in cases where the information base is severely limited, improvements are possible.

Fourth, the present formulation of paradigms is simply an initial step. As such it leaves a long list of critical questions unanswered. Given any action, an imaginative analyst should always be able to construct some rationale for the government's choice. By imposing, and relaxing, constraints on the parameters of rational choice (as in variants of Model I) analysts can construct a large number of accounts of any act as a rational choice. But does a statement of reasons why a rational actor would choose an action constitute an explanation of the *occurrence* of that action? How can Model I analysis be forced to make more systematic contributions to the question of the deterrninants of occurrences? Model II's explanation of t in terms of $t - 1$ is explanation. The world is contiguous. But governments sometimes make sharp departures. Can an organizational process model be modified to suggest where change is likely? Attention to organizational change should afford greater understanding of why particular programs and SOPs are maintained by identifiable types of organizations and also how a manager can improve organizational performance. Model III tells a fascinating 'story.' But its complexity is enormous, the information requirements are often overwhelming, and many of the details of the bargaining may be superfluous. How can such a model be made parsimonious? The three models are obviously not exclusive alternatives. Indeed, the paradigms highlight the partial emphasis of the framework – what each emphasizes and what it leaves out. Each concentrates on one class of variables, in effect, relegating other important factors to a *ceteris parabus* clause. Model I concentrates on 'market factors: ' pressures and incentives created by the 'international strategic marketplace.' Models II and III focus on the internal mechanism of the government that chooses in this environment. But can these relations be more fully specified? Adequate synthesis would require a typology of decisions and actions, some of which are more amenable to treatment in terms of one model and some to another. Government behavior is but one cluster of factors relevant to occurrences in foreign affairs. Most students of foreign policy adopt this focus (at least when explaining and predicting). Nevertheless, the dimensions of the chess board, the character of the pieces, and the rules of the game – factors considered by international systems theorists – constitute the context in which the pieces are moved.

3.4 Removing the Obstacles to Effective Strategic Planning

By Thomas Marx[1]

From its origins in the early 1960s through the late 1970s, strategic business planning held the business community spellbound with its promise of 'sustainable competitive advantage' and the superior financial returns that would flow from it. No insignificant amount of this appeal was traceable to the veiled hint that these superior returns were the inevitable result of adhering strictly to the logical process being prescribed.

The strength of planning's appeal to the business community could be measured by the magnitude of the resources committed to the process by companies large and small. Huge amounts were expended for training managers in the methods of strategic planning, for compiling and analyzing the mountains of information that lie below the business plans sitting on desk tops like the tips of icebergs, and for writing, reviewing and monitoring the business plans. Entirely new organizations (strategic business units) were created to develop the plans and entirely new staffs (corporate strategic planning) were created to lead them through this process. The consumption of resources was enormous but so were the promised benefits.

Today, strategic business planning is in considerable disarray. The total resources devoted to planning at most companies steadily declined throughout the 1980s as the promised benefits often failed to materialize. Many companies at the forefront of strategic business planning only a few

---

[1] Source: Reprinted with permission from *Long Range Planning*, 'Removing the Obstacles to Effective Strategic Planning', August 1991, Vol. 24, Pergamon Press Ltd. Oxford, England.

years ago have now substantially reduced the scope of their planning activity or abandoned it altogether. Those abandoning strategic business planning are comforted by the new conventional wisdom that 'the Japanese don't plan.'

Strategic business planning frequently has not delivered the promised benefits because it has failed to overcome the numerous bureaucratic obstacles that lie in its path. These obstacles are illustrated aptly by Jack Welch's description of the problems encountered with strategic business-planning at General Electric – the company that pioneered the strategic business planning process in the 1960s:

> Our planning system was dynamite when we first put it in. The thinking was fresh, the form mattered little – the format got no points. It was idea-oriented. We then hired a head of planning and he hired two vice presidents and then he hired a planner, and the books got thicker and the printing got more sophisticated, and the covers got harder and the drawings got better. The meetings kept getting larger. Nobody can say anything with 16 or 18 people there.

The premise of this article is that while substantial reform of the planning process is urgently needed, it would be a major mistake to abandon strategic business planning in the face of the twin competitive and regulatory challenges facing most companies in the 1990s. Simultaneously meeting the increasing challenges of global competition, responding to the opportunities created by the tumultuous political, social, and economic changes throughout Europe and addressing the growing concerns for the protection of the environment from ozone depletion, greenhouse gases, and toxic wastes will require a strategic planning capability few firms currently possess, and even fewer will possess in the near future if the abandonment of strategic business planning continues. At the same time, it is imperative that the bureaucratic obstacles to effective strategic planning be eliminated. The trick is to avoid throwing out the baby with the bath water.

Obstacles to Effective Strategic Business Planning

The obstacles to an effective planning process can best be explained in the context of the four classical development phases of strategic business-planning systems, as shown in Figure 3.4.1.

The promised benefits of strategic business planning are only realized in the latter stages of phase 3 and in the final phase in which planning is fully integrated with operating decision making and resource allocation throughout the company. Prior to this, management encounters the bulk of the cost of planning with only the promise of future benefits. Since management's tolerance for such a state of affairs is not without serious limits, the task is to move through the first three phases of planning as quickly as possible. Passage through the first two phases proceeds smoothly

FIGURE 3.4.1
Phases in the development of strategic planning (Gluck, Kaufman, and Walleck, 1982)

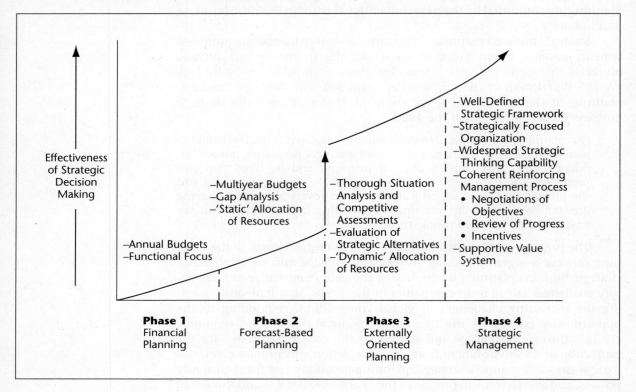

enough at most companies. The extension of annual financial planning to a three- to five-year horizon occurs naturally as the length of investment paybacks, contractual commitments, and product cycles grows with the success and maturity of the company. The introduction of forecasting techniques in phase 2 imposes no great burdens on the organization if one excludes the despair of those who expected to foretell the future with reasonable accuracy.

It is in phase 3 of the planning process that the difficult processes really begin. It is here that the company is organized, for planning purposes, into strategic business units (SBUs); extensive training is required; through analyses of competitors and the external environment and an inventory of internal strengths and weaknesses are undertaken; and formal business plans are written, reviewed, and monitored for the first time. It is also here that the organizational changes are most severe, and that the planning process becomes most vulnerable to its natural enemies – inertia, entrenched interests, and risk aversity. It is at this point that many companies, unable to steer the process safely through the many obstacles encountered in phase 3, abandon planning altogether.

The obstacles typically encountered in phase 3 of the planning process relate to the planning process itself, to the content of the business plans, and to the monitoring and reward processes essential to the successful implementation of the business plans. The basic obstacles encountered in phase 3 are shown in Table 3.4.1 where they are contrasted with the characteristics of an effective phase 4 strategic business-planning process.

Planning Processes

The planning processes themselves often raise numerous obstacles to effective planning in phase 3. When these processes are seriously flawed, they are incapable of producing sound strategic business plans.

Uniform procedures Effective strategic business-planning procedures must be flexible and relatively unstructured. They must be tailored to the individual needs of the SBU in terms of process and content. This customizing ensures that the unique strategic issues affecting each SBU are effectively analyzed, presented and reviewed. This cannot occur if each plan is forced into a rigid, uniform mold. An effective strategic plan cannot be developed by requiring the SBUs to answer standardized questions and to complete mass-produced forms. Thus, a uniform planning process imposed upon the

TABLE 3.4.1
Obstacles to effective strategic planning

Phase 3 Obstacles	Phase 4 Characteristics
Planning Processes	
Uniform procedures	Flexible procedures
Regularly scheduled reviews	Scheduled as needed
Strict time limits on reviews	As much time as needed
Formal presentations	Informal presentations
Numerous observers	Decision makers only
Massive paperwork	Ten-page plans
Restricted discussion	Open dialogue
No decisions	Decisions mandatory
Process emphasized	Results emphasized
Content of the Plans	
Data, numbers facts	Business intelligence
Financial analysis	Strategic analysis
Short-term focus	Long-term focus
Generic strategies	Strategic action plans
Monitoring and Reward Processes	
Random progress reviews	Regular progress reviews
Limited accountability	Strict accountability

SBUs without regard for their individual industry circumstances and competitive positions is the first and, perhaps, most common obstacle to effective strategic business planning incurred at the entrance to phase 3.

Regularly scheduled reviews The importance of flexibility to meet the unique needs of each SBU extends to the timing of the business plan reviews. Strategic business plan reviews should be scheduled as needed whether that is every three months or every three years. All SBU plans do not have to be reviewed every year or at the same time of year. Regularly scheduled, annual business plan reviews for every SBU elevate form over substance and serve as another obstacle to effective business planning.

Strict time limits on reviews The time allotted to the business plan reviews should be adequate to enable management to comprehend and to respond to the competitive issues facing the SBU, whether it be two hours or two days. Further, the initial time set aside for the business plan review should be determined by the SBU, which knows its situation and needs best. A failure by top management to make adequate time available for reviewing the plans results in hasty reviews and poor decisions (if any decisions are made), and signals a lack of commitment to the process by top management. The setting of strict (often two-hour) time limits for each business plan review thus becomes another obstacle to effective business planning.

Formal presentations The importance of informal presentations of the business plans cannot be overemphasized. Formal presentations, complete with slides and prepared text, are often crafted to limit discussion and to minimize the open probing needed to test the rigor of the business plans. Formal presentations are thus a major obstacle to effective planning.

Numerous observers Attendance at the business plan reviews should be strictly limited to key decision makers. The presence of numerous observers is another obstacle to effective planning because their presence discourages the candid discussion needed, and reduces the likelihood that any important decisions will be made. More often than not, these observers are not present to add value to the planning process, but rather are only there to protect the interests of other staffs and operating units.

Massive paperwork Planning by the pound (or kilo) is a common affliction that strikes companies entering phase 3 of the planning process. If the plan is much more than 15 to 20 pages, the value of the paper probably exceeds the value of the plan. A good plan goes right to the key competitive issues and strategic action plans. To be sure, a great deal of analysis lies behind the plans, but the analysis is not the plan, and 100 pages of analysis does not substitute for 10 pages of strategic actions. A company that is planning by the pound is not planning. Thick notebooks are the work of analysts, not of strategists. Massive paperwork thus only serves as another obstacle to effective business planning by often delaying strategic reviews.

Restricted discussion   The purpose of the business plan review is to elicit open discussion of the strategic opportunities and threats confronting the SBU, and to test the rigor of the SBU's strategic action plans. The SBU should be seeking top management's counsel, not trying to sell it a bill of goods. At the same time, top management should be trying to understand and assist the SBU in formulating the most effective strategic responses to its external opportunities and threats within the limits of the company's operating and capital budgets. A lack of such open dialogue and the shared understanding it creates thus becomes another obstacle to effective planning.

No decisions   Perhaps the most critical element of all in the review process is whether top management makes decisions based on the business plans. This is the bottom line as far as the effectiveness of the business-planning process is concerned. The most important decisions, of course, are the allocations of resources. If the business plan is reviewed favorably but no resources are committed, it becomes perfectly clear to all that the real decisions are being made outside the business-planning system.

Process counts   One of the most serious failings in the development of the planning process is the substitution of the process for the plans. This is perhaps more a symptom of a failing process than a cause of failure *per se* since the alleged value of the process serves as a ready justification for the continued expenditure of resources for planning when expected results are lacking. This perceived value of the process often results from a naive presumption that the process inexorably leads to superior financial performance. However, since the process provides employment and perhaps status and enhanced career opportunities for those charged with overseeing it, there is a built-in demand for the process regardless of actual results. Here, as with several instances above, the elevation of the process and thus of form over substance acts as a major obstacle to effective business planning. The process itself does not count. Only the quality of the plans count. If you hear 'but we learned a lot from the process,' strategic business planning at your company is starting to fail. If you hear this repeatedly, it has probably already failed.

Content of the Plans

Having established that it is the quality of the plans and not the process that counts, and that uniform, formal processes are major obstacles to effective planning, we must also be alert to several major obstacles that can result from the content of the plans themselves.

Data, numbers, facts   Strategic plans often lack the essential business intelligence needed to make major business decisions. Instead, one finds pages and pages of data, numbers, and facts that are often of very limited value to strategic decision making. Those responsible for developing the business plans are typically more secure presenting indisputable facts than they are in proposing strategic actions on the basis of specific assumptions and hypotheses, both of which arise because of the great uncertainty that necessitates strategic planning in the first place. Forecasts of the courses the economy and industry are likely to take, assumptions about the most important legislative issues likely to arise, and hypotheses about the strategic actions key competitors are likely to take and what the impacts of such possible actions might be on the SBU are essential to the formulation of strategic action plans. These forecasts, assumptions and hypotheses, however, can easily be challenged, unlike the underlying raw data, numbers, and facts. They are therefore often avoided, especially in companies with strong risk-averse cultures. However, without the business intelligence that is created from these hypotheses, management is poorly equipped to make the critical strategic decisions necessary. Thus, the substitution of basic data, numbers, and facts for business intelligence is a major obstacle to effective business planning.

Financial analysis   It is not uncommon for the strategic business plan to be little more than an elaborate budget. In this case, the plans consist largely of financial forecasts, often with the focus of management's attention on next year's budget. A preoccupation with the financial numbers, unfortunately, effectively precludes real strategic planning. If management is satisfied with the numbers, it pays no attention to the business plans or to the strategies for achieving the numbers. If it is not satisfied with the numbers, it again pays no attention to the business plan, but rather orders some recalculation of the numbers.

Since there is usually neither adequate time nor interest in re-doing the actual business plan, consistency between the planned strategic actions and the financial projections vanishes. Subsequent budget or head-count cutbacks may further increase the gulf between the plan and the numbers so that the plan may no longer be implementable or relevant. Management should, of course, be concerned with the financial implications of the business plan over the entire planning horizon. However, evey number in the budget should be supported with a set of actions for achieving it. The substitution of a five-year budget for a five-year business plan is thus a major, though not uncommon, obstacle to effective planning.

Short-term focus   While most business plans cover a three- to five-year time horizon or longer, many companies focus on the coming year; especially if the emphasis is on the budget as discussed above, then managers defer concerns about the later years. Of course, this serves only to perpetuate an annual business planning or budgeting process that in turn precludes the discussion of most topics strategic in nature. This short-term focus stems largely from the emphasis on budgeting, on quarterly financial reporting, and on the greater predictability of the near term.

Generic strategies   Business strategies range in level of detail from grand portfolios and generic strategies (compete on the basis of product differentiation, low cost, or niche marketing) to specific functional strategies (provide the fastest delivery in the industry) and detailed tactics (add three new delivery trucks at each zone office). While the appropriate level of strategic detail to include in the business plans varies with the size, diversity, and organizational structure of the company, a common obstacle to effective business planning is the substitution of generic strategies for a set of integrated strategic action plans.

Generic strategies, which could apply equally to any number of business units, seldom provide any clue about how the SBU will actually achieve competitive advantage, and thus offer no foundation for management's review of the business plan. For example, a generic strategy to compete on the basis of greater product differentiation provides no indication about how the SBU will achieve this differentiation, its ability to do so, or the impact on cost, quality, and other key success factors. What is needed for effective planning is a set of specific strategic actions integrated into a cohesive overall plan for gaining competitive supremacy.

Monitoring and Reward Processes

The monitoring and reward systems are critical elements in the business-planning process. The likelihood that the plan will be successfully implemented without effective monitoring and reward systems is remote. These two systems are also frequently the source of major obstacles to effective planning during phase 3 of the business-planning process.

Random progress reviews   While there is a need for substantial flexibility so that business plan reviews can be scheduled as needed, progress toward achieving the goals in the business plan should be reviewed on a regular basis – usually quarterly or semiannually, depending on business dynamics and management quality. If progress is not reviewed regularly, the plans are not likely to be effectively implemented because 'what counts gets counted.' With no systematic reviews to monitor progress and to discuss needed course corrections, the plans quickly become irrelevant to the operation of the business. Without effective monitoring, there is also no basis for accountability, which is essential to the successful implementation of the business plan.

Limited accountability   A successful planning process requires that those responsible for carrying out the plans be held accountable for doing so, and be rewarded or penalized accordingly. If rewards are not tied directly to business plan performance, the plans will not be implemented and the objectives will not be achieved, unless fortuitously. The managers of the SBUs respond to the reward system, not the business-planning system. The successful implementation of the business plans thus requires that the two be inextricably linked. SBU managers will quickly deviate from or abandon the business plans altogether to pursue those objectives for which they believe they will be rewarded.

In order to avoid or eliminate these obstacles, it is helpful to recognize that in most organizations they seem to originate from a small set of underlying or root causes that are rather easy to identify.

Avoiding the Obstacles

The numerous obstacles to effective strategic business planning typically encountered in phase 3 of the planning process have one of four basic root causes: a lack of commitment to the process by top management; staff, rather than line-management control of the process; entrenched self-interests that are threatened by the business-planning process and which thus result in turf wars; and a corporate culture that discourages entrepreneurship and risk taking. The impact of these four factors on the success of business planning is often greatly magnified by the fact that these factors can be highly interdependent and mutually reinforcing. Thus, avoiding or controlling these four root causes is essential to eliminating the many obstacles to strategic business planning. These interrelationships are shown in Table 3.4.2 where the obstacles discussed above are related to their root causes.

Management Commitment

The most fundamental cause of many of the obstacles to effective strategic business planning, and often the ultimate cause of its failure, is a lack of commitment to business planning by the top management of the company. This, not uncommon, lack of enthusiasm for strategic business planning by top management generates more problems than any other single factor. Further, it often results in staff control of the process by default, and the additional obstacles this creates. A lack of commitment by top management also permits entrenched interest groups, threatened by the planning process, to raise additional obstacles to the process. The lack of management commitment may also in part stem from a tradition of risk aversity, so there are likely to be major cultural obstacles to strategic business planning as well.

Given the significant consequences of inadequate executive support, the perplexing question arises why a company would commit substantial resources to strategic business planning without a solid commitment to the process from top management. There are several explanations for this apparent inconsistency. First, strategic business planning rapidly came to be considered a requirement of sound management by academics and management consultants. Many companies were therefore anxious to implement such a process even before they understood it fully. Managers were more prepared to spend money for a business-planning process than they were to change the way they managed the company, and often more interested in the visible trappings of business planning than in its sub-

TABLE 3.4.2

The root causes of failure in strategic planning

Lack of Management Commitment	Staff Control	Entrenched Interests	Corporate Culture
Strict time limits	Uniform process	Numerous observers	Data, numbers, facts
Restricted discussion	Regular schedule	No decisions	Generic strategies
Short-term focus	Formal presentation		Limited accountability
Financial emphases	Massive paperwork		
No decisions	Process emphasis		
Random progress reviews			
Limited accountability			

stance. As it became clear that managers' roles in the company might have to change, often very substantially, their enthusiasm for strategic planning typically waned considerably.

In the strategic business planning process, top management is responsible for determining which businesses the company should be in, for allocating resources among those businesses, and for developing synergies among them to maximize overall stockholder wealth rather than the profits of individual SBUs. The top executives are not directly involved in the management of the SBUs. This separation of SBU and corporate management responsibilities gives the top executives the time, perspective, and motivation to allocate resources among SBUs to maximize the total value of the company. For many executives, this transition from a more traditional operating to a strategic role represents a fundamental change that was not fully anticipated, and for which they are often not prepared.

In other companies, the planning process may have been urged on management from lower levels within the company, especially from staffs intrigued with the new analytical techniques, and may have never received more than tacit endorsement from the top management. And, of course, top management's initial enthusiasm for planning has generally waned as the financial results have failed to materialize as quickly as they may have been promised by zealous staffers or outside consultants. For any or all of these reasons, top management's commitment to strategic business planning at many companies is far less than appears to casual observers.

A lack of commitment to the strategic business planning process by top management is clearly evidenced by strict time limits on the business plan reviews, restricted discussion at these reviews, and a primary focus on the short term and on short-term financial performance in particular. The most direct and deleterious result of a lack of management commitment to the planning process, however, is the failure to make decisions based on the business plans. The approval of the plans without commitment of the resources needed to implement them is the most common, obvious, and condemning statement of management's lack of commitment to the process, regardless of the visible trappings, amount of expenditures, and size of the planning books. The lack of management commitment to strategic planning is also clearly manifest in a failure to conduct systematic performance reviews and to hold people accountable for achieving business plan goals.

To remove these major obstacles to effective strategic business planning, top management's absolute commitment to the planning process must be secured. This commitment is not measured so much by a willingness to spend money for planning but by a willingness to accept the strategic, as opposed to operating, role that the planning process defines for the top management, and to make decisions on the basis of the strategic business plans. This commitment must clearly be understood to represent a fundamental change in the way key resource decisions are made. Management must also be willing to make a long-term commitment to the business-planning process. Results should not be promised prematurely in order to sell the process to the top management.

Staff Control

Many of the obstacles noted earlier occur when staff, rather than line management, control the business-planning process. Staff are prone to placing more emphasis on the process, on the uniformity and formality of the process, and on massive amounts of analysis rather than strategic action plans and bottom-line results. This should not be surprising since the process is the result from the staff's perspective. The development and implementation of the actual strategic plans are the responsibility of line management – not staff. When line management is in control of the process, the focus will be on the bottom-line results for which they are responsible and will be held accountable. When staff control the process, business planning often takes on a life of its own quite unrelated to bottom-line results.

The most effective way to avoid staff control is to employ in the central planning group primarily people from operating units to which they will return shortly. Such personnel on temporary assignment to the planning staff will maintain their bottom-line focus. A few staff experts are needed to maintain the continuity of the planning process and to train managers and analysts in planning techniques, but their numbers should be kept to the minimum. Staff control can also be avoided by leaving much of the responsibility for the business-planning process – format, timing, instructions, and so on – with the operating units rather than with the central planning staff.

Entrenched Interests

The introduction of strategic business planning may be perceived as a serious threat to the power and status of numerous entrenched interest groups throughout the company. For example, business planning is often seen as a threat to the financial departments, which may control the budgeting process, because they foresee being replaced as an important decision-making unit as the company moves from phase 2 to phase 3 business planning. The creation of SBUs as planning organizations may also threaten the power of divisional managements or central office staffs that previously held more functional control over operations. Somewhat surprisingly, planning may also threaten the top management itself. Unfamiliarity with the new strategic roles, analytical techniques, and decision-making systems may threaten at least some members of top management. This is especially likely for top managers who are more accustomed to making operating as opposed to strategic decisions. The reduced scope of their direct involvement in the operations of the SBUs may be perceived as a serious loss of power and prestige by some top managers.

The presence of numerous observers at the business plan reviews is usually a reliable indicator of the amount of resistance to business planning from the entrenched interests that feel threatened by the new planning process. And the lack of decisions based on the business plans may be testimony to their ability to keep critical decisions outside the strategic business-planning process.

To avoid these obstacles, all of the major affected interests throughout the company should be invited to participate in the development of the strategic business-planning process, and each should be assigned an essential role in this new process. This should not prove difficult because, properly executed, strategic business planning is a process for effectively integrating all of the company's resources in the pursuit of common, corporate goals. Beyond this, an absolute commitment to the process by the top management is the most effective means of dispelling such resistance.

Corporate Culture

The company's attitude toward risk taking and entrepreneurship is a critical factor in the success of strategic business planning. Effective long-term business planning requires a culture that encourages entrepreneurial responses to risks and uncertainty. A highly risk-averse company will find it difficult to formulate explicit long-term plans, and to assign explicit accountability for carrying them out. Management, of course, cannot avoid risks by refusing to address them. Management can, however, avoid, or at least attempt to avoid, accountability for the mistakes and failures that are inevitable in an uncertain environment. If the culture will not tolerate such failures, entrepreneurialism and risk taking will be driven out of the business plans, and they will degenerate to nothing more than indisputable data, facts, and numbers, rather than valuable business intelligence. Implementation will be limited to generic strategies and ambiguous, qualitative, and easily achieved objecctives rather than specific action strategies and measurable goals against which the SBU management can be held accountable.

To avoid such sterile and defensive (protecting the SBU from failure and accountability) business plans, the corporate culture must visibly promote and reward entrepreneurialism and risk taking. It must permit failure – otherwise the SBUs will not try aggressively to succeed. Most SBUs will emphasize avoiding failures that are readily identifiable and for which they will be held accountable. Changing a risk-averse culture to one that promotes entrepreneurialism and risk taking is equally essential and difficult. As De Geus has articulated well, an effective planning process can aid the organizational learning so essential to developing new perspectives and attitudes toward the future. The company must clearly announce the new behaviour that is desired, it must explain the business context that makes this new behaviour essential to the continued success of the firm, and most importantly, it must visibly reward the desired behaviour.

Summary and Conclusions

Strategic business planning has not consistently delivered the promised financial benefits because it has often fallen victim to a number of formidable, bureaucratic obstacles. As a result, many firms today are seriously rethinking their prior commitments to the business-planning process. This, however, is not the time to abandon strategic business planning, especially for those companies simultaneously facing growing world-wide competition and social demands. This is the time to begin removing the obstacles to effective strategic business planning so that these demands can be met.

There is a subtle but significant danger in the process of removing the obstacles to effective strategic business planning. The elimination of these obstacles by such leading companies as General Electric may well be mistakenly interpreted as an abandonment of business planning by other companies who will then dismantle their own strategic business-planning processes. This is a serious danger because the bureaucratic obstacles to planning, described in the second section of this reading, have become so intricately embedded in the planning process that they are often seen as essential components of the process rather than obstacles to it. Nowhere is this better illustrated than in the mistaken notion that the Japanese do not plan. It is the lack of the most visible obstacles to effective strategic business planning in the Japanese systems that leads to this misperception. The elimination of formal presentations, large meetings, massive planning books, and regularly scheduled, annual reviews is not the abandonment of planning – it is the liberation of planning!

3.5   The Fall and Rise of Strategic Planning

By Henry Mintzberg[1]

When strategic planning arrived on the scene in the mid-1960s, corporate leaders embraced it as 'the one best way' to devise and implement strategies that would enhance the competitiveness of each business unit. True to the scientific management pioneered by Frederick Taylor, this one best way involved separating thinking from doing and creating a new function staffed by specialists: strategic planners. Planning systems were expected to produce the best strategies as well as step-by-step instructions for carrying out those strategies so that the doers, the managers of businesses, could not get them wrong. As we now know, planning has not exactly worked out that way.

While certainly not dead, strategic planning has long since fallen from its pedestal. But even now, few people fully understand the reason: strategic planning is not *strategic thinking*. Indeed, strategic planning often spoils strategic thinking, causing managers to confuse real vision with the manipulation of numbers. And this confusion lies at the heart of the issue: the most successful strategies are visions, not plans.

Strategic planning, as it has been practiced, has really been *strategic programming*, the articulation and elaboration of strategies, or visions, that already exist. When companies understand the difference between planning and strategic thinking, they can get back to what the strategy-making process should be: capturing what the manager learns from all sources (both the soft insights from his or her personal experiences and the experiences of others throughout the organization and the hard data from market research and the like) and then synthesizing that learning into a vision of the direction that the business should pursue.

Organizations disenchanted with strategic planning should not get rid of their planners or conclude that there is no need for programming. Rather, organizations should transform the conventional planning job. Planners should make their contribution *around* the strategy-making process rather than *inside it*. They should supply the formal analyses or hard data that strategic thinking requires, as long as they do it to broaden the consideration of issues rather than to discover the one right answer. They should act as catalysts who support strategy making by aiding and encouraging managers to think strategically. And, finally, they can be programmers of a strategy, helping to specify the series of concrete steps needed to carry out the vision.

By redefining the planner's job, companies will acknowledge the difference between planning and strategic thinking. Planning has always been about analysis – about breaking down a goal or set of intentions into

---

[1] Source: This article was adapted with permission from 'The Fall and Rise of Strategic Planning', *Harvard Business Review*, January/February 1994, pp. 107–114.

steps, formalizing those steps so that they can be implemented almost automatically, and articulating the anticipated consequences or results of each step. 'I favour a set of analytical techniques for developing strategy,' Michael Porter, probably the most widely read writer on strategy, wrote in the *Economist*.

The label 'strategic planning' has been applied to all kinds of activities, such as going off to an informal retreat in the mountains to talk about strategy. But call that activity 'planning,' let conventional planners organize it, and watch how quickly the event becomes formalized (mission statements in the morning, assessment of corporate strengths and weaknesses in the afternoon, strategies carefully articulated by 5 p.m.).

Strategic thinking, in contrast, is about synthesis. It involves intuition and creativity. The outcome of strategic thinking is an integrated perspective of the enterprise, a not-too-precisely articulated vision of direction, such as the vision of Jim Clark, the founder of Silicon Graphics, that three-dimensional visual computing is the way to make computers easier to use.

Such strategies often cannot be developed on schedule and immaculately conceived. They must be free to appear at any time and at any place in the organization, typically through messy processes of informal learning that must necessarily be carried out by people at various levels who are deeply involved with the specific issues at hand.

Formal planning, by its very analytical nature, has been and always will be dependent on the preservation and rearrangement of established categories – the existing levels of strategy (corporate, business, functional), the established types of products (defined as 'strategic business units'), overlaid on the current units of structure (divisions, departments, etc.). But real strategic change requires not merely rearranging the established categories, but inventing new ones.

Search all those strategic planning diagrams, all those interconnected boxes that supposedly give you strategies, and nowhere will you find a single one that explains the creative act of synthesizing experiences into a novel strategy. Take the example of the Polaroid camera. One day in 1943, Edwin Land's three-year-old daughter asked why she could not immediately see the picture he had just taken of her. Within an hour, this scientist conceived the camera that would transform his company. In other words, Land's vision was the synthesis of the insight evoked by his daughter's question and his vast technical knowledge.

Strategy making needs to function beyond the boxes, to encourage the informal learning that produces new perspectives and new combinations. As the saying goes, life is larger than our categories. Planning's failure to transcend the categories explains why it has discouraged serious organizational change. This failure is why formal planning has promoted strategies that are extrapolated from the past or copied from others. Strategic planning has not only never amounted to strategic thinking but has, in fact, often impeded it. Once managers understand this, they can avoid other costly misadventures caused by applying formal technique, without judgment and intuition, to problem solving.

The Pitfalls of Planning

If you ask conventional planners what went wrong, they will inevitably point to a series of pitfalls for which they, of course, are not responsible. Planners would have people believe that planning fails when it does not receive the support it deserves from top management or when it encounters resistance to change in the organization. But surely no technique ever received more top management support than strategic planning did in its heyday. Strategic planning itself has discouraged the commitment of top managers and has tended to create the very climates its proponents have found so uncongenial to its practice.

The problem is that planning represents a calculating style of management, not a committing style. Managers with a committing style engage people in a journey. They lead in such a way that everyone on the journey helps shape its course. As a result, enthusiasm inevitably builds along the way. Those with a calculating style fix on a destination and calculate what the group must do to get there, with no concern for the members' preferences. But calculated strategies have no value in and of themselves; to paraphrase the words of sociologist Philip Selznick, strategies take on value only as committed people infuse them with energy.

No matter how much lip service has been paid to the contrary, the very purpose of those who promote conventional strategic planning is to reduce the power of management over strategy making. George Steiner (1979) declared, 'If an organization is managed by intuitive geniuses there is no need for formal strategic planning. But how many organizations are so blessed? And, if they are, how many times are intuitives correct in their judgments?' Peter Lorange, who is equally prominent in the field, stated (Lorange, 1980b), 'The CEO should typically not be . . . deeply involved' in the process, but rather be 'the designer of [it] in a general sense.' How can we expect top managers to be committed to a process that depicts them in this way, especially when its failures to deliver on its promises have become so evident?

At lower levels in the hierarchy, the problem becomes more severe because planning has often been used to exercise blatant control over business managers. No wonder so many middle managers have welcomed the overthrow of strategic planning. All they wanted was a commitment to their own business strategies without having to fight the planners to get it!

The Fallacies of Strategic Planning

An expert has been defined as someone who avoids the many pitfalls on his or her way to the grand fallacy. For strategic planning, the grand fallacy is this: because analysis encompasses synthesis, strategic planning is strategy making. This fallacy itself rests on three fallacious assumptions: that prediction is possible, that strategists can be detached from the subjects of their strategies, and, above all, that the strategy-making process can be formalized.

The Fallacy of Prediction

According to the premises of strategic planning, the world is supposed to hold still while a plan is being developed and then stay on the predicted course while that plan is being implemented. How else to explain those lockstep schedules that have strategies appearing on the first of June, to be approved by the board of directors on the fifteenth? One can just picture competitors waiting for the board's approval, especially if they are Japanese and don't believe in such planning to begin with.

In 1965, Igor Ansoff wrote in his influential book *Corporate Strategy*, 'We shall refer to the period for which the firm is able to construct forecasts with an accuracy of, say, plus or minus 20 percent as the planning horizon of the firm.' What an extraordinary statement! How in the world can any company know the period for which it can forecast with a given accuracy?

The evidence, in fact, points to the contrary. While certain repetitive patterns, such as seasons, may be predictable, the forecasting of discontinuities, such as a technological innovation or a price increase, is virtually impossible. Of course, some people sometimes 'see' such things coming. That is why we call them 'visionaries.' But they create their strategies in much more personalized and intuitive ways.

The Fallacy of Detachment

In her book *Institutionalizing Innovation*, Mariann Jelinek (1979) developed the interesting point that strategic planning is to the executive suite what Taylor's work-study methods were to the factory floor – a way to circumvent human idiosyncrasies in order to systematize behavior. 'It is through administrative systems that planning and policy are made possible, because the systems capture knowledge about the task.' Thus 'true management by exception, and true policy direction are now possible, solely because management is no longer wholly immersed in the details of the task itself.'

According to this viewpoint, if the system does the thinking, then strategies must be detached from operations (or 'tactics'), formulation from implementation, thinkers from doers, and so strategists from the objects of their strategies.

The trick, of course, is to get the relevant information up there, so that senior managers on high can be informed about the details down below without having to immerse themselves in them. Planners' favored solution has been 'hard data,' quantitative aggregates of the detailed 'facts' about the organization and its context, neatly packaged and regularly delivered. With such information, senior managers need never leave their executive suites or planners their staff offices. Together they can formulate – work with their heads – so that the hands can get on with implementation.

All of this is dangerously fallacious. Innovation has never been institutionalized. Systems have never been able to reproduce the synthesis created by the genius entrepreneur or even the ordinary competent strategist, and they likely never will.

Ironically, strategic planning has missed one of Taylor's most important messages: work processes must be fully understood before they can be formally programmed. But where in the planning literature is there a shred of evidence that anyone has ever bothered to find out how it is that managers really do make strategies? Instead many practitioners and theorists have wrongly assumed that strategic planning, strategic thinking, and strategy making are all synonymous, at least in best practice.

The problem with the hard data that are supposed to inform the senior manager is they can have a decidedly soft underbelly. Such data take time to harden, which often makes them late. They tend to lack richness; for example, they often exclude the qualitative. And they tend to be overly aggregated, missing important nuances. These are the reasons managers who rely on formalized information, such as market-research reports or accounting statements in business and opinion polls in government, tend to be detached in more ways than one. Study after study has shown that the most effective managers rely on some of the softest forms of information, including gossip, hearsay, and various other intangible scraps of information.

My research and that of many others demonstrates that strategy making is an immensely complex process, which involves the most sophisticated, subtle, and, at times, subconscious elements of human thinking.

A strategy can be deliberate. It can realize the specific intentions of senior management, for example, to attack and conquer a new market. But a strategy can also be emergent, meaning that a convergent pattern has formed among the different actions taken by the organization one at a time.

In other words, strategies can develop inadvertently, without the conscious intention of senior management, often through a process of learning. A salesperson convinces a different kind of customer to try a product. Other salespeople follow up with their customers, and the next thing management knows, its products have penetrated a new market. When it takes the form of fits and starts, discoveries based on serendipitous events, and the recognition of unexpected patterns, learning inevitably plays *a*, if not *the*, crucial role in the development of novel strategies.

Contrary to what traditional planning would have us believe, deliberate strategies are not necessarily good, nor are emergent strategies necessarily bad. I believe that all viable strategies have emergent and deliberate qualities, since all must combine some degree of flexible learning with some degree of cerebral control.

Vision is unavailable to those who cannot 'see' with their own eyes. Real strategists get their hands dirty digging for ideas, and real strategies are built from the occasional nuggets they uncover. These are not people who abstract themselves from the daily details; they are the ones who immerse themselves in them while being able to abstract the strategic messages from them. The big picture is painted with little strokes.

The Fallacy of Formalization

The failure of strategic planning is the failure of systems to do better than, or even nearly as well as, human beings. Formal systems, mechanical or otherwise, have offered no improved means of dealing with the information overload of human brains; indeed, they have often made matters worse. All the promises about artificial intelligence, expert systems, and the like improving, if not replacing, human intuition never materialized at the strategy level. Formal systems could certainly process more information, at least hard information. But they could never *internalize* it, *comprehend* it, *synthesize* it. In a literal sense, planning could not learn.

Formalization implies a rational sequence, from analysis through administrative procedure to eventual action. But strategy making as a learning process can proceed in the other direction too. We think in order to act, to be sure, but we also act in order to think. We try things, and those experiments that work converge gradually into viable patterns that become strategies. This is the very essence of strategy making as a learning process.

Formal procedures will never be able to forecast discontinuities, inform detached managers, or create novel strategies. Far from providing strategies, planning could not proceed without their prior existence. All this time, therefore, strategic planning has been misnamed. It should have been called strategic programming, distinguished from other useful things that planners can do, and promoted as a process to formalize, when necessary, the consequences of strategies that have already been developed. In short, we should drop the label 'strategic planning' altogether.

Planning, Plans, and Planners

Two important messages have been conveyed through all the difficulties encountered by strategic planning. But only one of them has been widely accepted in the planning community: business-unit managers must take full and effective charge of the strategy-making process. The lesson that has still not been accepted is that managers will never be able to take charge through a formalized process. What then can be the roles for planning, for plans, and for planners in organizations?

Planners and managers have different advantages. Planners lack managers' authority to make commitments, and, more important, managers' access to soft information critical to strategy making. But because of their time pressures, managers tend to favor action over reflection and the oral over the written, which can cause them to overlook important analytical information. Strategies cannot be created by analysis, but their development can be helped by it.

Planners, on the other hand, have the time and, most important, the inclination to analyze. They have critical roles to play alongside line managers, but not as conventionally conceived. They should work in the spirit of what I like to call a 'soft analyst,' whose intent is to pose the right questions rather than to find the right answers. That way, complex issues get opened up to thoughtful consideration instead of being closed down prematurely by snap decisions.

Planning as Strategic Programming

Planning cannot generate strategies. But given viable strategies, it can program them; it can make them operational. For one supermarket chain that a colleague and I studied, planning was the articulation, justification, and elaboration of the strategic vision that the company's leader already had. Planning was not deciding to expand into shopping centers, but explicating to what extent and when, with how many stores, and on what schedule.

An appropriate image for the planner might be that person left behind in a meeting, together with the chief executive, after everyone else has departed. All of the strategic decisions that were made are symbolically strewn about the table. The CEO turns to the planner and says, 'There they all are; clean them up. Package them neatly so that we can tell everyone about them and get things going.' In more formal language, strategic programming involves three steps: codification, elaboration, and conversion of strategies.

Codification means clarifying and expressing the strategies in terms sufficiently clear to render them formally operational, so that their consequences can be worked out in detail. This requires a good deal of interpretation and careful attention to what might be lost in articulation: nuance, subtlety, qualification. A broad vision, like capturing the market for a new technology, is one thing, but a specific plan – 35 percent market share, focusing on the high end – is quite another.

Elaboration means breaking down the codified strategies into substrategies and *ad hoc* programs as well as overall action plans specifying what must be done to realize each strategy: build four new factories and hire 200 new workers, for example.

And conversion means considering the effects of the changes on the organization's operations – effects on budgets and performance controls, for example. Here a kind of great divide must be crossed from the non-routine world of strategies and programs to the routine world of budgets and objectives. Objectives have to be restated and budgets reworked, and policies and standard operating procedures reconsidered, to take into account the consequences of the specific changes.

One point must be emphasized. Strategic programming is not 'the one best way' or even necessarily a good way. Managers don't always need to program their strategies formally. Sometimes they must leave their strategies flexible, as broad visions, to adapt to a changing environment. Only when an organization is sure of the relative stability of its environment and is in need of the tight coordination of a myriad intricate operations (as is typically the case of airlines with their needs for complicated scheduling), does such strategic programming make sense.

Plans as Tools to Communicate and Control

Why program strategy? The most obvious reason is for coordination, to ensure that everyone in the organization pulls in the same direction. Plans in the form of programs – schedules, budgets, and so on – can be prime media to communicate strategic intentions and to control the individual pursuit of them, in so far, of course, as common direction is considered to be more important than individual discretion.

Plans can also be used to gain the tangible as well as moral support of influential outsiders. Written plans inform financiers, suppliers, government agencies, and others about the intentions of the organization so that these groups can help it achieve its plans.

Planners as Strategy Finders

As noted, some of the most important strategies in organizations emerge without the intention or sometimes even the awareness of top managers. Fully exploiting these strategies, though, often requires that they be recognized and then broadened in their impact, like taking a new use for a product accidentally discovered by a salesperson and turning it into a major new business. It is obviously the responsibility of managers to discover and anoint these strategies. But planners can assist managers in finding these fledgling strategies in their organizations' activities or in those of competing organizations.

Planners can snoop around places they might not normally visit to find patterns amid the noise of failed experiments, seemingly random activities, and messy learning. They can discover new ways of doing or perceiving things, for example, spotting newly uncovered markets and understanding their implied new products.

Planners as Analysts

In-depth examinations of what planners actually do suggests that the effective ones spend a good deal of time not so much doing or even encouraging planning as carrying out analyses of specific issues. Planners are obvious candidates for the job of studying the hard data and ensuring that managers consider the results in the strategy-making process.

Much of this analysis will necessarily be quick and dirty, that is, in the time frame and on the *ad hoc* basis required by managers. It may include industry or competitive analyses as well as internal studies, including the use of computer models to analyze trends in the organization.

But some of the best models that planners can offer managers are simply alternative conceptual interpretations of their world, such as a new way to view the organization's distribution system. As Arie de Geus, the one-time head of planning at Royal Dutch/Shell, wrote in his HBR article 'Planning as Learning' (1988), 'The real purpose of effective planning is not to make plans but to change the . . . mental models that . . . decision makers carry in their heads.'

Planners as Catalysts

The planning literature has long promoted the role of catalyst for the planner, but not as I will describe it here. It is not planning that planners should be urging on their organizations so much as any form of behavior that can lead to effective performance in a given situation. Sometimes that may even mean criticizing formal planning itself.

When they act as catalysts, planners do not enter the black box of strategy making; they ensure that the box is occupied with active line managers. In other words, they encourage managers to think about the future in creative ways.

Such planners see their job as getting others to question conventional wisdom and especially helping people out of conceptual ruts (which managers with long experience in stable strategies are apt to dig themselves into). To do their jobs, they may have to use provocation or shock tactics like raising difficult questions and challenging conventional assumptions.

Left- and Right-Handed Planners

Two very different kinds of people populate the planning function. One is an analytic thinker, who is closer to the conventional image of the planner. He or she is dedicated to bringing order to the organization. Above all, this person programs intended strategies and sees to it that they are communicated clearly. He or she also carries out analytic studies to ensure consideration of the necessary hard data and carefully scrutinizes strategies intended for implementation. We might label him or her the *right-handed planner.*

The second is less conventional but present nonetheless in many organizations. This planner is a creative thinker who seeks to open up the strategy-making process. As a 'soft analyst,' this planner is prepared to conduct more quick and dirty studies. He or she likes to find strategies in strange places and to encourage others to think strategically. This person is somewhat more inclined toward the intuitive processes identified with the brain's right hemisphere. We might call him or her the *left-handed planner.*

Many organizations need both types, and it is top management's job to ensure that it has them in appropriate proportions. Organizations need people to bring order to the messy world of management as well as challenge the conventions that managers and especially their organizations develop. Some organizations (those big, machine-like bureaucracies concerned with mass production) may favor the right-handed planners, while others (the loose, flexible 'adhocracies,' or project organizations) may favor the left-handed ones. But both kinds of organization need both types of planners, if only to offset their natural tendencies. And, of course, some organizations, like those highly professionalized hospitals and educational systems that have been forced to waste so much time doing ill-conceived strategic planning, may prefer to have very few of either!

The Formalization Edge

We human beings seem predisposed to formalize our behavior. But we must be careful not to go over the formalization edge. No doubt we must formalize to do many of the things we wish to in modern society. That is why we have organizations. But the experiences of what has been labeled strategic planning teach us that there are limits. These limits must be understood, especially for complex and creative activities like strategy making.

Strategy making is not an isolated process. It does not happen just because a meeting is held with that label. To the contrary, strategy making is a process interwoven with all that it takes to manage an organization. Systems do not think, and when they are used for more than the facilitation of human thinking, they can prevent thinking.

Three decades of experience with strategic planning have taught us about the need to loosen up the process of strategy making rather than trying to seal it off by arbitrary formalization. Through all the false starts and excessive rhetoric, we have learned what planning is not and what it cannot do. But we have also learned what planning is and what it can do, and perhaps of greater use, what planners themselves can do beyond planning. We have also learned how the literature of management can get carried away and, more important, about the appropriate place for analysis in organizations.

The story of strategic planning, in other words, has taught us not only about formal technique itself but also about how organizations function and how managers do and don't cope with that functioning. Most significant, it has told us something about how we think as human beings, and that we sometimes stop thinking.

Strategy Formation in International Perspective

To plan, v. To bother about the best
method of accomplishing an accidental result.
(*The Devil's Dictionary*, Ambrose Bierce 1842–1914; American columnist)

From the preceding contributions it has become evident that views differ sharply as to whether strategies should be formed by means of planning or incrementalism. It is clear that a wide variety of approaches exists to deal with the paradox of deliberateness and emergentness. None of the authors, however, suggest that their views may be more appropriate in some countries than in others. Nor do any of them mention the possibility that an organization's choice of approach may be influenced by national circumstances. In other words, so far the international angle has been conspicuously absent. It has generally been assumed that international differences are a non-issue.

Yet, the question whether there are specific national preferences for the planning or the incrementalism perspective seems quite legitimate. In the past, a few international comparative studies have be done that show significantly different levels of formal planning across various industrialized countries. For instance, Steiner and Schollhammer (1975) reported that planning was found to be most common and most formalized in the United States, with other English-speaking countries (Britain, Canada and Australia) also exhibiting a high score. At the other extreme were Italy and Japan, where very little formal planning was witnessed. The low propensity to engage in formal planning in Japan has been noted by a number of other authors as well (e.g. Kagono *et al.*, 1985). Hayashi (1978: 221) remarks that Japanese firms 'distrust corporate planning in general,' while Ohmae (1982: 225) characterizes Japanese companies as 'less planned, less rigid, but more vision- and mission-driven' than Western companies. Unfortunately, there are no cross-cultural studies of a more recent date to confirm that these international dissimilarities still exist. However, many observers have suggested that there remain discernible national differences in approaches to strategy formation (e.g. Gilbert and Lorange, 1995; Mintzberg, 1994b; Schneider, 1989).

Although it is difficult to generalize at the national level, since there can be quite a bit of variance within a country, it is challenging to pursue these observed international dissimilarities. Are there really national strategy formation styles and what factors might influence their existence? As a stimulus to the international dimension of this debate, we put forward the following country characteristics as possible influences on how the paradox of deliberateness and emergentness is dealt with in different national settings. As we noted at the end of Chapter 2, these propositions are intended to encourage discussion, but more concrete international comparative research is needed to give this debate a firmer footing.

Level of Professionalization

The high incidence of formal planning systems in Australia, Britain, Canada, New Zealand, and the United States seems odd, given their high level of individualism and their strong preference for a market economy. One might expect that the English-speaking countries' fondness of unplanned markets would be a reflection of a general dislike of planning. Yet, strangely, 'most large US corporations are run like the Soviet economy' of yesteryear, with strong central plans and top-down control, Ohmae concludes (1982: 224).

One explanation might be that formalized planning and control systems are a logical consequence of having professional management (e.g. Mintzberg, 1994b). Nowhere in the industrialized world, with the exception of France, has there been a stronger development of a distinct managerial class than in the English-speaking countries (Hampden-Turner and Trompenaars, 1993; Lessem and Neubauer, 1994). These professional managers run companies on behalf of the owners, who are usually distant from the operations (i.e. often minority shareholders). In the division of labor, the managers perform the 'thinking' tasks – analyzing, planning, coordinating, leading, budgeting, motivating, controlling – while the workforce concentrates on performing the primary activities. This makes it possible for large, complex production processes to be controlled by a hierarchy of professional managers. It is commonly believed that these managers possess general skills that allow them to run a wide variety of different businesses.

In companies with professional management, the split between thinking and doing is made more explicit than in other organizations. The managers are the officers who formulate the strategies and the personnel on the workfloor are the troops that must implement them – 'management' has intentions that the 'employees' must realize. This requires formal planning to guide workers' actions and a tight control system to ensure compliance. This mechanism is usually employed all the way up the hierarchy, as higher level managers use a planning and control system to steer and coordinate the behavior of lower level managers. All the way at the top, senior management must also make plans to win the approval of the shareholders.

This stratified organizational model, that Mintzberg dubs the machine bureaucracy (1979), is also prevalent in France, where the distinction between *cadre* employees and *non-cadre* personnel is also very strong (Hofstede, 1993; reading 1.5 in this book). In many other countries, however, the split between managerial and non-managerial tasks is not as radical. For instance, in Germany and Japan, senior employees are expected to be involved in operational matters, while junior employees are expected to contribute to strategy formation, by coming up with ideas and passing on information to seniors. In such countries, there is less need to use formal planning and control mechanisms to manage employees, since the 'managers' have direct and informal links with those 'managed'. Usually these managers have risen through the ranks, giving them the richness of information and contacts needed to manage without highly formalized systems. In these nations, consensus-building and personal control are the important management skills, and these are not readily transferable to another industry or even another organization.

In yet other countries, the dominant form of organization is that of direct control by one person or a family. This usually means that organizations remain relatively small, although they can compensate by linking up into networks based on personal connections between the top bosses. This organizational model, common in Italy and among the overseas Chinese (see Hofstede, 1993; reading 1.5; Weidenbaum and Hughes, 1996; reading 7.5) will be further discussed in Chapter 7. Here it is sufficient to conclude that in such organizations there is also little need for formalized planning and control systems to manage employees. The top boss, who is usually also the owner, steers the firm personally, with little regard for 'professional' methods.

The conclusion is that the national propensity to engage in formal planning is probably influenced by the level of professionalization of management within the country. In nations where the machine bureaucracy is the predominant organizational model, a stronger inclination towards formal planning systems can be expected.

Preference for Internal Control

While the previous section discussed different *types* of internal control, and the related organizational models, it should be noted that countries can also differ with regard to the *level* of internal control their citizens prefer. In some cultures, people have a strong desire for order and structure – clear tasks, responsibilities, powers, rules and procedures. Ambiguous situations and uncertain outcomes are disliked and therefore management strives to control organizational processes. Management can reduce uncertainty in a number of ways. Structure can be offered by strictly following traditions or by imposing top-down paternalistic rule. However, uncertainty can also be reduced by planning (Kagono *et al.*, 1985; Schneider, 1989). By setting direction, coordinating initiatives, committing resources, and programming activities, structure can be brought to the organization. In this way, planning can help to alleviate people's anxiety about 'disorganization'. In cultures that are more tolerant towards ambiguity and uncertainty, one can expect a weaker preference for planning.

The importance of planning as a means for structuring and controlling is particularly important in cultures where there is little confidence in self-organization. This is especially true in individualistic cultures, where organizational members can not always be counted on to work towards the common good (Hofstede, 1993; reading 1.5). In these countries, extensive planning and control systems are often used as a formal means for getting people to cooperate, coordinate and serve the organization's interests. Strategic plans function as internal contracts, to limit dysfunctional opportunistic behavior (Allaire and Firsirotu, 1990; Bungay and Goold, 1991). In cultures with a stronger group-orientation, there is usually more trust that individuals will be team players, making formal control mechanisms redundant (Nonaka and Johansson, 1985). Therefore, in general, one can expect a weaker preference for planning in collectivist cultures.

Preference for External Control

Cultures also differ with regard to the level of control that organizational members prefer to have over their environment. At the one extreme are cultures in which people strive to manage or even dominate their surroundings. In these countries, there is a strong desire to create the future and a fear of losing control of one's destiny. George Bernard Shaw's famous remark that 'to be in hell is to drift, to be in heaven is to steer,' neatly summarizes these feelings. The consequence is that organizations in these nations are strongly drawn to proactive and deliberate strategy making, under the motto 'plan or be planned for' (Ackoff, 1980). Drawing up plans to actively engage the outside world meets people's need to determine their own fate. This cultural characteristic is particularly pronounced in Western countries (Trompenaars, 1993).

At the other extreme are cultures in which most people passively accept their destiny. They believe that most external events are out of their hands and that they exert no control over the future. In such highly fatalistic cultures people tend to approach opportunities and threats reactively, on a day to day basis. Such muddling through behavior rarely leads to emergent strategy, but more often to disjointed, unpatterned action.

In the middle are cultures in which people believe neither in domination of, nor submission to, external circumstances. In these cultures people accept that events are unpredictable and that the environment cannot be tightly controlled, yet trust that individuals and organizations can proactively seek their own path among these uncertainties. The environment and the firm, it is thought, co-evolve through interaction and mutual adjustment, often in unforeseen ways. This requires firms to 'develop an attitude of receptivity and high adaptability to changing conditions' (Maruyama, 1984). This way of thinking is particularly pronounced in South-East Asia, and leads to a stronger inclination towards the incrementalism perspective (Kagono *et al.*, 1985; Schneider, 1989).

Time Orientation

A culture's time orientation can also be expected to influence national preferences for dealing with the paradox of deliberateness and emergentness. There are a number of dimensions along which cultures' perception of time can differ. Cultures can be more involved with the past, the present or the future, whereby some make a strong linear separation between these phases, while others emphasize the continuity of time or even its cyclical nature. With regard to the future, a distinction can also be made between cultures with a more short-term or long-term orientation (Hofstede, 1993; reading 1.5).

In general, it can be expected that people in cultures that heavily accentuate the past, or the present, over the future, will be less inclined to think and act strategically. In cultures that emphasize the near future, however, it is likely that individuals and organizations will exhibit a preference for planning. A focus on the not-too-distant future, which is more predictable than the long-term future, fits well with a planning approach. In these countries, intentions are formulated, courses of action are determined and resources are committed, but with a relatively short planning horizon. Plans will only be adopted if results can be expected in the 'foreseeable' future. As Hofstede reports, the English-speaking countries belong to this category of short-term oriented cultures (see also Calori, Valla and De Woot, 1994; Kagono *et al.*, 1985).

In cultures with a stronger long term orientation, incrementalism can be expected to be a more predominant perspective. Since the long term future is inherently unknown, planning for the future is seen as an inappropriate response. In these countries, it is generally believed that the unpredictability of the long term future must be accepted and accommodated. This requires an attitude of caution and flexibility, linked to curiosity, learning and persistence. Actions are often taken that are not optimal in the short run, but point in the right long term direction. As Hofstede reports, many South-East Asian countries fall into this category, as do some European countries.

Further Readings

Readers interested in an overview of the strategy formation literature have a number of good, although rather academically-oriented, articles they can choose from. 'How Strategies Develop in Organisations,' by Andy Bailey and Gerry Johnson, and 'An Integrative Framework for Strategy-Making Processes,' by Stuart Hart, both present short reviews of the main approaches to the topic of strategy process. However, if readers have more time, Henry Mintzberg's much longer article 'Strategy Formation: Schools of Thought' is also highly recommended.

There are many books that give a detailed rendition of how strategic planning should be conducted within organizations. Igor Ansoff's well-known textbook *Implanting Strategic Management* is an excellent, yet taxing, description of strategy making from a planning perspective, while George Steiner's *Strategic Planning: What Every Manager Must Know* is a more down to earth prescription. Between these two extremes is a whole range of widely-sold textbooks, such as Arthur Thompson and A.J. Strickland's *Strategic Management: Concepts and Cases*, and Thomas Wheelen and David Hunger's *Strategic Management and Business Policy*. For further reading on formal planning systems, Balaji Chakravarthy and Peter Lorange's book *Managing the Strategy Process: A Framework for a Multibusiness Firm* is a good place to start. On the link between planning and forecasting, the book *Forecasting, Planning, and Strategy for the 21st Century*, by Spiro Makridakis, provides a useful introduction.

The most articulate critic of planning is probably Henry Mintzberg, whose book *The Rise and Fall of Strategic Planning* makes for thought-provoking reading. David Hurst's article 'Why Strategic Management is Bankrupt' also provides many interesting arguments against strategic planning. For a more extensive description of the incrementalism perspective, James Brian Quinn's book *Strategies for Change* is still a good starting point. Ralph Stacey's excellent *Strategic Management and Organizational Dynamics* is one of the only textbooks incorporating incrementalist approaches. Also highly recommended are Ikujiro Nonaka's article 'Toward Middle-Up-Down Management: Accelerating Information Creation' and Robert Burgelman's article 'Corporate Entrepreneurship and Strategic Management: Insights from a Process Study.'

For a better understanding of the political processes involved in strategy formation the reader might want to turn to Andrew Pettigrew's article 'Strategy Formulation as a Political Process,' or to Jeffrey Pfeffer's book *Power in Organizations*. Graham Allison's book *The Essence of Decision: Explaining the Cuban Missile Crisis* is also highly recommended. The cultural processes are vividly described in Gerry Johnson's *Strategic Change and the Management Process*, and more popularly in Rosabeth Moss Kanter's *The Change Masters*. Further readings that explore the link between strategy formation and strategic change are presented at the end of Chapter 4.

References

Ackoff, R.L. (1980) *Creating the Corporate Future*, Wiley, Chichester.

Allaire, Y., and Firsirotu, M. (1990) Strategic Plans as Contracts, *Long Range Planning*, Vol. 23, No. 1, pp. 102–15.

Allison, G.T. (1969) Conceptual Models and The Cuban Missile Crisis, *The American Political Science Review*, No.3, September pp. 689–718.

Allison, G.T. (1971) *Essence of Decision: Explaining the Cuban Missile Crisis*, Little Brown, Boston.

Andrews, K.R., (1987) *The Concept of Corporate Strategy*, Third Edition, Irwin, Homewood, IL.

Ansoff, H.I. (1965) *Corporate Strategy: An Analytic Approach to Business Policy for Growth and Expansion*, McGraw-Hill, New York, p. 44.

Ansoff, H.I. (1991) Critique of Henry Mintzberg's The 'Design School': Reconsidering the Basic Premises of Strategic Management, *Strategic Management Journal*, September pp. 449–61.

Ansoff, H.I., and McDonnell, E. (1990) *Implanting Strategic Management*, 2nd edn, Prentice Hall, New York.

Bailey, A., and Johnson, G. (1992) How Strategies Develop in Organizations, in: Faulkner, D., and Johnson, G. (eds), *The Challenge of Strategic Management*, Kogan Page, London.

Bungay, S., and Goold, M. (1991) Creating a Strategic Control System, *Long Range Planning*, Vol. 24, No. 6, pp. 32–9.

Burgelman, R.A. (1983) Corporate Entrepreneurship and Strategic Management: Insights from a Process Study, *Management Science*, Vol. 29, No. 12, pp. 1349–64.

Burgelman, R.A. (1991) Intraorganizational Ecology of Strategy Making and Organizational Adaptation: Theory and Field Research, *Organization Science*, Vol. 2, pp. 239–62.

Calori, R., Valla, J.-P. and de Woot, Ph. (1994) Common Characteristics: The Ingredients of European Management, in Calori, R., and de Woot, Ph. (eds), *A European Management Model: Beyond Diversity*, Prentice Hall, Hemel Hempstead.

Chaffee, E.E. (1985) Three Models of Strategy, *Academy of Management Review*, January, pp. 89–98.

Chakravarthy, B.S., and Lorange, P. (1991) *Managing the Strategy Process: A Framework for a Multibusiness Firm*, Prentice Hall, Englewood Cliffs, NJ.

Chandler, A.D. (1962) *Strategy and Structure: Chapters in the History of the American Industrial Enterprise*, MIT Press, Cambridge, MA.

Christensen, C.R., Andrews, K.R., Bower, J.L., Hamermesh, R.G., and Porter, M.E. (1982) (1987) *Business Policy: Text and Cases*, 5th and 6th edns, Irwin, Homewood, IL.

Cohen, M.D., March, J.G., and Olsen, J.P. (1972) A Garbage Can Model of Organization Choice, *Administrative Science Quarterly*, March, pp. 1–25.

De Geus, A. (1988) Planning as Learning, *Harvard Business Review*, March/April, pp. 70–4.

Eccles, M. (1951) *Beckoning Frontiers*, Knopf, New York, p. 336.

Evans, J.S. (1991) Strategic Flexibility for High Technology Manoeuvres: A Conceptual Framework, *Journal of Management Studies*, January, pp. 69–89.

Ghemawat, P. (1991) *Commitment: The Dynamic of Strategy*, Free Press, New York.

Gilbert, X., and Lorange, P. (1995) National Approaches to Strategic Management – A Resource-based Perspective, *International Business Review*, Vol. 3, No. 4, pp. 411–23.

Gluck, F.W., Kaufman, S.P., and Walleck, A.S. (1982) The Four Phases of Strategic Management, Journal of Business Strategy, Winter, pp. 9–21.

Godet, M. (1987) *Scenarios and Strategic Management*, Butterworths, London.

Hampden-Turner, C., and Trompenaars, A. (1993) *The Seven Cultures of Capitalism: Value Systems for Creating Wealth in the United States, Japan, Germany, France, Britain, Sweden and the Netherlands*, Doubleday, New York.

Hart, S.L. (1992) An Integrative Framework for Strategy-Making Processes, *Academy of Management Review*, Vol. 17, No. 2 (April), pp. 327–51.

Hax, A.C., and Maljuf, N.S. (1984) *Strategic Management: An Integrative Approach*, Prentice Hall, Englewood Cliffs.

Hayashi, K. (1978) Corporate Planning Practices in Japanese Multinationals, *Academy of Management Journal*, Vol. 21, No. 2, pp. 211–26.

Hayes, R.H. (1985) Strategic Planning – Forward in Reverse?, *Harvard Business Review*, November/December, pp. 111–19.

Hedberg, B.L., Nystrom, P.C. and Starbuck, W.H. (1976) Camping on Seesaws: Prescriptions for a Self-Designing Organization, *Administrative Science Quarterly*, Vol. 21, March, pp. 41–65.

Hofstede, G. (1993) Cultural Constraints in Management Theories, *Academy of Management Executive*, Vol. 7, No. 1.

Hurst, D.K. (1986) Why Strategic Management is Bankrupt, *Organizational Dynamics*, Vol. 15 (Autumn), pp. 4–27.

Jelinek, M. (1979) *Institutionalizing Innovation*, Praeger, New York.

Johnson, G. (1987) *Strategic Change and the Management Process*, Basil Blackwell, Oxford.

Johnson, G. (1988) Rethinking Incrementalism, *Strategic Management Journal*, January/February, pp. 75–91.

Kagono, T., Nonaka, I. Sakakibara, K. and Okumara, A. (1985) *Strategic vs. Evolutionary Management*, North-Holland, Amsterdam.

Kanter, R. (1983) *The Change Masters: Innovation for Productivity in the American Corporation*, Basic Books, New York.

Kiechel, W., III. (1984) Sniping at Strategic Planning, *Planning Review*, May, pp. 8–11.

Langley, A. (1995) Between 'Paralysis and Analysis' and 'Extinction by Instinct', *Sloan Management Review*, Spring, pp. 63–76.

Lenz, R.T., and Lyles, M. (1985) Paralysis by Analysis: Is Your Planning System Becoming Too Rational?, *Long Range Planning*, Vol. 18, pp. 64–72.

Lessem, R., and Neubauer, F.F. (1994) *European Management Systems*, McGraw-Hill, London.

Lindblom, C.E. (1959) The Science of Muddling Through, *Public Administration Review*, Spring, pp. 79–88.

Lorange, P. (1980a) *Corporate Planning: An Executive Viewpoint*, Prentice Hall, Englewood Cliffs.

Lorange, P. (1980b) *Roles of the CEO in Strategic Planning and Control Processes*, in a seminar on The Role of General Management in Strategy Formulation and Evaluation, cosponsored by E.S.S.E.C., E.I.A.S.M., and I.A.E., Cergy, France, April 28–30, pp. 2.

Lorange, P. and Vancil, R.F. (1977) *Strategic Planning Systems*, Prentice Hall, Englewood Cliffs.

Lyles, M.A. (1981) Formulating Strategic Problems, Empirical Analysis and Model Development, *Strategic Management Journal*, January/March, pp. 61–75.

MacMillan, I.C. (1978) *Strategy Formulation: Political Concepts*, West, St. Paul, MN.

Majone, G., and Wildavsky, A. (1978) Implementation as Evolution, *Policy Studies Review Annual*, pp. 103–117.

Makridakis, S. (1990) *Forecasting, Planning, and Strategy for the 21st Century*, Free Press, New York.

Maruyama, M. (1984) Alternative Concepts of Management: Insights from Asia and Africa, *Asia Pacific Journal of Management*, January, pp. 100–11.

Marx, T.G. (1991) Removing the Obstacles to Effective Strategic Planning, *Long Range Planning*, August, pp. 21–8.

Mason, R.O., and Mitroff, I.I. (1981) *Challenging Strategic Planning Assumptions*, Wiley, New York.

Mintzberg, H. (1978) Patterns in Strategy Formation, *Management Science*, vol. 24, pp. 934–48.

Mintzberg, H. (1979) *The Structuring of Organizations: A Synthesis of the Research*, Prentice-Hall, Englewood Cliffs.

Mintzberg, H. (1990a) The Design School: Reconsidering the Basic Premises of Strategic Management, *Strategic Management Journal*, XI, pp. 171–95.

Mintzberg, H. (1990b) Strategy Formation: Schools of Thought, in: Frederickson, J. (ed.), *Perspectives on Strategic Management*, Ballinger, Boston.

Mintzberg, H. (1991) Learning 1, Planning 0: Reply to Igor Ansoff, *Strategic Management Journal*, September, pp. 463–66.

Mintzberg, H. (1994a) The Fall and Rise of Strategic Planning, *Harvard Business Review*, January-February, pp. 107–14.

Mintzberg, H. (1994b) *The Rise and Fall of Strategic Planning*, Prentice-Hall, Englewood Cliffs.

Mintzberg, H., and Waters, J.A. (1985) Of Strategies: Deliberate and Emergent, *Strategic Management Journal*, July/September, pp. 257–72.

Morgenthau, H. (1960) *Politics Among Nations*, Third Edition, New York, pp. 191.

Noel, A. (1989) Strategic Cores and Magnificent Obsessions: Discovering Strategy Formulation through Daily Activities of CEO's, *Strategic Management Journal*, Summer, pp. 33–49.

Nonaka, I., and Johansson, J.K. (1985) Japanese Management: What about 'Hard' Skills?, *Academy of Management Review*, Vol. 10, No. 2, pp. 181–91.

Nonaka, I. (1988a) Toward Middle-Up-Down Management: Accelerating Information Creation, *Sloan Management Review*, Spring, pp. 9–18.

Nonaka, I. (1988b) Creating Organizational Order Out of Chaos: Self-Renewal in Japanese Firms, *California Management Review*, Spring, pp. 57–73.

Ohmae, K. (1982) *The Mind of the Strategist*, McGraw-Hill, New York.

Pascale, R.T. (1984) Perspectives on Strategy: The Real Story Behind Honda's Success, *California Management Review*, Vol. 26, No. 3 (Spring), pp. 47–72.

Pettigrew, A.M. (1977) Strategy Formulation as a Political Process, *International Studies of Management and Organization*, Summer, pp. 47–72.

Pettigrew, A.M. (1988) *The Management of Strategic Change*, Basil Blackwell, Oxford.

Pfeffer, J. (1981) *Power in Organizations*, Pitman, Marshfield, Mass.

Pinchot, G., III. (1985) *Intrapreneuring: Why You Don't Have to Leave the Company to Become an Entrepreneur*, Harper & Row, New York.

Porter, M.E. (1987) The State of Strategic Thinking, *Economist*, May 23, p. 21.

Quinn, J.B. (1978) Strategic Change: 'Logical Incrementalism', *Sloan Management Review*, Fall, pp. 7–21.

Quinn, J.B. (1980a) Managing Strategic Change, *Sloan Management Review*, Summer, pp. 3–20.

Quinn, J.B. (1980b) *Strategies for Change*, Irwin, Homewood, IL.

Quinn, J.B. (1985) Managing Innovation: Controlled Chaos, *Harvard Business Review*, Vol. 63, May/June, pp. 73–84.

Rittel, H.W., and Webber, M.M. (1973) Dilemmas in a General Theory of Planning, *Policy Sciences*, Vol. 4, pp. 155–69.

Rumelt, R.P. (1995) Inertia and Transformation, in: Montgomery, C.A. (ed.), *Resource-based and Evolutionary Theories of the Firm: Towards a Synthesis*, Kluwer Academic Publishers, Boston, pp. 101–32.

Schelling, T. (1960) *The Strategy of Conflict*, New York, p. 232.

Schneider, S.C. (1989) Strategy Formulation: The Impact of National Culture, *Organization Studies*, Vol. 10, No. 2, pp. 149–68.

Schrader, C.B., Taylor, I., and Dalton, D.R. (1984) Strategic Planning and Organizational Performance: A Critical Appraisal, Journal of Management, Summer, pp. 149–71.

Selznick, P. (1957) *Leadership in Administration: A Sociological Interpretation*, Harper & Row, New York.

Shrivastava, P., and Grant, J. (1985) Empirically Derived Models of Strategic Decision-Making Processes, *Strategic Management Journal*, Vol. 6, pp. 97–113.

Smircich, L., and Stubbart, C. (1985) Strategic Management in an Enacted World, *Academy of Management Review*, Vol. 10, pp. 724–36.

Stacey, R.D. (1993) Strategy as Order Emerging from Chaos, *Long Range Planning*, Vol. 26, No.1, pp. 10–17.

Stacey, R.D. (1996) *Strategic Management and Organisational Dynamics*, 2nd edn, Pitman, London.

Steiner, G.A. (1979) *Strategic Planning: What Every Manager Must Know*, Free Press, New York.

Steiner, G.A. and Schollhammer, H. (1975) Pitfalls in Multi-National Long-Range Planning, *Long Range Planning*, April, pp. 2–12.

Thompson, A.A., and Strickland III, A.J. (1995) *Strategic Management: Concepts and Cases*, 8th edn, Irwin, Chicago.

Trompenaars, A. (1993) *Riding the Waves of Culture: Understanding Cultural Diversity in Business*, The Economist Books, London.

Wack, P. (1985a) Scenarios: Uncharted Waters Ahead, *Harvard Business Review*, September/October, pp. 73–89.

Wack, P. (1985b) Scenarios: Shooting the Rapids, *Harvard Business Review*, November/December, pp. 139–50.

Weidenbaum, M., and Hughes, S. (1996) *The Bamboo Network: How Expatriate Chinese Entrepreneurs Are Creating a New Economic Superpower in Asia*, Free Press, pp. 23–59.

Wheelen, T.L., and Hunger, J.D. (1992) Strategic Management and Business Policy, 4th edn, Addison-Wesley.

Wildavsky, A. (1979) *Speaking Truth to Power: The Art and Craft of Policy Analysis*, Little, Brown & Co., Toronto.

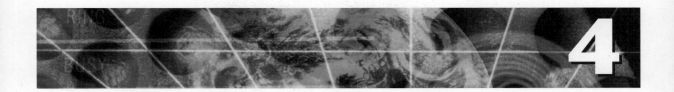

Strategic Change

*Every act of creation is first of all an
act of destruction.*

(Pablo Picasso 1881–1973; Spanish artist)

Slow and steady wins the race.

(*The Hare and the Tortoise*, Aesop c. 620–c. 560 BC; Greek writer)

The Paradox of Revolution and Evolution

As became clear in the previous chapter, strategy formation is concerned
with the realization of change. In a world of changing technologies, transforming economies, shifting demographics, reforming governments, fluctuating consumer preferences, and dynamic competition, making strategy
means making organizations change. In such a turbulent environment, an
organization's mission might remain unaltered for a long period of time, but
its objectives and behavior will repeatedly need to change. For strategists, it
is not an issue of whether organizations must change, but of where, how
and in what direction they must change.

In Chapter 3, the strategy formation debate focused on the question
whether realized strategic changes are arrived at deliberately or emergently.
Proponents of the planning perspective argued that strategic change should
be deliberately conceived, while supporters of the incrementalism perspective championed the case of emergent strategic change. The disagreement
between the two sides centered on the issue of *intentions* – should strategic
changes be planned in advance or unfold in the absence of intentions?

In this chapter, the discussion will move to the issue of *continuity* –
should strategic changes gradually evolve out of the current state of
affairs, or mark a radical departure from the organization's past? Should
strategic change be *evolutionary*, that is, piecemeal and continuous, or
revolutionary, which is dramatic and discontinuous? What is the nature

of effective strategic change processes? Again, opinions differ considerably, and the subject is hotly contested by both practitioners and theorists. There is a wide range of differing views, each dealing with the tension between revolution and evolution in a different way. However, at the extreme poles of this debate, two diametrically opposed positions can be identified. On the one hand, there are strategists who argue that strategic change in organizations should be pushed through in a revolutionary manner, by taking radical, comprehensive and swift action. We shall refer to this point of view as the *discontinuous change* perspective. On the other hand, there are strategists who argue that strategic change should not be a one-shot, big bang affair, but should be approached in an evolutionary manner, with an emphasis on permanent learning and constant upgrading. This point of view will be referred to as the *continuous change* perspective.

Following the familiar debate model, the inquiry in this chapter into the nature of effective strategic change will be structured by contrasting these two extremes. By comparing the two opposite ways of dealing with the paradox of revolution and evolution, a better understanding of the issues under discussion should be gained. In the next few pages, the discontinuous change and continuous change perspectives will be further explained, and finally summarized in Table 4.1.

The Discontinuous Change Perspective

According to advocates of the discontinuous change perspective, it is a common misconception that organizations develop gradually. It is often assumed that organizations move fluidly from one state to the next, encountering minimal friction. In reality, however, organizational change is arduous and encounters significant resistance. Pressure must be exerted, and tension must mount, before a major shift can be accomplished. Movement, therefore, is not steady and constant, as a current in the sea, but abrupt and dramatic, as in an earthquake, where resistance gives way and tension is released in a short shock. In general, the more significant a change is, the more intense the shock will be.

Proponents of this perspective argue that people and organizations exhibit a natural reluctance to change. Humans have a strong preference for stability. Once general policy has been determined, most organizations are inclined to settle into a fixed way of working. The organizational structure will solidify, formal systems will be installed, standard operating procedures will be defined, key competence areas will be identified, a distribution of power will emerge, and a corporate culture will become established. The stability of an organization will be especially high if all of these elements form a consistent and cohesive configuration (Mintzberg, 1991). Moreover, if an organization experiences a period of success, this usually strongly reinforces the existing way of working (Miller, 1990).

It must be emphasized that stability is not inherently harmful, as it allows people to 'get to work'. A level of stability is required to function efficiently (March and Simon, 1958; Thompson, 1967). Constant upheaval would only create an organizational mess. There would be prolonged confusion about tasks and authority, poorly structured internal communication and coordination, and a lack of clear standards and routines. The instability brought on by such continuously changing processes, procedures, and structures would lead to widespread insecurity, political manoevering, and interdepartmental conflicts.

Advocates of the discontinuous change perspective, therefore, argue that periods of relative stability are necessary for the proper functioning of organizations. However, the downside of stability is *inertia* – the unwillingness and/or inability to change, even when it is urgently required. An unwillingness to change can be due to the uncertainty and ambiguity that unavoidably accompany strategic shifts (e.g. Argyris, 1990; Pondy, Boland and Thomas, 1988). It is also common that individuals or departments resist change because they believe that their interests will be damaged (e.g. Allison, 1969, reading 3.3 in this book; Pettigrew, 1988). An inability to change can be caused by *lock-in* factors, such as fixed investments, inflexible standards and long-term commitments (e.g. Arthur, 1996; reading 8.5; Ghemawat, 1991). However, change is often also impeded by the tenacity of organizational belief systems – cognitive maps shared by members of an organization are not easily adapted, as discussed in Chapter 2.

When change is needed and inertia must be overcome, a series of small nudges will not be sufficient to get the organization into motion. A big shove will be needed. For strategic change to really happen, measures must be radical and comprehensive. A coordinated assault is usually required to decisively break through organizational defenses and 'shock therapy' is needed to fundamentally change people's cognitive maps. Solving lock-in problems generally also demands a quick, organization-wide switch-over to a new system. For instance, *business process reengineering* must involve all aspects of the value chain at once (Hammer, 1990; reading 4.1; Hammer and Champy, 1993). However, proponents of the discontinuous change perspective emphasize that the period of turmoil must not take too long. People cannot be indefinitely confronted with high levels of uncertainty and ambiguity, and a new equilibrium is vital for a new period of efficient operations.

Therefore, the long term pattern of organizational change is not gradual, but episodic. Periods of relative stability are interrupted by short and dramatic periods of instability, during which revolutionary changes take place (Greiner, 1972). This pattern of development has also been recognized in a variety of other sciences (Gersick, 1991). Following the natural historians Eldredge and Gould, it is often referred to as the *punctuated equilibrium* view.

Some authors taking this view argue that strategists proactively seek the benefits of discontinuous change. In a competitive environment, they state, many firms will attempt to gain an advantage over their rivals by innovating. Staying one step ahead of other companies in the competitive game by means of technological or organizational innovation is regarded by many as a key success factor (see Chapter 5). Firms that can pull off major innovations in a short period of time will be the winners in the competitive sweepstakes. Such innovation, it must be noted, is inherently revolutionary. Creating novel products, processes, and business formulas requires a sharp break with the past. Old ways must be discarded, before new methods can be adopted. This is the essence of what Schumpeter (1950) referred to as the process of *creative destruction*, inherent in the capitalist system. This process is not orderly and protracted, but disruptive and intense. Therefore, it is argued, to be a competitive success, firms must learn to master the skill of revolutionary change (e.g. D'Aveni, 1994; Hamel, 1996). Rapid implementation of system-wide change is an essential organizational capability.

Other authors argue that discontinuous change is usually the reaction to an organizational crisis. In their view, inertia is usually too strong to be overcome by will-power alone. Organizations tend to stay close to stability, making minor changes where necessary, but not upsetting the basic beliefs, processes, systems and power structures. For significant changes to take place, a crisis is needed – either real or induced. A major environmental jolt can be the reason for a sudden crisis (e.g. Meyer, 1982; Meyer, Brooks and Goes, 1990), but often a misalignment between the firm and its environment grows over a longer period of time (e.g. Johnson, 1988; reading 9.4; Strebel, 1992). As tension mounts, the organization becomes more receptive for painful changes. This increased willingness to change under crisis circumstances coincides with the physical law that 'under pressure things become fluid'. As long as the pressure persists, revolutionary change is possible, but as soon as the pressure lets up the organization will resolidify in a new form, inhibiting any further major changes (e.g. Miller and Friesen, 1984; Tushman, Newman and Romanelli, 1986; reading 4.3).

It can be concluded that strategic change, whether proactive or reactive, requires an abrupt break with the status quo. Change management demands strong leadership to rapidly push through stressful, discomforting and risky shifts in an organization's structure, culture, processes and behavior. Battling the sources of inertia and turning crisis into opportunity are the key qualities needed by strategists implementing strategic change. Ultimately, strategists should know when to change and when it is more wise to seek stability – they should know when to trigger an 'earthquake' and when to avoid one.

The Continuous Change Perspective

According to proponents of the continuous change perspective, if organizations shift by 'earthquake', it is usually their own 'fault'. The problem with revolution is that it commonly leads to the need for further revolution at a later time – discontinuous change creates its own boom-and-bust cycle. Revolutionary change is generally followed by a strong organizational yearning for stability. The massive, organization-wide efforts to implement agonizing changes can often only be sustained for a short period of time, after which change momentum collapses. Any positive inclination towards change among employees will have totally disappeared by the time the reorganizations are over. Consequently, the organization lapses back into a stable state, in which only minor changes occur. This stable situation is maintained until the next round of shock therapy becomes necessary, to jolt the organization out of its ossified state.

To supporters of the continuous change perspective, the boom-and-bust approach to strategic change is like running a marathon by sprinting and then standing still to catch one's breath. Yet, marathons are not won by good sprinters, but by runners with endurance and persistence, who can keep a steady pace – runners who are more inspired by the tortoise than by the hare. The same is true for companies in the marathon of competition. Some companies behave like the hare in Aesop's fable, showing off their ability to take great leaps, but burdened by a short span of attention. Other companies behave more like the tortoise, moving gradually and undramatically, but unrelentingly and without interruption, focusing on the long-term goal. In the short run, the hares might dash ahead, suggesting that making big leaps forward is the best way to compete. But in the long run, the most formidable contenders will be the diligent tortoise, whose ability to maintain a constant speed will help them to win the race.

Therefore, the 'big ideas', 'frame-breaking innovations' and 'quantum leaps' that so mesmerize proponents of the discontinuous change perspective, are viewed with suspicion by supporters of continuous change. Revolution not only causes unnecessary disruption and dysfunctional crises, but is usually the substitute of diligence. If organizations do not have the stamina to continuously improve themselves, quick fix discontinuous change can be used as a short-term remedy. Where organizations do not exhibit the drive to permanently upgrade their capabilities, revolutionary innovations can be used as the short cut to renewed competitiveness. In other words, the lure of revolutionary change is that of short-term results. By abruptly and dramatically making major changes, managers hope to rapidly book tangible progress – and instantly win recognition and promotion (Imai, 1986; reading 4.2).

To advocates of the continuous change perspective, a preference for revolution usually reflects an unhealthy obsession with the short term. Continuous change, on the other hand, is more long term in orientation. Development is gradual, piecemeal and undramatic, but as it is constantly maintained over a longer period of time, the aggregate level of change can still be significant. Three organizational characteristics are important for keeping up a steady pace of change. First, all employees within the firm should be committed to *continuously improve*. Everyone within the organization should be driven by constructive dissatisfaction with the status quo. This attitude, that things can always be done better, reflects a rejection of stability and the acceptance of bounded instability (Stacey, 1993; reading 9.2) – everything is open to change.

Second, everyone in the firm must be motivated to *continuously learn* (e.g. Argyris, 1990; Senge, 1990; reading 4.4). People within the organization must constantly update their knowledge-base, which not only means acquiring new information, but also challenging accepted company wisdom. Learning goes hand in hand with unlearning – changing the cognitive maps shared within the organization (McCaskey, 1982; reading 2.4). In this respect, it is argued that an atmosphere of crisis actually inhibits continuous change. In a situation of crisis, it is not a matter of 'under pressure things become fluid', but 'in the cold everything freezes'. Crisis circumstances might lower people's resistance to imposed change, but it also blunts their motivation for experimenting and learning, as they brace themselves for the imminent shock. Crisis encourages people to seek security and to focus on the short term, instead of opening up and working towards long-term development (Bate, 1994).

Third, everyone in the firm must be motivated to *continuously adapt*. Constant adjustment to external change and fluid internal realignment should be pursued. To this end, the organization must actively avoid inertia, by combating the forces of ossification. Strategists should strive to create flexible structures and systems, to encourage an open and tolerant corporate culture, and to provide sufficient job and career security for employees to accept other forms of ambiguity and uncertainty (e.g. Kagono *et al.*, 1985; Nonaka, 1988).

These three characteristics of an evolutionary organization – continuous improvement, learning and adaptation – have in common the fact that basically everyone in the organization is involved. Revolutionary change can be initiated by top management, possibly assisted and urged on by a few external consultants, and carried by a hand full of change agents or champions (e.g. Maidique, 1980; Day, 1994). Evolutionary change, on the other hand, requires an organization-wide effort. Leaders can not learn on behalf of their organizations, nor can they orchestrate all of the small improvements and adaptations needed for continuous change. Strategists must realize that evolution can be led from the top, but not imposed from the top. For strategists to realize change, hands-on guidance of organizational developments is more important than commanding organizational actions (see Bourgeois and Brodwin, 1983; reading 9.3).

The question within the field of strategic management is, therefore, whether strategic change is primarily a revolutionary or an evolutionary process. Should strategists strive to implement radical, comprehensive and dramatic changes, or should they emphasize continuous improvement, learning and adaptation? Not all strategists agree on the answers to these questions, leaving readers with the challenge of formulating their own conclusions with regard to the nature of strategic change. Readers will have to come to terms themselves with the paradox of revolution and evolution (see Table 4.1).

Defining the Issues: Magnitude and Pace

Before proceeding with the 'debate' between proponents of the discontinuous and continuous change perspectives, it is useful to clarify the key topics under discussion. As will be seen, the disagreements between the two extreme points of view revolve around two major issues: the *magnitude* of change and the *pace* of change. In the next paragraphs these two issues will be further explored, to set the stage for the debate articles that follow.

TABLE 4.1
Discontinuous change versus continuous change perspective

	Discontinuous Change Perspective	Continuous Change Perspective
Emphasis on	Revolution over evolution	Evolution over revolution
Strategic change as	Disruptive innovation/turnaround	Uninterrupted improvement
Strategic change process	Creative destruction	Organic adaptation
Magnitude of change	Radical, comprehensive and dramatic	Moderate, piecemeal and undramatic
Pace of change	Abrupt, unsteady and intermittent	Gradual, steady and constant
Fundamental change requires	Sudden break with status quo	Permanent learning and flexibility
Reaction to environmental jolts	Shock therapy	Continuous adjustment
View of organizational crises	Under pressure things becomes fluid	In the cold everything freezes
Long-term change dynamics	Stable and unstable states alternate	Persistent transient state
Long-term change pattern	Punctuated equilibrium	Gradual development

The Magnitude of Change

Change does not happen everywhere in the same way. Even to the casual observer, it is obvious that processes of change differ according to the thing being changed – the process of changing a satellite's orbit is inherently different than the process of changing one's socks. For anything useful to be said about change, it must be specified what the object is that is being changed. This is particularly true for the poorly defined topic of 'strategic change'. To have an insightful debate in this chapter, it is essential to clarify which elements of an organization are the objects of change, and what qualifies as 'strategic'. Only then can the discussion turn to the determination of the best type of strategic change process.

Organizations are complex systems, consisting of many different elements, each of which can be changed. Many frameworks exist that disassemble organizations into a number of components, to assist analysts in gaining an overview of an organization's complex composition. For instance, the 7S framework, put forward by Waterman, Peters and Phillips (1980), divides the organization into seven interconnected elements, that can all be changed: structure, strategy, systems, style, staff, skills and super-ordinate goals. For the discussion in this chapter, however, the simple framework proposed by Mintzberg and Westley (1992) is particularly insightful (see Table 4.2).

Mintzberg and Westley first distinguish between change in the spheres of organization and strategy. Altering the *state* of the organization has traditionally been the focus of the field of organizational behavior, while changing the *direction* of the organization has been central to the field of strategic management. Obviously the two spheres are linked and both must be discussed to understand organizational change. However, it is important

TABLE 4.2
Levels and spheres of
organizational change
(Mintzberg and Westley,
1992)

	Changes in Organization (State)	Changes in Strategy (Direction)
More Conceptual (Thought)	Culture	Vision
	Structure	Positions
	Systems	Programs
More Concrete (Action)	People	Facilities

to note that changes in one sphere are not always accompanied by full and simultaneous changes in the other.

Second, Mintzberg and Westley distinguish between different levels of change, from the broadest, most conceptual level, all the way down to the narrowest, most concrete. At the highest level, the collective mindset within the organization can be the object of change, both in the form of the organizational culture and the strategic vision. One level lower, it can be the organizational structure and corresponding strategic positions that need to be altered. Even more concrete is the next level of organizational systems and strategic programs, at which tangible change efforts can be directed. Finally, at the most concrete level, are the actual operations that can be the target of adjustment. At this level of action, it can be the actors (the people or their jobs) and the activities (the value-adding processes or the facilities) that are changed. Clearly, changes at the various levels are linked and understanding organizational change requires a holistic view of the entire range. However, not all organizational changes are strategic. Autonomous operational changes with no impact on the top two levels do not qualify as strategic. For instance, downsizing is usually not strategic, since vision and position (and culture and structure) are not altered. Only changes that affect the top two levels constitute strategic change.

If the elements in Table 4.2 are the major aspects of the organization that can be changed, the first question to be asked in this debate is how major the changes to these elements should be? What should be the *magnitude of change*? This issue can be divided into two component parts.

1   *Scope of change.* The first bone of contention is whether all eight aspects of the organization need to be shifted in unison, or whether bits and pieces can be changed one after the other. The two perspectives take diametrically opposed positions on this point. In the discontinuous change perspective, revolution demands comprehensive action on all eight fronts – the scope of change must be broad. In the continuous change perspective, evolution demands a high number of piecemeal adjustments to be made over a prolonged period of time. Therefore, while the accumulated changes might be broad in scope, the scope of each individual change is rather narrow.

2   *Amplitude of change.* The second point of disagreement is whether the eight aspects of Table 4.2 need to be changed in a radical or moderate manner.

Again the two perspectives express diametrically opposed opinions. In the discontinuous change perspective, revolution demands a radical departure from the present situation – the amplitude of change should be high. In the continuous change perspective, evolution demands gradual development out of the present situation by means of moderate steps – the amplitude of changes should be low.

These two dimensions together determine the magnitude of change, as illustrated in Figure 4.1. What this diagram emphasizes, is that in terms of magnitude, revolution and evolution are the two extreme cases of change. In practice, a wide variety of possibilities exist between these two poles.

The Pace of Change

The second question dividing the two perspectives is how change should take place over time. The two parties disagree on what the *pace of change* should be. This issue can also be decomposed into two related parts.

1   *Tempo of change.* The first matter of dispute is whether change should take place in short bursts or should be realized over a longer period of time. Again the two perspectives adopt opposing vantage points. In the discontinuous change perspective, revolution demands fast action within a short timespan, after which the rate of change tapers off, until the next 'storming' effort is needed. This leads to an unsteady tempo of change. In the continuous change perspective, evolution demands a constant rate of change that is maintained indefinitely, without interruption. In other words, the tempo of change should be steady.

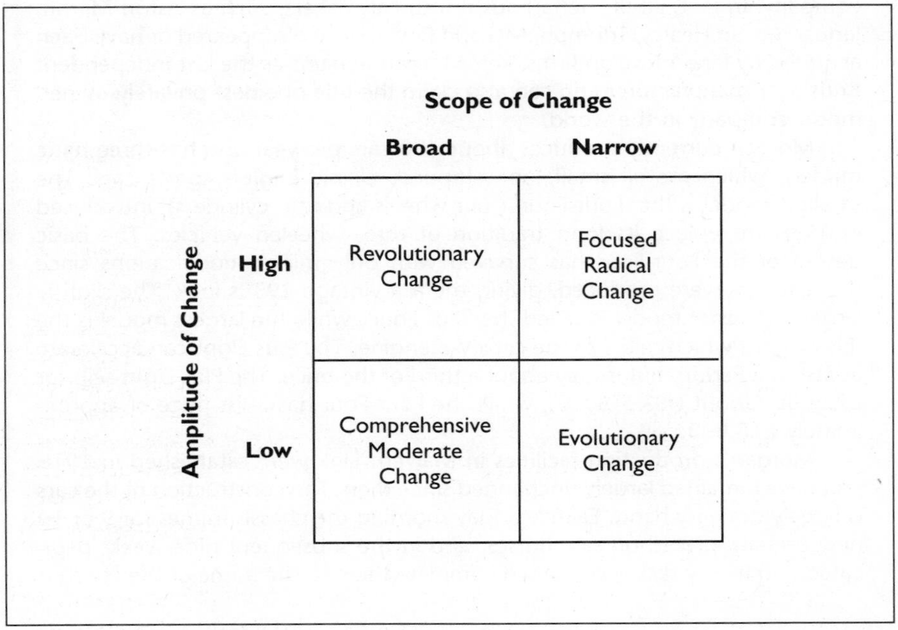

FIGURE 4.1
The magnitude of change

2   *Timing of change.* The second topic of debate has to do with the moment at which change should be realized. The question is whether change requires immediate action or can be gradually implemented over a longer period of time. Supporters of the discontinuous change perspective are inclined to view all strategic changes as highly urgent – the faster a change is pushed through, the sooner the competitive benefits of the change can be enjoyed. If a strategic change is a proactive innovation, then a rapid *transformation* can result in a major lead over rival firms. If the strategic change is a reaction to an organizational crisis, then a rapid *turnaround* is highly advantageous. Therefore, the timing of change should usually be 'as soon as possible'. Proponents of the continuous change perspective, on the other hand, tend to emphasize the need for persist change over the need for immediate change. In their view, getting off to a flying start is not that difficult, but carrying a change all the way through is the challenge. Therefore, enough time should be taken to gradually improve, learn and adapt. Crises requiring immediate action should avoided, where possible, by maintaining a flexible and proactive stance.

EXHIBIT 4.1
Morgan Motor Company
Short Case

MORGAN MOTOR COMPANY: (W)RECKLESS DRIVING?

Henry Fredrick Stanley Morgan was an apprentice engineer at the Great Western Railways works in Swindon, Great Britain, at the start of the 20th century, as were two other young men, whose names have become motor industry icons – Henry Royce and W.O. Bentley. All three went on to establish their own automobile manufacturing firms, but Morgan Motor Company, founded in 1909, is the only one that has survived as an independent company. In fact, all of the famous British car makers, such as Aston Martin, Jaguar, Austin Healey, Triumph, MG and Rover, have disappeared or have been acquired by larger foreign firms. Yet, Morgan remains as the last independent British car manufacturer and can also claim the title of oldest privately-owned motor company in the world.

Morgan currently produces about 480 cars per year and has three basic models, which are all small, open-topped, classic English sports cars. The smallest model is the 'Four-Four' (four wheels and four cylinders), introduced in 1936 to replace its long tradition of three-wheeled vehicles. The basic design of the Four-Four has survived with only minor modifications since the first cars were produced, giving them a vintage 1930s look. The slightly larger and faster model is called the 'Plus Four', while the largest model is the 'Plus Eight', which refers to the car's V-8 engine. The Plus Eight can accelerate as fast as a Ferrari, but is only about a third of the price. The Plus Eight sells for £26,000 (about US$ 50,000), while the Four-Four has a list price of approximately £18,000.

Morgan's production facilities in Malvern Link were established in 1919 and have remained largely unchanged since then. The construction of the cars is largely done by hand. Each Monday morning the chassis frames for 9 or 10 new cars are placed on saw horses, and in the subsequent nine weeks dedicated and highly skilled craftsmen complete the car. The frame of the coach is made of 100-year old ash wood, requiring precision carpentry. The exterior is finished with steel or aluminium sheet metal, demanding excellent metal working skills. All of this work is labor-intensive. Labor cost is estimated at 30–40 percent of the total cost. This mode of production also depends heavily on the abilities of the approximately 100 craftsmen employed by the company. Therefore, emphasis is placed on training and taking in a constant flow of apprentices. While a high proportion of the parts are made in-house, other components, such as the engine, rear axles, chassis, transmissions, windshields and electric parts, are all obtained from outside suppliers. By integrating these state-of-the-art components into its classic design, Morgan combines the best of both worlds – tradition and up-to-date technology.

In the market place, Morgan also seems to be cruising at a constant speed. While the company only has the capacity to produce 480 cars per year, there is a waiting list of about 3000 eager buyers, who on average have to wait six years before they can come to Malvern Link to see their car being produced. And these are the people who take the trouble to order and wait. Many more potential customers give up or change their minds once the long delivery time becomes apparent. The demand is so strong, that second-hand Morgans sell for almost the same price as new ones – sometimes even higher! Half of the cars are sold abroad, mostly in Western Europe, but also in Japan and North America. The other half is sold in Britain, and all quite profitably. Morgan earns a pre-tax profit of over £2000 (US$ 4000) per vehicle, while the large car manufacturers typically make a little over £300.

While Morgan sounds relatively successful, not everyone believes that the company is developing in the right way. Some analysts believe the company is squandering its enormous potential. One outspoken outsider has been Sir John Harvey-Jones, the well-known former CEO of ICI, the giant British chemical company. In the early 1990s, Harvey-Jones starred in a series of television programs produced by the BBC called 'The Troubleshooter'. In these programs Harvey-Jones went into small firms and made suggestions for improvement. One of the companies he visited for an episode was the Morgan Motor Company. His conclusion was that gradual modifications to Morgan's production system and market strategy would not be enough to secure the company's future. Radical changes would be needed for Morgan to remain prosperous. In the opinion of Harvey-Jones, the profits at Morgan were too low to give it the stamina to survive the shock of changes in the environment. His suggestion was to increase production to at least 600 cars per year by moving to a more up-to-date production facility. New production technologies could be introduced and the firm would be less dependent on scarce craftsmen. The investment in a new plant could be financed by significantly raising the price of the cars. The fact that people were willing to wait for years or pay more than the list price to obtain a Morgan, indicated to Harvey-Jones that the cars were underpriced and that the market would easily accept price increases. Using a waiting list to cushion the firm against swings in demand seemed to Harvey-Jones to be overly cautious.

Yet, Peter and Charles Morgan, the son and grandson of the firm's founder, have remained unrepentant. They have fiercely resisted the pressure to raise production levels and prices. 'Our objective is to be in business for another 50 years,' has been Charles Morgan's stern response. In reaction to the suggestions by Harvey-Jones in 'The Troubleshooter,' Charles Morgan sent an open letter to a newspaper, writing: 'It is Sir John's view that we should double production in a short time scale, paying for this by increasing the price of the car and investing in an expensive new plant. His methods would result in making many changes in the way the Morgan is built. We strongly disagree with his solution, and believe the Morgan policy of gradual and carefully considered change will enable us to maintain the car's qualities, and unique appeal, and thereby ensure its survival for the foreseeable future. Sir John's criticisms have been noted, but they are unworthy of us.'

Morgan's approach has been to strive for gradual improvement. For instance, the car designs have been modified to facilitate airbags and a computerized just-in-time stock control system has been introduced. Alterations in the plant layout and minor changes in production practices are considered, but Morgan is not receptive to any large-scale reengineering efforts or bold strategic initiatives. The question is, however, whether these minor adaptations will be enough to keep Morgan healthy in the long run. Are the changes being made adequate to keep up with shifts in the environment? If a downturn hits the industry, will Morgan be sufficiently robust to survive or will it then pay for its unwillingness to make big changes in the fat years? In short, is the pace and magnitude of change within Morgan high enough, or should Charles Morgan reconsider the value of revolutionary change?

Sources: Morgan Website; *The Economist*, December 25th 1993; Goulet and Rappaport, 1992.

The Debate and the Readings

As opening contribution in the 'virtual debate', Michael Hammer's 'Reengineering Work: Don't Automate, Obliterate' has been selected to represent the discontinuous change perspective. This paper was published in *Harvard Business Review* in 1990 and was followed in 1993 by the highly influential book *Reengineering the Corporation: A Manifesto for Business Revolution*, that Hammer co-authored with James Champy. In this article, Hammer explains the concept of reengineering in much the same way as in the best-selling book. 'At the heart of reengineering,' he writes, 'is the notion of discontinuous thinking – of recognizing and breaking away from the outdated rules and fundamental assumptions that underlie operations.' In his view, radically redesigning business processes 'cannot be planned meticulously and accomplished in small and cautious steps. It's an all-or-nothing proposition with an uncertain result.' He exhorts managers to 'think big,' by setting high goals, taking bold steps and daring to accept a high risk. In short, he preaches business revolution, and the tone of his article is truly that of a manifesto – impassioned, fervent, with here and there 'a touch of fanaticism.'

Equally impassioned is the argumentation in the second reading, 'Kaizen', by Masaaki Imai, which has been selected to represent the continuous change perspective. This article has been taken from Imai's famous book *Kaizen: The Key to Japan's Competitive Success*. Kaizen (pronounced Ky'zen) is a Japanese term, that is best translated as continuous improvement. Imai argues that it is this continuous improvement philosophy that best explains the competitive strength of so many Japanese companies. In his view, Western companies have an unhealthy obsession with one-shot innovations and revolutionary change. They are fixated on the great-leap forward, while disregarding the power of accumulated small changes. Imai believes that innovations are also important for competitive success, but that they should be embedded in an organization that is driven to continuously improve.

While the articles by Hammer and Imai clearly illustrate the fundamentals of the two change perspectives, both are strongly focused on operational changes, instead of strategic changes. To rectify this imbalance, two articles have been included that emphasize the strategic level. Reading 4.3 is 'Convergence and Upheaval: Managing the Unsteady Pace of Organizational Evolution,' by Michael Tushman, William Newman and Elaine Romanelli. This often-cited contribution, like Hammer, takes a discontinuous change perspective, but develops a more sophisticated argumentation. While Hammer presents revolution as the radical measure needed to break the shackles of antiquated business systems, it is unclear what the corporation must do after it is reengineered. Tushman, Newman and Romanelli look beyond a single episode of revolution, to the longer term pattern of organizational development. In their view, short periods of revolutionary upheaval are usually followed by longer periods of equilibrium during which only small adaptations are made. After several years of relative stability, which they call convergence, the next wave of frame-breaking changes sweep through the organization. This leads to a cyclical pattern of convergence and sharp upheavals, referred to as punctuated equilibrium. According to Tushman, Newman and Romanelli, this pattern of organizational development is commonplace in practice and understandably so. They argue that piecemeal approaches to major change tend to get bogged down in politics, individual resistance to change and organizational inertia. Therefore, an abrupt, all-at-once approach to change is needed. The big challenge to top management, they believe, is to initiate upheavals proactively, instead of having to respond in the face of an unfolding crisis.

Reading 4.4 is 'Building Learning Organizations' by Peter Senge. This article summarizes many of the major points of Senge's acclaimed book *The Fifth Discipline: The Art and Practice of the Learning Organization*. Although Senge does not explicitly argue in favor of the evolutionary approach to change, his emphasis on building organizations that can constantly learn and renew themselves place him within the continuous change tradition. Senge's main argument is that leaders cannot learn on behalf of their organizations and then push through the strategic changes they believe should be made. In his view, leaders must facilitate organizational learning – leaders 'are responsible for building organizations where people are continually expanding their capabilities to shape their future.' Creating organizations that want to adapt, learn and evolve, means avoiding the traditional sources of inertia. Senge believes that one of the keys to continuous learning is motivation. He suggests that the drive to learn can best be stimulated by establishing a creative tension between the current reality and a compelling vision of the future. Furthermore, learning requires a teacher. Not someone with the right answers, but a leader who can ask challenging questions and can shake up existing cognitive maps. Finally, Senge also argues that organizations must be designed in a way that they enable learning instead of impeding it.

Confusingly, many authors, including the above, speak of change and learning, revolution and evolution, and discontinuity and continuity, without much reference to the context. They present a generic approach to change, which is believed to be generally applicable. In the last contribution, 'Choosing the Right Change Path,' Paul Strebel challenges the implicit assumption that most change situations are similar and that one standard 'change path' can be followed. Strebel explores the wide variety of change circumstances by distinguishing between strong and weak forces of change, and also between strong and weak forces of resistance. These two dimensions are brought together in a diagram, which Strebel calls the change arena. Using this visual aid, Strebel outlines eight different change paths, each with their own magnitude and pace. Ultimately, the question raised by Strebel's arguments is whether the best approach to strategic change depends on the context. Is there one best way of dealing with the paradox of revolution and evolution, or will the answer depend on the circumstances?

4.1   Reengineering Work: Don't Automate, Obliterate

By Michael Hammer[1]

Despite a decade or more of restructuring and downsizing, many US companies are still unprepared to operate in the 1990s. In a time of rapidly changing technologies and ever-shorter product life cycles, product development often proceeds at a glacial pace. In an age of the customer, order fulfilment has high error rates and customer inquiries go unanswered for weeks. In a period when asset utilization is critical, inventory levels exceed many months of demand.

The usual methods for boosting performance – process rationalization and automation – haven't yielded the dramatic improvements companies need. In particular, heavy investments in information technology have delivered disappointing results – largely because companies tend to use

---

[1] Source: This article was adapted with permission from *Harvard Business Review*, July/August 1990.

technology to mechanize old ways of doing business. They leave the existing processes intact and use computers simply to speed them up.

But speeding up those processes cannot address their fundamental performance deficiencies. Many of our job designs, work flows, control mechanisms, and organizational structures came of age in a different competitive environment and before the advent of the computer. They are geared toward efficiency and control. Yet the watchwords of the new decade are innovation and speed, service and quality.

It is time to stop paving the cow paths. Instead of embedding outdated processes in silicon and software, we should obliterate them and start over. We should 'reengineer' our businesses: use the power of modern information technology to radically redesign our business processes in order to achieve dramatic improvements in their performance.

Every company operates according to a great many unarticulated rules. 'Credit decisions are made by the credit department.' 'Local inventory is needed for good customer service.' 'Forms must be filled in completely and in order.' Reengineering strives to break away from the old rules about how we organize and conduct business. It involves recognizing and rejecting some of them and then finding imaginative new ways to accomplish work. From our redesigned processes, new rules will emerge that fit the times. Only then can we hope to achieve quantum leaps in performance.

Reengineering cannot be planned meticulously and accomplished in small and cautious steps. It's an all-or-nothing proposition with an uncertain result. Still, most companies have no choice but to muster the courage to do it. For many, reengineering is the only hope for breaking away from the antiquated processes that threaten to drag them down. Fortunately, managers are not without help. Enough businesses have successfully reengineered their processes to provide some rules of thumb for others.

What Ford and MBL Did

Japanese competitors and young entrepreneurial ventures prove every day that drastically better levels of process performance are possible. They develop products twice as fast, utilize assets eight times more productively, respond to customers ten times faster. Some large, established companies also show what can be done. Businesses like Ford Motor Company and Mutual Benefit Life Insurance have reengineered their processes and achieved competitive leadership as a result. Ford has reengineered its accounts payable processes, and Mutual Benefit Life, its processing of applications for insurance.

In the early 1980s, when the American automotive industry was in a depression, Ford's top management put accounts payable – along with many other departments – under the microscope in search of ways to cut costs. Accounts payable in North America alone employed more than 500 people. Management thought that by rationalizing processes and installing new computer systems, it could reduce the head count by some 20 percent.

Ford was enthusiastic about its plan to tighten accounts payable – until it looked at Mazda. While Ford was aspiring to a 400-person department, Mazda's accounts payable organization consisted of a total of five people. The difference in absolute numbers was astounding, and even after adjusting for Mazda's smaller size, Ford figured that its accounts payable organization was five times the size it should be. The Ford team knew better than to attribute the discrepancy to callisthenics, company songs, or low interest rates.

Ford managers ratcheted up their goal: accounts payable would perform with not just a hundred but many hundreds fewer clerks. It then set out to achieve it. First, managers analyzed the existing system. When Ford's purchasing department wrote a purchase order, it sent a copy to accounts payable. Later, when material control received the goods, it sent a copy of the receiving document to accounts payable. Meanwhile, the vendor sent an invoice to accounts payable. It was up to accounts payable, then, to match the purchase order against the receiving document and the invoice. If they matched, the department issued payment.

The department spent most of its time on mismatches, instances where the purchase order, receiving document, and invoice disagreed. In these cases, an accounts payable clerk would investigate the discrepancy, hold up payment, generate documents, and all-in-all gum up the works.

One way to improve things might have been to help the accounts payable clerk investigate more efficiently, but a better choice was to prevent the mismatches in the first place. To this end, Ford instituted 'invoiceless processing.' Now when the purchasing department initiates an order, it enters the information into an on-line database. It doesn't send a copy of the purchase order to anyone. When the goods arrive at the receiving dock, the receiving clerk checks the database to see if they correspond to an outstanding purchase order. If so, he or she accepts them and enters the transaction into the computer system. (If receiving can't find a database entry for the received goods, it simply returns the order.)

Under the old procedures, the accounting department had to match 14 data items between the receipt record, the purchase order, and the invoice before it could issue payment to the vendor. The new approach requires matching only three items – part number, unit of measure, and supplier code – between the purchase order and the receipt record. The matching is done automatically, and the computer prepares the check, which accounts payable sends to the vendor. There are no invoices to worry about since Ford has asked its vendors not to send them.

Ford didn't settle for the modest increases it first envisioned. It opted for radical change – and achieved dramatic improvement. Where it has instituted this new process, Ford has achieved a 75 percent reduction in head count, not the 20 percent it would have gotten with a conventional program. And since there are no discrepancies between the financial record and the physical record, material control is simpler and financial information is more accurate.

Mutual Benefit Life, the country's eighteenth largest life carrier, has reengineered its processing of insurance applications. Prior to this, MBL handled customers' applications much as its competitors did. The long, multistep process involved credit checking, quoting, rating, underwriting, and so on. An application would have to go through as many as 30 discrete steps, spanning five departments and involving 19 people. At the very best, MBL could process an application in 24 hours, but more typical turnarounds ranged from five to 25 days – most of the time spent passing information from one department to the next. (Another insurer estimated that while an application spent 22 days in process, it was actually worked on for just 17 minutes.)

MBL's rigid, sequential process led to many complications. For instance, when a customer wanted to cash in an existing policy and purchase a new one, the old business department first had to authorize the treasury department to issue a check made payable to MBL. The check would then accompany the paperwork to the new business department.

The president of MBL, intent on improving customer service, decided that this nonsense had to stop and demanded a 60 percent improvement in productivity. It was clear that such an ambitious goal would require more than tinkering with the existing process. Strong measures were in order, and the management team assigned to the task looked to technology as a means of achieving them. The team realized that shared databases and computer networks could make many different kinds of information available to a single person, while expert systems could help people with limited experience make sound decisions. Applying these insights led to a new approach to the application-handling process, one with wide organizational implications and little resemblance to the old way of doing business.

MBL swept away existing job definitions and departmental boundaries and created a new position called a case manager. Case managers have total responsibility for an application from the time it is received to the time a policy is issued. Unlike clerks, who performed a fixed task repeatedly under the watchful gaze of a supervisor, case managers work autonomously. No more handoffs of files and responsibility, no more shuffling of customer inquiries.

Case managers are able to perform all the tasks associated with an insurance application because they are supported by powerful PC-based workstations that run an expert system and connect to a range of automated systems on a mainframe. In particularly tough cases, the case manager calls for assistance from a senior underwriter or physician, but these specialists work only as consultants and advisers to the case manager, who never relinquishes control.

Empowering individuals to process entire applications has had a tremendous impact on operations. MBL can now complete an application in as little as four hours, and average turnaround takes only two to five days. The company has eliminated 100 field office positions, and case managers can handle more than twice the volume of new applications the company previously could process.

The Essence of Reengineering

At the heart of reengineering is the notion of discontinuous thinking – of recognizing and breaking away from the outdated rules and fundamental assumptions that underlie operations. Unless we change these rules, we are merely rearranging the deckchairs on the Titanic. We cannot achieve breakthroughs in performance by cutting fat or automating existing processes. Rather, we must challenge old assumptions and shed the old rules that made the business underperform in the first place.

Every business is replete with implicit rules left over from earlier decades. 'Customers don't repair their own equipment.' 'Local warehouses are necessary for good service.' 'Merchandising decisions are made at headquarters.' These rules of work design are based on assumptions about technology, people, and organizational goals that no longer hold. The contemporary repertoire of available information technologies is vast and quickly expanding. Quality, innovation, and service are now more important than cost, growth, and control. A large portion of the population is educated and capable of assuming responsibility, and workers cherish their autonomy and expect to have a say in how the business is run.

It should come as no surprise that our business processes and structures are outmoded and obsolete: our work structures and processes have not kept pace with the changes in technology, demographics, and business objectives. For the most part, we have organized work as a sequence of separate tasks and employed complex mechanisms to track its progress. This arrangement can be traced to the Industrial Revolution, when specialization of labor and economies of scale promised to overcome the inefficiencies of cottage industries. Businesses disaggregated work into narrowly defined tasks, reaggregated the people performing those tasks into departments, and installed managers to administer them.

Our elaborate systems for imposing control and discipline on those who actually do the work stem from the postwar period. In that halcyon period of expansion, the main concern was growing fast without going broke, so businesses focused on cost, growth, and control. And since literate, entry-level people were abundant but well-educated professionals hard to come by, the control systems funneled information up the hierarchy to the few who presumably knew what to do with it.

These patterns of organizing work have become so ingrained that, despite their serious drawbacks, it's hard to conceive of work being accomplished any other way. Conventional process structures are fragmented and piecemeal, and they lack the integration necessary to maintain quality and service. They are breeding grounds for tunnel vision, as people tend to substitute the narrow goals of their particular department for the larger goals of the process as a whole. When work is handed off from person to person and unit to unit, delays and errors are inevitable. Accountability blurs, and critical issues fall between the cracks. Moreover, no one sees enough of the big picture to be able to respond quickly to new situations.

Managers desperately try, like all the king's horses and all the king's men, to piece together the fragmented pieces of business processes.

Managers have tried to adapt their processes to new circumstances, but usually in ways that just create more problems. If, say, customer service is poor, they create a mechanism to deliver service but overlay it on the existing organization. Bureaucracy thickens, costs rise, and enterprising competitors gain market share.

In reengineering, managers break loose from outmoded business processes and the design principles underlying them and create new ones. Ford had operated under the old rule that 'We pay when we receive the invoice.' While no one had ever articulated or recorded it, that rule determined how the accounts payable process was organized. Ford's reengineering effort challenged and ultimately replaced the rule with a new one: 'We pay when we receive the goods.'

Reengineering requires looking at the fundamental processes of the business from a cross-functional perspective. Ford discovered that reengineering only the accounts payable department was futile. The appropriate focus of the effort was what might be called the goods acquisition process, which included purchasing and receiving as well as accounts payable.

One way to ensure that reengineering has a cross-functional perspective is to assemble a team that represents the functional units involved in the process being reengineered and all the units that depend on it. The team must analyze and scrutinize the existing process until it really understands what the process is trying to accomplish. The point is not to learn what happens to form 73B in its peregrinations through the company but to understand the purpose of having form 73B in the first place. Rather than looking for opportunities to improve the current process, the team should determine which of its steps really add value and search for new ways to achieve the result.

The reengineering team must keep asking Why? and What if? Why do we need to get a manager's signature on a requisition? Is it a control mechanism or a decision point? What if the manager reviews only requisitions above $500? What if he or she doesn't see them at all? Raising and resolving heretical questions can separate what is fundamental to the process from what is superficial. The regional offices of an East Coast insurance company had long produced a series of reports that they regularly sent to the home office. No one in the field realized that these reports were simply filed and never used. The process outlasted the circumstances that had created the need for it. The reengineering study team should push to discover situations like this.

In short, a reengineering effort strives for dramatic levels of improvement. It must break away from conventional wisdom and the constraints of organizational boundaries and should be broad and cross-functional in scope. It should use information technology not to automate an existing process but to enable a new one.

Principles of Reengineering

Creating new rules tailored to the modern environment ultimately requires a new conceptualization of the business process – which comes down to someone having a great idea. But reengineering need not be haphazard. In fact, some of the principles that companies have already discovered while reengineering their business processes can help jump start the effort for others.

Organize Around Outcomes, Not Tasks

This principle says to have one person perform all the steps in a process. Design that person's job around an objective or outcome instead of a single task. The redesign at Mutual Benefit Life, where individual case managers perform the entire application approval process, is the quintessential example of this.

The redesign of an electronics company is another example. It had separate organizations performing each of the five steps between selling and installing the equipment. One group determined customer requirements, another translated those requirements into internal product codes, a third conveyed that information to various plants and warehouses, a fourth received and assembled the components, and a fifth delivered and installed the equipment. The process was based on the centuries-old notion of specialized labor and on the limitations inherent in paper files. The departments each possessed a specific set of skills, and only one department at a time could do its work.

The customer order moved systematically from step to step. But this sequential processing caused problems. The people getting the information from the customer in step one had to get all the data anyone would need throughout the process, even if it wasn't needed until step five. In addition, the many handoffs were responsible for numerous errors and misunderstandings. Finally, any questions about customer requirements that arose late in the process had to be referred back to the people doing step one, resulting in delay and rework.

When the company reengineered, it eliminated the assembly-line approach. It compressed responsibility for the various steps and assigned it to one person, the 'customer service representative.' That person now oversees the whole process – taking the order, translating it into product codes, getting the components assembled, and seeing the product delivered and installed. The customer service rep expedites and coordinates the process, much like a general contractor. And the customer has just one contact, who always knows the status of the order.

Have Those Who Use the Output of the Process Perform the Process

In an effort to capitalize on the benefits of specialization and scale, many organizations established specialized departments to handle specialized processes. Each department does only one type of work and is a 'customer' of other groups' processes. Accounting does only accounting. If it needs new pencils, it goes to the purchasing department, the group specially equipped with the information and expertise to perform that role. Purchasing finds vendors, negotiates price, places the order, inspects the goods, and pays the invoice – and eventually the accountants get their pencils. The process works (after a fashion), but it's slow and bureaucratic.

Now that computer-based data and expertise are more readily available, departments, units, and individuals can do more for themselves. Opportunities exist to reengineer processes so that the individuals who need the result of a process can do it themselves. For example, by using expert systems and databases, departments can make their own purchases without sacrificing the benefits of specialized purchasers. One manufacturer has reengineered its purchasing process along just these lines. The company's old system, whereby the operating departments submitted requisitions and let purchasing do the rest, worked well for controlling expensive and important items like raw materials and capital equipment. But for inexpensive and nonstrategic purchases, which constituted some 35 percent of total orders, the system was slow and cumbersome; it was not uncommon for the cost of the purchasing process to exceed the cost of the goods being purchased.

The new process compresses the purchase of sundry items and pushes it on to the customers of the process. Using a database of approved vendors, an operating unit can directly place an order with a vendor and charge it on a bank credit card. At the end of the month, the bank gives the manufacturer a tape of all credit card transactions, which the company runs against its internal accounting system.

When an electronics equipment manufacturer reengineered its field service process, it pushed some of the steps of the process on to its customers. The manufacturer's field service had been plagued by the usual problems: technicians were often unable to do a particular repair because the right part wasn't on the van, response to customer calls was slow, and spare-parts inventory was excessive.

Now customers make simple repairs themselves. Spare parts are stored at each customer's site and managed through a computerized inventory-management system. When a problem arises, the customer calls the manufacturer's field-service hot line and describes the symptoms to a diagnostician, who accesses a diagnosis support system. If the problem appears to be something the customer can fix, the diagnostician tells the customer what part to replace and how to install it. The old part is picked up and a new part left in its place at a later time. Only for complex problems is a service technician dispatched to the site, this time without having to make a stop at the warehouse to pick up parts.

When the people closest to the process perform it, there is little need for the overhead associated with managing it. Interfaces and liaisons can be eliminated, as can the mechanisms used to coordinate those who perform the process with those who use it. Moreover, the problem of capacity planning for the process performers is greatly reduced.

Subsume Information-Processing Work into the Real Work that Produces the Information

The previous two principles compress linear processes. This principle suggests moving work from one person or department to another. Why doesn't an organization that produces information also process it? In the past, people didn't have the time or weren't trusted to do both. Most companies established units to do nothing but collect and process information that other departments created. This arrangement reflects the old rule about specialized labor and the belief that people at lower organizational levels are incapable of acting on information they generate. An accounts payable department collects information from purchasing and receiving and reconciles it with data that the vendor provides. Quality assurance gathers and analyzes information it gets from production.

Ford's redesigned accounts payable process embodies the new rule. With the new system, receiving, which produces the information about the goods received, processes this information instead of sending it to accounts payable. The new computer system can easily compare the delivery with the order and trigger the appropriate action.

Treat Geographically Dispersed Resources as Though They Were Centralized

The conflict between centralization and decentralization is a classic one. Decentralizing a resource (whether people, equipment, or inventory) gives better service to those who use it, but at the cost of redundancy, bureaucracy, and missed economies of scale. Companies no longer have to make such trade-offs. They can use databases, telecommunications networks, and standardized processing systems to get the benefits of scale and coordination while maintaining the benefits of flexibility and service.

At Hewlett-Packard, for instance, each of the more than 50 manufacturing units had its own separate purchasing department. While this arrangement provided excellent responsiveness and service to the plants, it prevented H-P from realizing the benefits of its scale, particularly with regard to quantity discounts. H-P's solution is to maintain the divisional purchasing organizations and to introduce a corporate unit to coordinate them. Each purchasing unit has access to a shared database on vendors and their performance and issues its own purchase orders. Corporate purchasing maintains this database and uses it to negotiate contracts for the corporation and to monitor the units. The payoffs have come in a 150 percent improvement in on-time deliveries, 50 percent reduction in lead times, 75 percent reduction in failure rates, and a significantly lower cost of goods purchased.

Link Parallel Activities Instead of Integrating Their Results

H-P's decentralized purchasing operations represent one kind of parallel processing in which separate units perform the same function. Another common kind of parallel processing is when separate units perform different activities that must eventually come together. Product development typically operates this way. In the development of a photocopier, for example, independent units develop the various subsystems of the copier. One group works on the optics, another on the mechanical paperhandling device, another on the power supply, and so on. Having people do development work simultaneously saves time, but at the dreaded integration and testing phase, the pieces often fail to work together. Then the costly redesign begins.

Or consider a bank that sells different kinds of credit – loans, letters of credit, asset-based financing – through separate units. These groups may have no way of knowing whether another group has already extended credit to a particular customer. Each unit could extend the full $10 million credit limit.

The new principle says to forge links between parallel functions and to coordinate them while their activities are in process rather than after they are completed. Communications networks, shared databases, and teleconferencing can bring the independent groups together so that coordination is ongoing. One large electronics company has cut its product development cycle by more than 50 percent by implementing this principle.

Put the Decision Point Where the Work is Performed, and Build Control into the Process

In most organizations, those who do the work are distinguished from those who monitor the work and make decisions about it. The tacit assumption is that the people actually doing the work have neither the time nor the inclination to monitor and control it and that they lack the knowledge and scope to make decisions about it. The entire hierarchical management structure is built on this assumption. Accountants, auditors, and supervisors check, record, and monitor work. Managers handle any exceptions.

The new principle suggests that the people who do the work should make the decisions and that the process itself can have built-in controls. Pyramidal management layers can therefore be compressed and the organization flattened.

Information technology can capture and process data, and expert systems can to some extent supply knowledge, enabling people to make their own decisions. As the doers become self-managing and self-controlling, hierarchy – and the slowness and bureaucracy associated with it – disappears.

When Mutual Benefit Life reengineered the insurance application process, it not only compressed the linear sequence but also eliminated the need for layers of managers. These two kinds of compression – vertical and horizontal – often go together; the very fact that a worker sees only one piece of the process calls for a manager with a broader vision. The case managers at MBL provide end-to-end management of the process, reducing the need for traditional managers. The managerial role is changing from one of controller and supervisor to one of supporter and facilitator.

Capture Information Once and at the Source

This last rule is simple. When information was difficult to transmit, it made sense to collect information repeatedly. Each person, department, or unit had its own requirements and forms. Companies simply had to live with the associated delays, entry errors, and costly overhead. But why do we have to live with those problems now? Today when we collect a piece of information, we can store it in an on-line database for all who need it. Bar coding, relational databases, and electronic data interchange (EDI) make it easy to collect, store, and transmit information. One insurance company found that its application review process required that certain items be entered into 'stovepipe' computer systems supporting different functions as many as five times. By integrating and connecting these systems, the company was able to eliminate this redundant data entry along with the attendant checking functions and inevitable errors.

Think Big

Reengineering triggers changes of many kinds, not just of the business process itself. Job designs, organizational structures, management systems – anything associated with the process must be refashioned in an integrated way. In other words, reengineering is a tremendous effort that mandates change in many areas of the organization.

When Ford reengineered its payables, receiving clerks on the dock had to learn to use computer terminals to check shipments, and they had to make decisions about whether to accept the goods. Purchasing agents also had to assume new responsibilities – like making sure the purchase orders they entered into the database had the correct information about where to send the check. Attitudes toward vendors also had to change: vendors could no longer be seen as adversaries; they had to become partners in a shared business process. Vendors too had to adjust. In many cases, invoices formed the basis of their accounting systems. At least one Ford supplier adapted by continuing to print invoices, but instead of sending them to Ford threw them away, reconciling cash received against invoices never sent.

The changes at Mutual Benefit Life were also widespread. The company's job-rating scheme could not accommodate the case manager position, which had a lot of responsibility but no direct reports. MBL had to devise new job-rating schemes and compensation policies. It also had to develop a culture in which people doing work are perceived as more important than those supervising work. Career paths, recruitment and training programs, promotion policies – these and many other management systems are being revised to support the new process design.

The extent of these changes suggests one factor that is necessary for reengineering to succeed: executive leadership with real vision. No one in an organization wants reengineering. It is confusing and disruptive and affects everything people have grown accustomed to. Only if top-level managers back the effort and outlast the company cynics will people take reengineering seriously. As one wag at an electronics equipment manufacturer has commented, 'Every few months, our senior managers find a new religion. One time it was quality, another it was customer service, another it was flattening the organization. We just hold our breath until they get over it and things get back to normal.' Commitment, consistency – maybe even a touch of fanaticism – are needed to enlist those who would prefer the status quo.

Considering the inertia of old processes and structures, the strain of implementing a reengineering plan can hardly be overestimated. But by the same token, it is hard to overestimate the opportunities, especially for established companies. Big, traditional organizations aren't necessarily dinosaurs doomed to extinction, but they are burdened with layers of unproductive overhead and armies of unproductive workers. Shedding them a layer at a time will not be good enough to stand up against sleek startups or streamlined Japanese companies. US companies need fast change and dramatic improvements.

We have the tools to do what we need to do. Information technology offers many options for reorganizing work. But our imaginations must guide our decisions about technology – not the other way around. We must have the boldness to imagine taking 78 days out of an 80–day turnaround time, cutting 75 percent of overhead, and eliminating 80 percent of errors. These are not unrealistic goals. If managers have the vision, reengineering will provide a way.

4.2   Kaizen

By Masaaki Imai[1]

Back in the 1950s, I was working with the Japan Productivity Center in Washington, D.C. My job mainly consisted of escorting groups of Japanese businessmen who were visiting American companies to study 'the secret of American industrial productivity.' Toshiro Yamada, now Professor Emeritus of the Faculty of Engineering at Kyoto University, was a member of one such study team visiting the United States to study the industrial-vehicle industry. Recently, the members of his team gathered to celebrate the silver anniversary of their trip.

At the banquet table, Yamada said he had recently been back to the United States in a 'sentimental journey' to some of the plants he had visited, among them the River Rouge steelworks in Dearborn, Michigan. Shaking his head in disbelief, he said, 'You know, the plant was exactly the same as it had been 25 years ago.'

---

[1] Source: This article was adapted with permission from chapter 1 and 2 of *Kaizen: The Key to Japan's Competitive Success*, McGraw-Hill, New York, 1986.

These conversations set me to thinking about the great differences in the ways Japanese and Western managers approach their work. It is inconceivable that a Japanese plant would remain virtually unchanged for over a quarter of a century.

I had long been looking for a key concept to explain these two very different management approaches, one that might also help explain why many Japanese companies have come to gain their increasingly conspicuous competitive edge. For instance, how do we explain the fact that while most new ideas come from the West and some of the most advanced plants, institutions, and technologies are found there, there are also many plants there that have changed little since the 1950s?

Change is something which everybody takes for granted. Recently, an American executive at a large multinational firm told me his company chairman had said at the start of an executive committee meeting: 'Gentlemen, our job is to manage change. If we fail, we must change management.' The executive smiled and said, 'We all got the message!'

In Japan, change is a way of life, too. But are we talking about the same change when we talk about managing change or else changing management? It dawned on me that there might be different kinds of change: gradual and abrupt. While we can easily observe both gradual and abrupt changes in Japan, gradual change is not so obvious a part of the Western way of life. How are we to explain this difference?

This question led me to consider the question of values. Could it be that differences between the value systems in Japan and the West account for their different attitudes toward gradual change and abrupt change? Abrupt changes are easily grasped by everyone concerned, and people are usually elated to see them. This is generally true in both Japan and the West. Yet what about the gradual changes? My earlier statement that it is inconceivable that a Japanese plant would remain unchanged for years refers to gradual change as well as abrupt change.

Thinking all this over, I came to the conclusion that the key difference between how change is understood in Japan and how it is viewed in the West lies in the Kaizen concept – a concept that is so natural and obvious to many Japanese managers that they often do not even realize that they possess it! The Kaizen concept explains why companies cannot remain the same for long in Japan. Moreover, after many years of studying Western business practices, I have reached the conclusion that this Kaizen concept is non-existent, or at least very weak, in most Western companies today. Worse yet, they reject it without knowing what it really entails. It's the old 'not invented here' syndrome. And this lack of Kaizen helps explain why an American or European factory can remain exactly the same for a quarter of a century.

The essence of Kaizen is simple and straightforward: Kaizen means improvement. Moreover, Kaizen means ongoing improvement involving everyone, including both managers and workers. The Kaizen philosophy assumes that our way of life – be it our working life, our social life, or our home life – deserves to be constantly improved.

In trying to understand Japan's postwar 'economic miracle,' scholars, journalists, and businesspeople alike have dutifully studied such factors as the productivity movement, total quality control (TQC), small-group activities, the suggestion system, automation, industrial robots, and labor relations. They have given much attention to some of Japan's unique management practices, among them the lifetime employment system, seniority-based wages, and enterprise unions. Yet I feel they have failed to grasp the very simple truth that lies behind the many myths concerning Japanese management.

The essence of most 'uniquely Japanese' management practices – be they productivity improvement, TQC (Total Quality Control) activities, QC (Quality Control) circles, or labor relations – can be reduced to one word: Kaizen. Using the term Kaizen in place of such words as productivity, TQC, ZD (Zero Defects), *kamban*, and the suggestion system paints a far clearer picture of what has been going on in Japanese industry. Kaizen is an umbrella concept covering most of those 'uniquely Japanese' practices that have recently achieved such world-wide fame.

The implications of TQC or CWQC (Company-Wide Quality Control) in Japan have been that these concepts have helped Japanese companies generate a process-oriented way of thinking and develop strategies that assure continuous improvement involving people at all levels of the organizational hierarchy. The message of the Kaizen strategy is that not a day should go by without some kind of improvement being made somewhere in the company.

The belief that there should be unending improvement is deeply ingrained in the Japanese mentality. As the old Japanese saying goes, 'If a man has not been seen for three days, his friends should take a good look at him to see what changes have befallen him.' The implication is that he must have changed in three days, so his friends should be attentive enough to notice the changes.

After World War II, most Japanese companies had to start literally from the ground up. Every day brought new challenges to managers and workers alike, and every day meant progress. Simply staying in business required unending progress, and Kaizen has become a way of life. It was also fortunate that the various tools that helped elevate this Kaizen concept to new heights were introduced to Japan in the late 1950s and early 1960s by such experts as W. E. Deming and J. M. Juran. However, most new concepts, systems, and tools that are widely used in Japan today have subsequently been developed in Japan and represent qualitative improvements upon the statistical quality control and total quality control of the 1960s.

Kaizen and Management

Figure 4.2.1 shows how job functions are perceived in Japan. As indicated, management has two major components: maintenance and improvement. Maintenance refers to activities directed toward maintaining current

FIGURE 4.2.1
Japanese perceptions of
job functions

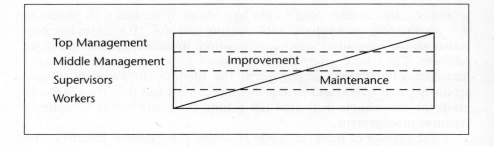

technological, managerial, and operating standards; improvement refers to those directed toward improving current standards.

Under its maintenance functions, management performs its assigned tasks so that everybody in the company can follow the established SOP (Standard Operating Procedure). This means that management must first establish policies, rules, directives, and procedures for all major operations and then see to it that everybody follows SOP. If people are able to follow the standard but do not, management must introduce discipline. If people are unable to follow the standard, management must either provide training or review and revise the standard so that people can follow it.

In any business, an employee's work is based on existing standards, either explicit or implicit, imposed by management. Maintenance refers to maintaining such standards through training and discipline. By contrast, improvement refers to improving the standards. The Japanese perception of management boils down to one precept: maintain and improve standards.

The higher up the manager is, the more he is concerned with improvement. At the bottom level, an unskilled worker working at a machine may spend all his time following instructions. However, as he becomes more proficient at his work, he begins to think about improvement. He begins to contribute to improvements in the way his work is done, either through individual suggestions or through group suggestions.

Ask any manager at a successful Japanese company what top management is pressing for, and the answer will be, 'Kaizen' (improvement). Improving standards means establishing higher standards. Once this is done, it becomes management's maintenance job to see that the new standards are observed. Lasting improvement is achieved only when people work to higher standards. Maintenance and improvement have thus become inseparable for most Japanese managers.

What is improvement? Improvement can be broken down between Kaizen and innovation. Kaizen signifies small improvements made in the status quo as a result of ongoing efforts. Innovation involves a drastic improvement in the status quo as a result of a large investment in new technology and/or equipment. Figure 4.2.2 shows the breakdown among maintenance, Kaizen, and innovation as perceived by Japanese management.

On the other hand, most Western managers' perceptions of job functions are as shown in Figure 4.2.2. There is little room in Western management for the Kaizen concept.

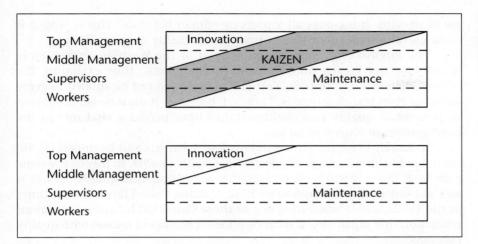

FIGURE 4.2.2
Japanese vs Western
perceptions of job
functions

Sometimes, another type of management is found in the high-technology industries. These are the companies that are born running, grow rapidly, and then disappear just as rapidly when their initial success wanes or markets change.

The worst companies are those which do nothing but maintenance, meaning there is no internal drive for Kaizen or innovation, change is forced on management by market conditions and competition and management does not know where it wants to go.

Implications of QC for Kaizen

While management is usually concerned with such issues as productivity and quality, the thrust of this article is to look at the other side of the picture – at Kaizen.

The starting point for improvement is to recognize the need. This comes from recognition of a problem. If no problem is recognized, there is no recognition of the need for improvement. Complacency is the arch-enemy of Kaizen. Therefore, Kaizen emphasizes problem-awareness and provides clues for identifying problems.

Once identified, problems must be solved. Thus Kaizen is also a problem-solving process. In fact, Kaizen requires the use of various problem-solving tools. Improvement reaches new heights with every problem that is solved. In order to consolidate the new level, however, the improvement must be standardized. Thus Kaizen also requires standardization.

Such terms as QC (Quality Control), SQC (Statistical Quality Control), QC circles, and TQC (or CWQC) often appear in connection with Kaizen. To avoid unnecessary confusion, it may be helpful to clarify these terms here.

The word *quality* has been interpreted in many different ways, and there is no agreement on what actually constitutes quality. In its broadest sense, quality is anything that can be improved. In this context, quality is associated not only with products and services but also with the way people work, the way machines are operated, and the way systems and procedures are dealt with. It includes all aspects of human behavior. This is why it is more useful to talk about Kaizen than about quality or productivity.

The English term *improvement* as used in the Western context more often than not means improvement in equipment, thus excluding the human elements. By contrast, Kaizen is generic and can be applied to every aspect of everybody's activities. This said, however, it must be admitted that such terms as quality and quality control have played a vital role in the development of Kaizen in Japan.

In March 1950, the Union of Japanese Scientists and Engineers (JUSE) started publishing its magazine *Statistical Quality Control*. In July of the same year, W. E. Deming was invited to Japan to teach statistical quality control at an eight-day seminar organized by JUSE. Deming visited Japan several times in the 1950s, and it was during one of those visits that he made his famous prediction that Japan would soon be flooding the world market with quality products.

Deming also introduced the 'Deming cycle,' one of the crucial QC tools for assuring continuous improvement, to Japan. The Deming cycle is also called the Deming wheel or the PDCA (Plan-Do-Check-Action) cycle. (See Figure 4.2.3) Deming stressed the importance of constant interaction among research, design, production, and sales in order for a company to arrive at better quality that satisfies customers. He taught that this wheel should be rotated on the ground of quality-first perceptions and quality-first responsibility. With this process, he argued, the company could win consumer confidence and acceptance and prosper.

In July 1954, J.M. Juran was invited to Japan to conduct a JUSE seminar on quality-control management. This was the first time QC was dealt with from the overall management perspective.

FIGURE 4.2.3
Deming wheel

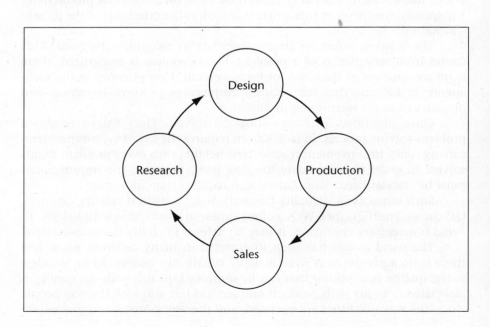

In 1956, Japan Shortwave Radio included a course on quality control as part of its educational programming. In November 1960, the first national quality month was inaugurated. It was also in 1960 that Q-marks and Q-flags were formally adopted. Then in April 1962 the magazine *Quality Control for the Foreman* was launched by JUSE, and the first QC circle was started that same year.

A QC circle is defined as a small group that *voluntarily* performs quality-control activities within the shop. The small group carries out its work continuously as part of a company-wide program of quality control, self-development, mutual education, and flow-control and improvement within the workshop. The QC circle is only *part* of a company-wide program; it is never the whole of TQC or CWQC.

Those who have followed QC circles in Japan know that they often focus on such areas as cost, safety, and productivity, and that their activities sometimes relate only indirectly to product-quality improvement. For the most part, these activities are aimed at making improvements in the workshop.

There is no doubt that QC circles have played an important part in improving product quality and productivity in Japan. However, their role has often been blown out of proportion by overseas observers who believe that QC circles are the mainstay of TQC activities in Japan. Nothing could be further from the truth, especially when it comes to Japanese management. Efforts related to QC circles generally account for only 10 percent to 30 percent of the overall TQC effort in Japanese companies.

What is less visible behind these developments is the transformation of the term quality control, or QC, in Japan. As is the case in many Western companies, quality control initially meant quality control applied to the manufacturing process, particularly the inspections for rejecting defective incoming material or defective outgoing products at the end of the production line. But very soon the realization set in that inspection alone does nothing to improve the quality of the product, and that product quality should be built at the production stage. 'Build quality into the process' was (and still is) a popular phrase in Japanese quality control. It is at this stage that control charts and the other tools for statistical quality control were introduced after Deming's lectures.

Juran's lectures in 1954 opened up another aspect of quality control: the managerial approach to quality control. This was the first time the term QC was positioned as a vital management tool in Japan. From then on, the term QC has been used to mean both quality control and the tools for overall improvement in managerial performance.

Initially, QC was applied in heavy industries such as the steel industry. Since these industries required instrumentation control, the application of SQC tools was vital for maintaining quality. As QC spread to the machinery and automobile industries, where controlling the process was essential in building quality into the product, the need for SQC became even greater.

At a later stage, other industries started to introduce QC for such products as consumer durables and home appliances. In these industries, the interest was in building quality in at the design stage to meet changing and increasingly stringent customer requirements. Today, management has gone beyond the design stage and has begun to stress the importance of quality product development, which means taking customer-related information and market research into account from the very start.

All this while, QC has grown into a full-fledged management tool for Kaizen involving everyone in the company. Such company-wide activities are often referred to as TQC (total quality control) or CWQC (company-wide quality control). No matter which name is used, TQC and CWQC mean company-wide Kaizen activities involving everyone in the company, managers and workers alike. Over the years, QC has been elevated to SQC and then to TQC or CWQC, improving managerial performance at every level. Thus it is that such words as QC and TQC have come to be almost synonymous with Kaizen. This is also why I constantly refer to QC, TQC, and CWQC in explaining Kaizen.

On the other hand, the function of quality control in its original sense remains valid. Quality assurance remains a vital part of management, and most companies have a QA (quality assurance) department for this. To confuse matters, TQC or CWQC activities are sometimes administered by the QA department and sometimes by a separate TQC office. Thus it is important that these QC-related words be understood in the context in which they appear.

Kaizen and TQC

Considering the TQC movement in Japan as part of the Kaizen movement gives us a clearer perspective on the Japanese approach. First of all, it should be pointed out that TQC activities in Japan are not concerned solely with quality control. People have been fooled by the term 'quality control' and have often construed it within the narrow discipline of product-quality control. In the West, the term QC is mostly associated with inspection of finished products, and when QC is brought up in discussion, top managers, who generally assume they have very little to do with quality control, lose interest immediately.

It is unfortunate that in the West TQC has been dealt with mainly in technical journals when it is more properly the focus of management journals. Japan has developed an elaborate system of Kaizen strategies as management tools within the TQC movement. These rank among this century's most outstanding management achievements. Yet because of the limited way in which QC is understood in the West, most Western students of Japanese QC activities have failed to grasp their real significance and challenge. At the same time, new TQC methods and tools are constantly being studied and tested.

TQC in Japan is a movement centered on the improvement of managerial performance at all levels. As such, it has typically dealt with:

1   quality assurance;

2   cost reduction;

3   meeting production quotas;

4   meeting delivery schedules;

5   safety;

6   new-product development;

7   productivity improvement;

8   supplier management.

More recently, TQC has come to include marketing, sales, and service as well. Furthermore, TQC has dealt with such crucial management concerns as organizational development, cross-functional management, policy deployment, and quality deployment. In other words, management has been using TQC as a tool for improving overall performance.

Those who have closely followed QC circles in Japan know that their activities are often focused on such areas as cost, safety and productivity, and that their activities may only indirectly relate to product-quality improvement. For the most part, these activities are aimed at making improvements in the workplace.

Management efforts for TQC have been directed mostly at such areas as education, systems development, policy deployment, cross-functional management and, more recently, quality deployment.

Kaizen and the Suggestion System

Japanese management makes a concerted effort to involve employees in Kaizen through suggestions. Thus, the suggestion system is an integral part of the established management system, and the number of workers' suggestions is regarded as an important criterion in reviewing the performance of these workers' supervisor. The manager of the supervisors is in turn expected to assist them so that they can help workers generate more suggestions.

Most Japanese companies active in Kaizen programs have a quality-control system and a suggestion system working in concert. The role of QC circles may be better understood if we regard them collectively as a group-oriented suggestion system for making improvements.

One of the outstanding features of Japanese management is that it generates a great number of suggestions from workers and that management works hard to consider these suggestions, often incorporating them into the overall Kaizen strategy. It is not uncommon for top management of a leading Japanese company to spend a whole day listening to presentations of activities by QC circles, and giving awards based on predetermined criteria. Management is willing to give recognition to employees' efforts for improvements and makes its concern visible wherever possible. Often, the number of suggestions is posted individually on the wall of the workplace in order to encourage competition among workers and among groups.

Another important aspect of the suggestion system is that each suggestion, once implemented, leads to a revised standard. For instance, when a special foolproof device has been installed on a machine at a worker's suggestion, this may require the worker to work differently and, at times, more attentively.

However, inasmuch as the new standard has been set up by the worker's own volition, he takes pride in the new standard and is willing to follow it. If, on the contrary, he is told to follow a standard imposed by management, he may not be as willing to follow it.

Thus, through suggestions, employees can participate in Kaizen in the workplace and play a vital role in upgrading standards. In a recent interview, Toyota Motor chairman Eiji Toyoda said, 'One of the features of the Japanese workers is that they use their brains as well as their hands. Our workers provide 1.5 million suggestions a year, and 95 percent of them are put to practical use. There is an almost tangible concern for improvement in the air at Toyota.'

Kaizen vs. Innovation

There are two contrasting approaches to progress: the gradualist approach and the great-leap-forward approach. Japanese companies generally favor the gradualist approach and Western companies the great-leap approach – an approach epitomized by the term 'innovation'.

Western management worships at the altar of innovation. This innovation is seen as major changes in the wake of technological breakthroughs, or the introduction of the latest management concepts or production techniques. Innovation is dramatic, a real attention-getter. Kaizen, on the other hand, is often undramatic and subtle, and its results are seldom immediately visible. While Kaizen is a continuous process, innovation is generally a one-shot phenomenon.

In the West, for example, a middle manager can usually obtain top management support for such projects as CAD (computer-aided design), CAM (computer-aided manufacture), and MRP (materials requirements planning), since these are innovative projects that have a way of revolutionizing existing systems. As such, they offer ROI (return on investment) benefits that managers can hardly resist.

However, when a factory manager wishes, for example, to make small changes in the way his workers use the machinery, such as working out multiple job assignments or realigning production processes (both of which may require lengthy discussions with the union as well as reeducation and retraining of workers), obtaining management support can be difficult indeed.

Table 4.2.1 compares the main features of Kaizen and of innovation. One of the beautiful things about Kaizen is that it does not necessarily

	Kaizen	Innovation
1. Effect	Long-term and long-lasting but undramatic	Short-term but dramatic
2. Pace	Small steps	Big steps
3. Timeframe	Continuous and incremental	Intermittent and non-incremental
4. Change	Gradual and constant	Abrupt and volatile
5. Involvement	Everybody	Select few 'champions'
6. Approach	Collectivism, group efforts, systems approach	Rugged individualism, individual ideas and efforts
7. Mode	Maintenance and improvement	Scrap and rebuild
8. Spark	Conventional know-how and state of the art	Technological break-throughs, new inventions, new theories
9. Practical requirements	Requires little investment but great effort to maintain it	Requires large investment but little effort to maintain it
10. Effort orientation	People	Technology
11. Evaluation criteria	Process and efforts for better results	Results and profits
12. Advantage	Works well in slow-growth economy	Better suited to fast-growth economy

TABLE 4.2.1
Features of Kaizen and innovation

require sophisticated technique or state-of-the-art technology. To implement Kaizen, you need only simple, conventional techniques. Often, common sense is all that is needed. On the other hand, innovation usually requires highly sophisticated technology, as well as a huge investment.

Kaizen is like a hotbed that nurtures small and ongoing changes, while innovation is like magma that appears in abrupt eruptions from time to time.

One big difference between Kaizen and innovation is that while Kaizen does not necessarily call for a large investment to implement it, it does call for a great deal of continuous effort and commitment. The difference between the two opposing concepts may thus be likened to that of a staircase and a slope. The innovation strategy is supposed to bring about progress in a staircase progression. On the other hand, the Kaizen strategy brings about gradual progress. I say the innovation strategy 'is supposed to' bring about progress in a staircase progression, because it usually does not. Instead of following the staircase pattern, the actual progress achieved through innovation will generally follow the pattern shown in Figure 4.2.4, if it lacks the Kaizen strategy to go along with it. This happens because a system, once it has been installed as a result of new innovation, is subject

FIGURE 4.2.4
Innovation alone

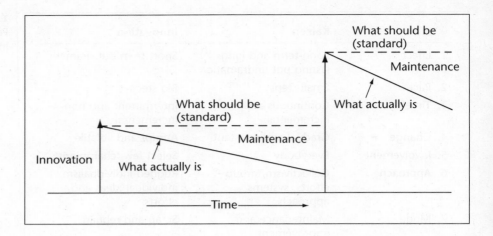

to steady deterioration unless continuing efforts are made first to maintain it and then to improve on it.

In reality, there can be no such thing as a static constant. All systems are destined to deteriorate once they have been established. One of the famous Parkinson's Laws is that an organization, once it has built its edifice, begins its decline. In other words, there must be a continuing effort for improvement to even maintain the status quo.

When such effort is lacking, decline is inevitable (see Figure 4.2.4). Therefore, even when an innovation makes a revolutionary standard of performance attainable, the new performance level will decline unless the standard is constantly challenged and upgraded. Thus, whenever an innovation is achieved, it must be followed by a series of Kaizen efforts to maintain and improve it (see Figure 4.2.5).

Whereas innovation is a one-shot deal whose effects are gradually eroded by intense competition and deteriorating standards, Kaizen is an ongoing effort with cumulative effects marking a steady rise as the years go by. If standards exist only in order to maintain the status quo, they will not be challenged so long as the level of performance is acceptable. Kaizen, on the other hand, means a constant effort not only to maintain but also to upgrade standards. Kaizen strategists believe that standards are by nature tentative, akin to stepping stones, with one standard leading to another as continuing improvement efforts are made. This is the reason why QC circles no sooner solve one problem than they move on to tackle a new problem. This is also the reason why the so-called PDCA (plan-do-check-action) cycle receives so much emphasis in Japan's TQC movement.

Another feature of Kaizen is that it requires virtually everyone's personal efforts. In order for the Kaizen spirit to survive, management must make a conscious and continuous effort to support it. Such support is quite different from the fanfare recognition that management accords to people who have achieved a striking success or breakthrough. Kaizen is concerned more with the process than with the result. The strength of Japanese management lies in its successful development and implementation of a system that acknowledges the ends while emphasizing the means.

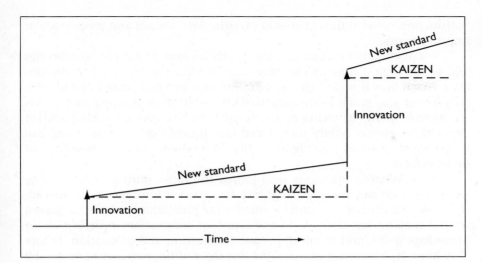

FIGURE 4.2.5
Innovation plus Kaizen

Thus Kaizen calls for a substantial management commitment of time and effort. Infusions of capital are no substitute for this investment in time and effort. Investing in Kaizen means investing in people. In short, Kaizen is people-oriented, whereas innovation is technology- and money-oriented.

Finally, the Kaizen philosophy is better suited to a slow-growth economy, while innovation is better suited to a fast-growth economy. While Kaizen advances inch-by-inch on the strength of many small efforts, innovation leaps upward in hopes of landing at a much higher plateau in spite of gravitational inertia and the weight of investment costs. In a slow-growth economy characterized by high costs of energy and materials, overcapacity, and stagnant markets, Kaizen often has a better payoff than innovation does.

As one Japanese executive recently remarked, 'It is extremely difficult to increase sales by 10 percent. But it is not so difficult to cut manufacturing costs by 10 percent to even better effect.'

I argued that the concept of Kaizen is nonexistent or at best weak in most Western companies today. However, there was a time, not so long ago, when Western management also placed a high priority on Kaizen-like improvement-consciousness. Older executives may recall that before the phenomenal economic growth of the late 1950s and early 1960s, management attended assiduously to improving all aspects of the business, particularly the factory. In those days, every small improvement was counted and was seen as effective in terms of building success.

People who worked with small, privately owned companies may recall with a touch of nostalgia that there was a genuine concern for improvement 'in the air' before the company was bought out or went public. As soon as that happened, the quarterly P/L (profit/loss) figures suddenly became the most important criterion, and management became obsessed with the bottom line, often at the expense of pressing for constant and unspectacular improvements.

For many other companies, the greatly increased market opportunities and technological innovations that appeared during the first two decades after World War II meant that developing new products based on the new technology was much more attractive or 'sexier' than slow, patient efforts for improvement. In trying to catch up with the ever-increasing market demand, managers boldly introduced one innovation after another, and they were content to ignore the seemingly minor benefits of improvement.

Most Western managers who joined the ranks during or after those heady days do not have the slightest concern for improvement. Instead, they take an offensive posture, armed with professional expertise geared toward making big changes in the name of innovation, bringing about immediate gains, and winning instant recognition and promotion. Before they knew it, Western managers had lost sight of improvement and put all their eggs in the innovation basket.

Another factor that has abetted the innovation approach has been the increasing emphasis on financial controls and accounting. By now, the more sophisticated companies have succeeded in establishing elaborate accounting and reporting systems that force managers to account for every action they take and to spell out the precise payout or ROI of every managerial decision. Such a system does not lend itself to building a favorable climate for improvement.

Improvement is by definition slow, gradual, and often invisible, with effects that are felt over the long run. In my opinion, the most glaring and significant shortcoming of Western management today is the lack of improvement philosophy. There is no internal system in Western management to reward efforts for improvement; instead, everyone's job performance is reviewed strictly on the basis of results. Thus it is not uncommon for Western managers to chide people with, 'I don't care what you do or how you do it. I want the results – and now!' This emphasis on results has led to the innovation-dominated approach of the West. This is not to say that Japanese management does not care about innovation. But Japanese managers have enthusiastically pursued Kaizen even when they were involved in innovation.

4.3   Convergence and Upheaval: Managing the Unsteady Pace of Organizational Evolution

By Michael Tushman, William Newman, and Elaine Romanelli[1]

A snug fit of external opportunity, company strategy, and internal structure is a hallmark of successful companies. The real test of executive leadership, however, is in maintaining this alignment in the face of changing competitive conditions. Consider the Polaroid or Caterpillar corporations. Both firms virtually dominated their respective industries for decades, only to be caught off guard by major environmental changes. The same strategic and organizational factors that were so effective for decades became the seeds of complacency and organization decline.

Recent studies of companies over long periods show that the most successful firms maintain a workable equilibrium for several years (or decades), but are also able to initiate and carry out sharp, widespread changes (referred to here as reorientations) when their environments shift. Such upheaval may bring renewed vigor to the enterprise. Less successful firms, on the other hand, get stuck in a particular pattern. The leaders of these firms either do not see the need for reorientation or they are unable to carry through the necessary frame-breaking changes. While not all reorientations succeed, those organizations which do not initiate reorientations as environments shift underperform.

This article focuses on reasons why for long periods most companies make only incremental changes, and why they then need to make painful, discontinuous, system-wide shifts. We are particularly concerned with the role of executive leadership in managing this pattern of convergence punctuated by upheaval. Here are four examples of the convergence/upheaval pattern:

■ Founded in 1915 by a set of engineers from MIT, the General Radio Company was established to produce highly innovative and high-quality (but expensive) electronic test equipment. Over the years, General Radio developed a consistent organization to accomplish its mission. It hired only the brightest young engineers, built a loose functional organization dominated by the engineering department, and developed a 'General Radio culture' (for example, no conflict, management by consensus, slow growth). General Radio's strategy and associated structures, systems, and people were very successful. By World War II, General Radio was the largest test equipment firm in the United States. After World War II, however, increasing technology and cost-based competition began to erode

[1] Source: This article was adapted with permission from *California Management Review*, Vol. 29, No. 1, Fall 1986, pp. 29–44.

General Radio's market share. While management made numerous incremental changes, General Radio remained fundamentally the same organization. In the late 1960s, when CEO Don Sinclair initiated strategic changes, he left the firm's structure and systems intact. This effort at doing new things with established systems and procedures was less than successful. By 1972, the firm incurred its first loss. In the face of this sustained performance decline, Bill Thurston (a long-time General Radio executive) was made President. Thurston initiated system-wide changes. General Radio adopted a more marketing-oriented strategy. Its product line was cut from 20 different lines to three; much more emphasis was given to product-line management, sales, and marketing. Resources were diverted from engineering to revitalize sales, marketing, and production. During 1973, the firm moved to a matrix structure, increased its emphasis on controls and systems, and went outside for a set of executives to help Thurston run this revised General Radio. To perhaps more formally symbolize these changes and the sharp move away from the 'old' General Radio, the firm's name was changed to GenRad. By 1984, GenRad's sales exploded to over $200 million (vs. $44 million in 1972). After 60 years of convergent change around a constant strategy, Thurston and his colleagues (many new to the firm) made discontinuous system-wide changes in strategy, structure, people, and processes. While traumatic, these changes were implemented over a two-year period and led to a dramatic turnaround in GenRad's performance.

■ Prime Computer was founded in 1971 by a group of individuals who left Honeywell. Prime's initial strategy was to produce a high-quality/high-price minicomputer based on semiconductor memory. These founders built an engineering-dominated, loosely structured firm which sold to OEMs and through distributors. This configuration of strategy, structure, people, and processes was very successful. By 1974, Prime turned its first profit; by 1975, its sales were more than $11 million. In the midst of this success, Prime's board of directors brought in Ken Fisher to reorient the organization. Fisher and a whole new group of executives hired from Honeywell initiated a set of discontinuous changes throughout Prime during 1975–1976. Prime now sold a full range of minicomputers and computer systems to OEMs and end-users. To accomplish this shift in strategy, Prime adopted a more complex functional structure, with a marked increase in resources to sales and marketing. The shift in resources away from engineering was so great that Bill Poduska, Prime's head of engineering, left to form Apollo Computer. Between 1975 and 1981, Fisher and his colleagues consolidated and incrementally adapted structure, systems, and processes to better accomplish the new strategy. During this convergent period, Prime grew dramatically to over $260 million by 1981. In 1981, again in the midst of this continuing sequence of increased volume and profits, Prime's board again initiated an upheaval. Fisher and his direct reports left Prime (some of whom founded Encore Computer), while Joe Henson and a set of executives from IBM initiated wholesale changes throughout the organization. The firm diversified into robotics, CAD/CAM, and office systems; adopted a divisional structure; developed a more market-driven orientation; and increased controls and systems. It remains to be seen how this 'new' Prime will fare. Prime must be seen, then, not as a 14-year-old firm, but as three very different organizations, each of which was managed by a different set of executives. Unlike General Radio, Prime initiated these discontinuities during periods of great success.

- The Operating Group at Citibank prior to 1970 had been a service-oriented function for the end-user areas of the bank. The Operating Group hired high school graduates who remained in the 'back-office' for their entire careers. Structure, controls, and systems were loose, while the informal organization valued service, responsiveness to client needs, and slow, steady work habits. While these patterns were successful enough, increased demand and heightened customer expectations led to ever decreasing performance during the late 1960s. In the face of severe performance decline, John Reed was promoted to head the Operating Group. Reed recruited several executives with production backgrounds, and with this new top team he initiated system-wide changes. Reed's vision was to transform the Operating Group to over $260 million by 1981. In 1981, again in the midst of this continuing sequence of increased volume and profits, Prime's board again initiated an upheaval. Fisher Group transformed itself from a service-oriented back office to a factory producing high-quality products. Consistent with this new mission, Reed and his colleagues initiated sweeping changes in strategy, structure, work flows, controls, and culture. These changes were initiated concurrently through-out the back office, with very little participation, over the course of a few months. While all the empirical performance measures improved substantially, these changes also generated substantial stress and anxiety within Reed's group.

- For 20 years, Alpha Corporation was among the leaders in the industrial fastener industry. Its reliability, low cost, and good technical service were important strengths. However, as Alpha's segment of the industry matured, its profits declined. Belt-tightening helped but was not enough. Finally, a new CEO presided over a sweeping restructuring: cutting the product line, closing a plant, trimming overhead; then focusing on computer parts which call for very close tolerances, CAD/CAM tooling, and cooperation with customers on design efforts. After four rough years, Alpha appears to have found a new niche where convergence will again be warranted.

These four short examples illustrate periods of incremental change, or convergence, punctuated by discontinuous changes throughout the organization. Discontinuous or 'frame-breaking' change involves simultaneous and sharp shifts in strategy, power, structure, and controls. Each example illustrates the role of executive leadership in initiating and implementing discontinuous change. Where General Radio, Citibank's Operating Group, and Alpha initiated system-wide changes only after sustained performance decline, Prime proactively initiated system-wide changes to take advantage of competitive/technological conditions. These patterns in organization evolution are not unique. Upheaval, sooner or later, follows convergence if a company is to survive; only a farsighted minority of firms initiate upheaval prior to incurring performance declines.

The task of managing incremental change, or convergence, differs sharply from managing frame-breaking change. Incremental change is compatible with the existing structure of a company and is reinforced over a period of years. In contrast, frame-breaking change is abrupt, painful to participants, and often resisted by the old guard. Forging these new strategy–structure–people–process consistencies and laying the basis for the next period of incremental change calls for distinctive skills.

Because the future health, and even survival, of a company or business unit is at stake, we need to take a closer look at the nature and consequences of convergent change and of differences imposed by frame-breaking change. We need to explore when and why these painful and risky revolutions interrupt previously successful patterns, and whether these discontinuities can be avoided and/or initiated prior to crisis. Finally, we need to examine what managers can and should do to guide their organizations through periods of convergence and upheaval over time.

Patterns in Organizational Evolution: Convergence and Upheaval

Successful companies wisely stick to what works well. At General Radio between 1915 and 1950, the loose functional structure, committee management system, internal promotion practices, control with engineering, and the high-quality, premium-price, engineering mentality all worked together to provide a highly congruent system. These internally consistent patterns in strategy, structure, people, and processes served General Radio for over 35 years.

Similarly, the Alpha Corporation's customer driven, low-cost strategy was accomplished by strength in engineering and production and ever more detailed structures and systems which evaluated cost, quality, and new product development. These strengths were epitomized in Alpha's chief engineer and president. The chief engineer had a remarkable talent for helping customers find new uses for industrial fasteners. He relished solving such problems, while at the same time designing fasteners that could be easily manufactured. The president excelled at production – producing dependable, low-cost fasteners. The pair were role models which set a pattern which served Alpha well for 15 years.

As the company grew, the chief engineer hired kindred customer-oriented application engineers. With the help of innovative users, they developed new products, leaving more routine problem-solving and incremental change to the sales and production departments. The president relied on a hands-on manufacturing manager and delegated financial matters to a competent treasurer-controller. Note how well the organization reinforced Alpha's strategy and how the key people fit the organization. There was an excellent fit between strategy and structure. The informal structure also fitted well – communications were open, the simple mission of the company was widely endorsed, and routines were well understood.

As the General Radio and Alpha examples suggest, convergence starts out with an effective dovetailing of strategy, structure, people, and processes. For other strategies or in other industries, the particular formal and informal systems might be very different, but still a winning combination. The formal system includes decisions about grouping and linking resources as well as planning and control systems, rewards and evaluation procedures, and human resource management systems. The informal system includes core values, beliefs, norms, communication patterns, and actual decision-making and conflict resolution patterns. It is the whole fabric of structure, systems, people, and processes which must be suited to company strategy.

As the fit between strategy, structure, people, and processes is never perfect, convergence is an ongoing process characterized by incremental change. Over time, in all companies studied, two types of converging changes were common: fine-tuning and incremental adaptations.

Converging Change: Fine-Tuning

Even with good strategy–structure–process fits, well-run companies seek even better ways of exploiting (and defending) their missions. Such effort typically deals with one or more of the following:

- Refining policies, methods, and procedures.

- Creating specialized units and linking mechanisms to permit increased volume and increased attention to unit quality and cost.

- Developing personnel especially suited to the present strategy – through improved selection and training, and tailoring reward systems to match strategic thrusts.

- Fostering individual and group commitments to the company mission and to the excellence of one's own department.

- Promoting confidence in the accepted norms, beliefs, and myths.

- Clarifying established roles, power, status, dependencies, and allocation mechanism.

The fine-tuning fills out and elaborates the consistencies between strategy, structure, people, and processes. These incremental changes lead to an ever more interconnected (and therefore more stable) social system.

Converging Change: Incremental Adjustments to Environmental Shifts

In addition to fine-tuning changes, minor shifts in the environment will call for some organizational response. Even the most conservative of organizations expect, even welcome, small changes which do not make too many waves. A popular expression is that almost any organization can tolerate a 'ten-percent change.' At any one time, only a few changes are being made; but these changes are still compatible with the prevailing structures, systems, and processes. Examples of such adjustments are an expansion in sales territory, a shift in emphasis among products in the product line, or improved processing technology in production.

The usual process of making changes of this sort is well known: wide acceptance of the need for change, openness to possible alternatives, objective examination of the pros and cons of each plausible alternative, participation of those directly affected in the preceding analysis, a market test or pilot operation where feasible, time to learn the new activities, established role models, known rewards for positive success, evaluation, and refinement.

The role of executive leadership during convergent periods is to re-emphasize mission and core values and to delegate incremental decisions to middle-level managers. Note that the uncertainty created for people affected by such changes is well within tolerable limits. Opportunity is provided to anticipate and learn what is new, while most features of the structure remain unchanged. The overall system adapts, but it is not transformed.

Converging Change: Some Consequences

For those companies whose strategies fit environmental conditions, convergence brings about better and better effectiveness. Incremental change is relatively easy to implement and ever more optimizes the consistencies between strategy, structure, people, and processes. At AT&T, for example, the period between 1913 and 1980 was one of ever more incremental change to further bolster the 'Ma Bell' culture, systems, and structure, all in service of developing the telephone network.

Convergent periods are, however, a double-edged sword. As organizations grow and become more successful, they develop internal forces for stability. Organization structures and systems become so interlinked that they only allow compatible changes. Further, over time, employees develop habits, patterned behaviors begin to take on values (e.g. 'service is good'), and employees develop a sense of competence in knowing how to get work done within the system. These self-reinforcing patterns of behavior, norms, and values contribute to increased organizational momentum and complacency and, over time, to a sense of organizational history. This organizational history – epitomized by common stories, heroes, and standards – specifies 'how we work here' and 'what we hold important here.'

This organizational momentum is profoundly functional as long as the organization's strategy is appropriate. The Ma Bell and General Radio culture, structure, and systems – and associated internal momentum – were critical to each organization's success. However, if (and when) strategy must change, this momentum cuts the other way. Organizational history is a source of tradition, precedent, and pride which are, in turn, anchors to the past. A proud history often restricts vigilant problem solving and may be a source of resistance to change. When faced with environmental threat, organizations with strong momentum

■   may not register the threat due to organization complacency and/or stunted external vigilance (e.g., the automobile or steel industries); or

- if the threat is recognized, the response is frequently heightened conformity to the status quo and/or increased commitment to 'what we do best.'

For example, the response of dominant firms to technological threat is frequently increased commitment to the obsolete technology (e.g. telegraph/telephone; vacuum tube/transistor; core/semiconductor memory). A paradoxical result of long periods of success may be heightened organizational complacency, decreased organizational flexibility, and a stunted ability to learn.

Converging change is a double-edged sword. Those very social and technical consistencies which are key sources of success may also be the seeds of failure if environments change. The longer the convergent period, the greater these internal forces for stability. This momentum seems to be particularly accentuated in those most successful firms in a product class (for example, Polaroid, Caterpillar, or US Steel), in historically regulated organizations (for example, AT&T, GTE, or financial service firms), or in organizations that have been traditionally shielded from competition (for example, universities, not-for-profit organizations, government agencies and/or services).

On Frame-Breaking Change

What, then, leads to frame-breaking change? Why defy tradition? Simply stated, frame-breaking change occurs in response to or, better yet, in anticipation of major environmental changes – changes which require more than incremental adjustments. The need for discontinuous change springs from one or a combination of the following:

- *Industry discontinuities*. Sharp changes in legal, political, or technological conditions shift the basis of competition within industries. Deregulation has dramatically transformed the financial services and airlines industries. Substitute product technologies (such as jet engines, electronic typing, microprocessors) or substitute process technologies (such as the planar process in semiconductors or float-glass in glass manufacture) may transform the bases of competition within industries. Similarly, the emergence of industry standards, or dominant designs (such as the DC-3, IBM 360, or PDP-8) signal a shift in competition away from product innovation and towards increased process innovation. Finally, major economic changes (e.g. oil crises) and legal shifts (e.g. patent protection in biotechnology or trade/regulator barriers in pharmaceuticals or cigarettes) also directly affect bases of competition.

- *Product life-cycle shifts*. Over the course of a product class life-cycle, different strategies are appropriate. In the emergence phase of a product class, competition is based on product innovation and performance, where in the maturity stage, competition centers on cost, volume, and efficiency. Shifts in patterns of demand alter key factors for success. For example, the demand and nature of competition for minicomputers, cellular telephones, wide-body aircraft, and bowling alley equipment was transformed as these products gained acceptance and their product classes evolved. Powerful international competition may compound these forces.

- *Internal company dynamics.* Entwined with these external forces are breaking points within the firm. Sheer size may require a basically new management design. For example, few inventor-entrepreneurs can tolerate the formality that is linked with large volume; even Digital Equipment Company apparently has outgrown the informality so cherished by Kenneth Olsen. Key people die. Family investors may become more concerned with their inheritance taxes than with company development. Revised corporate portfolio strategy may sharply alter the role and resources assigned to business units or functional areas. Such pressures especially when coupled with external changes, may trigger frame-breaking change.

Scope of Frame-Breaking Change

Frame-breaking change is driven by shifts in business strategy. As strategy shifts so too must structure, people, and organizational processes. Quite unlike convergent change, frame-breaking reforms involve discontinuous changes throughout the organization. These bursts of change do not reinforce the existing system and are implemented rapidly. For example, the system-wide changes at Prime and General Radio were implemented over 18–24-month periods, whereas changes in Citibank's Operating Group were implemented in less than five months. Frame-breaking changes are revolutionary changes of the system as opposed to incremental changes in the system. The following features are usually involved in frame-breaking change:

- *Reformed mission and core values.* A strategy shift involves a new definition of company mission. Entering or withdrawing from an industry may be involved; at least the way the company expects to be outstanding is altered. The revamped AT&T is a conspicuous example. Success on its new course calls for a strategy based on competition, aggressiveness, and responsiveness, as well as a revised set of core values about how the firm competes and what it holds as important. Similarly, the initial shift at Prime reflected a strategic shift away from technology and towards sales and marketing. Core values also were aggressively reshaped by Ken Fisher to complement Prime's new strategy.

- *Altered power and status.* Frame-breaking change always alters the distribution of power. Some groups lose in the shift while others gain. For example, at Prime and General Radio, the engineering functions lost power, resources, and prestige as the marketing and sales functions gained. These dramatically altered power distributions reflect shifts in bases of competition and resource allocation. A new strategy must be backed up with a shift in the balance of power and status.

- *Reorganization.* A new strategy requires a modification in structure, systems, and procedures. As strategic requirements shift, so too must the choice of organization form. A new direction calls for added activity in some areas and less in others. Changes in structure and systems are means to ensure that this reallocation of effort takes place. New structures and revised roles deliberately break business-as-usual behavior.

- *Revised interaction patterns.* The way people in the organization work together has to adapt during frame-breaking change. As strategy is different, new procedures, work flows, communication networks, and decision-making patterns must be established. With these changes in work flows and procedures must also come revised norms, informal decision-making/conflict-resolution procedures, and informal roles.

- *New executives.* Frame-breaking change also involves new executives, usually brought in from outside the organization (or business unit) and placed in key managerial positions. Commitment to the new mission, energy to overcome prevailing inertia, and freedom from prior obligations are all needed to refocus the organization. A few exceptional members of the old guard may attempt to make this shift, but habits and expectations of their associations are difficult to break. New executives are most likely to provide both the necessary drive and an enhanced set of skills more appropriate for the new strategy. While the overall number of executive changes is usually relatively small, these new executives have substantial symbolic and substantive effects on the organization. For example, frame-breaking changes at Prime, General Radio, Citibank, and Alpha Corporation were all spearheaded by a relatively small set of new executives from outside the company or group.

Why All at Once?

Frame-breaking change is revolutionary in that the shifts reshape the entire nature of the organization. Those more effective examples of frame-breaking change were implemented rapidly (e.g. Citibank, Prime, Alpha). It appears that a piecemeal approach to frame-breaking changes gets bogged down in politics, individual resistance to change, and organizational inertia (e.g. Sinclair's attempts to reshape General Radio). Frame-breaking change requires discontinuous shifts in strategy, structure, people, and processes concurrently – or at least in a short period of time. Reasons for rapid, simultaneous implementation include:

- *Synergy* within the new structure can be a powerful aid. New executives with a fresh mission, working in a redesigned organization with revised norms and values, backed up with power and status, provide strong reinforcement. The pieces of the revitalized organization pull together, as opposed to piecemeal change where one part of the new organization is out of synch with the old organization.

- *Pockets of resistance* have a chance to grow and develop when frame-breaking change is implemented slowly. The new mission, shifts in organization, and other frame-breaking changes upset the comfortable routines and precedent. Resistance to such fundamental change is natural. If frame-breaking change is implemented slowly, then individuals have a greater opportunity to undermine the changes and organizational inertia works to further stifle fundamental change.

■ Typically, there is a *pent-up need for change*. During convergent periods, basic adjustments are postponed. Boat-rocking is discouraged. Once constraints are relaxed, a variety of desirable improvements press for attention. The exhilaration and momentum of a fresh effort (and new team) make difficult moves more acceptable. Change is in fashion.

■ Frame-breaking change is an inherently *risky and uncertain venture*. The longer the implementation period, the greater the period of uncertainty and instability. The most effective frame-breaking changes initiate the new strategy, structure, processes, and systems rapidly and begin the next period of stability and convergent change. The sooner fundamental uncertainty is removed, the better the chances of organizational survival and growth. While the pacing of change is important, the overall time to implement frame-breaking change will be contingent on the size and age of the organization.

Patterns in Organization Evolution

This historical approach to organization evolution focuses on convergent periods punctuated by reorientation – discontinuous, organization-wide upheavals. The most effective firms take advantage of relatively long convergent periods. These periods of incremental change build on and take advantage of organization inertia. Frame-breaking change is quite dysfunctional if the organization is successful and the environment is stable. If, however, the organization is performing poorly and/or if the environment changes substantially, frame-breaking change is the only way to realign the organization with its competitive environment. Not all reorientations will be successful (e.g. People Express' expansion and up-scale moves in 1985–86). However, inaction in the face of performance crisis and/or environmental shifts is a certain recipe for failure.

Because reorientations are so disruptive and fraught with uncertainty, the more rapidly they are implemented, the more quickly the organization can reap the benefits of the following convergent period. High-performing firms initiate reorientations when environmental conditions shift and implement these reorientations rapidly (e.g. Prime and Citibank). Low-performing organizations either do not reorient or reorient all the time as they root around to find an effective alignment with environmental conditions.

This metamorphic approach to organization evolution underscores the role of history and precedent as future convergent periods are all constrained and shaped by prior convergent periods. Further, this approach to organization evolution highlights the role of executive leadership in managing convergent periods and in initiating and implementing frame-breaking change.

Conclusion

Our analysis of the way companies evolve over long periods of time indicates that the most effective firms have relatively long periods of convergence giving support to a basic strategy, but such periods are punctuated by upheavals – concurrent and discontinuous changes which reshape the entire organization. Managers should anticipate that when environments change sharply:

- Frame-breaking change cannot be avoided. These discontinuous organizational changes will either be made proactively or initiated under crisis/turnaround condition.

- Discontinuous changes need to be made in strategy, structure, people, and processes concurrently. Tentative change runs the risk of being smothered by individual, group, and organizational inertia.

- Frame-breaking change requires direct executive involvement in all aspects of the change, usually bolstered with new executives from outside the organization.

There are no patterns in the sequence of frame-breaking changes, and not all strategies will be effective. Strategy and, in turn, structure, systems, and processes must meet industry-specific competitive issues.

Effectiveness over changing competitive conditions requires that executives manage fundamentally different kinds of organizations and different kinds of change. An executive team's ability to proactively initiate and implement frame-breaking change and to manage convergent change seem to be important factors which discriminate between organizational renewal and greatness versus complacency and eventual decline.

4.4 Building Learning Organizations

By Peter Senge[1]

The Nature of Learning

Human beings are designed for learning. No one has to teach an infant to walk, or talk, or master the spatial relationships needed to stack eight building blocks that don't topple. Children come fully equipped with an insatiable drive to explore and experiment. Unfortunately, the primary institutions of our society are oriented predominantly toward controlling rather than learning, rewarding individuals for performing for others rather than for cultivating their natural curiosity and impulse to learn. The young child entering school discovers quickly that the name of the game is getting

---

[1] Source: Reprinted from 'The Leader's New Work: Building Learning Organizations,' *Sloan Management Review*, Fall, 1990, by permission of the publisher. Copyright © 1990 by the Sloan Management Review Association. All rights reserved.

the right answer and avoiding mistakes – a mandate no less compelling to the aspiring manager.

'Our prevailing system of management has destroyed our people,' writes W. Edwards Deming, leader in the quality movement. 'People are born with intrinsic motivation, self-esteem, dignity, curiosity to learn, joy in learning. The forces of destruction begin with toddlers – a prize for the best Halloween costume, grades in school, gold stars, and on up through university. On the job, people, teams, divisions are ranked – reward for the one at the top, punishment at the bottom. Management by Objectives (MBO), quotas, incentive pay, business plans, put together separately, division by division, cause further loss, unknown and unknowable.'

Ironically, by focusing on performing for someone else's approval, corporations create the very conditions that predestine them to mediocre performance. Over the long run, superior performance depends on superior learning.

If anything, the need for understanding how organizations learn and accelerating that learning is greater today than ever before. The old days when a Henry Ford, Alfred Sloan, or Tom Watson learned for the organization are gone. In an increasingly dynamic, interdependent, and unpredictable world, it is simply no longer possible for anyone to 'figure it all out at the top.' The old model, 'the top thinks and the local acts,' must now give way to integrating thinking and acting at all levels. While the challenge is great, so is the potential payoff.

Adaptive Learning and Generative Learning

The prevailing view of learning organizations emphasizes increased adaptability. Given the accelerating pace of change, or so the standard view goes, 'the most successful corporation of the 1990s,' according to *Fortune* magazine, 'will be something called a learning organization, a consummately adaptive enterprise.'

But increasing adaptiveness is only the first stage in moving toward learning organizations. The impulse to learn in children goes deeper than desires to respond and adapt more effectively to environmental change. The impulse to learn, at its heart, is an impulse to be generative, to expand our capability. This is why leading corporations are focusing on *generative* learning, which is about creating, as well as *adaptive* learning, which is about coping.

The total quality movement in Japan illustrates the evolution from adaptive to generative learning. With its emphasis on continuous experimentation and feedback, the total quality movement has been the first wave in building learning organizations. But Japanese firms' view of serving the customer has evolved. In the early years of total quality, the focus was on 'fitness to standard,' making a product reliably so that it would do what its designers intended it to do and what the firm told its customers it would do. Then came a focus on 'fitness to need,' understanding better what the customer wanted and then providing products that reliably met those needs. Today, leading-edge firms seek to understand and meet the 'latent need' of the customer – what customers might truly value but have never experienced or would never think to ask for.

Generative learning, unlike adaptive learning, requires new ways of looking at the world, whether in understanding customers or in understanding how to better manage a business. For years, US manufacturers sought competitive advantage in aggressive controls on inventories, incentives against overproduction, and rigid adherence to production forecasts. Despite these incentives, their performance was eventually eclipsed by Japanese firms who saw the challenges of manufacturing differently. They realized that eliminating delays in the production process was the key to reducing instability and improving cost, productivity, and service. They worked to build networks of relationships with trusted suppliers and to redesign physical production processes to reduce delays in materials procurement, production setup, and in-process inventory – much higher-leverage approach to improving both cost and customer loyalty.

As Boston Consulting Group's George Stalk has observed, the Japanese saw the significance of delays because they saw the process of order entry, production scheduling, materials procurement, production, and distribution as an integrated system (see chapter 5, for Stalk's original article). 'What distorts the system so badly is time,' observes Stalk – the multiple delays between events and responses. 'These distortions reverberate throughout the system, producing disruptions, waste, and inefficiency.' Generative learning requires seeing the systems that control events. When we fail to grasp the systemic source of problems, we are left to 'push on' symptoms rather than eliminate underlying causes. The best we can ever do is adaptive learning.

The Leader's New Work

Our traditional view of leaders – as special people who set the direction, make the key decisions, and energize the troops – is deeply rooted in an individualistic and nonsystemic worldview. Especially in the West, leaders are heroes – great men (and occasionally women) who rise to the fore in times of crisis. So long as such myths prevail, they reinforce a focus on short-term events and charismatic heroes rather than on systemic forces and collective learning.

Leadership in learning organizations centers on subtler and ultimately more important work. In a learning organization, leaders' roles differ dramatically from that of the charismatic decision maker. Leaders are designers, teachers, and stewards. These roles require new skills: the ability to build shared vision, to bring to the surface and challenge prevailing mental models, and to foster more systemic patterns of thinking. In short, leaders in learning organizations are responsible for building organizations where people are continually expanding their capabilities to shape their future – that is, leaders are responsible for learning.

Creative Tension: The Integrating Principle

Leadership in a learning organization starts with the principle of creative tension. Creative tension comes from seeing clearly where we want to be, our 'vision,' and telling the truth about where we are, our 'current reality.' The gap between the two generates a natural tension.

Creative tension can be resolved in two basic ways: by raising current reality toward the vision, or by lowering the vision toward current reality. Individuals, groups, and organizations who learn how to work with creative tension learn how to use the energy it generates to move reality more reliably toward their visions.

Without vision there is no creative tension. Creative tension cannot be generated from current reality alone. All the analysis in the world will never generate a vision. Many who are otherwise qualified to lead fail to do so because they try to substitute analysis for vision. They believe that, if only people understood current reality, they would surely feel the motivation to change. They are then disappointed to discover that people resist the personal and organizational changes that must be made to alter reality. What they never grasp is that the natural energy for changing reality comes from holding a picture of what might be that is more important to people than what is.

But creative tension cannot be generated from vision alone; it demands an accurate picture of current reality as well. Vision without an understanding of current reality will more likely foster cynicism than creativity. The principle of creative tension teaches that *an accurate picture of current reality is just as important as a compelling picture of a desired future.*

Leading through creative tension is different from solving problems. In problem solving, the energy for change comes from attempting to get away from an aspect of current reality that is undesirable. With creative tension, the energy for change comes from the vision, from what we want to create, juxtaposed with current reality. While the distinction may seem small, the consequences are not. Many people and organizations find themselves motivated to change only when their problems are bad enough to cause them to change. This works for a while, but the change process runs out of steam as soon as the problems driving the change become less pressing. With problem solving, the motivation for change is extrinsic. With creative tension, the motivation is intrinsic. The distinction mirrors the distinction between adaptive and generative learning.

New Roles

The traditional authoritarian image of the leader as 'the boss calling the shots' has been recognized as oversimplified and inadequate for some time. According to Edgar Schein, 'Leadership is intertwined with culture formation.' Building an organization's culture and shaping its evolution is the 'unique and essential function' of leadership. In a learning organization, the critical roles of leadership – designer, teacher, and steward – have antecedents in the ways leaders have contributed to building organizations in the past. But each role takes on new meaning in the learning organization and, as will be seen in the following sections, demands new skills and tools.

Leader as Designer

The functions of design, or what some have called social architecture, are rarely visible; they take place behind the scenes. The consequences that appear today are the result of work done long in the past, and work today will show its benefits far in the future. Those who aspire to lead out of a desire to control, or gain fame, or simply to be at the center of the action will find little to attract them to the quiet design work of leadership.

But what, specifically, is involved in organizational design? 'Organization design is widely misconstrued as moving around boxes and lines,' says Hanover's O'Brien. 'The first task of organization design concerns designing the governing ideas of purpose, vision, and core values by which people will live.' Few acts of leadership have a more enduring impact on an organization than building a foundation of purpose and core values.

If governing ideas constitute the first design task of leadership, the second design task involves the policies, strategies, and structures that translate guiding ideas into business decisions. Leadership theorist Philip Selznick calls policy and structure the 'institutional embodiment of purpose.' 'Policy making (the rules that guide decisions) ought to be separated from decision making,' says Jay Forrester. 'Otherwise, short-term pressures will usurp time from policy creation.'

Traditionally, writers like Selznick and Forrester have tended to see policy making and implementation as the work of a small number of senior managers. But that view is changing. Both the dynamic business environment and the mandate of the learning organization to engage people at all levels now make it clear that this second design task is more subtle. Henry Mintzberg has argued that strategy is less a rational plan arrived at in the abstract and implemented throughout the organization than an 'emergent phenomenon.' Successful organizations 'craft strategy' according to Mintzberg, as they continually learn about shifting business conditions and balance what is desired and what is possible. The key is not getting the right strategy but fostering strategic thinking.

Behind appropriate policies, strategies, and structures are effective learning processes; their creation is the third key design responsibility in learning organizations. This does not absolve senior managers of their strategic responsibilities. Actually, it deepens and extends those responsibilities. Now they are not only responsible for ensuring that an organization has well-developed strategies and policies but also for ensuring that processes exist whereby these are continually improved.

In the early 1970s, Shell was the weakest of the big seven oil companies. Today, Shell and Exxon are arguably the strongest, both in size and financial health. Shell's ascendance began with frustration. Around

1971 members of Shell's Group Planning in London began to foresee dramatic change and unpredictability in world oil markets. However, it proved impossible to persuade managers that the stable world of steady growth in oil demand and supply they had known for 20 years was about to change. Despite brilliant analysis and artful presentation, Shell's planners realized, in the words of Pierre Wack, that they 'had failed to change behavior in much of the Shell organization.' Progress would probably have ended there, had the frustration not given way to a radically new view of corporate planning.

As they pondered this failure, the planners' view of their basic task shifted: 'We no longer saw our task as producing a documented view of the future business environment five or ten years ahead. Our real target was the microcosm (the 'mental model') of our decision makers.' Only when the planners reconceptualized their basic task as fostering learning rather than devising plans did their insights begin to have an impact. The initial tool used was 'scenario analysis,' through which planners encouraged operating managers to think through how they would manage in the future under different possible scenarios. It mattered not that the managers believed the planners' scenarios absolutely, only that they became engaged in ferreting out the implications. In this way, Shell's planners conditioned managers to be mentally prepared for a shift from low prices to high prices and from stability to instability. The results were significant. When the Organisation of Petroleum Exporting Countries (OPEC) became a reality, Shell quickly responded by increasing local operating company control (to enhance maneuverability in the new political environment), building buffer stocks, and accelerating development of non-OPEC sources – actions that its competitors took much more slowly or not at all.

Somewhat inadvertently, Shell planners had discovered the leverage of designing institutional learning processes whereby, in the words of former planning director De Geus, 'Management teams change their shared mental models of their company, their markets, and their competitors.' Since then, 'planning as learning' has become a byword at Shell, and Group Planning has continually sought out new learning tools that can be integrated into the planning process. Some of these are described below.

Leader as Teacher

Leader as teacher does *not* mean leader as authoritarian expert whose job it is to teach people the 'correct' view of reality. Rather, it is about helping everyone in the organization, oneself included, to gain more insightful views of current reality. This is in line with a popular emerging view of leaders as coaches, guides, or facilitators. In learning organizations, this teaching role is developed further by virtue of explicit attention to people's mental models and by the influence of the systems perspective.

The role of leader as teacher starts with bringing to the surface people's mental models of important issues. No one carries an organization, a market, or a state of technology in his or her head. What we carry in our heads are assumptions. These mental pictures of how the world works have a significant influence on how we perceive problems and opportunities, identify courses of action, and make choices.

One reason that mental models are so deeply entrenched is that they are largely tacit. Ian Mitroff, in his study of General Motors, argues that an assumption that prevailed for years was that, in the United States, 'Cars are status symbols. Styling is therefore more important than quality.' The Detroit automakers didn't say, 'We have a *mental model* that all people care about is styling.' 'Few actual managers would even say publicly that all people care about is styling. So long as the view remained unexpressed, there was little possibility of challenging its validity or forming more accurate assumptions.

But working with mental models goes beyond revealing hidden assumptions. Reality, as perceived by most people in most organizations, means pressures that must be borne, crises that must be reacted to, and limitations that must be accepted. Leaders as teachers help people *restructure their views of reality* to see beyond the superficial conditions and events into the underlying causes of problems and therefore to see new possibilities for shaping the future.

Specifically, leaders can influence people to view reality at three distinct levels: events, patterns of behavior, and systemic structure.

Systemic Structure (Generative)
↓
Patterns of Behavior (Responsive)
↓
Events (Reactive)

The key question becomes 'Where do leaders predominantly focus their own and their organization's attention?'

Contemporary society focuses predominantly on events. The media reinforces this perspective, with almost exclusive attention to short-term, dramatic events. This focus leads naturally to explaining what happens in terms of those events: 'The Dow Jones average went up 16 points because high fourth-quarter profits were announced yesterday.'

Pattern-of-behavior explanations are rarer, in contemporary culture, than event explanations, but they do occur. Trend analysis is an example of seeing patterns of behavior. A good editorial that interprets a set of current events in the context of long-term historical changes is another example. Systemic, structural explanations go even further by addressing the question 'What causes the patterns of behavior?'

In some sense, all three levels of explanation are equally true. But their usefulness is quite different. Event explanations – who did what to whom – doom their holders to a reactive stance toward change. Pattern-of-behavior explanations focus on identifying long-term trends and assessing their implications. They at least suggest how, over time, we can respond to shifting conditions. Structural explanations are the most powerful. Only they address the underlying causes of behavior at a level such that patterns of behavior can be changed.

By and large, leaders of our current institutions focus their attention on events and patterns of behavior, and under their influence, their organizations do likewise. That is why contemporary organizations are predominantly reactive, or at best responsive – rarely generative. On the other hand, leaders in learning organizations pay attention to all three levels, but focus especially on systemic structure; largely by example, they teach people throughout the organization to do likewise.

Leader as Steward

This is the subtlest role of leadership. Unlike the roles of designer and teacher, it is almost solely a matter of attitude. It is an attitude critical to learning organizations.

While stewardship has long been recognized as an aspect of leadership, its source is still not widely understood. I believe Robert Greenleaf came closest to explaining real stewardship, in his seminal book *Servant Leadership*. There, Greenleaf argues that 'the servant leader *is* servant first. . . . It begins with the natural feeling that one wants to seve, to serve *first*. This conscious choice brings one to aspire to lead. That person is sharply different from one who is leader first, perhaps because of the need to assuage an unusual power drive or to acquire material possessions.'

Leaders' sense of stewardship operates on two levels: stewardship for the people they lead and stewardship for the larger purpose or mission that underlies the enterprise. The first type arises from a keen appreciation of the impact one's leadership can have on others. People can suffer economically, emotionally, and spiritually under inept leadership. If anything, people in a learning organization are more vulnerable because of their commitment and sense of shared ownership. Appreciating this naturally instills a sense of responsibility in leaders. The second type of stewardship arises from a leader's sense of personal purpose and commitment to the organization's larger mission. People's natural impulse to learn is unleashed when they are engaged in an endeavor they consider worthy of their fullest commitment. Or, as Lawrence Miller puts it, 'Achieving return on equity does not, as a goal, mobilize the most noble forces of our soul.'

New Skills

New leadership roles require new leadership skills. These skills can only be developed, in my judgment, through a lifelong commitment. It is not enough for one or two individuals to develop these skills. They must be distributed widely throughout the organization. This is one reason that understanding the disciplines of a learning organization is so important. These disciplines embody the principles and practices that can widely foster leadership development.

Three critical areas of skills (disciplines) are building shared vision, surfacing and challenging mental models, and engaging in systems thinking.

Building Shared Vision

The skills involved in building shared vision include the following:

- *Encouraging personal vision.* Shared visions emerge from personal visions. It is not that people only care about their own self-interest – in fact, people's values usually include dimensions that concern family, organization, community, and even the world. Rather, it is that people's capacity for caring is personal.

- *Communicating and asking for support.* Leaders must be willing to continually share their own vision, rather than being the official representative of the corporate vision. They also must be prepared to ask, 'Is this vision worthy of your commitment?' This can be difficult for a person used to setting goals and presuming compliance.

- *Visioning as an ongoing process.* Building shared vision is a never-ending process. At any one point there will be a particular image of the future that is predominant, but that image will evolve. Today, too many managers want to dispense with the 'vision business' by going off and writing the Official Vision Statement. Such statements almost always lack the vitality, freshness, and excitement of a genuine vision that comes from people asking, 'What do we really want to achieve?'

- *Blending extrinsic and intrinsic visions.* Many energizing visions are extrinsic – that is, they focus on achieving something relative to an outsider, such as a competitor. But a goal that is limited to defeating an opponent can, once the vision is achieved, easily become a defensive posture. In contrast, intrinsic goals like creating a new type of product, taking an established product to a new level, or setting a new standard for customer satisfaction can call forth a new level of creativity and innovation. Intrinsic and extrinsic visions need to coexist; a vision solely predicated on defeating an adversary will eventually weaken an organization.

- *Distinguishing positive from negative visions.* Many organizations only truly pull together when their survival is threatened. Similarly, most social movements aim at eliminating what people don't want: for example, antidrug, antismoking, or antinuclear arms movements. Negative visions carry a subtle message of powerlessness: people will only pull together when there is sufficient threat. Negative visions also tend to be short term. Two fundamental sources of energy can motivate organizations: fear and aspiration. Fear, the energy source behind negative visions, can produce extraordinary changes in short periods, but aspiration endures as a continuing source of learning and growth.

Surfacing and Testing Mental Models

Many of the best ideas in organizations never get put into practice. One reason is that new insights and initiatives often conflict with established mental models. The leadership task of challenging assumptions without invoking defensiveness requires reflection and inquiry skills possessed by few leaders in traditional controlling organizations.

■   *Seeing leaps of abstraction.* Our minds literally move at lightning speed. Ironically, this often slows our learning, because we leap to generalizations so quickly that we never think to test them. We then confuse our generalizations with the observable data upon which they are based, treating the generalizations as if they were data.

■   *Balancing inquiry and advocacy.* Most managers are skilled at articulating their views and presenting them persuasively. While important, advocacy skills can become counterproductive as managers rise in responsibility and confront increasingly complex issues that require collaborative learning among different, equally knowledgeable people. Leaders in learning organizations need to have both inquiry and advocacy skills.

■   *Distinguishing espoused theory from theory in use.* We all like to think that we hold certain views, but often our actions reveal deeper views. For example, I may proclaim that people are trustworthy, but never lend friends money and jealously guard my possessions. Obviously, my deeper mental model (my theory in use), differs from my espoused theory. Recognizing gaps between espoused views and theories in use (which often requires the help of others) can be pivotal to deeper learning.

■   *Recognizing and defusing defensive routines.* As one CEO (chief executive officer) in our research program puts it, 'Nobody ever talks about an issue at the eight o'clock business meeting exactly the same way they talk about it at home that evening or over drinks at the end of the day.' The reason is what Chris Argyris calls defensive routines, entrenched habits used to protect ourselves from the embarrassment and threat that come with exposing our thinking. For most of us, such defenses began to build early in life in response to pressures to have the right answers in school or at home. Organizations add new levels of performance anxiety and thereby amplify and exacerbate this defensiveness. Ironically, this makes it even more difficult to expose hidden mental models, and thereby lessens learning. The first challenge is to recognize defensive routines, then to inquire into their operation. Those who are best at revealing and defusing defensive routines operate with a high degree of self-disclosure regarding their own defensiveness.

Systems Thinking

We all know that leaders should help people see the big picture. But the actual skills whereby leaders are supposed to achieve this are not well understood. In my experience, successful leaders often are 'systems thinkers' to a considerable extent. They focus less on day-to-day events and more on underlying trends and forces of change. But they do this almost completely intuitively. The consequence is that they are often unable to explain their intuitions to others and feel frustrated that others cannot see the world the way they do.

One of the most significant developments in management science today is the gradual coalescence of managerial systems thinking as a field of study and practice. This field suggests some key skills for future leaders:

■ *Seeing interrelationships, not things, and processes, not snapshots.* Most of us have been conditioned throughout our lives to focus on things and to see the world in static images. This leads us to linear explanations of systemic phenomenon.

■ *Moving beyond blame.* We tend to blame each other or outside circumstances for our problems. But it is poorly designed systems, not incompetent or unmotivated individuals, that cause most organizational problems. Systems thinking shows us that there is no outside – that you and the cause of your problems are part of a single system.

■ *Distinguishing detail complexity from dynamic complexity.* Some types of complexity are more important strategically than others. Detail complexity arises when there are many variables. Dynamic complexity arises when cause and effect are distant in time and space, and when the consequences over time of interventions are subtle and not obvious to many participants in the system. The leverage in most management situations lies in understanding dynamic complexity, not detail complexity.

■ *Focusing on areas of high leverage.* Some have called systems thinking the 'new dismal science' because it teaches that most obvious solutions don't work – at best, they improve matters in the short run, only to make things worse in the long run. But there is another side to the story. Systems thinking also shows that small, well-focused actions can produce significant, enduring improvements, if they are in the right place. Systems thinkers refer to this idea as the principle of leverage. Tackling a difficult problem is often a matter of seeing where the high leverage lies, where a change – with a minimum of effort – would lead to lasting, significant improvement.

■ *Avoiding symptomatic solutions.* The pressures to intervene in management systems that are going awry can be overwhelming. Unfortunately, given the linear thinking that predominates in most organizations, interventions usually focus on symptomatic fixes, not underlying causes. This results in only temporary relief, and it tends to create still more pressures later on for further, low-leverage intervention. If leaders acquiesce to these pressures, they can be sucked into an endless spiral of increasing intervention. Sometimes the most difficult leadership acts are to refrain from intervening through popular quick fixes and to keep the pressure on everyone to identify more enduring solutions.

The consequences of leaders who lack systems-thinking skills can be devastating. Many charismatic leaders manage almost exclusively at the level of events. They deal in visions and in crises, and little in-between. Under their leadership, an organization hurtles from crisis to crisis. Eventually, the worldview of people in the organization becomes dominated by events and reactiveness. Many, especially those who are deeply committed, become burned out. Eventually, cynicism comes to pervade the organization. People have no control over their time, let alone their destiny.

Similar problems arise with the 'visionary strategist,' the leader with vision who sees both patterns of change and events. This leader is better prepared to manage change. He or she can explain strategies in terms of emerging trends, and thereby foster a climate that is less reactive. But such leaders still impart a responsive orientation rather than a generative one.

Many talented leaders have rich, highly systemic intuitions but cannot explain those intuitions to others. Ironically, they often end up being authoritarian leaders, even if they don't want to, because only they see the decisions that need to be made. They are unable to conceptualize their strategic insights so that these can become public knowledge, open to challenge and further improvement.

Developing Leaders and Learning Organizations

In a recently published retrospective on organization development in the 1980s, Marshall Sashkin and N. Warner Burke observe the return of an emphasis on developing leaders who can develop organizations. They also note Schein's critique that most top executives are not qualified for the task of developing culture. Learning organizations represent a potentially significant evolution of organizational culture. So it should come as no surprise that such organizations will remain a distant vision until the leadership capabilities they demand are developed. 'The 1990s may be the period,' suggest Sashkin and Burke, 'during which organization development and (a new sort of) management development are reconnected.'

I believe that this new sort of management development will focus on the roles, skills, and tools for leadership in learning organizations. Undoubtedly, the ideas offered above are only a rough approximation of this new territory. The sooner we begin seriously exploring the territory, the sooner the initial map can be improved – and the sooner we will realize an age-old vision of leadership:

> The wicked leader is he who the people despise.
> The good leader is he who the people revere.
> The great leader is he who the people say, 'We did it ourselves.'
>
> (Lao Tsu)

4.5   Choosing the Right Change Path

By Paul Strebel[1]

Change management is suffering from competing approaches. On the one hand, chief executives put their companies through radical restructuring, with little account taken of the time and process needed to change skills and behavior. Then they are surprised to find that they have to repeat the exercise a few years later, because once the restructuring is over, change stops. On the other hand, executives influenced by theories of organizational behavior encourage deep cultural change in their companies from the bottom up and are surprised to find that financial performance, rather than improving, is suffering from the impact of external change drivers.

Barring a fortuitous combination of events, these competing approaches to managing change are doomed to failure. Programs based primarily on the change drivers, ignoring the forces of resistance, are as prone to failure as those dealing primarily with the forces of resistance, ignoring the change drivers. What is needed is the choice of a change path based on a diagnosis of both the forces of change and resistance.

The importance of the forces of change and resistance was pointed out already in the 1940s by the psychologist, Kurt Lewin (1947), who showed how the force field, or the tension between environmental change and psychological resistance, can be used to explain human behavior. The same idea of a force field is frequently evoked in the context of change management and has resurfaced recently in the academic literature on organizational change (see e.g. Ginsberg and Bucholz, 1990; Meyer, Brooks, and Goes, 1990). But little, if anything, has been done to relate the force field to the choice of generic change paths.

By distinguishing between strong and weak forces of change, strong and weak forces of resistance, and the balance between them, eight different change paths can be identified. The choice of the most appropriate path can be made by using a series of questions about the forces of change and resistance to diagnose a particular change situation. A simple graphical tool called a change arena can be used to diagram the change paths. The change arena can be employed to depict corporate change campaigns, incorporating a sequence of change paths, that explicitly take account of the variations in the interplay between the forces of change and resistance.

---

[1] Source: This article was adapted with permission from *California Management Review*, Winter 1994, pp. 29–51.

Mapping out the Change Arena

When dealing with complex, multiphase change, the first step is to identify the forces for change and resistance acting on the company, as well as the generic change processes that might be used to deal with the forces. Change forces come in three basic forms:

- established trends in the socio-political, economic, technological, competitive, and organizational environments;

- turning points that reflect the limits to the established trends (limits to the existing resources, capacity, investment, growth) and the stimuli promoting new trends (innovation, life cycle shifts, new players);

- internal change drivers in the form of organizational shifts, new managers, and change agents.

The strength of a change force is reflected in the rate of change it is causing in the environment. From the company perspective, the strength of a change force is determined by its current or future impact on the company's performance (most frequently measured by market share, sales, or profits). A strong change force creates a substantial decline in the performance of a company that is not adapted to it, and improvement in the performance of a company that is adapted. Typically, the stronger the change force on an unadapted company, the larger the gap between what is needed for adapting to the force of change and where the company is today – that is, the greater the change requirements in terms of tangible and intangible resources, functional competencies and organizational capabilities.

The forces of resistance reflect the response of the company's internal and external stakeholders to the change requirements. Resistance comes in four basic forms:

- rigid structures and systems reflecting organizations, business technology, and stakeholder resources that are not consistent with the forces of change;

- closed mindsets reflecting business beliefs and strategies that are oblivious to the forces of change;

- entrenched cultures reflecting values, behaviors, and skills that are not adapted to the forces of change;

- counterproductive change momentum driven by historical or other change drivers that are not relevant to the most urgent forces of change.

There is a natural hierarchy in terms of the difficulty and time required to break down the various forms of resistance: internal structures and systems (excluding technology) typically can be altered most rapidly and readily; more time is required to convert closed business mindsets to the need for change; cultural change involving behaviors and skills is much more difficult and time consuming; counterproductive change typically constitutes the strongest form of resistance because it encompasses the other forms. (To get rid of the resistance, the supporting structure and systems have to be altered, mindsets have to be changed, and new behaviors and skills have to be learned.) Most change processes involve several, if not all the forms of resistance. The overall strength of the resistance can be summarized in terms of the time and resources needed to realign the company, or business unit, and its status quo agents, with the force of change.

Four generic change processes can be distinguished for dealing with the forces of change and resistance. Although these can be found in various forms in the literature on change management, in the present context they can be described most simply in terms of the four domains of the change arena shown in Figure 4.5.1, each domain corresponding to a different combination of strong/weak forces of change and resistance.

In the top left-hand corner, weak change forces hardly affect an industry or company with strong resistance. Since the resistance threshold has not been reached, the status quo prevails and no change occurs. Status quo agents set the tone by emphasizing continuity based on old behavior (Cyert and March, 1963). This is typical of closed, inward-looking systems such as regulated markets and bureaucratic government organizations subject only to weak forces of change. Provided the force does not increase, the system may continue with this posture indefinitely.

In the opposite, bottom right-hand corner of the arena, the forces of change are strong and the resistance is weak. The forces of change far exceed

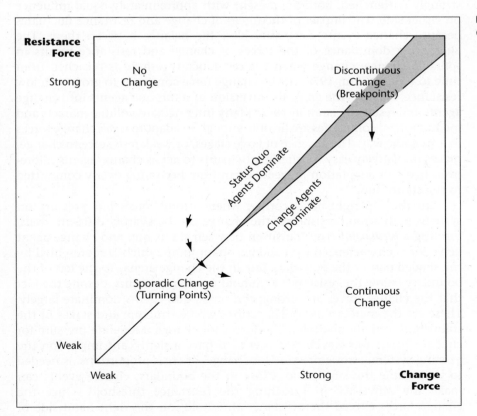

FIGURE 4.5.1
Change arena

the resistance threshold, so the system adapts continuously to the change forces. This represents a flexible industry or company that responds to strong forces in the environment, one in which there is little resistance to change. All the participants perceive the forces for change. There are few status quo agents; almost everyone is a change agent. Whenever adaptation is required, the full house of change agents ensures that the system responds accordingly (Lawrence and Lorsch, 1967). Small new companies and independent business units facing strong forces, especially those in high-tech and financial service industries, often come close to continuous adaptation. The closest are firms in high-volume, competitive markets for commodities and financial instruments, in which there are no obstacles to change.

Bisecting the change arena is a diagonal which marks the boundary between the dominance of the status quo agents and the forces of resistance on the one side, and the dominance of the change agents and forces of change on the other side. Along the diagonal the forces of change and resistance are finely balanced. A slight alteration in the balance can shift the dominant influence in the system between the status quo and change agents.

In the bottom left-hand corner of the arena where the forces of change are weak and the resistance is weak, the boundary between old and new behavior is easily crossed. Neither the status quo nor the change agents are strongly entrenched; both are present with approximately equal influence on either side. The impact of the forces of change and resistance fluctuates because chance events can easily alter the balance between them. The alternating dominance of the forces of change and resistance results in sporadic change: change when the resistance threshold is breached from time to time (Quinn, 1978). If the change force continues to grow with low resistance, it causes the gradual conversion of status quo agents into change agents and results in a *turning point*. Many intermediate-volume markets and medium-sized companies are flexible enough to adapt to weak change forces in a sporadic way. The absence of large stakes, or weak resistance to change, makes it relatively easy for their participants to act as change agents. Moreover, frequent adaptation prevents them from becoming overly committed to the status quo.

In the top right-hand corner, where strong forces put pressure on systems with strong resistance, the change can be sharply discontinuous, forming a *breakpoint*. The transition between status quo and change agent behavior is characterized by a sudden sharp jump which is represented by the shaded part of the boundary line in the change arena. To the left of the boundary below the resistance threshold no change occurs, despite the fact that the change forces are strong; the status quo agents dominate largely. These are the markets and organizations where structure and stakes in the status quo initially neutralize the forces for change. Moderate pressure for change creates too few change agents to have a significant impact on the existing system. Strong pressure for change, of crisis proportions, is needed to undermine the status quo. Close to the boundary, chance events can make the difference in breaching the resistance threshold. Once the change forces exceed the resistance threshold, on the right hand side of the boundary, the resistance breaks down. Domination by the change agents occurs all of a sudden when the balance of power tips in their favor. A massive shift takes place from status quo to change agent behavior, thereby triggering a breakpoint (Meyer, 1982).

Breakpoints in rigid systems are the stuff that revolutions, market crashes, and radical corporate reorganizations are made of. The abandonment of the Bretton Woods agreement and the oil price shocks of the 1970s, for example, introduced an era of sharply fluctuating exchange and interest rates, which completely changed competitive conditions in many industries from one moment to the next. The breakpoints in the financial markets in the late 1980s and the collapse of the command economies in the early 1990s have reinforced the trend toward more frequent radical shifts in the competitive environment and in organizations. As long as strong forces continue to confront strong resistance, breakpoints will be frequent.

However, the change arena suggests that all four change types are relevant. The continuing and varying tension between the forces of resistance and change, between the status quo and a new order, determines the type of change that occurs. Even if one change type is in the limelight because of overall economic conditions, the position of individual industries, companies, and business units differs and evolves over time. The location of a business in the change arena during a particular period shapes the kind of change that the business is likely to experience.

When managers intervene they typically alter the configuration of the forces for change and resistance. The company moves around in the change arena tracing out a change path. Viable change paths are those which successfully adapt the company to its environment. To identify a viable change path, a series of questions about the relative strength of the forces of change and resistance must be answered. These questions are summarized in Figure 4.5.2 in the form of an outline of the change path diagnostic.

The first question that must be answered is: How strong are the forces of change and what is their impact on the company's performance? It is important to distinguish between situations in which the forces of change are already having a strong negative impact on the performance of the company (these are situations calling for *reactive change*) and situations in which the company is doing well and the forces of change have yet to affect performance (those calling for *proactive change*).

Identifying Reactive Change Paths

In the case of reactive change, the manager and company have to respond to well developed forces of change and resistance. The company is close to the edge of a breakpoint (see Figure 4.5.1). To identify a viable change path under these conditions, the relevant question to be answered is: What is the balance between the forces of change and resistance? Or, more explicitly, can the forces of change be rolled back? The answer depends on the nature of the forces of change and the resources and time at the disposal of the

FIGURE 4.5.2
Change path diagnostic

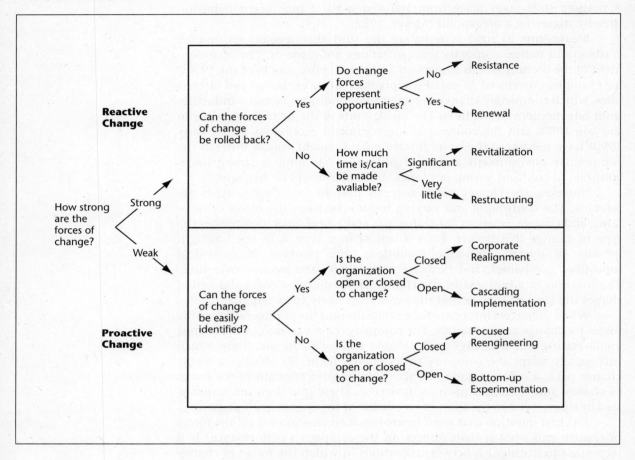

company. The characteristics of the corresponding reactive change paths are summarized in Table 4.5.1.

Change Forces Can Be Rolled Back

If the change force can be rolled back, then the less radical change associated with renewal or resistance will be appropriate (see Table 4.5.1). The key issue is whether the change force represents a business opportunity or threat? If the change force is a business threat, then the company is best off on a path of resistance using its resources and existing momentum to either avoid or role back the change force. By contrast, the company obviously should adapt to a change force that represents a business opportunity. Since the change force can be neutralized, adaptation typically is limited to parts of the organization on a path of renewal. Adaptation often removes the need for further change, until the pressure builds up again. If so, this results in sporadic, stepwise change.

TABLE 4.5.1
Reactive change paths

Interplay between forces of change and resistance	Change Path	Scope of Change	Pace of Change Process
Change force can be rolled back; represents a threat	Resistance	No internal change	Depends on ability to contain change force
Change force can be rolled back; but is an opportunity	Renewal	Change limited to parts of the organization	Periodic stepwise change
Change force cannot be rolled back; time is available	Revitalization	Ongoing change throughout the organization	Slow continuous adaptation
Change force cannot be rolled back; very little time available	Restructuring	Intense change on a few dimensions	Sudden change jump

Resistance path   A resistance path is appropriate when strong resistance that is closed to change confronts a change force that is a threat but can be contained. The resistance path presumes the firm can avoid a potential organizational breakpoint by working on its environment to create more stable conditions where the change force is weaker. What little change occurs internally is directed toward reducing the pressure exerted by the change force. The resistance path often involves interacting with government and public agencies, trade and industry associations, and other external groups that can channel and reduce the forces of change in the business environment.

A resistance path often involves the pursuit of a niche formula, designed to avoid need for sharp change by finding a corner of the market protected from the change force. This formula is generally more useful for smaller players. Rolex, Audemars-Piguet, and the other up-market Swiss watch companies carved out a high-quality niche that shielded them from the massive breakpoint created by Seiko, Citizen, and other East Asian competitors. As one of their managers put it, 'We have never heard of the Japanese.'

Niche formulas are common in the German-speaking world. Specialized, high-quality products represent the strategy of thousands of medium-sized and small German companies, the so-called 'Mittelstand.' They have created highly profitable, well-protected niches in the world market. From their niches, the Mittelstand contribute a great deal to Germany's record exports, despite the discontinuities faced by the more exposed major players.

Renewal path   A renewal path is appropriate when the change force represents an opportunity that can be exploited with stepwise change. The scope of the change is typically limited to parts of the company and the pace is sporadic. Both internal and external organization with various stakeholders may be involved. Through adaptation, renewal takes the pressure off and weakens the change force.

In the 1980s, Procter & Gamble (the detergent giant) and Frito-Lay (the potato chip maker owned by Pepsi) invaded the $2.2 million cookie market that Nabisco had dominated for almost a century. With a heavy barrage of advertising, Frito-Lay was said to have captured 20 percent of the Kansas City market in a few weeks. Procter & Gamble spent $20 million on advertising and promotion for a comfortable 25 percent share in six months. Nabisco's initial reaction was to add more chocolate chips to its 'Chips Ahoy' hard cookies. Stock analysts on Wall Street were not convinced by this lame response and their commentary increased the pressure for change. (See arrow 1 in Figure 4.5.3.)

Management then decided to shake up its complacent mindset and shake off Nabisco's reputation as 'a sleepy sales company that did little to push its products.' It initiated a renewal of the product range with the company's biggest cookie development project in years. Sixteen months after Frito-Lay's first attack, a new Nabisco line with fifteen varieties, called

FIGURE 4.5.3
Nabisco's renewal path

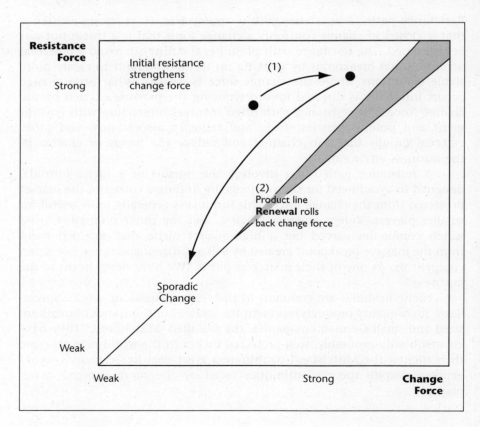

Almost Home, appeared on supermarket shelves. Presented as 'the moistest, chewiest, most perfectly baked cookies the world has ever tasted . . . well, almost,' the new line was supported by a $25 million advertising counter-attack. When the dust finally settled, Frito-Lay's market share had fallen back to 8 percent, Procter & Gamble's to 20 percent. Nabisco with its established warehousing, distribution, and sales strengths had renewed its product line and captured 35 percent of the soft cookie segment (arrow 2 in Figure 4.5.3).

The renewal path was appropriate for Nabisco, because the change force could be rolled back by exploiting the strengths of the company to attack the competition and enter the market for chewy cookies. The adaptation to the change force was limited to a change in mindset with only part of the organization being involved, in this case, the product development and marketing departments. Once this had been done, the competition dealt with, and the demand for chewy cookies satisfied, the force for change was much weaker.

Change Forces Cannot Be Rolled Back

If the change force cannot be rolled back, only the more radical change associated with restructuring and revitalization will be able to adapt the company to the change force. The key issue is how much time is, or can be made available before the change force overwhelms the resistance? (Fry & Killing, 1989). When enough time is available, entrenched cultural resistance and momentum can be reduced gradually to initiate a corporate turning point followed by a pervasive revitalization. When the time available is short, restructuring will be needed to break the resistance. The two paths are contrasted below.

Revitalization path   A revitalization path, involving a reactive turning point, is appropriate when resistance based on culture and momentum must be adapted to a strong and growing change force. The strong external change forces can be used indirectly to drive the internal organizational change processes. The pace of change is typically slow, but continuous and all-encompassing. Under these conditions, lowering the resistance usually stimulates the change forces by converting status quo agents into change agents. Revitalization can only be implemented if the firm can protect itself from the negative effects of the change force long enough to accomplish the necessary cultural turning point.

When Jan Carlson took over as president, the Scandinavian Airlines System (SAS) was struggling with the impact of a world-wide recession and an accumulated two-year deficit of $30 million after 17 consecutive years of profits. Carlson had enough accumulated resources, however, to initiate a change in strategic momentum plus a cultural revitalization. While competitors cut back on new product development in the face of sagging demand, SAS invested heavily in its Businessman's Airline Program. Among strategic initiatives were a cost reduction drive, a punctuality drive, a new corporate identity, and new marketing projects. These moves opened the company up and by improving performance reduced the external pressure, thereby, providing the time for more fundamental change (arrow 1 in Figure 4.5.4).

The centerpiece of the change process, however, was a cultural revolution. Responsibility for action was delegated downward to the front line, putting employees in charge. Management was asked to serve as consultants rather than as leaders of the organization. To implement the cultural revolution, Carlson and his team personally visited the front line all over the company and established a training program for 20,000 managers and employees on the new concept of service. According to Carlson, 'Giving a person freedom to take responsibility for his ideas, decisions, and actions is to release hidden resources.'

By encouraging the change agents both inside and outside SAS to move into action, Carlson stimulated a gradual process of fundamental change (arrow 2 in Figure 4.5.4). This turning point approach was facilitated by the time that could be made available and avoided the organizational trauma associated with breakpoint restructuring.

Restructuring path   A restructuring path, involving a reactive breakpoint, is appropriate when a strong and growing change force confronts strong resistance that is closed to change. On this path, because time is very limited, the organization is given a sharp shock to adapt it to the environment. The scope of the change is highly focused, typically on organizational hardware such as structure and systems. This facilitates control of the transition and avoids possible disintegration.

Organizational restructuring – via acquisition, divestment, reorganization, downsizing, and so on – is a common way of trying to respond to an external breakpoint, especially in the Anglo-Saxon world. In Continental Europe and Japan, the restructuring often takes place within a larger industrial group, where the parent company and related banks play a major role. For companies with strong forces of resistance, the shock created by a radical change imposed from the top down is often the only way of unfreezing existing structures before the forces of change overwhelm the company.

When Bob Horton took over as chairman of BP in early 1990, he initiated Project 1990, which was designed to transform the bureaucratic, civil service culture of the company. Its purpose was to make BP capable of discovering and unleashing corporate entrepreneurs to find new opportunities for the company's dwindling oil reserves. The number of businesses, layers of management, committees, head office staff, and so on were cut. This initial streamlining lowered the resistance to change somewhat and by reducing costs also lowered the change pressure. (See arrow 1 in Figure 4.5.5.)

Workshops, communication and training programs were used to promote a new culture based on values of 'openness, care, teamwork, empowerment and trust. People will be expected to take decisions themselves, rather than through committees,' said Horton. But costs had not been reduced enough to sustain this revitalization effort (arrow 2 in Figure 4.5.5).

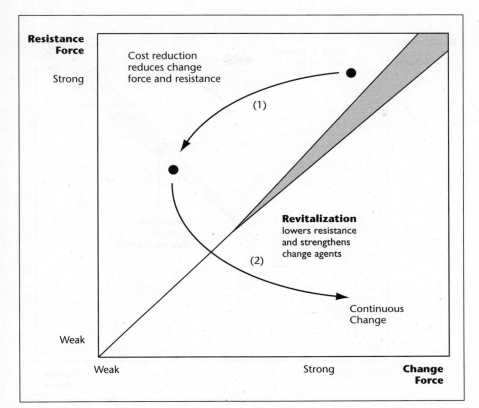

FIGURE 4.5.4
SAS's revitalization path

BP was facing a more immediate problem in the form of the worldwide economic downturn, which severely constrained the company's ability to maintain the tempo of exploration, debt repayments and dividends. The conflict between the longer run internal objectives of Project 1990, to create a more entrepreneurial culture, and the external market forces of contraction seriously compromised the whole change effort. BP announced its first historic loss in the first quarter of 1992. And on June 25th, Bob Horton resigned in 'what appeared to be a coup by his fellow directors.' In the presence of strong financial pressure, with an organization still closed to radical change and with time running out, the Board had little choice. It put BP through a forced process of restructuring based on radical cost reduction, as well a new financial policy of lower dividends and reduced investment in exploration (arrow 3 in Figure 4.5.5).

Putting Together a Change Campaign

A complete radical change campaign, as the BP example illustrates, may require several moves in the change arena. The initial position of the company and the constellation of forces may be such that, in the time

FIGURE 4.5.5
BP's restructuring path

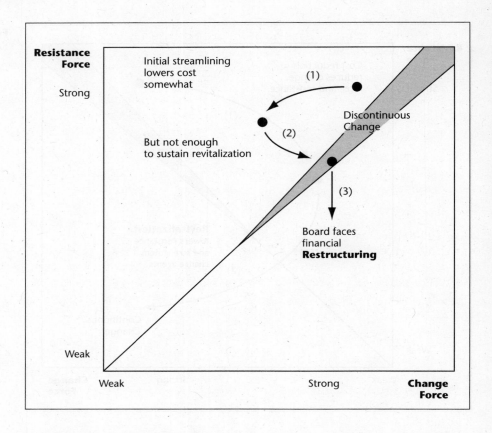

available, all the change requirements cannot be achieved with a single change path. There may be a set of change forces of differing urgency. To deal with a set of change forces, a change campaign is needed in the form of a sequence of change paths.

A reactive change campaign can be used to come from behind and leapfrog the competition. Under these conditions, there is often a company-specific change force with a strong financial impact, together with a competitive change force with somewhat longer run impact. Being the greatest threat to survival, the strongest change force must be dealt with in the first phase of the change campaign, while the weaker change force(s) is/are dealt with in the subsequent phase(s). Once the necessary resources and competence have been acquired to deal with the strongest change force, competence can be added to deal with the other forces.

A classic example of how such a reactive change campaign evolves is provided by the Harley Davidson story. 'At the start of the 1980s, few people gave Harley-Davidson much chance to survive. The last US motorcycle maker was being battered by the Japanese. Its share of the super heavy-weight motorcycle market had fallen from 75 percent in 1973 to 25 percent.' As Peter Reid pointed out in his book on Harley Davidson, more than half the machines coming off Harley's assembly line had missing parts; the dealers had to fix them up before they could be sold.

The first phase of the change campaign was triggered by the appointment of Vaugh Beals as CEO in 1975. He intervened immediately to protect Harley's operations from the immediate financial and competitive change forces in order to keep the company in business. He appealed to the banks for financial support to restructure the balance sheet; a quality control program was set up with the chief engineer to repair the bikes before selling them to the dealers; the design skills of William G. Davidson, grandson of one of the founders, were deployed in the form of styling innovations to stem the erosion of market share.

During the second phase, Beals and his team intervened to revitalize the production operations with new skills and behaviors. After a visit to Honda's plant in Marysville, Ohio, and a successful pilot program, they decided to introduce just-in-time inventory control and quality improvement. Some of the workers laughed at the idea of replacing Harley's computerized control system, overhead conveyors, and high-rise parts storage with just-in-time push carts. To deal with the resistance, Harley executives spent months meeting with employees from all departments. The employees were involved in planning the system and working out the details. 'No changes were implemented until the people involved understood and accepted them. It took two months before the consensus decision was made to go ahead. That was a Friday – and we started making the changes on Monday.' The employees responded with initiative. The company followed up by teaching workers the use of statistical tools needed for quality control, training plant managers to become team leaders, and helping suppliers to use similar methods.

Having laid the quality and cost foundation for its comeback, Harley turned to the third phase of the campaign: adding perceived value through renewal of marketing. First, it won five years of declining import tariff protection against the big Japanese bikes. Then to shape the mindset of its customers a series of TV commercials announced Super Ride, a demonstration program inviting bikers to try out a new Harley at any of the 600 or more dealers. As a result, potential buyers were increasingly convinced that Harley had solved its quality control problems. Super Ride became so successful that Harley takes a fleet of demo bikes to all motorcycle rallies. Money was also spent boosting dealers and forming the Harley Owners Group (HOG). The club sponsors bikers' events virtually every weekend from April to November all over the country and includes managers and their wives: 'HOG is one way we differentiate ourselves from our Japanese competitors.' Indeed, Honda tried and failed to create its own version of HOG.

In 1983, Harley moved from the red to the black in terms of profitability. Its market share started climbing again. By 1989, Harley had recaptured almost 50 percent of the super-heavyweight bike market, with profits of $26.9 million on sales of $810.1 million.

The overall change process can be summarized graphically by mapping out the intervention paths in the change arena as shown in Figure 4.5.6 for Harley-Davidson.

FIGURE 4.5.6
Harley Davidson leapfrog:
sequence of change paths

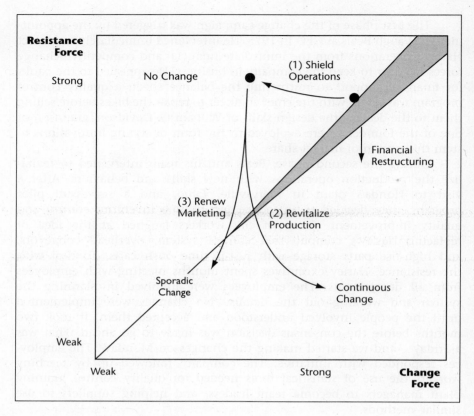

- *Path 1*. Resistance path to stay in the game by shielding operations from the most urgent change forces with financial restructuring and W. Davidson's designs.

- *Path 2*. Revitalizing to catch up with the Japanese by changing the culture and moving production toward continuous improvement.

- *Path 3*. Renewal to outperform the Japanese by incremental addition of value through marketing (Super Ride and HOG programs).

The key to the success of Harley's change campaign was the way in which the change paths were sequenced to deal with the stronger change forces first, thereby clearing the way for dealing with the weaker ones. Furthermore, each change path was consistent with the strength of the corresponding forces of change and resistance.

The timing of the transition between the paths is crucial. If the process moves too soon from one path to the next, the basis for supporting the next path may not be sufficient. On the other hand, if the process is too slow, the company may miss the window of opportunity that often opens up after an industry breakpoint.

Creating Proactive Breakpoints and Turning Points

In the case of proactive change, the change forces have yet to affect performance. Typically, there is enough time for whatever change path might be envisaged. However, the change requirements are often difficult to specify, because, as an industry leader, the company has no other example to follow. In addition, when a company is ahead of the competition, and when there is no performance crisis, it is much more difficult to mobilize the organization for change than when it has to react to the moves of others. In situations that call for proactive change, people may agree intellectually that something more is needed to stay ahead, but when things are going well, it is not easy to get an emotional commitment to change from comfortable status quo agents.

The main diagnostic question to be answered when selecting a proactive change path is whether the forces of change can be easily identified? When the change forces are easy to identify, action is called for to capitalize on the new environment as soon as possible before the competitors do so. By contrast, when the environmental change forces are difficult to identify, a more exploratory response is needed to give the organization the opportunity to discover the direction of the new change forces. The corresponding proactive change paths are described below and summarized in Table 4.5.2.

Change Forces Can Be Identified

The key to mobilizing for emerging change forces that can be identified is to bring the external change forces into the organization, to create a tension between where the organization is and where it should be going. Typically, status quo agents can only be converted into change agents if they feel the change force directly in the form of a threat to their position, or an opportunity to improve it. Successful proactive change managers have found numerous ways of converting the identifiable external change forces into internal change drivers. The question is whether the organization is open or closed to change?

Corporate realignment If the organization is closed to change, then it has to be jolted into recognizing the forces of change: for example, by challenging the company internally with another organization that is closer to the force of change – that is, by initiating a breakpoint in the form of an organizational realignment.

A common approach to an organizational realignment is through an acquisition or merger. Helmut Maucher of Nestlé anticipated the global consolidation of the food industry and tried to revitalize the company by streamlining procedures and shifting power from the head office on Lake

TABLE 4.5.2
Creating proactive change

Forces of change and resistance	Change Path	Nature of Path	Motivation to change
Change force easy to identify; organization closed to change	Corporate Realignment	Organizational contrast with another approach	Challenge to resolve organizational tension
Change force easy to identify; organization open to change	Cascading Implementation	Progressive adaptation to change forces	Participative commitment
Change force difficult to identify; organization closed to change	Focused Re-engineering	Benchmarking. Explicit focused comparisons	Threat implicit in performance of benchmark
Change force difficult to identify; organization open to change	Bottom-up Experimenting	Learning by example from successful internal change	Competition to match example

Geneva into the field. Although these actions improved performance somewhat, they also increased the resistance to globalization by strengthening the power of the geographic zones and the accompanying national cultures (arrow 1 in Figure 4.5.7).

Little else changed until Nestlé was exposed internally, through the acquisition of Rowntree, to a different way of doing things that reflected the globally oriented forces of change. The acquired Rowntree became Nestlé's first center for a global product line, in this case, confectionery. The tension between this new global product line and the zonal structure created dissatisfaction with the existing situation, thereby, providing the motivation for fundamental change (arrow 2 in Figure 4.5.7). In response to this tension, Nestlé put itself through a structural breakpoint – in the form of two new global, strategic product groups, one of which included confectionery – as part of a corporate realignment from a local to a global orientation (arrow 3 in Figure 4.5.7).

In the absence of the Rowntree acquisition (or some other motivating event), it would have been very difficult to generate the organizational energy to support fundamental change. The size and inertia in the Nestlé organization precluded the use of a more gradual turning point. On the other hand, relative to top-down reactive restructuring, Nestlé's proactive realignment provided much more time for the organization to take ownership of the need for change.

Cascading implementation   If the organization is open to change, then it can be asked to begin implementing. The key managers can be encouraged to become change agents to exploit the change force in their business units,

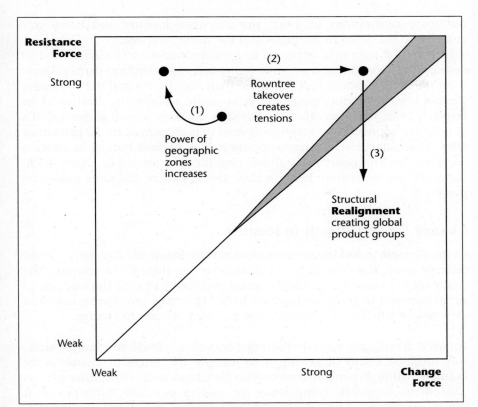

FIGURE 4.5.7
Nestlé's realignment path

both in a stepwise organizational turning point and in a cascading implementation from the top down through the organization.

When Seiko's planning department issued their report on market saturation and the increasing weakness in watch prices, Ichiro Hattori, the CEO, felt that the company should do something. The question was how to get a company with very healthy profits to respond to such a weak change force. Hattori first made the threat more real by highlighting Matsushita's plans for a TV watch in addition to the pressure on prices. He then began at the top by asking his fellow directors on the board what Daini Seikosha's response should be to the competitive situation. They opted for diversification into electronic equipment.

When he was satisfied with their answers he moved to the second stage, a company-wide conference for approximately 50 senior managers. Each was asked to 'propose a three-year strategic plan at the divisional and departmental levels relating to the corporate survival scenario for 1990 incorporating diversification into electronic equipment.'

In early 1982, once these plans had been accepted by the board, the third stage began with a three-day seminar for 250 junior managers who were asked to develop the implementation of the plan at their level. Finally, a Total Quality Control program was initiated to 'ensure the highest level of corporatewide implementation.' And at the time of the centenary celebrations in 1982, the corporate identity and name was changed to the Seiko Instruments and Electronics Co. Ltd.

It took longer than expected to get corporate-wide consensus and to develop the necessary new manufacturing and engineering expertise. Moreover, the diversification cost was more than anticipated and the customers wanted a wider product range. Yet Seiko easily achieved its diversification target in 1986, four years ahead of schedule. By then Seiko had developed a new line of sophisticated graphics devices that accounted for 50 percent of sales. The collaborative cascade approach had allowed Hattori to create a proactive turning point from above. (See the four arrows in Figure 4.5.8; these are not numbered, because they are all part of the same cascading process.)

Change Forces Difficult to Identify

Getting people to feel the external change force inside the company is most difficult when the change forces themselves are difficult to identify. The challenge is to create a mobilizing sense of discomfort with the way things are as opposed to the way they should be. How this can best be achieved depends on whether the organization is closed or open to change.

Focused re-engineering If the organization is closed to change, some way must be found of getting it to identify the forces of change – for example, through explicit comparison (benchmarking) with other players (customers, suppliers, competitors, or leaders in other industries with similar processes). The first key to success is a breakpoint in mindset. Then, based on the benchmarking or other analysis, processes and systems can be redesigned from scratch. This serves to improve efficiency and effectiveness by eliminating the waste of resources and time and focusing on the needs of the customer. Relative to corporate realignment, such re-engineering of the affected systems and processes leads to a more focused breakpoint.

Bottom-up experimenting If the organization is open to change, it can be stimulated to identify the forces of change by encouraging experimentation to find an example of successful internal change that embodies the change force. Once an example of successful change has been produced, it can be used as a cultural change driver to create an organizational turning point from the bottom up in the rest of the organization.

Such change often emerges in unexpected ways, at unexpected places. For example, in a move to cut costs, the manager of the Energy Chemicals Division of a major oil company temporarily stopped all field trips by the research and technology staff from the central laboratory. As anticipated, this decision produced strong reactions from both the sales force and the technology unit: the sales force complained that they could not do their work without a technologist on site; technology complained that they no longer had field trips to test their new products. Unintentionally, however,

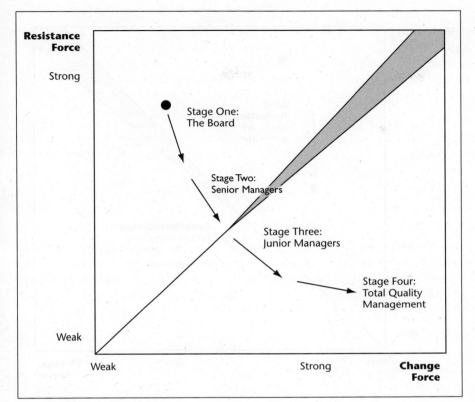

FIGURE 4.5.8
Seiko's cascading
implementation

this dissatisfaction provided the opening for more fundamental change (arrow 1 in Figure 4.5.9).

Since the technologists could not come on site, the sales force started trying to do the bottle and field tests itself. In Safniyah, one of the largest Saudi fields, the salesman spent time in the field lab, blending and trying new chemical combinations, calling the central lab by telephone for advice. Through this process he developed an innovative new blend. The client received a detailed report on the results of the new product trials within two days and the company quickly won a six-month contract. Samples of the new blend and copies of the test report were sent to the central lab for review. The central lab responded by sending new samples to the sales force for field trials. Gradually an exchange of ideas and methods developed, with the central lab concentrating on perfecting and developing fundamentally new chemicals, while in the field the sales force blended these to satisfy the specific needs of new customers.

As sales began to improve with new products and product adaptations visible in the lab and the field, the manager of the division and his team began to realize that the key to success was not only cost cutting, but also new products and customized service. Product development was then further encouraged in the central lab, while field labs were set up in all markets where they didn't already exist. The Energy Chemicals Division

FIGURE 4.5.9
Oil Chemical Co's bottom-up experimentation

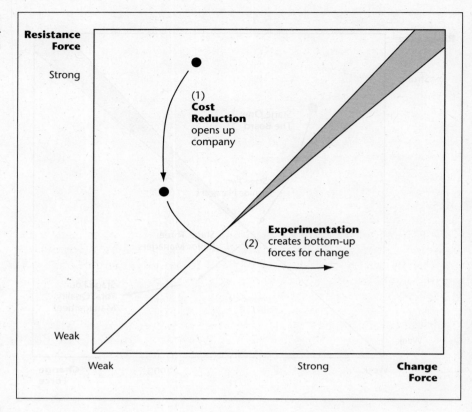

developed a reputation for providing good products in a short time with excellent after-sales service. Competitors were caught off guard, the division's market share expanded and its success began to be noticed in other parts of the corporation.

In effect, a proactive turning point had occurred from the bottom up. Management had inadvertently created the organizational space needed for experimentation in the field. It quickly recognized what was going on and encouraged the new process (arrow 2 in Figure 4.5.9).

Conclusion

Assessing the strength of the forces of change and resistance provides a framework for choosing between eight different change paths. Of the eight paths, seven (all but the resistance path) have to do with reducing the forces of resistance inside the organization to respond to the impact of the forces of change. The way in which this can best be done depends on the strength of the change forces. The main distinction is between reactive change paths (for dealing with strong change forces that have already affected performance) and proactive change paths (for taking advantage of weak change forces whose impact has yet to be felt).

When the change forces are strong, the key issue is whether, and when, the resistance will be overcome? Resistance that is capable of dominating the change force gives the company the choice of adapting with limited renewal, or resisting. By contrast, change forces that cannot be neutralized must be fully adapted to – either with slow deep revitalization when there is enough time and resources available, or with sharp, rapid restructuring when time is short.

When the change forces are weak and have yet to affect performance, the key question for initiating proactive change is whether the forces can be readily identified? If so, the most appropriate change path is determined by how open or closed the organization is to change. A radical realignment is typically needed in closed organizations to exploit the emerging opportunity in time; cascading implementation, or some other turning point approach, can be used in open organizations. By contrast, if the change forces themselves are difficult to identify, the challenge is to create a mobilizing sense of discomfort with thing as they are. In closed organizations, a way must be found of creating a breakpoint in the managerial mindset (by benchmarking, for example). Open organizations, on the other hand, can be stimulated to identify the forces of change with bottom-up experimentation.

To adapt to more than one change force, a change campaign is required in the form of a sequence of change paths, to deal with the stronger change forces first, thereby clearing the way for exploiting the weaker ones. Each of the change paths in the campaign should reflect the configuration of the forces acting on the part of the business to be changed. The transition between the paths must allow enough time to provide a sufficient basis for the next phase of the campaign, while being quick enough to capitalize on competitive opportunities. And the change campaign must be ongoing; as soon as companies stop dealing with change forces, they run into trouble, as illustrated by the recent experience of both SAS and Harley Davidson.

As they become more proficient at managing change, especially proactive change, leading companies become the force of change in the industry. Ideally, they develop the capability of managing internal turning points and breakpoints, both reactively and proactively, in order to exploit environmental change and outpace the competition.

Strategic Change in International Perspective

> Wisdom lies neither in fixity nor in change, but in the dialectic between the two.
>
> (Octavio Paz born 1914; Mexican poet and essayist)

Again it has become clear that there is little consensus within the field of strategic management. Views on the best way to accomplish strategic change differ sharply. Even authors from one and the same country exhibit strikingly divergent perspectives on how to deal with the paradox of revolution and evolution.

Provocatively, the article by Imai explicitly introduced the international dimension, suggesting that there are specific national preferences in approach to strategic change. He argues that 'Japanese companies generally favor the gradualist approach and Western companies the great-leap approach – an approach epitomized by the term innovation. Western management worships at the altar of innovation.' This general, yet fundamental, distinction is supported by other researchers such as Ouchi (1981), Pascale and Athos (1981) and Kagono *et al.* (1985), although all of these international comparative studies concentrate only on US–Japanese differences. The extensive study by Kagono and his colleagues among the top 1000 American and Japanese companies concludes that there are clearly different national change styles: 'The US-style elite-guided, logical, deductive approach achieves major innovation in strategies geared to surpass other companies. In contrast, the Japanese inductive, step-wise gradual adjustment approach seeks to steadily build upon the existing strengths to *evolve* strategy' (Kagono *et al.*, 1985: 89–90). Other authors suggest that the US and Japan seem to represent the two extremes, while most other industrialized countries seem to be somewhere in between (e.g. Calori and De Woot, 1994; Krueger, 1996).

Such pronounced international variance raises the question of cause. Why do firms in different countries prefer such significantly different approaches to strategic change? Which factors determine the existence of national strategic change styles? Answers to these questions might assist in defining the most appropriate context for discontinuous change, as opposed to circumstances in which continuous change would be more fitting. Understanding international dissimilarities and their roots should help to clarify whether firms in different countries can borrow practices from one another, or are limited by their national context.

As a stimulus to the international dimension of this debate, a short overview will be given of the country characteristics mentioned in the literature as the major influences on how the paradox of revolution and evolution is dealt with in different national settings. It should be noted, however, that cross-cultural research on this topic has not been extensive. Therefore, the propositions brought forward here should be viewed as tentative explanations, intended to encourage further discussion and research.

Prevalence of Mechanistic Organizations

At the end of Chapter 3, the international differences in organizing work were briefly discussed. It was argued that in some countries the machine bureaucracy is a particularly dominant form of organization, while in other countries organizations are more organic. The machine bureaucracy, that is more predominant in English-speaking countries and France, is characterized by clear hierarchical authority relationships, strict differentiation of tasks, and highly formalized communication, information, budgeting, planning and decision-making systems. In such organizations, there is a relatively clear line separating the officers (management) from the troops, and internal relationships are depersonalized and calculative. In more organic forms of organization, management and production activities are not strictly separated, leading to less emphasis on top-down decision-making, and more on bottom-up initiatives. Job descriptions are less strictly defined and control systems are less sophisticated. Integration within the organization is not achieved by these formal systems, but by extensive informal communication and consultation, both horizontally and vertically, and by a strong common set of beliefs and a shared corporate vision. Internal relationships are based on trust, cooperation and a sense of community, leading Ouchi (1981) to call such organizations clans. This type of organization is more prevalent in Japan, and to a lesser extent in, for example, Germany, the Netherlands and the Nordic countries.

Various researchers have suggested that machine bureaucracies exhibit a high level of inertia (e.g. Kanter, 1989; Mintzberg, 1994). Once formal systems have been created, they become difficult to change. As soon as particular tasks are specified and assigned to a person or group, it becomes their turf, while all else is 'not their business'. Once created, hierarchical positions, giving status and power, are not easily abolished. The consequence, it is argued, is that machine bureaucracies are inherently more resistant to change than clan-like organizations (Kagono *et al.*, 1985). Therefore, revolution is usually the potent mode of change needed to make any significant alterations. It can be expected that in countries where organizations are more strongly mechanistic, the preference for the discontinuous change perspective will be more pronounced.

Clan-like organizations, on the other hand, are characterized by a strong capacity for self-organization – the ability to exhibit organized behavior without a boss being in control (Nonaka, 1988; Stacey, 1993; reading 9.2 in this book). They are better at fluidly, and spontaneously, reorganizing around new issues because of a lack of rigid structure, the close links between management and production tasks, the high level of group-oriented information-sharing and consensual decision-making, and the strong commitment of individuals to the organization, and vice versa. In countries where organizations are more organic in this way, a stronger preference for the continuous change perspective can be expected. This issue will be discussed in more length in Chapter 9.

Position of Employees

This second factor is partially linked to the first. A mechanistic organization, it could be said, is a system, into which groups of people have been brought, while an organic organization is a group of people, into which some system has been brought. In a machine bureaucracy, people are human resources *for* the organization, while in a clan, people *are* the organization. These two conceptions of organization represent radically different views on the position and roles of employees within organizations.

In mechanistic organizations, employees are seen as valuable, yet expendable, resources utilized by the organization. Salaries are determined by the prices on the labor market and the value-added by the individual employee. In the contractual relationship between employer and employee, it is a shrewd bargaining tactic for employers to minimize their dependence on employees. Organizational learning should, therefore, be captured in formalized systems and procedures, to avoid the irreplaceability of their people. Employees, on the other hand, will strive to make themselves indispensable for the organization, for instance by not sharing their learning. Furthermore, calculating employees will not tie themselves too strongly to the organization, but will keep their options open to job-hop to a better paying employer. None of these factors contribute to the long-term commitment and receptiveness for ambiguity and uncertainty needed for continuous change.

In clan-like organizations the tolerance for ambiguity and uncertainty is higher, because employees' position within the organization is more secure. Information is more readily shared, as it does not need to be used as a bargaining chip and acceptance within the group demands being a team player. Employers can invest in people instead of systems, since employees are committed and loyal to the organization. These better trained people can consequently be given more decision-making power and more responsibility to organize their own work to fit with changing circumstances. Therefore, clan-like organizations, with their emphasis on employees as permanent co-producers, instead of temporary contractors, are more conducive to continuous change. It is in this context that Imai concludes that 'Investing in Kaizen means investing in people . . . Kaizen is people-oriented, whereas innovation is technology- and money-oriented.'

A number of factors have been brought forward to explain these international differences in the structuring of work and the position of employees. Some authors emphasize cultural aspects, particularly the level of individualism. It is argued that the mechanistic-organic distinction largely coincides with the individualism-collectivism division (e.g. Ouchi, 1981; Pascale and Athos, 1981). In this view, machine bureaucracies are the logical response to calculative individuals, while clans are more predominant in group-oriented cultures. Other authors point to international differences in labor markets (e.g. Kagono *et al.* 1985; Calori, Valla and De Woot, 1994). High mobility of personnel would coincide with the existence of mechanistic organizations, while low mobility (e.g. life time employment) fits with organic forms. Yet others suggest that the abundance of skilled workers is important. Machine bureaucracies are suited to dealing with narrowly trained individuals requiring extensive supervision. Clan-like organizations, however, need skilled, self-managing workers, that can handle a wide variety of tasks with relative autonomy. Kogut (1993: 11) reports that the level of workers within a country with these qualifications 'has been found to rest significantly upon the quality of education, the existence of programs of apprenticeship and worker qualifications, and the elimination of occupational distinctions.'

Based on these arguments it can be proposed that the discontinuous change perspective will be more prevalent in countries with a more individualistic culture, high labor mobility, and less skilled workers. Conversely, the continuous change perspective will be more strongly rooted in countries with a group-oriented culture, low labor mobility, and skilled, self-managing workers.

Role of Top Management

The third factor is also related to the previous points. Various researchers have observed important international differences in leadership styles and the role of top management. In some countries, top management is looked at as the 'central processing unit' of the company, making the key decisions and commanding the behavior of the rest of the organizational machine. Visible top-down leadership is the norm and, therefore, strategic innovation and change are viewed as top management responsibilities (e.g. Hambrick and Mason, 1984; Kotter, 1982). Strategic changes are formulated by top managers and then implemented by lower levels. Top managers are given significant power and discretion to develop bold new initiatives and to overcome organizational resistance to change. If organizational advances are judged to be insufficient or if an organization ends up in a crisis situation, a change of top management is often viewed as a necessary measure to transform or turnaround the company (e.g. Boeker, 1992; Fredrickson, Hambrick and Baumrin, 1988). In nations where people exhibit a strong preference for this commander type of leadership, an inclination towards the discontinuous change perspective can be expected.

In other countries, top managers are viewed as the captains of the team and leadership is less direct and less visible (e.g. Kagono *et al.*, 1985; Hofstede, 1993; reading 1.5). The role of top managers is to facilitate change and innovation among the members of the group. It is not necessarily the intention that top managers initiate entrepreneurial activities themselves (e.g. Senge, 1990; reading 4.4; Bourgeois and Brodwin, 1984, reading 9.3).

Change comes from within the body of the organization, instead of being imposed upon it by top management. Therefore, change under this type of leadership will usually be more evolutionary than revolutionary. In nations where people exhibit a strong preference for this servant type of leadership, an inclination towards the continuous change perspective is more likely.

Time Orientation

At the end of Chapter 3, a distinction was made between cultures that are more oriented towards the past, the present, and the future. Obviously, it can be expected that cultures with a past or present orientation will be much less inclined towards change, than future-oriented cultures. Among these future-minded cultures, a further division was made between those with a long-term and a short-term orientation.

Various researchers have argued that short-term oriented cultures exhibit a much stronger preference for fast, radical change than cultures with a longer time horizon. In short-term oriented cultures, such as the English-speaking countries, there are significant pressures for rapid results, which predisposes managers towards revolutionary change. The sensitivity to stock prices especially is often cited as a major factor encouraging firms to focus on short spurts of massive change and pay much less attention to efforts and investments with undramatic long term benefits. Other contributing factors mentioned include short-term oriented bonus systems, stock option plans and frequent job-hopping (e.g. Calori, Valla and De Woot, 1994; Kagono et al., 1985).

In long-term oriented cultures, such as Japan, China and South Korea, there is much less pressure to achieve short term results. There is broad awareness that firms are running a competitive marathon and that a high, but steady, pace of motion is needed. Generally, more emphasis is placed on facilitating long-term change processes, instead of intermittently moving from short-term change to short-term change. Frequently mentioned factors contributing to this long-term orientation include long-term employment relationships, the lack of short-term bonus systems and most importantly the accent on growth, as opposed to profit, as firms' prime objective (e.g. Abegglen and Stalk, 1985; Pascale and Athos, 1981). This topic will be discussed at more length in Chapter 11.

Further Readings

Many excellent writings on the topic of strategic change are available, although most carry other labels, such as innovation, entrepreneurship, reengineering, renewal, revitalization, rejuvenation and learning. For a good overview of the literature, readers can consult 'Environmental Jolts and Industry Revolutions: Organizational Responses to Discontinuous

Change,' by Alan Meyer, Geoffry Brooks and James Goes. Paul Strebel's book *Breakpoints: How Managers Exploit Radical Business Change* also provides broad introduction to much of the work on change.

In the discontinuous change literature, Larry Greiner's article 'Evolution and Revolution as Organizations Grow' is a classic well worth reading. Danny Miller and Peter Friesen's landmark book *Organizations: A Quantum View* is also stimulating, although not easily accessible. More readable books on radical change are *Rejuvenating the Mature Business* by Charles Baden-Fuller and John Stopford; *Sharpbenders: The Secrets of Unleashing Corporate Potential*, by Peter Grinyer, David Mayes and Peter McKiernan; *Crisis and Renewal*, by David Hurst. More 'hands-on' is Rosabeth Moss Kanter's *When Giants Learn to Dance*, and of course *Reengineering the Corporation: A Manifesto for Business Revolution*, by Michael Hammer and James Champy, which expands on the ideas discussed in Hammer's contribution in this chapter.

On the topic of innovation, Jim Utterback's book *Mastering the Dynamics of Innovation* provides a good overview, as does *Managing Innovation: Integrating Technological, Market and Organizational Change*, by Joe Tidd, John Bessant and Keith Pavitt. An excellent collection of cases is provided by Charles Baden-Fuller and Martyn Pitt, in their book *Strategic Innovation*.

Literature taking a continuous change perspective is less abundant, but no less interesting. Masaaki Imai's article in this chapter has been taken from his book *Kaizen: The Key to Japan's Competitive Success*, which is highly recommended. A more academic work that explains the continuous change view in detail is *Strategic vs. Evolutionary Management: A US-Japan Comparison of Strategy and Organization*, by Tadao Kagono, Ikujiro Nonaka, Kiyonori Sakakibara, and Akihiro Okumura. Ikujiro Nonaka's article 'Creating Organizational Order Out of Chaos: Self-Renewal in Japanese Firms' gives a good summary of this way of thinking. Peter Senge's book *The Fifth Discipline: The Art and Practice of the Learning Organization*, which further details his contribution to this chapter, can also be highly advised.

Finally, the award-winning article 'Ambidextrous Organizations: Managing Evolutionary and Revolutionary Change,' by Michael Tushman and Charles O'Reilly must be mentioned as a delightful reading, in particular with regard to the way in which the authors explicitly wrestle with the paradox of revolution and evolution. Their book *Winning Through Innovation: A Practical Guide to Leading Organizational Change and Renewal* is equally stimulating.

References

Abegglen, J.C., and Stalk, G. (1985) *Kaisha, The Japanese Corporation*, Basic Books, New York.

Allison, G.T. (1969) Conceptual Models and The Cuban Missile Crisis, *The American Political Science Review*, No.3, September, pp. 689–718.

Argyris, C. (1990) *Overcoming Organizational Defenses: Facilitating Organizational Learning*, Prentice Hall, Boston.

Arthur, W.B. (1996) Increasing Returns and the New World of Business, *Harvard Business Review*, July–August, pp. 100–9.

Baden-Fuller, C. and Pitt, M. (1996) *Strategic Innovation*, Routledge, London.

Baden-Fuller, C., and Stopford, J.M. (1992) *Rejuvenating the Mature Business*, Routledge, London.

Bate, P. (1994) *Strategies for Cultural Change*, Butterworth-Heinemann, Oxford.

Boeker, W. (1992) Power and Managerial Dismissal: Scapegoating at the Top, *Administrative Science Quarterly*, Vol. 27, pp. 538–47.

Bourgeois, L.J., and Brodwin, D.R. (1983) Putting Your Strategy into Action, *Strategic Management Planning*, March/May.

Calori, R., and de Woot, Ph. (eds) (1994) *A European Management Model: Beyond Diversity*, Prentice Hall, Hemel Hempstead.

Calori, R., Valla, J.-P. and de Woot, Ph. (1994) Common Characteristics: The Ingredients of European Management, in Calori, R., and de Woot, Ph. (eds), *A European Management Model: Beyond Diversity*, Prentice Hall, Hemel Hempstead.

Cyert, R.M., and March, J.G. (1963) *A Behavioral Theory of the Firm*, Prentice Hall, Englewood Cliffs, NJ.

D'Aveni, R. (1994) *Hypercompetition*: *Managing the Dynamics of Strategic Maneuvering*, Free Press, New York.

Day, D.L. (1994) Raising Radicals: Different Processes for Championing Innovative Corporate Ventures, *Organization Science*, Vol. 5, No. 2, May, pp. 148–72.

Fredrickson, J.W., Hambrick, D.C. and Baumrin, S. (1988) A Model of CEO Dismissal, *Academy of Management Review*, Vol. 13, pp. 255–70.

Fry, J.N., and Killing, J.R. (1989) *Strategic Analysis and Action*, 2nd edn, Prentice Hall, Englewood Cliffs, NJ.

Gersick, C.J.G. (1991) Revolutionary Change Theories: A Multilevel Exploration of the Punctuated Equilibrium Paradigm, *Academy of Management Review*, pp. 10–36.

Ghemawat, P. (1991) *Commitment: The Dynamic of Strategy*, Free Press, New York.

Ginsberg, A., and Bucholz, A. (1990) Converting to For-Profit Status: Corporate Responsiveness to Radical Change, *Academy of Management Journal*, Vol. 33, No.3, pp. 93–110.

Greenleaf, R.K. (1977) *Servant Leadership: A Journey into the Nature of Legitimate Power and Greatness*, Paulist Press, New York.

Greiner, L.E. (1972) Evolution and Revolution as Organizations Grow, *Harvard Business Review*, July/August, pp. 37–46.

Grinyer, P.H., Mayes, D. and McKiernan, P. (1987) *Sharpbenders: The Secrets of Unleashing Corporate Potential*, Blackwell, Oxford.

Grinyer, P.H., and McKiernan, P. (1990) Generating Major Change in Stagnating Companies, *Strategic Management Journal*, Summer, pp. 131–46.

Hambrick, D.C., and Mason, P. (1984) Upper Echelons: The Organization as a Reflection of Its Top Managers, *Academy of Management Review*, Vol. 9, pp. 193–206.

Hamel, G. (1996) Strategy as Revolution, *Harvard Business Review*, July–August, pp. 69–82.

Hammer, M. (1990) Reengineering Work: Don't Automate, Obliterate, *Harvard Business Review*, July/August, pp. 104–11.

Hammer, M., and Champy, J. (1993) *Reengineering the Corporation: A Manifesto for Business Revolution*, HarperCollins, New York.

Hofstede, G. (1993) Cultural Constraints in Management Theories, *Academy of Management Executive*, Vol. 7, No.1.

Hurst, D. (1995) *Crisis and Renewal*, Harvard Business School Press, Boston.

Imai, M. (1986) *Kaizen: The Key to Japan's Competitive Success*, McGraw-Hill, New York.

Jelinek, M., and Schoonhoven, C. (1990) *The Innovation Marathon*, Basil Blackwell, Cambridge, MA.

Johnson, G. (1987) *Strategic Change and the Management Process*, Basil Blackwell, Oxford.

Johnson, G. (1988) Rethinking Incrementalism, *Strategic Management Journal*, January/February, pp. 75–91.

Kagono, T., Nonaka, I. Sakakibara, K. and Okumura, A. (1985) *Strategic vs. Evolutionary Management: A US-Japan.Comparison of Strategy and Organization*, North Holland, Amsterdam.

Kanter, R.M. (1983) *The Change Masters: Innovation for Productivity in the American Corporation*, Basic Books, New York.

Kanter, R.M. (1989) *When Giants Learn to Dance*, Simon & Schuster, New York.

Kogut, B. (ed.) (1993) *Country Competitiveness: Technology and the Organizing of Work*, Oxford University Press, Oxford.

Kotter, J.P. (1982) *The General Managers*, Free Press, New York, 1982.

Krueger, W. (1996) Implementation: The Core Task of Change Management, *CEMS Business Review*, pp. 77–96.

Lawrence, P.R., and Lorsch, J.W. (1967) *Organization and the Environment*, Harvard Business School, Boston, MA.

Lewin, K. (1947) Frontiers in Group Dynamics, Concept Method and Reality in Social Science; Social Equilibria and Social Change, *Human Relations*, I, pp. 2–38.

Maidique, M.A. (1980) Entrepreneurs, Champions, and Technological Innovation, *Sloan Management Review*, 1980, pp. 18–31.

Majone, G., and Wildavsky, A. (1978) Implementation as Evolution, *Policy Studies Review Annual*, pp. 103–17.

March, J.G., and Simon, H.A. (1958) *Organizations*, Wiley, New York.

McCaskey, M.B. (1982) *The Executive Challenge: Managing Change and Ambiguity*, Pitman, Boston.

Meyer, A.D. (1982) Adapting to Environmental Jolts, *Administrative Science Quarterly*, Vol. 27, December, pp. 515–37.

Meyer, A., Brooks, G. and Goes, J. (1990) Environmental Jolts and Industry Revolutions: Organizational Responses to Discontinuous Change, *Strategic Management Journal*, Vol. 11, pp. 93–110.

Miller, D. (1990) *The Icarus Paradox: How Excellent Companies Bring About Their Own Downfall*, Harper Business, New York.

Miller, D., and Friesen, P. (1984) *Organizations: A Quantum View*, Prentice Hall, Englewood Cliffs.

Mintzberg, H. (1991) The Effective Organization: Forces and Forms, *Sloan Management Review*, Winter, pp. 54–67.

Mintzberg, H., and Westley, F. (1992) Cycles of Organizational Change, *Strategic Management Journal*, Vol. 13, pp. 39–59.

Mintzberg, H. (1994) *The Rise and Fall of Strategic Planning*, Prentice Hall, Englewood Cliffs.

Nelson, R.R., and Winter, S.G. (1982) *An Evolutionary Theory of Economic Change*, Harvard University Press, Cambridge, MA.

Nonaka, I. (1988) Creating Organizational Order Out of Chaos: Self-Renewal in Japanese Firms, *California Management Review*, Spring, pp. 9–18).

Ouchi, W. (1981) *Theory Z: How American Business Can Meet the Japanese Challenge*, Addison-Wesley, Reading, MA.

Pascale, R.T., and Athos, A.G. (1981) *The Art of Japanese Management*, Simon & Schuster, New York.

Pettigrew, A.M. (1988) *The Management of Strategic Change*, Basil Blackwell, Oxford.

Pondy, I.R., and Huff, A.S. (1985) Achieving Routine in Organizational Change, *Journal of Management*, Summer, pp. 102–16.

Pondy, L.R., Boland, J.R. and Thomas, H. (1988) (eds), *Managing Ambiguity and Change*, Wiley, New York.

Quinn, J.B. (1978) Strategic Change: Local Incrementalism, *Sloan Management Review*, Fall, pp. 7–21.

Schumpeter, J.A. (1950) *Capitalism, Socialism and Democracy*, 3rd edn, Harper and Brothers, New York.

Selznick, P. (1957) *Leadership in Administration: A Sociological Interpretation*, Harper & Row, New York.

Senge, P.M. (1990) The Leader's New Work: Building Learning Organizations, *Sloan Management Review*, Fall, pp. 7–23.

Stacey, R.D. (1993) Strategy as Order Emerging from Chaos, *Long Range Planning*, Vol. 26, No.1, pp. 10–17.

Stacey, R.D. (1993) *Strategic Management and Organizational Dynamics*, Pitman Publishing, London.

Stalk, G., Evans, P., and Schulman, L.E. (1992) Competing on Capabilities: The New Rules of Corporate Strategy, *Harvard Business Review*, March/April, pp. 57–69.

Strebel, P. (1992) *Breakpoints: How Managers Exploit Radical Business Change*, Harvard Business School Press, Boston.

Strebel, P. (1994) Choosing the Right Change Path, *California Management Review*, Winter, pp. 29–51.

Thompson, J.D. (1967) *Organizations in Action*, McGraw-Hill, New York.

Tidd, J., Bessant, J. and Pavitt, K. (1997) *Managing Innovation: Integrating Technological, Market and Organizational Change*, Wiley, Chichester.

Tushman, M.L., Newman, W.H. and Romanelli, E. (1986) Convergence and Upheaval: Managing the Unsteady Pace of Organizational Evolution, *California Management Review*, Vol. 29, No. 1, Fall, pp. 29–44.

Tushman, M.L., and O'Reilly III, C.A. (1996) Ambidextrous Organizations: Managing Evolutionary and Revolutionary Change, *California Management Review*, Vol. 38, No. 4, Summer, pp. 8–30.

Tushman, M.L., and O'Reilly III, C.A. (1997) *Winning Through Innovation: A Practical Guide to Leading Organizational Change and Renewal*, Harvard Business School Press, Boston.

Tushman, M., and Romanelli, E. (1985) Organizational Evolution: A Metamorphosis Model of Convergence and Reorientation, in Cummings, L.L., and Staw, B.M. (eds), *Research in Organizational Behavior*, JAI Press, Greenwich, CT, Vol. 7, pp. 171–222.

Utterback, J. (1994) *Mastering the Dynamics of Innovation*, Harvard Business School Press, Boston.

Waterman, R.H., Peters, T.J., and Phillips, J.R. (1980) Structure is Not Organization, *Business Horizons*, June, pp. 14–26.

Strategy Content

❏   5 Business Level Strategy
❏   6 Corporate Level Strategy
❏   7 Network Level Strategy

Strategy Content

5 Business Level Strategy

6 Corporate Level Strategy

7 Network Level Strategy

Business Level Strategy

One does not gain much by mere cleverness.

(Marquis de Vauvenargues 1715–1747; French soldier and moralist)

Drive thy business; let it not drive thee.

(Benjamin Franklin 1706–1790; American writer and statesman)

The Paradox of Markets and Resources

The central question in this chapter is quite simple: 'What is the basis of a good strategy?' Are there characteristics that effective strategies have in common, that could be used as criteria for developing new strategies? Are there fundamental laws of strategy that could function as guiding principles for strategists? In short, what are the qualities of a successful strategy?

While the question may be straight forward, the answer seems less so, if the diversity of opinions among strategy theorists is taken as a measure. The variety of views on the topic is dauntingly large. Yet, at a fundamental level, two different perspectives on strategy can be identified, that underlie the broad spectrum of views observed within the field of strategic management. These two opposing outlooks are the *outside-in perspective* and the *inside-out perspective*. As in previous chapters, these two poles are based on diametrically opposed assumptions and arrive at distinct interpretations of actual behavior and recommended action. It is the intention of this chapter to structure the debate on the basic characteristics of a good strategy by presenting a limited number of readings illuminating the major differences between these two perspectives.

To understand the differences between the outside-in and inside-out perspectives, it is useful to start with their similarities. Both views accept the four broad criteria that need to be met by a good strategy, as outlined by Rumelt in Chapter 1. In this reading, Rumelt argues that strategies must be *feasible* (implementable) and *consistent* (no mutually exclusive goals or policies). Rumelt also states that strategies must provide a competitive *advantage*. Finally, he also notes the necessity of *consonance* – a fit between the organization and its environment. It is the interpretation of these last two principles that forms the dividing line between the outside-in and inside-out perspectives.

While both views share the assumption that an alignment between the firm and the outside world must be established and maintained that assures competitive advantage, what divides them is their way of achieving such a fit. Should a company adapt itself to its surroundings or should it attempt to adapt the surroundings to itself? Should strategists take the environment as starting point, choose an advantageous market position and obtain the resources needed to implement this choice? Or should strategists take the organization's resource base (physical assets, competences and relationships) as starting point, selecting and/or adapting an environment to fit with these strengths? Creating alignment to achieve competitive advantage can go both ways, but which way is preferable?

This issue can also be expressed in terms of the classic SWOT framework, that suggests that a sound strategy should match the firm's strengths (S) and weaknesses (W) to the opportunities (O) and threats (T) encountered in the firm's environment. When striving for this match, should the firm be primarily strength driven or opportunity driven? What should be leading and what should be lagging?

The Outside-in Perspective

Strategists adopting an outside-in perspective believe that firms should not be self-centered, but should continuously take their environment as starting point when determining their strategy. Successful companies, it is argued, are *externally-oriented* and *market-driven* (e.g. Day, 1990; Webster, 1994). Such companies take their cues from customers and competitors, and use these signals to determine their own game plan (Jaworski and Kohli, 1993). Strategists analyze the environment to identify attractive market opportunities. They search for potential customers whose needs could be better satisfied than currently done by other firms. The most attractive buyers are those willing and able to pay a premium price, and whose loyalty could be won, despite the efforts of the competition. Once these customers have been won over and a market position has been established, the firm must consistently defend or build on this position by adapting itself to changes in the environment. Shifts in customers' demands must be met, challenges from rival firms must be countered, impending market entries by outside firms must be rebuffed and excessive pricing by suppliers must be resisted. In short, to the outside-in strategist the game of strategy is about market positioning and understanding and responding to external developments. For this reason, the outside-in perspective is sometimes also referred to as the *positioning approach* (Mintzberg, 1990a).

Positioning is not short-term opportunistic behavior, but requires a strategic perspective, because superior market positions are difficult to attain, but once conquered can be the source of sustained profitablility. Some proponents of the outside-in perspective argue that in each market a number of different positions can yield sustained profitability. For instance, Porter suggests that companies that focus on a particular niche, and companies that strongly differentiate their product offering, can achieve strong and profitable market positions, even if another company has the lowest cost position (Porter, 1980, 1985; reading 5.1 in this book). Other authors emphasize that the position of being market leader is particularly important (e.g. Buzzell and Gale, 1987; reading 5.3). Companies with a high market share profit more from economies of scale, benefit from risk aversion among customers, have more bargaining power towards buyers and suppliers, and can more easily flex their muscles to prevent new entrants and block competitive attacks.

Unsurprisingly, outside-in strategists argue that insight into markets and industries is essential. Not only the general structure of markets and industries needs to be analyzed, but also the specific demands, strengths, positions and intentions of all major forces need to be determined. For instance, buyers must be understood, with regard to their needs, wants, perceptions, decision-making processes and bargaining chips. The same holds true for suppliers, competitors, potential market and/or industry entrants, and providers of substitute products (Porter, 1980, 1985; reading 5.1). Once a strategist knows 'what makes the market tick' – sometimes referred to as the *rules of the game* – a position can be identified within the market that could give the firm bargaining power *vis-à-vis* suppliers and buyers, while keeping competitors at bay. Of course, the wise strategist will not only emphasize winning under the current rules with the current players, but will attempt to anticipate market and industry developments, and position the firm to benefit from these. Many outside-in advocates even advise firms to initiate market and industry changes, so that they can be the first to benefit from the altered rules of the game (this issue will be discussed in further length in Chapter 8).

Proponents of the outside-in perspective readily acknowledge the importance of firm resources for cashing in on market opportunities the firm has identified. If the firm does not have, or is not able to develop or obtain, the necessary resources to implement a particular strategy, then specific opportunities will be unrealizable. Therefore, strategists should always keep the firm's strengths and weaknesses in mind when choosing an external position, to ensure that it remains feasible. Yet, to the outside-in strategist, the firm's current resource base should not be the starting point when determining strategy, but should merely be acknowledged as a potentially limiting condition on the firm's ability to implement the best market strategy. In general, therefore, the outside-in approach can be summarized as that of 'resource base follows market position' – the organization's resource base is adapted to fit the market position selected.

The Inside-out Perspective

Strategists adopting an inside-out perspective argue that strategies should not be built around external opportunities, but around a company's strengths. They believe that organizations should focus on the development of difficult-to-imitate competences and/or on the acquisition of exclusive assets. This unique resource base should be used as the starting point of strategy formation. Markets should subsequently be chosen, adapted or created to exploit these specific strengths. Identifying which company resources have to be further developed and applying them to various environmental opportunities is what strategy is all about.

Many strategists taking an inside-out perspective tend to emphasize the importance of the firm's competences over its tangible resources (physical assets). Their views are more specifically referred to as *competence-based* (e.g. Prahalad and Hamel, 1990; reading 6.2; Sanchez, Heene and Thomas, 1996) or *capabilities-based* (e.g. Stalk, Evans and Shulman, 1992; reading 5.2; Teece, Pisano and Shuen, 1990) perspectives on strategy. They argue that building up unique abilities is a strenuous and lengthy process, that can have both positive and negative consequences. On the positive side, once a company has developed a distinctive ability, it is usually difficult for competitors to imitate such a strength. And while rivals try to catch up, a company with an initial lead can try to upgrade its competences in the race to stay ahead (e.g. Collis and Montgomery, 1995; Barney, 1991; reading 5.4). On the negative side, the laborious task of building up competences makes it difficult to switch to other competences if that is what the market demands (e.g. Leonard-Barton, 1995; Rumelt, 1996; reading 9.5). In the same way, few concert pianists are able (and willing) to switch to playing saxophone when they are out of a job. From an inside-out perspective, both companies and concert pianists should first try to build on their unique competences and attempt to find or create a more suitable market, instead of reactively adapting to the unpredictable whims of the current environment. In other words, the approach is that of 'market position follows resource base' – the market position selected is adapted to fit the organization's resource base.

The question for the field of strategic management is, therefore, whether business strategies are formed and should be formed outside-in or inside-out. Is it better to be market-driven or resource-driven? As in all previous paradoxes, it is compelling to want both at the same time, while their premises are contradictory and possibly even mutually exclusive. Therefore, strategists will have to somehow resolve the paradox of markets and resources (see Table 5.1).

Defining the Issues: Adaptation and Advantage

Most strategists agree that the key question of business level strategy is 'how should a firm be related to its environment to achieve success?' In other words, how can the current, and potential, strengths and weaknesses of the organization be aligned with the current, and potential, opportunities and threats in the environment, in such a way that the firm will be able to reach its aims? The answer to this question must be sought in the issues of *adaptation* and *advantage*. 'Alignment of firm and environment' entails

	Outside-in Perspective	**Inside-out Perspective**
Emphasis on	Markets over resources	Resources over markets
Orientation	Market/Industry-driven	Resource-driven
Starting point	Market/Industry structure	Firm's resource infrastructure
Fit through	Adaptation to environment	Adaptation of environment
Strategic focus	Attaining advantageous position	Attaining distinctive resources
Strategic moves	Market/Industry positioning	Developing resource base
Tactical moves	Attaining necessary resources	Industry entry and positioning
Competitive weapons	Bargaining power and mobility barriers	Superior resources and imitation barriers

TABLE 5.1
Outside-in versus inside-out perspective

that they must be adapted to one another, while 'achieving success' necessitates the existence of a advantage over the firm's rivals.

Before proceeding to the readings, the nature of these two issues will first be more closely examined. In particular, what is the environment that must be adapted or adapted to, and what are firm resources?

Positioning in Industries, Markets and Businesses

While strategists generally agree that a firm must be aligned to its environment, the question is which external factors are the most relevant for the firm – which part of the environment should the firm be positioning in? Here there is a difference in emphasis among strategists, which requires that a distinction be made between various parts of the environment. Unfortunately, there is not yet a generally accepted set of concepts within the field of strategic management with which to describe the external environment of the firm. Terms such as industry, market and business are defined differently, or more often, not defined at all. Many of the contributions in this book actually use some of these terms interchangeably. However, to aid the debate, we suggest that the following distinction between the concepts of industry, market and business could be made:

■ *Industry*. An industry is defined as a group of firms making a similar type of product or employing a similar set of value-adding processes or resources. In other words, an industry consists of producers that are much alike – there is *supply side similarity* (Kay, 1993). The simplest way to draw an industry boundary is to use product similarity as delineation criterion. For instance, British Airways can be said to be in the air transportation industry, along with many other providers of the same product, such as Delta, Singapore Airlines and Air UK. Porsche can be placed in the automobile industry. However, an industry can also be defined on the basis of value-chain similarity (e.g. consulting industry and retailing industry) or resource similarity (e.g. information technology industry and oil industry). Economic statisticians tend to favor industry categories based on product similarity and therefore most figures available about industries are product-category based. However, a strategist may want to define an industry on the basis of underlying value-adding processes or resources. For instance, in which industry should Swatch be classified? If one focuses on the physical product and the production process, one would be inclined to situate Swatch in the watch industry. However, if a Swatch is seen as a fashion accessory and emphasis is placed on the key value-adding activities of fashion design and marketing, then Swatch would have to be categorized as a member of the fashion industry. For the strategist, the realization that Swatch can be viewed in both ways is an important insight (Porac, Thomas and Baden-Fuller, 1989).

■   *Market*. While economists see the market as a place where supply and demand meet, in the business world a market is usually defined as a group of customers with similar needs. In other words, a market consists of buyers whose demands are much alike – *demand side similarity*. For instance, there is a market for air transportation between London and Jamaica, which is a different market than for air transportation between London and Paris – the customer needs are different and therefore these products can not be substituted for one another. But customers can substitute a British Airways flight London–Paris for one by Air France, indicating that both companies are serving the same market. Yet, this market definition (London–Paris air transport) might not be the most appropriate, if in reality many customers are willing to substitute air travel by rail travel, taking Le Shuttle through the channel tunnel, or by ship or hoovercraft. In this case, there is a broader London–Paris transportation market, and air transportation is a specific *market segment*. If many customers are willing to substitute physical travel by teleconferencing or other telecommunications methods, the market might need to be defined as the 'London-Paris meeting market'. For the strategist, the realization that all these market definitions might be useful is an important insight (see Figure 5.1).

■   *Business*. A business is defined as a set of related product-market combinations. The term 'business' refers neither to a set of producers nor a group of customers, but to the domain where the two meet. In other words, a business is a competitive arena where companies offering similar products serving similar needs rival against one another for the favor of the buyers. Hence, a business is delineated in both industry and market terms. Typically, a business is narrower than the entire industry and the set of markets served is also limited. For instance, within the airline industry the charter business is usually recognized as rather distinct. In the charter business, a subset of the airline services is offered to a number of tourist markets. Cheap flights from London to Jamaica and from London to Benidorm fall within this business, while service levels will be different than in other parts of the airline industry. It should be noted, though, that just as with industries and markets, there is no best way to define the boundaries of a business (Abell, 1980).

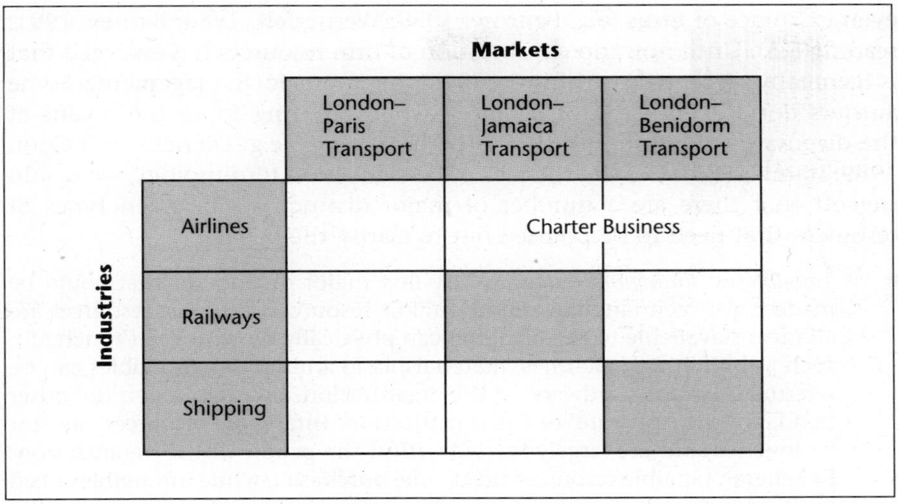

FIGURE 5.1
Industries, markets and businesses

Markets

Industries	London–Paris Transport	London–Jamaica Transport	London–Benidorm Transport
Airlines		Charter Business	
Railways			
Shipping			

A firm positioning itself in the external environment will need to define which industries, markets and businesses it is currently in and 'what makes them tick'. Based on this understanding, the strategist may want to strengthen the firm's existing position, or may prefer to reposition the firm within the current, or a newly-defined, industry, market or business.

An important distinction within the outside-in perspective can be made between strategists focusing on *positioning within a market* and those emphasizing *positioning within an industry*. When firms target a product or brand at a particular group of customers, they are positioning within a market. This is also referred to as *product positioning* and/or *brand positioning*. The key issue when positioning in a market is to meet customer demands in a manner that alternative products or services will not be selected. Emphasis is placed on the need to be market-driven, that is, responsive to the specific demands evolving within the market. This issue is central to the marketing discipline, and marketing strategists write extensively on such positioning challenges (e.g. Aaker, 1991; Day, 1994; reading 5.5).

On the other hand, when a firm more generally distinguishes itself from other firms producing similar goods or services, they are positioning within an industry. A strategist dealing with *firm positioning* necessarily takes a broader view than that of individual products and markets. The firm's overall position within its industry, and more particularly a business unit's position within its business, are of concern. While marketing writers have also contributed to this topic, much of the underlying theory has its origins in the economic discipline of industrial organization (e.g. Scherer, 1980; Porter, 1980; reading 5.1). In this chapter, both types of positioning will be considered.

Developing Tangible and Intangible Resources

Under the broad umbrella of *resource-based view of the firm*, there has been a wide range of research into the importance of resources for the success and even existence of firms (e.g. Penrose, 1959; Wernerfelt, 1984; Barney, 1991; reading 5.5). Until now, no classification of firm resources has emerged that is generally accepted within the field of strategic management. Some authors don't even speak of *resources*, when referring to all the means at the disposal of the firm, but prefer the term *assets* (e.g. Dierickx and Cool, 1989; Itami, 1986). Despite the lack of consensus on terminology, we would suggest that there are a number of major distinctions between types of resources that need to be pointed out to clarify the debate:

■ *Tangible vs. intangible resources.* The first major distinction that could be made is between tangible and intangible resources. Tangible resources are all means available to the firm that can physically be observed ('touched'), such as buildings, machines, materials, land and money. Tangibles can be referred to as the 'hardware' of the organization. Intangibles, on the other hand, are the 'software' of the organization. Intangible resources can not be touched, but are largely carried within the people in the organization. In general, tangible resources need to be purchased, while intangibles need to be developed. Therefore, tangible resources are often more readily transferable, easier to price and usually are placed on the balance sheet. For this reason, *assets* (with the connotation of ownership) is an appropriate term for tangible resources.

■ *Relational resources vs. competences.* Within the category of intangible resources, relational resources and competences can be distinguished. Relational resources are all of the means available to the firm derived from the firm's interaction with its environment (Lowendahl, 1997). The firm can cultivate specific *relationships* with individuals and organizations in the environment, such as buyers, suppliers, competitors and government agencies, that can be instrumental in achieving the firm's goals. As attested by the old saying 'it's not what you know, but who you know,' relationships can often be an essential resource (see Chapter 7 for a further discussion). Besides direct relationships, a firm's *reputation* among other parties in the environment can also be an important resource. Compe-

FIGURE 5.2
Types of firm resources

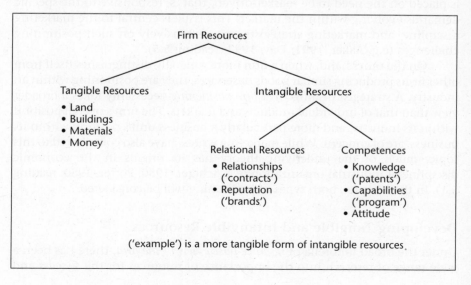

('example') is a more tangible form of intangible resources.

tence, on the other hand, refers to the firm's fitness to perform in a particular field. A firm has a competence if it has the knowledge, capabilities and attitude needed to successfully operate in a specific area.

This description of competences is somewhat broad and therefore difficult to employ. However, a distinction between knowledge, capability and attitude (Durand, 1996) can be used to shed more light on the nature of competences:

- *Knowledge.* Knowledge can be defined as the whole of rules (know-how, know-what, know-where and know-when) and insights (know-why) that can be extracted from, and help make sense of, information. In other words, knowledge flows from, and influences, the interpretation of information (Dretske, 1981). Examples of knowledge that a firm can possess are market insight, competitive intelligence, technological expertise, and understanding of political and economic developments.

- *Capability.* Capability refers to the organization's potential for carrying out a specific activity or set of activities. Sometimes the term *skill* is used to refer to the ability to carry out a narrow (functional) task or activity, while the term capability is reserved for the quality of combining a number of skills. For instance, a firm's capability-base can include narrower abilities such as market research, advertising and production skills, that if co-ordinated could result in a capability for new product development (Stalk, Evans and Shulman, 1992; reading 5.2).

- *Attitude.* Attitude refers to the outlook prevalent within an organization. Sometimes the terms *disposition* and *will* are used in the same sense, to indicate how an organization views and relates to the world. Although ignored by some writers, every sports coach will acknowledge the importance of attitude as a resource. A healthy body (tangible resource), insight into the game (knowledge), speed and dexterity (capabilities) – all are important, but without the winning mentality a team will not get to the top. Some attitudes may change rapidly within firms, yet others may be entrenched within the cultural fabric of the organization – these in particular can be important resources for the firm (Barney, 1986). A company's attitude can, for instance, be characterized as quality-driven, internationally-oriented, innovation-minded and/or competitively-aggressive.

It must be noted that in practice the term 'competences' is used in many different ways, partially due to the ambiguous definition given by its early proponents (Prahalad and Hamel, 1990; reading 6.2). It is often used as a synonym for capabilities, while Prahalad and Hamel seem to focus more on technologically-oriented capabilities ('how to coordinate diverse production skills and integrate multiple streams of technologies'). Others (e.g. Durand, 1996) have suggested that a firm has a competence in a certain area, when the firm's underlying knowledge-base, capabilities and attitude are all aligned. So, Honda's engine competence is built on specific knowledge, development capabilities and the right predisposition. Walmart's inventory control competence depends on specific information technology knowledge, coordination capabilities and a conducive state of mind. Virgin Airway's service competence combines customer knowledge, adaptation capabilities and a customer-oriented attitude.

As in the case of industries, markets, and businesses, employing the concepts of tangible and intangible resources is quite difficult in practice. Two problems need to be overcome – resources are difficult to categorize, but worse yet, often difficult to recognize. The issue of categorization is a minor one. For some resources it is unclear how they should be classified. Are *human resources* tangible or intangible? Problematically, both. In humans, hardware and software are intertwined – if an engineer's expertise is required, the physical person usually needs to be hired. Knowledge, capabilities and attitudes need human carriers. Sometimes it is possible to separate hardware and software, by making the intangibles more tangible. This is done by 'writing the software down'. In such a manner, knowledge can be codified, for instance in a patent, a capability can be captured in a computer program and a relationship can be formalized in a contract (see Figure 5.2 for further examples).

More important is the problem of resource identification. Tangible resources, by their very nature, are relatively easy to observe. Accountants keep track of the financial resources, production managers usually know the quality of their machinery and stock levels, while the personnel department will have an overview of all people on the pay role. Intangible resources, on the other hand, are far more difficult to identify (e.g. Grant, 1991; Itami, 1986). With whom does the firm have a relationship and what is the state of this relationship? What is the firm's reputation? These relational resources are hard to pin down. Competences are probably even more difficult to determine. How do you know what you know? Even for an individual it is a formidable task to outline areas of expertise, let alone for a more complex organization. Especially the *tacit* (non-articulated) nature of much organizational knowledge makes it difficult to identify the firm's knowledge-base (Polanyi, 1958; Nonaka, 1991). The same is true for a firm's capabilities, which have developed in the form of organizational *routines* (Nelson and Winter, 1982). Likewise, the firm's attitudes are difficult to discern, because all people sharing the same disposition will tend to consider themselves normal and will tend to believe that their outlook is 'a matter of common sense' (see Chapter 2). Hence, firms intent on identifying their competences find that this is not an easy task.

While an overview of the firm's resource-base is important in itself, a strategist will want to know how the firm's resources compare to other companies. In other words, are the firm's resources unique, superior to, or inferior to the resources of (potential) competitors? In which resource areas does the firm have a relative strength and where does it have a relative weakness? This type of analysis is particularly difficult, as comparison requires insight into other firms' resource-bases. Especially the identification of other firms' intangible resources can be quite arduous.

Creating a Sustainable Competitive Advantage

A firm has a competitive advantage when it has the means to edge out rivals when vying for the favor of customers. A competitive advantage is said to be sustainable if it cannot be copied or eroded by the actions of rivals, and is not made redundant by environment developments (Porter, 1980).

The question to be debated is how a sustainable competitive advantage can be created. Should generals create a sustainable competitive advantage by first selecting a superior environmental position (e.g. a mountain pass) and then adapting their military resources to this position, or should generals develop armies with unique resources and then try to let the battle take place where these resources can best be employed? Should football coaches first determine how they want the game to be played on the field and then attract and train players to fit with this style, or should coaches develop uniquely talented players and then adapt the team's playing style to make the best use of these resources? Whether a military, sports or business strategist, an approach to creating competitive advantage must be chosen.

EXHIBIT 5.1
Avon Short Case

AVON: KEEPING THOSE DOORBELLS RINGING?

When James Preston became chairman and CEO of Avon Products in 1989, the company was in dire straits. Many analysts doubted whether the well-known door-to-door vendor of cosmetics would make it into the 1990s as an independent company. Under Preston's predecessor, Avon had branched out of the mature cosmetics business, into the growing market for healthcare products, acquiring a number of companies along the way. However, this diversification move was not particularly successful, with the added disadvantage of tying up cash and siphoning off the profits made in cosmetics. As a consequence, Avon itself became an attractive candidate for acquisition and the company was forced to fight off some hostile take-over attempts. One of Preston's first tasks at the helm was to resist the aggressive bids by Mary Kay, one of Avon's most prominent cosmetics competitors, and Amway, a similar direct sales company, with a broad product portfolio. In an effort to retain Avon's independence, Preston also took drastic downsizing measures to restore profitability. The healthcare business was sold off and a number of production and distribution facilities in the cosmetics business were closed, putting over a thousand people out of a job. Preston realized, however, that recovery would not result from 'surgery' alone – Avon would need to strengthen its slipping position in the cosmetics markets of the US and Western Europe, as well as seek growth elsewhere. Naturally, the challenge facing Preston and his company was how this could be achieved. What competitive advantage would Avon have to concentrate on to return the firm to healthy profitability?

Avon did have a number of things going for it. Avon's direct sales system is probably its most valuable asset. Almost 100 percent of Avon's total turnover is generated through direct sales to consumers, using a network of over two million sales representatives around the world (445,000 in the US alone). These 'Avon ladies' are not employed by the company, but are 'independent entrepeneurs' paid on a commission basis. In 1995 this legion of sales reps took 650 million orders, in more than 120 countries, good for approximately

$4.5 billion worth of beauty products. Selling through this system of 'virtual stores', has some important advantages over traditional retailing methods. Expanding and maintaining a network of virtual stores can be done at a fraction of the cost, and within a fraction of the time, of opening real stores. It is possible to reach almost anyone anywhere, because the 'virtual' store' comes to the buyer, instead of vice versa. Selling Avon products can be done at home, but elsewhere as well. For instance, in the US 30 percent of sales are signed up at work. Furthermore, Avon's 'virtual stores' do not need a critical mass of potential buyers within a sales area. Avon ladies can sell as much as they want, wherever they want – and their straight commission income is a large incentive to ensure that they will be creative in seeking customers.

On the other hand, Avon's image in North America and Western Europe was stale and down market. While still popular among older women, more fashion-conscious younger women steered clear of Avon products. Preston himself recognized that this was a significant problem: 'I am well aware that there are many women who would not want to open their purses and pull out Avon lipstick.' Furthermore, customers increasingly demand instantaneous satisfaction. Ordering a product from Avon could take weeks, while products in the shop can be taken directly. This problem was aggravated by the growing trend toward 'recreational shopping'. Young women, especially, were exhibiting a growing preference for visiting stores as a leisure activity. By the early 1990s this had resulted in stagnant sales in the US and even declining sales in Western Europe.

Preston decided to counter these developments with a number of moves. First, slipping sales in mature markets could be more than off-set by expansion in fast-growing markets outside the developed economies. Demand for beauty products is booming in many 'emerging markets', as more women in these countries have enough cash at their disposal to make discretionary purchases. But even the lesser developed economies, where GNP growth is low, are in Preston's words 'Avon Heaven'. Where the retailing infrastructure is poor and conventional shops are difficult to set up, Avon's sales ladies have an even stronger advantage than usual. Avon needs only basic transportation and distribution facilities to get up and running. Moreover, there are usually plenty of eager sales people in less developed economies, willing to work hard to provide their family with some additional income. Between 1989 and 1995 Avon entered 14 new markets and plans to proceed at the same pace until it has global coverage. An interesting spin off has been that the company now has one of the best sales forces in many countries, so that many firms, such as Reader's Digest, use Avon as their local sales organization.

Yet, Preston also refused to give up on the established markets. Avon's image needed to be upgraded and Preston set a two-day order processing time as new standard. Emphasis was also placed on getting to know its customers better. 'We do not want to build transactions, we want to build relationships,' according to Preston. Avon wanted to strengthen relations by being *the* resource for women, helping them in any way possible, for instance by providing seminars on household management and by offering education about abuse and breast cancer.

By 1995, the company seemed at a crossroads. Despite the aforementioned efforts, growth in the mature markets remained lacklustre. Preston seemed to be faced with two major options for achieving further growth. One would be to abandon direct sales as the company's primary sales method and to develop multiple channels. Avon could actually go into traditional retailing, catalogue sales, direct mail, telephone sales or even internet sales, if this were what the market demanded. However, this partial repositioning would require the firm to develop many new skills. Alternatively, Avon could build on its direct sales ability and add related products to its sales portfolio. Glassware and bedware were suggested as potentially suitable product lines. The question facing Preston was which avenue of expansion to choose. What would be the advantages and disadvantages of each alternative, both in the short and in the long run? In a nutshell, he had to choose whether Avon would primarily be a cosmetics company or a direct sales company – which wasn't an easy choice to make.

Sources: *The Economist*, July 13 1996; *Forbes*, December 2 1996.

The Debate and the Readings

The opening reading in the debate, 'Competitive Strategy', has been taken from Michael Porter's 1985 book *Competitive Advantage*, but its central concepts were originally introduced in his first book, *Competitive Strategy*. Since Porter is considered by all to be the most important theorist in the positioning tradition, it seems only logical to start with him as representative of the outside-in perspective. In his contribution, Porter argues that 'two central questions underlie the choice of competitive strategy.' First, strategists must select a competitive domain with attractive characteristics and then they must position the firm *vis-à-vis* the five competitive forces encountered. These five forces impinging on the firm's profit potential are 'the entry of new competitors, the threat of substitutes, the bargaining power of buyers, the bargaining power of suppliers, and the rivalry among the existing competitors.' Long run above-average performance results from selecting one of the three defensible positions available to the strategist: *cost leadership*, *differentiation* or *focus*. According to Porter, these three options, or *generic strategies*, are the only feasible ways of achieving a sustainable competitive advantage. A firm that does not make a clear choice between one of the three generic strategies, is 'stuck in the middle' and will suffer below-average performance. For the debate in this chapter it is important to note that Porter does not explicitly advocate an exclusively outside-in approach. However, he strongly emphasizes competitive positioning as leading strategy principle and treats the development of firm resources as a derivative activity. Indirectly, therefore, his message to strategists is that in the game of strategy it is essential to be focused on the external dynamics.

As representative of the inside-out approach, the reading 'Competing on Capabilities,' by George Stalk, Philip Evans and Lawrence Shulman has been selected. They argue that the key to competitive success lies in identifying and developing 'the hard-to-imitate organizational capabilities that distinguish a company from its competitors in the eyes of the customers.' In their view, the positioning way of looking at the world is too static. Competition, they believe, is increasingly unlike chess, a 'war of position,' and more like an interactive video game, a 'war of movement.' Therefore, a company should not build static market share, but should develop organizational capabilities that allow the firm to 'move quickly in and out of products, markets, and even entire businesses.' The flexibility gained by superior capabilities can be used to consistently change the rules of the competitive game in one's own industry, but can also be employed to rewrite the rules in entirely different industries. Stalk, Evans and Shulman refer to companies seeking to transfer their most important business processes to different industries as *capabilities predators*. The capabilities-based approach is, therefore, not only an important approach to business strategy, but also to corporate strategy (in Chapter 6, Prahalad and Hamel expand on this point).

A key argument used by Stalk, Evans and Shulman to justify their support for the inside-out approach to business strategy, is that they believe that market share is becoming increasingly unimportant. This remark is a direct challenge to the researchers of the PIMS group, who are the most prominent exponents of the link between market share and profitability. The acronym PIMS stands for Profit Impact of Market Strategy, and refers to a fifteen-year-long, quantitative study of more than 3000 business units. For the PIMS data base, information was gathered on a large number of company characteristics, such as sales, costs, investments, prices, perceived quality, and market share, as well as on market and industry characteristics such as growth, concentration and investment-intensity. Many articles have been based on the PIMS data set, but the major work flowing from this enormous undertaking has been the book *The PIMS Principles: Linking Strategy to Performance*, by Robert Buzzell and Bradley Gale. From this book, the chapter reporting the link between market position and profitability has been included here as reading 5.3. Buzzell and Gale are very clear about the conclusions of their research: 'There is no doubt that market share and return on investment are strongly related.' In itself, market share does not cause profitability, they argue, but it does lead to economies of scale and experience advantages that improve a company's competitiveness and consequently its profits. Of course, without high quality products or services the advantages of high market share can easily be cancelled out. Yet, Buzzell and Gale reiterate, once a company has gained a strong market position, as measured in terms of relative market share, they will be difficult to dethrone. Their advice is, therefore, lead where possible. For followers it is often wise to position themselves in defensible niches. In the context of this chapter, their major conclusion is that resources and quality products are important, but far from sufficient to be highly profitable. Rather, gaining and maintaining a favorable market position is essential for continued profitability.

As mentioned earlier, much of the theoretical underpinning of the inside-out perspective comes from a stream of literature known under the umbrella term 'resource-based view of the firm'. Stalk, Evans and Shulman use some of the key ideas of this body of literature to build up their argument, but do not really explain the essence of this school of thought. To compensate and add further depth to the discussion, an often cited article by Jay Barney has been selected as a more thorough introduction to the resource-based view. In this contribution, 'Firm Resources and Sustained Competitive Advantage,' Barney differentiates resource-based models of competitive advantage from the Porter-like environmental models. He does not dismiss externally-oriented explanations of profitability, but wishes to explore the internally-oriented explanation that idiosyncratic firm resources are the basis of superior performance. He sets out on this task by pinpointing the two fundamental assumptions on which the resource-based view rests – that firms have different resources (resource heterogeneity) and that these resources cannot be easily transferred to, or copied by, other firms (resource immobility). He goes on to argue that these resources can be the basis of a competitive advantage if they meet four criteria: they must be valuable and rare, while being difficult to imitate and substitute.

Since the early 1990s, the resource-based view of the firm has increasing come to dominate the field of strategic management. Consequently, support for the inside-out perspective on business strategy has also grown strongly. Interestingly, on the other side of the fence, in the field of marketing, the outside-in perspective is still widely expounded. Almost simultaneously with the strategy field's emphasis on resource-driven strategies, the marketing field has huddled around the concept of market-driven strategy. In an effort to avoid disciplinary myopia and to keep the debate on the paradox of markets and resources open to all challenging points of view, one of the best contributions from the field of marketing has been incorporated into this chapter as reading 5.5. In this paper, 'The Capabilities of Market-Driven Organizations,' George Day argues that not all capabilities are inside-out in orientation. Capabilities in the areas of manufacturing, logistics, technology development, finances, and human resource management are deployed from the inside-out, but there are also outside-in capabilities, such as market sensing, customer linking, channel bonding and technology monitoring. He also distinguishes spanning capabilities, such as purchasing, new product development and strategy development, that link inside-out and outside-in capabilities. According to Day, in a market-driven organization outside-in capabilities should 'inform and guide both spanning and inside-out capabilities.' Although he just stops short of advocating a dominant role for outside-in capabilities, it is clear that he believes that in a market-driven organization all activities become more externally oriented. In the context of the discussion in this chapter, Day's article makes more tangible what an outside-in oriented company is like, and indirectly the profile of an inside-out oriented company. While Day's sympathies are clear, the question for the debate remains which of the two orientations is the most valuable? Or could the two seeming opposites be combined, to get the best of both worlds?

5.1   Competitive Strategy

By Michael Porter[1]

Competition is at the core of the success or failure of firms. Competition determines the appropriateness of a firm's activities that can contribute to its performance, such as innovations, a cohesive culture, or good implementation. Competitive strategy is the search for a favorable competitive position in an industry, the fundamental arena in which competition occurs. Competitive strategy aims to establish a profitable and sustainable position against the forces that determine industry competition.

Two central questions underlie the choice of competitive strategy. The first is the attractiveness of industries for long-term profitability and the factors that determine it. Not all industries offer equal opportunities for sustained profitability, and the inherent profitability of its industry is one essential ingredient in determining the profitability of a firm. The second central question in competitive strategy is the determinants of relative competitive position within an industry. In most industries, some firms are much more profitable than others, regardless of what the average profitability of the industry may be.

Neither question is sufficient by itself to guide the choice of competitive strategy. A firm in a very attractive industry may still not earn attractive profits if it has chosen a poor competitive position. Conversely, a firm in an excellent competitive position may be in such a poor industry that it is not very profitable, and further efforts to enhance its position will be of little benefit. Both questions are dynamic; industry attractiveness and competitive position change. Industries become more or less attractive over time, and competitive position reflects an unending battle among competitors. Even long periods of stability can be abruptly ended by competitive moves.

Both industry attractiveness and competitive position can be shaped by a firm, and this is what makes the choice of competitive strategy both challenging and exciting. While industry attractiveness is partly a reflection of factors over which a firm has little influence, competitive strategy has considerable power to make an industry more or less attractive. At the same time, a firm can clearly improve or erode its position within an industry through its choice of strategy. Competitive strategy, then, not only responds to the environment but also attempts to shape that environment in a firm's favor.

---

[1] Source: This article was adapted with permission from *Competitive Advantage: Creating and Sustaining Superior Performance*, Free Press, New York, 1985.

The Structural Analysis of Industries

The first fundamental determinant of a firm's profitability is industry attractiveness. Competitive strategy must grow out of a sophisticated understanding of the rules of competition that determine an industry's attractiveness. The ultimate aim of competitive strategy is to cope with and, ideally, to change those rules in the firm's favor. In any industry, whether it is domestic or international or produces a product or a service, the rules of competition are embodied in five competitive forces: the entry of new competitors, the threat of substitutes, the bargaining power of buyers, the bargaining power of suppliers, and the rivalry among the existing competitors.

The collective strength of these five competitive forces determines the ability of firms in an industry to earn, on average, rates of return on investment in excess of the cost of capital. The strength of the five forces varies from industry to industry, and can change as an industry evolves. The result is that all industries are not alike from the standpoint of inherent profitability. In industries where the five forces are favorable, such as pharmaceuticals, soft drinks, and database publishing, many competitors earn attractive returns. But in industries where pressure from one or more of the forces is intense, such as rubber, steel, and video games, few firms command attractive returns despite the best efforts of management. Industry profitability is not a function of what the product looks like or whether it embodies high or low technology, but of industry structure. Some very mundane industries such as postage meters and grain trading are extremely profitable, while some more glamorous, high-technology industries such as personal computers and cable television are not profitable for many participants.

The five forces determine industry profitability because they influence the prices, costs, and required investment of firms in an industry – the elements of return on investment. Buyer power influences the prices that firms can charge, for example, as does the threat of substitution. The power of buyers can also influence cost and investment, because powerful buyers demand costly service. The bargaining power of suppliers determines the costs of raw materials and other inputs. The intensity of rivalry influences prices as well as the costs of competing in areas such as plant, product development, advertising, and sales force. The threat of entry places a limit on prices, and shapes the investment required to deter entrants.

The strength of each of the five competitive forces is a function of *industry structure*, or the underlying economic and technical characteristics of an industry. Its important elements are shown in Figure 5.1.1. Industry structure is relatively stable, but can change over time as an industry evolves. Structural change shifts the overall and relative strength of the competitive forces, and can thus positively or negatively influence industry profitability. The industry trends that are the most important for strategy are those that affect industry structure.

If the five competitive forces and their structural determinants were solely a function of intrinsic industry characteristics, then competitive

FIGURE 5.1.1
Elements of industry structure

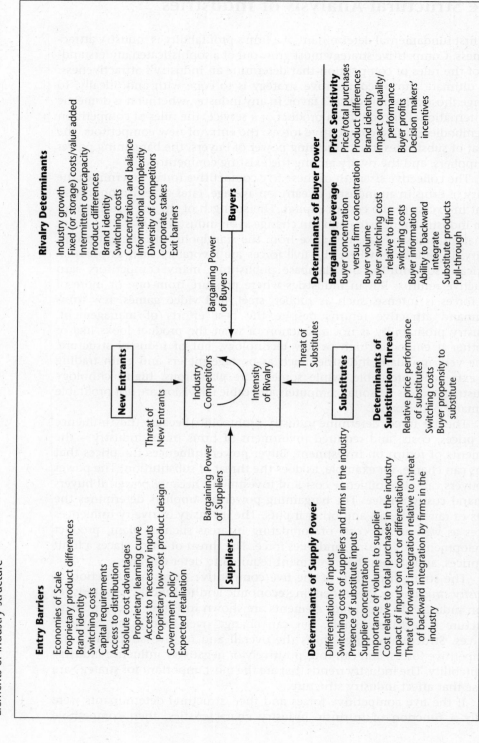

strategy would rest heavily on picking the right industry and understanding the five forces better than competitors. But while these are surely important tasks for any firm, and are the essence of competitive strategy in some industries, a firm is usually not a prisoner of its industry's structure. Firms, through their strategies, can influence the five forces. If a firm can shape structure, it can fundamentally change an industry's attractiveness for better or for worse. Many successful strategies have shifted the rules of competition in this way.

Figure 5.1.1 highlights all the elements of industry structure that may drive competition in an industry. In any particular industry, not all of the five forces will be equally important and the particular structural factors that are important will differ. Every industry is unique and has its own unique structure. The five-forces framework allows a firm to see through the complexity and pinpoint those factors that are critical to competition in its industry, as well as to identify those strategic innovations that would most improve the industry's – and its own – profitability. The five-forces framework does not eliminate the need for creativity in finding new ways of competing in an industry. Instead, it directs managers' creative energies toward those aspects of industry structure that are most important to long-run profitability. The framework aims, in the process, to raise the odds of discovering a desirable strategic innovation.

Strategies that change industry structure can be a double-edged sword, because a firm can destroy industry structure and profitability as readily as it can improve it. A new product design that undercuts entry barriers or increases the volatility of rivalry, for example, may undermine the long-run profitability of an industry, though the initiator may enjoy higher profits temporarily. Or a sustained period of price cutting can undermine differentiation. In the tobacco industry, for example, generic cigarettes are a potentially serious threat to industry structure. Generics may enhance the price sensitivity of buyers, trigger price competition, and erode the high advertising barriers that have kept out new entrants. Joint ventures entered into by major aluminum producers to spread risk and lower capital cost may have similarly undermined industry structure. The majors invited a number of potentially dangerous new competitors into the industry and helped them overcome the significant entry barriers to doing so. Joint ventures also can raise exit barriers because all the participants in a plant must agree before it can be closed down.

Often firms make strategic choices without considering the long-term consequences for industry structure. They see a gain in the competitive position if a move is successful, but they fail to anticipate the consequences of competitive reaction. If imitation of a move by major competitors has the effect of wrecking industry structure, then everyone is worse off. Such industry 'destroyers' are usually second-tier firms that are searching for ways to overcome major competitive disadvantages, firms that have encountered serious problems and are desperately seeking solutions, or 'dumb' competitors that do not know their costs or have unrealistic assumptions about the future. In the tobacco industry, for example, the Liggett Group (a distant follower) has encouraged the trend toward generics.

The ability of firms to shape industry structure places a particular burden on industry leaders. Leaders' actions can have a disproportionate impact on structure, because of their size and influence over buyers, suppliers, and other competitors. At the same time, leaders' large market shares guarantee that anything that changes overall industry structure will affect them as well. A leader, then, must constantly balance its own competitive position against the health of the industry as a whole. Often leaders are better off taking actions to improve or protect industry structure rather than seeking greater competitive advantage for themselves. Such industry leaders as Coca-Cola and Campbell's Soup appear to have followed this principle.

Industry Structure and Buyer Needs

It has often been said that satisfying buyer needs is at the core of success in business endeavor. How does this relate to the concept of industry structural analysis? Satisfying buyer needs is indeed a prerequisite to the viability of an industry and the firms within it. Buyers must be willing to pay a price for a product that exceeds its cost of production, or an industry will not survive in the long run.

Satisfying buyer needs may be a prerequisite for industry profitability, but in itself is not sufficient. The crucial question in determining profitability is whether firms can capture the value they create for buyers, or whether this value is competed away to others. Industry structure determines who captures the value. The threat of entry determines the likelihood that new firms will enter an industry and compete away the value, either passing it on to buyers in the form of lower prices or dissipating it by raising the costs of competing. The power of buyers determines the extent to which they retain most of the value created for themselves, leaving firms in an industry only modest returns. The threat of substitutes determines the extent to which some other product can meet the same buyer needs, and thus places a ceiling on the amount a buyer is willing to pay for an industry's product. The power of suppliers determines the extent to which value created for buyers will be appropriated by suppliers rather than by firms in an industry. Finally, the intensity of rivalry acts similarly to the threat of entry. It determines the extent to which firms already in an industry will compete away the value they create for buyers among themselves, passing it on to buyers in lower prices or dissipating it in higher costs of competing.

Industry structure, then, determines who keeps what proportion of the value a product creates for buyers. If an industry's product does not create much value for its buyers, there is little value to be captured by firms regardless of the other elements of structure. If the product creates a lot of value, structure becomes crucial. In some industries such as automobiles and heavy trucks, firms create enormous value for their buyers but, on average, capture very little of it for themselves through profits. In other industries such as bond rating services, medical equipment, and oil field services and equipment, firms also create high value for their buyers but have historically captured a good proportion of it. In oil field services and equipment, for example, many products can significantly reduce the cost of drilling. Because industry structure has been favorable, many firms in the oil field service and equipment sector have been able to retain a share of these savings in the form of high returns. Recently, however, the structural attractiveness of many industries in the oil field services and equipment sector has eroded as a result of falling demand, new entrants, eroding product differentiation, and greater buyer price sensitivity. Despite the fact that products offered still create enormous value for the buyer, both firm and industry profits have fallen significantly.

Industry Structure and the Supply/Demand Balance

Another commonly held view about industry profitability is that profits are a function of the balance between supply and demand. If demand is greater than supply, this leads to high profitability. Yet, the long-term supply/demand balance is strongly influenced by industry structure, as are the consequences of a supply/demand imbalance for profitability. Hence, even though short-term fluctuations in supply and demand can affect short-term profitability, industry structure underlies long-term profitability.

Supply and demand change constantly, adjusting to each other. Industry structure determines how rapidly competitors add new supply. The height of entry barriers underpins the likelihood that new entrants will enter an industry and bid down prices. The intensity of rivalry plays a major role in determining whether existing firms will expand capacity aggressively or choose to maintain profitability. Industry structure also determines how rapidly competitors will retire excess supply. Exit barriers keep firms from leaving an industry when there is too much capacity, and prolong periods of excess capacity. In oil tanker shipping, for example, the exit barriers are very high because of the specialization of assets. This has translated into short peaks and long troughs of prices. Thus industry structure shapes the supply/demand balance and the duration of imbalances.

The consequences of an imbalance between supply and demand for industry profitability also differs widely depending on industry structure. In some industries, a small amount of excess capacity triggers price wars and low profitability. These are industries where there are structural pressures for intense rivalry or powerful buyers. In other industries, periods of excess capacity have relatively little impact on profitability because of favorable structure. In oil tools, ball valves, and many other oil field equipment products, for example, there has been intense price cutting during the recent sharp downturn. In drill bits, however, there has been relatively little discounting. Hughes Tool, Smith International, and Baker International are good competitors operating in a favorable industry structure. Industry structure also determines the profitability of excess demand. In a boom, for example, favorable structure allows firms to reap extraordinary profits, while a poor structure restricts the ability to capitalize on it. The presence of powerful suppliers or the presence of substitutes, for example, can mean that the fruits of a boom pass to others. Thus industry structure is fundamental to both the speed of adjustment of supply to demand and the relationship between capacity utilization and profitability.

Generic Competitive Strategies

The second central question in competitive strategy is a firm's relative position within its industry. Positioning determines whether a firm's profitability is above or below the industry average. A firm that can position itself well may earn high rates of return even though industry structure is unfavorable and the average profitability of the industry is therefore modest.

The fundamental basis of above-average performance in the long run is *sustainable competitive advantage*. Though a firm can have a myriad strengths and weaknesses *vis-à-vis* its competitors, there are two basic types of competitive advantage a firm can possess: low cost or differentiation. The significance of any strength or weakness a firm possesses is ultimately a function of its impact on relative cost or differentiation. Cost advantage and differentiation in turn stem from industry structure. They result from a firm's ability to cope with the five forces better than its rivals.

The two basic types of competitive advantage combined with the scope of activities for which a firm seeks to achieve them lead to three *generic strategies* for achieving above-average performance in an industry: cost leadership, differentiation, and focus. The focus strategy has two variants, cost focus and differentiation focus. The generic strategies are shown in Figure 5.1.2.

Each of the generic strategies involves a fundamentally different route to competitive advantage, combining a choice about the type of competitive advantage sought with the scope of the strategic target in which competitive advantage is to be achieved. The cost leadership and differentiation strategies seek competitive advantage in a broad range of industry segments, while focus strategies aim at cost advantage (cost focus) or differentiation (differentiation focus) in a narrow segment. The specific actions required to implement each generic strategy vary widely from industry to industry, as do the feasible generic strategies in a particular industry. While selecting and implementing a generic strategy is far from simple, they are the logical routes to competitive advantage that must be probed in any industry.

The notion underlying the concept of generic strategies is that competitive advantage is at the heart of any strategy, and achieving competitive advantage requires a firm to make a choice – if a firm is to attain a competitive advantage, it must make a choice about the type of competitive advantage it seeks to attain and the scope within which it will attain it. Being all things to all people is a recipe for strategic mediocrity and below-average performance, because it often means that a firm has no competitive advantage at all.

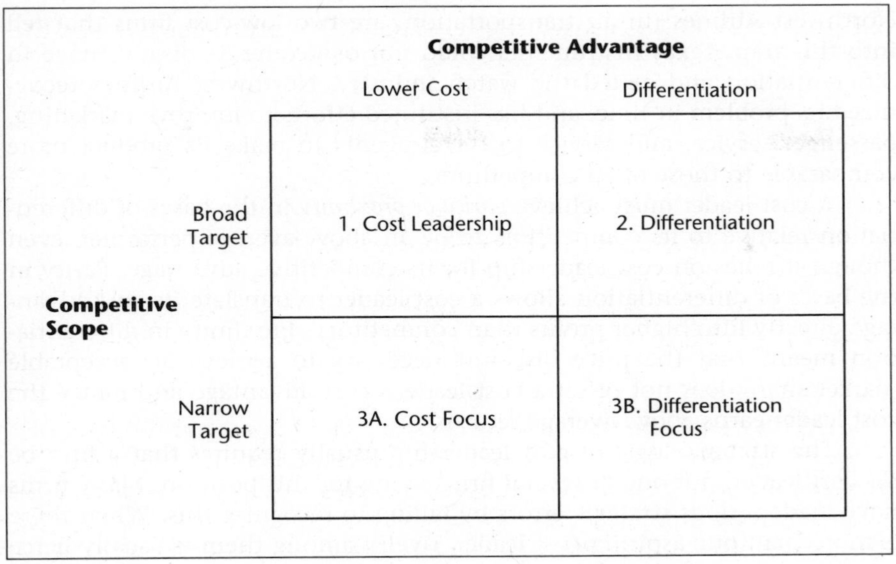

FIGURE 5.1.2
Three Generic Strategies

	Competitive Advantage	
	Lower Cost	Differentiation
Broad Target	1. Cost Leadership	2. Differentiation
Narrow Target	3A. Cost Focus	3B. Differentiation Focus

Competitive Scope (row label, left side)

Cost Leadership

Cost leadership is perhaps the clearest of the three generic strategies. In it, a firm sets out to become *the* low-cost producer in its industry. The firm has a broad scope and serves many industry segments, and may even operate in related industries – the firm's breadth is often important to its cost advantage. The sources of cost advantage are varied and depend on the structure of the industry. They may include the pursuit of economies of scale, proprietary technology, preferential access to raw materials, and other factors. In TV sets, for example, cost leadership requires efficient-size picture tube facilities, a low-cost design, automated assembly, and global scale over which to amortize research and development (R&D). In security guard services, cost advantage requires extremely low overhead, a plentiful source of low-cost labor, and efficient training procedures because of high turnover. Low-cost producer status involves more than just going down the learning curve. A low-cost producer must find and exploit all sources of cost advantage. Low-cost producers typically sell a standard, or no-frills, product and place considerable emphasis on reaping scale or absolute cost advantages from all sources.

If a firm can achieve and sustain overall cost leadership, then it will be an above-average performer in its industry provided it can command prices at or near the industry average. At equivalent or lower prices than its rivals, a cost leader's low-cost position translates into higher returns. A cost leader, however, cannot ignore the bases of differentiation. If its product is not perceived as comparable or acceptable by buyers, a cost leader will be forced to discount prices well below competitors' to gain sales. This may nullify the benefits of its favorable cost position. Texas Instruments (in watches) and

Northwest Airlines (in air transportation) are two low-cost firms that fell into this trap. Texas Instruments could not overcome its disadvantage in differentiation and exited the watch industry. Northwest Airlines recognized its problem in time, and has instituted efforts to improve marketing, passenger service, and service to travel agents to make its product more comparable to those of its competitors.

A cost leader must achieve *parity or proximity* in the bases of differentiation relative to its competitiors to be an above-average performer, even though it relies on cost leadership for its competitive advantage. Parity in the bases of differentiation allows a cost leader to translate its cost advantage directly into higher profits than competitors'. Proximity in differentiation means that the price discount necessary to achieve an acceptable market share does not offset a cost leader's cost advantage and hence the cost leader earns above-average returns.

The strategic logic of cost leadership usually requires that a firm be *the* cost leader, not one of several firms vying for this position. Many firms have made serious strategic errors by failing to recognize this. When there is more than one aspiring cost leader, rivalry among them is usually fierce because every point of market share is viewed as crucial. Unless one firm can gain a cost lead and 'persuade' others to abandon their strategies, the consequences for profitability (and long-run industry structure) can be disastrous, as has been the case in a number of petrochemical industries. Thus cost leadership is a strategy particularly dependent on preemption, unless major technological change allows a firm to radically change its cost position.

Differentiation

The second generic strategy is differentiation. In a differentiation strategy, a firm seeks to be unique in its industry along some dimensions that are widely valued by buyers. It selects one or more attributes that many buyers in an industry perceive as important, and uniquely positions itself to meet those needs. It is rewarded for its uniqueness with a premium price.

The means for differentiation are peculiar to each industry. Differentiation can be based on the product itself, the delivery system by which it is sold, the marketing approach, and a broad range of other factors. In construction equipment, for example, Caterpillar Tractor's differentiation is based on product durability, service, spare parts availability, and an excellent dealer network. In cosmetics, differentiation tends to be based more on product image and the positioning of counters in the stores.

A firm that can achieve and sustain differentiation will be an above-average performer in its industry if its price premium exceeds the extra costs incurred in being unique. A differentiator, therefore, must always seek ways of differentiating that lead to a price premium greater than the cost of differentiating. A differentiator cannot ignore its cost position, because its premium prices will be nullified by a markedly inferior cost position. A differentiator thus aims at cost parity or proximity relative to its competitors by reducing cost in all areas that do not affect differentiation.

The logic of the differentiation strategy requires that a firm choose attributes in which to differentiate itself that are *different* from its rivals'. A firm must truly be unique at something or be perceived as unique if it is to expect a premium price. In contrast to cost leadership, however, there can be more than one successful differentiation strategy in an industry if there are a number of attributes that are widely valued by buyers.

Focus

The third generic strategy is focus. This strategy is quite different from the others because it rests on the choice of a narrow competitive scope within an industry. The focuser selects a segment or group of segments in the industry and tailors its strategy to serving them to the exclusion of others. By optimizing its strategy for the target segments, the focuser seeks to achieve a competitive advantage in its target segments even though it does not possess a competitive advantage overall.

The focus strategy has two variants. In *cost focus* a firm seeks a cost advantage in its target segment, while in *differentiation focus* a firm seeks differentiation in its target segment. Both variants of the focus strategy rest on *differences* between a focuser's target segments and other segments in the industry. The target segments must either have buyers with unusual needs or else the production and delivery system that best serves the target segment must differ from that of other industry segments. Cost focus exploits differences in cost behavior in some segments, while differentiation focus exploits the special needs of buyers in certain segments. Such differences imply that the segments are poorly served by broadly targeted competitiors who serve them at the same time as they serve others. The focuser can thus achieve competitive advantage by dedicating itself to the segments exclusively. Breadth of target is clearly a matter of degree, but the essence of focus is the exploitation of a narrow target's differences from the balance of the industry. Narrow focus in and of itself is not sufficient for above-average performance.

A good example of a focuser who has exploited differences in the production process that best serves different segments is Hammermill Paper. Hammermill has increasingly been moving toward relatively low-volume, high-quality speciality papers, where the larger paper companies with higher volume machines face a stiff cost penalty for short production runs. Hammermill's equipment is more suited to shorter runs with frequent setups.

A focuser takes advantage of suboptimization in either direction by broadly targeted competitors. Competitors may be *underperforming* in meeting the needs of a particular segment, which opens the possibility for differentiation focus. Broadly targeted competitors may also be *overperforming* in meeting the needs of a segment, which means that they are bearing higher than necessary cost in serving it. An opportunity for cost focus may be present in just meeting the needs of such a segment and no more.

If a focuser's target segment is not different from other segments, then the focus strategy will not succeed. In soft drinks, for example, Royal Crown has focused on cola drinks, while Coca-Cola and Pepsi have broad product lines with many flavored drinks. Royal Crown's segment, however, can be well served by Coke and Pepsi at the same time they are serving other segments. Hence Coke and Pepsi enjoy competitive advantages over Royal Crown in the cola segment due to the economies of having a broader line.

If a firm can achieve sustainable cost leadership (cost focus) or differentiation (differentiation focus) in its segment and the segment is structurally attractive, then the focuser will be an above-average performer in its industry. Segment structural attractiveness is a necessary condition because some segments in an industry are much less profitable than others. There is often room for several sustainable focus strategies in an industry, provided that focusers choose different target segments. Most industries have a variety of segments, and each one that involves a different buyer need or a different optimal production or delivery system is a candidate for a focus strategy.

Stuck in the Middle

A firm that engages in each generic strategy but fails to achieve any of them is 'stuck in the middle.' It possesses no competitive advantage. This strategic position is usually a recipe for below-average performance. A firm that is stuck in the middle will compete at a disadvantage because the cost leader, differentiators, or focusers will be better positioned to compete in any segment. If a firm that is stuck in the middle is lucky enough to discover a profitable product or buyer, competitors with a sustainable competitive advantage will quickly eliminate the spoils. In most industries, quite a few competitors are stuck in the middle.

A firm that is stuck in the middle will earn attractive profits only if the structure of its industry is highly favorable, or if the firm is fortunate enough to have competitors that are also stuck in the middle. Usually, however, such a firm will be much less profitable than rivals achieving one of the generic strategies. Industry maturity tends to widen the performance differences between firms with a generic strategy and those that are stuck in the middle, because it exposes ill-conceived strategies that have been carried along by rapid growth.

Becoming stuck in the middle is often a manifestation of a firm's unwillingness to make *choices* about how to compete. It tries for competitive advantage through every means and achieves none, because achieving different types of competitive advantage usually requires inconsistent actions. Becoming stuck in the middle also afflicts successful firms, who compromise their generic strategy for the sake of growth or prestige. A classic example is Laker Airways, which began with a clear cost-focus strategy based on no-frills operation in the North Atlantic market, aimed at a particular segment of the traveling public that was extremely price sensitive. Over time, however, Laker began adding frills, new services, and new routes. It blurred its image, and suboptimized its service and delivery system. The consequences were disastrous, and Laker eventually went bankrupt.

The temptation to blur a generic strategy, and therefore become stuck in the middle, is particularly great for a focuser once it has dominated its target segments. Focus involves deliberately limiting potential sales volume. Success can lead a focuser to lose sight of the reasons for its success and compromise its focus strategy for growth's sake. Rather than compromise its generic strategy, a firm is usually better off finding new industries in which to grow where it can use its generic strategy again or exploit interrelationships.

Pursuit of More Than One Generic Strategy

Each generic strategy is a fundamentally different approach to creating and sustaining a competitive advantage, combining the type of competitive advantage a firm seeks and the scope of its strategic target. Usually a firm must make a choice among them, or it will become stuck in the middle. The benefits of optimizing the firm's strategy for a particular target segment (focus) cannot be gained if a firm is simultaneously serving a broad range of segments (cost leadership or differentiation). Sometimes a firm may be able to create two largely separate business units within the same corporate entity, each with a different generic strategy. A good example is the British hotel firm Trusthouse Forte, which operates five separate hotel chains each targeted at a different segment. However, unless a firm strictly separates the units pursuing different generic strategies, it may compromise the ability of any of them to achieve its competitive advantage. A suboptimized approach to competing, made likely by the spillover among units of corporate policies and culture, will lead to becoming stuck in the middle.

Achieving cost leadership and differentiation is also usually inconsistent, because differentiation is usually costly. To be unique and command a price premium, a differentiator deliberately elevates costs, as Caterpillar has done in construction equipment. Conversely, cost leadership often requires a firm to forego some differentiation by standardizing its product, reducing marketing overhead, and the like.

Reducing cost does not always involve a sacrifice in differentiation. Many firms have discovered ways to reduce cost not only without hurting their differentiation but while actually raising it, by using practices that are both more efficient and effective or employing a different technology. Sometimes dramatic cost savings can be achieved with no impact on differentiation at all if a firm has not concentrated on cost reduction previously. However, cost reduction is not the same as achieving a cost advantage. When faced with capable competitors also striving for cost leadership, a firm will ultimately reach the point where further cost reduction requires a sacrifice in differentiation. It is at this point that the generic strategies become inconsistent and a firm must make a choice.

If a firm can achieve cost leadership and differentiation simultaneously, the rewards are great because the benefits are additive – differentiation leads to premium prices at the same time that cost leadership implies lower costs. An example of a firm that has achieved both a cost advantage and differentiation in its segments is Crown Cork and Seal in the metal container industry. Crown has targeted the so-called hard-to-hold uses of cans in the beer, soft drink, and aerosol industries. It manufactures only steel cans rather than both steel and aluminium. In its target segments, Crown has differentiated itself based on service, technological assistance, and offering a full line of steel cans, crowns, and canning machinery. Differentiation of this type would be much more difficult to achieve in other industry segments that have different needs. At the same time, Crown has dedicated its facilities to producing only the types of cans demanded by buyers in its chosen segments and has aggressively invested in modern two-piece steel-canning technology. As a result, Crown has probably also achieved low-cost producer status in its segments.

Sustainability

A generic strategy does not lead to above-average performance unless it is sustainable *vis-à-vis* competitors, though actions that improve industry structure may improve industrywide profitability even if they are imitated. The sustainability of the three generic strategies demands that a firm's competitive advantage resist erosion by competitor behavior or industry evolution. Each generic strategy involves different risks, which are shown in Table 5.1.1.

The sustainability of a generic strategy requires that a firm possess some barriers that make imitation of the strategy difficult. Since barriers to imitation are never insurmountable, however, it is usually necessary for a firm to offer a moving target to its competitors by investing in order to continually improve its position. Each generic strategy is also a potential threat to the others – as Table 5.1.1 shows, for example, focusers must worry about broadly targeted competitors and vice versa.

Table 5.1.1 can be used to analyze how to attack a competitor that employs any of the generic strategies. A firm pursuing overall differentiation, for example, can be attacked by firms that open up a large cost gap, narrow the extent of differentiation, shift the differentiation desired by buyers to other dimensions, or focus. Each generic strategy is vulnerable to different types of attacks.

In some industries, industry structure or the strategies of competitors eliminate the possibility of achieving one or more of the generic strategies. Occasionally no feasible way for one firm to gain a significant cost advantage exists, for example, because several firms are equally placed with

TABLE 5.1.1
Risks of the Generic Strategies

Risks of Cost Leadership	Risks of Differentiation	Risks of Focus
Cost leadership is not sustained • competitors imitate • technology changes • other bases for cost leadership erode	Differentiation is not sustained • competitors imitate • bases for differentiation become less important to buyers	The focus strategy is imitated The target sement becomes structually unattractive • structure erodes • demand disappears
Proximity in differentiation is lost	Cost proximity is lost	Broadly targeted competitors overwhelm the segment • the segment's differences from other segments narrow • the advantages of a broad line increase
Cost focusers achieve even lower cost in segments	Differentiation focusers achieve even greater differentiation in segments	New focusers subsegment the industry

respect to scale economies, access to raw materials, or other cost drivers. Similarly, an industry with few segments or only minor differences among segments, such as low-density polyethylene, may offer few opportunities for focus. Thus the mix of generic strategies will vary from industry to industry.

In many industries, however, the three generic strategies can profitably coexist as long as firms pursue different ones or select different bases for differentiation or focus. Industries in which several strong firms are pursuing differentiation strategies based on different sources of buyer value are often particularly profitable. This tends to improve industry structure and lead to stable industry competition. If two or more firms choose to pursue the same generic strategy on the same basis, however, the result can be a protracted and unprofitable battle. The worst situation is where several firms are vying for overall cost leadership. The past and present choice of generic strategies by competitors, then, has an impact on the choices available to a firm and the cost of changing its position.

The concept of generic strategies is based on the premise that there are a number of ways in which competitive advantage can be achieved, depending on industry structure. If all firms in an industry followed the principles of competitive strategy, each would pick different bases for competitive advantage. While not all would succeed, the generic strategies provide alternate routes to superior performance. Some strategic planning concepts have been narrowly based on only one route to competitive advantage, most notably cost. Such concepts not only fail to explain the success of many firms, but they can also lead all firms in an industry to pursue the same type of competitive advantage in the same way – with predictably disastrous results.

5.2 Competing on Capabilities

By George Stalk, Philip Evans, and Lawrence Shulman[1]

In the 1980s, companies discovered time as a new source of competitive advantage. In the 1990s, they will learn that time is just one piece of a more far-reaching transformation in the logic of competition.

Companies that compete effectively on time–speeding new products to market, manufacturing just in time, or responding promptly to customer complaints–tend to be good at other things as well: for instance, the consistency of their product quality, the acuity of their insight into evolving customer needs, the ability to exploit emerging markets, enter new businesses, or generate new ideas and incorporate them in innovations. But all these qualities are mere reflections of a more fundamental characteristic: a new conception of corporate strategy that we call capabilities-based competition.

Four Principles of Capabilities-Based Competition

In industry after industry, established competitors are being outmaneuvered and overtaken by more dynamic rivals. In the years after World War II, Honda was a modest manufacturer of a 50cc engine designed to be attached to a bicycle. Today it is challenging General Motors and Ford for dominance of the global automobile industry. Xerox invented xerography and the office copier market. But between 1976 and 1982, Canon introduced more than 90 new models, cutting Xerox's share of the midrange copier market in half. Today Canon is a key competitor not only in midrange copiers but also in high-end color copiers.

The greatest challenge to department store giants like Macy's comes neither from other large department stores nor from small boutiques but from The Limited, a $5.25 billion design, procurement, delivery, and retail-

---

ing machine that exploits dozens of consumer segments with the agility of many small boutiques. Citicorp may still be the largest US bank in terms of assets, but Banc One has consistently enjoyed the highest return on assets in the US banking industry and now enjoys a market capitalization greater than Citicorp's.

These examples represent more than just the triumph of individual companies. They signal a fundamental shift in the logic of competition, a shift that is revolutionizing corporate strategy.

When the economy was relatively static, strategy could afford to be static. In a world characterized by durable products, stable customer needs, well-defined national and regional markets, and clearly identified competitors, competition was a 'war of position' in which companies occupied competitive space like squares on a chessboard, building and defending market share in clearly defined product or market segments. The key to competitive advantage was *where* a company chose to compete. *How* it chose to compete was also important but secondary, a matter of execution.

Few managers need reminding of the changes that have made this traditional approach obsolete. As markets fragment and proliferate, 'owning' any particular market segment becomes simultaneously more difficult and less valuable. As product life cycles accelerate, dominating existing product segments becomes less important than being able to create new products and exploit them quickly. Meanwhile, as globalization breaks down barriers between national and regional markets, competitors are multiplying and reducing the value of national market share.

In this more dynamic business environment, strategy has to become correspondingly more dynamic. Competition is now a 'war of movement' in which success depends on anticipation of market trends and quick response to changing customer needs. Successful competitors move quickly in and out of products, markets, and sometimes even entire businesses – a process more akin to an interactive video game than to chess. In such an environment, the essence of strategy is not the structure of a company's products and markets but the dynamics of its behavior. And the goal is to identify and develop the hard-to-imitate organizational capabilities that distinguish a company from its competitors in the eyes of customers.

Companies like Wal-Mart, Honda, Canon, The Limited, or Banc One have learned this lesson. Their experience and that of other successful companies suggest four basic principles of capabilities-based competition:

- The building blocks of corporate strategy are not products and markets but business processes.

- Competitive success depends on transforming a company's key processes into strategic capabilities that consistently provide superior value to the customer.

- Companies create these capabilities by making strategic investments in a support infrastructure that links together and transcends traditional strategic business units (SBUs) and functions.

■   Because capabilities necessarily cross functions, the champion of a capabilities-based strategy is the chief executive officer (CEO).

A capability is a set of business processes strategically understood. Every company has business processes that deliver value to the customer. But few think of them as the primary object of strategy. Capabilities-based competitors identify their key business processes, manage them centrally, and invest in them heavily, looking for a long-term payback.

What transforms a set of individual business processes into a strategic capability? The key is to connect them to real customer needs. A capability is strategic only when it begins and ends with the customer. Of course, just about every company these days claims to be 'close to the customer.' But there is a qualitative difference in the customer focus of capabilities-driven competitors. These companies conceive of the organization as a giant feedback loop that begins with identifying the needs of the customer and ends with satisfying them.

As managers have grasped the importance of time-based competition, for example, they have increasingly focused on the speed of new product *development*. But as a unit of analysis, new product development is too narrow. It is only part of what is necessary to satisfy a customer and, therefore, to build an organizational capability. Better to think in terms of new product *realization*, a capabilty that includes the way a product is not only developed but also marketed and serviced. The longer and more complex the string of business processes, the harder it is to transform them into a capability – but the greater the value of that capability once built because competitors have more difficulty imitating it.

Weaving business processes together into organizational capabilities in this way also mandates a new logic of vertical integration. At a time when cost pressures are pushing many companies to outsource more and more activities, capabilities-based competitors are integrating vertically to ensure that they, not a supplier or distributor, control the performance of key business processes. Even when a company doesn't actually own every link of the capability chain, the capabilities-based competitor works to tie these parts into its own business systems.

Another attribute of capabilities is that they are collective and cross-functional – a small part of many people's jobs, not a large part of a few. This helps explain why most companies underexploit capabilities-based competition. Because a capability is 'everywhere and nowhere,' no one executive controls it entirely. Moreover, leveraging capabilities requires a panoply of strategic investments across SBUs and functions far beyond what traditional cost-benefit metrics can justify. Traditional internal accounting and control systems often miss the strategic nature of such investments. For these reasons, building strategic capabilities cannot be treated as an operating matter and left to operating managers, to corporate staff, or still less to SBU heads. It is the primary agenda of the CEO. The prize will be companies that combine scale and flexibility to outperform the competition along five dimensions:

1   *Speed.* The ability to respond quickly to customer or market demands and to incorporate new ideas and technologies quickly into products.

2   *Consistency.* The ability to produce a product that unfailingly satisfies customers' expectations.

3   *Acuity.* The ability to see the competitive environment clearly and thus to anticipate and respond to customers' evolving needs and wants.

4   *Agility.* The ability to adapt simultaneously to many different business environments.

5   *Innovativeness.* The ability to generate new ideas and to combine existing elements to create new sources of value.

Becoming a Capabilities-Based Competitor

Few companies are fortunate enough to begin as capabilities-based competitors. For most, the challenge is to become one.

The starting point is for senior managers to undergo the fundamental shift in perception that allows them to see their business in terms of strategic capabilities. Then they can begin to identify and link together essential business processes to serve customer needs. Finally, they can reshape the organization – including managerial roles and responsibilities – to encourage the new kind of behavior necessary to make capabilities-based competition work.

The experience of a medical-equipment company we'll call Medequip illustrates this change process. An established competitor, Medequip recently found itself struggling to regain market share it had lost to a new competitor. The rival had introduced a lower-priced, lower-performance version of the company's most popular product. Medequip had developed a similar product in response, but senior managers were hesitant to launch it. Their reasoning made perfect sense according to the traditional competitive logic. As managers saw it, the company faced a classic no-win situation. The new product was lower priced but also lower profit. If the company promoted it aggressively to regain market share, overall profitability would suffer.

But when Medequip managers began to investigate their competitive situation more carefully, they stopped defining the problem in terms of static products and markets. Increasingly, they saw it in terms of the organization's business processes. Traditionally, the company's functions had operated autonomously. Manufacturing was separate from sales, which was separate from field service. What's more, the company managed field service the way most companies do – as a classic profit center whose resources were deployed to reduce costs and maximize profitability. For instance, Medequip assigned full-time service personnel only to those customers who bought enough equipment to justify the additional cost.

However, a closer look at the company's experience with these steady customers led to a fresh insight: at accounts where Medequip had placed one or more full-time service representatives on-site, the company renewed its highly profitable service contracts at three times the rate of its other accounts. When these accounts needed new equipment, they chose Medequip twice as often as other accounts did and tended to buy the broadest mix of Medequip products as well. The reason was simple. Medequip's on-site service representatives had become expert in the operations of their customers. They knew what equipment mix best suited the customer and what additional equipment the customer needed. So they had teamed up informally with Medequip's salespeople to become part of the selling process. Because the service reps were on-site full-time, they were also able to respond quickly to equipment problems. And of course, whenever a competitor's equipment broke down, the Medequip reps were on hand to point out the product's shortcomings.

This new knowledge about the dynamics of service delivery inspired top managers to rethink how their company should compete. Specifically, they redefined field service from a stand-alone function to one part of an integrated sales and service capability. They crystallized this new approach in three key business decisions.

First, Medequip decided to use its service personnel not to keep costs low but to maximize the life-cycle profitability of a set of targeted accounts. This decision took the form of a dramatic commitment to place at least one service rep on-site with selected customers – no matter how little business each account currently represented.

The decision to guarantee on-site service was expensive, so choosing which customers to target was crucial; there had to be potential for considerable additional business. The company divided its accounts into three categories: those it dominated, those where a single competitor dominated, and those where several competitors were present. Medequip protected the accounts it dominated by maintaining the already high level of service and by offering attractive terms for renewing service contracts. The company ignored those customers dominated by a single competitor – unless the competitor was having serious problems. All the remaining resources were focused on those accounts where no single competitor had the upper hand.

Next Medequip combined its sales, service, and order entry organizations into cross-functional teams that concentrated almost exclusively on the needs of the targeted accounts. The company trained service reps in sales techniques so they could take full responsibility for generating new sales leads. This freed up the sales staff to focus on the more strategic role of understanding the long-term needs of the customer's business. Finally, to emphasize Medequip's new commitment to total service, the company even taught its service reps how to fix competitor's equipment.

Once this new organizational structure was in place, Medequip finally introduced its new low-price product. The result: the company has not only stopped its decline in market share but also *increased* share by almost 50 percent. The addition of the lower-priced product has reduced profit margins, but the overall mix still includes many higher-priced products. And absolute profits are much higher than before.

This story suggests four steps by which any company can transform itself into a capabilities-based competitor.

Shift the Strategic Framework to Achieve Aggresive Goals

At Medequip, managers transformed what looked like a no-win situation – either lose share or lose profits – into an opportunity for a major competitive victory. They did so by abandoning the company's traditional function, cost, and profit-center orientation and by identifying and managing the capabilities that link customer need to customer satisfaction. The chief expression of this new capabilities-based strategy was the decision to provide on-site service reps to targeted accounts and to create cross-functional sales and service teams.

Organize around the Chosen Capability and Make Sure Employees Have the Necessary Skills and Resources to Achieve It

Having set this ambitious competitive goal, Medequip managers next set about reshaping the company in terms of it. Rather than retaining the existing functional structure and trying to encourage coordination through some kind of matrix, they created a brand new organization – Customer Sales and Service – and divided it into 'cells' with overall responsibility for specific customers. The company also provided the necessary training so that employees could understand how their new roles would help achieve new business goals. Finally, Medequip created systems to support employees in their new roles. For example, one information system uses CD-ROMs to give field-service personnel quick access to information about Medequip's product line as well as those of competitors.

Make Progress Visible and Bring Measurements and Reward into Alignment

Medequip also made sure that the company's measurement and reward systems reflected the new competitive strategy. Like most companies, the company had never known the profitability of individual customers. Traditionally, field-service employees were measured on overall service profitability. With the shift to the new approach, however, the company had to develop a whole new set of measures – for example, Medequip's 'share-by-customer-by-product,' the amount of money the company invested in servicing a particular customer, and the customer's current and estimated lifetime profitability. Team members' compensation was calculated according to these new measures.

Do Not Delegate the Leadership of the Transformation

Becoming a capabilities-based competitor requires an enormous amount of change. For that reason, it is a process extremely difficult to delegate.

Because capabilities are cross-functional, the change process can't be left to middle managers. It requires the hands-on guidance of the CEO and the active involvement of top line managers. At Medequip, the heads of sales, service, and order entry led the subteams that made the actual recommendations, but it was the CEO who oversaw the change process, evaluated their proposals, and made the final decision. His leading role ensured senior management's commitment to the recommended changes.

This top-down change process has the paradoxical result of driving business decision making down to those directly participating in key processes – for example, Medequip's sales and service staff. This leads to a high measure of operational flexibility and an almost reflexlike responsiveness to external change.

EXHIBIT 5.2.1

HOW CAPABILITIES DIFFER FROM THE CORE COMPETENCIES: THE CASE OF HONDA

In their influential 1990 HBR article, 'The Core Competencies of the Corporation,' (see chapter 6) Gary Hamel and C.K. Prahalad mount an attack on traditional notions of strategy that is not so dissimilar from what we are arguing here. For Hamel and Prahalad, however, the central building block of corporate strategy is 'core competence.' How is a competence different from a capability, and how do the two concepts relate to each other?

Hamel and Prahalad define core competence as the combination of individual technologies and production skills that underly a company's myriad product lines. Sony's core competence in miniaturization, for example, allows the company to make everything from the Sony Walkman to videocameras to notebook computers. Canon's core competencies in optics, imaging, and microprocessor controls have enabled it to enter markets as seemingly diverse as copiers, laser printers, cameras, and image scanners.

As the above examples suggest, Hamel and Prahalad use core competence to explain the ease with which successful competitors are able to enter new and seemingly unrelated businesses. But a closer look reveals that competencies are not the whole story.

Consider Honda's move from motorcycles into other businesses, including lawn mowers, outboard motors, and automobiles. Hamel and Prahalad attribute Honda's success to its underlying competence in engines and power trains. While Honda's engine competence is certainly important, it alone cannot explain the speed with which the company has successfully moved into a wide range of businesses over the past 20 years. After all, General Motors (to take just one example) is also an accomplished designer and manufacturer of engines. What distinguishes Honda from its competitors is its focus on capabilities.

One important but largely invisible capability is Honda's expertise in 'dealer management'–its ability to train and support its dealer network with operating procedures and policies for merchandising, selling floor planning, and service management. First developed for its motorcycle business, this set of business processes has since been replicated in each new business the company has entered.

Another capability central to Honda's success has been its skill at 'product realization.' Traditional product development separates planning, proving, and executing into three sequential activities: assessing the market's needs and whether existing products are meeting those needs; testing the proposed product; then building a prototype. The end result of this process is a new factory or organization to introduce the new product. This traditional approach takes a long time – and with time goes money.

Honda has arranged these activities differently. First, planning and proving go on continuously and in parallel. Second, these activities are clearly separated from execution. At Honda, the highly disciplined execution cycle schedules major product revisions every four years and minor revisions every two years. The 1990 Honda Accord, for example, which is the first major redesign of that model since 1986, incorporates a power train developed two years earlier and first used in the 1988 Accord. Finally, when a new product is ready, it is released to existing factories and organizations, which dramatically shortens the amount of time needed to launch it. As time is reduced, so are cost and risk.

Consider the following comparison between Honda and GM. In 1984, Honda launched its Acura division; one year later, GM created Saturn. Honda chose to integrate Acura into its existing organization and facilities. In Europe, for example, the Acura Legend is sold through the same sales force as the Honda Legend. The Acura division now makes three models – the Legend, Integra, and Vigor – and is turning out 300,000 cars a year. At the end of 1991, seven years after it was launched, the division had produced a total of 800,000 vehicles. More important, it had already introduced eight variations of its product line.

By contrast, GM created a separate organization and a separate facility for Saturn. Production began in late 1990, and 1991 will be its first full model year. If GM is lucky, it will be producing 240,000 vehicles in the next year or two and will have two models out.

As the Honda example suggests, competencies and capabilities represent two different but complementary dimensions of an emerging paradigm for corporate strategy. Both concepts emphasize 'behavioral' aspects of strategy in contrast to the traditonal structural model. But whereas core competence emphasizes technological and production expertise at specific points along the value chain, capabilities are more broadly based, encompassing the entire value chain. In this respect, capabilities are visible to the customer in a way that core competencies rarely are.

Like the 'grand unified theory' that modern-day physicists are searching for to explain physical behavior at both the subatomic level and that of the entire cosmos, the combination of core competence and capabilities may define the universal model for corporate strategy in the 1990s and beyond.

A New Logic of Growth: The Capabilities Predator

Once managers reshape the company in terms of its underlying capabilities, they can use these capabilities to define a growth path for the corporation. At the center of capabilities-based competition is a new logic of growth.

In the 1960s, most managers assumed that when growth in a company's basic business slowed, the company should turn to diversification. This was the age of the multibusiness conglomerate. In the 1970s and 1980s, however, it became clear that growth through diversification was difficult. And so, the pendulum of management thinking swung once again. Companies were urged to 'stick to their knitting' – that is, to focus on their core business, identify where the profit was, and get rid of everything else. The idea of the corporation became increasingly narrow.

Competing on capabilities provides a way for companies to gain the benefits of both focus and diversification. Put another way, a company that focuses on its strategic capabilities can compete in a remarkable diversity of regions, products, and businesses and do it far more coherently than the typical conglomerate can. Such a company is a 'capabilities predator' – able to come out of nowhere and move rapidly from nonparticipant to major player and even to industry leader.

Capabilities-based companies grow by transferring their essential business processes–first to new geographic areas and then to new businesses. Wal-Mart CEO David Glass alludes to this method of growth when he characterizes Wal-Mart as 'always pushing from the inside out; we never jump and backfill.'

Strategic advantages built on capabilities are easier to transfer geographically than more traditional competitive advantages. Honda, for example, has become a manufacturer in Europe and the United States with relatively few problems. The quality of its cars made in the United States is so good that the company is exporting some of them back to Japan.

But the big payoff for capabilities-led growth comes not through geographical expansion but through rapid entry into whole new businesses. Capabilities-based companies do this in at least two ways. The first is by 'cloning' their key business processes. Again, Honda is a typical example.

Most people attribute Honda's success to the innovative design of its products or the way the company manufactures them. These factors are certainly important. But the company's growth has been spearheaded by less visible capabilities. For example, a big part of Honda's original success in motorcycles was due to the company's distinctive capability in 'dealer management,' which departed from the traditional relationship between motorcycle manufacturers and dealers. Typically, local dealers were motorcycle enthusiasts who were more concerned with finding a way to support their hobby than with building a strong business. They were not particularly interested in marketing, parts-inventory management, or other business systems.

Honda, by contrast, managed its dealers to ensure that they would become successful businesspeople. The company provided operating procedures and policies for merchandising, selling, floor planning, and service management. It trained all its dealers and their entire staffs in these new management systems and supported them with a computerized dealer-management information system. The part-time dealers of competitors were no match for the better prepared and better financed Honda dealers.

Honda's move into new businesses, including lawn mowers, outboard motors, and automobiles, has depended on recreating this same dealer-management capability in each new sector. Even in segments like luxury cars, where local dealers are generally more service oriented than those in the motorcycle business, Honda's skill at managing its dealers is transforming service standards. Honda dealers consistently receive the highest ratings for customer satisfaction among auto companies selling in the United States. One reason is that Honda gives its dealers far more autonomy to decide on the spot whether a needed repair is covered by the warranty (see Exhibit 5.1.1).

But the ultimate form of growth in the capabilities-based company may not be cloning business processes so much as creating processes so flexible and robust that the same set can serve many different businesses.

The Future of Capabilities-Based Competition

For the moment, capabilities-based companies have the advantage of competing against rivals still locked into the old way of seeing the competitive environment. But such a situation won't last forever. As more and more companies make the transition to capabilities-based competition, the simple fact of competing on capabilities will become less important than the specific capabilities a company has chosen to build. Given the necessary long-term investments, the strategic choices managers make will end up determining a company's fate.

5.3   PIMS: Market Position and Profitability

By Robert Buzzell and Bradley Gale[1]

Large market share is both a reward for providing better value to the customer and a means of realizing lower costs. Under most circumstances, enterprises that have achieved a large share of the markets they serve are

---

[1] Source: This article was adapted with permission from chapter five of *The PIMS Principles: Linking Strategy to Performance*, Free Press, New York, 1987.

considerably more profitable than their smaller-share rivals. This connection between market share and profitability has been recognized by corporate executives and consultants, and it is clearly demonstrated in the results of our research over the last 15 years.

We use several measures of market position – absolute market share, market-share rank, and relative market share. Each measure captures a particular nuance of market position, but their similarities far outweigh their differences. Absolute market share compares a business unit's sales to the sales of its served market. The served market's boundaries must realistically reflect customers' feelings about which companies, products, and services actually compete head-to-head in the marketplace.

Since businesses compete in many different kinds of served markets, an absolute market share of 15 may represent the market leader in a fragmented market or the number four competitor in a concentrated market. In light of this, we use market-share rank to make comparisons across the many served markets in the data base. Even in situations where the size of the served market (and therefore absolute market shares) cannot be determined accurately, managers typically have a good feel for the market-share rank of each competitor. For purposes of comparing a portfolio of businesses that compete in many different served markets, market-share rank is the simplest measure to use. But, a market-share rank of number one may represent a dominant leader with 70 percent of the market, or a first-among-equals position. Share relative to three largest competitors has been shown by our research to be the most useful measure of relative share for calibrating competitive advantage.

There is no doubt that market share and return on investment are strongly related (see Figure 5.3.1). On average, market leaders earn rates of

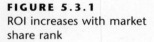
FIGURE 5.3.1
ROI increases with market share rank

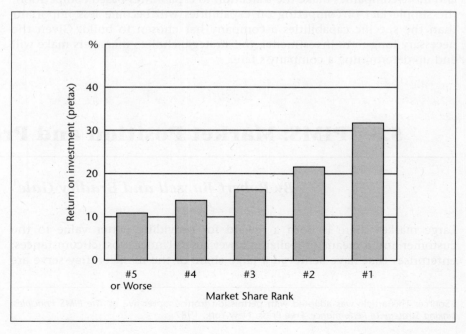

return that are three times greater than businesses with a market share rank of fifth or worse. We can put these typical performance levels in perspective by comparing them to a pretax profit 'hurdle rate' of 20 percent. We find that, on average, businesses ranked number one in market share beat this hurdle by 10 percentage points, but businesses ranked fifth or worse fall short by 10 percentage points.

The PIMS database is the world's most extensive and detailed source of information on the share/profitability relationship, but additional evidence helps to confirm its existence. For instance, companies enjoying strong competitive positions in their primary product markets tend to be highly profitable. Consider, for example, such major companies as IBM, Gillette, Kellogg, and Coca-Cola, as well as smaller, more specialized corporations like Dr. Scholl (foot care products), Dexter (specialty chemicals and materials), and Sonoco Products (industrial packaging). Research on the Federal Trade Commission's line-of-business database also supports the share/profitability relationship.

Why Is Market Share Profitable?

The data demonstrate that market leaders and small-market-share businesses have very different ROIs (Figure 5.3.1). This evidence that the relationship exists, does not, however, tell us why there is a link between market share and profitability. There are at least four possible reasons:

■ economies of scale;

■ risk aversion by customers;

■ market power;

■ a common underlying factor.

The most obvious rationale for the high rate of return enjoyed by large-share businesses is that they have achieved economies of scale in procurement, manufacturing, marketing, R&D, and other cost components. A business with a 40 percent share of its served market is simply twice as big as one with 20 percent of the same market, and it can attain, to a much greater degree, more efficient methods of operation within a particular type of technology. The effects of economies of scale represent the primary direct causal mechanism that links share to profitability. Related to scale economies is the so-called 'experience curve' phenomenon widely publicized by the Boston Consulting Group (BCG). Interpretation of the experience curve will be discussed in a later section of this article.

If a business has achieved (or is expected to achieve) the leading market-share position, risk-averse buyers may favor its products because they don't want to take the chances sometimes associated with buying from a smaller-share competitor. The customer preference comes as a direct consequence of share: a person placing an order with a dominant supplier feels he/she won't be challenged to defend that decision. IBM enjoys this kind of advantage in many of its business units. Many household consumers have the same kind of confidence in Kodak film, Gillette razor blades, and Bayer aspirin.

Many economists, especially in the antitrust field, believe that economies of scale have relatively little importance in most industries. These economists argue that if large-scale businesses earn higher profits than their smaller competitors, it is a result of their greater market power: their size permits them to bargain more effectively, 'administer' prices, and, in the end, realize significantly higher prices for a particular product.

The simplest of all explanations for the share/profitability relationship suggests that both share and ROI reflect a common underlying factor, for example, the quality of management. Good managers (including, perhaps, lucky ones!) succeed in achieving large shares of their respective markets; they are also skillful in controlling costs, getting maximum productivity from employees, and so on. Moreover, once a business achieves a leadership position – possibly by developing a new field – it is much easier for it to retain its lead than for others to catch up.

These varied explanations of why the share/profitability relationship exists are not mutually exclusive. To some degree, a large-share business may benefit from all four kinds of relative advantages. It is important, however, to understand how much of the increased profitability that accompanies large market share comes from each of these or other sources.

Dissecting the Relationship

Analyzing the PIMS database sheds light on the driving forces behind the strong relationship between market share and ROI. The database allows us to observe real-life relationships between share and financial and operating ratios (Table 5.3.1) and between share and measures of relative prices and relative quality (Table 5.3.2). As you examine these figures, remember that the PIMS sample of businesses includes a wide variety of products and industries. Consequently, when we compare businesses with market-share rank of five or worse, say, with those having the number one share position, we are not observing difference in costs and profits within a single industry. Each subgroup contains a diversity of industries, types of products, kinds of customers, and so on.

The data reveal important differences between large-share businesses and those with smaller shares. ROI depends, of course, on both the rate of net profit on sales and the amount of investment required to support a given volume of sales. Differences in ROI can result from differences in return on sales, investment to sales, or both.

The data show that the major reason for the share/profitability relationship is the dramatic difference in pretax profit margins on sales (Table 5.3.1). Market leaders average a return on sales of 12.7 percent, while businesses with market-share ranks of five or worse earn only 4.5 percent. In

Financial and Operating Ratios	Market Share Rank (%)				
	#5 or worse	#4	#3	#2	#1
Capital Structure:					
Investment/Sales	54.9	51.4	52.5	52.1	46.3
Receivables/Sales	15.3	14.8	14.7	14.7	14.7
Inventory/Sales	22.3	20.6	20.5	19.6	18.5
Operating Ratios:					
Pretax Profit/Sales	4.5	5.5	7.1	9.1	12.7
Purchases/Sales	51.3	48.9	45.8	43.4	41.8
Manufacturing/Sales	24.5	26.5	26.8	26.8	26.0
Marketing/Sales	9.2	9.3	9.5	9.5	8.9
R&D/Sales	1.9	1.8	1.9	2.3	2.1
Capacity Utilization	73.1	73.7	75.8	75.7	77.1

TABLE 5.3.1
How market leaders differ from small-share businesses

	Market Share Bank				
	#5 or worse	#4	#3	#2	#1
Relative Quality (Percentile)	43	45	47	51	69
Relative Price (%)	103.0	103.2	103.4	103.8	105.7
Number of Businesses	301	240	347	549	877

TABLE 5.3.2
Market leaders have higher perceived quality and command higher prices

the PIMS sample, the average return on sales exhibits a strong, smooth, upward trend as market share increases. By contrast, the ratio of investment to sales declines only slightly with increased market share.

Quality is extremely important to market leaders. Looking back at Tables 5.3.1 and 5.3.2, the data do not always show smooth, continuous relationships between market share and the various components of quality, price, cost, and investment. Indeed, it appears that one pattern operates as share rank moves from five or worse to number two, but a somewhat different pattern applies to market leaders. In particular, there are substantial differences in relative quality (and also in relative prices) between market leaders and followers (Table 5.3.2). Market leaders not only command higher prices but also maintain their leadership position by offering products and services that are superior relative to those offered by their competitors.

Here is how Tom Peters summarized this subject in his best-selling book, *A Passion For Excellence*:

> The PIMS paradigm is diametrically opposite to the experience curve from a cause-and-effect standpoint: It says, First achieve a 'relative perceived product-quality' edge over your competitors. If you do so, you will gain

share. By gaining share (via relatively higher perceived product quality) you can, indeed, then take advantage of economies of scale as appropriate, and achieve low-cost distinction.

The difference is radical. By the PIMS logic, you start from quality and achieve low cost as a result. According to the traditional experience curve approach, you buy your way in with low prices, achieve low cost, and may or may not have acceptable service and quality. If you don't have them, then you're constantly vulnerable to any higher-quality attacker who comes your way; the edge you scrambled so hard for is not likely to be sustainable. We call the distinction 'earning your way in' (via quality and service) versus 'buying your way in' (via heavy discounting). Only the former, it would appear, is sustainable.

In the experiences of PIMS businesses, attaining a superior quality position does not seem to involve many of the strategic trade-offs, such as higher relative direct costs or marketing expenditures, that business analysts often attribute to quality strategies. Superior quality does, however, support higher prices.

Can Small-Share Businesses Prosper?

The fact that market share and profitability generally go hand in hand (as shown in Figure 5.3.1) led some consultants and corporate executives to adopt the extreme position that small-share businesses cannot be profitable. Reacting to this, several investigators have demonstrated that some small-share competitors can and do earn very attractive returns. Two articles in the *Harvard Business Review* have reported these studies:

- Richard Hamermesh, M.J. Anderson, and J.E. Harris (1978) analyzed the performance of companies whose results are published in the annual *Forbes* magazine financial surveys. They found 'numerous successful low-share businesses' and discussed three examples of this phenomenon in some detail. One of these, Burroughs, was praised for focusing on selected segments of the computer market. As a result, the company's profits grew during the early 1970s at a rate faster than IBM's despite a huge disadvantage in overall market share.

- Carolyn Woo and Arnold Cooper (1984) examined the performance of low-share businesses in the PIMS database. They identified 40 low-share businesses that enjoyed pretax ROIs of 20 percent or more and compared their strategies with those of 'ineffective' low-share businesses Among other things, the successful low-share businesses were found to be characterized by high relative quality, narrow product lines, and low total costs.

As these two studies show, small-share businesses can indeed be profitable. This is hardly surprising in light of the fact, noted earlier, that share is just one of approximately two dozen key profit influences that have been documented in PIMS-based research – and that other profit determinants, such as 'corporate culture,' also play important roles. A small-share business that is favorably positioned on most other key strategic dimensions should earn satisfactory profits. PIMS research shows, for example, the average ROI of small-share businesses whose products or services ranked in the top third in terms of relative quality was 18 percent. If a business in this group also benefited from low investment intensity, high labor productivity, and rapid market growth, its expected rate of return could easily be 25 percent or better. But it should be emphasized that most small-share businesses don't fit this description. Of the 641 businesses in the PIMS database with shares of 10 percent or less, only about one in four achieved an ROI of 20 percent or more. In contrast, three-fourths of the businesses with shares of 40 percent or more had rates of return over 20 percent. It is useful to recognize and understand the exceptions to the general rule – but it is also important to remember that they are exceptions.

Is It Better To Be Small Than 'Stuck In The Middle?'

The examples of profitable small-share businesses cited by Hamermesh *et al.* and by Woo and Cooper don't contradict the general rule that share and profitability usually go together. A stronger dissent, however, has been expressed by Michael Porter in his best-selling book, *Competitive Strategy* (1980; reading 5.1 in this book). Porter suggests that while there may be a positive share-profitability relationship in 'some' industries, in others the relationship is inverse and in still others it is U-shaped, i.e. high on both ends and low in the middle. Citing the automobile and electric motor industries as examples of the U-shaped pattern, he warns of the dangers of being 'stuck in the middle.' The clear implication is that in such industries, it is better to have a small share than to be, say, the second or third-ranked competitor. In the industries where the relationship is inverse, it would even be better to be a small-share competitor than to be the market leader!

Can Porter's views be reconciled with the positive share-profitability relationship shown in Figure 5.3.1? We should note, first, that there is an important conceptual difference between Porter's concept of share and ours. He defines 'share' as a business unit's sales in relation to a broadly-defined industry such as computers or automobiles. (Hamermesh *et al.* followed the same approach, defining the Burroughs Corporation's market share as its fraction of total computer industry shipments.) In contrast, all of our market-share figures are measured in relation to each business unit's served market. The served market is defined as that part or segment of an industry (in terms of products, kinds of customers, and geographic areas) in which a business actually competes. For most businesses, the market defined in this way is considerably smaller than the overall industry in which it participates. For example, one of the successful small-share competitors cited by Porter is Mercedes-Benz.

This highly profitable firm has a very small share of total world-wide automobile sales. But, applying our concept of its relevant served market, Mercedes-Benz has a large share of the luxury car market. Put another way, we don't believe that Mercedes-Benz really competes with Honda, Toyota, or Volkswagen, and only to a very limited extent with General Motors. Its sales relative to these much larger producers is not, therefore, a meaningful measure of Mercedes-Benz's competitive position.

By defining market share in relation to a business unit's actual served market, we do not mean to encourage executives to limit their attention only to current customers, products, and geographic markets. Competitors operating in neighboring markets often can enter a market and overcome even the strongest incumbent, especially when capabilities developed in one sector are easily transferred to another. For example, Briggs & Stratton Corporation has long dominated the US market for small engines of the types used in lawn mowers and garden tractors. Beginning in 1984, Honda began an aggressive campaign to promote its line of lawn and garden equipment in the US, utilizing its experience in manufacturing engines for motorcycles. If Briggs & Stratton had been oblivious to the possibility of Honda's entry into its served market (which they were not), they could have been highly vulnerable. Thus, having a large share of a particular served market is not a guarantee of invulnerability to competition. But, we believe, a business unit's share of its served market is nevertheless a better measure of its current competitive position than its share of a broad and heterogeneous industry.

There is a more fundamental flaw in Porter's notion of a U-shaped relationship between share and profitability. By suggesting that small-share businesses typically earn high rates of return, he implies that this performance is caused by having a small share. In fact, the examples he cites illustrate how successful product differentiation can offset the disadvantages of a low share. As Figure 5.3.2 demonstrates, high quality can indeed yield high profits, even for small-share competitors – but it yields even bigger returns for those with strong market positions, and the latter is a much more common combination. A PlMS-based study by Lynn Phillips, Dae Chang, and Robert Buzzell showed that in the majority of cases superior quality, large share, and low costs relative to competition go together. This contradicts the idea that so-called 'generic strategies' aimed at low cost are incompatible with those based on product differentiation.

Even if market share is defined and measured in relation to industries rather than served markets, the available evidence shows that share is generally positively related to profitability. If the relationship really varied from positive to negative to U-shaped, we would expect the average of a broad sample of industries to show a very weak connection, if any, between share and profit performance. But this is not the case: in the Federal Trade Commission's Line of Business research program, the profitability of business segments was related to a variety of factors including each segment's 'share of industry sales.' The results showed a strong, positive relationship between share and profits. This is hardly what we would expect

FIGURE 5.3.2
A business that is 'caught in the corner' is in an extremely poor strategic position

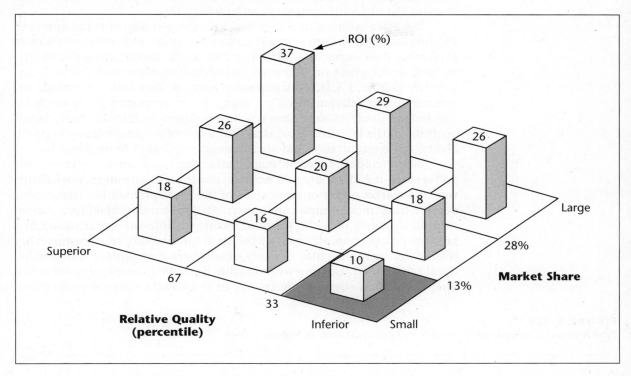

if there were an appreciable number of industries characterized by U-shaped or down-sloping share-profitability relationships.

An analogy may help to put the seeming anomaly of successful small-share businesses into perspective. In 1985 a nationally-televised 'slam dunk' competition featured some of the most talented players in the National Basketball Association. Almost all of the contestants were at least 6'8' tall. But the winner, incredibly, was 5'5' Spud Webb of the Atlanta Hawks! Webb's performance certainly showed that small people can win at a big person's game. But no one, presumably, would conclude from it that small players are usually or even often better at slamdunking than tall players. In the same way, we find the occasional success of small-share competitors unconvincing as the basis for any general argument for preferring a weak market position.

Other Views Of Cause And Effect

Some economists believe concentrated market structures facilitate 'oligopolistic coordination,' a rather friendly, nonaggressive kind of competition, resulting in lower output, higher prices, and thereby higher rates of return than are typical in 'competitive' markets. Therefore, they expect to see a direct relation between 'industry concentration' (the combined market share of the top four companies) and profitability.

The PIMS business unit data base provides a straightforward approach to comparing the relative power of market share and concentration in explaining differences in profitability. The result: market share shows a far more dramatic effect on ROI than concentration when they are looked at together (Figure 5.3.3). Concentration actually does little to explain the structure-profit relationship. Our findings are supported by research on the Federal Trade Commission's line-of-business (LOB) data base. When analyzed in the LOB data base, share has a strong positive relation to profitability, but concentration has a weak negative relation to profitability.

We conclude that even though market share and concentration usually go together, it is the share that matters, not the concentration. Put another way, the market power interpretation of the share/profitability relationship doesn't have much empirical support. Is the share/profitability relationship all a matter of luck? Many academic technicians are attracted to a random-process interpretation of the share/profitability relationship. They reason, for example, that if many small-share competitors start out on equal terms, the lucky one will probably gain both share and profitability. They focus their attention on change in share and change in profitability,

FIGURE 5.3.3
Which determines profitability – industry concentration or market share?

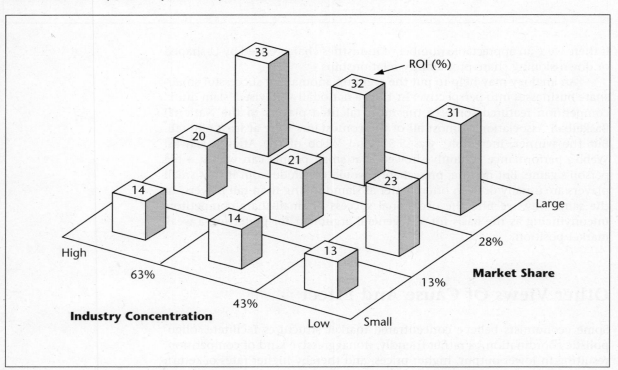

rather than on how share differences affect profit differences in more stable market environments. Often they forget that many served markets are created by a pioneer rather than by a horde of small-share competitors awaiting the start of a random process. The pioneer starts with 100 percent share and subsequently faces challenges from early followers and late entrants.

We don't dispute that the assumptions of random process are logically sufficient to explain a dynamic share/profitability relationship. Indeed, one can find examples of businesses that (by skill or luck) were in the right place at the right time and gained in both share and profitability. But the random process view is not very interesting from a strategy perspective. If random events cause the share/profitability relationship, the action implication is to 'be lucky.' That advice is easy to understand, but hard to implement. Still, it is useful to know to what extent the observed share/profitability relationship is due to economies of scale versus random events.

In 1977 Caves, Gale, and Porter demonstrated that the random process hypothesis is probably not the primary explanation for the observed relationship. Here we will present a simplified update of one of their tests.

If the share/profitability relationship is due mostly to luck, it would show up more strongly in unstable markets where shares are shifting dramatically. Changing shares suggest that investment decisions by competing suppliers carry a great deal of risk. And the very fact that market shares are changing indicates that investments that succeed are capable of increasing a business's market share as well as its profit rate.

If the share/profitability relationship is stronger in markets where shares are stable, however, it is difficult to credit this result to the random-process view that luck causes share and profit to move together.

The evidence? The share/profitability relation turns out to be stronger where shares are stable as Caves, Gale, and Porter found in their 1977 study. In stable markets, market leaders on average reap 25 percentage points more ROI than small-share businesses. In markets where shares are unstable, the ROI difference is significantly less – only 17 percentage points. These results contradict the random process interpretation of the share/profitability relationship. We conclude, therefore, that the random process hypothesis not only offer little help from a strategy perspective, but also doesn't explain much of the relationship between profitability and market share.

The whole question of 'spurious' versus 'causal' relationships between share and profit performance is, we believe, a red herring. Market share in itself doesn't 'cause' anything. How can it? A business unit's market share is nothing more than a measurement. It reflects two kinds of forces, however, that do cause high or low profits: (1) relative scale and/or experience-based cost advantages or disadvantages and (2) relative success or lack of it in designing, producing, and marketing products that meet the needs of the customers in a particular served market. We have shown that both factors are important – large-share businesses do typically have lower costs, and they also typically have product quality advantages that translate into bigger profit margins.

Our interpretation of how the share-profitability relationship typically works is summarized in these key steps:

- Superior relative quality is achieved by a combination of skillful product or service design and proper selection of market(s) to serve.

- Providing superior quality enables a successful business to charge premium prices (within reason, of course) and to gain market share.

- By gaining share, the business attains scale and/or experience-based cost advantages over its competitors. (As noted earlier, these kinds of cost advantages are not generally incompatible with successful differentiation.)

- Higher profitability follows as a result of premium prices, costs equal to or lower than those of competitors, and advantages in procurement and utilization of invested capital, as noted earlier.

If this is a valid picture of the typical linkage between share and profitability, then the key 'causal' factors operating are scale and quality. Market share is, in effect, a convenient kind of shorthand that reflects some combination of these underlying profit influences.

When Is Market Share Most Important?

Given that market leaders have a large relative market share and thus the profitability that goes with it, it is natural to question whether the share and profitability relationship shifts from industry to industry. What kinds of businesses will find market share most critical to their success? What industries need to think most carefully about share position?

Our analyses of the PIMS database clearly demonstrate a strong general relationship between ROI and market share. But while these general findings are interesting, more specific analyses are necessary if you wish to reposition your business so that it will outperform its competitors. The importance of share does vary considerably from one type of industry or market situation to another. We have already seen that share is more important in stable markets than it is in unstable markets. Two other interesting variations focus on the functional components of value added and the degree of investment intensity

R&D and Marketing versus Manufacturing

High-tech industries are characterized by heavy doses of R&D and marketing. Others carry out most of their value adding activities in the manufacturing function. Is market share more important in high-tech or smokestack industries?

People who follow the experience curve explanation of the share/ profitability relationship invariably answer that share is most important in manufacturing-intensive industries. By contrast, those who believe that economies of scale are the main reason behind the share/profitability relationship feel that share matters more in industries where fixed costs are large relative to variable costs.

We used the ratio of R&D and marketing costs relative to manufacturing costs, to split the PIMS data base into two groups. For R&D and marketing intensive businesses the ROI of the average market leader is 26 percentage points greater than the ROI of the average small-share business (Figure 5.3.4). For manufacturing-intensive businesses the corresponding ROI differential is only 12 points. So, we conclude that market share is more important in high-tech industries.

Why? Compared to manufacturing costs, R&D and marketing costs tend to be relatively fixed. In most markets you need a certain amount of expenditure on innovation and marketing to remain a viable competitor. R&D and marketing activities are thus more subject to scale effects than are manufacturing costs.

Initially one might, therefore, expect R&D and marketing costs to decline as we move from small-share businesses to large-share businesses. But, we find that R&D-to-sales and marketing-to-sales ratios are about the same for large-share and small-share businesses (Table 5.3.1). There are two reasons why we don't observe a decline. First, as noted earlier, large-share businesses are more vertically integrated (they 'make' rather than 'buy'). Second, and related, since R&D and marketing costs are more subject to scale effects, market leaders often pursue competitive strategies of developing product and service superiority and of introducing new products that are R&D and marketing intensive. This strategy makes it difficult for small-share competitors to keep pace. The vertical integration and innovation activities that tend to increase the R&D and marketing-to-sales ratios of

FIGURE 5.3.4
Market share is more important in high-tech or marketing-intensive industries

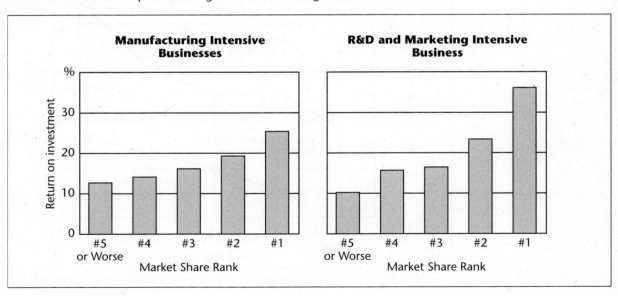

large-share businesses are offset by economies of scale in marketing and R&D. This yields the flat pattern of average cost ratios we have observed (Table 5.3.1).

Heavy versus Light Investment Intensity

Market leadership has a greater payoff in industries that are not very investment intensive. For businesses with low investment to sales the ROI of the average market leader soars 25 percentage points above the ROI of the average small-share business. For investment intensive businesses the corresponding ROI differential is only 11 points. Why? Market share helps return on sales (ROS) via economies of scale that reduce unit costs. Since ROI = ROS × (Sales/investment), the ROS differential between share leaders and followers is greatly leveraged in industries where investment-to-sales is very low.

In investment-intensive industries, on average, only the market leaders come close to earning a 20 percent pre-tax ROI . . . and even they fall a little short (see Figure 5.3.5). By contrast, in low-investment situations all but the smallest-share competitors average returns well above 20 percent, and even the smallest-share competitors come close.

In addition to these industry differences (high-tech versus low-tech, investment-intensity light versus heavy) we have noted previously that the positive effect of absolute market share on ROI diminishes as market share gets larger because the drops in unit costs don't come as fast when market share is already large.

FIGURE 5.3.5
Market leadership pays off most in industries that are not investment intensive

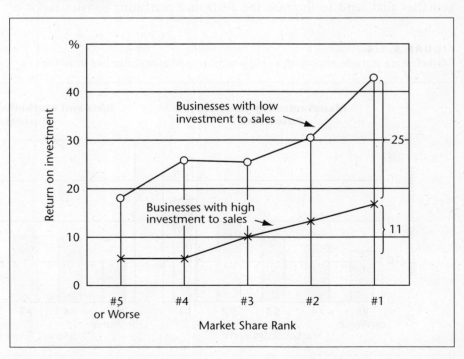

Market Share And Competitive Strategy

The importance of market share has, no doubt, been exaggerated by some commentators, especially those who linked the advantages of a large share to experience-based cost differentials. But the available evidence from PIMS and other sources clearly shows that share and profitability are strongly related. The relationship has been confirmed repeatedly, in analyses of the actual experiences of businesses in different kinds of industries, different time periods, and various parts of the world. Market share is not the only key to profitability, but it is certainly one of the most important. In light of this, how should market share be treated in the process of developing and evaluating competitive strategies?

First, the pursuit of market share is not in itself a strategy. It is often an important strategic objective; but it is much easier to state such a goal than it is to determine how it can be attained. In this article we have emphasized the importance of relative quality, both as a means of staking out a strong market position and, later, of maintaining or improving one. Other important weapons in competing for market share include product innovation and spending levels for sales forces and advertising and sales promotion. All of these play a role: the special appeal of quality is that, in many cases, it offers a means of building share without incurring any short-term penalty.

When a business doesn't have a significant quality advantage over its rivals, adopting a share-building strategy can be very costly. An example of this is Yamaha's disastrous effort in the early 1980s to overtake Honda as the leader in motorcycle production. Yamaha's president, Hisao Koike, adopted the slogan 'Take the Lead' and pursued an aggressive program of new model introductions. By April 1983 the company was heavily in debt to finance its inventories and more than 2,000 workers had been laid off. Koike was removed as president and the 'kamikaze attack' was called off.

Efforts to wrest market share away from a well-established leader are unlikely to pay off unless the leader is complacent or distracted by other problems. Considerable attention has therefore been given to the question of alternative strategies for market followers. Several of the critics of the share-profitability relationship have cited the successes of small competitors who focused their efforts on particular market segments or niches. There is no doubt that this kind of market focusing is an important strategic option for many enterprises, especially those that have no possibilities of becoming leaders in more broadly-defined industries. It is for this reason that we, in the PIMS research program, have so strongly emphasized the idea of carefully defining and selecting a business unit's served market. Making the proper choices of products or services to offer, types of customers to serve, and geographic areas in which to operate are among the most important decisions that managers make.

Defining the served market is not, however, something that managers can control completely. Who competes with whom is an issue that is also affected by what other companies do and, ultimately, by the underlying economics of an industry. Consider, for example, the three examples of successful small-share competitors cited by Hamermesh *et al.* in 1978: the Burroughs Corporation (computers), Crown Cork & Seal (metal containers), and Union Camp (paper). All three had outstanding records of growth and profitability in the early 1970s. A decade later, the picture had changed considerably. During the years 1981–85, Crown Cork & Seal's average return on equity (ROE) was 11.3 percent; it ranked 12th among 13 companies in the packaging industry. Union Camp, with an ROE of 14.8 percent, placed near the middle of the rankings in the paper industry. Burroughs' ROE had declined to 7.1 percent (23rd out of 24 computer manufacturers) and the company was attempting to acquire Sperry in an effort to create a viable competitor to IBM in the large-computer business.

These illustrations suggest that what constitutes a distinct sub-market within an industry at one time may not be so distinct at a later time. A particular product variation or customer group may, for example, simply have been neglected by larger competitors, leaving it available to a smaller rival despite the latter's inherently inferior cost position or technology. Serving such a niche may be highly profitable for some years, but eventually it is likely to become much less so. The moral would appear to be: either take steps to accentuate the differences between a sub-market and the overall market (for instance, through product development) or be prepared to move on to another one.

Many of the criticisms of the market-share profitability relationship stem from the perception that it was being used, a decade ago, as a basis for overly simplistic strategic formulas. This is unfortunate; the share-profitability relationship is a fact of life that should be recognized and understood. It does not, in itself, provide any general prescriptions for management, but it does yield insights into the likely consequences of strategic choices.

The strategic implications of the market-share/profitability relationship do vary according to the circumstances of the individual business. But there is no doubt that the relationship can be translated into dynamic strategies for all companies trying to set market share goals. The PIMS data base is often used to calibrate the cost of growing against the benefits of growing, with some precision, for specific business situations and then translate this knowledge into action plans.

One example of a company pursuing strategic objectives that are consistent with the concepts and findings of this chapter is General Electric under the leadership of John F. Welch. Jr. He has said that 'Our strategic aim is to evolve into a company that's either number one or number two in its arenas . . .' Major steps in this evolution include the disposition of Utah Mining and the acquisition of RCA and some financial service companies. GE is shifting its portfolio away from investment-intensive arenas toward high-tech and service arenas. Welch is attempting to become number one or number two in situations where being number one or number two matters most.

5.4   Firm Resources and Sustained Competitive Advantage

By Jay Barney[1]

Understanding sources of sustained competitive advantage for firms has become a major area of research in the field of strategic management. Since the 1960s, a single organizing framework has been used to structure much of this research. This framework, summarized in Figure 5.4.1, suggests that firms obtain sustained competitive advantages by implementing strategies that exploit their internal strengths, through responding to environmental opportunities, while neutralizing external threats and avoiding internal weaknesses. Most research on sources of sustained competitive advantage has focused either on isolating a firm's opportunities and threats (Porter, 1980, 1985), describing its strengths and weaknesses (Hofer and Schendel, 1978; Penrose, 1958), or analyzing how these are matched to choose strategies.

Research by Porter and his colleagues (Caves and Porter, 1977; Porter, 1980, 1985) has attempted to describe the environmental conditions that favor high levels of firm performance. Porter's 'five forces model,' for example, describes the attributes of an attractive industry and thus suggests that opportunities will be greater, and threats less, in these kinds of industries.

To help focus the analysis of the impact of a firm's environment on its competitive position, much of this type of strategic research has placed little emphasis on the impact of idiosyncratic firm attributes on a firm's competitive position. Implicitly, this work has adopted two simplifying assumptions. First, these environmental models of competitive advantage have assumed that firms within an industry (or firms within a strategic group) are identical in terms of the strategically relevant resources they control and the strategies they pursue. Second, these models assume that should resource heterogeneity develop in an industry or group (perhaps through new entry) that this heterogeneity will be very short lived because the resources that firms use to implement their strategies are highly mobile (i.e. they can be bought and sold in factor markets).

There is little doubt that these two assumptions have been very fruitful in clarifying our understanding of the impact of a firm's environment on performance. However, the resource-based view of competitive advantage, because it examines the link between a firm's internal characteristics and performance, obviously cannot build on these same assumptions. These assumptions effectively eliminate firm resource heterogeneity and immobility as possible sources of competitive advantage. The resource-based view of

---

[1] Source: This reading was adapted with permission from Firm Resources and Sustained Competitive Advantage, *Journal of Management*, March 1991, Vol. 17, No. 1, pp. 99–120.

FIGURE 5.4.1

The relationship between traditional 'strengths-weaknesses-opportunities-threats' analysis, the resource based model, and models of industry attractiveness

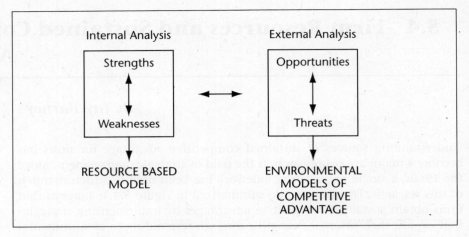

the firm substitutes two alternate assumptions in analyzing sources of competitive advantage. First, this model assumes that firms within an industry (or group) may be heterogeneous with respect to the strategic resources they control. Second, this model assumes that these resources may not be perfectly mobile across firms, and thus heterogeneity can be long lasting. The resource-based model of the firm examines the implications of these two assumptions for the analysis of sources of sustained competitive advantage.

Defining Key Concepts

To avoid possible confusion, three concepts that are central to the perspective developed in this reading are defined in this section. These concepts are firm resources, competitive advantage, and sustained competitive advantage.

Firm Resources

In this reading, firm resources include all assets, capabilities, organizational processes, firm attributes, information, knowledge, etc. controlled by a firm that enable the firm to conceive of and implement strategies that improve its efficiency and effectiveness. In the language of traditional strategic analysis, firm resources are strengths that firms can use to conceive of and implement their strategies.

A variety of authors have generated lists of firm attributes that may enable firms to conceive of and implement value-creating strategies. For purposes of this discussion, these numerous possible firm resources can be conveniently classified into three categories: physical capital resources, human capital resources, and organizational capital resources. Those attributes of a firm's physical, human, and organizational capital that do enable a firm to conceive of and implement strategies that improve its efficiency and effectiveness are, for purposes of this discussion, firm resources. The purpose of this reading is to specify the conditions under which such firm resources can be a source of sustained competitive advantage for a firm.

Competitive Advantage and Sustained Competitive Advantage

A firm is said to have a competitive advantage when it is implementing a value creating strategy not simultaneously being implemented by any current or potential competitors. It is said to have a sustained competitive advantage when it is implementing a value creating strategy not simultaneously being implemented by any current or potential competitors and when these other firms are unable to duplicate the benefits of this strategy.

That a competitive advantage is sustained does not imply that it will 'last forever.' It only suggests that it will not be competed away through the duplication efforts of other firms. Unanticipated changes in the economic structure of an industry may make what was, at one time, a source of sustained competitive advantage, no longer valuable for a firm, and thus not a source of any competitive advantage. These structural revolutions in an industry redefine which of a firm's attributes are resources and which are not. Some of these resources, in turn, may be sources of sustained competitive advantage in the newly defined industry structure. However, what were resources in a previous industry setting may be weaknesses, or simply irrelevant, in a new industry setting. A firm enjoying a sustained competitive advantage may experience these major shifts in the structure of competition, and may see its competitive advantages nullified by such changes. However, a sustained competitive advantage is not nullified through competing firms duplicating the benefits of that competitive advantage.

Competition with Homogeneous and Perfectly Mobile Resources

Armed with these definitions, it is now possible to explore the impact of resource heterogeneity and immobility on sustained competitive advantage. This is done by examining the nature of competition when firm resources are perfectly homogeneous and mobile.

Resource Homogeneity and Mobility and Sustained Competitive Advantage

Imagine an industry where firms possess exactly the same resources. This condition suggests that firms all have the same amount and kinds of strategically relevant physical, human, and organizational capital. Is there a strategy that could be conceived of and implemented by any one of these firms that could not also conceived of and implemented by all other firms in this industry? The answer to this question must be no. The conception and implementation of strategies employs various firm resources. That one firm in an industry populated by identical firms has the resources to conceive of and implement a strategy means that these other firms, because they possess the same resources, can also conceive of and implement this strategy. Because these firms all implement the same strategies, they all will improve their efficiency and effectiveness in the same way, and to the same extent. Thus, in this kind of industry, it is not possible for firms to enjoy a sustained competitive advantage.

Resource Homogeneity and Mobility and First-Mover Advantages

One objection to this conclusion concerns so-called 'first mover advantages' (Lieberman and Montgomery, 1988). In some circumstances, the first firm in an industry to implement a strategy can obtain a sustained competitive advantage over other firms. These firms may gain access to distribution channels, develop goodwill with customers, or develop a positive reputation, all before firms that implement their strategies later. Thus, first-moving firms may obtain a sustained competitive advantage.

However, upon reflection, it seems clear that if competing firms are identical in the resources they control, it is not possible for any one firm to obtain a competitive advantage from first moving. To be a first mover by implementing a strategy before any competing firms, a particular firm must have insights about the opportunities associated with implementing a strategy that are not possessed by other firms in the industry, or by potentially entering firms (Lieberman and Montgomery, 1988). This unique firm resource (information about an opportunity) makes it possible for the better informed firm to implement its strategy before others. However, by definition, there are no unique firm resources in this kind of industry. If one firm in this type of industry is able to conceive of and implement a strategy, then all other firms will also be able to conceive of and implement that strategy, and these strategies will be conceived of and implemented in parallel, as identical firms become aware of the same opportunities and exploit that opportunity in the same way.

It is not being suggested that there can never be first-mover advantages in industries. It is being suggested that in order for there to be a first-mover advantage, firms in an industry must be heterogeneous in terms of the resources they control.

Resource Homogeneity and Mobility and Entry/ Mobility Barriers

A second objection to the conclusion that sustained competitive advantages cannot exist when firm resources in an industry are perfectly homogeneous and mobile concerns the existence of 'barriers to entry' (Bain, 1956), or more generally, 'mobility barriers' (Caves and Porter, 1977). The argument here is that even if firms within an industry (group) are perfectly homogeneous, if there are strong entry or mobility barriers, these firms may be able to obtain a sustained competitive advantage *vis-à-vis* firms that are not in their industry (group). This sustained competitive advantage will be reflected in above normal economic performance for those firms protected by the entry or mobility barrier (Porter, 1980).

However, from another point of view, barriers to entry or mobility are only possible if current and potentially competing firms are heterogeneous in terms of the resources they control and if these resources are not perfectly mobile. The heterogeneity requirement is self-evident. For a barrier to entry or mobility to exist, firms protected by these barriers must be implementing different strategies than firms seeking to enter these protected areas of competition. Firms restricted from entry are unable to implement the same strategies as firms within the industry or group. Because the implementation of strategy requires the application of firm resources, the inability of firms seeking to enter an industry or group to implement the same strategies as firms within that industry or group suggests that firms seeking to enter must not have the same strategically relevant resources as firms within the industry or group. Thus, barriers to entry and mobility only exist when competing firms are heterogeneous in terms of the strategically relevant resources they control.

The requirement that firm resources be immobile in order for barriers to entry or mobility to exist is also clear. If firm resources are perfectly mobile, then any resource that allows some firms to implement a strategy protected by entry or mobility barriers can easily be acquired by firms seeking to enter into this industry or group. Once these resources are acquired, the strategy in question can be conceived of and implemented in the same way that other firms have conceived of and implemented their strategies. These strategies are thus not a source of sustained competitive advantage.

Again, it is not being suggested that entry or mobility barriers do not exist. However, it is being suggested that these barriers only become sources of sustained competitive advantage when firm resources are not homogeneously distributed across competing firms and when these resources are not perfectly mobile.

Firm Resources and Sustained Competitive Advantage

Thus far, it has been suggested that in order to understand sources of sustained competitive advantage, it is necessary to build a theoretical model that begins with the assumption that firm resources may be heterogeneous and immobile. Of course, not all firm resources hold the potential of sustained competitive advantages. To have this potential, a firm resource must have four attributes:

- it must be valuable, in the sense that it exploits opportunities and/or neutralizes threats in a firm's environment;

- it must be rare among a firm's current and potential competition;

- it must be imperfectly imitable;

- there cannot be strategically equivalent substitutes for this resource that are valuable but neither rare or imperfectly imitable.

These attributes of firm resources can be thought of as empirical indicators of how heterogeneous and immobile a firm's resources are and thus how useful these resources are for generating sustained competitive advantages. Each of these attributes of a firm's resources are discussed in more detail below.

Valuable Resources

Firm resources can only be a source of competitive advantage or sustained competitive advantage when they are valuable. As suggested earlier, resources are valuable when they enable a firm to conceive of or implement strategies that improve its efficiency and effectiveness. The traditional 'strengths–weaknesses–opportunities–threats' model of firm performance suggests that firms are able to improve their performance only when their strategies exploit opportunities or neutralize threats. Firm attributes may have the other characteristics that could qualify them as sources of competitive advantage (e.g. rareness, inimitability, non-substitutability), but these attributes only become resources when they exploit opportunities or neutralize threats in a firm's environment.

That firm attributes must be valuable in order to be considered resources (and thus as possible sources of sustained competitive advantage) points to an important complementarity between environmental models of competitive advantage and the resource-based model. These environmental models help isolate those firm attributes that exploit opportunities and/or neutralize threats, and thus specify which firm attributes can be considered as resources. The resource-based model then suggests what additional characteristics that these resources must possess if they are to generate sustained competitive advantage.

Rare Resources

By definition, valuable firm resources possessed by large numbers of competing or potentially competing firms cannot be sources of either a competitive advantage or a sustained competitive advantage. A firm enjoys a competitive advantage when it is implementing a value-creating strategy not simultaneously implemented by large numbers of other firms. If a particular valuable firm resource is possessed by large numbers of firms, then each of these firms have the capability of exploiting that resource in the same way, thereby implementing a common strategy that gives no one firm a competitive advantage.

The same analysis applies to bundles of valuable firm resources used to conceive of and implement strategies. Some strategies require a particular mix of physical capital, human capital, and organizational capital resources to implement. One firm resource required in the implementation of almost all strategies is managerial talent (Hambrick, 1987). If this particular bundle of firm resources is not rare, then large numbers of firms will be able to conceive of and implement the strategies in question, and these strategies will not be a source of competitive advantage, even though the resources in question may be valuable.

To observe that competitive advantages (sustained or otherwise) only accrue to firms that have valuable and rare resources is not to dismiss common (i.e. not rare) firm resources as unimportant. Instead, these valuable but common firm resources can help ensure a firm's survival when they are exploited to create competitive parity in an industry. Under conditions of competitive parity, though no one firm obtains a competitive advantage, firms do increase their probability of economic survival.

How rare a valuable firm resource must be in order to have the potential for generating a competitive advantage is a difficult question. It is not difficult to see that if a firm's valuable resources are absolutely unique among a set of competing and potentially competing firms, those resources will generate at least a competitive advantage and may have the potential of generating a sustained competitive advantage. However, it may be possible for a small number of firms in an industry to possess a particular valuable resource and still generate a competitive advantage. In general, as long as the number of firms that possess a particular valuable resource (or a bundle of valuable resources) is less than the number of firms needed to generate perfect competition dynamics in an industry, that resource has the potential of generating a competitive advantage.

Imperfectly Imitable Resources

It is not difficult to see that valuable and rare organizational resources may be a source of competitive advantage. Indeed, firms with such resources will often be strategic innovators, for they will be able to conceive of and engage in strategies that other firms could either not conceive of, or not implement, or both, because these other firms lacked the relevant firm resources. The observation that valuable and rare organizational resources can be a source of competitive advantage is another way of describing first-mover advantages accruing to firms with resource advantages.

However, valuable and rare organizational resources can only be sources of sustained competitive advantage if firms that do not possess these resources cannot obtain them. These firm resources are imperfectly imitable. Firm resources can be imperfectly imitable for one or a combination of three reasons: (a) the ability of a firm to obtain a resource is dependent upon *unique historical conditions*, (b) the link between the resources possessed by a firm and a firm's sustained competitive advantage is *causally ambiguous*, or (c) the resource generating a firm's advantage is *socially complex*. Each of these sources of the imperfect imitability of firm resources are examined below.

Unique historical conditions and imperfectly imitable resources Another assumption of most environmental models of firm competitive advantage, besides resource homogeneity and mobility, is that the performance of firms can be understood independent of the particular history and other idiosyncratic attributes of firms. These researchers seldom argue that firms do not vary in terms of their unique histories, but rather that these unique histories are not relevant to understanding a firm's performance (Porter, 1980).

The resource-based view of competitive advantage developed here relaxes this assumption. Indeed, this approach asserts that not only are firms intrinsically historical and social entities, but that their ability to acquire and exploit some resources depends upon their place in time and space. Once this particular unique time in history passes, firms that do not have space- and time-dependent resources cannot obtain them, and thus these resources are imperfectly imitable.

Resource-based theorists are not alone in recognizing the importance of history as a determinant of firm performance and competitive advantage. Traditional strategy researchers often cited the unique historical circumstances of a firm's founding, or the unique circumstances under which a new management team takes over a firm, as important determinants of a firm's long term performance. More recently, several economists (e.g. Arthur, Ermoliev and Kaniovsky, 1987; David, 1985) have developed models of firm performance that rely heavily on unique historical events as determinants of subsequent actions. Employing path-dependent models of economic performance these authors suggest that the performance of a firm does not depend simply on the industry structure within which a firm finds itself at a particular point in time, but also on the path a firm followed through history to arrive where it is. If a firm obtains valuable and rare resources because of its unique path through history, it will be able to exploit those resources in implementing value-creating strategies that cannot be duplicated by other firms, for firms without that particular path through history cannot obtain the resources necessary to implement the strategy.

The acquisition of all the types of firm resources examined in this article can depend upon the unique historical position of a firm. A firm that locates it facilities on what turns out to be a much more valuable location than was anticipated when the location was chosen possesses an imperfectly imitable physical capital resource. A firm with scientists who are uniquely positioned to create or exploit a significant scientific breakthrough may obtain an imperfectly imitable resource from the history-dependent nature of these scientist's individual human capital. Finally, a firm with a unique and valuable organizational culture that emerged in the early stages of a firm's history may have an imperfectly imitable advantage over firms founded in another historical period, where different (and perhaps less valuable) organizational values and beliefs come to dominate.

Causal ambiguity and imperfectly imitable resources   Unlike the relationship between a firm's unique history and the imitability of its resources, the relationship between the causal ambiguity of a firm's resources and imperfect imitability has received systematic attention in the literature. In this context, causal ambiguity exists when the link between the resources controlled by a firm and a firm's sustained competitive advantage is not understood or understood only very imperfectly.

When the link between a firm's resources and its sustained competitive advantage is poorly understood, it is difficult for firms that are attempting to duplicate a successful firm's strategies through imitation of its resources to know which resources it should imitate. Imitating firms may be able to describe some of the resources controlled by a successful firm. However, under conditions of causal ambiguity, it is not clear that the resources that can be described are the same resources that generate a sustained competitive advantage, or whether that advantage reflects some other non-described firm resource. Sometimes it is difficult to understand why one firm consistently outperforms other firms. Causal ambiguity is at the heart of this difficulty. In the face of such causal ambiguity, imitating firms cannot know the actions they should take in order to duplicate the strategies of firms with a sustained competitive advantage.

To be a source of sustained competitive advantage, both the firms that possess resources that generate a competitive advantage and the firms that do not possess these resources but seek to imitate them must be faced with the same level of causal ambiguity (Lippman and Rumelt, 1982). If firms that control these resources have a better understanding of their impact on competitive advantage than firms without these resources, then firms without these resources can engage in activities to reduce their knowledge disadvantage. They can do this, for example, by hiring away well placed knowledgeable managers in a firm with a competitive advantage or by engaging in a careful systematic study of the other firm's success. Although acquiring this knowledge may take some time and effort once knowledge of the link between a firm's resources and its ability to implement certain strategies is diffused throughout competing firms, causal ambiguity no longer exists, and thus cannot be a source of imperfect imitability. In other words, if a firm with a competitive advantage understands the link between the resources it controls and its advantages, then other firms can also learn about that link, acquire the necessary resources (assuming they are not imperfectly imitable for other reasons), and implement the relevant strategies. In such a setting, a firm's competitive advantages are not sustained because they can be duplicated.

At first, it may seem unlikely that a firm with a sustained competitive advantage will not fully understand the source of that advantage. However, given the very complex relationship between firm resources and competitive advantage, such an incomplete understanding is not implausible. The resources controlled by a firm are very complex and interdependent. Often, they are implicit, taken for granted by managers, rather than being subject to explicit analysis. Numerous resources, taken by themselves or in combination with other resources, may yield sustained competitive advantage.

Although managers may have numerous hypotheses about which resources generate their firm's advantages, it is rarely possible to rigorously test these hypotheses. As long as numerous plausible explanations of the sources of sustained competitive advantage exist within a firm, the link between the resources controlled by a firm and sustained competitive advantage remains somewhat ambiguous, and thus which of a firm's resources to imitate remains uncertain.

Social complexity A final reason that a firm's resources may be imperfectly imitable is that they may be very complex social phenomena, beyond the ability of firms to systematically manage and influence. When competitive advantages are based in such complex social phenomena, the ability of other firms to imitate these resources is significantly constrained.

A wide variety of firm resources may be socially complex. Examples include the interpersonal relations among managers in a firm, a firm's culture (Barney, 1986), a firm's reputation among suppliers and customers. Notice that in most of these cases it is possible to specify how these socially complex resources add value to a firm. Thus, there is little or no causal ambiguity surrounding the link between these firm resources and competitive advantage. However, understanding that, say, an organizational culture with certain attributes or quality relations among managers can improve a firm's efficiency and effectiveness does not necessarily imply that firms without these attributes can engage in systematic efforts to create them. Such social engineering may be, for the time being at least, beyond the capabilities of most firms. To the extent that socially complex firm resources are not subject to such direct management, these resources are imperfectly imitable.

Notice that complex physical technology is not included in this category of sources of imperfectly imitable. In general, physical technology, whether it takes the form of machine tools or robots in factories or complex information management system, is by itself typically imitable. If one firm can purchase these physical tools of production and thereby implement some strategies, then other firms should also be able to purchase these physical tools, and thus such tools should not be a source of sustained competitive advantage.

On the other hand, the exploitation of physical technology in a firm often involves the use of socially complex firm resources. Several firms may all possess the same physical technology, but only one of these firms may possess the social relations, culture, traditions, etc. to fully exploit this technology in implementing strategies. If these complex social resources are not subject to imitation (and assuming they are valuable and rare and no substitutes exist), these firms may obtain a sustained competitive advantage from exploiting their physical technology more completely than other firms, even though competing firms do not vary in terms of the physical technology they possess.

Substitutability

The last requirement for a firm resource to be a source of sustained competitive advantage is that there must be no strategically equivalent valuable resources that are themselves either not rare or imitable. Two valuable firm resources (or two bundles of firm resources) are strategically equivalent when they each can be exploited separately to implement the same strategies. Suppose that one of these valuable firm resources is rare and imperfectly imitable, but the other is not. Firms with this first resource will be able to conceive of and implement certain strategies. If there were no strategically equivalent firm resources, these strategies would generate a sustained competitive advantage (because the resources used to conceive and implement them are valuable, rare, and imperfectly imitable). However, that there are strategically equivalent resources suggests that other current or potentially competing firms can implement the same strategies, but in a different way, using different resources. If these alternative resources are either not rare or imitable, then numerous firms will be able to conceive of and implement the strategies in question, and those strategies will not generate a sustained competitive advantage. This will be the case even though one approach to implementing these strategies exploits valuable, rare, and imperfectly imitable firm resources.

Substitutability can take at least two forms. First, though it may not be possible for a firm to imitate another firm's resources exactly, it may be able to substitute a similar resource that enables it to conceive of and implement the same strategies. For example, a firm seeking to duplicate the competitive advantages of another firm by imitating that other firm's high quality top management team will often be unable to copy that team exactly. However, it may be possible for this firm to develop its own unique top management team. Though these two teams will be different (different people, different operating practices, a different history, etc.), they may likely be strategically equivalent and thus be substitutes for one another. If different top management teams are strategically equivalent (and if these substitute teams are common or highly imitable), then a high quality top management team is not a source of sustained competitive advantage, even though a particular management team of a particular firm is valuable, rare and imperfectly imitable.

Second, very different firm resources can also be strategic substitutes. For example, managers in one firm may have a very clear vision of the future of their company because of a charismatic leader in their firm. Managers in competing firms may also have a very clear vision of the future of their companies, but this common vision may reflect these firms' systematic, company-wide strategic planning process. From the point of view of managers having a clear vision of the future of their company, the firm resource of a charismatic leader and the firm resource of a formal planning system may be strategically equivalent, and thus substitutes for one another. If large numbers of competing firms have a formal planning system that generates this common vision (or if such a formal planning is highly imitable), then firms with such a vision derived from a charismatic leader will not have a sustained competitive advantage, even though the firm resource of a charismatic leader is probably rare and imperfectly imitable.

Of course, the strategic substitutability of firm resources is always a matter of degree. It is the case, however, that substitute firm resources need not have exactly the same implications for an organization in order for those resources to be equivalent from the point of view of the strategies that firms can conceive of and implement. If enough firms have these valuable substitute resources (i.e. they are not rare), or if enough firms can acquire them (i.e. they are imitable), then none of these firms (including firms whose resources are being substituted for) can expect to obtain a sustained competitive advantage.

The Framework

The relationship between resource heterogeneity and immobility; value, rareness, imitability, and substitutability; and sustained competitive advantage is summarized in Figure 5.4.2. This framework can be applied in analyzing the potential of a broad range of firm resources to be sources of sustained competitive advantage. These analyses not only specify the theoretical conditions under which sustained competitive advantage might exist, they also suggest specific empirical questions that need to be addressed before the relationship between a particular firm resource and sustained competitive advantage can be understood.

That the study of sources of sustained competitive advantage focuses on valuable, rare, imperfectly imitable, and non-substitutable resource endowments does not suggest – as some population ecologists would have it (e.g., Hannan and Freeman, 1977; reading 8.3 in this book) – that managers are irrelevant in the study of such advantages. In fact, managers are important in this model, for it is managers that are able to understand and describe the economic performance potential of a firm's endowments. Without such managerial analyses, sustained competitive advantage is not likely. This is the case even though the skills needed to describe the rare, imper-

FIGURE 5.4.2
Firm resources and sustained competitive advantage

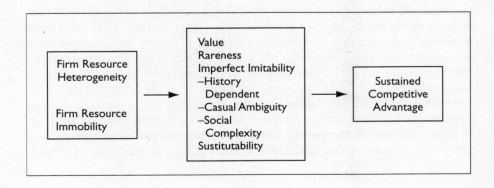

fectly imitable, and non-substitutable resources of a firm may themselves not be rare, imperfectly imitable, or non-substitutable.

Indeed, it may be the case that a manager or a managerial team is a firm resource that has the potential for generating sustained competitive advantages. The conditions under which this will be the case can be outlined using the framework presented in Figure 5.4.2. However, in the end, what becomes clear is that firms cannot expect to 'purchase' sustained competitive advantages on open markets. Rather, such advantages must be found in the rare, imperfectly imitable, and non-substitutable resources already controlled by a firm.

5.5   The Capabilities of Market-Driven Organizations

By George Day[1]

The marketing concept has been a paradox in the field of management. For over 40 years managers have been exhorted to 'stay close to the customer,' 'put the customer at the top of the organizational chart,' and define the purpose of a business as the creation and retention of satisfied customers. Companies that are better equipped to respond to market requirements and anticipate changing conditions are expected to enjoy long-run competitive advantage and superior profitability.

Throughout much of its history, however, the marketing concept has been more an article of faith than a practical basis for managing a business. Little was known about the defining features or attributes of this organizational orientation, and evidence as to the antecedents and performance consequences was mainly anecdotal. Consequently, managers had little guidance on how to improve or redirect their organizations' external orientation toward their markets.

Fortunately, this situation is changing following a 'rediscovery' in the late 1980s (Dickson 1992; Webster 1992). In the last five years, a number of conceptual and empirical studies have appeared that more clearly describe what a market orientation is and what it consists of. According to this emerging literature market orientation represents superior skills in understanding and satisfying customers (Day 1990). Its principal features are the following:

■   a set of beliefs that puts the customer's interest first;

---

[1] Source: This article was adapted with permission from The Capabilities of Market-Driven Organizations, *Journal of Marketing*, Vol. 58 (October 1994), pp. 37–52.

- the ability of the organization to generate, disseminate, and use superior information about customers and competitors;

- the coordinated application of interfunctional resources to the creation of superior customer value.

In addition, a modest but growing body of empirical evidence supports the proposition that a market orientation is positively associated with superior performance. Despite the recent progress in understanding what a market-driven organization does and identifying who they are, troubling gaps and shortcomings remain. Little is known, for example, about the characteristics of successful programs for building market orientation. How should these programs be designed? Should management emphasize fundamental culture change, revised work processes, organizational restructuring, new systems, redirected incentives, or some other set of plausible initiatives?

I address these issues by examining the role of capabilities in creating a market-oriented organization. Capabilities are complex bundles of skills and collective learning, exercised through organizational processes, that ensure superior coordination of functional activities. I propose that organizations can become more market oriented by identifying and building the special capabilities that set market-driven organizations apart.

Classifying Capabilities

It is not possible to enumerate all possible capabilities, because every business develops its own configuration of capabilities that is rooted in the realities of its competitive market, past commitments, and anticipated requirements. None the less, certain types of capabilities can be recognized in all businesses, corresponding to the core processes for creating economic value.

Some capabilities are easier to identify than others, usually because their activities are contained within the organization. Thus, Pitney-Bowes's ability to solve customers' mail-handling problems and McDonald's Corporation's achievement of unparalleled consistency of service delivery in dispersed outlets are pointed to as distinctive capabilities that explain their durable advantages. The visibility and prevalence of these examples of capabilities that have been successfully deployed from the inside out have led some observers to argue that firms should be defined by what they are capable of doing, rather than by the needs they seek to satisfy. This perspective is unbalanced, because it is the ability of the business to use these inside-out capabilities to exploit external possibilities that matters. Thus, there has to be a matching 'outside-in' capability to sense these possibilities and decide how best to serve them.

Consider the Corning, Inc. division that manufactures fiber optic products. Its challenge was to balance demands for increased product customization and faster delivery while reducing costs to stay ahead of aggressive competition. Originally, its objective was to be the most efficient mass producer of standard fiber optics. As the fiber optic market evolved and customers began to demand more specialized products, it was necessary to convert the manufacturing capabilities from a rigid, standard-production system to a flexible manufacturing platform capable of building customized fiber products to order. This transition required both an inside-out capability to produce the low-cost, custom products on a timely basis and an outside-in capability for understanding the evolving requirements of customers and energizing the organization to respond to them.

Capabilities can be usefully sorted into three categories, depending on the orientation and focus of the defining processes (see Figure 5.5.1). At one end of the spectrum are those that are deployed from the *inside-out* and activated by market requirements, competitive challenges, and external opportunities. Examples are manufacturing and other transformation activities, logistics, and human resource management, including recruiting, training, and motivating employees. At the other end of the spectrum are those capabilities whose focal point is almost exclusively outside the organization. The purpose of these *outside-in* capabilities is to connect the processes that define the other organizational capabilities to the external environment and enable the business to compete by anticipating market requirements ahead of competitors and creating durable relationships with customers, channel members, and suppliers. Finally, spanning capabilities are needed to integrate the inside-out and outside-in capabilities. Strategy development, new product/service development, price setting, purchasing,

FIGURE 5.5.1
Classifying capabilities

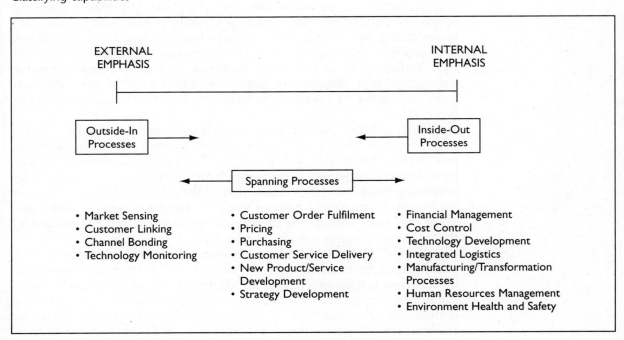

and customer order fulfillment are critical activities that must be informed by both external (outside-in) and internal (inside-out) analyses.

Market-driven organizations have superior market sensing, customer linking, and channel bonding capabilities. The processes underlying their superior capabilities are well understood and effectively managed and deliver superior insights that inform and guide both spanning and inside-out capabilities. The effect is to shift the span of all processes further toward the external end of the orientation dimension. Consider what happens when human resources are managed by the belief that customer satisfaction is both a cause and a consequence of employee satisfaction. Key policies become market oriented: rewards are based on measurable improvements in customer satisfaction and retention, employees are empowered to resolve customer problems without approvals, recruiting is based on customer problem-solving skills, and so forth. By contrast, the spanning and inside-out capabilities of internally oriented firms will be poorly guided by market considerations, which confines them to a narrow band toward the internal end of the orientation dimension. One reason is that the necessary outside-in processes that comprise the market sensing, customer linking, and channel bonding capabilities are likely to be poorly understood, badly managed, or deficient.

The Role of Spanning Capabilities

Spanning capabilities are exercised through the sequences of activities that comprise the processes used to satisfy the anticipated needs of customers identified by the outside-in capabilities and meet the commitments that have been made to enhance relationships. Order fulfillment, new product development, and service delivery processes all play this role. Managing these horizontal processes so they become distinctive capabilities that competitors cannot readily match is very different from managing a vertical function in a traditional hierarchical organization.

First, process management emphasizes external objectives. These objectives may involve customers' satisfaction with the outcome of the process, whether quality, delivery time, or installation assistance, or may be based on competitive performance benchmarks (e.g. cycle time, order processing time). This helps ensure that all those involved with the process are focused on providing superior value to external or internal customers. These objectives become the basis for a measurement and control system that monitors progress toward the objective.

Second, in coordinating the activities of a complex process, several jurisdictional boundaries must be crossed and horizontal connections made. These interactions require an identifiable owner of the process who can isolate sources of delay and take action to eliminate them. When no one understands the total flow of activities in an order-entry process, for example, critical time-consuming steps such as credit checks may be undertaken separately in sequence when they could have been done in parallel to save time.

Third, information is ready available to all team members, unfiltered by a hierarchy. If a question arises concerning order requirements, delivery status, or parts availability, everyone who is affected by the answer can get the information directly without having to go through an intermediary.

The order fulfillment process in Figure 5.5.2 illustrates both the problems and benefits of managing a process so it becomes a distinctive capability rather than simply a sequential series of necessary activities. Often this process is obscured from top management view because it links activities that take place routinely as sales forecasts are made, orders are received and scheduled, products are shipped, and services are provided. Things can go awry if unrealistic promises are made to customers, these promises are not kept, blame is passed around, and inventories expand as each function seeks to protect itself from the shortcomings of another (in part because no one incurs a cost for holding excess inventories).

Furthermore, the order fulfillment process has a wealth of connections to other processes. It brings together information from the outside-in processes and depends on their ability to forecast and generate a flow of orders. It depends even more on the inside-out manufacturing and logistics processes to fulfill the scheduled orders or have capacity in place to service requests and transactions. Finally, there is the allied process of cost estimation and pricing of orders. The management of this activity will significantly improve profitability, if the customer value of each order is clearly recognized and the costs of filling each order are known.

FIGURE 5.5.2
Order fulfillment processes: basis of a critical spanning capability

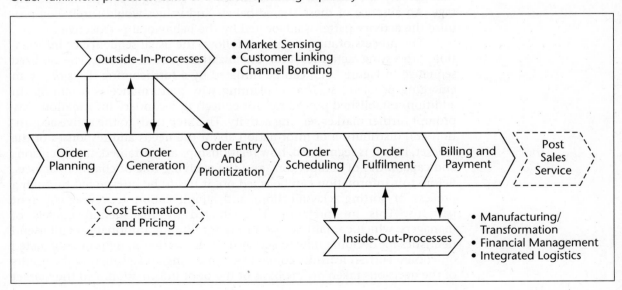

Market Sensing as a Distinctive Capability

Every discussion of market orientation emphasizes the ability of the firm to learn about customers, competitors, and channel members in order to continuously sense and act on events and trends in present and prospective markets. In market-driven firms the processes for gathering, interpreting, and using market information are more systematic, thoughtful, and anticipatory than in other firms. They readily surpass the ad hoc, reactive, constrained, and diffused efforts of their internally focused rivals.

A behavioral definition of a market orientation as 'the organization-wide generation of market intelligence, dissemination of its intelligence across departments, and organization-wide responsiveness to it' (Kohli and Jaworski 1990), captures the essence of a market sensing capability. Each element of this definition describes a distinct activity having to do with collecting and acting on information about customer needs and the influence of technology, competition, and other environmental forces. Narver and Slater (1990) offer another definition in the same spirit. They distinguish three behavioral components: customer orientation – the firm's understanding of the target market; competitor orientation – the firm's understanding of the longrun capabilities of present and prospective competitors; and interfunctional coordination – the coordinated utilization of company resources to create superior customer value.

An alternative to this behavioral perspective holds that a market orientation is part of a more deeply rooted and pervasive culture. For this purpose, Deshpandé and Webster (1989) define culture as 'the pattern of shared values and beliefs that gives the members of an organization meaning, and provides them with the rules for behavior.' A market-driven culture supports the value of thorough market intelligence and the necessity of functionally coordinated actions directed at gaining a competitive advantage. An absence of these shared beliefs and values would surely compromise the activity patterns advocated by the behavioral perspective.

The process of market sensing follows the usual sequence of information processing activities that organizations use to learn. The stylized sequence in Figure 5.5.3 can be initiated by a forthcoming decision or an emerging problem, such as explaining why performance is declining. In addition, established procedures for collecting secondary information may prompt further market-sensing activity. This step leads to the active acquisition and distribution of information about the needs and responses of the market, how it is segmented, how relationships are sustained, the intentions and capabilities of competitors, and the evolving role of channel partners. Before this information can be acted on, it has to be interpreted through a process of sorting, classification, and simplification to reveal coherent patterns. This interpretation is facilitated by the mental models of managers, which contain decision rules for filtering information and useful heuristics for deciding how to act on the information in light of anticipated outcomes. Further learning comes from observing and evaluating the results of the decisions taken on the basis of the prior information. Did the market

FIGURE 5.5.3
Market sensing: processes for learning about markets

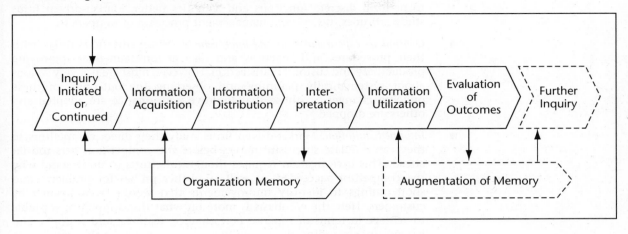

respond as expected, and if not, why not? Organizational memory plays several roles in this process: it serves as a repository for collective insights contained within policies, procedures, routines, and rules that can be retrieved when needed; a source of answers to ongoing inquiries; and a major determinant of the ability to ask appropriate questions.

Market-driven firms are distinguished by an ability to sense events and trends in their markets ahead of their competitors. They can anticipate more accurately the responses to actions designed to retain or attract customers, improve channel relations, or thwart competitors. They can act on information in a timely, coherent manner because the assumptions about the market are broadly shared. This anticipatory capability is based on superiority in each step of the process. It is achieved through opened-minded inquiry, synergistic information distribution, mutually informed interpretations, and accessible memories.

Open-minded inquiry All organizations acquire information about trends, events, opportunities, and threats in their market environment through scanning, direct experience, imitation, or problem-solving inquiries. Market-driven organizations approach these activities in a more thoughtful and systematic fashion, in the belief that all decisions start with the market. The most distinctive features of their approach to inquiry are the following:

■ *Active scanning.* All organizations track key market conditions and activities and try to learn from the departures from what is normal and expected. However, this learning is usually a top-down effort because information from the front-line employees is blocked. In market-driven organizations, these front-line contacts, who hear complaints or requests for new services and see the consequences of competitive activity, are motivated to inform management systematically.

- *Self-critical benchmarking.* Most firms do regular tear-down analyses of competitors' products and occasionally study firms for insights into how to perform discrete functions and activities better. Market-driven firms study attitudes, values, and management processes of nonpareils.

- *Continuous experimentation and improvement.* All organizations tinker with their procedures and practices and take actions aimed at improving productivity and customer satisfaction. However, most are not very serious about systematically planning and observing the outcomes of these ongoing changes, so those that improve performance are adopted and others are dropped.

- *Informed imitation.* Market-driven firms study their direct competitors so they can emulate successful moves before the competition gets too far ahead. This investigation requires thoughtful efforts to understand why the competitor succeeded, as well as further probes for problems and shortcomings to identify improvements that would be welcomed by customers. Here the emphasis is more on what the competitor was able to achieve in terms of superior performance, features, and so forth, and less on understanding the capabilities of the competitor that resulted in the outcome.

Synergistic information distribution Firms often do not know what they know. They may have good systems for storing and locating 'hard' routine accounting and sales data, but otherwise managers have problems figuring out where in the organization a certain piece of information is known or assembling all the needed pieces in one place. This is especially true of competitor information, in which, for example, manufacturing may be aware of certain activities through common equipment suppliers, sales may hear about initiatives from distributors and collect rumors from customers, and the engineering department may have hired recently from a competitor.

Market-driven firms do not suffer unduly from organizational chimneys, silos, or smokestacks, which restrict information flows to vertical movements within functions. Instead, information is widely distributed, its value is mutually appreciated, and those functions with potentially synergistic information know where else it could be used beneficially.

Mutually informed interpretations The simplifications inherent in the mental models used by managers facilitate learning when they are based on undistorted information about important relationships and are widely shared throughout the organization. These mental models can impede learning when they are incomplete, unfounded, or seriously distorted by functioning below the level of awareness, they are never examined. A market-driven organization avoids these pitfalls by using scenarios and other devices to force managers to articulate, examine, and eventually modify their mental models of how their markets work, how competitors and suppliers will react, and the parameters of the response coefficients in their marketing programs.

Accessible memory   Market-driven inquiry, distribution, and interpretation will not have a lasting effect unless what is learned is lodged in the collective memory. Organizations without practical mechanisms to remember what has worked and why will have to repeat their failures and rediscover their success formulas over and over again. Collective recall capabilities are most quickly eroded by turnover through transfers and rapid disbanding of teams. Data banks that are inaccessible to the entire organization can also contribute to amnesia. Here is where information technology can play an especially useful role.

Customer Linking as a Distinctive Capability

As buyer-seller relationships continue their transformation, a customer-linking capability – creating and managing close customer relationships – is becoming increasingly important. At one time, standard purchasing practice emphasized arm's length adversarial bargaining with suppliers, aimed at achieving the lowest price for each transaction or contract. Not surprisingly, suppliers focused on individual transactions and gave little attention to the quality of the interface with the customer. They had little incentive to be open with buyers or develop superior or dedicated capabilities because they could easily lose the business to a competitor. The buyer, in turn, was unlikely to be aware of a supplier's costs and capabilities.

Now customers, as well as major channel members such as Ikea and Wal-Mart, are seeking closer, more collaborative relationships with suppliers based on a high level of coordination, participation in joint programs, and close communication links. They want to replace the adversarial model, which assumes that advantages are gained through cutting input costs, with a co-operative model that seeks advantage through total quality improvement and reduced time to market. This way of doing business suits their better suppliers, who confront intense competition that quickly nullifies their product advantages and powerful channels that control access to the market.

Despite recent emphasis on the establishment, maintenance, and enhancement of collaborative relationships, few firms have mastered this capability and made it a competitive advantage. Successful collaboration requires a high level of purposeful cooperation aimed at maintaining a trading relationship over time. The activities to be managed start with the coordination of inside-out and spanning capabilities, although these are not the means by which the relationship is managed. Instead, new skills, abilities, and processes must be mastered to achieve mutually satisfactory collaboration. These include the close communication and joint problem solving, and coordinating activities.

Close communication and joint problem solving

Suppliers must be prepared to develop team-based mechanisms for continuously exchanging information about needs, problems, and emerging requirements and then taking action. In a successful collaborative relationship, joint problem solving displaces negotiations. Suppliers must also be prepared to participate in the customer's development processes, even before the product specifications are established.

Communications occur at many levels and across many functions of the customer and supplier organizations, requiring a high level of internal coordination and a new role for the sales function. When the focus is on transactions, the salesperson is pivotal and the emphasis is on persuading the customer through features, price, terms, and the maintenance of a presence. The sales function adopts a very different – and possibly subordinate – role in a collaborative relationship. It is responsible for coordinating other functions, anticipating needs, demonstrating responsiveness, and building credibility and trust.

Coordinating activities

In addition to the scheduling of deliveries, new management processes are needed for (1) joint production planning and scheduling; (2) management of information system links so each knows the other's requirements and status and orders can be communicated electronically; and (3) mutual commitments to the improvement of quality and reliability.

Manufacturer-reseller relations has become a fertile area for the development of collaborative management capabilities, with the major grocery product firms taking the lead. The objective of each party used to be to transfer as much of their cost to the other as possible. This approach lead to dysfunctional practices such as forward buying to take advantage of manufacturer's promotional offers, resulting in excessive warehousing expenses and costly spikes in production levels. Traditionally, contacts between parties were limited to lower-level sales representatives calling on buyers who emphasized prices, quantities, and deals. Increasingly, manufacturers like Procter & Gamble and retailers like KMart are assigning multifunctional teams to deal with each other at many levels, including harmonizing systems, sharing logistics and product movement information, and jointly planning for promotional activity and product changes. The objectives of this collaborative activity are to cut total system costs while helping retailers improve sales.

Firms that have developed a distinctive capability for managing collaborative relationships find they have more integrated strategies. The integration begins with a broad-based agreement on which customers serve collaboratively. No longer is this choice left to the sales function, without regard to the impact on the manufacturing and service functions. The cross-functional coordination and information sharing required to work collaboratively with customers enhances shared understanding of the strategy and role of the different functions.

Although collaborative relationships are becoming increasingly important, they are not appropriate for every market or customer. Some customers want nothing more than the tamely exchange of the product or service with minimum hassle and a competitive price. And because of the effort and resources required to support a tightly linked relationship, it may not be possible to do this with more than a few critical customers. Yet even when most relationships are purely transactional, there are still possibilities for gaining advantages by nurturing some elements of a linking capability within the organization. This process begins by analyzing which customers are more loyal or easier to retain and proceeds by seeking ways to maintain continuity with these customers through customized services or incentives.

Developing the Capabilities of Market-Driven Organizations

Initiatives to enhance market sensing and customer linking capabilities are integral to broader efforts to build a market-driven organization. The overall objective is to demonstrate a pervasive commitment to a set of processes, beliefs, and values, reflecting the philosophy that all decisions start with the customer and are guided by a deep and shared understanding of the customer's needs and behavior and competitors' capabilities and intentions, for the purpose of realizing superior performance by satisfying customers better than competitors.

Many firms have aspired to become market driven but have failed to instill and sustain this orientation. Often these aspirants underestimate how difficult a task it is to shift an organization's focus from internal to external concerns. They apparently assume that marginal changes, a few management workshops, and proclamations of intent will do the job, when in fact a wide-ranging cultural shift is necessary. To have any chance for success, change programs will have to match the magnitude of the cultural shift.

Preliminary insights into how to design change programs come from empirical research on why some organizations are more market oriented than others. For example, Jaworski and Kohli (1993) confirm the long-standing belief that top management commitment is essential. Strong affirmation of the notion that market-driven organizations have superior capabilities comes from three of their findings. First, they found that formal and informal connectedness of functions facilitates the exchange of information whereas interdepartmental conflicts inhibit the communications that are necessary to effective market sensing. This confirms the desirability of managing this capability as a set of organization-spanning activities. Second, there was solid evidence that centralization was antithetical to market orientation. This mind-set appears to flourish when there is delegation of decision making authority and extensive participation in decision making. Finally, the use of market-based factors such as customer satisfaction for evaluating and rewarding managers was the single most influential determinant of market orientation.

Summary and Conclusions

It is almost an article of faith within marketing that superior business performance is the result of superior skills in understanding and satisfying customers. This proposition has been partially validated by a growing body of research on the impact of a market orientation on business performance. This work has helped give a fuller picture of the attributes of market-driven organizations, highlighting the roles of culture, information utilization, and interfunctional coordination. These insights are not sufficient for managers, because they do not reveal how the superior skills were developed. All we see is the results of the organizational transformation. Now managers seek guidance on how to enhance the market orientation of their organization.

The emerging capabilities approach to strategy offers a valuable new perspective on how to achieve and sustain a market orientation. This approach seeks the sources of defensible competitive positions in the distinctive, difficult-to-imitate capabilities the organization has developed. The shift in emphasis to capabilities does not mean that strategic positioning is any less important. On the contrary, the choice of which capabilities to nurture and which investment commitments to make must be guided by a shared understanding of the industry structure, the needs of the target customer segments, the positional advantages being sought, and the trends in the environment.

Two capabilities are especially important in bringing these external realities to the attention of the organization. One is the market sensing capability, which determines how well the organization is equipped to continuously sense changes in its market and to anticipate the responses to marketing actions. The second is a customer-linking capability, which comprises the skills, abilities, and processes needed to achieve collaborative customer relationships so individual customer needs are quickly apparent to all functions and well-defined procedures are in place for responding to them.

Business-Level Strategy in International Perspective

> Whoever is winning at the moment will always seem to be invincible.
> (George Orwell 1903–1950; English novelist)

Just as in the previous debates, it has become clear that there are various ways of dealing with the paradox of markets and resources. Each of the authors has argued a particular point of view, and it is the reader's task to judge which approach will yield the highest strategic dividends, under which set of circumstances. And as before, the chapter is concluded by explicitly looking at the issue from an international angle.

The difference between this and other chapters is that comparative management researchers have not reported specific national preferences for an inside-out or an outside-in perspective. This may be due to the fact that there actually are no distinct national inclinations when dealing with this paradox. However, it might also be the case that the late emergence of resource-based theories (starting in the early 1990s) has not yet allowed for cross-national comparisons.

As a stimulus to the debate whether there are national differences in the approach to business level strategies, we would like to bring forward a number of factors that might be of influence on how the paradox of markets and resources is tackled in different countries. It goes almost without saying that more international research is needed to give this issue a firmer footing.

Mobility Barriers

In general, industry and market positions will be of more value if there are high mobility barriers within the environment (Porter, 1980). Some of these mobility barriers can be specifically national in origin. Government regulation, in particular, can be an important source of mobility barriers. For instance, import quotas and duties, restrictive licensing systems, and fiscal regulations and subsidies, can all – knowingly or unknowingly – result in protection of incumbent firms. Such government intervention enhances the importance of obtained positions.

Other national sources of mobility barriers can be unions' resistance to change and high customer loyalty. In some economies high mobility barriers might also be imposed by powerful groups or families.

In such economies, which are more rigid due to high mobility barriers, strategists might have a strong preference to think in terms of market positions first, since these are more difficult to obtain than the necessary resources. The opposite would be true in more dynamic economies, where market positions might easily be challenged by competitors, unless they are based on distinctive and difficult to imitate resources.

Resource Mobility

A second international difference might be found in the types of the resources employed across countries. In nations where the dominant industries are populated by firms using relatively simple and abundant resources, market positions are far more important, since acquisition of the necessary resources is hardly a worry. However, if a national economy is composed of industries using complex bundles of resources, requiring many years of painstaking development, there might be a tendency to emphasize the importance of resources over market positions.

Further Readings

Although many textbooks give an overview of the variety of approaches to the topic of business level strategy, none of these introductions are as crisp as John Kay's book *Foundations of Corporate Success: How Corporate Strategies Add Value*, which can be highly recommended as further reading. In the category of textbooks, Robert Grant's *Contemporary Strategy Analysis* is suggested as a good overview of business strategy approaches.

Most of what has been published on the topic of business level strategy has implicitly or explicitly made reference to the work of Michael Porter. Therefore, any follow up readings should include his benchmark works *Competitive Strategy* and *Competitive Advantage*. It is also interesting to see how his thinking as developed and has embraced some of the resource-based concepts. In particular his articles 'Towards a Dynamic Theory of Strategy,' and 'What is Strategy?' are stimulating works. Also highly recommended is the book by Robert Buzzell and Bradley Gale, *The PIMS Principles: Linking Strategy to Performance*, from which the contribution in this chapter was taken.

For a better insight into the resource-based approach, readers might want to go back to Edith Penrose's classic book *The Theory of the Growth of the Firm*, which has recently been republished. For a more recent introduction, Robert Grant's article 'The Resource-Based Theory of Competitive Advantage: Implications for Strategy Formulation' can be advised. David Collis and Cynthia Montgomery have also written an accessible article explaining the resource-based view, titled 'Competing on Resources: Strategy in the 1990s.' Other important works that are more academically-oriented are 'A Historical Comparison of Resource-Based Theory and Five Schools of Thought Within Industrial Organization Economics: Do We Have a New Theory of the Firm?' by Kathleen Conner; 'Strategic Assets and Organizational Rent' by Raphael Amit and Paul Schoemaker; 'The Cornerstones of Competitive Advantage: A Resource-Based View' by Margaret Peteraf.

Last, but not least, the works of Gary Hamel and C.K. Prahalad should be mentioned. Many of their articles in *Harvard Business Review*, such as 'Strategic Intent,' 'Strategy as Stretch and Leverage,' and 'The Core Competence of the Corporation' (reading 6.2 in this book) have had a major impact, both on practitioners and academics, and are well worth reading. Many of the ideas expressed in these articles have been brought together in their book *Competing for the Future*, which is therefore highly recommended.

References

Aaker, D.A. (1995) *Strategic Market Management*, 4th edn, John Wiley & Sons, New York.

Abell, D. (1980) *Defining the Business – The Starting Point of Strategic Planning*, Prentice Hall, Englewood Cliffs, NJ.

Amit, R. and Schoemaker, P.J.H. (1993) Strategic Assets and Organizational Rent, *Strategic Management Journal*, Vol. 14, pp. 33–45.

Arthur, W.B., Emoliev, Y.M., and Kaniovsky, Y.M. (1987) Path Dependent Processes and the Emergence of Macro Structure, *European Journal of Operations Research*, 30, pp. 294–303.

Bain, J. (1956) *Barriers to New Competition*, Harvard University Press, Cambridge, MA.

Barney, J.B. (1986) Organizational Culture: Can It Be a Source of Sustained Competitive Advantage?, *Academy of Management Review*, 11, pp. 656–65.

Barney, J.B. (1991) Firm Resources and Sustained Competitive Advantage, *Journal of Management*, Vol. 17, No. 1, pp. 99–120.

Buzzell, R.D., and Gale, B.T. (1987) *The PIMS Principles: Linking Strategy to Performance*, Free Press, New York.

Caves, R.E., Gale, B.T., and Porter, M.E. (1977) Interfirm Profitability Differences: Comment, *Quarterly Journal of Economics*, November.

Caves, R.E., and Porter, M.E. (1977) From Entry Barriers to Mobility Barriers: Conjectural Decisions and Contrived Deterrence to New Competition, *Quarterly Journal of Economics*, 91, pp. 241–62.

Collis, D.J., and Montgomery, C.A. (1995) Competing on Resources: Strategy in the 1990s, *Harvard Business Review*, July–August, pp. 118–28.

Conner, K.R. (1991) A Historical Comparison of Resource-Based Theory and Five Schools of Thought Within Industrial Organization Economics: Do We Have a New Theory of the Firm?, *Journal of Management*, Vol. 17, pp. 121–54.

David, P.A. (1985) Clio and the Economics of QWERTY, *American Economic Review Proceedings*, 75, pp. 332–37.

Day, G.S. (1990) *Market Driven Strategy, Processes for Creating Value*, The Free Press: New York.

Day, G.S. (1994) The Capabilities of Market-Driven Organizations, *Journal of Marketing*, Vol. 58, October, pp. 37–52.

Demsetz, H. (1988) The Theory of the Firm Revisited, *Journal of Law, Economics, and Organization*, vol. 4, pp. 141–61.

Deshpandé, R., and Webster Jr., F.E. (1989) Organizational Culture and Marketing: Defining the Research Agenda, *Journal of Marketing*, 53, January, pp. 3–15.

Dickson, P.R. (1992) Toward A General Theory of Competitive Rationality, *Journal of Marketing*, 56, January, pp. 69–83.

Dierickx, I., and Cool, K. (1989) Asset Stock Accumulation and Sustainability of Competitive Advantage, *Management Science*, December, pp. 1504–11.

Dretske, F. (1981) *Knowledge and the Flow of Information*, MIT Press, Cambridge, MA.

Durand, T. (1996) Revisiting Key Dimensions of Competence, Paper presented to the SMS Conference, Phoenix.

Ghemawat, P. (1991) *Commitment: The Dynamic of Strategy*, Free Press, New York.

Grant, R.M. (1991) The Resource-Based Theory of Competitive Advantage:

Implications for Strategy Formulation, *California Management Review*, Spring, pp. 114–35.

Grant, R.M. (1995) *Contemporary Strategy Analysis: Concepts, Techniques, Applications*, 2nd edn, Blackwell Business, Oxford.

Hambrick, D. (1987) Top Management Teams: Key to Strategic Success, *California Management Review*, 30, pp. 88–108.

Hamel, G., and Prahalad, C.K. (1994) *Competing for the Future*, Harvard Business School Press.

Hamel, G., and Heene, A. (eds) (1994) *Competence-Based Competition*, Wiley, Chicester.

Hamermesh, R.G., Anderson Jr., M.J., and Harris, J.E. (1978) Strategies for Low Market Share Businesses, *Harvard Business Review*, May/June, pp. 95–102.

Hannan, M.T. and Freeman, J. (1977) The Population Ecology of Organizations, *American Journal of Sociology*, March, pp. 929–64.

Hofer, C., and Schendel, D. (1978) *Strategy Formulation: Analytical Concepts*, West, St. Paul, MN.

Itami, H. (1986) *Mobilizing Invisible Assets*, Harvard University Press, Cambridge, MA.

Jaworski, B., and Kohli, A.K. (1993) Market Orientation: Antecedents and Consequences, *Journal of Marketing*, 57, July, pp. 53–70.

Kay, J. (1993) *Foundations of Corporate Success: How Business Strategies Add Value*, Oxford University Press, Oxford.

Kogut, B., and Zander, U. (1992) Knowledge of the Firm, Combinative Capabilities, and the Replication of Technology, *Organization Science*, Vol. 3, pp. 383–97.

Kohli, A.K., and Jaworski, B. (1990) Market Orientation: The Construct, Research Propositions, and Managerial Implications, *Journal of Marketing*, 54, April, pp. 1–18.

Leonard-Barton, D. (1995) *Wellsprings of Knowledge*, Harvard Business School Press, Boston.

Lieberman, M.B., and Montgomery, D.B. (1988) First Mover Adavantages, *Strategic Management Journal*, 9, pp. 41–58.

Lippman, S., and Rumelt, R. (1982) Uncertain Imitability: An Analysis of Inter-firm Differences in Efficiency under Competition, *Bell Journal of Economics*, 13, pp. 418–38.

Lowendahl, B.R. (1997) *Strategic Management of Professional Business Service Firms*, Copenhagen Business School Press, Copenhagen.

Mintzberg, H. (1990a) Strategy Formation: Schools of Thought, in Frederickson, J. (ed.), *Perspectives on Strategic Management*, Harper & Row, New York.

Mintzberg, H. (1990b) The Design School: Reconsidering the Basic Premises of Strategic Management, *Strategic Management Journal*, March, pp. 171–95.

Narver, J.C., and Slater, S.F. (1990) The Effect of a Marketing Orientation on Business Profitability, *Journal of Marketing*, Vol. 54, October, pp. 20–35.

Nelson, R., and Winter, S. (1982) *An Evolutionary Theory of Economic Change*, Harvard University Press, Cambridge, MA.

Nonaka, I. (1991) The Knowledge-Creating Company, *Harvard Business Review*, November–December, pp. 96–104.

Penrose, E.T. (1958) *The Theory of the Growth of the Firm*, Wiley, New York, 1958.

Peteraf, M.A. (1993) The Cornerstones of Competitive Advantage: A Resource-based View, *Strategic Management Journal*, Vol. 14, pp. 179–91.

Polanyi, M. (1958) *Personal Knowledge*, University of Chicago Press, Chicago.

Porac, J.F., Thomas, H. and Baden-Fuller, Ch. (1989) 'Competitive Groups as

Cognitive Communities: The Case of Scottish Knitwear Manufacturers,' *Journal of Management Studies*, No. 26, pp. 397–416.

Porter, M.E. (1980) *Competitive Strategy: Techniques for Analyzing Industries and Competitors, Free Press*, New York.

Porter, M.E. (1985) *Competitive Advantage: Creating and Sustaining Superior Performance*, Free Press, New York.

Porter, M.E. (1996) What is Strategy?, *Harvard Business Review*, November/December, pp. 61–78.

Prahalad, C.K., and Hamel, G. (1990) The Core Competence of the Corporation, *Harvard Business Review*, May/June, pp. 79–91.

Quinn, J.B. (1992) *Intelligent Enterprise: A Knowledge and Service Based Paradigm for Industry*, Free Press, New York.

Rumelt, R.P. (1996) Inertia and Transformation, in: Montgomery, C.A. (ed.) *Resource-based and Evolutionary Theories of the Firm: Towards a Synthesis*, Kluwer, Boston, pp. 101–32.

Sanchez, R., Heene, A. and Thomas, H. (eds) (1996) *Dynamics of Competence-Based Competition*, Elsevier, London.

Scherer, F.M. (1980) *Industrial Market Structure and Economic Performance*, 2nd Edition, Houghton-Mifflin, Boston.

Stalk, G., Evans, P., and Schulman, L.E. (1992) Competing on Capabilities: The New Rules of Corporate Strategy, *Harvard Business Review*, March/April, pp. 57–69.

Teece, D.J., Pisano, G., and Shuen, A. (1990) *Firm Capabilities, Resources, and the Concept of Strategy: Four Paradigms of Strategic Management*, CCC Working Paper, December.

Webster Jr., F.E. (1992) The Changing Role of Marketing in the Corporation, *Journal of Marketing*, 56, October, pp. 1–17.

Webster, F. (1994) *Market Driven Management: Using the New Marketing Concept to Create a Customer-oriented Company*, John Wiley, New York.

Wernerfelt, B. (1984) A Resource-Based View of the Firm, *Strategic Management Journal*, April/June, pp. 171–80.

Woo, C.Y., and Cooper, A.C. (1982) The Surprising Case for Low Market Share, *Harvard Business Review*, November–December, pp. 106–13.

Woo, C.Y. (1984) Market-Share Leadership – Not Always So Good, *Harvard Business Review*, January–February, pp. 2–4.

6

Corporate Level Strategy

Consider the little mouse, how sagacious
an animal it is which never entrusts its
life to one hole only.

(Plautus 254–184 BC; Roman playwright)

None ever got ahead of me
except the man of one task

(Azariah Rossi 1513–1578; Italian physician)

The Paradox of Responsiveness and Synergy

Just as mice see the benefit of more than one hole, so many companies believe in the virtue of being active in more than one business. These firms have chosen to diversify based on the assumption that multibusiness involvement will lead to synergies that outweigh the extra costs of managing a more complex organization. *Multibusiness level*, or *corporate*, strategy deals with the identification and realization of these synergies. Or as Porter (1987) puts it, 'corporate strategy is what makes the corporate whole add up to more than the sum of its business unit parts.'

Synergies occur when firms are able to productively share resources among two or more businesses (also referred to as *economies of scope*). If resource productivity gains are achieved by such sharing, this is called *resource leveraging* (Hamel and Prahalad, 1993). All types of company resources can potentially be leveraged. For example, if two business units use the same production facilities, savings might be achieved. Other tangible resources may also be jointly employed, such as buildings, equipment, materials, land and money. Besides these tangibles, business units may share intangible resources as well. Joint use can be made of relational resources (e.g. bargaining power *vis-à-vis* suppliers, reputation among customers, contacts with regulatory agencies), while competences can also be leveraged (sharing knowledge, capabilities and business outlook).

Synergies can also be achieved by linking the market strategies of two or more business units. Such coordination of business units' externally oriented behavior, with the intention of creating added-value, can be referred to as *strategy alignment*. Both vertically and horizontally-related business units might benefit from aligning their market strategies with one another. Two vertically related business units might develop a symbiotic supplier-buyer relationship between them, with a high level of specialized investment and dependence, without the threat of one misusing this power over the other. Two horizontally related business units (i.e. selling similar types of products) might, for example, coordinate their attack on a common competitor, join forces to create market entry barriers and build acceptance for a common standard in the market.

To realize such synergies, a firm must to some extent coordinate the activities carried out in its various business units. The autonomy of the business units must be partially limited, in the interest of concerted action. However, coordination comes with a price tag. An extra level of management is required, more meetings, extra complexity, potential conflicts of interest, turf wars, additional bureaucracy – alignment costs money and diminishes a business unit's ability to precisely tailor its strategy to its specific business environment. In other words, *coordination* with other business units and meddling by the corporate center can blunt a business unit's *responsiveness* to its own business (e.g. Lawrence and Lorsch, 1967; Prahalad and Doz, 1987).

Multibusiness level strategy is concerned with realizing more value creation by means of synergy than value destruction through loss of responsiveness (Campbell, Goold and Alexander, 1995; reading 6.4 in this book). To achieve this, corporate strategists must wrestle with the paradox of responsiveness and synergy. Although there are many different views on how these two objectives might be balanced or pursued simultaneously, two opposite perspectives stand out in the debate. These two views, the *portfolio* and the *core competence* perspectives, are almost at opposite ends of the spectrum, with many other strategists taking up intermediate positions. While these two perspectives do not monopolize the real-life debate, they do represent the two extremes to which strategists are willing to go. Therefore, the debate in this chapter will start with these two poles.

The Portfolio Perspective

In the portfolio perspective, responsiveness is strongly emphasized over synergy. Strategists taking this perspective usually argue that each business has its own unique characteristics and demands. Firms operating in different businesses must therefore develop a specific strategy for each business and assign the responsibility for each business strategy to a specific part of the organization – a *strategic business unit* (SBU). In this manner, the (strategic) business units can be highly responsive to the competitive dynamics in the business, while being a clear unit of accountability towards the corporate center. High responsiveness, however, requires freedom from corporate center interference and freedom from cross-business coordination. Hence, a high level of business unit autonomy is required, with the corporate center's influence limited to arm's length financial control.

In the portfolio perspective, the main reason for a number of highly autonomous business units to be in one firm is to *leverage financial resources*. The only synergies emphasized are financial synergies. Actually, the term 'portfolio' entered the business vocabulary via the financial sector, where it refers to an investor's *collection of shareholdings* in different companies, purchased to spread investment risks. Transferred to corporate strategy, the portfolio perspective views the corporate center as an active investor with financial stakes in a number of stand-alone business units. The role of the center is one of selecting a promising portfolio of businesses, keeping tight financial control, and allocating available capital – redirecting flows of cash from business units where prospects are dim ('cash cows' or 'dogs'), to other business units where higher returns can be expected ('stars' or 'question marks'). The strategic mission of each business unit is, therefore, also financial in orientation – grow, hold, milk or divest, depending on the business unit's position on the portfolio grid (e.g. Henderson, 1979; Hedley, 1977). A good corporate strategy strives for a balanced portfolio of mature cash producers and high potential ROI cash users, at an acceptable level of overall risk. The business units do not necessarily need to be 'related' in any other way than financial. In practice, the business units can be related, that is, there can be resource leveraging and strategy alignment opportunities that are seized. The portfolio perspective does not reject the pursuit of other forms of synergy, but neither does it accommodate such efforts (Haspeslagh, 1982).

New businesses can be entered by means of internal growth, but the portfolio approach to corporate strategy is particularly well suited to diversification through acquisition. In a multibusiness firm run on portfolio principles, acquired companies are simple to integrate into the corporation, because they can be largely left as stand alone units and only need to be linked to corporate reporting and control systems. Proponents of the portfolio perspective argue that such nonsynergistic acquisitions can be highly profitable (Kaplan, 1989; Long and Ravenscraft, 1993). Excess cash can be routed to more attractive investment opportunities than the corporation has internally. Moreover, the acquiring corporation can shake up the management of the acquired company and can function as a strategic sounding board for the new people (Anslinger and Copeland, 1996).

The portfolio perspective is particularly well known for the analytical techniques that have been developed to support it. A large number of portfolio grids are in widespread use as graphical tools for visualizing the composition of the corporation and for determining the position of each of the business units. All of these portfolio grids are based on the same fundamental concept, that the profit and growth potential of individual business units can be measured along two dimensions – attractiveness of the business, and competitive strength of the business unit. For instance, the Boston Consulting Group matrix (Hedley, 1977; reading 6.1) uses business growth as a measure of attractiveness and relative market share as a measure of competitive strength. The General Electric business screen uses a larger number of factors to determine a score on both dimensions (Hofer and Schendel, 1978). The Arthur D. Little matrix, on the other hand, uses industry maturity instead of industry attractiveness as one of its two dimensions (see the Oldelft case in Section VI). These portfolio tools have proven to popular and much used (Goold and Lansdell, 1997), even among strategists who are not proponents of the portfolio perspective.

The Core Competence Perspective

The core competence perspective is fundamentally at odds with the portfolio perspective's minimalist interpretation of corporate strategy. In the core competence perspective, multibusiness firms should be more than a loose federation of businesses held together by a common investor. Actually, corporations should be quite the opposite – a common resource-base that is applied to various businesses. As the name of the perspective indicates, it is a set of shared competences that is believed to be the best central core for a multibusiness company. It is argued that these core competences should be leveraged as much as possible, by using them in all of the firm's business units. Such use in a specific business setting will, in turn, improve the core competence, leading to a virtuous circle of competence upgrading, profiting the entire corporation.

As all business units should both tap into, and contribute to, the corporation's core competences, the business units' autonomy is necessarily limited. The creation and leveraging of core competences requires that the business units remain close team players. Prahalad and Hamel's (1990; reading 6.2) metaphor for the corporation is not an investor's portfolio, but a large tree – 'the trunk and major limbs are core products, the smaller branches are business units, the leaves, flowers and fruit are end products; the root system that provides nourishment, sustenance and stability is the core competence.' Business unit branches can be cut off and new ones can grow on, but all spring from the same tree. And it is the corporate center's role to nurture this tree, building up the core competences and ensuring that the firm's critical resources and competence carriers can easily be redeployed across business units. Unavoidably, the responsiveness to the specific characteristics of each business does suffer from this emphasis on coordination.

Yet the loss of responsiveness to business demands is more than compensated by the benefits of resource leveraging. In line with the inside-out perspective discussed in Chapter 5, proponents of the core competence perspective argue that long-term competitiveness depends more on the continual upgrading of unique bundles of resources within a corporation, than on occupying specific market positions. Competitive wars are fought out between corporations, each trying to build better competence bases – skirmishes in particular markets are only battles in this broader war. From this angle, building the corporation's core competences is strategic, while engaging other corporations in specific markets is tactical. The corporate center is therefore the nexus of competitive strategy, instead of the business units, that are literally divisions in the overall campaign. It follows that some loss of responsiveness to specific business pressures is an acceptable price to pay.

The question for the field of strategic management is, therefore, whether multibusiness level strategies should be formed based on the portfolio or the core competence perspective. Should corporate strategists limit themselves to achieving financial synergies, leaving SBU managers to 'mind their own business'? Or should corporate strategists strive to build a multibusiness firm around a shared set of competences, intricately weaving all business units into a highly coordinated whole? In short, strategist have to deal with yet another fundamental challenge, the paradox of responsiveness and synergy.

Defining the Issues: Composition and Coordination

Most strategists agree that the two key questions of corporate strategy are: What businesses should the corporation be in and how should this array of businesses be managed? These two central questions can be referred to as

TABLE 6.1
Portfolio versus core competence perspective

	Portfolio Perspective	Core Competence Perspective
Emphasis on	Responsiveness over synergy	Synergy over responsiveness
View of competition	Firms compete within a business	Corporations compete across businesses
Competitive strategy at	Business level	Corporate level
Key success factor	Responsiveness to business demands	Competence leveraging
Corporate composition	Potentially unrelated (diverse)	Shared competence-base (focused)
Multibusiness synergy	Cash flow optimization	Rapid competence building
Primary task corporate center	Capital allocation to SBUs	Competence development and application
Position of business units	Highly autonomous (independent)	Highly integrated (interdependent)
Coordination between SBU's	Low, incidental	High, structural
Corporate control style	Setting financial objectives	Joint strategy development
Diversification acquisitions	Simple to accommodate	Difficult to integrate

the issues of *composition* and *coordination*. Before proceeding to the readings, the nature of these two issues will first be more closely examined.

The Issue of Corporate Composition

A multibusiness firm is composed of two or more businesses. When a corporation enters yet another line of business, either by starting up new activities (*internal growth*) or by buying another firm (*acquisition*), this is referred to as *diversification*. There are two general categories of diversification moves, *vertical* and *horizontal*. Vertical diversification, usually called *vertical integration*, is when a firm enters other businesses within its own business system – it can strive for backward integration by getting involved in supplier businesses or it can initiate forward integration by entering the businesses of its buyers. When a firm expands outside of its current business system(s), this is referred to as horizontal diversification (see Figure 6.1).

The issue of corporate composition deals with the question whether a firm should diversify, and if so, into which businesses. This issue can be examined by looking at the conditions under which diversification results in value creation. According to Porter (1987) entering into another business (by acquisition or internal growth) can only lead to increased shareholder value if three essential tests are passed:

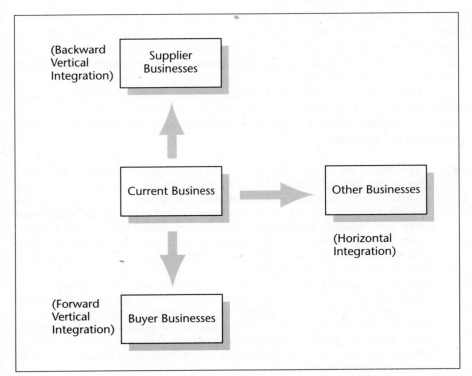

FIGURE 6.1
Directions of diversification

- *The attractiveness test*. The business 'must be structurally attractive, or capable of being made attractive.' In other words, the business must be potentially profitable (see Chapter 5).

- *The cost-of-entry test*. 'The cost of entry must not capitalize all the future profits.' In other words, it must be possible to recoup the investment made.

- *The better-off test*. 'Either the new unit must gain competitive advantage from its link with the corporation or vice versa.' In other words, it must be possible to create synergy.

It is around this last test that the debate in the area of corporate strategy revolves. What types of synergies can realistically be achieved, without paying a heavier penalty in terms of coordination costs? To answer this question, it must first be clear what synergy is.

For quite some time, strategists have known that potential for synergy has something to do with *relatedness* (Rumelt, 1974). Diversification moves that were 'unrelated', for example a food company's entrance into the bicycle rental business, were deemed to be less profitable, in general, than moves that were related, such as car makers' diversification into the car rental business. However, the problem has been to determine the nature of 'relatedness'. Superficial signs of relatedness do not indicate that there is potential for synergy. Drilling for oil and mining might seem highly related (both are 'extraction businesses'), but Shell found out the hard way that they are not, selling the acquired mining company Billiton to Gencor after they were unable to add value (see the Shell case in Section VI). Chemicals and pharmaceuticals seem like similar businesses (especially if pharmaceuticals are labelled 'specialty chemicals'), but ICI decided to split itself in two (into ICI and Zeneca), because it couldn't achieve sufficient synergy between these two business areas.

Strategists have therefore attempted to pin down the exact nature of relatedness (e.g. Prahalad and Bettis, 1986; Chatterjee, 1986; Ramanujam and Varadarajan, 1989). Two areas of 'potential relatedness' (Nayyar, 1992) are generally identified:

- *Opportunities for resource leveraging*. Two businesses are related if resources can be productively shared between them. All types of resources can be shared, both tangible and intangible. Resource leveraging can be achieved in three ways. First, resources can be physically transferred from one business unit to the other, where better use can be made of them (*resource reallocation*). For instance, money and personnel are often shifted between business units, depending on where they are needed. Second, resources can be copied from one business unit to the other, so that the same resource can be used many times over (*resource replication*). This happens, for example, when competences are copied between business units. Third, resources can be employed simultaneously by two or more business units, where joint use is more efficient and/or more effective (*resource pooling*). For instance, business units can initiate shared activities, such as production or marketing, or can make use of the same brand name.

■ *Opportunities for strategy alignment.* Two businesses are related if the alignment of their market strategies creates added-value. Coordinated behavior
   between business units can be preferable to independent, uncoordinated
   behavior under a number of circumstances. Horizontally related business
   units working together as a team can often multiply their effective market
   power by 'ganging up' on competitors, buyers or suppliers. Coordination
   within one firm can also prevent a number of business units from fighting
   fiercely amongst one another, which might have happened if all units
   were independent companies. Vertically related business units linked to
   each other in one firm may also be preferable to independent buyers and
   suppliers. Especially where close vertical cooperation is needed and
   relation-specific investments need to be made, *vertical integration* has a
   high potential for synergy, by avoiding the threats of mistrust and power
   misuse.

In this chapter the focus is on the potential for resource leveraging across
business units. The advantages and disadvantages of strategy alignment
across businesses are studied in more depth in Chapter 7.

The Issue of Corporate Coordination

Coordination is about attaining the potential synergies. In other words, the
question is how the business units must be managed to achieve the
envisioned added value. Recognizing the possible benefits of working
together under a corporate umbrella is one thing, but developing coordination mechanisms that do not cost more than they yield is another. Therefore, corporate strategists need to carefully design organizational systems
that facilitate resource leveraging and/or strategy alignment, without
excessive costs in terms of overhead, bureaucracy, slow decision-making,
political infighting and bland compromises.

Many forms of coordination exist and many classifications have been
put forward (e.g. Mintzberg, 1979; Govindarajan, 1988). For the debate in
this chapter, however, the most important distinction is between cooperation and control mechanisms (see Figure 6.2).

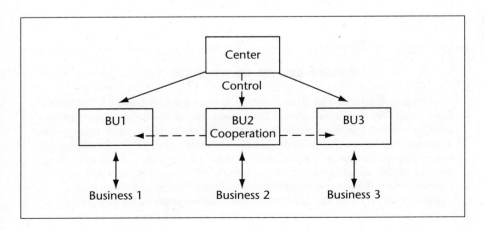

FIGURE 6.2
Corporate coordination
mechanisms

- *Control mechanisms*. An obvious way to facilitate resource leveraging and strategy alignment across businesses is to appoint someone as coordinator and to place that person hierarchically above the units that need to be coordinated. Such a central figure (a division-level or corporate-level manager), with formal power over the individual business units, can then enforce coordination by hierarchical control. Such control can be exerted in many ways. It can be *direct* (telling business units what to do), but often it is more indirect, by giving business units objectives that must be met. Campbell and Goold (1988; reading 6.5) distinguish between financial and strategic objectives. The negotiation, setting and monitoring of financial objectives is referred to as *financial control*, while they speak of *strategic control* when the guiding objectives are of a strategic nature.

- *Cooperation mechanisms*. Coordination between business units can also be achieved without the use of hierarchical authority. Business units might be willing to cooperate because it is in their interest to do so, or because they recognize the overall corporate interests. If business units believe in the importance of certain synergies, sometimes identifying these potential synergies themselves, this can be a powerful impetus to coordinate. Corporate strategists interested in such coordination by mutual adjustment will focus on creating the organizational circumstances under which such *self-organization* can take place (see Chapters 3 and 4). For instance, they might strengthen formal and informal ties between the business units, to enhance mutual understanding and encourage the exchange of ideas and joint initiatives. They may also support cross-business career paths and try to instil a corporation-wide culture, to facilitate the communication between business units.

It is the task of the corporate strategist to determine the right mix of control and cooperation mechanisms, needed to bring about the synergies envisioned. Of course, which mechanisms are emphasized depends on the perspective taken by the corporate center. Advocates of the portfolio perspective, arguing that very little coordination is needed at all, strongly prefer arm's length financial control over more direct interference and 'fuzzy' cooperation. Proponents of the core competence perspective, believing in the importance of tight coordination, stress the need for directer control by the corporate center, supported by strong cooperation mechanisms.

EXHIBIT 6.1
Philips Short Case

PHILIPS: REWIRE OR SHORTCIRCUIT?

On October 1st 1996, Cor Boonstra took over as president and CEO of Philips Electronics NV, headquartered in Eindhoven, the Netherlands. Boonstra had only joined the top management team at Philips in 1994, after leaving the American fast-moving consumer goods company, Sara Lee. His appointment was a surprise to many, both in and outside the company, as he edged out internal Philips candidates and other recently hired industry outsiders, such as Pierre Everaert (from food-retailing multinational Ahold) and Henk Bodt (from copier-maker Océ van der Grinten). In the business press it was suggested that

Boonstra had been selected because of his strong marketing background, ability to make tough decisions and lack of emotional and political attachment to the current Philips businesses and way of doing things.

Boonstra succeeded Jan Timmer, under whose leadership Philips had been pulled back from the brink of collapse. When taking the helm in 1990, Timmer had been confronted with a severe crisis, brought on by intense competition in most of the industries in which Philips was active, and compounded by a high level of bureaucracy and political infighting. Timmer, a long-time company man, had built up a reputation for restructuring ailing divisions and was appointed to apply the same medicine to the entire company. He initiated a major restructuring plan, code-named 'Operation Centurion,' involving major cost and job cutting programs. Throughout its world-wide operations, Philips chopped 59,000 jobs, most of them in high-cost regions, such as North America and Europe, reducing the work force to a level of 238,000 at the beginning of 1995. Timmer also gave the company some financial breathing space by divesting non-core activities. The white goods division (mainly refrigerators and washing machines) was sold to Whirlpool and a minority stake in the Japanese electronics giant Matsushita was sold back to this company.

Due to these efforts, the $2.3 billion loss (including restructuring costs) suffered in 1990, had been transformed into a modest profit by 1994, allowing Philips to pay a small dividend to its shareholders for the first time in four years. Three of the five product sectors (Light, Other Consumer Products, and Components and Semiconductors) were profitable, while the other two product sectors (Consumer Electronics and Professional Products) still showed negative results (for a large part due to problems within their German Grundig subsidiary).

While the emphasis of the Centurion program had been on operational efficiency, Timmer had also endorsed a number of high profile new product initiatives, to ensure future areas of growth. Especially in Philips' key consumer electronics division new products were needed to compensate for the low growth and cut-throat competition in the 'traditional' product groups, such as televisions, radios, and audio and video equipment. In this area, three new initiatives were launched. To reinvigorate sales in the area of television, Philips took a leading role in the development of high definition television (HDTV); to bring cassette players into the digital age, Philips introduced the digital compact cassette (DCC) player; and as a venture into the world of multimedia, Philips created the interactive CD player (CD-I). However, as Boonstra took over from Timmer, he was forced to conclude that none of these innovations had evolved into the blockbuster products needed to revive Philips', and the industry's, fortunes. Neither did Timmer's decision to pour hundreds of millions of guilders into the fast-growing mobile telephones market result in a strong profit-generator for the future. As a late entrant into this industry, Philips was finding it just too difficult to catch up with the top three, Ericsson, Nokia and Motorola.

Unfortunately, Philips' move into 'software' creation and distribution hadn't proven to be particularly successful either. The purchase in 1991 of Superclub, the video rental chain with 430 stores in the US and 86 stores in Europe (mostly in Belgium) was very costly, especially due to unforeseen reorganization costs. In 1993 the American stores were sold. Philips also invested in the acquisition of television cable companies, particularly in the Netherlands, spending approximately a billion guilders ($600 million). However, these holdings were fragmented geographically, and didn't help to turn Timmer's pet project, a cable sports channel called Sport7, into a success. The channel, in which Philips had a minority stake, and of which Timmer was chairman, went bankrupt in 1996, after only a few months. Only Philips' music company PolyGram, already in the business of 'content,' was moderately successful in its diversification into the motion picture industry. When compared to the track records of Philips' arch rivals Sony and Matsushita, who both lost billions of dollars by acquiring major Hollywood film studios, PolyGram's results look even better.

Given these developments, it was clear to Boonstra that besides continued cost cutting, significant strategic changes would have to be made. Obviously, at the business level Philips would need to improve its competitive position and find growth oppportunities, despite the intense rivalry and sluggish demand in many of its markets. Particularly worrying were the comsumer electronics business units and the medical products (due to reduced health care budgets). At the corporate level, the tough choices confronting Boonstra were even more challenging. Overseeing this strongly diversified company, with 60 different units, Boonstra had to ask himself why the company existed in its current composition. What was the 'wiring' keeping the corporation together and was it actually creating added-value? Wouldn't Philips be worth more to its shareholders split up and sold to the highest bidder, than kept together as one firm? Maybe less drastically than a split up, Philips should divest certain business units or even entire divisions?

In other words, Boonstra had to grapple with the task of determining what Philips' core businesses should be and what types of synergies he wished to pursue between these businesses. The company's array of businesses was quite wide. Within the product sector consumer electronics (34 percent of sales), Philips was divided into Sound & Vision (television, audio, video and personal communication), Car Systems (car stereo, car navigation, automotive electronics), Business Electronics (monitors, broadcast TV systems, video distribution networks, digital video communication, dictation systems), and Grundig (TV, audio, video, car stereo and professional electronics). The Other Consumer Products sector (19 percent of sales) consisted of Domestic Appliances and Personal Care (vacuum cleaners, irons, air cleaners, shavers, hair dryers, electric toothbrushes, etc.), Philips Media (software, services, interactive media systems and cable television systems) and PolyGram. Professional Products and Systems (13 percent of sales) was another diverse product sector, spanning Medical Systems (x-ray, tomography, magnetic resonance, ultrasound, and radiotherapy), Communication Systems (business communication, personal communication, wide-area paging, smart cards and private mobile radio), and Industrial Electronics (x-ray, communication and security systems, electronic manufacturing technology, electron optics, automation systems, weighing systems and integrated projects). The sector Components and Semiconductors (17 percent of sales), true to its name, contained Components (display, passive components, magnetic products, active-matrix LCDs, LCD cells, and key modules) and Semiconductors. Lighting (13 percent of sales) was a distinct sector (lamps, luminaries, lighting electronics, automotive lamps and batteries), while the company also had a category Miscellaneous (e.g. ASM Lithography, Philips Plastics and Metalware Factories).

Could resources be leveraged more effectively across such a variety of businesses without succumbing to even more bureaucracy than already burdening Philips? One of the first things Boonstra had noticed when entering Philips was that there were too many layers of middle management 'clay' in which initiatives tended to get stuck. Should the solution be to de-emphasize cross-business coordination and to liberate the business units from the shackles of corporate interference, so that they can get on with their own business? In short, should Boonstra attempt to 'rewire' Philips into a more integrated company, or would a 'shortcircuiting' of the company be fine, leaving each business to operate autonomously as a stand alone unit? Which ever way it went, it promised to be an electrifying time.

Sources: *Fortune*, March 31, 1997; *Advertising Age*, November, 1996; *Electronic Business Today*, February, 1997.

The Debate and the Readings

To open the debate on behalf of the portfolio perspective, Barry Hedley's reading 'Strategy and the Business Portfolio' has been selected. Hedley was an early proponent of the portfolio perspective, together with other consultants from the Boston Consulting Group (BCG), such as Bruce Henderson (1979). In this contribution, he explains the strategic principles underlying the famed growth-share grid, that it commonly known as the BCG matrix. His argument is based on the premise that a complex corporation can be viewed as a portfolio of businesses, that each have their own competitive arena to which they must be responsive. By disaggregating a corporation into its business unit components, separate strategies can be devised for each. The overarching role of the corporate level can then be defined as that of portfolio manager. The major task of the corporate head-quarters is to manage the allocation of scarce financial resources over the business units, to achieve the highest returns at an acceptable level of risk. Each business unit can be given a strategic mission to grow, hold or milk, depending on their prospects compared to the businesses in the corporate portfolio. This is where portfolio analysis comes in. Hedley argues that the profit and growth potential of each business unit depends on two key variables: the growth rate of the total business and the relative market share of the business unit within its business. When these two variables are put together in a grid, this forms the BCG matrix. This graphical tool can be used to visualize the composition of the corporation and to determine the position of each of the business units. For the discussion in this chapter, the precise details of the BCG portfolio technique are less relevant than the basic corporate strategy perspective that Hedley advocates – running the multi-business firm as a hands-on investor.

Selecting a representative for the core competence perspective was a simple choice. In 1990, C.K. Prahalad and Gary Hamel published an article in *Harvard Business Review* with the title 'The Core Competence of the Corporation.' This has had a profound impact on the debate surrounding the topic of corporate strategy, and has inspired a considerable amount of research and writing taking a core competence perspective. Obviously, this article has been selected as reading 6.2. In this contribution, and in their subsequent book, *Competing for the Future*, Prahalad and Hamel explicitly dismiss the portfolio perspective as a viable approach to corporate strategy. Prahalad and Hamel acknowledge that diversified corporations have a portfolio of businesses, but they do not believe that this implies the need for a portfolio management approach, in which the business units are highly autonomous. In their view, 'the primacy of the SBU – an organizational dogma for a generation – is now clearly an anachronism.' Drawing mainly on Japanese examples, they carry on to argue that corporations should be built around a core of shared competences (note that one of the few Western companies they mention is Philips, featured in Exhibit 6.1 above). Business units should use and help to further develop these core competences. The consequence is that the role of the corporate level is much more far reaching than in the portfolio perspective. The corporate center must 'establish objectives for competence building' and must ensure that this 'strategic architecture' is carried through.

To complement the initial arguments brought forward by the first discussants, three additional readings have been included in this chapter. The first of these is intended to bring forward the issue of acquisitions, to which both opening articles pay less attention. Mergers and acquisitions, and their opposites, demergers and divestments, are an important – maybe the most important – method for changing a corporation's composition. Understanding whether growth through acquisition is a feasible approach, and if so, how it should be carried out, is a prominent aspect of the corporate strategy debate. The reading selected to stir up the debate on the merits of acquisition has been taken from Mark Sirower's provocative book *The Synergy Trap: How Companies Lose the Acquisition Game.* Sirower skilfully combines strategic management theory with insights from financial economics and industrial organization literature, to explore the meaning of the term synergy. The conclusion he reaches, based on his quantitative research, is that on average acquisitions do not lead to synergy – acquisitions are a trap. 'Acquiring firms destroy shareholder value. This is a plain fact.' Sirower reports that this sobering finding has also been confirmed by researchers in the field of industrial organization (e.g. Ravenscraft and Scherer, 1989). He then goes on to outline the criteria that strategists must meet to make a successful acquisition. For the discussion in this chapter, Sirower raises an important issue. If it is difficult to predict the potential benefits of an acquisition and even more difficult to realize them, should corporations get involved in 'the acquisition game' at all? And what would that mean for their choice of corporate strategy perspective?

Reading 6.4 is 'The Value of the Parent Company,' by Andrew Campbell, Michael Goold and Marcus Alexander. These researchers from the Ashridge Strategic Management Centre have been responsible for a constant stream of work on corporate strategy. One of their most recent publications has been the book *Corporate-Level Strategy: Creating Value in the Multibusiness Company,* of which this contribution is a summary. Their contribution to the debate is that they focus attention on the role of the corporate center. They pose the question under what circumstances it is justified to bring a business unit under the wings of a 'parent company.' In their view, it is only to the benefit of business units to be part of a larger corporate whole if the parent company can create value – preferably more value than any other parent company could. They argue that parent companies that have a superior ability to create additional value for a business possess a parenting advantage. They continue by outlining the ways in which parent organizations can create value and what the consequences are for the issues of composition and coordination. In the context of this debate, it is important to note that Campbell, Goold and Alexander do not necessarily side with either of the two perspectives. Their examples of successful corporations include a core competence-oriented company such as Canon, but also a portfolio-oriented company such as BTR. Both approaches can be successful, if the corporate center has the parenting capabilities needed to create the value envisioned.

Reading 6.5, 'Adding Value from Corporate Headquarters,' is also by Andrew Campbell and Michael Goold, and is a summary of their influential book *Strategies and Styles: The Role of the Centre in Managing Diverse Corporations.* This has been selected to place a stronger emphasis on the issue of corporate coordination in the debate. Many of the authors on the topic of corporate strategy focus their attention on the issue of composition – should diversification be related and is acquisition the best means? The issue of how a multibusiness firm should actually be structured and managed has been much less studied. In this article, however, Campbell and Goold pay explicit attention to the variety of possible corporate management styles. Their view is that there are 'many best ways to make corporate strategy.' In their study of 16 large, diversified British companies, they witnessed the successful application of different corporate management styles, spanning the spectrum between portfolio-oriented autonomous business units and core competence-oriented integration. Their conclusion is that there are circumstances where a *financial control* style is more fitting (roughly coinciding with the portfolio perspective, while other situations require more interdependencies between the business units and hence a stronger involvement of the corporate center in managing coordination (the *strategic control* and *strategic planning* styles). Goold and Campbell stress that each style of managing corporate strategy has benefits and drawbacks, of which the strategist should be aware when deciding which style to adopt. For the debate, however, the question remains whether each approach is equally valid, or whether one perspective should be preferred over the other when dealing with the paradox of responsiveness and synergy.

6.1   Strategy and the Business Portfolio

By Barry Hedley[1]

All except the smallest and simplest companies comprise more than one business. Even when a company operates within a single broad business area, analysis normally reveals that it is, in practice, involved in a number of product-market segments which are distinct economically. These must be considered separately for purposes of strategy development.

The fundamental determinant of strategy success for each individual business segment is relative competitive position. As a result of the experience curve effect the competitor with high market share in the segment relative to competition should be able to develop the lowest cost position and hence the highest and most stable profits. This will be true regardless of changes in the economic environment. Hence relative competitive position the appropriately defined business segment forms a simple but sound strategic goal. Almost invariably, any company which reviews its various businesses carefully in this light will discover that they occupy widely differing relative competitive positions. Some businesses will be competitively strong already, and may appear to present no strategic problem; others will be weak, and the company must face the question of whether it would be worthwhile to attempt to improve their position, making whatever investments might be required to achieve this; if this is not done, the company can only expect poor performance from the business and the best option economically will be divestment.

Even in quite small companies, the total number of possible combinations of individual business strategies can be extremely large. The difficulty of making a firm final choice on strategy for each business is normally compounded by the fact that most companies must operate within constraints established by limited resources, particularly cash resources.

The Business Portfolio Concept

At its most basic, the importance of growth in shaping strategy choice is twofold. First, the growth of a business is a major factor influencing the

[1] Source: This article was adapted with permission from 'Strategy and the "Business Portfolio"', *Long Range Planning*, Vol. 10, February 1977, pp. 9–15.

likely ease – and hence cost of gaining market share. In low-growth businesses, any market share gained will tend to require an actual volume reduction in competitors' sales. This will be very obvious to the competitors and they are likely to fight to prevent the throughput in their plants dropping. In high-growth businesses, on the other hand, market share can be gained steadily merely by securing the largest share of the growth in the business: expanding capacity earlier than the competitors, ensuring product availability and effective selling support despite the strains imposed by the *growth*, and so forth. Meanwhile competitors may even be unaware of their share loss because their actual volume of throughput has been well maintained. Even if aware of their loss of share, the competitors may be unconcerned by it given that their plants are still well loaded. This is particularly true of competitors who do not understand the strategic importance of market share for long term profitability resulting from the experience curve effect.

An unfortunate example of this is given by the history of the British motorcycle industry. British market share was allowed to erode in motorcycles world-wide for more than a decade, throughout which the British factories were still fairly full: British motorcycle production volumes held up at around 80,000 units per year throughout the sixties; in sharp contrast, Japanese export volumes leapt from only about 60,000 in 1960 to 2.5 million in 1973; their total production volumes roughly tripled in the same period. The long term effect was that while Japanese real costs were falling rapidly British costs were not: somewhat oversimplified, this is why the British motorcycle industry faced bankruptcy in the early seventies.

The second important factor concerning growth is the opportunity it provides for investment. Growth businesses provide the ideal vehicles for investment, for ploughing cash into a business in order to see it compound and return even larger amounts of cash at a later point in time. Of course this opportunity is also a need: the faster a business grows, the more investment it will require just to maintain market share. Yet the experience curve effect means that this is essential if its profitability is not to decline over time.

Whilst these growth considerations affect the rate at which a business will use cash, the relative competitive position of the business will determine the rate at which the business will generate cash: the stronger the company's position relative to its competitors the higher its margins should be, as a result of the experience curve effect. The simplest measure of relative competitive position is, of course, relative market share. A company's relative market share in a business can be defined as its market share in the business divided by that of the largest other competitor. Thus only the biggest competitor has a relative market share greater than one. All the other competitors should enjoy lower profitability and cash generation than the leader.

The Growth-Share Matrix

Individual businesses can have very different financial characteristics and face different strategic options depending on how they are placed in terms of growth and relative competitive position. Businesses can basically fall into any one of four broad strategic categories, as depicted schematically in the growth-share matrix in Figure 6.1.1.

■   *Stars*. High growth, high share – are in the upper left quadrant. Growing rapidly, they use large amounts of cash to maintain position. They are also leaders in the business, however, and should generate large amounts of cash. As a result, star businesses are frequently roughly in balance on net cash flow, and can be self-sustaining in growth terms. They represent probably the best profit growth and investment opportunities available to the company, and every effort should therefore be made to maintain and consolidate their competitive position. This will sometimes require heavy investment beyond their own generation capabilities and low margins may be essential at times to deter competition, but this is almost invariably worthwhile for the longer term: when the growth slows, as it ultimately does in all businesses, very large cash returns will be obtained if share has been maintained so that the business drops into the lower left quadrant of the matrix, becoming a cash cow. If star businesses fail to hold share, which frequently happens if the attempt is made to net large amounts of cash from them in the short and medium term (e.g. by cutting back on investment and raising prices, creating an 'umbrella' for competitors), they will ultimately become dogs (lower right quadrant). These are certain losers.

FIGURE 6.1.1
The business portfolio or growth–share matrix

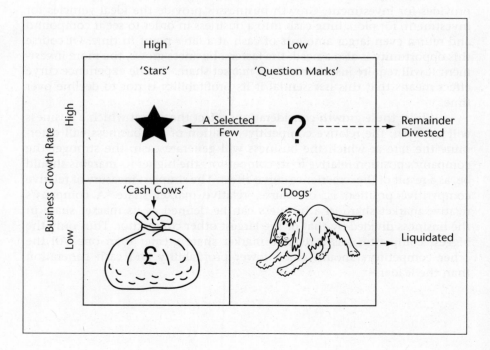

- *Cash cows*. Low growth, high share – should have an entrenched superior market position and low costs. Hence profits and cash generation should be high, and because of the low growth reinvestment needs should be light. Thus large cash surpluses should be generated by these businesses. Cash cows pay the dividends and interest, provide the debt capacity, pay for the company overhead and provide the cash for investment elsewhere in the company's portfolio of businesses. They are the foundation on which the company rests.

- *Dogs*. Low growth, low share – represent a tremendous contrast. Their poor competitive position condemns them to poor profits. Because the growth is low, there is little potential for gaining sufficient share to achieve a viable cost position at anything approaching a reasonable cost. Unfortunately, the cash required for investment in the business just to maintain competitive position, though low, frequently exceeds that generated, especially under conditions of high inflation. The business therefore becomes a 'cash trap' likely to absorb cash perpetually unless further investment in the business is rigorously avoided. The colloquial term dog describing these businesses, though undoubtedly pejorative, is thus rather apt. A company should take every precaution to minimize the proportion of its assets that remain in this category.

- *Question marks*. High growth, low share – have the worst cash characteristics of all. In the upper right quadrant, their cash needs are high because of their growth, but their cash generation is small because of their low share. If nothing is done to change its market share, the question mark will simply absorb large amounts of cash in the short term and later, as the growth slows, become a dog. Following this sort of strategy, the question mark is a cash loser throughout its existence. Managed this way, a question mark becomes the ultimate cash trap.

In fact there is a clear choice between only two strategy alternatives for a question mark, hence the name. Because growth is high, it should be easier and less costly to gain share here than it would be in a lower growth business. One strategy is therefore to make whatever investments are necessary to gain share, to try to fund the business to dominance so that it can become a star and, ultimately a cash cow when the business matures. This strategy will be very costly in the short term – growth rates will be even higher than if share were merely being maintained, and additional marketing and other investments will be required to make the share actually change hands – but it offers the only way of developing a sound business from the question mark over the long term. The only logical alternative is divestment. Outright sale is preferable; but if this is not possible, then a firm decision must be taken not to invest further in the business and it must be allowed simply to generate whatever cash it can while none is reinvested. The business will then decline, possibly quite rapidly if market growth is high, and will have to be shut down at some point. But it will produce cash in the short term and this is greatly preferable to the error of sinking cash into it perpetually without improving its competitive position.

These then, are the four basic categories to which businesses can belong. Some companies tend to fit almost entirely into a single quadrant.

General Motors and English China Clays are examples of predominantly cash cow companies. Chrysler, by comparison, is a dog which compounded its fundamental problem of low share in its domestic US market by acquiring further mature low share competitors in other countries (e.g. Rootes which became Chrysler UK). IBM in computers, Xerox in photocopiers, BSR in low cost record autochangers, are all examples of predominantly star businesses. Xerox's computer operation, XDS, was clearly a question mark, however, and it is not surprising that Xerox recently effectively gave it away free to Honeywell, and considered itself lucky to escape at that price! When RCA closed down its computer operation, it had to sustain a write-off of about $490m. Question marks are costly.

Portfolio Strategy

Most companies have their portfolio of businesses scattered through all four quadrants of the matrix. It is possible to outline quite briefly and simply what the appropriate overall portfolio strategy for such a company should be. The first goal should be to maintain position in the cash cows, but to guard against the frequent temptation to reinvest in them excessively. The cash generated by the cash cows should be used as a first priority to maintain or consolidate position in those stars which are not self sustaining. Any surplus remaining can be used to fund a selected number of question marks to dominance. Most companies will find they have inadequate cash generation to finance market share-gaining strategies in all their question marks. Those which are not funded should be divested either by sale or liquidation over time.

Finally, virtually all companies have at least some dog businesses. There is nothing reprehensible about this, indeed on the contrary, an absence of dogs probably indicates that the company has not been sufficiently adventurous in the past. It is essential, however, that the fundamentally weak strategic position of the dog be recognized for what it is. Occasionally it is possible to restore a dog to viability by a creative business segmentation strategy, rationalizing and specializing the business into a small niche which it can dominate. If this is impossible, however, the only thing which could rescue the dog would be an increase in share taking it to a position comparable to the leading competitors in the segment. This is likely to be unreasonably costly in a mature business, and therefore the only prospect for obtaining a return from a dog is to manage it for cash, cutting off all investment in the business. Management should be particularly wary of expensive 'turn around' plans developed for a dog if these do not involve a significant change in fundamental competitive position. Without this, the dog is a sure loser. An indictment of many corporate managements is not the fact that their companies have dogs in the portfolio, but rather that these dogs are not managed according to logical strategies. The decision to liquidate a business is usually even harder to take than that of entering a new business. It is essential, however, for the long-term vitality and performance of the company overall that it be prepared to do both as the need arises.

Thus the appropriate strategy for a multibusiness company involves striking a balance in the portfolio such that the cash generated by the cash cows, and by those question marks and dogs which are being liquidated, is sufficient to support the company's stars and to fund the selected question marks through to dominance. This pattern of strategies is indicated by the arrows in Figure 6.1.1. Understanding this pattern conceptually is, however, a far cry from being able to implement it in practice. What any Company should do with its own specific businesses is of course a function of the precise shape of the company's portfolio, and the particular opportunities and problems it presents. But how can a clear picture of the company's portfolio be developed?

The Matrix Quantified

Based on careful analysis and research it is normally possible to divide a company into its various business segments appropriately defined for purposes of strategy development. Following this critical first step, it is usually relatively straightforward to determine the overall growth rate of each individual business (i.e. the growth of the market, not the growth of the company within the market), and the company's size (in terms of turnover or assets) and relative competitive position (market share) within the business.

Armed with these data it is possible to develop a precise overall picture of the company's portfolio of businesses graphically. This can greatly facilitate the identification and resolution of the key strategic issues facing the company. It is a particularly useful approach where companies are large, comprising many separate businesses. Such complex portfolios often defy description in more conventional ways.

The nature of the graphical portfolio display is illustrated by the example in Figure 6.1.2. In this chart, growth rate and relative competitive position are plotted on continuous scales. Each circle in the display represents a single business or business segment, appropriately defined. To convey an impression of the relative significance of each business, size is indicated by the area of the circle, which can be made proportional to either turnover or assets employed. Relative competitive position is plotted on a logarithmic scale, in order to be consistent with the experience curve effect, which implies that profit margin or rate of cash generation differences between competitors will tend to be related to the ratio of their relative competitive positions (market shares). A linear axis is used for growth, for which the most generally useful measure is volume growth of the business concerned, as in general rates of cash use should be directly proportional to growth.

The lines dividing the portfolio into four quadrants are inevitably somewhat arbitrary. 'High growth', for example, is taken to include all businesses growing in excess of 10 percent per annum in volume terms. Certainly, above this growth rate market share tends to become fairly fluid and can be made to change hands quite readily. In addition many companies have traditionally employed a figure of 10 percent for their discount rate

FIGURE 6.1.2
Growth rate and relative competitive position

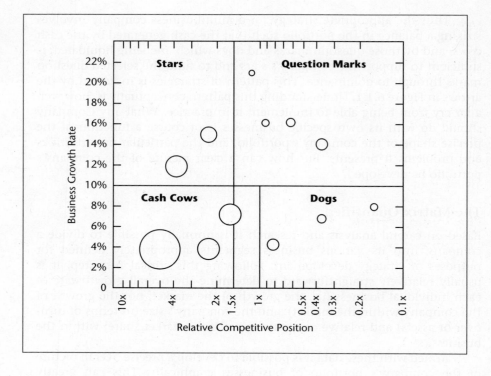

in times of low inflation, and so this also tends to be the growth rate above which investment in market share becomes particularly attractive financially.

The line separating areas of high and low relative competitive position is set at 1.5 times. Experience in using this display has been that in high-growth businesses relative strengths of this magnitude or greater are necessary in order to ensure a sufficiently dominant position that the business will have the characteristic of a star in practice. On the other hand, in low-growth businesses acceptable cash generation characteristics are occasionally, but not always, observed at relative strengths as low as 1 times; hence the addition of a second separating line at 1 times in the low growth area, to reflect this. These lines should, of course, be taken only as approximate guides in characterizing businesses in the portfolio as dogs and question marks, cash cows and stars. In actuality, businesses cover a smooth spectrum across both axes of the matrix. There is obviously no 'magic' which transforms a star into a cash cow as its growth declines from 10.5 to 9.5 percent. It is undeniably useful, however, to have some device for broadly indicating where the transition points occur within the matrix, and the lines suggested here have worked well in practical applications of the matrix in a large number of companies.

Portfolio Approaches in Practice

The company shown in Figure 6.1.2 would be a good example of a potentially well-balanced portfolio. With a firm foundation in the form of two or three substantial cash cows, this company has some well-placed stars to provide growth and to yield high cash returns in the future when they mature. The company also has some question marks, at least two of which are probably sufficiently well placed that they offer a good chance of being funded into star positions at a reasonable cost, not out of proportion to the company's resources. The company is not without dogs, but properly managed there is no reason why these should be a drain on cash.

The Sound Portfolio, Unsoundly Managed

Companies with an attractive portfolio of this kind are not rare in practice. In fact Figure 6.1.2 is a disguised version of a representation of an actual UK company analyzed in the course of a Boston Consulting Group assignment. What is much rarer, however, is to find that the company has made a clear assessment of the matrix positioning and appropriate strategy for each business in the portfolio.

Ideally, one would hope that the company in Figure 6.1.2 would develop strategy along the following lines. For the stars, the key objectives should be the maintenance of market share; current profitability should be accorded a lower priority. For the cash cows, however, current profitability may well be the primary goal. Dogs would not be expected to be as profitable as the cash cows, but would be expected to yield cash. Some question marks would be set objectives in terms of increased market share; others, where gaining dominance appeared too costly, would be managed instead for cash.

The essence of the portfolio approach is therefore that strategy objectives must vary between businesses. The strategy developed for each business must fit its own matrix position and the needs and capabilities of the company's overall portfolio of businesses. In practice, however, it is much more common to find all businesses within a company being operated with a common overall goal in mind. 'Our target in this company is to grow at 10 percent per annum and achieve a return of 10 percent on capital'. This type of overall target is then taken to apply to every business in the company. Cash cows beat the profit target easily, though they frequently miss on growth. Nevertheless, their managements are praised and they are normally rewarded by being allowed to plough back what only too frequently amounts to an excess of cash into their 'obviously attractive' businesses. Attractive businesses, yes: but not for growth investment. Dogs on the other hand rarely meet the profit target. But how often is it accepted that it is in fact unreasonable for them ever to hit the target? On the contrary, the most common strategic mistake is that major investments are made in dogs from time to time in hopeless attempts to turn the business around without actually shifting market share. Unfortunately, only too often question marks are regarded very much as dogs, and get insufficient investment funds ever to bring them to dominance. The question marks usually do receive some investment, however, possibly even enough to maintain share. This is throwing money away into a cash trap. These businesses should either receive enough support to enable them to achieve segment dominance, or none at all.

These are some of the strategic errors which are regularly committed even by companies which have basically sound portfolios. The result is a serious sub-optimization of potential performance in which some businesses (e.g. cash cows) are not being called on to produce the full results of which they are actually capable, and resources are being mistakenly squandered on other businesses (dogs, question marks) in an attempt to make them achieve performance of which they are intrinsically incapable without a fundamental improvement in market share. Where mismanagement of this kind becomes positively dangerous, is when it is applied within the context of a basically unbalanced portfolio.

The Unbalanced Portfolio

The disguised example in Figure 6.1.3 is another actual company. This portfolio is seriously out of balance. As shown in Figure 6.1.3(a), the company has a very high proportion of question marks in its portfolio, and an inadequate base of cash cows. Yet at the time of investigation this company was in fact taking such cash as was being generated by its mature businesses and spreading it out amongst all the high-growth businesses, only one of which was actually receiving sufficient investment to enable it even to maintain share! Thus the overall relative competitive position of the portfolio was on average declining. At the same time, the balance in the portfolio was shifting: as shown in the projected portfolio in Figure 6.1.3(b), because of the higher relative growth of the question marks their overall weight in the portfolio was increasing, making them even harder to fund from the limited resources of the mature businesses.

If the company continued to follow the same strategy of spreading available funds between all the businesses, then the rate of decline could only increase over time leading ultimately to disaster.

This company was caught in a vicious circle of decline. To break out of the circle would require firm discipline and the strength of will to select only one or two of the question marks and finance those, whilst cutting off investment in the remainder. Obviously the choice of which should receive investment involves rather more than selection at random from the portfolio chart. It requires careful analysis of the actual nature of the businesses concerned and particularly the characteristics and behavior of the competitors faced in those businesses. However, the nature of the strategic choice facing the company is quite clear, when viewed in portfolio terms. Without the clarity of view provided by the matrix display, which focuses on the real

FIGURE 6.1.3
An unbalanced portfolio

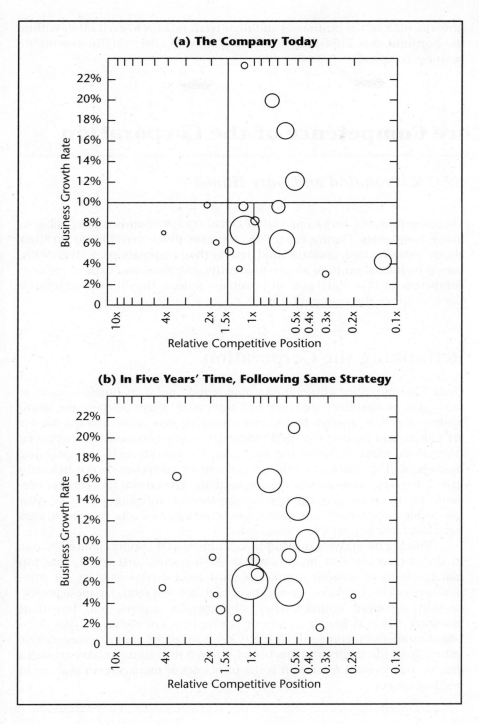

(a) The Company Today

(b) In Five Years' Time, Following Same Strategy

fundamentals of the businesses and their relationships to each other within the portfolio, it is impossible to develop strategy effectively in any multi-business company.

6.2   The Core Competence of the Corporation

By C.K. Prahalad and Gary Hamel[1]

The most powerful way to prevail in global competition is still invisible to many companies. During the 1980s, top executives were judged on their ability to restructure, declutter, and delayer their corporations. In the 1990s, they'll be judged on their ability to identify, cultivate, and exploit the core competencies that make growth possible – indeed, they'll have to rethink the concept of the corporation itself.

Rethinking the Corporation

Once, the diversified corporation could simply point its business units at particular end-product markets and admonish them to become world leaders. But with market boundaries changing ever more quickly, targets are elusive and capture is at best temporary. A few companies have proven themselves adept at inventing new markets, quickly entering emerging markets, and dramatically shifting patterns of customer choice in established markets. These are the ones to emulate. The critical task for management is to create an organization capable of infusing products with irresistible functionality or, better yet, creating products that customers need but have not yet even imagined.

This is a deceptively difficult task. Ultimately, it requires radical change in the management of major companies. It means, first of all, that top managements of western companies must assume responsibility for competitive decline. Everyone knows about high interest rates, Japanese protectionism, outdated antitrust laws, obstreperous unions, and impatient investors. What is harder to see, or harder to acknowledge, is how little added momentum companies actually get from political or macroeconomic 'relief.' Both the theory and practice of Western management have created a drag on our forward motion. It is the principles of management that are in need of reform.

The Roots of Competitive Advantage

In the short run, a company's competitiveness derives from the price/ performance attributes of current products. But the survivors of the first wave of global competition, western and Japanese alike, are all converging on similar and formidable standards for product cost and quality – minimum hurdles for continued competition, but less and less important as sources of differential advantage. In the long run, competitiveness derives from an ability to build, at lower cost and more speedily than competitors, the core competencies that spawn unanticipated products. The real sources of advantage are to be found in management's ability to consolidate corporate-wide technologies and production skills into competencies that empower individual businesses to adapt quickly to changing opportunities.

Senior executives who claim that they cannot build core competencies either because they feel the autonomy of business units is sacrosanct or because their feet are held to the quarterly budget fire should think again. The problem in many western companies is not that their senior executives are any less capable than those in Japan or that Japanese companies possess greater technical capabilities. Instead, it is their adherence to a concept of the corporation that unnecessarily limits the ability of individual businesses to fully exploit the deep reservoir of technological capability that many American and European companies possess.

The diversified corporation is a large tree. The trunk and major limbs are core products, the smaller branches are business units; the leaves, flowers, and fruit are end products. The root system that provides nourishment, sustenance, and stability is the core competence. You can miss the strength of competitors by looking only at their end products, in the same way you miss the strength of a tree if you look only at its leaves (see Figure 6.2.1).

Core competencies are the collective learning in the organization, especially how to coordinate diverse production skills and integrate multiple streams of technologies. Consider Sony's capacity to miniaturize or Philips's optical-media expertise. The theoretical knowledge to put a radio on a chip does not in itself assure a company the skill to produce a miniature radio no bigger than a business card. To bring off this feat, Casio must harmonize know-how in miniaturization, microprocessor design, materials science, and ultrathin precision casing – the same skills it applies in its miniature card calculators, pocket TVs, and digital watches.

If core competence is about harmonizing streams of technology, it is also about the organization of work and the delivery of value. Among Sony's competencies is miniaturization. To bring miniaturization to its products, Sony must ensure that technologists, engineers, and marketers have a shared understanding of customer needs and of technological possibilities. The force of core competence is felt as decisively in services as in manufacturing. Citicorp was ahead of others investing in an operating system that allowed it to participate in world markets 24 hours a day. Its competence in

FIGURE 6.2.1
Competencies as the roots
of competitiveness

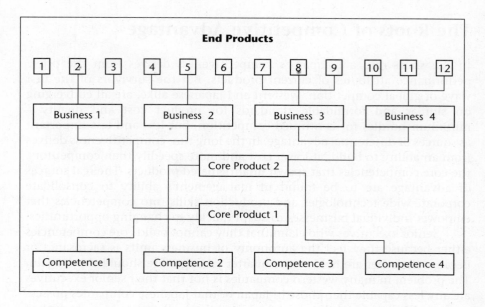

systems has provided the company the means to differentiate itself from many financial service institutions.

Core competence is communication, involvement, and a deep commitment to working across organizational boundaries. It involves many levels of people and all functions. World-class research in, for example, lasers or ceramics can take place in corporate laboratories without having an impact on any of the businesses of the company. The skills that together constitute core competence must coalesce around individuals whose efforts are not so narrowly focused that they cannot recognize the opportunities for blending their functional expertise with those of others in new and interesting ways.

Core competence does not diminish with use. Unlike physical assets, which do deteriorate over time, competencies are enhanced as they are applied and shared. But competencies still need to be nurtured and protected; knowledge fades if it is not used. Competencies are the glue that binds existing businesses. They are also the engine for new business development. Patterns of diversification and market entry may be guided by them, not just by the attractiveness of markets.

Consider 3M's competence with sticky tape. In dreaming up businesses as diverse as 'Post-it' note pads, magnetic tape, photographic film, pressure-sensitive tapes, and coated abrasives, the company has brought to bear widely shared competencies in substrates, coatings, and adhesives and devised various ways to combine them. Indeed, 3M has invested consistently in them. What seems to be an extremely diversified portfolio of businesses belies a few shared core competencies.

In contrast, there are major companies that have had the potential to build core competencies but failed to do so because top management was unable to conceive of the company as anything other than a collection of discrete businesses. General Electric sold much of its consumer electronics business to Thomson of France, arguing that it was becoming increasingly difficult to maintain its competitiveness in this sector. That was undoubtedly so, but it is ironic that it sold several key businesses to competitors who were already competence leaders – Black & Decker in small electrical motors, and Thomson, which was eager to build its competence in microelectronics and had learned from the Japanese that a position in consumer electronics was vital to this challenge.

Management trapped in the strategic business unit (SBU) mind-set almost inevitably finds its individual businesses dependent on external sources for critical components, such as motors or compressors. But these are not just components. They are core products that contribute to the competitiveness of a wide range of end products. They are the physical embodiments of core competencies.

How Not to Think of Competence

Since companies are in a race to build the competencies that determine global leadership, successful companies have stopped imagining themselves as bundles of businesses making products. Canon, Honda, Casio, or NEC may seem to preside over portfolios of businesses unrelated in terms of customers, distribution channels, and merchandising strategy. Indeed, they have portfolios that may seem idiosyncratic at times: NEC is the only global company to be among leaders in computing, telecommunications, and semiconductors *and* to have a thriving consumer electronics business.

But looks are deceiving. In NEC, digital technology, especially VLSI and systems integration skills, is fundamental. In the core competencies underlying them, disparate businesses become coherent. It is Honda's core competence in engines and power trains that gives it a distinctive advantage in car, motorcycle, lawn mower, and generator businesses. Canon's core competencies in optics, imaging, and microprocessor controls have enabled it to enter, even dominate, markets as seemingly diverse as copiers, laser printers, cameras, and image scanners. Philips worked for more than 15 years to perfect its optical-media (laser disc) competence, as did JVC in building a leading position in video recording. Other examples of core competencies might include mechantronics (the ability to marry mechanical and electronic engineering), video displays, bioengineering, and microelectronics. In the early stages of its competence building, Philips could not have imagined all the products that would be spawned by its optical-media competence, nor could JVC have anticipated miniature camcorders when it first began exploring videotape technologies.

Unlike the battle for global brand dominance, which is visible in the world's broadcast and print media and is aimed at building global 'share of mind,' the battle to build world-class competencies is invisible to people who aren't deliberately looking for it. Top management often tracks the cost and quality of competitors' products, yet how many managers untangle the web of alliances their Japanese competitors have constructed to acquire competencies at low cost? In how many western boardrooms is there an explicit, shared understanding of the competencies the company must build for world leadership? Indeed, how many senior executives discuss the crucial distinction between competitive strategy at the level of a business and competitive strategy at the level of an entire company?

Let us be clear. Cultivating core competence does not mean outspending rivals on research and development. In 1983, when Canon surpassed Xerox in world-wide unit market share in the copier business, its R&D budget in reprographics was but a small fraction of Xerox's. Over the past 20 years, NEC has spent less on R&D as a percentage of sales than almost all of its American and European competitors.

Nor does core competence mean shared costs, as when two or more SBUs use a common facility – a plant, service facility, or sales force – or share a common component. The gains of sharing may be substantial, but the search for shared costs is typically a post hoc effort to rationalize production across existing businesses, not a premeditated effort to build the competencies out of which the businesses themselves grow.

Building core competencies is more ambitious and different than integrating vertically, moreover. Managers deciding whether to make or buy will start with end products and look upstream to the efficiencies of the supply chain and downstream toward distribution and customers. They do not take inventory of skills and look forward to applying them in nontraditional ways. (Of course, decisions about competencies *do* provide a logic for vertical integration. Canon is not particularly integrated in its copier business, except in those aspects of the vertical chain that support the competencies it regards as critical.)

Identifying Core Competencies – And Losing Them

At least three tests can be applied to identify core competencies in a company. First, a core competence provides potential access to a wide variety of markets. Competence in display systems, for example, enables a company to participate in such diverse businesses as calculators, miniature TV sets, monitors for laptop computers, and automotive dashboards – which is why Casio's entry into the handheld TV market was predictable. Second, a core competence should make a significant contribution to the perceived customer benefits of the end product. Clearly, Honda's engine expertise fills this bill.

Finally, a core competence should be difficult for competitors to imitate. And it will be difficult if it is a complex harmonization of individual technologies and production skills. A rival might acquire some of the technologies that comprise the core competence, but it will find it more difficult to duplicate the more-or-less comprehensive pattern of internal coordination and learning. JVC's decision in the early 1960s to pursue the development of a videotape competence passed the three tests outlined here. RCA's decision in the late 1970s to develop a stylus-based video turntable system did not.

Few companies are likely to build world leadership in more than five or six fundamental competencies. A company that compiles a list of 20 to 30 capabilities has probably not produced a list of core competencies. Still, it is probably a good discipline to generate a list of this sort and to see aggregate capabilities as building blocks. This tends to prompt the search for licensing deals and alliances through which the company may acquire, at low cost, the missing pieces.

Most western companies hardly think about competitiveness in these terms at all. It is time to take a tough-minded look at the risks they are running. Companies that judge competitiveness, their own and their competitors', primarily in terms of the price/performance of end products are courting the erosion of core competencies – or making too little effort to enhance them. The embedded skills that give rise to the next generation of competitive products cannot be 'rented in' by outsourcing and original equipment manufacturer (OEM) supply relationships. In our view, too many companies have unwittingly surrendered core competencies when they cut internal investment in what they mistakenly thought were just 'cost centers' in favor of outside suppliers.

Of course, it is perfectly possible for a company to have a competitive product line up but be a laggard in developing core competencies – at least for a while. If a company wanted to enter the copier business today, it would find a dozen Japanese companies more than willing to supply copiers on the basis of an OEM private label. But when fundamental technologies changed or if its supplier decided to enter the market directly and become a competitor, that company's product line, along with all of its investments in marketing and distribution, could be vulnerable. Outsourcing can provide a shortcut to a more competitive product, but it typically contributes little to building the people-embodied skills that are needed to sustain product leadership.

Nor is it possible for a company to have an intelligent alliance or sourcing strategy if it has not made a choice about where it will build competence leadership. Clearly, Japanese companies have benefited from alliances. They've used them to learn from western partners who were not fully committed to preserving core competencies of their own. Learning within an alliance takes a positive commitment of resources – travel, a pool of dedicated people, test-bed facilities, time to internalize and test what has been learned. A company may not make this effort if it doesn't have clear goals for competence building.

Another way of losing is forgoing opportunities to establish competencies that are evolving in existing businesses. In the 1970s and 1980s, many American and European companies – like General Electric, Motorola, GTE, Thorn, and General Electric Company (GEC) – chose to exit the color television business, which they regard as mature. If by 'mature' they meant that they had run out of new product ideas at precisely the moment global rivals had targeted the TV business for entry, then yes, the industry was mature. But it certainly wasn't mature in the sense that all opportunities to enhance and apply video-based competencies had been exhausted.

In ridding themselves of their television businesses, these companies failed to distinguish between divesting the business and destroying their video media-based competencies. They not only got out of the TV business but they also closed the door on a whole stream of future opportunities reliant on video-based competencies.

There are two clear lessons here. First, the costs of losing a core competence can be only partly calculated in advance. The baby may be thrown out with the bath water in divestment decisions. Second, since core competencies are built through a process of continuous improvement and enhancement that may span a decade or longer, a company that has failed to invest in core competence building will find it very difficult to enter an emerging market, unless, of course, it will be content simply to serve as a distribution channel.

American semiconductor companies like Motorola learned this painful lesson when they elected to forgo direct participation in the 256k generation of DRAM chips. Having skipped this round, Motorola, like most of its American competitors, needed a large infusion of technical help from Japanese partners to rejoin the battle in the 1-megabyte generation. When it comes to core competencies, it is difficult to get off the train, walk to the next station, and then reboard.

From Core Competencies to Core Products

The tangible link between identified core competencies and end products is what we call the core products – the physical embodiments of one or more core competencies. Honda's engines, for example, are core products, linchpins between design and development skills that ultimately lead to a proliferation of end products. Core products are the components or sub-assemblies that actually contribute to the value of the end products. Thinking in terms of core products forces a company to distinguish between the brand share it achieves in end product markets (for example, 40 percent of the US refrigerator market) and the manufacturing share it achieves in any particular core product (for example, five percent of the world share of compressor output).

It is essential to make this distinction between core competencies, core products, and end products because global competition is played out by different rules and for different stakes at each level. To build or defend leadership over the long term, a corporation will probably be a winner at each level. At the level of core competence, the goal is to build world leadership in the design and development of a particular class of product functionality – be it compact data storage and retrieval, as with Philips's optical-media competence, or compactness and ease of use, as with Sony's micromotors and microprocessor controls.

To sustain leadership in their chosen core competence areas, these companies *seek to maximize their world manufacturing share in core products*. The manufacture of core products for a wide variety of external (and internal) customers yields the revenue and market feedback that, at least partly, determines the pace at which core competencies can be enhanced and extended. This thinking was behind JVC's decision in the mid-1970s to establish VCR supply relationships with leading national consumer electronics companies in Europe and the United States. In supplying Thomson, Thorn, and Telefunken (all independent companies at that time) as well as US partners, JVC was able to gain the cash and the diversity of market experience that ultimately enabled it to outpace Philips and Sony. (Philips developed videotape competencies in parallel with JVC, but it failed to build a world-wide network of OEM relationships that would have allowed it to accelerate the refinement of its videotape competence through the sale of core products.)

JVC's success has not been lost on Korean companies like Goldstar, Samsung, Kia, and Daewoo, who are building core product leadership in areas as diverse as displays, semiconductors, and automotive engines through their OEM-supply contracts with Western companies. Their avowed goal is to capture investment initiative away from potential competitors, often US companies. In doing so, they accelerate their competence-building efforts while 'hollowing out' their competitors. By focusing on competence and embedding it in core products, Asian competitors have built up advantages in component markets first and have then leveraged off their superior products to move downstream to build brand share. And they are not likely to remain the low-cost suppliers forever. As their reputation for brand leadership is consolidated, they may well gain price leadership. Honda has proven this with its Acura line, and other Japanese carmakers are following suit.

Control over core products is critical for other reasons. A dominant position in core products allows a company to shape the evolution of applications and end markets. Such compact audio disc-related core products as data drives and lasers have enabled Sony and Philips to influence the evolution of the computer-peripheral business in optical-media storage. As a company multiplies the number of application arenas for its core products, it can consistently reduce the cost, time, and risk in new product development. In short, well-targeted core products can lead to economies of scale and scope.

The Tyranny of the SBU

The new terms of competitive engagement cannot be understood using analytical tools devised to manage the diversified corporation of 20 years ago, when competition was primarily domestic (GE versus Westinghouse, General Motors versus Ford) and all the key players were speaking the language of the same business schools and consultancies. Old prescriptions have potentially toxic side effects. The need for new principles is most obvious in companies organized exclusively according to the logic of SBUs. The implications of the two alternate concepts of the corporation are summarized in Table 6.2.1.

Obviously, diversified corporations have a portfolio of products and a portfolio of businesses. But we believe in a view of the company as a portfolio of competencies as well. United States companies do not lack the technical resources to build competencies, but their top management often lacks the vision to build them and the administrative means for assembling resources spread across multiple busiinesses. A shift in commitment will inevitably influence patterns of diversification, skill deployment, resource allocation priorities, and approaches to alliances and outsourcing.

We have described the three different planes on which battles for global leadership are waged: core competence, core products, and end products. A corporation has to know whether it is winning or losing on each plane. By sheer weight of investment, a company might be able to beat its rivals to blue-sky technologies yet still lose the race to build core competence leadership. If a company is winning the race to build core competencies (as opposed to building leadership in a few technologies), it will almost certainly outpace rivals in new business development. If a company is winning the race to capture world manufacturing share in core products, it will probably outpace rivals in improving product features and the price/performance ratio.

TABLE 6.2.1
Two concepts of the corporation

	SBU	Core Competence
Basis for competition	Competiveness of today's products	Interfirm competition to build competencies
Corporate structure	Portfolio of businesses related in product-market terms	Portfolio of competencies, core products, and businesses
Status of the business unit	Autonomy is sacrosanct; the SBU 'owns' all resources other than cash	SBU is a potential reservoir of core competencies
Resource allocation	Discrete businesses are the unit of analysis; capiital is allocated business by business	Businesses and competencies are the unit of analysis: top management allocates capital and talent
Value added of top management	Optimizing corporate returns through capital allocation trade-offs among businesses	Enunciating strategic architecture and building competencies to secure the future

Determining whether one is winning or losing end-product battles is more difficult because measures of product market share do not necessarily reflect various companies' underlying competitiveness. Indeed, companies that attempt to build market share by relying on the competitiveness of others, rather than investing in core competencies and world core-product leadership, may be treading on quicksand. In the race for global brand dominance, companies like 3M, Black & Decker, Canon, Honda, NEC, and Citicorp have built global brand umbrellas by proliferating products out of their core competencies. This has allowed their individual businesses to build image, customer loyalty, and access to distribution channels.

When you think about this reconceptualization of the corporation, the primacy of the SBU – an organizational dogma for a generation – is now clearly an anachronism. Where the SBU is an article of faith, resistance to the seductions of decentralization can seem heretical. In many companies, the SBU prism means that only one plane of the global competitive battle, the battle to put competitive products on the shelf *today*, is visible to top management. What are the costs of this distortion?

Underinvestment in Developing Core Competencies and Core Products

When the organization is conceived of as a multiplicity of SBUs, no single business may feel responsible for maintaining a viable position in core products or be able to justify the investment required to build world leadership in some core competence. In the absence of a more comprehensive view imposed by corporate management, SBU managers will tend to underinvest. Recently, companies such as Kodak and Philips have recognized this as a potential problem and have begun searching for new organizational forms that will allow them to develop and manufacture core products for both internal and external customers.

SBU managers have traditionally conceived of competitors in the same way they've seen themselves. On the whole, they've failed to note the emphasis Asian competitors were placing on building leadership in core products or to understand the critical linkage between world manufacturing leadership and the ability to sustain development pace in core competence. They've failed to pursue OEM-supply opportunities or to look across their various product divisions in an attempt to identify opportunities for co-ordinated initiatives.

Imprisoned Resources

As an SBU evolves, it often develops unique competencies. Typically, the people who embody this competence are seen as the sole property of the business in which they grew up. The manager of another SBU who asks to borrow talented people is likely to get a cold rebuff. SBU managers are not only unwilling to lend their competence carriers but they may actually hide talent to prevent its redeployment in the pursuit of new opportunities. This may be compared to residents of an underdeveloped country hiding most of their cash under their mattresses. The benefits of competencies, like the benefits of the money supply, depend on the velocity of their circulation as well as on the size of the stock the company holds.

Western companies have traditionally had an advantage in the stock of skills they possess. But have they been able to reconfigure them quickly to respond to new opportunities? Canon, NEC, and Honda have had a lesser stock of the people and technologies that compose core competencies but could move them much quicker from one business unit to another. Corporate R&D spending at Canon is not fully indicative of the size of Canon's core competence stock and tells the casual observer nothing about the velocity with which Canon is able to move core competencies to exploit opportunities.

When competencies become imprisoned, the people who carry the competencies do not get assigned to the most exciting opportunities, and their skills begin to atrophy. Only by fully leveraging core competencies can small companies like Canon afford to compete with industry giants like Xerox. How strange that SBU managers, who are perfectly willing to compete for cash in the capital budgeting process, are unwilling to compete for people – the company's most precious asset. We find it ironic that top management devotes so much attention to the capital budgeting process yet typically has no comparable mechanism for allocating the human skills that embody core competencies. Top managers are seldom able to look four or five levels down into the organization, identify the people who embody critical competencies, and move them across organizational boundaries.

Bounded Innovation

If core competencies are not recognized, individual SBUs will pursue only those innovation opportunities that are close at hand – marginal product-line extensions or geographic expansions. Hybrid opportunities like fax machines, laptop computers, handheld televisions, or portable music keyboards will emerge only when managers take off their SBU blinkers. Remember, Canon appeared to be in the camera business at the time it was preparing to become a world leader in copiers. Conceiving of the corporation in terms of core competencies widens the domain of innovation.

Developing Strategic Architecture

The fragmentation of core competencies becomes inevitable when a diversified company's information systems, patterns of communication, career paths, managerial rewards, and processes of strategy development do not transcend SBU lines. We believe that senior management should spend a significant amount of its time developing a corporate-wide strategic architecture that establishes objectives for competence building. A strategic architecture is a road map of the future that identifies which core competencies to build and their constituent technologies.

By providing an impetus for learning from alliances and a focus for internal development efforts, a strategic architecture like NEC's C&C (computers and communication) can dramatically reduce the investment needed to secure future market leadership. How can a company make partnerships intelligently without a clear understanding of the core competencies it is trying to build and those it is attempting to prevent from being unintentionally transferred?

Of course, all of this begs the question of what a strategic architecture should look like. The answer will be different for every company. But it is helpful to think again of that tree, of the corporation organized around core products and, ultimately, core competencies. To sink sufficiently strong roots, a company must answer some fundamental questions: How long could we preserve our competitiveness in this business if we did not control this particular core competence? How central is this core competence to perceived customer benefits? What future opportunities would be foreclosed if we were to lose this particular competence?

The architecture provides a logic for product and market diversification, moreover. An SBU manager would be asked: Does the new market opportunity add to the overall goal of becoming the best player in the world? Does it exploit or add to the core competence? At Vickers, for example, diversification options have been judged in the context of becoming the best power and motion control company in the world.

The strategic architecture should make resource allocation priorities transparent to the entire organization. It provides a template for allocation decisions by top management. It helps lower-level managers understand the logic of allocation priorities and disciplines senior management to maintain consistency. In short, it yields a definition of the company and the markets it serves. 3M, Vickers, NEC, Canon, and Honda all qualify on this score. Honda knew it was exploiting what it had learned from motorcycles – how to make high-revving, smooth-running, lightweight engines – when it entered the car business. The task of creating a strategic architecture forces the organization to identify and commit to the technical and production linkages across SBUs that will provide a distinct competitive advantage.

It is consistency of resource allocation and the development of an administrative infrastructure appropriate to it that breathes life into a strategic architecture and creates a managerial culture, teamwork, a capacity to change, and a willingness to share resources, to protect proprietary skills, and to think long term. That is also the reason the specific architecture cannot be copied easily or overnight by competitors. Strategic architecture is a tool for communicating with customers and other external constituents. It reveals the broad direction without giving away every step.

Redeploying to Exploit Competencies

If the company's core competencies are its critical resource and if top management must ensure that competence carriers are not held hostage by some particular business, then it follows that SBUs should bid for core competencies in the same way they bid for capital. We've made this point glancingly. It is important enough to consider more deeply.

Once top management (with the help of divisional and SBU managers) has identified overarching competencies, it must ask businesses to identify the projects and people closely connected with them. Corporate officers should direct an audit of the location, number, and quality of the people who embody competence.

This sends an important signal to middle managers: core competencies are corporate resources and may be reallocated by *corporate* management. An individual business doesn't own anybody. SBUs are entitled to the services of individual employees so long as SBU management can demonstrate that the opportunity it is pursuing yields the highest possible payoff on the investment in their skills. This message is further underlined if each year in the strategic planning or budgeting process, unit managers must justify their hold on the people who carry the company's core competencies.

Also, reward systems that focus only on product-line results and career paths that seldom cross SBU boundaries engender patterns of behavior among unit managers that are destructively competitive. At NEC, divisional managers come together to identify next-generation competencies. Together they decide how much investment needs to be made to build up each future competency and the contribution in capital and staff support that each division will need to make. There is also a sense of equitable exchange. One division may make a disproportionate contribution or may benefit less from the progress made, but such short-term inequalities will balance out over the long term.

Incidentally, the positive contribution of the SBU manager should be made visible across the company. An SBU manager is unlikely to surrender key people if only the other business (or the general manager of that business who may be a competitor for promotion) is going to benefit from the redeployment. Cooperative SBU managers should be celebrated as team players. Where priorities are clear, transfers are less likely to be seen as idiosyncratic and politically motivated.

Transfers for the sake of building core competence must be recorded and appreciated in the corporate memory. It is reasonable to expect a business that has surrendered core skills on behalf of corporate opportunities in other areas to lose, for a time, some of its competitiveness. If these losses in performance bring immediate censure, SBUs will be unlikely to assent to skills transfers next time.

Finally, there are ways to wean key employees off the idea that they belong in perpetuity to any particular business. Early in their careers, people may be exposed to a variety of businesses through a carefully planned rotation program.

Competence carriers should be regularly brought together from across the corporation to trade notes and ideas. The goal is to build a strong feeling of community among these people. To a great extent, their loyalty should be to the integrity of the core competence area they represent and not just to particular businesses. In traveling regularly, talking frequently to customers, and meeting with peers, competence carriers may be encouraged to discover new market opportunities.

Core competencies are the wellspring of new business development. They should constitute the focus for strategy at the corporate level. Managers have to win manufacturing leadership in core products and capture global share through brand-building programs aimed at exploiting economies of scope. Only if the company is conceived of as a hierarchy of core competencies, core products, and market-focused business units will it be fit to fight.

Nor can top management be just another layer of accounting consolidation, which it often is in a regime of radical decentralization. Top management must add value by enunciating the strategic architecture that guides the competence acquisition process. We believe an obsession with competence building will characterize the global winners of the 1990s. With the decade underway, the time for rethinking the concept of the corporation is already overdue.

6.3   The Synergy Trap

By Mark Sirower[1]

The 1990s will go down in history as the time of the biggest merger and acquisition (M&A) wave of the century. Few, if any, corporate resource decisions can change the value of a company as quickly or dramatically as a major acquisition. Yet the change is usually for the worse. Shareholders of acquiring firms routinely lose money right on announcement of acquisitions. They rarely recover their losses. But shareholders of the target firms, who receive a substantial premium for their shares, usually gain.

Here's a puzzle. Why do corporate executives, investment bankers, and consultants so often recommend that acquiring firms pay more for a target company than anybody else in the world is willing to pay? It cannot be because so many acquisitions turn out to be a blessing in disguise. In fact,

---

[1] Source: This article was adapted with permission from chapter 1 and 2 of *The Synergy Trap: How Companies Lose the Acquisition Game*, Free Press, New York, 1997.

when asked recently to name just one big merger that has lived up to expectations, Leon Cooperman, the former co-chairman of Goldman Sachs's investment policy committee, answered, 'I'm sure that there are success stories out there, but at this moment I draw a blank.'

It doesn't make sense. For over 30 years, academics and practitioners have been writing books and articles on managing mergers and acquisitions. Corporations have spent billions of dollars on advisory fees. The platitudes are well known. Everyone knows that you should not pay 'too much' for an acquisition, that acquisitions should make 'strategic sense,' and that corporate cultures need to be 'managed carefully.' But do these nostrums have any practical value?

Consider. You know you've paid too much only if the acquisition fails. Then, *by definition*, you have overpaid. But how do we predict upfront whether a company is overpaying for an acquisition – in order to prevent costly failures? What exactly does the acquisition premium represent, and when is it too big? What is the acquirer paying for? These are the details, and the devil is in them.

Like a major R&D project or plant expansion, acquisitions are a capital budgeting decision. Stripped to the essentials, an acquisition is a purchase of assets and technologies. But acquirers often pay a premium over the stand-alone market value of these assets and technologies. They pay the premium for something called *synergy*.

Dreams of synergy lead to lofty acquisition premiums. Yet virtually no attention has been paid to how these acquisition premiums affect performance. Perhaps this is because the concept of synergy itself has been poorly defined. The common definition of synergy is $2 + 2 = 5$. This reading will show just how dangerous that definition is. Pay attention to the math. The easiest way to lose the acquisition game is by failing to define synergy in terms of real, measurable improvements in competitive advantage.

A quantifiable post-merger challenge is embedded in the price of each acquisition. Using the acquisition premium, we can calculate what the required synergies must be. Often this calculation shows that the required performance improvements are far greater than what any business in a competitive industry can reasonably expect.

By analyzing the acquisition premium, we can determine in advance when the price is far above the potential value of an acquisition. We can also show why most purported synergies are like the colorful petals of the Venus flytrap – dangerous deceivers. But managers who analyze the acquisition premium and understand the concept of synergy will not get caught. They can predict the probability and the amount of shareholder losses or gains. My claim is that most major acquisitions are *predictably* dead on arrival – no matter how well they are 'managed' after the deal is done.

The M&A Phenomenon

Mergers and acquisitions are arguably the most popular and influential form of discretionary business investment. On the single day of April 22, 1996, with the announcement of the Bell Atlantic-NYNEX merger and Cisco Systems' acquisition of Stratacom, over $27 billion of acquisitions were announced. For 1995, the total value of acquisition activity was over $400 billion. By comparison, in the aggregate managers spent only $500 billion, on average, over the past several years on new plant and equipment purchases and a mere $130 billion on R&D.

Acquisition premiums can exceed 100 percent of the market value of target firms. Evidence for acquisitions between 1993 and 1995 shows that shareholders of acquiring firms lose an average of 10 percent of their investment on announcement. And over time, perhaps waiting for synergies, they lose even more. A major McKinsey & Company study found that 61 percent of acquisition programs were failures because the acquisition strategies did not earn a sufficient return (cost of capital) on the funds invested. Under the circumstances, it should be natural to question whether it is economically productive to pay premiums at all.

Logically, we should expect that managers choose an acquisition strategy only when it offers a better payoff than other strategic alternatives. But there are several pitfalls inherent in acquisitions because they are, in fact, a very unique investment.

First, since acquirers pay a premium for the business, they actually have two business problems to solve: (1) to meet the performance targets the market already expects, and (2) to meet the even higher targets implied by the acquisition premium. This situation is analogous to emerging technology investments where investors pay for breakthroughs that have not yet occurred, knowing that competitors are chasing the same breakthroughs. However, in acquisitions, the breakthroughs are called 'synergies.'

I define synergy as *increases in competitiveness and resulting cash flows beyond what the two companies are expected to accomplish independently*. In other words, managers who pay acquisition premiums commit themselves to delivering more than the market already expects from current strategic plans. The premium represents the value of the additional performance requirements.

Second, major acquisitions, unlike major R&D projects, allow no test runs, no trial and error and, other than divesting, no way to stop funding during the project. Acquirers must pay up front just for the right to 'touch the wheel.'

Finally, once companies begin intensive integration, the costs of exiting a failing acquisition strategy can become very high. The integration of sales forces, information and control systems, and distribution systems, for example, is often very difficult to reverse in the short term. And in the process, acquirers may run the risk of taking their eyes off competitors or losing their ability to respond to changes in the competitive environment.

Legendary and successful acquirers such as Cooper Industries and Emerson Electric have learned over time and implicitly understand the fundamentals of the game. But most companies make very few major acquisitions and often hire outside advisers to do the acquisition valuations (called *fairness opinions*). A Boston Consulting Group study found that during the pre-merger stage, eight of ten companies did not even consider how the acquired company would be integrated into operations following the acquisition. It is no wonder that often the acquirer loses the entire premium – and more. Escalating the commitment by pouring more money into a doomed acquisition just makes things worse, perhaps even destroying the acquirer's pre-existing business.

The objective of management is to employ corporate resources at their highest-value uses. When these resources are committed to acquisitions, the result is not simply failure or not failure. Instead there is a whole range of performance outcomes.

Shareholders can easily diversify themselves at existing market prices without having to pay an acquisition premium. Acquisition premiums have little relation to potential value and the losses we observe in the markets to acquisition announcements are predictable. What do acquiring firm executive teams and advisers see that markets do not?

The most obvious answer to this question is synergy, yet anecdotal evidence suggests that managers are somewhat reluctant to admit that they expect synergy from acquisitions. In the battle for Paramount, synergy became the embarrassing unspoken word. And Michael Eisner has stated that he does not like to use the 's' word regarding Disney's acquisition of CapCities/ABC. So why do these executives pay premiums? Is it that those who do not remember the past are thoughtlessly repeating it?

The 1980s set all-time records for the number and dollar value of corporate mergers and takeovers in the United States, firmly displacing the famous merger wave of the 1960s. More than 35,000 deals worth almost $2 trillion were completed during the 1980s, with the average size of a deal reaching over $200 million in 1988 and 1989. Advisory fees alone totaled over $3.5 billion in the peak years, 1988 and 1989.

The merger and acquisition field is well established. Since 1980, managers have allocated over $20 billion to investment banking and other advisory fees to help formulate and ensure the success of their acquisition strategies. In addition to professional advisers, there are academic courses: leading universities give week-long seminars to packed houses all over the world, and the American Management Association has an extensive program on M&A. Yet despite all of this advice, many fail.

As Bruce Greenwald, a professor at Columbia Business School has said: 'Once you see the truth about something it is obvious, but there are many seemingly obvious things that simply are not true.' Obvious but untrue advice and folklore about acquisitions has led to bad business decisions. Why in fact do some acquisitions lose more money than others?

Back To First Principles: The Acquisition Game

A bad acquisition is one that does not earn back its cost of capital. Stock market reactions to mergers and acquisitions are the aggregate forecasts of investors and analysts around the world of the expectations of the value of the investment. What does it mean when these sophisticated capitalists bid down the stock of acquiring firms and bid up the stock of targets?

The theory of the acquisition game and the synergy trap is rooted in the Nobel Prize-winning research of Professors Franco Modigliani and Merton Miller (M&M). The M&M propositions and their pathbreaking research on valuation (1958) begin with the assumption that the value of a firm (V) is equal to the market value of the debt (D) plus the market value of the equity (E):

$$V = D + E$$

Think of this as an economic balance sheet where the market value of claims (the debt and equity) is a function of the expected earnings stream coming from the assets. You can divide the claims any way you like, but the value of the firm will remain the same. In the words of Merton Miller, 'Think of the firm as a gigantic pizza, divided into quarters. If now you cut each quarter in half or in eighths, the M&M proposition says that you will have more pieces but not more pizza.'

The application of this principle is crucial to understanding what it means for acquiring firms to lose huge chunks of market value following acquisition announcements. When you make a bid for the equity of another company (we will call this the target company), you are issuing claims or cash to the shareholders of that company. If you issue claims or cash in an amount greater than the economic value of the assets you purchase, you have merely transferred value from the shareholders of your firm to the shareholders of the target-right from the beginning. This is the way the economic balance sheet of your company stays balanced.

Markets give estimates of this range of value transfer through changes in share prices. The idea of the transfer of value is the stepping-off point for the development of the acquisition game. In short, playing the acquisition game is a business gamble where you pay up front for the right to control the assets of the target firm, and earn, you hope, a future stream of payoffs. But while the acquisition premium is known with certainty, the payoffs are not. What, then, is synergy?

Investors around the world have already valued the future expected performance of the target firm. That value equals the pre-acquisition share price. These investors' livelihoods are based on paying what the performance is worth. So synergy must translate into performance gains beyond those that are already expected. Simply put, achieving synergy means competing better. But in current hypercompetitive markets, it is a difficult challenge just to achieve the expected performance that is already built into existing share prices – at a zero premium. *What happens when we raise the bar?*

Because markets have already priced what is expected from the stand-alone firms, the net present value (NPV) of playing the acquisition game can be simply modeled as follows:

NPV = Synergy − Premium

Companies that do not understand this fundamental equation risk falling into the synergy trap. To quote G. Bennett Stewart of Stern Stewart & Co., 'Paying unjustified premiums is tantamount to making charitable contributions to random passersby, never to be recouped by the buying company no matter how long the acquisition is held.'

It is the NPV of the acquisition decision – the expected benefits less the premium paid – that markets attempt to assess. The more negative the assessment is, the worse the damage is to the economic balance sheet and to the share price. Folklore says that the share price of acquirers inevitably drops on the announcement of acquisitions – but in a properly valued acquisition, that does not have to be true.

To visualize what synergy is and what exactly the premium represents in performance terms, imagine being on a treadmill. Suppose you are running at 3 mph but are required to run at 4 mph next year and 5 mph the year after. Synergy would mean running even harder than this expectation while competitors supply a head wind. Paying a premium for synergy – that is, for the right to run harder – is like putting on a heavy pack. Meanwhile, the more you delay running harder, the higher the incline is set. This is the acquisition game.

For most acquisitions, achieving significant synergy is not likely. When it does occur, it usually falls far short of the required performance improvements priced into the acquisition premium. Putting together two businesses that are profitable, well managed, and even related in every way is not enough to create synergy. After all, competitors are ever present.

What can a manager do with the new business that will make it more efficient for the new business to compete or harder for competitors to contest their markets? When the managers of Novell acquired WordPerfect for $1.4 billion, did they calculate what WordPerfect was already required to accomplish given the first bid for WordPerfect by Lotus for $700 million? Did they ask what Novell, the parent, could do to make it more competitive against the office suite products of Microsoft or Lotus? If they asked, their answers apparently left something out. Novell lost $550 million of market value on announcement of the acquisition. Since then, Microsoft has continued to gain market share and Novell recently sold WordPerfect, less than two years later, to Corel for less than $200 million – a loss of over $1.2 billion.

A Brief History of the Research on Acquisitions

Faced with the facts of acquisition performance, academics have struggled to explain them. The explanations fall into two broad categories:

1   managers attempt to maximize shareholder value by either replacing in-efficient management in the target firm or achieving synergies between the two firms;

2   managers pursue their own objectives such as growth or empire building at the expense of shareholder value.

These hypotheses are an attempt to understand the average results of acquisitions and can be of use to policymakers.

Interestingly, there were good old days in the acquisition business. Research examining mergers from the 1960s and 1970s found that target firm shareholders on average experienced significant gains and acquirers either gained or, at worst, broke even. These results were consistent with the reasonable economic expectation that buyers would bid up asset prices to their fair value.

Then something went wrong. The evidence from the merger wave of the 1980s shows significantly negative results to the shareholders of acquiring firms upon announcement of the acquisition. These negative results extended beyond the initial announcement; shareholder returns declined as much as 16 percent over the three years following the acquisition.

The evidence documenting the destruction of value to the shareholders of acquiring firms came as no surprise to industrial-organization economists who for more than 30 years have studied the effects of mergers on issues such as accounting profitability, market share, and growth. The overwhelming evidence is that mergers do not improve profitability. Indeed, many studies show decreases in profitability at the line-of-business level. And these disappointing results hold also for market share and growth. These results are consistent with the hypothesis that managers are pursuing objectives other than wealth maximization for their shareholders.

Richard Roll, a finance professor at UCLA, explained value-destructive acquisitions with a dramatic template, suggesting that managers actually believe there are synergies that can be achieved from acquisitions but that they are infected with a classic tragic flaw – *hubris* (Roll, 1986). They are overconfident and thus pay too much when they win a bidding contest. In this scenario, overinflated egos cause acquisitions to fail.

This type of proposition can generate great notoriety for an academic and is exactly what the popular press looks for: the chance to pin a big failed decision on the ego of a CEO. How do you explain the difference between a failed acquisition and a successful one? The CEO had a bigger ego. Yet the hypothesis fails to explain why the premiums paid over the past 10 to 15 years are as much as five times the premiums paid during the 1960s and early 1970s when acquisitions on average created value for shareholders. Are we to understand that managers today are five times more confident or have an ego five times bigger than it was during the conglomerate era of the 1960s? And what about big-ego executives who do not make acquisitions?

In the end it is impossible to test whether the hubris hypothesis or the hypothesis that managers simply pursue their own objectives is the true explanation. As Dennis Mueller of the University of Vienna so insightfully states, 'Whether the premium paid actually represents the underlying beliefs of managers is inherently unanswerable in the absence of testimony at the time of the acquisition by managers under the influence of truth serum.'

My objective here is to describe thoroughly what senior executives are getting their companies and their shareholders into when they enter the acquisition game, regardless of their motives. Reaching the decision to approve an acquisition is a complex process with a multitude of players, advisers, opinions, and interests. Major acquisitions are actually rare decisions for most companies. The problem is not necessarily hubris or even self-interest but may simply be unfamiliarity with the fundamentals of the problem. Acquisitions must be compared to other strategic alternatives. The real concern for managers is not the personal motivations of the players or the size of their ego but the mechanics of why the acquisition either works or does not work. What does the range of outcomes to acquirers mean? There have been many hypotheses, but no explanations.

Whether acquisition premiums are fair values needs to be challenged. Because acquisitions are complex processes involving different levels of management, different political agendas, investment bankers, law firms, and accounting firms, it is altogether too easy for executives to pay too much. Many acquisition premiums require performance improvements that are virtually impossible to realize, even for the best of managers in the best of industry conditions.

The first step in understanding the acquisition game is to admit that price may have nothing at all to do with value. I call this the *synergy limitation* view of acquisition performance. In this view, synergy has a low expected value and, thus, the level of the acquisition premium predicts the level of losses in acquisitions.

For the past two decades, the premiums paid for acquisitions – measured as the additional price paid for an acquired company over its pre-acquisition value – have averaged between 40 and 50 percent, with many regularly surpassing 100 percent (e.g. IBM's acquisition of Lotus). The higher the premium is, the greater is the value destruction from the acquisition strategy.

Restating the definition of performance, NPV = Synergy − Premium, we see that if synergies are predictably limited, the premium becomes an up-front predictor of the returns to acquirers. My objective is to explain the range of performance outcomes we observe, no matter how acquisitions perform on average. For example, in the sample of acquisitions from my study, the range of market reactions just on announcement ranges from a positive 30 percent to a negative 22 percent. Since the average size of acquirers in the sample is over $2 billion, we are talking about a significant range of changes in value.

If price represented value, then synergy would generally occur in the amount dictated by the premium. But suppose that price in acquisitions is *not* correlated with potential value. Further, suppose that *potential* is limited even in acquisitions where no post-merger problems occur. Predictions about overpayment up front would then be possible, and integration issues could be considered within a performance context.

Synergy and the Acquisition Game

When executives play the acquisition game, they pay, in addition to the current market price, an up-front premium for an uncertain stream of pay-offs sometime in the future. Since shareholders do not have to pay a premium to buy the shares of the target on their own, these payoffs, the synergies, must represent something that shareholders cannot get on their own. They must mean improvements in performance greater than those already expected by the markets. If these synergies are not achieved, the acquisition premium is merely a gift from the shareholders of the acquirer to the shareholders of the target company.

Current share prices at various market multiples already have substantial projected improvements in profitability and growth built into them. Hence, our operational definition of synergy is this: *synergy is the increase in performance of the combined firm over what the two firms are already expected or required to accomplish as independent firms.*

In management terms, synergy means competing better than anyone ever expected. It means gains in competitive advantage over and above what firms already need to survive in their competitive markets.

One reason that synergy is difficult to achieve is that the current strategic plans and resources of the target do have value. The easiest trap to fall into occurs when acquirers forget about this value. Acquirer management must maintain and manage this value while making changes in operations. It may be unrealistic to hope to gain two customers, but it is very easy to lose two customers after an acquisition. As Unisys (the merger of Burroughs and Sperry), Novell (with its acquisition of WordPerfect), and so many other acquirers have learned the hard way, all the cultural management in the world will not generate synergies and will not save an acquisition that reduces the competitiveness of the underlying businesses. Most of the problems that have been considered in managing acquisitions are important with regard to maintaining value rather than creating it. But acquisitions at a premium demand ever more.

Recall that acquisitions are a unique investment decision for some important managerial reasons:

1   there are no dry runs, and all the money is paid up front;

2   the exit costs following integration can be extremely high, in both reputation and dollars;

3   managing synergy is in many ways like managing a new venture or a new business.

Putting the idea of managing above what is already expected into an earnings per share (EPS) context, we can think of the management challenge of synergy in this way:

$$\text{EPS (tomorrow)} = \text{EPS (today)} + \text{EPS (today)} \times \text{Expected growth} + \text{Synergy}$$

The management challenge of any business is the base business today plus the expected growth of the future business. The expected future growth and profitability improvements are already embedded in current share prices. Adding synergy means creating value that not only does not yet exist but is not yet expected. So achieving synergy – improvements above what is already expected or required – is like starting a new business venture. There might be improvements in performance following an acquisition, but if they were already expected, that is not synergy. And if it costs a lot more to run this new venture after the acquisition, funds may be diverted from pre-acquisition strategic plans, and value may be destroyed rather than created.

So where is the new value going to come from? If cultures are managed correctly and all employees receive hats with the new corporate name and logo, will that create synergy? If two large companies are put together that are already operating well above minimum efficient scale and already have to run hard just to stay in place, will cost savings be generated? And if there are cost savings, how much will they be?

The synergy problem must be tackled within a competitive context. At the end of the day, acquirers need to be able to show where additional cash will be available to suppliers of capital. How exactly will they generate higher revenues or lower costs less additional required capital investment in a competitive market?

The Competitive Challenge of Synergy

In acquisitions, managers must show what will be different before they can actually value the strategy. They must be prepared to answer how and in what ways it will be more difficult for competitors to compete in the businesses of both the target and the acquirer. They must consider whether competitors will be able to challenge successfully – or what I call 'contest' – the improvements that the acquirer will attempt in order to generate performance gains. Whether merging firms have valuable resources or competencies as stand-alones reveals little about the ability to create synergy. By contrast, the contestability approach that I present here puts the questions that acquirers must ask in competitive terms.

Using the value chain concept advanced by Michael Porter of the Harvard Business School, we can think of a business as consisting of input markets, processes, and output markets. In any competitive business, competitors are already attempting to contest each other's markets by finding the most efficient means of producing a given set of products and services and/or offering a more attractive set of products and services at a given cost structure. In a competitive environment, the only way to earn economic returns is by preventing rivals (current and potential) from winning along the value chain. At least one of the following conditions is necessary:

1   acquirers must be able to further limit competitors' ability to contest their or the targets' current input markets, processes, or output markets;

2   acquirers must be able to open new markets and/or *encroach* on their competitors' markets where these competitors cannot respond.

This is the starting point. Condition 1 involves the ability of the acquirer to sustain advantages or decrease vulnerabilities. Condition involves the ability of the acquirer to engage competitors in current or new markets in ways that were not previously possible. The following examples illustrate these conditions.

Anheuser-Busch/Campbell Taggart/Eagle Snacks   Anheuser-Busch (A-B) is a distribution and marketing giant. In 1979, A-B started Eagle Snacks, and in 1982, A-B paid $560 million (about a 20 percent premium) for Campbell Taggart, a major manufacturer of bread and snacks. What could be more natural than combining the distribution and sales of beer, bread, and salty snacks? After all, they all use yeast. In fact, however, beer and snacks go into different areas of supermarkets and convenience stores, and they have different ordering schedules. Although A-B devised a distribution strategy using Eagle distributors, Campbell Taggert distributors, and its regular beer distributors, it failed to achieve synergy. What's more, A-B's beer distributors refused to detract from their own core business to support A-B's emerging and inevitable fight with snack-food leader Frito-Lay.

Anheuser-Busch's distributors laid the blame for the failure squarely at the feet of Frito-Lay, which did not sit still to watch while A-B generated synergies at its expense. Indeed, as A-B expanded the Eagle product line, Frito-Lay attacked with an array of new products and price cuts on existing products. A-B's snack market share never topped six percent, while Frito's increased from 40 percent to 50 percent. For 1995 alone, the Eagle brand lost $25 million on sales of $400 million. After 17 years of losses, A-B put the Eagle brand to rest. Interestingly, A-B sold its four Eagle Snacks plants to none other than Frito-Lay, and Campbell Taggart was spun off to shareholders. The lesson is that if the strategic moves of an acquirer are easily contestable, competitive gains, and thus synergy, will not occur.

Lockheed Martin/Loral Corporation   Vertical integration acquisitions present other interesting competitor reactions. Lockheed Martin paid $9.1 billion for most of the electronics supplier Loral Corporation. The result is that Loral, as a captive supplier of Lockheed, is now perceived and treated as a competitor by its erstwhile customers.

In a move that surprised Loral's chairman, Bernard Schwartz (now a vice chairman of Lockheed Martin), Harry Stonecipher, CEO of McDonnell Douglas (M-D), announced that M-D would switch its business away from Loral to other potential suppliers of electronic systems such as Litton Industries or Raytheon. Clearly McDonnell Douglas has little incentive to support the operations of a major rival for defense contracts when there are alternative suppliers. So before Lockheed Martin can realize any net synergies from the Loral acquisition, it will need to make up for the substantial lost business resulting from M-D's decision to switch suppliers. A similar scenario may play out in the entertainment business, where former suppliers are now owned by competitors. Such relationships may cause serious problems for Viacom, Disney, Time Warner, and others.

Achieving synergy is a brand new competitive problem for executive teams of acquirers, and their competitors will be watching and reacting in anticipation of changes. Acquirers need to ask which of their competitors will stand by silently while the attempt is made to generate synergy at their expense. In hypercompetitive environments, this expectation is simply unrealistic.

Unfortunately for acquirers, these contestability conditions are necessary but not sufficient. For example, customers may not value the new products or may not want to change their buying habits. The acquisition may require substantial additional investments in the business, even beyond the target's price, that negate any additional operating profitability. If the executives of an acquirer do not understand the target's businesses well enough to consider these issues, they will be extremely hard-pressed to develop a credible outlook for potential performance gains.

The Cornerstones of Synergy

How can acquirers know when they are likely to realize little value gain from an acquisition even at a zero acquisition premium? Here, we put the contestability conditions within a managerial framework.

Figure 6.3.1 illustrates the cornerstones of synergy. The four cornerstones represent the major elements of an acquisition strategy that must be in place for there to be any likelihood of synergy. The diagram is presented in the context of the premium decision (tackled in the next chapter) and competitor reactions. If any of these four cornerstones is missing when the deal is done, synergy will be a trap; the premium is likely to represent a total loss for the shareholders of the acquirer.

As with the contestability conditions, these cornerstones are necessary but not sufficient components to ensure performance gains. Achieving significant synergy is fundamentally difficult even when the essential cornerstones are in place – so even at a zero acquisition premium, synergy will be limited.

Acquirers can easily destroy value in the stand-alone businesses by attempting to gain synergies that have little chance of occurring. Executives who are making the costly mistake of throwing additional resources at a failing acquisition strategy can decrease the value of their businesses and make them more vulnerable to competitive attacks.

A poor understanding of the fundamentals of synergy can hurt acquirers in three important ways:

1   Post-acquisition planning will be a disappointing waste of managerial resources.

FIGURE 6.3.1
The cornerstones of
synergy

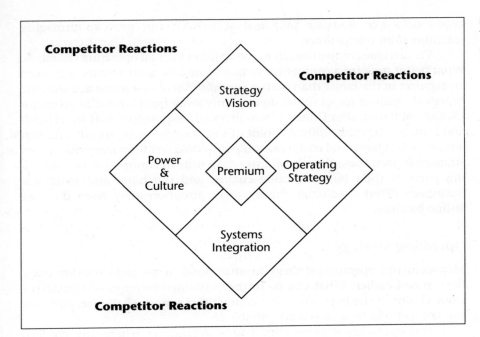

2   The limits to performance improvements will not be understood, so over-payment will be predictable; valuation will consist of hollow and spurious assumptions.

3   Original values of the acquiring and target firms will be severely jeopardized. The premium will be lost, and additional investments to achieve synergy will subtract shareholder value.

Strategic Vision

Strategic vision is where all acquisitions begin. Management's vision of the acquisition is shared with suppliers, customers, lenders, and employees as a framework for planning, discussions, decisions, and reactions to changes. The vision must be clear to large constituent groups and adaptable to many unknown circumstances. Viacom's vision to be the 'premier globally branded content provider' is a clear communicable vision, as was AT&T's vision for the NCR acquisition to 'link people, organizations and their information in a seamless global computer network.' Sears's one-stop shopping concept in financial services was really a wonderful vision. Unfortunately for Sears, the vision that customers actually wanted to or would buy these different products and services in one place and improve the core merchandising business was a mirage.

Investment bankers and executives are usually very good at coming up with a compelling and attractive strategic vision statement. Without the other three cornerstones, however, the vision has little use. The vision must be a continuous guide to the actual operating plans of the acquisition. If the vision does not translate into real actions, it can provoke damaging reactions from competitors.

Visions clue competitors in to the acquirer's actual operating strategies. What better time for a competitor to launch an attack on a major market of an acquirer or the target than on the announcement of a major acquisition? American Airlines took critical share points away from United in its major Chicago hub soon after United's (now divested) acquisitions of Hilton Hotels and Hertz in the mid-1980s. At point of sale it might seem intuitive that an airline, hotel chain, and rental car company could create an integrated travel strategy. In fact, these three businesses have little in common in the preceding parts of their business value chains, and the hotel and rental car businesses diverted valuable management attention away from the core airline business.

Operating Strategy

Management's operating strategy must respond to the contestability questions posed earlier: What can be further sustained or improved along the value chains of the businesses that competitors cannot challenge, and how can competitors be attacked and disabled?

The operating strategy cornerstone determines where any contestability gains can occur. Given that most major acquisitions involve little pre-acquisition planning, most acquisitions have no real operating strategy on the day the deal is completed. Instead there is a restatement of the vision with comments about how good the 'fit' is between the assets of the acquirer and the target. But actions speak louder than words, and without an operating strategy the vision is just words.

For example, Time Warner's acquisition of Turner Broadcasting System leaves much in doubt concerning the changes in the competitive strength of the companies. Chairman Gerald Levin has claimed that 35 percent of the new company will be owned by people who 'understand the media business and the powerful nature of where it's going.' Does this mean that the companies will be managed better than before? An operating strategy arising out of the acquisition must address how it will be more difficult for Viacom, Westinghouse, Disney, and News Corp. to attack Time Warner-TBS along the value chains of the businesses in which they all compete.

Shareholders lost over $2.2 billion of market value in just two months following the announcement of this acquisition (over $1 billion on announcement), so the challenge for Levin is to convince the markets, current and potential customers, and competitors that positive change will occur. Simply having a 'compelling fit' among the businesses, even where the businesses may have great competitive competencies, will not generate improvements in performance.

The operating strategy must address how the new company will be more competitive along the entire value chain of the businesses. Acquisitions are often an attempt to divert attention away from a failing core business with the hope that the acquisition might provide a miracle for the acquirer. If answers are not forthcoming to the contestability questions, what becomes obvious is a vision with no strategy that will increase competitiveness or generate performance gains. The following example clearly illustrates this problem.

AT&T/NCR   The AT&T acquisition of NCR in 1991 is a lesson on the absence of the operating strategy cornerstone. It is a mystery why, after losing an estimated $2 billion in its own computer business between 1985 and 1990, AT&T directors were willing to approve the payment of a $4.2 billion premium for the NCR acquisition – a 125 percent premium above the pre-bid share price of the company. Charles Exley, chairman and CEO of NCR at the time, accused AT&T of merely trying to bail out its own failed strategy for marketing computers.

He may have been right on target. After paying the extraordinary premium for NCR, AT&T voluntarily left NCR executives in place to conduct business as usual for two years after the acquisition. In fact, they were even put in charge of AT&T's old computer production and marketing business. NCR executives were merely asked by AT&T to 'look' for synergy. The vision was that there would be 'convergence' between computers and communications, but AT&T's Technological advantage was in telecom switches, not in the corporate or consumer computer business.

By 1993, when earnings began to decline, AT&T signaled somewhat belatedly that it had a strategy for NCR after all. It appointed its own executive, Jerre Stead, to run the computer division but synergies did not materialize. In fact, between 1993 and 1995 most of NCR's top managers left the company. Costs increased dramatically as hundreds of new sales teams in over one hundred countries were set up and the company was pushed into new markets and industries where it had little experience. The result was that AT&T shareholders lost the entire premium that was paid to NCR shareholders and racked up losses of $720 million in 1995 alone.

Vision and operating strategy are necessary but not sufficient to ensure performance gains from an acquisition. The other two cornerstones – systems integration, and power and culture are closely related. Systems integration focuses on the physical integration plans that must be in place to implement the strategy (such as integration of sales forces, distribution systems, information and control systems, and R&D and marketing efforts). Power and culture focuses on the reward and incentive systems and the control of information and decision processes at various levels of the organization. When these cornerstones are missing, the consequences go far beyond a failure to generate synergy.

Systems Integration

The problem of systems integration is a component of the implementation side of acquisitions. Systems integration must be carefully considered before the acquisition and must support a clearly defined operating strategy. Management must decide which operations will be integrated and which will be stand-alone, while maintaining awareness of the preexisting performance targets. It is much like driving a car 100 miles per hour and trying to make adjustments to the engine while moving.

The folklore that mergers that are strategically related should out-perform those that are not is rooted in systems integration. If synergies are expected to come from cost savings in large organizations, they must emerge from eliminating duplication. Systems integration planning must lie at the heart of this strategy. This means that future systems integration plans must be planned in advance, and in considerable detail, before the acquirer calculates a bid price for the target. Otherwise the acquirer will not know what it is paying for and, even worse, will not know when the acquisition is simply a resource drain on stand-alone operations.

Acquirers must understand that there can be very distinct post-acquisition integration environments. There are several possible scenarios:

- The company is acquired as a stand-alone.

- The company is acquired as a stand-alone but with a change in strategy.

- The target is to become part of the acquirer's operations.

- The target and acquirer are to be completely integrated.

- The target takes over the acquirer's existing business and is integrated into the target's operations.

Different degrees of integration can pose different types of problems. If they are poorly considered, they can damage the underlying businesses.

Northwest Airlines/Republic Airlines In 1986, Northwest Airlines (NWA) completed what was the largest acquisition ever in the airline industry: the $884 million acquisition of Republic Airlines. The acquisition nearly doubled the size of NWA, making it the fifth largest domestic airline. But within two hours of completion of the acquisition, the airline's Twin Cities operation had ground to a standstill.

NWA and Republic had been prohibited from engaging in detailed pricing and scheduling discussions prior to the acquisition because of federal antitrust regulations. Senior management had little idea how the two computer systems interfaced, and when they put the two systems together, neither pilots nor passengers knew what was going on.

But integration of crew and gate scheduling was only the beginning of a long-term problem. Human resources integration was a disaster. The unions representing NWA employees were different from those representing Republic, and power struggles ensued. Having only recently made severe wage concessions, Republic's employees came to the merger with lower pay schedules than those of NWA. At the Detroit hub, disgruntled baggage handlers tore off destination tags, and employees in Memphis mounted an unofficial work slowdown that destroyed on-time performance. A story even emerged that former Republic employees in Detroit shut down the sewage system by simultaneously flushing their 'People, Pride, Performance' buttons down the toilets.

Northwest was dubbed 'Northworst' by frequent flyers. Less than a year after the merger, it topped the government's list of passenger complaints. Complicating these matters, on August 16, 1987, Northwest flight 255 crashed after takeoff from Detroit due to pilot error – the second worst disaster in American aviation history. In 1989, NWA was bought out by a group of private investors, and senior management resigned.

Sony/Columbia-TriStar   Vertical integration acquisitions carry with them a unique integration problem, as Sony learned with its $3.4 billion acquisition of Columbia Pictures Entertainment from Coca-Cola in 1989.

In vertical integration acquisitions, the integration begins at the link between the two companies. Since this is almost by definition a new business, the acquirer may not have an executive team or an appropriate control system in place to run the acquisition – and costs can veer out of control. Sony's strategy rested on the assumption that having a commanding position in the software business (movies) could influence consumption patterns in the hardware market, such as high-definition television. But first, Sony needed executives to run Columbia.

Sony hired Peter Guber and Jon Peters at a cost of $700 million – $200 million in salary plus $500 million to settle a breach of a long-term production agreement Guber and Peters had with Warner Brothers. Guber and Peters, neither having studio management experience, went out to find executives with experience to run Columbia and TriStar (which was acquired along with Columbia). Their spending did not stop there.

As part of the settlement with Warner Brothers, Columbia had to trade its Burbank studios for an old M-G-M production facility, which cost an additional $100 million to upgrade at the lavish standard of Guber and Peters. Additional expenses included a fleet of jets and the purchase of a florist shop so that Columbia's executives could enjoy fresh flowers delivered daily.

Synergies never materialized between hardware and software. The company ranked last in market share among the large Hollywood studios. And in November 1994, only five years later, Sony announced that it was taking a loss of $3.2 billion on the studios.

Power and Culture

For almost 30 years numerous articles, both academic and popular, have discussed the potential troubles of power and culture clashes between merging organizations. Most of these, however, lament that managers are more concerned about the financials than the soft side of acquisition management. The danger of isolated power and culture approaches to acquisitions is that they can often be used as an alibi for anything that goes wrong.

In fact, the issue of culture in acquisitions has not been studied in the context of how it would improve performance. The implicit assumption has been that if only the cultures were managed well, performance gains would occur. Thus culture and power issues have remained soft issues, easily dismissed by many parties involved.

We need to consider the 'why' (the economics) of culture to put this cornerstone in the context of synergy. Cultural tensions can undercut mergers and imperil synergies. Anthropologists and sociologists have over a hundred definitions of culture, but the classic definition is a 'shared set of norms, values, beliefs, and expectations.' This shared set of norms, values, beliefs, and expectations is developed over time and passed down or forward through the generations of managers. Although a corporate culture may have developed slowly, it is acquired as a whole, on the spot, in a merger. And these companies may have very different information and decision processes and incentive and reward systems. But the issue for acquirers is not whether the cultures are similar or different but whether the changes necessary to support the strategy will clash with either culture.

Two questions about culture are particularly relevant to mergers and acquisitions: (1) When will problems of conflict and cooperation arise? (2) How will they be solved? Some problems may arise from what would be considered differences in standard operating procedures, such as conduct of performance evaluations, chain of command, methods of communication, and capital allocation approvals.

The larger problems stem from the reshuffling of power and the unwritten expectations of payoffs of cooperating versus competing in the course of doing business in the new company. It is the uncertainty and ambiguity surrounding acquisition events that will cause executives and employees in general to defend positions they may have taken years to build. Key executives or knowledge workers who are crucial to the business as a stand-alone may leave in anticipation of these problems and join the competition.

The solution to the problems will lie in the incentive and other reward systems established for the new company. Are there clearly defined incentives that will drive the desired cooperation and coordination between previously independent businesses? In other words, if one side cooperates, will the other side honor its implied commitment or will it cheat when there is an incentive? That people will defect in anticipation of others' defection spells disaster in acquisitions where cooperation may be essential.

Unless rewards and incentives support a real strategy with real integration plans, management of culture means little with regard to generating performance improvements. As Gerald Levin of Time Warner has said, 'My philosophy is to let things happen naturally so that they make sense from the ground up instead of hammering it in from the top down.' Cooperation will not magically occur in entrepreneurial-based cultures unless incentives and rewards are created that will induce changes in behavior.

On the other hand, the inappropriate change of incentive systems can cause problems of its own. In 1990, two years after the Commercial Credits acquisition of Primerica, Sandy Weill, chairman and CEO, moved to change the incentive systems of the 110,000–strong part-time sales organization of the A. L. Williams insurance division by establishing specific targets and comparative evaluations by which to measure performance. It backfired immediately, and for two years, the writing of new insurance business was in a free fall. An A. L. Williams manager explained: 'Controls don't work here because they imply a downside – they don't just reward good performance, but imply negative consequences for low performance. That doesn't sit well with most of our agents. If they feel that they're going to be subjected to quotas and performance evaluations, they might as well stay home.'

Careless changes in decision authority can also result in unexpected changes in profitability, as AT&T learned in its NCR acquisition. In 1993, when AT&T executives took over the NCR division after having been left under the control of former NCR management, Jerre Stead moved to flatten the old NCR hierarchy and 'empower' more people. Sales representatives then had more authority to approve contracts that actually represented lower-margin business. Previously these contracts would have been rejected, but sales representatives who were compensated on revenues and not on margin had tremendous incentive to push through the business. The result was more business but lower profits.

Predictable Overpayment

The intensity of the challenge of generating synergies should now be apparent. *Price does not represent potential value* – and thus it becomes a predictor of acquisition value losses. This conclusion goes well beyond the simple prediction that acquirers overpay because of a winner's curse in a bidding auction.

Let us consider the following five acquisitions with two different synergy scenarios:

Premium	Synergy A	Synergy B
100%	80%	15%
80	60	15
60	40	15
40	20	15
20	0	15

The two scenarios (A and B) represent two categories of post-acquisition performance gains expressed as a percentage of the premium recovered. If price on average represents value, then synergy should occur in the amount dictated by the premium. In other words, a 60 percent premium should be associated, on average, with a 60 percent increase in value through actual performance gains. But suppose that, in acquisitions, price is not correlated with potential value. In other words, suppose that this potential is in fact limited across acquisitions. Predictions about overpayment up front (ex ante) would then be possible, and integration issues could be considered within more of a performance context.

From an after-the-fact (ex post) perspective, 'overpayment' occurs in each of the five cases in both scenarios. However, in synergy scenario A, the level of the premium gives no information about the amount of up-front risk of failure. A loss of 20 percent occurs in each acquisition. In this scenario, synergy is highly correlated with the premium, as would be predicted by the assumption of a competitive markets view. The result is consistent with what is often called the winner's curse: you win the contest but don't like the prize. Acquirers tend to overpay, but there seems to be good reason to make the acquisition if they paid just a little less.

On the other hand, if synergy does not occur or there are limits to the realization of synergy, as in synergy scenario B, then the predictive power of the premium becomes meaningful. That is, the level of the acquisition premium predicts the amount of losses. It is scenario B that represents the likely payoffs of the acquisition game.

6.4 The Value of the Parent Company

By Andrew Campbell, Michael Goold, and Marcus Alexander[1]

Many corporate parent companies destroy value. Businesses in corporate portfolios would, often, be better off as independent companies or as part of other corporate portfolios. This is the disturbing conclusion we have reached after nearly 10 years of research and consulting on the subject of corporate-level strategy and the role of the corporate center.

The main evidence for our conclusion lies in the hundreds of stories and situations we have come across where the corporate parent's influence over a business unit has caused the managers in the unit to make the wrong decisions, or at least to make poorer decisions than they would have made without the parent's influence. It is these value-destroying interventions that lead to the groundswell of complaint and resentment that business unit managers express when talking about their corporate centers. This body of anecdotal evidence is supported by analyst's reports, as well as by the activities of raiders, which show that many large companies have a market value lower than their break-up value. The continuing success of management buy-outs, where business units blossom when freed from the grasp of some large corporation, also demonstrates how widespread is value destruction by corporate parents.

---

[1] Source: This article was adapted with permission from *California Management Review*, Vol. 38, No. 1, Fall 1995, pp. 79–97.

On the other hand, there are some companies where the parent is clearly creating value, where the business unit managers have high respect for the corporate center and the influence it has over their businesses, and where the company's market value is greater than the sum of its parts. The stories, the atmosphere and the results in these successful corporate parents are completely different, underlining both the shortcomings in many large companies and the opportunities for those who get their corporate-level strategies right.

In this reading, we shall therefore focus on the role and influence of corporate parents in multi-business companies. The corporate parent consists of all managers and staff not assigned to a business unit, including not only the corporate headquarters but also division, group, region and other intermediate levels of management. Do these parent managers and staff create or destroy value? This issue lies at the heart of the justification for multi-business companies. Unless the parent company is creating value greater than its cost, the business units would be better off as independent companies. Our observation that many parent companies today are actually destroying value adds urgency to the need to identify the conditions under which value is likely to be created.

Four Ways to Destroy Value

Parent companies affect value in four ways – through stand-alone influence, through linkage influence, through central functions and services, and through corporate development activities. In each of these areas, it is possible for parent companies to create value. It is more common, however, for these areas of influence to result in value destruction.

Stand-Alone Influence

After the 1970s' oil crisis, many of the oil majors decided to diversify into new businesses, which would provide more growth and opportunity than their core oil businesses. A popular new area was minerals, which was seen as drawing on skills in natural resource exploration and extraction that were related to their base businesses. However, almost all the oil companies have found that they destroyed shareholder value through their minerals diversifications. The root cause of the problem was that parent company managers from the oil industry did not understand the subtle differences between the oil businesses and the minerals businesses, and ended up by influencing the strategies of their minerals businesses in ways that caused them to perform worse, not better. For example, we were told by a manager who had been part of British Petroleum's (BP's) minerals business:

> The problem was that the BP managing directors couldn't really get to grips with the minerals business or feel that they understood it. There was always that vestige of suspicion about the business, that in turn led to a

temptation to say no to proposals from the business, or, alternatively, if they said yes, to say yes for the wrong reasons.

The impact on performance was dramatic. During the mid-1980s, the minerals businesses of Atlantic Richfield, BP, Exxon, Shell and Standard Oil had an average pre-tax return on sales of 17 percent, while the independent minerals companies (i.e. companies not parented by the oil majors) achieved an average positive return on sales of 10 percent.

This is an example of what we call stand-alone influence. Stand-alone influence is about the parent's impact on the strategies and performance of each business in the parent's ownership, viewed as a stand-alone profit center. All parents exert considerable stand-alone influence on their businesses. At a minimum, they are involved in agreeing and monitoring performance targets, in approving major capital expenditures, and in selecting and replacing the business unit chief executives. These activities, in themselves, are powerful influences on the businesses. Many parents, however, go further, exercising influence on a wider range of issues, such as product-market strategies, pricing decisions, and human resource development.

While corporate parents can create value through stand-alone influence, they often destroy value instead. By pressing for inappropriate targets, by starving businesses of resources for worthwhile projects, by encouraging wasteful investment, and by appointing the wrong managers, the parent can have a serious adverse effect on its businesses. The potential for value creation must therefore always be balanced against the risk of value destruction.

Linkage Influence

Linkage influence can be just as destructive. Through linkage influence, the corporate parent seeks to create value by fostering cooperation and synergy between its businesses. But the search for linkages and synergies so often leads to problems that Guy Jillings, Head of Strategic Planning of Shell International Petroleum, has coined the term 'anergy.' He believes that avoiding anergy is often a more essential goal than pursuing synergy.

The problem of anergy is illustrated by a global consulting company that had made acquisitions in two new areas of consulting services to add to its traditional core. Senior managers believed that synergy could be created in a number of ways. First, economies of scale could be achieved by sharing back-office systems such as client billing and data processing. Second, a more powerful identity could be established by sharing a brand name. Third, more business could be generated by appointing client managers for the company as a whole who could deepen client relationships, coordinate approaches, and cross-sell a broad range of consulting services.

In reality, the pressure for linkages nearly destroyed one of the acquisitions, and hampered the efforts of all the other businesses. The shared billing system was complicated by the different needs of each business; after several million dollars of development cost, a compromise solution was reached which most units felt was inferior to their original systems, and which was no cheaper to run. Attempts at joint branding were abandoned because the individual brands were each strong and associated with particular services, whereas the amalgam brand was hard for clients to relate to and was rejected by staff who felt loyal to the brand values of the specific organization they had joined. Cross-selling was not increased by the new layer of client managers, who were insufficiently familiar with the full range of services available. Worse still, clients resented the imposition of a gatekeeper between them and the specialist service providers they were used to dealing with, and few valued the supposed advantages of one-stop shopping. Eventually, poor performance forced the company to drop many of its linkage initiatives and to reaffirm clearly distinct lines of business.

In many companies, the problems associated with linkage initiatives have made business managers so cynical about the efforts of their parent that they deliberately conceal linkage opportunities. To avoid the risk of parental intervention, managers in these companies prefer to do business with outsiders rather than with insiders.

Central Functions and Services

Parents can also destroy value through establishing central functions and services that undermine, rather than support, business effectiveness. This is not simply a matter of excessive overhead costs. It is also about delayed decisions and sub-standard or unresponsive support. ABB's chief executive, Percy Barnevik, has acquired many companies where these problems had been rife. His dramatic response in cutting headquarters staff has led to an ABB rule of thumb: by taking out 90 percent of the center, you can usually improve business performance as well as save cost. This rule has been applied to Brown Boveri's headquarters, and to acquisitions such as Combustion Engineering in the US and Strömberg in Finland. Typically, Barnevik removes 30 percent of the central functions and staff on the grounds that they are adding little except cost. A further 30 percent are set up as service units that must compete directly with outside suppliers. If they are cost effective, their services are purchased. Otherwise, they rapidly shrink or are disbanded. Another 30 percent of the central staff are put under the direct control of the individual businesses. If they fulfill a valid role in the business, they stay. If not, they are replaced or fired.

This approach addresses one of the main problems of central functions and services: that their privileged status protects them from the rigors of the market. By treating the divisions as clients whose business must be won, service levels are sharpened and improved. Unless this sort of relationship exists, the hoped-for economies of scale in central functions often prove illusory, and their influence can hamper rather than help the businesses.

Corporate Development

The final way in which parents destroy value is through corporate development activities – acquisitions, divestments, alliances, business redefinitions and new ventures. Many corporate parents believe that they create substantial value in their corporate development activities, for example by spotting opportunities to buy businesses cheaply, by creating new ventures that provide profitable future growth opportunities, or by redefining businesses in ways that lead them to be more competitive in their market places. We have found, however, that such initiatives frequently misfire. Parents overpay for acquisitions, support losing ventures and redefine businesses in the wrong way. The weight of research evidence indicates that the majority of corporately sponsored acquisitions, alliances, new ventures, and business redefinitions fail to create value. In particular, corporate histories are littered with stories of acquired businesses which turned out to be worth much less than expected, and so were sold subsequently for a fraction of the purchase price.

An extreme case concerns Ferranti, a medium-sized electronics company. During the 1980s, Ferranti performed well, developing a variety of sound businesses in defense electronics and other areas. However, in 1987, Ferranti paid $670 million to acquire the US International Signal and Communication (ISC) Group, with a view to becoming a major player in international defense markets. In 1989, it was discovered that ISC had entered into various fraudulent contracts, which led to losses of around $500 million for Ferranti. As a result, Ferranti was severely weakened and eventually forced into receivership after GEC had offered to buy the company for only one penny a share. A single acquisition brought Ferranti to its knees and wiped out all of the value created during the previous decades.

Why Value Destruction Is So Common

While corporate managers recognize that mistakes can be made at the headquarters in the same way as they can be made at other levels of management, few would accept our proposition that many corporate centers are systematically destroying value. They point to economies of scale in financial reporting, fund raising, liaising with the shareholders, tax and other areas. They identify the lower cost of debt that large companies can provide. They talk about the value of providing an informed challenge and second opinion to the narrow perspective of business unit managers. They refer to the task of allocating resources across the portfolio. Clearly, they argue, the corporate center has a valid role and can contribute to performance.

We agree. There are economies of scale. The cost of debt can be lowered. An informed second opinion and a wise allocation of capital can add value. However, for reasons we will explain, the net influence of the parent in many companies is still negative. Inappropriate interference on linkage issues can outweigh the economies of scale in financial reporting. Wise resource allocation decisions can be fewer than foolish ones. Damage from over-ambitious or under-ambitious performance targets can be more significant than the benefits of lower interest on debt. Value-destroying influences can be greater than value-creating ones. Why is this so?

The reason why value destruction occurs is that it is hard for parent organizations to influence their businesses in ways that improve on the decisions of the managers running the businesses. As can be seen from examining each of the four ways parent organizations affect value, it is not as surprising as it might seem that the parent's influence will make decisions worse, not better. In fact, it is only under particular conditions that we can expect the parent's influence to be positive.

With stand-alone influence, the assumption is that parent managers know better what is right for a business than the unit's own managers. Is this a realistic assumption? In a multi-business organization, managers in the parent can devote only a small percentage of their attention to the affairs of each business, while the managers in the businesses are fully engaged in their own units. Why should the parent managers, in 10 percent of their time, be able to improve on the decisions being made by competent managers who are giving 100 percent of their efforts to the business? The idea that part-time managers at one remove (or more) will be able to enhance the performance of the business's own dedicated management is, in some sense, paradoxical. We refer to this as the '10 percent versus 100 percent' paradox.

The 10 percent vs. 100 percent paradox is compounded by principal/agent problems arising from placing a parent organization between the business managers and the providers of capital. In a hierarchy, the business level managers are not motivated primarily by the objective of maximizing the performance of their businesses. They are motivated primarily by the objective of gaining favor, rewards, and career opportunities from their parent bosses. Unless the parent can mimic the influence of the providers of capital, the ownership relationship will result in different motivations and different objectives. Altering the motivations and objectives of business-level managers is one of the ways the parent can add value, but it can also result in value destruction as the business managers play a game of cat and mouse, hiding information and disguising outcomes, to persuade parent managers that they are high quality individuals.

With linkage influence, the assumption is that the parent managers can identify benefits of linkages between businesses that would not be perceived or implemented by the businesses' own managers. But, given the business managers' much greater understanding of their businesses, it is likely that they will have more knowledge about linkage opportunities and how to realize them than parent managers do. The difficulty of value creation from linkage influence therefore stems from another paradox. Why should the parent managers be able to perceive linkage opportunities if they have not already been perceived as a result of mutual self-interest on the part of energetic business unit managers? We call this the 'enlightened self-interest' paradox. The existence of this paradox explains why corporately inspired synergy initiatives often prove unsatisfactory.

With central functions and services influence, the assumption is that central staffs can provide better functional guidance or better value-for-money services, than are available from businesses' own staff or from outside suppliers. But the trend in many large companies is now to decentralize or outsource central functions and services. This trend brings out another paradox. A specialist, external supplier stands or falls by its ability to provide the most responsive and cost-effective expertise in its chosen field, whether it be market research, manufacturing advice, or strategic planning. Why should an in-house staff department be able to create more value than specialist competitors who undertake similar tasks and services on a third-party basis? It is this 'beating the specialists' paradox that has led many companies to disband large parts of their corporate functions and services.

Finally, with corporate development activities, the assumption is that the parent can buy businesses for less than they are worth, sell businesses for more than they are worth, and launch new ventures or redefined businesses in ways that increase value. Yet the odds are against this happening. Given that the market for buying and selling businesses is sophisticated, and the competition to develop businesses in new areas is usually fierce, why should the parent expect to be able to create value through corporate development? We refer to this as the 'beating the odds' paradox.

Successful Parent Companies

These four paradoxes – 10 percent vs. 100 percent, enlightened self-interest, beating the specialists, and beating the odds – explain why it is hard to create value from the corporate center. Nevertheless, the best corporate parents do create substantial value. What conditions must exist to overcome the paradoxes? What conditions lead to value creation?

The first condition is that the businesses in the company's portfolio must have some opportunity to improve performance with which the parent company can help. If the businesses are performing at their optimum, there is no opportunity to add value. The parent can only add something if the business offers a 'parenting opportunity.'

Second, the parent must possess some special capabilities or resources that will enable it to improve performance and exploit the parenting opportunity. These parenting characteristics are the engine of value creation.

Third, the parent must have a sufficient understanding of the critical success factors in the business to make sure that it does not influence the business in inappropriate ways. Managers often refer to this understanding as having a 'feel for the business.' We have observed that it can take a parent manager a number of years, typically including experience of a business over a complete economic cycle, before a sufficient feel develops.

With these three conditions, we can see some analogy between the roles of the corporate parent and of medical experts. Medical spedalists can only make a contribution if there are people whose health could be improved. Without this 'opportunity,' their expertise is not valuable. To make a contribution, the medical expert must have skills and resources that match the patient's needs. An ear, nose, and throat specialist is unlikely to contribute much to a patient with depression. Moreover, a specialist on depression must possess sufficient understanding about the overall health of this patient to be sure that the drugs he prescribed will not have side effects that will make the patient worse off. For the medical expert to succeed, the same three conditions must exist: there must be an opportunity, the expert must have skills and resources that fit the opportunity, and the expert must understand the patient well enough to avoid negative side-effects that outweigh the beneficial influences.

Successful parent companies not only meet these basic conditions for value to be created, they are particularly good at creating value. The best parents have unusual insights about certain kinds of parenting opportunities and focus their influence and activities on creating value from these insights. They have what we call 'value creation insights.' The best parents also have special skills and resources that fit particularly well with their value creation insights. These skills and resources are normally superior to those of other similar parents. They have what we call 'distinctive parenting characteristics.' Finally, the best parents limit their portfolios to businesses where their parenting will create a substantial amount of value. They are more effective at doing this because they have clear criteria defining which businesses fit well with the parent and which do not. They have what we call 'heartland' criteria.

ABB, Canon, and Emerson are good illustrations of these concepts. They represent a cross-section of the successful diversified companies in our research sample. All three are recognized as world leaders and exemplars of their particular management styles. All three also have excellent performance records (see Table 6.4.1). We will, therefore, illustrate our concepts by explaining the value creation insights these companies have, the distinctive parenting characteristics that support their insights, and the heartland criteria these companies use to limit their portfolios.

One value creation insight at ABB involves linking nationally focused businesses into a global network: rationalizing production across countries, cross-selling products, sharing technical developments and transferring best practice. ABB focuses much of its parental influence on getting previously isolated national managers to work together across borders.

A second value creation insight at ABB concerns raising the commercial skills and orientation of managers. In large, engineering-dominated companies, managers can become more interested in their engineering prowess and in being involved in prestigious projects than they are in profit. Such companies often do not calculate profit except at high levels of aggregation. Most units are cost centers. The ABB parent has discovered that commercial performance can be transformed if the profit ethic can be driven into the hearts of the managers and engineers in the local businesses. Many of ABB's parenting activities are, therefore, focused on achieving this value creating objective.

A third value creation insight at ABB concerns overheads. Proud, previously rich, and nationally prominent companies have a tendency to build large central overheads that can cost as much as 20 percent or more of profit. Much of ABB's parent activity, in the first year or two following an acquisition, is designed to reduce these overheads and release the value they

TABLE 6.4.1
Three cases

	ABB	Canon	Emerson
Corporate HQ	Switzerland	Japan	USA
Origins	Merger of ASEA (Sweden) and Brown Boveri (Switzerland) (1988)	Research laboratory focusing on precision optics (1933)	Electrical manufacturing (1890)
Industries	Power plants, power transmission, power distribution, transportation, general industrial	Business machines, cameras, other optical equipment	Electrical-electronic products and systems such as motors, process control instruments, appliance components, etc.
Size			
• sales (£bn)	30	15	8
• employees (000)	210	67	69
Performance (10 yrs)			
• sales growth	NA*	250%	200%
• earnings growth	200%**	150%	200%
• share price growth	300%**	150%	300%

* ASEA and Brown Boveri merged in 1988   ** Based on ASEA (ASEA owns 50% of ABB)

have trapped. In later years, the parent maintains the pressure on overheads ensuring that excessive costs do not build up again.

In Canon, one value creation insight is about developing new products. Technologists and product developers normally see themselves within the confines of a particular technology or product type. This puts bounds on their thinking defined by the accepted wisdom of the areas they are working in. Canon managers, however, discovered that it is possible to develop more creative products by blending and mixing technologies in, for example, fine optics and precision mechanics, and by challenging product development teams to produce customer solutions well beyond the scope of existing products.

Canon's second value creation insight is based on another parenting opportunity resulting from the bounded thinking of managers. In companies with traditional business unit structures, managers are influenced by the competitors and critical success factors of the industry they see themselves competing in. They are influenced by the accepted industry logic and, therefore, play into the hands of the industry leaders. Canon managers discovered that it is possible to break out of the accepted logic and develop winning strategies by avoiding traditional business unit structures and challenging managers to find new ways of competing.

Emerson's value creation insights are based on sharpening the strategic thinking of sound and profitable businesses. Emerson has found that, in certain electrical and electronic businesses, it can often push profit margins up from 5–10 percent to in excess of 15 percent at the same time as gaining market share. These improvements stem from reassessments of competitive positions and growth opportunities, detailed analysis of the components of cost and revenue in the businesses, and Emerson's special focus on manufacturing cost reductions. Emerson drives these improvements through business strategy reviews, which have been gradually refined to focus on the issues of greatest potential. Emerson is by no means unusual in conducting strategy reviews with its businesses: what is unusual is the way in which the process zeroes in on opportunities to improve performance, rather than simply being a routine re-examination of the businesses' plans.

ABB, Canon, and Emerson have value creation insights that provide a focus for the parent's activities. All three companies have a specific understanding of how the parent can create value. This understanding is built on insights they have gained both about opportunities to build or improve businesses and also about how the parent can contribute. The insights affect the focus of parenting activities, the design of the parent organization and the type of businesses in the company's portfolio. Moreover, successful companies frequently have insights that are unique, giving them an advantage over other parent companies.

The second feature of successful diversified companies is their distinctive parenting. Emerson's distinctive parenting characteristics start with its planning process. At the heart of the process is the 'planning conference,' an annual meeting between parent managers and businesses that is unusually combative and challenging. The degree of preparation done by both sides is unusual; the 40 required charts and analyses are unusual; and the expertise of Chuck Knight, Emerson's CEO, based on 20 years' experience with running these meetings and monitoring Emerson's kind of businesses, is unusual. It is through the planning conference that Knight tests the thinking and the goals of the businesses, pressing for improvements and helping to identify ways of achieving them. By design, the atmosphere is confrontational. 'Emerson is a contact sport,' commented one manager. 'Knight invites people to punch back. He takes positions to provoke a response and expects one.' The debates are often heated, but the parent managers have the skills to make them open and constructive.

Canon has many distinctive parenting characteristics. Probably most important is Canon's uncompromising corporate commitment to developing its core technologies that goes back to its roots as a research laboratory. Professor Yamanouchi, previously a Canon employee, explained, 'R&D drives Canon's strategic thinking and is central to Canon's behavior. As an example, the medium range plan of each product group is drawn up by the development center of the product group. Canon's R&D staff, therefore, believe that their work is essential for the growth of Canon.' This commitment is linked to Canon's very large corporate staff which includes over 1,000 central research staff. Commitment to technology is also revealed in Canon frequently being among the top three companies registering new US patents.

Another distinctive parenting characteristic is Canon's ability to reduce rigidity in organizational boundaries by encouraging networking and cross-company linkages. The organization operates as a 'hub and spoke' system, with matrix lines that bind the spokes together. At the center there is a 22–man corporate executive committee which meets weekly, bringing together the central managers, the heads of product divisions, the heads of sales organizations and the heads of functions. This level of contact is unusual and greatly helps the effective management of the matrix. Canon also has many other mechanisms, such as heavyweight task forces, product development teams and career management processes, designed to bring people together and move them across functional and organizational boundaries.

ABB, our third example, also has distinctive parenting characteristics. Percy Barnevik, ABB's chief executive, developed his parenting approach by turning round ASEA in the late 1970s and early 1980s. ABB's 'lean matrix' of business areas and country managers topped by a corporate center with around 100 staff has been written about frequently. It is designed to break previously monolithic, national companies into small, focused business units linked to similar units in other countries, but still benefiting from a strong national presence. Business area managers are part of the parent organization. They make decisions about rationalizing production across countries and spend their lives visiting business units to persuade unit managers to share technical developments, cross-sell products and pick up on best practice.

Supporting this highly decentralized structure is a central monitoring and control system, Abacus, that provides profit statements and balance sheet information for every business unit and profit center (5,000 in total). Units can compare themselves, and senior managers can rapidly identify anomalies or problem areas. This profit focused information system combined with the small size of most business units, often less than 200 people and sometimes as few as 50, helps drive a commercial, profit-focused attitude into the culture of the lowest level engineer or manager. ABB's parenting systems and structures are distinctive and are linked to the value creation insights that provide a focus for all of ABB's parenting activities.

Successful parent companies, therefore, have a clear focus for their parenting activities, based on value creation insights. They also have distinctive parenting characteristics that enable them to create the value they focus on. In addition, successful companies have a portfolio of businesses that fit with their parenting. They are clear about the criteria that define what we call their 'heartland businesses,' the businesses that will benefit most from the center's parenting influence, and they focus their portfolios on such businesses. In these businesses, they are able to create high value and to avoid value destruction.

Emerson's heartland is businesses that manufacture electrical, electro-mechanical or electronic products of medium technology and capital intensity where there is potential to raise performance. Emerson avoids consumer markets: 'Our ability to strategize in consumer products is less good. We like a slower rhythm. We don't like advertising and short product cycles.' Canon's heartland includes businesses where precision mechanics, fine optics, and micro-electronics are important technologies, where technical innovation and creative market positioning are important sources of advantage, and where there is a sufficiently large market to justify intensive technical development. ABB's heartland includes engineering intensive, electro-technical businesses where there is potential to create linkages across national borders and which involve selling complex systems to large industrial companies or to governments.

Developing Successful Corporate Strategies

ABB, Canon and Emerson are successful parent companies with value-creating corporate strategies. They have value creation insights and distinctive parenting characteristics, and by focusing on a clearly defined heartland they avoid the value destroying pitfalls that afflict many companies. But how can other companies that are currently less successful develop similarly powerful corporate strategies? We will end this reading by proposing a criterion, parenting advantage, that should guide companies, and a framework that can be used to structure their search for successful corporate strategies.

We have argued that success is dependent on the value created or destroyed by the parent organization. By doing so we are identifying the parent as an organization that is separate from the business units, and that stands between the business units and the investors. This separate organization needs to justify its existence as an intermediary. Moreover, the parent organization is in competition with other parent organizations and other intermediaries for the ownership of businesses. To succeed, a parent organization needs to create value and it needs to be better at creating value than rivals – it needs to have what we call 'parenting advantage.'

Parenting advantage is a criterion for guiding corporate strategy development, in the same way that competitive advantage is a criterion for guiding business strategy development. In business strategy, the key objective is to outperform competitors, and the concept of competitive advantage has proved immensely useful in assessing and developing business strategies. In corporate strategy, the key objective is to outperform rivals and other intermediaries, and the concept of parenting advantage has similar power to help assess and develop corporate strategies.

In the increasingly active market for corporate control that exists in Anglo-Saxon economies, parenting advantage is the only robust logic for a parent company to own a business. Without parenting advantage, a company is potentially exposed to the hostile attentions of other, superior rivals, and can often enhance shareholder value simply by selling businesses to other owners. Parenting advantage is the goal and criterion that should guide both the selection of businesses to include in the portfolio and the design of the parent organization.

As companies search for parenting advantage, they need to analyze and assess a number of inputs. They need to understand the strengths and weaknesses of the existing parent organization: What are the current characteristics of the parent? They need to understand the nature of the businesses currently owned by the parent: What are the parenting opportunities in these businesses? They need to know enough about rival parents to be able to assess which parents might be better owners of any of the current businesses. Finally, they need to understand the trends and possible scenarios for the future that might affect the other three inputs. Developing corporate strategy, therefore, involves four inputs (Figure 6.4.1).

These inputs do not provide answers. Rather they provide understandings that are useful in the search for value creation insights. This search is an essentially creative process guided by the objective of parenting advantage: the strategist is searching for a strategy that will give the company parenting advantage. The outputs of this strategy development process are decisions about which businesses to include in the portfolio and decisions about how the parent organization should be designed.

A useful first step in developing a new corporate strategy is to identify areas where the parent is currently destroying value. By divesting businesses or changing the parent's behavior these situations can be avoided. For many companies this first step greatly enhances shareholder value.

The second step is to start searching for 'parenting opportunities.' These are opportunities to improve performance through the involvement of a parent company. For example, a business may have low levels of manufacturing skills because it is dominated by marketing managers. A parent company with a manufacturing capability can, therefore, help redress the balance. Or a business may be too small, causing its costs to be too high. By combining it with another business, a parent company can cure the scale problem, Table 6.4.2 describes some of the common reasons why businesses under-perform in ways that provide parenting opportunities.

The third step is to assess whether and how the company can grasp the

FIGURE 6.4.1
Corporate strategy
framework

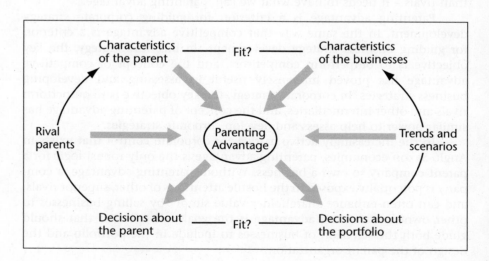

TABLE 6.4.2
Typical reasons for
parenting opportunities

Wrongly Defined Business	The managers in the business have a wrong conception of what the business should be and, therefore, have too narrow or too broad a product market scope, and too much or too little vertical integration. The trend to outsourcing and alliances is changing the definitions of many businesses, creating new parenting opportunities.
Size and Age	Old, large, successful businesses often build up bureaucracies and overheads that are hard to eliminate from the inside. Small, young businesses may have insufficient functional skills, managerial succession problems and lack of financial resources to ride a recession. In both cases parenting opportunities exist.
Temptations	Some businesses tempt their managers to make mistakes. Mature businesses often lead managers into over-diversifying. Businesses with long product cycles cause managers to rely too much on old products. Cyclical businesses cause managers to over-invest in the upswing. In all cases there are opportunities for a parent to provide corrective influence.
Linkages	Where businesses can create value through linking with other businesses, blockages often exist preventing this from happening between independent companies. Parent organizations can remove these blockages.
Major Changes	Industries undergoing change, for example from local to international or from single product to system, require managers with real expertise at making these changes. A parent organization that develops this expertise can provide important assistance to businesses it owns.
Special Expertise	Special expertise can be created by exposing managers to a number of businesses either facing similar strategic issues, such as declining sales or the need to professionalize management, or involved in similar products and markets, but in different countries. A parent organization owning these similar businesses can build the expertise.

parenting opportunities. This involves creating groupings of businesses with similar parenting opportunities. Each grouping is then assessed for its fit with the parent organization. Could the capabilities and resources in the parent fit with the parenting opportunities in the group of businesses? If fit does not currently exist, the question is what changes would be necessary in the parent organization to create a fit. Achieving a good fit may take a number of years of searching for parenting opportunities and developing capabilities and resources to match.

Once a concept of parenting advantage has been developed and the basis for a corporate strategy agreed, we have found it useful to capture this in a parenting advantage statement (see statement for ABB, Table 6.4.3). This statement identifies the value creation insights and distinctive parenting

TABLE 6.4.3
Parenting advantage
statement

Value Creation Insights	Most companies make direct trade-offs between centralization and decentralization, or scale and focus. There are opportunities for a parent that can combine the various benefits in new ways.
	Many European engineering businesses have been relatively fragmented in global terms. Consolidation can reduce costs while increasing coverage and global muscle.
	Many engineering businesses do not have a strong commercial focus, and are prone to increase sales volume and product range at the expense of margin. A parent can help redress the balance.
Distinctive Parenting Characteristics	Ability to combine decentralized small business units into a global network through the ABB matrix structure.
	Systems and corporate initiatives that focus on profitability, customer needs, and simplification of operations.
	Ability to integrate acquisitions and improve their performance rapidly.
	Ruthless approach to cutting of overhead costs.
Heartland Businesses	Engineering-intensive, electro-technical businesses, usually involving complex integration into systems. Customers are large industrial or governmental institutions.

characteristics on which the strategy will be built, and the heartland businesses within which parenting advantage will be sought. The parenting advantage statement captures the essence of a value-creating corporate strategy and provides a succinct view of how and why parenting advantage will be achieved.

The chosen strategy can then be converted into an action plan, involving decisions about the parent organization and decisions about the portfolio of businesses. The implementation of these decisions will, in turn, feed back into changes in the parenting characteristics and the business characteristics. The ongoing corporate strategy development process thus requires continuous adjustment of the parent company and the portfolio of businesses to bring about a closer fit, and to adjust to unplanned changes in any of the important factors.

For companies whose corporate-level plan has traditionally been little more than an aggregation of the plans of the businesses, together with a page or two describing the company's overall ambitions and objectives, the corporate strategy development process we are suggesting is radically different. It puts the role of the parent in creating, and destroying, value at center stage; it insists that decisions that impact the capabilities and resources of the parent are just as essential components of corporate strategy as portfolio choices; and it derives choices about the corporate strategy from assessment of their likely impact on net value creation and parenting advantage. As such, it forces companies to face up to the fact that they are likely to be destroying value in many of their businesses, and to search for ways in which they can become better parents for all of their businesses.

The parenting advantage framework can also lead to very different conclusions from other, more conventional theories of corporate strategy. For example, objectives such as portfolio balance, spread of risk, and growth take second place to parenting advantage. Decisions that improve balance, or increase spread of risk, or raise the rate of corporate growth cannot, in our view, be justified if they at the same time damage parenting advantage. Many of the large chemical companies that diversified away from bulk chemicals into specialty chemicals, in search of faster growth, more spread and greater balance, have subsequently regretted their decisions. They have found that they were not able to parent the specialty businesses well, and that their results have therefore been disappointing. A focus on parenting advantage in corporate strategy development would have prevented many of these decisions.

Parenting advantage thinking has more in common with core competences thinking. But there are important differences. The parenting advantage framework puts the emphasis on the capabilities and resources of the parent (parenting competences), and the impact of these on the businesses. The core competences logic does not distinguish so clearly between parent competences and business competences, and simply encourages companies to base their corporate strategies on competences that are or could become common across the portfolio. As a result, the development of core competences can sometimes conflict with the pursuit of parenting advantage. Texas Instruments, for example, attempted to exploit technical competences it had developed in its semi-conductor businesses in areas such as calculators, watches, and home computers. It failed in these new areas not because it did not possess the requisite technical skills, but because senior managers in the parent company lacked experience and skills in parenting such consumer-oriented businesses. Similarly, Minebea, the Japanese leader in miniature ball bearings, attempted to move into semi-conductors, on the basis of its skills in precision manufacturing of miniature components. It has found, however, that this undoubted competence has not proved sufficient to allow it to become successful in the semi-conductor business, and in 1991 it reported a loss of ¥5 billion from its semi-conductor subsidiary. In both cases, although the diversifications drew on common technical competences, they were not successful because the corporate center lacked the appropriate parenting competences to avoid the mistakes that were made.

Conversely, corporate strategies that build on powerful capabilities and resources in the parent company, but do not involve the sharing of operating competences between the businesses, can be less easy to understand from a core competences perspective. BTR, the highly successful British-based industrial manufacturing company, voted best-managed company in Britain in 1993, has a corporate strategy based on clear sources of parenting advantage, but it does not go in for sharing marketing, technical, or engineering skills across its businesses. BTR's success with a portfolio of more than 1,000 business units in more than 50 countries is not based on core comperences. Like Emerson, it is based on the influence the parent organization exerts to raise performance in its businesses.

The parenting advantage framework that we propose therefore represents a new approach to the familiar issues of corporate strategy. Our conviction is that its use will help many corporate parents avoid destroying value through their corporate strategies, and move them towards the objective of becoming the best parent for the businesses they own.

6.5   Adding Value from Corporate Headquarters

By Andrew Campbell and Michael Goold[1]

Introduction

The key issue for the chief executive of a diversified company is: Do the separate businesses gain from membership of the whole? Is the whole greater than the sum of the parts? The test is whether business units perform better as part of the corporate portfolio than they would as independent companies. This is the harsh criterion that all central management groups should apply in rating their own effectiveness.

The same question also arises in comparing different companies. Often the issue is not only whether a business would be better off as part of a group than as an independent company, but also whether the business would prosper more in one group than another. In acquisition battles, such as the fight between Hanson Trust and United Biscuit for control of Imperial, the option of continued independence was ruled out early, and the outcome turned on judgements about which contender would make the better parent organization.

For the last four years we have been studying the way that the corporate centre adds value to the business units. By looking at 16 major British companies we have defined three broad categories of management style used by the centre – Strategic Planning (such as BP and UB), Strategic Control (such as Courtaulds and ICI), and Financial Control (such as Hanson and BTR).

We have found that the different styles cause value to be added in different ways. None of them proved to be inherently best. Each has strengths and weaknesses. Each adds value in a specific way and each can subtract value (i.e. make the business unit perform less well than it would as an independent company). Corporate managers faced with the problem of

---

[1] Source: This article was originally published in the *London Business School Journal* (Summer 1988). Reprinted by permission of the authors.

maximizing their effectiveness need to understand the strengths and weaknesses of the different styles and how to get the best from the style they have chosen.

This article summarizes the results of our research, explaining the differences between the styles and the different ways in which they add value to the portfolio of business units.

Why Different Styles Exist

We identified important tensions or trade-offs confronting corporate level managers. For example, the chief executive would like to help the business units by giving strong leadership from the centre, providing clear direction about which products and markets are suitable and how the units should compete. On the other hand, the chief executive would like to release the energies and entrepreneurial commitment of managers lower down by giving them wide autonomy to run their businesses as they please and to feel a sense of ownership. These two objectives are in conflict. The centre cannot simultaneously provide strong leadership and give autonomy to the business units. Hence we labeled it a tension facing corporate-level managers. The chief executive needs to decide where, on the scale of leadership versus autonomy, he wants to be positioned.

We identified four other similar tensions – coordination and cooperation versus clear responsibilities and accountability; thorough analysis and planning versus entrepreneurial speed of response; long-term strategic targets versus short-term financial targets; and flexible strategies (i.e. strategies that can be changed quickly to meet competitor moves) versus tight controls.

The three different styles (strategic planning, strategic control, and financial control) exist because it is possible to develop three different positionings against these tensions (see Figure 6.5.1, 'The Styles Matrix'). Hence, managers in the headquarters of Hanson Trust believe in autonomy for business units, clear accountability, entrepreneurial decision making, short-term financial targets, and tight controls. Alternatively, managers at the centre of BP believe in leadership from the centre, coordination and cooperation between different business units, thorough analysis and review of major decisions, long-term strategic targets, and flexible strategies. Figure 6.5.2 summarizes the choices underlying each of the styles and compares these to the style used by the capital markets in relation to an independent company.

We also defined eight mechanisms through which the centre can add value to its business units. We recognized that the centre can only add value if it successfully influences (for the better) the strategies and actions of managers in the business units. The eight mechanisms are tools that the centre uses to influence strategy and actions. They are the organization structure; the planning process; the use of themes, thrusts, or suggestions to guide managers; the degree to which the centre managers overlap between units; the resource allocation decisions taken by the centre; the objectives set for each unit; the closeness of monitoring against objectives;

FIGURE 6.5.1
The Styles Matrix

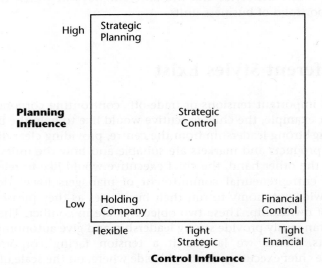

The strategic planning, strategic control, and financial control styles form part of a continuum of ways headquarters can influence business units. The continuum has two dimensions: (1) planning influence, which expresses the degree to which strategy is centralized, and (2) control influence, which shows the importance companies attach to short-term financial targets.

Companies that fall in the bottom left-hand corner con be labeled holding companies. In such organizations the centre has little influence over the subsidiaries. Our research found that successful companies moved away from the holding company style to one of the three alternatives.

The top right-hand corner of the matrix is blank because this style appears to be infeasible. Some companies in our research tried to combine a high degree of planning influence with tight short-term controls, but they have moved away from it. Either business unit managers became demotivated by a seemingly oppressive corporate centre, or headquarters failed to maintain sufficient objectivity to keep the controls tight.

and the types of incentives and sanctions applied to managers who meet or fail to meet targets.

Each style uses these mechanisms in different ways and to different degrees, depending on the choices that have been made on the tensions. For example, a company that prizes coordination and cooperation, such as BP, has a matrix organization structure in its oil business that forces managers to coordinate over the big decisions. A company that believes in strong leadership, such as the Lex Service Group, guides business unit managers by often repeated themes, by defining the main thrusts of the organisation, and by making frequent suggestions or instructions. The choices managers make about the tensions affect the way the company uses these mechanisms.

In this reading, we summarize the key features of each style against the eight mechanisms and we show how the features can both add value to the subsidiaries as well as subtract value. Some of the negative consequences of a style are intrinsic and unavoidable; others are pitfalls that can be avoided. While we recognize that no style is superior for all situations, we believe

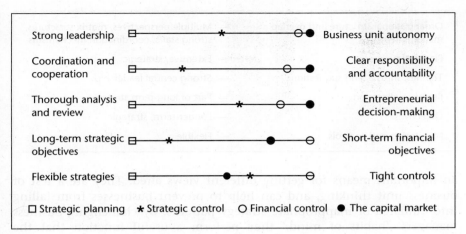

FIGURE 6.5.2
Tensions in corporate level management

that managers who understand the style they are using will be able to avoid the pitfalls and make sure that the net contribution of the centre is positive rather than negative.

Strategic Planning

The strategic planning style is characterized by an emphasis on strategy, on long-term objectives, and on a cooperative, flexible management approach. Figure 6.5.3 summarizes the key features.

The complex and overlapping organisational structures of these companies ensure that a variety of views on strategy will be expressed. They also allow the centre to inject its ideas into the formulation of strategy. So they bring the judgement and experience of a cross-section of senior managers into play to help define the best ways forward. This allows a wider discussion of issues and a more comprehensive search for new strategy options than would occur in an independent company. Coordinating committees and devices also allow strategies to be drawn together across a variety of businesses (or countries), to achieve benefits of synergy and integration that would not be available to separate companies. And strong staff groups at the centre allow economies of scope in the provision of central services.

The drawback of this structure is that business managers have less clear-cut individual responsibilities, less control over their own destinies. The emphasis on cooperation between businesses and across levels, and the need to coordinate strategies, means that they have less unilateral authority to take decisions for their businesses that they personally feel are right. The inevitable price of multiple viewpoints and synergy is some loss of autonomy. This, in turn, can reduce motivation, unless a sense of shared purpose compensates for the loss of individual responsibility.

The *extensive planning processes* of the Strategic Planning companies are

FIGURE 6.5.3
Strategic planning: key
features

Organizational structure and overlap management	— Multiple perspectives, matrix structures, strong staffs, coordination mechanisms
Planning process	— Extensive, strategic
Themes, thrusts, and suggestions	— Strong central leadership
Resource allocation	— Part of long-term strategy
Objectives	— Longer-term, strategic
Monitoring and controls	— Flexible

an important means for getting different views aired. They are a test of business unit thinking, and can help to prevent businesses from falling into outdated or inappropriate strategy patterns. By challenging business managers' 'habits of mind,' they perform a useful function that the independent company lacks. The questions posed by the central management in a Strategic Planning company should be much more informed, much more 'strategic' than is possible for the outside investors and bankers to whom the independent company reports. This is a prime value of the planning processes of the Strategic Planning company. They also constitute a vehicle for the exercise of central leadership in strategic decision making, and a means by which the centre can learn more about the businesses. But extensive planning processes cannot avoid constraining business managers. As one line manager explained:

> The decision-making and planning process in our company is very professional. We are very open about discussing things. We chew over important decisions at great length. My boss will get involved and his boss will join in the thinking. It's all very constructive and I am sure we make a better decision as a result. But somehow after all the discussion, I don't feel it's my decision anymore.

The need to communicate and justify plans to the center inhibits freedom of action, slows down the decision process, and takes some ownership from lower levels of management. The independent company can be swifter and more entrepreneurial.

Furthermore, Strategic Planning processes are often cumbersome and confusing rather than probing and insightful. At their worst, they degenerate into rigid, bureaucratic exercises. The drawbacks of bureaucracy in planning may not be intrinsic to the Strategic Planning style, but it is an occupational hazard – a potential pitfall.

By providing *strong central leadership* through themes, thrusts, and suggestions, the Strategic Planning companies are able to embark on bolder, more aggressive strategies than would otherwise emerge. Central sponsorship can enlarge the ambitions of business management, ensure that resources are available to support investments, and help to overcome risk aversion. We have given examples in each Strategic Planning company of the sorts of business-building strategies that result, often looking toward the building of long-term advantage in major international businesses. It is doubtful whether these strategies would have been adopted by independent companies without a supportive and well-resourced parent in the background to underwrite the effort. It is in this context that mission statements and broad policies can be valuable, by defining what will receive priority from the centre.

The downside of strong leadership is equally clear. Close involvement by the centre in strategy development inevitably reduces both the objectivity of the centre in reviewing strategy, and the sense of personal 'ownership' at the business level. This is the strong leadership-business autonomy tension.

Moreover, strong leadership can lead to a number of pitfalls. It can be seen as autocratic or ill-informed interference that overrules business-level ideas; bold strategies can become risky and overoptimistic; sound opportunities in noncore businesses may be turned down because they do not fit with the grand design. These pitfalls are frequently associated with the Strategic Planning style, although the best exponents of the style are able to avoid them. In companies such as BP, strong leadership blends into a cooperative attempt to work together for a common aim, thereby generating a sense of shared purpose and commitment that goes far to offset the disadvantages we have listed.

Resource allocation and objective setting in the Strategic Planning companies are aimed at the long-term development of the business. The centre acts as a sort of buffer to the capital market, protecting the business units from the need to satisfy the shorter-term performance criteria applied by the outside investor. This allows business managers to concentrate on building the core businesses, rather than trimming their sails with a view to meeting half-yearly earnings targets. It also means that they can make major acquisitions to support existing activities, or to build new ones, without an expectation that the payoff to such moves will come immediately. Clear priority can be given to long-term objectives.

There are a number of businesses in the Strategic Planning companies that have benefited from this strategic, long-term resource allocation process. Without it, BOC would be a weaker force in the world-wide gases business; Lex would not have built up its electronic component distribution business, BP would not have achieved its successes in oil and gas exploration. But there are others that, it can be argued, might have reacted more quickly to adversity, or avoided risky and unpromising investments, if they *had* been exposed to the disciplines of the external capital market.

Several managers in Strategic Planning companies made us aware of the dangers of too much emphasis on strategy and the long term. 'The pressure on the long term took our eye off the short-term issues. They [corporate] and we undervalued the short-term profit impact of what we were doing,' said one manager. 'Too much strategy and not enough graft,' was the conclusion of another.

We have also pointed out the difficulty in defining clear, objective, and measurable goals for monitoring long-term performance. This means that long-term performance measures open up the possibility of excuses. As Dick Giordano of BOC put it: 'This is probably one of the most difficult challenges. How do you have milestones that measure strategic progress without allowing excuse making from business management?' But to point to these shortcomings is only to underline the tension that exists between giving priority to profits now or profits later, to short-term controls or long-term objectives. All Strategic Planning companies must accept some sacrifice in the clarity and enforceability of short-term objectives in order to allow for the allocation of resources to long-term aims.

Linked to this tension we noted that Strategic Planning companies are also prone to undue optimism about the future or to personal incentives that are not linked to strategies. Lacking both market disciplines and clear internal targets, the atmosphere can become too cosy. As one divisional manager put it: 'As part of the corporate entity, we have this shield and blanket around us to protect us.' This can mean that flexibility becomes tolerance, and tolerance becomes looseness. Motivation to perform is then at risk. The fact that the Strategic Planning companies have been relatively inactive in divestments, closures, and portfolio rationalisations, and that some have overextended themselves through rapid growth, is all evidence of this.

Furthermore, replacing the verdict of the stock market with subjective corporate assessments of strategic progress may not be an unmitigated gain. If second guessing what will impress the centre becomes the major goal, this can be even less conducive to strategic thinking than the short-term financial pressures of the City. It is in these circumstances that corporate 'politics' flourish, with decisions taken to reinforce personal positions in the hierarchy, rather than to improve the strategies of the business.

Finally, the *flexible control system* in the Strategic Planning companies adds value. By accepting that precise, short-term targets may have to be compromised in order to stay on track to build a business, it encourages a more tenacious pursuit of long-term goals. Furthermore, it is more tolerant of innovative strategies that carry with them the risk of failure, and of strategies that evolve continuously to meet the needs of rapidly changing markets. The centre in the Strategic Planning company is more sympathetic than the capital market to the manager who is struggling to create a major new business in a highly competitive and uncertain world.

Flexible controls, however, can never provide clear and objective standards of performance. Hence it is harder for both the centre and the business manager to know whether results are 'on target.' An element of judgement enters into the assessment of performance, and increases the scope for discretion. The price of flexibility is ambiguous performance measures and a reduced sense of personal accountability.

Table 6.5.1 summarizes the key features and the added and subtracted value of the Strategic Planning style. We have divided the negative features of the style between those that are intrinsic and those that represent pitfalls that can be avoided. With skilful management the negative features of the style can be minimized or avoided by:

■   sensitive, flexible, and selective planning processes;

■   leadership;

■   well-informed central management;

■   shared purpose and commitment;

TABLE 6.5.1
The strategic planning style

Key Features	Added Value	Intrinsic Subtracted Value	Common But Avoidable Pitfalls
Complex, coordinated structure	Wider discussion of issues Synergy Central services	Less individual responsibility and authority	Can reduce motivation
Extensive, strategic planning process	More thorough search for best strategies	Less freedom of action Slower decisions	Can be cumbersome, confusing, bureaucratic
Strong central leadership	Bolder strategies Shared purpose and commitment	Less 'ownership' by business Less objectivity by centre	Can become interference Can lead to risky and overambitious strategies
Long-term criteria	Building core businesses 'Buffer' to capital market	Slower reactions to adversity Less clear targets	Can lead to overoptimism, 'lip service'
Flexible controls	More tenacious pursuit of long-term goals More innovative, responsive strategies	Subjective assessments Less accountability	Can lead to politics

- avoiding overoptimism;
- incentives aligned with strategy;
- strenuous efforts to identify, measure, and act on strategic milestones.

But the style will always give less priority to individual accountability, responsibility, and incentives, and to short-term measures of performance.

Financial Control

At the opposite extreme to Strategic Planning lies Financial Control. Figure 6.5.4 summarizes the key features of this style.

The *organizational structures* of the Financial Control companies stress *multiple, separate profit centres*, each with independent responsibilities. As far as possible, these structures replicate, for the profit centres, the circumstances of independent companies. The profit centres are set up to overlap as little as possible, and no attempt is made by the centre to coordinate between them. The profit centre manager is largely free to run his own show without interference from other parts of the company. 'We believe in the

FIGURE 6.5.4
Financial control: key
features

Organizational structure and overlap management	— Clearly separate, profit centre responsibilities
Planning process	— Budgets
Themes, thrusts, and suggestions	— Business autonomy stressed
Resource allocation	— Project-based, short payback criteria
Objectives	— Shorter-term, financial
Monitoring and controls	— Very tight

importance of the individual line manager in achieving success for his business and for the group as a whole. The management system has been devised to give maximum responsibility to the line management,' said Martin Taylor of Hanson Trust. There are advantages in the simplicity and clarity of this structure. In particular it gives early general management responsibility, thereby developing the skills needed for the long-term success of the company.

But the structure is less ambitious than that of the Strategic Planning companies. It adds no value in comparison to the independent company situation; but at least it avoids the negatives that are also associated with the more complex structures of Strategic Planning companies.

The *planning process* in the Financial Control companies *concentrates on budgets*. The emphasis is on the short term, and on agreeing targets rather than on the means by which they are going to be achieved. As with Strategic Planning companies, the centre probes the plans of business managers, but the nature of the questioning is very different. For Financial Control companies the primary value arises from the pressure it creates for 'high-wire' standards of profitability and growth in profits, not from probing underlying strategic logic. As Lionel Stammers of BTR put it: 'Many managers do not know what they can achieve until you ask them.' The Financial Control companies add value by asking for performance that is more demanding than that insisted on by stockholders or bankers, and they exert pressure for performance much more continuously. An independent company can produce unexciting results for long periods, in some cases for many years, before market pressure will cause a change in management. But in Financial Control companies controls are tight.

As a by-product of the budgeting process, managers may also have to think again about the validity of the strategies they are following. If they are unable to satisfy corporate requirements, they may be forced to consider changes of direction. But the centre will not typically question strategies directly, or expect to make much contribution to the definition of new and preferable strategy options. And the emphasis is on next year's results, 'the road ahead,' not the long term. The focus on results not strategies leaves managers more free to make their own decisions, provided they turn in the required performance. Furthermore, the planning process can be simpler and therefore less prone to 'bureaucracy' than in Strategic Planning companies.

The major drawback of the planning process is that it cannot claim to add much value to the business manager in probing and thinking through his strategy options. Indeed, the short-term results orientation may distract him from tackling long-term issues. If the stock market is felt to create an unduly short-term orientation, the Financial Control style serves to reinforce this bias. We noted, for example, that a number of the subsidiaries of Financial Control companies are losing market share. Their managers explained that they are retreating from less profitable sections of the market, and that market share is not a useful objective. As one BTR manager put it: 'We don't pride ourselves on market share. In fact, we don't like to refer to market share at all.' It is this focus on the short term that causes critics of Financial Control companies to claim that they are gradually harvesting their competitive positions. Taken to extremes the style can encourage managers to milk their businesses by cutting back too far on investment.

Although the centre may make occasional suggestions, *business autonomy* is preserved. In the Financial Control companies by insisting that the final decision rests with business management and by avoiding any broad, top-down corporate themes, missions, or thrusts. This philosophy attempts to replicate the freedom of the independent company, and hence can obviously add little value when compared to it. If, however, constructive suggestions are made, but not imposed, the business manager may gain something that is denied to his fully independent counterpart. Nevertheless, it is clear that Financial Control does not attempt to add as much value in this respect as Strategic Planning; equally, however, it runs fewer risks of subtracting value.

The resource allocation process in the Financial Control companies adopts *objectives and criteria similar to the capital market*. There is no attempt to buffer the businesses from requirements for short-term profit. Rather, the Financial Control style sees itself as applying capital market criteria but in a much more thoroughgoing and efficient manner. With detailed information on each business and the ability to discriminate between them in resource allocation, the centre can ensure that funds flow only to those businesses whose proposals meet corporate criteria, and whose track records give confidence in their ability to deliver. The system reviews each investment on its merits, rather than as part of a long-term business strategy. It adds value by insisting that proposals will only be funded if they project high returns and fast paybacks, and if business managers appear committed to achieving their forecasts and have a track record of doing so in the past. By exposing all individual investments to this test, it goes much further than the capital markets in applying tough standards. The centre, however, does not pretend to have a detailed knowledge of each business's products and markets, or to be able to criticize, shape, and add value to the strategies behind the investment proposals.

The centre is more directly active in acquisitions and divestments. The search is for acquisition candidates whose assets are underperforming. Value is added to these acquisitions by increasing their profitability through the application of Financial Control disciplines. Conversely, divestments are made of businesses that do not respond to these criteria.

The clear emphasis on *short-term* profit *objectives* in resource allocation and acquisitions simplifies the management task. But it can also result in missed opportunities. We were told of a number of opportunities that had been considered and rejected because of the risk or the length of payback of the investment. Although it is not clear that the opportunities rejected would have resulted in substantial profit growth, it is probable that many more of these opportunities would have been taken up by Strategic Planning (or even Strategic Control) companies. One example is the market for standard gate arrays. Both GEC and Ferranti had the opportunity to enter the fast-growing MOS-technology segment at the early stages. Both rejected the opportunity. Ferranti chose to stay with its proven bipolar technology and GEC, after examining options, passed up the opportunity altogether. The bold strategies they rejected were pursued by LSI Logic, which now has a leading position world-wide. The short-term focus does preclude longer-term, more speculative investments. The tension remains and means that the Financial Control style will always create problems in businesses where long timescales are needed.

The main strength of the Financial Control style, however, is in the *tight controls* it imposes. Not only are budgets stretching; not only do investments demand short paybacks; but also the monitoring of results achieved and the feedback and follow through from the centre create strong incentives to deliver. The knowledge that there will be a speedy reaction to under- (or over-) achievement of monthly targets does create more motivation, more pressure for performance than is brought to bear on the managing director of an independent company. The simplicity of the criteria for judging performance also makes it easier for line managers to know where to focus their attention, and makes it perfectly clear who is doing a good job and succeeding, and who is not. Indeed, the knowledge that demanding standards have been set and can be seen to have been met is one of the prime motivating factors for successful managers in the Financial Control companies. A BTR division head commented that he would be willing to forgo £10,000 in salary in exchange for the psychological satisfaction of knowing he was going to be able to deliver on his budgeted objectives.

Those who do meet their objectives can be confident that they have earned the respect of the centre, and grow in self-confidence themselves. This has two benefits. It makes for a more open discussion of business issues with the centre, since the line manager can rely on his results rather than his words to impress the centre; and it creates a 'winner's' psychology among business managers which makes them feel more capable of overcoming obstacles and pushing on to further peaks of performance.

But the tight control process also has its downside. It can stifle creativity, snuff out experimentation, and eliminate the entrepreneurial skunk works activities. There is less flexibility to respond to opportunities. The point was made by a Hanson Trust group chairman in this way:

> Our business chief executives tend to be quite conservative in assessing the payback of potential investments. In order to preserve credibility with Hanson Trust, they will typically only promise what they are certain they can deliver. The chief executive knows he will be hung on it, and is therefore cautious rather than overambitious.

At its worst, tight control can mean that everything is sacrificed to meeting specified control objectives at whatever cost to the underlying health of the business. The system can become a straitjacket, not a source of added value.

Table 6.5.2 summarizes the key features and the added and subtracted value of the Financial Control style, again distinguishing between intrinsic problems and avoidable pitfalls. The negative features of this style can be minimized by:

■ targets that require year-on-year *growth* in profits;

■ leaving business managers in post long enough that they have to live with the consequences of the strategies they adopt;

■ informed central managers who will offer constructive advice and suggestions but without imposing their views;

■ willingness to question and override control objectives if it is clear that they will damage the health of the business;

■ a winner's psychology to provide energy to maintain growth momentum;

■ acceptance that, in some businesses, the Financial Control style may be inappropriate.

But the style cannot avoid problems in businesses where long-term, coordinated strategies are needed, and cannot claim to provide much constructive help to business managers in the search for optimum strategies.

TABLE 6.5.2
The financial control style

Key Features	Added Value	Intrinsic Subtracted Value	Common But Avoidable Pitfalls
Separate profit centres	Simplifies task Early general management responsibility	No coordination synergy	
Budgetary planning	Higher standards Challenges strategies that won't deliver Avoids 'potholes'	Distracts from strategic issues	Can encourage milking the business
Business autonomy	Advice, not instructions	No cooperation, no 'help' for businesses	
Short-term criteria	Clearer criteria 'Efficient' internal capital market	Missed opportunities 'Control games'	
Tight controls	Faster reaction More motivation 'Winner's' psychology	Less flexibility and creativity	Can become a straitjacket

Strategic control

Figure 6.5.5 shows the key features of the Strategic Control style, again expressed in terms that relate to our discussion of tensions. Strategic Control is a blend of the features found in Strategic Planning and Financial Control. By structuring themselves around individual profit centre businesses that are grouped into divisions, Strategic Control companies claim to achieve the motivational benefits of decentralization, while allowing important business overlaps to be managed at the business level. There is some added value from divisional coordination, but a minimum of interference with business managers.

This view may justify the divisional structure. But even if the divisional level is able to achieve synergies between businesses that would not be achieved independently, it is less clear how the corporate level adds value, structurally, to the divisions. Put simply, what would the divisions lose if they were set up as independent companies? As in Financial Control companies, the decentralized structure leaves little room for the centre to orchestrate the several businesses in the portfolio.

Strategic Control companies argue that they have a prime contribution to divisional thinking via the quality controls in the *strategic review process*. The disciplines provide a continuing challenge that sharpens the thinking in the divisions and businesses. By its probing, the centre raises minimum standards of thinking and analysis, and prevents 'habits of mind' from forming. The intention is similar to that of the Strategic Planning companies, although Strategic Control companies limit themselves to a questioning role, and do not propose their own views from the centre.

Although we have found some evidence to support these contentions, our research suggests that in reality the challenge to divisional thinking is not always helpful. Extensive planning processes run into the same problem of acting as a constraint that we described for the Strategic Planning companies. Moreover, bureaucracy grows quickly in Strategic Control companies because the centre is that much more distant from the businesses. One manager explained that the planning reviews in his company were a 'whole series of rakings over, all of them too shallow.' This means either that the centre may fail to be well-enough informed to ask useful questions, or

FIGURE 6.5.5
Strategic control: key features

Organizational structure and overlap management	— Decentralized profit centres; some divisional coordination
Planning process	— Extensive, strategic
Themes, thrusts, and suggestions	— Avoided; business autonomy stressed
Resource allocation	— Part of long-term strategy
Objectives	— Longer-term, strategic and shorter-term financial
Monitoring and controls	— Tight

that any benefits may be more than offset by the time-consuming and costly processes that they involve. 'Net' added value is not always delivered by corporate planning processes. Only if these processes are sensitively designed and administered, and if the businesses in the portfolio are likely to respond to a second view can value be added by the centre.

Strategic Control companies generally *avoid major suggestions and initiatives* and are not active in coordinating between divisions or businesses. The emphasis on *business autonomy* is well caught by the chairman of a Vickers division, who said:

> In giving freedom, it's a bit nerve-racking at times because you feel you're not in control, not in charge. But the result is that they take more initiative and they perform better. And they feel responsible for their actions whereas if you at the centre always ask questions, always try and monitor things very, very carefully, you get a reaction that they're not really responsible for the decisions, that you're really controlling things, and so if it goes wrong, it's as much your fault as it is theirs.

Strategic Control companies recognize that direction from the centre can subtract value. They stress the responsibility and independence of the business manager. However, this means that they are unlikely to add value by steering the development of strategy. Where *ad hoc* interventions do take place, our research would indicate that value was subtracted at least as often as it was added.

It is in *a resource allocation process that balances long- and short-term goals* that many Strategic Control companies add the most value. The centre provides access to a pool of resources, which can be made available for investment in long-term, large or risky projects. These projects might be turned down by outside investors, who have little knowledge of the business and who are often short-term or fashion driven in their attitudes, focusing more on past results than future prospects, and failing to assess technically complex or strategically innovative ideas. As Sir John Clark of Plessey argued: 'City pressures make life difficult if you're trying to balance short-term profit pressure and the requirements of the business in terms of competitive advantage.' Many of the business and divisional managements also see real value in this access to funding. 'Probably the greatest benefit of being part of ICI is that they were willing to fund us through seventeen years of losses in getting the business going' (chairman, ICI Pharmaceuticals). 'We were able to take a major step forwards in investment in new production capacity that would have been beyond us as an independent company' (chief executive, Howson Algraphy division, Vickers).

The downside of the long-term investment attitude is, of course, the same as in the Strategic Planning companies: a danger of undervaluing the importance of next year's profits. But the Strategic Control companies attempt to defend against this problem by balancing long-term objectives with short-term profit pressures. The ability of companies such as Courtaulds, ICI and Vickers to cut back drastically in some areas of their portfolios, while preserving growth momentum elsewhere, is evidence of their ability to make trade-offs of this sort. Indeed major corporate resource allocation decisions in the Strategic Control companies have concentrated at least as much on portfolio rationalization and profitability improvement as on long-term investment.

In practice, however, there are numerous difficulties in achieving the right balance of objectives. Assessing more speculative, longer-term investments is hard. If the centre lacks close familiarity with the business, it may be forced to rely on the credibility of the sponsoring management team together with formal financial evaluations – much the same criteria as used by the outside investor. Where long-term projects *are* backed by the centre, the reason may be personal commitments to a business rather than clear-sighted strategic thinking. We encountered several examples of long-term and continued support for a business by the centre that cost the company far more than a hard-nosed and early closure would have done.

Reliance on corporate funds for investment can also be a source of problems since capital scarcity can cut out investments that might have been funded by the outside market. During the years of financial crisis, Vickers was unable to finance good proposals that were coming forward and Courtaulds was short of funds for investments even in growth areas. During this period Courtaulds applied across-the-board cash targets to all its businesses regardless of previous success or failure. Now the company has set up its major business groups with capital structures to resemble as closely as possible the conditions of the publicly quoted parent company. It believes that the groups should be better placed to identify the consequences of their investment plans to their own balance sheets and take proper action in a more differentiated fashion to control the financing consequences of their business performance. This is a long way from viewing the value of corporate management mainly in terms of its ability to allocate resources.

Lastly, although portfolio rationalization has improved profitability ratios for the Strategic Control companies, it is less clear that divisions of these companies would have moved any less speedily to take corrective measures had they been independently set up. Strategic Control companies may move more decisively on rationalization and exit decisions than Strategic Planning or Holding companies, but the discipline of the outside capital markets would in some cases have been more pressing than that provided by corporate management.

The resource allocation process in the Strategic Control companies therefore attempts to combine the 'buffer' function of the Strategic Planning companies and the 'efficiency' function of the Financial Control companies. In some respects this achieves the best of both worlds; but in others it encounters the disadvantages that come from the lack of a clear commitment to either. This follows from the basic tension between short- and long-term goals. Furthermore, uninformed long-term investments, naive portfolio pruning, and partisan preference for particular businesses are all potential – if avoidable – pitfalls for Strategic Control.

It is therefore only if the centre is genuinely better informed, closer to the businesses, and as objective as the outside investor that value is likely to be added.

Detailed monitoring and reporting allow the centre to pinpoint shortcomings more precisely; and incentives and *tight strategic and financial controls* create personal motivation in a much less blunt fashion than the outside capital market, where takeovers or palace revolutions are effectively the only sanctions against nonperforming management. Provided, therefore, that the control objectives are conducive to the prosperity of the business, Strategic Control adds value.

Our research suggests, however, that the definition of strategic control objectives is fraught with difficulty. First, the objectives that Strategic Control companies establish do not always embody the strategies they have agreed. Financial controls can crowd out strategic objectives, thereby damaging the long-term interests of the business. Or vague strategic goals can become an excuse for nonperformance. This means that the control process becomes bogged down in arguments over trade-offs, and the intention to create tight control languishes. Second, as in Financial Control, tight controls can subtract values through causing inflexibility and risk aversion in strategies.

There is an intrinsic conflict between encouraging long-term, creative, strategic thinking, and imposing tight, short-term controls. Two quotes from divisional managing directors in Strategic Control companies are relevant. The first illustrates the tension between strategy and control: 'The centre is pressing us to grow. But it is unwilling to accept the negative impact on profitability this may entail.' The second illustrates the uneasy balance between strategic and financial control, and the difficulty of being poised between them: 'I asked the chief executive when I was appointed whether the company was a financial conglomerate or an industrial company. After four years the question still seems relevant, and the answer is always: "Ask me again in six months' time."' This remark found echoes in almost all the Strategic Control companies.

Making the controls supportive of flexible and innovative strategies is not easy. It can even be that the stock market, whose control process is less precise and rigorous, allows more latitude for business building than strategic controls that are poorly defined and insensitively applied.

Table 6.5.3 summarizes the key features and the added and subtracted value of the Strategic Control style. The negative features of the style can be minimized by:

- flexible planning processes;
- willingness by the centre to spend the time necessary to get close to business unit strategies, to be knowledgeable about their competitive environments, and to discuss issues thoroughly;
- avoiding overoptimism;
- personal incentives aligned with strategy;
- strenuous efforts to identify, measure, and act on strategic milestones.

But the style will always encounter difficulties in setting priorities between different sorts of objectives, and in encouraging business initiatives, while at the same time providing a check on strategic thinking from the centre.

TABLE 6.5.3
The strategic control style

Key Features	Added Value	Intrinsic Subtracted Value	Common But Avoidable Pitfalls
Decentralized profit centres; divisional coordination	Little by centre	No central coordination	
Extensive, strategic planning process	Raises minimum standards of thinking and analysis Challenges habits of mind	Constraining	Can be bureaucratic; add cost, but little value
Business autonomy			Gratuitous suggestions
Long- and short-term criteria	Acceptance of longer-term investments Balanced objectives	Ambiguous objectives	Tolerance for low performers Capital rationing Uninformed investments and divestments
Tight controls	More motivation to perform	Risk aversion Subjective balancing of objectives	'Politics' 'Lip service'

Summary

The best corporate parents have an understanding of the issues, trade-offs, and tension we have raised in this reading. Companies like Tarmac and ICI have clearly chosen the style they want to use at the centre. They recognize the strengths and weaknesses of the style and work hard to get the most added value from the strengths and to minimize the negative consequences of the style's weak points. They are also articulate on the subject, explaining the management processes they use in terms of the benefits given to units in the portfolio.

It is common for managers in subsidiaries to complain about the interference and overhead burden of headquarters. Most corporate level managers think that this is to be expected. 'Well of course they complain about the paperwork and fight the overhead allocations,' said one planning manager, 'I would do the same if I was in their shoes.'

Yet we have found companies where the units praise the centre; where managers value the review meetings and budget planning meetings and where there is an atmosphere of trust and cooperation between layers in the hierarchy. This should be an objective of all companies. By understanding the differences between styles and the strengths and weaknesses of each style, we believe managers will be better able to create the trust and cooperation that some companies have achieved.

Corporate Level Strategy in International Perspective

> Growth for the sake of growth is the
> ideology of the cancer cell.
>
> (Edward Abbey 1927–1989; American author)

As with the topic in the previous chapter, scarce attention has been paid to international differences in multibusiness level strategies. Despite the high media profile of major corporations from different countries and despite researchers' fascination with large companies, little comparative research has been done. Yet, it seems not unlikely that corporate strategy practices and preferences vary across national boundaries, although these differences are not blatant. Casual observation of the major corporations around the globe quickly makes clear that one cannot easily divide the world into portfolio-oriented and core competence-oriented countries. However, Campbell, Goold and Alexander do observe that in their research they have found 'there are relatively few companies in the United Kingdom, the United States, and other Western countries that pursue a full-fledged Strategic Planning style,' while it is 'the most popular style among leading Japanese companies' (1994: 413).

As an input to the debate whether there are international differences in corporate strategy perspectives, we would like to put forward a number of factors that might be of influence on how the paradox of responsiveness and synergy is managed in different countries. It should be noted, however, that these propositions must be viewed as tentative explanations, intended to encourage further discussion and research.

Functioning of Capital and Labor Markets

One of the arguments levelled against the portfolio perspective is that there is no need for corporations that merely act as investors. With efficiently-operating capital markets, investing should be left to 'real' investors. Stock markets are an excellent place for investors to spread their risks and for growing firms to raise capital. Start-up companies with viable plans can easily find venture capitalists to assist them. And all these capital providers can perform the task of financial control – portfolio-oriented corporations have nothing else to add but overhead costs. Add to this the argument that large corporations no longer have an advantage in terms of professional management skills. While in the past large firms could add value to smaller units by injecting more sophisticated managers, flexible labor markets now allow small firms to attract the same talent themselves.

Even if this general line of argumentation is true, the extent to which capital and labor markets are 'efficient' varies widely across countries. Porter (1987), an outspoken detractor of the portfolio perspective, acknowledges that 'in developing countries, where large companies are few, capital markets are undeveloped, and professional management is scarce, portfolio management still works.' However, he quickly adds that portfolio thinking 'is no longer a valid model for corporate strategy in advanced economies.' But are capital and labor markets equally efficient across all so-called advanced economies? Few observers would argue that venture capital markets in Asia and Europe work as well as in the US, and the terms under which large corporations can raise capital on these continents are usually far better than for smaller companies. Neither does holding shares of a company through the stock markets of Asia and Europe give investors as much influence over the company as in the US. In short, even in the group of developed economies, various gradations of capital market efficiency seem to exist, suggesting varying degrees to which corporations can create value by adopting the role of investors.

The same argument can be put forward for the efficiency of 'managerial labor' markets. Even if Porter is right when stating that smaller companies can attract excellent professional managers through flexible labor markets, this conclusion is not equally true across advanced economies. Life time employment might be a declining phenomenon in most of these countries, but not to the same extent. Job-hopping between larger and smaller companies is far more common in the US, than in many European and Asian countries (e.g. Calori, 1994). In many advanced economies large corporations still command a more sophisticated core of professional managers, through superior recruiting and training practices, higher compensation and status, and greater perceived career opportunities and job security. Hence, even within this group of countries, different degrees of labor market flexibility exist, suggesting that corporations in some countries might be able to create more value as developers and allocators of management talent than in other countries.

Leveraging of Relational Resources and Strategy Alignment

With the portfolio perspective focusing on the leveraging of financial resources and the core competence perspective favoring the leveraging of competences, the leveraging of relational resources is a topic receiving far less attention within the field of strategic management. It is widely acknowledged that 'umbrella' brands can often be stretched to include more product categories and that the corporation's reputation can commonly be employed to the business units' benefit. However, in the areas of political science and industrial organization much more attention is paid to the corporation as leverager of contacts and aligner of power. In many circumstances knowing the right people, being able to bring parties together, being able to force compliance and having the power to influence government regulations, are essential aspects of doing business. Often, corporations, either by their sheer size, or by their involvement in many businesses, will have more clout and essential contacts than can be mustered by individual businesses.

Here the international differences come in. As put forward at the end of Chapter 5, in some countries relational resources are more important than in others. Influence over government policy making, contacts with the bureaucrats applying the rules, power over local authorities and institutions, connections with the ruling elite, access to informal networks of companies – the importance of these factors can differ from country to country. Therefore, it stands to reason that the clustering of businesses around key external relationships and power bases will vary strongly across nations.

Costs of Coordination

Coordination comes at a cost, it is argued. Individual business units usually have to participate in all types of corporate systems, file reports, ask permission, attend meetings and adapt their strategy to fit with the corporate profile. This can result in time delays, lack of fit with the market, less entrepreneurial action, a lack of accountability and a low morale. On top of this, business units have to pay a part of corporate overhead as well. The benefits of coordination should be higher than these costs.

This argument might be suffering from a cultural bias, as it assumes that individuals and businesses are not naturally inclined to coordinate. However, control by the corporate center and cooperation with other business units is not universally viewed as a negative curtailment of individual autonomy. In many countries coordination is not an unfortunate fact of life, but a natural state of affairs. Coordination within the corporate whole is often welcomed as motivating, not demotivating, especially in cultures that are more group-oriented (Hofstede, 1993; reading 1.5 in this book). As observed in Chapter 4, if the common form of organization in a country resembles a clan, coordination might not be as difficult and costly as in other nations. Therefore, on the basis of this argument, it is reasonable to expect a stronger preference for the portfolio perspective in countries that favor mechanistic organizations.

Preference for Control

The last point of international difference ties into the discussion of the next chapter. If the essence of corporate strategy is about realizing synergies between businesses, is it not possible for these businesses to coordinate with one another and achieve synergies without being a part of the same corporation? In other words, is it necessary to be owned and controlled by the same parent in order to leverage resources and align strategies? Or could individual businesses band together and work as if they were one company – acting as a *virtual corporation*?

In Chapter 7 it will be argued that there are significant international differences on this account. In some countries there is a strong preference to have hierarchical control over two businesses that need to be coordinated. In other countries there is a preference for businesses to use various forms of cooperation to achieve synergies with other businesses, while retaining the flexibility of independent ownership. Preference for control, it will be argued, depends on how managers deal with the paradox of competition and cooperation.

Further Readings

Readers who would like to gain a better overview of the literature on the topic of corporate level strategy have a number of good sources from which to choose. Two scholarly reviews are 'Strategy and Structure in the Multi-product Firm' by Charles Hill and Robert Hoskisson, and 'Research on Corporate Diversification: A Synthesis,' by Vasudevan Ramanujam and P. Varadarajan, although both have become somewhat dated. A more recent review is 'Why Diversify? Four Decades of Management Thinking,' by Michael Goold and Kathleen Luchs. Mark Sirower's book *The Synergy Trap: How Companies Lose the Acquisition Game* also has an excellent overview of the literature as appendix.

Much of the strategy literature taking a portfolio perspective is from the end of the 1970s and the beginning of the 1980s. Bruce Henderson's popular book *On Corporate Strategy*, that explains the basic principles of the portfolio perspective, is from this period. However, a better review of the portfolio approach, and especially portfolio techniques, is given by Charles Hofer and Dan Schendel in *Strategy Formulation: Analytical Concepts*. Recently, there has been renewed interest in viewing the corporation as investor and restructurer. In this crop, the article 'Growth Through Acquisitions: A Fresh Look,' by Patricia Anslinger and Thomas Copeland is particularly provocative.

For further reading on the core competence perspective, Gary Hamel and C.K. Prahalad's book *Competing for the Future* is an obvious choice. The literature on the resource-based view of the firm mentioned at the end of Chapter 5 is also interesting in the context of this chapter. Also highly stimulating is Hiroyuki Itami's book *Mobilizing Invisible Assets*, in which he also argues for sharing intangible resources throughout a multibusiness firm.

On the topic of acquisitions, a good overview of the arguments and quantitative research is provided by Anju Seth, in his article 'Value Creation in Acquisitions: A Re-Examination of Performance Issues.' Mark Sirower's earlier mentioned book is also an excellent choice. When it comes to issues in the area of post-acquisition integration, Philippe Haspeslagh and David Jemison's *Managing Acquisitions: Creating Value Through Corporate Renewal* is the authoritative work in the field.

On the role of the corporate center, *Corporate-Level Strategy: Creating Value in the Multibusiness Company*, by Michael Goold, Andrew Campbell and Marcus Alexander, is highly recommended. Also stimulating is Charles Hill's article 'The Functions of the Headquarters Unit in Multibusiness Firms.' For a more academic analysis, readers are advised to turn to Vijay Govindarajan's article 'A Contingency Approach to Strategy Implementation at the Business-Unit Level: Integrating Administrative Mechanisms with Strategy.'

References

Anslinger, P.L., and Copeland, T.E. (1996) Growth Through Acquisitions: A Fresh Look, *Harvard Business Review*, January-February, pp. 126–35.

Bower, J.L. (1972) *Managing the Resource Allocation Process: A Study of Corporate Planning and Investment*, Irwin, Homewood, IL.

Buzzell, R.D. (1983) Is Vertical Integration Profitable? *Harvard Business Review*, January/February, pp. 92–102.

Calori, R. (1994) The Diversity of Management Systems, in Calori, R., and de Woot, Ph. (eds), *A European Management Model: Beyond Diversity*, Prentice-Hall, Hemel Hempstead.

Campbell, A., and Goold, M. (1988) Adding Value from Corporate Headquarters, *London Business School Journal*, Summer, pp. 219–40.

Campbell, A., Goold, M., and Alexander, M. (1994) *Corporate-Level Strategy: Creating Value in the Multibusiness Company*, John Wiley & Sons, New York.

Campbell, A., Goold, M., and Alexander, M. (1995) The Value of the Parent Company, *California Management Review*, Vol. 38, No.1, Fall, pp. 79–97.

Campbell, A., and Luchs, K. (1992) *Strategic Synergy*, Butterworth Heinemann, London.

Chatterjee, S. (1986) Types of Synergy and Economic Value: The Impact of Acquisitions on Merging and Rival Firms, *Strategic Management Journal*, Vol. 7, pp. 119–39.

Chatterjee, S., and Wernerfelt, B. (1991) The Link between Resources and Type of Diversification: Theory and Evidence, *Strategic Managment Journal*, January, pp. 33–48.

Ghoshal, S., and Mintzberg, H. (1994) Diversifiction and Diversifact, *California Management Review*, Vol. 37, No. 1, Fall, pp. 8–27.

Goold, M., and Campbell, A. (1987) *Strategies and Styles: The Role of the Centre in Managing Diverse Corporations*, Basil Blackwell, Oxford.

Goold, M., and Lansdell, S. (1997) *Survey of Corporate Strategy Objectives, Concepts and Tools*, Ashridge Strategic Management Centre, November.

Goold, M., and Luchs, K. (1993) Why Diversify? Four Decades of Management Thinking, *Academy of Management Executive*, August, pp. 7–25.

Govindarajan, V. (1988) A Contingency Approach to Strategy Implementation at the Business-Unit Level: Integrating Administrative Mechanisms with Strategy, *Academy of Management Journal*, Vol. 31, pp. 828–53.

Hamel, G., and Prahalad, C.K. (1993) Strategy as Stretch and Leverage, *Harvard Business Review*, March/April, pp. 75–84.

Hamel, G., and Prahalad, C.K. (1994) *Competing for the Future*, Harvard Business School Press, Boston.

Hampden-Turner, C., and Trompenaars, A. (1983) *The Seven Cultures of Capitalism: Value Systems for Creating Wealth in the United States, Japan, Germany, France, Britain, Sweden and the Netherlands*, Doubleday, New York.

Harrigan, K.R. (1983) *Strategies for Vertical Integration*, D.C. Heath, Lexington, MA.

Harrigan, K.R. (1985) Vertical Integration and Corporate Strategy, *Academy of Management Journal*, June, pp. 397–425.

Haspeslagh, P. (1982) Portfolio Planning: Uses and Limits, *Harvard Business Review*, January/February, pp. 58–73.

Haspeslagh, P., and Jemison, D. (1991) *Managing Acquisitions: Creating Value through Corporate Renewal*, Free Press, New York.

Hedley, B. (1977) Strategy and the 'Business Portfolio', *Long Range Planning*, Vol. 10, February, pp. 9–15.

Henderson, B.D. (1979) *On Corporate Strategy*, Abt Books, Cambridge, MA.

Hill, C.W.L. (1994) The Functions of the Headquarters Unit in Multibusiness Firms, in Rumelt, R., Teece, D. and Schendel, D. (eds), *Fundamental Issues in Strategy Research*, Harvard University Press, Cambridge, Mass.

Hill, C.W.L., and Hoskisson, R.E. (1987) Strategy and Structure in the Multiproduct Firm, *Academy of Management Review*, Vol. 2, pp. 331–41.

Hofer, C., and Schendel, D. (1978) *Strategy Formulation: Analytical Concepts*, West, St. Paul.

Hofstede, G. (1980) *Culture's Consequences*, Sage, London.

Hofstede, G. (1993) Cultural Constraints in Management Theories, *Academy of Management Executive*, Vol. 7, No.1.

Itami, H. (1987) *Mobilizing Invisible Assets*, Harvard University Press, Cambridge, MA.

Kaplan, S. (1989) The Effects of Management Buyouts on Operating Performance and Value, *Journal of Financial Economics*, Vol. 24, pp. 217–31.

Lawrence, P.R., and Lorsch, J.W. (1967) *Organization and Environment*, Harvard University Press, Cambridge, MA.

Long, W.F., and Ravenscraft, D.J. (1993) Decade of Debt: Lessons from LBOs in the 1980s, in Blair M.M. (ed.), *The Deal Decade: What Takeovers and Leveraged Buyouts Mean for Corporate Governance*, Brookings Institution, Washington.

Mintzberg, H. (1979) *The Structuring of Organizations: A Synthesis of Research*, Prentice-Hall, Englewood Cliffs.

Modigliani, F., and Miller, M.H. (1958) The Cost of Capital, Corporation Finance and the Theory of Investment, *American Economic Review*, Vol. 48, pp. 261–97.

Nayyar, P.R. (1992) On the measurement of corporate diversification strategy: Evidence from large US service firms, *Strategic Management Journal*, 13 (3), pp. 219–35.

Porter, M.E. (1987) From Competitive Advantage to Corporate Strategy, *Harvard Business Review*, May/June, pp. 43–59.

Prahalad, C.K., and Bettis, R.A. (1986) The Dominant Logic: A New Linkage between Diversity and Performance, *Strategic Management Journal*, November/December, pp. 485–601.

Prahalad, C.K., and Doz, Y. (1987) *The Multinational Mission: Balancing Local Demands and Global Vision*, Free Press, New York.

Prahalad, C.K., and Hamel, G. (1990) The Core Competence of the Corporation, *Harvard Business Review*, May/June, pp. 79–91.

Ramanujam, V., and Varadarajan, P. (1989) Research on Corporate Diversification: A Synthesis, *Strategic Management Journal*, November/December, pp. 523–51.

Ravenscraft, D.J., and Scherer, F.M. (1989) The Profitability of Mergers, *International Journal of Industrial Organization*, Vol. 7, pp. 101–16.

Roll, R. (1986) The Hubris Hypothesis of Corporate Takeovers, *Journal of Business*, Vol. 59, pp. 197–216.

Rumelt, R.P. (1974) *Strategy, Structure, and Economic Performance*, Harvard University Press, Cambridge, MA.

Rumelt, R.P. (1982) Diversification Strategy and Profitability, *Strategic Management Journal*, October/December, pp. 359–69.

Seth, A. (1990) Value Creation in Acquisitions: A Re-Examination of Performance Issues, *Strategic Management Journal*, Vol. 11, pp. 99–115.

Sirower, M.L. (1997) *The Synergy Trap: How Companies Lose the Acquisition Game*, Free Press, New York.

Trautwein, F. (1990) Merger Motives and Merger Prescriptions, *Strategic Management Journal*, Vol. 11, pp. 283–95.

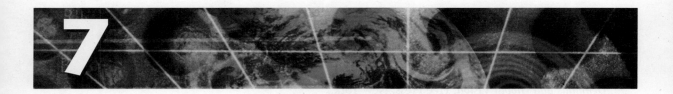

Network Level Strategy

The strong one is most powerful alone.

(Friedrich von Schiller 1759–1805; German writer)

All for one, one for all.

(*The Three Musketeers* by Alexandre Dumas Jr. 1824–1895; French novelist)

The Paradox of Competition and Cooperation

Strategists generally agree that for an effective *business level* strategy it is necessary to integrate *functional level* strategies into a consistent whole. Marketing, operations, finance, logistics, human resource, procurement and research and development strategies need to be systematically aligned for a business to be successful. It is also generally accepted that when a number of businesses reside together in one corporation an overarching *multibusiness level* strategy is required. However, while the business strategy and corporate strategy concepts are largely uncontroversial, widespread consensus is lacking when the next level of aggregation is discussed. The issue arises whether or not an overarching strategy is required for a group of interacting companies. In other words, the question is posed whether a *network* or *multicompany level* strategy is necessary to align the strategies of a network of firms. The alternative to such a network strategy would be for all firms to 'go it alone,' without explicit coordination of their strategies and to interact with one another at arm's length.

This issue of developing strategy together with other firms has an impact on all aspects of a company's functioning. For example, should a company work closely with its suppliers on a common production strategy or is it better to keep one's distance and shop around for the best deals? Should a company build up long-term partnerships with its customers, or is it more sensible not to become a captive supplier? Should a company get involved in joint ventures with other firms to develop new technologies and products, or is it wiser to do all research and development independently? Is it beneficial for a company to determine its strategy together with its bankers or is it preferable to keep the money lenders at a distance? In each case the question is what type of *relationship* a company wants or needs to have with other organizations in its environment.

On the one hand, interorganizational relationships can be primarily *competitive*. Such antagonism between organizations can vary from open 'warfare' to more subtle forms of friction, tension and strain. Under conditions of competition, behavior between rivals is characterized by calculation, bargaining, manoevering and the use of power to achieve results. Usually conflicting interests and/or objectives are the root of competitive relationships.

On the other hand, interorganizational relationships can be primarily *cooperative*. Such symbiosis between organizations can vary from occasional collaboration to virtual integration. Under conditions of cooperation, behavior between partners is characterized by trust, commitment, reciprocity and the use of coordination to achieve results. Usually the opportunity for mutual gain lies at the heart of cooperative relationships.

So, should strategists prefer more competitive or more cooperative relationships with the organizations in their environment? As before, two diametrically opposed positions can be identified on this issue. On the one side of the spectrum, there are strategists who believe that it is best for companies to be primarily competitive in their relationships to all outside forces. They argue that firms should remain independent and interact with other companies under market conditions. We shall refer to this point of view as the *discrete organization* perspective. At the other end of the spectrum, there are strategists who believe that companies should build up more cooperative relationships with key organizations in their environment. They argue that firms can reap significant benefits by surrendering a part of their independence and developing close relationships with a group of other organizations. This will be referred to as the *embedded organization* perspective.

Following the familiar debate model, this chapter will explore the nature of successful interfirm relationships by contrasting these two extreme views. By comparing the two opposite ways of dealing with the paradox of competition and cooperation, a better understanding of the issues under discussion should be gained. In the next few pages the discrete organization and embedded organization perspectives will be further explained, and finally summarized in Table 7.1.

The Discrete Organization Perspective

Strategists employing the discrete organization perspective view companies as independent entities competing with other organizations in a hostile market environment. Inspired by neo-classical economics, this perspective commonly emphasizes that individuals, and the organizations they form, are fundamentally motivated by aggressive self-interest and therefore that competition is the natural state of affairs. Suppliers will try to enhance their bargaining power *vis-à-vis* buyers with the aim of getting a better price, while conversely buyers will attempt to improve their negotiation position to attain better quality at lower cost. Competing firms will endeavour to gain the upperhand against their rivals if the opportunity arises, while new market entrants and manufacturers of substitute products will consistently strive to displace existing firms (e.g. Porter, 1980, 1985; reading 5.1 in this book).

In such a hostile environment it is a strategic necessity for companies to strengthen their competitive position in relation to the external forces. The best strategy for each organization is to obtain the market power required to get good price/quality deals, ward off competitive threats and even determine the development of the industry. Effective power requires independence and therefore heavy reliance on specific suppliers, buyers, financiers or public organizations should be avoided. Coalitions are occasionally formed to create power blocks, if individual companies are not strong enough on their own, but such alliances of convenience are usually second best to doing things independently. In most cases, collaboration is the strategy of the weak, to be engaged in at one's own peril. Collaborative efforts, it is argued, are fraught with the hazard of opportunism. Due to the ultimately competitive nature of relationships, allies will be tempted to serve their own interests to the detriment of the others, by manoevering, manipulating or cheating. The collaboration might even be a useful ploy, to cloak the company's aggressive intentions and moves. Collaboration, it is therefore concluded, is merely 'competition in a different form' (Hamel, Doz and Prahalad, 1989; reading 7.1).

Where collaboration is not the tool of the weak, it is often a conspiracy of the strong to inhibit competition. If two or more formidable companies collaborate, chances are that the alliance is actually ganging up on a third party, for instance on buyers. In such cases, it is argued, the term 'collaboration' is just a euphemism for collusion and not in the interest of the economy at large.

Worse yet, collaboration is usually also bad for a company's long-term health. A highly competitive environment is beneficial for a firm, because it provides the necessary stimulus for companies to continually improve and innovate. Strong adversaries push companies towards competitive fitness. As expressed by Porter (1990; reading 10.4), 'alliances are rarely a solution . . . no firm can depend on another independent firm for skills and assets that are central to its competitive advantage . . . Alliances tend to ensure mediocrity, not create world leadership.'

The label 'discrete organization' given to this perspective refers to the fact that each organization is seen as being entirely on its own in a game with a large number of other players. The competitive situation is believed to be *atomistic*, that is, each 'selfish' individual firm strives to satisfy its own interests, leading to rivalry and occasionally to shifting coalitions between antagonists. Furthermore, the competitive game is assumed to be largely of a *zero-sum* nature, that is, a fight for who gets how much of the pie. Under these circumstances, collaboration is tactical; strategically each individual firm tries to retain its independence.

The Embedded Organization Perspective

Strategists taking an embedded organization perspective are fundamentally at odds with the assumption that competition is the predominant factor determining the interaction between organizations. Business isn't war, so to approach all interactions from a conflictual angle is seen as overly pessimistic, even cynical. On the contrary, it is argued that relations between organizations are characterized by a dynamic mix of competitive and cooperative behavior. Rarely are the interests of firms completely opposed or entirely aligned. The natural state of affairs is that firms must balance competitive and cooperative postures in their relationships towards other organizations, depending on the circumstances. In some interactions a predominantly competitive posture might prevail, while in other situations a genuinely cooperative posture may be deemed more suitable. For example, a company may have a long-standing partnership with the supplier of one input, while the suppliers of another input are forced to compete fiercely for every new contract. Each relationship with a buyer, supplier, competitor, institution or government agency can be placed on the continuum from competitive to cooperative. Collaboration is not competition in disguise, but a real alternative means of dealing with other organizations (e.g. Contractor and Lorange, 1988; Piore and Sabel, 1984).

In the embedded organization perspective it is argued that firms can, and many do, intentionally embed themselves in a web of durable collaborative relationships (e.g. Axelsson and Easton, 1992; Lorenzoni and Baden-Fuller; reading 7.5). In the most simple case, a firm can have a number of bilateral collaborative relationships, in the form of joint ventures, strategic alliances and value-adding partnerships. However, loose multilateral webs or tight federations of cooperating companies can also develop. These collaborative clusters of organizations, which can also include not-for-profit institutions such as government agencies and universities, are referred to as networks. The companies in such networks align their strategies, or even develop their strategies jointly, in an effort to accrue system-wide benefits to the advantage of all network participants (e.g. Best, 1990; Jarillo, 1988; reading 7.2).

The fact that strategic coordination takes place within networks makes them an organizational form at a higher level of aggregation than the individual company. Networks are neither *markets* or *hierarchies*, to use Williamson's (1975, 1985) classic distinction. The term 'hierarchies' is used to refer to regular companies, where internal relationships are governed by a central authority that has the formal power to coordinate strategy and solve interdepartmental disputes. 'Markets,' on the other hand, refers to the situation where transactional relationships are not governed by the 'visible,' but by the 'invisible hand.' Independent firms interact with one another under competitive conditions, without any explicit coordination or dispute settlement mechanism. A network is in between markets and hierarchies (e.g. Thorelli, 1986; Powell, 1990). Strategies are coordinated and disputes resolved, not through formal top-down power, but by mutual

TABLE 7.1
Discrete organization
versus embedded
organization perspective

	Discrete Organization Perspective	Embedded Organization Perspective
Emphasis on	Competition over cooperation	Cooperation over competition
Structure of the environment	Discrete organizations (atomistic)	Embedded organizations (networked)
Firm boundaries	Distinct	Fuzzy
Preferred position	Independence	Interdependence
Interaction outcomes	Mainly zero-sum (win/lose)	Often positive-sum (win/win)
Source of advantage	Bargaining power	Specialization and coordination
Multicompany level strategy	No	Yes
Use of collaboration	Temporary arrangement (tactical)	Durable partnership (strategic)
Basis of collaboration	Power and calculation	Trust and reciprocity
Structure of collaboration	Limited, well-defined, contract-based	Broad, open, relationship-based

adaptation. To extend the above metaphor, networks rely neither on the visible nor invisible hand to guide relationships, but rather employ the continuous handshake (Gerlach, 1992).

To proponents of the embedded organization perspective, therefore, atomistic competition is a neo-classical theoretical abstraction, that seriously mischaracterizes the nature of relationships between organizations. In reality, companies have some competitive relationships, but they are also characterized by their *embeddedness* in webs of durable partnerships, whereby the game is potentially *positive-sum*, that is, a win-win situation. In turn, networks can compete against other networks (e.g. Gomes-Casseres, 1994; Weidenbaum and Hughes, 1996; reading 7.5), or build up cooperative relationships where appropriate. Collaboration can be tactical, but also strategic; companies can accept a measure of interdependence if the cooperating network achieves more than the companies independently.

The question for the field of strategic management is, therefore, whether network level strategies are formed and should be formed. Is market power and independence the best approach to the environment? Or is a web of durable cooperative relationships the best way forward for companies? In short, strategists must grapple with the paradox of competition and cooperation.

Defining the Issues: Boundaries and Relationships

The two major issues under discussion in this chapter are to which activities the firm wishes to limit itself and how it wishes to interact with organizations or individuals in its environment. These are referred to as the issues of *boundaries* and *relationships*. The issue of organizational boundaries revolves around the questions of *scope* and *scale* (Chandler, 1990) – how many different activities should a firm be involved in and how much of each activity should a firm want to perform? The issue of interorganizational relationships deals with the nature of the interactions that a firm would like to have with external parties. Before launching into the debate, both issues will be examined more closely.

Relationships between the Firm and Its Environment

In Figure 7.1 an overview is given of the eight major groups of external parties with which the firm can, or must, interact. A distinction has been made between *market* and *contextual* actors. The market actors are those individuals and organizations that perform value-adding activities and/or consume the outputs of these activities. The contextual actors are those parties whose behavior, intentionally or unintentionally, sets the conditions under which the market actors must operate. The four main categories of relationships between the firm and other market parties are the following (adapted from Porter, 1980, 1985; reading 5.1; and Reve, 1990):

- *Upstream vertical (supplier) relations*. Every company has suppliers of some sort. In a narrow definition these include the providers of raw materials, parts, machinery, and business services. In a broader definition the providers of all production factors (land, capital, labor, technology, information and entrepreneurship) can be seen as suppliers, if they are not part of the firm itself. All these suppliers can either be the actual producers of the input, or an intermediary (distributor or agent) trading in the product or service. Beside the suppliers with which the firm transacts directly (first-tier suppliers), the firm may also have relationships with suppliers further upstream in the business (value) system (Porter, 1985). All these relationships are traditionally referred to as upstream vertical relations, because economists commonly draw the business system as a column.

- *Downstream vertical (buyer) relations*. On the output side, the firm has relationships with its customers. These clients can either be the actual users of the product or service, or intermediaries trading the output. Besides the buyers with which the firm transacts directly, it may also have relationships with parties further downstream in the business system.

- *Direct horizontal (competitor) relations*. This category includes the relations between the firm and other industry incumbents. Because these competitors produce similar goods or services, they are said to be at the same horizontal level in the industry column.

STRATEGY CONTENT

- *Indirect horizontal (industry outsider) relations.* Where a firm has a relationship with a company outside its industry, this is referred to as an indirect horizontal relation (or a diversification relation). For instance, the joint venture between Mercedes-Benz and Swatch discussed in Exhibit 2.1 is a straightforward example of a relationship between two firms with roots in different industries. An indirect horizontal relation can develop between a firm and a potential industry entrant, whereby the incumbent firm can assist or attempt to block the entry of the industry outsider. A relation can also exist with the producer of a substitute good or service, either as an adversary or an ally. Furthermore, a firm can establish a relationship with a firm in another industry, with the intention of diversifying into that, or a third, industry. In reality, where industry boundaries are not clear, the distinction between direct and indirect horizontal relations is equally blurry.

Besides relationships with these market actors, there can be many contacts with condition-setting parties in the broader environment. Employing the classic SEPTember distinction, the following rough categories of contextual actors can be identified:

FIGURE 7.1
The firm and its relationships

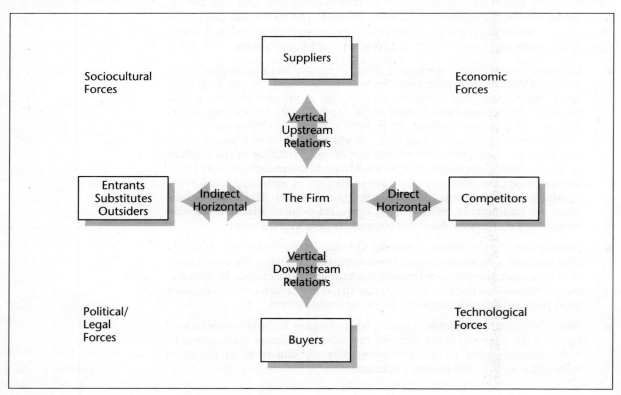

- *Sociocultural forces.* Individuals or organizations that have a significant impact on societal values, norms, beliefs and behaviors may interact with the firm. These could include the media, community groups, religious organizations, and opinion leaders.

- *Economic forces.* There can also be organizations influencing the general economic state of affairs, with which the firm interacts. Among others tax authorities, central banks, employers' federations, stock exchanges and unions may be of importance.

- *Political/legal forces.* The firm may also interact with organizations setting or influencing the regulations under which companies must operate. These could include governments, political parties, special interest groups, regulatory bodies and international institutions.

- *Technological forces.* There are also many organizations that influence the pace and direction of technological development and the creation of new knowledge. Among others, universities, research institutes, government agencies and standardization bodies may be important to deal with.

As Figure 7.1 visualizes, companies can choose, or are often forced, to interact with a large number of organizations and individuals in the environment. In the further discussion in this chapter, however, the focus will be primarily on the vertical and horizontal relationships between market parties.

Boundaries Between the Firm and its Environment

Closely tied to the issue of interorganizational relationships is the question of interorganizational boundaries. While the first topic deals with the 'how' of the interface between organizations, the second topic deals with the 'where.' Where should the firm end and the environment begin? Which activities should the firm carry out and which should be left to others? Where should the boundary of the firm be drawn?

The boundary issue, it could be said, revolves around the optimal level of *vertical* and *horizontal integration*. Vertically, the firm must determine which activities in the business system it deems necessary to perform itself, leaving all other activities to suppliers and buyers. Horizontally, the firm must assess what size it needs to have within the business (scale) and in which businesses it wishes to participate (scope).

Scale has already been a topic of discussion in Chapter 5. It was made clear by Porter in reading 5.1 and Buzzell and Gale in reading 5.3 that in many industries potential scale advantages exist that pressure companies to increase their size. These advantages include cost savings per unit produced, leveraging of resources, and increased bargaining power. Furthermore, large companies can set industry standards and influence regulatory agencies. However, it has also been acknowledged that severe scale disadvantages may exist, such as bureaucratic inertia, excessive coordination costs and lagging innovativeness. Moreover, antitrust authorities may intervene to cut companies down to size. Bigger is, therefore, not always better, but neither is small always beautiful. Each company must decide what its size within the industry should be and strive to achieve this optimal scale. The company's intended scale, in turn, will have a significant impact on the type of relationships the company will have with the other industry players. In general, the more intrusive a firm's size ambitions, the more conflictual will be its direct horizontal relations.

Scope has been discussed at length in Chapter 6. The central question was in what array of businesses a company should be involved. It was argued that there are potential scope advantages, that is, synergies between units operating in different businesses. Depending on the perspective taken, the leveraging of competences, the sharing of activities and financial synergies were mentioned as possible gains. On the other side of the balance, however, were the scope disadvantages, including coordination costs, slower decision-making and the corporate center's lack of specific business know-how. It was concluded that each company must continuously assess its optimal scope, and may need to enter and exit businesses accordingly. The company's intended scope, in turn, will have an impact on its relationships with other firms. Particularly in those businesses that a company is considering to enter, it must determine whether to cooperate with others, or to challenge all the incumbents.

An essential aspect of organizational scope, that was only touched on in Chapter 6, is that of vertical integration. In each business system there are a number of major production and distribution stages that take place between raw materials and final consumer. Each of these major stages consists of an enormous number of value-adding activities. Few companies are fully integrated 'from the mine to the customer's front door,' producing all goods and services *in-house*. Alternatively, it is also rare that a firm performs only one specific business system activity, *outsourcing* all other activities to outsiders. Companies seek the optimal level of activity *internalization* somewhere between these two extremes. Advantages of vertical integration, pressuring the firm to expand its boundaries upstream or downstream, may include (e.g. Harrigan 1985; Mahoney, 1992):

- *Avoidance of contracting costs.* Reaching a deal with a supplier or buyer and transferring the goods or services to the required location may be accompanied by significant direct costs. These can include the costs of negotiations, drawing up a contract, financial transfers, packaging, distribution and insurance. If a firm vertically integrates, many of these costs can be avoided, leading to potential savings.

- *Economies of scale.* Costs per unit can often be reduced by combining similar administrative, production, transport and information-processing activities. For instance, vertical integration can allow for the investment in more efficient large scale systems and can help to achieve learning curve savings.

- *Operational coordination.* Often it is necessary for various parts of the business system to be tightly coordinated, to ensure that the right components, meeting the right specification, are available in the right quantities, at the right moment, so that high quality and timely delivery can be achieved. To realize this level of coordination it might be necessary to gain control over a number of key activities in the business system.

- *Implementing system-wide changes*. Besides continual operational coordination, there may be a need to coordinate strategic changes throughout the business system. Switching over to new technologies, new production methods and new standards can sometimes only be implemented if there is commitment and a concerted effort in various parts of the business system. Vertical integration can give a firm the formal control needed to push through such changes.

- *Exploitation of dissipation-sensitive knowledge*. Know-how that is readily codifiable and transferable, but difficult to protect by means of patents, might best be exploited by applying it to a number of activities within the confines of one firm. Vertical integration minimizes the risk that such knowledge will quickly leak out to rival firms.

- *Exploitation of non-marketable capabilities*. Other knowledge may be tacit, that is, difficult to codify and transfer. This knowledge and the capabilities resulting from it, may be valuable to other activities, but difficult to sell, because they are wrapped up in the management systems, routines and culture of the firm. Vertical integration can be the best way to exploit these non-marketable capabilities. By internalizing various activities, a firm may be able to leverage these 'wrapped up' capabilities.

- *Increased bargaining power*. If a firm is facing a supplier or buyer with a disproportionately high level of bargaining power (for instance, a monopolist), vertical integration can be used to weaken or neutralize such a party. By fully or partially performing the activities in-house, the firm can lessen its dependence on a strong buyer or supplier. Alternatively, the firm may strive to acquire the other party, to avoid the bargaining situation altogether.

Counterbalancing these advantages of vertical integration are a number of important disadvantages. These drawbacks to internalization can include:

- *High governance costs*. Coordinating activities within a firm requires managers. Layers of management, and the bureaucratic processes that might entail, can lead to higher costs than if activities were outsourced.

- *Dulled incentives*. Operating units carrying out activities within the firm may not be as motivated to perform optimally, as when they would have to sell their wares on the open market. Internalizing activities can thus dull the incentive to excel, compared to the competitive stimulus offered by the market.

- *High capital investment*. Vertical integration requires extra capital to be invested. These funds may not be available, or may need to be withdrawn from investments in the core business. The additional risk of investing within one value system may also be judged to be too high.

- *Reduced flexibility*. Once integrated into one firm, operating units can become fully dependent on each other. However, each unit may be exposed to different environmental and technological changes, requiring different strategic responses. Their interdependence will limit the extent to which adaptation to these changes will be possible.

■   *Reduced exposure to external know-how.* If the firm is more or less a closed system, it will be infrequently exposed to new insights and technologies adopted elsewhere. There may be a real threat of missing important external developments.

It is often argued that all of these reasons for not internalizing activities can be regarded as the strengths of the market system. In many situations, markets are the most efficient mechanism of conducting transactions. Where activities are performed by autonomous parties and sold in the market place, costs will often be lowest. As summarized by Ouchi (1980: 130), 'in a market relationship, the transaction takes place between the two parties and is mediated by a price mechanism in which the existence of a competitive market reassures both parties that the terms of exchange are equitable.'

Integration of activities into the firm is only necessary where markets do not function properly. All of the advantages of integration mentioned above refer to such cases of *market failure*. The firm must internalize activities, despite the disadvantages, because the invisible hand of the market cannot be trusted to be equitable and effective. Control over transactions by means of formal authority – the visible hand – is needed under these conditions (these ideas about firm boundaries have been worked out in more detail in transaction cost economics, see suggested readings).

Between Markets and Hierarchies

In the previous paragraphs, the firm and its environment have been presented as a clear dichotomy for argumentation's sake. Within a firm (a hierarchy, in transaction cost jargon) cooperative relationships were assumed to be prevalent, while in the market environment competitive relationships were assumed to be the norm. In reality, however, there are many organizational forms between markets and hierarchies. These are referred to as *hybrids*, *alliances* or *collaborative arrangements*. In Table 7.2, an overview of the most common types of collaborative arrangements is presented.

The intent of these collaborative arrangements is to profit from some of the advantages of vertical and horizontal integration, without incurring its costs. These organizational forms are truly hybrids, as they attempt to combine the benefits of integration with the benefits of the market. However, they might also combine the weaknesses of both, making their use an issue for heated debate.

Strategists taking a discrete organization perspective are not particularly fond of these collaborative arrangements. After all, they believe that the relationships between firms are fundamentally competitive and that other firms can never be fully trusted. Companies run the risk of opportunism, that is, '. . . self-interest seeking with guile. This includes but is scarcely limited to more blatant forms, such as lying, stealing and cheating . . . More generally, opportunism refers to the incomplete or distorted disclosure of information, especially to calculated efforts to mislead, distort,

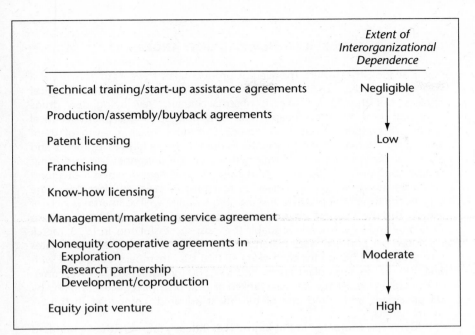

	Extent of Interorganizational Dependence
Technical training/start-up assistance agreements	Negligible
Production/assembly/buyback agreements	
Patent licensing	Low
Franchising	
Know-how licensing	
Management/marketing service agreement	

Nonequity cooperative agreements in
  Exploration
  Research partnership
  Development/coproduction
	Moderate

Equity joint venture	High

TABLE 7.2
Types of cooperative arrangements

Source: Contractor and Lorange 1988

disguise, obfuscate, or otherwise confuse' (Williamson, 1985: 47). Therefore, collaborative arrangements must be approached with caution and only used tactically under a limited set of circumstances. In particular, it is argued that collaborative efforts should be restricted to a well-defined area, with clear objectives, responsibilities, authority and results spelled out ahead of time, preferably in an explicit contract.

In the embedded organization perspective, collaborative arrangements can evolve to such an extent that a group of cooperating companies actually functions as a *virtual corporation* (e.g. Chesbrough and Teece, 1996; Quinn, 1992). A firm can become so embedded in a web of collaborative relationships, that the boundary between the firm and the environment is entirely fuzzy. This enthusiasm for collaborative forms is based on the belief that organizations can develop relationships based on trust, and that durable partnerships can grow. The more trust that exists between the partners, the more open-ended the collaboration can become. Objectives, responsibilities, authority and results needn't be fully determined in advance in a written contract, but can evolve and be adjusted over time, given all parties' sincere willingness to 'work on their relationship' (Kanter, 1994). This is what economists call an implicit contract and legal theorists refer to as a relational contract (Kay, 1993).

EXHIBIT 7.1
Merck Short Case

MERCK: A MEDICINE AGAINST ANOREXIA?

Name an industry in which the average product takes 15 years to develop, at a cost of more than US$350 million a shot. Aerospace? Robotics? Logical choices, but the right answer is pharmaceuticals. Developing new drugs does not come easily or cheaply. The R&D budgets of the pharmaceutical giants are typically about 10–12 percent of sales, placing seven of them among the 25 biggest R&D spenders in the US. These high investments and long lead times make the pharmaceutical industry a competitive arena that should be avoided by the short-winded and faint-hearted. Raymond Gilmartin, however, does not need to reach for Prilosec, an ulcer drug – he only needs to sell the product and is doing so quite well. Gilmartin is CEO of Merck, the third largest pharmaceutical company in the world, after Glaxo Wellcome and Novartis, and arguably the most successful one. In 1996, Merck produced net profits of $3.9 billion on sales of $19.8 billion, which translates into profits of $79,000 for each of its 49,000 staff members, compared with $64,500 for the Swiss giant Roche and $57,500 for Britain's Glaxo Wellcome. In the same year, Merck was also ranked as best pharmaceutical company by US physicians and voted one of the 'most admired' companies in the US by managers.

Merck has competed in this high-stakes industry for more than a hundred years, initially as the US subsidiary of the German Merck company. During World War I the Merck subsidiary became separated from the parent company in Darmstadt, and to this day both companies use the Merck name (the German E. Merck has sales of approximately $4 billion, half of which in pharmaceuticals). Gilmartin was placed at the helm of Merck in 1994, as the first outsider in the company's history, coming from Becton Dickinson & Co., a modest-sized manufacturer of medical equipment. While the retirement of ex-CEO Roy Vagelos had been planned far in advance, the appointment of Gilmartin, and the bypassing of all senior managers within Merck by the board of directors had come as quite a shock. The resulting exodus of top management was accepted by the board as the necessary price for shaking up the company. It was the board's belief that Merck had become accustomed to easy expansion in the late 1980s, growing annually by 20 to 30 percent. Costs had risen sharply, while by the early 1990s growth was declining and competitive pressures were increasing. In the board's view, a sharp break with the past was needed and a more cost-conscious CEO was required to push through changes.

Since Gilmartin's arrival pressures for change at Merck have only increased, as the pharmaceutical industry has entered a tumultuous period. After years of unchallenged price hikes, governments now look at the drug firms as partially responsible for the soaring cost of health care. In the US, the rise of 'managed care' organizations has further enhanced the bargaining power of buyers, placing more pressure on prices. In the mean time, the pharmaceutical industry has had to double its spending on R&D in the five years between 1991 and 1996 to make up for the slowing stream of new products. Development costs per new drug are rapidly increasing, while the profitable 'monopoly' period after introduction is becoming ever shorter. Companies are not waiting to see whether their competitors' new drugs are successful before following in their footsteps, but are quickly investing in emerging areas as soon as others do. Therefore, innovative drugs are soon joined by similar products.

The high cost of getting the scientists' chemical compounds out of the test tube and on to the pharmacists' shelves is only partially attributable to the process of actually discovering a potential new drug. In general it takes about one to three years for a new preparation to be synthesized and tested. But once a preparation is in the pipeline, many further steps need to be taken before it becomes a sellable product. First, the preparation enters the pre-clinical development phase, which might involve animal testing. If, after a few years of tests, the results are promising, permission can be gained to proceed with clinical trials on human volunteers. At first, these are conducted on small groups, but if successful, they are enlarged to full-scale tests. The clinical trials can take 5 to 10 years before a drug is approved for broader use and sales can begin. On average, of the 20 preparations entering preclinical development, only one has come out of the pipeline as a marketable drug. Obviously, pharmaceutical companies would like to increase this yield and shorten the process, but this is not proving to be easy.

Merck has followed the industry trend by investing more heavily in R&D. In 1997, its R&D budget was more than $1.7 billion, compared to $1.1 billion in 1992. What Merck has consciously not done, is to follow the industry trend towards more alliances with small biotech firms. Merck's philosphy towards R&D is decidedly do-it-yourself. Not more than 5 percent of Merck's total research spending ends up outside of its own laboratories. This emphasis on doing everything in-house contrasts sharply with the direction being taken by the rest of the industry. All of Merck's rivals reserve between 10 and 20 percent of their R&D budgets for external work. In some cases only the laborious task of conducting clinical trials is outsourced, but increasingly the pharmaceutical giants are contracting out the development of new drugs to specialist firms. Some analysts are predicting that the proportion of R&D performed outside of the big companies could reach 80 percent. Sir Richard Sykes, head of Glaxo Wellcome, has suggested that the major drug firms will increasingly become 'virtual' companies, as they concentrate on the marketing of drugs developed by the legions of small independent biotech firms.

The enthusiasm of Merck's competitors for alliances with the creative independents is based on the view 'if you can't beat them, join them'. The number of small biotech firms has grown rapidly – in the United States alone there are more than 1200 firms active. All of these firms are so specialized, that at any one moment at least one of them will be ahead of any given big firm in any given technology. Most pharmaceutical giants believe that it is wise to tap in to this source of new products, especially if this speeds up the process of getting new drugs into their product portfolio. Moreover, licensing in new drugs from the small biotech firms can usually be achieved at a fraction of the cost of doing it in-house. Most biotech firms do not have the financial stamina to shepherd their products through the years of development and trials, nor do they have the marketing and distribution infrastructure needed to reap the benefits of their labors. This gives the big firms the negotiation position to snap up promising products for considerably less than they are worth. In 1996, over 170 deals were struck between small biotech firms and big drug companies, more than double the amount of just three years before.

Merck, however, is strongly opposed to this policy of hollowing out.

According to Ed Scolnick, Merck's combative head of research and only remaining member of Vagelos' original top management team, the type of corporate anorexia its rivals are suffering from might end up to be fatal. He argues that without first class in-house scientific talent, a drug firm cannot tell which biotech ideas are worth buying. In his view, competitors are taking the easy route of shopping for new products simply because they are not clever enough to come up with their own.

Of course, the question is whether Scolnick and Gilmartin are right, while the rest of the industry is wrong. Is it necessary to keep all key activities in-house and to remain largely self-contained and independent from the outside world? Or are Merck's competitors right, when they argue that the pharmaceutical industry will come to resemble Hollywood, where the big studios are focusing more on marketing and distribution, while the films are increasingly being made by small production companies. Time will tell who is right, but maybe Gilmartin should keep a bottle of Prilosec handy, just in case.

Sources: *The Economist*, May 24 1997; *Medical Marketing and Media*, May 1996; *Drug Topics*, July 24 1995.

The Debate and the Readings

In Table 7.1 the two perspectives were summarized, to sharply contrast their divergent assumptions. As before, the first two readings in this chapter have been chosen as well-known representatives of these two perspectives, while the following three contributions add further depth to the debate.

As representative of the discrete organization perspective, Michael Porter's reading in Chapter 5 could easily have been selected. In this reading, Porter states that 'the essence of strategy formulation is coping with competition,' and that there are five sources of competitive pressure, all impinging on a firm's profit potential. These competitive forces are the threat of new entrants, powerful buyers and suppliers, rivalry among existing competitors and the threat of substitute products. Porter asserts that a company's profitability depends on how well it is able to defend itself against these 'opponents'. It is this view of the firm, as a lone organization surrounded by hostile forces, that places this contribution clearly within the discrete organization perspective. While Porter does not denounce or warn against cooperative arrangements in this reading (as he does in reading 10.4), neither does he recognize cooperation as a possibility. His message is that of *realpolitik* – in inter-organizational relationships, conflict and power is the name of the game.

Because Porter's reading is already a part of Chapter 5, another classic, 'Collaborate with Your Competitors – and Win,' has been selected as the opening contribution for this chapter. In this piece, the authors, Gary Hamel, Yves Doz and C.K. Prahalad, basically take the same stance as Porter, in assuming that interfirm relations are largely competitive and governed by power and calculation. However, while Porter makes little mention of, or is apprehensive about, collaboration with other organizations, Hamel, Doz and Prahalad see collaboration as a useful tool for improving the firm's competitive profile. They argue that alliances with competitors 'can strengthen both companies against outsiders even if it weakens one partner *vis-à-vis* the other,' and therefore that the net result can be positive. Yet they emphasize that companies should not be naive about the real nature of alliances – 'collaboration is competition in a different form.' An alliance is 'a constantly evolving bargain,' in which each firm will be fending for itself, trying to learn as much as possible from the other, while attempting to limit the partner's access to its knowledge and skills. The authors advise firms to proceed cautiously with alliances, only when they have clear objectives of what they wish to learn from their allies, a well-developed capacity to learn, and defenses against their allies' probing of their skills and technologies. While Hamel, Doz and Prahalad only focus on horizontal relationships in this article, their message is similar to that of Porter – competition in the environment is paramount and cooperation is merely an opportunistic move in the overall competitive game.

As representative of the embedded organization perspective, Carlos Jarillo's reading, 'On Strategic Networks', has been selected. Jarillo argues that parallel to the acceptance of the importance of competitive behavior, 'the realization is growing that cooperative behavior among firms is at the root of many success stories in today's management.' In his view, competition and cooperation jointly govern inter-firm behavior, in different mixes under different circumstances. In this reading, he is specifically concerned with vertical relationships, and outlines in which situations it makes strategic sense to invest in durable partnerships. Of particular interest in Jarillo's argumentation is his use of transaction cost economics to explain the rationale of networks. Furthermore, he emphasizes the importance of trust in the development of networks. He stresses that economic cooperative relationships can not evolve without social relationships between the partners. In a nutshell, his message is that of *symbiosis* – in inter-organizational relations, interdependence is the name of the game.

The third reading, 'Incorporating International Strategic Alliances into Overall Firm Strategy', by Stephen Preece, presents a thorough overview of the strategic objectives driving cooperative arrangements. As Preece points out, discussions on competition and cooperation often deal with the merits of various organizational structures, instead of focusing on the strategic objectives of collaboration in the first place. Preece, therefore, analyzes the various potential benefits of inter-organizational cooperation, that motivate organizations to form alliances. He identifies six categories of cooperation objectives: learning, leveraging, leaping, leaning, linking and locking out. His contribution to the discussion is that his framework helps to focus the debate on the possible reasons for collaboration, instead of only dwelling on its mechanisms. Furthermore, by identifying six different cooperation objectives, he has made it possible to distinguish different types of alliances, and to ask the question whether some alliances are more beneficial or more dangerous than others.

In the fourth reading, 'Creating a Strategic Center to Manage a Web of Partners', Gianni Lorenzoni and Charles Baden-Fuller clearly employ an embedded organization perspective. Just as in Jarillo's article, Lorenzoni and Baden-Fuller argue that a network of firms can closely work together as a virtual company, without the disadvantages of integration. But while Jarillo's contribution is more abstract, Lorenzoni and Baden-Fuller are quite concrete, outlining how a network of firms can be created and maintained. Interestingly, they believe that networks can be deliberately assembled and require a strategic center to effectively coordinate activities. Of course, the question is whether this is always the case. Are networks designed by a central coordinating body, or might they gradually emerge, without any party being in control?

What all four of these articles have in common is that competition and cooperation are viewed from an economic vantage point. Both competitive and cooperative conduct are largely explained as rational economic behavior. Relationships between parties are primarily economic, although social bonds might be needed to facilitate cooperation and social dislikings might intensify competition. However, in many settings relationships between parties may be simultaneously social and economic, or even primarily social ('first we become trusting friends – then we might do business'). The social ties between parties may be based on family relationships, religious loyalties, ideological bonds, educational connections, regional sympathies, political affinities, ethnic links, and personal friendships. Networks or intense rivalries may develop more along these social lines than economically-oriented analysts might assume. By exclusively focusing on the economic side of relationships, an important driver of competition and cooperation might be underestimated. To bring this point into the discussion, 'The Bamboo Network,' has been selected as the final reading in this chapter. In this contribution, Murray Weidenbaum and Samuel Hughes describe the tight connections between expatriate Chinese entrepreneurs spread throughout Southeast Asia as an interesting example of a network, whose 'glue' is just as much social as economic. For the broader discussion, the question is whether the bamboo network is the exception or the rule. Are socio-economic networks common place or are they merely the last vestiges of an outdated mode of business?

7.1 Collaborate with Your Competitors – and Win

By Gary Hamel, Yves Doz, and C. K. Prahalad[1]

Collaboration between competitors is in fashion. General Motors and Toyota assemble automobiles, Siemens and Philips develop semiconductors, Canon supplies photocopiers to Kodak, France's Thomson and Japan's JVC manufacture videocassette recorders. But the spread of what we call 'competitive collaboration' – joint ventures, outsourcing agreements, product licensings, cooperative research – has triggered unease about the long-term consequences. A strategic alliance can strengthen both companies against outsiders even as it weakens one partner *vis-à-vis* the other. In particular, alliances between Asian companies and western rivals seem to work against the western partner. Cooperation becomes a low-cost route for new competitors to gain technology and market access.

Yet the case for collaboration is stronger than ever. It takes so much money to develop new products and to penetrate new markets that few companies can go it alone in every situation. ICL, the British computer company, could not have developed its current generation of mainframes without Fujitsu. Motorola needs Toshiba's distribution capacity to break into the Japanese semiconductor market. Time is another critical factor. Alliances can provide shortcuts for western companies racing to improve their production efficiency and quality control.

We have spent more than five years studying the inner workings of 15 strategic alliances and monitoring scores of others. Our research involves cooperative ventures between competitors from the United States and Japan, Europe and Japan, and the United States and Europe. We did not judge the success or failure of each partnership by its longevity – a common mistake when evaluating strategic alliances – but by the shifts in competitive strength on each side. We focused on how companies use competitive collaboration to enhance their internal skills and technologies while they guard against transferring competitive advantages to ambitious partners.

There is no immutable law that strategic alliances *must* be a windfall for Japanese or Korean partners. Many western companies do give away more than they gain – but that's because they enter partnerships without knowing what it takes to win. Companies that benefit most from competitive collaboration adhere to a set of simple but powerful principles.

■   *Collaboration is competition in a different form.* Successful companies never forget that their new partners may be out to disarm them. They enter

---

alliances with clear strategic objectives, and they also understand how their partners' objectives will affect their success.

- *Harmony is not the most important measure of success.* Indeed, occasional conflict may be the best evidence of mutually beneficial collaboration. Few alliances remain win-win undertakings forever. A partner may be content even as it unknowingly surrenders core skills.

- *Cooperation has limits.* Companies must defend against competitive compromise. A strategic alliance is a constantly evolving bargain whose real terms go beyond the legal agreement or the aims of top management. What information gets traded is determined day to day, often by engineers and operating managers. Successful companies inform employees at all levels about what skills and technologies are off-limits to the partner and monitor what the partner requests and receives.

- *Learning from partners is paramount.* Successful companies view each alliance as a window on their partners' broad capabilities. They use the alliance to build skills in areas outside the formal agreement and systematically diffuse new knowledge throughout their organizations.

Why Collaborate?

Using an alliance with a competitor to acquire new technologies or skills is not devious. It reflects the commitment and capacity of each partner to absorb the skills of the other. We found that in every case in which a Japanese company emerged from an alliance stronger than its western partner, the Japanese company had made a greater effort to learn.

Strategic intent is an essential ingredient in the commitment to learning. The willingness of Asian companies to enter alliances represents a change in competitive tactics, not competitive goals. NEC, for example, has used a series of collaborative ventures to enhance its technology and product competences. NEC is the only company in the world with a leading position in telecommunications, computers, and semiconductors – despite its investing less in research and development (R&D) (as a percentage of revenues) than competitors like Texas Instruments, Northern Telecom, and L.M. Ericsson. Its string of partnerships, most notably with Honeywell, allowed NEC to leverage its in-house R&D over the last two decades.

Western companies, on the other hand, often enter alliances to avoid investments. They are more interested in reducing the costs and risks of entering new businesses or markets than in acquiring new skills. A senior US manager offered this analysis of his company's venture with a Japanese rival: 'We complement each other well – our distribution capability and their manufacturing skill. I see no reason to invest upstream if we can find a secure source of product. This is a comfortable relationship for us.'

An executive from this company's Japanese partner offered a different perspective: 'When it is necessary to collaborate, I go to my employees and say, "This is bad, I wish we had these skills ourselves. Collaboration is second best. But I will feel worse if after four years we do not know how to do what our partner knows how to do.'' We must digest their skills.'

The problem here is not that the US company wants to share investment risk (its Japanese partner does too) but that the US company has no ambition beyond avoidance. When the commitment to learning is so one-sided, collaboration invariably leads to competitive compromise.

Many so-called alliances between western companies and their Asian rivals are little more than sophisticated outsourcing arrangements. General Motors buys cars and components from Korea's Daewoo. Siemens buys computers from Fujitsu. Apple buys laser printer engines from Canon. The traffic is almost entirely one way. These original equipment manufacturer (OEM) deals offer Asian partners a way to capture investment initiative from Western competitors and displace customer-competitors from value-creating activities. In many cases this goal meshes with that of the Western partner: to regain competitiveness quickly and with minimum effort.

Consider the joint venture between Rover, the British automaker, and Honda. Some 25 years ago, Rover's forerunners were world leaders in small car design. Honda had not even entered the automobile business. But in the mid-1970s, after failing to penetrate foreign markets, Rover turned to Honda for technology and product development support. Rover has used the alliance to avoid investments to design and build new cars. Honda has cultivated skills in European styling and marketing as well as multinational manufacturing. There is little doubt which company will emerge stronger over the long term.

Troubled laggards like Rover often strike alliances with surging late-comers like Honda. Having fallen behind in a key skills area (in this case, manufacturing small cars), the laggard attempts to compensate for past failures. The latecomer uses the alliance to close a specific skills gap (in this case, learning to build cars for a regional market). But a laggard that forges a partnership for short-term gain may find itself in a dependency spiral: as it contributes fewer and fewer distinctive skills, it must reveal more and more of its internal operations to keep the partner interested. For the weaker company, the issue shifts from, 'Should we collaborate?' to 'With whom should we collaborate?' to 'How do we keep our partner interested as we lose the advantages that made us attractive to them in the first place?'

There's a certain paradox here. When both partners are equally intent on internalizing the other's skills, distrust and conflict may spoil the alliance and threaten its very survival. That's one reason joint ventures between Korean and Japanese companies have been few and tempestuous. Neither side wants to 'open the kimono.' Alliances seem to run most smoothly when one partner is intent on learning and the other is intent on avoidance – in essence, when one partner is willing to grow dependent on the other. But running smoothly is not the point; the point is for a company to emerge from an alliance more competitive than when it entered it.

One partner does not always have to give up more than it gains to ensure the survival of an alliance. There are certain conditions under which mutual gain is possible, at least for a time:

- *The partners' strategic goals converge while their competitive goals diverge.* That is, each partner allows for the other's continued prosperity in the shared business. Philips and Du Pont collaborate to develop and manufacture compact discs, but neither side invades the other's market. There is a clear upstream/downstream division of effort.

- *The size and market power of both partners is modest compared with industry leaders.* This forces each side to accept that mutual dependence may have to continue for many years. Long-term collaboration may be so critical to both partners that neither will risk antagonizing the other by an overtly competitive bid to appropriate skills or competences. Fujitsu's 1 to 5 size disadvantage with IBM means it will be a long time, if ever, before Fujitsu can break away from its foreign partners and go it alone.

- *Each partner believes it can learn from the other and at the same time limit access to proprietary skills.* JVC and Thomson, both of whom make VCRs, know that they are trading skills. But the two companies are looking for very different things. Thomson needs product technology and manufacturing prowess; JVC needs to learn how to succeed in the fragmented European market. Both sides believe there is an equitable chance for gain.

How to Build Secure Defenses

For collaboration to succeed, each partner must contribute something distinctive: basic research, product development skills, manufacturing capacity, access to distribution. The challenge is to share enough skills to create advantage *vis-à-vis* companies outside the alliance while preventing a wholesale transfer of core skills to the partner. This is a very thin line to walk. Companies must carefully select what skills and technologies they pass to their partners. They must develop safeguards against unintended, informal transfers of information. The goal is to limit the transparency of their operations.

The type of skill a company contributes is an important factor in how easily its partner can internalize the skills. The potential for transfer is greatest when a partner's contribution is easily transported (in engineering drawings, on computer tapes, or in the heads of a few technical experts); easily interpreted (it can be reduced to commonly understood equations or symbols); and easily absorbed (the skill or competence is independent of any particular cultural context).

Western companies face an inherent disadvantage because their skills are generally more vulnerable to transfer. The magnet that attracts so many companies to alliances with Asian competitors is their manufacturing excellence – a competence that is less transferable than most. Just-in-time inventory systems and quality circles can be imitated, but this is like pulling a few threads out of an oriental carpet. Manufacturing excellence is a complex web of employee training, integration with suppliers, statistical process controls, employee involvement, value engineering, and design for manufacture. It is difficult to extract such a subtle competence in any way but a piecemeal fashion.

So companies must take steps to limit transparency. One approach is to limit the scope of the formal agreement. It might cover a single technology rather than an entire range of technologies; part of a product line rather than the entire line; distribution in a limited number of markets or for a limited period of time. The objective is to circumscribe a partner's opportunities to learn.

Moreover, agreements should establish specific performance requirements. Motorola, for example, takes an incremental, incentive-based approach to technology transfer in its venture with Toshiba. The agreement calls for Motorola to release its microprocessor technology incrementally as Toshiba delivers on its promise to increase Motorola's penetration in the Japanese semiconductor market. The greater Motorola's market share, the greater Toshiba's access to Motorola's technology.

Many of the skills that migrate between companies are not covered in the formal terms of collaboration. Top management puts together strategic alliances and sets the legal parameters for exchange. But what actually gets traded is determined by day-to-day interactions of engineers, marketers, and product developers: who says what to whom, who gets access to what facilities, who sits on what joint committees. The most important deals ('I'll share this with you if you share that with me') may be struck four or five organizational levels below where the deal was signed. Here lurks the greatest risk of unintended transfers of important skills.

Consider one technology-sharing alliance between European and Japanese competitors. The European company valued the partnership as a way to acquire a specific technology. The Japanese company considered it a window on its partner's entire range of competences and interacted with a broad spectrum of its partner's marketing and product development staff. The company mined each contact for as much information as possible.

For example, every time the European company requested a new feature on a product being sourced from its partner, the Japanese company asked for detailed customer and competitor analyses to justify the request. Over time, it developed a sophisticated picture of the European market that would assist its own entry strategy. The technology acquired by the European partner through the formal agreement had a useful life of three to five years. The competitive insights acquired informally by the Japanese company will probably endure longer.

Limiting unintended transfers at the operating level requires careful attention to the role of gatekeepers, the people who control what information flows to a partner. A gatekeeper can be effective only if there are a limited number of gateways through which a partner can access people and facilities. Fujitsu's many partners all go through a single office, the 'collaboration section,' to request information and assistance from different divisions. This way the company can monitor and control access to critical skills and technologies.

We studied one partnership between European and US competitors that involved several divisions of each company. While the US company could only access its partner through a single gateway, its partner had unfettered access to all participating divisions. The European company took advantage of its free rein. If one division refused to provide certain information, the European partner made the same request of another division. No single manager in the US company could tell how much information had been transferred or was in a position to piece together patterns in the requests.

Collegiality is a prerequisite for collaborative success. But *too much* collegiality should set off warning bells to senior managers. CEOs or division presidents should expect occasional complaints from their counterparts about the reluctance of lower level employees to share information. That's a sign that the gatekeepers are doing their jobs. And senior management should regularly debrief operating personnel to find out what information the partner is requesting and what requests are being granted.

Limiting unintended transfers ultimately depends on employee loyalty and self-discipline. This was a real issue for many of the western companies we studied. In their excitement and pride over technical achievements, engineering staffs sometimes shared information that top management considered sensitive. Japanese engineers were less likely to share proprietary information.

There are a host of cultural and professional reasons for the relative openness of western technicians. Japanese engineers and scientists are more loyal to their company than to their profession. They are less steeped in the open give-and-take of university research since they receive much of their training from employers. They consider themselves team members more than individual scientific contributors. As one Japanese manager noted, 'We don't feel any need to reveal what we know. It is not an issue of pride for us. We're glad to sit and listen. If we're patient we usually learn what we want to know.'

Controlling unintended transfers may require restricting access to facilities as well as to people. Companies should declare sensitive laboratories and factories off-limits to their partners. Better yet, they might house the collaborative venture in an entirely new facility. IBM is building a special site in Japan where Fujitsu can review its forthcoming mainframe software before deciding whether to license it. IBM will be able to control exactly what Fujitsu sees and what information leaves the facility.

Finally, which country serves as 'home' to the alliance affects transparency. If the collaborative team is located near one partner's major facilities, the other partner will have more opportunities to learn – but less control over what information gets traded. When the partner houses, feeds, and looks after engineers and operating managers, there is a danger they will 'go native.' Expatriate personnel need frequent visits from headquarters as well as regular furloughs home.

Enhance the Capacity to Learn

Whether collaboration leads to competitive surrender or revitalization depends foremost on what employees believe the purpose of the alliance to be. It is self-evident: to learn, one must want to learn. Western companies won't realize the full benefits of competitive collaboration until they overcome an arrogance borne of decades of leadership. In short, western companies must be more receptive.

We asked a senior executive in a Japanese electronics company about the perception that Japanese companies learn more from their foreign partners than vice versa. 'Our western partners approach us with the attitude of teachers,' he told us. 'We are quite happy with this, because we have the attitude of students.'

Learning begins at the top. Senior management must be committed to enhancing their companies' skills as well as to avoiding financial risk. But most learning takes place at the lower levels of an alliance. Operating employees not only represent the front lines in an effective defense but also play a vital role in acquiring knowledge. They must be well briefed on the partner's strengths and weaknesses and understand how acquiring particular skills will bolster their company's competitive position.

This is already standard practice among Asian companies. We accompanied a Japanese development engineer on a tour through a partner's factory. This engineer dutifully took notes on plant layout, the number of production stages, the rate at which the line was running, and the number of employees. He recorded all this despite the fact that he had no manufacturing responsibility in his own company, and that the alliance didn't encompass joint manufacturing. Such dedication greatly enhances learning.

Collaboration doesn't always provide an opportunity to fully internalize a partner's skills. Yet just acquiring new and more precise benchmarks of a partner's performance can be of great value. A new benchmark can provoke a thorough review of internal performance levels and may spur a round of competitive innovation. Asking questions like, 'Why do their semiconductor logic designs have fewer errors than ours?' and 'Why are they investing in this technology and we're not?' may provide the incentive for a vigorous catch-up program.

Competitive benchmarking is a tradition in most of the Japanese companies we studied. It requires many of the same skills associated with competitor analysis: systematically calibrating performance against external targets; learning to use rough estimates to determine where a competitor (or partner) is better, faster, or cheaper; translating those estimates into new internal targets; and recalibrating to establish the rate of improvement in a competitor's performance. The great advantage of competitive collaboration is that proximity makes benchmarking easier.

Indeed, some analysts argue that one of Toyota's motivations in collaborating with GM in the much-publicized NUMMI venture is to gauge the quality of GM's manufacturing technology. GM's top manufacturing people get a close look at Toyota, but the reverse is true as well. Toyota may be learning whether its giant US competitor is capable of closing the productivity gap with Japan.

Competitive collaboration also provides a way of getting close enough to rivals to predict how they will behave when the alliance unravels or runs its course. How does the partner respond to price changes? How does it measure and reward executives? How does it prepare to launch a new product? By revealing a competitor's management orthodoxies, collaboration can increase the chances of success in future head-to-head battles.

Knowledge acquired from a competitor-partner is only valuable after it is diffused through the organization. Several companies we studied had established internal clearinghouses to collect and disseminate information. The collaborations manager at one Japanese company regularly made the rounds of all employees involved in alliances. He identified what information had been collected by whom and then passed it on to appropriate departments. Another company held regular meetings where employees shared new knowledge and determined who was best positioned to acquire additional information.

Proceed with Care – But Proceed

After World War II, Japanese and Korean companies entered alliances with western rivals from weak positions. But they worked steadfastly toward independence. In the early 1960s, NEC's computer business was one-quarter the size of Honeywell's, its primary foreign partner. It took only two decades for NEC to grow larger than Honeywell, which eventually sold its computer operations to an alliance between NEC and Group Bull of France. The NEC experience demonstrates that dependence on a foreign partner doesn't automatically condemn a company to also-ran status. Collaboration may sometimes be unavoidable; surrender is not.

Managers are too often obsessed with the ownership structure of an alliance. Whether a company controls 51 percent or 49 percent of a joint venture may be much less important than the rate at which each partner learns from the other. Companies that are confident of their ability to learn may even prefer some ambiguity in the alliance's legal structure. Ambiguity creates more potential to acquire skills and technologies. The challenge for western companies is not to write tighter legal agreements but to become better learners.

Running away from collaboration is no answer. Even the largest western companies can no longer outspend their global rivals. With leadership in many industries shifting toward the East, companies in the United States and Europe must become good borrowers – much like Asian companies did in the 1960s and 1970s. Competitive renewal depends on building new process capabilities and winning new product and technology battles. Collaboration can be a low-cost strategy for doing both.

7.2   On Strategic Networks

By J. Carlos Jarillo[1]

In parallel with a theoretical acceptance of the importance of the laws of competition to formulate strategy, the realization is growing that cooperative behavior among firms is at the root of many success stories in today's management. This situation calls for an effort to develop a theoretical framework to study both aspects of firm behavior (cooperative and competitive) as compatible, complementary aspects of a unique reality. Indeed, the cooperative relationships of a firm can be the source of its competitive strength.

This paper develops the concept of strategic network, as a tool to understand those cooperative relationships and their role in the strategy of the firm. There are three main tasks of the paper: first, to show that strategic networks are but a 'mode of organization'; second, to study the economic conditions of existence of a network; finally, to analyze the conditions of existence of a network from the point of view of its internal consistency. In a final section some of the most obvious strategic implications of the framework are outlined

Networking is a fashionable topic. But, important as the topic may be, it lacks a generally accepted conceptual framework, with enough theoretical depth to help understand the plentiful anecdotal evidence, and particularly to put the phenomenon in a context consistent with the overall strategic paradigm.

The reason for such 'lack of depth', from a strategic point of view, might be found in the fact that the concept of network was coined outside the strategy field. Thus, the seminal work on inter-organizational relationships was performed by researchers in the organizational theory tradition. The empirical research was, in all instances, conducted in non-profit organizations. This is an important consideration: strategy scholars have had little use for the concept of networks. They do not use the network construct precisely because it is very hard to harmonize with the basic postulates of competitive behavior. This 'problem' to conceptualize the realities of networks has been probably aggravated by the preeminence of models of strategy based on microeconomic theory (Porter, 1981). And yet the anecdotal evidence of phenomena classifiable as networking abounds. Among the best-known cases is the use of suppliers by Japanese manufacturing firms. Practically all studies of industrial suppliers and industrial markets touch on this point. Von Hippel (1985) has shown how a close relationship with suppliers and customers provides firms with the most important source of innovation.

---

[1] Source: This article was adapted with permission from 'On Strategic Networks', *Strategic Management Journal*, June–July 1988.

In spite of this conceptual difficulty, scholarly articles are appearing on the topic, mostly from Europe, and ideas are emerging that can be used as building blocks in a theory of strategic networks. Thorelli (1986) sees networks as something between markets and hierarchies. Firms act in a complex environment, where no firm can really be understood without a reference to its relationships with many others. He recognizes that, instead of network, he could have used the term 'system', but thought it was a 'tired term'. In this sense he is basically describing reality, more than conceptualizing it. Johanson and Mattson (1987) use the concept of network to define industrial markets. Networks are seen as complex arrays of relationships between firms. Firms establish those relationships through interactions with each other. These interactions imply investments to build the relationships, which gives consistency to the network. Competing is more a matter of positioning one's firm in the network than attacking the environment. The care of the relationships becomes a priority for management. Along similar lines, MacMillan and Farmer (1979) talk about expanding the theory of the firm to include what they call 'managed economic systems'. Lorenzoni goes a step further. He bases his work on the changes of deintegration which have occurred in the textile industry in northern Italy. A strong process of deintegration is documented, whereby 700 firms in 1951 'deintegrate into 9,500 in 1976, with a decrease in average employment per firm from 30 to five. Total employment has more than doubled: the industry is very healthy, the most competitive in the world'. Analyzing the phenomenon, he describes the rich web of relationships that constitute the networks of small firms ('constellations'), and how these networks go from a phase of 'reaction' (realized constellation), to one of efficiency (rationalized constellation) to its current phase of effectiveness (planned constellation). The step made by Lorenzoni over the previous work is that he sees the network, in this last step, as the product of a determined entrepreneur, bent on obtaining the best (most efficient) organizational arrangement to compete in his or her chosen market. This understanding of the network arrangement as something that entrepreneurs use purposefully to obtain a competitive advantage for their firms, instead of as a 'metaphor' to describe business transactions, constitutes the theoretical thrust of this reading. (See Lorenzoni and Baden-Fuller, 1995; reading 7.4.)

In this reading, networks are conceptualized as a mode of organization that can be used by managers or entrepreneurs to position their firms in a stronger competitive stance. That is why the term 'strategic' has been added to 'networks': I see strategic networks as long-term, purposeful arrangements among distinct but related for-profit organizations that allow those firms in them to gain or sustain competitive advantage *vis-à-vis* their competitors outside the network. Firms in the network are independent along some dimensions (i.e. they are not completely dependent on each other). Otherwise they would fall into a case of 'vertical quasi-integration'. The relationships enjoyed by the firms in the network are, however, essential to their competitive position. It is a mode of organization that is not based strictly on the price mechanism, or on 'hierarchical fiat', but on coordination through adaptation. Essential to this concept of strategic network is that of 'hub firm', which is the firm that, in fact, sets up the network, and takes a pro-active attitude in the care of it.

The main theoretical difficulty is that networks do not fit well the basic models of strategy, as has been said. Firms are normally regarded as 'complete entities', operating in an environment that is implicitly defined in a rather negative way, as 'everything that is not the firm'. The problem of establishing the 'boundaries of the organization' has always vexed the 'open system model' (MacMillan and Farmer, 1979). And yet real-life firms, particularly in some highly relevant contexts, are very far from that proto-typical 'firm' that buys raw materials, processes them and sells them in an almost completely isolated way.

The theoretical thrust of this paper consists of trying to understand the economic basis for the relationships established in a network, how those relationships can enhance the competitive stance of the particular firms involved in the network, and what the conditions for the stability of the relationships are. Briefly, we must understand under which circumstances a network arrangement can be more efficient than both a purely 'market' relationship or an integrated solution. If it is more efficient, it can easily be turned into strategically superior.

Networks as a Mode Of Organization

Williamson's (1975) main insight, derived from Coase (1937), was to see 'markets' and 'hierarchies' as two alternative modes of organizing economic activities. It is assumed that the most efficient mode, for a particular kind of transaction, will prevail. In the classical theory the advantages of a total 'deintegration' seem clear. So much so that the original question posed by Coase was, indeed, why are there firms at all, instead of just a market of separate economic atomistic units. Consider a firm that contemplates different cost curves in the different sub-components that make up its final product. Some of these curves fall indefinitely, some go up, and some are U-shaped. If there are several firms in the market producing the same good, the (a priori) most efficient way to organize production would consist of one firm specializing in one of the subcomponents of the product that has a descending cost curve, and supplying it to the other firms, which would get it at a lower cost than if they had to perform that function by themselves. Why does this not happen? Williamson's answer is that there are trans-actions costs associated with such an arrangement, that make it actually more expensive than the production of the subcomponent by each firm. In this particular case it is not difficult to imagine what these costs are: oppor-tunism, early-mover advantages, and other strategic considerations. The other firms simply cannot let one of their competitors take care in a mono-polistic fashion of an activity that is needed for their 'smooth functioning.'

By definition, in the absence of transactions costs, firms would not integrate functions. That would allow them not only to reap economies of scale, but also all the well-known benefits of internal focus, plus the flexibility to switch suppliers whenever technological or market developments so advised. If, however, there are transactions costs, firms will integrate activities that could have been subcontracted. But if an entrepreneur is able to lower those transactions costs (relative to its competitors), the resulting firm will be less integrated and more efficient (ceteris paribus): the firm can concentrate exclusively on its comparative advantages. There is, of course, an assumption here, not discussed by Williamson: transactions costs can be affected by conscious actions of the entrepreneur. We shall see that this is the case, and how this is the foundation for the concept of 'strategic network'.

It cannot be taken for granted that a 'hierarchical relationship', from a practical point of view, avoids the theoretical transactions costs, however. We see, for instance, many management-labor relationships that 'should' fit into the hierarchical mode and are not different from any arms-length market relationship with a non-cooperative supplier. Thus Williamson's distinction, although extremely useful from a theoretical point of view, cannot be naively translated into actual corporate realities.

Ouchi (1980) has addressed this problem. He proposed to break 'hierarchies' down into two different categories: 'bureaucracies' and 'clans'. The first type would have some of the characteristics of markets: the 'congruence of goals' could be very low, but the organizational form would still be that of a firm. Clans, on the other hand, would be much closer to eliminating transactions costs, because the congruence of goals would allow the firm to do without much of the supervision inherent in a 'bureaucratic' company. The main 'transaction cost' avoided by a clan would be the need to ascertain how much each participant should get paid. Since it is impractical, in many settings, to do that through a market mechanism, because there is joint effort, a hierarchical arrangement is arrived at.

But we can go a step further. 'Markets' can also be broken down into two different categories, according to the 'approach' both parties take to the relationship (to their degree of 'goal congruence', or, in other words, to the perceived opportunity for joint value creation). Whether the relationship is seen by the two parties as a zero-sum game (competitive) or not (cooperative) is the criterion which cuts across the two kinds of legal organization, 'markets' and 'hierarchies'. Figure 7.2.1 represents the four possibilities.

Thus the different 'modes' of organizing complex economic activity come determined by two variables: the 'legal' organization (i.e. whether the entities act as separated units) and the 'kind of relationship' (i.e. where there is goal congruence, inseparability of returns). Of course, the two extremes of these variables must be seen as poles in a continuum. Thus, more than four 'pure' forms, we have four 'prototypes'.

The upper-left corner of the matrix thus formed would truly be what Williamson called 'markets', i.e. an organizational arrangement where many players interact on a spot basis. The lower-left quadrant would be exemplified by the antagonistic labor-management relationship. It is, from a formal point of view, a hierarchical organization, but many of its char-

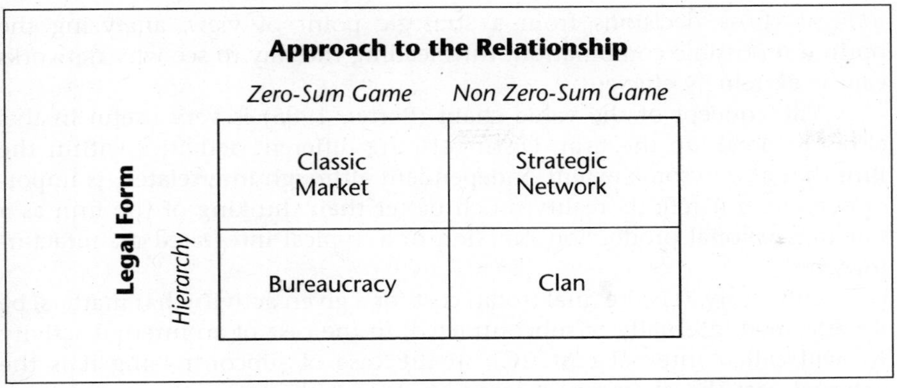

FIGURE 7.2.1
The four modes of
organizing economic
activity

acteristics – particularly those referring to transactions costs – are those of an open market.

The third quadrant, 'clans' as Ouchi called it, is probably the closest thing to what a Williamsonian hierarchy would be in real life: long-term relationships, carried out through nonspecified contracts within the formal environment of an organization.

Finally, I have called the upper-right quadrant 'strategic networks'. In them, a 'hub' firm has special relationships with the other members of the network. Those relationships have most of the characteristics of a 'hierarchical' relationship: relatively unstructured tasks, long-term point of view, relatively unspecified contracts. These relationships have all the characteristics of 'investments', since there is always a certain 'asset specificity' to the know-how of, say, dealing with a given supplier instead of a new one. And yet the 'contracting parties' remain as independent organizations, with few or no points of contact along many of their dimensions.

I contend that the entrepreneur can affect the way the relationship is shaped and, the same way a conscientious manager can create a 'clan' atmosphere, an inter-organizational relationship can be based on perceived goal congruence and trust. When the relationship is viewed as valuable in itself because of future, unforeseen developments, keeping it alive becomes much easier. We will expand on this in the remaining sections.

How can a Network be Economically Efficient?

I have explained so far what a strategic network is. The task now is to understand how can it be efficient, in the competitive sense; i.e. how can it be more efficient than any other mode of organization. This takes us back to Williamson's original question of why economic activities are organized along different modes.

In order to understand the way firms structure themselves (which activities are integrated and which are farmed out) we must break up the firm into smaller units of analysis. In this section a framework is provided to look at those decisions from a strategic point of view, analyzing the optimum possible combination, thus leading the way to see why networks can be extremely efficient.

The concept of the value chain (Porter, 1985) is very useful in this effort to break up the firm. Distinguishing different activities within the firm that are, to some extent, independent although interrelated, is important because it reflects reality much better than thinking of the firm as a one-dimensional production function or a 'typical integrated manufacturing firm'.

Obviously, it is the final (total) cost for a given activity that matters, be it performed internally or subcontracted. In the case of an internal activity we will call it internal cost (IC); in the case of subcontracting it is the external cost (EP, the price charged by the supplier) plus the transactions cost (TC). The total external cost will then be called EC, and it is EP + TC. An activity will be integrated (thus shaping a hierarchy) when EP + TC > IC. This, obviously, can hold even in the case of EP < IC. Remember that TC is dependent on structural characteristics (assets specificity, small numbers bargaining, etc.). It is expected, then, that all competitors will make a similar choice and integrate, or else be driven out of business.

But let us assume for a moment that a given entrepreneur can in fact lower TC for activities supplied to (or by) his or her firm. If TC is lowered up to a point where EC + TC < IC, the entrepreneur will not integrate that activity and, precisely by doing so, will be more efficient than its competitors. This is the essence of the effectiveness of the network arrangement. The hub firm in the network can enjoy lower costs because it captures economies of scale (or whatever source of efficiency) from its associated firms, which other competitors cannot obtain because TC forces them to integrate. Obviously, this will be the case if and only if EP < IC (a technological consideration) and TC can in fact be lowered enough so that (part of) the savings can be realized by subcontracting. Thus the condition for the economic efficiency of a network is that EP be lower than IC, for some activities necessary for the production of the good delivered by the network Of course, without a lowering of TC the network will not exist (or will be competed out of the market). But this point will be dealt with in the next section.

The strategic implications of a network arrangement are important. It allows a firm to specialize in those activities of the value chain that are essential to its competitive advantage, reaping all the benefits of specialization, focus and, possible, size. The other activities are then farmed out to members of the network, that carry them out more efficiently than the 'hub' firm would, since they are specialized in them. At the same time, all the firms in the network enjoy the added flexibility of not having fixed commitments to activities which are not essential to them. A very important benefit of a networking arrangement over an integrated solution is that efficiency is fostered because 'the market test is still applicable. No matter how close the relationship between buyers and sellers, no matter how long it has endured, if better trading terms (considering quality, quantity, timing and price) can be obtained elsewhere, there is no permanent tie to stop either party making alternative arrangements' (MacMillan and Farmer, 1979). Thus networking introduces a cost discipline that may be absent in an integrated firm, with its captive internal markets. Finally it must be remarked that, by farming out activities to other members of the network, a firm can lower its costs for those activities it keeps inside, because it can reap economies of scale and develop distinctive competences. Thus, when deciding the allocation of an activity (assessing internal and external costs), the real complete internal cost must be calculated. It is often higher than it seems at first look, because performing a given activity inside may imply a loss of efficiency for the overall firm. This is well known to many successful real-life entrepreneurs who refuse to be distracted by activities other than the essential ones.

How can a Network be Created and Sustained?

The conditions for the existence of stable networks are the same as the conditions for the existence of organizations, using this word now in the traditional sense of organization theory. It has been accepted that, at a maximum level of abstraction, an organization has to meet two character-istics to come into existence, and then survive: it must be effective and it must be efficient. An organization is effective if it achieves the desired end. It is efficient if it does so while, at the same time, offering more inducements to the members of the organization than efforts they have to put into it. This can directly be translated to interorganizational relationships. That a networking arrangement can be effective has been argued in the previous section. In fact it can be the most effective arrangement in many circum-stances. The basic condition for effectiveness is technological (that external costs be lower than internal costs), plus the possibility of lowering trans-actions costs. But to actually come into existence and, especially, to survive, a network must be efficient. The basic condition for efficiency is that the gain to be accrued by being part of the network is seen as superior, over the long term, to the profits that can be obtained by going alone (or by estab-lishing short-term, changing relationships). This can be achieved through the realization of two points: first, that belonging to the network gives superior performance (thus there is more pie to share, because the network is effective); and second, that the sharing mechanisms are 'fair'.

Efficiency and effectiveness are, then, the basic conditions of existence of networks. We shall see now what mechanisms are used by actual entre-preneurs to ensure that those conditions apply.

It will be remembered that Williamson argues that markets fail, and therefore hierarchies have to be established to perform their functions, because of costs that make market transactions inefficient. Those costs stem from four reasons: man's 'bounded rationality', uncertainty about the future, the presence of a 'small number' of players for a given kind of transaction, and the possibility of 'opportunistic behavior' on the part of (at least) some of the players. These are precisely the reasons why trust might be lacking in a relationship. In other words, lack of trust is the quintessential cause of transactional costs: 'Opportunism is a central concept in the study of transaction costs' (Williamson, 1979), for it poses a real danger whenever there are 'appropriable quasi-rents of specialized assets' a situation intrinsically characteristic of networks, as we have seen. Being able to generate trust, therefore, is the fundamental entrepreneurial skill to lower those costs and make the existence of the network economically feasible.

Thorelli (1986) has defined trust as 'an assumption or reliance on the part of A that if either A or B encounters a problem in the fulfillment of his implicit or explicit transactional obligations, B may be counted on to do what A would do if B's resources were at A's disposal.' Observe that trust dissolves the need to specify unforeseeable consequences, for it is assumed that the decision rule to be followed will be identical to my own decision rule. The same can be said of the problem of 'fair sharing'. Thus trust is a critical component of both effectiveness and efficiency.

The importance of trust for the smooth and effective functioning of organizations has been argued, among many others, by Barnes (1981). Driscoll (1978) found evidence that a trustful environment is more important for work satisfaction than participation in decision-making. Zand (1972) found empirical evidence, confirmed by Boss (1978), that an atmosphere of trust is actually conducive to more efficient problemsolving. The reason is that, in such an atmosphere, information is exchanged freely, and more solutions to a given problem are explored, since the decision-makers do not feel they must protect themselves from the others' opportunistic behavior. These arguments deal with the function of trust within organizations, but they can be easily applied to networks. In the words of Williamson (1979: 241), 'other things being equal, idiosyncratic exchange relations [i.e., transactions involving specific assets] which feature personal trust will survive greater stress and display greater adaptability'.

How can trust be generated? Let us take the situation of the business-person who needs to generate trust in order to build a network, i.e. in order to lower TC arising from opportunism and asset-specificity. He or she will have to act on two variables: the assumptions of the owner of the resources (the other party) regarding the entrepreneur's motivations and intrinsic situation.

The first variable can be addressed through choosing carefully the partners to the different relationships, searching explicitly for people the entrepreneur can 'relate to', i.e. with similar values. This identity of values and motivations will certainly facilitate the emergence of trust

The second variable is the intrinsic situation. The entrepreneur cannot expect 'blind trust' if it means the members of the network must put themselves at high risk. Trustful behavior can only be generated by showing that the entrepreneur would be worse off if he or she behaved opportunistically. A typical way of doing this is by showing a track record, a reputation that is valuable and has to be protected. The entrepreneur, it is assumed, will behave correctly because, even if in this particular circumstance he or she could gain from opportunistic behavior, such behavior would destroy his or her reputation, thus making the total outcome of the opportunistic behavior undesirable.

An emphasis on long-term relationships is also essential to the development of trust, because it makes it clear that the relationship itself is considered valuable. Therefore, opportunistic behavior, which would cause a severance of the relationship, will be considered less likely.

Strategic Implications

Much work has been done on analytical tools to help a firm analyze the attractiveness of a given market, i.e. to help them choose where to compete. But it is much more important to decide which segments of the value chain of a given product or sets of products are to be emphasized in a firm, and which ones are to be downplayed or even subcontracted altogether. Whether a firm is a low-cost manufacturer or a niche marketer within the same industry is, at least, as radical a distinction, with as many implications, as whether the firm is competing in a given market, or another similar to it – concentrating on the same activities of the value chain. Shaping the value chain is really shaping the firm.

A good example of this point can be seen in the huge success many Japanese corporations have had diversifying widely in their product ranges, going from cameras to office equipment to electronics (Canon). It is contended that a reason for that success – so elusive for many western corporations – may be that they have concentrated on their 'distinctive competences', those being the activities of the value chain where the firm excels. The amount of subcontracting by those firms tends to be very large, again compared with their western counterparts.

Establishing an efficient network implies the ability to lower transactions costs, for it is precisely those costs that lead firms to integrate, shunning the flexibility offered by a market relationship, together with the advantages of specialization, both their own and their suppliers'. This ability is, then, considered a critical element of success when managing. After all, what the 'hub firm' is doing is establishing an external relationship for a set of transactions that other firms must internalize, given the high cost for them of having those transactions performed outside. The flexibility and focus that result from deintegration, made possible by the existence of a network that takes care of the other functions, can be extremely powerful competitive weapons, especially in environments that experience rapid change, due to increasingly rapid technological pace, globalization of competition, or the apparition of new, flexible, focused, deintegrated competitors.

As we saw above, the critical component that makes a relationship take the shape of 'strategic network', instead of that of a 'typical market' is the high degree of (perceived) 'opportunity for joint value creation' between the two organizations. An important component of that perception is the time frame being considered. The relationship of a supplier with a customer is, for a given transaction, a zero-sum game: each dollar gained by the supplier is a dollar lost by the buyer. But, over the long term, the situation may be different: the success of the supplier may be linked to the success of the buyer. A clear case of this is the relationship between management and a trade union or a car dealer and the automobile manufacturer. A given contract may be viewed as a zero-sum game but, over the long run, the destinies of both parties are intertwined. Thus, specific actions must be implemented to ensure that the firm is taking the appropriate long-term outlook, and that it is being seen to do so. The need to build and maintain a reputation in order to be able to establish relationships that can result in an overall decrease of costs has specific implications for management, and can seriously alter priorities.

It has been said that subcontracting practices are simply a mechanism by which large firms would export some of their risk in business to smaller, defenseless subcontractors. The larger firms would, for instance, keep production in-house when there is a slack in demand, thus avoiding lay-offs. The agency relationship would then be based on the exporting of all the risk to the subcontractors. That would certainly go against the trust-building practices that we should expect in efficient networks. In a real networking arrangement the 'principal' should take on some of the risk of the relationship, through an agreement that shifts (at least) part of the random variance in the subcontractor's costs to the principal, i.e. there should be a factor α that represents the share of variance taken up by the principal. Thus, if $\alpha = 0$, then the subcontractor bears all the risk (it is a purely fixed-price contract); if $\alpha = 1$ the principal bears all the risk (it is a cost-plus contract). The problem with $\alpha = 0$ is that there is no real network relationship (it would be the case of buying something at a given, fixed price, with no further involvement between the firms). The problem with $\alpha = 1$ is that there is no incentive whatsoever for the subcontractor to be efficient. Efficient networks, therefore, should show a fact $1 > \alpha > 0$. There is some evidence of this. Kawasaki and MacMillan (1986) examine a large sample of subcontracting arrangements among Japanese firms, and find the following: first, the subcontractors are indeed risk-averse (as may be expected from their small size, compared to the principals); second, the contracts have the principal absorbing some of the risk on behalf of the subcontractor ($\alpha > 0$); third, α grows, among other things, with the degree of risk-aversion of the subcontractor and the size of the fluctuations in costs; finally, the average α is 0.69, with many of them being above 0.75. This means that the contracts are closer to the cost-plus end of the spectrum.

Although an in-depth analysis of Japanese subcontracting practices is clearly outside the scope of this paper, and would have to include considerations from many different fields, the previous points let us realize that some of the most successful industrial networks do behave in a way consistent with the previous analysis. Thus the risk-sharing agreement is basic to the long-term success of the relationship, and the 'principal' has to be willing to take it. The supposed 'exploitation' is certainly nowhere to be found. The arrangement gives flexibility to the large firm while the subcontractor is better off because of the risk absorbed by the big firm, presumably more neutral with respect to it.

An area where the use of networks is of the utmost importance is in entrepreneurship. It is an essential characteristic of entrepreneurs to end up using more resources than they control, for they are motivated primarily by the pursuit of opportunity, rather than feeling constrained by using the resources they control. Networking is, in most instances, the method entrepreneurs use to get access to external resources, necessary in the pursuit of their opportunities. Thus the realization of the importance of networking, and the understanding of the skills involved in making it succeed, are two of the most important 'entrepreneurial skills' that can be taught and developed. Something similar can be said of the process of 'professionalization' of the entrepreneurial firm, once it has succeeded in the start-up phase. The risk of losing the 'entrepreneurial spirit' through paying too much attention to what has already been achieved goes together with the tendency to do more and more things inside, losing the initial advantages that served the firm so well.

7.3 Incorporating International Strategic Alliances into Overall Firm Strategy

By Stephen Preece[1]

In response to global competitive forces, business leaders are increasingly turning to cooperative arrangements to advance their competitive edge internationally. Popularly called international strategic alliances, it appears that this trend represents a permanent fixture in the portfolio of strategic options available to global managers, as opposed to what has sometimes been described as a passing fad in the managerial transition to international maturity.

The rise of international strategic alliance formation has brought about both euphoria over the potential of such arrangements to meet the intensifying demands of global competition, as well as disappointment over the challenges inherent in their implementation. Important to the success of these arrangements is that managers be clear about their overall strategic purpose. Alliances are often spoken of in terms of specific functions performed (i.e. market extension, technology sharing). However, the decision to engage a company in a major alliance often represents a substantive

[1] Source: This article was adapted with permission from 'Incorporating International Strategic Alliances into Overall Firm Strategy: A Typology of Six Managerial Objectives,' *The International Executive*, Vol. 37 (3), May/June 1995, pp. 261–277.

strategic alternative having wide-ranging implications for overall firm competitiveness, both positive and negative. The way in which international strategic alliances are incorporated into the overall firm strategy, the long-run strategic objective assumed by management, is critical to the effectiveness of this competitive tool. This article suggests that there are multiple objectives managers can take regarding the integration of international strategic alliances into the strategic management of the organization, with varying consequences.

Conceptualization of Strategic Alliances

The three ways to conceptualize international strategic alliances are: structures, functions, and objectives (see Table 7.3.1). Perhaps the most common way of thinking about international strategic alliances focuses on alliance organizational structures. The most prevalent organizational structure is the joint venture, where two firms contribute equity in order to create a new and separate entity; some have described this new organization as the 'child' with contributing firms assuming the role of 'parents.' A variation on the joint venture is the minority-equity investment, where one firm takes a minority-equity position in another ongoing firm. Non-equity co-operative arrangements are also possible where firms agree to share efforts, assets, and profits without engaging in equity ties.

A second conceptualization of international strategic alliances relates to the various functions of alliances. The primary areas targeted for alliance formation are often collapsed into four primary categories: technology, finance, markets, and production. Technology-driven alliances include such activities as technology development, commercialization, sharing, or licensing. Finance-driven alliances focus on gaining access to financial markets at least cost and the sharing of risk where the product gestation period is long. Market-driven alliances emphasize the penetration of new foreign markets, sharing distribution channels, or extending a brand name. Production-driven alliances include the sharing of production facilities, rationalizing manufacturing, or integrating supplier relationships.

Although the structure and functional conceptualizations address important elements of collaborative activity, it is the third category,

TABLE 7.3.1
Structures, functions, and objectives of international strategic alliances

Structures	The organizational form chosen for the collaboration. May include joint venture, minority-equity, licensing, nonequity contractual, etc.
Functions	The specific activities to be performed by the alliance. May include market access, technology development, production sharing, financial access, risk sharing, etc.
Objectives	The overall contribution the alliance is intended to have on the strategic direction and capabilities of the firm, i.e. its long-run significance.

TABLE 7.3.2
Six objectives of international strategic alliances

Objective	Description	Positive Aspects	Negative Aspects
Learning	Acquire needed know-how (markets, technology, management)	Inexpensive and efficient acquisition	Partner opportunism, organizational challenges
Leaning	Replace value-chain activities, fill in missing firm infrastructure	Specialization advantages	Partner dependency
Leveraging	Fully integrate firm operations with partner	Entirely new portfolio of resources	Decision paralysis, evolving environment
Linking	Closer links with suppliers and customers	Closer coordination of vertical activities	Greater inflexibility in vertical relations
Leaping	Pursue radically new area of endeavor	Expanding universe of market opportunity	Cultural incompatibility
Locking out	Reduce competitive pressure from non-partners	Temporary competitive hiatus	Static strategic position, ephemeral advantage

strategic objectives of international strategic alliances, that will potentially have the greatest impact on the overall strategic direction and future organizational capabilities of the firm. This reading presents a typology defining six cooperative objectives, in hopes that it will assist managers in assessing their own vision of strategic alliances and contribute to the understanding of how such relationships can work to their advantage both cooperatively and competitively.

It is important to emphasize that both structural and functional issues are important, and inextricably linked, to the various strategic objectives (see Table 7.3.2) that will be discussed. It is also evident that while one alliance objective will likely dominate, others may play secondary roles.

Learning

The first strategic objective is *learning*. In this case the firm enters into the alliance with the intention of acquiring needed know-how from the partner through the learning process.

Learning becomes attractive when a firm is incapable of performing certain value-chain activities that have the potential to make it either more powerful or more profitable. Two important assumptions linked to this objective are: there is an advantage to maintaining the function/technology within the firm hierarchy; and the function/technology is embedded within the firm, making an arm's-length (market) transaction difficult.

It is unlikely that the learning alliance will actually be described by the participants in these terms. The stated rationale will be defined as an agreement to combine R&D efforts, jointly manufacture a product, and/or share distribution outlets (all functional arrangements). However, one or both sides may aggressively use the alliance to acquire valuable know-how, gradually becoming independent of the 'teaching' partner once the learning process is complete.

Learning in cooperative relationships has received important attention in the research on international strategic alliances. A common theme is the 'intractability' of learning mechanisms. It is difficult to isolate specific areas of the alliance interface, leaving a variety of processes, technologies, and practices up for grabs for the would-be 'student.' The fundamental risk in alliance learning is the issue of 'leakage' where unintended knowledge or expertise is passed on, with the worst-case scenario leading to the student coming back to compete with the teacher.

When learning is a primary motivation, alliance longevity is naturally determined by the time it takes to acquire the needed skills; the alliance essentially becomes a 'race to learn' between partners. The three key determinants of learning capabilities in alliances are:

- intent – the objectives the partners have for systematic learning;

- transparency – the organizational barriers to learning;

- receptivity – the willingness or ability of firm employees to learn.

Instilling the necessary learning capabilities in organizational actors can pose a major challenge to architects of interorganizational relationships. The positive elements of pursuing alliances as a learning vehicle are speed, efficiency, and cost. Rather than developing a new capability (process, market, or technology) by trial and error through internal development, the alliance provides immediate access to the desired skill. An alternative to alliance learning would be to acquire a firm that carries the needed know-how. However, this strategy can prove to be confrontational and ultimately result in losing the desired skills by way of workplace disruptions, distrust, and defections. Licensing can also serve as an alternative for developing needed know-how; however, some of the most valuable technologies (management, process, and product) are often so embedded in the organizational framework that they are difficult to separate and transfer effectively to a new organization. In short, the strategic alliance relationship with learning as a primary intent has many advantages over the alternatives – acquisition, in-house development, or licensing.

The negative elements of learning alliances primarily accrue to the nonlearner. If an alliance partner does not have a learning motive, it may view partner learning efforts to be predatory or in bad faith, resulting in conflict or even dissolution. Further, the learning alliance assumes an organizational ability to learn and a willingness of the partner to allow learning to take place.

Leaning

The second objective in relationships of international strategic alliances is *leaning*. In this case the alliance is entered with the intention of having the partner replace an element of the firm's value-chain activities that was previously performed internally. An important assumption is that by ceding out certain operational segments, firms will be able to focus on what they do best, placing an emphasis on their core competence. The firm picking up the value-chain activity is assumed to have its own core competence in that particular area. Leaning objectives, to the extent that the firm is moving away from unattractive value-chain activities, may be considered to be the opposite of the learning objective that seeks to take on particular activities and competencies.

A natural opportunity for leaning in international strategic alliances occurs through cooperative relationships with firms located in countries that provide a comparative advantage in specific value-added activities. US companies, for example, may shift production assignments to overseas alliance partners where labor costs are significantly cheaper, while maintaining basic R&D and marketing functions in the United States. The effect is to enable US companies to focus on the higher value-added value-chain activities while ceding out more labor-intensive segments to alliance partners. The general rationale for this type of partnership is to delegate out a central business function to an alliance partner, thereby freeing resources for more appropriate uses.

The advantage of such a strategy can result in substantial short-term gains in a production cost structure. Both parties benefit through specialization in the functions that are most amenable to their environments or organizations. The risk in a leaning strategy is in determining which activities are not critical to the core competence of the firm. If a firm mistakenly cedes out crucial activities it can severely cripple its long-term strategy.

A central problem to this alliance objective is functional impotence resulting from a loss of skills. When a set of operations is removed from the 'vocabulary' of the firm, the organization may forget how to use it and end up losing it forever. Employees who were once engaged in a specific function that is later ceded out to the alliance partner either move to another company or are reassigned. This can lead to a dependency relationship where the original firm can no longer perform production or other functions internally without incurring substantial costs.

Another problem with the leaning strategy is associated with the geographic and organizational separation of value-chain functions. Performing design and research functions in one country while production takes place on the other side of the world can lead to inefficiencies and slower response times. In addition, important feedback and interactive development and production processes are noticeably absent.

Finally, the risk of creating a competitor is great. The number of industries that have relied on cooperative relationships to substitute internal processes only to be later overtaken by the partners are numerous. Once the production process falls into the hands of another producer, it then has all the opportunities to achieve productivity and technological gains from improvements and innovation.

Leveraging

The third strategic objective to be addressed in relationships of international strategic alliances is *leveraging*. In this case the alliance represents a major integration of firm functions between partners in order to benefit from size and/or scope advantages. The competitive structure of numerous global industries often requires a critical mass in areas such as market reach, R&D dollars, and product offerings to compete with other dominant global players. While the costs of amassing the necessary size or scope may be prohibitive for an individual firm, two or more smaller firms can enter into an international strategic alliance to achieve similar results. The outcome is the leveraging of individual firm strengths with those of a partner for size and/or scope advantages.

An illustration of the leveraging objective is as follows. In early 1991, the Eastman Kodak Co. subsidiary, Sterling Drug (US), and Sanofi S.A. (France) joined their pharmaceutical operations in what could be considered a leveraging alliance. The arrangement, which involved no equity exchange, enabled Sanofi to market its products through the extensive Sterling distribution system in both North and Latin America, while Sterling gained access to the extensive Sanofi distribution system throughout Europe. In addition to market sharing arrangements, the alliance included a significant R&D component.

Traditionally, Sterling held a strong over-the-counter expertise while Sanofi maintained strengths in prescription drugs. The combination of their R&D efforts and budgets was considered by many to give their joint operations the critical mass necessary to be major players in the global pharmaceuticals industry.

The strategic rationale behind this specific alliance illustrates the leveraging concept. Two medium-sized pharmaceutical companies with complementary markets, product capabilities, and research budgets, combined efforts to become a powerhouse in a global industry. The extensiveness of this relationship was such that the two companies had to co-ordinate activities on virtually every level of business practice. The obvious advantage of this kind of alliance objective is the opportunity to expand assets, resources, capabilities, and opportunities significantly in a very short time frame. With the stroke of a pen (to a 150–page document requiring six months of negotiations) two medium-sized pharmaceutical firms, one based in France and one in the United States, each with extensive regional operations and specific expertises, combined operations in a world-wide competitive effort.

Two negative elements stand out in the leveraging strategy. Organizational inertia and bureaucratic stagnation is possible when any organization reaches the point of having multiple management layers and departments; combining two large bureaucracies increases complexity and the potential for decision hang-ups. Procedural issues as well as trust, reciprocity, and monitoring issues affect the commitment and durability of the relationship.

The other negative aspect of this strategy is the problem of a changing world. The top management of two major companies may see eye-to-eye regarding industry and competitive factors that make such an alliance favorable today. However, the question becomes, will this consensus in 'world view' exist one, two, or five years from now? Extensive research suggests that industry evolution and the shifting of the competitive landscape are major contributors to alliance instability. In her analysis of almost 900 joint ventures, Kathryn Harrigan identifies several important 'change forces' that significantly alter the environment for strategic alliances and lead to either reconfiguration, dismantling, or renegotiation of the agreement. Some of the most important change forces include the actual and perceived market performance of the joint venture, changes in industry structure, changes in competitor make-up, changes in the perceived mission of the parents, and changes in relative worth of individual assets, including technology (Harrigan, 1985).

Linking

The fourth objective of international strategic alliances considered in this analysis is *linking*. This particular relationship approach is most frequently associated with vertical relationships (as opposed to horizontal) and are often singular in their functional scope. Strategic supplier and customer relationships are becoming much more prevalent as a specific example of this relationship type.

The traditional model in the United States has been to maintain multiple suppliers for any given component and then to foster an environment that makes them compete against one another. Annual or biannual bidding arrangements would lead to constant competitive pressure through low-price seeking and the willingness to shift suppliers with virtually interchangeable component parts. A changing trend, however, is for manufacturers to seek tighter links with supplier companies, based on the belief that closer cooperation and coordination will lead to a more effective relationship, because the sharing of information, specifications, and expertise over time will result in shorter lead times, higher quality, and greater control in the manufacturing process. The advantage to the linking strategic objective is that it brings about opportunities for greater coordination and a tighter relationship between partners than would be available in an arm's-length supplier relationship.

The major negative element of this strategy is inflexibility. When a traditional supplier relationship is reevaluated annually or biannually, there is little problem in severing a relationship when it becomes necessary; with an alliance relationship it becomes much more difficult. As the relationship deepens and intensifies over time, specific assets and personnel are exclusively devoted to the relationship. If the firm encounters a downturn in business or a reduction in customer orders, it is much more difficult to sever the relationship with the one supplier with which the firm has developed an involved relationship than it would be otherwise, and the damage to both may be severe.

Leaping

The fifth alliance objective is *leaping*. In this case a company benefits from the expertise of another firm whose core competency is substantially different, thereby allowing the former to expand into largely disparate but potentially viable areas in which it would otherwise not venture. This objective is called leaping because the areas of expertise sought for in the partner enable the firm to explore product or market opportunities, leaping over otherwise formidable entry barriers, that would be difficult to exploit internally due to a lack of specific firm capabilities.

Successful firms develop deep and abiding expertise areas that enable them to compete with the best in their field. Branching into a wholly unrelated field does not match with the description of 'what we do around here' and is likely an unfruitful, if not excessively costly, proposition. Leaping alliances make this possible.

Similarly, leaping may represent cultural or geographic expansions necessary to access foreign markets. In many cases companies may have products that are appropriate for a particular country or market, but may have little expertise in the cultural practices of the residents. This is particularly true of less-developed countries, and may explain why culturally sensitive sectors such as retailing involve alliances. An illustration is the expansion of both K-Mart and Wal-Mart into Mexico; both use joint-venture partners instead of wholly owned subsidiaries. This is different, for example, from the subsidiary strategies pursued by both Wal-Mart and K-Mart in Canada where cultural differences are not as extreme.

The leaping strategy has some overlap with learning and leveraging but the extent of substantive differences merits a separate category. Leaping differs from learning in that the leaping firm is not likely to have the desire to internalize the expertise of its partner. The technological infrastructure is so different that this would be a far too onerous task. Leaping differs from leveraging in that the leaping segment of the firm typically does not represent the core technological thrust and integration that the leveraging relationship would encompass.

The negatives associated with leaping alliances are primarily those of cultural incompatibility. Any international strategic alliance arrangement presents challenges to the successful integration of management styles as well as bridging the cultural gap between nations. However, efforts to cooperate between companies that occupy *radically* different industry and technological capabilities can prove to be particularly difficult to manage due to organizational cultural differences. Organizational traditions in such areas as decision-making processes, risk preferences, and managerial styles can represent enormous invisible barriers to the successful implementation of desired alliance objectives. Such cultural distance can be extreme between industry groups, for example consumer nondurables versus high technology. However, when cultural differences from international firms are added, the potential for cultural distances increase geometrically. Parkhe (1991) makes an important distinction between differences in alliance partners that are technologically complimentary, and differences that are culturally based and emphasize variances in managerial outlook. The former represent the actual opportunity inherent to leaping alliances; the latter may represent the greatest threat to their successful implementation.

Locking Out

The sixth strategic objective of international strategic alliances to be considered is *locking out*. In this scenario two or more partners come together in order to thwart competition and benefit from the combined market power or structural relationship of the cooperating firms. The intention is not particularly to advance a new technology, innovation, or market, but rather to protect existing advantages from potential competition. Harrigan (1985) identifies strategic alliances as a primary means by which firms can coopt outsiders as potential competitors in an effort to protect established 'turf' that may otherwise be at risk. There is some overlap between the leveraging and locking-out objectives in that both may involve economies of scale. However, the following primary difference distinguishes them sufficiently. Leveraging enables the participating firms to participate in markets and activities that they were otherwise unable to, particularly in industries where global strategic advantages are present. Locking out merely preserves a competitive advantage that already exists.

Examples of such alliances may include large manufacturers consolidating supplier networks to make it more difficult for competing firms to gain access. Consolidating a customer network may also be a motive for firms to join forces rather than compete with one another. The recent alliance between two northern European hotel chains is illustrative. Scandic Hotels, operating in Sweden, Norway, Denmark, and Germany (among other countries) combined its hotel booking and marketing system with Arctia Hotels, which also operates in Scandinavia as well as Russia and Estonia. Management of the hotels remains separate, but the booking advantage makes their network the largest in Northern Europe and keeps the two chains from having to build new hotels and aggressively conquer each other's markets through price wars and other competitive measures.

The hotel example represents the locking-out strategy from a horizontal perspective. From a vertical perspective, restrictive contracts between manufacturers and retailers can also serve as a locking-out alliance strategy. Selective dealership arrangements are restrictions that allow only those retailers who are willing to service a brand in specified ways (i.e. service or sales method) to deal in a product line. Exclusive dealerships require that only one brand be sold. Requirements for stocking a full line of merchandise may also be stipulated by the manufacturer.

The primary negative element of locking-out alliances is their ephemeral nature. The antitrust issues related to strategic alliances are often complex and untested in many countries. As potential competitors fall to unfair market obstructions and as customers complain about the lack of competition, governments may quickly disallow an alliance and threaten a competitive advantage stronghold. Additionally, alliances used to neutralize competition may make the involved firms enjoy a false sense of competitive advantage, ultimately making them vulnerable to more innovative and nimble competitors.

Managerial Implications

Once an alliance objective has been selected, it is important to consider how it fits with the overall strategic objectives of the firm. Short- and long-term implications should be considered, along with the commitment of firm resources and the bearing such an objective will have on overall firm capabilities.

Once the appropriate alliance strategy has been identified, the next step is to analyze how the alliance partner is approaching the relationship. The mismatch of strategic objectives in approaching international strategic alliances can lead to miscommunication, misunderstanding, and ultimately dissolution of the partnership. For example, if one partner views an alliance as primarily learning, while the other views it as leaning, incompatible assumptions of permanence, sharing, and competition will likely lead to unfortunate outcomes. The leaning firm will tend to see the arrangement as a long-term, stable relationship, but the learning firm will view it as a short-term means to an end. Another possible scenario would be one partner assuming the alliance objective to be linking while the other as primarily locking out. In this case the linking firm will be seeking to coordinate operations to the extent that efficiencies can be realized. The locking-out firm will be potentially placing more demands on the partnership with respect to competitor relationships than the linking firm is comfortable with.

7.4 Creating a Strategic Center to Manage a Web of Partners

By Gianni Lorenzoni and Charles Baden-Fuller[1]

Strategic alliances and inter-firm networks have been gaining popularity with many firms for their lower overhead costs, increased responsiveness and flexibility, and greater efficiency of operations. Networks that are *strategically guided* are often fast-growing and on the leading edge. In 10 years, Sun Microsystems (founded in 1982) grew to $3.2 billion in sales and

[1] Source: This article was adapted with permission from 'Creating A Strategic Center to Manage a Web of Partners,' *California Management Review*, Vol. 37, No. 3, Spring 1995.

$284 million in profits. This remarkable growth has been achieved by Sun's strategic direction of a web of alliances.

Few would expect such rapid growth and technological success in an older and mature industry such as textiles. Yet Benetton, the famous global textile empire, is in many ways like Sun. Founded in 1964, it had by 1991 achieved more than $2 billion in sales and $235 million in profits. Benetton is widely admired in Europe and the Far East for its rapid growth and ability to change the industry's rules of the game through its strategy of 'mass fashion to young people.'

What creates and guides the successful, innovative, leading-edge inter-firm network? Most research into inter-firm networks has emphasized how they can reconcile the flexibility of market relationships with the long-term commitment of hierarchically centralized management. Although all networks reflect the conscious decisions of some managers, it is becoming increasingly apparent that those networks that are not guided strategically by a 'center' are unable to meet the demanding challenges of today's markets. In this article, we are concerned with those strategic centers that have had a very significant impact on their sectors, especially as regards innovation. They are not confined to just a few isolated sectors, but have been observed in a wide variety of circumstances, some of which are listed in Table 7.4.1.

In this reading, we examine three dimensions of the strategic center:

■   as a creator of value for its partners;

■   as leader, rule setter, and capability builder;

■   as simultaneously structuring and strategizing.

The Role of The Strategic Center

The strategic center (or central firm) plays a critical role as a creator of value. The main features of this role are:

■   *Strategic outsourcing.* Outsource and share with more partners than the normal broker and traditional firm. Require partners to be more than doers, expect them to be problemsolvers and initiators.

■   *Capability.* Develop the core skills and competencies of partners to make them more effective and competitive. Force members of the network to share their expertise with others in the network, and with the central firm.

■   *Technology.* Borrow ideas from others which are developed and exploited as a means of creating and mastering new technologies.

■   *Competition.* Explain to partners that the principle dimension of competition is between value chains and networks. The network is only as strong as its weakest link. Encourage rivalry between firms inside the network, in a positive manner.

TABLE 7.4.1
Some central firms and their activities

Name of Company and its Industry	Activities of Strategic Center	Activities of the Network
Apple (Computers)	Hardware Design Software Design Distribution	Principal subcontractors manufacture 3,000 software developers
Benetton (Apparel)	Designing Collections Selected Production Developing New Technology Systems	6,000 shops 400 subcontractors in production Principal joint ventures in Japan, Egypt, India, and others
Corning (Glass, Medical Products and Optical Fibers)	Technology Innovation Production	More than 30 joint ventures world-wide
Genentech (Biotechnology/DNA)	Technology Innovation	J.V.s with drug companies for production and distribution, licensing in from universities
McDonald's (Fast Food)	Marketing Prototyping Technology and Systems	9,000 outlets, joins ventures in many foreign countries
McKesson (Drug Distribution)	Systems Marketing Logistics Consulting Advice	Thousands of retail drug outlets, and ties with drug companies, and government institutions
Nike (Shoes and Sportswear)	Design Marketing	Principal subcontractors world-wide
Nintendo (Video Game)	Design Prototyping Marketing	30 principal hardware subcontractors 150 software developers
Sun (Computers and Computer Systems)	Innovation of Technology Software Assembly	Licensor/licensees for software and hardware
Toyota (Automobiles)	Design Assembly Marketing	Principal subcontractors for complex components Second tier for other components Network of agents for distribution

From Subcontracting to Strategic Outsourcing

All firms that act as brokers or operate networks play only a limited role in undertaking the production and delivery of the good or service to the markets in which the system is involved. What distinguishes central firms is both the extent to which they subcontract, and the way that they collect together partners who contribute to the whole system and whose roles are clearly defined in a positive and creative way.

Many organizations see their sub-contractors and partners as passive doers or actors in their quest for competitive advantage. They typically specify exactly what they want the partners to do, and leave little to the creative skills of others. They reserve a special creative role for only a few 'critical' partners. In strategic networks, it is the norm rather than an exception for partners to be innovators.

Typically each of these partnerships extends beyond a simple subcontracting relationship. Strategic centers expect their partners to do more than follow the rules, they expect them to be creative. For example, Apple worked with Canon and Adobe to design and create a laser jet printer which then gave Apple an important position in its industry. In all the cases we studied, the strategic center looked to the partners to be creative in solving problems and being proactive in the relationships. They demanded more – and obtained more – from their partners than did their less effective counterparts that used traditional subcontracting.

Developing the Competencies of the Partners

How should the central firm see its own competencies *vis-à-vis* its partners? Most writers ague that current competencies should guide future decisions. Many have warned of the dangers in allowing the other partners in a joint venture or alliance to exploit the skills of the host organization. For example, Reich and Mankin (1986) noted that joint ventures between Japanese and US firms often result in one side (typically the Japanese) gaining at the expense of the other. Bleeke and Ernst (1991) found similar disappointment in that in only 51 percent of the cases they studied did both firms gain from alliances. In a study of cross border alliances, Hamel (1991) found that the unwary partner typically found that its competencies were 'hollowed out' and that its collaborator became a more powerful competitor. Badaracco (1991) examined the experiences of GM and IBM, who have signed multiple agreements, and explored the difficulties they face.

Traditional brokers and large integrated firms do not 'hand out' core skills, but the central firms we studied have ignored this advice and won. While keeping a very few skills and assets to themselves, the central firms were remarkable in their desire to transfer skill and knowledge adding value to their partners. Typically, they set out to build up the partners' ability and competencies. At Benetton, site selection and sample selection were skills which Benetton would offer to the new retail partners, either directly or through the agents. Skill transfers were also evident in the machinery networks and at Apple.

Nike brings its partners to its research site at Beaverton to show them the latest developments in materials, product designs, technologies, and markets. Sometimes the partners share some of the costs, but the prime benefit is to shorten cycle times and create a more vibrant system. Toyota's subcontractors may receive training from Toyota and are helped in their development of expertise in solving problems pertaining to their particular component. Not only does this encourage them to deliver better quality parts to the Toyota factories, but it also allows the Toyota system to generate an advantage over other car manufacturers.

In contrast to these companies, the less successful organizations we studied did not have groups of specialists to transfer knowledge to partners – nor, it seems, did they appreciate its importance. They did not enlist all their suppliers and customers to fight a common enemy. Moreover, their experiences did not encourage exploration of this approach. They spoke of past difficulties in alliances. Skill transfers between parties did not always result in mutual benefit. One defense contractor explained that their experience of skill transfers nearly always meant that the partner was strengthened and became a stronger rival.

Borrowing–Developing–Lending New Ideas

While all firms bring in new ideas from outside, the central firms we studied have adopted an unusual and aggressive perspective in this sphere. They scan their horizons for all sorts of opportunities and utilize a formula we call *borrow–develop–lend*. 'Borrow' means that the strategic center deliberately buys or licenses some existing technological ideas from a third party; 'develop' means that it takes these outside ideas and adds value by developing them further in its own organization. This commercialization can then be exploited or 'lent' with great rapidity through its stellar system, creating new adjuncts to leverage to the greatest advantage. Borrowing ideas, which are subsequently developed and exploited, stretches the organization and forces it to grow its capabilities and competencies. It demands a new way of thinking.

In the Italian packaging machinery sector, lead producers follow this strategy. They borrow designs of a new machine from specialist designers or customers. These designs are then prototyped. From these prototypes, small and medium-sized partners or specialists often improve the design in a unique way, such as improving the flows and linkages, The focal firm then re-purchases and exploits the modified design, licensing to producers for the final development and marketing phase. Thus we see a 'to-and-fro' pattern of development between the central firm and its many partners.

Sun also used the borrow-develop-lend approach in their project to build a new workstation delivering 'more power with less cost.' They borrowed existing technology from other parties, recombined and developed them further inside Sun, and then licensed them to third parties for development and sale under the Sun brand.

The borrow–develop–lend principle helps the central firm reduce the cost of development, make progress more quickly, and, most importantly, undertake projects which would normally lie outside its scope. This approach contrasts with the procedures used by other large firms. Although these firms may buy ideas from other sources, large firms usually have a slower pace of development and rarely match the speed of exploitation achieved through networking and re-lending the idea to third parties. The strategic center seems to avoid the *not-invented-here* syndrome, where innovations and ideas are rejected because they are not internally created and developed.

From the view of independent inventors, the strategic center is an attractive organization with which to do business. The central firms have a track record of rapid commercialization (usually offering large incentives to those with ideas). They emphasize moving quickly from ideas to market by a simultaneous learning process with partners, thereby offering a competitive advantage over other developers. Finally, the willingness to involve others means rapid diffusion with fast payback, thus lessening the risks.

Perceptions of the Competitive Process

Firms in the same industry experience varying degrees of competitive rivalry. The joint venture, formal agreements, or the use of cross share-holdings are mechanisms used to create common ties, encourage a common view, and unite firms against others in the industry. Strategic centers also create this sense of cooperation across competing enterprises.

Competitive success requires the integration of multiple capabilities (e.g. innovation, productivity, quality, responsiveness to customers) across internal and external organizational boundaries. Such integration is a big challenge to most organizations. Strategic centers rise to this challenge and create a sense of common purpose across multiple levels in the value chain and across different sectors. They achieve a combination of specialized capability and large-scale integration at the same time, despite the often destructive rivalry between buyers and customers. Strategic purchasing partnerships are commonly used to moderate this rivalry, but few firms are able to combine both horizontal and vertical linkages.

	Single Units Within the Sector	**Multiple Units Within the Sector or Across Related Sectors**
Multiple Stages of the Value Chain	Vertical Integration or Value-Added Partnerships	Strategic Centers and Their Webs of Partners or Large Integrated Multi-Market Organizations
Single Stages of the Value Chain	Traditional Adversarial Firm	Chain Stores or Simple Networks

TABLE 7.4.2
Different kinds of competition across sectors and stages of the value chain

In building up their partner's capabilities and competencies, strategic centers convey an unusual perspective to their partners on the nature of the competitive process. This perspective permits the partners to take a holistic view of the network, seeing the collective as a unit that can achieve competitive advantage. In this respect, the whole network acts like a complex integrated firm spanning many markets.

Table 7.4.2 illustrates how the actions of the strategic center differ from other organizations. Chain stores are a good example of organizations that coordinate activities across many actors, yet at a single stage of the value chain. In contrast, the narrowly defined, vertically integrated firm coordinates across many stages but not across many markets or actors. Only the strategic center and the large multi-market, vertically integrated organization are able to coordinate across many markets and many stages of the value chain.

Beyond the Hollow Organization

Although the strategic center outsources more activities than most organizations, it is not hollow. Unlike the traditional broker that is merely a glorified arranger, the central firms we studied understand that they have to develop some critical core competencies. These competencies are, in general, quite different from those stressed by most managers in traditional firms. The agenda for the central firm consists of:

- *The idea.* Creating a vision in which partners play a critical role.

- *The investment.* A strong brand image and effective systems and support.

- *The climate.* Creating an atmosphere of trust and reciprocity.

- *The partners.* Developing mechanisms for attracting and selecting partners.

Sharing a Business Idea

Most of the central firms we studied are small, lean, and focused operations. They employ comparatively few people and are very selective in what they do. Yet, they have an unusual ability to conceptualize a business idea that can be shared not only internally, but with other partners. In the case of Benetton, this idea has a few key elements such as: mass fashion for young people, and the notion of a strategic network to orchestrate and fulfill this vision. In food-machinery, the key idea of the central firms is to solve the client's problems, rather than selling existing competencies, while new partners are developed in response to customer needs – a novel notion in this sector. These simple ideas are not easy to create or sustain.

These ideas have been able to capture the imagination of the employees and their partners. They also encapsulate strategy and so contain, in the language of Prahalad and Hamel (1990; reading 6.2), the features of a clear strategic intent. Common to all the business ideas we studied, there is a notion of partnership which includes the creation of a learning culture and the promotion of systems experiments so as to outpace rival competing organizations. The strategic centers view their role as one of leading and orchestrating their systems. Their distinctive characteristics lie in their ability to perceive the full business idea and understand the role of all the different parties in many different locations across the whole value chain. The managers in the strategic center have a dream and they orchestrate others to fulfill that dream.

This vision of the organization is not just an idea in the minds of a few managers, it is a feature that is shared throughout the organization. Many of the strategic centers we studied admit that their visions have emerged over time, they are not the work of a moment. Their vision is dynamic, for as their network grows and as the environment changes, the organizational vision also changes. This is not the case in the less successful alliances. They showed the typical characteristics of most organizations, multifaceted views of the world and a less-than-clear expression of their vision.

Clearly, vision is reinforced by success. The ability of central firms to deliver profits and growth for the partners helps cement a vision in their minds and makes their claims credible. It creates a cycle where success breeds clarity, which in turn helps breed more success.

Brand Power and Other Support

To maintain the balance of power in the network, all central firms retain certain activities. The control of the brand names and the development of the systems that integrate the network are two activities that give the organization a pivotal role and allow it to exercise power over the system.

Some of the firms we observed were involved in consumer markets where branding is important. The brand name, owned by the central firm, was promoted by the activities of the partners, who saw the brand as a shared resource. They were encouraged to ensure its success, and quite often these efforts helped the brand become famous in short period of time. While the brand and marketing are not so vital in producer goods markets, they are still important – and the strategic center neglects these at its peril. Its importance is highlighted by the experiences of one of the less successful organizations we studied. This aerospace firm had problems as a result of the inability of its members to relinquish many of the aspects of marketing to a single central firm.

To retain its power, the central firm must ensure that the information between partners flows freely and is not filtered. Communication is a costly activity, and developing effective communication systems is always the responsibility of the strategic center. These systems are not only electronically based, but include all other methods of communication. Often there is a style for meeting among the partners, which is set and monitored by the central firm. The quality of information is a key requirement if the central firm is to mandate effectively the stream of activities scattered among different firms.

Trust and Reciprocity

Leveraging the skills of partners is easy to conceive but hard to implement. The difficulties occur because it takes many partners operating effectively to make the system work, but the negative behavior of only a few can bring the whole system to a halt. The strategic vision requires all its members to contribute all the time without fail. This is a considerable demand. The typical organizational response to such a need is to circumscribe the contracts with outsiders in a tight legalistic manner. But this is not always wise; contract making and policing can be difficult and expensive. Formal contracts are relatively inflexible and are suitable only where the behavior is easy to describe and is relatively inflexible. But the relationships are creative and flexible and so very difficult to capture and enforce contractually.

The approach of the central firms we studied is to develop a sense of trust and reciprocity in the system. This trust and reciprocity is a dynamic concept and it can be very tight. The tightness is apparent in each party agreeing to perform its known obligations. This aspect has similarities to contracts in the sense that obligations are precisely understood. But Anglo-Saxon contracts are typically limited in the sense that partners are not expected to go beyond the contract. In contrast, in a network perspective, the behavior is prescribed for the unknown, each promising to work in a particular manner to resolve future challenges and difficulties as they arise. This means that each partner will promise to deliver what is expected, and that future challenges will also be addressed positively. If there are uncertainties and difficulties in the relationships, these will be resolved after the work is done. If one party goes beyond (in the positive sense) the traditional contract, others will remember and reciprocate at a later date.

Trust and reciprocity are complements, not substitutes, to other obligations. If partners do not subscribe to the trust system, they can hold the whole system hostage whenever they are asked to do something out of the ordinary, or even in the normal course of events. Such behavior will cause damage to all, and the system will break up. Only with trust can the system work in unison.

The Benetton franchising system is perhaps an extreme version of this trust system. In the continent of Europe, Benetton does not use legal contracts, rather it relies on the unwritten agreement. This, it claims, focuses everyone's attention on making the expectations clear. It also saves a great deal of time and expense. Many other strategic centers also rely on trust, but utilize contracts and formal controls as a complement. Central firms develop rules for settling disputes (for there will be disputes even in a trust system). The central firm also ensures that rewards are distributed in a manner which encourages partners to reinforce the positive circle. Benetton has encountered limits to its approach in the US, where the cultural emphasis on law and contracts has come into conflict with Benetton's strategy.

In sharp contrast are the other less successful systems we studied. There, trust was used on a very limited scale, since most organizations had difficulty in getting partners to deliver even that which was promised.

Broken promises and failed expectations were common in the defense systems. Very low anticipated expectations of partner reciprocity were a common feature of the Scottish network and appliance sectors. Most organizations believed that anything crucial had to be undertaken in-house.

Trust is delicate, and it needs fostering and underpinning. One of the ways in which positive behavior is encouraged is to ensure that the profit-sharing relationships gives substantial rewards to the partners. None of the central firms we studied seeks to be the most profitable firm in the system; they are happy for others to take the bulk of the profit. In Benetton, a retailer may find his or her capital investment paid back in three years. In Corning, some partners have seen exceptional returns. This seemingly altruistic behavior, however, does not mean that the rewards to the central firm are small.

Partner Selection

The central firms we studied recognize that creating success and a long-term perspective must begin with the partner selection process. In building a network, partners must be selected with great care. Initially, the central firms followed a pattern of trial and error, but following successful identification of the key points the selection process, they became more deliberate. The many new styles of operation and new ways of doing things are not easy to grasp, and they are quite difficult to codify – especially at the early stages of the selection process. As time passes, a partner profile emerges together with a selection procedure aimed at creating the correct conditions for the relationships. These relationships require coordination among all the partners, a common long-term perspective, an acceptance of mutual adaptation, and incremental innovation.

When we looked at the details of the selection procedure, there was a difference between those central firms that had a few large partners and those that had many small-scale partners. In the case of the network composed of a few, large firm alliances, the selection criterion is typically based on careful strategic considerations. There is the question of matching capabilities and resources, as well as considerations of competition. However, most important are the organizational features based on a compatibility of management systems, decision processes, and perspectives – in short, a cultural fit.

The selection process must also be tempered by availability. Typically, there are few potential partners to fit the ideal picture. Perhaps it is for this reason that some Japanese and European firms start the process early on by deliberately spinning off some of their internal units to create potential partners. Typically these units will contain some of their best talents. However, these units will have a cultural affinity and a mutual understanding, which makes the partnership easier.

In the case of the large network composed of many small partners, the center acts as a developer of the community. Its managers must assume a different role. Apple called some of its managers 'evangelists' because they managed the relationships with 3,000 third-party developers. So that they could keep constant contact with them, they used images of the 'Figure-head' and the 'Guiding Light.'

Simultaneous Structuring and Strategizing

Of all the battles firms face, the most difficult is not the battle for position, nor is it even the battle between strong firms and weak firms following the same strategic approaches. Rather, it is the battle between firms adopting different strategies and different approaches to the market. In these battles, the winners are usually those who use fewer and different resources in novel combinations. The central firms we studied fit this category, for they have typically dominated their sectors by stretching and leveraging modest resources to great effect. In trying to understand these battles of stretch and leverage, others have stressed the technical achievements of central firms such as lean production, technical innovation, or flexible manufacturing and service delivery. To be sure, these advances are important and provide partial explanations for the success of Sun, Nintendo, Benetton, Apple, and others. Equally important, if not more important, are new ideas on the nature of strategizing and structuring. Strategizing is a shared process between the strategic center and its partners; structuring of the relationships between the partners goes hand in hand and is seen as a key part of the strategy.

Strategy conception and implementation of ideas is shared between central firms and their webs of partners. Here they differ from most conventional organizations, which neither share their conceptions of strategy with other organizations nor insist that their partners share their ideas with them in a constructive dialogue. While all firms form partnerships with some of their suppliers and customers, these linkages rarely involve sharing ideas systematically. Subcontracting relationships are usually deeper and more complex, and many firms share their notions of strategy with their subcontractors, but the sharing is nearly always limited. Alliances demand even greater levels of commitment and interchange, and it is common for firms involved in alliances to exchange ideas about strategy and to look for strategic fit and even reshaping of strategic directions. Networks can be thought of as a higher stage of alliances, for in the strategic center there is a conscious desire to influence and shape the strategies of the partners, and to obtain from partners ideas and influences in return.

This conscious desire to share strategy is reflected in the way in which central firms conceive of the boundaries of their operations. Most organizations view their joint ventures and subcontractors as beyond the boundaries of their firm, and even those involved in alliances do not think of partners as an integral part of the organization. Even firms that are part of a franchise system (and thus have a more holistic perspective) do not view their relationships as a pattern of multilateral contracts. Going beyond the franchise view, central firms and their participants communicate multi-laterally across the whole of the value chain. In the words of Johanson and Mattsson (1992), they have a 'network theory,' a perception of governing a whole system.

Strategizing and structuring in the central firms we studied reverses Chandler's famous dictum about structure following strategy. When partner's competencies are so crucial to the developments of the business idea of the strategic center, the winners are building strategy and structure simultaneously whereas the losers are signing agreements without changing their organizational forms to match them. When each partner's resources and competencies are so essential to the success of the enterprise, new forms must be designed. To achieve this, structuring must come earlier, alongside strategizing, and both require an interaction among partners to create a platform of flexibility and capability This behavior challenges much of what is received managerial practice and avoids some of the traps that webs of alliances face.

Like the large integrated cohesive organization, networked firms are able to believe as a single competitive entity which can draw on considerable resources. However, the network form avoids many of the problems of large integrated firms, who typically find themselves paralyzed in the struggle between freedom and control. By focusing attention on the matters where commonality is important (e.g. product design) and by allowing each unit to have freedom elsewhere, cooperation is fostered, time and energy spent in monitoring is reduced, and resources are optimized. In this way, the networked organization succeeds in bridging the gap between centralization and decentralization. But cooperation can dull the edge of progress, and the organizations in our study, have avoided this trap by fostering a highly competitive spirit.

Marketing and Information Sharing

The way in which information is collected and shared in the system reveals how structure and strategy go hand in hand. The gathering of information is a central activity in any organization. A strategic feature of a network of alliances is that the firms in the system are closely linked for the sharing of information. Members of the network exchange not only hard data about best practice, but also ideas, feelings, and thoughts about customers, other suppliers, and general market trends.

The central firm structures the information system so that knowledge is funneled to the areas that need it the most. Members specializing in a particular function have access to others in the system performing similar tasks, and share their knowledge. This creates a level playing field within the network system. It also provides the opportunity for the members to focus and encourage the development of competitive advantage over rivals.

One of the basic premises in our network view is that new information leading to new ways of doing things emerges in a process of interaction with people and real-life situations. It follows that the 'information ability' of the firm depends critically on a scheme of interactions. The difficulty is that the generation of new information cannot be planned, but has to emerge. Thus, the task of the manager is one of designing a structure which provides an environment favorable for interactions to form, and for new information to be generated. Such a structure is a network.

Our study found, as have others, that the availability of large amounts of high quality information on many aspects of the business facilitated more rapid responses to market opportunities. Information condensed through the network is 'thicker' than that condensed through the brokerage market, but is 'freer' than in the hierarchy.

The need for a sophisticated system was clear when we contrasted the central firms we studied with other firms. In these other firms, we often found that critical information was guarded, not shared. As is so common among organizations, individual players are either afraid of being exploited or they have a desire to exploit the power they have through knowledge. Even in traditional franchise systems, information is typically passed to the center for filtering before being shared. In the large integrated firm, centralization also causes unnecessary filtering. With centralization, the process of collecting and distributing information can be cumbersome and slow. Moreover, power to manipulate the information can be accidentally or intentionally misused by a small central group.

Some of the 'control group' of firms we studied did share their information, with adverse consequences. For example, defense contractors, unable to create an effective strategic network, found the partners sometimes used the shared information to their own advantage, and then did not reciprocate. The knowledge was exploited by partners to create superior bargaining positions. Opportunities to foster collective interest were missed, and in extreme cases, partners used the information to bolster a rival alliance to the detriment of the original information provider.

Learning Races

Whereas identifying opportunities for growth is facilitated by information sharing, responding to the opportunity is more difficult. Here we see some of the clearest evidence that structure and strategy go hand in hand. First and foremost, the central firms we studied reject the idea of doing everything themselves. Instead, they seek help from others to respond to the opportunities they face. When the knowledge and capabilities exist within the network, the role of the center is to orchestrate the response so that the whole system capitalizes on the opportunity.

It frequently happens that opportunities require an innovative response, and it is common for strategic centers to set up 'learning races.' Here, partners are given a common goal (say a new product or process development) with a prize for the first to achieve the target. The prize may be monetary, but more commonly it is the opportunity to lead off the exploitation of the new development. There is a catch, the development must be shared with others in the network. Learning races create a sense of competition and rivalry, but within an overall common purpose.

Nintendo uses carefully nurtured learning races with its partners to create high quality rapid innovation. Partners are typically restricted in the number of contributions they can make. In the case of software design, the limit may be three ideas a year. These restrictions force a striving for excellence, and the consequence is a formidable pace of progress.

Learning races can be destructive rather than constructive if the partners do not have the skills and resources. The strategic centers we studied get around these difficulties by sharing knowledge and in effect allowing the whole network to 'borrow' skills and competencies from each other.

It is important to understand the role of new members in the process of creating innovations. Many central firms follow the twin strategies of internal and external development. Internal development involves offering existing partners a possibility of sharing in the growth markets. External development involves the finding of new partners to fill the gaps and accelerate the possibilities. New partners typically fit the pattern set by existing partners. These newly found 'look alike' firms allow the strategic center to truncate development of the necessary capabilities, leveraging off earlier experiences developed by the existing partners. By making growth a race between old and new partners, speed is assured and scale effects exploited. Our strategic centers fostered positive rivalry rather than hostility by ensuring that both old and new partners share in the final gains. When pursuing rapid growth, the twin tracks of internal and external development can lessen tensions. Because they are independent, existing members can respond to the new demands as they wish. But, if they do not respond positively, the central firm can sign up new partners to fill the gaps. The stresses and strains of growth can thus be reduced for each of the members of the network.

Conclusions

The strategically minded central firms in our study view the boundaries of the organization differently because their conception and implementation of strategy are shared with a web of partners. This attitude contrasts sharply with most organizations, which view their joint ventures and subcontractors as existing beyond the boundaries of their firm. Even those involved in alliances typically do not think of partners as an integral part of their organization; they rarely share their conceptions of strategy and even fewer insist that their partners share their strategy with them in a constructive dialogue. In contrast, strategic centers communicate strategic ideas and intent multilaterally across the whole of the value chain. They have a network view of governing a whole system.

Strategic centers reach out to resolve classic organizational paradoxes. Many subcontracting and alliance relationships seemed to be mired in the inability to reconcile the advantages of the market with those of the hierarchy. Strategic centers are able to create a system that has the flexibility and freedom of the market coupled with long-term holistic relationships, ensuring the requisite strategic capabilities across the whole system. Another paradox exists between creativity and discipline. Most organizations oscillate between having ample creativity and little discipline, or too much discipline and not enough creativity. Through their unusual attitude to structuring and strategizing, strategic centers attain leading-edge technological and market developments while retaining rapid decision-making processes.

All organizations have much to learn from studying strategic centers and their unusual conception of the managerial task. Strategic centers have taken modest resources and won leadership positions in a wide variety of sectors. They have brought a new way of thinking about business and organizing. Much of what they do is at the cutting edge, and they are shining examples of how firms can change the rules of the game by creative and imaginative thinking.

7.5 The Bamboo Network

By Murray Weidenbaum and Samuel Hughes[1]

Since the 1500s, southern China has served as a springboard for emigrants to Vietnam, Thailand, Indonesia, and elsewhere in Southeast Asia. These overseas Chinese have developed a bamboo network that transcends national boundaries. This informal array of complementary business relationships extends throughout the region, where entrepreneurs, business executives, traders, and financiers of Chinese background are major players in local economies. The heart of the Chinese network is Hong Kong, Taiwan, and the China coast. Singapore, with a predominantly Chinese population, is also an important factor in cross-border Chinese business relationships.

Companies owned by overseas Chinese dominate the private business sectors of every Southeast Asian country. Typically, the founders of these overseas Chinese businesses possessed little wealth and built their firms from scratch, contributing substantially to the development of the local economy in the process.

Today, many of these small family firms have grown into enormous conglomerates, each of which maintains interests in dozens of highly diversified companies. In 1994, the total assets of the 500 largest public companies in Asia controlled by overseas Chinese exceeded $500 billion (see Table 7.5.1 below). These numbers exclude the many privately owned enterprises controlled by the same families.

As S. Gordon Redding (1990) notes in his landmark study, *The Spirit of Chinese Capitalism*, it is difficult to recognize the true significance of the overseas Chinese in Southeast Asia because their impact is spread across so many boundaries. Thus, they cannot as a total be represented in any national statistics. 'Even adding together Taiwan, Hong Kong, and

---

[1] Source: This article was adapted with permission from chapter 2 of *The Bamboo Network: How Expatriate Chinese Entrepreneurs Are Creating a New Economic Superpower in Asia*, The Free Press, 1996, pp. 23–59.

Location	Number of Companies	Market Capitalization (in billions)	Total Assets (in billions)
Hong Kong	123	$155	$173
Taiwan	159	111	89
Malaysia	83	55	49
Singapore	52	42	92
Thailand	39	35	95
Indonesia	36	20	33
Philippines	8	6	8
Total	500	424	539

TABLE 7.5.1
The total assets of the 500 largest public companies in Asia controlled by overseas Chinese, 1994.

Singapore is grossly inadequate, as it leaves out much going on in Malaysia, Indonesia, Thailand, and the Philippines, to say nothing of China or of Vancouver, Toronto, New York, San Francisco, London, Sydney, etc.' The World Bank estimates that the combined economic output of the overseas Chinese was nearly $400 billion in 1991, an impressive sum for 40 million people. Today, considering the explosive economic growth of Southeast Asia, the figure is probably closer to $600 billion.

In Indonesia, overseas Chinese make up only three to four percent of the population, yet they own about 70 percent of private domestic capital and run more than 160 of the 200 largest businesses. Liem Sioe Liong's Salim Group alone is estimated to account for five percent of the country's gross domestic product. In 1995, every reported Indonesian billionaire was ethnic Chinese.

In Thailand, overseas Chinese account for about 10 percent of the population and control the four largest private banks. One of these, the Bangkok Bank, is the largest and most profitable in the region, and a key lender to the bamboo network. In Malaysia, ethnic Chinese control roughly half of that nation's corporate assets. In the Philippines, they make up less than two percent of the population, but control over one-third of the 1,000 largest corporations.

The economic dominance of the bamboo network within these countries is a source of great tension. The overseas Chinese are often seen as profiteers, stealing the wealth of a country from its indigenous people. This misguided view often results in discrimination, both formal and informal, as well as outright violence. From the late 1930s to the mid-1950s, the Thai government took over large numbers of private Chinese firms. During the 1960s and 1970s, Indonesia and the Philippines formally blocked Chinese businesses from operating in certain sectors of the economy, a type of affirmative action for the majority. In Indonesia, tens of thousands of ethnic Chinese were killed in 1965 during an attempted communist coup. In Malaysia, ethnic tension in May 1969 fueled riots that resulted in massive property damage and nearly 200 deaths.

Events such as these provide further incentive for overseas Chinese to deal primarily with other members of the bamboo network, and foster an 'us against them' mentality that is not completely unjustified. Parallels with Jewish business leaders, historical targets of discrimination, are hard to avoid. Indeed, sensationalistic Japanese newspapers have reported off-the-wall conspiracy theories that blame overseas Chinese and Jewish business-people for engineering declines in Tokyo's stock market during the early 1990s. These stories are indicative of the widespread hostility faced by overseas Chinese throughout Asia.

Partly in response to such discrimination, the overseas Chinese have attempted to blend in with their local cultures. Many change their names to avoid persecution. Corazon Aquino's maiden name – Cojuangco – appears to be Spanish but in reality is derived from her immigrant grandfather's name – Ko Hwan Ko. In Thailand, ethnic Chinese were required to take Thai names from a government list.

As further protection against discrimination and violence, the overseas Chinese have diversified their wealth outside of their home countries. In the process, they have become the largest cross-border investors in Thailand, Malaysia, Indonesia, Hong Kong, the Philippines, and Vietnam. In recent years, much of this investment capital has been flowing into the Chinese mainland, especially the southern coastal region. Since Deng Xiaoping launched his economic open door policy in 1978, overseas Chinese have invested more than $50 billion in their motherland, representing about 80 percent of all foreign investment.

To date, the members of what we call the bamboo network have formed more than 100,000 joint ventures in China. In the process, they have generated export industries, brought in management skills and technology, and provided international connections to the mainland. William Overholt, a senior official in the Hong Kong office of Bankers Trust, describes the ongoing phenomenon of overseas Chinese executives training mainland Chinese in capitalist methods as 'the biggest business school for managers ever created in the world.'

The Rise of Chinese Businesses

One of the most striking characteristics of the typical overseas Chinese business is its international diversification. A good example of such geographic diversification is furnished by Hong Kong entrepreneur Lee Shau Kee, who owns a controlling interest in the Henderson Land Development Company (with an estimated market value in 1995 of $9.1 billion). That wealthy firm invests in Beijing, Shanghai, Guangdong, and Hong Kong. It also has interests in a Singapore convention center, as well as in residential developments in the United States and Canada. In 1995, Lee's personal net worth was estimated at $6.5 billion.

Many of these cross-border enterprises have a fundamentally different organizational structure than their Western counterparts. In large measure, the bamboo network consists of crossholdings of privately owned family-run, trade-oriented firms, rather than the huge publicly owned manufacturing corporations that are typical in the United States, Japan, and Western Europe. Of the world's 500 largest corporations in 1994, only six were located in Greater China: one in Hong Kong, two in Taiwan, and three on the mainland. In comparison, 149 Japanese enterprises made the list, as did 151 US companies.

The tendency of Chinese merchants to establish themselves at locations away from their home country is a long-standing practice, going back at least several centuries. As Americans traditionally migrated to the West, the Chinese moved south into Malaysia, Thailand, and Indonesia. However, despite this migratory tradition, these individuals remain Chinese in some deep and significant sense. According to Redding, 'the majority of them have not psychologically left China, or at least . . . some ideal and perhaps romanticized notion of Chinese civilization.'

Ever since the fifth century BC, every generation of students in China has learned the sayings of Confucius (K'ung fu-tzu) by rote. The Confucian tradition is remarkably persistent. Most Chinese who have emigrated to other nations have carried these principles with them and preserved them as they adapt to the values of their new countries. Traditional Chinese thought continues to be marked by acceptance of the course of events and pragmatism with regard to order. The common core of Confucian teaching includes such values as loyalty to a hierarchical structure of authority, a code of defined conduct between children and adults, and trust among friends.

Other characteristics of the Confucian tradition are beneficial to a market economy. A sense of collective responsibility, pride in the work ethic, and a disdain for conspicuous consumption make for high saving rates, an especially valuable trait in fostering rapid industrialization. As we will see, the resultant state of mind is expressed in business dealings, networks, and family management of companies.

More than half of today's overseas Chinese population can be traced to only two southeastern coastal provinces: Guangdong (located next to Hong Kong) and Fujian (across the strait from Taiwan). Another large portion fled from Shanghai to Hong Kong in the late 1940s to avoid being swept up in the Communist Revolution. Many of these refugees were owners of textile factories who helped provide the British colony with the technical know-how that fueled its first industrial boom.

Wary of government, the expatriate Chinese found that kinship, dialect, or a common origin (in a clan, a village, or even a county) provided a basis for mutual trust in business transactions, even ones conducted at great distances. Hakka tended to deal with Hakka, Chiu Chownese with Chiu Chownese. These relationships provided both certainty and informality, facilitating transactions that at times may have skirted the letter of the law.

Traditionally, overseas Chinese businesses have tried to develop close ties with the leaders of the government of their host country. Unlike the expatriate managers of Japanese and Western firms, Chinese family members frequently become citizens of the countries in which they do business. This gives them a critical advantage in assimilating, understanding, and adopting the local culture, as well as the nuances of local politics and economics. It also helps them to circumvent discriminatory legislation or to seek the protection needed by a productive but unpopular minority. In Malaysia, the phenomenon known as the 'Ali Baba' business arose in response to the official discrimination against foreign businesses. 'Ali' refers to the native partner whose main contribution is to help the firm qualify for the special government subsidy available only to native Malays. 'Baba' is the Chinese entrepreneur with the capital and skill to really run the enterprise.

The overseas Chinese network is often 'maddeningly impenetrable' to outsiders, according to *Institutional Investor* magazine. Ross H. Munro of the Foreign Policy Research Institute, who worked in Beijing and Hong Kong for many years, concludes that Chinese businesses in Southeast Asia are extremely secretive about their business activities at home and abroad. He notes especially that, in China, empathetic local officials cater to their secretiveness.

Capital moves throughout the network in circuitous ways, providing safety against unforeseen political and economic events. Bankers speak of transactions that involve six or seven countries, with the funds flowing back to their original source at the end of it all. Even when Taiwan had strict exchange controls, it was possible for an individual in the network to deposit a large sum with a gold shop in Taipei and for a relative to withdraw the equivalent on the next day from an affiliated gold dealer in Hong Kong. Such 'underground' transactions still take place.

The Family Business in Operation

Sociologist Peter L. Berger, who has studied in depth the relation between Chinese culture and economics, concludes that the 'absolutely central institution' for understanding Chinese business is the overseas Chinese family. Berger (1994) notes that Chinese firms are almost always family firms because, within traditional Chinese culture, 'you can only trust close relatives.' After interviewing the people in many Chinese businesses, Berger concluded that managers who were not family members were the most unhappy people he encountered. The reasons were all interrelated: nobody trusted them, they knew they were not going to get anywhere, and their constant thought was to leave the business as soon as possible and start their own.

Because so much of the typical overseas Chinese business is privately held, very little information is released about the firm's operations – in contrast to the vast amounts of public information available regarding the standard US corporation. Nevertheless, some of the holdings of the larger overseas Chinese firms are publicly held and listed on stock exchanges, providing some idea of their size and structure.

Charoen Pokphand Group of Thailand

The Charoen Pokphand (CP) Group, a Thai agribusiness conglomerate, is a typical example of the overseas Chinese family business. The CP Group had its beginnings in a small seed company named Chia Tai, founded in 1921 by two Chinese brothers – Chia Ek Chor and Chia Seow Nooy. Although originally headquartered in Shantou, a seaport in China's southeastern Guangdong province, Chia Tai developed a network of seed outlets with locations in Bangkok, Hong Kong, Taipei, Kuala Lumpur, and Singapore. After the 1949 Communist Revolution, Chia Ek Chor moved his company headquarters to Bangkok and, as is the custom in Thailand, took a Thai name – Chearavanont (which means 'long-established wealth' in Thai).

Today, although its primary specialty continues to be agribusiness, CP has expanded into nine other divisions, including such disparate enterprises as petrochemicals and property development. One of CP's largest ventures outside of its agribusiness core is its stake in TelecomAsia, a joint venture with the US telecommunications giant NYNEX. In 1990, TelecomAsia was granted a 25–year license to build and operate two million telephone lines in Bangkok. More recently, it has acquired interests in satellite launch, cable television, and mobile telephone services.

In all, CP controls more than 200 affiliated companies, of which only 14 are listed on stock exchanges. The fact that so much of the group is privately held by the family (all of the founders' sons sit on the board of directors) makes it difficult to ascertain its true wealth or structure.

Officially, CP reports that its 1993 revenues exceeded $5 billion (only half of which came from operations in Thailand). Chia Ek Chor's son, Dhanin Chearavanont, controls the family empire. Contrary to custom, Dhanin took over at the age of only 25 despite being the youngest of Chia's four sons. Dhanin's older brother, Sumet Jiaravanon, is vice chairman and operates out of Hong Kong. In 1995, the family wealth was estimated at $5.5 billion.

It is not surprising that most Westerners are unfamiliar with conglomerates such as CP, because these business groups have specialized almost exclusively in Southeast Asian operations, particularly the rapidly growing Chinese market. CP is reportedly the single largest investor in the mainland, where each one of its divisions has established a joint venture. Its agribusiness division operates in 26 of China's 30 provinces. CP currently commands five percent of China's enormous (and growing) feed meal market, and derives over one-fifth of its total revenue from the mainland. According to Prasert Poongkumain, group president in charge of agro-industry, 'We have an advantage because we are of Chinese origin. We speak the language and look the same.'

There seems to be more to it than common culture, however. The equity of most of CP's dozens of joint ventures in China is divided rather evenly with partners on the mainland. These diverse business partners range from the provincial grain bureau to provincial and municipal govern-ments to NORINCO – a state-owned industrial conglomerate controlled by the army. The exact contribution of these PRC partners is difficult to assess.

We must wonder whether the local party receives its ownership share by virtue of the influence it brings to bear at crucial points in the business relationship – rather than in exchange for any contribution of funds or physical assets. In return for their stake in the partnership, local officials are often hired as employees of the joint venture. These types of arrangements replace the commissions that are often paid under such circumstances, and thus may obviate the need for outright bribery.

Salim Group of Indonesia

The Salim Group, founded by Liem Sioe Liong (also known by his Indonesian name, Sudono Salim), exemplifies the transnational nature of the bamboo network. Witness the group's major holdings in Hong Kong and Singapore, in addition to its home base in Indonesia. The Salim Group controls and owns more than 60 enterprises, including the majority of Indonesia's blue chip companies: Indocement, Indosteel, Indomilk, Unggul Indah Chemical, and Bogasari Flour. In 1995, Indocement alone reported a market value of $4.4 billion.

A penniless Liem left Fuqing, China, in 1938 for Kudus, a county in Java. The very next year, he and a friend started a company dealing in local products. During the 1947–1949 Indonesian war of independence, Liem supplied the rebels with clothing, food, and arms, forging links with the native forces that would rise to power after the Dutch left. In free Indonesia, he founded companies trading in everything from nails to bicycle parts. In 1957, he acquired Bank Central Asia, now the country's largest private-sector bank. Subsequently, he befriended army general Suharto, whose relatives joined him in many ventures. After Suharto took power in 1965, Liem acquired state licenses to control much of the logging, clove, flour milling, and cement industries.

Salim's flagship enterprise in Hong Kong is the First Pacific Group, which, in turn, has two listed companies on the local stock exchange – First Pacific Company Ltd. and FPB Bank Holding Company. With a market capitalization of $1.2 billion, First Pacific operates in 25 countries in Asia, North America, and Europe and maintains business interests in marketing and distribution, property, and financial services. Salim's interests in Hong Kong include cellular telephone, paging, and telepoint services.

In Singapore, the Salim Group's chief investment vehicle is the United Industrial Corporation, whose activities range from property development to trade to manufacturing. Its Singapore Land subsidiary is one of the largest property firms in the country, holding a sizable portfolio in the central business district. The group also controls property interests and business development activities in China, Britain, Canada, Thailand, and Turkey. In 1995, Salim founder Liem Sioe Liong and family had a reported net worth of $4.6 billion, making him one of the richest members of the bamboo network.

The scope of Liem's business activities continues to expand. In 1994, he joined forces with Malaysia's Robert Kuok to form a new holding company in the Sumatran sugar business. Kuok is one of the largest sugar

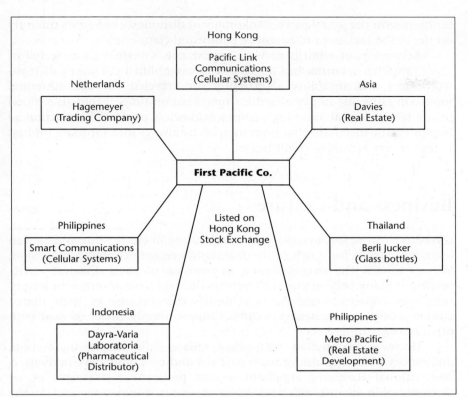

FIGURE 7.5.1
Major holdings of First
Pacific Company

producers in Malaysia and the Indonesian undertaking is estimated, in the aggregate, to cover an area twice the size of Singapore.

Most new overseas investments by the Liem family are not undertaken directly by the Salim Group in Jakarta. Rather, foreign-based associates are used to offset accusations of capital flight. For example, a three-times-removed Salim unit went into a joint venture with CWT, a listed Singapore government-linked company, to manage two ports in Fuqing. The Salim Group operated through a company owned by the Netherlands-listed Hagemeyer Group which, in turn, is owned by its Hong Kong-listed company, First Pacific Company (see Figure 7.5.1 for a display of the major holdings of First Pacific). In 1994, First Pacific reported profits of over $120 million on sales of approximately $3.5 billion.

Smaller enterprises rely on more formal overseas Chinese mutual aid associations. These organizations are typically based on family, clan, province, or dialect (Cantonese, Hakka, Hokkien, or Chiu Chow). The associations act like banks through which members can borrow money, trade information, recruit workers, and receive business introductions. They help enforce the 'handshake' deals on which much of Chinese business is based. If a business owner violates an agreement, he is blacklisted. This is far worse than being sued, because the entire Chinese network will refrain from doing business with the guilty party. Bankruptcy or dishonesty redounds not only on the individual, but on the entire family and clan.

Keeping your word is of vital importance. Overseas Chinese tell of Qiao Tanming, a tanner in Calcutta, who exemplified the ideals of trustworthiness and reliability. Apparently, he traveled through torrential monsoon rains just to pay a rawhide merchant on time. If there is a moral to the tale, it is that Tanming's conscientiousness paid off. This action so impressed the merchant that from then on he always sold Tanming his best hides on very favorable credit terms.

Business and Culture

Overseas Chinese businesses – particularly those in Hong Kong and Taiwan – are responsible for much of the mainland's recent economic expansion. What explains the overwhelming dominance of these Chinese entrepreneurs? Many believe that the overseas Chinese have an inherent advantage over Western investors. This implies that because of their shared culture, ethics, and language, ethnic Chinese simply prefer to deal with other ethnic Chinese.

However, economists traditionally place little weight on cultural differences when explaining trade patterns and economic development. A conventional economic argument is that preferential treatment of, or discrimination against, a certain group of people is expensive and, in the long run, unsustainable. The logic is this: such treatment creates opportunities for individuals who do not discriminate to acquire resources or sell their products on more favorable terms than those who do.

Although they may be theoretically appealing, such explanations are not very helpful in explaining the sustained success over time of ethnically homogenous trading groups, such as the Jews in medieval Europe, the Lebanese in West Africa, the Indians in East and Central Africa, and the Chinese in Southeast Asia. These important examples cannot be dismissed as either insignificant or the product of a primitive, irrational society.

But if we acknowledge that there *are* costs associated with the preferential treatment of certain trading parties, the long-term existence of these trading groups implies that there must be benefits that outweigh these costs. Specifically, members of the extensive intra-Chinese trading network are able to economize on the high 'transaction costs' associated with doing business in China and elsewhere in Southeast Asia.

Throughout Southeast Asia, where many markets are underdeveloped and law is often unpredictable, informal networks have become the preferred vehicle for many complex transactions. The financing for a $100 million property deal can be arranged in a matter of days within the bamboo network. Under such circumstances, personal trust replaces formal – as well as more expensive and time-consuming – 'due diligence' reviews. In the process, the cost of doing business is lowered substantially. Without these informal arrangements, many business transactions would be impossible or prohibitively expensive. Seen in this light, the extensive trade among overseas Chinese is a direct response to the high transactions costs inherent in many economies in Southeast Asia – particularly China – that lack sophisticated political and economic institutions.

These transnational trading networks are very much in accord with Chinese tradition. They allow for the flexible and efficient transmission of information, finance, goods, and capital in what are often informal agreements and transactions. Confidence and trust replace contracts as the major guarantees that commitments will be met satisfactorily. In a region where capital markets are rudimentary, financial disclosure is limited, and contract law very weak, interpersonal networks are critical to moving economic resources across political boundaries.

The Power of Family and Personal Relationships

A traditional – and perhaps the oldest – method to economize on contract enforcement costs is to maintain strong kinship ties that promote repeated interaction among the same people. Although family-controlled business empires are encountered in the United States and Europe, the scale and scope of modern overseas Chinese family businesses are unprecedented. Kinship ties are extremely important and family control over firms is the rule. Most Chinese family firms are extremely reluctant to appoint outsiders to key positions.

These examples are not isolated instances. Indeed, the family enterprise tends to be the basic economic unit in Southeast Asia. In an in-depth survey of more than 150 Chinese entrepreneurs conducted by Professor John Kao of the Harvard Business School (1993), 90 percent of the Chinese entrepreneurs he surveyed had experienced war, 40 percent had weathered a political disaster, and 32 percent had lost a home. As we would expect, such experiences have strongly influenced the investment decisions of the bamboo network.

Indeed, Kao's survey identified many common beliefs among ethnic Chinese businesspeople. One is that the only people you can trust are family members. An incompetent relative in the family business is considered to be more reliable than a competent stranger. Also, obedience to patriarchal authority is deemed essential to maintaining the enterprise.

A high level of savings is considered desirable, regardless of immediate need. In turn, investment must be based on kinship or clan affiliations, rather than more general business principles. Hard work is seen as necessary to ward off the hazards present in an unpredictable world. A favorite maxim is the widespread admonition to 'keep your bags packed at all times.'

In the typical ethnic Chinese family firm, there is little separation between owner and management. The head of a Chinese company typically is an all-powerful 'paterfamilias' who entrusts key activities and positions to members of the family. Within the family, confidence in his judgment borders on the absolute.

This extreme centralization of authority avoids many of the 'agency' problems that Western businesses must overcome in ensuring that managers promote the interests of the owners rather than themselves. Yet there are also disadvantages associated with the family-run business. Keeping control within the family almost inevitably restricts the size, or at least the complexity, to which it can grow. That is not so much a problem for lowtech firms as it is for high-tech companies that require sophisticated organizational structures.

The track record of second- and third-generation overseas Chinese managers is mixed. Frequently, these sons and daughters must manage the transition of the family firm from an entrepreneurial start-up to a modern corporation. Family ties can be so strong that incompetent relatives are preferred to competent outside professionals. The best and brightest Chinese entrepreneurs are trying to finesse the succession problem by taking their companies public, hiring professional managers, and sending their offspring to Western business schools.

Conclusion

As competitors to Western business, the overseas Chinese bring to the arena a number of specific advantages including intense managerial effort, financial shrewdness, and production efficiency. Most important, however, is the high degree of flexibility made possible within a network of companies allied by ties of mutual obligation. As competitors or partners with this network, Western firms should remember some useful generalizations about its operations.

1   *Most overseas Chinese take a low profile in the commercial world and shy away from publicity.* As a result, rather than produce consumer goods with a Chinese brand name, the members of the bamboo network operate in the interstices of the trading world. They make components, manufacture for others, and perform subassembly work. They are also heavily involved in wholesaling, financing, sourcing, and transporting. Most of these operations are behind the scenes, minimizing the need to market products to end users. The leading businessmen know each other personally and do deals together, with information spreading through an informal network rather than through more conventional channels.

2   *Ethnic Chinese family firms rely on strict, centralized control and informal transactions to minimize company bureaucracy and paperwork.* Key information is obtained in conversation and retained in the heads of the senior managers, which helps to eliminate the need for formal reporting. Considering the tremendous flow of studies, reports, and memoranda in the typical Western business of any size, the implicit economies of time and effort achieved by the bamboo network are impressive. Money is

borrowed from family and friends on trust. Transactions of great size are often dealt with by common understanding and a note jotted in a diary.

3   *The successful overseas Chinese business family operates through a network of enterprises rather than the unitary company (e.g. Ford, Wal-Mart) characteristic of US family firms.* Most US family business dynasties grew out of a single firm's dominance in a single market or area. For example, the Ford Motor Company, despite its enormous size, has to this day retained its 'core competency' as a motor vehicle manufacturer. Its business structure follow a clear hierarchy, with the parent company maintaining full ownership and tight control of its subordinate businesses. Diversification is generally accomplished by internationalization or by obtaining an interest in firms that provide necessary parts for automobile assembly.

In sharp contrast, the typical overseas Chinese business family maintains varying percentage interests in a galaxy of small to medium-sized firms, many of which have little relationship to the parent company's core competency. For example, although the ascension of Thailand's CP Group from feed mills to poultry farming may have been predictable, the group's tremendous success in motorcycle manufacturing and telecommunications joint ventures is more difficult to explain. The *guanxi* of the overseas Chinese family business provides a perfect complement to high-tech Western firms that lack the necessary economic and political connections to navigate a treacherous foreign business environment.

Overseas Chinese firms have eschewed traditional business structures in order to capitalize on the weak system of contracting and law throughout Southeast Asia, particularly on the mainland. Core business groups develop varying degrees of ownership in dozens, if not hundreds, of small to medium-sized businesses. In turn, many of these businesses maintain cross-holdings with other family-controlled firms. The resulting web of holdings, when combined with the insertion of family members into key management positions, allows the family to maintain ultimate, albeit circuitous, control. This structure ensures the secrecy and diversification necessary in a region where the threat of governmental expropriation and ethnic discrimination is still pervasive.

A fundamental shortcoming, however, is that the Chinese family business structure makes it extremely difficult to develop the high-tech products and systems that will provide the foundation for future business growth and national economic progress.

4   *Overseas Chinese business leaders utilize a management style that is more informal and intuitive than that practiced in a typical Western corporation.* The extensive – and expensive – due diligence efforts conducted by US corporations before making major investments are streamlined in the overseas Chinese firm. Senior management performs the analysis itself, rather than delegating the task to technical experts. Decision making is more practical than theoretical, more intuitive than bureaucratic. The resulting rapidity of action allows opportunities to be seized as they arise, creating a fundamentally different organizational structure than is present in most Western firms. The fortunes of the wealthy overseas Chinese are usually based on a variety of activities, such as shipping, hotels, textiles, toys, property management, and trade. There is no Chinese equivalent of such complex, decentralized companies as America's Procter & Gamble, Japan's Sony, or Korea's Daewoo. The exception is in Taiwan, which has

cultivated the ability to make long-term investments and to manage complex manufacturing operations.

Some of the younger members of the overseas Chinese community have emigrated to the West, especially to the United States and Canada. Portions of this group, particularly those trained in California's Silicon Valley electronics industry, are now returning with their Western ideas. Those who possess MBAs from American universities are loosening their ties to the ancestral cultural heritage and adopting more modern business techniques. Over time, traditional cultural factors will play a reduced role in Southeast Asian business, especially as the reins of power are passed to a younger generation of business leaders who lack their parents' emotional ties to the mainland.

The ability to rely on personal contacts may also become less significant if – or when – mainland decisionmakers adopt more modern political and legal institutions in order to participate more fully in the global marketplace. In the long run, such adaptation will be essential to maintaining competitiveness in an increasingly high-tech global marketplace. In the short run, family control will continue to be an essential ingredient in dealing effectively with the rudimentary and often chaotic institutional structure that typifies the economies of Southeast Asia.

Network Level Strategy in International Perspective

Do as adversaries in law, strive mightily, but eat and drink as friends.
(William Shakespeare 1564 – 1616; English dramatist and poet)

Of all of the debates in the field of strategic management, this one has received the most attention from comparative management researchers. Almost all of these researchers have concluded that firms from different countries display widely divergent propensities to compete and cooperate. Many authors suggest that there are recognizable national inclinations, even national styles, when it comes to establishing interfirm relationships. For instance, Kanter (1994) notes that

North American companies, more than others in the world, take a narrow, opportunistic view of relationships, evaluating them strictly in financial terms or seeing them as barely tolerable alternatives to outright acquisition. Preoccupied with the economics of the deal, North American companies frequently neglect the political, cultural, organizational, and human aspects of the partnership. Asian companies are the most comfortable with relationships, and therefore they are the most adept at using and exploiting them. European companies fall somewhere in the middle.

Although Kanter's 'classification' is somewhat rough, most strategic management researchers who have done international comparative studies agree with the broad lines of her remark (e.g. Contractor and Lorange, 1988; Kagono *et al.*, 1985).

While it is difficult to generalize at the national level, since there can be quite a bit of variance within a country, it is challenging to debate these observed international dissimilarities. Are there really national interfirm relationship styles and what factors might influence their existence? As a stimulus to the international dimension of this debate, a number of country characteristics are put forward as possible influences on how the paradox of competition and cooperation is dealt with in different national settings. As noted before, it is the intention of these propositions to encourage further discussion and cross cultural research on the topic of interorganizational relationships.

Level of Individualism

At the most fundamental level, cultural values can place more emphasis on competition or cooperation. Some researchers (e.g. Hofstede, 1993; reading 1.5; Hampden-Turner and Trompenaars, 1993) point out that this has much to do with a culture's orientation toward individuals or groups. More individualist cultures accentuate the position of each single person as a distinct entity, while more collectivist cultures stress people's group affiliations. In Hofstede's research, the United States surfaced as highest scoring nation in the world on the individualism scale, closely followed by the other English-speaking countries, Australia, Great Britain, Canada and New Zealand respectively. Hofstede argues that 'in the US individualist conception, the relationship between the individual and the organization is essentially calculative, being based on enlightened self-interest,' while in more collectivist cultures the relationship 'is not calculative, but moral: it is based not on self interest, but on the individual's loyalty toward the clan, organization, or society – which is supposedly the best guarantee of that individual's ultimate interest.' The willingness of individuals to forgo self-interested behavior for the good of the group, is believed to be the same cultural value spurring individual firms to cooperate for the good of an entire network (e.g. Gerlach, 1992). Pascale and Athos (1981) agree that in the highly group-oriented culture of Japan, interdependence is valued, while the 'self' is regarded as an obstacle to joint development. Group members feel indebted and obligated toward one another, and trust results from a shared understanding and acceptance of interdependence.

The strong orientation of the English-speaking ('Anglo-Saxon') cultures toward individualism and the Japanese cultural emphasis on group-affiliation, is also recognized by Lessem and Neubauer (1994), who place these two cultures at the extreme ends of a continuum. In the socially atomistic Anglo-Saxon nations, individuals are seen as the building blocks of society and each person is inclined to optimize her/his own interests. In the socially symbiotic Japanese culture, the whole is more important than the individual parts, so that individuals are more likely to strive towards a group's common good. Interestingly, Lessem and Neubauer (following Albert, 1991) argue that, on this point, German and Japanese culture are strikingly similar. Both cultures exhibit a 'wholist' world view, in which 'management and banker, employer and employee, government and industry combine forces rather than engage in adversarial relations,' to the benefit of the entire system. This collectivist bent can be observed at the multi-company level (industrial networks/*keiretsu*), but also at the industry and national levels of aggregation, leading many analysts to speak of Japan Incorporated and Germany Incorporated.

Other cultures fall somewhere between these two extremes. Italy, for instance, is often cited for its high number of networked companies (Piore and Sabel, 1984). Besides the well-known example of Benetton, there are many networks in the textile industry of Prato, the ceramics industry of Sassuolo, the farm machine industry of Reggio-Emilia and motorcycle industry of Bologna. Similar to the Germans and Japanese, Italian culture is also characterized by a strong group-orientation, but the affiliations valued by Italians tend to be mostly family-like, based on blood-ties, friendships or ideological bonds between individuals. There is often a strong loyalty and trust within these family-like communities, but distrust toward the outside world. Therefore, cooperation tends to be high within these communities, but competition prevails beyond.

In France the situation is again different. In French culture, according to Lessem and Neubauer (1994), there is 'an ingrained mistrust of the natural play of forces of a free economy.' People have a strong sense that cooperation in economic affairs is important, similar to the Japanese, Germans and Italians. However, the French are unwilling to depend on the evolution of cooperation between (semi-)independent firms. Generally, there is a preference to impose cooperation top-down, by integrating companies into efficiently working bureaucracies. Such structuring of the economy usually takes place under influence, or by direct intervention, of the French government. Such *dirigisme* is based on the opposite assumption as Williamson's work (1975, 1985): hierarchical coordination is usually preferable to market transactions. Former prime minister, Edouard Balladur, summarized this assumption far more graciously, when he remarked: 'What is the market? It is the law of the jungle, the law of nature. And what is civilisation? It is the struggle against nature' (*The Economist*, March 15th 1997). Based on this view, even relationships with firms not absorbed into the hierarchy are of a bureaucratic nature, that is, formal, rational and depersonalized.

Type of Institutional Environment

Of course, the cultural values described above are intertwined with the institutional structures that have developed in each country. Some comparative management researchers focus on these institutional forces, such as governments, banks, universities and unions, to explain the divergent national views on competition and cooperation. It is generally argued that most countries have developed an idiosyncratic economic system, that is, their own distinct brand of capitalism, with a different emphasis on competition and cooperation.

One prominent analysis is that of business historian Chandler (1986, 1990), who has described the historical development of 'personal capitalism' in the United Kingdom, 'managerial capitalism' in the United States, 'cooperative capitalism' in Germany and 'group capitalism' in Japan from 1850 to 1950. The legacy of these separately evolving forms of capitalism is that, to this day, there are significantly different institutional philosophies, roles and behaviors in each of these countries. In the English-speaking nations, governments have generally limited their role to the establishment and maintenance of competitive markets (Hampden-Turner and Trompenaars, 1993). A shared belief in the basic tenets of classical economics has lead these governments to be suspect of competition-undermining collusion masquerading under the term 'cooperation.' For instance, in the United States the Sherman Antitrust Act was passed in 1890 and has been applied with vigor since then to guard the functioning of the market. Many companies that would like to cooperate have been discouraged from doing so (e.g. Teece, 1992; Dyer and Ouchi, 1993).

In the German 'cooperative capitalism' system, the situation has been quite different. The government has major shareholdings in hundreds of companies outside the public services. According to Lessem and Neubauer (1994) 'the attitude to government participation in industry is based not on ideology but on a sense of partnership with the business community. It extends to the local level where local authorities, schools, banks and businesses combine to establish policies of mutual benefit.' Especially the large German banks play an important role in guiding industrial development, promoting cooperation and defusing potentially damaging conflicts between companies. They have an intimate knowledge of the business and have a long-term stake in each relationship, which is often expressed by a minority shareholding of the bank in the client company and/or a seat on its supervisory board. The officers of the largest bank, Deutsche Bank, hold roughly 400 seats on other companies' supervisory boards. It should be noted, however, that trade associations and unions also employ a long term, cooperative perspective.

The Japanese 'group capitalism' system is somewhat akin to the German model. In Japan, too, business and social institutions have formed a partnership to promote mutually beneficial developments. However, in Japan, the government plays a more prominent role than in Germany, through its national industrial strategies (Best, 1990). As Thurow (1991) points out, the Japanese government is actively involved in the indirect protection of some domestic industries, the selection of other sectors as development priorities and the funding of related research and development. Furthermore, the keiretsu industry groups, such as Mitsui, Mitsubishi, Sanwa, Hitachi and Sumitomo, also form long-term networks of cooperating companies. While some consortia are formed to deal with a particular task at hand, firms within a keiretsu are familiar with one another through long historical association and have durable, opened-ended relationships, partially cemented by multilateral minority shareholdings.

In France, the dirigiste state planners play an even more prominent role than in Japan. The French model, which could be dubbed 'bureaucratic capitalism,' focuses sharply on the State as industrial strategist, coordinating all major developments in the economy. It is the planners' job 'to maintain a constant pressure on industry – as part industrial consultant, part banker, part plain bully – to keep it moving in some desired direction' (Lessem and Neubauer, 1994). The unions, on the other hand, tend to be more antagonistic, particularly in their relationship to the government. On the work floor, however, a more cooperative attitude prevails.

Finally, in the 'familial capitalism' system of Italy, local networks of economic, political and social actors cooperate to create a mutually beneficial environment. Trade associations, purchasing cooperatives, educational institutions and cooperative marketing are often created to support a large number of small specialized firms working together as a loose federation. Trust within the network is often large, but institutions outside of these closed communities are mistrusted, especially the central government, tax authorities, bankers and the trade unions.

Market for Corporate Control

Linked to the general institutional environment, is how the issue of mergers, acquisitions and take-overs is viewed in each nation. In countries such as the United States and Britain, companies whose shares are traded on the stock exchange are exposed to the threat of a take-over. This relatively open market for corporate control facilitates vertical and horizontal integration. Companies can contemplate acquiring another firm, if they believe that internal coordination is preferable to a market-based relationship. In other countries, however, the market for corporate control is less open, if not entirely absent. Where horizontal or vertical integration is difficult to achieve, but working together is still beneficial, potential acquirers often only have collaborative arrangements as an alternative.

Type of Career Paths

Finally, a more down to earth reason why competition or cooperation might be more prevalent in a particular country may be found at the level of personnel policy. In general, the longer people know each other and the more they interact, the more trust and cooperativeness that evolves (Axelrod, 1984; Teece, 1992). In countries such as Japan and Germany, where stable, long-term employment is common, individuals are in a better position to build up durable personal relationships with people in other firms. In nations where employees frequently shift between positions and companies, establishing personal ties and gradually building mutual trust is more difficult to achieve.

Another relationship-building mechanism can be the exchange of personnel, on a temporary or permanent basis. In Japan, for instance, it is not unusual to send an employee 'on assignment' to a partner firm for a long period of time, often simultaneously accepting 'external' employees in return. In some countries, the transfer of employees between partner organizations is more permanent. France and Japan are known for their public servants' mid-career shifts to the private sector (*pantouflage* and *amakudari*, respectively), which makes building public-private partnerships much easier.

Further Readings

No one who wishes to delve more deeply into the topic of organizational boundaries and inter-organizational relationships can avoid running into references to the classic in this area, Oliver Williamson's *Markets and Hierarchies: Analysis and Antitrust Implications*. Williamson's writings have inspired many researchers, especially economists. Others have remarked that Williamson's transaction cost economics largely ignores the political, social and psychological aspects of business relationships. As an antidote to Williamson's strongly rationalist view of the world, another classic can be advised. Jeffrey Pfeffer and Gerald Salancik's *The External Control of Organizations: A Resource Dependency Perspective* is an excellent book that emphasizes the political aspects of interorganizational relationships. However, both books are quite academic and not for the faint-hearted.

A more accessible overview of the topic of interorganizational co-operation is provided by Farok Contractor and Peter Lorange in their book *Cooperative Strategies in International Business*. For further reading on the subject of vertical relationships, Michael Best's *The New Competition*, and Carlos Jarillo's *Strategic Networks: Creating the Borderless Organization*, are both excellent choices. For horizontal relationships a good starting point would be *Strategic Alliances: Formation, Implementation and Evolution*, by Peter Lorange and Johan Roos, or *The Knowledge Link: How Firms Compete through Strategic Alliances*, by J. Badaracco. If the reader is interested in moving beyond dyadic relationships, B. Axelsson and G. Easton's *Industrial Networks: A New View of Reality* is recommended.

All of the above works are positively inclined towards collaboration, largely adopting the embedded organization perspective. For a more critical appraisal of networks, alliances and close relationships, by authors taking the discrete organization perspective, readers are advised to start with the article 'Outsourcing and Industrial Decline,' by Richard Bettis, Stephen Bradley and Gary Hamel. Other critical accounts are John Hendry's article 'Culture, Community and Networks: The Hidden Cost of Outsourcing,' and S. MacDonald's 'Too Close for Comfort?: The Strategic Implications of Getting Close to the Customer.'

For a more thorough understanding of networks within the Japanese context, Michael Gerlach's *Alliance Capitalism: The Social Organization of Japanese Business* is a good book to begin with. T. Nishiguchi's book *Strategic Industrial Sourcing: The Japanese Advantage* is particularly interesting on the topic of Japanese supplier relationships. For the Chinese view on networks Murray Weidenbaum and Samuel Hughes book *The Bamboo Network: How Expatriate Chinese Entrepreneurs Are Creating a New Economic Superpower in Asia* is recommended, as is S. Redding's *The Spirit of Chinese Capitalism*. For an overview of European views, Ronnie Lessem and Fred Neubauer's *European Management Systems* is an excellent book, but also Roland Calori and Philippe de Woot's collection *A European Management Model: Beyond Diversity* provides challenging insights.

References

Albert, M. (1991) *Capitalisme contre Capitalisme*, Seuil, Paris.

Aoki, M., Gustafsson, B., and Williamson, O.E. (1990) *The Firm as a Nexus of Treaties*, Sage, London.

Axelrod, R. (1984) *The Evolution of Cooperation*, Basic Books, New York.

Axelsson, B., and Easton, G. (1992) *Industrial Networks: A New View of Reality*, Wiley, New York.

Badaracco, J.L. (1991) *The Knowledge Link: How Firms Compete Through Strategic Alliances*, Harvard Business School Press, Boston, MA.

Barnes, L.B. (1981) Managing the Paradox of Organizational Trust, *Harvard Business Review*, March/April, pp. 107–16.

Berger, P.L. (1994) Our Economic Culture, in Boxx, T.W., and Quinlivan, G.M. (eds), *The Cultural Context of Economics and Politics*, University Press of America, Lanham, MD, p. 72.

Best, M.H. (1990) *The New Competition: Institutions of Industrial Restructuring*, Polity, Cambridge.

Bettis, R.A., Bradley, S.P. and Hamel, G. (1992) Outsourcing and Industrial Decline, *Academy of Management Executive*, February, pp. 7–22.

Bleeke, J., and Ernst, D. (1991) The Way to Win in Cross Border Alliances, *Harvard Business Review*, November/December, pp. 127–35.

Boisot, M. (1986) Markets and Hierarchies in a Cultural Perspective, *Organization Studies*, Vol. 7, pp. 135–58.

Borys, B., and Jemison, D.B. (1989) Hybrid Arrangements as Strategic Alliances: Theoretical Issues in Organizational Combinations, Academy of Management Review, April pp. 234–49.

Boss, R.W. (1978) Trust and Managerial Problem Solving Revisited, *Group and Organizational Studies*, September, pp. 331–42.

Calori, R. and de Woot, Ph. (eds) (1994) *A European Management Model: Beyond Diversity*, Prentice-Hall, Hemel Hempstead.

Chandler, A.D. (1986) The Evolution of Modern Global Competition, in Porter, M.E. (ed.), *Competition in Global Industries*, Harvard Business School Press, Boston, pp. 405–48.

Chandler, A.D. (1990) *Scale and Scope*, Belknop, Cambridge, MA.

Chesbrough, H.W., and Teece, D.J. (1996) Organizing for Innovation: When is Virtual Virtuous?, *Harvard Business Review*, January-February, pp. 65–73.

Coase, R.H. (1937) The Nature of the Firm, *Economica*, Vol. 4, pp. 386–405.

Contractor, F.J., and Lorange, P. (1988) *Cooperative Strategies in International Business*, Lexington Books, Lexington, MA.

Driscoll, J.W. (1978) Trust and Participation in Organizational Decision Making as Predictors of Satisfaction, *Academy of Management Journal*, Vol. 21 (1), pp. 44–56.

Dyer, J.H., and Ouchi, W.G. (1993) Japanese-Style Partnerships: Giving Companies a Competitive Edge, *Sloan Management Review*, Fall, pp. 51–63.

Dyer, J.H. (1996) Specialized Supplier Networks as a Source of Competitive Advantage: Evidence from the Auto Industry, *Strategic Management Journal*, Vol. 17, No. 4, pp. 271–91.

Gambetta, D. (ed.) (1988) *Trust: Making and Breaking Cooperative Relations*, Blackwell, New York.

Gerlach, M. (1992) *Alliance Capitalism*, University of California Press, Berkeley, CA.

Ghoshal, S., and Moran, P. (1996) Bad for Practice: a Critique of the Transaction Cost Theory, *Academy of Management Review*, Vol. 21, No. 1, pp. 13–47.

Gomes-Casseres, B. (1994) Group versus Group: How Alliance Networks Compete, *Harvard Business Review*, July/August, pp. 62–74.

Grabher, G. (ed.) (1993) *The Embedded Firm: On the Socioeconomics of Industrial Networks*, Routledge, London.

Granovetter, M.S. (1972) The Strength of Weak Ties, *American Journal of Sociology*, Vol. 78, No. 6, pp. 1360–80.

Granovetter, M.S. (1985) Economic Action and Social Structure: The Problem Of Embeddedness, *American Journal of Sociology*, Vol. 91, pp. 481–501.

Granovetter, M.S. (1995) Coase Revisited: Business Groups in the Modern Economy, *Industrial and Corporate Change*, Vol. 4, No.1, pp. 93–130.

Hamel, G. (1991) Competition for Competence and Inter-Partner Learning Within International Strategic Alliances, *Strategic Mangement Journal*, Vol. 12, Summer Special Issue, pp. 83–103.

Hamel, G., Doz, Y.L., and Prahalad, C.K. (1989) Collaborate with Your Competitors-and Win, *Harvard Business Review*, January/February, pp. 133–9.

Hampden-Turner, C., and Trompenaars, A. (1993) *The Seven Cultures of Capitalism: Value Systems for Creating Wealth in the United States, Japan, Germany, France, Britain, Sweden and the Netherlands*, Doubleday, New York.

Handy, C. (1989) *The Age of Unreason*, Business Books, London.

Harrigan, K.R. (1985) *Strategies for Joint Ventures*, D.C. Heath, Lexington, MA.

Hendry, J. (1995) Culture, Community and Networks: The Hidden Cost of Outsourcing, *European Management Journal*, Vol. 13, No. 2, pp. 193–200.

Hill, C.W.L. (1990) Cooperation, Opportunism, and the Invisible Hand: Implications for Transaction Cost Theory, *Academy of Management Review*, Vol. 15 No. 3, pp. 500–13.

Hofstede, G. (1993) Cultural Constraints in Management Theories, *Academy of Management Executive*, Vol. 7, No. 1.

Jarillo, J.C. (1988) On Strategic Networks, *Strategic Management Journal*, Vol. 9, No. 1, pp. 31–41.

Jarillo, J.C. (1993) *Strategic Networks: Creating the Borderless Organization*, Butterworth-Heinemann, Oxford.

Johanson, J., and Mattson, L.G. (1987) Interorganisational Relations in Industrial Systems: A Network Approach Compared with the Transaction Cost Approach, *International Studies in Management and Organisation*, Vol. 17, No.1, pp. 34–48.

Johanson, J., and Mattson, L.G. (1992) Network Position and Strategic Action – An Analytical Framework, in Axelsson, B., and Easton, G. *Industrial Networks: A New View of Reality*, Routledge, London.

Johnston, R., and Lawrence, P.R. (1988) Beyond Vertical Integration – The Rise of the Value-Adding Partnership, *Harvard Business Review*, July/August, pp. 94–101.

Kagono, T., Nonaka, I. Sakakibara, K. and Okumara, A. (1985) *Strategic vs. Evolutionary Management*, North-Holland, Amsterdam.

Kanter, R.M. (1994) Collaborative Advantage: The Art of Alliances, *Harvard Business Review*, July/August, pp. 96–108.

Kao, J. (1993) The Worldwide Web of Chinese Business, *Harvard Business Review*, March/April, pp. 25, 39.

Kawasaki, S., and MacMillan, J. (1986) *The Design of Contracts: Evidence from Japanese Subcontracting*, mimeo, University of Western Ontario.

Kay, J.A. (1993) *Foundations of Corporate Success*, Oxford Universtity Press, Oxford.

Kogut, B. (1988) Joint Ventures: Theoretical and Empirical Perspectives, *Strategic Management Journal*, Vol. 9, pp. 319–32.

Lessem, R., and Neubauer, F.F. (1994) *European Management Systems*, McGraw-Hill, London.

Lewis, J.D. (1990) *Partnerships for Profit: Structuring and Managing Strategic Alliances*, Free Press, New York.

Lorange, P., and Roos, J. (1992) *Strategic Alliances: Formation, Implementation, and Evolution*, Blackwell, Cambridge, MA.

Lorenzoni, G., and Baden-Fuller, C. (1995) Creating a Strategic Center to Manage a Web of Partners, *California Management Review*, Vol. 37, Spring, pp. 146–63.

Macdonald, S. (1995) Too Close for Comfort?: The Strategic Implications of Getting Close to the Customer, *California Management Review*, Vol. 37, Summer, pp. 8–27.

MacMillan, K., and Farmer, D. (1979) Redefining the Boundaries of the Firm, *Journal of Industrial Economics*, Vol. 27, pp. 277–85.

Mahoney, J.T. (1992) The Choice of Organizational Form: Vertical Financial Ownership versus Other Methods of Vertical Integration, *Strategic Management Journal*, Vol. 13, No. 8, pp. 559–84.

Miles, R.E., and Snow, C.C. (1986) Network Organizations: New Concepts for New Forms, *California Management Review*, Vol. 28, Spring, pp. 62–73.

Miles, R.E., and Snow, C.C. (1992) Causes of Failure in Network Organizations, *California Management Review*, Summer, pp. 53–72.

Nishiguchi, T. (1994) *Strategic Industrial Sourcing: The Japanese Advantage*, Oxford University Press, New York.

Norman, R., and Ramirez, R. (1993) From Value Chain to Value Constellation:

Designing Interactive Strategy, *Harvard Business Review*, July/August, pp. 65–77.

Osborn, R., and Baughn, C. (1990) Forms of Interorganizational Governance for Multinational Alliances, *Academy of Management Journal*, Vol. 33, pp. 503–19.

Ouchi, W.G. (1980) Markets, Bureaucracies, and Clans, *Administrative Science Quarterly*, Vol. 25, pp. 129–42.

Parkhe, A. (1991) Interfirm Diversity, Organizational Learning, and Longevity in Global Strategic Alliances, *Journal of International Business Studies*, Vol. 22, pp. 579–601.

Pascale, R.T., and Athos, A.G. (1981) *The Art of Japanese Management*, Simon & Schuster, New York.

Pfeffer, J., and Salancik, G.R. (1978) *The External Control of Organizations: A Resource Dependency Perspective*, Harper & Row, New York.

Piore, M., and Sabel, C.F. (1984) *The Second Industrial Divide*, Basic Books, New York.

Porter, M.E. (1979) How Competitive Forces Shape Strategy, *Harvard Business Review*, March/April, pp. 137–45.

Porter, M.E. (1980) *Competitive Strategy: Techniques for Analyzing Industries and Competitors*, Free Press, New York.

Porter, M.E. (1981) The Contributions of Industrial Organization to Strategic Management, *Academy of Management Review*, Vol. 6, pp. 609–20.

Porter, M.E. (1985) *Competitive Advantage*, Free Press, New York.

Porter, M.E. (1990) *The Competitive Advantage of Nations*, Macmillan, London.

Powell, W. (1990) Neither Market nor Hierarchy: Network Forms of Organization, *Research in Organizational Behavior*, Vol. 12, pp. 295–336.

Preece, S.B. (1995) Incorporating International Strategic Alliances into Overall Firm Strategy: A Typology of Six Managerial Objectives, *The International Executive*, Vol. 37, May/June, pp. 261–77.

Quinn, J.B. (1992) *The Intelligent Enterprise: A Knowledge and Service Based Paradigm for Industry*, Free Press, New York.

Rappaport, A.S., and Halevi, S. (1991) The Computerless Company, *Harvard Business Review*, July/August, pp. 69–80.

Redding, S.G. (1990) *The Spirit of Chinese Capitalism*, Walter de Gruyter, Berlin.

Reich, R., and Mankin, E. (1986) Joint Ventures with Japan Give Away Our Future, *Harvard Business Review*, March/April, pp. 78–86.

Reve, T. (1990) The Firm as a Nexus of Internal and External Contracts, in Aoki, M., Gustafsson, B., and Williamson, O.E. *The Firm as a Nexus of Treaties*, Sage, London.

Ring, P.S., and van de Ven, A.H. (1992) Structuring Cooperative Relationships between Organizations, *Strategic Management Journal*, Vol. 13, No. 7, pp. 483–98.

Teece, D.J. (1992) Competition, Cooperation, and Innovation: Organizational Arrangements for Regimes of Rapid Technological Progress, *Journal of Economic Behavior and Organization*, Vol. 18, pp. 1–25.

Thorelli, H.B. (1986) Networks: Between Markets and Hierarchies, *Strategic Management Journal*, Vol. 7, No. 1, pp. 37–51.

Thurow, L. (1991) *Head to Head*, MIT Press, Cambridge, MA.

Von Hippel, E. (1985) *User Innovation: An Analysis of the Functional Sources of Innovation*, Sloan School of Management, Massachusetts Institute of Technology, Cambridge, MA.

Weidenbaum, M., and Hughes, S. (1996) *The Bamboo Network: How Expatriate*

Chinese Entrepreneurs Are Creating a New Economic Superpower in Asia, Free Press, pp. 23–59.

Welch, J.A., and Nayak, P.R. (1992) Strategic Outsourcing: A Progressive Approach to the Make-or-Buy Decision, *Academy of Management Executive*, February, pp. 23–31.

Williamson, O.E. (1975) *Markets and Hierarchies: Analysis and Antitrust Implications*, Free Press, New York.

Williamson, O.E. (1979) Transaction Cost Economics: The Governance of Contractual Relations, *Journal of Law and Economics*, Vol. 22, pp. 223–61.

Williamson, O.E. (1985) *The Economic Institutions of Capitalism*, Free Press, New York.

Williamson, O.E. (1991) Strategizing, Economizing, and Economic Organization, *Strategic Management Journal*, Vol. 12, pp. 75–94.

Zand, D. (1972) Trust and Managerial Problem Solving, *Administrative Science Quarterly*, Vol. 17, June, pp. 229–39.

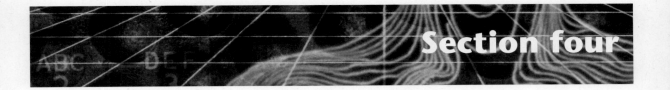

Strategy Context

❑ 8 The Industry Context
❑ 9 The Organizational Context
❑ 10 The International Context

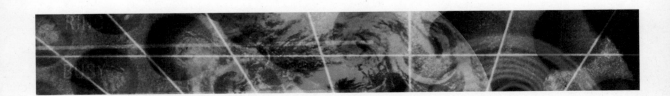

Strategy Context

☐ 8 The Industry Context
☐ 9 The Organizational Context
☐ 10 The International Context

The Industry Context

The pilot cannot mitigate the billows
or calm the winds.

(Plutarch c.46–c.120; Greek biographer and philosopher)

The reasonable man adapts himself to
the world; the unreasonable one
persists in trying to adapt the world
to himself. Therefore, all progress
depends on the unreasonable man.

(George Bernard Shaw 1856–1950; Irish playwright and critic)

The Paradox of Compliance and Choice

Is it unreasonable to want to change the world? Your answer to this question will largely depend on how adaptable you think the world is. Those who believe that the world develops following its own dynamics will argue that individuals must adapt to the world – it is better to buy an umbrella than to attempt to change the weather. If individuals do not 'follow the laws of nature' or 'play by the rules of the game', they do so at their own peril. On the other hand, those who believe that there are no unchangeable rules or laws, will argue that the world is actually quite adaptable – it is better to invent a new cure than to get used to the illness. Individuals who expose the 'rules' as mere conventions and show that the 'laws' are merely habits, can do so to their own (and others') advantage.

This chapter looks at the issue of environment adaptability at the industry level. The issue is the *malleability* of the industry context – the extent to which the industry context can be modified by a firm (or group of collaborating firms). If firms cannot influence the structure of the industry they are in, *compliance* to the rules of the game is the strategic imperative. Under these circumstances, wise strategists will adapt the firm to the industry environment. However, if firms do have the ability to manipulate the industry structure, they can try to change the 'terms of competition' in their own favor. In this type of situation, wise strategists will not comply to the existing industry rules, but exercise their freedom of *choice* to break the rules or create new rules.

How malleable are industries in practice? Should strategists take a predominantly compliance- or choice-oriented view? Opinions on this matter differ considerably. As in the previous debates, two diametrically opposed points of view can be identified, while many others take in intermediate positions. On the one hand, some argue that industry development is an autonomous process, to which firms must adjust or risk being selected out. We shall refer to this point of view as the *industry evolution* perspective. On the other hand, many strategists believe that the industry context can be moulded in an infinite variety of ways by innovative firms. This point of view will be referred to as the *industry creation* perspective.

As before, this chapter has been structured as a debate between the two opposite points of view. By comparing these two contradictory views on how the paradox of compliance and choice should be dealt with, a better understanding of the issues under discussion should be gained. In the next few pages, the industry evolution and industry creation perspectives will be further explained, and finally summarized in Table 8.1.

The Industry Evolution Perspective

To those taking an industry evolution perspective, the popular notion that individual firms have the power to shape their industry is an understandable, but quite misplaced, belief. Of course, the illusion of control is tempting – most people, especially managers, would like to control their own destiny. Most individuals assume they have a free will and can decide their own future. Many governments suppose that they can shape society and many cultures assume that they control nature. In the same way, it is seductive to believe that the individual firm can matter, by influencing the development of its industry.

Unfortunately, this belief is largely a fallacy, brought on by a poor understanding of the underlying industry dynamics. In reality, according to advocates of the industry evolution perspective, industries are complex systems, with a large number of forces interacting simultaneously, none of which can significantly direct the long-term development of the whole. Firms are relatively small players in a very large game – their behaviors may have some impact on industry development, but none can fundamentally shape the direction of changes. On the contrary, as industries evolve, all firms that do not meet the changing demands of the environment are weeded out. Firms not suited to the new circumstances die, while firms complying to the changing rules prosper. Hence, through *selection* the industry context determines the group of industry survivors and through the pressures for *adaptation* the behavior of the remaining firms is determined. In short, the industry shapes the firm, not the other way around.

The label 'industry evolution perspective' is derived from the parallel often drawn with biological evolution. Both evolutionary processes, it is argued, share a number of basic characteristics. In nature, as in business, the survival and growth of entities depends on their fit with the environment. Within each environment variations to a successful theme might come about. These new individuals will thrive, as long as they suit the existing circumstances, but as the environment changes, only those that meet the new demands will not be selected out. Hence, Darwin's well-known principle of 'survival of the fittest' is based on a cycle of *variation* and *environmental selection*. Some proponents of the industry evolution perspective think that this biological view of evolution is a good model for what happens in industries – new organizations arise as mutations and only the fittest mutations survive (e.g. Aldrich, 1979; Hannan and Freeman, 1977; reading 8.3 in this book). Others adopting the industry evolution perspective argue that there is a significant difference with biological evolution. Organizations do not vary 'at random,' but purposefully, and they possess the ability to adapt to selection pressures during the evolution process (e.g. Nelson and Winter, 1982; Baum and Singh, 1994).

The upshot of the industry evolution perspective is that there is actually not very much that a strategist can do to improve the performance of a company. Industries follow an evolutionary trajectory, that no one controls. The current and future industry structure cannot be influenced, however cunning strategists believe they can be. With immutable rules of the game, strategy is reduced to playing well within the rules. This leaves only small margins within which to manoeuver and predetermines the general level of profitability that a firm can achieve. Once in a poor industry, a firm's growth and profit potential are significantly limited (Porter, 1980; reading 8.1). The best a firm can do is to score slightly above the industry average, by adapting better, and anticipating changes better, than competitors.

The Industry Creation Perspective

Strategists taking an industry creation perspective fundamentally disagree with the determinism inherent in the industry evolution perspective. Even in biology, breeders and genetic engineers consistently attempt to shape the natural world. Of course, in industries, as in biology, some rules are immutable. Certain economic, technological, social and political factors have to be accepted as hardly influenceable. But the remaining environmental factors that can be manipulated leave strategists with an enormous scope for moulding the industry of the future. This belief is reflected in the remark by the Dutch poet Jules Deelder that 'even within the limits of the possible, the possibilities are limitless.' It is up to the strategist to identify which rules of the game must be respected and which can be ignored in the search for new strategic options. The strategist must recognize both the limits on the possible and the limitless possibilities.

In the industry creation perspective, both the *strictness* and *rigidity* of the industry rules can be challenged. The 'strictness of rules' refers to the degrees of freedom available to the strategist. Strict rules imply that only very specific behavior is allowed – firms must closely follow the rules or face severe consequences. However, those taking an industry creation perspective argue that rules are usually not as strict as they seem. There is plenty of room for firms to 'do their own thing' within the existing industry structure. The 'rigidity of rules' refers to the extent to which strategists can actually alter the industry rules. Rigid rules cannot easily be changed, but must be accepted as a given. In the industry creation perspective, however, it is argued that rules can usually be broken by those who know where to apply pressure. In this way rule breakers can become the new rule makers, unless these new rules are again challenged by others.

It must be emphasized that, while rules are rooted in the underlying economics, technologies, politics and social structures of an industry, it is perception of the rules that guides firms' behavior. Companies make strategies based on their understanding of the rules. Over time, firms within an industry often tend to develop a common definition of the rules, also referred to as an *industry recipe* (Spender, 1989; Baden-Fuller and Stopford, 1992; reading 8.2). Proponents of the industry creation perspective argue that such shared beliefs are often a more significant barrier to changing the industry rules, than the underlying economic, technological, political and social factors themselves. In this manner, industry incumbents can become the victims of their own experience (e.g. Hamel, 1996; Hamel and Prahalad, 1994; reading 8.4). They lose the ability to question their own beliefs about the industry rules and therefore lose their ability to be innovative (see Chapter 2). Industry rule breaking therefore starts with mental frame breaking. Strategists striving to shape the rules must violate industry conventions by challenging their own cognitive preconceptions. Industry creation requires a significant amount of creativity.

Advocates of the industry creation perspective do not deny that in many industries developments are largely evolutionary. For an understanding of the dynamics in these industries, the industry evolution perspective offers a powerful explanatory 'lens.' However, these industries only followed an evolutionary path because no firms were creative and powerful enough to actively shape the direction of change. An evolutionary trajectory isn't a strategic given, but the result of a lack of strategy by the industry incumbents. Industry developments can be shaped, but it does require innovative companies (Baden-Fuller and Stopford, 1992; reading 8.2).

The question for the field of strategic management is, therefore, whether the future of industries evolves or can be created. Must firms conform to the environmental demands placed upon them or can they shape their own environment (e.g. Bettis and Donaldson, 1990)? Should the industry context be understood from a determinist or a voluntarist point of view (Astley and Van der Ven, 1983; Hrebiniak and Joyce, 1985; Wilson, 1992)? In short, strategists must come to terms with the paradox of compliance and choice (see Table 8.1).

	Industry Evolution Perspective	Industry Creation Perspective
Emphasis on	Compliance over choice	Choice over compliance
Industry changes	Uncontrollable evolutionary processes	Controllable creation processes
Change dynamics	Environment selects fit firms	Firm creates fitting environment
Firm success due to	Fitness to industry demands	Manipulation of industry demands
Industry malleability	Low, slow	High, fast
Normative implication	Play by the rules (adapt)	Change the rules (innovate)
Firm profitability	Industry-dependent	Firm-dependent
Point of view	Deterministic	Voluntaristic

TABLE 8.1
Industry evolution versus industry creation perspective

Defining the Issues: Rules and Recipes

Debates between people with a voluntaristic inclination and those with a more deterministic perspective, are not limited to the field of strategy. In many areas, thinkers are in disagreement about the malleability of the environment. Macroeconomists, for example, debate to what extent governments can influence economic growth, inflation and unemployment, sociologists wrangle about the ability of political and social action groups to change society and historians argue about the power of great individuals to shape the course of history. In all cases, it cannot be simply and unambiguously established how much impact individuals or organizations can have on their environments and vice versa. Therefore, assumptions must be made – a perspective must be taken on the question of malleability.

Two issues are central to this discussion on 'who shapes whom'. The first issue, as already indicated above, is that of *industry rules* (Prahalad and Doz, 1987). Industry rules are the demands dictated to the organization by the industry context, that limit the scope of economically rational behavior. In other words, industry rules stipulate what must be done to survive and thrive in the chosen line of business – they determine under what conditions the competitive game will be played. Failure to adhere to the rules leads to being selected out.

The industry rules arise from the structure of the industry (Porter, 1980, 1985; reading 5.1). All five forces can impose constraints on a firm's freedom of action. The main question for strategists is how strict and rigid these rules actually are. Are a firm's possibilities for maneuvering within the rules and changing the rules severely restricted, or should strategists be inspired by Napoleon's famous remark: 'Circumstances? I make circumstances!'?

The second issue in the debate is that of *industry recipes* (Spender, 1989). An industry recipe is a widely held perception with regard to the industry rules. In other words, an industry recipe is the cognitive map that people have about the structure and demands of an industry (see Chapter 2). Industry recipes usually develop over time through shared experiences and interaction. A common understanding of the rules of the game grows among those involved. The issue in this chapter is whether most of the perceived industry rules are 'real' – that is, rooted in the underlying economics of the industry – or merely conventions. Does the industry recipe reflect actual constraints or largely the constraints of habit?

EXHIBIT 8.1
CarMax Short Case

CARMAX: TO THE MAX!?

Picture this. After 150,000 miles (240,000 kilometers) of faithful service, your old car is ready to roll over and die. So you drive down the road to the local car dealer to look at the used cars on offer. As you kick the tires on the 50 vehicles on the lot – all of the same make – you suddenly hear a voice behind you: 'That one belonged to a little old lady. She hardly drove over 30mph with it.' Great, a used-car salesman. You're thrilled by the prospect of spending the rest of the day visiting other dealer's, listening to unlikely stories and haggling over prices.

Richard Sharp and Austin Ligon are counting on this story sending a shiver down your spine. In 1993 they founded CarMax, a used car retailing company with a twist. Realizing that most people hate the hassle and uncertainty that seem so inherent to buying a second hand car, Sharp and Ligon introduced a different retailing concept: the auto superstore. Similar to food and electronics superstores, the giant CarMax outlets offer an enormous choice of 500 to 1500 cars of all makes, each no more than five model years old, with a past of no more than 70,000 miles (112,000 km). To be salesworthy, a car must pass the extensive CarMax 110-point inspection program. CarMax does not sell bottom line used cars because the small margins on these items are not sufficient to cover all service-related expenses. And service there is: the showroom floor is scattered with touch-screen computer terminals in which customers can enter their preferences, and there are supervised playrooms for the kids. While the potential buyers make a test drive in the vehicle of their choice, the salesperson checks out whether CarMax's own financing subsidiary can give them an accreditation for a loan, according to the customers' wishes. When the customers return, they can sign up for an extended service plan with warranty that covers all mechanical and electrical parts. When the customers climb into their clean, shiny used car, ready to drive off, the salesperson snaps their picture with a Polaroid.

But probably the most important difference is that CarMax outlets offer no room for haggling, by using fixed prices for their vehicles. The salespersons receive a fixed commission per car, independent of the price of the vehicle. That is why CarMax calls them 'consultants', using their time to smooth the process for the customer, instead of using it for bargaining over prices. Potential customers do not have to fear getting stuck with a lemon: each car comes with a 30-day warranty and is always sold below NADA's (National Automotive Dealers Association) prices. Sharp himself says: 'Once you remove the price negotiation process, the salesperson becomes someone who can assist you in making the right purchase.'

Results so far seem to indicate that CarMax is on to something big. Customers are giving CarMax a 90 percent favorable rating, a level that most dealers can only dream of. In its first operational year, 1993, the 'pilot' outlet in Richmond, Virginia, alone turned over more than 4000 cars to the tune of $55m. By 1995 there were seven CarMax locations, with sales of $288m. Driven by this success, Sharp is aiming for a nationwide retail chain by the end of the decade, consisting of 55 outlets, generating approximately $3.3bn in revenues. Eventually, CarMax hopes to go abroad and introduce its auto superstores to other parts of the world, starting in Europe.

Richard Sharp and Austin Ligon are not the young penniless entre-preneurs who are stereotypically associated with 'frame-breaking' innovations. Sharp is the CEO of Circuit City stores, the largest chain of brand name consumer electronics in the US, and Ligon is Circuit City's senior vice president of corporate planning and automotive. The first CarMax outlet Richmond is less than a mile from Circuit City's 'big box' stores.

Sharp and Ligon had some convincing arguments for diversifying from electronics retailing (consumer electronics and computers) to used car retail-ing. The used-car market is the third largest market in the USA, after food and housing, but ahead of new cars. Total demand in the market for used cars is about $150bn a year. This demand is being boosted by all time high new car prices, on average $20,270 in 1995. The prices for used vehicles are signifi-cantly lower, with an average of $10,980 in 1995. Yet the profit margin per vehicle sold is almost the same, regardless of whether it is new or used. Furthermore, by selling used vehicles, CarMax can sell any brand it wants, without restrictions or commitments towards the producers or importers. The supply of used cars is tremendous due to the boom in leasing practices, each leasing company releasing its vehicles after just two or three years of use. Adding to this constant supply, CarMax buys its inventory from auctions, fleet holders (e.g. rental companies) and even from customers trading in their vehicles when they are looking for something else.

A $150 billion market, buoyant demand and a good bargaining position towards suppliers are all quite attractive, but could easily be overshadowed by cut-throat competition. However, Sharp and Ligon concluded that the compe-tition was heavily fragmented, and that there was no 'category killer' chain, such as Toys 'R' Us or Walmart, that could spoil the fun. The main competitors were relatively small car dealerships, usually with an exclusive contract to sell one auto maker's new products in a certain geographic area. To aid the selling of new cars, dealers accept trade-ins of various makes, which they in turn will try to sell. The average dealer in the US has about 150 used vehicles on offer, com-pared to CarMax's 500 to 1500. So far, the response by the big three auto makers in Detroit has not been to come to the rescue of their dealers. Officially, CarMax's entry into the business has been welcomed by the car manufacturers as a needed stimulus to improve the service quality in the dealerships.

Unfortunately for CarMax, it is hard to keep a good idea to yourself nowadays, and they have to deal with other entrants. Blockbuster Entertain-ment's Wayne Huizenga, a man who can only get excited when the stakes are high, intends to go nationwide with his AutoNation USA second-hand car retailing chain, after the successful start of two Florida sites in 1996. And there is more to come. Waad J. Nadhir, an established shopping-mall developer, intends to copy the CarMax concept with his CarChoice.

Of course, the question is whether the launching of CarMax and other secondhand vehicle megastores heralds the structural transformation of the used car retailing industry, or whether this is all a storm in a glass of water. Has CarMax fundamentally changed the rules of the game, to which all other retailers must now comply? Or can the traditional car dealerships continue on the same footing, surrendering a small segment to these newcomers? Alternatively, could the dealerships innovate themselves and try to find new methods for competing against the megastores? In other words, how much room do the dealerships have to manoeuvre? And what can CarMax do to make its concept the predominant formula? It was not at all certain how the industry would evolve in the coming years, but the score so far was clear: CarMax 7 – traditional dealers NADA.

Sources: *The Economist*, July 12, 1997; *Forbes*, February 10, 1997; *Stores*, June 1996

The Debate and the Readings

Few strategists like to hear that they have little influence over their industry and that they should play by the rules. This message is hardly inspiring, if not outright frustrating. And it definitely does not sell books. This might partially explain why few proponents of the industry evolution perspective have written for an audience of practicing managers. Most contributions to the strategic management literature by researchers taking an industry evolution view have been written in academic journals and are hardly comprehensible to outsiders. There are many excellent works, but none that are accessible enough to act as opening reading in this debate.

As a compromise, therefore, the debate in this chapter will be started off by an author who is strongly affiliated with the industry evolution perspective, but who is not fully in their camp. This author is Michael Porter, and the contribution selected is appropriately titled 'Industry Evolution.' In this reading taken from his classic book *Competitive Strategy*, Porter expands on his basic premises that were discussed in Chapter 5. In his view, a company's profitability is heavily influenced by the structure of the industry in which it competes. Some industries have a poor structure, making it difficult for even the best firms to make a profit. Other industries, however, have a more advantageous structure, making it much easier to show a good performance. In Porter's opinion, how the game of competition is played in each industry is largely determined by the underlying economics. The industry structure presents the strict rules to which companies must comply. As an industry's structure evolves, Porter sees two processes at work that determine which companies will survive and profit over the longer term. On the one hand, Porter recognizes 'natural selection' processes, whereby only the fittest survive and firms that are not suited to the new environment become extinct. For instance, Porter argues that the selection of fit companies is particularly strong as industries move into a mature phase of development: 'when growth levels off in an industry (. . .) there is a period of turmoil as intensified rivalry weeds out the weaker firms.' On the other hand, Porter also believes that companies can adapt themselves to changes in the industry's structure, although he emphasizes that they first must understand the drivers of change. So far, Porter's arguments fully coincide with the industry evolution perspective. However, besides compliance to the industry context, Porter mentions the possibility of 'co-makership' as well. Or, in his own terms, he believes that firms can have some influence on the evolution of the industry's structure. Thus, each company does have a certain degree of strategic freedom to determine its own fate, but ultimately the autonomous development of the industry structure is crucially important to the survival and profitability of the company.

To open the debate on behalf of the industry creation perspective, a reading by Charles Baden-Fuller and John Stopford has been selected, with the telling title 'The Firm Matters, Not the Industry.' In a direct reference to Porter, they state that their view 'contrasts sharply with the popular, but misguided, school of thought that believes that the fortune of a business is closely tied to its industry.' They point out that only a fraction of the differences in profitability between companies can be attributed to industry characteristics, while more than half of the profit variations are due to the choice of strategy. Their conclusion is that the given industry circumstances are largely unimportant – it's how a firm plays the game that matters. In their opinion, high profitability is not the consequence of complying with some preset rules, but the result of acting creatively and imaginatively. For instance, they challenge the widely held belief that high market share is important for profitability (Buzzell and Gale, 1987; reading 5.3). Nor do they agree that the competitive game dictates generic strategies, as Porter suggested in Chapter 5. They do not even believe that there is such a thing as a mature industry. In their view, the industry environment does not present any fixed rules, that can not be avoided or changed by innovative companies. Their advice, therefore, is to remain imaginative and to adopt approaches that counter traditional solutions.

To complement the initial arguments brought forward by the first discussants, three additional contributions have been included in this chapter. Reading 8.3 is the famous article 'The Population Ecology of Orga-nizations,' by Michael Hannan and John Freeman. This classic article was the first important work in a stream of literature, that is known under the label 'population ecology approach'. More so than Porter, population ecologists argue from an industry evolution perspective, drawing their inspiration from theories of biological evolution. They believe that to understand the pattern of survival and demise of *organizations*, it is useful to borrow concepts developed to understand the survival and demise of *organisms*. In biology, the authors stress, scientists have long been research-ing why certain members of a population of organisms survive environ-mental changes, while others do not. Two mechanisms seem to be at play simultaneously – *adaptation* and *selection*. Viewed at the level of the individual organisms, some are flexible enough to adapt themselves to new environmental circumstances, while other individuals do not have this ability. Viewed at the level of the entire population, however, among the variety of individuals there will usually be some that by chance fit the new circumstances, while others will never be suited to the changed environment. In other words, survivors are 'selected' from the population by environmental influences. Transferring these ideas to organizational studies, Hannan and Freeman argue that most management literature takes an adaptation view, while there are many reasons to doubt organizations' ability to learn and adapt to industry evolution. They believe that the environment's power to select is very strong and therefore that a population ecology approach can be very useful in understanding which organizations survive in the process of industry evolution. It is clear that in their perspective the industry matters, not the firm.

Reading 8.4 is 'Competing for the Future,' by Gary Hamel and C.K. Prahalad. In this contribution, taken from their highly influential book of the same name, Hamel and Prahalad go a step further than the arguments of Baden-Fuller and Stopford in Reading 8.2. While Baden-Fuller and Stopford argue that imaginative firms are free to choose their own future and not limited by any preset rules, Hamel and Prahalad believe that firms should proactively create the industries of the future and set the rules that others must follow. In their own words, 'in this race to the future there are drivers, passengers, and road kill . . . Those who drive industry revolution – companies that have a clear, premeditated view of where they want to take their industry and are capable of orchestrating resources inside and outside the company to get there first – will be handsomely rewarded.' With an indirect reference to Porter, Hamel and Prahalad criticize strategists who focus solely on competing within present industry structures, while paying little attention to the (re)writing of the rules for the industries' future. They conclude that 'conceiving of strategy as a quest to proactively configure nascent industries, or fundamentally reconfigure existing industries to one's own advantage, is a very different perspective than a view of strategy as positioning individual businesses and products within today's competitive environment.' They believe that managers should spend more time 'creating the future.'

The last contribution to this chapter is a thought-provoking reading by Brian Arthur, with the mysterious title 'Increasing Returns and the New World of Business.' Arthur is a well-known economist and in this reading he transfers some of the recent economic thinking on the development of industries to the area of business strategy. His point of view falls between the industry evolution and creation perspectives. He argues that in many industries companies have the ability to influence developments in the early stages of a new technological wave. But then something odd happens. Once a particular product, standard or technology gets ahead of the rest, however marginally, the market can tilt in its favor, causing it to move further ahead. This leads to a positive feedback loop, pushing the early front-runner further and further ahead. Early success leads to more and more success, which is referred to as *increasing returns*. Within a short period the further development of the industry is locked into a particular course, even if later better products, standards or technologies would emerge. This property, that economists call *path dependency*, is also known as the QWERTY phenomenon, after the well-known example of how the world has been locked into a standard keyboard layout ever since the early days of the typewriter. Therefore, Arthur concludes that firms in an increasing returns world can only really shape their environments during the incubation phase of the next technological wave. However, Arthur does point out that not all industries are characterized by increasing returns. In traditional smoke-stack industries, that process bulk resources into physical products, diminishing returns are more common. Increasing returns are typical for knowledge-based design and reproduction industries.

With so many competing opinions on the nature of the industry context, readers may now want to 'select the fittest one'. Or maybe readers will have to conclude that one view has rewritten the rules of competition in the strategy industry. Whichever way, it is up to individual readers to form their own judgement on how to deal with the paradox of compliance and choice.

8.1 Industry Evolution

By Michael Porter[1]

Structural analysis gives us a framework for understanding the competitive forces operating in an industry that are crucial to developing competitive strategy. It is clear, however, that industries' structures change, often in fundamental ways. Entry barriers and concentration have gone up significantly in the US brewing industry, for example, and the threat of substitutes has risen to put a severe squeeze on acetylene producers.

Industry evolution takes on critical importance for formulation of strategy. It can increase or decrease the basic attractiveness of an industry as an investment opportunity, and it often requires the firm to make strategic adjustments. Understanding the process of industry evolution and being able to predict change are important because the cost of reacting strategically usually increases as the need for change becomes more obvious and the benefit from the best strategy is the highest for the first firm to select it. For example, in the early post-war farm equipment business, structural

[1] Source: Reprinted with the permission of The Free Press, a Division of Macmillan, Inc., from *Competitive Strategy: Techniques for Analyzing Industries and Competitiors*, pp. 156–164, 184–188, by Michael E. Porter. Copyright © 1980 by The Free Press.

change elevated the importance of a strong exclusive dealer network backed by company support and credit. The firms that recognized this change first had their pick of dealers to choose from.

This article will present analytical tools for predicting the evolutionary process in an industry and understanding its significance for the formulation of competitive strategy.

Basic Concepts in Industry Evolution

The starting point for analyzing industry evolution is the framework of structural analysis (see chapter 5). Industry changes will carry strategic significance if they promise to affect the underlying sources of the five competitive forces; otherwise changes are important only in a tactical sense. The simplest approach to analyzing evolution is to ask the following question: Are there any changes occurring in the industry that will affect each element of structure? For example, do any of the industry trends imply an increase or decrease in mobility barriers? An increase or decrease in the relative power of buyers or suppliers? If this question is asked in a disciplined way for each competitive force and the economic causes underlying it, a profile of the significant issues in the evolution of an industry will result.

Although this industry-specific approach is the place to start, it may not be sufficient, because it is not always clear what industry changes are occurring currently, much less which changes might occur in the future. Given the importance of being able to predict evolution, it is desirable to have some analytical techniques that will aid in anticipating the pattern of industry changes we might expect to occur.

The Product Life Cycle

The grandfather of concepts for predicting the probable course of industry evolution is the familiar product life cycle. The hypothesis is that an industry passes through a number of phases or stages – introduction, growth, maturity, and decline – illustrated in Figure 8.1.1. These stages are defined by inflection points in the rate of growth of industry sales. Industry growth follows an S-shaped curve because of the process of innovation and diffusion of a new product. The flat introductory phase of industry growth reflects the difficulty of overcoming buyer inertia and stimulating trials of the new product. Rapid growth occurs as many buyers rush into the market once the product has proven itself successful. Penetration of the product's potential buyers is eventually reached, causing the rapid growth to stop and to level off to the underlying rate of growth of the relevant buyer group. Finally, growth will eventually taper off as new substitute products appear.

As the industry goes through its life cycle, the nature of competition will shift. I have summarized in Table 8.1.1 the most common predictions about how an industry will change over the life cycle and how this should affect strategy.

The product life cycle has attracted some legitimate criticism:

- The duration of the stages varies widely from industry to industry, and it is often not clear what stage of the life cycle an industry is in. This problem diminishes the usefulness of the concept as a planning tool.

- Industry growth does not always go through the S-shaped pattern at all. Sometimes industries skip maturity, passing straight from growth to decline. Sometimes industry growth revitalizes after a period of decline, as has occurred in the motorcycle and bicycle industries and recently in the radio broadcasting industry. Some industries seem to skip the slow takeoff of the introductory phase altogether.

- Companies can *affect* the shape of the growth curve through product innovation and repositioning, extending it in a variety of ways. If a company takes the life cycle as given, it becomes an undesirable self-fulfilling prophesy.

- The nature of competition associated with each stage of the life cycle is *different* for different industries. For example, some industries start out highly concentrated and stay that way. Others, like bank cash dispensers, are concentrated for a significant period and then become less so. Still others begin highly fragmented; of these some consolidate (automobiles) and some do not (electronic component distribution). The same divergent patterns apply to advertising, research and development (R&D) expenditures, degree of price competition, and most other industry characteristics. Divergent patterns such as these call into serious question the strategic implications ascribed to the life cycle.

The real problem with the product life cycle as a predictor of industry evolution is that it attempts to describe *one* pattern of evolution that will invariably occur. And except for the industry growth rate, there is little or no underlying rationale for why the competitive changes associated with the life cycle will happen. Since actual industry evolution takes so many different paths, the life cycle pattern does not always hold, even if it is a common or even the most common pattern of evolution. Nothing in the concept allows us to predict when it will hold and when it will not.

A Framework for Forecasting Evolution

Instead of attempting to describe industry evolution, it will prove more fruitful to look underneath the process to see what really drives it. Like any evolution, industries evolve because some forces are in motion that create incentives or pressures for change. These can be called *evolutionary processes*.

Every industry begins with an *initial structure* – the entry barriers, buyer

FIGURE 8.1.1
Stages of the life cycle

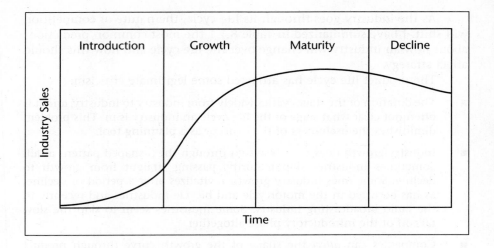

and supplier power, and so on that exist when the industry comes into existence. This structure is usually (though not always) a far cry from the configuration the industry will take later in its development. The initial structure results from a combination of underlying economic and technical characteristics of the industry, the initial constraints of small industry size, and the skills and resources of the companies that are early entrants. For example, even an industry like automobiles with enormous possibilities for economies of scale started out with labor-intensive, job-shop production operations because of the small volumes of cars produced during the early years.

The evolutionary processes work to push the industry toward its *potential structure*, which is rarely known completely as an industry evolves. Embedded in the underlying technology, product characteristics, and nature of present and potential buyers, however, there is a range of structures the industry might possibly achieve, depending on the direction and success of research and development, marketing innovations, and the like.

It is important to realize that instrumental in much industry evolution are the investment decisions by both existing firms in the industry and new entrants. In response to pressures or incentives created by the evolutionary process, firms invest to take advantage of possibilities for new marketing approaches, new manufacturing facilities, and the like, which shift entry barriers, alter relative power against suppliers and buyers, and so on. The luck, skills, resources, and orientation of firms in the industry can shape the evolutionary path the industry will actually take. Despite potential for structural change, an industry may not actually change because no firm happens to discover a feasible new marketing approach; or potential scale economies may go unrealized because no firm possesses the financial resources to construct a fully integrated facility or simply because no firm is inclined to think about costs. Because innovation, technological developments, and the identities (and resources) of the particular firms either in the industry or considering entry into it are so important to evolution, industry evolution will not only be hard to forecast with certainty but also an industry can potentially evolve in a variety of ways at a variety of different speeds, depending on the luck of the draw.

Evolutionary Processes

Although initial structure, structural potential, and particular firms' investment decisions will be industry-specific, we can generalize about what the important evolutionary processes are. There are some predictable (and interacting) dynamic processes that occur in industry in one form or another, though their speed and direction will differ from industry to industry:

- long-run changes in growth;

- changes in buyer segments served;

- buyer's learning;

- reduction of uncertainty;

- diffusion of proprietary knowledge;

- accumulation of experience;

- expansion (or contradiction) in scale;

- changes in input and currency costs;

- product innovation;

- marketing innovation;

- process innovation;

- structural change in adjacent industries;

- government policy change;

- entries and exits.

Key Relationships in Industry Evolution

In the context of this analysis, *how* do industries change? They do not change in a piecemeal fashion, because an industry is an *interrelated system*. Change in one element of an industry's structure tends to trigger changes in other areas. For example, an innovation in marketing might develop a new buyer segment, but serving this new segment may trigger changes in manufacturing methods, thereby increasing economies of scale. The firm reaping these economies first will also be in a position to start backward integration, which will affect power with suppliers – and so on. One industry change, therefore, often sets off a chain reaction leading to many other changes.

It should be clear from the discussion here that whereas industry evolution is always occurring in nearly every business and requires a strategic response, there is no one way in which industries evolve. Any single model for evolution such as the product life cycle should therefore

TABLE 8.1.1
Predictions of product life-cycle theories about strategy, competition, and performance

	Introduction	Growth	Maturity	Decline
Buyers and Buyer Behavior	High-income purchaser Buyer inertia Buyers must be convinced to try the product	Widening buyer group Consumer will accept uneven quality	Mass market Saturation Repeat buying Choosing among brands is the rule	Customers are sophisticated buyers of the product
Products and Product Change	Poor quality Product design and development key Many different product variations; no standards Frequent design changes Basic product designs	Products have technical and performance differentiation Reliability key for complex products Competitive product improvements Good quality	Superior quality Less product differentiation Standardization Less rapid product changes – more minor annual model changes Trade-ins become significant	Little product differentiation Spotty product quality
Marketing	Very high advertising/sales (a/s) Creaming price strategy High marketing costs	High advertising, but lower percent of sales than introductory Most promotion of ethical drugs Advertising and distribution key for nontechnical products	Market segmentation Efforts to extend life cycle Broaden line Service and deals more prevalent Packaging important Advertising competition Lower a/s	Low a/s and other marketing
Manufacturing and Distribution	Overcapacity Short production runs High skilled-labor content High production costs Specialized channels	Undercapacity Shift toward mass production Scramble for distribution Mass channels	Some overcapacity Optimum capacity Increasing stability of manufacturing process Lower labor skills Long production runs with stable techniques Distribution channels pare down their lines to improve their margins High physical distribution costs due to broad lines Mass channels	Substantial over-capacity Mass production Specialty channels

R&D	Changing production techniques			
Foreign Trade	Some exports	Significant exports Few imports	Falling exports Significant imports	No exports Significant imports
Overall Strategy	Best period to increase market share R&D, engineering are key functions	Practical to change price or quality image Marketing the key function	Bad time to increase market share, particularly if low-share company Having competitive costs becomes key Bad time to change price image or quality image 'Marketing effectiveness' key	Cost control key
Competition	Few companies	Entry Many competitors Lots of mergers and casualties	Price competition Shakeout Increase in private brands	Exits Fewer competitors
Risk	High risk	Risks can be taken here because growth covers them up	Cyclicality sets in	
Margins and Profits	High prices and margins Low profits Price elasticity to individual seller not as great as in maturity	High profits Highest profits Fairly high prices Lower prices than introductory phase Recession resistant High P/Es Good acquisition climate	Falling prices Lower profits Lower margins Lower dealer margins Increased stability of market shares and price structure Poor acquisition climate – tough to sell companies Lowest prices and margins	Low prices and margins Falling prices Prices might rise in late decline

be rejected. However, there are some particularly important relationships in the evolutionary process that I will examine here.

Will the Industry Consolidate?

It seems to be an accepted fact that industries tend to consolidate over time, but as a general statement, it simply is not true. In a broad sample of 151 four-digit US manufacturing industries in the 1963–72 time period, for example, 69 increased in four-firm concentration more than two percentage points, whereas 52 decreased more than two percentage points in the same period. The question of whether consolidation will occur in an industry exposes perhaps the most important interrelationships among elements of industry structure – those involving competitive rivalry, mobility barriers, and exit barriers.

Industry Concentration and Mobility Barriers Move Together

If mobility barriers are high or especially if they increase, concentration almost always increases. For example, concentration has increased in the US wine industry. In the standard-quality segment of the market, which represents much of the volume, the strategic changes (high advertising, national distribution, rapid brand innovation, and so on) have greatly increased barriers to mobility. As a result, the larger firms have gotten further ahead of smaller ones, and few new firms have entered to challenge them.

No Concentration Takes Place if Mobility Barriers are Low or Falling

Where barriers are low, unsuccessful firms that exit will be replaced by new firms. If a wave of exit has occurred because of an economic downturn or some other general adversity, there may be a temporary increase in industry concentration. But at the first signs that profits and sales in the industry are picking up, new entrants will appear. Thus a shakeout when an industry reaches maturity does not necessarily imply long-run consolidation.

Exit Barriers Deter Consolidation

Exit barriers keep companies operating in an industry even though they are earning subnormal returns on investment. Even in an industry with relatively high mobility barriers, the leading firms cannot count on reaping the benefits of consolidation if high exit barriers hold unsuccessful firms in the market.

Long-Run Profit Potential Depends on Future Structure

In the period of very rapid growth early in the life of an industry (especially after initial product acceptance has been achieved), profit levels are usually high. For example, growth in sales of skiing equipment was in excess of 20 percent per year in the late 1960s, and nearly all firms in the industry enjoyed strong financial results. When growth levels off in an industry, however, there is a period of turmoil as intensified rivalry weeds out the weaker firms. All firms in the industry may suffer financially during this adjustment period. Whether or not the remaining firms will enjoy above-average profitability will depend on the level of mobility barriers, as well as the other structural features of the industry. If mobility barriers are high or have increased as the industry has matured, the remaining firms in the industry may enjoy healthy financial results even in the new era of slower growth. If mobility barriers are low, however, slower growth probably means the end of above-average profits for the industry. Thus mature industries may or may not be as profitable as they were in their developmental period.

Changes in Industry Boundaries

Structural change in an industry is often accompanied by changes in industry boundaries. Industry evolution has a strong tendency to shift these boundaries. Innovations in the industry or those involving substitutes may effectively enlarge the industry by placing more firms into direct competition. Reduction in transportation cost relative to timber cost, for example, has made timber supply a world market rather than one restricted to continents. Innovations increasing the reliability and lowering the cost of electronic surveillance devices have put them into effective competition with security guard services. Structural changes making it easier for suppliers to integrate forward into the industry may well mean that suppliers effectively become competitors. Or buyers purchasing private label goods in large quantities and dictating product design criteria may become effective competitors in the manufacturing industry. Part of the analysis of the strategic significance of industry evolution is clearly an analysis of how industry boundaries may be affected.

Firms Can Influence Industry Structure

Industry structural change can be influenced by firms' strategic behavior. If it understands the significance of structural change for its position, the firm can seek to influence industry change in ways favorable to it, either through the way it reacts to strategic changes of competitors or in the strategic changes it initiates.

Another way a company can influence structural change is to be very sensitive to external forces that can cause the industry to evolve. With a head start, it is often possible to direct such forces in ways appropriate to the firm's position. For example, the specific form of regulatory changes can be influenced; the diffusion of innovations coming from outside the industry can be altered by the form that licensing or other agreements with innovating firms take; positive action can be initiated to improve the cost or supply of complementary products through providing direct assistance and help in forming trade associations or in stating their case to the government; and so on for the other important forces causing structural change. Industry evolution should not be greeted as a fait accompli to be reacted to, but as an opportunity.

8.2   The Firm Matters, Not the Industry

By Charles Baden-Fuller and John Stopford[1]

It is the firm that matters, not the industry. Successful businesses ride the waves of industry misfortunes; less successful business are sunk by them. This view contrasts sharply with the popular, but misguided, school of thought that believes that the fortune of a business is closely tied to its industry. Those who adhere to this view believe that some industries are intrinsically more attractive for investment than others. They (wrongly) believe that if a business is in a profitable industry, then its profits will be greater than if the business is in an unprofitable industry.

The Role of the Industry in Determining Profitability

Old views

■   Some industries are intrinsically more profitable than others.

■   In mature environments it is difficult to sustain high profits.

■   It is environmental factors that determine whether an industry is successful, not the firms in the industry.

New views

■   There is little difference in the profitability of one industry versus another.

■   There is no such thing as a mature industry, only mature firms; industries

---

[1] Source: This article has been adapted from chapter 2 of *Rejuvenating the Mature Business*, Routledge, 1992, pp. 13–34. Used with permission.

inhabited by mature firms often present great opportunities for the innovative.

■   Profitable industries are those populated by imaginative and profitable firms; unprofitable industries have unusually large numbers of uncreative firms.

This notion that there are 'good' and 'bad' industries is a theme that has permeated many strategy books. As one famous strategy writer put it:

> The state of competition in an industry depends on five basic competitive forces. . . . The collective strength of these forces determines the ultimate profit potential in the industry, where profit potential is measured in terms of long-run return on invested capital. . . . The forces range from intense in industries like tires, paper and steel – where no firm earns spectacular returns – to relatively mild like oil-field equipment and services, cosmetics and toiletries – where high returns are quite common.
>
> (Porter, 1980)

Unfortunately, the writer overstates his case, for the evidence does not easily support his claim. Choosing good industries may be a foolish strategy; choosing good firms is far more sensible. As noted in Table 8.2.1, recent statistical evidence does not support the view that the choice of industry is important. At best only 10 per cent of the differences in profitability between one business unit and another can be related to their choice of industry. By implication, nearly 90 per cent of profitability variations are not explained by the choice of industry, and *at least half appear to be attributable to the choice of strategy.* Put simply, the correct choice of strategy appears to be at least five times more important than the correct choice of industry.

Mature Industries Offer Good Prospects for Success

It is often stated that market opportunities are created rather than found. Thus market research would never have predicted the large potential of xerography, laptop computers, or the pocket cassette recorder. Leaps of faith may be required. By analogy, low-growth mature markets or troubled industries are arguably ones that may offer greater chances of rewards

Percentage of Business Units' Profitability Explained by	
Choice of industry	8.3 percent
Choice of strategy	46.4 percent
Parent company	0.8 percent
Not explained – random	44.5 percent

Abstracted from Rumelt (1991).

TABLE 8.2.1
The role of industry factors determining firm performance

than ones that appear to be glamorous and profitable. Our reasoning is simple. In general, profitable industries are more profitable because they are populated by more imaginative and more creative businesses. These businesses create an environment that attracts customers, grows the industry revenues, and makes the industry attractive. But creative and innovative businesses are also more fiercely competitive. To win in such environments may be difficult, as the pace of change may be rapid and the minimum standards high. In contrast, many less profitable industries are populated by sleepy, uncreative businesses that fail to innovate. In such environments, the potential for success by a creative newcomer is greater. The demands of competition may be less exacting and the potential for attracting customers is better.

We do not wish to overstate our case, but rather to force the reader to focus attention away from the mentality of labelling and prejudging opportunities based only on industry profitability. For example, outsiders often point to low-growth industries and suggest that the opportunities are less than those in high-growth industries. Yet the difference in growth rates may be dependent on the ability of businesses in these industries to be creative and innovative. Until Honda came, the motorcycle market was in steady decline. By their innovations – of new bicycles with attractive features sold at reasonable prices – the market was once again revived. Thus we suggest that the growth rate of the industry is a reflection of the kinds of businesses in the industry, not the intrinsic nature of the environment.

Large Market Share is the Reward, not the Cause of Success

We believe that many managers are mistaken in the value they ascribe to market share. A large share of the market is often the symptom of success, but it is not always its cause. Banc One and Cook achieved significant positions in their industries because they were successful. For these organizations the sequence of events was success followed by growth, which was then cemented into greater success. Banc One has been doing things differently from many of its competitors for many years. It emphasized operational efficiency and it quickly captured a significant position as a low cost, high quality data processor for other banks and financial service companies. It also emphasized service, in particular service to retail and commercial customers, which contrasted with the approach of many other banks that sought to compete solely on price or failed to appreciate what the customer really wanted. Mergers and growth have been an important part of Banc One's strategy, but in every case, the merged organizations have been changed to fit the philosophy of Banc One.

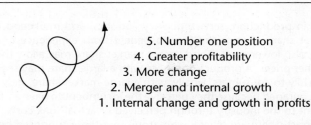

FIGURE 8.2.1
Upward spiral of creative business

5. Number one position
4. Greater profitability
3. More change
2. Merger and internal growth
1. Internal change and growth in profits

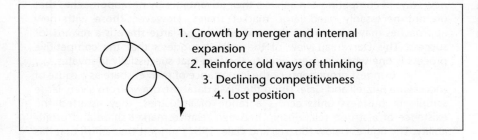

FIGURE 8.2.2
Downward spiral of unchanging business

1. Growth by merger and internal expansion
2. Reinforce old ways of thinking
3. Declining competitiveness
4. Lost position

Market Share and Profitability

Old views

■ Large market share brings lower costs and higher prices and so yields greater profits.

■ Small-share firms cannot challenge leaders.

New views

■ Large market share is the reward for efficiency and effectiveness.

■ If they do things better, small-share firms can challenge the leaders.

For creative organizations we see an upward spiral (Figure 8.2.1), and for organizations that are not creative, we see the cycles shown in Figure 8.2.2.

EXHIBIT 8.1.1
Market share and profitability

MARKET SHARE AND PROFITABILITY

There is a lively debate on the importance of market share in *explaining* business unit profitability. By *explaining* we do not mean *causing*. High market share could be the consequence of profitability, or the cause of both.

Those who advocate that large market share *leads* to greater profits point to the importance of several causal factors. First, large market share gives rise to the need to deliver large volumes of the service or good. These increased volumes in turn give rise to opportunities for costs savings by exploiting scale economies in production, service delivery, logistics, and marketing. Second, large market share permits the firm to benefit from experience or learning effects that also lower costs. Third, larger market share may allow the firm to charge higher prices. A product or service with a large share may seem intrinsically less risky to consumers. Finally, with a large market share, new entrants may be discouraged because they perceive the incumbent to have a substantial commitment to the industry through perceived or actual sunk costs.

In contrast, there are several who argue that these supposed benefits of large share are overrated. It is innovation that matters, innovators that realize new ways of competing can achieve their advantages by new approaches that do not necessarily need large market shares. However, those with new approaches may win market share, in which case large share is a reward for success. This Darwinian view of the market suggests that the competitive process is one where success goes to the firm that successfully innovates.

The strongest proponents of the importance of market share as a cause of success are Buzzell and Gale. Using the PIMS database drawn from a very large sample of business units across a range of industries, they asserted the existence of a strong relationship between relative market share and profitability. The figures below (Buzzell and Gale, 1987) suggest that a firm that has first rank in an industry will be more than twice as profitable as one of fourth rank.

Industry rank (by market share)	1	2	3	4	≤5
Pretax profits/sales (per cent)	12.7	9.1	7.1	5.5	4.5

However, these figures are misleading, for in a very large proportion of the industries studied, the firm with largest rank was *not* the most profitable. Often the picture is quite different; indeed according to the statistics published in Buzzell and Gale (1987) only 4 percent of the differences in profitability of one business unit versus another could be explained by differences in market share. Schmalensee (1985) in his extensive study of more than 400 firms in US manufacturing, found that less than 2 percent of the variations in profitability between one business and another could be explained by differences in market share. Market share effects appear to be relatively unimportant across a wide sample of industries. Of course, market share may be important in specific instances, but this only goes to reinforce our basic point that the critical success is dependent on getting the right strategy.

Our assertions run counter to much of what has been written in conventional books on strategy, and what is believed in many corporate boardrooms (see Exhibit 8.1.1). There is a common but incorrect belief among managers that being number one or number two in an industry gives the business unique advantages and that these are greatest in industries characterized by slow growth. With a large market share, it is often argued, the business can achieve lower costs and charge higher prices than its rivals. In slow-growth markets, it is argued, this may prove to be a decisive factor. This thinking ignores the importance of innovation, and believes that it is the size of the business that confers the advantage, not the new ways of doing things.

These false beliefs are widespread. They appear in many guises. At one extreme there are chief executives who say, 'We are only interested in industries where we hold a number one or number two position.' Such statements, if unaccompanied by an emphasis on innovation, will give out the wrong signal that high share will lead to success. At a more mundane level, managers are encouraged to write in their plans, 'We should dominate the industry and seek success by capturing a number one position.' Again, such statements are dangerous where the writer and reader believe that share by itself will bring success.

Growing market share is not the panacea for an organisation's ills, not even in mature slow-growing markets. The belief that gaining market share will lead to greater profitability comes from confusing cause and effect. Many successful businesses do have a large market share, but the causality is usually from success to share, not the other way. Successful businesses often (but not always) grow because they have discovered an overwhelming source of competitive advantage, such as quality at low cost. Such advantages can be used to displace the market share of even the most entrenched incumbents.

Competing Recipes

The crucial battles amongst firms in an industry are often centered around differing approaches to the market. Even in the so-called mature industries, where incumbent strategies have evolved and been honed over long time periods, it is new ideas that displace the existing leaders. Traditional wisdom has overstated the power of the generic approach (see Exhibit 8.2.2) and underplayed the role of innovation. Banc One established its premier position by rejecting conventional orthodoxy and emphasizing aspects hitherto neglected by industry leaders. Cook won in the steel castings industry by emphasizing quality and service to the customer. Hotpoint emphasized variety and quality in its approach to both the retailers and the final consumers. No single approach works well in all industries, but rather a multiple set of approaches. Here we emphasize the more fundamental point: the real competitive battles are fought out between firms with a diversity of approaches to the market.

EXHIBIT 8.2.2
The fallacy of the generic strategy

THE FALLACY OF THE GENERIC STRATEGY

It has been fashionable to suggest that there are a few *stable generic strategies* that offer fundamental choices to the organization. Typically these are described as a choice between a *low cost strategy* or a *differentiated strategy*. The low cost strategy involves the sacrifice of something – speed, variety, fashion, or even quality – in order to keep costs low, the lowest in the industry. In contrast, the high cost, differentiated strategy involves the focus on the very factors ignored by the others. The advocates of generic strategy make an (implicit or explicit) assertion: that the opposites cannot be reconciled. According to the generic strategists, it is not possible to be both low cost and high quality, or low cost and fashionable, or low cost and speedy. Trying to reconcile the opposites means being *stuck in the middle*. This, it is suggested, is the worst of both worlds.

Generic strategies are a fallacy. The best firms are striving all the time to reconcile the opposites. Cook did find a way to be both high quality and low cost, so, too, many of the other creative firms we studied. At any point in time, there are some combinations that have not yet been resolved, but firms strive to resolve them. Until McDonald's, the idea of consistency and low price for fast food had not been achieved on a large scale. McDonald's solved that problem. Benetton was but one of many firms that resolved the dilemma of fashion at low cost. Given the enormous rewards that accrue to those who can resolve the dilemmas of the opposites, it is not surprising that there are no *lasting or enduring generic strategies*.

The Dynamics of Competition in Traditional Industries

Old view

- Competition is based on firms following well-defined traditional (or generic) approaches to the market.

New view

- The real battles are fought among firms taking different approaches, especially those that counter yesterday's ideas.

Conclusions

Organizations that have become mature and suffer from poor performance typically view themselves as prisoners of their environment. Often their managers blame everyone but themselves for their poor performance. Labelling their environment as mature or hostile, they identify excess capacity, unfair competition, adverse exchange rates, absence of demand, and a host of other factors to explain why they are doing badly. Alas, too often these external factors are not really the causes of their demise but rather the symptoms of their failure. This conclusion is not so new; others have made the point before, yet their words appear to have been forgotten. Hall (1980) in an article in the *Harvard Business Review* noted

> Even a cursory analysis of the leading companies in the eight basic industries leads to an important observation: survival and prosperity are

possible even when the business environment turns hostile and industry trends change from favourable to unfavourable. In this regard, the casual advice frequently offered to competitors in basic industries – that is diversify, dissolve or be prepared for below average returns – seems over-simplified and even erroneous.

Of course all industries experience the roller coaster of economic upswings and downswings, but there are organizations that appear to ride the waves and others that appear to be submerged by them.

Those who are submerged all too often clutch at the wrong things in trying to escape their drowning. Seeking simple solutions such as industry recipes, the value of market share, or the need to amass large resources, they fail to appreciate the extent to which the rules of the game in an industry are always changing.

8.3   The Population Ecology of Organizations

By Michael Hannan and John Freeman[1]

Introduction

Analysis of the effects of the environment on organizational structure has moved to a central place in organizations theory and research in recent years. This shift has opened a number of exciting possibilities. As yet nothing like the full promise of the shift has been realized. We believe that the lack of development is due in part to a failure to bring ecological models to bear on questions that are preeminently ecological. We argue for a reformulation of the problem in population ecology terms.

Although there is a wide variety of ecological perspectives, they all focus on selection. That is, they attribute patterns in nature to the action of selection processes. The bulk of the literature on organizations subscribes to a different view, which we call the adaptation perspective. According to the adaptation perspective, subunits of the organization, usually managers or dominant coalitions, scan the environment for opportunities and threats, formulate strategic responses, and adjust organizational structure appropriately.

The adaptation perspective is seen most clearly in the literature on management. Contributors to it usually assume a hierarchy of authority and control that locates decisions concerning the organization as a whole at the top. It follows then, that organizations are affected by their environments

[1] Source: Reprinted from *American Journal of Sociology*, March 1977, Vol. 82, pp. 929–964. Used with permission from the University of Chicago Press.

according to the ways in which managers or leaders formulate strategies, make decisions, and implement them. Particularly successful managers are able either to buffer their organizations from environmental disturbances or to arrange smooth adjustments that require minimal disruption of organizational structure.

Clearly, leaders of organizations do formulate strategies and organizations do adapt to environmental contingencies. As a result at least some of the relationship between structure and environment must reflect adaptive behavior or learning. But there is no reason to presume that the great structural variability among organizations reflects only or even primarily adaptation.

There are a number of obvious limitations on the ability of organizations to adapt. That is, there are a number of processes that generate structural inertia. The stronger the pressures, the lower the organizations' adaptive flexibility and the more likely that the logic of environmental selection is appropriate. As a consequence, the issue of structural inertia is central to the choice between adaptation and selection models.

Inertial pressures arise from both internal structure arrangements and environmental constraints. A minimal list of the constraints arising from internal considerations follows.

- An organization's investment in plant, equipment, and specialized personnel constitutes assets that are not easily transferable to other tasks or functions. The ways in which such sunk costs constrain adaptation options are so obvious that they need not be discussed further.

- Organizational decision makers also face constraints on the information they receive. Much of what we know about the flow of information through organizational structures tells us that leaders do not obtain anything close to full information on activities within the organization and environmental contingencies facing the subunits.

- Internal political constraints are even more important. When organizations alter structure, political equilibria are disturbed. As long as the pool of resources is fixed, structural change almost always involves redistribution of resources across subunits. Such redistribution upsets the prevailing system of exchange among subunits (or subunit leaders). So at least some subunits are likely to resist any proposed reorganization. Moreover, the benefits of structural reorganization are likely to be both generalized (designed to benefit the organization as a whole) and long run. Any negative political response will tend to generate short-run costs that are high enough that organizational leaders will forgo the planned reorganization.

- Finally, organizations face restraints generated by their own history. Once standards of procedure and the allocation of tasks and authority have become the subject of normative agreement, the costs of change are greatly increased. Normative agreements constrain adaptation in at least two ways. First, they provide a justification and an organizing principle for those elements that wish to resist reorganization (i.e. they can resist in terms of a shared principle). Second, normative agreements preclude the serious consideration of many alternative responses. For example, few research-oriented universities seriously consider adapting to declining enrollments by eliminating the teaching function. To entertain this option would be to challenge central organizational norms.

The external pressures toward inertia seem to be at least as strong. They include at least the following factors.

- Legal and fiscal barriers to entry and exit from markets (broadly defined) are numerous. Discussions of organizational behavior typically emphasize barriers to entry (state-licensed monopoly positions, and so on). Barriers to exit are equally interesting. There are an increasing number of instances in which political decisions prevent firms from abandoning certain activities. All such constraints on entry and exit limit the breadth of adaptation possibilities.

- Internal constraints upon the availability of information are paralleled by external constraints. The acquisition of information about relevant environments is costly, particularly in turbulent situations where the information is most essential. In addition, the type of specialists employed by the organization constrains both the nature of the information it is likely to obtain and the kind of specialized information it can process and utilize.

- Legitimacy constraints also emanate from the environment. Any legitimacy an organization has been able to generate constitutes an asset in manipulating the environment. To the extent that adaptation (e.g. eliminating undergraduate instruction in public universities) violates the legitimacy claims, it incurs considerable costs. So external legitimacy considerations also tend to limit adaptation.

- Finally, there is the collective rationality problem. One of the most difficult issues in contemporary economics concerns general equilibria. If one can find an optimal strategy for some individual buyer or seller in a competitive market, it does not necessarily follow that there is a general equilibrium once all players start trading. More generally, it is difficult to establish that a strategy that is rational for a single decision maker will be rational if adopted by a large number of decision makers.

A number of these inertial pressures can be accommodated within the adaptation framework. That is, one can modify and limit the perspective in order to consider choices within the constrained set of alternatives. But to do so greatly limits the scope of one's investigation. We argue that in order to deal with the various inertial pressures the adaptation perspective must be supplemented with a selection orientation.

Population Thinking in the Study of Organization-Environment Relations

The comparison of unit choice facing the organizational analyst with that facing the bioecologist is instructive. To oversimplify somewhat, ecological analysis is conducted at three levels: individual, population, and community.

Events at one level almost always have consequences at other levels. Despite this interdependence, population events cannot be reduced to individual events (since individuals do not reflect the full genetic variability of the population) and community events cannot be simply reduced to population events. Both the latter employ a population perspective that is not appropriate at the individual level.

The situation faced by the organizations analyst is more complex. Instead of three levels of analysis, he faces at least five: (1) members, (2) subunits, (3) individual organizations, (4) populations of organizations, and (5) communities of (populations of) organizations. Levels 3–5 can be seen as corresponding to the three levels discussed for general ecology, with the individual organization taking the place of the individual organism. The added complexity arises because organizations are more nearly decomposable into constituent parts than are organisms. Individual members and subunits may move from organization to organization in a manner that has no parallel in nonhuman organization.

Instances of theory and research dealing with the effects of environments on organizations are found at all five levels. But, the common focus is on *the* organization and *its* environment. In fact, this choice is so widespread that there appears to be a tacit understanding that individual organizations are the appropriate units for the study of organization-environment relations.

We use the term *population* to refer to aggregates of organizations rather than members. Populations of organizations must be alike in some respect; that is, they must have some unit character. Unfortunately, identifying a population of organizations is no simple matter. The ecological approach suggests that one focus on common fate with respect to environmental variations. Since all organizations are distinctive, no two are affected identically by any given exogenous shock. Nevertheless, we can identify classes of organizations that are relatively homogeneous in terms of environmental vulnerability. Notice that the populations of interest may change somewhat from investigation to investigation depending on the analyst's concern. Populations of organizations referred to are not immutable objects in nature but are abstractions useful for theoretical purposes.

Taking our lead from distinguished ecologists, we suggest that a population ecology of organizations must seek to understand the distributions of organizations across environmental conditions and the limitations on organizational structures in different environments, and more generally seek to answer the question, Why are there so many kinds of organizations? Phrasing the question in this way opens the possibility of applying a rich variety of formal models to the analysis of the effects of environmental variations on organizational structure.

Hawley's formulation of Human Ecology

We begin with Hawley's classic formulation of human ecology. However, we recognize that ecological theory has progressed enormously since sociologists last systematically applied ideas from bioecology to social organization. None the less, Hawley's theoretical perspective remains a very useful point of departure. In particular we concentrate on the principle of isomorphism. This principle asserts that there is a one-to-one correspondence between structural elements of social organization and those units that mediate flows of essential resources into the system. It explains the variations in organizational forms in equilibrium. But any observed isomorphism can arise from purposeful adaptation of organizations to the common constraints they face or because nonisomorphic organizations are selected against. Surely both processes are at work in most social systems. We believe that the organizations literature has emphasized the former to the exclusion of the latter.

We suspect that careful empirical research will reveal that for wide classes of organizations there are very strong inertial pressures on structure arising both from internal arrangements (e.g. internal politics) and the environment (e.g. public legitimation of organizational activity). To claim otherwise is to ignore the most obvious feature of organizational life. Failing churches do not become retail stores; nor do firms transform themselves into churches. Even within broad areas of organizational action, such as higher education and labor union activity, there appear to be substantial obstacles to fundamental structural change. Research is needed on this issue. But until we see evidence to the contrary, we will continue to doubt that the major features of the world of organizations arise through learning or adaptation. Given these doubts, it is important to explore an evolutionary explanation of the principle of isomorphism. That is, we wish to embed the principle of isomorphism within an explicit selection framework.

Lotka-Volterra Models

In order to add selection processes we propose a competition theory using Lotka-Volterra models. This theory relies on growth models that appear suitable for representing both organizational development and the growth of populations of organizations. Recent work by bioecologists on Lotka-Volterra systems yields propositions that have immediate relevance for the study of organization-environment relations. These results concern the effects of changes in the number and mixture of constraints upon systems with regard to the upper bound of the diversity of forms of organization. We propose that such propositions can be tested by examining the impact of varieties of state regulation both on size distributions and on the diversity of organizational forms within broadly defined areas of activity (e.g. medical care, higher education, and newspaper publishing).

A more important extension of Hawley's work introduces dynamic considerations. The fundamental issue here concerns the meaning of isomorphism in situations in which the environment to which units are adapted is changing and uncertain. Should 'rational' organizations attempt to develop specialized isomorphic structural relations with one of the possible environmental states? Or should they adopt a more plastic strategy and institute more generalized structural features? The isomorphic principle does not speak to these issues.

We suggest that the concrete implication of generalism for organizations is the accumulation and retention of varieties of excess capacity. To retain the flexibility of structure required for adaptation to different environmental outcomes requires that some capabilities be held in reserve and not committed to action. Generalists will always be outperformed by specialists who, with the same levels of resources, happen to have hit upon their optimal environment. Consequently, in any cross section the generalists will appear inefficient because excess capacity will often be judged waste. None the less, organizational slack is a pervasive feature of many types of organizations. The question then arises, What types of environments favor generalists? Answering this question comprehensively takes one a long way toward understanding the dynamic of organization-environment relations.

Levins's Fitness-Set Theory

We begin addressing this question in the suggestive framework of Levins's fitness-set theory. This is one of a class of recent theories that relate the nature of environmental uncertainty to optimal levels of structural specialism. Levins argues that along with uncertainty one must consider the grain of the environment or the lumpiness of environmental outcomes. The theory indicates that specialism is always favored in stable or certain environments. When the environment shifts uncertainly among states that place very different demands on the organization, and the duration of environmental states is short relative to the life of the organization (variation is fine grained), populations of organizations that specialize will be favored over those that generalize. This is because organizations that attempt to adapt to each environmental outcome will spend most of their time adjusting structure and very little time in organizational action directed at other ends.

We doubt that many readers will dispute the contention that failure rates are high for new and/or small organizations. However, much of the sociological literature and virtually all of the critical literature on large organizations tacitly accepts the view that such organizations are not subject to strong selection pressures. While we do not yet have the empirical data to judge this hypothesis, we can make several comments. First, we do not dispute that the largest organizations individually and collectively exercise strong dominance over most of the organizations that constitute their environments. But it does not follow from the observation that such organizations are strong in any one period that they will be strong in every period. Thus, it is interesting to know how firmly embedded are the largest and most powerful organizations. Consider the so called Fortune 500, the largest publicly owned industrial firms in the United States. We contrasted the lists for 1955 and 1975 (adjusting for pure name changes). Of those on the list in 1955, only 268 (53.6 percent) were still listed in 1975. One hundred twenty-two had disappeared through merger, 109 had slipped off the '500,' and one (a firm specializing in Cuban sugar!) had been liquidated. The number whose relative sales growth caused them to be dropped from the list is quite impressive in that the large number of mergers had opened many slots on the list. So we see that whereas actual liquidation was rare for the largest industrial firms in the United States over a 20-year period, there was a good deal of volatility with regard to position in this pseudo-dominance structure because of both mergers and slipping sales.

Second, the choice of time perspective is important. Even the largest and most powerful organizations fail to survive over long periods. For example, of the thousands of firms in business in the United States during the Revolution, only 13 survive as autonomous firms and seven as recognizable divisions of firms. Presumably one needs a longer time perspective to study the population ecology of the largest and most dominant organizations.

Third, studying small organizations is not such a bad idea. The sociological literature has concentrated on the largest organizations for obvious design reasons. But if inertial pressures on certain aspects of structure are strong enough, intense selection among small organizations may greatly constrain the variety observable among large organizations. At least some elements of structure change with size, and the pressure toward inertia should not be overemphasized. None the less we see much value in studies of the organizational life cycle that would inform us as to which aspects of structure get locked in during which phases of the cycle. For example, we conjecture that a critical period is that during which the organization grows beyond the control of a single owner/manager. At this time the manner in which authority is delegated, if at all, seems likely to have a lasting impact on organizational structure. This is the period during which an organization becomes less an extension of one or few dominant individuals and more an organization *per se* with a life on its own. If the selection pressures at this point are as intense as anecdotal evidence suggests they are, selection models will prove very useful in accounting for the varieties of forms among the whole range of organizations.

The optimism of the previous paragraph should be tempered by the realization that when one examines the largest and most dominant organizations, one is usually considering only a small number of organizations. The smaller the number, the less useful are models that depend on the type of random mechanisms that underlie population ecology models.

Fourth, we must consider what one anonymous reader, caught up in the spirit of our paper, called the antieugenic actions of the state in saving firms such as Lockheed from failure. This is a dramatic instance of the way in which large dominant organizations can create linkages with other large and powerful ones so as to reduce selection pressures. If such moves are effective, they alter the pattern of selection. In our view the selection pressure is bumped up to a higher level. So instead of individual organizations failing, entire networks fail. The general consequence of a large number of linkages of this sort is an increase in the instability of the entire system, and therefore we should see boom and bust cycles of organizational outcomes. Selection models retain relevance, then, when the systems of organizations are tightly coupled.

8.4   Competing for the Future

By Gary Hamel and C.K. Prahalad [1]

We are standing on the verge, and for some it will be the precipice, of a revolution as profound as that which gave birth to modern industry. It will be the environmental revolution, the genetic revolution, the materials revolution, the digital revolution, and, most of all, the information revolution. Entirely new industries, now in their gestation phase, will soon be born. Such prenatal industries include microrobotics – miniature robots built from atomic particles that could, among other things, unclog sclerotic arteries; machine translation telephone switches and other devices that will provide real-time translation between people conversing in different languages; digital highways into the home that will offer instant access to the world's store of knowledge and entertainment; urban underground automated distribution systems that will reduce traffic congestion; 'virtual' meeting rooms that will save people the wear and tear of air travel; biomimetic materials that will duplicate the wondrous properties of materials found in the living world; satellite-based personal communicators that will allow one to 'phone home' from anywhere on the planet; machines capable of emotion, inference, and learning that will interact with human beings in entirely new ways; and bioremediation – custom designed organisms – that will help clean up the earth's environment.

Existing industries – education, health care, transportation, banking, publishing, telecommunications, pharmaceuticals, retailing, and others – will be profoundly transformed. Cars with on-board navigation and collision avoidance systems, electronic books and personally tailored multimedia educational curricula, surgeries performed in isolated locales by a remote-controlled robot, and disease prevention via gene replacement therapy are just some of the opportunities that are emerging to reshape existing products, services, and industries.

Many of these mega-opportunities represent billions of dollars in potential future revenues. One company has estimated the potential market for information services in the home, via interactive TV, to be worth at least $120 billion per year in 1992 dollars – home video ($11 billion), home catalog shopping ($51 billion), video games ($4 billion), broadcast advertising ($27 billion), other information services ($9 billion), and more. Many of these mega-opportunities have the potential to fundamentally transform the way we live and work, in much the same way that the telephone, car, and airplane transformed twentieth-century lifestyles.

Each of these opportunities is also inherently global. No single nation or region is likely to control all the technologies and skills required to turn

[1] Source: This article was adapted with permission from chapter 2 of *Competing for the Future*, Harvard Business School Press, Boston, 1994.

these opportunities into reality. Markets will emerge at different speeds around the world, and any firm hoping to establish a leadership role will have to collaborate with and learn from leading-edge customers, technology providers, and suppliers, wherever they're located. Global distribution reach will be necessary to capture the rewards of leadership and fully amortize associated investments.

The future is now. The short term and the long term don't abut one another with a clear line of demarcation five years from now. The short term and long term are tightly intertwined. Although many of tomorrow's mega-opportunities are still in their infancy, companies around the world are, at this moment, competing for the privilege of parenting them. Alliances are being formed, competencies are being assembled, and experiments are being conducted in nascent markets – all in hopes of capturing a share of the world's future opportunities. In this race to the future there are drivers, passengers, and road kill. (Road kill, an American turn of phrase, is what becomes of little creatures who cross the highway in the path of an on-coming vehicle.) Passengers will get to the future, but their fate will not be in their own hands. Their profits from the future will be modest at best. Those who drive industry revolution – companies that have a clear, premeditated view of where they want to take their industry and are capable of orchestrating resources inside and outside the company to get there first – will be handsomely rewarded.

Thus, the question of which companies and countries create the future is far from academic. The stakes are high. The wealth of a firm, and of each nation in which it operates, largely depends on its role in creating tomorrow's markets and its ability to capture a disproportionate share of associated revenues and profits.

Perhaps you have visited the Henry Ford Museum at Greenfield Village in Dearborn, Michigan. Although the home of Ford Motor Co.'s world headquarters, Dearborn's additional claim to fame is Greenfield Village and the museum where you can see the industrial history of the United States. The exhibits are a testimony to pioneers who created new industries and revolutionized old ones: Deere, Eastman, Firestone, Bell, Edison, Watson, the Wright brothers and, of course, Ford. It was the foresight of these pioneers that created the industries that created the unprecedented prosperity that created the American lifestyle. Any visitor strolling through the museum who has enjoyed the material comforts of a middle-class American lifestyle can't help but recognize the enormous debt he or she owes to these industrial pioneers. Similarly, any German citizen owes much to the pioneers who built that country's innovative, globe-spanning chemical companies, world-class machine tool industry, and automakers that set the benchmarks for excellence for nearly a century. The success of Japanese firms in redefining standards of innovation and performance in the electronics and automobile industries propelled Japan from an industrial also-ran into a world economic superpower and paid for all those Waikiki holidays and Louis Vuitton handbags.

Failure to anticipate and participate in the opportunities of the future impoverishes both firms and nations. Witness Europe's concern over its abysmal performance in creating high-wage jobs in new information technology-related businesses, or Japan's worry over the inability of its financial institutions to capture the high ground of innovation and new business creation, or America's anxiety that Japanese companies may steal a march in the commercialization of superconductivity. Even protectionist-minded politicians realize that a nation that can do little more than protect the industries of the past will lose its economic standing to countries that help create the industries of the future.

The future is not an extrapolation of the past. New industrial structures will supersede old industrial structures. Opportunities that at first blush seem evolutionary will prove to be revolutionary. Today's new niche markets will turn out to be tomorrow's mass markets Today's leading edge science will become tomorrow's household appliance. At one time IBM described the personal computer as an 'entry system' – the expectation was that anyone buying a PC would move up to more powerful computers, and that PCs could happily coexist with mainframes. Ten years later, desktop workstations and local client-server computers were displacing mainframes from more and more applications. Although today's wireless telephones – both cellular and cordless – may seem no more than an adjunct to traditional tethered telephones, in ten years all wired phones will likely seem anachronistic. Twenty years ago few observers expected mutual funds to significantly erode the 'share of savings' captured by banks and savings and loans. But savers became investors and by 1992, mutual funds in the United States represented 96 percent of the money that private investors put into the stock market. Mutual funds accounted for 11.4 percent of total financial assets in the United States, up from only 2.0 percent in 1975, whereas the share taken by commercial banks and savings and loans fell from 56.2 percent in 1975 to 37.3 percent in 1992. Again, there is no way to create the future, no way to profit from the future, if one cannot imagine it.

To compete successfully for the future, senior managers must first understand just how competition for the future is different from competition for the present. The differences are profound. They challenge the traditional perspectives on strategy and competition. We will see that competing for the future requires not only a redefinition of strategy, but also a redefinition of top management's role in creating strategy.

Competition for Today versus Competition for Tomorrow

Pick up a strategy textbook or marketing handbook and the focus will almost certainly be on competition within extant markets. The tools of segmentation analysis, industry structure analysis, and value chain analysis are eminently useful in the context of a clearly defined market, but what help are they when the market doesn't yet exist? Within an existing market most of the rules of competition have already been established: what price-performance trade-offs customers are willing to make, which channels have proved most efficient, the ways in which products or services can be differentiated, and what is the optimal degree of vertical integration. Yet in emerging opportunity arenas like genetically engineered drugs, multimedia publishing, and interactive television, the rules are waiting to be written. (In existing industries, the rules are waiting to be rewritten.) This vastly complicates the business of making strategic choices. So how is the context for strategy making different when the focus is on tomorrow rather than today, and when there is little or no clarity about industry structure and customer preferences?

Market Share versus Opportunity Share

Strategy researchers and practitioners have focused much attention on the problem of getting and keeping market share. For most companies, market share is the primary criterion for measuring the strength of a business's strategic position. But what is the meaning of market share in markets that barely exist? How can one maximize market share in an industry where the product or service concept is still underdefined, where customer segments have yet to solidify, and customer preferences are still poorly understood?

Competition for the future is competition for opportunity share rather than market share. It is competition to maximize the share of future opportunities a company could potentially access within a broad opportunity arena, be that home information systems, genetically engineered drugs, financial services, advanced materials, or something else.

The question that must be answered by every company is, given our current skills, or competencies as we will call them, what share of future opportunities are we likely to capture? This question leads to others: which new competencies would we have to build, and how would our definition of our 'served market' have to change, for us to capture a larger share of future opportunities? Whether for a country or a company, the issue is much the same: how to attract and strengthen the skills that form the competencies (e.g. opto-electronics, biomimetics, genetics, systems integration, financial engineering) that provide a gateway to future opportunities.

To gain a disproportionate share of future profits it is necessary to possess a disproportionate share of the requisite competencies. Because such competencies represent the patient and persistent accumulation of intellectual capital rather than a God-given endowment, governments can legitimately play a role in strengthening such competencies (through educational policy, tax incentives, recruitment of inward investment, government-sanctioned private-sector joint ventures, etc.). Singapore, for example, has employed just such means to enhance the range and quality of nationally resident competencies. But to know which competencies to build, policy-makers and corporate strategists must be prescient about the broad shape of tomorrow's opportunities. Top management must be just as obsessed with maximizing opportunity share as with maximizing market share. As we will see, this means a commitment to build competence leadership in new areas, long before the precise form and structure of future markets comes completely into view.

Business Units versus Corporate Competencies

Competition for the future is not product versus product or business versus business, but company versus company – what we term 'interfirm competition.' This is true for several reasons. First, because future opportunities are unlikely to fit neatly within existing SBU boundaries, competing for the future must be a corporate responsibility, and not just the responsibility of individual business unit heads. (This responsibility may be exercised by a group of corporate officers or, preferably, a cohort of SBU heads working horizontally across the organization.) Second, the competencies needed to access the new opportunity arena may well be spread across a number of business units, and it is up to the corporation to bring these competencies together at the appropriate point within the organization. Third, the investment and timeframe required to build the new competencies necessary to access tomorrow's markets may well tax the resources and patience of a single business unit.

It is important that top managers view the firm as a portfolio of competencies, for they must ask, 'Given our particular portfolio of competencies, what opportunities are we uniquely positioned to exploit?' The answer points to opportunity arenas that other firms, with different competence endowments, may find difficult to access. For example, it would be hard to imagine any other firm than Eastman Kodak creating a product like Photo-CD, which required an in-depth understanding of both chemical film and electronic imaging competencies. Canon may understand electronic imaging and Fuji may understand film, but only Kodak had a deep understanding of both.

So the question for top managers is, 'How do we orchestrate all the resources of the firm to create the future?' This was the question George Fisher faced when he left Motorola to become Kodak's new chief executive. At IBM, Lou Gerstner put together a top team to look for transcendent opportunities. Given IBM's still impressive set of competencies, the question was, 'What can we do that other companies might find difficult to do?' Companies like Matsushita and Hewlett-Packard, long champions of bottom-up innovation and business unit autonomy, have recently been searching for opportunities that blend the skills of multiple business units. Even Sony, which has traditionally granted near total autonomy to individual product development teams, has realized that more and more of its products must function as part of complex systems. It has therefore moved to restructure its audio, video, and computer groups for better coordination of new product development.

Creating the future often requires that a company build new core competencies, competencies that typically transcend a single business unit – both in terms of the investment required and the range of potential applications. Within Sharp, for example, it is not up to each business unit to decide how much to invest in perfecting flat screen displays. Sharp competes as a corporation against Toshiba, Casio, and Sony to build world leadership in this area.

The sheer size, scope, and complexity of future opportunities may also require a corporate rather than an individual unit perspective. Mega-opportunities don't yield easily to 'skunk works' or undirected entrepreneurship. A lone employee with a bit of free time and access to a small slush fund may create Post-it Notes but is unlikely to bring the interpreting telephone from conception to reality or make much progress on creating a new computing architecture. Consistent, focused competence-building requires something more than 'thriving on chaos.'

Stand-Alone versus Integrated Systems

Most textbooks on the management of innovation and new product development assume that the company controls most of the resources needed for the commercialization of that innovation. Such an assumption is increasingly likely to be wrong. Many of the most exciting new opportunities require the integration of complex systems rather than innovation around a stand-alone product. Not only does no single business unit have all the necessary capabilities, neither does a single company or country. Few companies can create the future single-handedly; most need a helping hand. Motorola, IBM, and Apple banded together to create a new semiconductor-based computer architecture. Hoping to take advantage of the potential convergence between the videogame industry and the telecommunications industry, AT&T has formed partnerships with, or taken small equity stakes in, a number of computer game makers. Even Boeing has often found it necessary to reach out to foreign partners for the development of its next-generation aircraft.

The need to bring together and harmonize widely disparate technologies, to manage a drawn-out standards-setting process, to conclude alliances with the suppliers of complementary products, to co-opt potential rivals, and to access the widest possible array of distribution channels, means that competition is as much a battle between competing and often overlapping coalitions as it is a battle between individual firms. Competition for the future is both intercorporate and intercoalition.

Speed versus Perseverance

Yet another way in which competition for the future is different from competition for the present is the timeframe. Today speed is of the essence. Product life cycles are getting shorter, development times are getting tighter, and customers expect almost instantaneous service. Yet the relevant timeframe for exploring and conquering a new opportunity arena may be 10 years, 20 years, or even longer. AT&T first built a prototype of a videophone in its labs in 1939, first demonstrated a videophone to the public at the New York World's Fair in 1964, and finally introduced a model for home use in 1992, 53 years after its first prototype. And even now, video telephony has yet to become a mass market product. Marc Porat, president and CEO of

General Magic, a company that is developing the software for tomorrow's personal communication devices, believes it may take a decade or more to turn his company's vision of intelligent, ubiquitous, mobile personal communications into a reality. Leadership in fundamentally new industries is seldom built in anything less than 10 or 15 years, suggesting that perseverance may be just as important as speed in the battle for the future.

Obviously, no company is likely to persevere for 20 years unless it has a deep, visceral commitment to the particular opportunity. JVC, a subsidiary of Matsushita and the world leader in VCRs, began developing videotape competencies in the late 1950s and early 1960s, yet it wasn't until the late 1970s, nearly 20 years later, that JVC hit the jackpot with its VHS-standard machines. What keeps a company going for this length of time? Just what did JVC see in the VCR, or AT&T in the video telephone, or Apple Computer in the Lisa and then the Macintosh, that compelled them to pick themselves up time and time again when they stumbled on the inevitable hurdles, and keep pressing on toward the finish line? What they saw was the potential to deliver new and profound customer benefits. For JVC, it was the desire to 'take control [of program scheduling] away from the broadcasters and give it back to the viewers.' An engineer would term this 'time-shift,' but a technical description of the opportunity dramatically underplays its potential impact on lifestyles. Such commitment was also evident at Apple (making computers user friendly), at Ford in its early years (putting a car in every garage), at Boeing (bringing air travel to the masses), at CNN (providing the news around the clock), and at Wal-Mart (offering friendly service and rock-bottom prices to rural Americans).

Organizational commitment and perseverance are driven by the desire to make a difference in people's lives – the bigger the difference, the deeper the commitment. This suggests another difference between competition for the future and competition for the present, namely, the prospect of making an impact, rather than the certitude of immediate financial returns. In contrast, strategic moves within the confines of existing markets are likely to be predicated on traditional financial analysis. But this is not possible in the early stages of competition for the future. No one in the early 1960s could have produced a meaningful set of pro formas around the VCR opportunity. By the early 1970s, when one might have legitimately made a stab at developing a business case, it was too late for anyone who had not been working on videotape competencies since the early 1960s to catch up without help from one of the pioneers.

This is not to say that commitment to a new opportunity arena is based solely on gut feeling, or that companies at work to create the future are not hoping for substantial financial rewards. A commitment substantial enough to beget the perseverance required to create the future must be based on something more than a hunch. There are ways of judging the potential impact of a market-creating innovation that may still be many years in the future. Questions to consider might include: How many people will be affected by this innovation? How valuable will they find this innovation? What is the potential scope for the application of this innovation? In the case of the VCR, there were a host of specific indicators one might have considered: How many people had televisions? How fast was the penetration of televisions in the home growing? How many hours did the average person watch television? How often were they away when some potentially interesting program was being broadcast? How often were they forced to choose between two appealing shows broadcast simultaneously? Were there programs they would like to watch more than once? Would they find it more convenient to watch movies at home than at the cinema? Would movie studios and other software providers be willing to release movies not shown on TV as prerecorded software? Might video-cameras be attractive to consumers? And so on.

There should be no mushy-headed wishfulness involved in competing for the future. The absence of a business case does not mean that one commits to a whopping great investment in some hair-brained scheme. As we will see, the investment commitments in the early stages of competition for the future may be quite modest; small as they may be, however, the emotional and intellectual commitment to the future needs to be near absolute. Steve Jobs and Steve Wozniak had virtually no money, but their commitment to creating a computer for every 'man, woman, and child' was unshakable.

One of President Reagan's favorite stories provides an illustration. Waking up to her tenth birthday, a young farm girl rises before the sun and runs out to the barn, hoping her parents have bought her a pony. She flings open the barn door, but in the dim light can see no pony, just mounds of horse manure. Being an optimist she declares, 'With all this manure around, there must be a pony in here somewhere.' Similarly, companies that create the future say to themselves, 'With all this potential customer benefit, there must be a way to make some money in here somewhere.' A company that cannot commit emotionally and intellectually to creating the future, even in the absence of a financially indisputable business case, will almost certainly end up as a follower.

Think of the people who left Europe in the nineteenth century or Asia in the twentieth century to start a new life in the United States. At the outset of their journeys, few immigrants could have foretold exactly when and how they would achieve economic success in the new world, yet they set out for the 'land of opportunity' nevertheless. More than that, many of them willingly accepted great hardship during the journey itself. The important point is that the commitment to be a pioneer precedes an exact calculation of financial gain. A company that waits around for the numbers to 'add up' will be left flat-footed in the race to the future. Without a clear-eyed view of the ultimate prize, a company is all too likely to abandon the race when unexpected hazards are encountered en route. Nevertheless, as we will emphasize again and again, a company must ultimately find a profitable route to the future.

Structured versus Unstructured Arenas

We now come to what are the two most important ways in which competition for the future is different from competition for the present: (1) It often takes place in 'unstructured' arenas where the rules of competition have yet to be written, and (2) it is more like a triathlon than a 100-meter sprint. We will see that these differences demand a very different way of thinking about strategy and the role of senior management.

Some industries are more 'structured' than others, in that the rules of competition are more clear-cut, product concepts better defined, industry boundaries more stable, technology change more predictable, and customer needs more precisely measurable. Unpredictable and turbulent change can come to any industry today (think of how long the three big US television networks dominated their cozy little industry), and new opportunity arenas like genetic engineering are almost universally unstructured. More and more industries, by their very nature, seem to be perpetually underdefined, or even undefinable.

Take the 'digital industry.' It is not one industry, but a collection of industries that are simultaneously converging and disintegrating. It is an industry that has been around since the invention of the transistor, but is now, more than ever, underdefined. Figure 8.4.1 depicts the digital industry, circa 1990. While some firms like AT&T spanned several industry groupings, the industry could be broadly partitioned into seven more or less-distinct components:

1   computer system suppliers (from Compaq to IBM, and Apple to Hewlett-Packard);

2   information technology service companies (EDS, Cap Gemini, Andersen Consulting);

3   companies whose primary interest was in operating systems and application software for computers (Microsoft and Lotus, most notably, but also Novell, Computer Associates, Oracle, and a myriad of smaller companies focused on specific 'vertical' markets);

4   the owners and operators of the digital networks that transmit data and voice (including AT&T, McCaw, MCI, cable television companies, television and radio broadcasters, and regional telephone operating companies);

5   the providers of information content (Time Warner, Bertelesmann, MCA, Bloomberg Financial Markets, Polygram, Columbia Pictures, Dow-Jones, Reed International, and McGraw-Hill to name a few);

6   the manufacturers of professional electronics gear (Xerox, Canon, Kodak, and Motorola; defense electronics companies like Rockwell; and factory automation equipment manufacturers);

7   the familiar consumer electronics producers (Sony, Philips, Matsushita, and Samsung among others).

In the early 1990s, industry observers, corporate strategists, trade journals, and consultants mapped the digital industry more or less along these lines (see Figure 8.4.1)

The problem, for any company intent on getting to the future first, is that this is a map of the past and not of the future. For companies looking forward, it had become clear by the early 1990s that the labels used to distinguish among the different components of the digital industry were

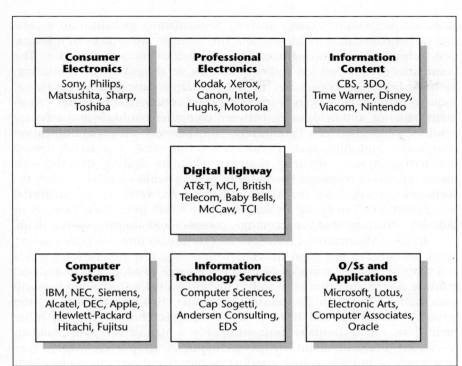

FIGURE 8.4.1
The evolving digital space

fast losing their descriptive power. It seemed unlikely that the future digital industry would be usefully partitioned into software versus hardware, computing versus communications, professional versus consumer, content versus conduit, services versus products, and horizontal markets versus vertical markets. Was the Macintosh a hardware or software innovation? How could one call Sharp's Personal Organizer a hardware product when software accounted for the biggest part of its development budget? What about all those hardware companies – Sony, Matsushita, and Toshiba – buying their way into the entertainment software industry? Did it make sense to distinguish between computing and communications when more and more personal computers were using the local telephone network to hook up to Prodigy or Compuserve, or when corporate customers demanded integrated networking of data, voice, and video? What was the distinction between professional versus consumer electronics when Motorola, because of the success of its cellular phones, was compelled to admit that it had become, de facto, a consumer electronics company? And when Time Warner wired homes in Orlando for two-way, interactive video and information services, just where was the dividing line between content and conduit? Pummeled by regulatory changes, advances in digital technology, changes in lifestyles, the raw ambition of companies intent on getting to the future first and those paranoid at the prospect of being left behind, the digital industry seemed to be in a state of permanent turmoil.

The digital industry may be more complex and variegated than most, but it is certainly not unique in the challenges it poses to the traditional tools and methods of strategy analysis. Deregulation, globalization, fundamental breakthroughs in science, and the strategic importance of information technology are blurring boundaries in a wide variety of industries. The boundaries between ethical and over-the-counter drugs have been blurring, as have been the boundaries between pharmaceuticals and cosmetics. Industry borders have been blurring between commercial banking, investment banking, and brokerages; between computer hardware and software vendors; and between publishers, broadcasters, telecommunication companies, and film studios. Adding to this stew is a trend toward disintermediation – whether that be Wal-Mart dealing directly with manufacturers or corporate borrowers bypassing banks – and a trend toward corporate confederacies and away from pervasive vertical and horizontal integration, like Toyota and its suppliers. The result, in all these cases, is an industry 'structure' that is exceedingly complex and almost indeterminate.

In an environment of turbulent and seemingly unpredictable change, being 'adaptive' is not good enough. A rudderless ship in gale force winds will simply go round in circles. Neither is it enough to adopt a 'wait-and-see' attitude. A company that pulls in its sails and waits for the calmer seas will find itself becalmed in an industry backwater. However tumultuous the industry, executives still have to make strategic choices. On the other hand, how can a company, possessing only a map of the past, make an intelligent decision about which technologies to pursue, which core competencies to build, which product or service concepts to back, which alliances to form, and what kind of people to hire?

Strategy, as taught in many business schools and practiced in most companies, seems to be more concerned with how to position products and businesses within the existing industry structure than how to create tomorrow's industries. Of what use are the traditional tools of industry and competitor analysis to executives caught up in the mêlée to create the world's digital future, or to managers trying to understand the opportunities presented by the collapsing boundaries of the financial services industry or the genetics revolution? Of what use are the principles of competitive interaction, drilled into the heads of countless MBA students as they worked their way through the comparatively simple cases of Coca-Cola versus Pepsi, the chain saw industry, DuPont in titanium dioxide, and Procter & Gamble versus Kimberly-Clark in the disposable diaper business? At least in these cases one could easily determine where the industry began and ended. It's not that difficult to determine who is making soft drinks, for example, and who is not. But where does the digital industry begin and end? Or the genetics industry? Or the entertainment industry? Or the retail financial services industry? On any given day, for example, AT&T might find Motorola to be a supplier, a buyer, a competitor, and a partner. In well-established industries it is easy to identify product and customer segments. With no preexisting 'value chain,' how can one anticipate where and how money can be made in the industry, decide which activities to 'control,' and know how vertically or horizontally integrated to be?

Traditional industry structure analysis, of the kind that is the subject of strategy textbooks, is of little help to executives competing in unstruc-

FIGURE 8.4.2
The digital industry space
without boundaries

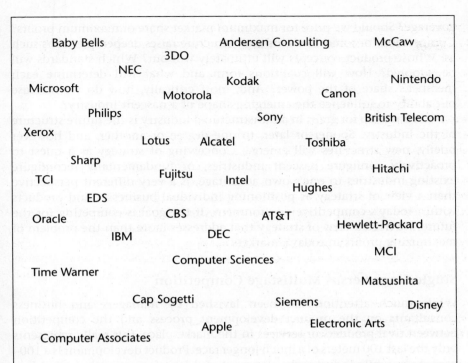

tured industries. On the other hand, simply doing away with existing industry boundaries, as we have done in Figure 8.4.2, provides no more help to companies trying to make sense of such a tumultuous industry.

Strategic planning typically takes, as its point of departure, the extant industry structure. Traditional planning seeks to position the firm optimally within the existing structure by identifying which segments, channels, price points, product differentiators, selling propositions, and value chain configurations will yield the highest profits. Although a view of strategy as a positioning problem is certainly legitimate, it is insufficient if the goal is to occupy the high ground in tomorrow's industries. If strategy is seen only as a positioning game, it will be difficult for a company to avoid becoming trapped in an endless game of catch-up with farsighted competitors.

Usually, the current industry structure and the rules of competitive engagement therein have been defined by the industry leader. Although it may be possible to find a profitable niche within the present industry terrain – as Japanese mainframe computer makers did for a while, mimicking IBM – there is typically little growth and prosperity to be found in the shadow of the industry leader. Companies that see strategy as primarily a positioning exercise are industry rule-takers rather than rule-breakers and rule-makers; they are unlikely to be the defining entity in their industry, now or ever.

In short, strategy is as much about competing for tomorrow's industry structure as it is about competing within today's industry structure. Competition within today's industry structure raises issues such as: What new features should be added to a product? How can we get better channel coverage? Should we price for maximum market share or maximum profits? Competition for tomorrow's industry structure raises deeper questions such as: Whose product concepts will ultimately win out? Which standards will be adopted? How will coalitions form and what will determine each member's share of the power? And, most critically, how do we increase our ability to influence the emerging shape of a nascent industry?

What is up for grabs in an unstructured industry is the future structure of the industry. Sooner or later, to one degree or another, and however briefly, new structures will emerge. Conceiving of strategy as a quest to proactively configure nascent industries, or fundamentally reconfigure existing industries to one's own advantage, is a very different perspective than a view of strategy as positioning individual businesses and products within today's competitive environment. If the goal is competing for the future, we need a view of strategy that addresses more than the problem of maximizing profits in today's markets.

Single-Stage versus Multistage Competition

While much attention has been lavished by managers and business consultants on the product development process and the competition between rival products or services in the marketplace, this really represents only the last 100 meters of a much longer race. Product development is a 100–yard dash, while industry development and transformation is a triathlon, where contestants cycle for 100 miles, swim a mile or two, and then run a marathon. Each event represents a distinct challenge to the triathelete.

Competition for the future of the digital industry is still in its early stages, but by reviewing one particular race, the race to develop the VCR, we can observe the distinct stages of competition for the future. We use the VCR as an example both because enough time has passed so that objective judgments can be made about who won and why, and because the VCR was the first major innovation in consumer electronics that was commercialized first in mass markets by Japanese, rather than US or European companies. And although companies like Motorola and Apple today are attempting to resurrect a consumer electronics industry led by US firms, it was the VCR that established the unequivocal dominance of Japanese companies in consumer electronics. The VCR also added billions of largely uncontested profits to the coffers of its Japanese pioneers. Like many other industry development marathons, the race to commercialize the VCR spanned decades, rather than years. The first videotape recorder was produced by a California company, Ampex, in 1959, but it wasn't until the late 1970s that Matsushita introduced its VHS standard and broke the tape at the finish line.

The first hurdle for any would-be pioneer was to commit to the videotape opportunity arena. Three companies saw clearly the potential for videotape – Philips, Sony, and Matsushita (JVC) – and each worked diligently for close to two decades to produce a VCR for home use. At JVC, what was initially the commitment of a small team to the videotape opportunity soon became a corporatewide commitment. Neither RCA, the color television pioneer, nor Ampex, the inventor of videotape, ever demonstrated the same unflinching commitment to the VCR, although both companies made aborted attempts to produce a home machine.

The second hurdle was to acquire the competencies that would be necessary to shape and profit from the future. The challenge of creating a compact videocassette that would pack two, four, or six hours of color recording onto a tape that was a fraction of the length and width of tapes used to produce a half hour of black and white recording time on reel-to-reel video recorders was a daunting one – what engineers call a 'nontrivial technical problem.' For more than 15 years Philips, Sony, and Matsushita raced to perfect their videotape competencies. Learning how to manufacture the extremely precise, revolving video-recording heads presented a major competence-building challenge to all comers. An executive at JVC believed that making a VCR was at least 10 times more complex than making a television set.

The third hurdle was to discover what configuration of price, features, size, and software was necessary to unlock the mass market. After all, consumers had never seen a VCR before. They could hardly be relied on to provide manufacturers with precise product development specs. How much record time did consumers want? Would they pay as much as $2,500 for a machine? Was slow motion an important feature? The only way to answer those questions was to go into the market again and again, each time improving the product, and coming that little bit closer to the demands of the consumer.

Matsushita launched several VCR models into the market before the company struck gold with VHS. Sony's U-matic VCR, which ultimately became a standards-setter in the professional VCR market, was originally introduced as a 'consumer video.' But the machine's size and price made it unattractive to home users. The more rapid the pace of market experimentation, the quicker the learning about what customers really want in a product. While Japanese competitors were experimenting in the marketplace, RCA was experimenting only in the lab. RCA didn't launch its consumer videoplayer until 1980. Therefore, it was not surprising that RCA's product, which lacked a record capability, missed the mark badly with consumers.

A fourth hurdle was to establish one's own technical approach to video recording as the industry standard. The battle here was among Sony's Beta, JVC's VHS, and Philips's V2000, each incompatible with the other. It was clear that whoever won the standards battle would reap great benefits in terms of software availability, licensing income, and economies of scale in component production. The losers would find themselves, millions of R&D dollars later, in a technological cul-de-sac that they could escape only by switching to a competitor's standard. Sony took an early lead, and had 85 percent of the US VCR market by the end of 1976. But when JVC introduced a machine with a two-hour record time, compared to Sony's one-hour, Sony's lead began to evaporate. The *coup de grâce* came when JVC succeeded in co-opting a number of key partners into its battle with Sony. Telefunken in Germany, Thomson in France, Thorn in Great Britain, and RCA and GE in the United States were all early VHS licensees, initially sourcing components and finished VCRs from JVC and Matsushita.

The wide selection of VHS brands and models, relative to Beta, soon convinced software suppliers to put their money behind VHS, and within two years the market battle between Beta and VHS was over. Philips's V2000, launched in Europe some 18-months after VHS, was dead on arrival despite the fact that Philips had more or less kept pace with its Japanese competitors over the 15-year competence acquisition phase. But in the 18–month gap between the launch of VHS and the launch of V2000, Matsushita managed to sell several million VCRs around the world, making it almost impossible for Philips to catch up with Matsushita's blistering pace of cost reduction and feature improvement. Thus, although the VCR marathon was a full 26 miles, the winner didn't emerge until the last mad scramble for the finish line. But in a marathon, winning by a nose is often as good as winning by a mile. Indeed, attempting to far outdistance a competitor too early in the race may well lead a company into spending too much too soon or running out of resources before the future arrives – the fate that befell Ampex (even though Ampex and Sony were roughly the same size in 1959 when Ampex invented videotape recorders). Although JVC won only by a yard or two, no one who wasn't in the race at the beginning was anywhere near the finish line when it ended.

The final challenge was to keep up in the battle for market share (as opposed to the battle for standards share). The weapons were fast-paced feature enhancement and cost reduction. Sony and Philips ultimately converted to the VHS camp, but Matsushita's early volume advantage gave it an edge in the race to steadily improve price and performance. In 1993, more than 15 years after the launch of VHS and more than 30 years after Matsushita began its pursuit of the videotape opportunity, Matsushita retained its title as the world leader in VCRs.

Whether the race to shift the pharmaceutical industry toward gene-engineered drugs, to allow customers to bank and shop via their PCs or televisions, or to produce cars with noncombustion engines, the race to the future occurs in three distinct, overlapping stages: *competition for industry foresight* and *intellectual leadership, competition to fore-shorten migration paths,* and *competition for market position and market share.*

Competition for industry foresight and intellectual leadership   This is competition to gain a deeper understanding than competitors of the trends and discontinuities – technological, demographic, regulatory, or lifestyle – that could be used to transform industry boundaries and create new competitive space. This is competition to be prescient about the size and shape of tomorrow's opportunities. This is competition to conceive fundamentally new types of customer benefits, or to conceive radically new ways of delivering existing customer benefits. In short, it is competition to imagine the future.

Competition to foreshorten migration paths   In between the battle for intellectual leadership and the battle for market share is typically a battle to influence the direction of industry development (the battle to control and foreshorten migration paths). Many years may elapse between the conception of a radically transformed industry future and the emergence of a real and substantial market. Dreams don't come true overnight, and the path between today's reality and tomorrow's opportunities is often long and tortuous.

In the second stage of competition there is a race to accumulate necessary competencies (and overcome technical hurdles), to test and prove out alternate product and service concepts (by progressively discovering what customers really want), to attract coalition partners who have critical complementary resources, to construct whatever product or service delivery infrastructure may be required, and to get agreement around standards, if necessary. If competition in the first stage is competition to imagine a new opportunity arena, competition in the second stage is competition to actively shape the emergence of that future industry structure to one's own advantage.

Competition for market position and market share   Finally, one gets to the last stage of competition. By this stage, competition between alternate technological approaches, rival product or service concepts, and competing channel strategies has largely been settled. Competition shifts to a battle for market share and market position within fairly well-defined parameters of value, cost, price, and service. Innovation is focused on product line extensions, efficiency improvement, and what are usually marginal gains in product or service differentiation. (Figure 8.4.3 shows the three stages of competition for the future.)

Competition for the future can be likened to pregnancy. Like competition for the future, pregnancy has three stages – conception, gestation, and labor and delivery. These three stages correspond to competition for foresight and intellectual leadership, competition to foreshorten migration paths, and competition for market position and share. It is the third phase of competition that is the focus of attention in most strategy textbooks and strategic planning exercises. Typically, the assumption is that the product or service concept is well established, the dimensions of competition are well-defined, and the boundaries of the industry have stabilized. But focusing on the last stage of market-based competition, without a deep understanding of premarket competition, is like trying to make sense of the process of childbirth without any insight into conception and gestation.

The question for managers to ask themselves at this point is which stage receives the bulk of our time and attention: conception, gestation, or labor and delivery? Our experience suggests that most managers spend a disproportionate amount of time in the delivery room, waiting for the miracle of birth. But as we all know, the miracle of birth is most unlikely, unless there's been some activity nine months previously. Again, we believe that managers are spending too much time managing the present, and not enough creating the future.

FIGURE 8.4.3
Three phases of competition for the future

Intellectual Leadership	**Management of Migration Paths**	**Competition of Market Share**
Gaining industry foresight by probing deeply into industry drivers	Preemptively building core competencies, exploring alternate product concepts, and reconfiguring the customer interface.	Building a world-wide supplier network.
Developing a creative point of view about the potential evolution of: • Functionality • Core competencies • Customer interface	Assembling and managing the necessary coalition of industry participants.	Crafting an appropriate market positioning strategy.
		Preempting competitors in critical markets.
		Maximizing efficiency and productivity.
Summarizing this point of view in a 'strategic architecture.'	Forcing competitors onto longer and more expensive migration paths.	Managing competitive interaction.

8.5 Increasing Returns and the New World of Business

***By W. Brian Arthur*[1]**

Our understanding of how markets and businesses operate was passed down to us more than a century ago by a handful of European economists – Alfred Marshall in England and a few of his contemporaries on the continent. It is an understanding based squarely upon the assumption of diminishing returns: products or companies that get ahead in a market eventually run into limitations, so that a predictable equilibrium of prices and market shares is reached. The theory was roughly valid for the bulk-processing, smokestack economy of Marshall's day. And it still thrives in today's economics textbooks. But steadily and continuously in this century, Western economies have undergone a transformation from bulk-material manufacturing to design and use of technology – from processing of resources to processing of information, from application of raw energy to application of ideas. As this shift has occurred, the underlying mechanisms

---

[1] Source: Reprinted by permission of *Harvard Business Review.* 'Increasing Returns and the New World of Business' by W. Brian Arthur, July–August 1996.

that determine economic behavior have shifted from ones of diminishing to ones of increasing returns.

Increasing returns are the tendency for that which is ahead to get further ahead, for that which loses advantage to lose further advantage. They are mechanisms of positive feedback that operate within markets, businesses, and industries – to reinforce that which gains success or aggravate that which suffers loss. Increasing returns generate not equilibrium but instability: if a product or a company or a technology-one of many competing in a market-gets ahead by chance or clever strategy, increasing returns can magnify this advantage, and the product or company or technology can go on to lock in the market. More than causing products to become standards, increasing returns cause businesses to work differently, and they stand many of our notions of how business operates on their head.

Mechanisms of increasing returns exist alongside those of diminishing returns in all industries. But roughly speaking, diminishing returns hold sway in the traditional part of the economy – the processing industries. Increasing returns reign in the newer part – the knowledge-based industries. Modern economies have therefore bifurcated into two interrelated worlds of business corresponding to the two types of returns. The two worlds have different economics. They differ in behavior, style, and culture. They call for different management techniques, strategies, and codes of government regulation. They call for different understandings.

Alfred Marshall's World

Let's go back to beginnings – to the diminishing-returns view of Alfred Marshall and his contemporaries. Marshall's world of the 1880s and 1890s was one of bulk production: of metal ores, aniline dyes, pig iron, coal, lumber, heavy chemicals, soybeans, coffee – commodities heavy on resources, light on know-how. In that world it was reasonable to suppose, for example, that if a coffee plantation expanded production it would ultimately be driven to use land less suitable for coffee. In other words, it would run into diminishing returns. So if coffee plantations competed, each one would expand until it ran into limitations in the form of rising costs or diminishing profits. The market would be shared by many plantations, and a market price would be established at a predictable level – depending on tastes for coffee and the availability of suitable farmland. Planters would produce coffee so long as doing so was profitable, but because the price would be squeezed down to the average cost of production, no one would be able to make a killing. Marshall said such a market was in perfect competition, and the economic world he envisaged fitted beautifully with the Victorian values of his time. It was at equilibrium and therefore orderly, predictable and therefore amenable to scientific analysis, stable and therefore safe, slow to change and therefore continuous. Not too rushed, not too profitable. In a word, mannerly. In a word, genteel.

With a few changes, Marshall's world lives on a century later within that part of the modern economy still devoted to bulk processing: of grains, livestock, heavy chemicals, metals and ores, foodstuffs, retail goods – the part where operations are largely repetitive day to day or week to week. Product differentiation and brand names now mean that a few companies rather than many compete in a given market. But typically, if these companies try to expand, they run into some limitation: in numbers of consumers who prefer their brand, in regional demand, in access to raw materials. So no company can corner the market. And because such products are normally substitutable for one another, something like a standard price emerges. Margins are thin and nobody makes a killing. This isn't exactly Marshall's perfect competition, but it approximates it.

The Increasing-Returns World

What would happen if Marshall's diminishing returns were reversed so that there were increasing returns? If products that got ahead thereby got further ahead, how would markets work?

Let's look at the market for operating systems for personal computers in the early 1980s when CP/M, DOS, and Apple's Macintosh systems were competing. Operating systems show increasing returns: if one system gets ahead, it attracts further software developers and hardware manufacturers to adopt it, which helps it get further ahead. CP/M was first in the market and by 1979 was well established. The Mac arrived later, but it was wonderfully easy to use. DOS was born when Microsoft locked up a deal in 1980 to supply an operating system for the IBM PC. For a year or two, it was by no means clear which system would prevail. The new IBM PC – DOS's platform – was a kludge. But the growing base of DOS/IBM users encouraged software developers such as Lotus to write for DOS. DOS's prevalence – and the IBM PC's – bred further prevalence, and eventually the DOS/IBM combination came to dominate a considerable portion of the market. That history is now well known. But notice several things: it was not predictable in advance (before the IBM deal) which system would come to dominate. Once DOS/IBM got ahead, it locked in the market because it did not pay for users to switch. The dominant system was not the best: DOS was derided by computer professionals. And once DOS locked in the market, its sponsor, Microsoft, was able to spread its costs over a large base of users. The company enjoyed killer margins.

These properties, then, have become the hallmarks of increasing returns: market instability (the market tilts to favor a product that gets ahead), multiple potential outcomes (under different events in history, different operating systems could have won), unpredictability, the ability to lock in a market, the possible predominance of an inferior product, and fat profits for the winner. They surprised me when I first perceived them in the late 1970s. They were also repulsive to economists brought up on the order, predictability, and optimality of Marshall's world. Glimpsing some of these properties in 1939, English economist John Hicks warned that admitting increasing returns would lead to 'the wreckage of the greater part of economic theory.' But Hicks had it wrong: the theory of increasing returns does not destroy the standard theory – it complements it. Hicks felt repugnance not just because of unsavory properties but also because in his day no mathematical apparatus existed to analyze increasing-returns markets. That situation has now changed. Using sophisticated techniques from qualitative dynamics and probability theory, I and others have developed methods to analyze increasing-returns markets. The theory of increasing returns is new, but it already is well established. And it renders such markets amenable to economic understanding.

In the early days of my work on increasing returns, I was told they were an anomaly. Like some exotic particle in physics, they might exist in theory but would be rare in practice. And if they did exist, they would last for only a few seconds before being arbitraged away. But by the mid 1980s, I realized increasing returns were neither rare nor ephemeral. In fact, a major part of the economy was subject to increasing returns-high technology. Why should this be so? There are several reasons:

- *Up-front costs*. High-tech products – pharmaceuticals, computer hardware and software, aircraft and missiles, telecommunications equipment, bio-engineered drugs, and suchlike – are by definition complicated to design and to deliver to the marketplace. They are heavy on know-how and light on resources. Hence they typically have R&D costs that are large relative to their unit production costs. The first disk of Windows to go out the door cost Microsoft $50 million; the second and subsequent disks cost $3. Unit costs fall as sales increase.

- *Network effects*. Many high-tech products need to be compatible with a network of users. So if much downloadable software on the Internet will soon appear as programs written in Sun Microsystems' Java language, users will need Java on their computers to run them. Java has competitors. But the more it gains prevalence, the more likely it will emerge as a standard.

- *Customer groove-in*. High-tech products are typically difficult to use. They require training. Once users invest in this training – say, the maintenance and piloting of Airbus passenger aircraft – they merely need to update these skills for subsequent versions of the product. As more market is captured, it becomes easier to capture future markets. In high-tech markets, such mechanisms ensure that products that gain market advantage stand to gain further advantage, making these markets unstable and subject to lock-in. Of course, lock-in is not forever. Technology comes in waves, and a lock-in such as DOS's can last only as long as a particular wave lasts.

So we can usefully think of two economic regimes or worlds: a bulk-production world yielding products that essentially are congealed resources with a little knowledge and operating according to Marshall's principles of diminishing returns, and a knowledge-based part of the economy yielding products that essentially are congealed knowledge with a little resources and operating under increasing returns. The two worlds are not neatly split. Hewlett-Packard, for example, designs knowledge-based devices in Palo Alto, California, and manufactures them in bulk in places like Corvallis,

Oregon, or Greeley, Colorado. Most high-tech companies have both knowledge-based operations and bulk-processing operations. But because the rules of the game differ for each, companies often separate them-as Hewlet-Packard does. Conversely, manufacturing companies have operations such as logistics, branding, marketing, and distribution, which belong largely to the knowledge world. And some products – like the IBM PC – start in the increasing-returns world but later in their life cycle become virtual commodities that belong to Marshall's processing world.

The Halls of Production and the Casino of Technology

Because the two worlds of business – processing bulk goods and crafting knowledge into products – differ in their underlying economics, it follows that they differ in their character of competition and their culture of management. It is a mistake to think that what works in one world is appropriate for the other.

There is much talk these days about a new management style that involves flat hierarchies, mission orientation, flexibility in strategy, market positioning, reinvention, restructuring, reengineering, repositioning, reorganization, and re-everything else. Are these new insights or are they fads? Are they appropriate for all organizations? Why are we seeing this new management style?

Let us look at the two cultures of competition. In bulk processing, a set of standard prices typically emerges. Production tends to be repetitive – much the same from day to day or even from year to year. Competing therefore means keeping product flowing, trying to improve quality, getting costs down. There is an art to this sort of management, one widely discussed in the literature. It favors an environment free of surprises or glitches – an environment characterized by control and planning. Such an environment requires not just people to carry out production but also people to plan and control it. So it favors a hierarchy of bosses and workers. Because bulk processing is repetitive, it allows constant improvement, constant optimization. And so, Marshall's world tends to be one that favors hierarchy, planning, and controls. Above all, it is a world of optimization.

Competition is different in knowledge-based industries because the economics are different. If knowledge-based companies are competing in winner-take-most markets, then managing becomes redefined as a series of quests for the next technological winner – the next cash cow. The goal becomes the search for the Next Big Thing. In this milieu, management becomes not production oriented but mission oriented. Hierarchies flatten not because democracy is suddenly bestowed on the workforce or because computers can cut out much of middle management. They flatten because, to be effective, the deliverers of the next-thing-for-the-company need to be organized like commando units in small teams that report directly to the

CEO or to the board. Such people need free rein. The company's future survival depends upon them. So they – and the commando teams that report to them in turn – will be treated not as employees but as equals in the business of the company's success. Hierarchy dissipates and dissolves.

Does this mean that hierarchy should disappear in meatpacking, steel production, or the navy? Contrary to recent management evangelizing, a style that is called for in Silicon Valley will not necessarily be appropriate in the processing world. An aircraft's safe arrival depends on the captain, not on the flight attendants. The cabin crew can usefully be 'empowered' and treated as human beings. This approach is wise and proper. But forever there will be a distinction – a hierarchy – between cockpit and cabin crews.

In fact, the style in the diminishing-returns Halls of Production is much like that of a sophisticated modern factory: the goal is to keep high-quality product flowing at low cost. There is little need to watch the market every day, and when things are going smoothly the tempo can be leisurely. By contrast, the style of competition in the increasing-returns arena is more like gambling. Not poker, where the game is static and the players vie for a succession of pots. It is casino gambling, where part of the game is to choose which games to play, as well as playing them with skill. We can imagine the top figures in high tech – the Gateses and Gerstners and Groves of their industries – as milling in a large casino. Over at this table, a game is starting called multimedia. Over at that one, a game called Web services. In the corner is electronic banking. There are many such tables. You sit at one. 'How much to play?' you ask. 'Three billion', the croupier replies. Who'll be playing? We won't know until they show up. What are the rules? Those'll emerge as the game unfolds. What are my odds of winning? We can't say. Do you still want to play? High technology, pursued at this level, is not for the timid.

In fact, the art of playing the tables in the Casino of Technology is primarily a psychological one. What counts to some degree – but only to some degree – is technical expertise, deep pockets, will, and courage. Above all, the rewards go to the players who are first to make sense of the new games looming out of the technological fog, to see their shape, to recognize them. Bill Gates is not so much a wizard of technology as a wizard of precognition, of discerning the shape of the next game.

We can now begin to see that the new style of management is not a fad. The knowledge-based part of the economy demands flat hierarchies, mission orientation, above all a sense of direction. Not five-year plans. We can also fathom the mystery of what I've alluded to as re-everything. Much of this 're-everything' predilection – in the bulk-processing world – is a fancy label for streamlining, computerizing, downsizing. However, in the increasing-returns world, especially in high tech, re-everything has become necessary because every time the quest changes, the company needs to change. It needs to reinvent its purpose, its goals, its way of doing things. In short, it needs to adapt. And adaptation never stops. In fact, in the increasing-returns environment I've just sketched, standard optimization makes little sense. You cannot optimize in the casino of increasing-returns games. You can be smart. You can be cunning. You can position. You can observe. But when the games themselves are not even fully defined, you cannot optimize. What you can do is adapt. Adaptation, in the proactive sense, means watching for the next wave that is coming, figuring out what shape it will take, and positioning the company to take advantage of it. Adaptation is what drives increasing-returns businesses, not optimization.

Playing the High-Tech Tables

Suppose you are a player in the knowledge-industry casino, in this increasing-returns world. What can you do to capitalize on the increasing returns at your disposal? How can you use them to capture markets? What strategic issues do you need to think about? In the processing world, strategy typically hinges upon capitalizing on core competencies, pricing competitively, getting costs down, bringing quality up. These are important also in the knowledge-based world, but so, too, are other strategies that make use of the special economics of positive feedbacks.

Two maxims are widely accepted in knowledge-based markets: it pays to hit the market first, and it pays to have superb technology. These maxims are true but do not guarantee success. Prodigy was first into the on-line services market but was passive in building its subscriber base to take advantage of increasing returns. As a result, it has fallen from its leading position and currently lags the other services. As for technology, Steve Jobs's NeXT workstation was superb. But it was launched into a market already dominated by Sun Microsystems and Hewlett-Packard. It failed. A new product often has to be two or three times better in some dimension – price, speed, convenience – to dislodge a locked-in rival. So in knowledge-based markets, entering first with a fine product can yield advantage. But as strategy, this is still too passive. What is needed is active management of increasing returns.

One active strategy is to discount heavily initially to build up an installed base. Netscape handed out its Internet browser for free and won 70 percent of its market. Now it can profit from spin-off software and applications. Although such discounting is effective – and widely understood – it is not always implemented. Companies often err by pricing high initially to recoup expensive R&D costs. Yet even smart discounting to seed the market is ineffective unless the resulting installed base is exploited later. America Online built up a lead of more than 4.5 million subscribers by giving away free services. But because of the Internet's dominance, it is not yet clear whether it can transform this huge base into later profits.

Let's get a bit more sophisticated. Technological products do not stand alone. They depend on the existence of other products and other technologies. The Internet's World Wide Web operates within a grouping of businesses that include browsers, on-line news, E-mail, network retailing, and financial services. Pharmaceuticals exist within a network of physicians, testing labs, hospitals, and HMOs. Laser printers are part of a grouping of products that include computers, publishing software, scanners, and photo-input devices. Unlike products of the processing world, such as soybeans or rolled steel, technological products exist within local groupings of products that support and enhance them. They exist in mini-ecologies.

This interdependence has deep implications for strategy. When, in the mid-1980s, Novell introduced its network-operating system, NetWare, as a way of connecting personal computers in local networks, Novell made sure that NetWare was technically superior to its rivals. It also heavily discounted NetWare to build an installed base. But these tactics were not enough. Novell recognized that NetWare's success depended on attracting software applications to run on NetWare – which was a part of the ecology outside the company's control. So it set up incentives for software developers to write for NetWare rather than for its rivals. The software writers did just that. And by building NetWare's success, they ensured their own. Novell managed these cross-product positive feedbacks actively to lock in its market. It went on to profit hugely from upgrades, spin-offs, and applications of its own.

Another strategy that uses ecologies is linking and leveraging. This means transferring a user base built up upon one node of the ecology (one product) to neighboring nodes, or products. The strategy is very much like that in the game Go: you surround neighboring markets one by one, lever your user base onto them, and take them over – all the time enhancing your position in the industry. Microsoft levered its 60-million-person user base in DOS onto Windows, then onto Windows 95, and then onto Microsoft Network by offering inexpensive upgrades and by bundling applications. The strategy has been challenged legally. But it recognizes that positive feedbacks apply across markets as well as within markets.

In fact, if technological ecologies are now the basic units for strategy in the knowledge-based world, players compete not by locking in a product on their own but by building webs – loose alliances of companies organized around a mini-ecology – that amplify positive feedbacks to the base technology. Apple, in closing its Macintosh system to outsiders in the 1980s, opted not to create such a web. It believed that with its superior technology, it could hold its increasing-returns market to itself. Apple indeed dominates its Mac-based ecology. But this ecology is now only eight percent of the personal computer business. IBM erred in the other direction. By passively allowing other companies to join its PC web as clones, IBM achieved a huge user base and locked in the market. But the company itself wound up with a small share of the spoils. The key in web building is active management of the cross-company mutual feedbacks. This means making a careful choice of partners to build upon. It also means that, rather than attempting to take over all products in the ecology, dominant players in a web should allow dependent players to lock in their dependent products by piggybacking on the web's success. By thus ceding some of the profits, the dominant players ensure that all participants remain committed to the alliance.

Important also to strategy in knowledge-based markets is psychological positioning. Under increasing returns, rivals will back off in a market not only if it is locked in but if they believe it will be locked in by someone else. Hence we see psychological jockeying in the form of preannouncements, feints, threatened alliances, technological preening, touted future partnerships, parades of vapor-ware (announced products that don't yet exist). This posturing and puffing acts much the way similar behavior does in a primate colony: it discourages competitors from taking on a potentially dominant rival. No moves need be made in this strategy of premarket face-down. It is purely a matter of psychology.

What if you hold a losing hand? Sometimes it pays to hold on for residual revenue. Sometimes a fix can be provided by updated technology, fresh alliances, or product changes. But usually under heavy lock-in, these tactics do not work. The alternatives are then slow death or graceful exit-relinquishing the field to concentrate on positioning for the next technology wave. Exit may not mean quitting the business entirely. America Online, Compuserve, Prodigy, and Microsoft Network have all ceded dominance of the on-line computer networking market to the Internet. But instead of exiting, they are steadily becoming adjuncts of the Net, supplying content services such as financial quotations or games and entertainment. They have lost the main game. But they will likely continue in a side game with its own competition for dominance within the Net's ecology.

What About Service Industries?

So far, I've talked mainly about high tech. Where do service industries such as insurance, restaurants, and banking fit in? Which world do they belong to? The question is tricky. It would appear that such industries belong to the diminishing-returns, processing part of the economy because often there are regional limits to the demand for a given service, most services do consist of 'processing' clients, and services are low-tech.

The truth is that network or user-base effects often operate in services. Certainly, retail franchises exist because of increasing returns. The more McDonald's restaurants or Motel 6 franchises are out there geographically, the better they are known. Such businesses are patronized not just for their quality but also because people want to know exactly what to expect. So the more prevalent they are, the more prevalent they can become. Similarly, the larger a bank's or insurance company's customer base, the more it can spread its fixed costs of headquarters staff, real estate, and computer operations. These industries, too, are subject to mild increasing returns.

So we can say more accurately that service industries are a hybrid. From day to day, they act like bulk-processing industries. But over the long term, increasing returns will dominate – even though their destabilizing effects are not as pronounced as in high tech. The US airline business, for example, processes passengers day to day. So it seemed in 1981 that deregulation should enhance competition, as it normally does under diminishing returns. But over the long term, airlines in fact experience a positive feedback: under the hub-and-spoke system, once an airline gets into trouble, it cannot work the feeder system for its routes properly, its fleet ages, it starts a downward spiral, and it loses further routes. The result of deregulation over the long term has been a steady decline in large carriers, from 15 airlines in 1981 to approximately six at present. Some routes have become virtual monopolies, with resulting higher fares. None of this was intended. But it should have been predicted – given increasing returns.

In fact, the increasing-returns character of service industries is steadily strengthening. One of the marks of our time is that in services everything is going software – everything that is information based. So operations that were once handled by people – designing fancy financial instruments or automobiles or fashion goods, processing insurance claims, supplying and inventorying in retail, conducting paralegal searches for case precedents – are increasingly being handled by software. As this reengineering of services plays out, centralized software facilities come to the fore. Service providers become hitched into software networks, regional limitations weaken, and user-base network effects kick in.

This phenomenon can have two consequences. First, where the local character of service remains important, it can preserve a large number of service companies but clustered round a dominant software provider – like the large numbers of small, independent law firms tied in to the dominant computer-search network, Lexis-Nexis. Or physicians tied in to an HMO. Second, where locality is unimportant, network effects can transform competition toward the winner-take-most character we see in high tech. For example, when Internet-based retail banking arrives, regional demand limitations will vanish. Each virtual bank will gain in advantage as its network increases. Barring regulation, consumer banking will then become a contest among a few large banking networks. It will become an increasing-returns business. Services belong to both the processing and the increasing-returns world. But their center of gravity is crossing over to the latter.

Thoughts for Managers

Where does all this leave us? At the beginning of this century, industrial economies were based largely on the bulk processing of resources. At the close of the century, they are based on the processing of resources and on the processing of knowledge. Economies have bifurcated into two worlds – intertwined, overlapping, and different. These two worlds operate under different economic principles. Marshall's world is characterized by planning, control, and hierarchy. It is a world of materials, of processing, of optimization. The increasing-returns world is characterized by observation, positioning, flattened organizations, missions, teams, and cunning. It is a world of psychology, of cognition, of adaptation.

Many managers have some intuitive grasp of this new increasing-returns world. Few understand it thoroughly. Here are some questions managers need to ask themselves when they operate in knowledge-based markets:

■ *Do I understand the feedbacks in my market?* In the processing world, understanding markets means understanding consumers' needs, distribution channels, and rivals' products. In the knowledge world, success requires a thorough understanding of the self-negating and self-reinforcing feed-backs in the market – the diminishing and increasing-returns mechanisms. These feedbacks are interwoven and operate at different levels in the market and over different time frames.

■ *Which ecologies am I in?* Technologies exist not alone but in an interlinked web, or ecology. It is important to understand the ecologies a company's products belong to. Success or failure is often decided not just by the company but also by the success or failure of the web it belongs to. Active management of such a web can be an important magnifier of increasing returns.

■ *Do I have the resources to play?* Playing one of the increasing-returns games in the Casino of Technology requires several things: excellent technology, the ability to hit the market at the right time, deep pockets, strategic pricing, and a willingness to sacrifice current profits for future advantage. All this is a matter not just of resources but also of courage, resolution, will. And part of that resolution, that courage, is also the decisiveness to leave the market when increasing returns are moving against one. Hanging on to a losing position that is being further eroded by positive feedbacks requires throwing reinforcements into a battle already lost. Better to exit with financial dignity.

■ *What games are coming next?* Technology comes in successive waves. Those who have lost out on this wave can position for the next. Conversely, those who have made a killing on this cycle should not become complacent. The ability to profit under increasing returns is only as good as the ability to see what's coming in the next cycle and to position oneself for it – technologically, psychologically, and coopera-tively. In high tech, it is as if we are moving slowly on a ship, with new technologies looming, taking shape, through a fog of unknowingness. Success goes to those who have the vision to foresee, to imagine, what shapes these next games will take.

These considerations appear daunting. But increasing-returns games provide large payoffs for those brave enough to play them and win. And they are exciting. Processing, in the service or manufacturing industries, has its own risks. Precisely because processing is low-margin, operations must struggle to stay afloat. Neither world of business is for the fainthearted.

In his book *Microcosm*, technology thinker George Gilder remarked, 'The central event of twentieth century is the overthrow of matter. In technology, economics, and the politics of nations, wealth in the form of physical resources is steadily declining in value and significance. The powers of mind are everywhere ascendant over the brute force of things.' As the economy shifts steadily away from the brute force of things into the powers of mind, from resource-based bulk processing into knowledge-based design and reproduction, so it is shifting from a base of diminishing returns to one of increasing returns. A new economics – one very different from that in the textbooks – now applies, and nowhere is this more true than in high technology. Success will strongly favor those who understand this new way of thinking.

The Industry Context in International Perspective

How many things are looked upon as quite impossible until they have been actually effected.

(Pliny the Elder 23–79; Roman writer)

As stated in the introduction, debates between people with a deterministic predisposition and those favoring a more voluntaristic view can be witnessed in quite a few scientific fields. In the field of strategy, perspectives on the malleability of the industry context also differ sharply, although often implicitly – few authors or practicing strategists make a point of expounding their assumptions about the nature of the environment. For this reason, it is difficult to identify whether there are national preferences when it comes to industry context perspective. Yet, it seems not unlikely that strategists in different countries have different inclinations on this issue. Although it is always difficult to generalize, it seems that strategists in some nations gravitate more towards an industry creation perspective than in other nations.

As an input to the debate whether there are international differences in industry context perspective, we would like to put forward a number of factors that might be of influence on how the paradox of compliance and choice is viewed in different countries. It should be noted, however, that these propositions are intended to encourage discussion and constitute only tentative explanations for cross-cultural differences in perspective. More specific international research is needed to give this debate a firm footing.

Locus of Control

Culture researchers have long recognized international differences in how people perceive the power of individuals to shape their environments. In some cultures the view that an individual is at the mercy of external events is more predominant, while in other cultures there is a stronger belief in the freedom of individuals to act independent of the environment and even to create their own circumstances. Psychologists refer to this as the perceived *locus of control* (e.g. Miller, Kets de Vries and Toulouse, 1982). People with an internal locus of control believe that they largely control their own fate. Their efforts will shape their circumstances – success is earned and failure is one's own fault. People with an external locus of control, on the other hand, believe that their fate is largely the result of circumstances beyond their control. Any effort to improve one's position, if at all possible, should be directed toward complying to external demands – fortune favors those who go with the flow. In the most extreme case, however, people with an external locus of control are fatalistic, that is, they assume no efforts will change that which is inevitable.

Obviously, in countries where the culture is more inclined towards an internal locus of control, it is reasonable to expect that the industry creation perspective will be more widespread. It is in such nations that one might expect remarks, such as that by the 19th century English essayist Sydney Smith: 'When I hear any man talk of an unalterable law, the only effect it produces on me is to convince me that he is an unalterable fool.' In cultures with a strong emphasis on external locus of control, the industry evolution perspective is likely to be more predominant.

Time Orientation

As was identified in Chapter 4, cultures can also differ with respect to their time orientation. Some cultures are directed towards the past, while others are more focused on the present or on the future. In countries with a future-orientation, the belief is widespread that change is progress. People generally welcome change as an opportunity for advancement. Therefore, in future-oriented cultures, people are even willing to initiate painful change processes, in the expectation that this will lead to future benefits. In these countries a strong inclination towards the industry creation perspective is most likely.

In past-oriented cultures, the belief is widespread that change is decay. People generally actively resist change and protect the status quo. In these cultures, external changes will only be adapted to if strictly necessary. In present-oriented cultures, the belief is widespread that change is relatively unimportant. People live for the day and adapt to changes as they come. In both types of culture, the industry evolution perspective is more likely to be more predominant.

Role of Government

Internationally, opinions also differ on the role that governments can play in encouraging the shaping of industries. In some countries the predominant view is that governments should facilitate industry change by creating good business circumstances and then staying out of the way of company initiatives. Governments are needed to set basic rules of business conduct, but firms should not be impeded by other governmental intervention in the functioning of industries and markets. Individual companies are seen as the primary drivers of industry innovation and if companies are given enough leeway, excellent ones can significantly shape their industry context. Such *economic liberalism* is particularly strong in the English-speaking nations, and it is here that governments attempt to actually facilitate firm's industry creation efforts. Unsurprisingly, the industry creation perspective is rather pronounced in these countries.

In other nations the predominant view is that Adam Smith's free market ideal often proves to be dysfunctional. A fully liberal market, it is believed, can lead to short-termism, negative social consequences, mutually-destructive competition, and an inability to implement industry-wide changes. Governments must therefore assume a more proactive role. They must protect weaker parties, such as workers and the environment, against the negative side-effects of the capitalist system, and actively create a shared infrastructure for all companies. Furthermore, the government can develop an industrial policy to encourage the development of new industries, force companies to work together where this is more effective, and push through industry-wide changes, if otherwise a stalemate would occur. Such a *managed competition* view is prevalent in Japan and France, and to a lesser extent in Germany (e.g. Hampden-Turner and Trompenaars, 1993; Lessem and Neubauer, 1994). In these countries the industry creation perspective is not as strongly held as in the English-speaking nations – industries can be shaped, but few companies have the power to do so without a good national industrial policy and government backing.

Network of Relationships

This factor is linked to the discussion in the previous chapter. In countries where the discrete organization perspective is predominant, companies often strive to retain their independence and power position *vis-à-vis* other companies. As these firms are not embedded in complex networks, but operate free from these constraining relationships, they are more at liberty to challenge the existing rules of the game. In other words, where firms are not entangled in a web of long-term relationships, they are better positioned for industry revolution – every firm can make a difference. In these countries an industry creation perspective is more prevalent.

However, in nations where firms are more inclined to operate in networks, each individual firm surrenders a part of its freedom in exchange for long-term relationships. The ability of the individual firm to shape its industry thus declines, as all changes must be discussed and negotiated with its partners. Hence, in these countries, the industry creation perspective is generally less strongly held than in the countries favoring discrete organizations. It should be noted that a group of firms, once in agreement, is often more powerful than each individual firm and therefore more capable of shaping the industry. However, it is acknowledged that getting the network partners to agree is a formidable task and a significant limit on the firm's ability to shape its environment.

Further Readings

For a good academic overview of the debate on 'who shapes whom' readers are advised to consult the special edition of *Academy of Management Review*

(July 1990), that focused on this issue. Especially the article 'Market discipline and the discipline of management,' by Richard Bettis and Lex Donaldson, which is very insightful. For a broader discussion on the issue of determinism and voluntarism, good readings are 'Central perspectives and debates in organization theory,' by W. Graham Astley and Andrew van der Ven, and 'Organizational adaptation: Strategic choice and environmental determinism,' by Lawrence Hrebiniak and William Joyce. Also useful is the recent work on managerial discretion, that attempts to measure how much leeway top managers have in shaping the future of their firm in different industries. Of these, the article 'Managerial Discretion: A Bridge Between Polar Views of Organizational Outcomes,' by Donald Hambrick and Sydney Finkelstein, is interesting for its theoretical base, while 'Assessing the Amount of Managerial Discretion in Different Industries: A Multimethod Approach,' by Donald Hambrick and Eric Abrahamson is interesting for its analysis of various industry environments. All of these readings, it should be mentioned, do not have an audience of practitioners in mind.

The same is true for all further readings taking an industry evolution perspective. A good follow up to Michael Hannan and John Freeman's article is their book, *Organizational Ecology*. The collection of articles edited by Joel Baum and Jitendra Sigh, *Evolutionary Dynamics of Organizations*, is also a stimulating, yet arduous, work. Other constraints on the freedom of firms to shape their own fate are brought forward by institutional theory and resource dependence theory, both of which have not been represented in this debate. A good overview of these two approaches is given by Christine Oliver, in her article 'Strategic responses to institutional processes.' The classic in the field of institutional theory is Paul DiMaggio and Walter Powell's article 'The Iron Cage Revisited: Institutional Isomorphism and Collective Rationality in Organizational Fields.' The classic work in the field of resource dependence is Jeffrey Pfeffer and Gerald Salancik's book *The External Control of Organizations*.

Readers interested in the industry creation perspective might want to start by looking at J.C. Spender's book *Industry Recipe – An Enquiry into the Nature and Sources of Managerial Judgement*. The book from which Charles Baden-Fuller and John Stopford's article was taken, *Rejuvenating the Mature Business*, is also an excellent follow up reading. The same is true of Gary Hamel and C.K. Prahalad's book *Competing for the Future*. In this context, Richard D'Aveni's book *Hypercompetition* is also worth reviewing. As a stimulating reading on the topic of increasing returns, Brian Arthur's book *Increasing Returns and Path Dependence in the Economy* can be recommended.

References

Aldrich, H.E. (1979) *Organizations and Environments*, Prentice Hall, Englewood Cliffs, NJ.

Arthur, W.B. (1994) *Increasing Returns and Path Dependence in the Economy*, University of Michigan Press.

Arthur, W.B. (1996) Increasing Returns and the New World of Business, *Harvard Business Review*, July–August, pp. 100–109.

Astley, W.G., and Fombrun, C.J. (1983) Collective Strategy: Social Ecology of Organizational Environments, *Academy of Management Review*, October, pp. 576–87.

Astley, W.G., and van der Ven, A.H. (1983) Central perspectives and debates in organization theory, *Administrative Science Quarterly*, no. 28, pp. 245–73.

Baden-Fuller, C.W.F., and Stopford, J.M. (1992) *Rejuvenating the Mature Business*, Routledge, London, pp. 13–34.

Baum, A.C., and Singh, J.V. (1994) (eds), *Evolutionary Dynamics of Organizations*, Oxford University Press, New York.

Bettis, R.A., and Donaldson, L. (1980) Market discipline and the discipline of management, *Academy of Management Review*, pp. 367–68.

Buzzell, R.D., and Gale, B.T. (1987) *The PIMS Principles: Linking Strategy to Performance*, Free Press, New York.

Buzzell, R.D., Gale, B.T., and Sultan, R.G.M. (1975) Market-Share – A Key to Profitability, *Harvard Business Review*, January/February, pp. 97–106.

Chakravarthy, B., and Lorange, P. (1991) *Managing the Strategy Process: A Framework for a Multibusiness Firm*, Prentice Hall, Englewood Cliffs.

D'Aveni, R. (1994) *Hypercompetition: Managing the Dynamics of Strategic Maneuvering*, Free Press, New York.

Di Maggio, P. and Powell, W.W. (1983) The Iron Cage Revisited: Institutional Isomorphism and Collective Rationality in Organizational Fields, *American Sociological Review*, Vol. 48, pp. 147–60.

Duncan, R., (1972) Characteristics of Organizational Environments and Perceived Environmental Uncertainty, *Administrative Science Quarterly*, September, pp. 313–27.

Freeman, J., and Boeker, W. (1984) The Ecological Analysis of Business Strategy, *California Management Review*, Spring, pp. 73–86.

Gilbert, X., and Strebel, P. (1989) Taking Advantage of Industry Shifts, *European Management Journal*, December, pp. 398–402.

Hall, W.K., (1980) Survival Strategies in a Hostile Environment, *Harvard Business Review*, September/October, pp. 75–85.

Hambrick, D.C. and Abrahamson, E. (1995) Assessing the Amount of Managerial Discretion in Different Industries: A Multimethod Approach, *Academy of Management Journal*, Vol. 38, pp. 1427–41.

Hambrick, D.C. and Finkelstein, S. (1987) Managerial Discretion: A Bridge between Polar Views of Organizations, in Cummings, L.L. and Staw, B.M. (eds) *Research in Organizational Behavior*, Vol. 9, pp. 369–406, JAI.

Hamel, G. (1996) Strategy as Revolution, *Harvard Business Review*, July/August.

Hamel, G., and Prahalad, C.K. (1994) *Competing for the Future*, Harvard Business School Press, Boston.

Hampden-Turner, C., and Trompenaars, A. (1993) *The Seven Cultures of Capitalism: Value Systems for Creating Wealth in the United States, Japan, Germany, France, Britain, Sweden and the Netherlands*, Doubleday, New York.

Hannan, M.T., and Freeman, J. (1977) The Population Ecology of Organizations, *American Journal of Sociology*, March, pp. 929–64.

Harrigan, K.R. (1980) *Strategies for Declining Businesses*, D.C. Health, Lexington, MA.

Hawley, A. (1950) Human Ecology: A Theory of Community Structure, Ronald, New York.

Hrebiniak, L.G., and Joyce, W.F. (1985) Organizational adaptation: Strategic choice and environmental determinism, *Administrative Science Quarterly*, No. 30, pp. 336–49.

Lawrence, P.R., and Lorsch, J.W. (1967) *Organization and Environment*, Harvard University Press, Cambridge, MA.

Lele, M.L. (1992) *Creating Strategic Leverage*, Wiley, New York.

Lessem, R., and Neubauer, F.F. (1994) *European Management Systems*, McGraw-Hill, London.

Levenhagen, M., J.F. Porac, and Thomas, H. (1993) Emergent Industry Leadership and the Selling of Technological Visions: A Social Constructionist View, in Hendry, J., Johnson, G. and Newton J. (eds), *Strategic Thinking: Leadership and the Management of Change*, Wiley, Chichester.

Levin, S.A. (1970) Community Equilibrium and Stability: An Extension of the Competitive Exclusion Principle, *American Naturalist*, September/October, pp. 413–23.

McKiernan, P. (1992) *Strategies for Growth*, Routledge, London.

Miller, D., Kets de Vries, M. and Toulouse, J.M. (1982) Top Executive Locus of Control and Its Relationship to Strategy-making Structure and Environment, *Academy of Management Journal*, Vol. 25, pp. 237–53.

Moore, J.F. (1993) Predators and Prey: A New Ecology of Competition, *Harvard Business Review*, May/June, pp. 75–86.

Nelson, R.R., and Winter, S.G. (1982) *An Evolutionary Theory of Economic Change*, Harvard University Press.

Oliver, C. (1991) Strategic Responses to Institutional Processes, *Academy of Management Review*, Vol. 16, pp. 145–79.

Pfeffer, J., and Salancik, G. (1978) *The External Control of Organizations: A Resource Dependency Perspective*, Harper & Row, New York.

Porter, M.E. (1980) *Competitive Strategy: Techniques for Analyzing Industries and Competitors*, Free Press, New York.

Porter, M.E. (1985) *Competitive Advantage: Creating and Sustaining Superior Performance*, Free Press, New York.

Prahalad, C.K., and Doz, Y.L. (1987) *The Multinational Mission: Balancing Local Demands and Global Vision*, Free Press, New York.

Rumelt, R. (1991) How Much Does Industry Matter?, *Strategic Management Journal*, March, pp. 167–86.

Scherer, F.M. (1980) *Industrial Market Structure and Market Performance*, 2nd edn, Houghton Mifflin, Boston.

Schmalensee, R. (1985) Do Markets Differ Much?, *American Economic Review*, June, pp. 341–51.

Schofield, M., and Arnold, D. (1988) Strategies for Mature Businesses, *Long Range Planning*, October, pp. 69–76.

Schumpeter, J.A. (1950) *Capitalism, Socialism and Democracy*, 3rd edn, Harper & Row, New York.

Spender, J.C. (1989) *Industry Recipe – An Enquiry into the Nature and Sources of Managerial Judgment*, Basil Blackwell, New York.

Strebel, P.J. (1992) *Breakpoints*, Harvard Business School Press, Boston.

Weick, K.E. (1979) *The Social Psychology of Organizing*, Random House, New York.

Wilson, D.C. (1992) *A Strategy of Change*, Routledge, London.

Woo, C.Y.Y. and Cooper, A.C. (1981) Strategies of Effective Low Share Businesses, *Strategic Management Journal*, July/September, pp. 301–18.

9

The Organizational Context

An institution is the lengthened
shadow of one man.

(Ralph Waldo Emerson 1803–1882; American essayist and poet)

We shape our environments, then
our environments shape us.

(Winston Churchill 1874–1965; British statesman and writer)

The Paradox of Control and Chaos

This chapter is the mirror image of Chapter 8. While the previous chapter dealt with the malleability of the company's *external* environment, this chapter focuses on the malleability of the company's *internal* environment. In other words, to what extent can strategists adapt the organization to fit with their wishes? Can the strategist shape the organization at will or does the organization have dynamics all its own, that can actually even shape the strategist?

If the firm's leader, responsible for deciding on strategy, is in absolute *control*, the organization can be fully geared to implement the strategy chosen. In such a case, the organization resembles a mechanical system, with the leader at the control panel. The leader has full command over the machine, within the limits of what is technically feasible. Under these circumstances, the wise strategist will first develop a strategy and then push through the necessary organizational changes. If, on the other hand, the strategist has hardly any influence on developments within the organization, there is a state of *chaos*. In such a case, the organization resembles a complex system, like the weather, in which events gradually evolve out of the current situation, depending on the intricate interactions between large numbers of influencing factors. The strategy is not selected by the strategist, but emerges from the complex dynamics within the organization. Strategy is not the result of free choice, but determined by the organizational context. Under these circumstances, even the wise strategist can do little more than marginally influence the unfolding system.

How malleable are organizations in practice? Should strategists take a predominantly control- or chaos-oriented view? Predictably, opinions on the matter are heavily divided. As in the previous debates, two opposite points of view can be identified, while many other authors take up intermediate positions. On the one hand, many strategists assume that leaders can have considerable control over organizations and therefore that leaders need not be restricted by the organizational context. We shall refer to this point of view as the *organizational leadership* perspective. On the other hand, some believe that leaders are actually the product of the organizational context and that they can have only a marginal impact on the strategy of the organization. This point of view will be referred to as the *organizational dynamics* perspective.

As in previous chapters, these two opposite points of view will be contrasted with one another to explore the real nature of the organizational context. By staging a debate between these two contradictory views on the paradox of control and chaos, a better understanding of the issues under discussion should be gained. In the next few pages, the organizational leadership and organizational dynamics perspectives will be further explained, and finally summarized in Table 9.1.

The Organizational Leadership Perspective

To proponents of the organizational leadership perspective, individual managers, especially those at the top, can make a big difference. *Organizational inertia* (see Hannan and Freeman, reading 8.3; Rumelt, reading 9.5) and *strategic drift* (Johnson, 1988; reading 9.4) are not normal and inevitable conditions, but result from a failure of leadership. Bureaucracy, organizational fiefdoms, hostile relationships, resilient corporate cultures, rigid competences, resistance to change – all of these organizational diseases exist, but they are not inherent to organizational life. Healthy organizations try to avoid falling prey to such degenerative illnesses, and when symptoms do arise, it is a task of the leader to address them. If organizations do go 'out of control', it is because weak leadership has failed to deal with a creeping ailment. The fact that there are many sick, poorly controllable, companies does not mean that sickness should be accepted as the natural state of affairs.

At the basis of the organizational leadership perspective lies the belief in the power of individuals to steer organizational processes, in particular strategy formation (e.g. Child, 1972; Christensen *et al.*, 1987; reading 9.1). It is usually argued that this power does not only stem from the formal position occupied by managers, but also from the forcefulness of their personality and the persuasiveness of their vision. Having a formal position of power, therefore, does not necessarily make someone a leader. Effective leaders must be able to get other people to follow them (e.g. Bennis and Nanus, 1985; Kelley, 1988), by setting an appealing organizational direction, and aligning and motivating people to move together in that direction (e.g. Kotter, 1990; Nanus, 1992). To gain control over the organization, and to 'lead the troops into battle', it is essential to convince the troops to let themselves be led.

This does not mean that the leader of an organization needs to engage in simple top-down management. Of course, there are circumstances where the CEO or the top management team design strategies in isolation and then impose them on the rest of the organization. This type of direct control is sometimes necessary to push through reorganizations or to make major acquisitions. In other circumstances, however, the top managers can control organizational behavior more indirectly. Initiatives can be allowed to emerge bottom-up, as long as top management retains its power to approve or 'kill' projects as soon as they become serious proposals (e.g. Bourgeois and Brodwin, 1983; reading 9.3; Quinn, 1980; reading 3.2). Some authors suggest that top management might even delegate decision-making powers to lower level managers, but still control outcomes by setting clear goals, developing a conducive incentive system and fostering a particular culture (e.g. Tichy and Devanna, 1987; Senge, 1990; reading 4.4).

What leaders should not do, however, is to relinquish control over the direction of the organization. The strategies do not have to be their own ideas, nor do they have to carry everything out themselves. But they should take upon themselves the responsibility for leading the organization in a certain direction and achieving results. If leaders let go of the helm, organizations will be set adrift, and will be carried by the prevailing winds and currents in directions unknown. Someone has to be in control of the organization, otherwise its behavior will be erratic. Leadership is needed to ensure that the best strategy is followed.

In conclusion, the organizational leadership perspective holds that the upper echelons of management can, and should, control the strategy process, and by extension, the strategy content. The CEO, or the top management team (e.g. Finkelstein, 1992; Hambrick and Mason, 1984), should have a grip on the organization's process of strategy formation and should be able to impose their will on the organization. Leaders should strive to overcome organizational inertia and adapt the organization to the strategic direction they intend. This type of controlled strategic behavior is what Chandler (1962) had in mind when he coined the aphorism *structure follows strategy* – the organizational structure should be adapted to the strategy intended by the decision-maker. In the organizational leadership perspective it would be more fitting to expand Chandler's maxim to *organization follows strategy* – all aspects of the company should be matched to the strategist's intentions.

The Organizational Dynamics Perspective

To proponents of the organizational dynamics perspective, such an heroic depiction of leadership is understandable, but usually more myth than reality. There might be a few great, wise, charismatic managers that rise to the apex of organizations, but unfortunately, all other organizations have to settle for regular mortals. Strong leaders are an exception, not the norm, and even their ability to mould the organization at will is highly exaggerated – good stories for a best-selling (auto)biography, but legend nevertheless (e.g. Chen and Meindl, 1991; Kets de Vries, 1994). Yet, the belief in the power of leadership is quite popular, among managers and the managed alike (e.g. Meindl, Ehrlich and Dukerich, 1985; Pfeffer, 1977). Managers like the idea that as leaders of an organization or organizational unit, they can make a difference. To most, 'being in control' is what management is about. They have a penchant for attributing organizational results to their own efforts (e.g. Calder, 1977; Sims and Lorenzi, 1992). Most other people in the organization, the managed, assume that they will be led and therefore have expectations about the characteristics of good leaders and the actions such leaders should take. In fact, both parties are subscribing to a seductively simple model of how organizations work. They see organizations as straightforward mechanical systems, whose behavior can be governed by a simple 'cause-and-effect' control system – to get an effect, one has to push the right button.

However seductive, this view of organizational functioning is rarely a satisfactory model. A top manager does not resemble a jockey riding a thoroughbred horse, but is more like a cowboy herding mules. Organizations are complex social systems, made up of many 'stubborn individuals' with their own ideas, interests, and agendas. Strategy formation is therefore an inherently political process (e.g. Allison, reading 3.3; Pettigrew, 1985), that leaders can only influence depending on their power base. The more dispersed the political power, the more difficult it is for a leader to control the organization's behavior. Even if leaders are granted, or acquire, significant political power to push through their favored measures, there may still be considerable resistance and guerrilla activities. Political processes within organizations do not signify the derailment of strategic decision-making – politics is the normal state of affairs.

Besides such political dynamics, a top manager's ability to control the direction of a company is also severely constrained by the organization's culture. Social norms will have evolved, relationships will have been formed, aspirations will have taken root and cognitive maps will have been shaped. A leader cannot ignore the cultural legacy of the organization's history, as this will be deeply etched into the minds of the organization's members. Any top manager attempting to radically alter the direction of a company will find out that changing the underlying values, perceptions, beliefs and expectations is extremely difficult, if not next to impossible. As Weick (1979) puts it, an organization does not have a culture, it is a culture – shared values and norms are what make an organization. And just as it is difficult to change someone's character, it is difficult to change an organization's culture (e.g. Johnson, 1988; reading 9.4; Smircich and Stubbart, 1985; reading 2.5). Moreover, as most top managers rise through the ranks to the upper echelons, they themselves are a product of the existing organizational culture. Changing your own culture is like pulling yourself up by your own bootstraps – a great trick, too bad that nobody can do it.

In Chapters 5 and 6, a related argument was put forward, as part of the resource-based view of the firm. One of the basic assumptions of the resource-based view is that building up competences is an arduous task, requiring a relatively long period of time. Learning is a slow process under the best of circumstances, but even more difficult if learning one thing means unlearning something else. The stronger the existing cognitive maps (knowledge), routines (capabilities) and disposition (attitude), the more challenging it is to 'teach an old dog new tricks.' The leader's power to direct and speed up such processes, it was argued, is quite limited (e.g. Barney, 1991; reading 5.4; Leonard-Barton, 1995).

Taken together, the political, cultural and learning dynamics leave top managers with relatively little power over the system the want to steer, according to advocates of the organizational dynamics perspective. A leader might be able to nudge, but on the whole the strategy will be the result of the chaotic internal dynamics of the organizational system. Some leaders might think that they are in control and that they are consciously choosing the future direction of the organization, but this is often only an illusion. In reality, they are limited by a cognitive map of which they are not aware, trapped in a culture they think is normal, reigned in by the political interests of diverse groups, and stuck with competences and investments that are difficult to change. Under these circumstances, one could say *strategy follows organization*, instead of the other way around.

The question for the field of strategic management is, therefore, whether organization follows strategy or strategy follows organization (e.g. Pfeffer, 1982; Leavy and Wilson, 1994). Can the top management of a firm shape the organization to fit with their intended strategy or does the organizational context determine the strategy actually followed? In short, strategists must come to terms with the paradox of control and chaos (see Table 9.1).

Defining the Issues: Inheritance and Initiative

As in Chapter 8, the debate between proponents of the organizational leadership perspective and supporters of the organizational dynamics perspective rests on the age-old question of voluntarism versus determinism. Are humans free to make their own choices and shape their own future, or is free will an illusion and is the future shaped by forces beyond an individual's grasp? Where people have the power to mould their direct environment as they see fit, they have control. Where their direct environment is shaped by dynamics that no one controls, there is a state of chaos. Whether control or chaos prevails – or whether both are simultaneously in evidence – is essential to the approach one takes to strategy process and strategy content. However, it is clear that the paradox of control and chaos is not easily resolved and therefore hotly disputed.

Two issues are central to this discussion on 'who shapes whom'. The first issue is that of *organizational inheritance* (e.g. Nelson and Winter, 1982; Baum and Singh, 1994). In organizations, just as in families, each new

TABLE 9.1
Organizational leadership
versus organizational
dynamics perspective

	Organizational Leadership Perspective	Organizational Dynamics Perspective
Emphasis on	Control over chaos	Chaos over control
Organizational changes	Controllable creation processes	Uncontrollable evolutionary processes
Change process	Leader commands behavior	Behavior emerges from history
Change determinants	Leader's vision and skill	Political, cultural and learning dynamics
Form of change	Top-down, mechanistic	Interactive fermentation
Organizational malleability	High, fast	Low, slow
Direction of adaptation	Organization follows strategy	Strategy follows organization
Normative implication	Strategize, then organize	Strategizing and organizing intertwined
Point of view	Voluntaristic	Deterministic

generation does not start from scratch, but inherits properties that belong to the group. In families, a part of this inheritance is in the form of genetic properties, but other elements are also passed on such as family traditions, myths, connections, feuds, titles, and possessions. Each person might think of themselves as a unique individual, but to some degree they are an extension of the family line, and their behavior is influenced by their inheritance. In organizations the same phenomenon is observable. New top managers may arrive on the scene, but they inherit a great deal from their predecessors. They inherit traditions and myths in the form of a culture. Internal and external connections and feuds shape the political constellation in which new leaders must function. And brands, skills and other resources are passed down to them.

The question is how heavily organizational inheritance predetermines an organization's future path. Can top managers, if necessary, compel the organization to break with its past, and transform it into something new? This would assume weak pressures of inheritance and high malleability. Or must top managers accept the fact that the influence of inherited characteristics is pervasive, and hence malleability limited?

The second issue in the debate is that of *managerial initiative*. While organizational inheritance refers to the 'momentum' present in the organizational system (e.g. Miller and Friesen, 1980; Tushman, Newman and Romanelli, 1986; reading 4.3), managerial initiative refers to the power of managers to intervene in organizational processes. Only where managers lose all ability to take initiatives do they truly become mere spectators of organizational development. The more power that managers have to move proactively, the greater the chance of gaining control over organizational behavior. If top managers are able to accumulate enough political power, it might be possible to neutralize opposing coalitions in the organization and impose a new agenda. If leaders are capable of critical thought and dialogue, they might have the intellectual power to challenge the organizational belief system, and forge a new paradigm. If they are skilled in capturing the hearts and minds of the employees, they might be able to change the corporate culture and push the organization in a new direction. Even if organizational inheritance is a major factor, the power of top managers to take initiatives might be a sufficiently strong counterpressure to give leaders a real impact on shaping the organizational context.

EXHIBIT 9.1
Kodak Short Case

KODAK: MANUAL OR AUTOFOCUS?

George Fisher was somewhat of a corporate celebrity in the US when he took over as Chairman, President, and Chief Executive Officer of Kodak in October 1993. His fame had been acquired while leading the restructuring of Motorola from a troubled firm into one of America's leading high-tech companies. Particularly eye-catching was how Fisher moved Motorola into the embryonic markets for cellular telephones and pagers just in time to ride the wave of exponential growth. Fisher had also gained widespread public attention in his efforts to combat what he believed to be unfair trade practices by Motorola's Japanese competitors. By intensively lobbying Washington, Fisher was able to extract concessions from the Japanese government to open up the Japanese market for Motorola's products, while Washington instituted measures to curb the 'dumping' of Japanese products on the American market. This success made Fisher one of the obvious choices to lead the necessary restructuring of Kodak.

The task facing Fisher was formidable. Kodak was a lumbering giant, with more than $12 billion in sales and over 100,000 employees world-wide. While the company, founded in 1881, had one of the world's most valuable brand names, it was slowly losing terrain in its core photographic film business and had not been particularly successful in its diversification efforts. Its main competitor in the photo film industry, the Japanese company Fuji, had been steadily nibbling away market share for years and Kodak had not demonstrated that it had the innovative capabilities to counter this trend. Moreover, the photographic film technology, on which Kodak's predominance in consumer markets rests, was being threatened by substitute technologies. Especially the emergence of digital imaging, using high resolution scanners and printers, posed a significant danger to Kodak's 'analog imaging' business. The company had been slow in its response to these developments, and the efforts that were been made resulted in lacklustre performance at best.

Between 1983 and 1993 Kodak had restructured several times, under changing leadership, but with little effect. In August 1993 a group of outside directors removed CEO, Kay Whitmore, because it was believed that not enough had been done to improve the company's performance and future outlook. It was felt that it was time to attract an outsider without Kodak photo chemicals in his veins. An outsider without an emotional attachment to the Kodak culture, without a stake in the current strategy and without political debts to repay, would have the freedom to reshape the firm as he saw fit. This person would be given *carte blanche* to wield the ax where necessary to bring about a rapid transformation of Kodak. Preferably this outsider would have a track record in transforming bogged down high-tech companies. According to the board of directors George Fisher fit the bill exactly. Or as Roberto C. Goizueta, Kodak board member and Chairman of Coca Cola, put it at the time: 'When we began this search, our No.1 candidate was God, and we stepped down from that'.

Fisher's mandate was to carry out all necessary changes at Kodak and turn around the company within three years. By 1996, Fisher had booked some impressive results. He had sold off $8.9 billion in non-core businesses, including Eastman Chemical Co. and a copier company. This had helped to reduce Kodak's debt from $7.5 billion to $1.5 billion. Sales grew to $16 billion and earnings reached $1.29 billion, more than double that of 1994. Investor confidence in Kodak's potential had also increased, as its stock reached a record high of $94 in January 1997, up 80 per cent since Fisher's arrival. In the 1996 annual report Fisher could reflect with satisfaction that 1996 had been a 'watershed' in his efforts to turn around the company. 'The picture at Kodak is clearly changing,' a proud Fisher reported to his shareholders.

However, as 1997 progressed, it became clear that all was not well at Kodak. On October 14 the firm announced results that shocked investors, and sent share prices in a nose dive to $63. Operating profits over 1997 were expected to be down by 25 per cent, with no immediate improvement foreseen. As a consequence, Fisher reduced the number of senior managers in the company by 20 per cent and unveiled plans to chop 16,000 of the company's 100,000 jobs. Analysts were quick to point out that massive bloodletting was long overdue. Kodak had been known for its bloated cost structure for years, yet during Fisher's reign the number of employees in continuing operations had actually grown by 3000. It is a tell-tale sign that Kodak's major rival, Fuji, accomplished twice the level of sales per employee. Furthermore, Kodak's overhead and administrative costs were at 27.5 per cent of sales, which was higher than most of its competitors.

While Kodak's efforts to significantly revamp its cost structure grabbed the headlines, other problems were dogging Fisher. Most importantly, Fisher's core strategy of expanding from analog to digital imaging, making Kodak an allround imaging company, was not running smoothly. Just as he had guided Motorola into the promising market for cellular phones, it was Fisher's intention to move Kodak into the emerging market for digital imaging. Yet, despite investments of some $500 million a year into research and product development, results were mixed at best. In terms of sales volume Fisher could point to a promising trend. In 1996 sales of digital products, such as digital cameras and scanners, went up 25 per cent to $1.5 billion, putting them ahead of the competition. The downside was that this lead was costing Kodak mountains of cash – in 1997 alone the losses were estimated at $200 million. Furthermore, Kodak was up against such ferocious competitors as Sony, Hewlett-Packard, Epson and Canon, as well as a pack of smaller companies, all accustomed to the break-neck pace of technological development in the information technology industry. Analysts point out that in this emerging business, where dominant formats for things like image compression and low-cost photo-quality printers still need to surface, competitors need to be fast and nimble. According to high-tech consultant Robert Krinsky 'to win at this game will require speed and flexibility – and that's not what I think of when I think of Kodak.'

Critics argue that this is the major difference between Kodak and Motorola. At Kodak Fisher has faced a far more ingrained and bureaucratic culture, more oriented to old-line manufacturing than to high-tech innovation. 'Fisher has been able to change the culture at the very top,' remarks one industry analyst in *Business Week*, 'but he hasn't been able to change the huge mass of middle managers, and they just don't understand this [digital] world.' Moreover, there is a fear among many Kodak managers that digital products will cannibalize the company's core business. This had lead to caution, suspicion and sometimes even hostility towards the new direction.

To make things worse, Fisher could find no effective response to Fuji's continued onslaught in Kodak's core photo film business. Fuji's market share in the US market jumped from 11 per cent in 1996 to 16 per cent in 1997, due to extensive marketing efforts, steep price cuts, and an exclusive deal for Wal-Mart's photofinishing business. In 1997, Fuji also boldly opened a plant in South Carolina with a capacity to produce 100 million rolls of color film a year, which equals about 14 per cent of the US annual demand. While Kodak's US market share has dropped to about 70 per cent, it cannot afford to get caught up in a price war with Fuji to recover lost ground, as this would cut into the profits it needs to fuel its digital activities. Fisher's only ace in his poker game with Fuji was to lobby Washington again to seek action against unfair trade barriers in the Japanese market for photo film and paper. Fisher argued that hidden barriers in this second largest photo market in the world had limited Kodak's market share to 10 per cent, while Fuji enjoyed a profitable market share of 70 per cent, allowing Fuji to cross-subsidize aggressive pricing in other markets. However, while in his Motorola days Fisher pulled off a success, the World Trade Organization rejected Kodak's claims due to lack of proof, leaving Fisher furious, but empty handed.

All these developments have left many analysts wondering whether Fisher is the leader who can get Kodak back on track again. Or as *Business Week* titled an article on the company's problems: 'Can George Fisher Fix Kodak?' Is Fisher in control and can he push through the necessary changes, or is it time to unleash the headhunters again? Or is it an illusion to believe that anyone can 'fix Kodak' and must more attention be paid to influencing the organizational dynamics that are propelling the company? Whichever is the case, for the next little while few people at Kodak will be saying 'smile'.

Sources: *Business Week*, October 20, 1997; *New York Times*, May 5, 1994

The Debate and the Readings

The economic sociologist Duesenberry once remarked that 'economics is all about how people make choices; sociology is all about how they don't have any choices to make.' Although half in jest, his comment does ring true.

Much of the literature within the field of economics assumes that people in organizations can freely make choices and have the power to shape their strategy – possible restraints on their freedom usually come from the environment. Sociological literature, but also psychological and political science work, often feature the limitations on individual's freedom. These different disciplinary inclinations are not absolute, but can be clearly recognized in the debate.

To open the debate on behalf of the organizational leadership perspective, a classic reading has been selected, 'The CEO: Leadership in Organizations,' by Roland Christensen, Kenneth Andrews, Joseph Bower, Richard Hamermesh and Michael Porter. This contribution is a part of the same well-known Harvard textbook, *Business Policy*, as is Kenneth Andrew's reading in Chapter 2. In line with the organizational leadership literature, this reading emphasizes the role of the organization's leader as main strategic planner and chief strategy implementor. But while many other authors taking this perspective accord a large measure of importance to the broader top management team, Christensen and his colleagues focus on the pivotal position of the CEO. In their view, the president of the company is essential to the organization's success. They are skeptical of research, such as Henry Mintzberg's, that portray managers as 'harried, improvisatory, overworked performers of ten roles [who] do not really know what they are doing.' In their opinion, this says little about how effective leaders should work. CEOs are crucial in their roles as organizational leaders, personal leaders and chief architects of organizational purpose. Where organizations are led by individuals of 'great human skill, sensitivity, administrative capability . . . [and] analytic intelligence of a higher order,' above average organizational performance is much more likely. The organization is a vehicle in need of a driver, who knows where to go, how to get there and is capable of roadside repairs if anything breaks down on the way. Christensen and colleagues recognize that the organizational context is sometimes not entirely malleable and can limit the freedom of the CEO to make and implement strategy. However, this is not viewed as a disqualification of the organizational leadership perspective, but as a failure of the CEO to lead. In short, the leader matters, not the organizational context.

For an opening reading to represent the organizational dynamics perspective, the same problem exists as in Chapter 8 – most authors arguing that managers have little freedom to shape their future usually do not write for a managerial audience. Almost all of the literature with a strong determinist bent is quite academic, and therefore less suitable as initial reading in this chapter. Therefore, an accessible contribution has been selected that is very close to the extreme pole of organizational dynamics, but is not fully deterministic. This reading by Ralph Stacey is mysteriously entitled 'Strategy as Order Emerging from Chaos.' Stacey argues that top managers cannot, and should not even try, to control the organization and its strategy. In his view, the organizational dynamics involved in strategy formation, learning and change are too complex to simply be controlled by managers. He states that 'sometimes the best thing a manager can do is to let go and allow things to happen.' The resulting *chaos*, he argues, does not mean that the organization will be a mess – a lack of control does not mean that the organization will be adrift. His reasoning is that non-linear feedback systems, such as organizations, have a self-organizing ability, which 'can produce controlled behaviour, even though no one is in control.' In his view, real strategic change requires the chaos of contention and conflict to destroy old recipes and to seek for new solutions. The 'self-organizing processes of political interaction and complex learning' ensure that chaos does not result in disintegration. Hence, in Stacey's opinion, it is management's task to help create a situation of bounded instability in which strategy can emerge. The role of leaders is to influence the organizational context in a way, that new and unexpected strategies can develop spontaneously.

To complement the two 'opening statements' in the debate, three additional readings have been selected for this chapter. Reading 9.3, 'Linking Planning and Implementation,' by L.J. Bourgeois and David Brodwin, has been chosen to bring forward the broad range of leadership styles that exist. In reading 9.1, Christensen and his Harvard colleagues seem to favor what Bourgeois and Brodwin regard as a traditional leadership approach. This traditional view, according to Bourgeois and Brodwin, separates the 'thinkers,' who formulate, from the 'doers,' who implement. Often the thinking is limited to the CEO, while the rest of the organization must execute the plans handed down to them. There are situations, Bourgeois and Brodwin believe, where it makes sense to have this top-down approach to the strategy process ('the CEO as master planner'). However, they argue that there are many more circumstances in which a bottom-up approach would be more effective ('the CEO as guide and judge'). Such a bottom-up approach, which the authors call *crescive*, would make it possible to address formulation and implementation simultaneously, allowing strategies to be created interactively. The fundamental reason why the crescive approach might be needed, Bourgeois and Brodwin conclude, is that the chief executives are often constrained by factors in the organizational context that do not let them command strategic change at will. For the debate in this chapter, Bourgeois and Brodwin major contribution is that they point out that a leader's ability to shape the organization's strategy might vary and that the leadership style might need to vary accordingly.

Reading 9.4, 'Rethinking Incrementalism,' by Gerry Johnson, has been added to this chapter as a more clear-cut representative of the organizational dynamics perspective than Stacey. Johnson argues that managers usually believe that they are making rational strategic choices, but that in fact the strategic outcomes should be understood as 'the product of the political, cognitive and cultural fabric of the organization.' According to Johnson, strategic decisions can

> 'be explained better in terms of political processes than analytical procedures; . . . cognitive maps of managers are better explanations of their perceptions of the environment and their strategic responses than are analysed position statements and evaluative techniques; and that the legitimacy of these cognitive maps is likely to be reinforced through the myths and rituals of the organization.'

In Johnson's view, organizations are entangled in a cultural web, with at the center a core of shared beliefs, which at best can be marginally adjusted. Therefore, Johnson is not optimistic about the ability of managers to shape the organizational context – it clearly shapes them.

The last contribution, 'Inertia and Transformation,' by Richard Rumelt, has been added to the debate to further clarify the forces hindering leaders to shape their organizations at will. The question Rumelt asks is essentially the same as in this chapter: are there barriers to reshaping an organization? However, there is a subtle distinction between Rumelt's angle and focus in this debate. Here, the pivotal issue has been on *organizational malleability* – the extent to which an organization can be moulded by the strategist(s). Rumelt is interested in *organizational plasticity* – the extent to which organizations can change at all. Despite this minor difference, his overview of the potential sources of inertia is very informative for the debate on the nature of the organizational context. His extensive list of 'frictions' and forms of inertia once again underline the challenge facing strategists – they must come to terms with the paradox of control and chaos.

9.1   The CEO: Leadership in Organizations

By Roland Christensen, Kenneth Andrews, Joseph Bower, Richard Hamermesh, and Michael Porter[1]

Management we regard as leadership in the informed, planned, purposeful conduct of complex organized activity. *General management* is, in its simplest form, the management of a total enterprise or of an autonomous subunit. The senior general manager in any organization is its chief executive officer, who for the purposes of simplicity we will often call the *president*.

We will begin by considering the *roles* that presidents must play. We will examine the *functions* or characteristic and natural actions that they perform in the roles they assume. We will try to identify *skills* or abilities that put one's perceptions, judgment, and knowledge to effective use in executive performance. As we look at executive roles, functions and skills, we may be able to define more clearly aspects of the *point of view* that provide the most suitable perspective for high-level executive judgment.

Many attempts to characterize executive roles and functions come to very little. Henri Fayol, originator of the classical school of management

---

[1] Source: This article has been adapted from 'The CEO: Leadership in Organization,' in *Business Policy: Text and Cases*, Sixth Edition, Irwin, Homewood, IL, 1987. Used with permission.

theory, identified the roles of planner, organizer, coordinator, and controller, initiating the construction by others of a later vocabulary of remarkable variety. Present-day students reject these categories as vague or abstract and indicative only of the objectives of some executive activity. Henry Mintzberg, who among other researchers has observed managers at work, identifies three sets of behavior – interpersonal, informational, and decisional. The interpersonal roles he designates as *figurehead* (for ceremonial duties), *leader* (of the work of his organization or unit), and *liaison agent* (for contacts outside his unit). Information roles can be designated as *monitor* (of information), *disseminator* (internally), and *spokesman* (externally). Decisional roles are called *entrepreneur, disturbance handler, resource allocator*, and *negotiator.*

Empirical studies of what managers do are corrective of theory but not necessarily instructive in educating good managers. That most unprepared managers act intuitively rather than systematically in response to unanticipated pressures does not mean that the most effective do so to the same extent. If in fact the harried, improvisatory, overworked performers of 10 roles do not really know *what* they are doing or have any priorities besides degree of urgency, then we are not likely to find out what more effective management is from categorizing their activities. On the other hand it is futile to offer unrealistic exhortations about long-range planning and organizing to real-life victims of forced expediency.

The simplification that will serve our approach to policy best will leave aside important but easily understood activities. The executive may make speeches, pick the silver pattern for the executive lunchroom, negotiate personally with important customers, and do many things human beings have to do for many reasons. Roles we may study in order to do a better job of general management can be viewed as those of *organization leader, personal leader*, and *chief architect of organization purpose*. As leader of persons grouped in a hierarchy of suborganizations, the president must be taskmaster, mediator, motivator, and organization designer. Since these roles do not have useful job descriptions saying what to do, one might better estimate the nature of the overlapping responsibility of the head of an organization than to draw theoretical distinctions between categories. The personal influence of leaders becomes evident as they play the role of communicator or exemplar and attract respect or affection. When we examine finally the president's role as architect of organization purpose, we may see entrepreneurial or improvisatory behavior if the organization is just being born. If the company is long since established, the part played may be more accurately designated as manager of the purpose-determining process or chief strategist.

The CEO as Organization Leader

Chief executives are first and probably least pleasantly persons who are responsible for results attained in the present as designated by plans made previously. Nothing that we will say shortly about their concern for the people in their organizations or later about their responsibility to society can gainsay this immediate truth. Achieving acceptable results against expectations of increased earnings per share and return on the stockholder's investment requires the CEO or president to be continually informed and ready to intervene when results fall below what had been expected. Changing circumstances and competition produce emergencies upsetting well-laid plans. Resourcefulness in responding to crisis is a skill that most successful executives develop early.

But the organizational consequences of the critical taskmaster role require presidents to go beyond insistence upon achievement of planned results. They must see as their second principal function the creative maintenance and development of the organized capability that makes achievement possible. This activity leads to a third principle – the integration of the specialist functions that enable their organizations to perform the technical tasks in marketing, research and development, manufacturing, finance, control, and personnel that proliferate as technology develops and tend to lead the company in all directions. If this coordination is successful in harmonizing special staff activities, presidents will probably have performed the task of getting organizations to accept and order priorities in accordance with the companies' objectives. Securing commitment to purpose is a central function of the president as organization leader.

The skills required by these functions reveal presidents not solely as taskmasters but as mediators and motivators as well. They need ability in the education and motivation of people and the evaluation of their performance, two functions that tend to work against one another. The former requires understanding of individual needs, which persist no matter what the economic purpose of the organization may be. The latter requires objective assessment of the technical requirements of the task assigned. The capability required here is also that required in the integration of functions and the mediation of the conflict bound to arise out of technical specialism. The integrating capacity of the chief executive extends to meshing the economic, technical, human, and moral dimensions of corporate activity and to relating the company to its immediate and more distant communities. It will show itself in the formal organizational designs that are put into effect as the blueprint of the required structured cooperation.

The perspective demanded of successful organization leaders embraces both the primacy of organizational goals and the validity of individual goals. Besides this dual appreciation, they exhibit an impartiality toward the specialized functions and have criteria enabling them to allocate organizational resources against documented needs. The point of view of the leader of an organization almost by definition requires an overview of its relations not only to its internal constituencies but to the relevant institutions and forces of its external environment. We will come soon to a conceptual solution of the problems encountered in the role of organization leader.

The CEO as Personal Leader

The functions, skills, and appropriate point of view of chief executives hold true no matter who they are or who makes up their organizations. The functions that accompany presidential performance of their role as communicator of purpose and policy, as exemplar, and as the focal point for the respect or affection of subordinates vary much more according to personal energy, style, character, and integrity. Presidents contribute as persons to the quality of life and performance in their organizations. This is true whether they are dynamic or colorless. By example they educate junior executives to seek to emulate them or simply to learn from their behavior what they really expect. They have the opportunity to infuse organized effort with flair or distinction if they have the skill to dramatize the relationship between their own activities and the goals of corporate effort.

All persons in leadership positions have or attain power that in sophisticated organizations they invoke as humanely and reasonably as possible in order to avoid the stultifying effects of dictatorship, dominance, or even markedly superior capacity. Formally announced policy, backed by the authority of the chief executive, can be made effective to some degree by clarity of direction, intensity of supervision, and the exercise of sanctions in enforcement. But in areas of judgment where policy cannot be specified without becoming absurdly overdetailed, chief executives establish in their own demeanor even more than in policy statements the moral and ethical level of performance expected.

The skills of the effective personal leader are those of persuasion and articulation made possible by saying something worth saying and by understanding the sentiments and points of view being addressed. Leaders cultivate and embody relationships between themselves and their subordinates appropriate to the style of leadership they have chosen or fallen into. Some of the qualities lending distinction to this leadership cannot be deliberately contrived, even by an artful schemer. The maintenance of personal poise in adversity or emergency and the capacity for development as an emotionally mature person are essentially innate and developed capabilities. It is probably true that some personal preeminence in technical or social functions is either helpful or essential in demonstrating leadership related to the president's personal contribution. Credibility and cooperation depend upon demonstrated capacity of a kind more tangible and attractive than, for example, the noiseless coordination of staff activity.

The CEO as Architect of Organization Purpose

To go beyond the organizational and personal roles of leadership, we enter the sphere of organization purpose, where we may find the atmosphere somewhat rare and the going less easy. We think students will note, as they see president after president cope or fail to cope with problems of various economic, political, social, or technical elements, that the contribution presidents make to their companies goes far beyond the apparently superficial activities that clutter their days.

The attention of presidents to organizations' needs must extend beyond answering letters of complaint from spouses of aggrieved employees to appraisal (for example) of the impact of their companies' information, incentive, and control systems upon individual behavior. Their personal contribution to their company goes far beyond easily understood attention to key customers and speeches to the Economic Club to the more subtle influence their own probity and character have on subordinates. We must turn now to activities even further out – away from immediate everyday decisions and emergencies. Some part of what a president does is oriented toward maintaining the development of a company over time and preparing for a future more distant than the time horizon appropriate to the roles and functions identified thus far.

The most difficult role – and the one we will concentrate on henceforth – of the chief executive of any organization is the one in which he serves as custodian of corporate objectives. The entrepreneurs who create a company know at the outset what they are up to. Their objectives are intensely personal, if not exclusively economic, and their passions may be patent protection and finance. If they succeed in passing successfully through the phase of personal entrepreneurship, where they or their bankers or families are likely to be the only members of the organization concerned with purpose, they find themselves in the role of planner, managing the process by which ideas for the future course of the company are conceived, evaluated, fought over, and accepted or rejected.

The presidential functions involved include establishing or presiding over the goal-setting and resource-allocation processes of the company, making or ratifying choice among strategic alternatives, and clarifying and defending the goals of the company against external attack or internal erosion. The installation of purpose in place of improvisation and the substitution of planned progress in place of drifting are probably the most demanding functions of the chief executive. Successful organization leadership requires great human skill, sensitivity, and administrative ability. Personal leadership is built upon personality and character. The capacity for determining and monitoring the adequacy of the organization's continuing purposes implies as well analytic intelligence of a high order. The president we are talking about is not a two-dimensional poster or television portrait.

The crucial skill of the president concerned with corporate purpose includes the creative generation or recognition of strategic alternatives made valid by developments in the marketplace and the capability and resources of the company. Along with this, in a combination not easily come by, runs the critical capacity to analyze the strengths and weaknesses of documented proposals. The ability to perceive with some objectivity corporate strengths and weaknesses is essential to sensible choice of goals, for the most attractive goal is not attainable without the strength to open the way to it through inertia and intense opposition, with all else that lies between.

Probably the skill most nearly unique to general management, as opposed to the management of functional or technical specialties, is the intellectual capacity to conceptualize corporate purpose and the dramatic skill to invest it with some degree of magnetism. As we will see, the skill can be exercised in industries less romantic than space, electronics, or environmental reclamation. No sooner is a distinctive set of corporate objectives vividly delineated than the temptation to go beyond it sets in. Under some circumstances it is the president's function to defend properly focused purpose against superficially attractive diversification or corporate growth that glitters like fool's gold. Because defense of proper strategy can be interpreted as mindless conservatism, wholly appropriate defense of a still valid strategy requires courage, supported by detailed documentation.

Continuous monitoring, in any event, of the quality and continued suitability of corporate purpose is over time the most sophisticated and essential of all the functions of general management alluded to here. The perspective that sustains this function is the kind of creative discontent that prevents complacency even in good times and seeks continuous advancement of corporate and individual capacity and performance. It requires also constant attention to the future, as if the present did not offer problems and opportunities enough.

9.2   Strategy as Order Emerging from Chaos

By Ralph Stacey[1]

Chaos and Self-Organization in Business

There are four important points to make on the recent discoveries about the complex behaviour of dynamic systems, all of which have direct application to human organizations.

Chaos is a Form of Instability Where the Specific Long-Term Future is Unknowable

Chaos in its scientific sense is an irregular pattern of behavior generated by well-defined nonlinear feedback rules commonly found in nature and

[1] Source: Reprinted with permission from *Long Range Planning*, Vol. 26, No. 1, 'Strategy as Order Emerging from Chaos,' pp. 10–17. © 1993, Pergamon Press Ltd. Oxford, England.

human society. When systems driven by such rules operate away from equilibrium, they are highly sensitive to selected tiny changes in their environments, amplifying them into self-reinforcing virtuous and vicious circles that completely alter the behavior of the system. In other words, the system's future unfolds in a manner dependent upon the precise detail of what it does, what the systems constituting its environments do, and upon chance. As a result of this fundamental property of the system itself, specific links between cause and effect are lost in the history of its development, and the specific path of its long-term future development is completely unpredictable. Over the short term, however, it is possible to predict behavior because it takes time for the consequences of small changes to build up.

Is there evidence of chaos in business systems? We would conclude that there was if we could point to small changes escalating into large consequences; if we could point to self-reinforcing vicious and virtuous circles; if we could point to feedback that alternates between the amplifying and the damping. It is not difficult to find such evidence.

Creative managers seize on small differences in customer requirements and perceptions to build significant differentiators for their products. Customers may respond to this by switching from other product offerings, leading to a virtuous circle; or they may switch away, causing the kind of vicious circle that Coca-Cola found itself caught up in when it made that famous soft drink slightly sweeter.

Managers create, or at the very least shape, the requirements of their customers through the product offerings they make. Sony created a requirement for personal hi-fi systems through its Walkman offering, and manufacturers and operators have created requirements for portable telephones. Sony and Matsushita created the requirement for video recorders, and when companies supply information systems to their clients, they rarely do so according to a complete specification – instead, the supplier shapes the requirement. When managers intentionally shape customer demands through the offerings they make, this feeds back into customer responses, and managers may increase the impact by intentionally using the copying and spreading effects through which responses to product offerings feed back into other customers' responses. When managers do this, they are deliberately using positive feedback – along with negative feedback controls to meet cost and quality targets, for example – to create business success.

A successful business is also affected by many amplifying feedback processes that are outside the control of its managers and produce effects that they did not intend. Successful businesses are quite clearly characterized by feedback processes that flip between the negative and the positive, the damping and the amplifying; that is, they are characterized by feedback patterns that produce chaos. The long-term future of a creative organization is absolutely unknowable, and no one can intend its future direction over the long term or be in control of it. In such a system long-term plans and visions of future states can be only illusions.

But in Chaos there are Boundaries Around the Instability

While chaos means disorder and randomness in the behavior of a system at the specific level, it also means that there is a qualitative pattern at a general, overall level. The future unfolds unpredictably, but it always does so according to recognizable family-like resemblances. This is what we mean when we say that history repeats itself, but never in the same way. We see this combination of unpredictable specific behavior within an overall pattern in snowflakes. As two nearby snowflakes fall to the earth, they experience tiny differences in temperature and air impurities. Each snowflake amplifies those differences as they form, and by the time they reach the earth they have different shapes – but they are still clearly snowflakes. We cannot predict the shape of each snowflake, but we can predict that they will be snowflakes. In business, we recognize patterns of boom and recession, but each time they are different in specific terms, defying all attempts to predict them.

Chaos is unpredictable variety within recognizable categories defined by irregular features, that is, an inseparable intertwining of order and disorder. It is this property of being bounded by recognizable qualitative patterns that makes it possible for humans to cope with chaos. Numerous tests have shown that our memories do not normally store information in units representing the precise characteristics of the individual shapes or events we perceive. Instead, we store information about the strength of connection between individual units perceived. We combine information together into categories or concepts using family resemblance-type features. Memory emphasizes general structure, irregular category features, rather than specific content. We remember the irregular patterns rather than the specific features and we design our next actions on the basis of these memorized patterns. And since we design our actions in this manner, chaotic behavior presents us with no real problem. Furthermore, we are adept at using analogical reasoning and intuition to reflect upon experience and adapt it to new situations, all of which is ideally suited to handling chaos.

Unpredictable New Order can Emerge from Chaos through a Process of Spontaneous Self-Organization

When nonlinear feedback systems in nature are pushed far from equilibrium into chaos, they are capable of creating a complex new order. For example, at some low temperature the atoms of a particular gas are arranged in a particular pattern and the gas emits no light. Then, as heat is applied, it agitates the atoms causing them to move, and as this movement is amplified through the gas it emits a dull glow. Small changes in heat are thus amplified, causing instability, or chaos, that breaks the symmetry of the atoms' original behavior. Then at a critical point, the atoms in the gas suddenly all point in the same direction to produce a laser beam. Thus, the system uses chaos to shatter old patterns of behavior, creating the opportunity for the new. And as the system proceeds through chaos, it is confronted with critical points where it, so to speak, makes a choice between different options for further development. Some options represent yet further chaos and others lead to more complex forms of orderly behavior, but which will occur is inherently unpredictable. The choice itself is made by spontaneous self-organization amongst the components of the system in which they, in effect, communicate with each other, reach a consensus, and commit to a new form of behavior. If a more complex form of orderly behavior is reached, it has what scientists call a dissipative structure, because continual attention and energy must be applied if it is to be sustained – for example, heat has to be continually pumped into the gas if the laser beam is to continue. If the system is to develop further, then the dissipative structure must be short-lived; to reach an even more complex state, the system will have to pass through chaos once more.

It is striking how similar the process of dealing with strategic issues in an organization is to the self-organizing phenomenon just outlined. The key to the effectiveness with which organizations change and develop new strategic directions lies in the manner in which managers handle what might be called their strategic issue agenda. That agenda is a dynamic, unwritten list of issues, aspirations, and challenges that key groups of managers are attending to. Consider the steps managers can be observed to follow as they handle their strategic issue agenda:

- *Detecting and selecting small disturbances.* In open-ended strategic situations, change is typically the result of many small events and actions that are unclear, ambiguous, and confusing, with consequences that are unknowable. The key difficulty is to identify what the real issues, problems, or opportunities are, and the challenge is to find an appropriate and creative aspiration or objective. In these circumstances the organization has no alternative but to rely on the initiative of individuals to notice and pursue some issue, aspiration, or challenge. In order to do this, those individuals have to rely on their experience-based intuition and ability to detect analogies between one set of ambiguous circumstances and another.

- *Amplifying the issues and building political support.* Once some individual detects some potential issue, that individual begins to push for organizational attention to it. A complex political process of building special interest groups to support an issue is required before it gains organizational attention and can thus be said to be on the strategic issue agenda.

- *Breaking symmetries.* As they build and progress strategic issue agendas, managers are in effect altering old mental models, existing company and industry recipes, to come up with new ways of doing things. They are destroying existing perceptions and structures.

- *Critical points and unpredictable outcomes.* Some issues on the agenda may be dealt with quickly, while others may attract attention, continuous or periodic, for a very long time. How quickly an issue is dealt with depends upon the time required to reach enough consensus and commitment to proceed to action. At some critical point, an external or internal pressure in effect forces a choice. The outcome on whether and how to proceed to action over the issue is unpredictable because it depends upon the context of power, personality, and group dynamic within which it is being handled. The result may or may not be action, and action will usually be experimental at first.

■ *Changing the frame of reference.* Managers in a business come to share memories of what worked and what did not work in the past – the organizational memory. In this way they build up a business philosophy, or culture, establishing a company recipe and in common with their rivals an industry recipe too. These recipes have a powerful effect on what issues will subsequently be detected and attended to; that is, they constitute a frame of reference within which managers interpret what to do next. The frame of reference has to be continually challenged and changed because it can easily become inappropriate to new circumstances. The dissipative structure of consensus and commitment is therefore necessarily short-lived if an organization is to be innovative.

These phases constitute a political and learning process through which managers deal with strategic issues, and the key point about these processes is that they are spontaneous and self-organizing: no central authority can direct anyone to detect and select an open-ended issue for attention, simply because no one knows what it is until someone has detected it; no one can centrally organize the factions that form around specific issues; nor can anyone intend the destruction of old recipes and the substitution of new ones since it is impossible to know what the appropriate new ones are until they are discovered. The development of new strategic direction requires the chaos of contention and conflict, and the self-organizing processes of political interaction and complex learning.

Chaos is a Fundamental Property of Nonlinear Feedback Systems, a Category that Includes Human Organizations

Feedback simply means that one action or event feeds into another; that is, one action or event determines the next according to some relationship. For example, one firm repackages its product and its rival responds in some way, leading to a further action on the part of the first, provoking in turn yet another response from the second, and so on. The feedback relationship may be linear, or proportional, and when this is the case, the first firm will repackage its product and the second will respond by doing much the same. The feedback relationship could be nonlinear, or nonproportional, however, so that when the first firm repackages its product, the second introduces a new product at a lower price; this could lead the first to cut prices even further, so touching off a price war. In other words, nonlinear systems are those that use amplifying (positive) feedback in some way. To see the significance of positive feedback, compare it with negative feedback.

All effective businesses use negative or damping feedback systems to control and regulate their day-to-day activities. Managers fix short-term targets for profits and then prepare annual plans or budgets, setting out the time path to reach the target. As the business moves through time, outcomes are measured and compared with annual plan projections to yield variances. Frequent monitoring of those variances prompts corrective action to bring performance indicators back onto their planned paths; that is, variances feed back into corrective action and the feedback takes a negative form, so that when profit is below target, for example, offsetting action is taken to restore it. Scheduling, budgetary, and planning systems utilize negative feedback to keep an organization close to a predictable, stable equilibrium path in which it is adapted to its environment. While negative feedback controls a system according to prior intention, positive feedback produces explosively unstable equilibrium where changes are amplified, eventually putting intolerable pressure on the system until it runs out of control.

The key discovery about the operation of nonlinear feedback systems, however, is that there is a third choice. When a nonlinear feedback system is driven away from stable equilibrium toward explosive unstable equilibrium, it passes through a phase of bounded instability – there is a border between stability and instability where feedback flips autonomously between the amplifying and the damping to produce chaotic behaviour; a paradoxical state that combines both stability and instability.

All human interactions take the form of feedback loops simply because the consequences of one action always feed back to affect a subsequent one. Furthermore, all human interactions constitute nonlinear feedback loops because people under- and overreact. Since organizations are simply a vast web of feedback loops between people, they must be capable of chaotic, as well as stable and explosively unstable, behavior. The key question is which of these kinds of behaviours leads an organization to success. We can see the answer to this question if we reflect upon the fundamental forces operating on an organization.

All organizations are powerfully pulled in two fundamentally different directions:

- *Disintegration.* Organizations can become more efficient and effective if they divide tasks, segment markets, appeal to individual motivators, empower people, promote informal communication, and separate production processes in geographic and other terms. These steps lead to fragmenting cultures and dispersed power that pull an organization toward disintegration, a phenomenon that can be seen in practice as companies split into more and more business units and find it harder and harder to maintain control.

- *Ossification.*To avoid this pull to disintegration, and to reap the advantages of synergy and coordination, all organizations are also pulled to a state in which tasks are integrated, overlaps in market segments and production processes managed, group goals stressed above individual ones, power concentrated, communication and procedures formalized, and strongly shared cultures established. As an organization moves in this direction it develops more and more rigid structures, rules, procedures, and systems until it eventually ossifies, consequences that are easy to observe as organizations centralize.

Thus, one powerful set of forces pulls every organization toward a stable equilibrium (ossification) and another powerful set of forces pulls it toward an explosively unstable equilibrium (disintegration). Success lies at the border between these states, where managers continually alter systems and structures to avoid attraction either to disintegration or to ossification. For example, organizations typically swing to centralization in one period, to decentralization in another, and back again later on. Success clearly lies in a nonequilibrium state between stable and unstable equilibria; and for a nonlinear feedback system, that is chaos.

Eight Steps to Create Order Out of Chaos

When managers believe that they must pull together harmoniously in pursuit of a shared organizational intention established before they act, they are inevitably confined to the predictable – existing strategic directions will simply be continued or innovations made by others will simply be imitated. When, instead of this, managers create the chaos that flows from challenging existing perceptions and promote the conditions in which spontaneous self-organization can occur, they make it possible for innovation and new strategic direction to emerge. Managers create such conditions when they undertake actions of the following kind.

Develop New Perspectives on the Meaning of Control

The activity of learning in a group is a form of control that managers do not normally recognize as such. It is a self-organizing, self-policing form of control in which the group itself discovers intention and exercises control. Furthermore, we are all perfectly accustomed to the idea that the strategic direction of local communities, nation-states, and international communities is developed and controlled through the operation of political sytems, but we rarely apply this notion to organizations. When we do, we see that a sequence of choices and actions will continue in a particular direction only while those espousing that direction continue to enjoy sufficient support. This constitutes a form of control that is as applicable to an organization when it faces the conflicts around open-ended change, as it is to a nation. The lesson is that self-organizing processes can produce controlled behavior even though no one is in control – sometimes the best thing a manager can do is to let go and allow things to happen.

Design the Use of Power

The distribution of power and the way in which it is used provide very important boundaries around the group learning process from which new strategic directions emerge. The application of power in particular forms has fairly predictable consequences for group dynamics. Where power is applied as force and consented to out of fear, the group dynamic will be one of submission, or where such power is not consented to, the group dynamic will be one of rebellion, either covert or overt. Power may be applied as authority, and the predictable group dynamic here is one in which members of the group suspend their critical faculties and accept instructions from those above them. Groups in states of submission, rebellion, or conformity are incapable of complex learning, that is, the development of new perspectives and new mental models.

The kind of group dynamics that are conducive to complex learning occur when highly competitive win/lose polarization is removed, and open questioning and public testing of assertions encouraged. When this happens, people use argument and conflict to move toward periodic consensus and commitment to a particular issue. That consensus and commitment cannot, however, be the norm when people are searching for new perspectives – rather, they must alternate between conflict and consensus, between confusion and clarity. This kind of dynamic is likely to occur when they most powerfully alternate the form in which they use their power: sometimes withdrawing and allowing conflict; sometimes intervening with suggestions; sometimes exerting authority.

Encourage Self-Organizing Groups

A group will be self-organizing only if it discovers its own challenges, goals, and objectives. Mostly, such groups need to form spontaneously – the role of top managers is simply to create the atmosphere in which this can happen. When top managers do set up a group to deal with strategic issues, however, they must avoid the temptation to write terms of reference, set objectives, or prod the group to reach some predetermined view. Instead top managers must present ambiguous challenges and take the chance that the group may produce proposals they do not approve of. For a group of managers to be self-organizing, it has to be free to operate as its members jointly choose, within the boundaries provided by their work together. This means that when they work together in this way, the normal hierarchy must be suspended for most of the time. Members are there because of the contributions they are able to make and the influence they can exert through those contributions and their own personalities. This suspension of the normal hierarchy can take place only if those on higher levels behave in a manner that indicates that they attach little importance to their position for the duration of the work of the group.

Provoke Multiple Cultures

One way of developing the conflicting countercultures required to provoke new perspectives is to rotate people between functions and business units. The motive here is to create cultural diversity as opposed to the current practice of using rotation to build a cadre of managers with the same management philosophy. Another effective way of promoting countercultures is that practiced by Canon and Honda, where significant numbers of managers are hired at the same time, midway through their careers in other organizations, to create sizeable pockets of different cultures that conflict with the predominant one.

Present Ambiguous Challenges Instead of Clear Long-Term Objectives or Visions

Agendas of strategic issues evolve out of the clash between different cultures in self-organizing groups. Top managers can provoke this activity by setting ambiguous challenges and presenting half-formed issues for others to develop, instead of trying to set clear long-term objectives. Problems without objectives should be intentionally posed to provoke the emotion and conflict that lead to active search for new ways of doing things. This activity of presenting challenges should also be a two-way one, where top executives hold themselves open to challenge from subordinates.

Expose the Business to Challenging Situations

Managers who avoid taking chances face the certainty of stagnation and therefore the high probability of collapse in the long term, simply because innovation depends significantly on chance. Running for cover because the future is unknowable is in the long run the riskiest response of all. Instead, managers must intentionally expose themselves to the most challenging of situations. In his study of international companies, Michael Porter concludes that those who position themselves to serve the world's most sophisticated and demanding customers, who seek the challenge of competing with the most imaginative and competent competitors, are the ones who build sustainable competitive advantage on a global scale (see Michael Porter's article in Chapter 10).

Devote Explicit Attention to Improving Group Learning Skills

New strategic directions emerge when groups of managers learn together in the sense of questioning deeply held beliefs and altering existing mental models rather than simply absorbing existing bodies of knowledge and sets of techniques. Such a learning process may well be personally threatening and so arouse anxiety that leads to bizarre group dynamics – this is perhaps the major obstacle to effective organizational learning. To overcome it, managers must spend time explicitly exploring how they interact and learn together – the route to superior learning is self-reflection in groups.

Create Resource Slack

New strategic directions emerge when the attitudes and behavior of managers create an atmosphere favourable to individual initiative and intuition, to political interaction, and to learning in groups. Learning and political interaction are hard work, and they cannot occur without investment in spare management resources. A vital precondition for emergent strategy is thus investment in management resources to allow it to happen.

Conclusion

Practicing managers and academics have been debating the merits of organizational learning as opposed to the planning conceptualization of strategic management. That debate has not, however, focused clearly on the critical unquestioned assumptions upon which the planning approach is based, namely, the nature of causality. Recent discoveries about the nature of dynamic feedback systems make it clear that cause and effect links disappear in innovative human organizations, making it impossible to envision or plan their long-term futures. Because of this lack of causal connection between specific actions and specific outcomes, new strategic directions can only emerge through a spontaneous, self-organizing political and learning process. The planning approach can be seen as a specific approach applicable to the short-term management of an organization's existing activities, a task as vital as the development of a new strategic direction.

9.3 Linking Planning and Implementation

By L.J. Bourgeois and David Brodwin[1]

Most discussions of strategic planning focus on how to formulate strategy. There are several tools and techniques in widespread use. Management consulting firms offer strategic planning on a commodity basis, and business-school programs are adorned with methodologies for choosing the 'best' strategy.

By contrast, scant attention has been given to how to implement those strategies. Yet many people have recognized that problems with implementation in many companies have resulted in failed strategies and abandoned planning efforts. This article will identify many of these implementation problems and then offer some remedies for them.

---

[1] Source: This article was originally published as 'Putting Your Strategy into Action,' in *Strategic Management Planning* (March/May 1983). Reprinted by permission of the authors.

Five Ways Companies Implement Strategy

In studying the management practices of a variety of companies, we have found that their approaches to strategy implementation can be categorized into one of five basic descriptions. In each one, the chief executive officer plays a somewhat different role and uses distinctive methods for developing and implementing strategies. We have given each description a title to distinguish its main characteristics.

The first two descriptions represent traditional approaches to implementation. Here the CEO (chief executive officer) formulates strategy first, and thinks about implementation later.

- *The Commander Approach.* The CEO concentrates on formulating the strategy, giving little thought to how the plan will be carried out. He either develops the strategy himself or supervises a team of planners. Once he's satisfied that he has the best strategy, he passes it along to those who are instructed to 'make it happen.'

- *The Organizational Change Approach.* Once a plan has been developed, the executive puts it into effect by taking such steps as reorganizing the company structure, changing incentive compensation schemes, or hiring staff.

The next two approaches involve more recent attempts to enhance implementation by broadening the bases of participation in the planning process.

- *The Collaborative Approach.* Rather than develop the strategy in a vacuum, the CEO enlists the help of his senior managers during the planning process in order to ensure that all the key players will back the final plan.

- *The Cultural Approach.* This is an extension of the collaborative model to involve people at middle and sometimes lower levels of the organization. It seeks to implement strategy through the development of a corporate culture throughout the organization.

The final approach takes advantage of managers' natural inclination to develop opportunities as they are encountered.

- *The Crescive Approach.* In this approach, the CEO addresses strategy planning and implementation simultaneously. He is not interested in planning alone, or even in leading others through a protracted planning process. Rather, he tries, through his statements and actions, to guide his managers into coming forward as champions of sound strategies.

In studying these five approaches we noticed several trends. First, the two traditional methods are gradually being supplanted by the others. Second, companies are focusing increasingly on organizational issues involved in getting a company to adapt to its environment and to pursue new opportunities or respond to outside threats. Finally, we see a trend toward the CEO playing an increasingly indirect and more subtle role in strategy development.

Method 1: The Commander Approach

The typical scenario depicting the most traditional approach to strategy formulation and implementation is as follows: After the CEO approves the strategic plan, he calls his top managers into a conference room, presents the strategy and tells them to implement it.

The CEO is involved only with formulating the strategy. He assumes that an exhaustive analysis must be completed before any action can be taken, so the CEO typically authorizes an extensive study of the firm's competitive opportunities. In general, focusing on the planning succeeds in at least giving the CEO a sense of direction for his firm, which helps him make difficult day-to-day decisions and also reduces uncertainty within the organization.

However, this approach can be implemented successfully only if several conditions are met. First, the CEO must wield a great deal of power so he can simply command implementation. Otherwise, unless the proposed strategy poses little threat to organizational members, implementation cannot be achieved very easily.

Second, accurate information must be available to the strategist before it becomes obsolete. Since good strategy depends on high-quality information, it is important that critical information entering the firm at lower levels is being compiled, digested, and transmitted upward quickly.

Third, the strategist must be insulated from personal biases and political influences that can impinge on the plan. Managers are likely to propose strategies favorable to their own divisions but not necessarily to the corporation as a whole.

One problem with this approach is that it often splits the firm into 'thinkers' and 'doers,' and those charged with the doing may not feel that they are part of the game. The general manager must dispel any impression that the only acceptable strategies are those developed by himself and his planning staff, or he may find himself faced with an extremely un-motivated, uninnovative group of employees.

Method 2: The Organizational Change Approach

With this approach, the CEO makes the strategy decisions and then paves the way for implementation by redesigning the organizational structure, personnel assignments, information systems, and compensation scheme.

This method goes beyond the first one by having the CEO consider how to put the plan into action. The CEO basically uses two sets of tools: (1) changing the structure and staffing to focus attention on the firm's new priorities and (2) revising systems for planning, performance measurement, and incentive compensation to help achieve the firm's strategic goals.

The first set of tools – changing the organizational structure and staffing – has been the traditional approach espoused in most business strategy texts.

The second set of tools involves adjusting administrative systems. Various planning, accounting, and control tools, such as those governing capital and operating budgets, can be used to help achieve desired goals. For example, if the firm's strategy calls for investing certain businesses and harvesting others, or for channeling profits from one national unit into funding others, these goals should be featured prominently in the capital budgeting procedures so that business-unit managers can effectively plan their resource requests and others can effectively evaluate them.

Performance measures should be designed so that they target meaningful short-term milestones in order to monitor progress toward strategic goals. The incentive compensation scheme should then be tied into the clear-cut numerical terms of the performance measures. At a minimum, the general manager must ensure that the current compensation plan isn't thwarting the achievement of the strategy in ways such as rewarding short-term profitability at the expense of longer-term growth.

Unlike the first approach, in this method the CEO doesn't merely command his subordinates to put the plan into action. He supervises the implementation and may only reveal the strategy gradually, rather than in one bold proclamation.

However, it usually is inadequate for the CEO simply to tack implementation onto strategy. This approach doesn't deal with problems of obtaining accurate information nor does it buffer the planner from political pressures. Also, as in the first approach, imposing the strategy downward from the top executives still causes motivational problems among the doers at lower levels.

In addition, another problem can develop when the CEO manipulates the systems and structures of the organization in support of a particular strategy. The general manager may be losing important strategic flexibility.

Some of these systems, particularly incentive compensation, take a long time to design, install, and become effective. If a dramatic change in the environment suddenly demands a major shift in the strategy, it may be very difficult to change the firm's course, since all the 'levers' controlling the firm have been set firmly in support of the now-obsolete game plan.

Method 3: The Collaborative Approach

In contrast to the two earlier approaches in which the chief executive makes most of the strategic and organizational decisions, the collaborative approach extends strategic decision making to the organization's top management team. The purpose here is to get the top managers to help develop and support a good set of goals and strategies.

In this model, the CEO employs group dynamics and brainstorming, techniques to get managers with different points of view to contribute to the strategic process. Our research indicates that in effective top management teams the executives will have conflicting goals and perceptions of the external environment, so the CEO will want to extract whatever group wisdom is inherent in these different perspectives.

The typical scenario depicting this approach should be familiar to readers: With key executives and division managers, the CEO embarks on a weeklong planning retreat. At the retreat, each participant presents his or her own ideas of where the firm should head. Extensive discussions follow, until the group reaches a consensus around the firm's longer-range mission and near-term strategy. Upon returning to their respective offices, each participant charges ahead in the agreed-upon direction.

The collaborative approach overcomes two key limitations of the previous two methods. By incorporating information from executives who are closer to the line operations and by engaging several points of view, it helps provide better information than the CEO alone would have. Also, because participation breeds commitment, this method helps overcome any resistance from top managers – which improves the possibility of successful implementation.

However, what the collaborative approach gains in team commitment may come at the expense of 'strategic perfection.' That is, it results in a compromise that has been negotiated among players with different points of view. The strategy may not be as dynamic as one CEO's vision, but it will be more politically feasible.

A second criticism of the collaborative approach is that it is not 'real' collective decision making from an organizatonal standpoint, because the managers – the organizational elite – cannot or will not give up centralized control. In effect, this approach still retains the wall separating thinkers from doers, and it fails to draw upon the resources of personnel throughout the organization. Our fourth approach to strategy implementation overcomes that shortcoming.

Method 4: The Cultural Approach

The cultural approach extends the benefits of collective participation into lower levels of the organization in order to get the entire organization committed to the firm's goals and strategies.

In this approach, the CEO sets the game plan and communicates the direction in which the firm should move, but he then gives individuals the responsibility of determining the details of how to execute the plan. To a large extent, the cultural approach represents the latest wave of management techniques promulgated to (and, in some cases, enthusiastically adopted by) American managers seeking the panacea to our current economic woes in the face of successful Japanese competition.

The implementation tools used in building a strong corporate culture range from such simple notions as publishing a company creed and singing a company song to much more complex techniques. The complex – and usually effective – tools involve implementing strategy by employing the concept of 'third-order control.'

Since implementation involves controlling the behavior of others, we can think of three levels of control. First-order control involves direct supervision. Second-order control involves using rules, procedures, and organizational structure to guide the behavior of others. Third-order control is a much more subtle – and potentially more powerful – means of influencing behavior through shaping the norms, values, symbols, and beliefs that managers and employees use in making day-to-day decisions.

The key distinction between managers using the cultural approach and those simply engaged in 'participative management,' is that these executives understand that corporate culture should serve as the handmaiden to corporate strategy, rather that proselytize 'power equalization' and the like for its own sake.

Some of the tools used in the cultural approach involve some readily identifiable personnel practices, such as long-term employment, slow promotion of employees, less-specialized career paths, and consensus decision making. For many managers, the cultural approach will also lead to change in their management style; it will involve much more interaction where subordinates will be seen as planners.

Once an organizational culture is established that supports the firm's goals, the chief executive's implementation task is 90 percent done. With a cadre of committed managers and workers, the organization more or less carries itself through cycles of innovation in terms of new products and processes at the workbench, followed by assimilation and implementation at the lower levels.

The most visible cost of this system also yields its primary strength: consensus decision making and other culture-inculcating activities consume enormous amounts of time. But the payoff can be speedy execution and reduced gamesmanship among managers. At Westinghouse, as William Coates, executive vice president of the corporation construction group, described it, 'We spend a lot of time trying to get a consensus, but once you get it, the implementation is instantaneous. We don't have to fight any negative feelings.'

Based on our assessment of the nature of the companies generally held up as examples of this approach to strategic management, we have reached some tentative conclusions about the organizational characteristics for which it is best suited. The cultural approach works when power is decentralized, where there are shared goals between the organization and its participants, and where the organization is stable and growing.

But the cultural method has several limitations. For one, it works only with informed and intelligent people (note that most of the examples are firms in high-technology industries). Second, it consumes enormous amounts of time to implement. Third, it can foster such a strong sense of organizational identity among employees that it becomes almost a handicap – that is, it can be difficult to have outsiders at top levels because the executives won't accept the infusion of alien blood.

In addition, companies with excessively strong cultures often will suppress deviance, impede attempts to change, and tend to foster homogeneity and inbreeding. The intolerance of deviance can be a problem when innovation is critical to strategic success. But a strong culture will reject inconsistency.

To handle this conformist tendency, companies such as IBM, Xerox, and General Motors have separated their ongoing research units and their new product-development efforts, sometimes placing them in physical locations far enough away to shield them from the corporation's culture.

Homogeneity can stifle creativity, encouraging nonconformists to leave for more accepting pastures and thereby robbing the firm of its innovative talent. The strongest criticism of the cultural approach is that it has such an overwhelming indoctrinal air about it. It smacks of faddism and may really be just another variant of the CEO-centered approaches (i.e. the previously discussed commander and organizational change approaches). As such, it runs the risk of maintaining the wall between the thinkers and doers.

Although each of the approaches discussed can be effective in certain companies and business environments, none has proved adequate for complex companies in highly diversified or rapidly changing environments. The best way to implement strategy in this challenging situation is by what we have identified as the crescive approach. The name means 'growing,' indicating that under this method the CEO cultivates or allows strategies to grow from *within* the company instead of imposing the strategies of top management onto the firm.

Method 5: The Crescive Approach

The crescive approach differs from others in several respects. First, instead of strategy being delivered downward by top management or a planning department, it moves upward from the doers (salespeople, engineers, production workers) and lower middle-level managers. Second, strategy becomes the sum of all the individual proposals that surface throughout the year. Third, the top management team shapes the employees' premises, that is, their notions of what would constitute strategic projects. Fourth, the chief executive functions more as a judge, evaluating the proposals that reach his desk, than as a master planner.

Why Did the Crescive Approach Arise?

At first, the crescive approach may sound too risky. After all, it calls for the chief executive to relinquish a lot of control over the strategy-making process, seemingly leaving to chance the major decisions that determine the long-term competitive strength of the company.

To understand why the crescive approach is sometimes appropriate, you need to recognize five constraints that impinge on the chief executive as he sets out to develop and implement a strategy.

1   *The chief executive cannot monitor all significant opportunities and threats.* If the company is highly diversified, it is impossible for senior management to stay abreast of developments in all of the firm's different industries. Similarly, if an industry is shifting very quickly (e.g. personal computers), information collected at lower levels often becomes stale before it can be assimilated, summarized, and passed up the ranks. Even in more stable industries, the time required to process information upward through many management levels can mean that decisions are being made based on outdated information.

   As a result, in many cases the CEO must abandon the effort to plan centrally. Instead, an incentive scheme or 'free-market' environment is established to encourage operating managers to make decisions that will further the long-range interests of the company.

2   *The power of the chief executive is limited.* The chief executive typically enjoys substantial power derived from the ability to bestow rewards, allocate resources, and reduce uncertainty for members of the organization. Thus, to an extent, the executive can impose his or her will on other members of the organization.

However, the chief executive is not omnipotent. Employees can always leave the firm, and key managers wield control over information and important client relationships. As a result, the CEO must often compromise on programs he wishes to implement.

Research indicates that new projects led by managers who were coerced into the leadership role fail, regardless of the intrinsic merit of the proposal. In contrast, a second-best strategy championed by a capable and determined advocate may be far more worthwhile than the optimum strategy with only lukewarm support.

3   *Few executives have the freedom to plan.* Although it is often said that one of the most important jobs of an executive is to engage in thoughtful planning, research shows that few executives actually set aside time to plan. Most spend the majority of their work days attending to short-range problems.

Thus, any realistic approach to strategic planning must recognize that executives simply don't plan much. They are bombarded constantly by requests from subordinates. So they shape the company's future more through their day-to-day decisions – encouraging some projects and discouraging others – than by sweeping policy statements or written plans. This process has been described as logical incrementalism because it is a rational process that proceeds in small steps rather than by long leaps.

4   *Tight control systems hinder the planning process.* In formulating strategies, top managers rely heavily on subordinates for up-to-date information, strategic recommendations, and approval of the operating goals.

The CEO's dependence on his subordinate managers creates a thorny control problem. In essence, if managers know they'll be accountable for plans they formulate or the information they provide, they have an incentive to bias their estimates of their division's performance.

A branch of decision science called agency theory, suggests how this situation should be handled. First, if the CEO wants his managers to deliver unbiased estimates, he cannot hold them tightly accountable for the successful implementation of each strategic proposal. Without such accountability, he places great emphasis on commitment as a force for getting things done.

Second, in order to assess the true ability and motivation of any subordinate, the CEO must observe him over a long period of time on a number of different projects. Occasional failures should be expected, tolerated, and not penalized.

One means to promote the ongoing flow of strategic information is to establish a special venture capital fund to take advantage of promising ideas that arise after the strategic and operating plans have been completed. Like the IBM Fellows or the Texas Instruments Idea programs, this approach allows opportunities to be seized and developed by their champions within the company.

5   *Strategies are produced by groups, not individuals.* Strategies are rarely created by single individuals. They are usually developed by groups of people, and they incorporate different perspectives on the business. The problem with group decisions is that groups tend to avoid uncertainty and to smooth over conflicts prematurely.

To reduce the distortions that can result from group decision making, the CEO can concentrate on three tools: first, encouraging an atmosphere that tolerates expression of different opinions; second, using organizational development techniques (such as group dynamics exercises) to reduce individual defensiveness and to increase the receptivity of the group to discrepant data; and third, establish separate planning groups at the corporate level and in the line organization.

How the CEO Can Use the Crescive Approach

As the preceding discussion indicates, the CEO of a large corporation simply cannot be solely responsible for forming and implementing strategy. The crescive approach suggests that the CEO can solicit and guide the involvement of lower-level managers in the planning and implementation process in five ways:

1   By keeping the organization open to new and potentially discrepant information.

2   By articulating a general strategy of superordinate goals to guide the firm's growth.

3   By carefully shaping the premises by which managers at all levels decide which strategic opportunities to pursue.

4   By manipulating systems and structures to encourage bottom-up strategy formulations.

5   By approaching day-to-day decisions as part of strategy formulation in the logical incrementalist manner described above.

One of the most important and potentially elusive of these methods is the process of shaping managers' decision-making premises. The CEO can shape these premises in at least three ways. First, the CEO can emphasize a particular theme or strategic thrust ('We are in the information business') to direct strategic thinking. Second, the planning methodology endorsed by the CEO can be communicated to affect the way managers view the business. Third, the organizational structure can indicate the dimensions on which strategies should focus. A firm with a product-divisional structure will probably encourage managers to generate strategies for domination in certain product categories, whereas a firm organized around geographical territories will probably evoke strategies to secure maximum penetration of all products in particular regions.

To conclude, a summary of the five approaches, the strategic question each addresses, and the CEO's role in each is given in Table 9.3.1. The choice

Approach	The CEO's Strategic Question	CEO's Role
I. Commander Approach	'How do I formulate the optimal strategy?'	Master Planner
II. Change Approach	'I have a strategy in mind – now how do I implement it?'	Architect of Implementation
III. Collaborative Approach	'How do I involve top management in planning so they will be committed to strategies from the start?'	Coordinator
IV. Cultural Approach	'How do I involve the whole organization in implementation?'	Coach
V. Crescive Approach	'How do I encourage managers to come forward as champions of sound strategies?'	Premise Setter and Judge

TABLE 9.3.1
The five approaches to strategic management

of method should depend on the size of the company, the degree of diversification, the degree of geographical dispersion, the stability of the business environment, and finally, the managerial style currently embodied in the company's culture.

9.4 Rethinking Incrementalism

By Gerry Johnson[1]

There are a number of models to account for the process of strategic management. One such framework is provided by Chaffee, who proposes three generic categories. Her first is the 'linear' model corresponding to what others have called the planning (Mintzberg), rational (Peters and Waterman), rational comprehensive or synoptic (Fredrickson) approach. It is a model of strategy making that assumes a progressive series of steps of goal setting, analysis, evaluation, selection, and the planning of implementation to achieve an optimal long-term direction for the organization.

Chaffee's second category is the 'adaptive' model of strategic management, a term also used by Mintzberg. This model corresponds to the idea of incremental strategic change discussed previously and, as we have seen, the explanations for this phenomenon vary considerably from those who see incrementalism as essentially logical or rational to those who accounted for

[1] Source: This article was originally published in *Strategic Management Journal* (January/February 1988). Reproduced by permission of John Wiley and Sons Limited.

the phenomenon in terms of satisficing behavior in a political, or pro-grammed, context or within the cognitive limits of management.

It is this cognitive view of strategy formulation that leads us to Chaffee's third category – the 'interpretative' model. Weick argues that there is a 'presumption of logic' in meeting a complex situation; this logic is rooted in the beliefs and assumptions that managers hold, a cognitive map that provides a view of the world, helps interpret the changes the organization faces, and provides appropriate responses. These organizational sets of beliefs and assumptions have been variously referred to in management literature as paradigms, interpretative schemes, and ideational culture. The result of the application of such cognitive maps is well documented: the danger is of 'groupthink' as the application of 'collective cognitive resources to develop rationalisations in line with shared illusions about the invulnerability of . . . organizations' (Janis, 1985). Other researchers have shown the extent to which symbolic aspects of the organization – stories and myths, rituals and ceremonies, and the language of the organization – act to legitimize and preserve such core beliefs and assumptions held within the organization.

Arguably these three models more generally embrace two broad thrusts about views on strategy formulation. The one is that strategy formulation can be accounted for by logical, rational processes either through the planning mode or through the adaptive, logical incremental mode. In either event the manager is a proactive strategy formulator consciously seeking to understand a complex environment, so as to establish causal patterns and formulate strategy by configuring organizational resources to meet environmental needs. The other view is an 'organizational action' view of strategy formulation where strategy is seen as the product of political, programmatic, cognitive, or symbolic aspects of management. In what follows we will take a closer look at a case, the retail clothing company Coopers, in order to assess the extent to which these differing views explain the strategic development of the company.

Explaining Strategic Management Processes

A Rational View of Strategy Formulation

It might appear that the notion of strategy as a logical response to environmental change is supported at least insofar as over the period 1970–1985 the company did apparently try to make strategic changes in response to a changing business environment. However, the observation that strategies change with environmental changes tells us little about the processes of strategic decision making. If we were to account for such decisions in terms of linear, rational planning models, we would expect to find strong evidence and a significant impact of systematic environmental scanning, clear objective setting and evaluation of strategic options against such objectives, and probably a planning infrastructure through which this took place. In fact, in Coopers throughout the period studied there was little evidence of any of this, and as will be seen, when such activity did take place, it had relatively little impact. We have to account for the observed strategic changes in other ways.

However, the managers themselves expressed views about the management of strategy which square well with rational but incremental models of strategic management – views that mirror closely Quinn's notion of logical incrementalism. These views included the following:

■ Small movements in strategy allow deliberate experimentation and sensing of the environment through action; if such small movements prove successful, then further development of strategy can take place.

■ Shareholders expect short-term returns; therefore it is not sensible to commit large sums of money or other resources to major shifts in strategy.

■ It is better to make continual adjustments to strategy so as to keep in line with market changes; if this is not done, then the company's strategy will become atrophied and over time will lead to the need for radical repositioning.

■ Opportunistic managements are able to search for ways in whcih they can take advantage of the matching of a historic and developing strategy with a developing market.

■ The nature of retailing is particularly suited to incremental adjustment, since there are few really fixed costs and assets. It is much less of a commitment and risk to try out a new strategy, because it can be done by opening a few new shops, or adjusting merchandise in shops; if this does not work, then the shops can be disposed of, or the merchandise sold off with relatively little loss.

■ In a business in which there is high regard for people it is important not to 'rock the boat' too much; people will go along with change much more readily if it is gradual and they can become used to it.

The danger is that of assuming that the logic of the processes described by the managers is necessarily a reasonable description of the processes that account for strategy formulation. This research was concerned with studying strategic changes as a longitudinal, contextual process, rather than as the espoused theory of managers. It will be shown that a somewhat different picture of the process of strategic management emerges if patterns of development of strategy in the business are examined in terms of the events, dramas, and routines of organization life and the belief systems of managers.

An 'Organizational Action' View of Strategy Formulation and Implementation

An 'organizational action' view of strategy formulation argues that strategy can best be seen as the product of the political, cognitive and cultural fabric of the organization. The expectation would be that strategic decisions could be explained better in terms of political processes than analytical procedures;

that cognitive maps of managers are better explanations of their perceptions of the environment and their strategic responses than are analyzed position statements and evaluative techniques; and that the legitimacy of these cognitive maps is likely to be reinforced through the myths and rituals of the organization.

Discernible from the analysis of the interviews with managers was a common set of beliefs and assumptions taken for granted by those managers; it was tacit knowledge, primarily about the modes of operation in the organization, typically in terms of trading procedures, organization, and control, seen as bestowing beneficial competences and capabilities on the organization. For Coopers this set of beliefs and assumptions could be characterized and summarized thus: low cost, good value, merchandise bought in bulk by experienced buyers, yielding high margins, linked to the tight centralized control of stock and distribution provides a secure position in our particular market niche. Moreover, we can take decisions fast because of centralized 'entrepreneurial' top management and rely on speedy implementation by loyal staff with years of experience in the business.

This set of beliefs amounts to what other writers have referred to as a paradigm: those sets of assumptions, usually implicit, about what sort of things make up the world, how they act, how they hang together, and how they may be known.

In Coopers over most of the years under study the buyers in particular exercised high degrees of power in the business. The link between the paradigm and the power bases in the company is an observation made by many researchers: 'power accrued to those sub-units which could best deal with organisational uncertainty' (Pfeffer and Salancik, 1978). The merchandise strategy was perceived to have the effect of insulating the company from market threats; the price and margin advantages reduced the likelihood of competitive incursions and buffered them against downturns in demand. Changes in fashion were seen to be less important than for some other companies because they had elected to concentrate on 'commodity' merchandise policies. It was the merchandise strategy that became the mechanism through which company profits were to be guaranteed, and this became central within the set of assumptions about the basis on which the business could compete in an uncertain world.

The dominance of buying and merchandise could be seen in the shop window displays of the 1970s, crowded with every item of merchandise the shop stocked with an emphasis given to what the buyers had procured. The assumption of the dominant importance of merchandise and buying was also symbolized in the greater freedom and discretion enjoyed by buyers in an otherwise tightly controlled business. The rituals of socialization ensured that everyone knew of the company way of retailing and acknowledged organizational features of loyalty, long service, and deference to senior executives not only as proper but beneficial. The nature of top management in the firm, its perceived entrepreneurial flair, the speed of decision making, and the centrality of the chief executive were enshrined in myths showing how this had been so throughout the history of the company. In short, the tenets of the paradigm were, indeed, legitimized symbolically.

Cases in the Formulation and Implementation of Strategy

The extent to which these characteristics of organizational action help explain the formulation of strategy in the company, and in so doing the observed phenomenon of incremental strategic change, can best be shown by using some brief examples from the company's history.

Younger fashions: a process of lobbying and incremental adjustment

Prior to the mid-1970s the company had concentrated on what managers described as a 'pile it high and sell it cheap' approach to clothes for the working man. However, there were managers in the business well aware of fashion changes in the market early in the 1970s; junior management, mainly from the relatively lower power base of the retail side of the company, were lobbying for merchandise changes over a period of years, but their appeals for change were ignored or blocked by senior managers. It was these senior managers, and in particular senior merchandise executives, who were most wedded to, and arguably derived power from, the established and hitherto successful strategy. Moreover, those resisting change could draw on a whole raft of justifications for such resistance, usually embedded in organizational routines: lead times on high-volume purchasing were long; more fashionable items might jeopardize volume purchases and hence margins; it would be more difficult to control a widening merchandise range; in any case, profit growth was continuing, and there was no other serious competitor in their market sector. In short, they could draw upon well-established bases of the strategic success of the business to defend the legitimacy of the approach upon which their power had been built.

However, it has to be noted that those from within the business who were advocating change were also conceiving of problems and solutions within much the same paradigm constraints. To them the customer was much the same as he always had been: he just wanted access to some more fashionable goods. Moreover it was seen as a merchandise problem that could be resolved through a change in merchandise by buyers whose ability was highly regarded. It was not, for example, seen as a problem to do with shop ambience, or requiring a change in definition of target market.

The resolution of the problem was through the mechanism of what managers saw as logically incremental action. It can also be seen as a change in strategy defined in terms of the paradigm and implemented gradually so as not to interfere with what was 'known to work.' Fashion was defined as imitating what other fashionable retailers demonstrated they could sell in volume. There was to be no loss of control on stocks: distribution was retained at the centre and shops had to 'qualify' for new stock on the evidence of past sales of the limited range of fashion merchandise available. The shops themselves were hardly changed.

The response to declining performance: 1980–81 By the middle of 1981 the company was in a state of serious performance decline. The period provides some examples of a management team faced with a problem it found difficult to understand, making sense of it through, and exerting greater efforts within, its paradigm, whilst seeking to preserve the legitimacy of that paradigm from the threats of growing counterevidence.

Performance decline had to do with an economic downturn regarded as temporary. In the meantime, the paradigm offered a menu of responses to the problems the business faced. This included tightening controls and cutting controllable costs. It also meant that managers sought to do better what they had always done: to stack the merchandise higher, pack windows more fully, and make sure staff were selling more aggressively.

Whilst most managers may have accepted that the market would return, a newly arrived marketing director was convinced, through market research he had commissioned, of the dubious reliability of Coopers' traditional market. The research report not only questioned the validity of management's conception of the clothing market but attacked their way of operating within it. The response to such questioning was much as Pfeffer has indicated: 'Attacks on the dominant beliefs or paradigm of the organization are likely to be met with counter argument and efforts to reinforce the paradigm.' The resistance was concerned with more than the report itself: it was also addressed at the new director.

Formalizing Explanatory Models

Examination of the processes of strategic change in Coopers bears out many of the phenomena that characterize incremental strategic change explained in terms of an organizational action perspective. The patterns of change are indeed evolutionary; strategic decisions build upon history and what managers at least perceive to be the core strength of the business. Decisions came about after long periods of incubation following identification of problems or opportunities through highly qualitative assessment. High levels of solicitation and bargaining characterized both problem definition and the selection of solutions. The primacy of cognitive maps in the interpretation of environmental stimuli, the configuration of responses, and strategy implementation is also evident; and it becomes clear that these belief sets are relatively commonly held within the organization and persistent, forming an organizational paradigm. Moreover, the mediatory and legitimizing role of symbolic aspects of the organization is also borne out. Building on all this we can move toward more integrated explanatory models of strategic management that arguably help in understanding the complexity of strategic management.

The Nature of the Paradigm

We need to start by distinguishing between what is meant by the paradigm and what is meant by strategy. Following Mintzberg we can distinguish between intended and realized strategy. Realized strategy is taken to mean the observable output of an organization's activity in terms of its positioning over time. Intended strategy means the strategy that managers espouse, perhaps in some sort of formal plan, public statement or explanation. The paradigm, on the other hand, is a more generalized set of beliefs about the organization and the way it is or should be and, since it is taken for granted and not problematic, may be difficult to surface as a coherent statement. It is more likely to emerge in the explanations and stories of managers. The point is that both intended and realized strategies are likely to be configured within the parameters of the paradigm.

There were discernible reasons why the paradigm would be resistant to rapid change. First, the internal consistency of the paradigm as observed was self-preserving and self-legitimizing. It is not an easy matter to challenge or repudiate a construct of an internally supportive and consistent whole. Second, and particularly significant in terms of understanding management implications, we need to understand the paradigm not just as a system of beliefs and assumptions; it is preserved and legitimized in a 'cultural web' of organizational action in terms of myths, rituals, symbols, control systems, and formal and informal power structures that support and provide relevance to core beliefs (see Figure 9.4.1). At Coopers the assumptions about the approach to buying and merchandising, and the emphasis on centralized control of current costs and assets, were not only linked themselves, but institutionalized, indeed capitalized, in the stock control and distribution systems. This is the inertia of technical organizational commitment, and is not likely to be ignored or overturned.

Further, the constructs of the paradigm are closely linked to the power structures in the organization. In effect, the paradigm represents the internally constructed belief set about uncertainty reduction, so it is likely that those most associated with operationalizing these beliefs will be most powerful in the organization. This point is of some significance. Strategic change processes traditionally advocated in the literature are linked to rational analytical planning models. The notion that it is through analysis of the business environment and the competitive position of the firm that managers yield insights into strengths and weaknesses that help identify the need and opportunities for change overlooks the political implications of such analysis. Such analysis was undertaken in Coopers. In the period following the analysis the evidence it provided was either denied by management, discredited, or led to minimal change. The reason for this was not that the analysis lacked clarity or cogency; quite the reverse: it pointedly questioned tenets of beliefs fundamental to the strategies being followed by the organization; in other words it raised explicit challenges to the paradigm and, as such, constituted not an intellectual analytical questioning of strategy, but a political threat to those whose power was most

FIGURE 9.4.1
The cultural web of an organization

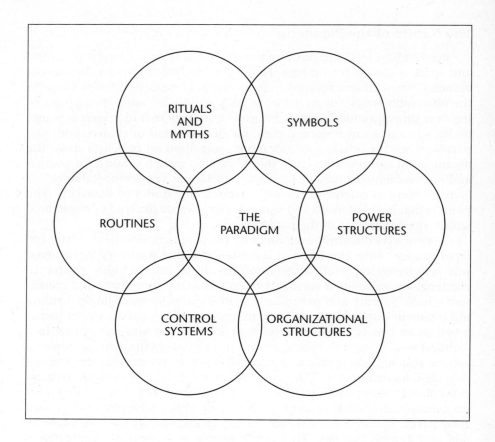

associated with it. Clarity of analysis is not, in itself, a sufficient basis to break the powerful momentum of the fundamental assumptions embraced within the paradigm, and indeed can actually increase resistance to change.

An Integrated Model of Process

The proposition arising from the analysis of the events at Coopers is that environmental signals will be reordered in terms of the paradigm. Some environmental signals will simply not be seen as relevant in terms of the paradigm, and will be ignored. Signals from the environment might also be seen as 'dissonant' with the paradigm; that is they might be actual or potential perceived threats to its basis, or not capable of being dealt with strictly within its bounds. Dissonance with the paradigm is potentially threatening to its integrity, and responses to such a threat follow a pattern:

- Dissonance will be mediated symbolically; that is, the symbolic mechanisms within which the paradigm is embedded will perform the role of maintaining the legitimacy of the paradigm in the face of the apparent threat.

- Since the threat may take the form of a political challenge to those most associated with core constructs of the paradigm, it may well be strongly resisted.

- Managers will seek to resolve the extent to which elements of the environment and the paradigm are in a state of dissonance. It is here that the most significant acts of strategic adaptation take place. The evidence throughout the period under study here is that such consonance might be achieved by (1) making sense of counterstimuli in terms of the paradigm rather than questioning or reconstructing the paradigm; or (2) where necessary marginally adjusting the paradigm, but from within its own bounds, and whilst maintaining its essential form.

The Notion of Strategic Drift

The paradigm effectively defines environmental 'reality' and responses to environmental change. Quinn's logical notion is that strategic change, through environmental sensing by managers within subsystems and the interplay between subsystems, and continual testing out of new strategies, results in a learning and readjustment process in organization by which the organization keeps itself in line with environmental changes. This notion is summarized in Figure 9.4.2a. The argument here is different: that managers may well see themselves as managing logically incrementally, but that such consciously managed incremental change does not necessarily succeed in keeping pace with environmental change. Indeed, it is argued that there is a high risk that it will not. The situation at Coopers as it evolved through the 1970s was not as shown in figure 9.4.2a, but rather as shown in Figure 9.4.2b. Gradually the incrementally adjusted strategic changes and the environmental, particularly market, changes moved apart.

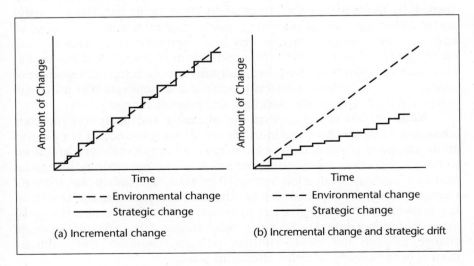

FIGURE 9.4.2
Incremental change and 'strategic drift'

Conclusions and Normative Implications

The question remains how it might be possible to achieve more nearly effective adaptive incremental strategic management and avoid strategic drift.

If strategy is to be managed effectively, a 'constructive tension' must exist between what is necessary to preserve and what must be changed – a tension, for example, between the need for managers to question and challenge and the preservation of core values and organizational mission; between the need for new ideas and directions and the need for continuity and preservation of the core business. This necessary tension is what Peters and Waterman call 'simultaneous loose-tight properties' or 'the coexistence of firm central direction and maximum individual autonomy.' It is a view echoed elsewhere but more specifically at the cultural and cognitive levels. Meyer has argued that the reason one organization is more likely to adopt strategies divergent from its previous strategies than another is because it has a more heterogeneous organizational 'ideology,' as manifested, for example, in terms of organizational images and symbols. A number of writers have argued that such ideological heterogeneity can be built into management systems in a variety of ways, for example, through organic management styles with a removal or reduction of hierarchical lines of reporting and communication; through deliberate challenging and assumption-surfacing devices, either formally promulgated or as part of the organizational culture; through the active involvement of 'outsiders' with less adherence to organizational culture or the organization's paradigm; and through the avoidance of 'segmentalist' structures.

Findings here also bear out those who argue the power of symbolic mechanisms for strategic management and change. The point they argue is that strategic issues have traditionally been seen as linked to analytical and planning mechanisms of management, and as such run the risk of not being 'owned' by those within the organization. They point out that successful organizations are good at managing change, not by talking about it at an analytical level but by demonstrating it at a symbolic and therefore more meaningful level in terms of the interpretative models suggested here and as illustrated in Figure 9.4.1. Such organizations approach the management of change through the very artifacts (symbolic and political) that otherwise preserve the integrity of the paradigm and prevent change.

None of this is to say that the planning and analytical methods advocated in so much of the literature are of no relevance. It is rather to argue that planning and analysis are necessary but not sufficient, and need to be understood as mechanisms for problem and opportunity identification and strategy evaluation rather than as a mechanism for strategic change. Indeed, the argument can be advanced that planning and analytical mechanisms are likely to give rise to resistance to change unless they take place within a context where the mechanisms for managing strategic change through the social, cultural, political, cognitive and symbolic devices of the organization are already in place.

Overall, the results of the study emphasize the importance of under-standing strategic management processes essentially in terms of organization action perspectives, and argue for the continued development of models that more precisely explain both strategy formulation and implementation in these terms.

9.5   Inertia and Transformation

By Richard Rumelt[1]

Roughly 15 years ago the field of business and corporate strategy began to incorporate economic reasoning into its research program. The first step was the adoption of traditional industrial organization economics, with its emphasis on barriers to entry and collusive reductions in rivalry. Subsequently, strategy researchers developed what is now called the resource-based view of the firm. This theory sees firms as collections of resources and sees performance differences as largely reflecting differences in resource quality. Whereas traditional industrial organization saw high profits as stemming from collusive reductions in competition or strategies of entry deterrence, the resource-based view sees high profits as the rents accruing to specialized and difficult-to-replicate or non-imitable resources.

Thus, today strategy researchers work with a complex amalgam of economic and quasi-economic reasoning. We envision the firm as striving to maximize value, but also see it as working with factors of production that are far from mobile, as dealing with ambiguous production functions, and as possessing or controlling collections of tacit knowledge and externally held attributions (reputation) that evolve over time in response to investment, activity and imitation.

There are a number of erroneous assumptions that most economically-oriented strategy researchers continue to borrow from economics. At this moment those that are clearest are plasticity, rationality of collective action, and homogeneity of beliefs. I believe that the most important of these is plasticity – the assumption that firms readily respond to exogenous shocks and changes in competitive conditions. The centerpiece of microeconomics is the deduction of the total economy's autonomous responsiveness (mediated by self-interest) to changes in prices, technology, taxes, etc. Yet the truth is that firms change only with difficulty. Changing

[1] Source: This article was adapted with permission from 'Inertia and Transformation', in: Montgomery, C.A. (Ed.), *Resource-based and Evolutionary Theories of the Firm: Towards a Synthesis*, Kluwer Academic Publishers, Boston, 1995, pp. 101–132.

strategy and the structural forms and administrative procedures that undergird strategy is difficult, costly, risky, and time consuming.

I shall call this lack of plasticity *inertia*. Inertia is the strong persistence of existing form and function. If the form is efficient, inertia is costless and arguably beneficial. However, if the firm's form or practices are inefficient, inertia is a problem. Indeed, the most direct evidence of inertia is the persistence of inefficient forms and practices.

A widely cited example of organizational inertia is General Motors. Once the world leader in automobile production efficiency, General Motors was eclipsed in this regard by leading Japanese manufacturers during the 1970s. Senior management understood the nature of the productivity gap by 1979, yet, despite a joint venture with Toyota in which world-class methods were used, the company has been unable to change its overall productivity in any substantial way. In fact, many GM plants became less productive during the 1980s, while Chrysler and Ford made broad and significant gains. Clearly, the basic problem facing the senior management of General Motors is not product-market strategy, but organizational change. Their challenge is not really competition, but their company's own inertia.

The fact of organizational inertia is not simply an 'implementation' problem. If firms lack plasticity then the formulation of product-market and corporate strategy is itself fundamentally altered:

- Good product-market strategy must take into account a firm's inertia and not create new inertia without sufficient reason.

- The important strategy problem facing a firm may well be internal inertia rather than product-market conditions.

- Leaving inertia out of an analysis underestimates, perhaps drastically, the payoff to strategic change and innovation. Modern economic analysis of strategy presumes alert responsive competitors who will compete away a firm's profits unless there are the protections afforded by property rights, reputation, tacit know-how, or other strategic resources and isolating mechanisms. But if competitors are subject to inertia, this analysis is incorrect. Some of the great strategic success stories are due as much to the (temporary) inertia of competitors as to the cleverness of the innovator (e.g. Timex, Federal Express).

A basic question motivating much of the research into the resource-based point of view was 'Why are firms different?' The question I suggest requires equal attention is 'What are the sources of organizational inertia?' Or, 'Why is change so difficult?'

The Five Frictions

With a nod to Michael Porter, I have organized the main sources of inertia into five groups, called the five frictions:

1   Distorted perception;

2   Dulled motivation;

3   Failed creative response;

4   Political deadlocks;

5   Action disconnects.

In many cases, the components of these frictions are well known or easily comprehended. In other cases the issues are novel or subtle. I shall pass swiftly over many the straightforward issues in order to concentrate on those that are novel or complex.

Distorted Perception

Change begins with perception. If perception is distorted, then change may be impeded. The fundamental sources of perceptual distortion inducing organizational inertia are: myopia, hubris and denial, and grooved thinking.

Myopia   A firm suffering from myopia is unable to look into the future with clarity. Various individuals within the firm may be aware of the future consequences of current action or inaction, but the organization, taken as a whole, acts as if only the short term matters.

   Myopia is to be expected in a firm that has employed high-intensity short-term controls. In such a case individuals bias their allocations of attention and effort toward problems that effect current performance. Less obvious is the fact that myopia is characteristic of a firm which is 'forgetful.' That is, when individuals do not expect the organization to remember the connections between current actions and future results. In forgetful firms, characterized by mergers, reorganizations, frequent personnel changes, etc. individuals have no realistic expectation that future results will be attributed to their current actions or decisions.

   When managers are myopic, the subtle consequence is that senior management will also behave myopically, expressing a rational disbelief in the claims of future threat or opportunity expressed by lower level managers. Thus the expectation of myopia in others leads, in turn, to further myopic behavior.

   A final source may be the failure of planning systems to counteract normal human myopia. Empirical evidence suggests that people's time-discount functions are steeper than exponential, leading to time-inconsistent behavior. Well-functioning organizational systems, it may be argued, help counteract short-term impulsiveness. And, by contrast, poorly functioning planning and review systems fail in this regard, fostering organizational myopia.

Hubris and denial   A serious source of perceptual distortion is denial – the rejection of information that is contrary to what is desired or what is believed to be true. Denial may stem from hubris-overweening pride in past accomplishments – or it may derive from fear. In his work on barriers to organizational learning, Argyris (1990) has argued that a virtually universal organizational response to information or analysis which threaten a loss of face is *defensive behavior*: denial of the validity of the data, cover-up of the situation, and cover-up of the cover-up. For example, for years the senior management of General Motors refused to admit that Japanese firms had higher absolute levels of productivity, denying the existence of the problem. In part, management could not believe that another company knew more about producing cars than did GM (hubris), and in part it was less embarrassing to believe other theories about the rising tide of imports.

Hubris is also explainable as *superstitious learning* – learning based on associating past success with factors that were coincidental with it but bear no causal relationship to the success. Skinner (1948) showed that when pigeons receive random reinforcements (feedings), they become conditioned to repeat some behavior that is accidentally correlated with the stimulus. Similarly, managers in highly uncertain environments (e.g. the entertainment industry) may cling steadfastly to policies that were only accidentally correlated with some past success.

A related syndrome is information filtering – the selective rejection of information that is unpopular, unpleasant, or contrary to doctrine. During the Vietnam war, for example, US commanders defined the conflict as a war of attrition which was being won over time and systematically withheld from Washington information which contradicted their vision (Sheehan 1988).

Grooved thinking Janis (1972) has described as 'groupthink' the restricted thinking that groups impose, punishing or rejecting ideas and information that deviate too much from orthodoxy. A somewhat different perspective is provided by Margolis (1993) who views patterns of thinking as mental habits whose structure and function are the same as physical habits. Finally, a third type of grooved thinking comes from the use of the 'wrong' metaphor. Just as policy makers may struggle to decide whether the situation in Bosnia is 'another Kuwait' or 'another Vietnam,' a metaphor, once accepted, acts as a powerful restriction on future thought.

Dulled Motivation

Even if perception is accurate, organizations may resist change because the need is not felt with sufficient sharpness. The lack of sufficient motivation may be rational, or it may reflect agency or psychological problems. The most important motivational dampers are: direct costs of change, cannibalization costs, and cross-subsidy comforts.

Direct costs of change It is likely that change temporarily increases the risk of organizational failure (mortality), disrupts operations, and involves a great deal of expensive effort. Even more importantly, change may imply the abandonment of costly sunk specific investments. If these considerations apply to the firm as a whole, they are rational impediments to change. Applied to individuals or groups, they point to agency problems.

Note that an impediment to change may be rational. When Timex created the disposable watch, there were no imitators for ten years. Some of the inertia was surely wasteful, but some may have been rational. Were a quality Swiss manufacturer to produce disposable watches it would risk damage to its reputation. Similarly, whereas firms making new investments may be able to justify an expensive new technology, a firm with adequate though less efficient capacity may not be able to economically justify switching to the newer technology.

Cannibalization costs   When a new product's success eats into the sales and profits of an older product, the older product is said to have been cannibalized. Cannibalization problems may be rational or simply reflect sub-group interests. Rational cannibalization problems occur under conditions of buyer loyalty (or switching costs). Loyal buyers will stay with a firm's old product despite competitors' introductions of new versions, but will switch to the new version when offered by the firm they favor.

This asymmetry in buyer response, when coupled with the fact of lower profits on the newer products, can induce a firm to exploit its buyers' loyalties by withholding introduction of the new product. For example, when interest rates rose sharply in the late 1970s, many banks and S&Ls began to offer new money-market accounts and other innovative services. However, those institutions with the largest volume of savings account deposits (paying five percent interest when market rates were 17 percent) were least likely to market the new products. They did, of course, lose some customers to other banks. But they also reasoned that they would lose even more savings account customers were they to market the new products heavily themselves – the new products would cannibalize the very high profits being earned on the old products.

Cross subsidy comforts   The motivation to change is inhibited when a problem business is subsidized by rents from another business. The subsidy may be direct, in the form of management's toleration of losses in a business that is compensated for by gains elsewhere. Or, it may be indirect, obtained through artificial transfer prices or through bundling businesses together so that separate measures are not obtained.

Failed Creative Response

If perception is acute and motivation sharp, change may still be blocked by other forces. In particular, it may be difficult for the organization to choose a direction out of its difficulties. The impediment may be in the analysis of the situation or in choice itself. The major categories of friction in this area are: speed and complexity, reactive mind-set, and inadequate strategic vision.

Speed and complexity   In the 1970s John Boyd, a captain in the US Air Force, concluded a study of why US aviators had been so successful in air combat in Korea. He found that although the MiG-15 was faster, quicker in the turn, and could climb faster than the US F-86, the critical factor was that the F-86 provided better visibility and faster control. Thus the US pilot could remain a step ahead, maintaining the initiative. Most importantly, Boyd found that once the MiG pilot found himself outmaneuvered, he froze or panicked.

Analysis is blocked or frozen when things happen too fast. If a competitor can go around the 'Boyd loop' of observation, orientation, decision, and action faster than an opponent, the opponent may not simply struggle along, he may freeze-up or collapse. The 'Boyd loop' phenomena is one form of what is known to everyone as 'having the initiative' in a game.

When the decision situation is very complex, there may also be a similar blockage. For example, US firms all dropped out of the liquid crystal flat-screen technology race when Japanese firms jumped too far ahead. The pace of events overtook their resource allocation systems and the complexity of the judgments to be made exacerbated the situation.

Reactive mind-set   Change is inhibited when people adhere to the view that their problems are natural and inevitable. The most common reactive mind-sets are that the industry is 'mature,' that the problems are industry problems and not the fault of the firm. These points of view have great validity behind them – the weight of expert advice and analysis. They are also self-fulfilling. If all competitors define their market as mature they will surely be correct.

Senior management may also be stuck in a reactive mind-set if they possess too little detailed understanding of the business to take a proactive creative stance. Entrepreneurial creativity requires a closeness to issues of commerce, technology, and/or buyer behavior that may be lacking in a senior management group that came to power in a different era or who have backgrounds unconnected to current business issues.

Inadequate strategic vision   Even when analysis and choice have not been blocked, the direction chosen and especially its articulation may be so flawed that change is blocked. Vision (direction) also may be inadequate because it is hypocritical. Hypocritical vision is dishonest, claiming values and goals that are known to be false. Announcing 'We are a community . . .' is a lie for a firm that is about to lay off one-third of its workforce. Managers know when goals of 'quality' or of being 'ecologically sound' are hypocritical and cannot help but treat the rest of the vision with cynicism.

Vision can be inadequate because it is unresponsive to the clear challenges facing the firm. An unresponsive vision can hardly inspire commitment and change. Finally, vision can be ineffective because there is no trust in senior management's commitment to the vision. If people believe that this 'vision' is simply today's plan, only to be replaced by another tomorrow, there will be no willing followers. If managers are to commit their energy, careers, time, and attention to a program of change, there must be trust that the direction chosen will not be lightly altered. Here we touch the central paradox that change may require the promise of future inertia.

Political Deadlocks

Politics, especially organizational politics, is frequently seen as somehow tainted or improper. But politics is simply about influence on decisions and is absent only in absolute dictatorships. The three main sources of disagreement among men are differences in personal interest, differences in belief, and differences in fundamental values. These are also the underlying themes of the three types of political deadlocks: departmental politics, incommensurable beliefs, and vested values.

Departmental politics   This is one of the most obvious sources of inertia and little more need be said. Managers rarely act to unseat themselves or to terminate their own departments. Yet change inevitably involves winners and losers; some people and departments will gain resources and prestige and others will be lessened. Change will be fought by those who will clearly lose thereby and departmental wrangling over who will win and lose can slow change to a crawl.

Incommensurable beliefs   More interesting than the politics of self interest is the problem that arises when different individuals or groups hold sincere but differing beliefs about the nature of the problem or its solution. Figure 9.5.1 illustrates the classic Condorcet paradox. Here three managers face three alternatives (downsize, merge, and R&D), and each ranks the three differently. The problem here is that the group's preferences are intransitive. If any of the three alternatives is taken to be the status quo, there is always an alternative preferred to it by a 2–to-1 majority. Here 'R&D' beats 'downsize,' 'merge' beats 'R&D,' and 'downsize' beats 'merge.' There is no stable resting place among the cyclic preference mix.

This sort of problem in aggregating individual preferences led Arrow (1963) to his 'Impossibility Theorem' and has inspired a stream of related work. It all points to the fact that traditional concepts of 'public interest' or the 'organization's goals' are empty of rigorous meaning unless there is uniformity of opinion.

What happens when these managers are asked to reach a 'consensus?' Modern political theory establishes that here (and in general) there is no 'rational' outcome, and that any of the outcomes can be obtained by manipulation of the agenda. My belief is that there are four basic patterns that can emerge. First, a leader may simply impose a decision, eliminating the illusion of group choice. Second, the choice process may cycle for some time without generating an outcome. Third, the managers may recognize the 'irrationality' of the situation and withdraw from participation (essentially colluding to avoid choice). Finally, other considerations or 'games' may change the relative influence the managers have, resolving the paradox.

FIGURE 9.5.1
Condorcet preferences

	Manager		
	John	Jan	Jon
Downsize	1	2	3
Merge	2	3	1
R&D	3	1	2

When managers disagree, there is no 'rational' way to combine their beliefs. If speed is important, leadership may have to abandon group decision processes. When process is important, and beliefs differ, inertia may well be the outcome.

Vested values The third source of political deadlock is the presence of vested values. Unlike the cases of differing interests or beliefs, here individuals and departments are taken to have strong emotional or value attachments to products, policies, or ways of doing things. These vested values and interests can easily be the greatest impediments to change.

For many years a central concept in the strategy field was the experience curve – the idea that the cost of doing something falls as cumulative experience (production) increases. By analogy, I suggest that there is a vested value 'curve': the more one does a task the more one sees value in that activity. I am careful not to say one 'likes' the activity, for that is another issue.

The psychology of vested value is dissonance reduction – the repetition of something difficult makes sense if it is valued. If one has been rewarded for doing the task, it will not only be valued, but liked as well.

Vested values lie at the heart of institutions. The defenders of vested values are usually the informal leadership network – the defenders of the society and of its norms. The paradox of change is that these same people, perhaps the best and the brightest, easily become the source of inertia. The problem of vested values is not with simple foot dragging, but with the organizational equivalent of patriotism.

Action Disconnects

The fifth source of friction concerns those forces which prevent action. Even if perception has been sound, analysis and choice have proceeded, and the problems of politics overcome, there may still be no change. The basic reasons for action blockades and disconnects are: leadership inaction, embedded routines, collective action problems, and capabilities gaps.

Leadership inaction   For change to begin, the leadership must articulate a vision for change, must alter incentives, must take direct action where possible, and must shift power. If it fails to do these things, change will be inhibited. The need for direct action is particularly worth emphasizing. The concept of leadership comes from the military notion of being 'in front,' of providing courage and energy by example. In business, the analog is for the senior management group to lead by example. If a new emphasis on service is the centerpiece of the strategy, and the marketing manager keeps on an old friend, the head of market research, despite a wide reputation for providing bad service to the product groups, there has been a failure of leadership by example.

Leadership may also fail to act because of its attachment to the status quo. In business, radical change in strategy or structure rarely happens without a change in leadership. Leaders may inaugurate change, but that change itself then becomes the new status quo.

Leadership is committed to the status quo for several reasons. The first is simple ego-involvement. If the current leaders were the architects of the status quo, then they will feel a special attachment to it as well as having a deep appreciation for its (original) functionality. The second reason is that the status quo is known whereas new structures and strategies are not. As Burke pointed out in his critique of the French revolution, new and as yet untried systems generally have terrible and as yet unimagined flaws. The third and most subtle reason is that leadership, by its nature, involves commitment. The leadership of an organization must be the guarantor of explicit contracts, both internal and external. In particular, organizational members give energy and their own commitment to broad goals only to the extent that they perceive that the leadership itself has made a strong commitment to a particular set of priorities and ways of doing things. Major change requires a leader to repudiate prior commitments, thus lessening his or her ability to lead in the future. Hence, entrenched leadership is normally a source of inertia.

Embedded routines   The life functions of a business are its processes – its ways of doing things. Complex processes possess great inertia. The knowledge of how certain steps are performed may be tacit, no one may have a complete understanding of the process, and changing one aspect of a process may have significant unanticipated consequences on other parts of the organization. Finally, the various routines that make up the process take on the force of habit. From a purely economics perspective, organizational change only requires a change in incentives. However, the habitual patterns of work have an inertial force that can be much stronger than any practical incentives.

Process inertia arises not only through the attraction of the habitual, but also because change may mean doing things for which the organization has no process experience. If change simply requires substituting one known process for another, things are relatively straightforward. But taking the organization beyond its repertoire of routines is difficult. In general, one cannot ask an organization to do something which has not been reduced to a routine. If novel routines are required, then macro-routines for creating novelty, with all their slowness and cost, are required.

Collective action problems   Action can be blocked by a variety of collective action problems. The simplest is the first mover problem: if senior management has called for new initiatives, does it pay to be a first-mover? In many situations the incentives are clearly in favor of waiting to see how the first mover does. In such cases, the equilibrium is for no one to move at all. There are also analogous problems of free-riders that inhibit change even when first-movers have led the way.

The more complex collective action problem is that best described as *cultural*. A dysfunctional culture may block change and itself be virtually impervious to alteration. Consider, for example, the simple question of cooperation (coordination) versus competition among departments. As a step towards a model, suppose that individuals in an organization meet in pairs and must each decide whether to cooperate or compete. Each individual has information that the other does not and each controls some resources that the other does not. Cooperation means trying to act for the good of the company as a whole. In particular, it means making claims on the other person's resources that are justified by one's private information and accepting the other person's claims on one's own resources as valid. Competition means trying to act (covertly) for the good of the local unit. Concessions from the other are sought that will benefit one's own unit. Because culture depends on mutual expectations, it is not easily changed. A culture that resists change or that does not fit the direction the firm needs to take can be an insurmountable source of inertia.

Capabilities gaps   The final action blockade is simply a gap or disconnect between the tasks that need to be performed and the competencies and capabilities within the firm. Prahalad and Hamel have introduced the term 'stretch' for the sense of tension between reality and aspiration, and have argued that healthy organizations are in a constant state of stretch. But too great a gap is discouraging and is more likely to inhibit than induce change.

Key Inertias

The description of the five frictions was intended to explore the range and depth of forces at work. Now, in order to facilitate reasoning within a simple model, it is useful to make some simplifying assumptions. Accordingly, I make the reasonable assumption that resistance to change is embodied in the following five inertias:

1   Cross-subsidy comforts from bundled businesses.

2   Departmental politics rooted in self-interest.

3   Embedded processes that link departments.

4   Cultural inertia.

5   Vested values in current methods and products.

If firms are not easily changed, there are important implications for strategy. The overwhelming evidence is that organizations possess considerable inertia, yet strategy content models, including the resource-based view of the firm, tend to sidestep this issue. A complete strategic theory of the firm must deal squarely with the issue of inertia.

Whereas the resource-based theory of the firm has had the advantage of using as a foil a corresponding model of the firm, there is no clear simple model of management or organizational process. Hence the study of inertia and transformation is complex and requires looking into a variety of disciplines.

The Organizational Context in International Perspective

Chaos often breeds life, when order breeds habit.

(Henry Brooks Adams 1838–1919; American writer and historian)

Again it has become clear that there is little consensus within the field of strategic management. Views on the nature of the organizational context vary sharply. Even authors from one and the same country have contrasting opinions on the paradox of control and chaos. However, looking back on the articles in the sections on strategy process and strategy content, it is striking how few of the authors make a point of expounding their outlook on organizational malleability. The assumptions on which their theories are built are largely left implicit.

For this reason, it is difficult to identify whether there are national preferences when it comes to organizational context perspective. Yet, it seems not unlikely that strategists in different countries have different inclinations on this issue. In recent large-scale field work done by researchers at Cranfield Business School in the UK (Kakabadse *et al.*, 1995), significantly different 'leadership styles' were recognized among European executives. The predominant approach in Sweden and Finland was typified as the 'consensus' style (low power distance, low masculinity), while executives in Germany and Austria had a style that was labelled 'working towards a common goal' (specialists working together within a rule-bound structure). In France, the most popular style was 'managing from a distance' (focus on planning, high power distance), while executives from the UK, Ireland, and Spain preferred 'leading from the front.' This last leadership style, according to the researchers, relies 'on the belief that the charisma and skills of some particular individuals will lead to either the success or the failure of their organizations.' This finding suggests that the organizational leadership perspective will be more popular in these three countries (as well as in other 'Anglo-Saxon' and 'Latin' cultures), than in the rest of Europe. Other cross-cultural theorists also support this supposition (e.g. Hampden-Turner and Trompenaars, 1993; Lessem and Neubauer, 1994).

As an input to the debate whether there are international differences in perspective, we would like to put forward a number of factors that might be of influence on how the paradox of control and chaos is viewed in different countries. It should be noted, however, that these propositions are intended to encourage discussion and constitute only tentative explanations for cross-cultural differences in perspective. More specific international research is needed to give this debate a firm footing.

Locus of Control

This point can be kept short, as it was also raised in Chapter 8. People with an internal locus of control believe that they can shape events and have an impact on their environment. People with an external locus of control believe that they are caught up in events that they can hardly influence. Cross-cultural researchers have argued that cultures can differ significantly with regard to the perceived locus of control that is predominant among the population.

Obviously, in countries where the culture is more inclined towards an internal locus of control, it is reasonable to expect that the organizational leadership perspective will be more widespread. Managers in such 'just do it' cultures will be more strongly predisposed to believe that they can shape organizational circumstances. In cultures that are characterized by a predominantly external locus of control, more support for the organizational dynamics perspective can be expected.

Level of Uncertainty Avoidance

A cultural characteristic related to the previous point, is the preference for order and structure that prevails in some countries. Hofstede (1993; reading 1.5) refers to this issue as uncertainty avoidance. In some cultures, there is a low tolerance for unstructured situations, poorly defined tasks and responsibilities, ambiguous relationships and unclear rules. People in these nations exhibit a distinct preference for order, predictability and security – they need to feel that things are 'in control'. In other cultures, however, people are less nervous about uncertain settings. The tolerance for situations that are 'unorganized', or 'self-organizing', is much higher – even in relatively chaotic circumstances, the call for 'law and order' will not be particularly strong. It can be expected that there will be a more pronounced preference for the organizational leadership perspective in countries that score high on uncertainty avoidance, than in nations with a low score.

Prevalence of Mechanistic Organizations

In Chapters 3 and 4, different international views on the nature of organizations were discussed. A simple distinction was made between mechanistic and organic conceptions of organizations. In the mechanistic view, organizations exist as systems that are staffed with people, while in the organic view organizations exist as groups of people, into which some system has been brought.

When it comes to malleability, people taking a mechanistic view will see organizational leaders as mechanics – the organizational system can be redesigned, reengineered and restructured to pursue another course of action where necessary. Success will depend on leaders' design, engineering and structuring skills, and their ability to overcome resistance to change by the system's inhabitants. If a leader does not function well, a new one can be installed, and if employees are too resistant, they can be replaced. In countries where the mechanistic view of organizations is more predominant, a leaning towards the organizational leadership perspective can be expected.

People taking an organic view will see a leader as the head of the clan, bound by tradition and loyalty, but able to count on the emotion commitment of the members. Success in reshaping the organization will depend on reshaping the people – changing beliefs, ideas, visions, skills and interests. Important in reorienting and rejuvenating the organization is the leader's ability to challenge orthodox ideas, motivate people and manage the political processes. In countries where the organic view of organizations is more predominant, a leaning towards the organizational dynamics perspective can be expected.

Further Readings

Readers interested in pursuing the topics of leadership and organizational dynamics have a rich body of literature from which to choose. An excellent overview of the subject is provided by Sydney Finkelstein and Donald Hambrick, in their book *Strategic Leadership: Top Executives and Their Effects on Organizations*. Also highly recommended as overview of the leadership literature is *Bass and Stogdill's Handbook of Leadership*, by Bill Bass. In the category of more academically oriented works, the special issue of *Organization Studies* entitled 'Interpreting Organizational Leadership,' and edited by Susan Schneider gives a rich spectrum of ideas. The same is true for the special edition of the *Strategic Management Journal* entitled 'Strategic Leadership,' and edited by Donald Hambrick.

For more specific readings taking an organizational leadership perspective, the classics with which to start are John Kotter's *The General Managers* and Gordon Donaldson and Jay Lorsch's *Decision Making at the Top: The Shaping of Strategic Direction*. Good follow up readings are the book by Warren Bennis, *On Becoming a Leader*, and the book by Burt Nanus, *Visionary Leadership: Creating a Compelling Sense of Direction for Your Organization*. For leadership literature further away from the voluntarist extreme, readers are advised to turn to Peter Senge's book *The Fifth Discipline: The Art and Practice of the Learning Organization* and Edward Schein's *Organizational Culture and Leadership*. The book by Henry Sims and Peter Lorenzi, *The New Leadership Paradigm: Social Learning and Cognition in Organizations*, is also a challenging book, but not easy to read.

For a critical reaction to the leadership literature, Manfred Kets de Vries has many excellent contributions. His article 'The Leadership Mystique' is very good, as are his books with Danny Miller, entitled *The Neurotic Organization* and *Unstable at the Top*. Miller also has many thought-provoking works to his name, of which *The Icarus Paradox: How Excellent Companies Can Bring About Their Own Downfall* is highly recommended. In the more academic literature, stimulating commentaries are given in the articles 'The Romance of Leadership' by James Meindl, S. Ehrlich and J. Dukerich, and in 'The Ambiguity of Leadership,' by Jeffrey Pfeffer.

For a good reading highlighting the importance of organizational dynamics for both strategy process and strategy content, Ralph Stacey's book *Strategic Management and Organizational Dynamics* is a good place to start. Gerry Johnson's *Strategic Change and the Management Process* also provides provocative ideas about the relationship between strategy and the organizational context. Richard Pascale's *Managing on the Edge: How Successful Companies Use Conflict to Stay Ahead* is also stimulating reading. Finally, for the academically more adventurous, Joel Baum and Jitendra Singh's volume, *Evolutionary Dynamics of Organizations*, gives plenty of food for thought.

References

Allison, G. (1969) Conceptual Models and The Cuban Missile Crisis, *The American Political Science Review*, No. 3, September, pp. 689–718.

Argyris, C. (1990) *Overcoming Organizational Defenses: Facilitating Organizational Learning*, Allyn & Bacon, Needham, MA.

Arrow, K.J. (1963) *Social Choice and Individual Values*, Yale University Press, New Haven, CT.

Barney, J.B. (1986) Organizational Culture: Can It Be a Source of Sustainable Competitive Advantage? *Academy of Management Review*, July, pp. 656–65.

Barney, J.B. (1991) Firm Resources and Sustained Competitive Advantage, *Journal of Management*, Vol. 17, No. 1, pp. 99–120.

Bass, B.M. (1990) *Bass and Stogdill's Handbook of Leadership*, 3rd edn, The Free Press, New York.

Baum, J.A.C., and Singh, J.V. (1994) Organizational Hierarchies and Evolutionary Processes: Some Reflections on a Theory of Organizational Evolution, in Baum, J.A.C., and Singh, J.V. (eds), *Evolutionary Dynamics of Organizations*, Oxford University Press, Oxford.

Bennis, W. (1989) *On Becoming a Leader*, Addison-Wesley, Reading, MA.

Bennis, W., and Nanus, B. (1985) *Leaders: The Strategies for Taking Charge*, Harper & Row, New York.

Bourgeois, L.J., and Brodwin, D.R. (1983) Putting Your Strategy into Action, *Strategic Management Planning*, March/May.

Bower, J.L. (ed) (1991) *The Craft of General Management*, Harvard Business School Publications, Boston.

Burrell, G., and Morgan, G. (1979) *Sociological Paradigms and Organizational Analysis*, Heinemann, London.

Calder, B. (1977) An Attribution Theory of Leadership, in Staw, B., and B. Salanck (eds.), *New Directions in Organizational Behavior*, St. Clair, Chicago.

Chaffee, E.E. (1985) Three Models of Strategy, *Academy of Management Review*, January, pp. 89–98.

Chandler, A.D. (1962) *Strategy and Structure: Chapters in the History of the American Industrial Enterprise*, MIT Press, Cambridge, MA.

Chandler, A.D. (1977) *The Visible Hand*, Harvard University Press, Cambridge, MA.

Channon, D. (1973) *The Strategy and Structure of British Enterprise*, Harvard University Press, Cambridge, MA.

Chen, C.C., and Meindl, J.R. (1991) The Construction of Leadership Images in the Popular Press: The Case of Donald Burr and People Express, *Administrative Science Quarterly*, Vol. 36, pp. 521–51.

Child, J. (1972) Organizational Structure, Environment, and Performance: The Role of Strategic Choice, *Sociology*, January, pp. 2–22.

Christensen, C.R., Andrews, K.R., Bower, J.L., Hamermesh, R.G., and Porter, M.E. (1982) (1987) *Business Policy: Text and Cases*, 5th and 6th edns, Irwin, Homewood, IL.

Cyert, R.M., and March, J.G. (1992) *A Behavioral Theory of the Firm*, Second Edition, Prentice-Hall, Englewood Cliffs.

Donaldson, G., and Lorsch, J.W. (1983) *Decision Making at the Top: The Shaping of Strategic Direction*, Basic Books, New York.

Drucker, P. (1973) *Management: Tasks, Responsibilities, Practices*, Harper & Row, New York.

Finkelstein, S. (1992) Power in Top Management Teams: Dimensions, Measurement, and Validation, *Academy of Management Journal*, Vol. 35, pp. 505–38.

Finkelstein, S., and Hambrick, D.C. (1996) *Strategic Leadership: Top Executive and Their Effects on Organizations*, West, St. Paul.

Frederickson, J.W. (1983) Strategic Process: Questions and Recommendations, *Academy of Management Review*, October, pp. 565–75.

Galbraith, J.R. (1983) Strategy and Organization Planning, *Human Resource Management*, Spring/Summer, pp. 63–77.

Greiner, L.E. (1972) Evolution and Revolution as Organizations Grow, *Harvard Business Review*, July/August, pp. 37–46.

Hambrick, D.C. (ed) (1989) Strategic Leadership, *Strategic Management Journal* (Special Issue), Vol. 10.

Hambrick, D.C., and Mason, P.A. (1984) Upper Echelons: The Organization as a Reflection of Its Top Managers, *Academy of Management Review*, 9, pp. 193–206.

Hampden-Turner, C. (1990) *Charting the Corporate Mind*, Free Press, New York.

Hampden-Turner, C., and Trompenaars, A. (1993) *The Seven Cultures of Capitalism: Value Systems for Creating Wealth in the United States, Japan, Germany, France, Britain, Sweden, and the Netherlands*, Doubleday, New York.

Hannan, M.T., and Freeman, J. (1977) The Population Ecology of Organizations, *American Journal of Sociology*, March, p. 929–64.

Hoffman, R.C. (1989) Strategies for Corporate Turnarounds: What Do We Know about Them?, *Journal of General Management*, Spring, pp. 46–66.

Hofstede, G. (1980) Motivation, Leadership and Organization: Do American Theories Apply Abroad?, *Organizational Dynamics*, Summer, pp. 42–63.

Janis, I.L. (1985) Sources of Error in Strategic Decision Making, in Pennings, J.M. (ed), *Organizational Strategy and Change*, Jossey-Bass, San Francisco.

Janis, I. (1972) *Groupthink*, The Free Press, New York.

Johnson, G. (1987) *Strategic Change and the Management Process*, Blackwell, Oxford.

Johnson, G. (1988) Rethinking Incrementalism, *Strategic Management Journal*, January/February, pp. 75–91.

Kakabadse, A., Myers, A., McMahon, T. and Spony, G. (1995) Top Management Styles in Europe: Implications for Business and Cross-National Teams, *European Business Journal*, Vol. 7, pp. 17–27.

Kelley, R.E. (1988) In Praise of Followers, *Harvard Business Review*, November–December.

Kets de Vries, M.F.R. (1994) The Leadership Mystique, *Academy of Management Executive*, Vol. 8, pp. 73–92.

Kets de Vries, M.F.R., and Miller, D. (1984) *The Neurotic Organization*, Jossey-Bass, San Francisco.

Khandwalla, P.N. (1977) *The Design of Organizations*, Harcourt, Brace, Jovanovich, New York.

Kotter, J.P. (1982) *The General Managers*, Free Press, New York.

Kotter, J.P. (1990) What Leaders Really Do, *Harvard Business Review*, May–June, pp. 103–11.

Lawrence, P.R., and Lorsch, J.W. (1967) Differentiation and Integration in Complex Organizations, *Administrative Science Quarterly*, March, pp. 1–47.

Leavy, B., and Wilson, D. (1994) *Strategy and Leadership*, Routledge, London.

Leonard-Barton, D. (1995) *Well-Springs of Knowledge: Building and Sustaining the Sources of Innovation*, Harvard Business School Press, Boston.

Lessem, R., and Neubauer, F.F. (1994) *European Management Systems*, McGraw-Hill, London.

March, J.G., and Simon, H.A. (1958) *Organizations*, Wiley, New York.

Margolis, H. (1993) *Paradigms and Barriers: How Habits of Mind Govern Scientific Beliefs*, University of Chicago Press, Chicago.

Meindl, J.R., Ehrlich, S.B. and Dukerich, J.M. (1985) The Romance of Leadership, *Administrative Science Quarterly*, 30, March, pp. 78–102.

Meyer, A.D. (1982) Adapting to Environmental Jolts, *Administrative Science Quarterly*, Vol. 27, December, pp. 515–37.

Meyer, J.W., and Zucker, L.G. (1989) *Permanently Failing Organizations*, Sage Publications, Newbury Park.

Miles, R.E., and Snow, C.C. (1978) *Organizational Strategy: Structure and Process*, McGraw-Hill, New York.

Miller, D. (1990) *The Icarus Paradox: How Excellent Companies Can Bring About Their Own Downfall*, Harper Business, New York.

Miller, D. (1993) The Architecture of Simplicity, *Academy of Management Review*, January, pp. 116–38.

Miller, D., and Friesen, P.H. (1980) Momentum and Revolution in Organizational Adaptation, *Academy of Management Journal*, Vol. 23, pp. 591–614.

Miller, D., and Friesen, P. (1984) *Organizations: A Quantum View*, Prentice Hall, Englewood Cliffs, NJ.

Miller, D., and Kets de Vries, M. (1987) *Unstable at the Top*, New American Library, New York.

Mintzberg, H. (1975) *The Structuring of Organizations*, Prentice Hall, Englewood Cliffs, NJ.

Mintzberg, H. (1978) Patterns of Strategy Formation, *Management Science*, May, pp. 934–48.

Mintzberg, H. (1991) The Effective Organization: Forces and Forms, *Sloan Management Review*, Winter, pp. 54–67.

Mitroff, I.I. (1983) *Stakeholders of the Organizational Mind: Toward a New View of Organizational Policy Making*, Jossey-Bass, San Francisco.

Nanus, B. (1992) *Visionary Leadership: Creating a Compelling Sense of Direction for Your Organization*, Jossey-Bass, San Francisco.

Nelson, R.R., and Winter, S.G. (1982) *An Evolutionary Theory of Economic Change*, Harvard University Press, Reading, MA.

Nonaka, I. (1988) Creating Order out of Chaos: Self Renewal in Japanese Firms, *California Management Review*, Spring, pp. 57–73.

Pascale, R.T. (1990) *Managing on the Edge: How Successful Companies Use Conflict to Stay Ahead*, Viking Penguin, London.

Pearson, A.E. (1991) Muscle-Build the Organization, in: Bower J.L. (ed.), *The Craft of General Management*, Harvard Business School Publications, Boston, MA.

Peters, T., and Austin, N. (1985) A Passion for Excellence, *Fortune*, 13 May, pp. 16, 20.

Peters, T.J., and Waterman, R.H. (1982) *In Search of Excellence*, Harper & Row, New York.

Pettigrew, A. (1985) *The Awakening Giant*, Blackwell, Oxford.

Pfeffer, J. (1977) The Ambiguity of Leadership, *Academy of Management Review*, Jaunuary, pp. 104–12.

Pfeffer, J. (1982) *Organizations and Organization Theory*, Pitman, Boston.

Pfeffer, J., and Salancik, G.R. (1974) Organizational Decision Making as a Political Process: The Case of a University Budget, *Administrative Science Quarterly*, June, pp. 135–51.

Pfeffer, J., and Salancik, G. (1978) *The External Control of Organizations: A Resource Dependency Perspective*, Harper & Row, New York.

Porter, M.E. (1980) *Competitive Strategy: Techniques for Analyzing Industries and Competitors*, Free Press, New York.

Quinn, J.B. (1977) Strategic Change: 'Logical Incrementalism', *Sloan Management Review*, Fall, pp. 7–21.

Rumelt, R.P. (1995) Inertia and Transformation, in: Montgomery, C.A. (ed.), *Resource-based and Evolutionary Theories of the Firm: Towards a Synthesis*, Kluwer Academic Publishers, Boston, pp. 101–32.

Schein, E.H. (1985) *Organizational Culture and Leadership*, Jossey-Bass, San Francisco.

Schneider, S.S. (ed.) (1991) Interpreting Organizational Leadership, *Organization Studies* (Special Issue), Vol. 12.

Schwartz, H., and Davis, S.M. (1981) Matching Corporate Culture and Business Strategy, *Organizational Dynamics*, Summer, pp. 30–48.

Selznick, P. (1957) *Leadership in Administration: A Sociological Interpretation*, Harper & Row, New York.

Senge, P. (1990) *The Fifth Discipline: The Art and Practice of the Learning Organization*, Doubleday, New York.

Sheehan, N. (1988) *A Bright and Shining Lie*, Vantage, New York.

Sims, H.P. and Lorenzi, P. (1992) *The New Leadership Paradigm: Social Learning and Cognition in Organizations*, Sage, London.

Skinner, B.F. (1948) Superstition in the Pigeon, *Journal of Experimental Psychology*, No.38, pp. 168–72.

Smircich, L., and Stubbart, C. (1985) Strategic Management in an Enacted World, *Academy of Management Review*, Vol. 10, pp. 724–36.

Stacey, R.D. (1992) *Managing Chaos: Dynamic Business Strategies in an Unpredictable World*, Kogan Page, London.

Stacey, R.D. (1993) Strategy as Order Emerging from Chaos, *Long Range Planning*, Vol. 26, No.1, pp. 10–17.

Stacey, R.D. (1993) *Strategic Management and Organizational Dynamics*, Pitman, London.

Stopford, J.M., and Baden-Fuller, C. (1990) Corporate Rejuvenation, *Journal of Management Studies*, July, pp. 399–415.

Tichy, N., and Devanna, M. (1987) *The Transformational Leader*, Wiley, New York.

Toynbee, A. (1947) *A Study of History*, Oxford University Press, London.

Tushman, M.L., Newman, W.H., and Romanelli, E. (1986) Convergence and Upheaval: Managing the Unsteady Pace of Organizational Evolution, *California Management Review*, Vol. 29, No. 1, Fall, pp. 29–44.

Weick, K.E. (1979) *The Social Psychology of Organizing*, Random House, New York.

10

The International Context

*You may say I'm a dreamer, but I'm not
the only one; I hope some day you'll join us,
and the world will live as one.*

(John Lennon 1940–1980; British musician and songwriter)

*When I am at Milan, I do as they do at
Milan; but when I go to Rome, I do as
Rome does.*

(St. Augustine 354–430; Roman theologian and philosopher)

The Paradox of Globalization and Localization

The subtitle to this book is 'an international perspective.' The question being addressed throughout the book is that of *international variety* – to what extent do people from different countries have divergent views on strategy? To explore this issue, each chapter has concluded by looking at the debate among strategists from this international angle.

While there may be national preferences when it comes to strategy perspectives, countries can also be different from one another on more mundane aspects. Nations can vary with regard to consumer behavior, language, legal system, technological infrastructure, business culture, educational system, labor relations, political ideology, distribution structures and fiscal regime, to name just a few. In other words, the pluriformity of the international context is multi-facetted. The question is, however, how significant are these international differences? Do strategists need to adapt the organization's behavior to the international diversity encountered, or can strategists find ways of overcoming the constraints imposed by cross-border variety? This is one of the issues that will be discussed in this chapter.

A second issue with regard to the international context is that of *international linkages* – to what extent do events in one country have an impact on what happens in other countries? Countries might be quite different, yet developments in one nation might significantly influence developments elsewhere. For instance, if interest rates rise in the United States, this cannot be ignored by central bankers in most other countries. If the price of oil goes down on the spot market in Rotterdam, this will have a 'spill over effect' towards most other nations. And if a breakthrough chip technology is developed in Japan, this will send a shockwave through the computer industry around the world. When a number of nations are tightly linked to one another in a particular area, this is referred to as *international integration*. If, on the other hand, there are very weak links between developments in one country and developments elsewhere, this is referred to as a situation of *international fragmentation*. The question for the strategist is how tightly linked are nations around the world? In the case of international fragmentation, a strategist can approach each country independently – as an isolated strategic issue. If nations are highly integrated, the strategist must view all countries as part of the same system – as squares on a chess board, not to be judged in isolation.

When looking at the variety and linkages within the international context, the question arises how these have been developing, and will develop further, over time. As might be expected by now, opinions on this matter, too, differ quite sharply. As in the previous debates, two opposite points of view can be identified, while many other strategists take up intermediate positions. On the one hand, there are strategists who believe that countries are becoming increasingly similar and more closely interrelated. This development towards lower international variety and tighter international linkages on a world-wide scale is referred to as the process of *globalization*. These strategists argue that globalization is already far advanced and will continue into the future, wiping out the importance of nations as it progresses. Therefore, it is wise to anticipate, and even encourage, a 'nationless' world. We shall refer to this point of view as the *global convergence* perspective. On the other hand, some strategists point out that important international differences will not change easily and that on many issues nations will not integrate with one another. In some circumstances, international variety might actually increase and international linkages might loosen, which is referred to as *localization*. Therefore, wise strategists should be willing to adapt themselves to the complex variety and fragmentation that characterizes our world. We shall refer to this point of view as the *international diversity* perspective.

Hence, the debate in this chapter revolves around the current and future nature of the international context. Where are processes of globalization taking place, at what speed and with which consequences? And are there countercurrents of localization that need to be taken into account? While there are quite a few different answers to these questions, the discussion in this chapter will start by considering the two opposite poles in the debate, the global convergence and international diversity perspectives.

The Global Convergence Perspective

According to proponents of the global convergence perspective, the growing similarity and integration of the world can be argued by pointing to extensive economic statistics, showing significant rises in foreign direct investment and international trade. Yet, it is simpler to observe things directly around you. For instance, are you wearing clothing unique to your country, or could you mingle in an international crowd without standing out? Are the television you watch, the vehicle you drive, the telephone you use and the timepiece you wear specific to your nation, or based on the same technology and even produced by the same companies as those in other countries? Is the music you listen to made by local bands, unknown outside your country, or is this music also popular abroad? Is the food you eat unique to your region, or is even this served in other countries? Now compare your answers to what your parents would have answered 30 years ago – the difference is due to global convergence.

Global convergence, it is argued, is largely driven by the ease, low cost and frequency of international communication, transport and travel. This has diminished the importance of distance. In the past world of large distances, interactions between countries were few and international differences could develop in relative isolation. But the victory of technology over distance has created a 'global village', in which goods, services and ideas are easily exchanged, new developments spread quickly and the 'best practices' of one nation are rapidly copied in others. Once individuals and organizations interact with one another as if no geographic distances exist, an unstopable process towards cultural, political, technological and economic convergence is set in motion – countries will become more closely linked to one another and local differences will be superseded by new global norms.

Of course, in the short run there will still be international differences and nations will not be fully integrated into a 'world without borders'. Strategists taking a global convergence perspective acknowledge that such fundamental and wide ranging changes take time. There are numerous sources of inertia – e.g. vested interests, commitment to existing systems, emotional attachment to current habits, fear of change. The same type of change inhibitors could be witnessed during the industrial revolution, as well. Yet, these change inhibitors can only slow the pace of global convergence, not reverse its direction – the momentum caused by the shrinking of distance can only be braked, but not stopped. Therefore, firms thinking further than the short term, should not let themselves be guided too much by current international diversity, but rather by the emerging global reality (Ohmae, 1990).

For individual firms, global convergence is changing the rules of the competitive game. In the past, most countries had their own distinct characteristics and there were few international economies of scale, while pressures to be locally responsive were high. But growing similarity between nations offers the enormous opportunity of leveraging resources across borders – e.g. production can be standardized to save costs, new product development can be done on an international scale to reduce the total investments required, and marketing knowledge can easily be exchanged to avoid reinventing the wheel in each country. In other words, growing international similarity allows firms to reap global scale economies through *standardization*.

Simultaneously, international integration facilitates the pursuit of global scale economies through *centralization*. Firms can centralize production in large-scale facilities at the most attractive locations, and supply world markets from there, unrestrained by international borders. In the same manner, all types of activities, such as R&D, marketing, sales and procurement, can be centralized to profit from world-wide economies of scale.

An equally important aspect of international integration is that suppliers, buyers and competitors can also increasingly operate as if there are no borders. The ability of buyers to shop around internationally makes the world one *global market*, in which global bargaining power is very important. The ability of suppliers and competitors to reap global economies of scale and sell everywhere around the world creates *global industries*, in which competition takes place on a world-wide stage, instead of in each nation separately. To deal with such global industries and global markets, the firm must be able to coordinate its strategy and activities across nations. In other words, firms must be capable of global *strategy alignment*.

These demands of standardization, centralization and alignment require a global firm, with a strong center responsible for the global strategy, instead of a federation of autonomous national subsidiaries focused on being responsive to their local circumstances. According to proponents of the global convergence perspective, such *global organizations*, or 'centralized hubs' (Bartlett and Ghoshal, 1995; reading 10.5 in this book), will become increasingly predominant over time. And as more companies switch to a global strategy and a global organizational form, this will in turn speed up the general process of globalization. By operating in a global fashion, these firms will actually contribute to a further decrease of international variety and fragmentation. In other words, globalizing companies are both the consequence and a major driver of further global convergence.

The International Diversity Perspective

To strategists taking an international diversity perspective, the 'brave new world' outlined above is largely science fiction. People around the world might be sporting a Swatch or a Rolex, munching Big Macs and drinking Coke, while sitting in their Toyota or Nissan, but to conclude that these are symptoms of global convergence is a leap of faith. Of course, there are some brand names and products more or less standardized around the world, and their numbers might actually be increasing. The question is whether these manufacturers are globalizing to meet increasing world-wide similarity, or whether they are actually finally utilizing the similarities between countries that have always existed. The actual level of international variety may really be quite consistent.

It is particularly important to recognize in which respects countries remain different. For instance, the world might be drinking the same soft drinks, but they are probably doing it in different places, at different times, under different circumstances and for different reasons in each country. The product might be standardized world-wide, but the cultural norms and values that influence its purchase and use remain diverse across countries. According to proponents of the international diversity perspective, it is precisely these fundamental aspects of culture that turn out to be extremely stable over time – habits change slowly, but cultural norms and values are outright rigid. Producers might be lucky to find one product that fits in with such cultural diversity, but it would be foolish to interpret this as world-wide cultural convergence.

Other national differences are equally resilient against the tides of globalization. No countries have recently given up their national language in favor of Esperanto or English. On the contrary, there has been renewed emphasis on the local language in many countries (e.g. Ireland and the Baltic countries) and regions (e.g. Catalonia and Quebec). In the same way, political systems have remained internationally diverse, with plenty of examples of localization, even within nations. For instance, in Russia and the US the shift of power to regional governments has increased policy diversity within the country. Similar arguments can be put forward for legal systems, fiscal regimes, educational systems and technological infra-structure – each is extremely difficult to change due to the lock-in effects (see Chapters 5 and 8), vested interests, psychological commitment and complex decision-making processes. For each example of increasing similarity, a counterexample of local initiatives and growing diversity could be given. Some proponents of the international diversity perspective argue that it is exactly this interplay of divergence and convergence forces that creates a dynamic balance preserving diversity. While technologies, organizing principles, political trends and social habits disperse across borders, resulting in global convergence, new developments and novel systems in each nation arise causing international divergence (Dosi and Kogut, 1993). Convergence trends are usually easier to spot than divergence – international dispersion can be more simply witnessed than new localized developments. To the casual observer, this might suggest that convergence trends have the upper hand, but after more thorough analysis, this conclusion must be cast aside.

Now add to this enduring international diversity the reality of international economic relations. Since World War II attempts have been made to facilitate the integration of national economies. There have been some regional successes (e.g. the North American Free Trade Association and the European Union) and some advances have been made on a world-wide scale (e.g. the World Trade Organization). However, progress has been slow and important political barriers remain.

The continued existence of international diversity and political obstacles, it is argued, will limit the extent to which nations can become fully integrated into one borderless world. International differences and barriers to trade and investment will frustrate firms' attempts to standardize and centralize, and will place a premium on firms' abilities to adapt and decentralize. Of course, there will be some activities for which global economies of scale can be achieved and for which strategy alignment is needed, but this will not become true for all activities. Empowering national managers to be responsive to specific local conditions will remain an important ingredient for international success. Balancing globalization and localization of the firm's activities will continue to be a requirement in the future international context.

Ideally, the internationally operating company should neither deny nor regret the existence of international diversity, but regard it as an opportunity that can be exploited. Each country's unique circumstances will pose different challenges, requiring the development of different competences. Different national 'climates' will create opportunities for different innovations. If a company can tap into each country's opportunities and leverage the acquired competences and innovations to other countries, this could offer the company an important source of competitive advantage. Naturally, these locally-leveraged competences and innovations would subsequently need to be adapted to the specific circumstances in other countries. This balancing act would require an organization that combined strong local responsiveness with the ability to exchange and coordinate internationally, even on a world-wide scale (globally-networked). International organizations blending these two elements are referred to as *transnational* (Bartlett and Ghoshal, 1995; reading 10.5), or *heterarchical* (Hedlund, 1986).

The question for the field of strategic management is, therefore, whether the international context is moving towards similarity and integration, or will it remain as diverse and fragmented as at the moment? Should strategists anticipate and encourage global convergence by emphasizing global standardization, centralization and strategy alignment, or should strategists acknowledge and exploit international diversity by emphasizing local adaptation, decentralization and international networking? In short, strategists must wrestle with the paradox of globalization and localization (see Table 10.1).

Defining the Issues: Dimensions and Subjects

Globalization is a term used by many, but specified by few. This lack of definition often leads to an unfocused debate, as different people employ the same term, but actually refer to different phenomena. To have a more structured debate, the term globalization (and its opposite, localization) needs to be explored and a broad common definition needs to be established. This stage-setting work will concentrate on two key questions, namely, what does globalization encompass? (*dimensions*) and what actually globalizes? (*subjects*).

	Global Convergence Perspective	International Diversity Perspective
Emphasis on	Globalization over localization	Localization over globalization
International variety	Growing similarity	Remaining diversity
International linkages	Growing integration	Remaining fragmentation
Major drivers	Technology and communication	Cultural and institutional inertia
Diversity and fragmentation	Costly, convergence can be encouraged	Reality, can be exploited
Strategic focus	Global-scale efficiency	Local responsiveness
Organizational preference	Standardize/centralize unless	Adapt/decentralize unless
Innovation process	Center-for-global	Locally-leveraged
Organizational structure	Global (centralized hub)	Transnational (globally-networked)

TABLE 10.1
Global convergence versus international diversity perspective

Globalization as Increasing International Scope, Similarity and Integration

Clearly, globalization refers to the process of becoming more global. But what is global? Although there is not full agreement on a single definition, most writers use the term to refer to one or more of the following elements:

■ *International scope*. 'Global' can simply mean world-wide. For instance, a firm with operations around the world can be labeled a global company, to distinguish it from firms that are national (local) or regional in scope. In such a case, the term 'global' is primarily intended to describe the *spatial* dimension – the broadest possible international scope is to be global. When this definition of global is employed, globalization is the process of international expansion on a world-wide scale (e.g. Patel and Pavitt, 1991).

■ *International similarity*. 'Global' can also refer to homogeneity around the world. For instance, if a company decides to sell the same product in all of its international markets, it is often referred to as a global product, as opposed to a locally-tailored product. In such a case, the term 'global' is primarily intended to describe the *variance* dimension – the ultimate level of international similarity is to be global. When this definition of global is employed, globalization is the process of declining international variety (e.g. Levitt, 1983; reading 10.1).

■ *International integration*. 'Global' can also refer to the world as one tightly-linked system. For instance, a global market can be said to exist if events in one country are significantly impacted by events in other geographic markets. This as opposed to local markets, where price levels, competition, demand and fashions are hardly influenced by developments in other nations. In such a case, the term 'global' is primarily intended to describe the *linkages* dimension – the ultimate level of international integration is to be global. When this definition of global is employed, globalization is the process of increasing international interconnectedness (e.g. Porter, 1986).

So, is for example McDonald's a global company? That depends along which of the above three dimensions the company is measured. When judging the international scope of McDonald's, it can be seen that the company is globalizing, but far from global. The company operates in approximately half the countries in the world, but in many of these only in one or a few large cities. Of McDonald's world-wide revenues, more than half is still earned in the United States. This predominance of the home country is even stronger if the composition of the company's top management is looked at (Ruigrok and Van Tulder, 1995). However, when judging McDonald's along the dimension of international similarity, it is simple to observe that the company is relatively global, as it takes a highly standardized approach to most markets around the world. Although, it should be noted that on some aspects as menu and interior design there is leeway for local adaptation. Finally, when judging McDonald's along the dimension of international integration, the company is only slightly global, as it is not very tightly linked around the world. Some activities are centralized or coordinated, but in general there is relatively little need for concerted action.

In this chapter, all three possible dimensions of globalization will be examined. The opposites – localization as decreasing international scope, similarity and integration – will also be discussed. The reader is advised, however, to consider which dimension of globalization or localization each of the contributing authors place centrally in their analyses.

Globalization of Companies, Businesses and Economies

The second factor complicating the debate on the nature of the international context is that the concept of globalization is applied to a variety of subjects, while the differences are often not made explicit. Some people discuss globalization as a development in the economy at large, while others debate globalization as something potentially happening to industries, markets, products, technologies, fashions, production, competition and organizations. For the reader it is essential to identify the actual subject(s) under discussion. In general, debates on globalization tend to concentrate on one of three levels of analysis:

■ *Globalization of companies*. Some authors focus on the *micro* level, debating whether individual companies are becoming more global. Issues are the extent to which firms have a global strategy, structure, culture, workforce, management team and resource base. In more detail, the globalization of specific products and value-adding activities is often discussed. Here it is of particular importance to acknowledge that the globalization of one product or activity (e.g. marketing) does not necessarily entail the globalization of all others (see Prahalad and Doz, 1987; reading 10.3; Bartlett and Ghoshal, 1987; reading 10.5).

■ *Globalization of businesses*. Other authors are more concerned with the *meso* level, debating whether particular businesses are becoming more global. Here it is important to distinguish those who emphasize the globalization of markets, as opposed to those accentuating the globalization of industries (see Chapter 5 for this distinction). The issue of globalizing markets has to do with the growing similarity of world-wide *customer demand* and the growing ease of world-wide product flows (see Levitt, 1983; reading 10.1; Douglas and Wind, 1987; reading 10.2). For example, the crude oil and foreign currency markets are truly global – the same commodities are traded at the same rates around the world. The markets for accountancy and hairdressing services, on the other hand, are very local – demand differs significantly, there is little cross-border trade and consequently prices vary sharply. The globalization of industries is quite a different issue, as it has to do with the emergence of a set of *producers* that compete with one another on a world-wide scale (see Prahalad and Doz, 1987; reading 10.3; Porter, 1990; reading 10.4). So, for instance, the automobile and consumer electronics industries are quite global – the major players in most countries belong to the same set of companies that compete against each other all around the world. Even the accountancy industry is relatively global, even though the markets for accountancy services are very local. On the other hand, the construction and retail banking industries are very local – the competitive scene in each country is relatively uninfluenced by competitive developments elsewhere.

■ *Globalization of economies*. Yet other authors take a *macro* level of analysis, arguing whether or not the world's economies in general are experiencing a convergence trend. Many authors are interested in the macro economic dynamics of international integration and its consequences in terms of growth, employment, inflation, productivity, trade and foreign direct investment (e.g. Kay, 1989; Krugman, 1990). Others focus more on the political realities constraining and encouraging globalization (e.g. McGrew *et al.*, 1992; Milner, 1988; Reich, 1991). Yet others are interested in the underlying dynamics of technological, institutional and organizational convergence (e.g. Dunning, 1986; Kogut, 1993). None of these authors has been included in this chapter due to space limits, but it should be noted that the discussions at this level of analysis are also important to the debate on the future of the international context.

Ultimately, the question in this chapter is not only whether economies, businesses and companies are actually globalizing, but whether these developments are a matter of choice. In other words, is global convergence or continued international diversity an uncontrollable evolutionary development to which firms (and governments) must comply, or can firms actively influence the globalization or localization of their environment?

EXHIBIT 10.1
IKEA Short Case

IKEA: GLOBALIZATION BY DESIGN?

IKEA's bright yellow and blue home furnishing stores have become a common sight in most western countries. With more than 125 stores in 25 countries, frequented by over 120 million people spending approximately $4.5 billion each year, IKEA is the world's largest home furnishing retailer. Their strong international presence is even more remarkable when compared to competitors and retailers in general. Retailing is a very local industry, with only a handful of companies that have successfully branched out to foreign markets, and in the home furnishings segment IKEA is virtually the only international player.

IKEA's success formula has remained surprisingly constant over the years, ever since founder Ingvar Kamprad set up a warehouse showroom in a disused factory in Almhult, Sweden, in 1953. Then, as now, furniture retailing was highly fragmented, split between department stores and small family-owned shops. Market power was in the hands of the furniture manufacturers and prices were high. Kamprad aimed to counter this situation and decided 'to offer a wide range of home furnishing items of good design and function at prices so low, that the majority of people can afford to buy them'. IKEA's way of achieving this was highly innovative. Instead of pushing a manufacturer's traditional wares, IKEA discussed with new and open-minded suppliers what types of products it could sell and at what prices. Manufacturers were encouraged to switch from hand-crafted items made of expensive woods, to mass-produced basic furniture of good quality, using local inexpensive softwoods such as pine and spruce, and new wood-based materials such as plywood and particle boards. Such pieces of furniture IKEA could sell in large quantities at low prices.

Long-term production agreements are still a hallmark of the IKEA concept. IKEA does not 'shop around for deals', but has established close relationships with more than 2000 suppliers around the world. These long-term partners are supported by IKEA when needed, but are also required to adapt to IKEA specifications and be very responsive to IKEA's needs. This is particularly important because the design and engineering of most products is carried out by IKEA itself in Sweden. Almost all of the 20,000 product items carried by IKEA have been specifically designed by or for the company. And all share a typical Scandinavian design – simple elegance achieved by clear lines and natural materials.

This is probably one of the most interesting aspects of IKEA's expansion outside of Scandinavia, which started in 1973, when the company entered the Swiss market. Although internationalizing, IKEA has remained quintessentially Swedish. Most products are of Swedish design, all have Swedish names, the store restaurants serve Swedish food and the company culture strongly reflects such Swedish values as equality, honesty, openness, modesty, reliability and simplicity. The company's home market provides IKEA with both image and identity – towards the marketplace IKEA's Swedishness is employed as a distinctive quality, while internally it provides much of the cultural glue keeping the company together. Approximately 90 percent of senior managers around the world are Swedes. The current CEO Anders Moberg is very clear about the importance of the Swedish culture within the organization: 'I would advise any foreign employee who really wants to advance in this company to learn Swedish. They will then get a completely different feeling for our culture, our mood, our values. We encourage them to have as much contact with Sweden as possible, for instance by going there for their holidays.'

One important reflection of the Swedish egalitarian culture is that there are only four levels of management separating Moberg from Willy the stock-boy, even though IKEA employs more than 27,000 people. The company is flat, open and informal. Employees are encouraged to take initiatives and creatively challenge the status quo. IKEA managers operate with a large measure of autonomy from headquarters. The Swedish emphasis on ethical behavior is also highly valued and is expressed in such conduct as rigorous product safety measures, environmental responsibility and employment conditions.

IKEA's store formula reflects many of these qualities. While the aircraft-hangar-sized stores benefit from scale efficiencies, IKEA has been able to create a quality atmosphere through human-scale dimensions in the store lay-out. Visiting an IKEA store is intended to be more like a day out than a shopping trip. Fun and excitement for the entire family are paramount – there are play areas for the kids, changing rooms for babies, and a family restaurant. Customers are lead by a one-way lay-out through the entire store, past articles that are either self-service (can be taken off the self) or full-service (can be picked up on the way out from the warehouse). If necessary, customers can find assistance at information desks, but pay when exiting the store through supermarket-style check-outs. IKEA stores are normally situated outside cities on cheap land, but close to major roads and with plenty of space for parking, so that customers can easily transport most items home in their own vehicle (delivery is available for a fee). Transportation is made easy by presenting most furniture as flat-packs, that is, in its unassembled state. This also saves IKEA labor-intensive assembly and the cost of shipping and storing air.

Within the international organization the functions of purchasing, and product range and development are strongly controlled by headquarters. The functions of physical distribution and retailing are regionally divided (Northern Europe, Southern Europe, East Central Europe, North America, Australasia). Within this structure the Market Unit North America has a special status, due to the need to do things differently on the other side of the Atlantic. When IKEA first entered the American market in 1985, the American stores were set up and run in the same way as the European stores. Most of the products were also sourced from European suppliers. But after five years and five new stores, operations were still not breaking even. Then in 1991 the US dollar strongly depreciated and IKEA's low cost position became threatened. After a thorough diagnosis, Moberg concluded that IKEA had been 'behaving like all Europeans, as exporters, which meant that we are not really in the country.' Supply lines from Europe to the US were too long and too currency dependent, and many products clashed with American standards and tastes. For instance, all products were made in metric sizes and often did not fit with other American products (e.g. kitchens did not fit with appliances, beds did not fit customer's sheets). Many products were also too small (e.g. beds and kitchen cupboards were perceived as too narrow and glasses as too small). To remedy this situation, the new US chief executive Goran Carstedt was given more autonomy and he quickly moved to more closely adapt to US practices and by 1994 about half of IKEA's furniture sales were locally produced.

Now IKEA wants to grow further by moving to markets outside the western industrialized group of nations. In particular, Moberg believes that South-East Asia and Eastern Europe represent an enormous potential for IKEA. Moberg's vision is to gradually transform the company into a more global player. One of the first moves he has announced is the opening of ten stores in mainland China. This might seem like a radical step in the dark, but IKEA has gained some indirect experience in Asia, through a number of franchise stores in Hong Kong (6), Taiwan (1) and Singapore (1). In these markets IKEA is perceived as very western and very trendy, and they have been able to lure young urban professionals into the stores. These experiences, together with the existing contacts with Chinese suppliers, have now emboldened IKEA to set up fully owned stores in mainland China. Yet the question is whether this move is foresight or fallacy. If global convergence is truly happening, IKEA might be at its forefront, actually even speeding up the process. Of course, IKEA would still need to make adjustments to the local circumstances, but it could transplant most of the IKEA formula to non-Western countries and benefit from being the first global home furnishing retailer. However, if international diversity remains high, IKEA will have to make enormous adaptations to its formula to be successful in China – possibly to the extent that one might wonder whether they will bring any competitive advantage with them at all. IKEA's entry into China might be an open invitation for local competitors to copy those aspects of IKEA's concept that are transferable, while retaining their stronger local responsiveness. Therefore the question facing IKEA is whether to enter China at all, and if they do choose to do so, whether they should take a more globally-integrated or locally-responsive approach.

Sources: *Financial Times*, various issues; *The Economist*, November 19 1994; Pitt, 1996.

The Debate and the Readings

The international context has long been a topic receiving significant academic attention. It was not until the early 1980s, however, that the subject of globalization developed into a full-fledged debate at the center of strategic management. The article that has probably been the most influential at focusing this debate, by boldly advocating a global convergence perspective, has been 'The Globalization of Markets' by Theodore Levitt. For this reason, Levitt's forceful article has been selected as the opening essay in this chapter, representing the global convergence perspective. In this contribution, Levitt provocatively predicts that the world is quickly moving towards a converging commonality. He believes that 'the world's needs and desires have been irrevocably homogenized.' The force driving this process is technology, which has facilitated communication, transport and travel, while allowing for the development of superior products at low prices. His conclusion is that 'the commonality of preference leads inescapably to the standardization of products, manufacturing, and the institutions of trade and commerce.' The old-fashioned multinational corporation, that adapted itself to local circumstances, is 'obsolete and the global corporation absolute.'

While a clear proponent of the global convergence perspective, it should be noted that Levitt's inspired prediction of global convergence is focused on the globalization of *markets*. In particular, he is intent on pointing out that converging consumer demand in international markets facilitates – even necessitates – the reaping of economies of scale through the standardization of products, marketing and production. With this emphasis on the demand side, Levitt pays far less attention to the supply side – the globalization of industries and the competition within industries – which other global convergence proponents tend to accentuate (see readings 10.3 and 10.4). And although he strongly advises companies to become 'global corporations,' he does not further detail what a global company should look like (see readings 10.5). Overall, Levitt views globalization more as growing international similarity, while paying less attention to the possibility of growing international integration, as some other authors do.

As a direct response to 'the sweeping and somewhat polemic character' of Levitt's argumentation, Susan Douglas and Yoram Wind have written 'The Myth of Globalization,' that has been selected as representative of the international diversity perspective. Douglas and Wind believe that many of the assumptions underlying Levitt's global standardization philosophy are contradicted by the facts. They argue that the convergence of customer needs is not a one way street; *divergence* trends are also noticeable. Furthermore, they believe that Levitt is mistaken in arguing that economies of scale in production and marketing is an irreversible force driving globalization. According to Douglas and Wind, many new technologies have actually lowered the minimum efficient scale of operation, while there are also plenty of industries where economies of scale are not an important issue. The authors conclude by outlining the specific circumstances under which a strategy of global standardization might be effective. Under all other circumstances, Douglas and Wind reiterate, the international strategist will have to deal with the existence of international diversity and search for the right balance between global standardization and local adaptation.

In the third contribution, 'The Dynamics of Global Competition', C.K. Prahalad and Yves Doz move beyond the standardization-adaptation issue surrounding international market similarity, which they see as only one of the questions posed by globalization. In their discussion, they take a broader view than Levitt and Douglas and Wind, by analyzing both the globalization of markets and industries, and by paying attention to international integration as well as international similarity. Their purpose is, as their title indicates, to understand the dynamics of global competition. In their view international convergence of consumer demand and opportunities for cross-border economies of scale can promote world-wide integrated competition, but many other factors can also bring this about. Even in a business where international market similarity is low – requiring extensive local adaptation – the industry players and the competition among the players can be global. For instance, if an aggressive company uses the cash and competences it develops in one country to attack its competitors in other countries, competition becomes a cross-border game. The national markets might be rather dissimilar, but they become integrated by international companies coordinating their strategies across national boundaries. To counter such a 'global' competitor, that aligns its strategy in each national market, a company must realize that a country-by-country response would be ineffective and that it too must play the game at the global level.

The importance of Prahalad and Doz's contribution to the discussion in this chapter is that in their broad view of the globalization issue, they outline all of the business characteristics that pressure a company to strive for international standardization, centralization and alignment, while also identifying the factors pressuring firms to be locally responsive. Furthermore, they convincingly argue that the level of globalization or localization of each business must be judged separately, and that a distinction should even be made for each of the business's functional areas. With regard to the global convergence and international diversity perspectives, their view is not as outspoken as in the first two readings in this chapter. Yet, their arguments seem to imply that global convergence, in particular global integration, is to be expected as soon as one strong competitor in a business formulates the strategic intent to strive for global dominance.

In the fourth reading, 'The Competitive Advantage of Nations,' Michael Porter introduces a different angle to the debate on globalization. Porter agrees with proponents of the global convergence perspective that the world is becoming highly integrated, although in some industries more than others (see Porter, 1986). However, Porter does not agree that the world is in all ways becoming more similar. In fact, Porter argues the opposite – growing international integration encourages international diversity. Global integration, according to Porter, does not make geographic location and nationality unimportant, as some authors seem to suggest (e.g. Ohmae, 1989), but in some ways more important. This is due to the process of local specialization, by which clusters of interconnected buyers, suppliers, competitors, and related and supporting industries evolve, that reinforce each other in innovating and becoming more competitive. Porter argues that such local clusters of firms operating in a particular sector will develop if there is a strong *national diamond*, that is, a challenging competitive environment with advantageous factor and demand conditions, and a strong infrastructure of related and supporting industries. And once a strong diamond has been established, it can have a self-perpetuating momentum, by winning in global competition and by attracting excellent companies and individuals from other countries. Porter therefore concludes that companies should recognize the specific characteristics of the national diamond in their home country and try to exploit and improve its unique strengths. He also advises companies to seek out and tap into strong local clusters abroad, to supplement their home-based advantages and to compensate for any home-based disadvantages. In short, international diversity is a reality, but can be exploited by the internationally-operating company.

In the last reading, 'Transnational Management', Christopher Bartlett and Sumantra Ghoshal bring the issue of organization into the debate on globalization. In this reading, Bartlett and Ghoshal do not take a direct stance on the issue of global convergence and international diversity. They are more concerned with clarifying the various pressures on international organizations and outlining the different organizational forms that can be adopted. The thrust of their argument is that globalization has forced the international company to manage across borders, as opposed to the old multinational corporation, that was organized on a country-by-country basis. In the old multinational, emphasis was placed on strong *geographic management* to be *responsive* to the local circumstances. But to deal with, and benefit from, international integration and similarities, companies have to be able to do more. *Global functional management* is needed to *learn* and transfer competencies world-wide, while *global business management* with global product responsibilities is needed to achieve world-wide *efficiency*. Bartlett and Ghoshal argue that optimizing learning, efficiency and responsiveness simultaneously is the challenge facing the new *transnational* organization. They believe that every organization must find its own dynamic balance between these forces; there is not one best organizational response to globalization, because the extent of globalization is never the same.

10.1   The Globalization of Markets

By Theodore Levitt [1]

A powerful force drives the world toward a converging commonality, and that force is technology. It has proletarianized communication, transport, and travel. It has made isolated places and impoverished peoples eager for modernity's allurements. Almost everyone everywhere wants all the things they have heard about, seen, or experienced via the new technologies.

The result is a new commercial reality – the emergence of global markets for standardized consumer products on a previously unimagined scale of magnitude. Corporations geared to this new reality benefit from enormous economies of scale in production, distribution, marketing, and management. By translating these benefits into reduced world prices, they can decimate competitors that still live in the disabling grip of old assumptions about how the world works.

Gone are accustomed differences in national or regional preference. Gone are the days when a company could sell last year's models – or lesser versions of advanced products – in the less developed world. And gone are the days when prices, margins, and profits abroad were generally higher than at home.

The globalization of markets is at hand. With that, the multinational commercial world nears its end, and so does the multinational corporation.

The multinational and the global corporation are not the same thing. The multinational corporation operates in a number of countries, and adjusts its products and practices in each – at high relative costs. The global corporation operates with resolute constancy – at low relative cost – as if the entire world (or major regions of it) were a single entity; it sells the same things in the same way everywhere.

Which strategy is better is not a matter of opinion but of necessity. World-wide communications carry everywhere the constant drumbeat of modern possibilities to lighten and enhance work, raise living standards, divert, and entertain. The same countries that ask the world to recognize and respect the individuality of their cultures insist on the wholesale transfer to them of modern goods, services, and technologies. Modernity is not just a wish but also a widespread practice among those who cling, with unyielding passion or religious fervor, to ancient attitudes and heritages.

Who can forget the televized scenes during the 1979 Iranian uprisings of young men in fashionable French-cut trousers and silky body shirts thirsting with raised modern weapons for blood in the name of Islamic fundamentalism?

In Brazil, thousands swarm daily from preindustrial Bahian darkness into exploding coastal cities, there quickly to install television sets in crowded corrugated huts and, next to battered Volkswagens, make sacrificial offerings of fruit and fresh-killed chickens to Macumban spirits by candlelight.

A thousand suggestive ways attest to the ubiquity of the desire for the most advanced things that the world makes and sells – goods of the best quality and reliability at the lowest price. The world's needs and desires have been irrevocably homogenized. This makes the multinational corporation obsolete and the global corporation absolute.

Living in the Republic of Technology

Daniel J. Boorstin, author of the monumental trilogy *The Americans*, characterized our age as driven by 'the Republic of Technology (whose) supreme law . . . is convergence, the tendency for everything to become more like everything else.'

In business, this trend has pushed markets toward global commonality. Corporations sell standardized products in the same way everywhere – autos, steel, chemicals, petroleum, cement, agricultural commodities and equipment, industrial and commercial construction, banking and insurance services, computers, semiconductors, transport, electronic instruments, pharmaceuticals, and telecommunications, to mention some of the obvious.

Nor is the sweeping gale of globalization confined to these raw material or high-tech products, where the universal language of customers and users facilitates standardization. The transforming winds whipped up by the proletarianization of communication and travel enter every crevice of life.

Commercially, nothing confirms this as much as the success of McDonald's from the Champs Elysées to the Ginza, of Coca-Cola in Bahrain and Pepsi-Cola in Moscow, and of rock music, Greek salad, Hollywood movies, Revlon cosmetics, Sony televisions, and Levi jeans everywhere. 'High-touch' products are as ubiquitous as high-tech.

Starting from opposing sides, the high-tech and the high-touch ends of the commercial spectrum gradually consume the undistributed middle in their cosmopolitan orbit. No one is exempt and nothing can stop the process. Everywhere everything gets more and more like everything else as the world's preference structure is relentlessly homogenized.

Consider the cases of Coca-Cola and Pepsi-Cola, which are globally standardized products sold everywhere and welcomed by everyone. Both successfully cross multitudes of national, regional, and ethnic taste buds trained to a variety of deeply ingrained local preferences of taste, flavor, consistency, effervescence, and aftertaste. Everywhere both sell well. Cigarettes, too, especially American-made, make year-to-year global inroads in territories previously held in the firm grip of other, mostly local, blends.

These are not exceptional examples. (Indeed their global reach would be even greater were it not for artificial trade barriers.) They exemplify a general drift toward the homogenization of the world and how companies distribute, finance, and price products. Nothing is exempt. The products and methods of the industrialized world play a single tune for all the world, and all the world eagerly dances to it.

Ancient differences in national tastes or modes of doing business disappear. The commonality of preference leads inescapably to the standardization of products, manufacturing, and the institutions of trade and commerce. Small nation-based markets transmogrify and expand. Success in world competition turns on efficiency in production, distribution, marketing, and management, and inevitably becomes focused on price.

The most effective world competitors incorporate superior quality and reliability into their cost structures. They sell in all national markets the same kind of products sold at home or in their largest export market. They compete on the basis of appropriate value – the best combinations of price, quality, reliability, and delivery for products that are globally identical with respect to design, function, and even fashion.

That, and little else, explains the surging success of Japanese companies dealing world-wide in a vast variety of products – both tangible products like steel, cars, motorcycles, hi-fi equipment, farm machinery, robots, microprocessors, carbon fibers, and now even textiles, and intangibles like banking, shipping, general contracting, and soon computer software. Nor are high-quality and low-cost operations incompatible, as a host of consulting organizations and data engineers argue with vigorous vacuity. The reported data are incomplete, wrongly analyzed, and contradictory. The truth is that low-cost operations are the hallmark of corporate cultures that require and produce quality in all that they do. High quality and low costs are not opposing postures. They are compatible, twin identities of superior practice.

To say that Japan's companies are not global because they export cars with left-side drives to the United States and the European continent, while those in Japan have right-side drives, or because they sell office machines through distributors in the United States but directly at home, or speak Portuguese in Brazil is to mistake a difference for a distinction. The same is true of Safeway and Southland retail chains operating effectively in the Middle East, and to not only native but also imported populations from Korea, the Philippines, Pakistan, India, Thailand, Britain, and the United States. National rules of the road differ, and so do distribution channels and languages. Japan's distinction is its unrelenting push for economy and value enhancement. That translates into a drive for standardization at high quality levels.

Vindication of the Model T

If a company forces costs and prices down and pushes quality and reliability up – while maintaining reasonable concern for suitability – customers will prefer its world-standardized products. The theory holds at this stage in the evolution of globalization, no matter what conventional market research and even common sense may suggest about different national and regional tastes, preferences, needs, and institutions. The Japanese have repeatedly vindicated this theory, as did Henry Ford with the Model T. Most important, so have their imitators, including companies from South Korea (television sets and heavy construction), Malaysia (personal calculators and microcomputers), Brazil (auto parts and tools), Colombia (apparel), Singapore (optical equipment), and yes, even from the United States (office copiers, computers, bicycles, castings), Western Europe (automatic washing machines), Rumania (housewares), Hungary (apparel), Yugoslavia (furniture), and Israel (pagination equipment).

Of course, large companies operating in a single nation or even a single city don't standardize everything they make, sell, or do. They have product lines instead of a single product version, and multiple distribution channels. There are neighborhood, local, regional, ethnic, and institutional differences, even within metropolitan areas. But although companies customize products for particular market segments, they know that success in a world with homogenized demand requires a search for sales opportunities in similar segments across the globe in order to achieve the economies of scale necessary to compete.

Such a search works because a market segment in one country is seldom unique; it has close cousins everywhere precisely because technology has homogenized the globe. Even small local segments have their global equivalents everywhere and become subject to global competition, especially on price.

The global competitor will seek constantly to standardize his offering everywhere. He will digress from this standardization only after exhausting all possibilities to retain it, and he will push for reinstatement of standardization whenever digression and divergence have occurred. He will never assume that the customer is a king who knows his own wishes.

Trouble increasingly stalks companies that lack clarified global focus and remain inattentive to the economics of simplicity and standardization. The most endangered companies in the rapidly evolving world tend to be those that dominate rather small domestic markets with high value-added products for which there are smaller markets elsewhere. With transportation costs proportionately low, distant competitors will enter the now-sheltered markets of those companies with goods produced more cheaply under scale-efficient conditions. Global competition spells the end of domestic territoriality, no matter how diminutive the territory may be.

When the global producer offers his lower costs internationally, his patronage expands exponentially. He not only reaches into distant markets, but also attracts customers who previously held to local preferences and now capitulate to the attractions of lesser prices. The strategy of standardization not only responds to world-wide homogenized markets but also expands those markets with aggressive low pricing. The new technological juggernaut taps an ancient motivation – to make one's money go as far as possible. This is universal – not simply a motivation but actually a need.

The Hedgehog Knows

The difference between the hedgehog and the fox, wrote Sir Isaiah Berlin in distinguishing between Dostoevski and Tolstoy, is that the fox knows a lot about a great many things, but the hedgehog knows everything about one great thing. The multinational corporation knows a lot about a great many countries and congenially adapts to supposed differences. It willingly accepts vestigial national differences, not questioning the possibility of their transformation, not recognizing how the world is ready and eager for the benefit of modernity, especially when the price is right. The multinational corporation's accommodating mode to visible national differences is medieval.

By contrast, the global corporation knows everything about one great thing. It knows about the absolute need to be competitive on a world-wide basis as well as nationally and seeks constantly to drive down prices by standardizing what it sells and how it operates. It treats the world as composed of few standardized markets rather than many customized markets. It actively seeks and vigorously works toward global convergence. Its mission is modernity and its mode, price competition, even when it sells top-of-the-line, high-end products. It knows about the one great thing all nations and people have in common: scarcity.

Nobody takes scarcity lying down; everyone wants more. This in part explains division of labor and specialization of production. They enable people and nations to optimize their conditions through trade. The median is usually money.

Experience teaches that money has three special qualities: scarcity, difficulty of acquisition, and transience. People understandably treat it with respect. Everyone in the increasingly homogenized world market wants products and features that everybody else wants. If the price is low enough, they will take highly standardized world products, even if these aren't exactly what mother said was suitable, what immemorial custom decreed was right, or what market-research fabulists asserted was preferred.

The implacable truth of all modern production – whether of tangible or intangible goods – is that large-scale production of standardized items is generally cheaper within a wide range of volume than small-scale production. Some argue that CAD/CAM (computer aided design/computer aided manufacturing) will allow companies to manufacture customized products on a small scale – but cheaply. But the argument misses the point. If a company treats the world as one or two distinctive product markets, it can serve the world more economically than if it treats it as three, four, or five product markets.

Different cultural preferences, national tastes and standards, and business institutions are vestiges of the past. Some inheritances die gradually; others prosper and expand into mainstream global preferences. So-called ethnic markets are a good example. Chinese food, pitta bread, country and western music, pizza, and jazz are everywhere. They are market segments that exist in world-wide proportions. They don't deny or contradict global homogenization but confirm it.

Many of today's differences among nations as to products and their features actually reflect the respectful accommodation of multinational corporations to what they believe are fixed local preferences. They believe preferences are fixed, not because they are but because of rigid habits of thinking about what actually is. Most executives in multinational corporations are thoughtlessly accommodating. They falsely presume that marketing means giving the customer what he says he wants rather than trying to understand exactly what he'd like. So they persist with high-cost, customized multinational products and practices instead of pressing hard and pressing properly for global standardization.

I do not advocate the systematic disregard of local or national differences. But a company's sensitivity to such differences does not require that it ignore the possibilities of doing things differently or better.

With persistence and appropriate means, barriers against superior technologies and economics have always fallen. There is no recorded exception where reasonable effort has been made to overcome them. It is very much a matter of time and effort.

A Failure in Global Imagination

Many companies have tried to standardize world practice by exporting domestic products and processes without accommodation or change – and have failed miserably. Their deficiencies have been seized on as evidence of bovine stupidity in the face of abject impossibility. Advocates of global standardization see them as examples of failures in execution.

In fact, poor execution is often an important cause. More important, however, is failure of nerve – failure of imagination.

Consider the case for the introduction of fully automatic home laundry equipment in Western Europe at a time when few homes had even semiautomatic machines.

The growing success of small, low-powered, low-speed, low-capacity, low-priced Italian machines, even against the preferered but highly priced and highly promoted brand in West Germany, was significant. It contained a powerful message that was lost on managers confidently wedded to a distorted version of the marketing concept according to which you give the customer what he says he wants. In fact the customers said they wanted certain features, but their behavior demonstrated they'd take other features provided the price and the promotion were right.

In this case it was obvious that under prevailing conditions, people preferred a low-priced automatic over any kind of manual or semiautomatic machine and certainly over higher priced automatics, even though the low-priced automatics failed to fulfil all their expressed preferences. The supposedly meticulous and demanding German consumers violated all expectations by buying the simple, low-priced Italian machines.

This case illustrates how the perverse practice of the marketing concept and the absence of any kind of marketing imagination let multinational attitudes survive when customers actually want the benefits of global standardization. People were asked what features they wanted in a washing machine rather than what they wanted out of life. Selling a line of products individually tailored to each nation is thoughtless. Managers who took pride in practicing the marketing concept to the fullest did not, in fact, practice it at all. Data do not yield information except with the intervention of the mind. Information does not yield meaning except with the intervention of imagination.

Cracking the Code of Western Markets

Since the theory of the marketing concept emerged a quarter of a century ago, the more managerially advanced corporations have been eager to offer what customers clearly want rather than what is merely convenient. They have created marketing departments supported by professional market researchers of awesome and often costly proportions. And they have proliferated extraordinary numbers of operations and product lines – highly tailored products and delivery systems for many different markets, market segments, and nations.

Significantly, Japanese companies operate almost entirely without marketing departments or market research of the kind so prevalent in the West. Yet, in the colorful words of General Electric's chairman John F. Welch Jr., the Japanese, coming from a small cluster of resource-poor islands, with an entirely alien culture and an almost impenetrably complex language, have cracked the code of Western markets. They have done it not by looking with mechanistic thoroughness at the way markets are different but rather by searching for meaning with a deeper wisdom. They have discovered the one great thing all markets have in common – an overwhelming desire for dependable, world-standard modernity in all things, at aggressively low prices. In response, they deliver irresistible value everywhere, attracting people with products that market-research technocrats described with superficial certainty as being unsuitable and uncompetitive.

The wider a company's global reach, the greater the number of regional and national preferences it will encounter for certain product features, distribution systems, or promotional media. There will always need to be some accommodation to differences.

In its highly successful introduction of Contac 600 (the timed-release decongestant) into Japan, SmithKline Corporation used 35 wholesalers instead of the 1000-plus that established practice required. Daily contacts with the wholesalers and key retailers, also in violation of established practice, supplemented the plan, and it worked.

Denied access to established distribution institutions in the United States, Komatsu, the Japanese manufacturer of lightweight farm machinery, entered the market through over-the-road construction equipment dealers in rural areas of the Sunbelt, where farms are smaller, the soil sandier and easier to work. Here inexperienced distributors were able to attract customers on the basis of Komatsu's product and price appropriateness.

In cases of successful challenge to prevailing institutions and practices, a combination of product reliability and quality, strong and sustained support systems, aggressively low prices, and sales-compensation packages, as well as audacity and implacability, circumvented, shattered, and transformed very different distribution systems. Instead of resentment, there was admiration.

The differences that persist throughout the world despite its globalization affirm an ancient dictum of economics – that things are driven by what happens at the margin, not at the core. Thus, in ordinary competitive analysis, what's important is not the average price but the marginal price, what happens not in the usual case but at the interface of newly erupting conditions. What counts in commercial affairs is what happens at the cutting edge. What is most striking today is the underlying similarities of what is happening now to national preferences at the margin. These similarities at the cutting edge cumulatively form an overwhelming, predominant commonality everywhere.

To refer to the persistence of economic nationalism (protective and subsidized trade practices, special tax aids, or restrictions for home market producers) as a barrier to the globalization of markets is to make a valid point. Economic nationalism does have a powerful persistence. But, as with the present almost totally smooth internationalization of investment capital, the past alone does not shape or predict the future.

Reality is not a fixed paradigm, dominated by immemorial customs and derived attitudes, heedless of powerful and abundant new forces. The world is becoming increasingly informed about the liberating and enhancing possibilities of modernity. The persistence of the inherited varieties of national preferences rests uneasily on increasing evidence of, and restlessness regarding, their inefficiency, costliness, and confinement. The historic past, and the national differences respecting commerce and industry it spawned and fostered everywhere, is now subject to relatively easy transformation.

Cosmopolitanism is no longer the monopoly of the intellectual and leisure classes; it is becoming the established property and defining characteristic of all sectors everywhere in the world. Gradually and irresistibly it breaks down the walls of economic insularity, nationalism, and chauvinism. What we see today as escalating commercial nationalism is simply the last violent death rattle of an obsolete institution.

The successful global corporation does not abjure customization or differentiation for the requirements of markets that differ in product preferences, spending patterns, shopping preferences, and institutional or legal arrangements. But the global corporation accepts and adjusts to these differences only reluctantly, only after relentlessly testing their immutability, after trying in various ways to circumvent and reshape them.

10.2 The Myth of Globalization

By Susan Douglas and Yoram Wind[1]

In recent years, globalization has become a key theme in every discussion of international strategy. Proponents of the philosophy of 'global' products and brands, such as Professor Theodore Levitt of Harvard, and the highly successful advertising agency, Saatchi and Saatchi, argue that in a world of growing internationalization, the key to success is the development of global products and brands, in other words, a focus on standardized products and brands world-wide. Others, however, point to the numerous

---

[1] Source: *Columbia Journal of World Business*, Winter 1987. Copyright © 1987. Reprinted with permission.

barriers to standardization, and suggest that greater returns are to be obtained from adapting products and marketing strategies to the specific characteristics of individual markets.

The growing integration of international markets as well as the growth of competition on a world-wide scale implies that adoption of a global perspective has become increasingly imperative in planning strategy. However, to conclude that this mandates the adoption of a strategy of universal standardization appears naive and oversimplistic. In particular, it ignores the inherent complexity of operations in international markets, and the formulation of an effective strategy to penetrate these markets. While global products and brands may be appropriate for certain markets and in targeting certain segments, adopting such an approach as a universal strategy in relation to all markets may not be desirable, and may lead to major strategic blunders. Furthermore, it implies a product orientation, and a product-driven strategy, rather than a strategy grounded in a systematic analysis of customer behavior and response patterns and market characteristics.

The purpose of this article is thus to examine critically the notion that success in international markets necessitates adoption of a strategy of global products and brands. Given the restrictive characteristic of this philosophy, a somewhat broader perspective in developing global strategy is proposed which views standardization as merely one option in the range of possible strategies which may be effective in global markets.

The Traditional Perspective on International Strategy

Traditionally, discussion of international business strategy has been polarized around the debate concerning the pursuit of a uniform strategy world-wide versus adaptation to specific local market conditions. On the one hand, it has been argued that adoption of a uniform strategy world-wide enables a company to take advantage of the potential synergies arising from multicountry operations, and constitutes the multinational company's key competitive advantage in international markets. Others however, have argued that adaptation of strategy to idiosyncratic national market characteristics is crucial to success in these markets.

Fayerweather in his seminal work in international business strategy described the central issue as one of conflict between forces toward unification and those resulting in fragmentation. He pointed out that within a multinational firm, internal forces created pressures toward the integration of strategy across national boundaries. On the other hand, differences in the sociocultural, political, and economic characteristics of countries as well as the need for effective relations with the host society, constitute fragmenting influences that favor adaptation to the local environment.

Recent discussion of global competitive strategy echoes the same theme of the dichotomy between the forces that have triggered the globalization of markets and those that constitute barriers to global competition. Factors such as economies of scale in production, purchasing, faster accumulation of learning from operating world-wide, decrease in transportation and distribution costs, reduced costs of product adaptation, and the emergence of global market segments have encouraged competition on a global scale. However, barriers such as governmental and institutional constraints, tariff barriers and duties, preferential treatment of local firms, transportation costs, differences in customer demand, and so on, call for nationalistic or 'protected niche' strategies.

Compromise solutions such as 'pattern standardization' have also been proposed. In this case, a global promotional theme or positioning is developed, but execution is adapted to the local market. Similarly, it has been pointed out that even where a standardized product is marketed in a number of countries, its positioning may be adapted in each market. Conversely, the positioning may be uniform across countries, but the product itself adapted or modified.

Although this debate first emerged in the 1960s, it has recently taken on a new vigor with the widely publicized pronouncements of proponents of 'global standardization' such as Professor Levitt and Saatchi & Saatchi.

The sweeping and somewhat polemic character of their argument has sparked a number of counterarguments as well as discussion of conditions under which such a strategy may be most appropriate. It has, for example, been pointed out that the potential for standardization may be greater for certain types of products such as industrial goods or luxury personal items targeted to upscale consumers, or products with similar penetration rates. Opportunities for standardization are also likely to occur more frequently among industrialized nations, and especially the Triad countries where customer interests as well as market conditions are likely to be more similar than among developing countries.

The role of corporate philosophy and organizational structure in influencing the practicality of implementing a strategy of global standardization has also been recognized. Here, it has been noted that few companies pursue the extreme position of complete standardization with regard to all elements of the marketing mix, and business functions such as R&D, manufacturing, and procurement in all countries throughout the world. Rather, some degree of adaptation is likely to occur relative to certain aspects of the firm's operations or in certain geographic areas. In addition, the feasibility of implementing a standardized strategy will depend on the autonomy accorded to local management. If local management has been accustomed to substantial autonomy, considerable opposition may be encountered in attempting to introduce globally standardized strategies.

An examination of such counterarguments suggests that there are a number of dangers in espousing a philosophy of global standardization for all products and services, and in relation to all markets world-wide. Furthermore, there are numerous difficulties and constraints to implementing such a strategy in many markets, stemming from external market conditions (such as government and trade regulation, competition, the marketing infrastructure, and so on), as well as from the current structure and organization of the firm's operations.

The Global Standardization Philosophy: The Underlying Assumptions

An examination of the arguments in favor of a strategy of global products and brands reveals three key underlying assumptions:

- Customer needs and interests are becoming increasingly homogeneous world-wide.

- People around the world are wiling to sacrifice preferences in product features, functions, design, and the like for lower prices at high quality.

- Substantial economies of scale in production and marketing can be achieved through supplying global markets.

There are, however, a number of pitfalls associated with each of these assumptions. These are discussed here in more detail.

Homogenization of the World's Wants

A key premise of the philosophy of global products is that customers' needs and interests are becoming increasingly homogeneous world-wide. But while global segments with similar interests and response patterns may be identified in some product markets, it is by no means clear that this is a universal trend. Furthermore, there is substantial evidence to suggest an increasing diversity of behavior within countries, and the emergence of idiosyncratic countryspecific segments.

Lack of evidence of homogenization   In a number of product markets ranging from watches, perfume, and handbags to soft drinks and fast foods, companies have successfully identified global customer segments, and developed global products and brands targeted to these segments. These include such stars as Rolex, Omega and Le Baume & Mercier watches, Dior, Patou or Yves St. Laurent perfume. But while these brands are highly visible and widely publicized, they are often, with a few notable exceptions such as Classic Coke or McDonald's, targeted to a relatively restricted upscale international customer segment.

Numerous other companies, however, adapt lines to idiosyncratic country preferences, and develop local brands or product variants targeted to local market segments. The Findus frozen food division of Nestlé, for example, markets fish cakes and fish fingers in the United Kingdom, but beef bourguignon and coq au vin in France, and vitello con funghi and braviola in Italy. Similarly, Coca-Cola in Japan markets Georgia, cold coffee in a can, and Aquarius, a tonic drink, as well as Classic Coke and Hi-C.

Growth of intracountry segmentation price sensitivity Furthermore, there is a growing body of evidence that suggests substantial heterogeneity within countries. In the United States, for example, the VALS (Value of American Lifestyles) study has identified nine value segments, while other studies have identified major differences in behavior between regions and subcultural segments. Many other countries are also characterized by substantial regional differences as well as different lifestyle and value segments.

Similarly, in industrial markets, while some global segments, often consisting of firms with international operations, can be identified, there also is considerable diversity within and between countries. Often local businesses constitute an important market segment and, especially in developing countries, may differ significantly in technological sophistication, business philosophy and strategy, emphasis on product quality, and service and price, from large multinationals.

The evidence thus suggests that the similarities in customer behavior are restricted to a relatively limited number of target segments, or product markets, while for the most part, there are substantial differences between countries. Proponents of standardization counter that the international strategist should focus on similarities among countries rather than differences. This may, however, imply ignoring a major part of a local market, and the potential profits that may be obtained from tapping other market segments.

Universal Preference for Low Price at Acceptable Quality

Another critical component of the argument for global standardization is that people around the world are willing to sacrifice preferences in product features, functions, design, and the like for lower prices, assuming equivalent quality. Aggressive low pricing for quality products that meet the common needs of customers in markets around the world is believed to further expand the global markets facing the firm. Although an appealing argument, this has three major problems.

Lack of evidence of increased price sensitivity Evidence to suggest that customers are universally willing to trade off specific product features for a lower price is largely lacking. While in many product markets there is invariably a price-sensitive segment, there is no indication that this is on the increase. On the contrary, in many product and service markets, ranging from watches, personal computers, and household appliances to banking and insurance, an interest in multiple product features, product quality, and service appears to be growing.

Low price positioning is a highly vulnerable strategy Also, from a strategic point of view, emphasis on price positioning may be undesirable, especially in international markets, since it offers no long-term competitive advantage. A price-positioning strategy is always vulnerable to new technological developments that may lower costs, as well as to attack from competitors with lower overhead, and lower operating or labor costs. Government subsidies to local competitors may also undermine the effectiveness of a price-positioning strategy. In addition, price-sensitive customers typically are not brand or source loyal.

Standardized low price can be overpriced in some countries and underpriced in others Finally, a strategy based on a combination of a standardized product at a low price, when implemented in countries that vary in their competitive structure as well as the level of economic development, is likely to result in products that are overdesigned and overpriced for some markets and underdesigned and underpriced for others. Cost advantages may also be negated by transportation and distribution costs as well as tariff barriers and/or price regulation.

Economies of Scale of Production and Marketing

The third assumption underlying the philosophy of global standardization is that a key force driving strategy is product technology, and that substantial economies of scale can be achieved by supplying global markets. This does, however, neglect three critical and interrelated points:

1 Technological developments in flexible factory automation enable economies of scale to be achieved at lower levels of output and do not require production of a single standardized product.

2 Cost of production is only one and often not the critical component in determining the total cost of the product.

3 Strategy should not be solely product driven but should take into account the other components of a marketing strategy, such as positioning, packaging, brand name, advertising, PR, consumer and trade promotion and distribution.

Developments in flexible factory automation Recent developments in flexible factory automation methods have lowered the minimum efficient scale of operation and have thus enabled companies to supply smaller local markets efficiently, without requiring operations on a global scale. However, diseconomies may result from such operations due to increased transportation and distribution costs, as well as higher administrative overhead, and additional communication and coordination costs.

Furthermore, decentralization of production and establishment of local manufacturing operations enables diversification of risk arising from political events, fluctuations in foreign exchange rates, or economic instability. Recent swings in foreign exchange rates, coupled with the growth of offshore sourcing have underscored the vulnerability of centralizing production in a single location. Government regulations relating to local component and/or offset requirements create additional pressures for local manufacturing. Flexible automation not only implies that decentralization of manufacturing and production may be cost efficient but also makes minor modifications in products of models in the latter stages of production feasible, so that a variety of model versions can be produced without major retooling. Adaptations to product design can thus be made to meet differences in preferences from one country to another without loss of economies of scale.

Production costs are often a minor component of total cost   In many consumer and service industries, such as cosmetics, detergents, pharmaceuticals, or financial institutions, production costs are a small fraction of total cost. The key to success in these markets is an understanding of the tastes and purchase behavior of target customers' distribution channels, and tailoring products and strategies to these rather than production efficiency. In the detergent industry, for example, mastery of mass-merchandising techniques and an effective brand management system are typically considered the key elements in the success of the giants in this field, such as Procter & Gamble (P&G) or Colgate-Palmolive.

The standardization philosophy is primarily product driven   The focus on product- and brand-related aspects of strategy in discussions of global standardization is misleading since it ignores the other key strategy variables. Strategy in international markets should also take into consideration other aspects of the marketing mix, and the extent to which these are standardized across country markets rather than adapted to local idiosyncratic characteristics.

Requisite Conditions for Global Standardization

The numerous pitfalls in the rationale underlying the global standardization philosophy suggests that such a strategy is far from universally appropriate for all products, brands, or companies. Only under certain conditions is it likely to prove a 'winning' strategy in international markets. These include:

- the existence of a global market segment;
- potential synergies from standardization;
- the availability of a communication and distribution infrastructure to deliver the firm's offering to target customers world-wide.

Existence of Global Market Segments

As noted previously, global segments may be identified in a number of industrial and consumer markets. In consumer markets these segments are typically luxury- or premium-type products. Global segments are, however, not limited to such product markets, but also exist in other types of markets, such as motorcycle, record, stereo equipment, and computer, where a segment with similar needs and wants can be identified in many countries.

In industrial markets, companies with multinational operations are particularly likely to have similar needs and requirements world-wide. Where the operations are integrated or coordinated across national boundaries, as in the case of banks or other financial institutions, compatibility of operational systems and equipment may be essential. Consequently, they may seek vendors who can supply and service their operations world-wide, in some cases developing global contrasts for such purchases. Similarly, manufacturing companies with world-wide operations may source globally in order to ensure uniformity in quality, service and price of components, and other raw materials throughout their operations.

Marketing of global products and brands to such target segments and global customers enables development of a uniform global image throughout the world. In some markets such as perfume or fashions, association with a specific country of origin or a foreign image in general may carry a prestige connotation. In other cases, for example, Sony electronic equipment, McDonald's hamburgers, Hertz or Avis car rental, IBM computers, or Xerox office equipment, it may help to develop a world-wide reputation for quality and service. Just as multinational corporations may seek uniformity in supply world-wide, some consumers who travel extensively may be interested in finding the same brand of cigarettes and soft drinks, or hotels, in foreign countries. This may be particularly relevant in product markets used extensively by international travelers.

While the existence of a potential global segment is a key motivating factor for developing a global product and brand strategy, it is important to note that the desirability of such a strategy depends on the size and economic viability of the segment in question, the strength of the segment's preference for the global brand, as well as the ability to reach the segment effectively and profitably.

Synergies Associated with Global Standardization

Global standardization may also have a number of synergistic effects. In addition to those associated with a global image noted above, opportunities may exist for the transfer of good ideas for products or promotional strategies from one country to another.

The standardization of strategy and operations across a number of countries may also enable the acquisition or exploitation of specific types of expertise that would not be feasible otherwise. Expertise in assessing country risk or foreign exchange risk, or in identifying and interpreting information relating to multiple country markets, for example, may be developed.

Such synergies are not, however, unique to a strategy of global standardization, but may also occur wherever operations and strategy are coordinated or integrated across country markets. In fact, only certain scale economies associated with product and advertising copy standardization, and the development of a global image as discussed earlier, are unique to global standardization.

Availability of an International Communication and Distribution Infrastructure

The effectiveness of global standardization also depends to a large extent on the availability of an international infrastructure of communications and distribution. As many corporations have expanded overseas, service organizations have followed their customers abroad to supply their needs world-wide.

Advertising agencies such as Saatchi & Saatchi, McCann Erickson, and Young & Rubicam now have an international network of operations throughout the world, while many research agencies can also supply services in major markets world-wide. With the growing integration of financial markets, banks, investment firms, insurance and other financial institutions are also becoming increasingly international in orientation and are expanding the scope of their operations in world markets. The physical distribution network of shippers, freight forwarding, export and import agents, customs clearing, invoicing and insurance agents is also becoming increasingly integrated to meet demand for international shipment of goods and services.

Improvements in telecommunications and in logistical systems have considerably increased capacity to manage operations on a global scale and hence facilitate adoption of global standardization strategies. The spread of telex and fax systems, as well as satellite linkages and international computer linkages, all contribute to the shrinking of distances and facilitate globalization of operations. Similarly, improvements in transportation systems and physical logistics such as containerization and computerized inventory and handling systems have enabled significant cost savings as well as reducing time required to move goods across major distances.

Operational Constraints to Effective Implementation of a Standardization Strategy

While adoption of a standardized strategy may be desirable under certain conditions, there are a number of constraints that severely restrict the firm's ability to develop and implement a standardized strategy.

External Constraints to Effective Standardization

The numerous external constraints that impede global standardization are well recognized. Here, three major categories are highlighted, namely

1   government and trade restrictions;

2   differences in the marketing infrastructure, such as the availability and effectiveness of promotional media;

3   the character of resource markets, and differences in the availability and costs of resources;

4   differences in competition from one country to another.

Government and trade restrictions   Government and trade restrictions, such as tariff and other trade barriers, product, pricing or promotional regulation, frequently hamper standardization of the product line, pricing, or promotional strategy. Tariffs or quotas on the import of key materials, components, or other resources may, for example, affect production costs and thus hamper uniform pricing or alternatively result in the substitution of other components and modifications in product design. Local content requirements or compensatory export requirements, which specify that products contain a certain proportion of components manufactured locally or that a certain volume of production is exported to offset imports of components or other services, may have a similar impact.

The existence of cartels such as the European steel cartel, or the Swiss chocolate cartel, may also impede or exclude standardized strategies in countries covered by these agreements. In particular, they may affect adoption of a uniform pricing strategy as the cartel sets prices for the industry. Cartel members may also control established distribution channels, thus preventing use of a standardized distribution strategy. Extensive grey markets in countries such as India, Hong Kong, and South America may also affect administered pricing systems, and require adjustment of pricing strategies.

The nature of the marketing infrastructure   Differences in the marketing infrastructure from one country to another may hamper use of a standardized strategy. These may, for example, include differences in the availability and reach of various promotional media, in the availability of certain distribution channels or retail institutions, or in the existence and efficiency of the communication and transportation network. Such factors may, therefore, require considerable adaptation of strategy of local market conditions.

Interdependencies with resource markets   Yet another constraint to the development of standardized strategies is the nature of resource markets, and their operation in different countries throughout the world as well as the interdependency of these markets with marketing decisions. Availability and cost of raw materials, as well as labor and other resources in different locations, will affect not only decisions regarding sourcing of and hence the location of manufacturing activities but also marketing strategy decisions such as product design. For example, in the paper industry, availability of cheap local materials such as jute and sugar cane may result in their substitution for wood fiber.

Cost differentials relative to raw materials, labor, management, and other inputs may also influence the trade-off relative to alternative strategies. For example, high packaging cost relative to physical distribution may result in use of cheaper packaging with a shorter shelf life and more frequent shipments. Similarly, low labor costs relative to media may encourage a shift from mass media advertising to labor-intensive promotion such as personal selling and product demonstration.

Availability of capital, technology, and manufacturing capabilities in different locations will also affect decisions about licensing, contract manufacturing, joint ventures, and other 'make-buy' types of decisions for different markets, as well as decisions about countertrade, reciprocity, and other long-term relations.

The nature of the competitive structure Differences in the nature of the competitive situation from one country to another may also suggest the desirability of adaptation strategy. Even in markets characterized by global competition, such as agricultural equipment and motorcycles, the existence of low-cost competition in certain countries may suggest the desirability of marketing stripped-down models or lowering prices to meet such competition. Even where competitors are predominantly other multinationals, preemption of established distribution networks may encourage adoption of innovative distribution methods or direct distribution to short-circuit an entrenched position. Thus, the existence of global competition does not necessarily imply a need for global standardization.

All such aspects thus impose major constraints on the feasibility and effectiveness of a standardized strategy, and suggest the desirability or need to adapt to specific market conditions.

Internal Constraints to Effective Standardization

In addition to such external constraints on the feasibility of a global standardization strategy, there are also a number of internal constraints that may need to be considered. These include compatibility with the existing network of operations overseas, as well as opposition or lack of enthusiasm among local management toward a standardized strategy.

Existing international operations Proponents of global standardization typically take the position of a novice company with no operations in international markets, and hence fail to take into consideration the fit of the proposed strategy with current international activities. In practice, however, many companies have a number of existing operations in various countries. In some cases, these are joint ventures, or licensing operations or involve some collaboration in purchasing, manufacturing or distribution with other companies. Even where foreign manufacturing and distribution operations are wholly owned, the establishment of a distribution network will typically entail relationships with other organizations, for example, exclusive distributor agreements.

Such commitments may be difficult if not impossible to change in the short run, and may constitute a major impediment to adoption of a standardized strategy. If, for example, a joint venture with a local company has been established to manufacture and market a product line in a specific country or region, resistance from the local partner (or government authorities) may be encountered if the parent company wishes to shift production or import components from another location. Similarly, a licensing contract will impede a firm from supplying the products covered by the agreement from an alternative location for the duration of the contract, even if it becomes more cost efficient to do so.

Conversely, the establishment of an effective dealer or distribution network in a country or region may constitute an important resource to a company. The addition of new products to the product line currently sold or distributed by this network may therefore provide a more efficient utilization of company resources than expanding to new countries or geographic regions with the existing line, as this would require substantial investment in the establishment of a new distribution network.

In addition, overseas subsidiaries may currently be marketing not only core products and brands from the company's domestic business, but may also have added or acquired local or regional products and brands in response to local market demand. In some cases, therefore, introduction of a global product or brand may be likely to cannibalize sales of local or regional brands.

Advocates of standardization thus need to take into consideration the evolutionary character of international involvement, which may render a universal strategy of global products and brands suboptimal. Somewhat ironically, the longer the history of a multinational corporation's involvement in foreign or international markets, and the more diversified and far-flung its operations, the more likely it is that standardization will not lead to optimal results.

Local management motivation and attitudes Another internal constraint concerns the motivation and attitudes of local management with regard to standardization. Standardized strategies tend to facilitate or result in centralization in the planning and organization of international activities. Especially if input from local management is limited, this may result in a feeling that strategy is 'imposed' by corporate headquarters, and/or not adequately adapted or appropriate in view of specific local market characteristics and conditions. Local management is likely to take the view 'it won't work here – things are different,' which will reduce their motivation to implement a standardized strategy effectively.

A Framework for Classifying Global Strategy Options

The adoption of a global perspective should not be viewed as synonymous with a strategy of global products and brands. Rather, for most companies such a perspective implies consideration of a broad range of strategic options of which standardization is merely one.

In essence, a global perspective implies planning strategy relative to markets world-wide rather than on a country-by-country basis. This may result in the identification of opportunities for global products and brands and/or integrating and coordinating strategy across national boundaries to exploit potential synergies of operating on an international scale. Such opportunities should, however, be weighed against the benefits of adaptation to idiosyncratic customer characteristics.

The development of an effective global strategy thus requires a careful examination of all international options in terms of standardization versus adaptation open to the firm.

A firm's international operations are likely to be characterized by a mix of strategies, including not only global products and brands, but also some regional products and brands and some national products and brands. Similarly, some target segments may be global, others regional, and others national. Hybrid strategies of this nature thus enable a company to take advantage of the benefits of standardization and potential synergies from operating on an international scale, while at the same time not losing those afforded by adaptation to specific country characteristics and customer preferences.

10.3   The Dynamics of Global Competition

By C.K. Prahalad and Yves Doz[1]

As the emerging patterns of competition in a wide variety of businesses become of increasing concern, especially the intense competition brought about by overseas competitors, the words *global business* and *global competition* have entered the lexicon of most managers. However, the distinction between the intrinsic characteristics of a business – its cost structure, technology, and customers, for example, at a given point in time – and the characteristics of competition in that business is not always well understood. Further, labeling businesses as 'global' or 'multidomestic' may hide broad variations in the underlying managerial tasks. We shall develop a methodology for capturing the characteristics of a wide range of businesses or for understanding the 'existing rules of the game' in a business. Then we shall go beyond the analysis of existing rules and examine how determined competitors often change those rules.

The Building Blocks

The building blocks of the methodology for mapping the characteristics of a business start with the managerial demands that it imposes on senior management.

Global Integration of Activities

Integration refers to the centralized management of geographically dispersed activities on an ongoing basis. Managing shipments of parts and subassemblies across a network of manufacturing facilities in various countries is an example of integration of activities.

The need for integration arises in response to pressures to reduce costs and optimize investment. Pressures to reduce cost may force location of plants in countries with low labor costs, such as South Korea, Taiwan, and Malaysia. Products are then shipped from those plants to the established markets of the United States and Europe. The same pressures may also lead to building large-scale, highly specialized plants to realize economies of scale. Ford's European operations and IBM's world-wide manufacturing operations are examples of the phenomenon. In either case, the goal is leveraging the advantages of low manufacturing cost. Managerially, that translates into a need for ongoing management of logistics that cut across multiple national boundaries.

Global Strategic Coordination

Strategic coordination refers to the central management of resource commitments across national boundaries in the pursuit of a strategy. It is distinct from the integration of ongoing activities across national borders. Typical examples would involve coordinating research and development (R&D) priorities across several laboratories, coordinating pricing to global customers, and facilitating transfers of technology from headquarters to subsidiaries and across subsidiaries. Unlike activity integration, strategic coordination can be selective and nonroutine.

Strategic coordination is often essential to provide competitive and strategic coherence to resource commitments made over time by head-quarters and various subsidiaries in multiple countries. The goal of strategic coordination is to recognize, build, and defend long-term competitive advantages. For example, headquarters may assign highly differentiated goals to various subsidiaries in the same business in order to develop a coherent response to competition.

Strategic coordination, like integration of activities, often involves headquarters and one or several subsidiaries. Coordination decisions transcend a single subsidiary.

Local Responsiveness

Local responsiveness refers to resource commitment decisions taken autonomously by a subsidiary in response to primarily local competitive or customer demands. In a wide variety of businesses, there may be no competitive advantage to be gained by coordinating actions across subsidiaries; in fact, that may prove to be detrimental.

Typically, businesses where there are no meaningful economies of scale or proprietary technology (e.g. processed foods) fall into this category. The need for significant local adaptation of products or differences in distribution across national markets may also indicate a need for local responsiveness.

Mapping the Characteristics of a Business

Let us take the case of Corning Glass. As of 1975 it operated internationally in six business categories with more than 60,000 line items. The businesses were:

■ Television products, which included supplying TV bulbs to original equipment manufacturers (OEM) like RCA, Philips, and Sylvania.

■ Electronic products, which consisted of components like resistors and capacitors used by computer, communication, and military equipment manufacturers.

■ Consumer products, chiefly Corning Ware, the leading cookware products in the United States.

■ Medical products, consisting of scientific instruments such as blood gas analyzers and diagnostic reagents.

■ Science products, specifically laboratory glassware.

■ Technical products, mostly ophthalmic products, which consisted of photochromatic eye-glass blanks, produced in a variety of thickness, curvatures, and so forth.

Corning's overseas activities comprised 14 major foreign manufacturing operations and a host of licensees. Its products were produced abroad, and the overseas sales volume was significant.

With such a spread of overseas activities in both manufacturing and marketing, should Corning treat all its businesses as global? Are there differences among those businesses that transcend the location of plants and the distribution of markets around the world?

It is a great temptation to categorize businesses as diverse as Corning Ware and electronic products as either global (meaning their activities can and should be integrated across borders) or multidomestic (meaning that they are local businesses in multiple countries). However, each business is subject to varying degrees of economic, competitive, and technological pressures that push it toward becoming global or toward remaining locally responsive. Some of the Corning businesses have to accommodate both pressures simultaneously.

The Integration-Responsiveness Grid

The Integration-Responsiveness (IR) grid provides us with a way of capturing the pressures on a given business–pressures that make *strategic coordination* and *global integration of activities* critical, as well as the pressures that make being sensitive to the diverse demands of various national markets and achieving *local responsiveness* critical.

We can use the following criteria for evaluating the pressures for global coordination and integration, as well as local responsiveness.

Pressures for Global Strategic Coordination

Importance of multinational customers   The dependence of a business on multinational original equipment manufacturer (OEM) customers imposes a need for global strategic coordination. For example, in the TV bulbs business, a significant portion of the total sales went to multinational original equipment manufacturer (OEM) customers like Philips and Sylvania. Multinational customers can, and often do, compare prices charged them by their suppliers around the world, demand the same level of service and product support, and have centralized vendor certification. The product is often sold at the center, say, to the OEM's product division, and delivered around the world – wherever the multinational customer may need it. The percentage of sales to multinational OEM customers and their importance to the business can thus dictate the need for global coordination. In the case of Corning Ware, the opposite was true. Its customers were mostly local, and it was primarily a mass-marketed item.

Presence of multinational competitors   The presence of competitors who operate in multiple markets indicates the potential for global competition. Consequently, it is crucial to gather intelligence on competitors across national markets, to understand their strategic intent, and to be ready to respond to their actions wherever most appropriate. The presence of multinational competitors calls for global strategic coordination. Competitors for Corning's various businesses ranged from global competitors in electronic products, to regional competitors in TV products, to local competitors in lab ware and Corning cookware.

Investment intensity   If an aspect of the business is investment intensive (e.g. R&D, manufacturing), the need to leverage that investment increases the need for global coordination. World-wide product strategies have to be developed and implemented quickly to make the large initial investments profitable.

At Corning, the intensity of the R&D effort in the medical products business and the intensity of investment in manufacturing and product development in the electronics business indicated that a high level of global coordination and integration was required in those two businesses. In the lab ware business, the pressure for international strategic coordination was not felt.

Technology intensity   Technology intensity and the extent of proprietary technology often encourage firms to manufacture in only a few selected locations. Having fewer manufacturing sites allows easier control over quality, cost, and new product introduction. Centralized product development and manufacturing operations in a few locations result in global integration, particularly when the markets are widely dispersed.

Again, at Corning the technological intensity differed from business to business. For example, the lab ware required a very low technology as compared to the medical products business. Medical products had short life cycles, with constantly renewed markets, whereas lab ware had stable products and applications.

Pressure for cost reduction   Global integration is often a response to pressure for cost reduction. Cost reduction requires sourcing the product from low-factor-cost locations (global sourcing), or exploiting economies of scale and experience by building large plants that serve multiple national markets. Either approach to lowering costs imposes a need for global integration.

Some of Corning's businesses, such as electronic products, were subject to severe cost pressures, while others, like Corning Ware, were less so.

Universal needs   If the product meets a universal need and requires little adaptation across national markets, global integration is obviously facilitated.

Electronic products – capacitors, resistors – are good examples of universal products. They do not vary by country. On the other hand, Corning Ware is not universal. It must be adapted to suit various market needs. For example, the 'oven-to-freezer' feature may be a big hit in the United States but may not be appropriate in France; a soufflé dish popular in France may not have a big market in the Midwest.

Access to raw materials and energy   Access to raw materials and a cheap and plentiful supply of energy can force manufacturing to be located in a specific area. Aluminium smelters, paper mills, and, increasingly, petrochemicals tend to be located where the raw materials are available. That tendency in some businesses suggests global coordination and integration. None of Corning's businesses had to contend with this issue.

Pressures for Local Responsiveness

Differences in customer needs Businesses that thrive on satisfying a diverse set of customer needs, most of which is nation or region specific, require a locally responsive strategy.

Several businesses within Corning have satisfied country-specific needs. Corning Ware, technical materials, and to some extent chemical systems were designed with specific customers of individual countries in mind. On the other hand, electronic products met a universal need.

Differences in distribution channels Differences in distribution channels in various countries and the differences in pricing, product positioning, promotion, and advertising that those differences entail indicate the need for local responsiveness.

In the lab ware business at Corning, the distribution system used to access the school systems in various countries varied; comparable differences in distribution channels characterized Corning Ware. On the other hand, in the electronic and TV products businesses, which were primarily serving OEM customers, the differences among national markets were only marginal.

Availability of substitutes and the need to adapt If a product function is being met by local substitutes, with differing price-performance relationships in a given national market, or if the product must be significantly adapted to be locally competitive, then a locally responsive strategy is indicated.

Corning Ware had a significant number of substitutes – cooking ware made from other materials, as well as cooking ware promoted differently. It also needed to be adapted to suit local conditions. In the case of electronic products, neither condition was important: products were universal and faced no differentiated local substitutes.

Market structure Market structure includes the importance of local competitors as compared to multinational ones, as well as the extent of their concentration. If local competitors tend to control a significant portion of the market and/or if the industry is not concentrated, then a locally responsive posture is most usually indicated (unless there are merits to competing globally to make the industry structure evolve in your favor). A fragmented industry with local competitors indicates that there may be no inherent advantages to size and scale, unless product and process technology can be changed.

Again, among Corning's businesses, lab ware had to compete in each national market with a large number of local competitors in a fragmented industry, while TV products had to cope with only a handful of large competitors in a globally concentrated industry.

Host government demands Demands imposed by host governments for local self-sufficiency for a variety of reasons – from concerns of national development to concerns of national security – can force a business to become locally responsive.

Mapping Corning's Businesses in the Integration-Responsiveness Grid

It is obvious that Corning does not operate in any one type of business – either global or multidomestic. Each of its businesses is subject to a different combination of pressures toward global coordination and integration and toward local responsiveness – pressures that elude a simple either/or classification. We can identify the differences using the criteria we have developed, as shown in Table 10.3.1.

The characteristics of the three businesses can now be captured in an Integration-Responsiveness Grid, as shown in Figure 10.3.1. From the foregoing analysis, the following generalizations can be drawn:

1   The mapping of the characteristics of the various businesses illustrates the differences among them, even though all six businesses share the same corporate logo and all evolved out of the same broad glass technology. Because of those differences, managers must examine each business individually to develop strategies rather than treat them all alike.

2   Classifying businesses broadly as either global or local can be misleading. There are few businesses that are totally local. If there were no advantages to be gained in that business by a multinational corporation (MNC), then it is likely to be very fragmented with no scope for leveraging knowledge, products, financial muscle, or brands across markets. On the other hand, few businesses are totally global. A variety of factors, including the need for a responsive and differentiated local presence in various countries, make it difficult to ignore totally the demands of various national markets.

3   The purpose of the IR framework is to assess the *relative importance* of the two sets of conflicting demands on a business and to determine which of the two provides strategic leverage at a given point in time.

4   In the case of Corning, some businesses tend toward global integration (e.g. electronics, medical products). In those businesses, strategic advantage will accrue to the competitor who is organized to exploit the benefits of strategic coordination in investments, product policy, product development, pricing, monitoring competitors, and so forth. In businesses that tend toward local responsiveness (e.g. Corning Ware, lab ware), strategic advantage accrues to the firm that is sensitive to the need for decentralized pricing, promotion, and product policy. There may be little benefit in strategic coordination.

5   In Corning's case the real challenge to management is not in managing the extremes; it is in managing multifocal businesses, which demand sensitivity to both dimensions *at the same time*, as is the case with the TV products business. This implies that in such businesses it is unwise to make a one-time trade-off in favor of either global integration or local responsiveness. Both demands have to be managed simultaneously.

TABLE 10.3.1

Comparison of three businesses within Corning

Criteria	Electronics	TV Products	Corning Ware
Pressures for Global Strategic Coordination			
Importance of multinational customers	high	high	low
Importance of multinational competitors	high	medium/high	low
Investment intensity	high	high	low/medium
Pressures for Global Operational Integration			
Technology intensity	medium	medium	low
Pressure for cost reduction	high	high	low
Universal needs	high	medium	low
Access to raw materials and energy	n/a	n/a	n/a
Need for Global Integration	*high*	*medium*	*low*
Pressures for Local Responsiveness			
Differences in customer needs	low	medium?	high
Differences in distribution	low	low	high
Need for substitutes and product adaptation	low	low	high
Market structure	concentrated	concentrated	fragmented
Host government demands	n/a	n/a	n/a
Need for Local Responsiveness	*low*	*medium*	*high*

Some Implications

Several managerial conclusions can be derived from mapping the characteristics of a business on the IR grid.

1 Corning's electronic components, which is high on the need for global integration and low on the need for local responsiveness, suggests that managers developing strategies for that business must pay considerably more attention to leveraging aspects like economies of scale, product development, global customers, and global competitors than to issues of local responsiveness. This also implies that resource allocation decisions with respect to key elements of strategy for that business (such as plant location and investment, pricing, product development, and key account management) may have to be centralized. In other words, for the electronic components business, the locus of strategic management is the central world-wide business management group. On the other hand, for Corning Ware or lab ware, the key strategic choices (pricing, promotion, choice of channels) have to be managed in a decentralized mode. The center for strategy making is the regional or the national subsidiary managers, as contrasted with the center for the electronic components business, as shown in Figure 10.3.2.

2 In both those businesses representing the extremes – electronic components and Corning Ware – managers can make 'clear one-time choices' of

what aspects of the business to leverage. Therefore, a clear and simple organizational form – world-wide business management in the case of electronic components and area management in the case of Corning Ware – is possible. In other words, the relative simplicity of the strategic priorities enables a clear-cut choice of simple organization.

3   In the case of the TV business the strategic choice is not all that clear-cut. Some elements of strategy, like plant size and technology, may have to be managed centrally. On the other hand, deliveries, competitors, and some key customers may have to be managed both regionally and locally. That implies that managers cannot make a 'one-time choice' on which of the two dimensions to leverage. They must *simultaneously focus their attention* on aspects of the business that require global integration and aspects that demand local responsiveness, and on varying degrees of strategic co-ordination. This need for *multiple focal points for managing* suggests that managers must reflect the need for multiple points of view – the need to integrate and be responsive at the same time – in the way that business is organized. That requires the organization to be multifocal or matrix.

In general, many businesses that have the characteristics of Corning's TV business will need a *multifocal* or matrix organization, despite all the problems of managing such an organization.

The IR grid is not just a tool for discovering the essential orientation of a business for strategy making. It also enables managers to decide on the appropriate form of organization to manage the strategic orientation desired.

Mapping the Dynamics of a Business on the IR Grid

While taking Corning to illustrate the basic approach to mapping the characteristics on the IR grid, we have assumed our data and have assessed the characteristics of a business at a given point in time, rather than the way it might change over time. For the strategist, the direction of possible change in the characteristics of a business is even more interesting than the situation at a given point in time. Now we shall identify the factors that can change the location of a business in the IR grid over time as well as suggest the type of data that might be useful in understanding such trends early.

Changes in Underlying Industry Economics

Shifts in the location of a business on the IR grid are often a result of shifts in the underlying economics of the industry. Let us take the example of ethylene oxide. During the early 1970s, most chemical firms operated plants of an annual capacity of 50 million to 75 million pounds. In most markets of the world, especially in the United States and Europe, that meant firms could dedicate a plant (or more) to each important national market. As each market could afford its own manufacturing and marketing facilities, and as ethylene oxide was a commodity product, managers could be very sensitive to local

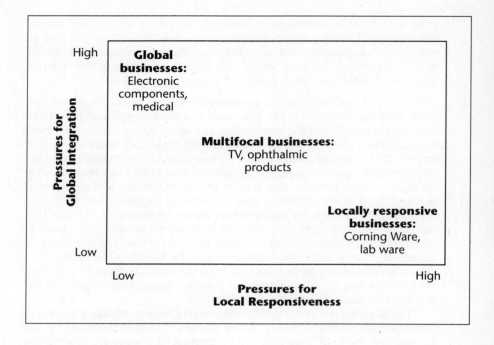

needs. In the early 1970s most firms operated with considerable local responsiveness and a low level of global integration. However, over the period 1972–75, several chemical firms, especially ICI in the United Kingdom, started building plants with a capacity as large as 250 million to 400 million pounds. The cost advantage arising from the economies of scale was around 12 to 15 percent over traditional, smaller plants. Because a single national market could not absorb the output of the large-scale plants, the firm had to coordinate prices, product specifications, logistics, and, most importantly, investments across several, so far autonomous, national markets. In a very short time, the center of gravity for strategy making in the ethylene oxide business for several chemical firms had shifted toward high need for integration and low need for responsiveness. Given a 12 to 15 percent cost advantage in a commodity chemical, few competitors could resist the pressure to build large plants in order to remain competitive. On the IR grid, the ethylene oxide business would be depicted as locally responsive until 1972.

Impact of Governments

During the same period drug companies also faced a shift in their business. The proprietary drug business, involving significant investment in R&D and requiring strict quality controls in manufacturing, is best managed centrally, from a few locations. However, the politics of health care in many countries around the world force drug firms to manufacture in multiple locations. They are also subject to local clinical testing, registration procedures, and

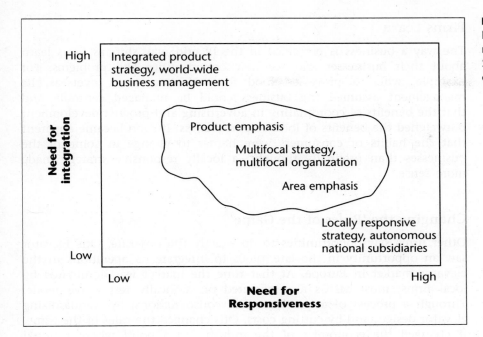

FIGURE 10.3.2
Integration –
responsiveness grid:
Strategic focus and
organizational adaptation

pricing restrictions. As governments and quasi-government agencies control a significant portion of the health care budget in most countries, they are in a position to demand a high level of local responsiveness. That has forced most drug firms into simultaneously facing a high need for global integration and a high need for local responsiveness.

Shifts in the Competitive Focus of Customers

Supplier industries tend to follow the shifts in the industries they serve. For example, the automobile industry has become global in terms of its sourcing and design, as well as manufacturing. That trend has had impact on suppliers to the auto industry. For example, paint manufacturers, who manufacture paints for household use as well as car finishes, have typically operated on a locally responsive basis. The trend in the auto industry has forced one segment of their operations, car finishes, to become globally integrated. Product planners and purchasing agents in the auto industry would like to contract with a set of suppliers who can supply the same quality of car finish around the world. Yet the home paint segment is still locally responsive. Paint manufacturers who saw their business as essentially locally responsive had to contend with the realization that the auto industry internationalization was changing the nature of customer relations in a segment of their business; they had to recognize that they could no longer treat both segments of their business – car finishes and home paints – alike.

Firms Learn

The way a business is perceived in the IR grid may shift as firms learn about their businesses and see new opportunities and problems. For example, when a processed food firm, Nabisco, went overseas, its management assumed the business could be managed centrally and that the benefits of coordinating in advertising and product development outweighed the benefits of local responsiveness. It soon became apparent that the habits of consumers were harder to change in some of the businesses than originally thought; a locally responsive strategy made more sense.

Changing the 'Rules of the Game'

Other firms saw opportunities to do exactly the opposite. Otis Elevator saw an opportunity in the late 1960s to integrate its operations in the elevator market in Europe. At that time the market was dominated by local firms; most MNCs also operated on a locally responsive mode. Through a process of acquisitions and consolidations, by standardizing elevator design, and by cutting costs, Otis changed the rules of the game. It changed the economics of the industry to a point where regional integration, if not global integration, became the dominant mode. The first company to initiate and exploit that change can gain a considerable advantage over its competitors, who are slower to move toward international integration.

The success of Japanese competitors in a variety of industries can be attributed to their ability to pick primarily locally responsive industries, even those populated by MNCs, and change them to globally integrated businesses. Examples abound. Traditional competitors who were multinational prior to the Japanese competitive thrust in the auto industry (e.g. General Motors), ball bearings (e.g. SKF), and television sets (e.g. Philips) operated on a locally responsive basis. They were caught off guard. Once a determined competitor changes the rules of the game, the degrees of freedom available to others may be limited, as in the case of ethylene oxide or in the auto and elevator industries.

The movement of a business within the IR grid is very much influenced by the perceptions, judgments, and ambitions of managers on how it can be resegmented or changed. Significant shifts in the location of a business in the IR grid imply that the key success factors in that business have changed dramatically, leading to shifts in strategy. Strategy development is therefore not just an exercise in assessing the 'rules of the game' in a given business, at a given point in time (i.e. the location of a business in the IR grid); it is as much developing viable new rules of the game (i.e. identifying opportunities for mobility within the IR grid). That calls for marrying analysis of objective data and current industry patterns and managerial perceptions together with judgments on how the business can be changed.

IR Pressures May Affect Functions within a Business Differently

We have assumed, so far, in identifying the pressures for global integration and local responsiveness that the unit of analysis is a discrete business. In some cases, however, functions within a business may respond differently to those pressures. For example, in the computer industry, integrated R&D is common. Manufacturing may be somewhat decentralized, and marketing fairly locally responsive.

Functions such as R&D, manufacturing, marketing, and service may be used to identify pressures for global integration and local responsiveness, when each function represents a significant commitment of distinct types of resources and different underlying cost structures (significant economies of scale in R&D and the need for differentiated marketing tasks by country), and when internal mechanisms exist or can be developed to coordinate the functions that are managed differently.

Global Business versus Global Competition

We have so far examined the characteristics of a business using the IR grid and have identified factors that cause mobility of a business within that framework. However, the location of a business in the IR framework does not always identify the pattern of competition in a business. It is likely that if a business is high on global integration and low on local responsiveness, (e.g. semiconductors), it will be run, by most firms participating in that business, on a world-wide basis. On the other hand, a business high on local responsiveness and low on global integration (e.g. processed foods), is likely to be run with significant local autonomy. Businesses that are high on both dimensions (e.g. telecommunications, ethical drugs), may require a complex structure that accommodates the pressures of both integration and responsiveness. But those patterns do not identify the nature of competition that may exist in a given business. For example, the detergents business would be seen as locally responsive in the IR grid. There are no overwhelming economies of scale in the manufacture of detergents. The technology is well known. Managing differences in distribution, promotion, and pricing across national markets are crucial. Based on that analysis, can we conclude that Unilever and Procter & Gamble are not involved in global competition? The computer industry will be regarded as a global business in the IR grid. Does that mean that all computer firms have to be global in their scope of operations or compete across the world? Computer firms like Nixdorf, ICL, Bull, and until recently Hitachi and Fujitsu competed primarily in their national markets, protected by privileged access to the public sector or to nationally defined customers. If we believe that the structural characteristics of a business – such as cost, technology, scale, customer profiles – *determine rather than influence* the pattern of a global competition, then the analysis developed before is adequate. However, if we believe that competitors influence the patterns of competition as much as the underlying characteristics of a business and that often they change those characteristics through competitive innovation, then we need to pay special attention to the role of *key competitors' strategic intentions in determining the patterns of global competition.*

Cost Structure versus Cash Flow

Most managers believe that cost reduction (or gaining cost parity with Japanese and Korean competitors) is the essence of the competitive problem faced by western MNCs. We would like to suggest that global competition is not about cost reduction per se but about managing *global cash flows.* Consider, for example, the following scenario:

Let us assume that CPC, the consumer products MNC, has a dominant market share in the cooking oil business in Brazil. The product and the brand name are well established. Because of CPC's dominant share and the absence of large and viable competitors in that business in Brazil, CPC typically enjoys very high levels of profitability. Let us further assume that Unilever, sensing the profit potential in Brazil for packaged and branded cooking oil, introduces a similar product. To gain market entry, Unilever prices its product about 5 to 8 percent lower and promotes it heavily with the trade. What should the manager of CPC Brazil do? Obviously there are no great economies of scale in manufacturing in the packaged cooking oil business, and CPC does not enjoy a competitive advantage based purely on size in Brazil. Switching costs to customers are almost negligible. By the criteria we developed, packaged cooking oil is a 'locally responsive' business.

We have posed this question to a large number of executives. In our experience, the response to the question is almost always 'I will also lower prices and defend my market share' or 'I will give better discounts to the trade and advertise more heavily' or 'I am willing to sacrifice some profit margin in Brazil to defend my market share.' When pushed to recognize the reality that any actions in Brazil – be it more advertising, more discounts, or price reductions – will all lead to deterioration of profits, managers typically would concede market share to the aggressor, in this case to Unilever. What are the lessons of this example?

1   Even though packaged cooking oil is a locally responsive business, it cannot be defended locally (in Brazil) against a determined global competitor like Unilever without a significant profit penalty. Unilever, in reducing prices and increasing discounts to the trade in Brazil, exposed only a very small percentage of its world-wide cash flow in that business. On the other hand, CPC exposed a significant percentage of its world-wide cash flow. Any price reduction by CPC in Brazil to counter Unilever's actions would hurt CPC more than it is likely to hurt Unilever. The only viable strategy for CPC is to search for Unilever's cash sanctuaries – whether in Germany or in the United Kingdom – and take price action there. That is likely to put a 'monkey wrench in Unilever's money machine' and reduce its ability to continue to fund market share battles in Brazil. Even though the characteristics of that business suggest that the

business ought to be locally responsive, the ability of multimarket firms like Unilever and CPC to coordinate strategies and cash flows across markets creates a competitive arena that is global.

2   The essence of global competition, as illustrated by the CPC-Unilever example, is the *management of international cash flows and strategic coordination*, even when global integration across subsidiaries in terms of product flows does not take place. If CPC is to become an effective competitor against Unilever, it has to have viable operations in markets like Germany and the United Kingdom – Unilever's profit sanctuaries. The ability to retaliate against Unilever is conditional on CPC's having operations in Unilever's profit sanctuaries as well as the ability to coordinate actions strategically between the two subsidiaries – say Brazil and Germany. It assumes that the CPC manager in Germany is willing or can be persuaded to take a short-term profit penalty in order to support the Brazilian operations. As every MNC manager knows, few organizations have the ability to coordinate subsidiaries' actions – as, for example, in Brazil and Germany. Moreover, the internal systems (planning, performance measurement, and compensation) in most MNCs act as impediments to such strategic behavior.

3   MNCs that are preoccupied with costs may find themselves strategically vulnerable. In the example above, even if CPC had lower costs than Unilever in Brazil, Unilever's actions would erode CPC's profit margin. Unilever could take a profit penalty in Brazil as long as its profit sanctuaries remained uncontested in Germany and the United Kingdom. CPC's lower costs in Brazil allow it to sustain a competitive battle and to outlast Unilever only if Unilever also competes on a market-by-market basis and does not coordinate its strategies across markets.

Managing Cash Flows

The game of global competition revolves around cash flows. Recognition of that fact allows managers to emphasize not just the cost side of the equation but also the price side.

Managing the Cost Side

The goal of the strategist in managing the cost side is simply this: How do I get the lowest possible systemwide cost in this business? The factors to consider in determining the lowest possible net cost are the following:

Factor costs   Factor costs refer to the location-specific advantages that accrue to a manufacturer. Included in factor costs are labor cost differentials between alternative manufacturing locations, availability of cheap sources of raw materials or semifinished materials, and availability and access to low-cost capital, as well as preferential tax treatment in specific locations.

Exchange rate advantages   The volatility of exchange rates during the last decade has brought an additional dimension to the problem of a competitor's cost advantage.

Scale advantages   Cost advantages can accrue to manufacturers from the average age of plants and the level of their technological sophistication. Further, productivity advantages accruing from better utilization of equipment, materials, and labor can add an additional layer of cost advantage.

The Manufacturing System

The manufacturing system has to balance the three dimensions of the cost equation – labor costs, manufacturing scale and technology, and exchange rate fluctuations.

The strategist's task is not to reduce the impact of any one of those dimensions to the exclusion of others but to strike a balance among the three factors, as well as to manage the system flexibly. That entails the following:

1   The business must have a portfolio of manufacturing locations that allows the firm to exploit both factor cost advantages and the exchange rate differentials.

2   While the logic of a portfolio of manufacturing locations and flexible loading of those locations is appealing, there are several impediments to accomplishing that goal. The first impediment is the difficulty of integrating the activities of various national subsidiaries and varying the load assigned to them in the short term. Issues of performance evaluation, incentive compensation, national pride, and the stability of the work force interfere seriously with the ability to be flexible. National policies in various countries also restrict flexibility in the short term.

Managing the Price Side

The concern of the strategist in managing the price side is simply this: How do I get the highest net price in this business? Because there are significant price differentials for the same product and 'functionality' in different markets, by developing a portfolio of markets the strategist can maximize the bet prices for the system as a whole. The factors to consider are as follows.

Structure of markets   The market of each country is unique in terms of its competitive structure. The intensity of competition, which determines price levels in various markets, is dependent on the number and the type of competitors, and the demand structure in a market. The relative market share of competitors in the market of a given country may also give us clues as to competitors who are motivated to take price action and thus drive margins down. It is important to realize that prices are constrained by market structure, competitive rivalry, and competitors' strategic intentions in a given market and not by cost to the firm. Although that is obvious, firms continue to think of prices in cost-plus terms and miss opportunities to exploit the market asymmetries around the world. In order to exploit the market asymmetries, the firm should have a market presence in a portfolio of markets.

The value of distribution and brand presence Well-established brands with a quality image, like Sony in consumer electronics, command a premium. Further, control over the distribution channels brought about by a product line also allows for a premium.

The value of a product family While the analysis so far has assumed a single business as the basic unit of analysis for competitive profiling, the value of a product family cannot be underestimated. For example, just as a firm can use its multinational market presence to cross-subsidize competitive battles (e.g. Unilever versus CPC in the example outlined before), a firm with a large product family can subsidize a given business within a market.

The Marketing System

Managing net prices is critical to managing a business's overall cash flow. That means firms should manage the marketing system. The strategist's role is to balance the three sources of price advantages available to the firm.

Strategic Intent: The Motor Behind Global Competition

The discussion so far has concentrated on the nature of the armory that one needs to compete globally. It is important to recognize that the outcomes in global competition are determined not just by the size of the armory that the various players possess but also by how effectively and imaginatively they use their weapons. The strategic intent of various competitors, or their long-term vision, may be as important as the size and quality of their armories. We should distinguish the strategic intent from the strategies: *intent* is used here to describe long-term goals and aims, rather than detailed plans.

Building Layers of Competitive Advantage

In our research we can discern three types of firms – firms whose strategic intent is *global dominance*, even if, initially, they do not possess the strategic infrastructure to accomplish that goal; firms whose strategic intent is *defending domestic dominance*, even if they have operations in multiple markets; and those whose primary orientation is *local responsiveness*. The different strategic intents lead to very distinct approaches to competition and the use of competitive advantages, even if the strategic infrastructures appear not to be markedly dissimilar.

Loose bricks: building layers of competitive advantage   Japanese firms in the consumer electronics business started with the strategic intent of global dominance, even though their strategic infrastructure during the 1960s did not extend beyond a well-protected home market. During the 1960s they were major exporters of black-and-white TV sets. By 1967 they had become the largest producers of black-and-white TVs; by the 1970s they had closed the gap in color sets. Japanese producers used their cost advantage, derived primarily from their low labor costs, to gain volume in the United States. Once they had secured that initial volume, they moved quickly to invest heavily in process and product technology, from which they gained scale and quality advantages. By the early 1970s the Japanese advantage was not only low labor costs but also greater reliability and quality based on superior manufacturing technology.

Japanese manufacturers recognized the transience of low labor cost as well as technology-based advantages. Volatile exchange rates and increases in labor costs as well as newer manufacturing technologies were rendering the sources of competitive advantages they had quite vulnerable. Throughout the 1970s Japanese TV makers invested heavily in order to create a strong brand presence in global markets and a distribution presence, thus adding another layer of competitive advantage.

Making global distribution and brand presence pay for themselves meant a high level of channel utilization. The Japanese force-fed the distribution channels by speeding up product development cycles and expanding across contiguous product families. Thus by the early 1980s, the Japanese competitive advantage had evolved from low-cost sourcing, to a technological advantage resulting in lower costs and higher quality, then to a global distribution and brand presence across a spectrum of consumer electronic products. The strategic intent of global dominance provided a basis for building on tactical and short-term advantages, deploying resources in such a way as to build 'layers of competitive advantage.' The Japanese position today in consumer electronics is formidable.

Defending domestic dominance   RCA was prototypical of firms with a defend-domestic-dominance orientation. RCA owned most CTV patents and should rightly be regarded as the 'father of color TV.' However, RCA did not invest in overseas markets and was quite happy to concede the private label and the small CTV market to the Japanese. It saw itself as not only defending the US market – its domestic base – but also defending only segments of the market, primarily the market for higher-priced sets. As a result, RCA allowed a market position for the Japanese, was unaware of their long-term goals in the United States, and was blindsided.

The Japanese threat was obvious by 1975–76, and American producers who were primarily concerned about domestic dominance were unable to respond. Convinced that the sources of Japanese competitive advantage lay in low labor costs, they transferred most of their manufacturing overseas.

They also sought protection. Yet even with costs under control, these companies (RCA, GE, and Zenith) were still vulnerable because they had failed to understand the changing nature of the Japanese competitive advantage. Even as American producers closed the cost gap, the Japanese were cementing future profit foundations by investing in global brand positions. While Zenith and RCA dominated the color TV business in the United States, neither had a strong presence elsewhere. With no choice of competitive venue, US companies were forced to fight every market share battle in their home profit sanctuary.

When American TV makers reduced prices at home, they subjected 100 percent of their sales volume to margin pressure. Matsushita could force such price action while exposing only a fraction of its own world-wide profitability. TVs were no more than one loose brick in the American consumer electronic market. The Japanese goal appears to be to knock down the entire wall. For example, with margins under pressure in the TV business, no American manufacturer had the stomach to develop its own video recorder. Today video tape recorders are the mainstay of profitability for many Japanese consumer electronics companies.

Companies defending domestic positions are often shortsighted about their competitor's strategic intentions. A company can understand its own vulnerability to global competition only by first understanding its rivals' intentions, and then carefully reasoning back to potential tactics. With no appreciation of strategic intent, defense-minded competitors are doomed to a perpetual game of catch-up.

Local responsiveness   Philips of The Netherlands is well known virtually everywhere in the world. Like other long-standing MNCs, Philips has always benefited from the kind of international distribution system that US companies often lack. Yet our evidence suggests that this advantage alone was not enough. Philips had its own set of problems in responding to the Japanese challenge.

Because laws prohibited Japanese producers from supplying finished sets for private-label sale, they supplied picture tubes instead. By concentrating on such volume-sensitive manufacturing, Japanese manufacturers skirted protectionist sentiment while exploiting the economies of scale gained from US and Japanese experience.

Yet, just as they had not been content to remain private-label suppliers in the United States, Japanese companies were not content to remain component suppliers in Europe. They wanted to establish their own brand positions. Sony, Matsushita, and Mitsubishi set up local manufacturing operations in the United Kingdom. When the British began to fear a Japanese takeover of the local industry, Toshiba and Hitachi simply found UK partners. In moving the assembly line from the Far East to Europe, Japanese manufacturers incurred cost and quality penalties. Yet they regarded such penalties as acceptable costs for establishing strong European distribution and brand positions.

If we contrast Japanese entry strategies in the United States and Europe, it is clear that the tactics and timetables differed. Yet the long-term strategic intentions were the same, and the competitive advantage of Japanese producers evolved similarly in both markets. In both Europe and the United States, Japanese companies found an opening in the bottom half of the market – small-screen portables, along with other openings in the private label business in the United States and the picture tube business in Europe.

Philips was the only European manufacturer whose volume could fund the automation of manufacturing and the rationalization of product lines and components. Even though its volume was sufficient, Philips' manufacturing was spread across seven European countries. So it had to demonstrate (country by country, minister by minister, union by union) that the only alternative to protectionism was to support the development of Pan-European competitors. Philips also had to wrestle with independent subsidiaries not eager to surrender their autonomy in manufacturing and capital investment. By 1982 it was the world's largest color TV maker and had almost closed the cost gap with the Japanese producers. Even so, after 10 years, rationalization plans are still incomplete.

Philips remains vulnerable to global competition because of the difficulties inherent in weaving disparate national subsidiaries into a coherent global competitive team. Low-cost manufacturing and international distribution give Philips two of the critical elements needed for global competition. Still needed is coordination of national business strategies.

Philips's national managers are jealous of their autonomy in marketing and strategy. With their horizon of competition often limited to a single market, national managers are poorly placed to assess their global vulnerability. They can neither fully understand nor adequately analyze the strategic intentions and market entry tactics of global competitors. Nor can they estimate the total resources available to foreign competitors for local market share battles.

Under such management pressure, companies like Philips risk responding to global competition on a purely local basis. Its Japanese competitors can 'cherry pick' attractive national markets with little fear that their multinational rival will focus total company resources on retaliation in key markets.

The Concept of Critical Markets

Central to the arguments presented here is the notion of critical markets. In other words, to defend itself against determined global competitors who can cross-subsidize market share battles, a firm should be a multimarket competitor. That does not mean the firm should be present in all markets. Critical markets may be determined by seeking, at a minimum:

- markets that are the profit sanctuaries of the key competitors in that business;

- markets that provide volume and include the state-of-the-art customers;

- markets where the competitive intensity allows reasonable margins.

10.4   The Competitive Advantage of Nations

By Michael Porter[1]

Companies, not nations, are on the front line of international competition. Yet, the characteristics of the home nation play a central role in a firm's international success. The home base shapes a company's capacity to innovate rapidly in technology and methods and to do so in the proper directions. It is the place from which competitive advantage ultimately emanates and from which it must be sustained. A global strategy supplements and solidifies the competitive advantage created at the home base; it is the icing, not the cake. However, on the one hand, while having a home base in the right nation helps a great deal, it does not ensure success. On the other hand, having a home base in the wrong nation raises fundamental strategic concerns.

The most important sources of national advantage must be actively sought and exploited, unlike low factor costs obtainable simply by operating in the nation. Internationally successful firms are not passive bystanders in the process of creating competitive advantage. Those we studied were caught up in a never-ending process of seeking out new advantages and struggling with rivals to protect them. They were positioned to benefit the most from their national environment. They took steps to make their home nation (and location within the nation) an even more favorable environment for competitive advantage. Finally, they amplified their home-based advantages and offset home-based disadvantages through global strategies that tapped selectively into advantages available in other nations.

Competitive advantage ultimately results from an effective combination of national circumstances and company strategy. Conditions in a nation may create an environment in which firms can attain international competitive advantage, but it is up to a company to seize the opportunity.

The Context for Competitive Advantage

These imperatives of competitive advantage constitute a mind-set that is not present in many companies. Indeed, the actions required to create and sustain advantage are unnatural acts. Stability is valued in most companies, not change. Protecting old ideas and techniques becomes the preoccupation, not creating new ones.

The long-term challenge for any firm is to put itself in a position where it is most likely to perceive, and best able to address, the imperatives of

[1] Source: Reprinted with the permission of The Free Press, a Division of Macmillan, Inc. from *The Competitive Advantage of Nations* by Michael E. Porter. Copyright © 1990 by Michael E. Porter.

competitive advantage. One challenge is to expose a company to new market and technological opportunities that may be hard to perceive. Another is preparing for change by upgrading and expanding the skills of employees and improving the firm's scientific and knowledge base. Ultimately, the most important challenge is overcoming complacency and inertia to act on the new opportunities and circumstances.

The challenge of action ultimately falls on the firm's leader. Much attention has rightly been placed on the importance of visionary leaders in achieving unusual organizational success. But where does a leader get the vision, and how is it transmitted in a way that produces organizational accomplishment? Great leaders are influenced by the environment in which they work. Innovation takes place because the home environment stimulates it. Innovation succeeds because the home environment supports and even forces it. The right environment not only shapes a leader's own perceptions and priorities but provides the catalyst that allows the leader to overcome inertia and produce organizational change.

Great leaders emerge in different industries in different nations, in part because national circumstances attract and encourage them. Visionaries in consumer electronics are concentrated in Japan, chemicals and pharmaceuticals in Germany and Switzerland, and computers in America. Leadership is important to any success story, but is not in and of itself sufficient to explain such successes. In many industries, the national environment provides one or two nations with a distinct advantage over their foreign competitors. Leadership often determines which particular firm or firms exploit this advantage.

More broadly, the ability of any firm to innovate has much to do with the environment to which it is exposed, the information sources it has available – and consults – and the types of challenges it chooses to face. Seeking safe havens and comfortable customer relationships only reinforces past behavior. Maintaining suppliers who are captive degrades a source of stimulus, assistance, and insight. Lobbying against stringent product standards sends the wrong signal to an organization about norms and aspirations.

Innovation grows out of pressure and challenge. It also comes from finding the right challenges to meet. The main role of the firm's leader is to create the environment that meets these conditions. One essential part of the task is to take advantage of the national 'diamond' (see Figure 10.4.1 and Exhibit 10.4.1) that currently describes competition in the industry.

The New Rules for Innovation

A company should actively seek out pressure and challenge, not try to avoid them. Part of the task is to take advantage of the home nation in order to create the impetus for innovation. Some of the ways of doing so are:

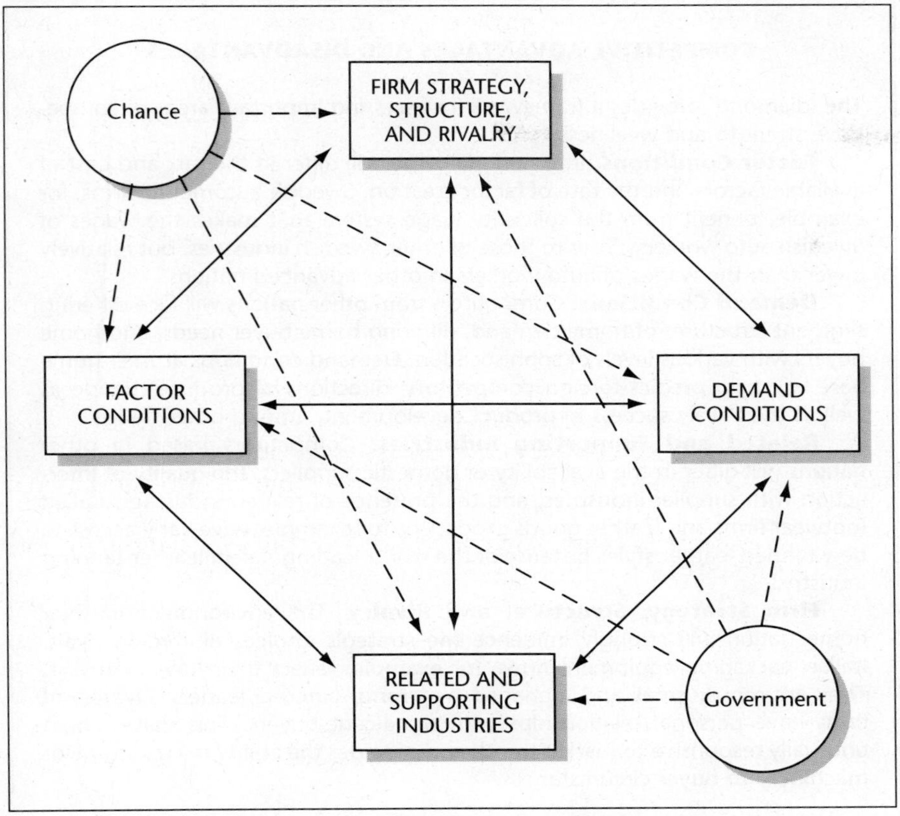

FIGURE 10.4.1
The diamond

- *Sell to the most sophisticated and demanding buyers and channels.* Some buyers (and channels) will stimulate the fastest improvement because they are knowledgeable and expect the best performance. They will set a standard for the organization and provide the most valuable feedback. However, sophisticated and demanding buyers and channels need not be the firm's only customers. Focusing on them exclusively may unnecessarily diminish long-term profitability. Nevertheless, serving a group of such buyers, chosen because their needs will challenge the firm's particular approach to competing, must be an explicit part of any strategy.

- *Seek out the buyers with the most difficult needs.* Buyers who face especially difficult operating requirements (such as climate, maintenance requirements, or hours of use), who confront factor cost disadvantages in their own businesses that create unusual pressures for performance, who have particularly tough competition, or who compete with strategies that place especially heavy demands on the firm's product or service, are buyers that will provide the laboratory (and the pressure) to upgrade performance and extend features and services. Such buyers should be identified and cultivated. They become part of a firm's R&D program.

EXHIBIT 10.4.1
Elements of the diamond

COMPETITIVE ADVANTAGES AND DISADVANTAGES

The 'diamond' provides a framework for assessing important areas of competitive strength and weakness.

Factor Conditions. International rivals will differ in the mix and cost of available factors and the rate of factor creation. Swedish automobile firms, for example, benefit from the solidarity wage system that makes the wages of Swedish auto workers closer to those of other Swedish industries, but relatively lower than the wages of auto workers in other advanced nations.

Demand Conditions. Competitors from other nations will face differing segment structures of home demand, differing home buyer needs, and home buyers with various levels of sophistication. Demand conditions at their home base will help predict foreign competitors' directions of product change as well as their likely success in product development, among other things.

Related and Supporting Industries. Competitors based in other nations will differ in the availability of domestic suppliers, the quality of interaction with supplier industries, and the presence of related industries. Italian footwear firms and leather goods producers, for example, have early access to new tanned leather styles because of the world-leading Italian leather tanning industry.

Firm Strategy, Structure, and Rivalry. The environment in their home nation will strongly influence the strategic choices of foreign rivals. Italian packaging equipment firms, for example, reflect their Italian context. They are mostly small and managed by strong, paternal leaders. Owners of firms have personal relationships with significant buyers. This makes them unusually responsive to market trends and provides the ability to custom-tailor machinery to buyer circumstances.

■ *Establish norms of exceeding the toughest regulatory hurdles or product standards.* Some localities (or user industries) will lead in terms of the stringency of product standards, pollution limits, noise guidelines, and the like. Tough regulating standards are not a hindrance but an opportunity to move early to upgrade products and processes. Older or simplified models can be sold elsewhere.

■ *Source from the most advanced and international home-based suppliers.* Suppliers who themselves possess competitive advantage, as well as the insight that comes from international activities, will challenge the firm to improve and upgrade as well as provide insights and assistance in doing so.

■ *Treat employees as permanent.* When employees are viewed as permanent instead of as workers who can be hired and fired at will, pressures are created that work to upgrade and sustain competitive advantage. New employees are hired with care, and continuous efforts are made to improve productivity instead of adding workers. Employees are trained on an ongoing basis to support more sophisticated competitive advantages.

■ *Establish outstanding competitors as motivators.* Those competitors who most closely match a company's competitive advantages, or exceed them, must become the standard of comparison. Such competitors can be a source of learning as well as a powerful focal point to overcome parochial concerns and motivate change for the entire organization.

The True Costs of Stability

These prescriptions may seem counterintuitive. The ideal would seem to be the stability growing out of obedient customers, captive and dependent suppliers, and sleepy competitors. Such a search for a quiet life, an understandable instinct, has led many companies to buy direct competitors or form alliances with them. In a closed, static world, monopoly would indeed be the most comfortable and profitable solution.

In reality, however, competition is dynamic. Complacent firms will lose to other firms who come from a more dynamic environment. Good managers always run a little scared. They respect and study competitors. Seeking out and meeting challenges is part of their organizational norm. By contrast, an organization that values stability and lacks self-perceived competition breeds inertia and creates vulnerabilities.

In global competition, the pressure of demanding local buyers, capable suppliers, and aggressive domestic rivalry are even more valuable and necessary for long-term profitability. These drive the firm to a faster rate of progress and upgrading than international rivals, and lead to sustained competitive advantage and superior long-term profitability. A tough domestic industry structure creates advantage in the international industry. A comfortable, easy home base, in contrast, leaves a firm vulnerable to rivals who enjoy greater dynamism at home.

Perceiving Industry Change

Beyond pressure to innovate, one of the most important advantages an industry can have is early insight into important needs, environmental forces, and trends that others have not noticed. Japanese firms had an early and clear warning about the importance of energy efficiency. American firms have often gotten a jump in seeing demand for new services, giving them a head start in many service industries. Better insight and early warning signals lead to competitive advantages. Firms gain competitive position before rivals perceive an opportunity (or a threat) and are able to respond.

Perceiving possibilities for new strategies more clearly or earlier comes in part from simply being in the right nation at the right time. Yet it is possible for a firm to more actively position itself to see the signals of change and act on them. It must find the right focus or location within the nation, and work to overcome the filters that distort or limit the flow of information.

- *Identify and serve buyers (and channels) with the most anticipatory needs*. Some buyers will confront new problems or have new needs before others because of their demographics, location, industry, or strategy.

- *Discover and highlight trends in factor costs*. Increases in the costs of particular factors or other inputs may signal future opportunities to leapfrog competitors by innovating to deploy inputs more effectively or to avoid the need for them altogether. A firm should know which markets or regions are likely to reflect such trends first.

- *Maintain ongoing relationships with centers of research and sources of the most talented people*. A firm must identify the places in the nation where the best new knowledge is being created that is now or might become relevant to its industry. Equally important is to identify the schools, institutions, and other companies where the best specialized human resources needed in the industry are being trained.

- *Study all competitors, especially the new and unconventional ones*. Rivals sometimes discover new ideas first. Innovators are often smaller, more focused competitors that are new to the industry. Alternatively, they may be firms led by managers with backgrounds in other industries not bound by conventional wisdom. Such 'outsiders,' with fewer blinders to cloud their perception of new opportunities and fewer perceived constraints in abandoning past practices, frequently become industry innovators.

- *Bring some outsiders into the management team*. The incorporation of new thinking in the management process is often speeded by the presence of one or more 'outsiders' – managers from other companies or industries or from the company's foreign subsidiaries.

Interchange within the National Cluster

A firm gains important competitive advantages from the presence in its home nation of world-class buyers, suppliers, and related industries. They provide insight into future market needs and technological developments. They contribute to a climate for change and improvement, and become partners and allies in the innovation process. Having a strong cluster at home unblocks the flows of information and allows deeper and more open contact than is possible when dealing with foreign firms. Being part of a cluster localized in a small geographic area is even more valuable.

Buyers, Channels, and Suppliers

The first hurdle to be cleared in taking advantage of the domestic cluster is attitudinal. It means recognizing that home-based buyers and suppliers are allies in international competition and not just the other side of trans-actions. A firm must also pursue:

- regular senior management contact;

- formal and ongoing interchange between research organizations;

- reciprocity in serving as test sites for new products or services;

- cooperation in penetrating and serving international markets.

Working with buyers, suppliers, and channels involves helping them upgrade and extend their own competitive advantages. Their health and strength will only enhance their capacity to speed the firm's own rate of innovation. Open communications with local buyers or suppliers, and early access to new equipment, services, and ideas, are important for sustaining competitive advantage. Such communication will be freer, more timely, and more meaningful than is usually possible with foreign firms.

Encouraging and assisting domestic buyers and suppliers to compete globally is one part of the task of upgrading them. A company's local buyers and suppliers cannot ultimately sustain competitive advantage in many cases unless they compete globally. Buyers and suppliers need exposure to the pressures of world-wide competition in order to advance themselves. Trying to keep them 'captive' and prevent them from selling their products abroad is ultimately self-defeating.

An orientation toward closer vertical relationships is only just starting to take hold in many American companies, though it is quite typical in Japanese and Swedish companies. Interchange with buyers, channels, and suppliers always involves some tension, because there is inevitably the need to bargain with them over prices and service. In global industries, however, the competitive advantage to be gained from interchange more than compensates for some sacrifice in bargaining leverage. Interchange should not create dependence but interdependence. A firm should work with a group of suppliers and customers, not just one.

Related Industries

Industries that are related or potentially related in terms of technology, channels, buyers, or the way buyers obtain or use products are potentially important to creating and sustaining competitive advantage. The presence in a nation of such industries deserves special attention. These industries are often essential sources of innovation. They can also become new suppliers, buyers, or even new competitors.

At a minimum, senior management should be visiting leading companies in related industries on a regular basis. The purpose is to exchange ideas about industry developments. Formal joint research projects, or other more structured ways to explore new ideas, are advisable where the related industry holds more immediate potential to affect com-petitive advantage.

Locating within the Nation

A firm should locate activities and its headquarters at those locations in the nation where there are concentrations of sophisticated buyers, important suppliers, groups of competitors, or especially significant factor-creating mechanisms for its industry (such as universities with specialized programs or laboratories with expertise in important technologies). Geographic proximity makes the relationships within a cluster closer and more fluid. It also makes domestic rivalry more valuable for competitive advantage.

Serving Home Base Buyers Who Are International and Multinational

To transform domestic competitive advantage into a global strategy, a firm should identify and serve buyers at home that can also serve abroad. Such buyers are domestic companies that have international operations, individuals who travel frequently to other nations, and local subsidiaries of foreign firms. Targeting such buyers has two benefits. First, they can provide a base of demand in foreign markets to help offset the costs of entry. More important, they will often be sophisticated buyers who can provide a window into international market needs.

Improving the National Competitive Environment

Sustaining competitive advantage is not only a function of making the most of the national environment. Firms must work actively to improve their home base by upgrading the national diamond (see Figure 10.4.1 and Exhibit 10.4.1). A company draws on its home nation to extend and upgrade its own competitive advantages. The firm has a stake in making its home base a better platform for international success.

Playing this role demands that a company understand how each part of the 'diamond' best contributes to competitive advantage. It also requires a long-term perspective, because the investments required to improve the home base often take years or even decades to bear fruit. What is more, short-term profits are elevated by foregoing such investments, and by shifting important activities abroad instead of upgrading the ability to perform them at home. Both actions will diminish the sustainability of a firm's competitive advantages in the long run.

Firms have a tendency to see the task of ensuring high-quality human resources, infrastructure, and scientific knowledge as someone else's responsibility. Another common misconception is that, because competition is global, the home base is unimportant. Too often, US and British companies in particular leave investments in the national diamond to others or to the government. The result is that companies are well managed but lack the human resources, technology, and access to capable suppliers and customers needed to succeed against foreign rivals.

Where and How to Compete

A firm's home nation shapes where and how it is likely to succeed in global competition. Germany is a superb environment for competing in printing equipment, but does not offer one conducive to international success in heavily advertised consumer packaged goods. Italy represents a remarkable setting for innovation in fashion and furnishing, but a poor environment for success in industries that sell to government agencies or infrastructure providers.

Within an industry, a nation's circumstances also favor competing in particular industry segments and with certain competitive strategies. Given local housing conditions, for example, Japan is a good home base for competing globally in compact models of appliances and in appliances that are inherently compact (such as microwave ovens) but a poor home base for competing in full-size refrigerators. Within compact appliances, the Japanese environment is particularly conducive to differentiation strategies based on rapid new model introduction and high product quality.

The national diamond becomes central to choosing the industries to compete in as well as the appropriate strategy. The home base is an important determinant of a firm's strengths and weaknesses relative to foreign rivals.

Understanding the home base of foreign competitors is essential in analyzing them. Their home nation yields them advantages and disadvantages. It also shapes their likely future strategies. The diamond serves as an important tool for competitor analysis in international industries.

Choosing Industries and Strategies

The likelihood that a firm can achieve breakthroughs or innovations of strategic importance in an industry is also influenced by its home nation. Innovation and entrepreneurial behavior is partly a function of chance. But it also depends to a considerable degree on the environment in which the innovator or entrepreneur works. The diamond has a strong influence on which nation (and even on which region within that nation) will be the source of an innovation.

Important innovations in Denmark, for example, have occurred in enzymes for food processing, in natural vitamins, in measuring instruments related to food processing, and in drugs isolated from animal organs (insulin and the anticoagulant heparin). These are hardly random in a nation whose exports are dominated by a large cluster of food-and-beverage-related industries. A firm or individual has the best odds of succeeding in innovation, or in creating a new business, where the national diamond provides the best environment.

The national circumstances most significant for competitive advantage depend on a firm's industry and strategy. In a resource-or basic factor-driven industry, the most important national attribute is a supply of superior or low-cost factors. In a fashion-sensitive industry, the presence of advanced and cutting-edge customers is paramount. In an industry heavily based on scientific research, the quality of factor-creating mechanisms in human resources and technology, coupled with access to sophisticated buyers and suppliers, is decisive.

Cost-oriented strategies are more sensitive to factor costs, the size of home demand, and conditions that favor large-scale plant investments. Differentiation strategies tend to depend more on specialized human resources, sophisticated local buyers, and world-class local supplier industries. Focus strategies rest on the presence of unusual demand in particular segments or on factor conditions or supplier access that benefits competing in a particular product range.

As competition globalizes, and as developments such as European trade liberalization and free trade between the United States and Canada promise to eliminate artificial distortions that have insulated domestic firms from market forces, firms must increasingly compete in industries and segments where they have real strengths. This must increasingly be guided by the national diamond.

A firm can raise the odds of success if it is competing in industries, and with strategies, where the nation provides an unusually fertile environment for competitive advantage. The questions in Figure 10.4.2 are designed to expose such areas. Of major importance is a forward-looking view in answering these questions. The focus must be on the nature of evolving competition, not the past requirements for success.

Diversification

While diversification is part of company strategy in virtually every nation, its track record has been mixed at best. Widespread diversification into unrelated industries was rare among the international leaders we studied. They tended instead to compete in one or two core industries or industry sectors, and their commitment to these industries was absolute. For every widely diversified Hitachi or Siemens, there were several Boeings, Koenig & Bauers, FANUCs, Novo Industries, and SKFs, who are global competitors but heavily focused on their core industry.

Internal diversification, not acquisition, has to a striking degree been the motivation for achieving leading international market positions. Where acquisitions were involved in international success stories, the acquisitions were often modest or focused ones that served as an initial entry point or reinforced an internal entry. The reasons for this track record in diversification are not hard to understand when viewed in light of my theory.

Internal diversification facilitates a transfer of skills and resources that is quite difficult to accomplish when acquiring an independent company with its own history and way of operating. Internal entry tends to increase the overall rate of investment in factor creation. There is also an intense commitment to succeed in diversification into closely related fields because of the benefits that accrue to the base business and the effect on the overall corporate image. Unrelated diversification, particularly through acquisition,

FIGURE 10.4.2
The home base diamond

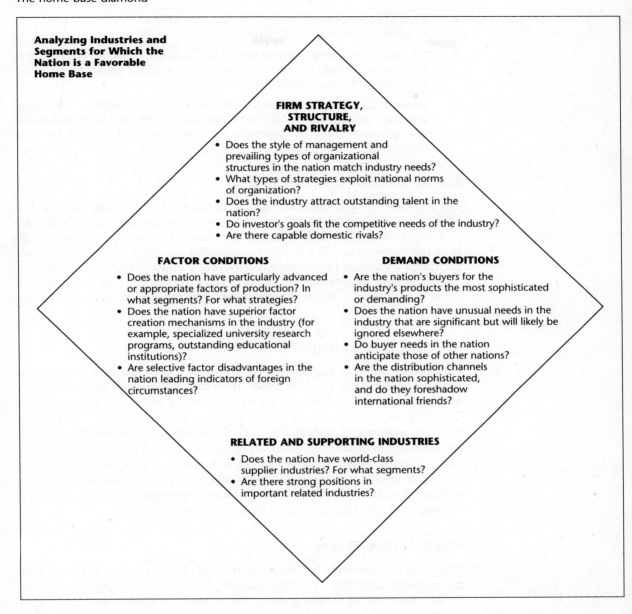

Analyzing Industries and Segments for Which the Nation is a Favorable Home Base

FIRM STRATEGY, STRUCTURE, AND RIVALRY

- Does the style of management and prevailing types of organizational structures in the nation match industry needs?
- What types of strategies exploit national norms of organization?
- Does the industry attract outstanding talent in the nation?
- Do investor's goals fit the competitive needs of the industry?
- Are there capable domestic rivals?

FACTOR CONDITIONS

- Does the nation have particularly advanced or appropriate factors of production? In what segments? For what strategies?
- Does the nation have superior factor creation mechanisms in the industry (for example, specialized university research programs, outstanding educational institutions)?
- Are selective factor disadvantages in the nation leading indicators of foreign circumstances?

DEMAND CONDITIONS

- Are the nation's buyers for the industry's products the most sophisticated or demanding?
- Does the nation have unusual needs in the industry that are significant but will likely be ignored elsewhere?
- Do buyer needs in the nation anticipate those of other nations?
- Are the distribution channels in the nation sophisticated, and do they foreshadow international friends?

RELATED AND SUPPORTING INDUSTRIES

- Does the nation have world-class supplier industries? For what segments?
- Are there strong positions in important related industries?

makes no contribution to innovation. The implications of my theory for diversification strategy are as follows:

■   New industries for diversification should be selected where a favorable national diamond is present or can be created. Diversification proposals should be screened for the attractiveness of the home base.

- Diversification is most likely to succeed when it follows or extends clusters in which the firm already competes.

- Internal development of new businesses, supplemented by small acquisitions, is more likely to create and sustain competitive advantage than the acquisition of large, establishment companies.

- Diversification into businesses lacking common buyers, channels, suppliers, or close technological connections is not only likely to fail but will also undermine the prospects for sustaining advantage in the core businesses.

Locating Regional Headquarters

The principles I have described carry implications for the choice of where to locate the regional headquarters responsible for managing a firm's activities in a group of nations. Regional headquarters are best placed not for administrative convenience but in the nation with the most favorable national diamond. Of special importance is choosing a location that will expose the firm to significant needs and pressures lacking at home. The purpose is to learn as well as raise the odds that information passes credibly back to the home base.

Selective Foreign Acquisitions

Foreign acquisitions can serve two purposes. One is to gain access to a foreign market or to selective skills. Here the challenge of integrating the acquisition into the global strategy is significant but raises a few unusual issues. The other reason for a foreign acquisition is to gain access to a highly favorable national diamond. Sometimes the only feasible way to tap into the advantages of another nation is to acquire a local firm because an outsider is hard-pressed to penetrate such broad, systemic advantages. The challenge in this latter type of acquisition is to preserve the ability of the acquired firm to benefit from its national environment at the same time as it is integrated into the company's global strategy.

The Role of Alliances

Alliances, or coalitions, are final mechanisms by which a firm can seek to tap national advantages in other nations. Alliances are a tempting solution to the dilemma of a firm seeking the home-base advantages of another nation without giving up its own. Unfortunately, alliances are rarely a solution. They can achieve selective benefits, but they always involve significant costs in terms of coordination, reconciling goals with an independent entity, creating a competitor, and giving up profits. These costs make many alliances temporary and destined to fail. They are often transitional devices rather than stable arrangements.

No firm can depend on another independent firm for skills and assets that are central to its competitive advantage. If it does, the firm runs a grave risk of losing its competitive advantage in the long run. Alliances tend to ensure mediocrity, not create world leadership. The most serious risk of alliances is that they deter the firm's own efforts at upgrading. This may occur because management is content to rely on the partner. It may also occur because the alliance has eliminated a threatening competitor.

10.5 Transnational Management

By Christopher Bartlett and Sumantra Ghoshal[1]

Changes in the international operating environment have forced MNCs to optimize global efficiency, national responsiveness, and world-wide learning simultaneously. For most companies, this new challenge implies not only a fundamental strategic reorientation, but also a major change in organizational capability.

Implementing such a complex three-pronged strategic objective would be difficult under any circumstances, but in a world-wide company the task is complicated even further. The very act of 'going international' multiplies a company's organizational complexity. Most companies find it difficult enough balancing product divisions that carry overall responsibility for achieving operating efficiency and strategic focus with corporate staffs whose functional expertise allows them to play an important counterbalance and control role. The thought of adding capable geographically oriented management and maintaining a three-way balance of organizational perspectives and capabilities among product, function, and area is intimidating. The difficulty is further increased because the resolution of tensions among the three different management groups must be accomplished in an organization whose operating units are often divided by distance and time and whose key members are separated by barriers of culture and language.

Beyond Structural Fit

Because the choice of a basic organizational structure has such a powerful influence on the management process in an MNC, much of the earlier

---

[1] Source: Reprinted with permission from chapter 5 of *Transnational Management: Text, Cases, and Readings in Cross-Border Management*, second edition., R.D. Irwin Inc, 1995.

attention of managers and researchers alike was focused on trying to find which formal structure provided the right 'fit' under various conditions. The most widely recognized study on this issue was John Stopford's research on the 187 largest US-based MNCs in the late 1960s (1972). His work resulted in a 'stages model' of international organization structure that became the benchmark for most work that followed.

Stopford defined two variables to capture strategic and administrative complexity that faced most companies as they expanded abroad: the number of products sold internationally ('foreign product diversity,' shown on the vertical axis in Figure 10.5.1) and the importance of international sales to the company ('foreign sales as a percentage of total sales,' shown on the horizontal axis). Plotting the structural change in his sample of 187 companies, he found that world-wide corporations typically adopt different organizational structures at different stages of international expansion.

According to this model, world-wide companies typically manage their international operations through an international division at the early stage of foreign expansion, when both foreign sales and the diversity of products sold abroad are limited. Subsequently, those companies that expand their sales abroad without significantly increasing foreign product diversity typically adopt an area structure. Other companies that expand by increasing their foreign product diversity tend to adopt the world-wide product division structure. Finally, when both foreign sales and foreign product diversity are high, companies resort to the global matrix.

Although these ideas were presented as a descriptive model, consultants, academics, and managers alike soon began to apply them

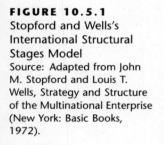

FIGURE 10.5.1
Stopford and Wells's International Structural Stages Model
Source: Adapted from John M. Stopford and Louis T. Wells, Strategy and Structure of the Multinational Enterprise (New York: Basic Books, 1972).

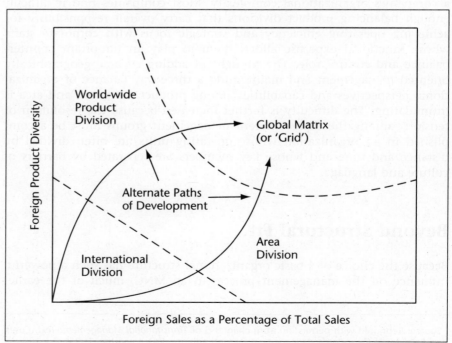

prescriptively. For many companies, it seemed that structure followed fashion more than strategy. And in the process, the debate was often reduced to generalized discussions of the comparative value of product-versus geography-based structures and to simplistic choices between 'centralization' and 'decentralization.'

Confronted with the increasing complexity, diversity, and change in the 1980s, managers in many world-wide companies looked for ways to restructure. Conventional wisdom provided a ready solution: the global matrix. But for most companies, the result was disappointing. The promised land of the global matrix turned out to be an organizational quagmire from which they were forced to retreat.

Failure Of The Matrix

In theory, the solution should have worked. Having front-line managers report simultaneously to different organizational groups (such as business managers reporting to both the area and the functional groups or area managers reporting along functional and business lines) should have enabled the companies to maintain the balance among centralized efficiency, local responsiveness, and world-wide knowledge transfer. The multiple channels of communication and control promised the ability to nurture diverse management perspectives, and the ability to shift the balance of power within the matrix theoretically gave it great flexibility. The reality turned out to be otherwise, however, and the history of companies that built formal global matrix structures was an unhappy one.

Dow Chemical, a pioneer of global matrix organization, eventually returned to a more conventional structure with clear lines of responsibility being given to geographic managers. Citibank, once a textbook example of the global matrix, similarly discarded this mode of dual reporting relationships after a few years of highly publicized experimentation. And so too did scores of other companies that experimented with this complex and rather bureaucratic structure.

Most encountered the same problems. The matrix amplified the differences in perspectives and interests by forcing all issues through the dual chains of command so that even a minor difference could become the subject of heated disagreement and debate. While this strategy had proven useful in highly concentrated domestic operations, the very design of the global matrix prevented the resolution of differences among managers with conflicting views and overlapping responsibilities. Dual reporting led to conflict and confusion; the proliferation of channels created informational logjams; and overlapping responsibilities resulted in turf battles and a loss of accountability. Separated by barriers of distance, time, language, and culture, managers found it virtually impossible to clarify the confusion and resolve the conflicts.

As a result, the management process was slow, acrimonious, and costly. Communications were routinely duplicated, approval processes were time-consuming, and constant travel and frequent meetings raised the company's administrative costs dramatically. In company after company, the initial appeal of the global matrix structure quickly faded into a recognition that a different solution was required.

Building Organizational Capability

The basic problem underlying a company's search for a structural fit was that it focused on only one organizational variable – formal structure – and this single tool proved to be unequal to the task of capturing the complexity of the strategic task facing most MNCs. First, as indicated earlier, this focus often forced managers to ignore the multidimensionality of the environmental forces as they made choices between product- versus geographically-based structures and debated the relative advantages of centralization versus decentralization. Furthermore, structure defined a static set of roles, responsibilities, and relationships in a dynamic and rapidly evolving task environment. And finally, restructuring efforts often proved harmful, as organizations were bludgeoned into a major realignment of roles, responsibilities, and relationships overnight.

In an increasing number of companies, managers now recognize that formal structure is a powerful but blunt instrument of strategic change. Moreover, given the complexity and volatility of environmental demands, structural fit is becoming both less relevant and harder to achieve. Success in coping with managers' multidimensional strategic task now depends rather more on building strategic and organizational flexibility.

To develop multidimensional and flexible strategic capabilities, a company must go beyond structure and expand its fundamental organizational capabilities. The key tasks become to reorient managers' thinking and reshape the core decision-making systems. In doing so, the company's entire management process – the administrative system, communication channels, and interpersonal relationships – become the tools for managing such change.

Administrative Heritage

While industry analysis can reveal a company's strategic challenges and market opportunities, its ability to fulfill that promise will be greatly influenced – and often constrained – by existing asset configurations, its historical definition of management responsibilities, and the ingrained organizational norms. A company's organization is shaped not only by current external task demands but also by past internal management biases. In particular, each company is influenced by the path by which it developed – its organizational history – and the values, norms, and practices of its management – its management culture. Collectively, these factors constitute a company's administrative heritage. It can be, at the same time, one of the company's greatest assets – the underlying source of its key competencies – and also a significant liability, since it resists change and thereby prevents realignment or broadening of strategic capabilities. As managers in many companies have learned, often at considerable cost, while strategic plans can be scrapped and redrawn overnight, there is no such thing as a zero-based organization. Companies are, to a significant extent, captives of their past, and any organizational transformation has to focus at least as much on where the company is coming from – its administrative heritage – as on where it wants to get to.

The importance of a company's administrative heritage can be illustrated by contrasting the development of a typical European MNC whose major international expansion occurred in the decades of the 1920s and 1930s, a typical American MNC that expanded abroad in the 1940s and 1950s, and a typical Japanese company that made its main overseas thrust in the 1960s and 1970s. Even if these companies were in the same industry, the combined effects of the different historical contexts in which they developed and the disparate internal cultural norms that influenced their management processes led to their adopting some very different strategic and organizational models.

Decentralized Federation

Expanding abroad in a period of rising tariffs and discriminatory legislation, the typical European company found its budding export markets threatened by local competitors. To defend its various market positions, it was forced to build local production facilities. With their own plants, various national subsidiaries were able to modify products and marketing approaches to meet widely differing local market needs. The increasing independence of these fully integrated national units was reinforced by the transportation and communications barriers that existed in that era, limiting the head-quarters' ability to intervene in the management of the company's spreading world-wide operations.

The emerging configuration of distributed assets and delegated responsibility fit well with the ingrained management norms and practices in many European companies. Because of the important role of owners and bankers in corporate-level decision making, European companies, particularly those from the United Kingdom, the Netherlands, and France, developed an internal culture that emphasized personal relationships rather than formal structures, and financial controls more than coordination of technical or operational detail. This management style, philosophy, and capability tended to reinforce companies' willingness to delegate more operating independence and strategic freedom to their foreign subsidiaries. Highly autonomous national companies were often managed more as a portfolio of offshore investments rather than as a single international business.

The resulting organization and management pattern was a loose federation of independent national subsidiaries, each focused primarily on its local market. As a result, many of these companies adopted what we have described as the multinational strategy and developed a decentralized federation organization model that is represented in Figure 10.5.2(a).

Coordinated Federation

US companies, many of which enjoyed their fastest international expansion in the 1950s and 1960s, developed under very different circumstances. Their main strength lay in the new technologies and management processes they had developed as a consequence of being located in the world's largest, richest, and most technologically advanced market. After the war, their foreign expansion focused primarily on leveraging this strength, particu-

FIGURE 10.5.2
Organizational Configuration Models

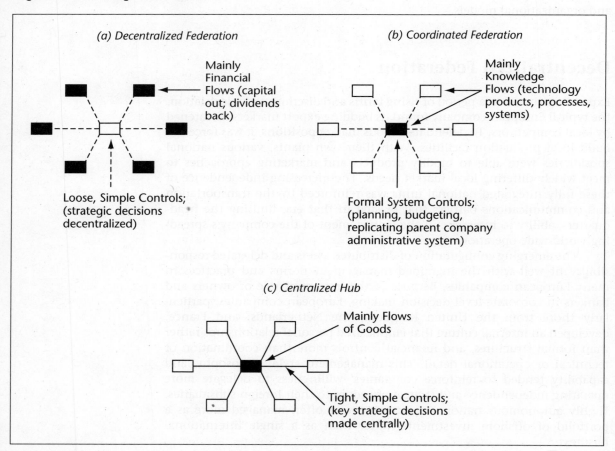

(a) Decentralized Federation

Mainly Financial Flows (capital out; dividends back)

Loose, Simple Controls; (strategic decisions decentralized)

(b) Coordinated Federation

Mainly Knowledge Flows (technology products, processes, systems)

Formal System Controls; (planning, budgeting, replicating parent company administrative system)

(c) Centralized Hub

Mainly Flows of Goods

Tight, Simple Controls; (key strategic decisions made centrally)

larly in response to demands generated by postwar reconstruction and the granting of independence to previously colonized nations.

Reinforcing this strategy was a professional managerial culture in most US-based companies that contrasted with the 'old boy network' that typified the European companies' processes. The management approach in most US-based companies was built on a willingness to delegate responsibility, while retaining overall control through sophisticated management systems and specialist corporate staffs. The systems provided channels for a regular flow of information, to be interpreted by the central staff. Holding the managerial reins, top management could control the free-running team of independent subsidiaries and guide the direction in which they were headed.

The main handicap such companies faced was that parent-company management often adopted a parochial and even superior attitude toward international operations, perhaps because of the assumption that new ideas and developments all came from the parent. Despite corporate management's increased understanding of its overseas markets, it often seemed to view foreign operations as appendages whose principal purpose was to leverage the capabilities and resources developed in the home market.

None the less, the approach was highly successful in the postwar decades, and many US-based companies adopted what we have described as the international strategy and a coordinated federation organizational model shown in Figure 10.5.2(b). Their foreign subsidiaries were often free to adapt products or strategies to reflect market differences, but their dependence on the parent company for new products, processes, and ideas dictated a great deal more coordination and control by headquarters than in the decentralized federation organization. This was facilitated by the existence of formal systems and controls in the headquarters-subsidiary link.

Centralized Hub

In contrast, the typical Japanese company, making its main international thrust since the 1970s, faced a greatly altered external environment and operated with very different internal norms and values. With limited prior overseas exposure, it chose not to match the well-established local marketing capabilities and facilities that its European and US competitors had built up. (Indeed, well-established Japanese trading companies often provided it with an easier means of entering foreign markets.) However, it had new, efficient, scale-intensive plants, built to serve its rapidly expanding domestic market, and it was expanding into a global environment of declining trade barriers. Together, these factors gave it the incentive to develop a competitive advantage at the upstream end of the value-added chain. Its competitive strategy emphasized cost advantages and quality assurance and required tight central control of product development, procurement, and manufacturing. A centrally controlled, export-based internationalization strategy represented a perfect fit with the external environment and the company's competitive capabilities.

Such an approach also fit the cultural background and organizational values in the emerging Japanese MNC. At the foundation of the internal processes were the strong national cultural norms that emphasized group behavior and valued interpersonal harmony. These values had been enhanced by the paternalism of the zaibatsu and other enterprise groups. They were also reflected in the group-oriented management practices of *nemawashi* and *ringi* that were at the core of Japanese organizational processes. By keeping primary decision making and control at the center, the Japanese company could retain this culturally dependent management system that was so communications intensive and people dependent.

Cultural values were also reflected in one of the main motivations driving the international expansion of Japanese MNCs. As growth in their domestic market slowed and became increasingly competitive, these companies needed new sources of growth so they could continue to attract and promote employees. In a system of lifetime employment, growth was the engine that powered organizational vitality and self-renewal. It was this motivation that reinforced the bias toward an export-based strategy managed from the center rather than the decentralized foreign investment approach of the European. As a result, these companies adopted what we have described as a global strategy, and developed a centralized hub organizational model, shown in Figure 10.5.2(c), to support this strategic orientation.

The Transnational Challenge

We advanced the hypothesis that many world-wide industries have been transformed in the 1980s from traditional multinational, international, and global forms toward a transnational form. Instead of demanding efficiency, responsiveness, or learning as the key capability for success. these businesses now require participating firms to achieve the three capabilities simultaneously to remain competitive.

Table 10.5.1 summarizes the key characteristics of the decentralized federation, coordinated federation, and centralized hub organizations as the supporting forms for companies pursuing the multinational, international, and global strategies. A review of these characteristics immediately reveals the problems each of the three archetypal company models might face in responding to the transnational challenge.

With its resources and capabilities consolidated at the center, the global company achieves efficiency primarily by exploiting potential scale economies in all its activities. In such an organization, however, the national subsidiaries' lack of resources and responsibilities may undermine their motivation and their ability to respond to local market needs. Similarly, while the centralization of knowledge and skills allows the global company to be highly efficient in developing and managing innovative new

TABLE 10.5.1
Organizational characteristics of decentralized federation, coordinated federation, and centralized hub organizations

	Decentralized Federation	Coordinated Federation	Centralized Hub
Strategic approach	Multinational	International	Global
Key strategic capability	National responsiveness	World-wide transfer of home country innovations	Global-scale efficiency
Configuration of assets and capabilities	Decentralized and nationally self-sufficient	Sources of core competencies centralized, others decentralized	Centralized and globally scaled
Role of overseas operations	Sensing and exploiting local opportunities	Adapting and leveraging parent-company competencies	Implementing parent-company strategies
Development and diffusion of knowledge	Knowledge developed and retained within each unit	Knowledge developed at the center and transferred to overseas units	Knowledge developed and retained at the center

products and processes, the central groups often lack adequate understanding of the market needs and production realities outside their home market. Limited resources and the narrow implementation role of its overseas units prevent the company from tapping into learning opportunities outside its home environment. These are problems that a global organization cannot overcome without jeopardizing its trump card of global efficiency.

The classic multinational company suffers from other limitations. While its dispersed resources and decentralized decision making allows national subsidiaries to respond to local needs, the fragmentation of activities also leads to inefficiency. Learning also suffers, because knowledge is not consolidated and does not flow among the various parts of the company. As a result, local innovations often represent little more than the efforts of subsidiary management to protect its turf and autonomy, or reinventions of the wheel caused by blocked communication or the not-invented-here (NIH) syndrome.

In contrast, the international company is better able to leverage the knowledge and capabilities of the parent company. However, its resource configuration and operating systems make it less efficient than the global company, and less responsive than the multinational company.

The Transnational Organization

There are three important organizational characteristics that distinguish the transnational organization from its multinational, international, or global counterparts. It builds and legitimizes multiple diverse internal perspectives able to sense the complex environmental demands and opportunities; its physical assets and management capabilities are distributed internationally but are interdependent; and it has developed a robust and flexible internal integrative process. In the following paragraphs, we will describe and illustrate each of these characteristics.

Multidimensional Perspectives

Managing in an environment in which strategic forces are both diverse and changeable, the transnational company must develop the ability to sense and analyze the numerous and often conflicting opportunities, pressures, and demands it faces world-wide. Having a limited or biased management perspective through which to view developments can constrain a company's ability to understand and respond to some potential problems or opportunities.

The transnational organization must have broad sensory capabilities able to reflect the diverse environmental opportunities and demands in the internal management process. Strong national subsidiary management is needed to sense and represent the changing needs of local consumers and the increasing pressures from host governments; capable global business management is required to track the strategy of global competitors and to provide the coordination necessary to respond appropriately; and influential functional management is needed to concentrate corporate knowledge, information, and expertise, and facilitate its transfer among organizational units.

Unfortunately, however, in many companies, power is concentrated with the particular management group that has historically represented the company's most critical strategic tasks – often at the cost of allowing other groups to represent different needs. For example, in multinational companies, key decisions were usually dominated by the country management group since they made the most critical contribution to achieving national responsiveness, which lay at the center of the strategic approach of such companies. In global companies, by contrast, managers in world-wide product divisions were typically the most influential, since strong business management played the key role in the company's efforts to seek global efficiency. And in international companies, functional management groups often came to assume this position of dominance because of their roles in building, accumulating, and transferring the company's skills, knowledge, and capabilities.

In transnational companies, however, biases in the decision-making process are consciously reduced by building up the capability, credibility, and influence of the less powerful management groups while protecting the morale and capabilities of the dominant group. The objective is to build a multidimensional organization in which the influence of each of the three management groups is balanced.

Distributed, Interdependent Capabilities

Having sensed the diverse opportunities and demands it faces, the transnational organization must then be able to make choices among them and respond in a timely and effective manner to those that are deemed strategically important. When a company's decision-making process and organizational capabilities are concentrated at the center – as they are in the global organization's centralized hub configuration – it is often difficult to respond appropriately to diverse world-wide demands. Being distant from the front-line opportunities and threats, the central group's ability to act in an effective and timely manner is constrained by its reliance on complex and intensive international communications. Furthermore, the volume and diversity of demands made on the central group often result in central capabilities being overloaded, particularly where scarce technological or managerial resources are involved.

On the other hand, multinational organizations with their response capabilities spread throughout the decentralized federation of independent operations suffer from duplication of effort (the reinventing-the-wheel syndrome), inefficiency of operations (the 'locally self-sufficing scale' problem), and barriers to international learning (the not-invented-here syndrome).

In transnational organizations, management breaks away from the restricted view that assumes the need to centralize activities for which global scale or specialized knowledge is important. They ensure that viable national units achieve global scale by giving them the responsibility of becoming the company's world source for a given product or expertise. And they tap into important technological advances and market developments wherever they are occurring around the globe. They do this by securing the cooperation and involvement of the relevant national units in upgrading the company's technology, developing its new products, and shaping its marketing strategy.

One major consequence of the distribution of assets and responsibilities is that the interdependence of world-wide units automatically increases. Simple structural configurations like the decentralized federation, the coordinated federation, and the centralized hub are inadequate for the task facing the transnational corporation. What is needed is a structure we term the *integrated network* (see Figure 10.5.3).

In the integrated network configuration, national units are no longer viewed only as the end of a delivery pipeline for company products, or as implementors of centrally defined strategies, or even as local adapters and modifiers of corporate approaches. Rather, the assumption behind this configuration is that management should consider each of the world-wide units as a source of ideas, skills, capabilities, and knowledge that can be harnessed for the benefit of the total organization. Efficient local plants may be converted into international production centers; innovative national or regional development labs may be designated the company's 'center of excellence' for a particular product or process development; and creative subsidiary marketing groups may be given a lead role in developing world-wide marketing strategies for certain products or businesses. The company becomes a truly integrated network of distributed and interdependent resources and capabilities.

FIGURE 10.5.3
Integrated Network Model

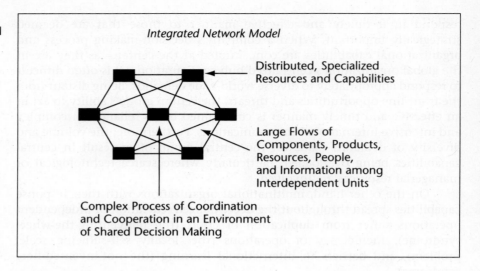

Integrated Network Model

Distributed, Specialized
Resources and Capabilities

Large Flows of
Components, Products,
Resources, People,
and Information among
Interdependent Units

Complex Process of Coordination
and Cooperation in an Environment
of Shared Decision Making

Flexible Integrative Process

Having established management groups representing multiple perspectives to reflect the variety of environmental demands and pressures and a configuration based on distributed and interdependent assets and organizational capabilities, the transnational organization requires a management process that can resolve the diversity of interests and perspectives and integrate the dispersed responsibilities. However, it cannot be bound by the symmetry of organizational process that follows when the task is seen in simplistic or static terms (e.g. 'Should responsibilities be centralized or decentralized?'). It is clear that the benefits to be gained from central control of world-wide research or manufacturing activities may be much more important than those related to the global coordination of the sales and service functions. We have also seen how the pattern of functional coordination varies by business and by geographic area (aircraft engine companies need central control of more decisions than multinational food packagers; operations in developing countries may need more central support than those in advanced countries). Furthermore, all coordination needs change over time due to changes in the international operating environment, the life cycles of products and technologies, or the company's stage of development.

Thus, management must be able to differentiate its operating relationships and change its decision-making roles by function, across businesses, among geographic units, and over time. The management process must be able to change from product to product, from country to country, and even from decision to decision.

This requires the development of rather sophisticated and subtle decision-making machinery based on three different but interdependent management processes. The first is a supportive but constrained escalation process that allows top management to intervene directly in the content of certain decisions – a subtle and carefully managed form of *centralization*. The second is a managed organizational process in which the key management task is to structure individual roles and supportive systems to influence specific key decisions through *formalization*. The third is a self-regulatory capability in which top management's role is to establish a broad culture and set of relationships that provide an appropriate organizational context for delegated decisions – a sophisticated management process driven by *socialization*.

The International Context in International Perspective

> There never were, since the creation of the world, two cases exactly parallel.
>
> (Philip Dormer Stanhope 1694–1773; English Secretary of State)

What a curious title, one might be inclined to think. 'The international context in international perspective' – isn't this a case of the snake biting itself in its own tail? Of course, the answer is no. Just as in all previous chapters, the debate between proponents of the global convergence perspective and those of the international diversity perspective can be viewed from an international angle. The question of interest is whether strategists in certain countries are more inclined towards a specific perspective on the international context than in others. In other words, are there nations where the global convergence perspective is more prevalent, while in other nations the international diversity perspective is more widespread?

This is a tantalizing question, but as before, it must be concluded that little comparative research has been done on the issue. As a stimulus to the debate whether there are national differences in international context perspective, we would like to put forward a number of factors that might be of influence on how the paradox of globalization and localization is dealt with in different countries. It goes without saying that more international comparative research is required before a clear picture can be formed about the actual international differences.

Of course, if the proponents of the global convergence perspective are entirely right, the factors mentioned below will become less and less important as countries grow more similar. All of the international differences in strategic management preferences discussed in the concluding pages of each of the preceding chapters will also wither away. However, if international diversity remains a characteristic of our world, the way strategic management paradoxes are dealt with differently in each country will continue to be an important issue to discuss.

Level of Nationalism

The prospect of global convergence is a dream to some, but a nightmare to others. It is inspiring for those who would like to see a borderless world, in which like-minded people would see eye-to-eye. It is frightening for those who prefer to keep a diverse world, in which local autonomy and the retainment of national culture are highly valued. Although global convergence enthusiasts and detractors can be found in each country, some nations seem more troubled by the prospect of further globalization than others. In some countries the belief is widespread that foreign values, norms, habits and behaviors are being imposed, that are undermining the national culture, and that the country's ability to decide its own fate is being compromised. This leads many to argue that global convergence should be, and will be, curtailed. In other countries such nationalism is far less pronounced, and the advantages of globalization are more widely accepted. In general, it can be expected that strategists from countries with a strong streak of nationalism will gravitate more toward the international diversity perspective, while strategists from less nationalist countries will be more inclined toward the global convergence perspective.

Size of Country

In general, smaller countries are more exposed to the international context than larger countries. Smaller countries commonly export more of their gross domestic product than larger countries, and import more as well. Hence, their companies are more used to dealing with, and adapting to, a high number of foreign suppliers, customers and competitors. Moreover, companies from smaller countries, confronted with a limited home market, are forced to seek growth in foreign markets earlier than their counterparts in larger countries. During this early internationalization, these companies do not have the benefit of scale economies in the home market and therefore are usually more inclined to adapt themselves to the demands of foreign markets. Companies in larger markets normally grow to a significant size at home, thereby achieving certain economies of scale through national standardization, while also establishing a domestically-oriented management style. When they do move abroad, as a more mature company, their international activities will tend to be modest compared to domestic operations and therefore they will be less inclined to be locally adaptive.

It stands to reason that this difference in exposure to the international context has an influence on how strategists from different countries perceive developments in the international context. Generally, strategists from smaller countries, to whom adaptation to international variety has become second nature, will favor the view that international diversity will remain. Strategists from larger countries will be more inclined to emphasize the growing similarities and to seek opportunities for international standardization.

Preference for Central Decision-Making

This point is linked to the debate in the previous chapter, where the paradox of control and chaos was discussed. It was argued that in some countries there is a stronger emphasis on the role of top management in running the firm. In these countries there is usually a strong chain of command, with clear authority and responsibilities, and a well-developed control system. To remain managable from the top, the organization must not become too complex to comprehend and steer. Usually this means that business units are structured along simple lines and that strategy is not too varied by product or geographic area. As soon as each product or geographic area requires its own specific strategy, the ability to run things centrally will diminish. Strategists with a strong preference for central decision-making will therefore be less inclined to acknowledge pressures for local responsiveness. Quite the opposite, they will be searching for opportunities to standardize their approach to different countries, which will allow for a more centralized decision-making structure. Strategists from countries with a tradition of more decentralized decision-making, are more likely to accept international diversity as a workable situation (e.g. Calori, Valla and De Woot, 1994; Turcq, 1994; Yoneyama, 1994).

Further Readings

There have been few writers as radical as Levitt, but quite a large number of stimulating works from the global convergence perspective. A good place for the interested reader to start would be Kenichi Ohmae's *The Borderless World: Power and Strategy in the Interlinked Economy* and George Yip's *Total Global Strategy*. For a stronger balancing of perspectives, the reader should turn to *The Multinational Mission*, by C.K. Prahalad and Yves Doz, and *Competition in Global Industries* by Michael Porter. For a critical review of the globalization literature, *The Logic of International Restructuring*, by Winfried Ruigrok and Rob van Tulder makes for stimulating reading.

Most of this literature emphasizes strategy content issues, while largely neglecting strategy process aspects. A well-known exception is the article 'Strategic Planning for a Global Business,' by Balaji Chakravarthy and Howard Perlmutter. With regard to the management of large international companies, *Managing Across Borders: The Transnational Solution*, by Christopher Bartlett and Sumantra Ghoshal, is highly recommended.

References

Bartlett, C.A., and Ghoshal, S. (1987) Managing across Borders: New Organizational Responses, *Sloan Management Review*, Fall, pp. 43–53.

Bartlett, C.A., and Ghoshal, S. (1989) *Managing Across Borders: The Transnational Solution*, Harvard Business School Press, New York.

Bartlett, C.A., and Ghoshal, S. (1995) *Transnational Management: Text, Cases, and Readings in Cross-Border Management*, second edition, R.D. Irwin Inc.

Calori, R., Valla, J.-P., and de Woot, Ph. (1994) Common Characteristics: The Ingredients of European Management, in Calori, R., and de Woot, Ph. (eds) *A European Management Model*, Prentice Hall, London.

Chakravarthy, B.S., and Perlmutter, H.W. (1985) Strategic Planning for a Global Business, *Columbia Journal of World Business*, Summer, pp. 3–10.

Dosi, G., and Kogut, B. (1993) National Specificities and the Context of Change: 'The Co-evolution of Organization and Technology, in Kogut, B. (ed.), *Country Competitiveness: Technology and the Organizing of Work*, Oxford University Press, Oxford.

Douglas, S.P., and Wind, Y. (1987) The Myth of Globalization, *Columbia Journal of World Business*, Winter, pp. 19–29.

Dunning, J. (1986) *Japanese Participation in British Industry: Trojan Horse or Catalyst for Growth?*, Croom Helm, Dover, NH.

Ghoshal, S., and Nohria, N. (1993) Horses for Courses: Organizational Forms for Multinational Companies, *Sloan Management Review*, Winter, pp. 23–35.

Hamel, G., and Prahalad, C.K. (1985) Do You Really Have a Global Strategy? *Harvard Business Review*, July/August, pp. 139–48.

Hedlund, G. (1986) The Hypermodern MNC – A Heterarchy? *Human Resource Management*, Vol. 25, pp. 9–35.

Hout, T.M., Porter, M.E., and Rudden, E. (1982) How Global Companies Win Out, *Harvard Business Review*, September/October, pp. 98–108.

Kay, J. (1989) Myths and Realities, in Davis, E. *et al*. (eds), *1992, Myths and Realities*, Centre for Business Strategy, London.

Krugman, P.R. (1990) *Rethinking International Trade*, MIT Press.

Kogut, B. (1985) Designing Global Strategies: Comparative and Competitive Value-Added Chains, *Sloan Management Review*, Summer, pp. 15–28.

Kogut, B. (ed.) (1993) *Country Competitiveness: Technology and the Organizing of Work*, Oxford University Press, Oxford.

Levitt, T. (1983) The Globalization of Markets, *Harvard Business Review*, May/June, pp. 92–102.

McGrew, A.G. *et al*. (eds) (1992) *Global Politics: Globalisation and the Nation-State*, Polity Press, Cambridge.

Milner, H. (1988) *Resisting Protectionism: Global Industries and the Politics of International Trade*, Princeton University Press, Princeton.

Morrison, A.J., Ricks, D.A., and Roth, K. (1991) Globalization versus Regionalization: Which Way for the Multinational?, *Organizational Dynamics*, Winter, pp. 17–29.

Ohmae, K. (1989) Managing in a Borderless World, *Harvard Business Review*, May/June, pp. 152–61.

Ohmae, K. (1990) *The Borderless World: Power and Strategy in the Interlinked Economy*, Fontana, London.

Patel, P., and Pavitt, K. (1991) Large Firms in the Production of the World's

Technology: An Important Case of 'Non-Globalisation', *Journal of International Business Studies*, no. 1, pp. 1–21.

Pitt, M. (1996) IKEA of Sweden: the Global Retailer, in Baden-Fuller, C., and Pitt, M. *Strategic Innovation*, Routledge, London.

Porter, M.E. (1986) *Competition in Global Industries*, Free Press, New York.

Porter, M.E. (1990) *The Competitive Advantage of Nations*, Macmillan, London.

Porter, M.E. (1990) New Global Strategies for Competitive Advantage, *Planning Review*, May/June, pp. 4–14.

Prahalad, C.K., and Doz, Y. (1987) *The Multinational Mission: Balancing Local Demands and Global Vision*, Free Press, New York.

Reich, R. (1991) *The Work of Nations: Preparing Ourselves for 21st Century Capitalism*, Alfred Knopf, New York.

Ruigrok, W., and van Tulder, R. (1995) *The Logic of International Restructuring*, Routledge, London.

Stopford, J.M., and Wells, L.T. (1972) *Strategy and Structure of Multinational Enterprise*, Basic Books, New York.

Teece, D.J. (1981) The Multinational Enterprise: Market Failure and Market Power Considerations, *Sloan Management Review*, Spring, pp. 4–17.

Turcq, D. (1994) Is There a US Company Management Style in Europe?, in Calori, R., and de Woot Ph. (eds), *A European Management Model*, Prentice Hall, London.

Vernon, R. (1966) International Investment and International Trade in the Product Life Cycle, *Quarterly Journal of Economics*, pp. 190–207.

Vernon, R., and Wells, L.T. (1986) *The Economic Environment of International Business*, 4th edn, Prentice Hall, Englewood Cliffs, NJ.

Welch, L.S., and Luostarinen, R. (1988) Internationalization: Evolution of a Concept, *Journal of General Management*, Winter, pp. 34–55.

Wortzel, L.H. (1990) Global Strategies: Standardization versus Flexibility, in Vernon-Wortzel, H., and Wortzel, L.H. (eds), *Global Strategic Management*, Wiley, New York.

Yip, G.S. (1993) *Total Global Strategy: Managing for Worldwide Competitive Advantage,* Prentice Hall, London.

Yoneyama, E. (1994) Japanese Subsidiaries: Strengths and Weaknesses, in Calori, R., and de Woot Ph. (eds), *A European Management Model*, Prentice Hall, London.

Purpose

❏   11 Organizational Purpose

Organizational Purpose

Corporation, *n. An ingenious device for*
obtaining individual profit without
individual responsibility.

(*The Devil's Dictionary*, Ambrose Bierce 1842 – 1914; American columnist)

A business that makes nothing but money
is a poor kind of business.

(Henry Ford 1863–1947; American industrialist)

The Paradox of Profitability and Responsibility

In Chapter 2 it was argued that strategy can be broadly conceived as a course of action for achieving an organization's purpose. Subsequently, nine chapters were spent looking at strategy from many different angles, but relatively little explicit attention was paid to the fundamental issue of organizational purpose – the focus was on means, not on ends. The various authors debated how to set a course for the organizational vessel through turbulent waters, but few raised the issue of why the journey was being undertaken in the first place. This lack of attention for the topic of organizational purpose may in part be due to the assumption by many that it is obvious why organizations exist. Others may avoid the topic because it is highly value-laden and somehow outside the realm of strategic management.

Yet, in practice, strategists must constantly seek solutions and make choices based on an understanding of what the organization is intended to achieve. Strategists are confronted by many different claimants, who believe that the organization exists to serve their interests. The demands placed on the organization by shareholders, employees, suppliers, customers, governments and communities must be weighed and priorities must be set, to guide organizational decision making. It is hardly possible for strategists to avoid taking a stance on what they judge to be the purpose of the organization. The topic of organizational purpose is not an irrelevant ivory tower subject, but an essential issue facing strategists. Therefore, a debate on organizational purpose in this chapter is justified and should prove valuable to both practitioners and academics.

Clearly, the debate on organizational purpose is not limited to the field of strategic management. Given the influential position of business organizations in modern society, the purpose they should serve is also discussed by theorists in the fields of economics, political science, sociology, ethics and philosophy. The enormous impact of corporations on the functioning of society also attracts political parties, labor unions, community representatives, environmentalists, the media and the general public to the debate. All take a position on the role that business organizations should play within society and the responsibilities that they ought to shoulder. In countries with a market economy, it is generally accepted that companies should pursue profitability, but also have certain responsibilities that must be fulfilled. But this is where the consensus ends. Opinions differ sharply with regard to the question to whom business organizations should be responsible and what the relative importance of profitability and responsibility should be.

Both within the field of strategic management, as in broader society, a wide variety of views exists on what the purpose of organizations should be. Although there are many aspects to this debate, the central tension appears to be between profitability and responsibility. These two elements seem to present a paradox, as they place partially conflicting and maybe even mutually exclusive pressures on firms. When focusing on this key aspect of the debate, a spectrum of opinions can be identified spanning the middle ground between two radically opposite points of view. At the one pole of the debate are those people who argue that corporations are established to serve the purposes of their owners. Generally, it is in the best interest of a corporation's shareholders to see the value of their stocks increase through the organization's pursuit of profitable business strategies. This point of view is commonly referred to as the *shareholder value* perspective. At the other end of the spectrum are those people who argue that corporations should be seen as joint ventures between shareholders, employees, banks, customers, suppliers, governments and the community. All of these parties hold a stake in the organization and therefore can expect that the corporation will take as its responsibility to develop business strategies that are in accordance with their interests and values. This point of view will be referred to as the *stakeholder values* perspective.

As before, this chapter will explore the topic under discussion by following a debate model. First, the two opposite ways of dealing with the paradox of profitability and responsibility will be compared, and then summarized in Table 11.1. Subsequently, five readings will be presented to kick off a 'virtual debate'.

The Shareholder Value Perspective

To proponents of the shareholder value perspective it is obvious that companies belong to their owners and therefore should act in accordance with the interests of the owners. Corporations are instruments, who's purpose it is to create economic value on behalf of those who invest risk-taking capital in the enterprise. This clear purpose should drive companies, irregardless of whether the are privately or publicly held. According to Rappaport (1986: xiii; see reading 11.1), 'the idea that business strategies should be judged by the economic value they create for shareholders is well accepted in the business community. After all, to suggest that companies be operated in the best interests of its owners is hardly controversial.'

There is some disagreement between advocates of this perspective with regard to the best way of advancing the interests of the shareholders, particularly in publicly held companies. Many people taking this point of view argue that the well-being of the shareholders is served if the strategy of a company leads to higher share prices and/or higher dividends (e.g. Hart, 1995; Rappaport, 1986, reading 11.1). Others are less certain of the stock markets' ability to correctly value long-term investments, such as R&D spending and capital expenditures. In their view, the stock markets are excessively concerned with the short term and therefore share prices myopically overemphasize current results and heavily discount investments for the future. To avoid being pressured into short-termism, these people advocate that strategists must keep only one eye on the share prices, while the other is focused on the long-term horizon (e.g. Charkham, 1994; Sykes, 1994).

According to supporters of the shareholder value perspective, one of the major challenges in large corporations is to actually get top management to pursue the shareholders' interests. Where ownership and managerial control over a company have become separated, it is often difficult to get the managers to work on behalf of the shareholders, instead of letting their self-interest prevail. This is known as the *principal–agent* problem (e.g. Jensen and Meckling, 1976; Eisenhardt, 1989) – the managers are agents, working to further the interests of their principals, the shareholders, but are tempted to serve their own interests, even when this is to the detriment of the principal. This has led to a widespread debate in the academic and business communities, especially in Britain and the United States, about the best form of *corporate governance*. The subject of corporate governance, as opposed to corporate management, deals with the issue of governing the behavior of top management. The most important players in corporate governance are the outside, or non-executive, members on the board of directors. It is one of the tasks of these outsiders to check whether the executives are truly running the company in a way that maximizes the shareholders' wealth. For this reason, many proponents of the shareholder value perspective call for a majority of independent-minded outside directors in the board, preferably owning significant amounts of the company's stock themselves.

The emphasis placed on profitability as the fundamental purpose of firms does not mean that supporters of the shareholder value perspective are blind to the demands placed on firms by other stakeholders. On the contrary, most exponents of this view argue that it is in the interest of the shareholders to do a stakeholder analysis and even to actively manage stakeholder relations. Knowing the force field of stakeholders constraining the freedom of the company is important information for the strategy process. It is never advisable to ignore important external claimants such as labor unions, environmental activists, bankers, governmental agencies and community groups. Few strategists would doubt that proactive engagement is preferable to 'corporate isolationism'. However, recognizing that it is expedient to pay attention to stakeholders does not mean that it is the corporation's purpose to serve them. If parties have a strong bargaining position, a firm might be forced into all types of concessions, sacrificing profitability, but this has little to do with any moral responsibility of the firm towards these other powers. The only duty of a company is to maximize shareholder value, within the boundaries of what is legally permissible.

The important conclusion is that in this perspective it might be in the interest of shareholders to treat stakeholders well, but that there is no moral obligation to do so. For instance, it might be a good move for a troubled company not to lay off workers if the resulting loyalty and morale improve the chances of recovery and profitability later on. In this case the decision not to fire workers is based on profit-motivated calculation, not on a sense of moral responsibility towards the employees. Generally, proponents of the shareholder value perspective argue that society is best served by this type of economic rationale. By pursuing enlightened self-interest and maintaining market-based relationships between the firm and all stakeholders, societal wealth will be maximized. Responsibility for employment, local communities, the environment, consumer welfare and social developments are not an organizational matter, but issues for individuals and governments (see Friedman, 1970, for the classic argument).

The Stakeholder Values Perspective

Advocates of the stakeholder values perspective do not see why the supplier of one ingredient in an economic value creation process has a stronger moral claim on the organization than the providers of other inputs. They challenge the assumption that individuals with an equity stake in a corporation have the right to demand that the entire organization work on their behalf. In the stakeholder values perspective, a company should not be seen as the instrument of shareholders, but as a coalition between various resource suppliers, with the intention of increasing their common wealth. An organization should be regarded as a joint-venture in which the suppliers of equity, loans, labor, management, expertise, parts and service all participate to achieve economic success. As all groups hold a stake in the joint-venture and are mutually dependent, it is argued that the purpose of the organization is to serve the interests of all parties involved (e.g. Berle and Means, 1932; Freeman and Reed, 1983; reading 11.2).

According to endorsers of the stakeholder values perspective, shareholders have a legitimate interest in the firm's profitability. However, the emphasis shareholders place on stock price appreciation and dividends must be balanced against the legitimate demands of the other partners. These demands are not only financial, as in the case of the shareholders, but also qualitative, reflecting different values held by different groups. For instance, employees might place a high value on job security, occupational safety, holidays and working conditions, while a supplier of parts might prefer secure demand, joint innovation, shared risk-taking and prompt payment. Of course, balancing these interests is a challenging task, requiring an ongoing process of negotiation and compromise. The outcome will in part depend on the bargaining power of each stakeholder – how essential is their input to the economic success of the organization? However, the extent to which a stakeholder's interests are pursued will also depend on the perceived legitimacy of their claim. For instance, employees usually have a strong moral claim because they are heavily dependent on the organization and have a relatively low mobility, while most shareholders have a spread portfolio and can exit the corporation with a phone call (e.g. Stone, 1975).

In this view of organizational purpose, strategists must recognize their responsibility towards all constituents (e.g. Clarkson, 1995; Alkhafaji, 1989). Maximizing shareholder value to the detriment of the other stakeholders would be unjust. Strategists in the firm have a moral obligation to consider the interests and values of all joint-venture partners. Managing stakeholder demands is not merely a pragmatic means to running a profitable business – serving stakeholders is an end in itself. These two interpretations of stakeholder management are often confused. Where it is primarily viewed as an approach or technique for dealing with the essential participants in the value-adding process, stakeholder management is *instrumental*. But if it is based on the fundamental notion that the organization's purpose is to serve the stakeholders, then stakeholder management is *normative* (e.g. Buono and Nichols, 1985; Donaldson and Preston, 1995).

Most proponents of the stakeholder values perspective argue that, ultimately, pursuing the joint interests of all stakeholders it is not only more just, but also more effective for organizations (e.g. Jones, 1995; Solomon, 1992). Few stakeholders are filled with a sense of mission to go out and maximize shareholder value, especially if shareholders bear no responsibility for the other stakeholders' interests (e.g. Campbell and Yeung, 1991; reading 11.5; Collins and Porras, 1994). It is difficult to work as a motivated team, if it is the purpose of the organization to serve only one group's interests. Furthermore, without a stakeholder values perspective, there will be a deep-rooted lack of trust between all of the parties involved in the enterprise. Each stakeholder will assume that the others are solely motivated by self-interest and are tentatively cooperating in a calculative manner. All parties will perceive a constant risk that the others will use their power to gain a bigger slice of the pie, or even rid themselves of their 'partners'. The consequence is that all stakeholders will vigorously guard their own interests and will interact with one another as adversaries. To advocates of the stakeholder values perspective, this 'every person for themselves' model of organizations is clearly inferior to the partnership model, in which sharing, trust and symbiosis are emphasized. Cooperation between stakeholders is much more effective than competition (note the link with the embedded organization perspective in Chapter 7).

Some exponents of the stakeholder values perspective argue that the narrow economic definition of stakeholders given above is too constrictive. In their view, the circle of stakeholders with a legitimate claim on the organization should be drawn more widely. Not only should the organization be responsible to the direct participants in the economic value creation process (the *primary stakeholders*), but also to all parties affected by the organization's activities. For example, an organization's behavior might have an impact on local communities, governments, the environment and society in general, and therefore these groups have a stake in what the organization does. Most supporters of the stakeholder values perspective acknowledge that organizations have a moral responsibility towards these *secondary stakeholders* (e.g. Carroll, 1993; Langtry, 1994). However, opinions differ whether it should actually be a part of business organizations' purpose to serve this broader body of constituents.

The implication of this view for corporate governance is that the board of directors should be able to judge whether the interests of all stakeholders are being justly balanced. This has led some advocates of the stakeholder values perspective to call for representatives of the most important stakeholder groups in the board (e.g. Guthrie and Turnbull, 1994). Others argue more narrowly for a stronger influence of employees on the choices made by organizations (e.g. Buchholz, 1986; Blair, 1995). Such *co-determination* of the corporation's strategy by management and workers can, for instance, be encouraged by establishing work councils (a type of organizational parliament or senate), as the European Union proposes. Yet others emphasize measures to strengthen corporate social responsibility in general. To improve *corporate social performance*, it is argued, companies should be encouraged to adopt internal policy processes that promote ethical behavior and responsiveness to societal issues (e.g. Epstein, 1987; Wartick and Wood, 1997). Corporate responsibility should not be, to quote Ambrose Bierce's sarcastic definition, 'a detachable burden easily shifted to the shoulders of God, Fate, Fortune, Luck, or one's neighbor.'

Given these arguments for the two perspectives – shareholder value versus stakeholder values – the question for strategists is which one to choose. Should it be the purpose of business organizations to pursue profitability on behalf of their owners? Or should firms serve the interests and promote the values of all of their stakeholders in a balanced way? It is clear that both theorists and practitioners sharply disagree, again placing readers in the position of needing to make up their own minds. Readers themselves will have to come to terms with the paradox of profitability and responsibility (see Table 11.1).

TABLE 11.1
Shareholder value versus
stakeholder values
perspective

	Shareholder Value Perspective	Stakeholder Values Perspective
Emphasis on	Profitability over responsibility	Responsibility over profitability
Organizations seen as	Instruments	Joint-ventures
Organizational purpose	To serve owner	To serve all parties involved
Measure of success	Share price & dividends (shareholder value)	Satisfaction among stakeholders
Major difficulty	Getting agent to pursue principal's interests	Balancing interests of various stakeholders
Corporate governance through	Independent outside directors with shares	Stakeholder representation
Stakeholder management	Means	End and means
Social responsibility	Individual, not organizational matter	Both individual and organizational
Society best served by	Pursuing self-interest (economic efficiency)	Pursuing joint-interests (economic symbiosis)

Defining the Issues: Mission and Governance

Before proceeding with the 'debate' between proponents of the shareholder value and stakeholder values perspectives, it is useful to clarify the key topics under dispute. As will be seen, the disagreements in this discussion revolve around two key issues. First, the two sides take a different view on the reasons why companies exist and the business philosophy that should guide strategic choices. This is referred to as the issues of *corporate mission*. Second, there is no agreement on who should determine the corporate mission and who should ensure that strategies pursued are in accordance with the mission. This is referred to as the issue of *corporate governance*. In the next few paragraphs, these two issues will be further explored, to set the stage for the 'debate readings' that follow.

Purpose, Mission and Vision

Organizational purpose can be defined as the reason for which an organization exists. It can be expected that the perception that strategists have of their organization's purpose will give direction to the strategy process and influence the strategy content. Sometimes strategists might consciously reflect on, or question, the organizational purpose as they make strategic choices. However, more often their view of the organization's purpose will be a part of the broader business philosophy that steers their decision making. This enduring set of fundamental principles guiding strategic decision making in a firm is referred to as the *corporate mission*.

The corporate mission encompasses the basic points of departure that send the organization in a particular direction (from the Latin *mittere* – to send; Cummings and Davies, 1994). The purpose of an organization is arguably the most important point of departure for strategy making, but also influential are the values embodied in an organization's culture (e.g. McCoy, 1985; Collins and Porras, 1994). The values shared by an organization's members will shape what is seen as ethical behavior and moral responsibilities, and therefore have an impact on strategic choices (e.g. Falsey, 1989; Hoffman, 1989). Other authors emphasize 'hard' strategy principles as points of departure for the strategy process. Often mentioned is the need to define the businesses on which the corporation wishes to focus its efforts (e.g. Abell, 1980; Pearce, 1982). Others mention competitive ambitions or intentions as an important part of the mission (e.g. Bartlett and Ghoshal, 1994; Hamel and Prahalad, 1989). Campbell and Yeung (1991; reading 11.5) bring all of these elements together in one framework.

The corporate mission can be articulated by means of a *mission statement*, but in practice not everything that is called a mission statement meets the above criteria (see David, 1989; Piercy and Morgan, 1994). However, firms can have a mission, even if it has not been explicitly encoded on paper, although this increases the chance of divergent interpretations within the organization.

In general, the corporate mission plays three important roles for a business organization. These roles are:

1   *Direction*. The corporate mission can point the organization in a certain direction, by defining the boundaries within which strategic choices and actions must take place. By specifying the fundamental principles on which strategies must be based, the corporate mission limits the scope of strategic options and sets the organization on a particular heading (e.g. Bourgeois and Brodwin, 1983; reading 9.3; Hax, 1990; reading 1.2).

2   *Legitimization*. The corporate mission can convey to all stakeholders inside and outside the company that the organization is pursuing valuable activities in a proper way. By specifying the business philosophy that will guide the company, it is hoped that stakeholders will accept, support and trust the organization (e.g. Klemm, Sanderson and Luffman, 1991; Freeman and Gilbert, 1988).

3   *Motivation*. The corporate mission can go a step further than legitimization, by actually inspiring individuals to work together in a particular way. By specifying the fundamental principles driving organizational actions, an *esprit de corps* can evolve, with the powerful capacity to motivate people over a prolonged period of time (e.g. Campbell and Yeung, 1991; reading 11.5; Peters and Waterman, 1982).

A concept that is often confused with mission is *vision*. Individuals or organizations have a vision if they picture a future state of affairs they wish to achieve (from the Latin *vide* – to see; Cummings and Davies, 1994). While the corporate mission outlines the basic points of departure, a corporate vision outlines the desired future at which the company hopes to arrive. In other words, vision provides a business aim, while mission provides a business philosophy.

Generally, a company vision is a type of goal that is less specific than an objective. Vision is usually defined as a broad conception of a desirable future state, of which the details must still be determined (e.g. Senge, 1990; reading 4.4; Collins and Porras, 1996). As such, corporate vision can play the same type of roles as corporate mission. A corporate vision can point the firm in a particular direction, can legitimize the organization's existence and actions, and can motivate individuals to work together towards a shared end.

Corporate Governance

While the first question in this debate is '*What* should be the corporate mission?', the second question is '*Who* should determine the corporate mission and regulate the activities of the corporation?'. This second issue is that of corporate governance. The subject of corporate governance, as opposed to corporate management, deals with the issue of governing the strategic choices and actions of top management. Popularly stated, corporate governance is about managing top management – building in checks and balances to ensure that the senior executives pursue strategies that are in accordance with the corporate mission. Corporate governance encompasses all tasks and activities that are intended to supervise and steer the behavior of top management.

In the common definition, corporate governance 'addresses the issues facing boards of directors' (Tricker, 1994: xi). In this view, corporate governance is the task of the directors and therefore attention must be paid to their roles and responsibilities (e.g. Cochran and Wartick, 1994; Keasey, Thompson and Wright, 1997). Others have argued that this definition is too narrow, and that in practice there are more forces that govern the activities of top management. In this broader view, boards of directors are only a part of the *governance system*. For instance, regulation by local and national authorities, as well as pressure from societal groups, can function as the checks and balances limiting top management's discretion (e.g. Mintzberg, 1984; Demb and Neubauer, 1992; reading 11.4).

Whether employing a narrow or broad definition, three important corporate governance functions can be distinguished (adapted from Tricker, 1994):

■ *Forming function.* The first function of corporate governance is to influence the forming of the corporate mission. The task of corporate governance is to shape, articulate and communicate the fundamental principles that will drive the organization's activities. Determining the purpose of the organization and setting priorities among claimants are part of the forming function. The board of directors can conduct this task by, for example, questioning the basis of strategic choices, influencing the business philosophy, and explicitly weighing the advantages and disadvantages of the firm's strategies for various constituents (e.g. Freeman and Reed, 1983; reading 11.2; Yoshimori, 1995; reading 11.3).

- *Performance function.* The second function of corporate governance is to contribute to the strategy process with the intention of improving the future performance of the corporation. The task of corporate governance is to judge strategy initiatives brought forward by top management and/ or to actively participate in strategy development. The board of directors can conduct this task by, for example, engaging in strategy discussions, acting as a sounding board for top management, and networking to secure the support of vital stakeholders (e.g. Baysinger and Hoskisson, 1990; Donaldson and Davis, 1995; Zahra and Pearce, 1989).

- *Conformance function.* The third function of corporate governance is to ensure corporate conformance to the stated mission and strategy. The task of corporate governance is to monitor whether the organization is undertaking activities as promised and whether performance is satisfactory. Where management is found lacking, it is a function of corporate governance to press for changes. The board of directors can conduct this task by, for example, auditing the activities of the corporation, questioning and supervising top management, determining remuneration and incentive packages, and even appointing new managers (e.g. Parkinson, 1993; Spencer, 1983).

To whom these functions should be given is the second issue central to the debate in this chapter. More than all other debates in this book, the disagreements between the proponents of the two perspectives are strongly influenced by national culture. Each country has its own system of corporate governance and the international differences are significant. Therefore, in this chapter the international perspective cannot be held back until the end of the debate, but must be dealt with from the very beginning. Two readings have been selected to explicitly introduce the international dimension to the debate, as will be explained in the next paragraph.

EXHIBIT 11.1
Daimler-Benz Short Case

DAIMLER-BENZ: BURNT AT THE STAKE?

On January 6, 1997, Jürgen Schrempp, Chairman of Daimler-Benz AG, stepped forward to address the members of the Economic Club of Detroit. He spoke at length of the major changes being implemented within Daimler-Benz, the largest industrial company in Germany. His message was clear:

> We have learned in Europe the same lessons you all have, there's no hiding from the global economy. We must go out to meet it, by unshackling the creativity of our employees and managers and encouraging them to be the best they can be.

He continued by explaining how his Stuttgart-based corporation was adopting measures to restructure after taking a $4.5 billion loss over 1995. This heavily disappointing financial result, the worst in the company's long history, had for a large part been due to major write-offs in the company's aerospace unit, DASA. The collapse of defense spending had hit DASA hard and had necessitated major reorganizations, the outsourcing of production to low wage US locations, wage concessions and a reduction in the DASA workforce from 40,000 to 25,000 employees. DASA had also been forced to halt financial support to its ailing regional aircraft manufacturing affiliate, Fokker, in which it held a 51 percent controlling stake. This withdrawal, which led to Fokker's bankruptcy, cost Daimler-Benz about $1.55 billion. Furthermore, Schrempp had divested Dornier aircraft and had pushed through a restructuring of the corporation's AEG electrical engineering subsidiary, which had cost another $1.1 billion. Luckily, the company's core business of Mercedes-Benz cars and trucks, good for 80 percent of the $75 billion in revenues, had been reasonably profitable. He carried on:

> All the changes I have mentioned were aggravating and painful for a German company and for our people. And, may I add, far from popular. The initial reaction demonstrated the obvious contrast in perceptions between the German public, trade unions, politicians and media on the one hand, and the international financial community on the other. Germany has been historically an economic success because we achieved a system of pragmatic consensus between labor and business. This emphasis on social stability paid off for the Germans. The model used to provide fast and continuously growing prosperity . . . I want to repeat that the German system of consensus should under no circumstances be abandoned . . . We need to modify the 'German model' so that we not only reap the benefits of consensus but also adapt ourselves successfully to a world that has significantly changed . . .
>
> While in Germany we initially faced criticism and there was a lack of understanding for our actions, the international financial markets responded positively. This year we achieved a 40 percent increase in the value of our shares. And I like to think that the consistent rise in our share price in recent months is a result of the growing trust of the financial markets.

A part of this trust was due to the promising strategies being pursued by Daimler-Benz and the wave of new products hitting the market. Schrempp could point to the sophisticated and stylish Mercedes-Benz CLK coupe being premiered in Detroit, but also to the new SLK roadster, which had just been awarded the title of 1997 North America car of the year. Schrempp was also proud of the new M-Class sport utility vehicle, set to be produced at Mercedes' brand new production facility in Tuscaloosa, Alabama. In the pipeline were also the A-Class compact Mercedes (more affectionately known as the 'Baby Benz') and the even smaller Smart car. The Mercedes-Benz truck division, together with its American Freightliner subsidiary, were also doing well and had the position of world market leader in sales. Daimler's railroad systems joint-venture with ABB, Adtranz, also occupied the global top spot. Furthermore, it was starting to look more likely that the Airbus consortium in which DASA participated, would be reformed into a stronger, unified company.

Daimler-Benz had also significantly improved its standing in the international financial community by boldly going where no German company had gone before – to Wall Street. In 1993 the company had negotiated a deal with the Securities and Exchange Commission to get a listing on the New York Stock Exchange. This deal pushed Daimler-Benz to adopt US generally accepted accounting principles (GAAP), in return for exemption from the rules requiring the publication of quarterly results. The importance of this switch in bean counting method became directly obvious in the first year of reporting. In 1994 Daimler's German accounts showed a DM500 million profit, while in the US a DM2 billion loss was reported. Since then, the company had introduced a new system of performance measurement and management accounting that aligns internal and external reporting based on US GAAP.

Even more importantly, Schrempp had openly professed his dedication to creating shareholder value. Each business unit within Daimler-Benz had been given the task of achieving a minimum return on capital employed of 12 percent by 1998 and were instructed to aim for profitability levels close to those of their most profitable competitors. According to analysts, this conversion to the importance of shareholder value was not only instigated by pressures from Wall Street, but also from Deutsche Bank, the company's largest shareholder. Deutsche Bank has a 24 percent share of Daimler-Benz, worth roughly $6 billion, and its chief executive, Hilmar Kopper, is the chairman of Daimler's *aufsichtsrat* (board of supervisors). Since Deutsche Bank has a poor return on capital of approximately 8 percent, compared to 20 percent at many large American banks such as Citicorp, Kopper is rumoured to be pressing Daimler-Benz to place more emphasis on profitability. To his Detroit audience Schrempp remarked:

> Profitability can no longer be a ghost word in Europe. Only profitable companies can ensure jobs and benefits. However, we do not think of profitability over the short-term . . . Value is not created just by paying out dividends to shareholders. Value creation is organic to a growing and profitable business.

However, Schrempp had to admit that the German labor unions, media, politicians and general public were slow at accepting Daimler's new message. In some circles, reactions had been vehement – just short of burning top management at the stake. At the other end, however, there were some shareholder activists, mainly in the US, arguing that Schrempp hadn't gone far enough. Criticisms were also levelled at the corporate governance structure at Daimler, where the twenty-person board of supervisors included only two people with experience in running a major manufacturer (half the board, by law, consists of labor representatives). Schrempp's position, he stated in his address, was to balance the two extremes:

> The imperatives that drive Anglo-American business are also making shareholder value an issue for European industry. However, we cannot simply graft Anglo-American business practices on to European industry. Rather, we must harness the best elements of both worlds.

As Schrempp concluded his speech, and the audience applauded, many in the room were impressed by Schrempp's words. But some wondered whether striving to get the 'best of both worlds' isn't a recipe for getting 'stuck in the middle'.

Sources: *The Economist*, February 15 1997; *Forbes*, April 22 1996; *Business Week*, February 5 1996

The Debate and the Readings

Selecting the first reading to represent the shareholder value perspective was a simple task. Alfred Rappaport's highly influential book *Creating Shareholder Value* is the classic reading in the field. Although the largest part of his book details how the shareholder value approach can be applied to planning and performance evaluation processes, the first chapter is a compelling exposition of his underlying views on the purpose of a business organization. This first chapter, entitled 'Shareholder Value and Corporate Purpose', has been reprinted here. Rappaport's argument is straightforward – the primary purpose of corporations should be to maximize shareholder value. Therefore, 'business strategies should be judged by the economic returns they generate for shareholders, as measured by dividends plus the increase in the company's share price.' Unlike some other proponents of the shareholder value perspective, Rappaport does not explicitly claim that shareholders have the moral right to demand the primacy of profitability. His argument is more pragmatic – failing to meet the objective of maximizing shareholder value will be punished by more expensive financing. A company's financial power is ultimately determined by the stock markets. Hence, management's ability to meet the demands of the various corporate constituencies depends on the continuing support of its shareholders. Creating shareholder value, therefore, precedes the satisfaction of all other claims on the corporation. It should be noted, however, that Rappaport's arrows are not directed at the demands of employees, customers, suppliers or debtholders, but at top management. He carefully states that senior executives may in some situations pursuit objectives that are not to the benefit of shareholders. His preferred solution is not to change corporate governance structures, but to more tightly align the interests of both groups, for example by giving top managers a relatively large ownership position and by tying their compensation to shareholder return performance (in later writings he does favor more structural reforms, e.g. Rappaport, 1990).

The opening reading on behalf of the stakeholder values perspective is also a classic, 'Stockholders and Stakeholders: A New Perspective on Corporate Governance,' by Edward Freeman and David Reed. This article in *California Management Review* and Freeman's subsequent book *Strategic Management: A Stakeholder Approach* were instrumental in popularizing the stakeholder concept. In their article, Freeman and Reed challenge 'the view that stockholders have a privileged place in the business enterprise.' They deplore the fact that 'it has long been gospel that corporations have obligations to stockholders . . . that are sacrosanct and inviolable.' They argue that there has also been a long tradition of management thinkers who believe that corporations have a broader responsibility towards other stakeholders than only the suppliers of equity financing. It is their conviction that such a definition of the corporation, as a system serving the interests of multiple stakeholders, is superior to the shareholder perspective. Their strong preference for the stakeholder concept is largely based on the pragmatic argument that in reality stakeholders have the power to seriously affect the continuity of the corporation. Stakeholder analysis is needed to understand the actual claims placed by constituents on the firm and to evaluate each stakeholder's power position. Stakeholder management is a practical response to the fact that corporations cannot afford to ignore or downplay the interests of the claimants. Only here and there do Freeman and Reed hint that corporations have the moral responsibility to work on behalf of all stakeholders (which Freeman does more explicitly in some of his later works, e.g. Freeman and Gilbert, 1988; Freeman and Liedtka, 1991). In their opinion, the consequence of the stakeholder concept for corporate governance is that 'there are times when stakeholders must participate in the decision-making process.' However, they believe that if boards of directors adopt a stakeholder outlook and become more responsive to the demands placed on corporations, structural reforms to give stakeholders a stronger role in corporate governance will not be necessary.

The third reading is intended to bring the international perspective directly into the debate, instead of introducing possible cross-cultural differences at the end of the chapter. The title of the article by Masaru Yoshimori, 'Whose Company Is It? The Concept of the Corporation in Japan and the West,' reflects the essence of the debate on corporate purpose. The ultimate issue dividing the shareholder value and stakeholder values perspectives is their conception of organization ownership. Yoshimori has looked at this issue by asking middle managers in Britain, France, Germany, the US, and Japan the simple question 'In whose interest should the firm be managed?'. He reports that the countries studied fall into three categories. In Britain and the US the shareholder value perspective, which he refers to as the monistic concept of the corporation, is most prevalent. In Japan, on the other hand, the stakeholder values perspective is by far the predominant outlook. In the Japanese pluralistic concept of the corporation, the employees' interests take precedence, closely followed by those of the main banks, major suppliers, subcontractors, and distributors. According to Yoshimori, most managers in Germany and France exhibit a dualistic concept of the corporation, in which shareholder and employee interests are both taken into consideration. Yoshimori carries on to explain the most important differences between these five countries, and he weighs the costs and benefits of each. He concludes that in all countries corporate governance is poorly developed, and that nations have a lot to learn from one another. In his opinion, international cross-fertilization will lead to a partial convergence of corporate governance systems in the various countries. However, 'the concept of the corporation is firmly rooted in the historic, economic, political and even socio-cultural traditions of the nation,' and therefore it is improbable 'that any one concept should drive out another at least in the foreseeable future.'

Another excellent contribution to the international debate on corporate governance is the book *The Corporate Board: Confronting the Paradoxes*, by Ada Demb and Friedrich Neubauer. From this book the introductory chapter on the nature of corporate governance, entitled 'Corporate Governance: Lifespace and Accountability,' has been selected as contribution to the discussion here. More than the previous three readings, this work by Demb and Neubauer explores the various aspects of corporate governance and relates them to the topic of organizational purpose. Demb and Neubauer take a broad view of corporate governance, as reaching 'far beyond the role of the board into the fundamental issue of the appropriate role for the corporation in today's society.' In their view, all nations have developed their own governance mechanisms to enforce corporate accountability to society at large. Boards of directors are one such mechanism of corporate governance, but other means are also employed to ensure that companies function in accordance with societal expectations. Governments can regulate corporate activities where necessary, or interest groups can attempt to pressure companies into a particular type of behavior. Various groups can also try to influence who owns corporations, with the intention of getting a better grip on corporate decision making. All of these elements together constitute a nation's governance system. According to Demb and Neubauer such national governance systems vary significantly from country to country, reflecting major differences in deeply held cultural values. They carry on by describing the most important international differences in approach to corporate governance. In the context of this chapter, the conclusion that can be drawn from this reading is that there are strong national inclinations towards the shareholder value or stakeholder values perspective. As came forward in Yoshimori's article, positions in the debate on organizational purpose differ sharply across cultures.

The final reading is 'Creating a Sense of Mission,' by Andrew Campbell and Sally Yeung. This article has been added to the debate to emphasize the importance of having a powerful mission. Campbell and Yeung argue that effective missions are capable of winning the 'hearts' and 'minds' of an organization's members. Winning the minds of people within a company requires the determination of strategy principles that will provide a compelling commercial logic for the firm. Winning the hearts of people requires the enshrining of values to which people can feel emotionally, morally, and ethically committed. If the commercial rationale, or left-brain reasoning, fits with the emotional, or right-brain reasoning, Campbell and Yeung believe a company may have a forceful mission. Essential in tying together the commercial and emotional elements of a mission, according to Campbell and Yeung, is a shared sense of corporate purpose. Where all of these elements of mission are linked tightly together, Campbell and Yeung expect members of the organization to be highly motivated to work toward a common direction – to be driven by a sense of mission. In the context of the debate in this chapter, the question is whether both perspectives are capable of eliciting the same sense of mission.

11.1   Shareholder Value and Corporate Purpose

By Alfred Rappaport[1]

Corporate mission statements proclaiming that the primary responsibility of management is to maximize shareholders' total return via dividends and increases in the market price of the company's shares abound. While the principle that the fundamental objective of the business corporation is to increase the value of its shareholders' investment is widely accepted, there is substantially less agreement about how this is accomplished.

On the cover of its 1984 annual report Coca-Cola states that 'to increase shareholder value over time is the objective driving this enterprise'. On the very next page the company goes on to say that to accomplish its objective 'growth in annual earnings per share and increased return on equity are still the names of the game.' In contrast, Hillenbrand Industries, a producer of caskets and hospital equipment, also declares its intention to provide a superior return to its shareholders, but to accomplish that objective management is focusing not on earnings but rather on creating 'shareholder value,' which, it explains in the 1984 annual report, 'is created when a company generates free cash flow in excess of the shareholders' investment in the business.'

Both Coca-Cola and Hillenbrand Industries acknowledge their responsibility to maximize return to their respective shareholders. However, Coca-Cola emphasizes accounting indicators, earnings-per-share growth, and return on equity, while Hillenbrand Industries emphasizes the cash-flow based shareholder value approach to achieve shareholder returns. There are material differences between these two approaches to assessing a company's investment opportunities. Maximizing earnings-per-share growth or other accounting numbers may not necessarily lead to maximizing return for shareholders.

The Growing Interest

Numerous surveys indicate that a majority of the largest industrial companies have employed the shareholder value approach in capital budgeting for some time. Capital budgeting applications deal with investment projects such as capacity additions rather than total investment at the business level. Thus, we sometimes see a situation where capital projects regularly exceed the minimum acceptable rate of return, while the business

---

[1] Source: This article was adapted with permission from Chapter 1 of *Creating Shareholder Value: The New Standard for Business Performance*, The Free Press, New York, 1986, pp. 1–13.

unit itself is a 'problem' and creates little or no value for shareholders. This situation can arise because capital expenditures typically represent only a small percentage of total company outlays. For example, capital expenditures amount to about 10 percent of total outlays at General Motors, a particularly capital intensive company.

During the past 10 years, the shareholder value approach has been frequently applied not only to internal investments such as capacity additions, but also to opportunities for external growth such as mergers and acquisitions. Recently a number of major companies such as American Hospital Supply, Combustion Engineering, Hillenbrand Industries, Libbey-Owens-Ford, Marriott, and Westinghouse have found that the shareholder value approach can be productively extended from individual projects to the entire strategic plan. A strategic business unit (SBU) is commonly defined as the smallest organizational unit for which integrated strategic planning, related to a distinct product that serves a well-defined market, is feasible. A strategy for an SBU may then be seen as a collection of product-market related investments and the company itself may be characterized as a portfolio of these investment-requiring strategies. By estimating the future cash flows associated with each strategy, a company can assess the economic value to shareholders of alternative strategies at the business unit and corporate levels.

The interest in shareholder value is gaining momentum as a result of several recent developments.

- The threat of corporate take-overs by those seeking undervalued, under-managed assets.

- Impressive endorsements by corporate leaders who have adopted the approach.

- The growing recognition that traditional accounting measures such as EPS and ROI are not reliably linked to increasing the value of the company's shares.

- Reporting of returns to shareholders along with other measures of performance in the business press such as Fortune's annual ranking of the 500 leading industrial firms.

- A growing recognition that executives' long-term compensation needs to be more closely tied to returns to shareholders.

Endorsements of the shareholder value approach can be found in an increasing number of annual reports and other corporate publications. One of the more thoughtful statements appears in Libbey-Owens-Ford's 1983 annual report and is reproduced as Table 11.1.1. Combustion Engineering's vice president for finance states that 'a primary financial objective for Combustion Engineering is to create shareholder value by earning superior returns on capital invested in the business. This serves as a clear guide for management action and is the conceptual framework on which CE's financial objectives and goals are based.'

Whether or not executives agree with the well-publicized tactics of raiders such as Carl Icahn and T. Boone Pickens, they recognize that the raiders characterize themselves as champions of the shareholders. The

TABLE 11.1.1
Libbey-Owens-Ford

A Greater Emphasis on Shareholder Value

Libbey-Owens-Ford's mission statement specifies that its primary responsibility is to its shareholders, and that the company has a continuing requirement to increase the value of our shareholders' investment in LOF. This is not just a contemporary business phrase, but the basis for a long-term company strategy. It evaluates business strategies and plans in terms of value to our shareholders, not just on the incremental income that the results will contribute to the bottom line. It requires a greater emphasis on developing strategies and plans that will increase shareholder value as measured by the market appreciation of our stock and dividends.

Traditional Accounting Measures May Not Tell the Entire Story

Traditionally, the most popular way to determine whether a company is performing well is through such accounting measurements as earnings per share (EPS) and return on investment. These measures do, of course, give an indication of a company's performance, but they can be misleading in that often they do not measure the increase or decrease in shareholder value. Sustained growth as measured by EPS does not necessarily reflect an increase in stock value.

This occurs because earnings do not reflect changes in risk and inflation, nor do they take into account the cost of added capital that may have been invested in the business to finance its growth. Yet these are critical considerations when you are striving to increase the value of the shareholders' investment.

Cash Flow Analysis is Emphasized

LOF stresses the importance of cash flow measurement and performance. Individual operating companies must analyze the cash flow effects of running their businesses. Where cash comes from and what cash is used for must be simply and clearly set forth. LOF's cash and short-term investments increased $46.3 million during 1983.

The Shareholder Value Approach

The shareholder value approach taken by LOF emphasized economic cash flow analysis in evaluating individual projects and in determining the economic value of the overall strategy of each business unit and the corporation as a whole. Management looks at the business units and the corporation and determines the minimum operating return necessary to create value. It then reviews the possible contribution of alternative strategies and evaluates the financial feasibility of the strategic plan, based on the company's cost of capital, return on assets, the cash flow stream and other important measurements.

This disciplined process allows LOF to objectively evaluate all its corporate investments, including internal projects and acquisitions, in light of our primary goal to increase shareholder value.

Libbey-Owens-Ford Company
1983 Annual Report

---

raiders attack on two fronts. First, they are constantly searching for poorly managed companies, where aggressive changes in strategic directions could dramatically improve the value of the stock. Second, they identify under-valued assets that can be redeployed to boost the stock price. As a result, many executives recognize a new and compelling reason to be concerned with the performance of their company's stock.

Executives have also become increasingly aware that many accrual-based accounting measures do not provide a dependable picture of the current and future performance of an organization. Numerous companies have sustained double-digit EPS growth while providing minimal or even *negative* returns to shareholders. Hillenbrand Industries, for example, points out in its 1984 annual report (p. 4) that 'public companies that focus on achieving short-term earnings to meet external expectations sometimes jeopardize their ability to create long-term value.'

Considerable attention has focused recently on the problems associated with rewarding executives on the basis of short-term accounting-based indicators. As a reflection of the increasing scrutiny under which executive compensation has come, business publications such as *Fortune* and *Business Week* have begun to publish compensation surveys that examine the correlation between the executives' pay and how well their companies have performed based on several measures-including returns to shareholders. For example, *Business Week*'s executive compensation score-board now includes a 'pay-performance index' for 255 companies in 36 industries. The index shows how well the top two executives in each company were paid relative to how shareholders fared. The index is the ratio of the executive's three-year total pay as a percent of the industry average to the shareholders' total three-year return as a percent of the industry average. If an executive's pay and shareholders' return are both at the industry average, the index is 100. The lower the index, the better shareholders fared. The broad range in the pay-performance index, even within industries, has further fueled the interest in achieving shareholder value. For the 1982–1984 period, for example, *Business Week* reported a pay-performance index of 59 for Roger Smith, CEO of General Motors, and an index of 160 for Phillip Caldwell, CEO of Ford Motor.

When the shareholder value approach first gained attention toward the end of the 1970s, even the executives who found the concept an intriguing notion tended to think that the approach would be very difficult to implement. The task of educating managers seemed substantial, and they were also not eager to develop a new planning system if it might involve upheaval in the corporate information system. Recent advances in technology have put impressive analytical potential at management's disposal. Managers' decisions are now greatly facilitated by microcomputer software. New approaches thus can more readily be incorporated without displacing existing information systems.

Management versus Shareholder Objectives

It is important to recognize that the objectives of management may in some situations differ from those of the company's shareholders. Managers, like other people, act in their self-interest. The theory of a market economy is, after all, based on individuals promoting their self-interests via market transactions to bring about an efficient allocation of resources. In a world in which principals (e.g. stockholders) have imperfect control over their agents (e.g. managers), these agents may not always engage in transactions solely in the best interests of the principals. Agents have their own objectives and it may sometimes pay them to sacrifice the principals' interests. The problem is exacerbated in large corporations where it is difficult to identify the interests of a diverse set of stockholders ranging from institutional investors to individuals with small holdings.

Critics of large corporations often allege that corporate managers have too much power and that they act in ways to benefit themselves at the expense of shareholders and other corporate constituencies. The argument is generally developed along the following lines. Responsibility for administering companies or 'control' is vested in the hands of professional managers and thereby has been separated from 'ownership.' Since the ownership of shares in large corporations tends to be diffused, individual shareholders are said to have neither influence on nor interest in corporate governance issues such as the election of board members. Therefore, boards are largely responsive to management which, in turn, can ignore shareholders and run companies as they see fit.

The foregoing 'separation of ownership and control' argument advanced by Berle and Means in 1932 has been a persistent theme of corporate critics during the intervening years. There are, however, a number of factors that induce management to act in the best interests of shareholders. These factors derive from the fundamental premise that the greater the expected unfavorable consequences to the manager who decreases the wealth of shareholders, the less likely it is that the manager will, in fact, act against the interests of shareholders.

Consistent with the above premise, at least four major factors will induce management to adopt a shareholder orientation: (1) a relatively large ownership position, (2) compensation tied to shareholder return performance, (3) threat of take-over by another organization, and (4) competitive labor markets for corporate executives.

Economic rationality dictates that stock ownership by management motivates executives to identify more closely with the shareholders' economic interests. Indeed, we would expect that the greater the proportion of personal wealth invested in company stock or tied to stock options, the greater would be management's shareholder orientation. While the top executives in many companies often have relatively large percentages of their wealth invested in company stock, this is much less often the case for divisional and business unit managers. And it is at the divisional and business unit levels that most resource allocation decisions are made in decentralized organizations.

Even when corporate executives own shares in their company, their viewpoint on the acceptance of risk may differ from that of shareholders. It is reasonable to expect that many corporate executives have a lower tolerance for risk. If the company invests in a risky project, stockholders can always balance this risk against other risks in their presumably diversified portfolios. The manager, however, can balance a project failure only against the other activities of the division or the company. Thus, managers are hurt by the failure more than shareholders.

The second factor likely to influence management to adopt a shareholder orientation is compensation tied to shareholder return performance. The most direct means of linking top management's interests with those of shareholders is to base compensation, and particularly the incentive portion, on market returns realized by shareholders. Exclusive reliance on shareholder returns, however, has its own limitations. First, movements in a company's stock price may well be greatly influenced by factors beyond management control such as the overall state of the economy and stock market. Second, shareholder returns may be materially influenced by what management believes to be unduly optimistic or pessimistic market expectations at the beginning or end of the performance measurement period. And third, divisional and business unit performance cannot be directly linked to stock price.

Rather than linking incentive compensation directly to the market returns earned by shareholders, most Fortune 500 companies tie annual bonuses and long-term performance plans to internal financial goals such as earnings or accounting return on investment. These accounting criteria can often conflict with the way corporate shares are valued by the market. If incentives were largely based on earnings, for example, management might well be motivated to pursue economically unsound strategies when viewed from the perspective of shareholders. In such a situation what is economically irrational from the shareholder viewpoint may be a perfectly rational course of action for the decision-making executives.

The third factor affecting management behavior is the threat of take-over by another company. Tender offers have become a commonly employed means of transferring corporate control. Moreover the size of the targets continues to become larger. During the 1979–1985 period, 77 acquisitions each in excess of $1 billion were completed. The threat of take-over is an essential means of constraining corporate managers who might choose to pursue personal goals at the expense of shareholders. Any significant exploitation of shareholders should be reflected in a lower stock price. This lower price, relative to what it might be with more efficient management, offers an attractive take-over opportunity for another company which in many cases will replace incumbent management. An active market for corporate control places limits on the divergence of interests between management and shareholders and thereby serves as an important counterargument to the 'separation of ownership and control' criticisms.

The fourth and final factor influencing management's shareholder orientation is the labor market for corporate executives. Managerial labor markets are an essential mechanism for motivating management to function in the best interests of shareholders. Managers compete for positions both within and outside of the firm. The increasing number of executive recruiting firms and the length of the 'Who's News' column in the *Wall*

Street Journal are evidence that the managerial labor market is very active. What is less obvious is how managers are evaluated in this market. Within the firm, performance evaluation and incentive schemes are the basic mechanisms for monitoring managerial performance. As seen earlier, the question here is whether these measures are reliably linked to the market price of the company's shares.

How managers communicate their value to the labor market outside of their individual firms is less apparent. While the performance of top-level corporate officers can be gleaned from annual reports and other publicly available corporate communications, this is not generally the case for divisional managers. For corporate level executives, the question is whether performance for shareholders is the dominant criterion in assessing their value in the executive labor market. The question in the case of division managers is, first, how does the labor market monitor and gain insights about their performance and second, what is the basis for valuing their services.

'Excellence' and Restructuring

Two of the most visible business phenomena of the first half of the 1980s have been the publication of Peters and Waterman's *In Search of Excellence* and the unprecedented surge in the restructuring of companies. The 'excellence phenomenon' certainly provided no obvious encouragement for management to link its decisions more closely with the objective of maximizing returns to shareholders. In contrast, the more recent restructuring movement is clearly a manifestation of top management's growing concern with its company's share price and shareholder returns.

As US corporations began the 1980s, saddled with a decade of inflation and lagging productivity, nothing could have come as better news than the idea that not all excellent companies are Japanese. It was in this climate that *In Search of Excellence*, published in 1982, became an absolute sensation. Its longevity on the top of the best-seller list along with its wide coverage in the business press provided an extraordinary platform for the authors' ideas.

The basic purpose of *In Search of Excellence* was to identify key attributes of corporate excellence that are common among successful American corporations. To choose the 'excellent' companies, Peters and Waterman began by assembling a list of 62 US companies that were considered 'successful' by business leaders, consultants, members of the business press, and business school professors. From that list they selected 36 'excellent' companies based on superior performance for such financial measures as return on total capital, return on equity, return on sales, and asset growth. Eight attributes of corporate excellence were identified – a bias for action; staying close to the customer; autonomy and entrepreneurship; productivity through people; hands-on, value-driven management; sticking to the knitting; simple organization form and lean staff; and simultaneous loose-tight properties.

Even though the 'excellent' firms exhibited superior financial (accounting) performance over the 1960–1980 period, they did not provide consistently superior returns to shareholder via dividends plus share price appreciation. The excellent companies did not perform significantly better than the market. Indeed, they did not consistently outperform their respective industry groups or closest competitors. These results once again raise questions about the use of accounting measures to gauge the economic performance of corporations. Since the eight attributes of corporate excellence are not associated with systematically superior returns to shareholders, efforts to emulate these attributes may be ill-advised.

While *In Search of Excellence* became 'must reading' in many organizations during 1982 and 1983, a certain degree of disenchantment set in during the following two years as a number of 'excellent' companies experienced strategic setbacks. Atari, Avon Products, Caterpillar Tractor, Digital Equipment, Hewlett-Packard, Levi Strauss, and Texas Instruments serve as examples.

But if emulating excellent companies has lost some of its luster, a new focal point of interest has captured the imagination of management during the past couple of years – restructuring. Hardly a day passes without some company announcing a major restructuring of its businesses or capital structure. Restructuring involves diverse activities such as divestiture of underperforming businesses or businesses that do not 'fit,' spinoffs directly to shareholders, acquisitions paid with 'excess cash,' stock repurchases, debt swaps, and liquidation of overfunded pension funds. In many cases, these restructurings are motivated by a desire to foil a take-over bid by so-called 'raiders' who look for undermanaged companies where changes in strategic direction could dramatically increase the value of the stock, and for companies with high liquidation values relative to their current share price. There is, of course, no better means of avoiding a take-over than increasing the price of the stock. Thus, increasing share price has become the fundamental purpose of corporate restructuring.

In contrast to the earlier euphoria over emulating excellent companies, the current restructuring movement is solidly based on shareholder value creation principles. In 1985, the Standard & Poor's 500 appreciated 26 percent in price. Goldman Sachs estimates that corporate restructuring accounted for about 30 percent of that price change. However, the early stage of the restructuring movement, which I call 'Phase I restructuring,' is largely based on one-time transactions such as those listed above rather than changes in day-to-day management of the business.

The necessary agenda for the second half of the 1980s seems clear. Companies need to move from Phase I restructuring to Phase II restructuring. In Phase II, the shareholder value approach is employed not only when buying and selling businesses or changing the company's capital structure, but also in the planning and performance monitoring of all business strategies on an ongoing basis. Frequently, the most difficult issue in this area is how to go about estimating the impact of strategies on shareholder value. Fortunately, relatively straightforward approaches do exist for estimating the shareholder value created by a business strategy, and an increasing number of major companies have begun to use them.

Most companies already use the same discounted cash-flow techniques used in the shareholder value approach to assess the attractiveness of capital investment projects and to value prospective acquisition targets. This approach can be extended to estimate the value creation potential of individual business units and the strategic plan for the entire company.

In Phase II restructuring it will also become increasingly important that executive compensation be tied closely to the shareholder value driven plans so that management will be strongly motivated to make decisions consistent with creating maximum returns to shareholders. A successful implementation of Phase II restructuring not only ensures that management has met its fiduciary responsibility to develop corporate performance evaluation systems consistent with the parameters investors use to value the company, but also minimizes the Phase I concern that a take-over of an undermanaged company is imminent.

Rationale for Shareholder Value Approach

Business strategies should be judged by the economic returns they generate for shareholders, as measured by dividends plus the increase in the company's share price. As management considers alternative strategies, those expected to develop the greatest sustainable competitive advantage will be those that will also create the greatest value for shareholders. The 'shareholder value approach' estimates the economic value of an investment (e.g. the shares of a company, strategies, mergers and acquisitions, capital expenditures) by discounting forecasted cash flows by the cost of capital. These cash flows, in turn, serve as the foundation for shareholder returns from dividends and share-price appreciation.

The case for why management should pursue this objective is comparatively straightforward. Management is often characterized as balancing the interests of various corporate constituencies such as employees, customers, suppliers, debtholders, and stockholders. As Treynor (1981) points out, the company's continued existence depends upon a financial relationship with each of these parties. Employees want competitive wages. Customers want high quality at a competitive price. Suppliers and debtholders each have financial claims that must be satisfied with cash when they fall due. Stockholders as residual claimants of the firm look for cash dividends and the prospect of future dividends which is reflected in the market price of the stock.

If the company does not satisfy the financial claims of its constituents, it will cease to be a viable organization. Employees, customers, and suppliers will simply withdraw their support. Thus, a going concern must strive to enhance its cash-generating ability. The ability of a company to distribute cash to its various constituencies depends on its ability to generate cash from operating its businesses and on its ability to obtain any additional funds needed from external sources.

Debt and equity financing are the two basic external sources. The company's ability to borrow today is based on projections of how much cash will be generated in the future. Borrowing power and the market value of the shares both depend on a company's cash-generating ability. The market value of the shares directly impacts the second source of financing, that is, equity financing. For a given level of funds required, the higher the share price, the less dilution will be borne by current shareholders. Therefore, management's financial power to deal effectively with corporate claimants also comes from increasing the value of the shares. Treynor, a former editor of the *Financial Analysts Journal*, summarizes this line of thinking best.

> Those who criticize the goal of share value maximization are forgetting that stockholders are not merely the beneficiaries of the corporation's financial success, but also the referees who determine management's financial power.
>
> Any management – no matter how powerful and independent – that flouts the financial objective of maximizing share value does so at its own peril.

11.2   Stockholders and Stakeholders: A New Perspective on Corporate Governance

By Edward Freeman and David Reed[1]

Management thought has changed dramatically in recent years. There have been, and are now underway, both conceptual and practical revolutions in the ways that management theorists and managers think about organizational life. The purpose of this article is to understand the implications of one of these shifts in world view; namely, the shift from 'stockholder' to 'stakeholder.'

The Stakeholder Concept

It has long been gospel that corporations have obligations to stockholders, holders of the firm's equity, that are sacrosanct and inviolable. Corporate

---

[1] Source: This article was adapted with permission from *California Management Review*, Vol. 25, No. 3, Spring 1993, pp. 88–106.

action or inaction is to be driven by attention to the needs of its stockholders, usually thought to be measured by stock price, earnings per share, or some other financial measure. It has been argued that the proper relationship of management to its stockholders is similar to that of the fiduciary to the *cestui gue trustent*, whereby the interests of the stockholders should be dutifully cared for by management. Thus, any action taken by management must ultimately be justified by whether or not it furthers the interests of the corporation and its stockholders.

There is also a long tradition of departure from the view that stockholders have a privileged place in the business enterprise. Berle and Means (1932) were worried about the 'degree of prominence entitling (the corporation) to be dealt with as a major social institution.' Chester Barnard argued that the purpose of the corporation was to serve society, and that the function of the executive was to instill this sense of moral purpose in the corporation's employees (Barnard, 1938). Public relations and corporate social action have a history too long to be catalogued here. However, a recent development calls for a more far-reaching change in the way that we look at corporate life, and that is the good currency of the idea of 'stakeholders.'

The stakeholder notion is indeed a deceptively simple one. It says that there are other groups to whom the corporation is responsible in addition to stockholders: those groups who have a stake in the actions of the corporation. The word *stakeholder*, coined in an internal memorandum at the Stanford Research Institute in 1963, refers to 'those groups without whose support the organization would cease to exist.' The list of stakeholders originally included shareowners, employees, customers, suppliers, lenders, and society. Stemming from the work of Igor Ansoff and Robert Stewart (in the planning department at Lockheed) and, later, Marion Doscher and Stewart (at SRI), stakeholder analysis served and continues to serve an important function in the SRI corporate planning process.

From the original work at SRI, the historical trail diverges in a number of directions. In his now classic *Corporate Strategy: An Analytic Approach to Business Policy for Growth and Expansion*, Igor Ansoff (1965) makes limited use of the theory:

> While as we shall see later, 'responsibilities' and 'objectives' are not synonymous, they have been made one in a 'stakeholder theory' of objectives. This theory maintains that the objectives of the firrn should be derived by balancing the conflicting claims of the various 'stakeholders' in the firm: managers, workers, stockholders, suppliers, vendors.

Ansoff goes on to reject the stakeholder theory in favor of a view which separates objectives into 'economic' and 'social' with the latter being a 'secondary modifying and constraining influence' on the former.

In the mid-1970s, researchers in systems theory, led by Russell Ackoff (1974) 'rediscovered' stakeholder analysis, or at least took Ansoff's admonition more seriously. Propounding essentially an open systems view of organizations, Ackoff argues that many social problems can be solved by the redesign of fundamental institutions with the support and interaction of stakeholders in the system.

A second trail from Ansoff's original reference is the work of William Dill, who in concert with Ackoff, sought to move the stakeholder concept from the periphery of corporate planning to a central place. In 1975 Dill argued:

> For a long time, we have assumed that the views and the initiative of stakeholders could be dealt with as externalities to the strategic planning and management process: as data to help management shape decisions, or as legal and social constraints to limit them. We have been reluctant, though, to admit the idea that some of these outside stakeholders might seek and earn active roles with management to make decisions. The move today is from *stakeholder influence towards stakeholder participation.*

Dill went on to set out a role for strategic managers as communicators with stakeholders and considered the role of adversary groups such as Nader's Raiders in the strategic process. For the most part, until Dill's paper, stakeholders had been assumed to be nonadversarial, or adversarial only in the sense of labor-management relations. By broadening the notion of stakeholder to 'people outside . . . who have ideas about what the economic and social performance of the enterprise should include,' Dill set the stage for the use of the stakeholder concept as an umbrella for strategic management.

A related development is primarily responsible for giving the stakeholder concept a boost; namely, the increase in concern with the social involvement of business. The corporate social responsibility movement is too diverse and has spawned too many ideas, concepts, and techniques to explain here. Suffice it to say that the social movements of the sixties and seventies – civil rights, the antiwar movement, consumerism, environmentalism, and women's rights – served as a catalyst for rethinking the role of the business enterprise in society. From Milton Friedman to John Kenneth Galbraith, there is a diversity of arguments. However, one aspect of the corporate social responsibility debate is particularly relevant to understanding the good currency of the stakeholder concept.

In the early 1970s the Harvard Business School undertook a project on corporate social responsibility. The output of the project was voluminous, and of particular importance was the development of a pragmatic model of social responsibility called 'the corporate social responsiveness model.' (Ackerman and Bauer, 1976) It essentially addressed Dill's question with respect to social issues: 'How can the corporation respond proactively to the increased pressure for positive social change?' By concentrating on responsiveness instead of responsibility, the Harvard researchers were able to link the analysis of social issues with the traditional areas of strategy and organization.

By the late 1970s the need for strategic management processes to take account of nontraditional business problems in terms of government, special interest groups, trade associations, foreign competitors, dissident shareholders, and complex issues such as employee rights, equal opportunity, environmental pollution, consumer rights, tariffs, government regulation, and reindustrialization had become obvious. To begin to develop these processes, The Wharton School began, in 1977 in its Applied Research

Center, a 'stakeholder project.' The objectives of the project were to put together a number of strands of thought and to develop a theory of management which enabled executives to formulate and implement corporate strategy in turbulent environments. Thus, an action research model was used whereby stakeholder theory was generated by actual cases.

To date the project has explored the implications of the stakeholder concept on three levels: as a management theory; as a process for practitioners to use in strategic management; and as an analytical framework.

At the theoretical level the implications of substituting *stakeholder* for *stockholder* needs to be explicated. The first problem at this level is the actual definition of *stakeholder*. SRI's original definition is too general and too exclusive to serve as a means of identifying those external groups who are strategically important. The concentration on generic stakeholders, such as society and customers, rather than specific social interest groups and specific customer segments produces an analysis which can only be used as a background for the planning process. Strategically useful information about the actions, objectives, and motivations of specific groups, which is needed if management is to be responsive to stakeholder concerns, requires a more specific and inclusive definition.

We propose two definitions of *stakeholder*: a wide sense, which includes groups who are friendly or hostile, and a narrow sense, which captures the essence of the SRI definition. but is more specific.

- *The wide sense of stakeholder.* Any identifiable group or individual who can affect the achievement of an organization's objectives or who is affected by the achievement of an organization's objectives. (Public interest groups, protest groups, government agencies, trade associations, competitors, unions, as well as employees, customer segments, shareowners, and others are stakeholders, in this sense.)

- *The narrow sense of stakeholder.* Any identifiable group or individual on which the organization is dependent for its continued survival. (Employees, customer segments, certain suppliers, key government agencies, shareowners, certain financial institutions, as well as others are all stakeholders in the narrow sense of the term.)

While executives are willing to recognize that employees, suppliers, and customers have a stake in the corporation, many resist the inclusion of adversary groups. But from the standpoint of corporate strategy, *stakeholder* must be understood in the wide sense: strategies need to account for those groups who can affect the achievement of the firm's objectives. Some may feel happier with other words, such as *influencers, claimants, publics, or constituencies*. Semantics aside, if corporations are to formulate and implement strategies in turbulent environments, theories of strategy must have concepts, such as the wide sense of *stakeholder*, which allow the analysis of all external forces and pressures whether they are friendly or hostile. In what follows we will use *stakeholder* in the wide sense, as our primary objective is to elucidate the questions of corporate governance from the perspective of strategic management.

A second issue at the theoretical level is the generation of prescriptive propositions which explain actual cases and articulate regulative principles for future use. Thus, a *post hoc* analysis of the brewing industry and the problem of beverage container legislation, combined with a similar analysis of the regulatory environments of public utilities have led to some simple propositions which serve as a philosophical guideline for strategy formulation (Freeman, 1981). For example:

- Generalize the marketing approach: understand the needs of each stakeholder, in a similar fashion to understanding customer needs, and design products, services, and programs to fulfill those needs.

- Establish negotiation processes: understand the political nature of a number of stakeholders, and the applicability of concepts and techniques of political science, such as coalition analysis, conflict management, and the use and abuse of unilateral action.

- Establish a decision philosophy that is oriented towards seizing the initiative rather than reacting to events as they occur.

- Allocate organizational resources based on the degree of importance of the environmental turbulence (the stakeholders' claims).

Other prescriptive propositions can be put forth, especially with respect to issues of corporate governance. One proposition that has been discussed is to 'involve stakeholder groups in strategic decisions,' or 'invite stakeholders to participate in governance decisions.' While propositions like this may have substantial merit, we have not examined enough cases nor marshalled enough evidence to support them in an unqualified manner. There are cases where participation is appropriate. Some public utilities have been quite successful in the use of stakeholder advisory groups in matters of rate setting. However, given the breadth of our concept of stakeholder we believe that co-optation through participation is not always the correct strategic decision.

The second level of analysis is the use of stakeholder concepts in strategy formulation processes. Two processes have been used so far: the *Stakeholder Strategy Process* and the *Stakeholder Audit Process*. The Stakeholder Strategy Process is a systematic method for analyzing the relative importance of stakeholders and their cooperative potential (how they can help the corporation achieve its objectives) and their competitive threat (how they can prevent the corporation from achieving its objectives). The process is one which relies on a behavioral analysis (both actual and potential) for input, and an explanatory model of stakeholder objectives and resultant strategic shifts for output. The Stakeholder Audit Process is a systematic method for identifying stakeholders and assessing the effectiveness of current organizational strategies. By itself, each process has a use in the strategic management of an organization. Each analyzes the stakeholder environment from the standpoint of organizational mission and objectives and seeks to formulate strategies for meeting stakeholder needs and concerns.

The use of the stakeholder concept at the analytical level means thinking in terms which are broader than current strategic and operational

FIGURE 11.2.1
Classical Grid

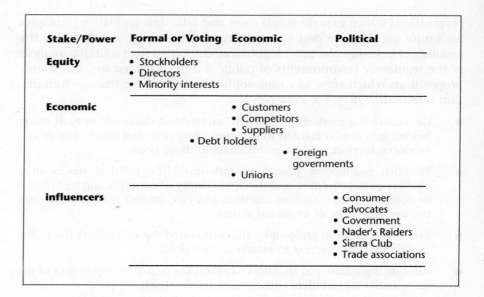

Stake/Power	Formal or Voting	Economic	Political
Equity	• Stockholders • Directors • Minority interests		

Economic		• Customers
		• Competitors
		• Suppliers
		• Debt holders
		    • Foreign
		      governments
		• Unions	

influencers			• Consumer advocates • Government • Nader's Raiders • Sierra Club • Trade associations

problems. It implies looking at public policy questions in stakeholder terms and trying to understand how the relationships between an organization and its stakeholders would change given the implementation of certain policies.

One analytical device depicts an organization's stakeholders on a two-dimensional grid map. The first dimension is one of 'interest' or 'stake' and ranges from an equity interest to an economic interest or marketplace stake to an interest or stake as a 'kibitzer' or influencer. Shareowners have an equity stake; customers and suppliers have an economic stake; and single-issue groups have an influencer stake. The second dimension of a stakeholder is its power, which ranges from the formalistic or voting power of stockholders to the economic power of customers to the political power of special interest groups. By *economic power* we mean 'the ability to influence due to marketplace decisions' and by *political power* we mean 'the ability to influence due to use of the political process.'

Figure 11.2.1 represents this stakeholder grid graphically. It is of course possible that a stakeholder has more than one kind of both stake and power, especially in light of the fact that there are stakeholders who have multiple roles. An employee may be at once shareholder, customer, employee, and even kibitzer. Figure 11.2.1 represents the prevailing world view. That is, shareholders and directors have formal or voting power; customers, suppliers, and employees have economic power; and government and special interest groups have political power. Moreover, management concepts and principles have evolved to treat this 'diagonal case.' Managers learn how to handle stockholders and boards via their ability to vote on certain key decisions, and conflicts are resolved by the procedures and

Stake/Power	Formal or Voting	Economic	Political
Equity	• Stockholders • Directors • Minority interests		• Dissident stockholders
Economic		• Suppliers • Debt holders • Customers • Unions	• Local governments • Foreign governments • Consumer groups • Unions
Influencers	• Government • SEC • Outside directors	• EPA/OSHA	• Nader's Raiders • Government • Trade associations

FIGURE 11.2.2
'Real World' Stakeholder Grid

processes written into the corporate charter or by methods which involve formal legal parameters. Strategic planners, marketers, financial analysts, and operations executives base their decisions on marketplace variables, and an entire tradition of management principles is based on the economic analysis of the marketplace. Finally, public relations and public affairs managers and lobbyists learn to deal in the political arena. As long as the real world approximately fits into the diagonal, management processes may be able to deal effectively with them. A more thoughtful examination, however, reveals that Figure 11.2.1 is either a straw man or that shifts of position have occurred. In the auto industry, for instance, one part of government has acquired economic power in terms of the imposition of import quotas or the trigger price mechanism. The Securities and Exchange Commission might be looked at as a kibitzer with formal power in terms of disclosure and accounting rules. Outside directors do not necessarily have an equity stake, especially those women, minorities, and academics who are becoming more and more normal for the boards of large corporations. Some kibitzer groups are buying stock and acquiring an equity stake, and while they also acquire formal power, their main source of power is still political. Witness the marshalling of the political process by church groups in bringing up, at annual meetings, issues such as selling infant formula in the Third World or investing in South Africa. Unions are using their political power as well as their formal clout as managers of large portions of pension funds to influence the company. Customers are being organized by consumer advocates to exercise the voice option and to politicize the marketplace. In short, the real world looks more like Figure 11.2.2. (Of course, each organization will have its own individual grid.) Thus, search for alternative applications of traditional management processes must begin, and new concepts and techniques are needed to understand the shifts that have occurred and to manage in the new environment.

There is a need to develop new and innovative management processes to deal with the current and future complexities of management issues. At the theoretical level, stakeholder analysis has been developed to enrich the economic approach to corporate strategy by arguing that kibitzers with political power must be included in the strategy process. At the strategic level, stakeholder analysis takes a number of groups into account and analyzes their strategic impact on the corporation.

Stakeholder Analysis and Corporate Democracy

The debate on corporate governance and, in particular, corporate democracy has recently intensified. Proposals have been put forth to make the corporation more democratic, to encourage shareholder participation and management responsiveness to shareholder needs, and to make corporations more responsive to other stakeholder needs and, hence, to encourage the participation of stakeholders in the governance process. Reforms from cumulative voting to audit committees have been suggested.

Corporate democracy has come to have at least three meanings over the years, which prescribe that corporations should be made more democratic: by increasing the role of government, either as a watchdog or by having public officials on boards of directors; by allowing citizen or public participation in the managing of its affairs via public interest directors and the like; or by encouraging or mandating the active participation of all or many of its shareholders. The analysis of the preceding section has implications for each of these levels of democratization.

The propositions of stakeholder analysis advocate a thorough understanding of a firm's stakeholders (in the wide sense) and recognize that there are times when stakeholders must participate in the decision-making process. The strategic tools and techniques of stakeholder analysis yield a method for determining the timing and degree of such participation. At the absolute minimum this implies that boards of directors must be aware of the impact of their decisions on key stakeholder groups. As stakeholders have begun to exercise more political power and as marketplace decisions become politicized, the need for awareness to grow into responsiveness has become apparent. Thus, the analytical model can be used by boards to map carefully the power and stake of each group. While it is not the proper role of the board to be involved in the implementation of tactical programs at the operational level of the corporation, it must set the tone for how the company deals with stakeholders, both traditional marketplace ones and those who have political power. The board must decide not only whether management is managing the affairs of the corporation, but indeed, what are to count as the affairs of the corporation. This involves assessing the stake and power of each stakeholder group.

Much has been written about the failure of senior management to think strategically, competitively, and globally. Some have argued that American businesspersons are 'managing [their] way to economic decline' (Hayes and Abernathy, 1980). Executives have countered the critics with complaints about the increase in the adversarial role of government and in the number of hostile external interest groups. Yet if the criteria for success for senior executives remains fixated on economic stakeholders with economic power and on short-term performance on Wall Street, the rise of such a turbulent political environment in a free and open society should come as no surprise. If the board sees itself as responsive only to the shareholder in the short term, senior management will continue to manage towards economic decline.[2] We have argued that the problem of governing the corporation in today's world must be viewed in terms of the entire grid of stakeholders and their power base. It is only by setting the direction for positive response and negotiation at the board level that the adversarial nature of the business-government relationship can be overcome.

If this task of stakeholder management is done properly, much of the air is let out of critics who argue that the corporation must be democratized in terms of increased direct citizen participation. Issues which involve both economic and political stakes and power bases must be addressed in an integrated fashion. No longer can public affairs, public relations, and corporate philanthropy serve as adequate management tools. The sophistication of interest groups who are beginning to use formal power mechanisms, such as proxy fights, annual meetings, the corporate charter, to focus the attention of management on the affairs of the corporation has increased. Responsive boards will seize these opportunities to learn more about those stakeholders who have chosen the option of voice over the Wall Street Rule. As boards direct management to respond to these concerns, to negotiate with critics, to trade off certain policies in return for positive support, the pressure for mandated citizen participation will subside.

---

[2] It is arguable whether responsiveness to nonmarket stakeholders is in the long-term interest of the corporation. We believe that there is no need to appeal to utilitarian notions of greatest social good or altruism or social responsibility. Rather the corporation fulfills its obligations to shareholders in the long term only through proper stakeholder management. In short we believe that enlightened self-interest gives both reasons why (personal motivation) and reasons for (social justification) taking stakeholder concerns into account. The development of this argument is, however, beyond our present scope.

11.3 Whose Company is it? The Concept of the Corporation in Japan and the West

By Masaru Yoshimori[1]

Available evidence seems to suggest that in terms of corporate governance countries may be divided into three groups: with monistic, dualistic and pluralistic concepts of the corporation. The monistic outlook is shareholder-oriented and looks at the firm as the private property of its owners. This concept is prevalent in the United States and the UK. The dualistic concept also puts a premium on the shareholder interest, but the interests of employees are taken into account as well. This is an adapted form of the monistic concept and is widely shared in Germany and to a lesser degree in France. The view that the firm is a social institution where people develop themselves freely ranked first among six alternative definitions, according to Albach's survey of leading German companies in 1975, though it slipped to the third rank in 1991 (Albach, 1994).

The pluralistic approach assumes that the firm belongs to all the stakeholders, with the employees' interests taking precedence. This is the concept specific to Japan which manifests itself in the form of long-term employment for employees and long-term trading relations among various other stakeholders (the main bank, major suppliers, subcontractors, distributors), loosely called *Keiretsu*.

This three-part categorization is supported by the results of a mail survey undertaken by the author with managers and executives in the five countries under review. The shareholder-centred Anglo–American outlook starkly contrasts with the employee-centred Japanese perspective, with Germany and France in between but significantly more oriented towards 'shareholder value' than Japan. The findings on Japan are consistent with the results of other studies. For instance, a survey carried out in 1990 by *Nippon Keizai Shimbun* on 104 employees of large corporations showed a majority of 80 percent replying that the company belongs to its employees; 70 percent believed that the company exists for the benefit of society as a whole. The concept that the firm is the property of shareholders ranked third with 67 percent.

Clearly Japan puts the interest of employees before that of shareholders. Her current unemployment rate of around three percent even in a prolonged recession is a testimony to this. Though increasingly challenged, job security is still defended as the mainstream ideology, as two major spokesmen of the Japanese business community recently proclaimed: Fumio Sato, Chairman of Toshiba Corporation, said that to

---

[1] Source: This article was adapted with permission from *Long Range Planning*, Vol. 28, No. 4, 1995, pp. 33–44.

FIGURE 11.3.1
Whose company is it?

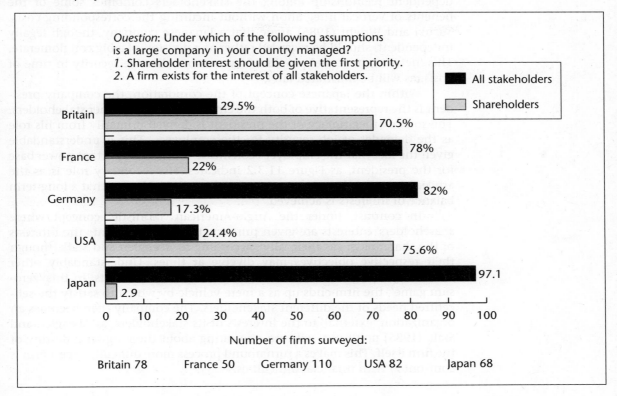

Question: Under which of the following assumptions
is a large company in your country managed?
1. Shareholder interest should be given the first priority.
2. A firm exists for the interest of all stakeholders.

- All stakeholders
- Shareholders

Britain — 29.5% / 70.5%
France — 78% / 22%
Germany — 82% / 17.3%
USA — 24.4% / 75.6%
Japan — 97.1 / 2.9

Number of firms surveyed:

Britain 78   France 50   Germany 110   USA 82   Japan 68

discharge employees is 'the most serious sin' a president can commit and
Takeshi Moroi, Chairman of Chichibu Cement, said that job security is the
'responsibility of the corporation'.

Key Implications of the Different Approaches

The central characteristic of the Japanese pluralistic concept is the alignment of the company's goals and interests with those of the stakeholders.
This leads to a higher degree of cohesion between the firm's stakeholders,
i.e. shareholders, management, employees, the main bank, major suppliers
and distributors. They pull together toward a common purpose: the
company's survival and prosperity. They share the implicit consensus that
their respective interests are realized and promoted through their long-term
commitment and cooperation with the firm. Maximization of general
benefit, or the firm's 'wealth maximizing capacity', as Drucker (1991) puts
it, and not self-interest, is the name of the game. Michael Porter characterizes such relationship as 'a greater community of interest' and categorizes

it as 'quasi integration', that is an intermediate form between long-term contracts and full ownership. According to Porter (1980), this type of inter-dependent relationship among the stakeholders combines some of the benefits of vertical integration without incurring the corresponding costs. Suzuki and Wright (1985) argue that a Japanese company, though legally independent, should be regarded rather as a division of a big conglomerate. This 'network structure' provides a system of collective security in time of crisis, as will be illustrated later.

Within the Japanese concept of the corporation, the company president is the representative of both the employees and the other stakeholders. The source of legitimacy of the president is derived primarily from his role as the defender of job security for the employees. This is understandable given the fact that the employees constitute the most important power base for the president, as Figure 11.3.2 indicates. His secondary role is as the arbitrator for the divergent interests of the stakeholders so that a long-term balance of interests is achieved.

In contrast, under the Anglo-American 'monistic' concept where shareholders' interests are given primacy, the CEO represents the interests of the shareholders as their 'ally', according to Abegglen and Stalk, though their respective objectives may diverge at times. Understandably other stakeholders also seek to maximize their respective interests. In this 'zero-sum game', the firm ends up as a mere vehicle by which to satisfy the self-centred needs of the different stakeholders. The company then becomes an organization 'external' to the interests of its stakeholders, as Abegglen and Stalk (1985) point out, with no one caring about the long-term destiny of the firm itself. This makes a turnaround process more difficult, once a firm is confronted with financial difficulties.

The Relationship Between the Firm and Its Main Bank

In the Japanese *Keiretsu* the main bank assumes a pivotal role owing to its monitoring and disciplinary function based on its financial and equity claims. The main bank is not to be confused with the *Zaibatsu*[2] institution, *as any bank, whether Zaibatsu or non-Zaibatsu in origin, can assume this role.* The firm's main bank relations are characterized as follows:

- The main bank is typically the largest or one of the largest providers of loans and makes available on a preferential basis long-term and comprehensive financial services covering deposits, discounting of notes, foreign exchange transactions, advice in financial planning, agents on other loans, etc.

---

[2] *Zaibatsu* is a prewar conglomerate under family ownership and control. Mitsubishi, Mitsui, Sumitomo, and other *Zaibatsu* controlled a majority of Japan's large industrial, financial and service firms before World War II. They were broken up by the Occupation forces after the war. Today the firms of a former *Zaibatsu* form a loose federation based on their common tradition and business relationship.

FIGURE 11.3.2
Job security or dividends?

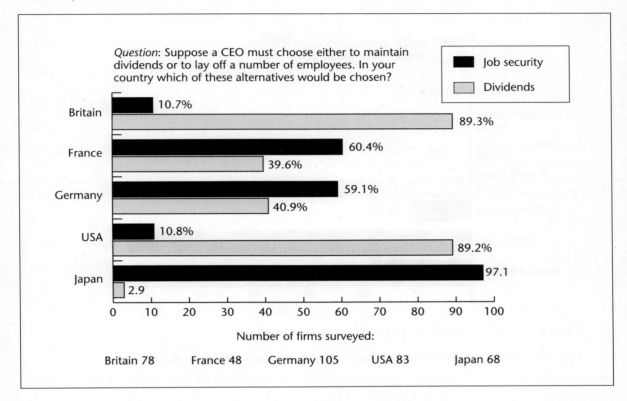

Question: Suppose a CEO must choose either to maintain dividends or to lay off a number of employees. In your country which of these alternatives would be chosen?

■ Job security
▢ Dividends

Britain — 10.7% / 89.3%
France — 60.4% / 39.6%
Germany — 59.1% / 40.9%
USA — 10.8% / 89.2%
Japan — 97.1 / 2.9

Number of firms surveyed:

Britain 78   France 48   Germany 105   USA 83   Japan 68

- Cross-shareholdings and interlocking directorships result in information sharing through official and personal contacts.

- The rescue of a client firm is attempted when it is targeted in a hostile take-over bid. Thus none of the hostile take-over attempts by a well-known raider, Minebea, were successful. An attempt to acquire Janome, a sewing machine maker, was thwarted by its main bank, Saitama Bank, another raid on Sankyo Seiki was frustrated by its main bank, Mitsubishi Bank who later arranged for an equity participation by Nippon Steel.

- Direct intervention in the turnaround process occurs in case the borrower company faces serious financial distress.

This main bank support is the most important motivation for Japanese firms to have a main bank. Typically the bailout measures range from the provision of emergency finance at an early stage in the crisis to, if the situation becomes more serious, the reduction of or exemption from interest payments, the engineering of a financial reorganization, the bank sending its own executives to supervise the reorganization, and finally the replacement of ineffectual management, the reorganization of the assets and an arrangement for an alliance or merger with another firm. The intervention by the main bank may have effects similar to an external take-over.

FIGURE 11.3.3
The Japanese CEO's most important power base

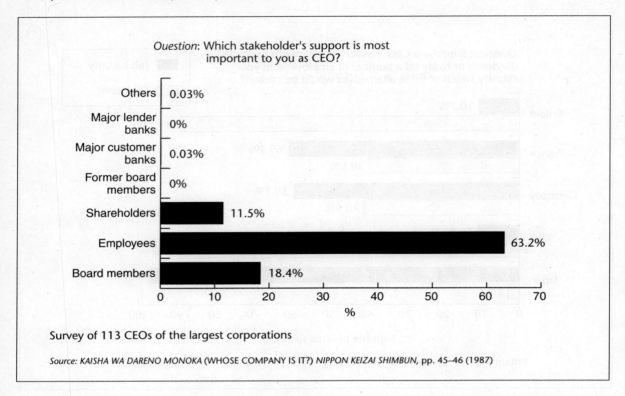

Question: Which stakeholder's support is most important to you as CEO?

Stakeholder	%
Others	0.03%
Major lender banks	0%
Major customer banks	0.03%
Former board members	0%
Shareholders	11.5%
Employees	63.2%
Board members	18.4%

Survey of 113 CEOs of the largest corporations

Source: KAISHA WA DARENO MONOKA (WHOSE COMPANY IS IT?) NIPPON KEIZAI SHIMBUN, pp. 45–46 (1987)

A recent mail survey of 305 listed companies excluding financial corporations suggests that 70 percent of them believe that their main bank would provide them with support in case of a crisis. The results of another poll of 354 corporations of Nikkeiren (The Japanese Federation of Employers' Associations) published in August 1994, indicated that 81.6 percent are in favour of maintaining the main bank system.

A Japan–US Comparison of Stakeholder Relations

The relations among stakeholders in Japan, in particular the firm-main bank relations, may be better understood when a firm faces a crisis. The turn-around processes of Toyo Kogyo, manufacturer of Mazda passenger cars, and of Chrysler are contrasted.

Toyo Kogyo

In 1974, Toyo Kogyo was confronted with a financial crisis due to its large stockpile of unsold cars. Mazda cars powered by Wankel rotary engines were less fuel-efficient, a serious disadvantage after the first oil crisis of 1973. Sumitomo Bank, the main bank, played a vital role in the bailout operations.

- Sumitomo Bank made a public assurance to stand by the distressed company, and a commitment to carry any new loans.

- Sumitomo Bank sent a team of seven directors to control and implement the reorganization process.

- Sumitomo Bank replaced the president with a new, more competent successor.

- Sumitomo Bank co-ordinated negotiations with the other lenders to establish a financial package.

- Sumitomo group companies switched their car purchases to Mazda and bought 8000 vehicles over six years.

- No lay-off of employees but factory operators joined the sales force.

- The suppliers and subcontractors agreed to extend payment terms from 189 to 210 days, resulting in estimated savings in interest payments of several billion Yen.

- They also agreed to price reductions of 14 percent over two and a half years. Joint cost reduction programmes were also implemented, with cost reductions of ¥123 billion over 4 years.

- The employees accepted rescheduling of bonus payments, contributing ¥4 billion in increased annual cash flow. They also agreed to restraints in wage and bonus increases.

Chrysler

In the turnaround process at Chrysler, the stakeholders – the banks, the union, and the dealers – distrusted each other, were afraid of being stuck with an unfair burden and shunned responsibility for saving the firm. Its lead bank, Manufacturers Hanover Trust, did not or could not make an assurance to bail Chrysler out, although the bank's chairman had been on the Chrysler board for years. The chairman declared that he would approve no more unguaranteed loans to Chrysler because of its fiduciary responsibility to its shareholders and depositors. Lack of solidarity of the lenders and other stakeholders made the turnaround process dependent on government guarantees. As Iacocca sarcastically wrote, 'it took longer to get $655 million in concessions from the four hundred lending institutions than it did to get the loan guarantees of $1.5 billion passed by the entire US Congress'. For him, 'the congressional hearings were as easy as changing a flat tire on a spring day, compared to dealing with the banks'. Such financial concerns occupied top management for most of one year.

- Manufacturers Hanover Trust arranged for an agreement on a $455 million revolving credit with 80 American banks.

- Manufacturers Hanover Trust's chairman pleaded in Congress for a Federal loan guarantee for Chrysler.

- Manufacturers Hanover Trust urged its colleagues to accept Chrysler's packages of concessions.

- The Labour union agreed to a wage restraint and curtailment of paid days off.

- Suppliers agreed to price reductions.

Legal Restrictions on Banks in the United States

Contrary to Japan and Germany, the United States traditionally put a premium on investor protection by insisting on complete and accurate disclosure of company information, portfolio diversification and on a sharp line of demarcation between investor and manager roles. Thus the Glass-Steagall Act, the Bank Holding Company Act of 1956, the Investment Company Act of 1940, the ERISA Act of 1974 and finally the rules against insider trading all combine to prohibit or inhibit investing funds of banks and pension plans in the stock of any single corporation, and participation in the management of the portfolio and borrower companies. This legal framework coupled with banks' preference for liquidity over investment has made the US financial market the most transparent, fair, efficient, liquid and low-cost in the world. The downside is fragmented equity holding, and arm's length or even antagonistic relations between shareholders and management.

The Roles of the German 'Hausbank'

In Germany where the Hausbank has a similar role to the Japanese main bank, many firms regard it as a kind of 'insurance, bearing appropriate premiums in good times and offering corresponding protection when things go less well', according to Schneider-Linné, a member of the Management Board of Deutsche Bank. German main banks do take initiatives to reorganize their client firms in financial distress. Their part in rescuing companies, however, seems to be more limited in scope and commitment than that of Japanese main banks. The most significant difference is that the German main bank does not get directly involved in the management of the distressed firm and that the rescue concept itself is usually left to management consultancy firms. The German bank usually confines itself to rescheduling interest and principal payments or reducing interest charges and debts, giving advice to management and bringing in suitable new management.

The Flaws in the Japanese Concept of the Corporation

Needless to say, Japan's close-knit, inward-looking concept of the corporation has its downsides. The most serious one is inefficient monitoring of top management. Indeed, there has been practically no control exercised over top management except through the product market. Through cross-shareholdings, cross-directorships and long-term business relations, Japanese managers have isolated themselves from take-over threats and shareholder pressures and thus have been able to pursue expansionist strategies throughout the post-war period, particularly during the high-growth period up until the mid-1970s. Certainly their growth-oriented strategies have been beneficial to companies, as many Japanese firms rose to dominant positions in the international market. In the process managers have not generally sought to maximize their personal income as in some other countries. The remuneration level of Japanese top executives is much lower than international levels.

But the potential risk of ineffective monitoring of top management was inherent in the Japanese governance system, as it is also in Germany. This flaw became apparent in the second half of the 1980s in horrendous wastes of capital through reckless and unrelated diversifications and investments, and illegal or unethical behaviour of many large firms. We now examine major dysfunctions of the Japanese monitoring system.

Ritualized General Meeting of Shareholders

The Japanese general meeting of shareholders is without doubt the least effective among the countries under review as a monitor over management. It has degenerated into a mere formality, as nearly everything is decided between the management and the major shareholders before the meeting takes place.

A mail survey carried out in June 1993 by the Japan Association of Statutory Auditors on 1106 public corporations revealed that nearly 80 percent of their general meetings of shareholders ended in less than half an hour including recess time. Less than three percent last for more than an hour. At the meeting not a single question was posed by shareholders in 87 percent of the companies studied, not to speak of shareholder proposals which were not made at all in 98 percent of the companies.

Limited Monitoring Power of the Chairman of the Board

Unlike in Anglo-American and French companies, board chairmanship and presidency of Japanese corporations are seldom assumed concurrently by the same person. At first sight, therefore, the supervisory function of the chairman and the executive function of the president seem to be clearly separated. Theoretically the chairman is expected to exercise control over the president. But this is not the case, because the Japanese board chairmanship is usually an honorary, symbolic or advisory position, the last step on the ladder before retirement from the company after having been president for several years. The chairman rarely interferes with the day-to-day managerial activities of the president, though his advice may be occasionally sought on major strategic decisions or on the appointment of key managerial positions. He spends most of his time representing the firm at external functions and activities, such as meetings of trade and economic associations, government commissions etc. This 'half-retired' position of the chairman of the board is well illustrated by the fact that in 96 percent of the firms the president, not the chairman, presides over the general meeting of shareholders.

Board Members Are Appointed by the President

The fundamental cause of the board's dysfunction is that in most large firms nearly all of the board members are appointed by the president and naturally pledge their allegiance to him. In addition there are no or very few outside directors. If any, they are typically representatives from affiliated companies such as suppliers, subcontractors, etc. with little influence on the president. There is no distinction, therefore, between directors and officers. The board members are supposed to monitor the president who is their immediate superior, with obvious adverse consequences.

Boards Are Too Large

The average board in Japanese companies is larger than in any of the other industrialized nations examined here. Sakura Bank, second largest bank in revenue in 1993, is the champion with 62 Board members. The average board size for the top three construction firms is about 52, for the top three trading companies close to 50, and for the three largest automobile and banking companies around 43.

This inflation of board sizes is due to the fact that board membership is often a reward for long and faithful service or major contributions to the company. The title of board member is useful to obtain business from major customers. In short, the Japanese board of directors has been transformed into a motivating and marketing tool. With such a large board with most directors engaged in day-to-day line activities, it is practically impossible to discuss any matter of importance in detail, let alone advise and sanction the president.

Ineffective Statutory Auditors

Large listed corporations are legally subject to two monitoring mechanisms: statutory auditors and independent certified public accountants. Neither is functioning properly. The primary auditing function of statutory auditors is to prevent any decisions by the directors to be taken or implemented which are judged to be in violation of laws or articles of incorporation, or otherwise detrimental to the company. Statutory auditors thus perform both accounting and operating audits to protect the interests of the company and the stakeholders by forestalling any adverse decisions and actions before it is too late. On paper they are given powerful authority, including the right to suspend illegal actions by a board member. But actual use of this power is unheard of. The root cause of the lack of monitoring by the statutory auditors is that they are selected by the president whom they are supposed to monitor.

A study conducted by Kobe University reveals that 57 percent of statutory auditors are selected by the president and 33 percent by directors or the executive committee and endorsed by the president. This shows that 90 percent of the statutory auditors are indeed chosen by the president for perfunctory approval at the shareholders' meeting.

Flawed Corporate Governance in the West

Nor do the monitoring capabilities of Western boards function perfectly due firstly to the CEO assuming the board chairmanship (except in Germany where this is legally prohibited), secondly due to the psychological and even economic dependence of outside (non-executive) directors on the CEO/chairman, and lastly due to multiple directorships.

CEO/Chairman Duality-USA, UK, and France

These three countries share the same problem as expressed by the chairman of Delta Metal; 'The problem with British companies is that the chairman marks his own papers'. In the United States, 75 percent of large manufacturing companies are run by the CEO-chairman, according to a survey by Rechner and Dalton (1989). CEO duality is also prevalent in the UK where in 60 percent of large firms including financial corporations the chairman is also the CEO, according to a Korn Ferry International survey. In France firms can opt either for the conventional single board or the two-tier board system inspired by the German model. An overwhelming majority of large firms have the traditional single board where in most cases the chairman is also the CEO, as the title Président Directeur-Général indicates.

In Germany the separation between the supervisory board and the management board is legally assured as no member of the one board is allowed to be a member of the other at the same time. Theoretically, the German system precludes the power concentration on the CEO-chairman as seen in other countries, thus assuring independent monitoring by the chairman of the supervisory board over the management board. But the reality does not altogether reflect the intention of the legislation. According to an empirical study by Gerum (1991) on 62 large firms, this monitoring mechanism functions effectively only in firms whose supervisory board is dominated by one or more blockvote holders. The study shows that in a majority of 64 percent of the sample firms the management board influences the supervisory board. Only in 13 percent of firms does the supervisory board discharge its oversight functions over the management board. In the remaining 23 percent of firms, the supervisory board is strongly involved in the decision making of the management board, a power concentration similar to the Anglo-American, French and Japanese situations. The researcher concludes that this represents 'pathological traits' in the light of the objectives sought by the law (Gerum, 1991).

Lack of Neutrality of Outside Directors-USA and Europe

In the United States the board chairman (who is often also the CEO as mentioned already) recommends candidates for outside directors in 81 percent of the 600 firms surveyed by Korn Ferry International. In the UK 80 percent of the non-executive (outside) directors are selected from among the 'old-boy network', reducing their monitoring potential, as reported by Sir Adrian Cadbury. A similar situation is observed in France where new candidates for board membership are recommended by the CEO-chairman in 93.5 percent of the firms controlled by owner-managers, and in 92 percent of firms under managerial control, according to a study by Charreaux and Pitol-Belin (1990). In Germany, no hard data are available, but the preceding findings of Gerum on the dominance of the management board over the supervisory board leads us to infer that in a majority of large firms it is the managers on the management board that effectively determine who will be the members of the supervisory board.

Multiple Directorships–USA and Europe

This is a phenomenon that does not exist in Japan. All the Western countries reviewed here share this convention. In the United States 72 percent of the CEOs of the largest 50 corporations serve on the board of other firms and 50 percent of them have more than 6 outside directorships, according to Bassiry and Denkmejian (1990). In Germany the maximum number of board memberships is set at 10 without counting directorships in subsidiary companies. Bleicher's study of directors (1987) shows that 36 percent of his sample assume directorship in more than three corporations. Whenever there is spectacular corporate mismanagement, further reduction in the maximum number of directorships is urged, often to five. In the UK 58 percent of directors assume non-executive directorship positions in other companies and 81 percent of them hold two to four directorships (Nash, 1990). In France the legal limit is eight directorships plus five at subsidiary firms. Of 13,000 directors, 47 percent have one to 13 outside director positions, two percent have 14 to 50 positions, according to a survey by Bertolus and Morin (1987).

The question is to what extent they can be counted on to be an effective monitor and advisor. They surely have enough problems in managing their own company. They do not have in-depth knowledge or information on the business and internal problems of the other companies where they serve as outside directors.

Which System Will Win Out?

The inevitable and tempting question which follows from this kind of international comparison is which system has superiority, if any at all, over the other in the long run in the light of two fundamental criteria: efficiency and equity.

As for efficiency we have limited evidence but one of the first empirical studies revealing a positive correlation between efficiency and the pluralistic concept of the corporation was offered by Kotter and Heskett (1992). They report that firms with cultures that emphasized the importance of all the stakeholders (customers, stockholders, and employees) outperformed by a huge margin firms that did not (see Table 11.3.1). If sufficient similar evidence is accumulated, we may conclude that the pluralistic concept does enhance a firm's efficiency.

The pluralistic concept seems to be more conducive to an equitable distribution of the firm's income, and fairer sharing of risk and power among the stakeholders. This will increase organizational cohesion and survivability, as we have seen in the comparative case studies. Under the monistic concept of the corporation, employees tend to incur a disproportionately higher risk, as their job security is jeopardized in favour of shareholder/manager interests. They are usually the first to bear the brunt of poor decision making by top management, even if they are not responsible for it. This makes it difficult to expect a high commitment from them, under normal conditions or in crisis situations.

Applicability of the Pluralistic Concept

The pluralistic concept of the corporation may find wider applicability in countries outside Japan and may be a more viable and universal way for the modern corporation to promote efficiency and equity. It is not an ideology unique to Japan. An almost identical concept of the corporation was put forward in 1917 in Germany by Walther Rathenau and in the United States by Adolf Berle/Gardiner Means in 1932, and by Ralph Cordiner in the 1950s.

TABLE 11.3.1
The pluralistic concept may bring better performance – a US study

Based on: John P. Kotter and James L. Heskett *Corporate Culture and Performance*, p. 11 (1992).

11-Year growth	Firms emphasizing value to customers, shareholders & employees	Other firms
	%	%
Revenue	682	166
Workforces	282	36
Stock prices	901	74
Income	756	1

Study carried out between August 1987 and January 1991 with 202 US firms.

Walther Rathenau, who was to become Foreign Minister later, succeeded his father as the CEO of the electric engineering firm AEG. In an influential article in 1917 he asserted that 'a big business is not only a product of private interests but it is, individually and collectively, a part of the national economy and of the whole community' (Rathenau, 1923). This thesis is believed to have been instrumental in the later development of the concept of 'the firm itself' (*Unternehmen an sich*), which is close to the pluralistic approach. It paved the way for a dilution of shareholder rights, the protection of management positions, the post-World War II co-determination, and the justification of 'hidden reserves' and shares with multiple votes.

Most probably influenced by Rathenau (quoted twice in their seminal work), Berle and Means (1932) conclude their book with exactly the same proposition. In the last chapter titled *'The New Concept of the Corporation'*, they suggest:

> neither the claims of ownership nor those of control can stand against the paramount interests of the community. . . . The passive property right (i.e. diffused ownership) . . . must yield before the largest interests of the society. It is conceivable indeed it seems almost essential if the corporate system is to survive that the 'control' of the great corporation should develop into a purely neutral technocracy, balancing a variety of claims by various groups in the community and assigning to each a portion of the income stream on the basis of the public policy rather than private cupidity.

A similar ideology was espoused by Ralph Cordiner, CEO of General Electric in the 1950s who advocated that top management, as a trustee, was responsible for managing the company 'in the best interest of shareholder, customers, employees, suppliers, and plant community cities'. This concept of the corporation did not last, however, primarily because of the rise of the hostile take-over in the late 1970s, according to Peter Drucker.

Emerging Convergence

The concept of the corporation is firmly rooted in the historic, economic, political and even socio-cultural traditions of the nation. Each approach has its own positive and adverse sides. It would be improbable nor would it be necessary, therefore, that any one concept should drive out another at least in the foreseeable future. Through the cross-fertilization process, nations will be correcting the flaws in their systems, while retaining the core norms. In the process different concepts of the corporation may slowly converge, but certainly not totally. Some signs of such partial convergence are already discernible.

Japan

Japan and Germany are edging towards the Anglo-American model for increased openness and transparency, emphasis of shareholder interest and shorttermism. In Japan the traditional emphasis on job security is being eroded and the process seems to be irreversible in the long run for various reasons: firms' tendency to place merit before seniority, perspectives of low growth economy, the changing industrial structure, competitive pressures from the rapidly developing Asian countries, the increasingly detached attitude of young employees to their company, and so on.

Yotaro Kobayashi, Chairman of Fuji Xerox, for instance, made an almost unprecedented declaration for a Japanese executive to the effect that Japanese management giving top priority to employees was no longer tenable. Several companies recently announced their target return on equity to show their emphasis on shareholder wealth. Mitsubishi Corporation has declared that it will raise ROE from currently 0.6 percent to eight percent by the year 2000. Other listed corporations such as Marubeni, Omron, Daikin, etc. are following suit.

The amended Commercial Code came into force on October 1993, albeit under the usual (salutary) pressure from the United States. Every large company is now required to increase the minimum number of statutory auditors from two to three. The newly introduced stockholders' representative action' makes it easier for shareholders to bring lawsuits against company directors as the court fee has been fixed at a flat rate of only ¥8,200 per case, regardless of the size of the claim. The number of shareholders eligible for access to confidential financial documents has been expanded to those with at least three percent ownership, down from the former 10 percent. This revision may be a small step forward but it is still progress.

USA

In the United States, conversely, the traditional restrictions on concentration of funds in a single investment and of board representation at portfolio companies are breaking down. Anti-take-over regulations have been introduced in a number of States, so that the interests of the company, i.e. all stakeholders and particularly employees, are taken into account. Employees are regarded as a major stakeholder and are involved in small group activities and share ownership. Long-term business relations are being introduced notably in the automobile industry between subcontractors and assemblers.

Germany

In Germany legislation against insider trading is finally being passed. The US style audit committee is advocated by senior executives and by scholars as one of the effective remedies to ensure the proper monitoring of the supervisory board. Shareholder activism by Anglo-American institutional shareholders as well as domestic individual shareholders is increasing. In an unprecedented move the CEO and CFO of Metallgesellschaft were simply fired for their responsibility in the alleged mismanagement of oil futures business. Increased reliance on the New York capital markets and the future location of the EU's central bank in Frankfurt am Main will certainly accelerate the Anglo–Americanization process. Disclosure by Daimler-Benz of its hidden assets to conform to the SEC regulations for listing on the New York Stock Exchange is symbolic.

Conclusion

The business organization is one of the few social institutions where the deficit of democracy is pronounced, compared with the national governance system. Lack of consensus as to whose interest the company should be promoting, and insufficient checks and balances among various corporate governance mechanisms are some of the evidence. As Prof. Rappaport (1990) of the Northwestern University stresses, corporate governance is 'the last frontier of reform' of the public corporation. This reform is a daunting challenge, but it will determine the economic fate of any industrialized nation in the next century.

11.4   Corporate Governance: Lifespace and Accountability

By Ada Demb and Friedrich Neubauer[1]

Corporate governance has always been a matter of enforcing 'accountability.' Initially, it was accountability to the merchants who financed the trading ships to the New World. In those years, the relationship was very direct and easily measured. Some continue to argue that accountability should only be expected where there is a direct legal relationship: companies and boards are accountable to the stockholders, and corporate governance is the exclusive responsibility of boards. This legalistic perspective fails to cope with the realities of the late twentieth century. The sheer scale of resources controlled and influenced by individual corporations has brought them into an implicit contract that defines accountability much more broadly. Employees, communities, even whole nations invest in corporations – directly and indirectly. More importantly, because people believe that companies are accountable to them and behave as if they were, in fact, they are. Perceptions, as much as legal constraints, define the reality of what we call the 'corporate lifespace.'

Like a horse fenced in a pasture, corporate activities are bounded by a set of performance standards that reflect the expectations of stakeholders.

---

[1] Source: This article was adapted with permission from chapter 2 of *The Corporate Board: Confronting the Paradoxes*, Oxford University Press, New York, 1992.

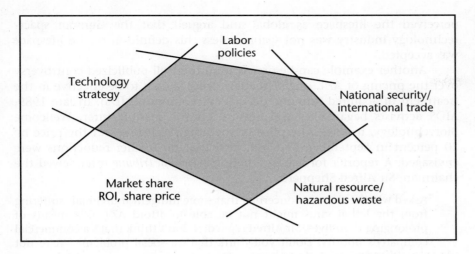

FIGURE 11.4.1
Corporate lifespace.
(Reprinted by permission
from Ada Demb and
F-Friedrich Neubauer, 'The
Board's Mandate: Defining
Corporate Lifespace,'
*European Management
Journal 7*, no. 3 [1989])

The expectations of employees, customers, creditors, neighbors, suppliers, shareholders, competitors, national and local governments, management, citizens, and others figuratively define a 'lifespace' within which a company must conduct its business (see Figure 11.4.1). The perimeters of the lifespace are defined by expectations, and the polygon has as many 'sides' as there are performance standards.

The shape of the lifespace is a matter of perspective. Those outside the corporation may perceive one lifespace; those inside, another. More often, stakeholders perceive only a subset of the boundaries with any clarity – for others the shape or implications, if noticed, remain indistinct. Corporate performance, thus, is in the eye of the beholder. Differences in perception of corporate lifespace can have important consequences, as is illustrated by the discussion in Germany in late 1989 surrounding the Daimler-Benz purchase of a majority of MBB, the aircraft and space-technology company. Among other activities, MBB was involved in international consortia building planes like the Airbus and the Tornado jetfighter. The German Cartel Office (Kartellamt) in Berlin refused approval on the grounds that the acquisition would eliminate competition for government defense orders in Germany. The majority of Dornier, the other German company with capabilities similar to MBB, was already owned by the Daimler-Benz group. The Daimler-Benz board argued that the Kartellamt missed the point: for MBB, business competition occurs only to a very limited extent within a country like Germany; its competition tends to be global. Edzard Reuter, president of Daimler-Benz, argued further that MBB and Dornier alone were too small to lead the multinational development of such large systems. The fate of the Daimler-Benz purchase rested with the German minister of economic affairs, who had the power to overrule the Kartellamt.

The acquisition was clearly a case where the lifespace was conceived quite differently by two stakeholders. German antitrust authorities (and a good portion of the German public) defined it as national; Daimler-Benz perceived the lifespace as global and argued that the German space-technology industry was not viable unless this definition of the lifespace was accepted.

Another example can be drawn from the well-publicized controversy over the pricing of AZT, one of the few drugs shown to be effective in the treatment of acquired immune deficiency syndrome (AIDS). In late 1989, AIDS activists began exerting pressure on the manufacturer, Wellcome Biotechnology, to lower the price of the drug. Wellcome cut the price by 20 percent in September, and indicated that no further reductions were envisaged. A reporter for the International *Herald Tribune* interviewed the chairman, Sir Alfred Shepperd:

> Asked whether he was concerned that some indigent individuals suffering from the lethal virus might not be able to afford AZT as a means of prolonging their lives, Sir Alfred replied: 'I don't think that's a commercial company's priority. Don't you think that's a social problem? We're not devoid of feeling. It doesn't mean to say the company doesn't take these things to heart.' He noted that the company had provided several millions of dollars worth of aid for a US government support program aimed at helping those AIDS sufferers unable to meet the costs of their debilitating disease. . . . He said it was not easy 'having to reconcile shareholders' concerns for an adequate return on their investments and the concern of terminally ill patients seeking medical palliatives. 'It's one of the issues of this industry,' he said. (Getler, 1989)

As these examples illustrate, to continue to equate corporate governance with the role of the board is to miss the point. It is much too narrow a focus. *A discussion of the meaning and purpose of corporate governance in the 1990s reaches far beyond the role of the board into the fundamental issue of the appropriate role for the corporation in today's society.* Changes in definitions of corporate governance during the past 30 years corroborate these shifts. In the 1960s, writers saw control of business power and authority as the purpose of corporate governance. More recent definitions create a broader focus and reflect the reality that standards for boards-definitions of corporate governance-have been adjusted to reflect changes in expectations for the roles that corporations play, or ought to play, in modern society. James Worthy and Robert Neuschel (1983) define corporate governance as a cluster of responsibilities:

> Governance . . . is concerned largely, though . . . not exclusively, with relating the corporation to the institutional environment within which it functions. Issues of governance include the legitimacy of corporate power, corporate accountability, to whom and for what the corporation is responsible, and by what standards it shall be governed and by whom.

In an era when companies and corporate activity shape the contours of physical, economic, and social environments to an overwhelming degree, existing 'ideologies' regarding the relationship between corporate activity and social welfare appear inadequate. Some, like George Cabot Lodge (1970), would argue that 'business cannot meet the transformational social needs of this society until political leadership provides the necessary ideology and structure.' Others prefer a more *laissez-faire* philosophy that leaves the output of business strictly to the marketplace. Whichever perspective one prefers, the profound and ubiquitous impacts of multinational and global businesses seem to demand that responsible leaders re-examine the fundamental assumptions on which the structures for corporate governance rest today (Mohn, 1989).

How Do Societies Enforce Corporate Accountability?

Every society has had to cope with the question of corporate accountability, and each has found its own variation of the solution. The approaches reflect deeply held cultural values. We can describe differences in the underlying structure of corporate lifespaces by grouping the governance mechanisms into the four clusters illustrated in Figure 11.4.2: the pattern of ownership in that national setting, the regulatory environment, the tendency of that society to exert direct pressure on corporations, and the structure of the board. The strength of the corporate governance 'system' derives from the combination of these four clusters. Each nation – and emerging regional units like the European Community – uses the elements differently. By examining them we can develop a more tangible appreciation of the national 'governance environments' encountered by corporations.

Conceptualizing corporate governance in these terms enables us to explore and understand the forces operating on a company. We can identify those forces that influence corporate behavior, and look at the conflicting demands that cause companies so much difficulty. Of course, the elements are constantly changing. The impact of these changes on corporate accountability and behavior is not always predictable. The following discussion explores each of the four elements of corporate accountability. Our resulting judgment about the shape of national governance configurations is, of

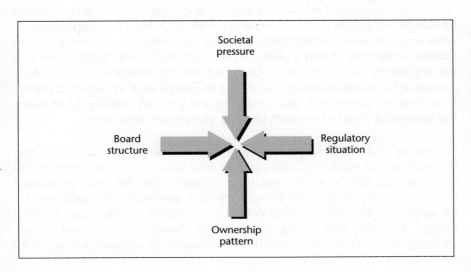

FIGURE 11.4.2
Elements of a national governance system. (Reprinted by permission from Ada Demb, 'East Europe's Companies: Thr Buck Stops Where?' *European Affairs* 4, no. 22 [1990])

necessity, impressionistic. There are no hard measures that permit 'ratings' of regulatory environments, ownership patterns, or societal habits *vis-à-vis* corporate influence. The discussion of board structures reflects our best understanding of the current legal frameworks. It is purposefully brief and intended to outline the major differences only.

The Broader Regulatory Framework

All countries have promulgated regulations that address the impacts of corporate activity. The purpose of the regulation is to ensure that corporations serve (or at least do not compromise) the greater public good, while pursuing corporate imperatives. The key questions in determining the influence of this element of the accountability system are:

1   What is the *scope* of the regulations?

2   How *stringent* are the regulations?

3   What are the *sources* of the regulations?

4   What are the *enforcement* mechanisms?

Scope   By and large the scope of most corporate legislation in market economies is similar. Hiring practices, labor relations, safety, health, plant siting standards, and waste management are among the operational matters regulated. Regulation addresses the structure of industries, how companies may be bought or sold, fair competition in markets, international and interstate trade, and requirements for the reporting and distribution of profits. Technical standards for product performance, responsibility, and relationships with customers come under regulatory purview. Companies that participate in the stock exchange face other reporting and structural requirements. The regulatory framework provides the primary reference point for management and the board because it specifies in very clear terms the nature of public expectations for corporate behavior.

The most marked differences in the scope of regulation can be observed by comparing planned or command economies – where the emphasis is on achieving universal employment, housing, medical care, and the like-with market economies. When a planned economy shifts to a market economy, the regulatory machinery must be broadened to incorporate dimensions particular to the functioning of a market economy, such as: antitrust regulation, truth-in-advertising, and consumer and product liability. Most likely, the range and detail of contract law will also require expansion.

Strictness   While the scope may be similar, we know from experience that the strictness of regulation varies enormously from country to country, and even from locality to locality within a country. Dramatic differences exist between environmental and natural resource management regulations in, for example, the industrialized countries of North America and Western Europe and the developing countries of South America and Africa. Differences in regulation, reflecting differences in attitude toward both safety and economic need, have led to the establishment of dumping sites for hazardous waste in Africa, and to bidding for toxic waste disposal sites among American towns. Different standards and beliefs about the use of growth hormones in beef production caused a serious rift between the United States and its European trading partners in early 1990. Industries also vary in their treatment of standards. For example, engineering firms involved in the design and construction of bridges, high-rise buildings, and aircraft usually incorporate a safety factor that is many times more strict than the public codes for stress. The reconciliator of differences in banking regulations, electrical appliance standards, auto emission, and so forth, is one of the greatest challenges to the EC in framing the regulations for a common market for member nations.

Sources   From a corporate perspective, the source of regulatory pressure is critically important. Whether codes are set at international, national, state, or industry levels, whether they represent formal regulation or informal codes of practice, affects the degree of corporate responsiveness. The source determines the consistency of compliance, as well as the 'management cost' of adhering to specific standards. Companies that wish to participate in seeking standards, or influencing the scope of regulation, generally find it easiest to do so at the national level. Local authorities, on the other hand, might be willing to grant more latitude to a corporation that is a major employer in the region.

Enforcement   Of course, a regulation is only as powerful as the enforcement mechanisms used to ensure corporate compliance-and enforcement mechanisms differ widely from one national setting to another. To assure that regulations are followed, corporations must expect that no one is exempt. Agency and government inspectors – the regulatory watchdogs – visit banks, food establishments, construction sites, and factories. The press and the public do their part by inquiring about corporate behavior – a point we will return to in the following section. Companies produce reports for their stockholders, the stock exchanges, and a wide variety of government agencies. Professional watchdogs, like Ralph Nader in the United States, can exert extraordinary pressures by mobilizing public opinion. A lawsuit filed against Burger King in March 1990 for abuse of US child labor laws reminds us that even 'good companies' can fall into bad practice in areas where there is little disagreement about 'correct' behavior.

The most salient aspect of the expansion in regulation that we have experienced during the past 20 years is the transfer of the control of corporate activities from the corporate domain to the public domain. Corporations must now respond to the public will. Although much room remains for business to exercise prerogatives and demonstrate leadership, government attorneys and regulatory agencies have taken the role of corporate watchdog. The scale, complexity, and geographic dispersion of corporate activity have led naturally to this situation. If government did not create these standards, we could argue that corporations would have had to create them. In some sense, then, the regulations make it easier for companies to manage themselves. There are clear sets of standards that must be applied across all company activity. Certainly, no single board could play the role of the dozen or more government agencies involved in monitoring corporate activity in the United States. The board now operates within an institutionalized framework for controlling corporate activity.

Societal Pressures

The regulatory framework would remain an empty shell without the public's willingness to bring direct pressure for corporate conformity. And the pressure would amount to little more than whistling in the wind if there were no consequences to the company. The societal habit – a vital force that is the result of much history and culture – speaks to fundamental matters of political will and responsibility: Do the governed or the governors take responsibility for the well-being of the community? By electing officials does one delegate the responsibility? Or, rather, does one simply designate a temporary focal point? Each country has its own special history in this regard.

The American mentality-established through the daring and independence of citizens who felt oppressed in their homelands, expanded through the grit and determination of the western pioneers, and articulated in the philosophy of John Stuart Mills – often seems to be grounded in contrariness. The elected government more often serves as a target for criticism than as the people's representatives. Some have characterized the Soviet Union as a nation that has always needed a strong and paternalistic leadership. The argument suggests that the Russian people are conditioned to servitude and thereby less able to resist the excesses of totalitarian regimes. There is a common saying in Scandinavia that 'you shouldn't be so tall that your head sticks up above the crowd – it might get cut off.' By contrast, in Switzerland the decisive entity is the canton; for example, the majority of tax money collected goes to the canton, rather than to the federal government.

These habits are expressed in the propensity to make use of a free press, public demonstrations, political and community action groups, and the like, to 'demand' corporate response on particular issues. The tradition of public pressure through the media developed early in US history. In the early part of this century, the impassioned books, newspaper stories, and magazine articles of Upton Sinclair and other 'muckrakers' about the early abuses of the Industrial Revolution resulted in child labor laws and other legislation regulating factor working conditions. Malcolm Forbes (father and son) continued this tradition in the business weekly, *Forbes*. Ironically, in September 1990, *Forbes* undertook an exposé of the organization and funding of popular corporate watchdog Ralph Nader. Organized consumer and environmental groups support well-respected publications today, such as *Consumer Reports*.

The mechanisms available to the public naturally affect the strength of the habit. In addition to an uncensored media, a judicial system that permits class-action suits creates a different accountability system than one that does not. While the use of class-action suits can clearly be abused, this mechanism contributes importantly to safer products (e.g. forcing companies to remove the Corvair and the Dalkon Shield from the market), safer work environments (e.g. the recognition of the health risk of exposure to asbestos fibers), and sound financial structures (e.g. the prosecution of insider trading). A liability structure that holds the board accountable as a collective has a different impact than one where liability is assessed on an individual basis.

In market economies, the marketplace provides the most direct mechanism for exerting pressure on the corporation. Loss of market share, decline in share price through stock market activity, or even direct access to capital are among the threats that can be imposed by an astute and active public. The stock market, particularly since the dramatic growth in mutual fund investment, provides a mechanism accessible to owners of all sizes. *Changing Times*, an investment magazine widely read in the United States, focused its lead article in February 1990 on 'Investing in a Cleaner Environment' and listed recently established mutual funds that invest only in companies whose environmental strategies meet certain criteria. Later in 1990, the merchant banking arm of Holland's ABN Amro Holding offered a new mutual fund, the Environment Growth Fund, which will 'initially invest in pollution control, purification and waste management companies, but its longer term objective will also include groups that produce systems and products that are not harmful to the environment.' Individual consumers, of course, can refuse to do business with a particular company, but maverick efforts are rarely compelling or irritating enough to change corporate behavior. Conversely, the managing director of a British company told us sadly of their need to divest their operation in South Africa in 1989 – the consequence of public pressure on their US operation, which accounted for some 30 percent of their market. The nature of the penalty, the size of the consequences to the corporation is the decisive aspect of this element in the governance system.

The willingness and ability of populations to exert pressure on business vary from country to country, and are the product of political and social evolution that is beyond the scope of this book. However, combined with the three other forces, they determine the real power of a governance system to elicit responsiveness and accountability from corporate enterprise.

The Ownership Patterns

In all societies, private and/or public ownership is the most basic and direct driving force for corporate accountability. 'Capitalism' has achieved success at least in part through its ability to support different philosophical orientations toward and forms of corporate ownership.

Public, or governmental, ownership The use of government ownership to ensure public accountability varies widely from country to country – and even within countries as economic and political circumstances change. The

US government prefers to regulate rather than own public utilities – the Tennessee Valley Authority being a rare exception to this policy. In Canada, Britain, France, and Finland we see much more systematic effort to bring the public interest (national security, in many cases) to bear through government ownership – through 'crown corporations' and state-owned enterprises. France and Britain seem to move through cycles of nationalization–privatization–nationalization somewhat regularly. In Great Britain, the histories of the major utilities – for example, British Rail, British Steel, British Telecom – provide a good illustration. In Germany, the federal government as well as individual states sometimes hold shares in major companies, such as Volkswagen. Examples of different approaches come most readily to hand from the oil companies.

National experience, east and west, has indicated that public ownership does not guarantee accountability. Rather, the pluralism endemic to all societies tends to ensure interest group interference with these bureaucracies – which leads to mixed signals and much inefficiency, as managers lose sight of primary service objectives.

Private ownership, shareholding   The private owner has always been a potent and mysterious force. At the turn of the century and through World War I, private owners (often families) and shareholders 'ran' European and American corporations and largely defined public accountability as they saw fit. As ownership – through private stockholders – became more diffuse, the impact of owners began to change, although it is difficult to judge whether they have become more or less influential. Certainly, current pressures through the American stock market dramatically affect most public companies, driving them to shorter-term perspectives than may be productive. As pictured in Figure 11.4.3, four types of ownership have been shifting in what seems to be a cyclical manner.

From the founding of the corporate form up through the early part of the twentieth century, ownership tended to be concentrated in the hands of a few investors: primarily families and banks, whose interests tended to focus on the long-term growth and development of corporate empires. The need for more substantial capital (usually for expansion) led to the sale of stock shares on the open market, bringing many more individuals into the ownership picture. By the early 1970s, as mutual funds became a common vehicle for investment, thousands of small investors became 'owners.' With increased pressure to raise capital for bigger and bigger deals, and pressure among the funds and brokerage houses to provide financial returns to investors, time horizons for performance grew shorter – at least in North America. Linkage of the major stock markets (in Tokyo, London, Frankfurt, New York) through electronic transfer capability heightened the thrill (and the risks) of manipulating stock for short-term gain. As corporate performance declined, the need for greater capital drove companies to more stock offerings (junk bonds for acquisitions), thereby further diffusing ownership and reinforcing the drive to short-term performance (Figure 11.4.4).

Concentrated ownership, which can exert control and accept a

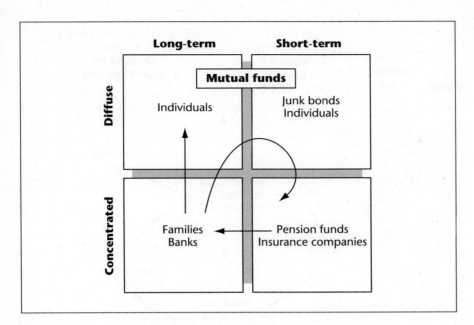

FIGURE 11.4.3
Shifts in the ownership
patterns

longer-term perspective on performance, is the only way to break this cycle. The Japanese, with their *Keiretsu*, and the Germans, through the role of the banks and insurance companies, present a more centrated ownership profile, which appears to be the basis for the greater stability and longer-term investment perspectives observed in those countries. Today in the United States and Britain, pension funds and insurance companies seem to be moving into direct and more concentrated investments in individual companies. Local pension funds, such as Alabama's Retirement Fund, control sufficient resources to enable them to guarantee an equity infusion to foreign companies that establish branches in the state. This growth in 'equity' holdings should lead, according to some, to greater stability for longer-term investment. Stephen Clark (1990), an analyst, says that 'the large-stake phenomenon may continue to evolve until it dominates some pension fund portfolios.' Quoting Tullio Cedraschi, of the $6 billion Canadian National Railway pension fund, Clark's article in *Institutional Investor* notes, 'Twenty-five stocks give you 85 to 90 percent of the diversification you need, and at some point, we should be willing to hold good companies forever. That's where I hope we're going.'

The key ingredient (new on the US scene) is the role – or potential role – institutional investors may play. The pension funds control huge assets in the United States, the Netherlands, Canada, Japan, Germany, Britain, and many other countries. Although we may be returning to the 'concentrated owners, long-term-perspective' phase of the ownership cycle, predicting the impact is hazardous (Holderness and Sheehan, 1988). Pension funds and insurance companies holding pension plans employ fund managers who also press for short-term performance from their stock portfolios. As we can

FIGURE 11.4.4
Dynamics of the
ownership cycle

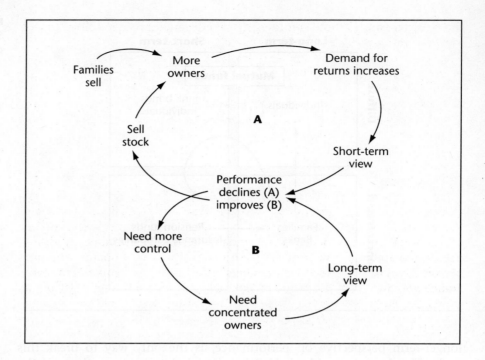

see from Figure 11.4.4, there is a built-in oscillation between the two performance loops, resulting in a constant swing from short-term to long-term as needs for capital increase. The multiple-investor loop (A) will stop driving down corporate performance only if this diffuse group can be persuaded to take the longer-term view.

Institutional investors may have the opportunity, and the will, to facilitate this shift in perspective. Institutional influence stems, most clearly, from the power that holding a major equity stake brings. Also, in Germany, and now in Canada and the United States, institutional investors hold seats on many corporate boards. The result is a strong personal and professional network of 'industrialists' who develop and act on shared values to directly influence corporate behavior. This network might be able to persuade the managers of stock funds to take the longer-term view, and to insist on corporate performance in areas of great public concern, such as the handling of toxic waste or environmental resources, thereby lending stability to the system. Whatever the structure of the ownership situation, it is clearly desirable that it support a governance system that demands performance accountability and allows for the longer-term perspectives necessary to develop both companies and societies.

The Structure and Functioning of Boards

Corporate boards remain an important element in these societal efforts to hold corporations accountable for their performance. Boards were set up as the mechanism to hold professional management accountable to the owners, and in some countries, to the employees. It is worth noting that most of the types of boards we will be discussing were structured before the proliferation of regulation, at a time when corporations were smaller and less diverse in scope, and prior to recent shifts in ownership profiles and behavior. The different legal frameworks found in the United States, France, Germany, Sweden, and Great Britain result in differing degrees and types of accountability. This is no accident. Political and economic histories helped shape the laws that established the current corporate form and board structures.

Tiers   Germany, the Netherlands, and Finland require two levels of boards: a management board of about five, usually the CEO and senior management team of the company, and supervisory board, consisting of outsiders (we return to the labor participants in Germany shortly). Canada, Great Britain, the United States and Venezuela operate with single-level boards. The ratio of executives to non-executive members differs from company to company. France and Switzerland provide companies with a choice. Our participants from France and Switzerland were both operating with single-level boards.

   One important difference between the countries with single, or two-tier boards involves the specification of board responsibilities. The two-tier structure is intended to clearly separate the 'supervisory' function from the 'management' function. In German law, for example, the membership of the supervisory board and requirements for involvement in decisions are specifically defined. While functions are clearly designated and separate, we note that for all three of our two-tier companies, the supervisory board always met with the management board. For our purposes, then, the 'body' of corporate governance is the combination of the supervisory and management boards. The management board, as the operating executive team, met much more often (up to weekly) and without the supervisory board. However, some executives told us that if the supervisory board were to call a separate meeting, they would assume a serious crisis of confidence. (For those countries with a two-tier structure, we will use the term 'board' to mean the combination of the supervisory and management boards, because we are making comparisons with single-tier or unitary boards, which combine the functions of both. When we wish to distinguish specifically, we will use the precise terminology.)

   This is quite by contrast with our British and French companies. The very broadly defined British and American board structures, evolving largely through legal precedent, create situations markedly different from that in Germany. Particularly in the United States, the law has evolved its definition of 'duty of care,' 'duty of loyalty,' and 'due diligence' through years of judicial proceedings that define case law. The statutes that delineate the requirement for a board differ from state to state. About a dozen states are fairly specific regarding director liabilities, while the others specify very little *vis-à-vis* responsibility, and nothing regarding structure. Structural requirements – such as the formation of an audit committee with a majority of outside directors – are mandated by the Securities and Exchange

Commission and necessary for listing on the New York Stock Exchange. Swiss law creates four specific mandates for the board: selecting management; providing adequate instructions for management; supervising management-ensuring compliance with instructions; and seeing that good control systems are in place.

The structural difference reflected in the laws masks essential similarities in operations, however. Our Canadian, Swiss, and British companies all have strong executive management teams that meet frequently-effectively constituting a 'management board' in practice. This operating reality does not diminish the very important differences in intent and liability in the German, Dutch, or Finnish situations.

Membership: executive, non-executive The British and North Americans use a board model that brings executives and outside directors onto the same board – albeit in different proportions. With no guidance from the law, the board is left largely to its own devices to determine the nature of interaction with management. Most Canadian and American boards are formed almost entirely with nonexecutives, plus the CEO. British boards tend to involve more executives. Many British multinationals constitute boards so that the mix is about 60: 40, perhaps seven outsiders and six executives, including the CEO. However, the majority of British companies still have a preponderance of executive directors on the board. More often than the North Americans, the British use 'outside,' non-executive chairmen in roles distinct from the CEO. In this, we hear an echo of the rationale behind the separation of the supervisory and management boards in other countries. For our British boards, it was usual procedure that the chairman met for dinner with some, or all, of the outside directors before the formal board meeting. A number of special committees on the Canadian, British, and Swiss boards involve only outside directors. We will return to this point.

Labor participation The Germans and Dutch have both established systems that bring labor into boardroom decision making in vital, but dramatically different ways. The German model creates a supervisory board (the Aufsichtsrat), in which half the membership represent shareholders (the owners) and the other half represents labor. The Dutch 'works council' system makes no requirements for direct board involvement, but calls for works council approval of certain key decisions. French companies with more than 50 employees are required to have labor observers on the board. Implicit in these systems is the essential point that 'ownership' is a necessary but insufficient definition of accountability. In some countries, those who give their lives to the company are as important as those who put their money into it.

The root of the difference between these countries and their North American, British, and Japanese counterparts can be attributed to at least two differences in history and philosophy. Much more so than in other countries, corporate activity on the continent is viewed as a partnership between labor and management. Germany's particular experience in rebuilding its industry and economy after World War II forged the very strong sense of partnership that undergirds the present board structure. In 1976, the German law shifted the ratio of labor-capital participation from 1/3: 2/3 to full 50: 50 codetermination.

Labor considerations in Britain, Canada, and the United States are incorporated through union activity and government regulation (minimum wage, work week, and health and safety, for example). Chrysler's experiment with direct labor representation on an American board was short lived. An elaborate negotiation cycle has been forged in various industries that enables the unions and management to make their way through this adversary process. Thus, the other agencies of this de facto governance system come into play to assure accountability on issues of concern to labor.

In Brussels, the EC is now addressing the knotty question of whether a structural requirement is necessary in order to involve labor fully in major corporate decisions. The practical reality is actually much the same the world over. In the Netherlands and Belgium, the works councils regulations bring labor into the picture on most critical decisions affecting their interests. In Britain, Canada, Japan, and the United States, companies seeking an energetic and motivated work force work with employees on issues of concern. The process may be less systematic, but the objective remains the same. From our point of view, for the EC Charter it seems much more important and practical to seek agreement on an outcome – a performance standard for management and labor – rather than a structural solution

Committees and number of meetings   The single-tier boards appear to use committee structures much more than do the two-tier boards. Those committee structures that isolate the nonexecutives accomplish to some degree a purpose similar to the legal separation between the management and supervisory boards. The use of an audit committee, which provides a means for outside directors to take a more active monitoring role, is a good case in point. Otherwise, the most common committees are structured to deal in detail with finance or strategy, and with the selection of senior management and nomination of board members. In Canada and the United States, audit committees are common, as are human resource, or management and compensation committees. Audit committees are becoming more common in Europe. Of our companies, four use audit committees.

The two-tier boards operate on dual frequency. Management boards meet formally, either twice monthly or once a week. As with most executive groups, informal interactions on a day-to-day basis are a way of life. The Dutch and German supervisory boards in our group of companies meet four times per year, usually for an evening and the following morning; the Finnish board meets 11 times annually. Among our unitary boards, frequency varied from a high of nine meetings per year, to a low of six. With such infrequent meetings, how does the company take action between meetings? Monthly meetings required little in-between organization, although we were told that telephone or fax votes could be taken, if needed, to approve an urgent acquisition. For the two-tier boards, quarterly meetings leave quite a gap. These structures provide for a presidium – variously constituted depending upon labor representation. In Germany, the presidium includes three people: the chairman of the supervisory board, the president of the management board, and the deputy chairman of the supervisory board, who is a labor representative. Our Dutch and Finnish CEOs indicated that they could take action 'conditional upon board approval' after consultation with the chairman.

The ability of a board to enforce accountability when it meets only four times a year is unclear. The power, influence, and judgment of outside directors relative to executives who meet continuously is another serious issue. We will examine these questions in more detail in the following chapters. It is very important at this point, however, to put the potential of the board as a mechanism for corporate governance in proper perspective. Is it strong or weak relative to the other elements of national governance structures?

Composite Lifespace

As we said earlier, the effective pressure for corporate governance comes from the cumulative effect of all four of the elements taken together. Nations work with different combinations. In some cases, elements of governance structure have been carefully designed to influence corporate behavior in specific directions. The philosophy, values, and culture of each country is reflected in these designs. More often, initiatives to change corporate behavior – an individual regulation, popular demonstrations regarding a particular issue – are taken independently. Thus our governance 'systems,' like our income tax structures, have grown into more of an inconsistent hodgepodge than we might wish.

Multinational, Global, or Hybrid ?

The lifespace diagram helps reveal the complexity of the governance environments of a multinational corporation. For a domestic company, there is one polygon – drawn to illustrate the performance standards the corporation must meet. For a multinational company, the lifespace is the cumulative result of adding together the polygons drawn for each national setting in which the company operates. Thus, a company is not only confronted with standards in one setting that may conflict, but with standards that are likely to vary across its settings. Board-level labor participation offers examples for German, Dutch, and French companies.

For Volkswagen, based in Germany, one unsettling inconsistency involves the responsibilities of the labor representatives on the supervisory board. Whom do these people actually represent? Volkswagen operates in many countries – for example, Brazil and South Africa – where labor participation is not required. The labor representatives participating in the Volkswagen board in Germany represent only German labor; while parallel structures on the subsidiary company boards might be desirable, such representation is required neither by host country corporate law nor practice. This structural anomaly creates the potential for awkward mis-understandings in labor relations in subsidiary locations. In the Netherlands the works councils, rather than board-level representation, provides the mechanism for responsiveness to labor concerns. The big Dutch multinationals have crafted structural solutions that focus (and limit) works council influence to operations within the domestic setting. Faced with a similar requirement, the French have the option of creating holding companies with fewer than 50 employees for their multinational operations, thereby avoiding the requirement for a local labor observer on the multinational board.

In addition to domestic and multinational lifespace, we can also identify certain 'hybrid' lifespace situations resulting from a mixture of global and locally defined standards. Growing global awareness of environmental impacts – including concern about acid rain and the deterioration of the ozone layer – has resulted in new standards for many corporations. Companies for whom environmental standards were previously defined domestically (albeit in multiple domestic situa-tions) now find they are facing global standards for this aspect of their lifespace. There is no simple solution when local standards for perfor-mance conflict with standards that relate to the global commons. For now the debate is in the hands of governments and corporate lenders to the Third World.

It is hardest to illustrate the 'pure' global form of lifespace because, in reality, corporate forms and public expectations are in transition, evolving from multi-domestic to global. While many aspects of a company's lifespace may be globally defined, others remain rooted in local customs and mores. Electronic technology has linked the major stock markets to such a degree that any company listed on the five major exchanges (New York, Tokyo, London, Amsterdam, Frankfurt) is effectively dealing with a set of global expectations regarding, for example, its share price. Yet employee compen-sation packages – wage rates and benefits – for the moment remain 'local,' although these have been the subject of intense discussion within the European Community.

In a May 1989 article in the *International Herald Tribune*, Colgate-Palmolive, Motorola, and Hewlett-Packard identified themselves as 'global enterprises whose futures are no longer dependent on the US economy.' The article continues, 'Inevitably, such views are putting American companies at odds with widely advocated national goals.' A union official commented, 'There is a decoupling of the corporation from the country . . . the country can be facing economic disaster and the global corporation can avoid it.' The American example illustrates that interest in a company contributing to the economy remains a strong national concern. There may always be a set of standards for, say, labor relations, strongly linked to locally held cultural values-which prevent (or save) us from evolving fully toward the 'pure' global lifespace.

Negotiating the Boundaries

How solid are the perimeters of the lifespace? How do they change? The diagram might give the impression that the lifespace is bounded by concrete fences when the perimeter is actually bounded by a permeable and changeable set of values. More like the membrane of a cell, the 'walls' connect the corporation to the other parts of society in a symbiotic and highly interdependent way. Laws, regulations, and general practice change with the evolution in community values. National differences reflect cultural preferences for social and economic values. However, changes are not simply imposed on the corporation from the outside, by stakeholders and the public; the corporation can also exert pressure from the inside to stimulate change. In theory, members of the corporation are best able to perceive the totality of this lifespace.

Should the board or management get involved in modifying, or negotiating, the perimeters – and if so, how? Reginald Jones, former Chairman and CEO of General Electric, argued strongly that companies must do so.

> I want to add my own conviction that business executives must participate personally in the formation of public policy. We cannot delegate this responsibility to our trade associations. We must study the issues, develop constructive positions, and then speak out in public forums, in congressional testimony and in personal contact with our representatives in government. These are the unavoidable responsibilities of business leadership today in companies large and small.

Negotiation can take at least two different forms: active involvement in public policy debates, and setting expectations by example. Tom Murphy, former chairman and CEO of General Motors, argued the second course in the late 1970s: 'Shoddy products, shoddy service and shoddy ethics are not acceptable. If we are not living up to legitimate public expectations, we must take corrective action without waiting to be told by the critics or the government.

A dozen years later, pollution and environmental regulation were again topics of heated public concern. An *International Wall Street Journal* article headlined 'Debate Over Pollution and Global Warming Has Detroit Sweating,' relates that

> Ford opposes strict tightening of the standards for tailpipe emissions on the grounds that pollutants from that source now are so minimal that further reductions may not be worth the cost. But the company is volunteering to redesign its cars' fuel tanks to reduce greatly the harmful emissions caused by the evaporation of gasoline.

Helen O. Petrauskas, Ford's vice president for environmental and safety engineering, was quoted in the article: 'If you want to participate in the shaping of public policy, you have to step forward and contribute to the solution, or else you can't be a player. That wasn't the attitude that the industry had in the '70s.' This new attitude reflects a change in posture toward Ford's lifespace. In the 1970s, the automobile industry took an adversary stance toward environmental activists and the government as they sought effective regulation of emissions. Today, the posture articulated by Petrauskas reflects a recognition that 'active negotiation' of the lifespace will likely result in a better solution – certainly for Ford, perhaps also for Ford's stakeholders.

National Comparisons

Using this framework, we can compare the overall strength of governance systems in different national settings (see Figure 11.4.5). While this is a highly subjective exercise, corporations do attempt these assessments in determining where to locate, or how to respond to various pressures.

Comparing board structures in the United States, France, Germany and Great Britain, we can say that German law probably makes for the strongest structures and US law makes for the weakest. Why weak? Until the very recent involvement of institutional investors, major shareholders were not represented on the boards of American companies, although boards are mandated to protect the owner's investment. By contrast, the banks and major shareholders hold board seats in Germany, as does labor. Thus, as mechanism for enforcing accountability, the board alone is not a particularly powerful structure in the United States, Great Britain, and France.

Similarly, a comparison of the influence of ownership patterns reveals important differences. Again, the German structure, because of the institutional shareholder role, appears quite influential. In Britain and France the diagram reflects the tendency to use government ownership as a vehicle. Although the stock market has seemed to drive American companies to short-term perspective, the diffusion of ownership makes this a less influential element of the system in the US context. The US ownership column in this diagram is the subject of much debate by our course participants. We can only guess at the size until we see how powerful a force the institutional investors become.

If US boards represent such a weak structure, why then does the system work? It works because, in the US context, when one part of the system fails to perform the necessary function, another part takes over (checks and balances). In recent years we have seen more and more court proceedings and regulation to ensure corporate accountability on key points. US corporate governance is currently in disarray because the structure of boards has lagged too far behind the operating definition of corporate governance: companies now are held accountable to a broader set of stakeholders than the owners. In fact, without the accompanying regulatory environment, judicial structure, and propensity for lawsuit, the United States (with or without boards) would have very poor ability indeed for forcing account-ability. Public attention and an active regulatory environment balance the board structure in the United States. In Europe, public habit plays an important, but lesser role in the governance system. Rather, ownership patterns in the United Kingdom and Germany play a more central role in creating a climate of accountability.

FIGURE 11.4.5
Relative governance
forces. (Reprinted by
permission from Ada
Demb, 'East Europe's
Companies: The Buck
Stops Where?' *European
Affairs 4*, no. 22 [1990])

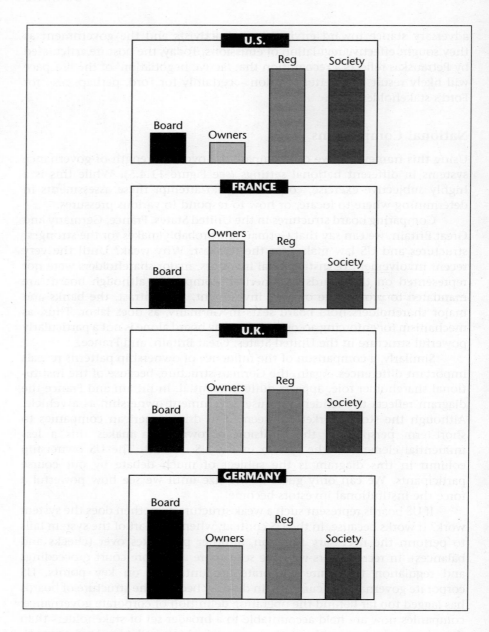

Boards in Perspective

The purpose of this discussion of governance systems is to provide a context for the central question: How can we create boards that add value with their role? Although they play an integral role, boards are no longer the primary mechanism for corporate governance. No group of eight, twelve, or twenty individuals can sensibly carry the full responsibility for assuring corporate accountability to its stakeholders. Rather, boards are one among a set of elements used by societies to make corporations responsive and account-able. Boards are designed to play an intervening role between the enterprise and society and to help resolve competing claims on the corporation. They have a dual role, as (1) one of four elements that shape the corporate life-space, and (2) an intermediary between the corporation and the other three governance forces-regulations, ownership, and societal pressures.

The question of accountability seems particularly crucial at this moment in corporate history. How do corporations resolve inconsistencies among stakeholder standards? Historically, shareholder interests were given priority. The logic was simple: ownership has its rights. For most publicly traded companies today ownership is diffuse and this makes it difficult to rely on ownership for guidance about priority interests.

Board members have commented to us that in take-over situations they must distance themselves from the company and give priority to shareholder interests. 'The company is an organic unit,' commented one non-executive board member. 'Usually you feel part of it. But when there is a take-over, you have to distance yourself from it.' Do we understand this to mean obtaining the highest 'share price,' a very short-term review of share-holder interest? In a company faced with a management buyout, the chair-man told us that, while he took very seriously his responsibility to obtain the best price for the business, he felt equally bound to assure that the employees of the business got a good deal. Having been in the business more than 30 years, he knew the people and knew they preferred the management buyout to being sold to a competitor.

The responsibility for choosing which stakeholders will get priority attention is at the core of corporate governance. Beyond those matters addressed by law, there remains enormous discretion, fraught with risks. In the words of George Cabot Lodge (1970):

> There is danger to itself, to the community, and to government in asking and expecting it [business] to do it. . . . The critical questions of which activities, how controlled, for what purposes, in whose interests are, finally, political or ideological questions having to do with the basic values of the community and its ends. They are questions for politicians to decide, preferably with the strong support and assistance of business.

Although those who are unhappy with current corporate performance may agree with Lodge, we find his comment inconsistent with the reality in the industrialized world, east and west. Corporations play a major role in shaping our societies and in managing the resources of this planet. Henry Mintzberg (1984) puts the opposing argument most forcefully:

> [T]he strategic decisions of large organizations inevitably involve social, as well as economic consequences that are inextricably intertwined. The neat distinction between economic goals in the private sector and social goals in the public sector just doesn't hold up in practice. Every important decision of the corporation – to introduce a new product line, to close an old plant, whatever – generates all kinds of social consequences. There is no such thing as purely economic decisions in big business. Only a conceptual ostrich, with his head deeply buried in the abstractions of

economic theory, could possibly use the distinction between economic and social goals to dismiss social responsibilities.

Whether or not corporations carry the legal mandate for this role, the sheer scale of their spheres of activity de facto decides the question. Corporations have as much responsibility for deciding 'which activities, how controlled, for what purposes, and in whose interests' as do public agencies and governments. We believe that there is a critical role here for boards of directors in shaping corporate response to the most fundamental question, and agree with Deming Whitman's (1989) comment:

> [It] is unlikely that the corporation can simultaneously meet all the expectations of these various groups. To do so would require such a proliferation of goals and consequent strategies that successful implementation would at best be confused and most likely impossible. Thus, some form of compromise is required. The choice of the form of the compromise is one of the more significant activities of the board of directors in conjunction with senior management.

Only corporate leaders – senior management or the board – are in a position to perceive all dimensions of the lifespace in which the corporation exists. Thus, they are the experts in understanding the opportunities, impacts, and dilemmas posed by the cumulative set of expectations that define their lifespace. Who do they tend to favor? Among directors participating in IMD programs, stockholders take primacy, but other stakeholders are given important weight. We asked IMD course participants to answer a simple written question: To whom do you feel accountable? Handwritten responses to this open-ended question, and subsequent rank-orderings of a list of twelve possibilities, generated the same result: shareholders, employees, and government/taxpayers/society were consistently named. There is a striking concurrence between the interview data and the program participants.

Forty-five board members participating in the IMD board and senior executive programs responded to an open-ended questionnaire with the phrases shown in Table 11.4.1. An additional thirty-two directors, responding to a request to rank-order a list of nine possibilities, and produced the prioritization shown in Table 11.4.2. The averages provide a clear rank-order from 1 to 9.

Many of these respondents recognized a loyalty to the company itself, for the well-being and continuity of the corporation. This was also true of many of our interviewees. As we can see, frequency of mention in the first list cannot be taken as an indication of priority. For example, although mentioned with great frequency by the first group in their open-ended responses, 'Government, People, and the Community' were given the lowest priorities by those responding to the rank-ordering. It is worthy of note that 'employees/labor' was among the top three mentioned by the first group, and ranked third by the second group. Very few respondents in this particular sample were from the Netherlands or Germany, so responses

Item	Frequency
Shareholders/owners	32
Government/society/community/taxpayers/law	17
Employees/labor	12
The board/nonexecutives	10
Chairman or CEO	10
Company	6
My staff	4
Suppliers	1
Myself	1

TABLE 11.4.1
Questionnaire responses on accountability

Item	Average
The company	2.72
Shareholders	3.84
Employees	4.50
The chairman	5.47
Clients/customers	5.78
Myself	5.78
The community	6.41
Other directors	6.53
Government/people	6.75

Note: 1 = high; 9 = low.

TABLE 11.4.2
Rank-order of 'To whom accountable'

were not biased by personal experience with direct labor participation in governance.

The only notable difference with interviewee comments came from chairmen or CEOs who more often indicated that they felt responsible to themselves. We feel this reflects the sense that they are the ultimate conscience for the company, the 'buck stops' with them, and therefore they must use their own judgment. When we asked the CEO of one company 'to whom do you feel accountable?' he responded immediately: 'To myself. I get mad at myself if I find out that I have let an unsatisfactory situation fester too long. I know that I am supposed to say that I am responsible to my shareholders, but in the first place I feels responsible to myself.' It is clear from this sampling that the 149 directors who considered the accountability question at our request take the broader view of corporate accountability.

11.5   Creating a Sense of Mission

By Andrew Campbell and Sally Yeung[1]

Many managers misunderstand the nature and importance of mission, while others fail to consider it at all. As far back as 1973, Peter Drucker observed: 'That business purpose and business mission are so rarely given adequate thought is perhaps the most important cause of business frustration and failure.' Unfortunately, his comment is as true today as it was then.

The reason for this neglect is due in part to the fact that mission is still a relatively uncharted area of management. Most management thinkers have given mission only a cursory glance, and there is little research into its nature and importance. What research there is has been devoted to analyzing mission statements and attempting to develop checklists of items that should be addressed in the statement. Indeed, a major problem is that mission has become a meaningless term — no two academics or managers agree on the same definition. Some speak of mission as if it is commercial evangelism, others talk about strong corporate cultures, and still others talk about business definitions. Some view mission as an esoteric and somewhat irrelevant preoccupation that haunts senior managers, while others see it as the bedrock of a company's strength, identity and success — its personality and character.

Despite the diversity of opinion about mission, it is possible to distinguish two schools of thought. Broadly speaking, one approach describes mission in terms of business strategy, while the other expresses mission in terms of philosophy and ethics.

The strategy school of thought views mission primarily as a strategic tool, an intellectual discipline that defines the business's commercial rationale and target market. Mission is something that is linked to strategy but at a higher level. In this context, it is perceived as the first step in strategic management. It exists to answer two fundamental questions: What is our business? and What should it be?

The strategy school of mission owes its birth to an article, 'Marketing Myopia,' that appeared in the *Harvard Business Review* in 1960. The author, Ted Levitt, a Harvard marketing professor, argued that many companies have the wrong business definition. Most particularly, companies define their businesses too narrowly. Levitt reasoned that a railroad company should see its business as moving people rather than railroading, an oil company should define its business as energy, and a company making tin cans should see itself as a packaging business. Managers, Levitt argued, should spend time carefully defining their business so that they focus on customer need rather than on production technology.

---

[1] Source: Reprinted with permission from *Long Range Planning*, August 1991, Pergamon Press Ltd. Oxford, England.

More recently, it has become common for companies to include a statement of what their business is in the annual report. Corning Glass states:

> We are dedicated to the total success of Corning Glass Works as a world-wide competitor. We choose to compete in four broad business sectors. One is Specialty Glass and Ceramics, our historical base, where our technical skills will continue to drive the development of an ever-broadening range of products for diverse applications. The other three are Consumer Housewares, Laboratory Sciences, and Telecommunications. Here we will build on existing strengths, and the needs of the markets we serve will dictate the technologies we use and the range of products and services we provide.

In contrast, the second school of thought argues that mission is the cultural 'glue' that enables an organization to function as a collective unity. This cultural glue consists of strong norms and values that influence the way in which people behave, how they work together, and how they pursue the goals of the organization. This form of mission can amount to a business philosophy that helps employees to perceive and interpret events in the same way and to speak a common language. Compared to the strategic view of mission, this interpretation sees mission as capturing some of the emotional aspects of the organization. It is concerned with generating cooperation among employees through shared values and standards of behaviour.

IBM seems to subscribe to the cultural view of mission. The company describes its mission in terms of a distinct business philosophy, which in turn produces strong cultural norms and values. For IBM, 'the basic philosophy, spirit and drive of the business' lies in three concepts: respect for the individual, dedication to service, and a quest for superiority in all things.

Is it possible to reconcile these two different interpretations? Are they conflicting theories or are they simply separate parts of the same picture? We believe these theories can be synthesized into a comprehensive single description of mission. We also believe that some of the confusion over mission exists because of a failure to appreciate that it is an issue that involves both the hearts (culture) and minds (strategy) of employees. It is something that straddles the world of business and the world of the individual.

Building a Definition of Mission

Our definition, which we have illustrated in Figure 11.5.1, includes four elements – purpose, strategy, behaviour standards, and values. A strong mission, we believe, exists when the four elements of mission link tightly together, resonating and reinforcing each other.

FIGURE 11.5.1
The Ashridge mission
model

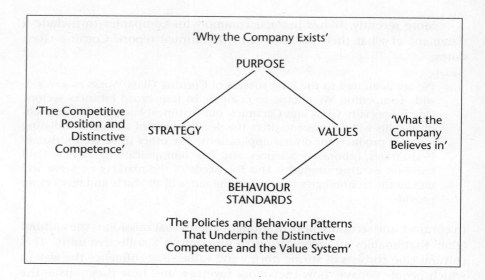

Purpose

What is the company for? For whose benefit is all the effort being put in? Why should a manager or an employee do more than the minimum required? For a company these questions are the equivalent of a person asking, Why do I exist? The questions are deeply philosophical and can lead boards of directors into heated debate. Indeed, many companies do not even attempt to reach a conclusion about the nature of their overall purpose.

However, where there does appear to be an overall idea of purpose, companies fall into three categories. First there is the company that claims to exist for the benefit of the shareholders. For these companies the purpose is to maximize wealth for the shareholders. All decisions are assessed against a yardstick of shareholder value. Hanson, a conglomerate focused on Britain and the United States, is one example. Lord Hanson repeatedly states, 'The shareholder is king.' Unlike many companies whose chairmen claim to be working primarily for the shareholders, Lord Hanson believes what he says and manages the business to that end. Hence Martin Taylor, a director, feels quite free to say: 'All of our businesses are for sale all of the time. If anyone is prepared to pay us more than we think they are worth we will sell. We have no attachment to any individual business.'

Most managers, however, are not as single-minded as Lord Hanson. They do not believe that the company's only purpose is to create wealth for shareholders. They acknowledge the claims of other stakeholders such as customers, employees, suppliers, and the community. Faced with the question: 'Is your company in business to make money for shareholders, make products for customers, or provide rewarding jobs for employees?' they will answer yes to all three.

The second type of company, therefore, is one that exists to satisfy all its stakeholders. In order to articulate this broader idea of purpose these companies have written down their responsibilities to each stakeholder group. Ciba-Geigy is an example. It has published the company's business principles under four headings – the public and the environment, customers, employees, and shareholders. Under the heading of the public and the environment it has five paragraphs describing principles such as: 'We will behave as a responsible corporate member of society and will do our best to cooperate in a responsible manner with the appropriate authorities, local and national.'

In practice it can be argued that the multiple-stakeholder view of purpose is more a matter of pragmatism than arbitrary choice. In a competitive labour market, a company that totally ignored its employees' needs would soon find its labour costs soaring as it fought to stem the tide of rising employee turnover. But what is important is the psychology of statements of purpose. Lord Hanson is saying that he is expecting his managers to put the allegiance of employees after the interests of shareholders in their list of priorities. Other companies say they have equal priority. For employees this makes them very different companies.

Managers in the third type of company are dissatisfied by a purpose solely aimed at satisfying stakeholder needs. They have sought to identify a purpose that is greater than the combined needs of the stakeholders, something to which all the stakeholders can feel proud of contributing. In short, they aim toward a higher ideal. The planning director in one company, operating in a depressed region of Britain, explained: 'I don't get excited about making money for shareholders. I like to help business succeed. That's something I can get excited about. I believe our future depends on it – I don't just mean this company, it's about the future of the nation, even the international community – it's about world peace and that sort of thing.'

At The Body Shop, a retailer of cosmetics, managers talk about 'products that don't hurt animals or the environment.' At Egon Zehnder the purpose is to be the world-wide leader in executive search. Whether these companies have an almost moral crusade, like The Body Shop, or whether they just aspire to be the best, like Egon Zehnder, they have all reached beyond the stakeholder definition of purpose. Each stakeholder, whether shareholder, employee, or supplier, can feel that doing business with the company supports some higher-level goal.

We believe that leaders will find it easier to create employees with commitment and enthusiasm if they choose a purpose aimed at a higher ideal. We have met individuals committed to shareholders or to the broader definition of stakeholders, but we believe that it is harder for this commitment to grow. Purposes expressed in terms of stakeholders tend to emphasize their different selfish interests. Purposes aimed at higher ideals seek to deny these selfish interests or at least dampen their legitimacy. This makes it easier to bind the organization together.

Strategy

To achieve a purpose in competition with other organizations, there needs to be a strategy. Strategy provides the commercial logic for the company. If the purpose is to be the best there must be a strategy explaining the principles around which the company will become the best. If the purpose is to create wealth, there must be a strategy explaining how the company will create wealth in competition with other companies.

Strategy will define the business that the company is going to compete in, the position that the company plans to hold in that business and the distinctive competence or competitive advantage that the company has or plans to create.

Behaviour Standards

Purpose and strategy are empty intellectual thoughts unless they can be converted into action, into the policy and behaviour guidelines that help people to decide what to do on a day-to-day basis.

Egon Zehnder's strategy is to be more professional than other executive search consultants. Connected with this it has a set of policies about how consultants should carry out assignments, called the systematic consulting approach. One of the policies is that consultants should not take on a search assignment unless they believe it will benefit the client. Another policy is that there should be a backup consultant for every assignment in order to ensure a quality service to the client. Supporting this systematic approach are behaviour standards about cooperation. These are ingrained into the culture rather than written on tablets of stone. An Egon Zehnder consultant willingly helps another consultant within his or her office or from other offices around the world.

The logic for the cooperation is a commercial logic. The firm wants to be the best. This means being better at cooperation than its competitors. As a result it needs a behaviour standard that makes sure consultants can help each other. This commercial logic is the left-brain logic of the firm.

Human beings are emotional, however, and are often driven more by right-brain motives than left-brain logic. To capture the emotional energy of an organization the mission needs to provide some philosophical or moral rationale for behaviour to run alongside the commercial rationale. This brings us to the next element of our definition of mission.

Values

Values are the beliefs and moral principles that lie behind the company's culture. Values give meaning to the norms and behaviour standards in the company and act as the 'right brain' of the organization.

In many organizations corporate values are not explicit and can only be understood by perceiving the philosophical rationale that lies behind management behaviour. For example, consultants in Egon Zehnder believe in cooperative behaviour because they are committed to the firm's strategy. But they also believe in cooperative behaviour because they feel that it is 'right'.

Egon Zehnder people can also be moral about certain aspects of the systematic approach. The policy of not taking on an assignment unless the consultant believes it is good for the client highlights a moral as much as a commercial rationale. Other executive search companies will take on any assignment, they argue. But Egon Zehnder puts the interests of the client first and will advise the client against an assignment even if it means lost revenues. It is a professional code of behaviour. As professionals they feel a moral duty to advise the client to do what is best for the client rather than what is best for Egon Zehnder. There is a commercial rationale for this behaviour, but the moral rationale is stronger.

Values can provide a rationale for behaviour that is just as strong as strategy. It is for this reason that the framework in Figure 11.5.1 has a diamond shape. There are two rationales that link purpose with behaviour. The commercial rationale or left-brain reasoning is about strategy and what sort of behaviour will help the company outperform competitors in its chosen arena. The emotional, moral, and ethical rationale or right-brain reasoning is about values and what sort of behaviour is ethical: the right way to treat people, the right way to behave in our society.

Our definition of mission includes both these rationales linked together by a common purpose.

A Sense of Mission: The Emotional Bond

A sense of mission is an emotional commitment felt by people toward the company's mission. But even in companies with very strong missions there are many people who do not feel an emotional commitment.

A sense of mission occurs, we believe, when there is a match between the values of an organization and those of an individual. Because organizational values are rarely explicit, the individual senses them through the company's behaviour standards. For example, if the behaviour standard is about cooperative working, the individual will be able to sense that helpfulness is valued above individual competition. If the individual has a personal value about the importance of being helpful and cooperative, then there is a values match between the individual and the organization. The greater the link between company policies and individual values, the greater the scope for the individual's sense of mission.

We see the values match as the most important part of a sense of mission because it is through values that individuals feel emotional about their organizations. Commitment to a company's strategy does not, on its own, constitute a sense of mission. It is not unusual for groups of managers to discuss their company's purpose and strategy and reach an intellectual agreement. However, this intellectual agreement does not necessarily translate into an emotional commitment, and hence the strategic plan does not get implemented. The emotional commitment comes when the individual personally identifies with the values and behaviours lying behind the plan, turning the strategy into a mission and the intellectual agreement into sense of mission.

Recognizing the personal nature of a sense of mission is important because it has two implications. First, no organization can hope to have 100 percent of its employees with a sense of mission, unless it is very small. People are too varied and have too many individual values for it to be possible for a large organization to achieve a values match for all its employees. Second, careful recruitment is essential. People's values do not change when they change companies. By recruiting people with compatible values, companies are much more likely to foster a sense of mission.

Mission and Sense of Mission

We have defined the terms *mission* and *sense of mission* at some length and been at pains to draw a distinction between these two concepts because we believe managers are frequently confused by them.

Mission is an intellectual concept that can be analysed and discussed unemotionally. Like strategy, mission is a set of propositions that can be used to guide the policies and behaviours of a company. However, mission is a larger concept than strategy. It covers strategy and culture. The strategy element of mission legislates what is important to the commercial future of the company. The values element of mission legislates what is important to the culture of the company. When the two are in tune, reinforcing each other and bound by a common purpose, the mission is strong. When there are contradictions and inconsistencies, the mission is weak.

Sense of mission is not an intellectual concept: it is an emotional and deeply personal feeling. The individual with a sense of mission has an emotional attachment and commitment to the company, what it stands for, and what it is trying to do.

A company with a clear mission does not necessarily have employees with a sense of mission. Some individuals may have a sense of mission with varying degrees of intensity. Many will not. Over time the number of employees with a sense of mission will increase as the policies of the mission become implemented and embedded in the company culture.

Mission and Vision

Warren Bennis and Burt Nanus identify vision as a central concept in their theory of leadership. 'To choose a direction, a leader must first have developed a mental image of a possible and desirable future state of the organization. This image, which we call a vision, may be as vague as a dream or as precise as a goal or mission statement,' they say. 'The critical point is that a vision articulates a view of a realistic, credible, attractive future for the organization, a condition that is better in some important ways than what now exists.' So far as the word *vision* has a meaning in business language, this quote captures its distinguishing features as well as its vagueness.

A vision and a mission *can* be one and the same. A possible and desirable future state of the organization can include all of the elements of mission – purpose, strategy, behaviour standards, and values. But vision and mission are not fully overlapping concepts. Vision refers to a future state, 'a condition that is better . . . than what now exists,' whereas mission more normally refers to the present. Marks and Spencer's mission, 'to raise the standards of the working man,' was being achieved throughout the 1950s and 1960s and is still being accomplished today. It is a timeless explanation of the organization's identity and ambition. When a vision is achieved, a new vision needs to be developed; but a mission can remain the same and members of the organization can still draw strength from their common and timeless cause.

A vision is, therefore, more associated with a goal, whereas a mission is more associated with a way of behaving. We believe that mission is the more powerful concept and we take issue with Bennis and Nanus for using the word *vision* without separating the two concepts. Vision is valuable because goals are valuable, but it is the clarity of mission rather than vision that we believe is the strength of a great leader.

In times of change, a new mission will be difficult to distinguish from a vision because the new mission will be a mental image of a desirable future state. Hence, our difference of opinion is not, in practice, a serious one. Nevertheless we have two concerns with vision as a concept. First, a vision begins to lose its power when it is achieved. It is no longer a driving force for action and the organization can begin to lose direction. This can happen to companies that strive for market leadership: once achieved, the ambition that drove the company drains away, leaving it directionless. Second, if a vision is so ambitious that it is unlikely to be achieved in the next five or ten years it loses its power to motivate and stimulate. It becomes too ambitious and unrealistic.

Mission is a much more timeless concept. It is concerned with the way the organization is managed today (behaviour standards) and its purpose. Both of these are enduring ideas and can supply an unbounded source of fulfillment and energy.

Mission and Strategic Intent

Strategic intent is another concept that overlaps with vision and mission. Hamel and Prahalad comment:

> On the one hand strategic intent envisions a desired leadership position and establishes the criterion the organization will use to chart its progress. Komatsu set out to 'encircle Caterpillar.' Canon sought to 'beat Xerox,' Honda strove to become a second Ford, an automotive pioneer. All are expressions of strategic intent. At the same time strategic intent is more than just unfettered ambition. (Many companies possess an ambitious strategic intent yet fall short of their goals.) The concept also encompasses an active management process that includes: focusing the organization's attention on the essence of winning; motivating people by communicating the value of the target; leaving room for individual and team contributions; sustaining enthusiasm by providing new operational definitions as

circumstances change; and using intent consistently to guide resource allocations.

Strategic intent is a concept that draws from both vision and mission. It includes a desired future state, a goal defined in competitive terms that is more a part of vision than of purpose. It also encompasses a definition of strategy that is fundamentally the same as the use of strategy within mission. Strategic intent is, therefore, closest in concept to the traditional definition of mission: What business are we in and what strategic position do we seek?

However, we see strategic intent as suffering from the same problem as vision, in that once the intent has been achieved, the organization is liable to lose direction. The problem with goals is that they have to be reset as they are achieved. Purpose has the advantage of being everlasting.

We also see strategic intent as being a left-brain concept. Hamel and Prahalad argue that intent should motivate people 'by communicating the value of the target.' We have not found many managers who are motivated by a target, unless it is a short-term objective or milestone. Managers we have spoken to are motivated more by the organization's current values than by some distant ambition. Strategic intent is, in our view, a less powerful concept than mission because it fails to include values and behaviour standards, the keys to long-standing employee commitment and enthusiasm.

Mission Planning

Our research has shown us that mission can be analyzed and discussed in as rigorous a way as strategy. In other words, managers can do mission planning in the same way that they do strategic planning. In fact, strategic planning is a subset of mission planning. Mission planning is more sophisticated than strategic planning; it helps managers formulate strategies that will fit their organization.

One of the reasons that so many strategies fail to get further than the pages of a beautifully bound planning document is that they are strategies, not mission: they fail to build on the values and behaviour standards that already exist in the organization and they do not inspire the emotions of the managers and employees who are expected to put them into practice.

Mission planning goes beyond strategic planning in three ways:

■ It involves an analysis of employee values and organization behaviour to assess the changes needed.

■ It focuses on identifying behaviour standards that are central to the implementation of strategy and symbolic of the new value system.

■ It encourages discussion of the organization's commitment to its stakeholders and to some higher-level purpose.

Mission planning forces managers to think through the behavioural implications of their plans; it prompts them to articulate an inspirational reason for any new plans; and it prevents them from sidestepping the issue of whether existing managers and employees are capable of responding to the challenge. Mission planning is where strategy, organization, and human resource issues come together. It asks managers to take a holistic view of their organization and its environment before developing a plan of action.

We believe that leaders of multibusiness companies should be promoting mission planning at the business unit level in the same way that most companies currently promote strategic planning. The first step is to extend mission thinking into the periodic strategic planning process:

■   Ask managers in charge of business units to include issues of purpose, values, and behaviour standards along with their presentation at the strategy review.

■   Ask them whether or not their organization is culturally aligned with their strategy.

■   Ask them what their three most important behaviour standards are.

Initially these questions will get little attention, superficial discussion, and insufficient analysis. But the process will have started. Managers at the centre will be able to identify issues of concern and ask for further clarification or follow-up with the business unit informally. The mission questions at the next strategy review can be more targeted, moving the thinking forward again.

In a highly developed process it may become necessary to separate the mission discussion from the strategy discussion in the same way that most companies have found it beneficial to separate the strategy discussion from the budget discussion.

Many managers at headquarters have argued to us that although they can see the relevance and importance of mission thinking at the business unit level, they can see no value in it at the headquarters level of a diversified company. A corporate-level mission would be considered an imposition, discouraging diverse business from developing their own diverse missions.

We do not disagree with this view, yet we still consider that it is possible to have a headquarters mission and a set of diverse business unit missions. Mission can be treated in the same way as strategy. Because it is possible, in fact necessary, to have a corporate strategy and a different strategy for each business unit, it is possible to have a corporate mission and a different mission for each business unit. With good strategic planning the strategies at different levels and between sister companies do not clash and can reinforce each other. In the same way, good mission planning ensures compatibility between the different missions.

Further Readings

Readers interested in delving deeper into the topic of organizational purpose have a richness of sources from which to choose. A good introductory work is the textbook *International Corporate Governance*, by Robert Tricker, which also contains many classic readings and a large number of interesting cases. One of the excellent readings reprinted in Tricker's book is Henry Mintzberg's article 'Who Should Control the Corporation?,' which provides a stimulating insight into the basic questions surrounding the topic of organizational purpose. Another good overview of the issues and literature in the area of corporate governance is presented in the book *Strategic Leadership: Top Executives and Their Effects on Organizations* by Sydney Finkelstein and Donald Hambrick.

Other worthwhile follow-up readings on the topic of corporate governance include the book by Ada Demb and Friedrich Neubauer, *The Corporate Board: Confronting the Paradoxes*, and an excellent comparison of five national governance systems given in the book *Keeping Good Company*, by Jonathan Charkham. Recent edited volumes well worth reading are *Capital Markets and Corporate Governance*, by Nicolas Dimsdale and Martha Prevezer, and *Corporate Governance: Economic, Management, and Financial Issues*, by Kevin Keasey, Steve Thompson and Mike Wright.

For further reading on the topic of shareholder value, Alfred Rappaport's book *Creating Shareholder Value* is the obvious place to start. A good follow-up reading is Michael Jensen's article 'Corporate Control and the Politics of Finance.' For a very fundamental point of view, Milton Friedman's classic article 'The Social Responsibility of Business is to Increase Its Profits,' is also highly recommended. For a stinging attack on the stakeholder concept, readers are advised to see 'The Defects of Stakeholder Theory,' by Elaine Sternberg.

For a more positive view of stakeholder theory, Edward Freeman's *Strategic Management: A Stakeholder Approach* is still the book at which to begin. Only recently has stakeholder theory really attracted significant academic attention. Excellent works in this new crop include 'Instrumental Stakeholder Theory: A Synthesis of Ethics and Economics,' by Thomas Jones, and 'The Stakeholder Theory of the Corporation: Concepts, Evidence, and Implications,' by Thomas Donaldson and Lee Preston.

On the topic of corporate social responsibility, there are a number good books that can be consulted. Archie Carroll's, *Business and Society: Ethics and Stakeholder Management* can be recommended, while the book *International Business and Society*, by Steven Wartick and Donna Wood, has a stronger international perspective. Good articles include 'The Corporate Social Policy Process: Beyond Business Ethics, Corporate Social Responsibility, and Corporate Social Responsiveness,' by Edwin Epstein, and the more academic 'A Stakeholder Framework For Analyzing and Evaluating Corporate Social Performance,' by Max Clarkson.

For an explicit link between strategy and ethics, the book *Corporate Strategy and the Search For Ethics*, by Edward Freeman and Daniel Gilbert, provides a good point of entry. The more recent article 'Strategic Planning As If Ethics Mattered,' by LaRue Hosmer, is also highly recommended. Many books on the general link between ethics and business, such as Thomas Donaldson's *The Ethics of International Business*, deal with major strategy issues as well.

Finally, on the topic of corporate mission a very useful overview of the literature is given in the reader *Mission and Business Philosophy*, edited by Andrew Campbell and Kiran Tawadey. Good follow-up works not in this reader are Derek Abell's book *Defining the Business – The Starting Point of Strategic Planning*, and the article 'Mission Analysis: An Operational Approach,' by Nigel Piercy and Neil Morgan. A interesting book emphasizing the importance of vision is *Built To Last: Successful Habits of Visionary Companies*, by James Collins and Jerry Porras.

References

Abbeglen, J., and Stalk, G. (1985) *Kaisha, the Japanese Corporation*, Basic Books, New York.

Abell, D. (1980) *Defining the Business – The Starting Point of Strategic Planning*, Prentice-Hall, Englewood Cliffs.

Ackermann, R.W., and Bauer, R.A. (1976) *Corporate Social Performance: The Modern Dilemma*, Reston, Reston, VA.

Ackoff, R.L. (1974) *Redesigning the Future*, John Wiley & Sons, New York.

Albach, H. (1994) Wertewandel Deutscher Manager, in Albach (Ed.), *Werte und Unternehmensziele im Wandel der Zeit*.

Alkhafaji, A.F. (1989) *A Stakeholder Approach to Corporate Governance: Managing a Dynamic Environment*, Quorum Books, Westport, CT.

Ansoff, I. (1965) *Corporate Strategy*, McGraw-Hill, New York, pp. 33–5.

Barnard, C. (1938) *The Function of the Executive*, Harvard University Press, Cambridge, MA.

Bartlett, C.A., and Ghoshal, S. (1994) Changing the Role of Top Management: Beyond Strategy to Purpose, *Harvard Business Review*, November-December, pp. 79–88.

Bassiry, G.R., and Denkmejian, H. (1990) The American Corporate Elite: A Profile, *Business Horizons*, May-June.

Baysinger, B.D., and Hoskisson, R.E. (1990) The Composition of Boards of Directors and Strategic Control: Effects of Corporate Strategy, *Academy of Management Review*, Vol. 15, pp. 72–81.

Berle, A.A., and Means, G.C. (1932) *The Modern Corporation and Private Property*, Transaction Publishers, (reprinted 1991).

Bertolus, J., and Morin, F. (1987) Conseil d'Administration, *Science et Vie Économie*, 33, November.

Blair, M. (1995) *Ownership and Control: Rethinking Corporate Governance for the Twenty-First Century*, Brookings Institution, Washington.

Bleicher, K. (1987) *Der Aufsichtsrat im Wandel*, Verlag Bertelsmann-Stiftung, Guetersloh.

Bourgeois, L.J., and Brodwin, D.R. (1983) Putting Your Strategy into Action, *Strategic Management Planning*, March/May.

Bowie, N. (1991) New Directions in Corporate Social Responsibility, *Business Horizons*, July-August, pp. 56–65.

Bucholz, R.A. (1986) *Business Environment and Public Policy*, Prentice-Hall, Englewood Cliffs.

Buono, A.F., and Nichols, L.T. (1985) *Corporate Policy, Values and Social Responsibility*, Praeger, New York.

Cadbury, A. (1990) *The Company Chairman*, Fitzwilliam Publishing, Cambridge.

Campbell, A., and Tawadey, K. (1990) *Mission and Business Philosophy*, Butterworth-Heinemann, Oxford.

Campbell, A., and Yeung, S. (1991) Creating a Sense of Mission, *Long Range Planning*, August, pp. 10–20.

Cannon, T. (1992) *Corporate Responsibility*, Pitman, London.

Carroll, A.B. (1993) *Business and Society: Ethics and Stakeholder Management*, 2nd edn, South-Western Publishing, Cincinnati.

Cavanagh, G.F. (1984) *American Business Values*, 2nd Edition, Prentice-Hall, Englewood Cliffs.

Charkham, J. (1994) *Keeping Good Company: A Study of Corporate Governance in Five Countries*, Oxford University Press, Oxford.

Charreaux, G., and Pitol-Belin, J. (1990) *Le Conseil d'Administration*.

Clark, S. (1990) Taking a Big Bite, *Institutional Investor*, August, pp. 69–70.

Clarkson, M.B.E. (1995) A Stakeholder Framework For Analyzing and Evaluating Corporate Social Performance, *Academy of Management Review*, Vol. 20, pp. 92–117.

Cochran, Ph.L., and Wartick, S.L. (1994) Corporate Governance – A Review of the Literature, in Tricker, R.I., *International Corporate Governance: Text, Readings and Cases*, Prentice-Hall, Singapore.

Collins, J.C., and Porras, J. (1994) *Built To Last: Successful Habits of Visionary Companies*, Random House, London.

Collins, J.C., and Porras, J. (1996) Building Your Company's Vision, *Harvard Business Review*, September-October, pp. 65–77.

Cummings, S., and Davies, J. (1994) Mission, Vision, Fusion, *Long Range Planning*, Vol. 27, No. 6, pp. 147–50.

David, F.R. (1989) How Companies Define Their Mission, *Long Range Planning*, Vol. 22, No. 1, pp. 90–7.

Demb, A., and Neubauer, F.F. (1992) *The Corporate Board: Confronting the Paradoxes*, Oxford University Press, Oxford.

Dill, W.R. (1975) Public Participation in Corporate Planning: Strategic Management in a Kibitzer's World, *Long Range Planning*, pp. 57–63.

Dimsdale, N., and Prevezer, M. (eds) (1994) *Capital Markets and Corporate Governance*, Oxford University Press, Oxford.

Donaldson, L., and Davis, J.H. (1995) Boards and Company Performance – Research Challenges the Conventional Wisdom, *Corporate Governance: An International Review*, Vol. 2, pp. 151–60.

Donaldson, T. (1989) *The Ethics of International Business*, Oxford University Press, New York.

Donaldson, T., and Preston, L.E. (1995) The Stakeholder Theory of the Corporation: Concepts, Evidence, and Implications, *Academy of Management Review*, Vol. 20, pp. 65–91.

Drucker, P.F. (1984) The New Meaning of Corporate Social Responsibility, *California Management Review*, Vol. 26, Winter, pp. 53–63.

Drucker, P.F. (1991) Reckoning with the Pension Fund Revolution, *Harvard Business Review*, March-April, pp. 106–14.

Eisenhardt, K.M. (1989) Agency Theory: An Assessment and Review, *Academy of Management Review*, Vol. 14, pp. 57–74.

Emshoff, J.R., and Freeman, R.E. (1979) Who's Butting Into Your Business?, *The Wharton Magazine*, Fall.

Emshoff, J.R., and Freeman, R.E. (1981) Stakeholder Management: A Case Study of the U.S. Brewers Association and the Container Issue, in Schultz, R., (ed.), *Applications of Management Science*, JAI Press, Greenwich.

Epstein, E.M. (1987) The Corporate Social Policy Process: Beyond Business Ethics, Corporate Social Responsibility, and Corporate Social Responsiveness, *California Management Review*, Vol. 29, Spring, pp. 99–114.

Falsey, T.A. (1989) *Corporate Philosophies and Mission Statements*, Quorum Books, New York.

Finkelstein, S., and Hambrick, D.C. (1996) *Strategic Leadership: Top Executives and Their Effects on Organizations*, West, St. Paul.

Freeman, R.E. (1984) *Strategic Management: A Stakeholder Approach*, Pitman/Ballinger, Boston.

Freeman, R.E., and Gilbert Jr., D.R. (1988) *Corporate Strategy and the Search for Ethics*, Prentice-Hall, Englewood Cliffs.

Freeman, R.E., and Liedtka, J. (1991) Corporate Social Responsibility: A Critical Approach, *Business Horizons*, July-August.

Freeman, R.E., and Reed, D.L. (1983) Stockholders and Stakeholders: A New Perspective on Corporate Governance, *California Management Review*, Vol. 25, No.3, Spring, pp. 88–106.

Friedman, M. (1970) The Social Responsibility of Business is to Increase Its Profits, *The New York Times Magazine*, September 13, (Reprinted in Hoffman, W.M., and J.M. Moore (eds), *Business Ethics*, McGraw-Hill, New York, 1990).

Gerum, E. (1991) Aufsichtratstypen – Ein Beitrag zur Theorie der Organisation der Unternehmungsführung, *Die Betriebswirtschaft*, No.6.

Getler, W. (1989) Wellcome Draws a Bottom Line, *International Herald Tribune*, 20, September, p. 13.

Goodpaster, K.E. (1991) Business Ethics and Stakeholder Analysis, *Business Ethics Quarterly*, January, pp. 53–73.

Guthrie, J., and Turnbull, S. (1994) Audit Committees: Is There a Role for Corporate Senates and/or Stakeholder Councils?, *Corporate Governance: An International Review*, Vol. 3, pp. 78–89.

Hamel, G., and Prahalad, C.K. (1989) Strategic Intent, *Harvard Business Review*, May/June, pp. 63–77.

Harrison, J.R. (1987) The Strategic Use of Corporate Board Committees, *California Management Review*, Vol. 30, pp. 109–25.

Hart, O.D. (1995) *Firms, Contracts and Financial Structure*, Clarendon Press, Oxford.

Hax, A.C. (1990) Redefining the Concept of Strategy and the Strategy Formation Process, *Planning Review*, May/June, pp. 34–40.

Hayes, R., and Abernathy, W. (1980) Managing Our Way to Economic Decline, *Harvard Business Review*, Vol. 58, No.4, pp. 67–77.

Hoffman, W.M. (1989) The Cost of a Corporate Conscience, *Business and Society Review*, Spring, pp. 46–7.

Holderness, C., and Sheehan, D. (1988) The Role of Majority Shareholders in Publicly Held Corporations, *Journal of Financial Economics*, 21/22, pp. 317–46.

Hosmer, L.T. (1994) Strategic Planning As If Ethics Mattered, *Strategic Management Journal*, Summer Special Issue, Vol. 15, pp. 17–34.

Jensen, M.C. (1991) Corporate Control and the Politics of Finance, *Journal of Applied Corporate Finance*, Vol. 4, pp. 13–33.

Jensen, M.C., and Meckling, W.H. (1976) Theory of the Firm, Managerial

Behavior, Agency Costs, and Ownership Structure, *Journal of Financial Economics*, October, pp. 305–60.

Jones, T.M. (1995) Instrumental Stakeholder Theory: A Synthesis of Ethics and Economics, *Academy of Management Review*, Vol. 20, pp. 404–37.

Keasey, K., Thompson, S. and Wright, M. (eds) (1997) *Corporate Governance: Economic, Management, and Financial Issues*, Oxford University Press, Oxford.

Klemm, M., Sanderson, S. and Luffman, G. (1991) Mission Statements, *Long Range Planning*, Vol. 24, No. 3, pp. 73–8.

Kotter, J.P., and Heskett, J.L. (1992) *Corporate Culture and Performance*.

Langtry, B. (1994) Stakeholders and the Moral Responsibilities of Business, *Business Ethics Quarterly*, Vol. 4, pp. 431–43.

Lodge, G.C. (1970) Top Priority: Renovating Our Ideology, *Harvard Business Review*, September-October, p. 54.

McCoy, C.S. (1985) *Management of Values*, Ballinger, Cambridge, MA.

Mintzberg, H. (1984) Who Should Control the Corporation?, *California Management Review*, Vol. 27, Fall pp. 90–115.

Mohn, R. (1989) *Success Through Partnership*, Bantam, London.

Nash, T. (1990) Bit Parts and Board Games, *Director*, October.

O'Connell, J.J. (1984) Corporate Governance: The European Challenge, in Hoffman, W.M., Moore, J.M. and Fedo, D.A. (eds), *Corporate Governance and Institutionalizing Ethics*, Lexington Books, Lexington, MA.

Parkinson, J.E. (1993) *Corporate Power and Responsibility*, Oxford University Press, Oxford.

Pearce, J.A. (1982) The Company Mission as a Strategic Tool, *Sloan Management Review*, Spring, pp. 15–24.

Peters, T.J., and Waterman, R.H. (1982) *In Search of Excellence*, Harper & Row, New York.

Piercy, N.F., and Morgan, N.A. (1994) Mission Analysis: An Operational Approach, *Journal of General Management*, Vol. 19, No. 3, pp. 1–16.

Porter, M.E. (1980) *Competitive Strategy: Techniques for Analyzing Industries and Competitors*, Free Press, New York.

Rappaport, A. (1986) *Creating Shareholder Value: The New Standard for Business Performance*, The Free Press, New York.

Rappaport, A. (1990) The Staying Power of the Public Corporation, *Harvard Business Review*, January-February.

Rathenau, W. (1923) *Vom Aktienwesen, eine geschäftliche Betrachtung*, Fischer, Berlin.

Rechner, P.L., and Dalton, D.R. (1989) The Impact of CEO as Board Chairperson on Corporate Performance: Evidence vs. Rhetoric, *The Academy of Management Executive*, Vol. III, No.2, pp. 141–3.

Solomon, R.C. (1992) *Ethics and Excellence: Cooperation and Integrity in Business*, Oxford University Press, New York.

Spencer, A. (1983) *On the Edge of the Organization: The Role of the Outside Director*, Wiley, New York.

Stark, A. (1993) What's the Matter with Business Ethics?, *Harvard Business Review*, May-June, pp. 38–48.

Sternberg, E. (1997) The Defects of Stakeholder Theory, *Corporate Governance*, Vol. 5, No. 1, January, pp. 3–10.

Stone, C.D. (1975) *Where the Law Ends*, Harper & Row, New York.

Suzuki, S., and Wright, R.W. (1985) Financial Structure and Bankruptcy Risk in

Japanese Companies, *Journal of International Business Studies*, Spring, pp. 97–110.

Sykes, A. (1994) Proposals for Internationally Competitive Corporate Governance in Britain and America, *Corporate Governance*, Vol. 2, No. 4, pp. 187–95.

Treynor, J.L. (1981) The Financial Objective in the Widely Held Corporation, *Financial Analysts Journal*, March-April, pp. 68–71.

Tricker, R.I. (1994) *International Corporate Governance: Text, Readings and Cases*, Prentice-Hall, Singapore.

Walsh, J.P., and Seward, J.K. (1990) On the Efficiency of Internal and External Corporate Control Mechanisms, *Academy of Management Review*, Vol. 15, pp. 421–58.

Wartick, S.L., and Wood, D.J. (1997) *International Business and Society*, Blackwell, Oxford.

Whitman, D. (1989) *The Role of the Board of Directors: To Whom Is the Board Responsible?*, Individual Research Project, MBA program, Geneva, IMI, p. 28.

Worthy, J.C., and Neuschel, R.P. (1983) *Emerging Issues in Corporate Governance*, Northwestern University Press, Chicago, p. 4.

Yoshimori, M. (1995) Whose Company Is It? The Concept of the Corporation in Japan and the West, *Long Range Planning*, Vol. 28, pp. 33–45.

Zahra, S.A., and Pearce, J.A. (1989) Boards of Directors and Corporate Financial Performance: A Review and Integrative Model, *Journal of Management*, Vol. 15, pp. 291–334.

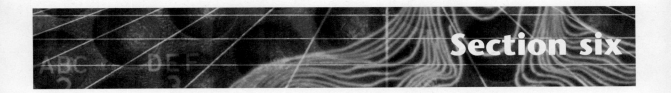

Cases

- Case 1 Honda
- Case 2 Swatch
- Case 3 Virgin
- Case 4 Stantret
- Case 5 Oldelft
- Case 6 Kao Corporation
- Case 7 Carl Zeiss Jena
- Case 8 Encyclopaedia Brittannica
- Case 9 Southwest Airlines
- Case 10 Canon
- Case 11 Shell & Billiton
- Case 12 Grand Metropolitan
- Case 13 KLM and the Alcazar Alliance
- Case 14 The Salim Group
- Case 15 The Champagne Industry
- Case 16 National Bicycle Industry
- Case 17 Teléfonos de Mexico
- Case 18 Cartier
- Case 19 Saatchi & Saatchi

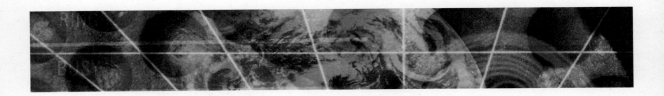

❑ **Case 20A and B Cap Gemini Sogeti**
❑ **Case 21   Burroughs Wellcome and AZT**
❑ **Case 22   The Body Shop International**

Case 1: Reconciling Managerial Dichotomies at Honda Motors

By Andrew Mair[1]

By following a corporate policy that stresses originality, innovation, and efficiency in every facet of its operations – from product development and manufacturing to marketing – Honda has striven to attain its goal of satisfying its customers (Honda Annual Report, 1997: i)

Honda Motor Co., the Japan-based manufacturer of cars, motorcycles and power products like lawnmowers and small boat engines, is one of the great success stories of the post-war Japanese economy (see Exhibit 1, Exhibit 2, Exhibit 3). Established in 1948, since the 1970s Honda has been widely recognized as a pioneering Japanese manufacturer and as one of the world's leading motor industry companies. Honda was the first Japanese manufacturer to make its products in Europe, when its Belgian motorcycle factory opened in 1963. Honda became the first Japanese firm to manufacture automobiles in North America when it opened its Ohio assembly plant in 1982. Honda took the risk of entering into a long and complex relationship during the 1980s with a European company universally considered to be one of the least capable automobile manufacturers in the West, British Leyland (now Rover Group).

By the late 1980s, only 25 years after the firm entered the automobile industry, the 'industry of industries', Honda had become one of the world's top ten producers. Indeed, automobile production had come to dominate Honda's activities, responsible for nearly four-fifths of its turnover. By the mid 1990s Honda also stood head and shoulders above other leading automobile producers in international sales (with 77 percent of its sales by volume outside its home market region), and had become the most international of all automobile companies in production, with 46 percent of its manufacturing output by volume outside its home market region (see Exhibit 4).

Compared to its Japanese rivals, Honda has remained a relatively small player in its domestic market, with market share consistently under 10 percent, on a par with Mazda and Mitsubishi, not far ahead of Daihatsu and Suzuki. But from a global perspective, Honda's early and rapid internationalization, first of sales during the 1970s, then of production during the 1980s, propelled the company spectacularly out of the ranks of mid-sized Japanese automobile producers to a status alongside Toyota and Nissan as one of the global Japanese 'Big Three' automobile producers. And Honda was now significantly more international than either Toyota or Nissan in both sales and production. Continued growth of sales and production during the first half of the 1990s was hindered – as in the early 1970s – by world recession. But the geographical spread of Honda's activities meant that, unlike some of its Japanese competitors, the firm was able to sustain profitability right through the post-'bubble economy' slump in the Japanese economy during the early 1990s (see Exhibit 5).

In the global automobile industry, Honda's achievements on the technology front are well recognized, ranging from its cutting-edge low pollution and low fuel consumption engine technologies to its achievement in powering World

[1] Source: This case was written by Andrew Mair, Birkbeck College, University of London. A previous version of this case study appeared as 'Honda Motors: a paradoxical approach to growth,' in C. Baden-Fuller and M. Pitt (eds.), *Strategic Innovation: An International Casebook*, Routledge, London, 1996, pp. 435–61. The author acknowledges the helpful comments of Charles Baden-Fuller and Martyn Pitt. This version has been updated and revised. Copyright 1997 by Andrew Mair.

EXHIBIT 1
Significant milestones in Honda's development

1946	Soichiro Honda sets up Honda Technical Research Institute in Hamamatsu, producing auxiliary engines for bicycles, and later, machine tools.
1948	Company renamed Honda Motor Co. Ltd. First production Honda vehicle, 90cc B-type motorcycle.
1952	Exports begin (to Philippines).
1954	Soichiro Honda visits European car manufacturers. First exports (of 200cc K-type 'Juno' scooter) to USA.
1955	Honda becomes largest Japanese motorcycle manufacturer.
1959	American Honda Motor Co. Inc. [sales subsidiary] established.
1961	European Honda GmbH (now Honda Deutschland GmbH) [sales subsidiary] established in Hamburg.
1962	NV Honda Motor SA (now Honda Belgium NV) established to assemble and sell mopeds in Europe (production begins 1963) [the first manufacturing facility opened by any Japanese company in the West].
1963	T360 lightweight truck and S360 sports car, first Honda 4–wheeled vehicles, go on sale.
1965	Honda UK Ltd. [sales subsidiary] established in London.
1968	First exports of N360 and N600 microcars. Cumulative motorcycle production passes 10 million.
1971	CVCC low emission automobile engine announced.
1972	First generation Civic automobile introduced.
1973	Soichiro Honda and Takeo Fujisawa retire to become Supreme Advisors.
1976	First generation Accord announced. Civic production reaches 1 million after 4 years.
1977	IAP Industriale SpA (now Honda Italia Industriale SpA) established in Italy [subsidiary to manufacture motorcycles].
1978	Honda of America Manufacturing, Inc. set up to make motorcycles in the USA (production begins 1979). Cumulative production of motorcycles exceeds 30 million. Cumulative car production exceeds 5 million.
1979	Company signs technical collaboration with British Leyland, [now Rover Group], covering BL production of Triumph Acclaim car (production in the United Kingdom begins 1981) [first of several joint car developments between the firms lasting until late 1990s].
1982	European Head Office established in Belgium. Honda of America begins car production.
1984	Plans to double Honda of America car manufacturing capacity to 300,000 units/year. Honda Research of America (now Honda R&D North America) established.
1985	Plans announced to double car production in Canada from 40,000 to 80,000 cars/year.
1986	Honda of America begins engine manufacture.
1988	Plans announced for second US car assembly plant. VTEC variable valve timing system principle announced. Plans announced to build R&D centre in Europe.
1989	Soichiro Honda inducted into America's Automotive Hall of Fame [as first Japanese]; Honda Accord becomes overall best selling automobile model in the United States.
1990	Agreement with Rover under which Honda acquires minority shareholding in Rover. Accord Aerodeck becomes the first American built car model to be exported both to Japan and to Europe.
1992	European production of Honda Accord begins at Swindon, United Kingdom.
1994	Honda unwinds formal relationship with Rover and BMW purchases Rover from it parent company; announcement of further investments in North America to take annual production capacity from 600,000 to 800,000 by 1999, with 150,000 of these vehicles exported.
1995–6	Successful entry into growing 'light truck' market niches in Japan and North America with Odyssey minivan and CR-V sports utility vehicle.
1997	Production of new 'Asian car' (City model) starts in Thailand as overseas production approaches half of total car production at Honda.

Source: Excerpted from Honda European Information Handbook (1991–1992) and Honda Annual Reports.

	Automobiles/Light Trucks (000 units)
1960	0
1965	52
1970	393
1975	414
1980	957
1985	1,363
1990	1,928
1995	1,794

* Honda projection

EXHIBIT 2
Growth of Honda's World-wide Automobile Production, 1960–1995

Source: Honda Annual Reports, Japan Automobile Manufacturers Association.

Product range	Annual unit sales (000s)	Percentage of sales by value
Motorcycles	5,198	13.0
Automobiles	2,184	79.9
Power products*	2,648	7.1

* General purpose engines, tillers, portable generators, outboard motors, lawnmowers, etc.

Focus on internal combustion engines

Honda produced over 10 million internal combustion engines world-wide in 1996–7, or about 40,000 per day.

Regional sales breakdown by value

Japan	34%
North America	42%
Europe	11%
Others	13%

Factories

Honda has a wide international production network, with 89 production facilities in 33 countries

Employees

Honda directly employs 101,100 people, approximately 1/3 of them in Japan

EXHIBIT 3
Snapshot of Honda activities, 1997

Source: Honda Annual Report 1996–7.

Champion Formula 1 (F-1) racing cars for six years in a row during the 1980s. In 1989 the company's founder, Soichiro Honda, became the first Japanese to be accepted into Detroit's symbolic Automotive Industry Hall of Fame.

It is perhaps not surprising that examples of strategic management practice at Honda became widely quoted in the management literature during the 1980s. An undoubtedly successful firm was attracting the attention it deserved. But was

EXHIBIT 4
Honda in global context

Producers	Production 1994 (output in 1,000s)	Geographic distribution of production				Geographic distribution of sales			
		North America	Europe	Japan	Others	North America	Europe	Japan	Others
Ford	3,959	54.6%	37.1%		8.3%	53.3%	35.8%	0.2%	10.7%
Ford (& Mazda)	4,928	46.6%	29.8%	16.7%	7.0%	49.3%	32.3%	5.5%	12.9%
General Motors	5,486	59.7%	30.1%		10.2%	61.4%	28.4%	0.4%	9.8%
GM (& Isuzu)	5,537	59.1%	29.9%	0.9%	10.1%	60.8%	28.1%	0.5%	10.6%
Honda	1,561	38.9%	3.3%	54.1%	3.7%	53.2%	10.7%	23.0%	13.0%
Nissan	2,081	22.0%	9.8%	64.5%	3.7%	31.7%	18.3%	36.5%	13.5%
Toyota	3,836	12.7%	2.2%	72.2%	12.9%	21.4%	8.2%	36.9%	33.5%
V.A.G.	2,980	8.2%	71.8%		20.1%	9.3%	63.3%	1.2%	26.2%
Fiat	2,137		62.7%		37.3%	0.1%	60.2%	0.2%	39.6%
Renault	1,613		86.5%		13.5%	0.0%	81.0%	0.1%	18.9%
PSA Peugot- Citroën	1,798		98.5%		1.5%	0.0%	84.9%	0.3%	14.7%
BMW-Rover	1,027	(*)	97.8%		2.2%	8.7%	75.6%	2.9%	12.8%
Mercedes	599	(*)	97.5%		2.5%	12.9%	69.9%	5.6%	11.6%

World production of passenger cars (only) in 1994
World sales of new passenger cars in 1994

Source: Bélis-Bergouignan, Bordenave and Lung (1998).
(*) New plants have been opened in North America since 1994.

that success a result of good management or was it due to a series of fortunate coincidences? One problem with the way Honda has been analyzed in the management literature is that its management innovations have been treated as a series of isolated stories frequently described in only a few sentences, and seemingly brought forth to justify or legitimate this or that new theory (Mair, 1998).

Is there anything more fundamental, more deep-seated, that underlies Honda's recognized proclivity for innovative and pioneering management strategies?

Reconciling Dichotomies: a Method for Innovative Strategic Thinking?

Underlying Honda's innovative strategic management, there appears to lie a process that might be described as 'reconciling dichotomies'. To see how it seems to work consider the dozens of dichotomous categories that pervade management thinking and permeate all aspects and functions. There are dichotomies in buyer-supplier relations (e.g. vertical integration and market relationships), work organization (e.g. efficient and humane), product development processes (e.g. sequential and simultaneous development), and business strategy (e.g. cost and differentiation), to name but a few.

Why are these dichotomies important? Strangely, although we can come up with lists of them, few western managers consider them to be of any significance. And yet if we were to consider them as paradoxes or poles that implicitly require to be solved, we would discover a novel method for developing new ideas about traditional management problems.

In the West, the traditional, ingrained and implicit approach to the puzzles that dichotomous concepts represent has been twofold:

EXHIBIT 5
Honda's recent financial
performance

Fiscal year*	Net sales + others as a revenue proportion (¥bn)	Net income of sales (%)	Research and development (¥bn)
1985	2,740	4.7	114
1986	3,009	4.9	135
1987	2,961	2.8	150
1988	3,229	3.1	164
1989	3,489	2.8	184
1990	3,853	2.1	186
1991	4,302	1.8	194
1992	4,391	1.4	192
1993	4,132	0.9	199
1994	3,863	0.6	189
1995	3,966	1.6	203
1996	4,252	1.7	221
1997	5,293	4.2	251

*Ends 28th February up to 1987, 31st March from 1988. Fiscal year therefore includes 9 or 10 months of previous calendar year. Figures for 1988 are author's estimate for comparative purposes, based on 12/13 of previous 13 months.

All yen conversions are at then-current exchange rates. During the above period, the value of the US dollar declined from 251 yen in February 1985 to 89 in March 1995 and then rose to 124 in March 1997. During the same period, Honda's unit automobile sales in North America remained roughly constant, proportionately, at approximately half of world-wide Honda sales.

1   Assume a trade-off between them: hence, to take the example of the group–individual dichotomy, to gain the advantages of individualism it is necessary to sacrifice some of the benefits of the group, and vice versa.

2   Conceive of change management in terms of switching from one dichotomized – and mutually exclusive – pole to the other. Any attempt to sit in the middle, (trying to keep elements of both group- and individual-oriented organizational forms, for instance) has been thought of as 'muddling through', ending up with 'the worst of both worlds'.

If these ways of thinking seem self-evidently true to many in the West, to Honda they do not. The case study examines Honda's very different way of thinking.

An Example: 'Right-first-time' or 'Build in quality'

To illustrate the Honda approach, let us look at a very significant instance of the thought process that characterizes dichotomy reconciliation and observe how it works. This example is well understood in Japan (it was not invented by Honda) and has also increasingly been accepted by many western managers in recent years.

Western management thinking has traditionally assumed trade-offs between product quality, cost and delivery: high quality cost more and took longer; low cost meant low quality too; fast delivery cost more and risked low quality. But the Japanese-developed 'right-first-time' principle inherent in the 'just-in-time' production system has revealed that there are better ways to manage these dichotomies. By focusing on how to 'build in quality' to products rather than 'test in quality' afterwards, it is possible to reduce costs (less waste and downtime) and to rationalize production with minimal stocks, hence reducing delivery lead times too.

This example involves a strategic approach to manufacturing, and it has widespread ramifications for marketing, product positioning and competitive strategy. Yet significant as the example is, it has been taken up almost in isolation in the West. Few realize that it represents just one example of a wholly different way of strategic thinking rather than a solution to one particular management problem. There are many more dichotomies waiting to be discovered and reconciled, thereby providing innovative impetus to strategic thinking across the range of management functions.

Nobuhiko Kawamoto's Reforms

Shortly after taking office as company president in 1991, Nobuhiko Kawamoto introduced significant reforms to the top management structure at Honda. Since the retirement in 1973 of the joint company founders, inventive engineer Soichiro Honda and financial mastermind Takeo Fujisawa, during their company's 25th anniversary year (see Exhibit 6), Honda had become well known in the business world for the collective decision-making process utilized by its top executives, a process in which few of them seemed to have clear individual responsibilities. The collective process was symbolized in the physical layout of the Honda headquarters 'board room', in which none of the executives had their own offices, but instead shared an open space where there were not only individual desks but also various areas for them to meet, sit and talk together.

There was no doubt that Kawamoto's new ideas were significant. He established a clear hierarchy at executive level, with two leading executives joining him to form an innermost leadership circle. He also announced that executives could have private offices if they so wished. Moreover, Honda's global management structure was reorganized with clear and direct lines of responsibility to the top management group.

Kawamoto's reforms made front page news in the western business press. *The Wall Street Journal* ran the headline 'Just as US Firms Try Japanese Management, Honda is Centralizing: Kawamoto Finds 'Teamwork' Is No Longer Enough To Boost Market Share: Coming Soon: Private Offices' (Chandler and Ingrassia, 1991). *Fortune* followed suit, with 'A US-Style Shakeup at Honda: CEO Kawamoto has abandoned consensus management for American-looking organization charts. Result: Communications and decision-making are getting faster' (Taylor, 1991). As far as strategic decision making was concerned, the clear impression given was that Honda's penchants for groupism and horizontal communication were on the way out, with individualism and vertical structure the order of the new day. Apparently a Japanese company with a particularly Japanese management style had now decided that a western style was superior after all.

But was this interpretation valid? Was Honda a firm whose strategic management decision making switched from a collectivist mode to an individualist mode? In fact, the true picture is

---

EXHIBIT 6
Honda's leaders

- Soichiro Honda, founded company 1948; retired 1973.
- Takeo Fujisawa, joined company 1949, in effect business manager, leaving Soichiro Honda free to concentrate on engineering and product strategy; retired 1973.
- Kiyoshi Kawashima, joined company 1947, before it was officially formed; ran works motor racing teams in 1960s; company president, 1973–83.
- Tadashi Kume, joined company 1953; ran works motor racing teams in 1960s; principal engineer in design and development of Life and Civic models; company president, 1983–90.
- Nobuhiko Kawamoto, joined company 1963; consecutively chief engineer, director and president of Honda R&D, 1970–91; company president and CEO, 1991–.

rather different, and the view presented in the western business press is, arguably, uninformed.

The joint board room had actually been set up in the mid 1960s by Takeo Fujisawa, who saw it as an adjunct structure to Soichiro Honda's highly individualistic style, a means of encouraging executives to talk about problems and solutions with each other, and to prepare younger managers for the day the founders would retire. In other words, the organizational structure to promote collective decision making existed alongside the individualist Honda (who is said once to have hit an engineer over the head with a spanner to drive home a point!).

Kawamoto's changes were only one of a series of periodic reorganizations at Honda. When Honda and Fujisawa retired in 1973, new president Kiyoshi Kawashima shifted Honda further towards a collective decision-making mode with the wide-ranging committee structure that he set up. When Tadashi Kume in turn succeeded Kawashima as president in 1983, he too instituted his own changes. Thus each new president has deliberately sent a shock wave of reorganization (of interrelationships as much as of people) through the firm. Indeed Kawamoto was by no means dispensing with collective decision making; what he was doing was injecting a strong dose of individual responsibility into the existing framework.

Kawamoto's changes are best interpreted less as a switch to a new type of structure, as the western press had it, from one pole of a dichotomy to another, than as a change in emphasis. A useful way to visualize this process is to think of the organization as a sailing ship on a narrow tack against the wind, progressing in a zig-zag fashion, first towards individualism and vertical structure, then back towards collectivism and horizontal structure, then back again. All the while, the ship moves forward despite sailing against the wind, as each tack builds on the achievements of the last, despite the apparently dramatic changes of direction (see Exhibit 7).

Reconciling Dichotomies at Honda

Honda's approach to the individual–group dichotomy in the strategic decision-making process is exemplary of Honda's approach to innovation in management. Honda appears to have implemented a systematic approach to resolving some of the great dilemmas of twentieth–century management.

Traditional dichotomous pairs of concepts are used in the West as an underlying framework to think about management. Thus in the case of Kawamoto's reforms, there is, first, the collective (or group) versus the individual, and second,

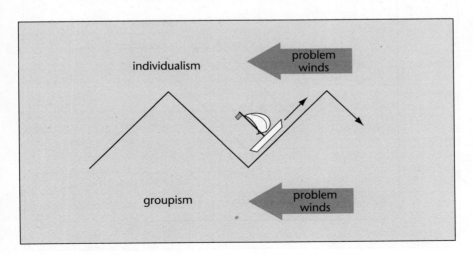

EXHIBIT 7
The 'tacking ship' vision of progress

vertical structure and horizontal structure. 'Reconciliation' in this context refers to an approach in which the two poles are somehow (and that is the challenge) made compatible with each other.

The way in which Kawamoto 'changed tacks' from a group-based to an individual-based trajectory (not structure) is a classic example of dichotomy reconciliation, Honda-style. Honda's strategic thinking rejects the typical western simple trade-off and emphatically rejects the typical western idea that failure to select clearly one or the other pole leads to indecision. Honda's solution to the group–individual dichotomy and the horizontal–vertical dichotomy is to progress flexibly with a 'tacking' motion along a well-defined and fairly narrow path. In other words, the reconciliation sought is always one which incorporates 'the best of both worlds' (see Exhibit 8).

The refusal to accept static trade-offs, and the rejection of any obligation to choose one pole or the other, lie behind many of Honda's strategic innovations. The process can be seen at work across a wide range of activities at Honda, and constitutes the hallmark of its strategic innovation.

Organizational Process: Competition and the Individual

Let us take a closer look at how the individual-group dichotomy is played out at Honda. Honda has a remarkable penchant for praising the successes of individual employees and for encouraging a sense of competition among them. Company-wide quality circle (called NH Circles; for New, Now, Next Honda) competitions have focused on the achievements of individual people (albeit, characteristically, working in small groups). Within Honda R&D, the subsidiary company that develops Honda products, competitive and individual-based basic research activities deliberately foster individual inventiveness. The competitive nature of employee suggestion schemes at Honda's North American operations, with awards given to annual 'winners', also fosters individualism.

In similar vein, individual managers remain closely associated with the projects and products for which they have been responsible; Tadashi Kume was lauded as the principal engineer behind the Life and Civic automobiles. Kawamoto has been known as 'Mr NSX' after the aluminium-bodied super-sports car Honda developed in the late 1980s, and he was also associated with Honda's

EXHIBIT 8
Visualizing dichotomy reconciliation

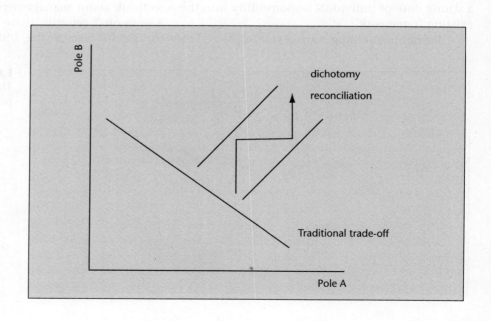

successes in the 1980s on the Grand Prix racing circuit.

What is most interesting, however, is that individualism and competition are not stressed over and above loyalty and cooperation; each 'pole' within the individual–group dichotomy is a tendency that 'has its place' in a way that maximizes the contribution each can make, while minimizing any negative impacts of over-emphasis on either individual or group. Hence alongside the stress on individual achievement can be observed the promotion of group processes: collective decision making, in the corporate board room for instance; team working, the tight and disciplined cooperation of the various people involved in F-1 racing being communicated as a model of behaviour for all employees; and interdepartmental cooperation in the product development process, which is organized into highly cooperative 'SED' (Sales-Engineering-Development) teams that are explicitly differentiated from the individualist and competitive character of the basic research process.

Organizational Structure

A classic dichotomy in organizational structures is between vertical and horizontal structures. Recently many consultants have been advising large companies to dispense with vertical, hierarchical structures in favour of process-oriented horizontal linkages. Indeed a driving force behind reform of organizational structure at Honda has been the avoidance of 'big business disease'. In the Honda view, when a company grows bigger and adopts overly rigid vertical structures of organizational control, it can lose the small-firm vitality and the horizontal linkages and communication that are so vital to innovation and dynamism.

At Honda there are regular drives to battle 'big business disease'. But significantly, these take place within, rather than replacing, a strongly hierarchical structural framework. Thus after he became Honda President in 1983, Tadashi Kume launched a series of initiatives to prevent bureaucratic structures from hardening. These included round-table meetings between executives and front-line supervisors to cut across layers of vertical hierarchy, regular round-table meetings between executives and middle-level managers, and the encouragement of 'diagonal' linkages whereby manufacturing managers, for instance, held discussions to share viewpoints with front-line sales staff.

In similar vein, strategic thinking about the career paths of individuals has been woven into organizational thinking to keep structure flexible and innovative. Honda's 'expert' system, developed during the 1950s and 1960s, allows technical experts to be promoted in a clearly vertical fashion without having to enter the ranks of management, on the grounds that the latter would be a sure-fire route to poor lower-level management since many technical experts desire promotion but do not actually want to manage other people. Moreover, managers can follow diagonal promotion paths (simultaneous vertical and horizontal moves). An example is the marketing manager who was put in charge of expanding one of Honda's North American factories in the late 1980s. One advantage Honda gained from this appointment was that manufacturing and engineering staff were obliged to be very clear about what they were doing and began to question taken-for-granted procedures.

Honda has pursued web-like organizational forms mixing group and individual processes, vertical and horizontal structures, and formal and informal relationships and positions to the point that it is well-nigh impossible for anyone entering the firm from outside to understand precisely what Honda's organizational structure is.

Is Honda a 'Japanese' Firm?

One dichotomy pervasive in the western management literature is the grand division between western firms and management methods, on the one hand, and Japanese firms and methods on the other hand. Many management theorists and practitioners have held to the idea that Japanese firms are fundamentally different from western firms: whether in organizational structures, company cultures, labour relations, inter-firm relationships, manufacturing systems, work

EXHIBIT 9
The 'Japanese management model' seen as diametrically opposed to the 'western management model'

'Western' model	'Japanese' model
Overall description	
mass	Lean
standardized	Flexible
Fordist	Post-Fordist
Work process	
Taylorist	Post-Taylorist
Do workers	Think workers
Unskilled	Polyvalent
Production organization and logistics	
Large-lot production	Small-lot production
Just-in-case	Just-in-time
Push system	Pull system
Organization	
Vertical	Horizontal
Fragmented duties	Broad duties
Individual as responsible	Group as responsible
Labour relations	
Job control focus	Employment conditions focus
Cross-company unions	Enterprise unions
Hire and fire	Job-for-life
Industry organization	
Separated firms	*Keiretsu* families
Distant inter-firm relations	Close inter-firm relations

organization, or marketing strategies. Analysts created a 'Japanese model' of management diametrically opposed, in classic dualist fashion, to the western model. Their argument was that adherence to this Japanese model explained much of Japan's economic successes during the 1970s and 1980s (see Exhibit 9).

It may therefore seem strange even to pose the question of whether Honda can be considered a 'Japanese' firm. But remember that only one third of Honda's turnover now derives from Japan, and the company runs over eighty manufacturing facilities throughout the world, nearly all of them outside Japan. The crux of the issue, however, is whether Honda is actually managed in

a 'Japanese' way. Many assume that it must be, given its roots in a country with a particularly strong and unique culture. And yet Japanese analysts agree that Honda does not easily fit the 'Japanese model'. In Japan Honda has deliberately set out to counter what it views as negative traits of 'Japanese-ness'. It deliberately stresses decentralized management structures, praises the achievements of individuals, makes merit the key to promotion, and awards responsibility to younger employees: all this in a Japanese society founded on centralization, collective decision making and responsibility, status and seniority, and respect for elders. The point to grasp is that Honda has struggled to overcome the innovation-deadening impacts of these cultural forces. Soichiro Honda himself has been the model, portrayed as exemplary of an individualist who cared nothing for the position of his supposed 'betters', deliberately crossed status barriers, and promoted younger individuals across seniority levels. The result is that in Japan Honda is commonly viewed as a peculiarly 'un-Japanese' firm.

Thus Honda has injected so-called western attributes into the way it functions, which co-exist with the 'Japanese' features that employees bring with them – the results of their upbringing in Japan – as they enter the firm. Rather than pursuing a 'Japanese model' distinct from a 'western model', the big picture reveals Honda's innovation to be its simultaneous incorporation of both models so as to work consciously and deliberately with elements of each: precisely what we saw earlier in Kawamoto's reforms.

Product Strategy: Guiding the Technology Development Process

A recognized source of competitive advantage for Honda has been its 'core competence' in the advanced internal combustion engines which power the whole range of its products. But Honda's product strength goes far deeper: a dichotomy-reconciling approach characterizes both the mental process of technology research and the philosophy behind the actual product designs. The technology and design features of Honda products are the embodiments of successful reconciliations of dichotomies which deliver direct and immediate competitive advantage.

The classic example of Honda's technology is the CVCC (compound vortex controlled combustion) engine, designed during the 1969–71 period. Indeed the CVCC engine is used within the firm to represent and communicate Honda's approach to technology. The compromise tackled and overcome by the CVCC engine was widely accepted in the world's automobile industry, namely a trade-off among the various pollutants emitted from internal combustion engines. According to the traditional view, attempts to reduce emissions of one chemical inevitably led

to increases in others. The only way out of the dilemma, it was believed, was to add a process (e.g. catalytic conversion) to clean up the pollutants after combustion.

Honda engineers proceeded from the assumption that it would be more rational not to create pollutants in the first place than to have to clean them up. The CVCC engine design therefore denied the taken-for-granted compromises. The technical solution was to place two connected combustion chambers in each cylinder. A fuel-thin mixture of fuel and air was injected into a main combustion chamber. A fuel-rich mixture was injected into a smaller chamber where the spark plug was located. When the spark ignited the mixture, combustion spread from the smaller to the main chamber, with the result that the fuel and oxygen burned more completely, and with less fuel used, compared to a conventional engine. Each of these characteristics helped reduce a different pollutant, resulting in an engine in which the old trade-offs were overcome (see Exhibit 10).

The thinking embodied in the VTEC (variable valve timing and lift electronic control) family of engines that Honda first introduced in 1989 derives from a similar approach. The conventional dichotomy and associated trade-off tackled by the VTEC engines was fuel economy versus engine power; to improve fuel economy meant losing power. However, in the VTEC engine the innovative variable valves (the mechanisms which let fuel and air in and out of the combustion chamber), in conjunction with the electronically controlled fuel injection system, control the ratio of fuel to air according to driving conditions. In normal mode, a fuel-thin mixture provides fuel economy. But at high engine speeds with the driver's foot pressed hard on the accelerator a fuel-richer mixture provides significantly more power. Exhibit 11 illustrates both the performance economy trade-off of Honda's conventional engines, and the dichotomy-reconciling leap achieved by VTEC engines in Honda Accord automobiles.

While in product terms Honda is perhaps best known for its technologically innovative engines, refusal to accept taken-for-granted

EXHIBIT 10
How the CVCC engine simultaneously reduced pollutants in a way previously thought impossible

Regular engine

- Supply of a denser mixture of air and fuel decreases NOx but increases CO and HC.
- Supply of a thinner mixture of air and fuel decreases CO and HC but increases NOx.
- As the mixture grows thinner, NOx and CO will decrease but the engine may die.

Sources of pollutants

- The higher the temperature of the gas in the cylinder, the greater the amount of NOx emitted.
- The more quickly the temperature of the gas in the cylinder falls in the process of expansion, the greater the amount of unignited fuel emitted as HC.
- The greater the amount of dense fuel supplied, the greater the amount of CO emitted due to lack of oxygen resulting from oxidation.

Merits of CVCC engine

- Decrease in NOx by lowering the maximum combustion temperature.
- Decrease in HC by prolonging the time the temperature of oxidation is maintained.
- Decrease in CO by supplying very thin mixed gas so as to make sufficient oxygen available.

Source: Mito (1990).

trade-offs characterizes all aspects of Honda's strategic approach to technological change. This is well illustrated in the revealing language used by a Honda engineer describing an apparently mundane technological advance made by Honda R&D at its North American operations (see Exhibit 12).

Designing Automobiles

In addition to its technologically innovative products, Honda's product development process is respected within the automobile industry for its sheer speed. During the 1970s and 1980s Honda led the Japanese automobile industry's drive to reduce development lead times: today automobiles are being manufactured only two years after the launch of their development process. Until recently five to six years or longer was the norm in the West, and few manufacturers achieve better than three to four years. Honda's

speed has been attained in two ways. The first is its organizational approach to the product development process, based on the SED teams mentioned above. The SED teams work together on projects from start to finish, in contrast to the traditional sequential development process utilized in the West where each function makes its specialized input in turn (marketing, design, product engineering, production engineering and manufacturing).

The second is Honda's particular model replacement system. What is most significant about this system is the way it challenges an important dichotomy observed in the western automobile industry. This is between the 'complete model change', in which the whole design process starts from scratch with every component redesigned for a totally new automobile, and the 'facelift', in which only a small number of components are redesigned to give an older model

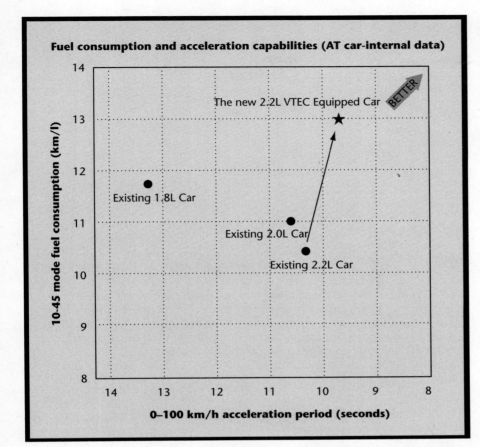

Fuel consumption and acceleration capabilities (AT car-internal data)

EXHIBIT 11
The VTEC engine
compared to the
conventional fuel
consumption-acceleration
trade-off in the Honda
Accord

Source: Japan Autotech
Report (1993).

a more modern image. As adherents of this dichotomous approach, for decades western automobile makers have made complete model changes perhaps every eight to ten years, and given facelifts to their models perhaps every two to four years. Most Honda models are changed every four years. Thus new Honda Accords were introduced in 1981, 1985, 1989, 1993 and 1997, and new Civics in 1979, 1983, 1987, 1991 and 1995. Western automobile makers, wedded to their traditional approach, claimed that Honda was not 'properly' replacing models in these short cycles, but simply giving its models a cosmetic facelift.

Yet Honda's strategic approach to model replacement means that it does not face the same dichotomous choices. The process at Honda can be described schematically as follows. Honda's model changes are neither complete changes nor mere facelifts. Instead, every four years, when a Honda model is 'officially' replaced, the components the driver can see or otherwise notice are replaced: the exterior body shape, the interior design, the lights. Then, also every four years with a two-year lag after the official model change, vital unseen components are changed, and new engines, gearboxes, braking systems, for instance, are introduced. The outcome is best described as a 'rolling' or 'iterative' model change programme with significant and regular changes to each model (and hence a regular boost to customer interest). The traditional distinction between complete change and facelift is dispensed with in favour of a smoother, more fluid and flexible approach. Manufacturing systems (for instance, sizes and shapes of machinery) and whole vehicle design configurations (for instance, sizes and shapes of components and the spaces

EXHIBIT 12
'We aren't interested in
trade-offs'

When it comes to weight reduction, the auto industry's appetite is insatiable. Honda is no exception.

As part of a corporate goal to reduce weight in its automobiles, Honda of America Manufacturing Inc. in Marysville, Ohio, is the first automaker in the United States to use a lightweight underbody coating, or sound deadener, with expanded polymeric microspheres supplied by Pierce & Stevens Corp. of Buffalo, NY.

Besides lightweight, Honda sought several other attributes from any new underbody coating, including reduced volatile organic compound emissions and an improved durability standard.

Honda also wanted improved 'line-side workability' – the ease-of-use characteristics judged by those who work with the product on the production line.

In addition, the product could not require any modifications to the existing sound-deadener delivery and application systems.

It was a tall order, but according to Trish Peters, assistant manager of the Marysville plant's auto paint department, reformulations either meet all of Honda's standards or they aren't used at all.

'We aren't interested in trade-offs', she said. 'We won't accept lesser performance in any aspect of a product to get improvement in some other aspect. Our sound-deadener suppliers – there are several – know this. They accepted our goals and came back to us with formulations that included polymeric microspheres – what we call 'plastic balloons'.' . . .

'We reduced the weight of the deadener by 30 to 40 percent,' said Lee Manville of the Marysville auto paint production staff. 'We got better adhesion of the product to the body surface and were able to reduce film build (the amount applied) while improving our durability standard' . . . .

'We're satisfied with the performance of the reformulated sound deadener – for now,' said Peters. 'Honda has trained us not to make or accept assumptions about the performance of anything we use. Our department's goals – to improve existing materials and find new materials – are like our corporate goals to improve quality and drive down costs. They never end'.'

Source: Fleming (1993).

they fit in) are pre-planned as far as possible to allow for the expected evolution of models and components.

This iterative process of model evolution is put into practice in three 'dimensions'. The first is over time, as described above. Thus the 1993 replacement for the Today model, sold in Japan, shared 40 percent of its components with its predecessor. Second, it is practiced laterally, in the development of parallel, 'sister' models for different market segments. The third dimension is geographical, in which models developed for different world markets are frequently spin-offs from existing models (neither entirely different,

nor mere cosmetic changes). Hence both the Accord and Civic models that Honda was manufacturing in Europe in the mid-1990s were spin-offs, with significant engineering changes, from automobiles first manufactured for the Japanese market.

Strategies for Production and Logistics: the Assembly Line

What philosophy guides how Honda actually makes its products? Honda has sought to combine the advantages inherent in what have normally been seen in the West as dichotomous and mutually exclusive production and logistics systems.

Honda first experimented with a 'free-flow' assembly line at its Kumamoto motorcycle plant on the Japanese island of Kyushu in the late 1970s. This system was an attempt to combine productive efficiency with human dignity. Efficiency and dignity have been treated as polar opposites in the traditional western strategy for manufacturing design which regarded the mind-numbing and alienating continuous assembly line, with its fragmentation of tasks carefully orchestrated by time-and-motion staff, as the epitome of efficiency, and viewed the efforts of the Swedish automobile manufacturers Volvo and Saab to develop more personally satisfying forms of 'group work' in the 1970s and 1980s as necessarily sacrificing efficiency.

Honda's free-flow assembly line, the first of its type in the Japanese motor industry, was based on a series of separate carriers upon which partially completed vehicles were placed (or hung). The carriers followed each other from work-station to work-station but their speed of movement was not controlled centrally as with the traditional chain-driven line. Advantages were sought in terms of efficiency and dignity. On the one hand both manual and automated assembly tasks could be undertaken more accurately since the separate carriers could stop at each work-station. Moreover, work could be completed satisfactorily before the carrier was sent on its way. On the other hand production workers could be given a sense of control over the production process since they could make the decision that the task had been executed properly and that the carrier should now move to the next work-station. The free-flow principle was later adopted for the new third automobile assembly line built at the Suzuka factory in the late 1980s, where Honda has continued to experiment with it.

Production Planning

Honda has also developed an innovative strategy for the planning of production, a strategy which exhibits characteristics of both the traditional dichotomous poles. One pole is 'large-lot mass production', in which manufacturing is organized so that thousands of identical or virtually identical products are made in a row, or series. This implies the use of dedicated machinery and, indeed, in the western automobile industry each factory frequently can make only a single automobile model, which is changed every few years. To many, the automobile industry is the epitome of large-lot mass production. In this system the goal is to reduce costs, achieved at the expense of product variety (the trade-off within the western mass production system).

At the other extreme is the 'one-piece-flow' production system said to characterize at least some firms in the Japanese automobile industry. In this system each assembly line can handle several different models with minimal if any changeover time, and the partly finished vehicles coming down the line are sequenced in 'lots of one', i.e. each vehicle is different from that preceding and following it (colours, options, engines, numbers of doors, models). The objective of this system is to permit far greater product variety (to the point of 'customized' products individually ordered). One drawback is the very complex logistics system needed to supply components to the assembly line in the correct order. In general terms, the Toyota-developed 'just-in-time' production and logistics system can be seen as a dichotomy reconciliation permitting both product variety and productive efficiency.

Honda's own innovative strategy for production planning has been to develop a 'small batch' production system based around the key number 60 and its factors (30, 15, 12, etc.). Automobiles are sent down the assembly lines in batches in which each vehicle is exactly the same (including colour). Workers therefore execute exactly the same tasks for each batch. Components are delivered to the assembly line in batches (lot sizes, colours, optional extras) which exactly match the vehicles they will be fitted into. The objective is to combine the advantages of large-lot production (simpler logistics and quality control, less likelihood of error, easier to programme production schedules) and of small-lot production (ability to offer a wider range of products to consumers and greater worker involvement and satisfaction).

Making Production Planning and Product Marketing Coherent

This small batch production system is closely linked to Honda's strategy towards marketing and sales. Honda has tended not to offer its customers the spectacular breadth of choice developed by other Japanese automobile manufacturers during the Japanese 'bubble economy' of the late 1980s. Some firms expanded product variety so far that Japanese customers could choose among several dozen different steering wheels per model, a level of consumer choice which was soon recognized to have got out of hand. Honda's strategy emphasizes the high technology built into all its products and it was quick to offer features like advanced engines (though often available in only two sizes per model), anti-lock brakes, electric windows and sun-roofs as standard rather than optional extras, thus simplifying product variety within each model type.

In operations management, an important dichotomy distinguishes 'push'-based production planning and logistical systems from 'pull'-based systems. In the former, said to be typically western, production schedules for particular models are set out months in advance, and alignment of output levels with customer demand tends to focus on sales strategy (e.g. discounting may be necessary). In the latter, said to be typically Japanese, automobiles are only made to customer order.

Honda's approach to production planning is to operate a combination push-pull system. When planning at the annual scale, production levels of particular models can be varied up or down as a function of demand, because flexible equipment means that production lines can be used for various models (in gross terms, a pull system). When undertaking monthly planning, an 'un-Japanese' push system fixes the total mix of products and appropriate schedules several months in advance, based on market forecasts. Simultaneously a small-scale inventory pull system is utilized for everyday production plan-

ning, where it helps deal with unforeseen difficulties: if, for instance, there is a problem with a certain colour of paint in the paint shops, components makers may be alerted in a matter of hours that the production schedule has been altered and they will need to respond accordingly. The outcome at Honda is the simultaneous operation of pull- and push-based production planning systems rather than dominance of one type over the other.

Relationships with Components Makers

In the analysis of inter-firm relationships, in particular buyer-supplier relations in the components supply chain, a distinction is traditionally made in the West between vertical integration and market relationships (reflected in the 'make or buy?' decision). Honda's approach to relationships with its components suppliers transcends this dichotomy and others associated with supply chain management. In Japan Honda has only a handful of components makers that might be considered to belong to its supplier 'family', and is the only firm in the Japanese automobile industry not to organize its own 'suppliers association' as a forum for suppliers to meet and solve common problems. Honda does build long-term relationships with its suppliers, but these are not buttressed by the institutional mechanisms (cross-shareholding, 'family' relationships, supplier associations) often said to govern long-term relationships in Japan.

In North America, where a substantial network of more than 80 Japanese 'transplant' component makers has developed to supply Honda with components, Honda invested its own capital in a number of the early arrivals as a means of reducing the risk for its smaller Japanese partners. Other than this, formal linkages in North America are non-existent. And yet in operational terms Honda intervenes directly in the 'internal' activities of its component makers when it believes this necessary. For a number of components Honda arranges the purchase of the raw materials, for example steel and aluminium, two or three tiers back along the supply chain, which will eventually find their way into Honda automobiles, gaining advantages in price and quality. Honda engineers also visit suppliers regularly, and may be stationed in their factories for a time if serious problems arise in components delivery and quality.

Thus relationships with component makers are based on complex combinations of close control and open, commercial relationships, creating a structure which defies the polar types in traditional views of buyer–supplier relations. The goal is clearly to reconcile the dichotomy to gain the advantages accruing from each polar type of organizing.

The same refusal to fit easily into traditional categories holds for the number of supplier firms from which Honda sources each component. The traditional dichotomous choice between 'dual/ multiple' sourcing strategy versus 'single' sourcing strategy is bypassed by Honda, where sourcing strategy is based on elements of both. Thus Honda sources a certain type of seat (the basic version, say) for its Accord model from supplier A, in single-sourcing fashion, and simultaneously sources a different type of seat (perhaps a high-tech electronic version) from supplier B, also in single-sourcing fashion. The two suppliers are not in direct competition, yet Honda can subtly play them off (in dual-sourcing fashion) since each is aware of the other's existence and willingness to expand its market share when plans are made for the next Accord model change. Honda gains the advantage of both single sourcing (stable relationships with one supplier) and dual sourcing (an element of competition).

Honda's ability to find solutions even reaches into the geographical pattern of its relationships with component makers in North America. The traditional approach is to choose between purchasing from component makers located very long distances away, often to allow cheap labour sources in other regions and countries to be exploited (a feature of the 'western model'), and the spatially concentrated production system at Toyota City in Japan, where hundreds of supplier companies and nearly all Toyota's production capacity are concentrated into a few square kilometres, which is particularly advantageous for just-in-time logistics.

In North America, where Honda has greatly influenced the general location choices made by its Japanese component makers, the geographical pattern reflects both spatial dispersal and spatial concentration. In Ohio, where Honda's main manufacturing base has been constructed, there are now more than 40 Japanese-owned firms making automobile components, nearly all of which supply Honda. Concentration within a two-hour travel-time permits just-in-time 'pull' logistics to be operated on a day-to-day basis. However, within Ohio the factories are dispersed to small town locations 10 to 20 miles apart; this way, their local labour markets are separated and the new investments and jobs they represent will not drive up local wages. Distant from Honda too, they can offer wages only half to two-thirds those paid at the automobile assembly plant. In other words, Honda's network of component makers is designed to combine the advantages of spatial concentration and spatial dispersal.

Honda's Strategic Challenges

How does Honda manage the key dichotomies of strategic management: planning vs. learning, market positioning vs. developing internal resources, and within the resource-based perspective, product-related core competencies vs. process-related core capabilities? The many western observers of Honda from the academic and consultancy worlds in recent years have tended to lay the emphasis on one pole to the exclusion of the other, and have battled it out among themselves to claim that Honda is *either* a planner *or* a learner, *either* a market positioner *or* a resource builder, *either* a competency-based diversifier *or* a capabilities predator. Similarly, followers of trends in multinational enterprise organization have been quick to claim that Honda exemplifies a polar position as a 'post-national' or 'stateless' corporation operating in a 'borderless' world (Mair, 1997, 1998).

Judging by the evidence of Honda's strategic capability to reconcile dichotomies, these analysts may be missing the point. As the energies of debate have been channelled into ceaseless either/or argument, meanwhile Honda may have been focusing its strategic effort, and mobilizing its dichotomy-reconciling strategic capability, precisely on reconciling the apparently incompatible poles of strategic dichotomies in a way that consigns these debates to the irrelevant margins.

Have Honda's strategists therefore implemented detailed planned strategies with precision whilst simultaneously learning and adjusting strategy to business environment change? One clue may be found by reversing the normal assumption that the formulation and execution of detailed strategic plans is inevitably a long-term process such that learning from environmental change can only extend to marginal tweaks. What if learning were the long term and planning the short term? A strategically agile company might be able to make operational (treat as short-term variables) parameters previously considered strategic (necessarily fixed in the short term). The strategy process would then consist of a series of rapid formulation-implementation pulses over time. And indeed Honda's rapid and iterative new product development process and flexifactory manufacturing infrastructure appear to support just such an approach.

Can a market positioning and resource-based view of strategy content be reconciled in innovative ways? Here Honda appears to have faced difficult challenges at a number of points in its history, without always succeeding, particularly in reconciling the company's core competencies in engine design as well as its engineers' pursuit of technological mastery to the evolution of market demand. Significantly, notwithstanding Honda's image as a designer of sporty and technically innovative cars, fully three-quarters of the company's global sales comprise the relatively conservative and simple Civic and Accord models, which, broadly speaking, occupy the market position (once thought unattainable) which combines high quality with low cost based on core capabilities residing at the heart of Honda's product design and production process. What core-competency related product technology breakthroughs might provide the basis for novel and successful market positions in future? Not surprisingly, along with other industry companies,

Honda has recently invested huge resources into developing new low-pollution power sources for its vehicles (electric, solar power, for example), in the drive to focus its competencies on potential breakthrough market positions.

Which matters most to the consumer, Hondas core competencies in mechanical technologies, or its core capabilities in managing the whole value chain from raw materials to dealer networks via product design and production processes? This dichotomy seems plainly false, at Honda at least. The company focuses on both resources because both matter to purchasers of its products: if to varying degrees. Purchasers of the top-of-the-range super sports NSX model are presumably attracted by the car's driving and handling characteristics, features intimately related to product technology, whereas purchasers of a small engine three-door Civic model may focus more on cost, quality, and reliability (hence in some countries, notably the United Kingdom, Honda has struggled to shake off a market image as a maker of cars for the over 60s), product features associated more with core design and production process capabilities.

The grand dichotomies of business and corporate strategy are clearly more complex, multilayered concepts and practices than those associated with operations, human resources and other functional-level strategies. Yet Honda seems destined to pitch the company's collective intellect full-force into the struggle to find ways of reconciling them for competitive advantage. Each time Honda succeeds in finding new solutions, the competitive map in its chosen industries will be redrawn, just as it has been at regular intervals over the past 50 years.

References

Bélis-Bergouignan, M-C., Bordenave, G., and Lung, Y. (1998) Global strategies in the automobile industry, *Regional Studies* (forthcoming).

Chandler, C. and Ingrassia, P. (1991) Just as US Firms Try Japanese Management, Honda is Centralizing: Kawamoto Finds 'Teamwork' Is No Longer

Enough To Boost Market Share: Coming Soon: Private Offices, *The Wall Street Journal*, 4th November, pp 1 and A10.

Fleming, A. (1993) Honda switches to lighter underbody coating, *Automotive News*, 12th April, p. 20.

Japan Autotech Report (1993) Vol. 175, p. 23.

Mair, A. (1998) Learning from Honda, *Journal of Management Studies* (forthcoming).

Mair, A. (1997) Strategic localization: the myth of the post-national enterprise, in Cox, K.R. (ed.), *Spaces of Globalization: Reasserting the Power of the Local*, Guildford, New York, pp. 64–88.

Mito, S. (1990) *The Honda Book of Management: A Leadership Philosophy for High Industrial Success*, Kogan Page, London.

Taylor III, A. (1991) A US-Style Shakeup at Honda: CEO Kawamoto has abandoned consensus management for American-looking organization charts. Result: Communications and decision-making are getting faster, *Fortune*, 20th December.

Case 2: The Swatch

By Arieh Ullmann[1]

In 1978 when Dr. Ernst Thomke became managing director of ETA after a 20-year leave of absence from the watch industry, the position of this Swiss flagship industry had changed dramatically. Just like other industries suffering from the competitive onslaught from the Far East, the Swiss watch industry faced the biggest challenge in its four hundred years of existence. Once the undisputed leaders in technology and market share – which the Swiss had gained thanks to breakthroughs in mechanizing the watch manufacturing process during the 19th century – the Swiss had fallen on hard times.

In 1980, Switzerland's share of the world market, which in 1952 stood at 56 percent, had fallen to a mere 20 percent of the finished watch segment while world production had grown from 61 million to 320 million pieces and movements annually. Even more troubling was the fact that the market share loss was more pronounced in finished watches compared to non-assembled movements (see Exhibit 1). Measured in dollars the decline was not quite as evident, because the Swiss continued to dominate the luxury segment of the market while withdrawing from the budget price and middle segments.

The Swiss, once the industry's leaders in innovation, had fallen behind. Manufacturers in the United States, Japan and Hong Kong had started to gain share especially since the introduction of the electronic watch. Although in 1967 the Swiss were the first to introduce a model of an electronic wristwatch at the Concours de Chronometrie of the Neuchatel Observatory (Switzerland) smashing all accuracy records, they dismissed the new technology as a fad and continued to rely on their mechanical timepieces where most of their research efforts were concentrated. While the Swiss dominated the watch segments based on older technologies, their market shares were markedly lower for watches incorporating recently developed technologies (see Exhibit 2). Thus, when electronic watches gained widespread acceptance the Swiss watch producers found themselves in a catch-up race against the Japanese who held the technological edge (see Exhibit 3).

The situation of the industry which exported more than 90 percent of its production was aggravated by adverse exchange rate movements relative to the US dollar, making Swiss watches more expensive in the United States – then the most important export market. Until the early 1970s, the exchange rate stood at US\$1 = SFr. 4.30; by the end of the decade it had dropped to about US\$1 = SFr. 1.90.

Structural Change in the Industry

Throughout its history the Swiss watch industry was characterized by an extreme degree of fragmentation. Until the end of the 1970s frequently up to thirty independent companies were involved in the production of a single watch. Skilled craftsmen called suppliers manufactured the many different parts of the watch in hundreds of tiny shops, each of them specializing on a few parts. The movements were either sold in loose

---

[1] Source: This case was written by Arieh A. Ullmann, State University of New York, Binghamton. All information in this case is from published sources. Unless indicated otherwise, exhibit information is from SMH and Swiss Watch manufacturers Federation annual reports. Distributed by the North American Case Research Association. © 1991. All rights reserved to the author and the North American Case Research Association.

EXHIBIT 1
World Watch Production
and Major Producing
Countries, 1980

Country	Production (Million Pieces) Electronic	Mechanic	Total	Market Share, %
Switzerland: watches	10.4	52.6	63.0	20
Incl. non-assembled movements	13.0	83.0	96.0	30
Japan: watches	50.4	17.1	67.5	21
Incl. non-assembled movements	53.8	34.1	87.9	28
United States: watches & movements	2.0	10.1*	12.1*	
Rest of Europe: watches & movements	4.5	57.2*	67.7*	
Rest of Asia: watches & movements	76.0	31.3*	113.0*	42†
Latin America: watches & movements		2.7*	2.7*	

*Includes unassembled movements.
†Without unassembled movements.

EXHIBIT 2
Switzerland's 1975 Share
of World Production by
Type of Technology

Technology	Year of Introduction	Stage of Product Life Cycle	Swiss Share, %
Simple mechanical	Pre-WWII	Declining	35
Automatic	1948	Mature	24
Electric	1953	Declining	18
Quartz (high frequency)	1970	Growing	10
Quartz (solid state)	1972	Growing	3

parts (*ebauche*) or assembled to chablons by termineurs which in turn supplied the etablisseurs, where the entire watch was put together. In 1975 63,000 empolyees in 12,000 workshops and plants were involved in the manufacture of watches and parts. Each etablisseur designed its own models and assembled the various pieces purchased from the many suppliers. Only a few vertically integrated manufacturers existed which performed most of the production stages in-house (see Exhibit 4). The watches were either exported bearing the assembler's or manufacturer's brand name (factory label) via wholly-owned distributors and independent importers, or sold under the name of the customer (private label). By the late 1970s private label sales composed about 75 percent of Swiss exports of finished watches. In addition, the Swiss also exported movements and unassembled parts to foreign customers (see Exhibit 5).

This horizontally and vertically fragmented industry structure had developed over centuries around a locally concentrated infrastructure and depended entirely on highly skilled craftsmen. Watch making encompassed a large number of sophisticated techniques for producing the mechanical watches and this complexity was exacerbated by the extremely large number of watch models. The industry was specialized around highly qualified labor, requiring flexibility, quality, and first-class styling at low cost.

This structure was, however, poorly suited to

EXHIBIT 3
Share of Electronic
Watches of Annual Output

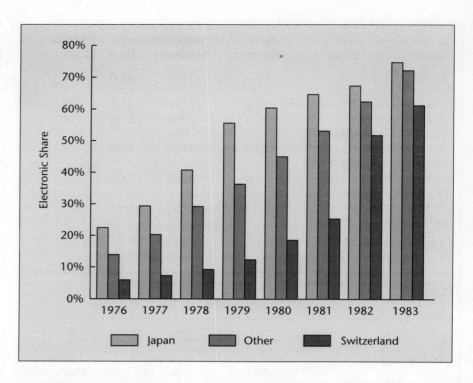

Electronic Share

| Japan | Other | Switzerland |

EXHIBIT 4
Traditional Structure of the
Swiss Watch Industry

Source: Bernheim, R.A. (1981)
*Koordination in Zersplitterten
Märkten* (Coordination in
Fragmented Markets), Paul
Haupt Publ., Berne.

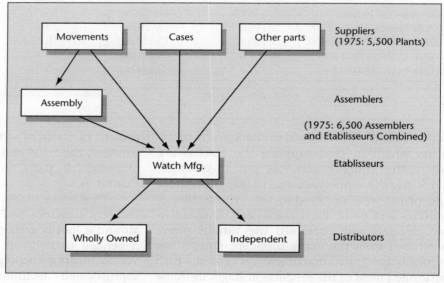

Movements | Cases | Other parts — Suppliers (1975: 5,500 Plants)

Assembly — Assemblers

(1975: 6,500 Assemblers and Etablisseurs Combined)

Watch Mfg. — Etablisseurs

Wholly Owned | Independent — Distributors

absorb the new electronics technology. Not only did electronics render obsolete many of the watchmaker's skills that had been cultivated over centuries, it also required large production volumes to take advantage of the significant scale and potential experience effects. Whereas the traditional Swiss manufacturing methods provided few benefits from mass production, the extreme fragmentation from the suppliers to the distributors prevented even these. Furthermore,

EXHIBIT 5
Swiss Exports of Watches,
Movements, and Parts,
1960–1990

Year	Finished Watches		Assembled Movements		Unassembled Movements	
	Pieces*	Francs†	Pieces*	Francs†	Pieces*	Francs†
1960	16.7	767.2	8.2	192.7	n/a	n/a
1965	38.4	1334.4	14.8	282.7	n/a	n/a
1970	52.6	2033.8	18.8	329.5	n/a	n/a
1975	47.2	2391.2	18.6	329.1	5.4	44.0
1976	42.0	2262.4	20.0	343.0	8.0	54.2
1977	44.1	2474.5	21.9	381.3	15.8	94.8
1978	39.7	2520.0	20.6	380.3	18.7	103.5
1979	30.3	2355.6	18.6	371.1	20.2	121.0
1980	28.5	2505.8	22.5	411.8	32.7	189.2
1981	25.2	2880.2	19.9	382.5	27.5	160.5
1982	18.5	2754.6	12.7	256.4	14.5	81.0
1983	15.7	2676.6	14.6	247.1	12.7	76.8
1984	17.8	3063.9	14.5	235.0	14.6	98.5
1985	25.1	3444.1	13.4	220.4	18.8	138.9
1986	28.1	3391.0	13.3	213.4	19.4	133.3
1987	27.6	3568.0	11.1	179.4	20.9	122.8
1988	28.0	4128.8	12.2	202.8	31.9	162.1
1989	29.9	5080.0	12.6	217.7	28.4	136.3

*In millions.
†In millions of current Swiss francs.

the critical stages in the value added chain of the watch shifted from parts and assembly – where the Swiss had their stronghold – to distribution where the Japanese concentrated their efforts. Encasement, marketing, wholesale and retail distribution, which the Japanese producers emphasized, represented over 80 percent of the value added.

Sales of mechanical watches in the budget and middle price segments dropped rapidly when electronic watches entered the market. Initially these were Instruments Inc., National Semiconductor Corp., Hughes Aircraft, Intel, and Time Computer. Due to rapidly rising production and sales volumes of electronic watches, prices dropped dramatically from $1,000 to $2,000 in 1970 to $40 in 1975 and less than $20 by the end of the 1970s. At this time most of the early American digital watch producers had started to withdraw from the watch business and it was the cheap digital watch from Hong Kong that flooded the market. As an indication of the eroded market

power of the Swiss, the sale of assembled and unassembled movements had started to rise while exports of finished watches declined (see Exhibit 5) – a trend which negatively affected domestic employment.

The industry's misfortune caused large-scale layoffs, and bankruptcies started to increase steeply in the 1970s. Since the watch industry was concentrated around a few towns in the western part of Switzerland, the ensuing job losses led to regional unemployment rates unknown in Switzerland since the 1930s (see Exhibit 6).

ETA, where Dr. Thomke became managing director, was a subsidiary of Ebauches SA, which in turn was a subsidiary of ASUAG (General Corporation of Swiss Horological Industries Ltd.) ASUAG had been created in 1931 during the first consolidation period in the industry. It was Switzerland's largest watch corporation (total sales in 1979 were SFr. 1,212 million) and combined a multitude of companies under its holding structure including such famous brands as Certina,

EXHIBIT 6
Swiss Watch Industry:
Companies and
Employment

Year	Number of Companies	Employment
1960	2,167	65,127
1965	1,927	72,600
1970	1,618	76,045
1975	1,169	55,954
1976	1,083	49,991
1977	1,021	49,822
1978	979	48,305
1979	867	43,596
1980	861	44,173
1981	793	43,300
1982	727	36,808
1983	686	32,327
1984	634	30,978
1985	634	31,949
1986	592	32,688
1987	568	29,809
1988	562	30,122

Eterna, Longines, and Rado. Ebauches, of which ETA was part, was the major producer of watch movements for ASUAG and most of the other Swiss etablisseurs. The other large Swiss manufacturer was SSIH (Swiss Watch Industry Corporation Ltd.) which also was a creation of the same 1931 consolidation and whose flagships were Omega and Tissot. During the second half of the 1970s ASUAG suffered from declining profitability and cash flow, poor liquidity, rising long-term debt, and dwindling financial reserves due to sluggish sales of outdated mechanical watches and movements which comprised about two thirds of ASUAG's watch sales. Diversified businesses outside the watch segment contributed less than five percent of total sales.

Turnaround at ETA

Ernst Thomke grew up in Bienne, the Swiss capital of watch making. After an apprenticeship in watch making with ETA he enrolled in the University of Berne where he first studied physics and chemistry and later medicine. After his studies he joined Beechams, a large British pharmaceuticals and consumer products company as a pharmaceutical salesman. In 1978, when his old boss at ETA asked him to return to his first love, he was managing director of Beecham's Swiss subsidiary and had just been promoted to Brussels. However, his family did not wish to move and so, after 18 years, he was back in watches.

When he took over, morale at ETA was at an all-time low due to the prolonged period of market share losses and continued dismissals of personnel. ETA's engineers and managers no longer believed in their capabilities of beating the competition from Japan and Hong Kong. Although ETA as the prime supplier of watch movements did not consider itself directly responsible for the series of failures, it was equally affected by the weakened position of the Swiss watch manufacturers. When Thomke assumed his role as managing director of ETA he clearly understood that, for a successful turnaround, his subordinates needed a success story to regain their self-confidence. But first a painful shrinking process had to be undertaken in order to bring costs under control. Production which used to be distributed over a dozen factories was concentrated in three centers and the number of movement models reduced from over 1,000 to about 250.

As a first step, a project called 'Delirium' was formulated with the objective to create the world's thinnest analogue quartz movement – a record which at that time was held by Seiko. When Thomke revealed his idea to ETA's engineers they were quick to nickname it 'Delirium Tremens' because they considered it crazy. But Thomke insisted on the project despite his staff's doubts. To save even the tiniest fraction of a millimeter some watch parts were for the first time bonded to the case instead of being layered on top of the watch back. Also, a new extra thin battery was invented. In 1979 the first watch was launched with Delirium movement and ETA had its first success in a long time. In that year, ASUAG sold more than 5,000 pieces at an average price of $4,700 with the top model retailing for $16,000.

The Delirium project not only helped to boost the morale of ETA's employees, it also led to a significant change in strategy and philosophy with ETA's parent, Ebauches SA. No longer was Ebauches content with its role as the supplier of movement parts. In order to fulfill its primary responsibility as the supplier of technologically advanced quality movements at competitive prices to Switzerland's etablisseurs, Ebauches argued, it was necessary to maintain a minimum sales volume that exceeded the reduced domestic demand. Therefore, in 1981 ETA expanded its movement sales beyond its then-current customers in Switzerland, France and Germany. This expansion meant sales to Japan, Hong Kong and Brazil. Ebauches thus entered into direct international competition with Japanese, French, German and Soviet manufacturers. In short, ETA claimed more control over its distribution channels and increased authority in formulating its strategy.

As a second step, the organizational culture and structure were revamped to foster creativity and to encourage employees to express their ideas. Management layers were scrapped and red tape reduced to a minimum. Communication across departments and hierarchical levels was stressed, continued learning and long-term thinking encouraged, playful trial-and-error and risk-taking reinforced. The intention was to boost morale and to create corporate heroes.

The third step consisted of defining a revolutionary product in the medium or low price category. By expanding even further into the downstream activities, Thomke argued, ETA would control more than 50 percent instead of merely 10 percent of the total value added. Since 1970 the watch segments below SFr. 200 had experienced the highest growth rates (see Exhibit 7). These were the segments the Swiss had ceded to the competitors from Japan and Hong Kong. As a consequence, the average price of Swiss watch exports had steadily risen, whereas the competitors exported at declining prices. Given the overall objective to reverse the long-term trend of segment retreat, it was crucial to reenter one or both of the formerly abandoned segments. Thomke decided to focus on the low price segment. 'We thought we'd leave the middle market for Seiko and Citizen. We would go for

Price Category	1970 Sales (Million Pieces)	1980 Sales (Million Pieces)	Growth, %
Less than 100 SFr.	110	290	264
100–200 SFr.	33	50	52
200–500 SFr.	20	20	0
More than 500 SFr.	7	10	43

EXHIBIT 7
World Watch Production by Price Category, 1970 vs. 1980

Source: Thomke, E. (1985) In der Umsetzung von der Produktidee Zur Marktreife liegt ein entscheidender Erfolgsfaktor ('In the translation from product idea to marketable product lies a key success factor'), *Management-Zeitschrift* No. 2, pp. 60–4.

the top and the bottom to squeeze the Japanese in the sandwich (Moynahan and Heumann 1985). The new concept was summarized in four objectives:

1 *Price*: Quartz-analogue watch, retailing for no more than SFr. 50.

2 *Sales target*: 10 million pieces during the first three years.

3 *Manufacturing costs*: Initially SFr. 15 – less than those of any competitor. At a cumulative volume of 5 million pieces, learning and scale economies would reduce costs to SFr. 10 or less. Continued expansion would yield long term estimated costs per watch of less than SFr. 7.

4 *Quality*: High quality, waterproof, shock resistant, no repair possible, battery only replaceable element, all parts standardized, free choice of material, model variations only in dial and hands.

The objectives were deliberately set so high that it was impossible to reach them by improving existing technologies; instead, they required novel approaches. When confronted with these parameters for a new watch, ETA's engineers responded with 'That's impossible,' 'Absurd,' 'You're crazy.' Many considered it typical of Thomke's occasionally autocratic management style which had brought him the nickname 'Ayatollah.' After all, the unassembled parts of the cheapest existing Swiss watch at that time cost more than twice as much! Also, the largest Swiss watch assembler – ETA's parent ASUAG – sold 750,000 watches annually scattered over several hundred models. In an interview with *The Sunday Times Magazine* Thomke told the story: 'A couple of kids, under 30, said they'd go away and look at the Delirium work and see if they could come up with anything. And they did. They mounted the moving parts directly on to a moulded case. It was very low cost. And it was new, and that is vital in marketing'. (ibid.) The concept was the brainchild of two engineers. Elmar Mock, a qualified plastics engineer, had recommended earlier that ETA acquire an injection moulding machine to investigate the possibilities of producing watch parts made of plastic.

Jacques Muller was a horological engineer and specialist in watch movements. Their new idea was systematically evaluated and improved by inter-disciplinary teams consisting of the inventors, product and manufacturing engineers, specialists from costing, marketing and accounting, as well as outside members not involved in the watch industry.

The fourth step required that ETA develop its own marketing. In the 1970s and early 1980s it did not have a marketing department. Thomke turned to some independent consultants and people outside the watch industry with extensive marketing experience in apparel, shoes and sporting goods to bring creative marketing to the project. Later, as Swatch sales expanded worldwide, a new marketing team was built up to cover the growing marketing, communications and distribution activities.

Product and Process Technology

A conventionally designed analogue watch consisted of a case in which the movement was mounted. The case was closed with a glass or crystal. The movement included a frame onto which the wheels, the micromotor needed for analogue display, other mechancial parts as well as the electronic module were attached with screws. First the movement was assembled and then mechanically fixed in the case. Later the straps were attached to the case.

The Swatch differed both with regard to its construction as well as the manufacturing process.

Construction

First, the case was not only an outer shell, it also served as the mounting plate. The individual parts of the movement were mounted directly into the case – the Delirium technology was perfected. The case itself was produced by a new, very precise injection-molding process which was specifically developed for this purpose. The case was made of extremely durable plastic which created a super-light watch.

Second, the number of *components* was reduced significantly from 91 parts for a conventional analogue quartz watch to 51 (see Exhibit 8). Unlike in conventional watch assembly, the individual parts of the movement – the electronic module and the motor module – were first assembled in subgroups before mounting and then placed in the case like a system of building blocks.

Third, the *method of construction* differed in that the parts were no longer attached with screws. Components were riveted and welded together ultrasonically. This eliminated screws and threads and reduced the number of parts and made the product rugged and shock-resistant. As the crystal was also welded to the case, the watch was guaranteed water-resistant up to 100 feet.

Fourth, the tear-proof *strap* was integrated into the case with a new, patented hinge system which improved wearing comfort.

Fifth, the *battery* – the only part with a limited life expectancy of about three years – was inserted into the bottom of the case and closed with a cover.

Production

First, as a special advantage the Swatch could be assembled from one side only.

Second, because of this it was possible to fully automate the watch-mounting process. Ordinary watches were assembled in two separate operations: the mounting of the movement and the finishing. The Swatch, however, was produced in one single operation (see Exhibit 9). According to representatives of the Swiss watch manufacturers, this technology incorporated advanced CAD/CAM technology as well as extensive use of robotics and was the most advanced of its kind in the world.

Third, due to the new design, the number of elements needed for the Swatch could be significantly reduced and the assembly process simplified. As a prerequisite for incoroprating this new product technology, new materials had to be developed for the case, the glass and the micro motor. Also, a new assembly technology was designed and the pressure diecasting process perfected.

Fourth, quality requirements had to be tightened, because the watch could not be reopened and therefore, except for the battery, not be repaired. Given these constraints, each step in the manufacturing process had to be carefully controlled including the parts, the pre-assembled modules, the assembly process itself as well as the final product. This was especially important because in the past high reject rates of parts and casings indicated that many Swiss manufacturers had difficulties with quality control which damaged their reputation.

Overall, the new product design and production technology reduced the costs significantly and raised product quality above watches in the same price category produced by conventional technology.

Marketing

The new marketing team came up with an approach that was unheard of in this industry dominated by engineers.

Product positioning Contrary to conventional wisdom in the industry it was not the product, its styling and technical value that were emphasized, but its brand name. Quality attributes such as water-proofness, shock resistance, color, preciseness were less important than the association of the brand name with positive emotions such as 'fun,' 'vacation,' 'joy of life.' The watch was positioned as a high-fashion accessory for fashion conscious people between 18 and 30. As it turned out many people outside this range started buying the Swatch. Jean Robert, a Zurich based designer, was responsible for Swatch's innovative designs.

Pricing The price was set at a level that allowed for spontaneous purchases yet provided the high margins needed for massive advertising.

Distribution As a high-fashion item competing in the same price range as some Timex and Casio

EXHIBIT 8
Swatch Components

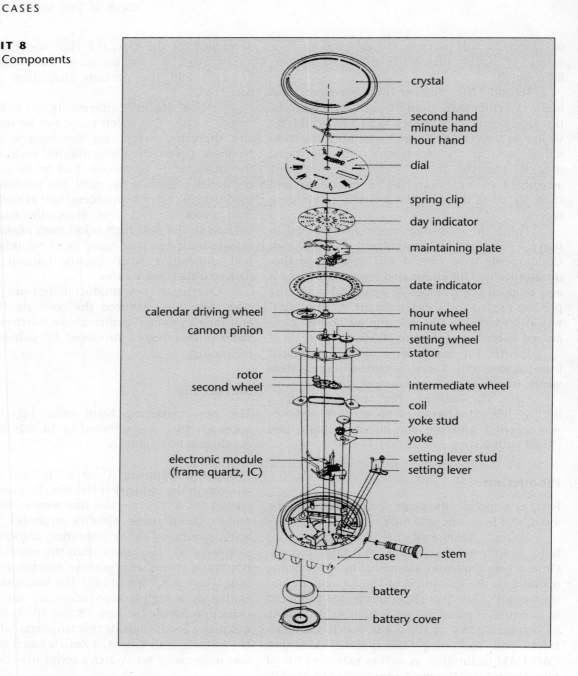

crystal
second hand
minute hand
hour hand
dial
spring clip
day indicator
maintaining plate
date indicator
calendar driving wheel
cannon pinion
hour wheel
minute wheel
setting wheel
stator
rotor
second wheel
intermediate wheel
coil
yoke stud
yoke
electronic module
(frame quartz, IC)
setting lever stud
setting lever
case — stem
battery
battery cover

models, the Swatch was not sold through drug-stores and mass retailers. Instead, department stores, chic boutiques and jewelry shops were used as distribution channels. Attractive distributor margins and extensive training of the retailers' sales personnel combined with innovative

advertising ensured the unique positioning of the product.

Brand name In 1982 20,000 prototypes of 25 Swatch models were pretested in the United States, which was viewed as the toughest market,

EXHIBIT 9
Swatch Assembly Process

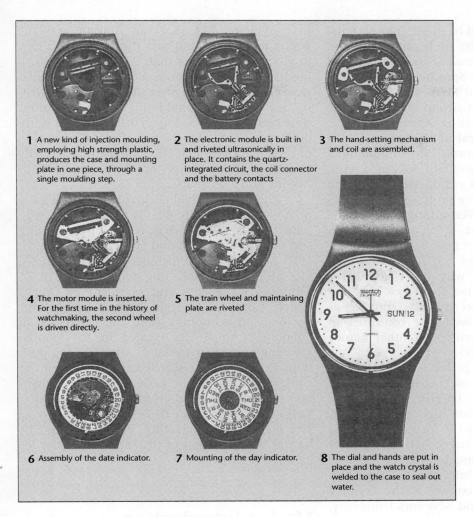

1 A new kind of injection moulding, employing high strength plastic, produces the case and mounting plate in one piece, through a single moulding step.

2 The electronic module is built in and riveted ultrasonically in place. It contains the quartz-integrated circuit, the coil connector and the battery contacts

3 The hand-setting mechanism and coil are assembled.

4 The motor module is inserted. For the first time in the history of watchmaking, the second wheel is driven directly.

5 The train wheel and maintaining plate are riveted

6 Assembly of the date indicator.

7 Mounting of the day indicator.

8 The dial and hands are put in place and the watch crystal is welded to the case to seal out water.

setting the trend for the rest of the world. The unisex models only differed in color of the cases and straps and the dial designs. It was during these pretests that Franz Sprecher, one of the outside consultants of the marketing team, came up with the name 'Swatch' (Swiss + Watch = Swatch) during a brainstorming session with the New York based advertising agency concerning the product's positioning and name. Up until then Sprecher's notes repeatedly mentioned the abbreviation S'Watch. During this meeting Sprecher took the abbreviation one step further and created the final name.

The Swatch Team

Besides Thomke, three individuals were crucial for the successful launching of the Swatch: Franz Sprecher, Max Imgrueth, and Jacques Irniger.

Franz Sprecher obtained a masters in economics and business from the University of Basle. Following one year as a research assistant and PhD student he decided to abandon academia and enter the international business world as a management trainee with Armour Foods in Chicago. After six months he returned to Switzerland and joined Nestlé in international marketing. Two years later he became sales and marketing director of a small Swiss/Austrian food additives company. Later Sprecher moved to the positions of International Marketing Director of Rivella and then Account Group Manager at the Dr. Dieter Jaeggi Advertising Agency in Basle. Sprecher took a sabbatical at this point in his career and planned to return to the international business world as a consultant within a year. Towards the end of this period while thinking of accepting a position as a professor at the Hoehere Wirtschafts- und Verwaltungschochschule in Lucerne he received a phone call from Thomke concerning the new watch. Thomke told Sprecher: 'You've got too much time and not enough money, so why don't you come and work for me.' Sprecher then took over the marketing of the, as of yet unnamed, product as a freelance consultant. Today, he continues to consult for Swatch as well as for other brands such as Tissot and Omega.

Another important person involved in the creation of the Swatch was Max Imgrueth. Max Imgrueth was born in Lucerne, Switzerland. Following graduation from high school in St. Maurice, a small town in the Valais surrounded by high mountains, he went to Italy and studied art history in Florence and fashion and leather design in Milan. After a brief stint in linguistics he enrolled in business courses at the Regency Polytechnic in England and New York University. In 1969 he left the United States because he had difficulties in obtaining a work permit and started to work in a women's specialty store in Zurich, Switzerland. Two years later he switched to apparel manufacturing and became manager for product development and marketing. In 1976 he was recruited by SSIH, owners of the Omega and Tissot brands. From 1976 to 1981 he was in charge of product development and design at Omega's headquarters in Bienne. Conflicts with the banks – which at that time de facto owned SSIH due to continued losses – over Omega's strategy led him to resign from his job and to start a consulting business. One of his first clients was ETA Industries which were just getting ready to test market the Swatch in San Antonio, Texas. He succeeded in convincing ETA that San Antonio was the wrong test market and that the Swatch as a new product required other than the traditional distributors. As a consequence New York and Dallas were chosen as primary test sites, and TV advertising and unconventional forms of public relations were tried. While working on debugging the introduction of the Swatch, he was offered the position of president of Swatch USA, a job which initially consisted of an office on Manhattan's Fifth Avenue and a secretary.

The third individual involved in the early phase of the Swatch was Jacques Irniger who joined ETA in 1983 as vice president of marketing and sales for both ETA and Swatch worldwide. In 1985 he was a board member of the Swatch SA, vice president of marketing and sales of ETA SA Fabriques d'Ebauches and president of Omega Watch Corp., New York. Irniger received his doctorate in economics from the University of Fribourg, a small city located in the French-speaking part of Switzerland. After training positions in marketing research and management at Unilever and Nestle he became marketing manager at Colgate Palmolive in Germany. After Colgate, he moved on to Beecham Germany as vice president of marketing. Before joining ETA he was vice president of marketing and sales for Bahksen international.

Market Introduction

The Swatch was officially introduced in Switzerland on March 1, 1983 – the same year that ASUAG and SSIH merged after continued severe losses that necessitated a SFr. 1.2 billion bailout by the Swiss banks. During the first four months 25,000 Swatch pieces were sold – more than a third of the initial sales objective of 70,000 for the first 12 months. According to some distinguished jewelry stores located on Zurich's famous Bahnhofstrasse where Switzerland's most prestigious and expensive watches were purchased by an endless stream of tourists from all over the world, the Swatch did not compete with the traditional models. On the contrary, some jewelers reported that the Swatch stimulated sales of their more expensive models. The success of the Swatch encouraged other Swiss manufacturers to develop similar models which, however, incorporated conventional quartz technology.

Subsequent market introductions in other countries used high-powered promotion. In Germany, the launching of the Swatch was accompanied by a huge replica of a bright yellow Swatch that covered the entire facade of the black Commerzbank skyscraper in Frankfurt's business district. The same approach was used in Japan. On Christmas Eve 1985 the front of a tall building in Tokyo was decorated with a huge Swatch that was 11 yards long and weighed more than 14,000 pounds. Japan, however, turned out to be a difficult market for the Swatch. The 7,000 Yen Swatch competed with domestic plastic models half the price. Distribution was restricted to eleven department stores in Tokyo only and carried out without a Japanese partner. After six months it became obvious that the original sales target of SFr. 25 million for the first year could not be reached. The head of the Japanese Swatch operation, the American Harold Tune, resigned. His successor was a Japanese.

In the United States, initial sales profited from the fact that many American tourists coming home from their vacation in Switzerland helped in spreading the word about this fancy product which quickly became as popular a souvenir as Swiss army knives. US sales of this $30 colorful watch grew from 100,000 pieces in 1983 to 3.5 million pieces in 1985 – a sign that Swatch USA, ETA's American subsidiary, was successful in changing the way time pieces were sold and worn. No longer were watches precious pieces given as presents on special occasions such as confirmation, bar mitzvahs, and marriages, to be worn for a lifetime. 'Swatch yourself,' meant wearing two, three watches simultaneously like plastic bracelets. Swatch managers traveling back and forth between the United States and Switzerland wore two watches, one showing EST time, the other Swiss time.

The initial success prompted the company to introduce a ladies' line one year after the initial introduction, thus leading to 12 models. New Swatch varieties were created about twice a year.

Also, special models were designed for the crucial Christmas season: In 1984 scented models were launched, a year later a limited edition watch called Limelight with diamonds sold at $100. The Swatch was a very advertising-intensive line of business. For 1985, the advertising budget of Swatch USA alone was $8 million, with US sales estimated at $45 million (1984 sales: $18 million). In 1985, Swatch USA sponsored MTV's New Year's Eve show; the year before it had sponsored a breakdancing festival offering $25,000 in prizes, and the Fresh Festival '84 in Philadelphia.

Swatch managers were, however, careful not to flood the market. They claimed that in 1984 an additional 2 million watches could have been sold in the United States. In England, 600,000 watches were sold in the first year and the British distributor claimed he could have sold twice as many.

Continued Growth

The marketing strategy called for complementing the $30 time piece with a range of Swatch accessories. The idea behind this strategy was to associate the product with a lifestyle and thereby create brand identity and distinction from the range of look-alikes which had entered the market and were copying the Swatch models with a delay of about three months. In late 1985 Swatch USA introduced an active apparel line called Funwear. T-shirts, umbrellas, and sunglasses should follow in the hope of adding an extra $100 million in sales in 1986. Product introduction was accompanied by an expensive and elaborate publicity campaign including a four-month TV commercial series costing $2.5 million, an eight-page Swatch insert featuring a dozen Swatch accessories in *Glamour*, *GQ*, *Vogue*, and *Rolling Stone*, and a $2.25 million campaign on MTV. In January 1985 Swatch AG was spun off from ETA. The purpose of the new Swatch subsidiary was to design and distribute watches and related consumer goods such as shoes, leather and leather imitation accessories, clothes, jewelry and perfumes, toys, sports goods, glasses and accessories, pens, lighters and cigarettes. Swatch production, however, remained with ETA. Furthermore, licenses were being considered for the distribution of the products. All of these products as well as the watches were designed in the United States with subsequent adaptations for European markets.

This strategy of broadening the product line was, however, not without risks, because it could dilute the impact of the brand name. *Forbes* mentioned the examples of Nike which failed miserably when it tried to expand from runningwear to leisure wear, and so did Lewis when it attempted to attach its brand recognition to more formal apparel (Heller 1986). Yet Max Imgrueth was quick to point to other examples such as Terence Conran, a designer and furniture maker who succeeded in building a retail empire ranging from kitchen towels to desk lamps around his inexpensive, well-designed home furnishings aimed at the young.

Ensuring Success

At the end of 1985, 45,000 Swatch units were produced daily and annual sales were expected to reach 8 million pieces (1984: 3.7 million). The Swatch was so successful that by the end of 1984 Swatch profits above recovering all product related investments and expenditures contributed significantly towards ETA's overhead. The Swatch represented 75 percent of SMH's unit sales of finished watches and made it SMH's number one brand in terms of unit sales and the number two brand in terms of revenues, topping such prestige brands as Longines and Rado. SMH (Swiss Corporation for Microelectronics and Watchmaking Industries Ltd.) was the new name of the Swatch parent after the ASUAG-SSIH merger in 1983. Thanks to the Swatch SMH was able to increase its share of the world market (1985: 400 million units) from one percent to three percent within four years. The success also invigorated the Swiss industry at large (see Exhibit 6). Despite this success the managers at Swatch continued to perfect and expand the Swatch line.

In 1986 The Maxi-Swatch was introduced which was ten times the size of the regular Swatch. Before the start of ths ski season during the same year the Pop-Swatch was launced which could be combined with different color wristbands. As a high-technology extravaganza the

Pop-Swatch could also be worn in combination with a 'Recco-Reflector' which had been developed by another SMH subsidiary. The Recco reflected radar waves emitted from a system and thus helped to locate skiers covered by avalanches.

In 1987 Swatch wall models were introduced, and the Swatch Twinphone. The latter was not just colorful. It had a memory to facilitate dialing and, true to its origin, provided an unconventional service in that it had a built-in 'party line,' so that two people could use it simultaneously. 1988 saw the successful introduction of the Twinphone in the USA, Japan and the airport duty-free business as well as the expansion of the Pop-Swatch product line. The Swatch accessories line was discontinued due to unmet profit objectives and negative impact on the Swatch brand image.

In its 1989 annual report SMH reported cumulative sales of over 70 million Swatch pieces. Over 450 models of the original concept had been introduced during the first seven years (see Exhibit 10). The Swatch had also become a collector's item. Limited edition models designed by well-known artists brought auction prices of SFr. 1,600, SFr. 3,900 and SFr. 9,400 – about 25 to 160 times the original price!

In 1990 the 'Swatch-Chrono' was launched to take advantage of the chronometer fashion. Except for the basic concept – plastic encasement and battery as the only replaceable part – it had little in common with the original model and represented a much more complex instrument. It had four micromotors instead of only one due to the added functions and was somewhat larger in diameter. Despite the added complexity it claimed to be as exact and robust as the original Swatch. As a special attraction the watch was available in six models and retailed for only SFr. 100. The company was also experimenting with a mechanical Swatch to be marketed in developing countries where battery replacement posed a problem. In this way the company hoped to boost sales in regions which represented only a minor export market for the Swiss.

The success of the Swatch at the market front was supported by a carefully structured organization. Just like the other major brands of SMH, the Swatch had its own organization in each

EXHIBIT 10
Swatch Sales

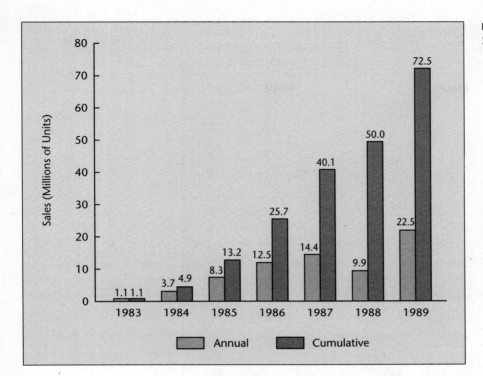

major market responsible for marketing, sales and communication. These regional offices were supported by SMH country organizations which handled services common to all brands such as logistics, finance, controlling, administration, EDP and after-sales service.

The Swatch also meant a big boost for Thomke's career. He was appointed general manager of the entire watch business of the reorganized SMH and became one of the decision makers of the new management team that took over in January 1985. The 'Swatch Story' was instrumental in the turnaround of SMH which only six years after the merger of two moribund companies showed a very healthy bottom line (see Exhibit 11).

The Future

Despite the smashing success of the Swatch and its contribution to the reinvigoration of the Swiss watch making industry, future success was by no means guaranteed.

First, competition remained as fierce as ever. The 1980s were characterized by an oversupply of cheap watches because many manufacturers had built capacity ahead of demand. Prices dropped, especially for the cheapest digital watches, a segment that the Swiss avoided. However, several competitors switched to the more sophisticated analogue models and thus created competition for the Swatch. Many look-alikes with names such as Action Watch, A-Watch, etc., flooded the market.

Second, the Swiss had to guard their brand recognition – not just because of the diversification of the Swatch line. It was not clear whether the Swatch brand name was strong enough to create a sustainable position against the imitations. Also, the quality advantage of the Swatch was neither evident to the consumer nor a top priority for the purchasing decision.

A third issue was for how long the Swatch could maintain its technological advantage. By the late 1980s all imitations were welded together. In addition, many competitors, especially the

	1989	1988	1987	1986	1985	1984
Income Statement Data						
Sales revenues:						
Gross sales	2,146	1,847	1,787	1,895	1,896	1,665
Costs:						
Materials	793	681	670	759	812	714
Personnel	646	580	577	593	556	541
External services	346	331	335	356	360	286
Depreciation	80	71	73	68	61	60
Total operating costs	1,865	1,663	1,655	1,776	1,789	1,758
Operating profit (loss)	236	142	117	103	66	51
Income before taxes	209	126	90	82	72	38
Net income	175	105	77	70	60	26
Balance Sheet Data						
Assets:						
Current assets	1,194	1,065	1,103	1,080	1,070	1,049
Inventories	602	562	528	568	513	524
Fixed assets	529	510	533	507	456	451
Total assets	1,723	1,575	1,636	1,587	1,526	1,500
Liabilities and stockholders' equity:						
Short-term debt	367	384	442	503	524	501
Long-term debt	295	302	798	801	862	898
Total liabilities	662	686	1,240	1,304	1,386	1,399
Total shareholders' equity	892	760	697	648	490	420
Total liabilities & equity	1,723	1,575	1,636	1,587	1,526	1,500
Other Data						
Personnel: in Switzerland	8,822	8,385	8,526	9,323	9,173	8,982
Personnel: abroad	2,963	2,893	2,597	2,611	2,353	2,311
Personnel: total	11,785	11,278	11,123	11,934	11,526	11,293
Stock price high (SFr.)	560	395	490	700	410	—
Stock price low (SFr.)	378	178	150	375	127	—

EXHIBIT 11
SMH: Financial Data
(in millions SFr.)

Japanese, were larger than SMH and therefore able to support larger R&D budgets.

A fourth threat was market saturation. While countries with a GDP per capita of over $5,000 comprised only 17 percent of the world's population, they absorbed 87 percent of Swiss watch exports. The changes in watch technology and pricing during the last 10 years had increased watch consumption. In England, consumption grew from 275 watches per 1,000 inhabitants in 1974 to 370 watches 10 years later. In the United States the respective figures were 240

and 425 units of which 90 percent was made up of low-price electronic models. While the average life of a watch was much shorter today and consumers had started to own several watches, market saturation could not be ruled out. Also, given the trendy nature of the Swatch it could fall out of fashion as quickly as it had conquered the market. For this situation SMH was not as well prepared as, say, Seiko or Casio, whose non-watch businesses were much stronger and contributed more in terms of overall sales and profits.

EXHIBIT 12
SMH Subsidiaries, 1990

SMH Swiss Corporation for Microelectronics and Watchmaking Industries Ltd. Neuchâtel (Holding Company)

Company Name, Registered Offices	Field of Activity	Shareholding SMH Direct or Indirect, %
Omega SA, Bienne	Watches	100
Compagnie des montres Longines	Watches	100
Francillon SA, Saint-Imier		100
SA Longines pour la vente en Suisse, Saint-Imier	Distribution	
Columna SA, Lausanne	Distribution	100
Longines (Singapore) PTE Ltd, Singapore	Distribution	100
Longines (Malaysia) Sdn, Kuala Lumpur	Distribution	100
Montres Rado Sa, Lengnau	Watches	100
Tissot SA, Le Locie	Watches	100
Certina, Kurth Freres SA, Grenchen	Watches	100
Mido G. Schaeren & Co SA, Bienne	Watches	100
Mido industria e Comercio de Relogios Ltda, Rio de Janeiro	Distribution	100
Swatch SA, Bienne	Watches	100
ETA SA Fabriques d'Ebauches, Grenchen	Watches, movements, electronic components and systems	100
ETA (Thailand) Co. Ltd, Bangkok	Watches and movements	100
Leader Watch Case Co. Ltd, Bangkok	Watch cases	100
Endura SA, Bienne	Watches	100
Lascor SpA, Sesto Calende (Italy)	Watch cases	100
Diantus Watch SA, Castel San Pietro	Watches and movements	100
Société Européenne de Fabrication d'Ebauches d'Annemasse (SEFEA) SA, Annemasse (France)	Watch components and electronic assembly	100
Ruedin Georges SA, Bassecourt	Watch cases	100
EM Microelectronic-Marin SA, Marin	Microelectronics	100
SMH Italia SpA Rozzano	Distribution (Omega, Rado, Tissot Swatch, Flik Flak)	100
SMH (UK) Ltd, Eastleigh	Distribution (Omega, Tissot)	100
SMH Australia Ltd, Prahran	Distribution (Omega, Tissot, Swatch, Flik Flak)	100
SMH Belgium SA, Bruxelles	Distribution (Omega, Tissot, Flik Flak)	100
SMH Ireland Ltd, Dublin	Distribution (Omega)	100
SMH Sweden AB, Stockholm	Distribution (Omega, Longines, Tissot, Certina, Swatch, Flik Flak)	100

Continued

EXHIBIT 12 – *Continued*
SMH Subsidiaries, 1990

SMH Uhren und Mikroelektronik GmbH, Bad Soden (Germany)	Distribution (Omega, Longines, Rado, Tissot, Certina, Swatch, Flik Flak)	100
SMH France SA, Paris	Distribution (Omega, Longines, Rado, Tissot, Certina, Swatch, Flik Flak)	100
SMH España SA, Madrid	Distribution (Omega, Tissot, Swatch, Flik Flak)	100
SMH Japan KK, Tokyo	Distribution (Longines, Tissot, Swatch)	100
SMH (HK) Ltd, Hong Kong	Distribution (ETA, Longines, Swatch, Flik Flak)	100
SMH (US) Inc., Dover Del.	Holding company	100
Hamilton Watch Co Inc., Lancaster Pa.	Distribution	100
Omega Watch Corp., New York	Distribution	100
Rado Watch Co Inc., New York	Distribution	100
Swatch Watch U.S.A. Inc., New York	Distribution (Swatch, Flik Flak)	100
ETA Industries Inc., New York	Distribution	
Unitime Industries Inc., Virgin Islands	Assembly	100
Movomatic USA Inc., Lancaster Pa.	Distribution (Movomatic, Farco)	100
Tissot (US) Inc., New York	Distribution	
Omega Electronics Equipment (US) Inc., Lancaster Pa.	Distribution	100
SMH (US) Services Inc., Lancaster Pa.	Service, watches	100
Technocorp Holding SA, Le Locie	Holding	100
Renata SA, Itingen	Miniature batteries	100
Oscilloquartz SA, Neuchâtel	High stability frequency sources	100
OSA-France Sarl, Boulogne-Billancourt	Distribution	100
Omega Electronics SA, Bienne	Sports timing equipment, score-board information systems	100
Omega Electronics Ltd, Eastleigh (UK)	Distribution	100
Lasag SA, Thun	Laser for industrial and medical application	100
Lasag USA, Inc., Arlington Heights Ill.	Distribution	100
Technica SA, Grenchen	Machine tools and tools	100
Meseitron SA, Corceiles	High precision length measurement (Cary) and automatic size control (Movomatic)	100
Farco SA, Le Locie	Bonding equipment	100
Comadur SA, la Chaux-de-Fonds	Products in hard materials	100
Nivarox-FAR SA, Le Locie	Watch components and thin wires	100

Continued

A. Michel SA, Grenchen	Industrial components and delay systems	100
Regis Mainier SA, Bonnetage (France)	Precision and watch components	97.5
Vuillemin Marc, Bonnetage (France)	Precision and watch components	70.1
Chronometrage Suisse SA (Swiss Timing), Bienne	Sports timing	100
Asulab SA, Bienne	Research and development	100
ICB Ingenieurs Conseils en Brevets SA, Bienne	Patents	100
SMH Marketing Services SA, Bienne	Services and licenses	100

A fifth threat was the continued rapid development of technology especially in the field of communications. Increasingly, time measurement was evolving into one of several features of an integrated communication system. Watches were already integrated in a wide variety of products including household durables, computers, telephones. Several SMH subsidiaries involved in microelectronics, electronic components and telecommunications were busy developing products in this area and searching for applications in other markets as well. In the late 1980s SMH started to test prototypes of a combined watch/pager. In late 1990 Motorola introduced a combined watch/pager. It was not clear how SMH and its Swatch subsidiary would fare in this evolving era despite its high-technology sector which, however, was smaller than that of its competitors (see Exhibit 12).

Finally, despite the success of the Swatch and of several mid-priced models under other brand names such as Tissot, the Swiss continued to experience higher than average unit prices for their watches. This was partially due to the success of their luxury mechanical watch pieces which were frequently encased in precious metal and adorned with precious stones. However, executives of Swiss comanpanies expressed concern about this trend.

References

Heller, M. (1986) Swatch Switches, *Forbes*, January, p. 87.

Moynahan, B. and Heumann, A. (1985) The Man Who Made the Cuckoo Sing, *The Sunday Times Magazine*, August 18, p. 25.

Case 3: Branson's Virgin: The Coming of Age of a Counter-cultural Enterprise

By Manfred Kets de Vries and Robert Dick[1]

The year 1994 was one of mixed success for Richard Branson. His $100 million deal with Delta, the US airline, to block purchase trans-atlantic seats on his airline, Virgin Atlantic, had been approved by the UK authorities but was later rejected by the US government; a submission to convert his rock radio station from the AM frequency to the more popular FM channel was not accepted. His bid to run the UK's new national lottery was rejected. However, approval was granted by the Office of Fair Trading for Virgin to acquire the Our Price chain to create the largest music retailer in the UK. In addition, a number of new projects were under development. Branson's opening salvo for 1995 was the announcement of a new 50–50 venture with Norwich Union to set up Virgin Direct Financial Services, an attempt to revolutionize financial services by selling cut-price insurance, personal equity plans, and pensions directly by phone, cutting out the middlemen. The latter venture was obviously influenced by the success of First Direct, an English company which pioneered telephone banking, and Direct Line, which now controls an increasing share of the market in automobile and household insurance. Branson also launched a challenge to the big beverage companies such as Coca-Cola and Pepsi-Cola by introducing his own Virgin brand beverage, Virgin Cola. In addition, after having won his first libel suit against British Airways, Branson was

suing his competitor again, this time claiming damages in the United States.

These are the issues that preoccupied Branson in 1994 and early 1995. There are also other long-term concerns that Branson will have to address in the coming years. As he approaches middle age, the question of succession arises. Market research has ranked Virgin among the top five brand names in the UK (among the top 25 in Europe) describing the company with words such as fun, innovative, daring, and successful. Branson's image, face and personality (the 'grinning pullover' to his detractors) are inextricably linked to his company. Entrepreneurs rarely pass on their heritage successfully. Without Branson, would his company lose the impetus and culture that has taken it to the position it now enjoys? Virgin has evolved over the years from a youthful enterprise to an established global corporation (see Exhibit 1). But is Branson capable of taking Virgin into the twenty-first century? What does the future hold? What potential dangers are out there, and what preventive steps should be taken to make the company better? Some observers of Virgin wonder whether the company, by engaging in ever newer ventures, will endanger the synergy between its various parts. Are the mechanisms currently in place still sufficient? Should Virgin's flamboyant chairman be 'controlled'? Is the risk-taking side of his personality a liability to the future of the company? Moreover, some analysts have raised the question about the extent to which the brand name could be affected as Virgin moves further and further away from its original core competencies. The late 1990s will undoubtedly prove to be a critical period in the development of the Virgin Group, as Branson faces

---

[1] Source: This case was written by Manfred Kets de Vries and Robert Dick, Associate of INSEAD. It is intended to be used as a basis for class discussion rather than to illustrate either effective or ineffective handling of an administrative situation. For further information on Virgin we refer to 'World Class Leadership in an Age of Discontinuity: A Study of Three Lives', by Manfred Kets de Vries and Elizabeth Treacy-Florent. Copyright © Jossey-Bass: San Francisco.

simultaneously the maturing of his business and himself.

'The Voice of Youth'

In the summer of 1967, the headmaster of Stowe School, an exclusive English boys' private school with a liberal reputation, faced a familiar dilemma. A 17-year-old student wished to leave before taking his final exams so that he could pursue non-academic interests. The young man wished to develop his growing magazine business which he operated in his spare time, using fellow students as workers and a nearby public pay phone as his office. Sensing the young man's determination, and having discussed the matter with his parents, the headmaster finally agreed to the boy's leaving. At the time he was not sanguine about Branson's prospects, saying, 'Richard, you will end up in prison or as a millionaire.' Both prophecies were to prove correct. Looking back today, the headmaster can claim a small part of the launch of one of Britain's most fast-growing private companies led by his ex-student, the unconventional and flamboyant Richard Branson.

Branson's brainchild, *Student* magazine, was a product of the 1960s, the decade when the post-war 'baby boomers' came of age. Across Western Europe and North America young people enjoyed educational, employment and lifestyle opportunities unknown to their parents, all made possible by rapid economic growth. The decade became known for its promotion of youth culture, in which authority was challenged, fashions changed rapidly and rock stars became the global gurus of a new age.

It was in such a climate that Richard Branson, tired of the boring inadequacies of the traditional school magazine and recognizing a 'gaping hole in the market,' founded his own publication. Aimed at people aged 16 to 25, *Student* was to be the 'Voice of Youth' and would 'put the world to rights.' Its eclectic style reflected its founder's ability to commission articles by celebrities and to identify subjects not touched by many well-established magazines. Norman Mailer, Vanessa Redgrave and Jean-Paul Sartre, for example, all contributed pieces which appeared among articles on sex and rock music, interviews with terrorists and proposals for educational reform.

The initial success of the magazine (Branson optimistically claimed a circulation of 100,000) prompted favorable notice in the national press. Branson was described in complimentary terms as 'the editor, publisher and sole advertisement manager . . ., a teenage professional whose enthusiasm gets things done to an extent that would shame his elders.' Certainly his energy and enthusiasm were needed to keep the organization going. The offices were transient, first located in a friend's basement flat, later in a disused church. The staff – who in effect were a loosely-organized co-operative of friends, acquaintances and hangers-on who turned up to help – distributed magazines, took copy and, frequently, avoided creditors. As Branson said at the time: 'The staff all work for nothing. I supply them with somewhere to sleep and some food. It's not so much they are working for you as working with you.'

Not yet 20 years old, Branson found himself with the responsibilities of a much older person, employing 10 people directly, walking a fine line between solvency and financial disaster, interviewing celebrities and appearing on television, rarely relaxing except to chase girls and indulge in escapades with his immediate circle.

Despite his hedonistic lifestyle, and the casual organization of the magazine, Branson was always focused on business. His drive and facility for promotion were not enough, however, and *Student* magazine was not the financial success that Branson had expected. Seeking new activities to boost his flagging business, he decided to try and tap the potential in the sale of records, still over-priced despite the abolition of retail price maintenance, a UK Government policy designed to support certain industries by allowing manufacturers and suppliers to 'recommend' prices to retailers.

Lacking the capital to start a retail outlet, Branson and his associates simply placed an advertisement in the last issue of *Student* to test the market, listing the records likely to appeal to

EXHIBIT I
Key Dates

1968	First issue of *Student* Magazine.
1970	Start of Virgin mail-order operation.
1971	First Virgin record shop opens in Oxford Street.
1972	First Virgin recording studio opens at The Manor near Oxford.
1973	Virgin record label launched.
	Music publishing operation established in the UK.
1977	Virgin signs the Sex Pistols.
1978	First Virgin nightclub opens, The Venue.
	Human League signed to Virgin.
1980	Virgin Records expands presence in overseas markets.
1981	Phil Collins signed to Virgin.
1982	Boy George and Culture Club signed to Virgin.
1983	Virgin Vision formed to distribute films and videos and to operate in television and broadcasting sector.
	Virgin Games (computer games software publisher) launched.
1984	Virgin Atlantic Airways and Virgin Cargo.
	Acquisition of interest in luxury hotel, Mallorca.
	Virgin Vision launches The Music Channel, a 24–hour satellite-delivered music station. Virgin Vision also produces the award-winning film *1984* starring Richard Burton and John Hurt.
1985	Virgin wins Business Enterprise Award for company of the year.
	Virgin Holidays formed.
1986	Virgin Group floated on London stock exchange.
1987	Virgin Records America launched.
	Establishment of subsidiary in Japan.
	Acquisition of Rushes Video.
	Opening of 525, Virgin Communications Los Angeles-based post-production facility.
1988	Olympic Recording Studios opened in Barnes, London.
	Virgin Classics established to specialize in high quality classical music repertoire.
	First Virgin Megastores in Australia, Glasgow and Paris.
	Smaller UK retail outlets sold to W.H. Smith for £23 million.
	Virgin Broadcasting formed to further develop Virgin's interests in radio and television.
	Virgin Atlantic Airways wins three major business class awards. Britain's second most popular long-haul carrier.
	Richard Branson announces management buyout following the 1987 October Stock Market crash.
1989	Virgin Atlantic announces doubled pre-tax profits at £10 million.
	Virgin Mastertronics signs long-term European distribution for Sega Video Games and Sega becomes the number one brand for video games in Europe.
	Virgin Vision sold to Management Company Entertainment Group (MCEG) of Los Angeles for $83 million.
	Virgin Atlantic Airways establishes its own engineering operations.

1990   Virgin Music Group launches second US record company based in New York.

Megastores open in Marseilles, Bordeaux and Belfast.

Virgin Communications creates West One Television, a post-production company to service the broadcast sector.

1991   Virgin Atlantic wins historic ruling by the Civil Aviation Authority (CAA) allowing it to operate extra services to Tokyo. Virgin Atlantic wins the right to operate services out of Heathrow (London) in addition to Gatwick (London).

Virgin Communications sells Virgin Mastertronic, its European computer games distributor to Sega of Japan for £40 million. It retains the publishing division and begins a rapid expansion of Virgin Games.

Virgins wins UK government approval to fly to South Africa, awaits outcome of bilateral talks in South Africa.

1992   Sale of Virgin Music Group to Thorn EMI PLC.

Virgin Games release first video-game software in Europe.

Acquires Westwood Studios Inc., a Las Vegas-based developer of award- winning computer software.

Virgin Games establishes Virgin Games SA in Paris.

Purchase of DC-3 announced to establish new US carrier Vintage Airtours which will initially operate a daily service from Orlando to the Florida Keys offering nostalgic trips in the finest vintage aircraft still flying.

Virgin announces its plan to participate in the operation of trains on the British Rail network.

Megastores in Barcelona, Amsterdam, Vienna, Kyoto and Yokohama.

1993   Virgin Atlantic Airways wins historic libel settlement of £610,000.

Virgin Atlantic voted Executive Travel's Airline of the Year for the third year running.

Virgin Games establishes Virgin Games K.K in Tokyo, Japan.

Virgin Euromagnetics enters the PC market by launching its first range of personal computers.

1994   Virgin City Jet service launched in January between Dublin and London City Airport.

Virgin Atlantic launches scheduled service to Hong Kong and San Francisco.

1995   Virgin Direct Financial Services opened in a 50–50 joint venture with Norwich Union.

Virgin takes on the big beverage companies with Virgin Cola.

Branson sues British Airways again, this time claiming damages, in the US.

young people. The product range was mostly that of bands and singers on the fringe of the music world whose recordings were often not available other than in London stores specializing in alternative music. Most importantly, prices discounted those offered in stores by as much as 15 percent. Orders (with cash) came flooding in. Using the cash to place volume orders with record companies prior to shipment to his customers, Branson found he had created a cut-price mail-order record supply business that required little initial investment or working capital which had a significant competitive advantage over established retail chains.

Casting around for a name for his new business, Branson rejected ideas for names that evoked the music and recording business, since even at that time he was thinking towards a future in which he would create a global brand not limited to entertainment. He finally accepted a suggestion made jokingly by one of his coterie that what they needed was a name that proclaimed their commercial innocence but which also had a certain shock value in keeping with the anti-establishment mood of the times. What better therefore, than 'Virgin'?

Virgin Records was not long in attracting the attention of the major recording companies, suspicious of the up-start's large orders and pricing policy. Investigations led to an immediate ban on direct credit sales, which Branson successfully circumnavigated by using a small retail chain as a purchasing agent. But other problems arose. Branson quickly realized that buying and selling records in bulk required proper controls and systems.

He turned therefore to a childhood friend, Nik Powell, to help him manage his new business, offering in return a 40 percent stake in the company. Methodical where Branson was erratic, cautious where Branson would overextend himself, Nik Powell became the ideal counterbalance in the record company, ensuring customers' orders were correct, payments were made and staff properly deployed. With a competitive advantage in a growing market and a semblance of administration on a low-cost base, the mail-order company seemed set for success. Branson, ever eager to expand, considered all the possibilities – recording studios, music publishing, retail shops, perhaps even record production and artist management. But his plans were upset by immediate problems brought about by hard luck and folly.

Branson's first set-back came early in 1971 when a national postal strike threatened to push the company into bankruptcy. Immediately Branson rented retail space in Oxford Street, London's main shopping thoroughfare, transferred his stock of records there, and launched Virgin Retail. True to the emerging Virgin style, the shop's decor was a mix of the outrageous and the shabby, attracting customers more bent on enjoying an experience than spending money. As the retail chain expanded into provincial towns and cities, Nik Powell, on periodic visits, found that, left to themselves, Virgin's shops would become the meeting place of pot-smoking music freaks.

Having reacted successfully to his company's first major challenge, Branson was stopped in his tracks when he made a misguided business decision that led to his temporary imprisonment. In the summer of 1971, Virgin received its first foreign order. A Belgian company ordered a vanload of records, which, since they were intended for export, could be purchased by Virgin tax-free. Branson, wanting to learn more about overseas markets, decided to make the delivery personally. However, due to a misunderstanding over shipment papers, he found himself back in England with the records and with documents showing that they had been 'exported.' Tempted by quick cash profit, Branson sold the 'exported' records through his London store.

Four or five bogus trips followed until the tax authorities pounced. Shocked and humiliated, Branson spent an uncomfortable night in Dover prison, to be released only after a tearful appeal to his parents to put up the £30,000 bail, using their home as security. Eventually formal charges were dropped in return for an out-of-court financial settlement (a down payment of £15,000, and taxes, duties and charges of £38,000 payable over the next three years), the usual procedure in such cases. Later, Branson would laughingly dismiss his night in a cell, but the pain and embarrassment he caused his parents made him resolve to 'avoid sleepless nights and pay taxes.' Even so, Branson remains an unwilling tax-payer and holds his Virgin shareholding in off-shore family trusts, preferring to reinvest all the profits in the business.

While these setbacks were taking place, Branson had a stroke of luck that was perhaps not evident at the time. Simon Draper, a distant relation from South Africa, arrived at Virgin looking for a job in England to avoid military service. A university graduate with left-of-center views, Draper was passionately interested in, and knowledgeable about, popular music. He joined Virgin as a record buyer, learning the record business from the bottom up.

In later years Draper earned himself the epithet of 'golden ears,' the industry's accolade for successful record producers in recognition of their ability to spot and develop bands and singers with potential. He earned his place at Virgin by persuading Branson to consider backing a nervous and troubled young musician who arrived at Virgin clutching a handful of recording tapes.

Already rejected by the major recording studios, the young man was looking for friends and supporters. At Virgin he found them, and his first recording, Tubular Bells, was to launch him and Virgin into the big time.

Tubular Bells

Mike Oldfield, the composer of Tubular Bells, was a talented and experienced musician with his own vision of popular music. Dismissive of stereotypical rock bands with a vocalist and backing musicians, Oldfield wanted to be known for music that met his artistic standards irrespective of its general appeal and commercial success. Not surprisingly, such an uncompromising attitude deterred potential backers.

Branson and Draper, however, were intrigued by the demonstration tapes he produced. They suggested to Oldfield that he develop his work while living at the Manor, a recording studio with the latest recording technology in a country house near Oxford that Virgin had recently purchased and converted. The result, after a year's endeavors, was 'Tubular Bells,' an original recording of instrumental sound effects, one overlaying another, to create a blended harmonic theme. Released in 1973, Tubular Bells was an immediate and substantial best seller, eventually selling over 5 million copies world-wide. For Branson, this was the ideal opportunity to launch the Virgin Record label and join the ranks of the small independent record producers that were active in the UK market at that time.

Oldfield contracted with Virgin to produce his music and with Branson to act as his manager – an unusual arrangement in the popular music industry where artists and record labels are frequently in dispute. Indeed, Oldfield was later to sue Virgin for imposition of unfair contracts, a tactic often employed by rock bands in an attempt to re-negotiate contract terms once success has been achieved. In Oldfield's case the matter was settled out of court and he remained with Virgin until 1992. He never repeated the huge success of his first title, although his music is still much in demand for film and television soundtracks.

With Oldfield, the Virgin Record label had had its first success and the massive inflow of funds transformed the company. No longer constrained by lack of capital, Branson began to diversify and rationalize his company, starting businesses as diverse as fashion retailing and catering, while closing down the mail-order operation. Popular music, however, remained Virgin's *raison d'être*.

Under Simon Draper's creative direction, the record label began to expand, initially focusing on artists outside the mainstream where Draper's interests lay. Such a policy fitted the Virgin image but restricted profit potential.

Within two years, however, financial pressure forced Virgin to reassess its position to avoid becoming a one-hit record label. Branson, by now anxious to sign up any artist likely to give his company credibility, put all his wheeler-dealer skills into creating deals with the financial backing and distribution rights that would be attractive to the bands he needed.

Serious attempts were made to sign up big names like David Bowie, Pink Floyd and The Who, as well as lesser artists who seemed to have breached the barrier between obscurity and fame. Never one to be deterred by reputation (or any other obstacle that would deter most people), Branson even approached the Rolling Stones. All these efforts, however, led nowhere and Branson became increasingly concerned. He needed something fast to re-establish the Virgin name with the record-buying public. He achieved his aim with a notorious punk rock band: the Sex Pistols.

Debauched and drug-crazed, foul-mouthed and obscene, the Sex Pistols cultivated a reputation of anarchical outrage, both on and off the stage. The public in general, and parents in particular, were scandalized and the band was angrily denounced by pundits, politicians and religious leaders. Their record 'God Save the Queen', which derided the British Royal Family, only added to the furore. Predictably, young people flocked to buy their records and attend their performances.

Draper had severe misgivings about associating the record label with a band of such notoriety and, in his view, dubious talent. But Branson was excited by the prospect, even though admitting privately that their music was dreadful. When the Sex Pistols were dropped in a panic by more conservative record labels, Virgin signed them up. For 18 months in 1977–78, Virgin and the Sex Pistols were the subject of intense media coverage and speculation, until in the band disintegrated when one of its members, already facing a murder charge, died of a drug overdose. Their short existence had been a considerable fillip for Virgin though.

The music business was in turn complemented by more recording studios and retail outlets, music and book publishing, nightclubs and cinemas as the company expanded. In the United States, by far the largest market for popular music, a Virgin subsidiary was formed in 1978, to promote Virgin's UK artists and attract new talent. Previously, many artists had been reluctant to sign with Virgin because they felt that without a significant US presence the company did not have the strength to successfully represent them worldwide.

All in all, Richard Branson could look back with some satisfaction as he prepared his company for the 1980s. Virgin had grown profitably, and his expansion plans all seemed to fit comfortably around the core of the business: popular music. But the music business was heading for a slump that would again test Branson's entrepreneurial skill. This time, however, his solutions included action that seemed the complete antithesis to the Virgin ethos: people would have to be fired.

Virgin in the 1980s

The record industry had shown average annual growth rates of 20 percent throughout most of the 1970s. But as the decade closed, recession and high inflation, combined with changing consumer tastes, severely affected the music business world wide. Sales contracted and few record companies earned profits. Virgin registered losses of £400,000 in 1980, and £900,000 in 1981.

Although well-established, the record company was still a small player in a business dominated by large multinationals. Moreover, it was still largely dependent on the UK market, lacking a broad geographical base that could have stabilized revenue.

Virgin was similarly positioned in the retail business. With 16 outlets, mostly in secondary positions, Virgin was the third largest specialist retailer in the UK, competing against other specialists as well as multiple stores.

With financial pressure mounting, Branson was forced to act. He looked to Nik Powell to find solutions which, inevitably, were likely to prove difficult. Working in conjunction with consultants, Powell recommended a series of cost-cutting measures, including the dismissal of some staff, a task that Branson has always found daunting and avoids, usually by delegation, if possible. Virgin personnel had grown accustomed to a degree of job security in return for modest salaries and their flexible approach to working, neither common in the music industry. Moreover, in keeping with the familial feeling Branson tried to encourage, people expected to be moved around until they found their niche rather than be dismissed. People were not fired, at least not until now. But on this occasion the unthinkable happened and the anxiety and ill-feeling that it caused led to talk of union representation. Virgin staff felt that Branson had become too isolated and knew little of their routine concerns. A shocked Branson immediately instigated staff meetings and a salary review, particularly for those with lower incomes. His response proved sufficient to dampen dissent.

To some extent Branson himself had inflamed the discontent in his company. His personal business philosophy was simple: why worry about the past, it is over and done; look to the future to solve difficulties through new opportunities, expansion and growth. While on one hand the company was firing staff, closing its US office, cutting its roster of bands and singers and writing off unprofitable capital investments, at the same Branson used scarce financial resources to purchase two nightclubs, Heaven, London's largest venue for homosexuals, and the struggling Roof Garden. He also launched a new London entertainment guide, *Event*, founded in response to the troubled rival magazine, *Time Out*. In the summer of 1981, *Time Out* had been off the streets for some time as a result of a strike. Branson saw an opportunity to challenge a monopoly supplier and return to publishing, a business activity for which he had particular enthusiasm. However, ill-prepared and requiring more cash than expected, *Event* quickly became a liability to Virgin when a revitalized *Time Out* and another new rival magazine entered the market. Within a year *Event* closed at a cost to Virgin of £750,000.

Branson's actions also created tension among his senior management. Simon Draper and other long-serving executives saw some of his moves as folly. Nik Powell especially was angered by what he saw as profligacy in straitened times and felt that Branson's actions could put the whole Virgin enterprise in jeopardy. His working relationship with Branson soured. He realized that his ambitions were likely to be unfulfilled while he was number two. Matters came to a head over creative policy.

Despite limited funds, Simon Draper wanted to invest in new bands and to carry on financing existing artists whom he believed would eventually be profitable. Nik Powell followed a more cautious, corporatist approach and pressed for the pruning of loss-making bands. Seeing the necessity to make a choice and settle matters, Branson, with some reluctance and sadness, backed Draper's artistic judgment rather than the traditional approach offered by Powell.

His instinct proved right since, within a short space of time, Virgin had signed up some of the most profitable bands of the 1980s: Phil Collins, Human League, Simple Minds and, in particular, the hugely successful Culture Club, led by the transvestite Boy George.

Virgin had successfully maneuvered itself out of the recession, nearly doubling its turnover from £48 million in 1982 to £94 million in 1983 with profits soaring to over £11 million. But Nik Powell was not around to share the success. Dissatisfied with his position, he had left the company in 1981, selling his share holding in return for £1 million, Virgin's cinema interests and a video recording studio, which later became the core of Palace Pictures, the UK's largest independent film production company in the 1980s.

Branson was once again the 100 percent owner of Virgin, with two trusted lieutenants, Simon Draper and Ken Berry, a long-standing collaborator. Branson depended on Draper for creative decisions and on Berry for contracts and management. Branson's own role was to talk to Draper and Berry several times a day, and to appear in person to sign stars to the record label. (Draper and Berry later acquired holdings in the company after lengthy negotiations.) Virgin was massively profitable and rapidly expanding. In France, Germany and Italy, Virgin distribution companies were established to add local artists to the company roster and to represent UK bands. In the US the Virgin label was re-established. Moreover, the huge success of Virgin artists attracted increasing numbers of established and emerging bands to the Virgin stable, creating a momentum that challenged the industry leaders. In circumstances such as these, traditional business practice would dictate that success should be consolidated and expansion restricted to complementary activities. Such, however, was not to be Branson's way. He wanted to expand his company in a completely new direction. To the astonishment of music industry observers, the horror of Simon Draper, and the ridicule of the music press, Richard Branson was off on a new path. He was going to found an airline.

'The Airline that Boy George Built'

In early 1984, Branson received a call from Randolph Fields, a 31-year-old Californian-born lawyer, who had founded British Atlantic, a cut-price, transatlantic airline that existed on paper only. Fields was seeking additional financing to get his airline airborne. Branson was all too aware of the dangers in entering the airline business: his company had no experience, it was capital intensive, revenue was highly seasonal. Perhaps most of all he recalled the recent experience of another UK cut-price airline, Laker Airlines, that had been pushed into bankruptcy by high debts, currency fluctuations and ferocious competition from established national airlines. The industry Goliaths had slaughtered the upstart David, the echoes of which still caused strain in UK/US trade diplomacy.

Yet, despite all these reservations and obstacles Branson was persuaded by Field's proposal. Within a week ('We can decide something in the morning and have it running in the afternoon' is Branson's proud boast) he had formed a partnership with him, renaming the airline Virgin Atlantic, later to be dubbed by jokers 'the airline that Boy George built,' a reference to the supposed source of cash injected by Branson into his new project.

In March 1984, the airline had neither a license to fly nor any aircraft; it had a staff of one but no offices. In the circumstances, Branson's target of a June inaugural flight to catch the summer season seemed to be unachievable. But after battles with regulatory authorities over a license, and protracted negotiations with Boeing to purchase an ex-Aerolinas Argentinas 747 on a sale or return contract, backed by a complex leasing agreement with a US bank, the airline gained some credibility.

Virgin Atlantic's low fares began to attract customers. They were served by nearly 100 staff, all rapidly recruited and trained, including several ex-Laker managers who brought with them their experience in running a low-cost operation. Branson's aim of launching an airline in three months seemed to be coming true. Pushing himself close to a breakdown, Branson drove the whole enterprise forward, involving himself in every detail of the airline. He was rewarded by a successful launch on 22 June 1984, which saw him playing to the cameras dressed as a World War I pilot in leather jacket and goggles – Virgin Atlantic was off the ground.

The creation of his airline took Branson into unfamiliar territory. For the first time his business required skills not previously required in the unregulated, open-market environment of the record industry. By contrast, the airline business is highly political: the awarding of jealously guarded international landing rights to (mostly) nationalized airlines involves protracted inter-government negotiations. To launch his airline, Branson was forced to lobby British Ministers to obtain their support and protection in his dealings with US government agencies and UK regulatory authorities.

Branson also had an eye to the future, expecting predatory pricing from the likes of British Airways and Pan Am that would jeopardize his cost advantage, particularly in the winter months. Such pricing, he knew, needed both US and UK government approval and could only be stopped by politicians. On his own, he would be powerless in a price war with the large transatlantic carriers who could subsidize one loss-making route from its other ticket revenues – the Laker scenario all over again.

As predicted, the winter of 1984 saw a transatlantic fares war between British Airways and Virgin Atlantic in the UK, and Pan Am and People Express (a similar operation to Virgin Atlantic that in some ways was the model for Branson's airline) in the US. British Ministers in the right-of-center Thatcher Government were in a dilemma. On the one hand they supported an open skies competition policy that benefited the consumer through lower fares, but equally they saw the need to protect new entrants to the market, without which there could be only limited competition. Branson used his newly-found diplomatic skills to exploit this dilemma and his lobbying, plus the threat of an anti-trust suit in the US, created sufficient uncertainty and confusion to force the UK transport minister to rescind cut-price fares already agreed with British Airways. It was a short-term victory but at least it had forced the large carriers to be circumspect in their opposition to Branson.

Due to the blunted competition, Virgin Atlantic attracted enough passengers in the difficult winter months to keep flying and to end its first financial year marginally in profit. Randolph Fields, the originator of the airline idea, did not stay with Virgin very long, however. His management style did not fit either the Virgin ethos or the detailed operation of an airline, although Branson recognized Fields' contribution in putting together the initial proposal. Press reports of a board room bust-up were publicly discounted by Branson. But, behind the scenes, relations were becoming increasingly acrimonious until Branson felt forced to act, ousting Fields from the board in late 1984, and later in 1985 buying out Field's share holding for £1 million. Fields later said that he had fallen in love with Branson on the day they met, but that Branson had only fallen in love with his, Fields', idea.

'From the Rock Market to the Stock Market'

In late 1986 a series of press and TV advertisements appeared in the UK under the title 'From the Rock Market to the Stock Market.' The advertisements invited the public to buy shares in the Virgin Group. Richard Branson, for so long a champion of private company status and the independence of entrepreneurs, had succumbed to the blandishments of City investment bankers to sell part of his company. Such deal-making was an intrinsic part of the investment banking process and in the mid 1980s, when the UK market was experiencing a powerful bull market, it was easy to understand the temptation for successful entrepreneurs to cash in part of their equity.

Branson saw his opportunity to raise capital quickly to reduce the company dependence on short-term bank borrowing and further expand without losing control of his company. (When the public company was eventually floated, Branson and his senior collaborators still controlled 63 percent of the voting stock.)

The flotation was not, in fact, the hasty decision it may have appeared. In anticipation of such an eventuality Branson had made overtures to City institutions in 1985, raising £25 million for acquisitions in the form of a convertible preference stock which, on conversion, gave holders a priority option to acquire equity in the company.

Much of the detail of this arrangement had been handled by Don Cruickshank, appointed Group Managing Director in 1984. A Scottish accountant with an MBA from Manchester Business School, Cruickshank had worked for McKinsey and had been in general management in the media industry. At ease in City circles, he was the kind of executive with whom bankers felt comfortable, an important factor in Branson's decision to recruit him. He complemented the skills and experience of the other long-serving executives: Simon Draper; Ken Berry, the Managing Director of Virgin Records who had started at Virgin as a junior accounts clerk; and Branson's brother-in-law Robert Devereux, the Cambridge-educated head of the then Virgin Vision company. To strengthen financial management, in particular debt management and banking facilities, Cruickshank recruited Trevor Abbott, a trained accountant with 10 years' management experience with MAM, the artist agency. This background smoothed his path into the new slot of Group Financial Director: 'I was not seen as an outsider.'

Cruickshank's primary task was to deconstruct the labyrinthine Virgin empire and create structure, systems and organizational discipline with which the City would feel comfortable. It was immediately apparent that Virgin Atlantic and the other travel interests, which had yet to show a steady income, would not meet City expectations. These and peripheral interests such as Heaven, the homosexual nightclub, were merged into a new private company, Voyager, to be owned by Branson and Draper. The remaining companies – Retail, Vision, and Music, by far the largest and most profitable part of the Virgin Group – were prepared to be floated on the London stock exchange. The flotation was carried out successfully using the rather unusual method of offer-by-tender whereby investors nominate a price which is then accepted or rejected. The striking price of 140p per share valued the public company at approximately £240 million. City institutions holding convertible preference stock took up their option to convert their holding to ordinary shares.

Other institutions acquired part of the new issue through subscription and trading in the after-market created by profit-taking among smaller shareholders, who initially numbered 85,000. Virgin artists and employees acquired seven percent of the new issue under the terms of the offer, which gave them priority access to up to ten percent.

Despite the demand for shares, the stock market flotation was not the success that Branson or the investors had expected. Although recording better-than-expected profits, Virgin's share price performed badly post-flotation and later fell precipitately when the London exchange crashed in October 1987. Moreover, relations between Virgin management and City analysts were at best uneasy. Branson was unsuited to cultivating the type of relationship that the chairman of a public company must have with institutional investors. While appreciating the discipline the public quotation had imposed on his company, he nevertheless felt the City undervalued Virgin and failed to understand the entrepreneurial nature of his business, especially the music division. The analysts in turn were uncomfortable with the vagaries of a business where most of the assets – rock musicians and their creative output – were valued against the ephemeral nature of current public taste. Their doubts and concerns were reinforced by the unpredictable nature of the Chairman and the demands on his time from his publicity stunts, airline business and charitable activities.

Unwilling to tolerate the constraints placed upon him but determined to help the many small investors who had seen the value of their investment diminish, Branson finally resolved to quit the stock market. In July 1988 he announced his decision to raise privately £200 million to be used to buy out the publicly-held shares at the original asking price, in effect compensating the original shareholders who at that point faced a considerable paper loss. Richard Branson thus honored a moral debt he felt he owed and was once more master of his own destiny.

'Too Old to Rock, Too Young to Fly'

With a major debt to repay and still in need of a substantial capital injection to finance his ambitions for the company, Branson recognized that he still needed external investors. His approach, however, in the light of his stock market experiences, was more circumspect this time.

In the years following privatization, Branson, while still an opportunistic, intuitive entrepreneur, nevertheless followed a path of rationalization through joint ventures with established companies. This approach permitted his company to expand, both in terms of products and geography. The most significant deal was the sale of 25 percent of Virgin records to Fujisankei, Japan's largest media company, for £115 million. Another Japanese company – Seibu-Saison, the hotel chain – paid £10 million for 10 percent of Voyager, which had recently acquired landing rights in Tokyo through Virgin Atlantic. He also gave minority share holdings to talented managers. (In Virgin Communications, for example, about 20 managers have equity options, in Retail a further 25.)

In the UK, Virgin's retail interests were consolidated around the Megastore concept in a joint venture with a major retailer. In prestige locations in major cities, Megastores sell home entertainment products music, videos, and books – on a large scale. They replaced the string of small secondary retail outlets for which Virgin had become known. The success of the Megastore concept was exported to major cities throughout the world, frequently through a joint venture.

Virgin entered many deals of this kind as it adjusted to Branson's new direction, although as usual Branson would probably have found it difficult to say precisely what that direction was. After turning 40, Branson experienced a period of introspection and self doubt, becoming more reflective about his business and other interests. He had long ago left the management of the music company to Simon Draper and Ken Berry; Robert Devereux was successfully running Virgin Communications with virtual autonomy, expanding its US activities; the retail division had never held any particular attraction for Branson.

Only the airline gave him the sense of excitement and involvement that he sought. Virgin Atlantic had advanced dramatically from the original low-cost low-fare operation envisaged by Randolph Fields. It now competed with the major carriers, winning awards for service and plaudits from vital business travelers. But the airline business is notoriously capital intensive and if Branson's target to fly to the world's major 20 cities was to be realized, more cash was needed.

By the early 1990s, Virgin Atlantic had become a serious threat to the major airlines, none more so than British Airways (BA), the UK's national carrier led by the ebullient and forthright Lord King. Despite the recession, the Gulf War and increasingly ferocious competition, Virgin Atlantic was able to exploit the UK government's competition policy to expand its routes, winning vital landing rights at the expense of BA. But Virgin remained a relatively small player in the airline business, still vulnerable to the tactics that had pushed Laker into bankruptcy. To defend his position, Branson constantly lobbied politicians as well as European and US officials, seeking assurances that unfair competition, however defined, would not be permitted.

Branson found politicking a tiring distraction from the main activity of getting people to fly Virgin Atlantic. The company had suffered financially and Branson was reconciled to finding a major capital investment to ensure the airline's long-term future. Such capital could only realistically come from the sale of the record business, the jewel in the Virgin crown, and the largest remaining independent record company in the world.

After long discussions with his immediate team, and a degree of soul searching, Branson entered into negotiations with Bertelsmann and Thorn EMI, realizing that he was currently in a strong enough position to achieve a sale on his own terms. Thorn's offer of cash or shares (Branson took the cash) to a value of £560 million won the day. Virgin Music, with tangible assets of £3 million, was sold in March 1992, creating a music business with 18 percent of the world market. City comments that Thorn had overpaid for Virgin were quickly discounted. A rationalization of Virgin staff and bands, improved Thorn's profits by more than £80 million in 1993–94.

At the time of the sale, some Virgin Music employees felt they had been misled by Branson. They had assumed they would share in the profits from the sale of the company. Branson had commanded great loyalty, providing opportunities for promotion, especially for women, that were unusual and generous for the industry. He had encouraged them to dream and forget about commercial details. However the employees had to admit that he had never made any concrete financial promises to them. Once again, he proved to be a brilliant leader who believes in putting employees first, but the same time, a tough negotiator who has learned that a positive cash flow is essential to Virgin's interests.

Simon Draper, who for some time had been losing interest in day-to-day management of the business, joined the new owners but gradually reduced his involvement to pursue private interests; Ken Berry remains as Managing Director of Virgin Music. Many of the long-serving staff attended an emotional farewell party after which Branson was quoted as saying, 'Too many entrepreneurs have gone down because they were not prepared to cash in their chips at the right time.'

The battle between British Airways and Virgin Atlantic became increasingly acrimonious and personalized around its two leaders. Lord King was quoted as saying that Richard Branson had discovered that he 'was too old to rock, and too young to fly.' Matters came to a head when a television program alleged that BA had used dirty tricks against Virgin Atlantic, breaking into its computer system to target its customers, spreading disinformation about Virgin's financial state and diverting its customers at US airports to BA flights. Branson immediately sued BA for damages, claiming £1 million. Lord King's denials were in terms that Branson found offensive. He sued King for libel and ultimately won substantial damages, humiliating the BA chairman and accelerating his retirement after an otherwise distinguished business career.

The sale of the record company saw the departure of many long-serving staff. This, combined with the evolutionary changes in retail, the growth of the airline and the creation of new companies, moved Virgin away from its roots and previous management structure. The Virgin Group is now overseen by a triumvirate: Richard

EXHIBIT 2
The Virgin Group

Richard Branson – Chairman
£1.4 billion

Managing Director
Virgin Atlantic Airways

Launched in 1984, now has 3 Airbus A-340S, 9 Boeing 747's
10 major city destinations, aviation services, franchised flights to Athens and Dublin

Trevor Abbott
Managing Director

Virgin Travel
£550 million
(including Virgin Atlantic Airways)

Virgin Holidays
Offers tours that boost business for the Airline, mostly to Florida, California, and the Caribbean

Virgin Retail
£650 million
Operates music and entertainments stores, including Megastores. New partnership with Blockbuster Entertainment is a key move in Branson's global expansion plans

Australia
5 Megastores in joint venture with Blockbuster
Britain and Ireland
24 Megastores and 305 smaller outlets. Recently merged with W.H. Smith's Our Price record chain
Continental Europe
12 Megastores in partnership with Blockbuster. Big expansion plans
Hong Kong
First Megastores in 1995 in partnership with Wheelock Pacific. Looking to expand into Southern China
Japan
7 Megastores with Marui department store group
North America
2 Megastores in California. Plans to open 20–30 more across the US with Blockbuster
South Korea
First Megastore in 1995 with Saehan Media Corp.

Virgin Investments
£20 million
Branson's private investments

Virgin Euromagnetics
computer products
Virgin Airship and Balloon
promotional blimps
Storm Model Agency
50% share in one of the world's hottest agencies
Property Development

Virgin Hotels Group
£40 million
Operates clubs and hotels in Britain and Spain, and Virgin Islands

Robert Devereux
Chief Executive

Virgin Communications
£150 million
Operates media and entertainment-related business. Small but profitable

Virgin Interactive Entertainment
Publishes computer and video games, interactive CD-ROM software
Virgin Publishing
Books – fiction and nonfiction
Virgin Radio
Virgin 1215 station in Britain, DG 90 St. Rushes
Virgin Television
Post production services for video, broadcast and advertising companies. Studios in London, Los Angeles, Mexico City and Madrid. 24% of super channel-Pan European; 45% of Oui FM Paris; 50% of Rapido TV
Entertainment holdings in Comic publication, Film/ Video production, Corporate Communications, Design

Branson, Trevor Abbott and Robert Devereux (see Exhibit 2), each with their own interests and fiefdoms.

Devereux runs Communications, now renamed Entertainment, at arm's length from the other activities in the Group. This separation is justified by the operational approach which is more akin to the former music division where a few people, through 'innovation and intellectual power add high value to a low capital base.' With his staff, all of whom are recruited locally, scattered around the world (50 percent in the USA, 30 percent in the UK, 20 percent in France and Germany), Devereux insists on a tight cash management system and detailed budgets to keep him in touch, a common theme throughout Virgin, which has a sophisticated centralized data-processing department to maintain information flow.

Abbott is the self-acknowledged hatchet man at Virgin, putting the many ideas that surface into a structured form that can be integrated into the Virgin organization. He spends much of his time 'creating business partnerships that equate to platonic marriages.' Once a partnership is set up with Virgin's interests tightly controlled one of his managing directors will run the project, a management philosophy that keeps the organization flat. His financial watchwords are 'build the balance sheet, watch the cash,' an approach justified, he believes, by the fact that Virgin is privately owned and has no need to maximize profits in the short term.

Branson's main business interest is Virgin Atlantic, where he is frequently involved in much of the detail of the operation. His commitment to the airline is total. It is the only company of his group of which he is Managing Director. He has even given his home phone number to all the airline's staff so they may ring him with ideas, difficulties and complaints – he will follow up any proposal that will give the airline a competitive edge.

Due in large part to Branson's drive and attention to detail, Virgin Atlantic has become an international leader in the small airline class. Branson believes that that Virgin can be both small and global, and he realizes that small air-

lines can and must compete on something other than price. This philosophy is reflected in Virgin's aggressive marketing style – one advertisement congratulated British Airways on lowering its fares to $51 higher than Virgin's – and emphasis on service and entertainment. From in-flight masseurs, tailors and underwear fashion shows (with Branson himself as a model) to transportation to the airport in London on the back of a motorcycle, Virgin has been at the forefront of innovative service and entertainment since its inception. Branson says, 'If you do something for fun and create the best possible product, then the profit will come.' And it has; Virgin Atlantic broke even in 1993, and sales in 1994 are projected to reach £600 million with a net profit of up to £10 million.

Branson also intends to expand his airline in the European domestic market. Here Branson's innovation is to franchise Virgin's name to other airlines who agree to meet Virgin's standards, thereby increasing revenues for Virgin with no further investment and little risk. In early 1994, two Virgin franchises were already in place London–Athens and London–Dublin – and more were in the negotiating stage.

As the franchise arrangement underscores, Virgin Atlantic has thrived because Branson is extremely cautious. He leases rather than buys airplanes, and has avoided major acquisitions. He often mentions the need to 'protect the downside,' and is looking for an equity partner for the airline.

Branson's cautiousness is also reflected in his belief in 'creative adaptation.' As the creation of Virgin Atlantic proved, he does not hesitate to pick up an idea which has been pioneered by someone else. He has constantly battled any signs of the not-invented-here syndrome in his organization.

Richard Branson's other principal activity is promoting the Virgin name to potential partners, customers and the world at large. Still impatient with traditional business practice, he rarely calls board meetings or has formal financial reviews, preferring to wait for problems to come to him for informal resolution with his senior collaborators. Always on the lookout for new opportunities, all he will say about the future is that he '[doesn't] want to run a conglomerate. People get lost and don't give their best . . . I expect we will sell off parts of the business, maybe to managers. I am always open to suggestions.'

Richard Branson: A Portrait

Family and Early Life

Richard Branson was born in July 1950, the first child and the only son of Ted Branson and his wife, Eve, nee Huntley-Flint. He was later joined by two sisters, Lindi and Vanessa. The family has remained close, all enjoying what Richard was later to describe as a 'happy and secure' childhood.

Both Ted and Eve came from comfortable Establishment backgrounds. Ted was the son and grandson of eminent lawyers, a fact impressed on young Richard when he visited Tussaud's wax-work museum in London with his father and saw models of murderers sentenced to hang by Sir George Branson, his grandfather. Following family tradition, Ted left his Quaker-run school to study law at Cambridge University. After military service in World War II, he eventually qualified as a lawyer but, perhaps because of his Quaker education or his naturally kindly disposition, his career in advocacy, where adversarial skills are vital, was slow to get started.

Eve Huntley-Flint came from a family of clerics, farmers and stockbrokers, whose women-folk were expected to have horizons beyond the home. While still a young girl, she trained as a dancer and appeared in London theaters, both in dance reviews and as an actress. By the time she met Ted Branson she had become an air stewardess, traveling to South America when air travel still contained a significant element of adventure and danger. Determined, self-assured and ambitious, at 27 Eve was an attractive, out-going young woman when she married Ted Branson, the reserved and fair-minded young lawyer.

Eve had decided views on child-rearing. While she was never a martinet, she pushed her children to be self-reliant and responsible, to take control of their own destinies rather than relying on others. One summer afternoon as she and four-year-old Richard were on their way home after visiting his grandparents, Eve told Richard to get out of the car and try to find his own way back. The farmhouse where they were staying was not far, but Richard got lost, ending up at the neighbor's farm. Eve Branson now admits that she may have been overly-enthusiastic about encouraging Richard's independence, but she has never regretted it. Clearly, Eve admired strength of character. She considered her children's ability to overcome challenges would encourage the kind of spirit she wanted to see in them. Accordingly, she used her own considerable energy to organize activities, games and projects for her children that were not only fun but also served a useful purpose. Holidays, weekends and other free time were used productively. The Branson household had no television since it was 'time wasting'; shyness in children was simply bad manners and a self indulgence to be discouraged; if money was short (as it was in the early days when Ted's father cut off his allowance in protest at his precipitate marriage) then a solution could always be found in small money-making schemes that Eve thought up. Bemoaning one's lot was never acceptable to Eve and she lived up to her own standards.

Ted Branson was never a strict and remote father figure. Rather, he acted as a calm and considerate backstop to Eve's daily management of the children. Sympathetic and supportive by preference, a half-hearted disciplinarian if really necessary, Ted was less directly ambitious for his children than Eve who expected, for example, that 'Richard [would] one day be Prime Minister.'

Richard grew up to be the archetypal naughty boy. Frequently in minor scrapes, scolded for innumerable misdemeanors and hyperactive in all he did, his parents found him both endearing and fatiguing. According to his father, Branson began his first business venture when he was around 11 or 12 years old. He planted a thousand seedlings and then went back to school convinced he would make a killing selling Christmas trees. Rabbits ate the trees. About a year later he tried again. This time the scheme involved budgerigars, a highly fecund type of small parrot. Another failure.

Richard's parents were particularly concerned about his progress at school, where his main accomplishments were on the sports field thanks to a strong physique and competitive spirit. His schoolboy heroes were sportsmen, particularly cricketers, and adventurers such as Scott of the Antarctic, the famous British explorer and a distant relation by marriage. A serious leg injury, however, forestalled a promising career in athletics, while a period of forced intensive study finally gained his admittance to Stowe School. His indifference to school work (not helped by long-undetected poor eyesight) continued, and he achieved only average results which ruled out a legal or other professional career. By contrast, *Student* magazine excited Branson with its possibilities and offered a timely and convenient exit. So, with his parents' reluctant blessing (his father's support was particularly influential) he quit school.

Branson left few friends behind him. While not unpopular, his energetic and single-minded pursuit of that which pleased him left little room for others. His indifference to the contemporary social mores and allegiances common in a school like Stowe left him somewhat isolated. His few friends were those inveigled into his varied and numerous projects. Commenting on the end of his schooldays, Branson said, 'Having left school without going to University, I decided to make money . . . I never considered failure.'

The 'Hippy Entrepreneur'

Having in some respects commercialized the anti-establishment lifestyle of the 1960s, it was not surprising that Branson was labeled 'the hippy entrepreneur' by the business and musical press. His alternative image was reinforced by the company's operating style where, from the start, informality and equality were essential principles rarely found in the business world at the time.

When Virgin started out, everyone received the same low salary, there was an absence of hierarchy (Branson was, and is, 'Richard' to everyone) and personal attire was casual to the point of idiosyncrasy. Even when the company had expanded massively this style was very much in evidence: Branson and staff are rarely seen in conventional business clothes, preferring sweaters and jeans even on formal occasions. Similarly, the company's offices, accumulated over time, were a collection of modest, often dilapidated, buildings scattered about northwest London from which the sound of rock music could usually be heard.

For a long time, Branson's office and home was a canal houseboat where he worked alone apart from two secretaries. One bedroom acted as their office while Branson operated from a dining table in the small sitting room. On occasion, it is reported, the bathroom served as the boardroom with Branson conducting meetings from his bath. Eventually, Branson was forced to move to a larger home, since his two children were 'starting to answer the phones,' but he kept the houseboat as an office.

His wife, a down-to-earth Glaswegian from a working-class background, has no interest or role in his business life. This is something of an anomaly at Virgin since Branson, contrary to conventional wisdom, is a great believer in working with family and friends, seeing only the advantages and not the risks. His cousins, aunts, school and childhood friends, parents and former girlfriends, have all been drawn into his various business activities. Only his first wife found the situation difficult to accept, but even she is now in a joint venture with Branson, developing hotels in Spain. The charges of nepotism that such arrangements usually engender were muted at Virgin because Branson adopted a promote-from-within policy, giving many of his staff opportunities that their lack of experience and training would have precluded in more conventional companies. Virgin was unconventional in other ways, too. Somehow, Branson created the impression that people worked at Virgin for fun and excitement rather than simply as a means of earning a living. Notoriously indifferent to material possessions and unconcerned about everyday financial matters, Branson saw no difficulty in paying modest salaries provided people were enjoying themselves, feeling part of an idiosyncratic enterprise that had a heart. If people were down, a party would revive spirits and, incidentally, give Branson the chance to play a practical joke on newcomers, an embarrassing rite of passage at Virgin that is maintained to this day.

Much of this operating style was established not so much by design but the exigencies of the time when Virgin was getting started. It has proved to be a successful model that Branson can replicate. His philosophy is to immerse himself in a new venture until he understands the ins and outs of the business, and then hand it over to a good managing director and financial controller, who are given a stake in it, and are then expected to make the company take off. He knows that expansion through the creation of additional discrete legal entities not only protects the Virgin Group, but also gives people a sense of involvement and loyalty, particularly if he trusts them with full authority and offers minority share holdings to the managers of subsidiaries. He is proud of the fact that Virgin has produced a considerable number of millionaires. He has said that he does not want his best people to leave the company to start a venture outside. He prefers to make millionaires within.

His use of joint ventures is an extension of this model and is reinforced by his dealings with the Japanese. Branson is impressed by the Japanese approach to business, admiring their commitment to the long term and the way they take time to build a business through organic growth rather than acquisitions. (He is proud to state that he has purchased only one major company, Rushes Video, for £6 million some years ago.)

He sees similarities in the Japanese *Keiretsu* system (small companies interlocking in a collaborative network) to the structure he has created at Virgin, with more than 500 small companies around the world operating quasi-independently: 'Small is beautiful.' He explained this and other business maxims that he believes are necessary for success in a speech to the Institute of Directors in 1993. 'Staff first, then customers and shareholders' should be the chairman's priority, according to Branson, if you want better performance. 'Shape the business around the people,' 'build

don't buy,' 'be best not biggest,' 'don't be a pioneer, follow the leader,' 'capture every fleeting idea,' 'drive for change' are other guiding principles in the Branson philosophy.

'Hero of the World'

In 1990, Richard Branson found himself in northern Japan preparing for take-off in an attempt to make the first ever trans-Pacific crossing in a hot-air balloon, an event timed to coincide with Virgin Atlantic's inaugural flight to Tokyo. His Japanese hosts had invited a huge crowd to witness the event and banners had been erected declaring him to be the 'Hero of the World.'

The attempt was the latest in a series of exploits undertaken by Branson. They began in 1985 when he attempted to cross the Atlantic in a high-powered speedboat to win the coveted Blue Riband, the prize awarded to the vessel and crew with the fastest time. The vessel sank off Ireland but a similar attempt the following year was successful. In 1987, he and Per Lindstrand, an experienced balloonist, attempted the fastest trans-Atlantic balloon crossing, an aim achieved but only after both barely escaped with their lives when the balloon made a forced landing in the Irish Sea.

Branson is happy to admit that these exploits were started as an inexpensive way of publicizing his trans-Atlantic airline but with time they seemed to gain a momentum of their own. Asked how the chairman of a major corporation can justify the risks and expense he replies, 'People who have to ask the question don't understand.'

Whatever his motives, Branson has come to be seen as a modern buccaneer with an attractive, devil-may-care attitude to physical danger as well as business risks. At the same time he supports charitable, radical and humanitarian causes. For example, he still funds a sex counseling clinic founded in his *Student* days when his girlfriend became pregnant and they had nowhere to turn to for advice. He also launched a new brand of condoms, Mates, as a response to the government's laissez-faire attitude towards AIDS and condom use. This was the kind of project that appealed to Branson; it would do good to society and raise money for charity, and he would have fun doing it. More controversially, he boycotted a magazine that refused to carry advertisements supporting the legalization of marijuana, although he personally dislikes illegal drugs following an ill-fated experiment with LSD. 'Richard could not stand to be out of control,' according to his girlfriend at the time.

Branson's exploits and causes are diverse, ranging from a health care foundation supporting AIDS research to financial support for a new political publication. He bought and published a banned video on security matters, used his aircraft to rescue people trapped by the Gulf War and led an initiative to help unemployed teenagers.

Branson's esteem in UK public opinion is regularly demonstrated. He was the darling of the former Prime Minister, Margaret Thatcher, although he has remained apolitical. He has been nominated for awards for enterprise, voted the most popular businessman, and in general is the point of reference whenever comparisons are made between the traditional business leader and emerging entrepreneurs of the 1980s and 1990s. He is, however, a man of contrasts. The public persona is that of a warm, friendly, idealistic, family man. At the same time, he is highly competitive and a workaholic, and an extremely tough negotiator who thrives on bargaining.

The 'Real' Richard Branson

Richard Branson has become an international celebrity, the subject of numerous profiles in gossip magazines, the business press and television programs. In the UK he has achieved folk-hero status. He is frequently cited as a role model by young people wanting a successful business career that does not compromise personal ethics.

In material terms Branson is undoubtedly successful. He became one of the UK's richest people before he turned 40, and recently he ranked as the 11th wealthiest person in the UK, with an estimated net worth of £895 million. Asked to explain the strategy that got him to this point he will talk of minimizing risks – 'Protect the downside, always be ready to walk away' – and seeking out opportunities to build 'the largest entertainment group outside the United States.' Over the years he has made a few strategic statements that, with hindsight, do not relate very much to subsequent events. Most frequently, however, he says he simply wants to enjoy himself.

But can a strategy for fun really explain the creation of a music company by a founder who, paradoxically, has little interest in or knowledge of music? Equally, it is difficult to explain how a shy man, ill at ease when speaking publicly or in private conversation with strangers, can become a supreme self-publicist? How an establishment-born figure with intrinsically conventional views can become the champion of radical and libertarian causes? Or how the man who is almost obsessive about fair play can negotiate ferociously for the last penny in a deal?

A London *Sunday Times* report on the British Airways affair quoted Lord King as saying: 'If Richard Branson had worn a pair of steel-rimmed glasses, a double-breasted suit and shaved off his beard, I would have taken him seriously. As it was I couldn't . . . . I underestimated him.' Perhaps Lord King is not alone in being misled by the hippy entrepreneur image that surrounds Branson. But if that image is not the real Richard Branson, then what is?

Case 4: Stantret: A Private Cargo Airline in the USSR

By Igor Touline, Abby Hansen and Derek Abell[1]

On a May evening in 1991, Sergei Sleptsov, the 25-year-old founder-director of Stantret Cargo Airlines, sat in his modest office in Moscow reviewing notes from an executive meeting and reflecting about his future. In less than a year he had transformed an idea for a private business into a highly profitable reality. Skirting massive obstacles in the government air transport bureaucracy by negotiating creative deals, Sleptsov had made money right from the start (a profit of 6,913,000 rubles in the latest quarter).

But lately, his luck seemed to have turned. He had recently been obliged to cover a 13,000,000 ruble loss incurred by his company's parent venture. And major competition had suddenly materialized: a joint venture with the funds to purchase many of the aircraft that Sleptsov leased for his cargo runs. But perhaps the most upsetting problem of all lay within his own company: he had begun to mistrust some of his own top managers.

The young businessman pondered his options. Should he overhaul Stantret and concentrate on longer term projects? Should he leave the company and start a new venture of his own? Should he accept a US commercial company's invitation to be its USSR representative?

[1] Source: This case was originally prepared by Dr Igor Touline of the Institute of World Economy and International Relations, Moscow, as the basis for class discussion rather than to illustrate either effective or ineffective handling of a business situation. It was subsequently edited by Dr Abby Hansen working in collaboration with Professor Derek F. Abell, IMD, to conform with EFER's case development project guidelines. Financial support for the original case and subsequent editorial work was provided by the European Foundation for Entrepreneurship Research (EFER). Copyright © 1992 EFER. Not to be altered or reproduced without permission.

Background: The Transport Industry in the USSR

By the early 1990s, all forms of ground and air transport in the USSR were severely inadequate. A third of the railway support facilities and a quarter of the rolling stock urgently needed modernization or replacement. Suppliers of all forms of equipment regularly failed to meet their contractual obligations for deliveries. In the trucking industry, lack of spare parts and gasoline, plus the disrepair of vehicles and roads, made the average range of Soviet vehicles 20 kilometers (compared to 700 kilometers in developed countries (*Delovye Livdi*, April 1991)). Civil aviation was in no better shape. Facilities and services were insufficient to accommodate the demand for civilian passenger and freight transport. Not only was there insufficient capacity to carry passengers, but across-the-board shortages of engines, spare parts, and (most often) fuel plagued every segment of the industry. One consulting firm ('Transaeroconsulting') estimated that shortages of cargo shipment services had doubled between 1980 and 1990, and would continue to worsen over the next two decades.

Government monopolies controlled civilian as well as military transport. The Ministry of Civil Aviation (MCA) functioned, in essence, as its own regulator, planner, supplier, and financier. It had authority to regulate, exercise supervision, control finances, planning, and other economic functions, and provide logistics for all civil aviation. By early 1991 such centralized control had created a situation in which virtually no cargo aircraft but those of the military met strict standards for intensive operation. The only airfields çapable of handling airplanes with a wide range of cargo capacities were those operated by an MCA subsidiary called the Ministry of Aviation Industries (MAI). The MAI was one of the largest defense contractors and a complete monopolist in the production of airplanes, including civilian aircraft. It had almost exclusive access to cargo planes and the technical services necessary to fly them.

The government airline, Aeroflot, was the largest air carrier in the world, with 50,000 employees, world-wide routes, and fleet of nearly a thousand aircraft (*Interavia*, 1990, vol. 45, No. 10). But, despite its enormous size and virtual monopoly on passenger and freight shipments in the USSR, Aeroflot suffered from persistent inefficiency and chronic fuel shortages. Centralized planning and distribution of spare parts and engines had prevented the company's managers

from developing long-term operational plans. Putting little emphasis on maintenance, Aeroflot flew its planes until they wore out. As a result, great numbers of Aeroflot planes stood idle for lack of either fuel or engines.

Years of inefficiency in the transport industry, characterized by increasing numbers of accidents and strikes and long waits for railway cars, had spurred the development of a 'parallel' aviation system. Some ministries and large enterprises had acquired their own air fleets. But the high cost of planes kept these small and extremely busy. Almost all of the aircraft in this category were in constant use, making emergency deliveries to enterprises threatened with shutdown for lack of vital supplies.

EXHIBIT 1
Chronological outline of Stantret's Air Link-Up Project

1990	
June:	Establishment of Stantret subsidiary of the Soviet-American joint venture Stanlet; appointment of Sergei Sleptsov as Stantret Director.
July, 1–10:	Negotiations with Aviation Research Institute (ARI) of the Ministry of aviation industry.
	Development of a feasibility study for Izdatbank.
	Signing of the credit agreement with Izdatbank involving a three-month R 600,000 loan at 18 percent interest.
	Signing of the three-month contract with the Aviation Research Institute on cooperation in cargo air shipments.
July, 10–20:	R 50,000 advertising contract with TASS and other publications.
	Payment to ARI for the first 80 flying hours of Ilyushin-76, of a total of R 400,000.
July, 15–24:	Placement of the first order.
	Sleptsov's trip to negotiate fuel, landing and ground services on the first order.
	Payment of first wages to Stantret staff.
July, 25:	Ilyushin-76 takeoff to fly the route of the first order.
August:	Payment of principal of the loan and interest.
October–November:	Strategic decision to establish a reliable network of Stantret air shipments.

1) Selection of personnel to be employed in the transportation technical maintenance system.
2) Organization of uninterrupted supplies of fuel, provision of crews and ground services. December – advertising campaign on ULC independent radio station owned by Stanlet.

The Entrepreneur and the Founding of Stantret Airlines

A native of a small township in the Urals, Sergei Sleptsov started as a factory worker, but soon rose to foreman, then supervisor, and then to a managerial post in a state-run architectural restoration concern, where he supervised 160 employees.

> I took orders, commissioned the necessary documentation, and sent the requisite personnel to the restoration project. My boss, the chief architect, taught me how to correlate the workload with the availability of specialists and support personnel. I learned to break projects down into stages and plan the operations for each stage. But, frankly, it got boring to do the same thing day after day, with the same rigid schedule and the same scope of responsibility.

At the beginning of 1990, Sleptsov became a senior marketing manager with a construction concern that was participating in the creation of a computer information network to disseminate supply and demand information about surpluses and shortages of construction materials all around the USSR. Working with this information gave Sleptsov an opportunity to learn how the centralized state distribution system produced shortages and surpluses in different parts of the country. He proposed that his firm set up a brokerage as a subdivision, but nothing came of his proposal.

> I had always wanted to start my own business, and the idea of organizing an effective brokerage activity got stuck in my mind. Nothing could be more straightforward. If someone has a surplus of something and another person or organization has a shortage of the same thing, all one has to do is organize a mutually beneficial exchange.

In the spring of 1990, popular articles about the 'unprecedented' harvest of grain, vegetables, and fruit gave Sleptsov an idea. The food storage, processing, and transportation facilities in the USSR were in poor condition. This meant that the bumper crop was in danger of rotting, unused. He realized that produce prices – especially for perishable goods – would fall in agricultural areas like the Crimea and rise in distant places like Siberia, where fresh fruits and vegetables were always scarce.

Thinking like a broker, Sleptsov saw that sellers and buyers could profit handsomely if swift transportation of produce could be ensured. This clinched his decision to go into business: he would organize an air transport service for perishable goods.

Alexander Subbota – who later became Sleptsov's Marketing Director for Air Carriage – recalled his first reaction to the idea:

> It seemed inconceivable. Who would provide not one, but several airplanes to some obscure venture, which had just come into being? Where would he get fuel, when one kept hearing about Aeroflot being unable to fly because of a huge shortage? Even state-owned collectives and farms could not obtain enough fuel to gather in their crops. How would the whole project operate?

Sleptsov found such skepticism amazing: 'It was simple: I just sized up the situation and adopted prompt and carefully considered solutions.' Within days of his conceiving the idea for an air transport service, friends introduced him to a potential backer: Ustas Lamin, a well-known composer-musician who was president of a large Soviet-American joint venture in the entertainment business, called 'Stanlet.'

Stanlet's main business was popular entertainment. It represented musicians (including 50 rock bands, music ensembles, and solo performers), and organized the release of their records. Its clients included dance and folk ensembles, athletes, and sports clubs. It arranged exhibitions, performances, tours, games, tournaments, and special contracts in the Soviet Union and abroad. In addition, it ran the Ustas Lamin Center, the biggest independent music corporation in the USSR.

Sleptsov recalled, 'When Ustas Lamin heard my idea for the air cargo service, he said: "I shall give you the possibility, but nothing else. We'll see what results you produce."'

The parent company established Stantret as

a subsidiary and gave it a two-room office in Moscow with a minimum of office equipment, including an old computer. By law, a subsidiary could have separate bank accounts and act independently, but only on behalf of the parent company. Furthermore Stantret accepted a statutory obligation to submit quarterly financial reports and contribute at least 25 percent of its net profits to the parent company.

In July, 1990, Sleptsov presented a business plan to Izdatbank, a commercial lender, and applied for a 600,000 ruble, 3 month credit. (See Exhibit 2.) He forecast that, given the difference in price between tomatoes in the southern and northern areas, one aircraft could make enough deliveries in three months to yield 141,000 rubles in earnings (see Exhibit 2). USSR law granted joint ventures two months of nearly tax-free operation, so gross earnings essentially equaled net earnings. The bank extended the credit at 18 percent.

(In fact, Stantret far exceeded the projected goal of its business plan. During the period forecast by the business plan, it flew aircraft for 160, not 80 hours a month. Often there were up to five Ilyushin-76s airborne simultaneously. As of September 30 1990, gross profit amounted to 6,430,000 rubles. The end of the harvest had virtually no impact on the company's profitability. First-time clients continued to hire Stantret's services. In the fourth quarter of 1990, gross profit reached 4,300,600 rubles, and in the first quarter of 1991, 18,410,100 rubles.)

The Market for Air Transport

When Sleptsov started up his business, he signed a contract with the ARI for a pre-paid lease of a cargo plane with a 40-ton capacity. He described how he went about setting his prices:

> I went to Aeroflot's marketing department posing as a prospective client with a cargo to transport quickly. They said they could transport the cargo quickly, but without a 100–percent guarantee, and at a very high rate: over 8,000 rubles per hour of flight time. If I did not take

this rate, I could wait like all other clients, with no guarantees. Very interesting indeed!

Sleptsov made another reconnaissance trip:

> I went to the cargo department of the Sheremetyevo-1 airport. They charged just as much, and asked for 10 percent in hard currency. I understood what a tough time customers were having.
>
> I was 100-percent, even 150-percent, sure that I could beat Aeroflot. It was just a matter of making the right estimate. I had an edge over my competitor in terms of speed, reliability, and, more often than not, prices.

Friends at TASS, the Soviet news bureau, helped Sleptsov advertise his transport services in a daily report that went out to all local newspapers and, in turn, to manufacturers all over the USSR.

In July, 1990, the popular business weekly *Ekonomika i Zhizn* carried a Stantret advertisement:

> Our firm will take your cargo to any place in or outside the Soviet Union . . . Services will be provided within three days upon request. This contrasts favorably with the Aeroflot practice; rapid transportation, especially when it comes to perishable goods, minimizes conveyance losses. Stantret is the fastest and the cheapest way to transport your cargo anywhere in the Soviet Union by 40 ton Ilyushin-76 planes.

Advertising ate up 50,000 rubles of Sleptsov's loan, but it introduced Stantret to business people all over the country – especially in the south and the north, Sleptsov's prime target markets – and triggered a four-month-long torrent of telephone calls. The deluge of information that flowed through the company – information about orders, prices, routes, tonnage, availability of fuel and the condition of runways – prompted Sleptsov to develop a scheduling system to reduce the number of empty flights and rationalize routes in terms of time and fuel. His marketing director took responsibility for this planning – combining orders to maximize revenues per hour of flight time. Only the most common routes and schedules had set prices.

Sleptsov crafted most deals individually.

EXHIBIT 2
Business plan for Izdatbank

	Rubles
Amount of required lending	600,000.00

Projected expenses from the loaned capital:

■	Advanced payment for 80 flying hours of Ilyushin-76 for the first month.	400,000.00
■	Advertising of air shipments by Stantret (Tass, printed publications).	50,000.00
■	Wages and salaries.	50,000.00
■	Overhead expenses (transportation costs, travel expenses, general business expenses, etc.).	40,000.00
■	Purchases of office equipment for Stantret.	60,000.00
TOTAL		**600,000.00**

PREMISES

■	Average purchasing price of transported tomatoes in the south of the USSR, ruble/kilo.	0.25
■	Average selling price of transported tomatoes in the north of the USSR, ruble/kilo.	10.00
■	Carrying capacity of Ilyushin-76 cargo plane, ton.	40 ton
■	Type of shipment.	charter for round-trip
■	Estimated profits of the client placing an order for air shipment (earned through a difference in prices) per one Ilyushin-76 plane, rubles.	390,000.00
■	Cost of one flying hour borne by Stantret customer, rubles.	7,000.00
■	Cost of one flying hour charged by the Aviation Research Institute and borne by Stantret (including fuel costs), rubles.	5,000.00
■	Number of Ilyushin-76 planes used.	1 plane
■	Number of flying hours per month.	1 hour
■	General term of operation for one airplane, month.	3 months

ESTIMATED EFFICIENCY OF STANTRET

■	Gross sales from operation of one Ilyushin-76 for a period of 3 months, rubles ($80 \times 7000 \times 3$).	1,680,000.00
■	Payment to the Aerospace Research Institute for operating Ilyushin-76 for a period of 2 months ($80 \times 5000 \times 2$), rubles*.	800,000.00
■	Gross profit of Stantret, rubles.	880,000.00
■	Repayment of credit, rubles.	600,000.00
■	Interest expense, rubles ($600,000 \times 0.015) \times 3$.	27,000.00
■	Wages for 2 months, rubles*.	100,000.00
■	Other expenses, rubles.	12,000.00
■	Earnings before income taxes, rubles.	141,000.00

* For the first month those payments should be made from the loaned capital.

Most of Stantret's customers bought a two-way flight, or a charter flight, just as with Aeroflot. He offered large discounts for providing cargo for the return flight, but as a rule, he took this job upon himself. Typically, planes carried fruits and vegetables from the south to north and returned south, often with stopovers in Syberia or central Russia, with machinery, equipment, and foreign-made consumer goods. Payments from clients in the north the return flights brought Stantret net profits.

Flexibility in pricing came from the terms of his lease payments to the ARI. Planes that flew up to 80 hours a month would cost Stantret 30 percent less than leasing from Aeroflot (which charged 7,000 rubles per hour of flight time). Flights in excess of 80 hours a month were four percent cheaper.

Sleptsov's Negotiation Methods

The first deal that Sleptsov arranged for his new air cargo operation turned out to be prototypical. He called the project, the 'Air Link-Up.' His work in the computer information network had acquainted Sleptsov with the existence of the MAI's glut of cargo airplanes. He also knew that an MAI subsidiary, the Aviation Research Institute (ARI) – located at an airport in the town of Zhukovsky, near Moscow – was one of the installations hit hardest by this glut. Several dozen of its planes – originally designed for test flights and government freight shipments – were sitting idle most of the time. Even when they made freight runs, usually only about 3–4 times a month they tended to return to Moscow empty.

Sleptsov went to Zhukovsky to ask the ARI managers, 'Why aren't you looking for customers and using planes to derive benefits?'

He recalled:

The first answer I got was: 'That's a great idea, but we don't know how to find customers.' I said, 'That's okay, I will line up clients, pay for aircraft and use them. You will help me with fuel, flight routes, air corridors, etc. But to begin with, talk with your people about routes, in terms of the necessary technological and organizational support for the flights.'

A couple of weeks passed. No one tried to get information. That's the Soviet bureaucratic system – it's typical to put off all decision-making indefinitely.

EXHIBIT 3
Stantret Cash Flow Statement

	Thousands of rubles		
	Year 1990		Year 1991
	IIIrd quarter	IVth quarter	Ist quarter
Gross profit*	6,430.0	4,300.2	18,410.1
Salaries & paid-in subcontracts	150.0	150.0	219.0
Loan repayments. including interest	627.0	—	4,210.0
Other expenses	27.5	30.6	34.8
Earnings before income taxes	5,625.5	4,119.6	13,946.3
Taxes	—	—	—
Earnings after taxes	5,625.5	4,119.6	13,946.3
Dividends to Stanlet	1,500.0	718.0	13,255.0
NET	3,125.5	3,401.6	691.3

*Gross profit equals the difference in price paid by customers to Stantret for charters and renting price of aircrafts owners for Stantret.

Sleptsov had an idea about how to break the log jam:

> I realized that it was impossible to understand the potential of this system, the real relations between its elements, or its bottle-necks without actually launching it into operation. But how could I launch it with no guarantees that it would work? I decided to have a dry run.

Sleptsov told the ARI managers that he had received a large order to ship fruit from the south to the north. If they could provide an equipped plane and arrange its reception along the route, they could share the profits.

> ARI staff members from Zhukovsky called the airport in the town of Tiksi (an interim stop on the route), to request that they receive and refuel the cargo plane. The Tiksi employees said, 'No fuel, runways busy.' This showed me some key problems: how to get fuel on site, how to ensure that the plane would be received on time at every point on its route, how to see that necessary services would be provided without delay?

The ARI managers approached the staffs of civilian airports along the proposed route, and they, too, raised objections. The ARI managers explained this by reminding Sleptsov that they had no authority over civilian airport personnel.

Sleptsov found this dry run informative.

> I now knew what these people could and could not do. The people in Zhukovsky could get planes ready for the flight and refuel. The civilian airfields in other areas could only ensure air corridors for the plane. But this was not bad – at least they could guarantee these things. I had learned that the major difficulties were getting fuel and having the plane received at other airports. All I had to do was overcome these, and I could enter the civilian air transport market. Now I needed some real orders to see how the project operated in practice and test all the links.

Lack of fuel posed a major difficulty. The existing distribution system allocated and rationed everything. It was summer, and Sleptsov knew that Aeroflot always had problems with fuel shortages in the summer. How could he get fuel, especially for an unscheduled flight to be conducted by a plane chartered from a different agency?

Despite official reports of shortages, Sleptsov suspected that he could find fuel. Such practices as report-padding and double counting had become routine under a system of quotas arbitrarily established by a central distribution authority. Sleptsov thought it more than likely that fuel reported as having been consumed was probably still available, somewhere. He also had an idea about how to get it. The severe depreciation of the ruble, combined with increasing inefficiencies of the central distribution system, had made it difficult to purchase spare parts, new equipment, consumer goods, and foodstuffs. Many people had turned to barter as their only possible option. Sleptsov would barter produce for fuel.

When his first order came – to carry fruit from the town of Simferopol (in the Crimea, on the Black Sea coast) to the town of Tiksi and then on to Nizhneyansk (Eastern Siberia, on the Arctic Ocean coast) – Sleptsov flew to meet the chiefs of airports and fueling services whose services he needed to put his route together.

> I did not know anyone out there, but I introduced myself. I said, 'Maybe you need peaches, tomatoes, or some other fruit and vegetables?' They said, 'It would be good to get some fresh fruit for my employees, but is this possible?' I said, 'Of course. You can have one ton of produce from an incoming plane.' At first they said it wasn't possible, but I simply refused to take the first 'no' for an answer. After a while, they said, 'Wonderful.' 'No' is the first reaction of a person in command of coveted resources. He does not want to know you until you have offered him something in exchange. Hardly anybody needs money today, but goods in shortage can always be exchanged for something else in shortage. In the northern parts of the country, fresh produce, particularly at reasonable prices, is in short supply. And this is what I offered.

In some airports, Sleptsov offered consumer goods like video and audio equipment. (He bought these at Moscow shops, using the company's bank credits.) When he returned to Moscow, he told the ARI authorities to phone the chiefs of the airports on his route, 'But do not ask on behalf of the Ministry, give my name.'

He commented, 'The main thing is to start informal relations with a person, learn about his problems, and help solve them. If you do that, he will also help you.'

When putting together a deal with a large-scale buyer of agricultural produce, Sleptsov often negotiated part of the shipment for himself He either subtracted the cost of his part from the amount of the contract paid by the client, or – primarily with frequent, large-scale clients – just arranged for the free use of one or two tons of a 40-ton shipment of fruit in the interests of 'ensuring the smooth operation of the air bridge.' The one to two tons cost little to the buyer in comparison with the selling price of these products in the North (see Exhibit 2), and the buyer got Sleptsov's guarantee of timely delivery of the remaining part of the consignment of a highly perishable product – an economic gain compared with alternative options. (Use of Aeroflot, the railways, or motor transport would mean loss of time and, consequently, loss of perishable products far in excess of one to two out of 40 tons.)

One of Sleptsov's clients, U. Umarov, the managing director of a large joint venture in Tashkent, attested to Stantret's superior service:

> When I attempted to use an Aeroflot plane, there was such a prolonged delay that I never dispatched the consignment of fruit. When I tried sending another consignment by motor transport, two trucks disappeared and I had to hire guards and sustain losses. With Sleptsov, there was no problem, nor any losses.

Umarov began by commissioning one planeload of tomatoes to be carried from Uzbekistan to the north, and stuck with Sleptsov throughout the harvest season, with contracts worth three million rubles overall. In the autumn of 1990, he also had Sleptsov's planes flying cargo abroad.

Sleptsov's dependability continued to impress Umarov:

> He honors his commitments, whatever the weather. In the event of force majeure he never fails to send notice of delay at least two days in advance, and he always sends a plane on the

same day. Aeroflot and Stantret operate identical planes with identical speed. But Sleptsov takes better care of the customers. With Aeroflot, arrival on time is an exception. Even when Sleptsov charges more than Aeroflot, I gain: what I spend on the plane I make up in preventing losses and accelerating turnover. Besides, when Sleptsov strikes a deal I can plan business in advance with certainty.

Sleptsov continued to arrange his company's cargo flights with creative deals that often involved an often ad hoc mix of regular payments and barter. Later, when his employees accompanied consignments in transit, he taught them to use the same negotiating tactics. Almost invariably, they solved fuel problems on the spot. 'Air Link-Up' was successful from its very first night. (It netted Stantret 40,000 rubles in gross profit.)

Sleptsov's Management Style

Sleptsov described how he ran the business:

> I devise, design, and define the specific stages and aims of every project personally. My employees work on a stage-by-stage basis, oriented towards specific goals, which I or Subbota set for each stage. When employees accomplish a particular goal, they think they have completed the entire mission. For example, men in charge of fuel supplies and fuel servicing focus on these tasks; they are responsible for fueling different aircraft, but they don't knew who has chartered them, on what terms, or what they are supposed to be carrying. When a team completes its stage of the work, as a rule, another team works on the next stage. Meanwhile, the first team has begun similar tasks on a different project.

He gave his rationale: 'Because each whole project exists only in my head, I can avoid rivals – for the time being, anyway. My employees cannot disclose the entire commercial secret of the project as a whole. This is my system of security.'

Even after giving his Marketing Director, Mr Subbota, authority to take orders from clients and distribute assignments among other managers, Sleptsov still negotiated practically all of the lucrative (over 1,000,000 rubles) or complicated contracts himself. Only after he had negotiated the price and defined the basic aspects of a major order, did he let Subbota take charge and execute the contract.

Side Ventures

Although Stantret's core business lay in the areas of air cargo carriage and brokerage-and-trade (see Exhibit 2), Sleptsov also branched into the entertainment business in 1991. In January, he used an Izdatbank credit of 4,000,000 rubles for three months at an annual interest rate of 21 percent and added part of fourth quarter, 1990, air cargo profits to buy the Soviet distribution rights for 10 Argentinian feature films for a period of five years.

> It cost 15,000 dollars for the distribution of one film over a period of 5 years. Converted into rubles at 40 rubles per dollar, my expenses were a mere 4.5 million rubles. I sold the distribution rights to each film to an independent Soviet film distributor for 1,900,000 rubles, and made 14,500,000 rubles by the end of March.

In March 1991, Sleptsov continued in this vein by commissioning, for 150,000 rubles, a documentary film about a well-known Soviet folk dance ensemble, whose Argentinian tour the parent company was planning for July, 1991. The film was ready in April, and Sleptsov had already received an offer from Argentinian TV that would yield 3,050,000 rubles in profit, but he thought that the price would rise dramatically if he waited until the dance troupe went to Argentina.

Expanding the Staff

By August, business was burgeoning and the physical pressure on Sleptsov was taking its toll. Constant flights to various parts of the country,

telephone conversations during the night, the need to monitor every flight, and numerous and exhausting negotiations with customers, airport authorities, and organizations – all of this produced insomnia and nervous fatigue. 'I could not any longer do everything myself. I needed people I could depend on – real leaders, capable of making decisions and implementing them within the framework of the aims assigned to them.' Sleptsov favored young employees:

> After 40, a man doesn't think about work any more. He thinks about easy profits, the size of his salary, and providing for old age. And most people who call themselves specialists are content simply with the title: in fact, they either cannot or will not work. This is probably related to the present system of employment. People are hired with no clear definitions of their rights and obligations, and the 'umbrella' of the social and labor legislation makes it difficult for a director to get rid of slack or negligent employees.

He decided to avoid 'professionals,' and hire, 'young guys with a flair for commerce, a creative thrust.' Until this point, his staff had included only himself, an accountant, a secretary, and a marketing director, whom Sleptsov had known since his work at the architectural restoration firm. All other people on his projects had come from the 'outside' and worked under contract in flexible groups of 20–25 people, whom Sleptsov usually assigned to finalize the technical details of particular projects and provide legal consulting on contracts and agreements under negotiations. Sleptsov conducted all negotiations with clients and aircraft owners and made all of the key decisions himself.

He explained this by citing a formative disappointment, 'When I tried to get my first marketing director to negotiate with customers, my attempts were unsuccessful. He had a colossal amount of knowledge, but couldn't conduct business talks. I had to replace him.'

In mid-August, 1990 Sleptsov hired Alexander Subbota, a man with a medical background, as his new Marketing Director. A week later, Subbota, on Sleptsov's approval, invited

EXHIBIT 4
Structure and members of staff of the Stantret Company

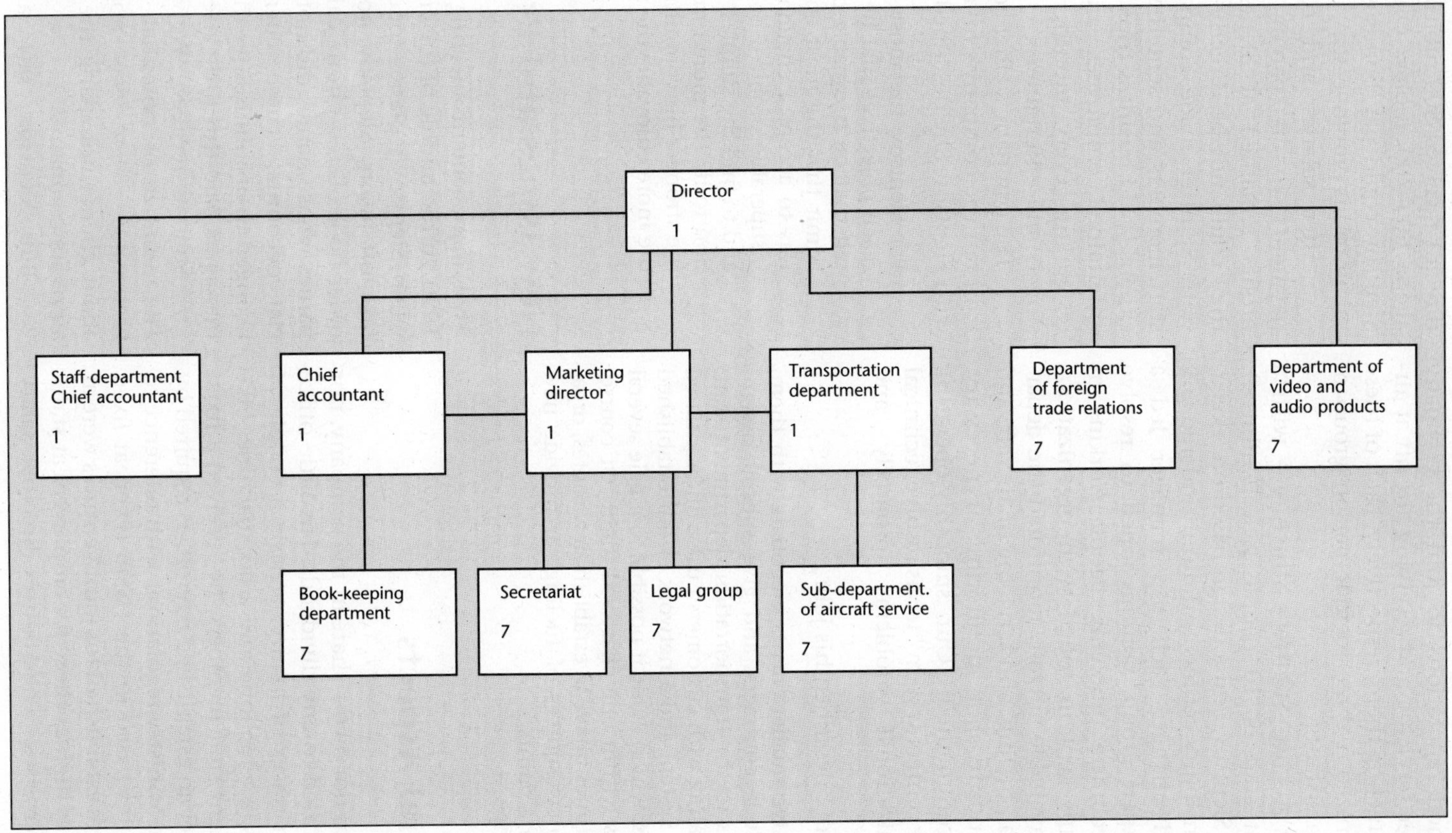

Staff department
Chief accountant
1

Director
1

Chief accountant
1

Book-keeping department
7

Marketing director
1

Secretariat
7

Legal group
7

Transportation department
1

Sub-department of aircraft service
7

Department of foreign trade relations
7

Department of video and audio products
7

two men who had worked under contract and earned good reputations to join the company and oversee servicing and receiving aircraft at airports and fueling them, respectively. Each of these men organized a three to four person group of non-staff assistants.

After August, Stantret's structure – with a permanent staff of 16 people (see Exhibit 4), including Sleptsov, and a design based on 'executive responsibility centers' – did not undergo any substantial change. Each top manager led a mobile expert group, commissioned to resolve specific technical problems. People working in such groups kept in touch with organizations that had available aircraft, monitored the departure, arrival, fueling, and servicing of aircraft, and provided on-the-spot monitoring, if necessary. Subbota commented: 'Our smoothly-operating "executive centers system" let us resolve technical or organizational problems promptly and efficiently.'

Subbota described his job:

I receive smaller clients, negotiate with them, conclude contracts, and give specific assignments to the transportation department staff. In dealing with customers I use a differentiated price system and a network of our established routes, which made it possible to juggle several orders within one chartered flight. Of course, sometimes I have to establish new routes, organize new sources of fueling, or provide new landing points.

Financial Aspects

Sleptsov did not own a share in the company, nor was he entitled to any dividends. His little office showed no traces of luxury: a desk, a couple of hard-chairs, a telephone and a fax machine. Like all permanent staff members, he received a fixed salary, under an established payroll, as required by the Finance Ministry regulations with reference to joint ventures based in the USSR. (Even at fixed rates, salaries established for joint ventures were at least twice as high as those for employees at state-owned enterprises.) The Stantret director's salary was set at 1,000 rubles a month. The commercial director received 800 rubles, and other key managers, 600–700 rubles. Once in every quarter, Sleptsov could pay bonuses of up to a month's salary to his employees.

After salaries and contractually required payments to its parent company, Stantret's profits remained at Sleptsov's disposal – but they could not be directly allocated among the staff. Stantret made company cars available to staff members and sent them on abroad on all-expense-paid business trips abroad. And Sleptsov entertained employees and their families at restaurants every month, inviting well-known singers and entertainers.

The company's chief accountant, E. Marmuzova ran the company's finances in collaboration with Sleptsov. She described her boss:

For Sleptsov the most important thing is to reach objectives that he sets, to prove to himself that he is capable of anything. He would admit that the most enjoyable thing for him was to accept a challenge that seems like an insuperable problem or a very daunting task, and to find the simplest and the quickest solution to it. The more formidable the challenge, the stronger his commitment to resolve it, and the more enjoyable the success.

New Issues and Pressures

At a management meeting in early September 1990, in the middle of the crop-harvesting season when Sleptsov's planes touched ground only to take off again, Sleptsov noticed that Subbota's order books listed phone calls from several companies whose names did not appear in the financial accounts. These clients had apparently changed their minds after the first call. The other managers paid this little attention.

Subbota recalled, 'We were doing very well. The number of potential clients was steadily increasing. There was nothing extraordinary about clients not liking the terms or distrusting a private company.'

But Sleptsov saw an opportunity for

improvement. The canceled orders involved two situations: either the client required a short-range flight to localities outside Stantret's standard routes, where the airports lacked runways for heavy planes, or he had a small shipment of goods to be transported and could not afford a whole plane.

Sleptsov commented, 'I understood the net we cast was meant only for large fish. At the peak of the crop-harvesting season major customers make the weather. But off-season, Air Link-Up might have to rely on an army of small private customers.' He set about reorganizing his operations.

> We did a bit of analysis and saw that, if loading is done rationally, planes always have some free space, however large the load. Besides, the MAI had a diversified stock of planes, so we could employ a variety of aircraft, from 3– ton midgets to 40–ton giants. We could combine two or three orders into a single package or 'supplement' a large order with a small order. If we could not do that, we would use a small plane. In both cases each individual customer would pay less than before.

In mid October, Sleptsov surprised his managers at a regular executive meeting by suddenly asking how they saw the future of their company and how they thought Stantret could retain the image of a fast, reliable air carrier. He had noticed that the situation with aircraft fuel and technical air services in the Soviet Union was deteriorating.

> On the face of it, everything seemed business as usual. Unlike Aeroflot's, our planes did not stand idle. They flew food, office equipment, computers, cars, and timber. But I had already felt tension in our system of fuel supplies – and, in fact, beginning in early November, we had to phone around practically all the airports to find fuel, and we were forced to change routes to include refueling points, and we experienced our first cases of falling behind delivery schedules. I realized the company was heading for a crisis.

Fuel wasn't the only scarce resource. Sleptsov had also encountered his first difficulties in providing aircraft for his orders. Stantret's heavy schedule of flights had increased the number of technical check-ups and engine certifications required to be conducted on planes operated by the ARI (regulations called for such inspections after every 2000 flying hours). This meant longer idle periods. It also led to the grounding of several ARI planes in October. Their engines had worn out.

Sleptsov brought an MAI executive, O. Mikoyan, to the October executive meeting. Mikoyan, director of a ten-month-old MAI subsidiary called 'Molniya,' was responsible for leasing and operating cargo planes that the MAI and other agencies owned. (The government allowed the MAI and the USSR Defense Ministry to make limited commercial use of planes when they weren't needed for military shipments.) Mikoyan knew the MAI personnel well, and was adept in the ins and outs of the Ministry's logistics and distribution system, and he had approached Sleptsov about working for Stantret.

At the meeting, Stantret managers argued in favor of turning the company into an independent cargo airline in the form of a joint-stock or limited company. Such a company could lease aircraft from manufacturers or owners, with a view to buying the planes, and make deals with aviation fuel distributors. The market niche seemed clear: Aeroflot was the only important competitor. Other organizations shipped air cargo from time to time, but as a rule they simply resold Aeroflot's freight flights to trading companies.

Sleptsov explained the attraction of forming a joint venture:

> Aside from state firms, economic laws favor only joint ventures with foreign firms, because the government wants to attract foreign exchange. The joint venture laws contain privileges like tax benefits. Such ventures present the only more or less stable and favorable area for business investment.

Sleptsov considered non-government companies highly insecure:

> Given the prevailing attitudes and existing legislation, the future of private and non-governmental corporations is more than precarious. Today you are a private business. Tomorrow a change of policy takes everything

away from you. There is no firm political commitment from the government to treat entrepreneurship as a priority concern.

He promised his managers that he would come back to the issue of forming a joint stock company in a couple of weeks.

> I had been told that somebody besides Aeroflot and me had been air-lifting cargoes, but I didn't see them as real competitors. Why? Because sooner or later their customers would turn to me. They were unhappy with the high rates (higher than Aeroflot's official prices), low reliability, and the long wait for a long time for their orders to be filled – problems similar to those of Aeroflot's clients. No wonder, because they used Aeroflot planes, and Aeroflot had problems keeping its own orders on schedule. Compounding the situation, 30–40 percent of planes were constantly grounded for lack of engines or fuel.

Sleptsov knew that the Council of Ministers had received two registration requests in the air cargo transport field. One was from a limited partnership called Transaero, founded in April, 1990 with equity of 1.5 million rubles. The other was from a joint-stock company called Volga-Dnieper, founded in August, 1990, with equity of 10 million rubles. Neither seemed particularly threatening. He and Mikoyan analyzed the situation for two weeks, then dropped the idea of setting up an independent airline.

Mikoyan explained:

> One must obtain permission from the USSR Council of Ministers to establish an independent airline company. I asked about the cost and availability of planes and learned that the market price of one Ilyushin-76 was exorbitant: 20 million rubles, compared to the state price of 7 million rubles. And even so, planes were very difficult to come by. Most of the aircraft produced in the country were distributed by state order to government ministries and agencies. The lion's share went to Aeroflot. Others had to wait 2–3 years to buy planes.

Sleptsov calculated pay-back at no less than two years. He told Mikoyan, 'I can't afford to tie up my capital for such a long time, especially when the very existence of our business as a private company is uncertain. The capital turnover period should be no longer than two or three months. I know a lot of ways to recoup the costs twice over within the same time frame.'

In early November, Sleptsov decided that Stantret would enter into a joint project with Molniya. Stantret would commission Molniya to conduct air shipments. Mikoyan would remain at Molniya, but combine his position with the leadership of Stantret's transportation department, on a part-time basis. In addition, Stantret signed contracts with other top executives at Molniya, and one of them, who was very well-connected in almost all Soviet airports and Military air fields, took a post at Stantret.

Stantret used the proceeds from its cargo operations to remit money to Molniya's bank account. Molniya provided the use of the aircraft, and did all the work required to line up planes, fuel, and airport ground services. As an enterprise of the MAI, Molniya had access to the Ministry's data systems.

Alexander Subbota recalled:

> As a result of this arrangement, after November 1990, we had no problems with obtaining planes or fuel. Molniya was turning a profit and thereby justifying its existence from the Ministry's standpoint. And its managers were actually being paid twice for doing one job – finding and leasing air planes and providing them with the necessary services on behalf of their company. The arrangement did not change the system of air shipments conducted with the MAI. It had the same functional relations, organizational principles and hierarchy. Stantret had simply used material incentives to galvanize the old system.

Molniya's established contacts with the Defense Ministry enabled Stantret to offer its customers giant Antonov-124s and permanent access to military airfields and fuel depots. In addition, Stantret hired the best pilots from both Ministries, capable of flying in all weather conditions and landing planes on poorly equipped runways. Stantret paid the pilots double their usual wages.

A Mounting Crisis

One big problem remained. Stantret's revenue continued to be 'gobbled up' by contractually-required dividend payments to the parent company, which used the money to finance tours of musicians in the Soviet Union and abroad and purchase musical instruments and studio equipment for new performers.

At the end of December, Sleptsov managed to persuade the Director of the parent company to modify their original contract. After January 1991, the parent company allowed Stantret to pay fixed monthly 'dividends' of 85,000 rubles rather than a percentage of earnings (see Exhibit 3).

Sleptsov lamented:

> My money had been disappearing in a bottomless barrel. They used the first million and a half, paid in September, to send the Ice Ballet to the US. The investment did not return any profit. They spent the second quarter payment of 1990 on equipment for a record studio – and there is a big question mark over when the first records are going to appear, and whether they will sell well.

> I explained to the Director that I would not be able to pay more than 85,000 a month because I was starting up new projects that would require large spending. It was the truth.

In late April, 1991, Sleptsov began to feel that luck was evading him. Stantret's parent company had failed to deliver a large shipment of imported consumer goods to Soviet customers on schedule. The consequence was a debt of 13 million rubles to repay a loan, plus interest and damages. Faced with the knowledge that defaulting on a major loan could jeopardize Stantret, among other assets of the parent company, Sleptsov paid the debt in early April. 'Thirteen million rubles down the drain. Left at Stantret's disposal, this money could have doubled our revenues within the next three to four months.'

This was bad, but something else upset Sleptsov even more: 'The worst of all was that I had started to lose support where I thought myself on firm ground: within my own company. I had become disenchanted with my managers.'

At the beginning of April, one of his managers had spoiled a major deal for Stantret. Sleptsov had signed a preliminary agreement with a Japanese trading company to produce Mitsubishi cars in the Soviet Union and sell them for hard currency. He had already bought the equipment for an assembly plant. He calculated that the project would quickly turn a profit.

> The million rubles in expenses, including the costs of setting up an assembly plant, could be recouped within two months at an exchange rate of 40 rubles to the dollar. The installation work would take about a month. All that remained was to close a deal with an enterprise in the Moscow area that had a plot of land on which we planned to build a assembly plant for a joint manufacturing project.

> I told the head of our foreign trade department to inspect the plot, find a construction company, and start building. We had the money in our bank accounts. A fairly simple task. Two weeks later, the landowners called to ask what happened to my representative. He had come to the site, looked at the land, and disappeared. I asked him what the matter was. He said they didn't have a deed. When I called them back, they told me that the deed had been ready for a week – obviously, we didn't mean business. They hung up on me. I had to break off relations with the Japanese. It was like a slap in the face.

At the end of April, while looking through the past two months' air shipment contracts, Sleptsov noticed something even more upsetting. Two large contracts for which he had participated in the preliminary negotiations stated customer prices five percent below the prices that he had negotiated. Subbota had signed both contracts. Upon closer inspection, Sleptsov saw that almost all the rest of the contracts included similar discounts. He confronted his employee. 'Subbota explained that the customers wanted a lower price now in exchange for a commitment to place larger orders later. We would make up the loss. But he was nervous during the explanation. I didn't believe him.'

Further checking, with friends at the bank, revealed to Sleptsov that over the past two months, large sums had been remitted to the accounts of managers responsible for his air shipment operations. 'It was a real blow. I didn't catch them red-handed, but I could no longer believe them. I still can't see what went wrong.'

The final ingredient in the crisis was serious competition, which Stantret hadn't experienced since beginning its operations. The documents from Sleptsov's May executive meeting showed that the Volga-Dnieper joint venture had accumulated equity capital of 270 million rubles – enough to buy several enormous cargo planes. Even more

worrisome, it had forged business relationships with the MAI, Stantret's regular supplier of rental aircraft.

Sleptsov faced a major strategic decision. Should he turn Stantret into a joint-stock company and orient it toward long-term projects? Should he accept the invitation of a US commercial company to become its official representative in the USSR? Should he quit the company, raise money on the strength of his own good name, and start a new business of his own? What should he do?

Case 5: Strategic Planning at Oldelft

By Ron Meyer[1]

It was September 16, 1986, as Kees van Hoeven put the final touches on the presentation he would be giving to MBA students at the Rotterdam School of Management the next day. As Oldelft's corporate planner, he had been requested to give a lecture on the way strategic planning had been implemented in his company since it was initiated in 1979. Without hesitation, he had agreed to come to the school, as he had good reason to believe that this would be a stimulating exercise for the students, as well as for himself.

For the students, he realized, Oldelft was an interesting example of a relatively small high-tech firm operating in a turbulent global market. The company, with its head office situated near The Netherlands' largest technical university in Delft, specialized in products requiring advanced knowledge of optics, electronics, electronoptics ('optronics'), and precision mechanics. These products, with relatively short product life cycles, fell into three categories, namely, medical, defense, and industrial products. In all three cases, Oldelft's competition was global and fierce. Van Hoeven recognized that it would be of great interest to the students to observe to what extent textbook planning processes had been adapted to fit the needs and constraints of such a company.

His visit to Rotterdam, however, was very interesting personally as well. He had already played a prominent role in guiding the 1985 planning cycle at Oldelft, but he was now in charge of running 'the circus,' as the planning process was generally referred to. Since the Oldelft strategic planning process was biannual, the first planning cycle under his supervision would lead to a final plan by the end of 1987. The first steps in this 1987 planning cycle would soon be taken, leaving him only a short period of time to review the manner in which the planning at Oldelft took place and to make changes where needed. Thus he welcomed the opportunity to exchange opinions on the strengths and weaknesses of the Oldelft planning process with a room full of MBA students. He was very curious to hear what kind of questions they would ask him and what kind of possible improvements they would propose.

The History of the Company

The Oldelft company was founded in 1939 by Oscar van Leer as the 'Optical Industry The Old Delft.' In its first years the company was quite small and specialized in handcrafted optical products, ranging from magnifying glasses and microscopes to cameras. At a very early stage, however, van Leer was able to lure an extremely capable man away from Philips to lead his company. This man was A. Bouwers, an engineer with a passion for research and development (R&D), who also proved to be a highly motivated entrepreneur.

Bouwers committed a large part of his time and a considerable portion of company funds to new product development, which in 1945 led to the first prototype of a photofluorographic camera with a concentric mirror system. This product, which was finally introduced in the market in

---

[1] Source: This case was prepared by Ron Meyer as a basis for class discussion rather than to illustrate either effective or ineffective handling of an administrative situation. Unless otherwise indicated, all information was obtained with the kind assistance of the Oldelft company. Some names in the text have been changed. This case was originally published as part of the strategic management course *Ondernemingsplanning II* (Corporate Planning) of the Dutch Open University. Copyright © 1991 Open Universiteit Heerlen.

1950 as the Odelca, allows expensive full-sized X-rays to be substituted by far cheaper postcard-size ones. This product was a great success because it made nationwide tuberculosis examinations financially feasible.

Fuelled by his success, Bouwers maintained his policy of remaining at the forefront of technological innovation in the field of optics. In 1952, for instance, Oldelft introduced advanced aerial cameras for both low- and high-altitude reconnaissance. During this period, Bouwers also followed an aggressive acquisitions strategy, buying up large numbers of smaller optical companies. As one Oldelft manager put it, 'No Dutch company with the word "optical" in its name was safe.'

By 1968, when Bouwers retired, Oldelft had expanded to a company with a turnover of about Dfl 35 million and more than a thousand employees. To the satisfaction of van Leer and the small number of other stockholders, Oldelft also proved to be very profitable, with a return on investment (ROI) ranging from 8 to 20 percent. To ensure that Oldelft would remain equally successful in future, Bouwers had also brought in an experienced R&D manager from outside the company to replace him. This was S. Duinker, head of the Philips laboratory in Hamburg, who has remained president of Oldelft since then.

The Years of Holding Course (1968–1975)

Duinker inherited a company operating in two very different markets, namely, the medical and defense markets. In the medical field Oldelft had developed radio therapy equipment, in addition to its Odelca X-ray cameras, and in the defense market Oldelft had established itself with reconnaissance cameras. Technology was the common theme linking these products and underlying Oldelft's R&D projects. In the late 1950s the company had supplemented its expertise in optics and precision mechanics with knowledge of the rapidly expanding field of electronics. The possibilities offered by these technologies by and large determined the thrust of Oldelft's product development strategy.

A second major factor determining Oldelft's

product line was the breathing space left to it by larger companies. A former member of the executive board described the strategy Oldelft employed by using the analogy of a guerrilla fighter – Oldelft was small and flexible, and only moved in areas left open to it by its powerful competitors; yet it was ready to strike at these opponents should weak points in their flanks show up.

Oldelft's relations to its competitors were, however, not as antagonistic as this analogy might suggest. Actually, the contrary was often true, it being the case that many competitors were also suppliers of Oldelft, while others purchased important components from the company. Philips, for instance, was simultaneously competitor, supplier, and customer of Oldelft, depending on the product in question. This meant that Oldelft was very dependent on the cooperative relationships it was able to establish with other companies. Oldelft's contacts were especially essential in the medical sector, since OEM (original equipment manufacturer) sales accounted for a large portion of turnover.

Besides OEM sales, Oldelft's major medical customers were all professional users, mostly hospitals, spread throughout the world, though concentrated in Europe and North America. Although the medical customers of Oldelft were easily identifiable, the company's competitors were somewhat harder to classify. Due to the highly specialized nature of the medical products Oldelft sold, the company was in fact operating in a number of small segments of a substantially fragmented market. To a large degree, the competitors Oldelft encountered in each segment differed in name, number, and strength.

In the defense business the same held true. The company had a small number of clearly identifiable customers, namely, national governments of western or developing nations, while the market niches in which the company operated were populated by a large number of nondominant competitors. This was where the similarities between the defense and medical markets ended, however. The defense industry, in which Oldelft participated, had characteristics all its own.

While the medical market could be said to be global due to the low level of protectionism practised by governments in this field, the defense market was quite the opposite. Governments are usually extremely hesitant to reward defense contracts to foreign companies, even though they might pay lip service to free trade. Moreover, in addition to discriminatory procurement policies, many governments are actively engaged in subsidizing and promoting nationally produced defense goods as well. This put Oldelft up against difficult competition in obtaining military contracts abroad. Yet being a Dutch company with a small home market, these foreign sales were essential for Oldelft. The company was severely export dependent, with 90 percent of its total turnover coming from abroad.

The defense market was also risky due to its sensitivity to shifting political winds. It is a Dutch law that all military products leaving the country require export permits, and these will not be granted if the country of destination is at war. This made Oldelft's exports vulnerable to political upheaval abroad. Especially since the lead time of a sale and the subsequent delivery can extend over a number of years, it could happen that a contract was signed with a country at peace and that war would break out before the products could be delivered.

The lead time of a sale in the defense industry could even be up to 10 years in the case of new products, introducing a variety of additional problems for a company such as Oldelft. The length of this lead time was due not only to the extra time involved in producing and 'debugging' new high-tech products but also to the government study groups in which defense contractors would need to invest years of their time before even being awarded the contract.

Despite these drawbacks, however, Oldelft made most of its profits in the defense market. Although winning a contract could prove extremely difficult, the margins on most contracts made all the trouble more than worthwhile. Company figures actually suggest that the medical products weren't profitable at all, although it can be difficult to do proper analysis in a small company. The medical products were retained, however, for a number of important reasons. The defense business tends to be rather cyclical and

the medical products could be used to counterbalance this, for instance, when planning production-capacity usage. Furthermore, Oldelft learned that the technological spin-off from medical to defense was considerable and could assist in strengthening the company's competitive advantage.

Besides the potentially rich financial rewards, the defense industry had a second attractive point. Military customers were far more interested in the quality of the product than in its price and delivery period. This was to Oldelft's advantage, since low cost and speed were not company strong points, while product reliability was a well-acknowledged Oldelft characteristic. This was largely due to the company's perfectionist culture, which was especially prevalent in the R&D department. This culture ensured a product of high quality and technological sophistication, yet also caused relatively high costs, both in terms of time and money.

It should come as no surprise that the vice president in charge of commercial affairs at the time expressed mixed feelings about the Oldelft culture. While it did facilitate the development of high-quality products, it weakened Oldelft's competitive position in the price-sensitive medical market. The perfectionist culture, with its inherently long R&D lead times, also reduced Oldelft's ability to quickly enter new high-tech markets not yet dominated by larger companies.

His concern was strengthened by the fact that by 1974 most of Oldelft's products were in a late phase of their product life cycle, while there were few promising civil products in the pipeline. At the same time, profits had dipped, and the 1974 annual report showed the first loss in years.

The Advent of Strategic Thinking (1975–1976)

By 1975, this decline in the company's fortunes led the executive board to point to a cost reduction drive as a necessary step toward profit recovery. There was, however, no staff group available at the time that could do an overhead analysis. It was therefore decided to institute a policy advice council (Beleids Advies Raad, BAR). This BAR was a voluntary group, mostly made up of young aggressive managers with new ideas who wanted to update the rather conservative corporate culture.

The BAR quickly obtained status as it developed beyond a cost-cutting group to a more general corporate think-tank. Being attuned to the newest management techniques, the BAR soon requested authority from the executive board to look into the possibilities of setting up a long-term planning approach, as this was one of the latest management developments at the time.

The BAR's initiative was accepted, and the seven-man team embarked on the task of designing a large-scale planning approach for Oldelft. The corporate plan they envisaged would be centered on turnover projections for the next seven to eight years. Sales managers would be asked to estimate the turnover they expected in their areas of responsibility, making it possible to synchronize all else to fit these forecasts. One would be able to derive everything, from capital requirements to personnel planning, from these figures, so that an overall business blueprint could be made. This would nicely solve a large number of important Oldelft problems at once, such as the need to level out production-capacity usage.

President Duinker was rather surprised by the farreaching BAR proposal, as he had a far more 'visionary' company plan in mind. He had expected a type of general SWOT analysis, followed by a number of corporate objectives and policy guidelines. After a period of discussion, however, a compromise was struck, whereby both planning options would be worked out.

By April 1976 Duinker's idea of drawing up a document outlining the company's 'objectives and policy principles' had taken shape. This hefty paper set out for the first time the company's long-term financial, social, commercial, and technological goals. It also laid down the fundamental policy guidelines that would be followed to achieve these goals. This was, in fact, the company's first attempt at explicitly formulating its mission and at putting to paper a number of its implicit strategic choices.

The foremost goal stated in this document was the primacy of continued independence over the goal of growth. This had never been a topic of discussion, as there had never been any reason to bring it up. It was realized, though, that the external environment was changing and that this would force the company to choose. The concentration ratio in many market segments was on the increase, and the funds needed to develop new products was also growing. This would put pressure on the company to merge or sell to a larger competitor in order to maintain growth. The executive board, however, clearly expressed that it would be its policy to remain independent, with company shares being widely spread.

While the intention was stated to periodically review the outlined objectives and policy principles, practice was that the document was neatly filed and rarely again exposed to daylight. The documents on stratgey that the BAR in the meantime had been working on were going to be concrete plans, including serious operational targets. By September 1976 the first 'strategic planning round' was started to obtain the turnover forecasts needed to work out the rest of the plans. There was but one problem in the BAR approach. No sales manager was willing to make a turnover prognosis eight years into the future. The extrapolation of current trends, it was realized, is dangerous in any case, but the unpredictability of the markets in which Oldelft operated made estimating impossible. The technological advances were seen as too fast and the number of competitors too unpredictable to even come close to an educated guess. No manager was willing to stick out his neck and try. The result was that the discussions dragged on an on, while very little was actually achieved.

The Impending Crisis (1976–1978)

In the meantime Oldelft's fortunes were slumping. In 1975 the company had been able to recover from the 1974 downturn, but by mid-1976 a sharp decline in sales had set in, and the short-term sales forecasts had taken a turn for the worse. By late 1977 it had become obvious that dramatic action would be necessary to prevent large-scale losses in the following years. An 'action plan' was drawn up to reduce overhead costs quickly. This plan led to a severe cutback in production capacity and consequently to a reduction in the workforce from 1600 to 1300 employees.

It was realized, however, that these short-term savings would not be sufficient to ensure the continued viability of the company. There were a number of more fundamental problems that would have to be addressed as well. First, there was 'serious doubt whether the present organizational structure, personnel and procedures would still fit the expected smaller scale of the company and whether they, in general, would be able to handle the commercial, technical and socio-economical problems.' Second, it was recognized that it was 'no longer self-evident that in the coming years Oldelft would be serving the same markets through the same distributing channels with the same products, developed and produced in the same way as before.'[2] The executive board decided to thoroughly reexamine both the structure of the company. To assist in this difficult process of self-analysis, the consultancy firm of Arthur D. Little (ADL) was called in.

The Introduction of Strategic Decision Making (1978–1979)

ADL started the two-front study in May 1978, looking both at the organizational structure of Oldelft, and at the strategy and the strategy-formulating process of the company. This large team of mostly American consultants was lead by John Niemans. It was his main task to teach this technology-oriented company to think in market terms and to develop its ability to effectively engage in strategic decision making. This was quite a challenge, one Oldelft manager later recalled, as Niemans had little to build on. Strategic thinking was still in its embryonic phase at Oldelft, and most strategic decision-making concepts were new to the company's management.

---

[2] Drawn from an internal company document announcing the hiring of ADL consultants.

By mid-1979 ADL had largely completed its task of reorganizing and reorienting Oldelft. This year-long process had led to a high number of important changes within the company. For instance, certain products were phased out, an important development program was cancelled, explicit make or buy decisions were made, and the company decided to substantially strengthen its position in electronics. Furthermore, strategic business units were implemented, in part to improve strategic decision-making ability.

Niemans had also given Oldelft the tools with which it would be able to carry out strategic planning on its own strength in future. He had given them a methodology and, in fact, had dragged the company through its very first strategic planning cycle. Not surprisingly, he also stressed the necessity for Oldelft to retain its ability to engage in strategic decison making. His advice, however, was not more concrete.

The First Attempts at Strategic Planning (1980–1981)

In 1980 the executive board decided to appoint the one-man market research department, presided over by the vice president for commercial affairs, as the coordinating body for the corporate strategic planning process. Mr. Verkade from this department was given the task of leading the first independent strategic planning cycle, generally along ADL lines. It was his opinion, however, that the ADL method was far too extensive to be implementable on a regular basis, so he introduced a simplified form. Before he could start with the actual process, though, Verkade left the company and was replaced by Mr. Jansen.

In the meantime, the last ADL people were finishing up their jobs of assisting in implementing the organizational changes, and Oldelft personnel were finally settling into the new situation. The years of upheaval, change, and uncertainty had left most employees with a desire just to get back to work. So when Jansen called on managers to participate in strategic planning meetings, very few had the time or the motivation to attend. The attractiveness that strategic planning had enjoyed due to its newness had also evaporated, making it even harder to get managers to come to planning sessions, especially since the sanctions for non-attendance were benign.

As gradually more and more managers dropped out of the strategic planning discussions, Jansen filled this vacuum by doing their strategic analyses for them. Within a short period of time, however, this task had become a full-time job, as the participation rate dropped ever lower. Jansen was pressed to write on and on. But as the company was actually far too large for one man to analyze, he got caught up in an endless writing process and never did catch up with the detailed facts. He was forced to generalize, and his analyses soon became too superficial for the line managers to consider seriously. This led these managers to dismiss strategic planning as a waste of time, justifying wholesale abandonment of meaningful cooperation. In this manner, in not more than a few months, Jansen had become isolated, and strategic planning had become nothing more than a one-man academic exercise.

The First Successful Independent Strategic Planning Cycle (1981)

During the same period, in 1981, the workers' council (Ondernemings Raad) proposed to have the head of the 1978 ADL team, John Niemans, appointed to the supervisory board. The executive board agreed, and thus invited a well-informed and outspoken person to join the company. Niemans, of course, was very interested to find out to what extent his recommendations had been carried out by the company. He was disappointed to see the strategic planning process being carried out so poorly.

The executive board agreed with this critique and took firm action to ensure that by the end of 1981 the first independent strategic planning cycle would be completed. The responsibility for accomplishing this was given to a man with more experience and weight than Jansen, namely, to the head of the commercial staff

offices, Ab Baas. Compared with most other Oldelft managers, Baas had a strong background in company planning, as he was one of the driving forces behind the old BAR. He also had a reputation for getting things done and, unlike Jansen, had the wholehearted backing of the executive board to strengthen his position. To the line managers it was clear that participation in the new planning cycle was no longer voluntary, but compulsory.

Baas introduced a planning process almost totally along ADL lines. This combination of both bottom-up and top-down approaches has, to this day, remained the way in which Oldelft conducts its strategic planning. This process consists of four general steps, namely:

- the drawing up of situation analyses per business segment of the business units;

- the formulation of plans and options per business segment;

- the evaluation of all plans and options by the company's top management;

- the communication of the decisions taken to all relevant personnel.

The Situation Analyses

Baas introduced a hard-nosed approach to obtaining the relevant data on the business segments' external environments. He started by handing out almost-empty booklets to the five business segment managers. The only things printed in each booklet were the headings on each page denoting what the managers should put in the space below. It was the duty of these line managers to hand the booklets back in with all the pages filled. The amount of information Baas requested from each business segment was extensive, and it was the responsibility of each manager to gather all relevant data himself.

A completed situation analysis was made up of two key elements, namely, an analysis of the industry's maturity and a weighing of the business segment's competitive position, which together determined the company's strategic position. The industry's maturity was ascertained by analyzing current and expected trends, threats, opportunities, market segmentation, customers, technological change, market growth, and growth potential. This analysis would place the industry's maturity somewhere on a continuum from embryonic to aging (see Exhibit 1).

The company's competitive position in each product market was determined by comparing Oldelft to its competitors on a large number of fronts. This assessment paid attention to differences between companies, as well as between products. Companies were checked for their strengths and weaknesses, for instance in the areas of R&D, finance, service and sales. Products were compared on the basis of price, quality and features. Together with the figures on the relative marketshares, this information placed each competitor somewhere on the continuum from weak to dominant.

In the ADL approach the industry maturity continuum and the competitive position continuum form the two axes of the strategic position matrix, displayed in Exhibit 1. The strategic position resulting from this whole situation analysis is the most important factor determining which strategies should be developed for each business segment in future.

This whole process of establishing the business segments' strategic position was a complex, yet vitally important, first step in the planning cycle. To ensure the quality of the business segment managers' output, Baas held a number of meetings with each manager on his situation analysis. Baas invited all other Oldelft managers who had a stake in the business unit to attend these meetings as well, as broad input usually increases the accuracy of an assessment. Besides the business segment manager, Baas also requested the presence of product managers, sales managers (from home and abroad), plant managers, project managers, production coordinators, development unit managers, as well as relevant staff members and an occasional external consultant. On average, between 10 and 15 participants came to each meeting.

Plans and Options

Once the situation analyses had been completed, the business segment managers were asked to evaluate past plans and to supply new plans and options. These new plans, Baas made clear, were to be developed using the strategic position of the business segment as a reference framework. Just as

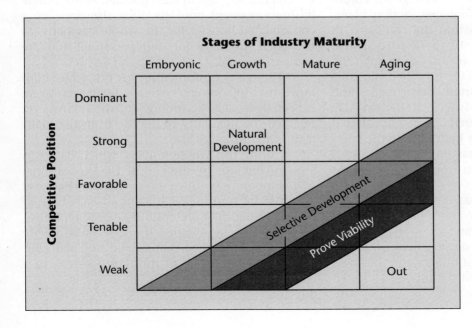

EXHIBIT 1
Strategic Option Zones

with the situation analysis, a number of meetings with a broad, representative group were held to discuss and finalize the proposed plans.

After all the meetings with the business segments had been concluded, it was Baas's task to reorganize all information into a presentable form. To facilitate decision-making by the company's top management, it was also necessary for him to 'translate' the business segments' options into comparable financial figures and to add a risk analysis to each of them. After considerable rewriting, this resulted in five business segment discussion papers, which were subsequently handed to top management.

The Corporate Scrums

These business segment analyses were the main input into the 'corporate scrums,' as the strategic decision-making discussions among the top managers are called in ADL-speak. The other two inputs provided by Baas were a financially and strategically consolidated view of the whole corporation and a socio-economic analysis of the outside world.

In total, three scrums were programmed to reach agreement on the strengths and weaknesses of the corporation, general goals, corporate strategies, business strategies, action plans, and resource allocation within the company. In each meeting there were 10 to 12 participants, including the president of the company, the executive vice presidents, the so-called directors (heads of the most important departments and business units), the company controller, an ADL consultant, and Baas himself. Each scrum lasted two to three days and was held outside the company offices to ensure that day-to-day business would not divert attention from the discussions at hand.

The first scrum evaluated past strategies and discussed strategic issues and financial performance. The second scrum drew conclusions about strategic issues and decided actions, strategies, and resource allocation to the business segments. Finally, the third scrum was dedicated to a discussion on socioeconomic analysis and the corporation's strengths, weaknesses, and general goals. This last scrum concluded with the selection of corporate strategies for the coming five year period.

While the planning horizon employed was five years, the emphasis of the plans was on the first two. Actions and resource allocations especially focused on the first two years. This was due to Baas having scheduled the following planning cycles to take place on a biennial basis (in 1983, 1985, 1987, and so on).

The Post-Scrum Booklets

After this decision-making process had been completed, Baas wrote up post-scrum booklets for each of the business segments. These documents each contained a finalized situation analysis, a list of the decisions taken on the business segments's proposed strategies and action plans, a forecast of the financial results for the next five years, and a specification of the amount of R&D resources allocated to each business segment. These booklets were subsequently sent to the 10 to 15 managers involved in the strategic planning process for each business segment. It was up to these managers to implement the plans along the general lines set out in each booklet. Besides these business segment booklets, Baas also drew up a consolidated booklet for the whole company, as well as a summary for staff personnel and the workers' council.

There was no formal review procedure built into the planning system. Managers were expected to act according to the plans, yet retained the flexibility to deviate from the plans if the circumstances arose.

During this whole process, which Baas was able to conclude by the end of 1981, occasional ADL support was called in, as no one had real expertise in 'running such a show.' Baas himself especially had few pretensions. It was typical of his style that he avoided the title of corporate planner, as he argued that he did not plan, but merely facilitated, the planning process. With a wink, he opted instead for the title of 'circus director.'

The Acceptance of Strategic Planning

While in 1981 the strategic planning process at times might have resembled a three-ring circus, by the third planning cycle, concluded in 1985, it had become well-rehearsed corporate practice. Gaining the acceptance of these production- and technology-oriented managers was a challenge for Baas. It was very difficult for him to motivate people to think and operate strategically, not only during the planning sessions but especially afterward. It was not only the corporate culture that frustrated Baas's attempts to gain acceptance for strategic planning but also the absence of both carrot and stick. There was no reward system geared to encourage participation in and compliance with the plans, nor was there any formal mechanism to control the managers' execution of them.

Despite these problems, by 1985 Baas had been able to embed the planning process in the company's way of running its business. By then, all fifty-odd participants had grown accustomed to the way Baas had implemented the ADL approach to strategic planning, and they had gotten used to the timetable Baas had drawn up for them to meet. This planning process timetable was spread out over a period of approximately one year. Baas started the process during November and used the period up until April to complete the pre-scrum booklets. The corporate scrums were subsequently planned for May and June. The period up until October was then used by the planning staff to draw up the post-scrum booklets for the business units (BUs), staff, and the worker's council.

Although Baas was the only person in the organization involved in guiding the planning process on a full-time basis, he was assisted during the busiest periods by three to four others. During the 1985 process, though, he did have a permanent assistant, namely, his young successor-to-be, Kees van Hoeven. Shortly after the completion of the third planning cycle, van Hoeven took over as corporate planner and Baas was promoted to head of the defense products business unit (see Exhibit 2).

The Fourth Strategic Planning Cycle

With the fourth planning cycle slated for completion by October 1987 and with a lead time of about one year, van Hoeven's visit to the Rotterdam School of Management on September 17, 1986 was really going to be on the eve of the next planning period. He would be planning for a company that had changed somewhat since the days of the ADL studies. One important step had been the divestment of two noncore businesses, namely, Cine (film-cutting equipment) and Deltronics (medical equipment merchandizing). This left Oldelft with two remaining BUs. The medical products BU was made up of three business segments, namely, X-ray (OEM), radio therapy, and ultrasound, while the other BU comprised the defense products.

All these products could be said to fit the 'mission definition,' formulated during the ADL consulting period, which was to 'reveal the invisible.' However, Oldelft did not feel restricted to a narrow interpretation of this mission, since it acted more as a good slogan that fit the range of products than as a guiding principle. In practice the company let itself be guided by the technologies involved in making certain products. Its lack of apprehension in interpreting its business-defining statement less strictly was demonstrated in 1984, when a new BU, industrial products, was created, and the Seampilot was introduced (see Exhibit 3). This laser-based seam-tracking system for arc-welding automation employed the unique combination of optronics, electronics, and precision mechanics in which Oldelft specialized. This diversification into another civil market, it was hoped, would help offset the destabilizing influence of the irregular large-scale defense contracts.

The introduction of the ACAL gas detection system in the same year entailed a further widening of the mission definition interpretation. This system for nerve gas detection actually 'reveals the unsmellable' and hence seems to fall outside Oldelft's traditional imaging business. The ACAL technology, however, is based on optronics' ability to identify discolorations caused by the gas and as such can be said to fall within a wider interpretation of 'revealing the invisible.'

EXHIBIT 2
Proposed Organization
Chart (as of January 1,
1987)

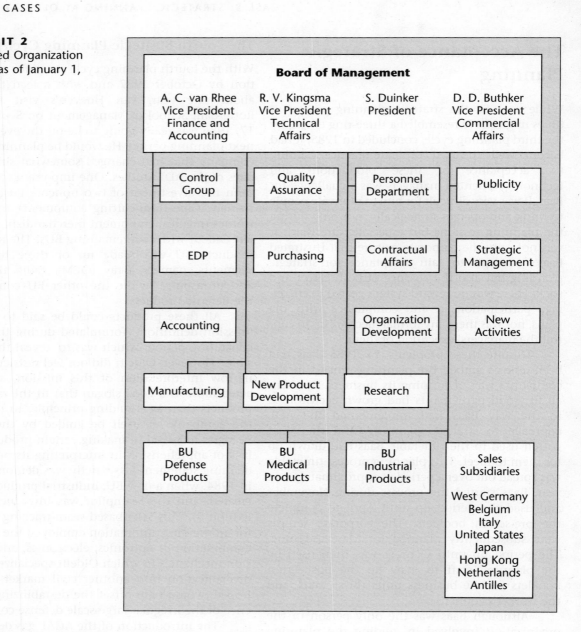

Board of Management

A. C. van Rhee Vice President Finance and Accounting	R. V. Kingsma Vice President Technical Affairs	S. Duinker President	D. D. Buthker Vice President Commercial Affairs
Control Group	Quality Assurance	Personnel Department	Publicity
EDP	Purchasing	Contractual Affairs	Strategic Management
Accounting		Organization Development	New Activities
Manufacturing	New Product Development	Research	
BU Defense Products	BU Medical Products	BU Industrial Products	Sales Subsidiaries

West Germany
Belgium
Italy
United States
Japan
Hong Kong
Netherlands
Antilles |

Besides new products, another important change was that of the company's fortunes. Since the ADL studies Oldelft had recovered its former profitability, with its return on equity ranging from 5 percent to a high of 37 percent (see Exhibits 4 and 5). These results had allowed the company to increase its R&D expenditures, and a number of promising new products had been introduced into the market.

Van Hoeven's position, too, was about to change. While he was still a member of the commercial staff office, as Baas had been, it had become obvious that an organizational reshuffling was in the making. The proposals within the executive board would have almost all commercial staff reporting under the individual business units instead of under the vice president for commercial affairs, Buthker, as now was the case. One of the few

EXHIBIT 3
Present Product Age Guide

	X-ray	Radio Therapy	Ultrasound	Defense	Industrial
				Defense	**Industrial**
1956	Oldelca				
1957	100-camera				
1958					
1959					
1960					
1961					
1962					
1963					
1964	Oldelca	Deccalix			
1965	70-camera				
1966					
1967					
1968					
1969					
1970	Anodica				
1971	2-camera			Night vision	
1972				equipment	
1973	Deltorax	Simulix			Indeca
1974	camera				(NDT)
1975					
1976					
1977					
1978				F-16 HUD	
1979		Simtomix			
1980				Laser	
1981	Anodica			range	
	6-camera			finders	
1982					
1983			Transducers		
1984			Small parts scanner	ACAL (gas detection)	Seampilot
1985	Electrodelca		Linear	arrays	

exceptions would be corporate planning, which would then no longer be reporting to the head of the commercial staff, but, rather, directly to the vice president for commercial affairs.

One of the things that was not altered much over the years was the company's approach to the planning process. Baas's attention during the first planning cycles had mainly been focused on getting strategic plans made. As mentioned before, he also exerted considerable effort at overcoming organizational resistance to planning and spent much time encouraging the highly product- and technology-oriented managers to think strategically. Only now that strategic planning had become more or less accepted was the time opportune for van Hoeven to review the planning methodology and implement improvements.

Hence, he welcomed the opportunity to

EXHIBIT 4
Financial Summary 1976–1985 in Dfl millions

	1976	1978	1980	1981	1982	1983	1984	1985
Results								
Sales	129.2	127.0	194.9	162.3	229.3	293.3	255.6	227.6
Salaries, wages and social security	(63.0)	(62.4)	(69.1)	(69.1)	(77.5)	(86.4)	(82.9)	(84.2)
Depreciation	(4.9)	(5.0)	(6.3)	(8.1)	(11.9)	(14.8)	(13.6)	(14.6)
Other operating cost	(48.9)	(60.0)	(103.9)	(68.9)	(99.9)	(146.3)	(122.7)	(111.9)
Operating result	12.4	(0.5)	15.7	16.2	40.0	45.8	36.4	16.9
Financial income and expenses	(8.4)	(9.5)	(11.7)	(11.4)	(11.8)	(6.3)	(3.5)	(4.1)
Taxation	(1.6)	(0.2)	—	(0.1)	(3.1)	(12.6)	(12.9)	(3.9)
Extraordinary income and expenses	0.6	0.6	(1.9)	—	(14.2)	(2.0)	(3.0)	(2.5)
Net income	3.0	(9.7)	2.1	4.7	10.9	25.0	17.1	6.4
Cashflow	7.9	(4.7)	9.7	13.2	38.0	43.0	41.2	14.0
Dividends	1.2	—	—	—	1.7	3.5	6.1	4.3
Assets								
Fixed assets	35.9	45.8	51.7	59.2	65.1	66.0	60.5	62.3
Inventories	71.9	72.7	75.4	79.1	74.5	74.7	96.0	67.4
Accounts receivable	40.0	72.3	80.8	56.9	67.2	86.0	116.6	93.2
Liquid resources	2.0	2.2	4.5	2.1	14.1	13.9	8.0	36.8
Total Assets	149.8	192.9	212.4	197.3	220.9	240.5	281.0	259.7
Liabilities								
Group equity	34.5	33.6	39.8	45.0	54.7	79.2	107.5	116.2
Long-term external liabilities	36.0	46.9	41.8	40.0	51.3	46.7	43.5	46.2
Short-term external liabilities	79.2	112.3	130.8	112.3	115.0	114.6	130.0	97.3
Total equity and liabilities	149.8	192.9	212.4	197.3	220.9	240.5	281.0	259.7

exchange opinions on the strengths and weaknesses of the Oldelft planning process with the students and professors of the school. He was very curious to hear what kind of questions they would ask him and what kinds of possible improvements they would propose.

EXHIBIT 5
Financial Ratios 1976–1985

	1976	1978	1980	1981	1982	1983	1984	1985
Sales and Results								
Sales increase over previous year in %	11.0	(14.2)	12.9	(16.7)	41.3	28.0	(3.0)	(11.0)
Net income as a % of sales	2.3	(7.6)	1.1	3.0	4.8	5.8	6.7	2.8
Net income as a % of average group equity	9.3	(28.8)	5.5	11.2	22.0	37.3	18.3	5.7
Dividend distribution as a % of net income	42	—	—	—	15	14	36	66
Equity								
Group equity as a % of total equity employed	22	17	19	23	25	33	38	45
Risk-bearing equity as a % of total equity employed	32	25	25	29	30	37	40	51
Working capital								
Inventory as a % of sales	56	57	39	39	32	25	38	30
Current assets/current liabilities	1.4	1.3	1.2	1.2	1.4	1.5	1.7	2.0
Working capital in Dfl. millions	34.7	34.8	29.9	26	41	60	90	100
Per share statistics								
Net income per share of Dfl. 10	4.82	(14.59)	n/a	7.12	16.43	36.11	21.05	7.55
Shareholders equity	53.37	50.46	n/a	67.53	82.18	114.53	132.56	136.58
Employees								
Number of employees at year end	1639	1448	1311	1319	1435	1412	1324	1321
Research and Development								
R&D costs as % of sales of own products	10.4	14.2	9.8	n/a	n/a	n/a	n/a	n/a
R&D costs as % of sales	n/a	n/a	n/a	6.5	6.8	8.9	8.4	11.0

Case 6: KAO Corporation

By Sumantra Ghoshal and Charlotte Butler[1]

Dr Yoshio Maruta introduced himself as a Buddhist scholar first, and as President of the Kao Corporation second. The order was significant, for it revealed the philosophy behind Kao and its success in Japan. Kao was a company that not only learned, but 'learned how to learn.' It was, in Dr Maruta's word's, 'an educational institution in which everyone is a potential teacher.'

Under Dr Maruta's direction, the scholar's dedication to learning had metamorphosed into a competitive weapon which, in 1990, had led to Kao being ranked ninth by Nikkei Business in its list of excellent companies in Japan, and third in terms of corporate originality (see Exhibit 1). As described by Fumio Kuroyanagi, Director of Kao's overseas planning department, the company's success was due not merely to its mastery of technologies nor its efficient marketing and information systems, but to its ability to integrate and enhance these capabilities through learning. As a result Kao had come up with a stream of new products ahead of its Japanese and foreign competitors and, by 1990, had emerged as the largest branded and packaged goods company in Japan and the country's second largest cosmetics company.

Since the mid 1960s Kao had also successfully used its formidable array of technological, manufacturing and marketing assets to expand into the neighbouring markets of SE Asia. Pitting itself against long established multinationals like Procter & Gamble and Unilever, Kao had made inroads into the detergent, soap and shampoo markets in the region. However, success in these small markets would not make Kao a global player, and since the mid-1980s, Kao had been giving its attention to the problem of how to break into the international markets beyond the region. There, Kao's innovations were being copied and sold by its competitors, not by Kao itself, a situation the company was keen to remedy. But would Kao be able to repeat its domestic success in the US and Europe? As Dr. Maruta knew, the company's ability to compete on a world-wide basis would be measured by its progress in these markets. This, then, was the new challenge to which Kao was dedicated: how to transfer its learning capability, so all-conquering in Japan, to the rest of the world.

The Learning Organization

Kao was founded in 1890 as Kao Soap Company with the prescient motto, 'Cleanliness is the foundation of a prosperous society.' Its objective then was to produce a high-quality soap that was as good as any imported brand, but at a more affordable price for the Japanese consumer, and this principle had guided the development of all Kao's products ever since. In the 1940s Kao had launched the first Japanese laundry detergent, followed in the 1950s by the launch of dishwashing and household detergents. The 1960s had seen an expansion into industrial products to which Kao could apply its technologies in fat and oil science, surface and polymer science. The 1970s and 1980s, coinciding with the presidency of Dr Maruta, had seen the company grow more rapidly than ever in terms of size, sales and profit, with the launching of innovative products

[1] Source: This case was written by Charlotte Butler, Research Assistant, under the supervision of Sumantra Ghoshal, Associate Professor at INSEAD. It is intended to be used as a basis for class discussion rather than to illustrate either effective or ineffective handling of an administrative situation. Unless otherwise indicated, all exhibits are based on information provided by Kao Corporation. Reprinted with the permission of INSEAD. Copyright © 1992 INSEAD-EAC, Fontainebleau, France.

EXHIBIT 1
The Ranking of Japanese
Excellent Companies 1990
(*Nikkei Business* April 9,
1990)

1.	Honda Motors	79.8
2.	IBM-Japan	79.4
3.	SONY	78.4
4.	Matsushita Electrics	74.5
5.	Toshiba	69.9
6.	NEC	69.8
7.	Nissan Motors	69.8
8.	Asahi Beer	67.4
9.	KAO	66.6
10.	Yamato Transportation	66.4
11.	Fuji-Xerox	66.3
12.	Seibu Department Store	66.2
13.	Suntory	65.8
14.	Nomura Security	65.4
15.	NTT (Nippon Telegraph & Telephone)	65.3
16.	Omron	65.1
17.	Ajinomoto	64.3
18.	Canon	64.3
19.	Toyota Motors	63.9
20.	Ohtsuka Medicines	63.8

Note: Points are calculated on the basis of the following criteria:
1. the assessment by Nikkei Business Committee's member corporate originality,
   corporate vision, flexibility, goodness;
2. the result of the researches among consumers.

and the start of new businesses. Between 1982 and 1985 it had successfully diversified into cosmetics, hygiene and floppy disks.

A vertically integrated company, Kao owned many of its raw material sources and had, since the 1960s, built its own sales organization of wholesalers who had exclusive distribution of its products throughout Japan. The 1980s had seen a consistent rise in profits, with sales increasing at roughly 10 percent a year throughout the decade, even in its mature markets (see Exhibit 2). In 1990, sales of Kao products had reached ¥620.4 billion ($3,926.8 million), an 8.4 percent increase on 1989. This total consisted of laundry and cleansing products (40 percent), personal care products (34 percent), hygiene products (13 percent), specialty chemicals and floppy disks (9 percent) and fatty chemicals (4 percent) (see Exhibit 3). Net income had increased by 1.7 percent, from ¥17.5 billion ($110 million) in 1989 to ¥17.8 billion ($112.7 million) in 1990.

Kao dominated most of its markets in Japan. It was the market leader in detergents and shampoo, and was vying for first place in disposable diapers and cosmetics. It had decisively beaten off both foreign and domestic competitors, most famously in two particular instances: the 1983 launch of its disposable diaper brand Merries which, within 12 months, had overtaken the leading brand, Procter & Gamble's Pampers and the 1987 launch of its innovative condensed laundry detergent, the aptly named Attack; as a result of which the market share of Kao's rival, Lion, had declined from 30.9 percent (1986) to 22.8 percent (1988), while in the same period Kao's share had gone from 33.4 percent to 47.5 percent.

The remarkable success of these two products had been largely responsible for Kao's reputation as a creative company. However, while the ability to introduce a continuous stream of innovative, high quality products clearly rested on Kao's repertoire of core competences, the wellspring behind these was less obvious: Kao's integrated learning capability.

EXHIBIT 2
The Trend of Kao's Performance

			Billions of Yen				Millions of US$
Years ended March 31	1985	1986	1987	1988	1989	1990	1990
Net Sales (Increase)	398.1	433.7	464.1	514.4	572.2	620.4	3,926.8
		+8.9%	+7.0%	+10.9%	+11.2%	+8.4%	
Operating Income (Increase)	16.5*	19.853*	31.7	36.5	41.4	43.5	275.5
				+15.2%	+13.5%	+5.1%	
Net Income (Increase)	9.4	10.5	12.9	13.4	17.5	17.8	112.7
		+12.3%	+22.5%	+4.2%	+30.4%	+1.7%	
Total assets	328.3	374.4	381.0	450.4	532.3	572.8	3,625.5
Total shareholders' equity	114.4	150.9	180.2	210.7	233.8	256.6	1,624.1

*non-consolidated
Note: The US dollar amounts are translated, for convenience only, at the rate of ¥156 = $1, the approximate exchange rate prevailing on March 30, 1990.

This learning motif had been evident from the beginning. The Nagase family, founders of Kao, had modeled some of Kao's operations, management and production facilities on those of United States corporations and in the 1940s, following his inspection of United States and European soap and chemical plants, Tomiro Nagase II had reorganized Kao's production facilities, advertising and planning departments on the basis of what he had learned. As the company built up its capabilities, this process of imitation and adaptation had evolved into one of innovation until, under Dr Maruta, a research chemist who joined Kao in the 1930s and became president in 1971, 'Distinct creativity became a policy objective in all our areas of research, production and sales, supporting our determination to explore and develop our own fields of activity.'

The Paperweight Organization

The organizational structure within which Kao managers and personnel worked embodied the philosophy of Dr Maruta's mentor, the 7th century statesman Prince Shotoku, whose Consitution was designed to foster the spirit of harmony, based on the principle of absolute equality; 'Human beings can live only by the Universal Truth, and in their dignity of living,

all are absolutely equal.' Article 1 of his Constitution stated that 'If everyone discusses on an equal footing, there is nothing that cannot be resolved.'

Accordingly, Kao was committed to the principles of equality, individual initiative and the rejection of authoritarianism. Work was viewed as 'something fluid and flexible like the functions of the human body,' therefore the organization was designed to 'run as a flowing system' which would stimulate interaction and the spread of ideas in every direction and at every level (see Exhibit 4). To allow creativity and initiative full rein, and to demonstrate that hierarchy was merely an expedient that should not become a constraint, organizational boundaries and titles were abolished.

Dr Maruta likened this flat structure to an old fashioned brass paperweight, in contrast to the pyramid structure of Western organizations: 'In the pyramid, only the person at the top has all the information. Only he can see the full picture, others cannot . . . The Kao organization is like the paperweight on my desk. It is flat. There is a small handle in the middle, just as we have a few senior people. But all information is shared horizontally, not filtered vertically. Only then can you have equality. And equality is the basis for trust and commitment.'

This organization practiced what Kao

EXHIBIT 3
Review of Operations

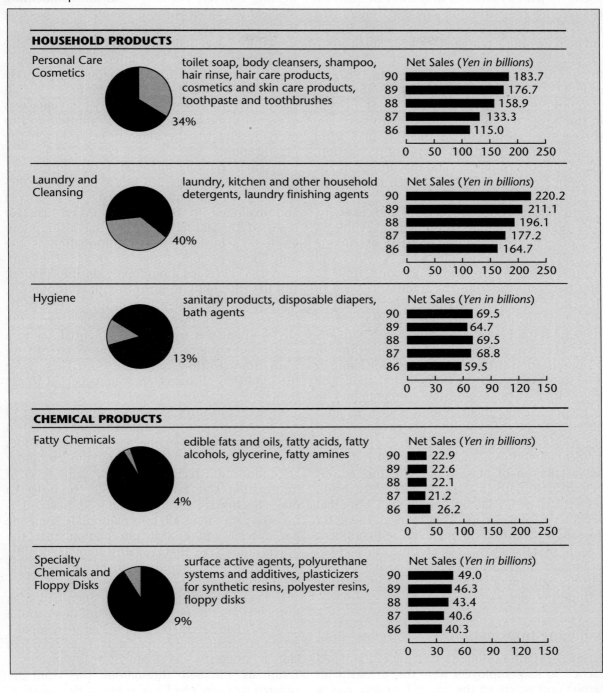

HOUSEHOLD PRODUCTS

Personal Care
Cosmetics

toilet soap, body cleansers, shampoo,
hair rinse, hair care products,
cosmetics and skin care products,
toothpaste and toothbrushes

34%

Net Sales (*Yen in billions*)

Year	
90	183.7
89	176.7
88	158.9
87	133.3
86	115.0

0 50 100 150 200 250

Laundry and
Cleansing

laundry, kitchen and other household
detergents, laundry finishing agents

40%

Net Sales (*Yen in billions*)

Year	
90	220.2
89	211.1
88	196.1
87	177.2
86	164.7

0 50 100 150 200 250

Hygiene

sanitary products, disposable diapers,
bath agents

13%

Net Sales (*Yen in billions*)

Year	
90	69.5
89	64.7
88	69.5
87	68.8
86	59.5

0 30 60 90 120 150

CHEMICAL PRODUCTS

Fatty Chemicals

edible fats and oils, fatty acids, fatty
alcohols, glycerine, fatty amines

4%

Net Sales (*Yen in billions*)

Year	
90	22.9
89	22.6
88	22.1
87	21.2
86	26.2

0 50 100 150 200 250

Specialty
Chemicals and
Floppy Disks

surface active agents, polyurethane
systems and additives, plasticizers
for synthetic resins, polyester resins,
floppy disks

9%

Net Sales (*Yen in billions*)

Year	
90	49.0
89	46.3
88	43.4
87	40.6
86	40.3

0 30 60 90 120 150

referred to as 'biological self control.' As the body reacted to pain by sending help from all quarters, 'If anything goes wrong in one department, the other departments should know automatically and help without having to be asked.' Small group activities were encouraged in order to link ideas or discuss issues of immediate concern. In 1987, for example, to resolve the problem of why Kao's Toyohashi factory could achieve only 50 percent of the projected production of Nivea cream, workers there voluntarily formed a small team consisting of the people in charge of production, quality, electricity, process and machinery. By the following year, production had been raised to 95 percent of the target.

In pursuit of greater efficiency and creativity, Kao's organization has continued to evolve. A 1987 programme introduced a system of working from home for sales people, while another will eventually reduce everyone's working time to 1800 hours a year from the traditional level of 2100 hours. Other programmes have aimed at either introducing information technology or re-vitalizing certain areas. 1971 saw the 'CCR move-ment,' aimed at reducing the workforce through computerization. 'Total Quality Control' came in 1974, followed in 1981 by Office Automation. The 1986 'Total Cost Reduction' programme to restructure management resources evolved into the 'Total Creative Revolution' designed to encou-rage a more innovative approach. For example, five people who were made redundant following the installation of new equipment, formed, on their own initiative, a special task force team, and visisted a US factory which had imported machinery from Japan. They stayed there for three months until local engineers felt confident enough to take charge. Over time, this group became a flying squad of specialists, available to help foreign production plants get over their teething troubles.

Managing Information

Just as Dr Maruta's Buddha was the enlightened teacher, so Kao employees were the 'priests' who learned and practiced the truth. Learning was 'a frame of mind, a daily matter,' and truth was sought through discussions, by testing and inves-tigating concrete business ideas until something was learned, often without the manager realizing it. This was 'the quintessence of information . . . something we actually see with our own eyes and feel with our bodies.' This internalized intuition, which coincides with the Zen Buddhist phrase *kangyo ichijo*, was the goal Dr Maruta set for all Kao managers. In reaching it, every individual was expected to be a coach; both to himself and to everyone else, whether above or below him in the organization.

Their training material was information. Information was regarded not as something life-less to be stored, but as knowledge to be shared and exploited to the utmost. Every manager repeated Dr Maruta's fundamental assumption: 'in today's business world, information is the only source of competitive advantage. The com-pany that develops a monopoly on information, and has the ability to learn from it continuously, is the company that will win, irrespective of its business.' Every piece of information form the environment was treated as a potential key to a new positioning, a new product. What can we learn from it? How can we use it? These were the questions all managers were expected to ask themselves at all times.

Access to information was another facet of Kao's commitment to egalitarianism: as described by Kuroyanagi, 'In Kao, the "classfied" stamp does not exist.' Through the development of computer communication technologies, the same level of information was available to all: 'In order to make it effective to discuss subjects freely, it is necessary to share all information. If someone has special and crucial information that the others don't have, that is against human equality, and will deprive us and the organization of real creativity.'

Every director and most salesmen had a fax in their homes to receive results and news, and a bi-weekly Kao newspaper kept the entire company informed about competitors' moves, new product launches, overseas development or key meetings. Terminals installed throughout the company ensured that any employee could, if they wished, retrieve data on sales records of any product for any of Kao's numerous outlets, or product development at their own or other branches. The latest findings from each of Kao's research laboratories were available for all to see, as were the details of the previous day's production and inventory at every Kao plant. 'They can even,' said Dr. Maruta, 'check up on the president's expense account.' He believed that the increase in creativity resulting from this pooling of data outweighed the risk of leaks. In any case, the prevailing environment of *omnes flux* meant that things moved so quickly 'leaked information instantly becomes obsolete.'

The task of Kao manager,s therefore, was to take information directly from the competitive environment, process it and, by adding value, transform it into knowledge or wisdom.

Digesting information from the market place in this way enabled the organization to maintain empathy with this fast moving environment. The emphasis was always on learning and on the future, not on following an advance plan based on previous experience. 'Past wisdom must not be a constraint, but something to be challenged,' Dr Maruta constantly urged. Kao managers were discouraged from making any historical comparisons. 'We cannot talk about history,' said Mr Takayama, Overseas Planning Director. 'If we talk about the past, they (the top management) immediately become unpleasant.' The emphasis was rather, what had they learnt today that would be useful tomorrow? 'Yesterday's success formula is often today's obsolete dogma. We must continuously challenge the

EXHIBIT 4
Organizational Structure

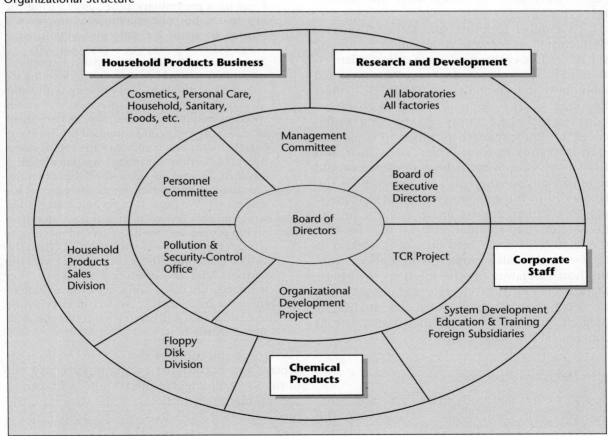

past so that we can renew ourselves each day,' said Dr Maruta.

'Learning through cooperation' was the slogan of Kao's research and development (R&D); the emphasis was on information exchange, both within and outside the department, and sharing 'to motivate and activate.' Glycerine Ether, for example, an emulsifier important for the production of Sofina's screening cream, was the product of joint work among three Kao laboratories. Research results were communicated to everyone in the company through the IT system, in order to build a close networking organization. Top management and researchers met at regular R&D conferences, where presentations were made by the researchers themselves, not their section managers. 'Open Space' meetings were offered every week by the R&D division, and people from any part of the organization could participate in discussions on current research projects.

A number of formal and informal systems were created to promote communication among the research scientists working in different laboratories. For example, results from Paris were fed daily into the computer in Tokyo. The most important of these communication mechanisms, however, were the monthly R&D working conferences for junior researchers which took place at each laboratory in turn. When it was their own laboratory's turn to act as host, researchers could nominate anyone they wished to meet, from any laboratory in the company, to attend that meeting. In addition, any researcher could nominate him or herself to attend meetings if they felt that the discussions could help their own work, or if they wanted to talk separately with someone from the host laboratory. At the meetings, which Dr Maruta often attended to argue and discuss issues in detail, researchers reported on studies in progress, and those present offered advice from commercial and academic perspectives.

The Decision Process

'In Kao, we try collectively to direct the accumulation of individual wisdom at serving the customer.' This was how Dr Maruta explained the company's approach to the decision process. At Kao, no one owned an idea. Ideas were to be shared in order to enhance their value and achieve enlightenment in order to make the right decision. The prevailing principle was *tataki-dai*; present your ideas to others at 80 percent completion so that they could criticize or contribute before the idea became a proposal. Takayama likened this approach to heating an iron and testing it on one's arm to see if it was hot enough. 'By inviting all the relevant actors to join in with forging the task,' he said, 'we achieve *zoawase*; a common perspective or view.' The individual was thus a strategic factor, to be linked with others in a union of individual wisdom and group strategy.

Fumio Kuroyanagi provided an illustration. Here is the process by which a problem involving a joint venture partner, in which he was the key person, was resolved:

> I put up a preliminary note summarizing the key issues, but not making any proposals. I wanted to share the data and obtain other views before developing a proposal fully . . . This note was distributed to legal, international controllers to read . . . then in the meeting we talked about the facts and came up with some ideas on how to proceed. Then members of this meeting requested some top management time. All the key people attended this meeting, together with one member of the top management. No written document was circulated in advance. Instead, we described the situation, our analysis and action plans. He gave us his comments. We came to a revised plan. I then wrote up this revised plan and circulated it to all the people, and we had a second meeting at which everyone agreed with the plan. Then the two of us attended the actual meeting with the partner. After the meeting I debriefed other members, discussed and circulated a draft of the letter to the partner which, after everyone else had seen it and given their comments, was signed by my boss.

The cross fertilization of ideas to aid the decision process was encouraged by the physical lay out of the Kao building. On the 10th floor, known as the top management floor, sat the chairman, the president, four executive vice presidents and a pool of secretaries (see Exhibit 5). A large part of the floor was open space, with one large conference table and two smaller ones, and chairs, blackboards and overhead projectors strewn around: this was known as the Decision Space, where all discussions with and among the top management took place. Anyone passing, including the president, could sit down and join in any discussion on any topic, however briefly. This layout was duplicated on the other floors, in the laboratories and in the workshop. Workplaces looked like large rooms; there were no partitions, but again tables and chairs for spontaneous or planned discussions at which everyone contributed as equals. Access was free to all, and any manager could thus find himself sitting round the table next to the president, who was often seen waiting in line in Kao's Tokyo cafeteria.

The management process, thus, was transparent and open, and leadership was practiced in daily behaviour rather than by memos and formal meetings. According to Takayama, top management 'emphasizes that 80 percent of its time must be spent on communication, and the remaining 20 percent on decision making.' While top mangement regularly visited other floors to join in discussions, anyone attending a meeting on the 10th floor then had to pass on what had happened to the rest of his colleagues.

Information Technology

Information Technology (IT) was one of Kao's most effective competitive weapons, and an integral part of its organizational systems and management processes. In 1982, Kao made an agreement to use Japan Information Service Co's VAN (Value Added Networks) for communication between Kao's head office, its sales companies and its large wholesalers. Over time, Kao built its own VAN, through which it connected upstream and downstream via information linkages. In 1986 the company added DRESS, a new network linking Kao and the retail stores receiving its support.

The objective of this networking capability was to achieve the complete fusion and interaction of Kao's marketing, production and R&D departments. Fully integrated information systems controlled the flow of materials and

products; from the production planning of raw materials to the distribution of the final products to local stores: no small task in a company dealing with over 1,500 types of raw materials from 500 different suppliers, and producing over 550 types of final products for up to 300,000 retail stores.

Kao's networks enabled it to maintain a symbiotic relationship with its distributors, the *hansha*. Developed since 1966, the Kao hansha (numbering 30 by 1990) were independent wholesalers who handled only Kao products. They dealt directly with 100,000 retail stores out of 300,000, and about 60 percent of Kao's products passed through them. The data terminals installed in the hansha offices provided Kao with up-to-date product movement and market information, which was easily accessible for analysis.

Kao's Logistics Information System (LIS) consisted of a sales planning system, an inventory control system and an on-line supply system. It linked Kao headquarters, factories, the hansha and Logistics centres by networks, and dealt with ordering, inventory, production and sales data (see Exhibit 6). Using the LIS, each hansha sales person projected sales plans on the basis of a head office campaign plan, an advertising plan and past market trends. These were corrected and adjusted at corporate level, and a final sales plan was produced each month. From this plan, daily production schedules were then drawn up for each factory and product. The system would also calculate the optimal machine load, and the number of people required. An on-line supply system calculated the appropriate amount of factory stocks and checked the hansha inventory. The next day's supply was then computed and automatically ordered from the factory.

A computerized ordering system enabled stores to receive and deliver products within 24 hours of placing an order. Through a POS (point of sale) terminal, installed in the retail store as a cash register and connected to the Kao VAN, information on sales and orders was transmitted to the hansha's computer. Via this, orders from local stores, adjusted according to the amount of their inventory, were transmitted to Kao's Logistics centre, which then supplied the product.

Two other major support systems, KAP and

EXHIBIT 5
Layout of Kao Offices

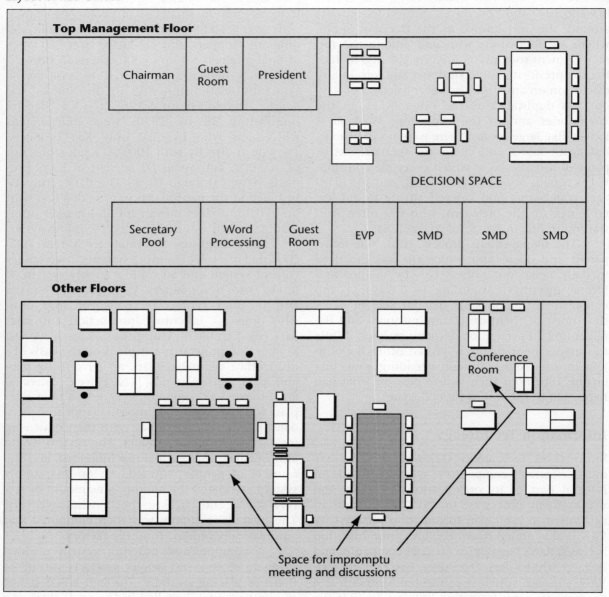

RRS, respectively helped the wholesale houses in ordering, stocking and accounting, and worked with Kao's nine distribution information service companies: the Ryutsu Joho Service Companies (RJSs). Each RJS had about 500 customers, mainly small and medium-sized supermarkets who were too small to access real-time information by themselves. The RJSs were essentially consulting outfits, whose mandate was to bring the benefits of information available in Kao VAN to those stores that could not access the information directly. They guided store owners by offering analysis of

EXHIBIT 6
Kao's Information Network (*Nikkei Computer* Oct. 9, 1989)

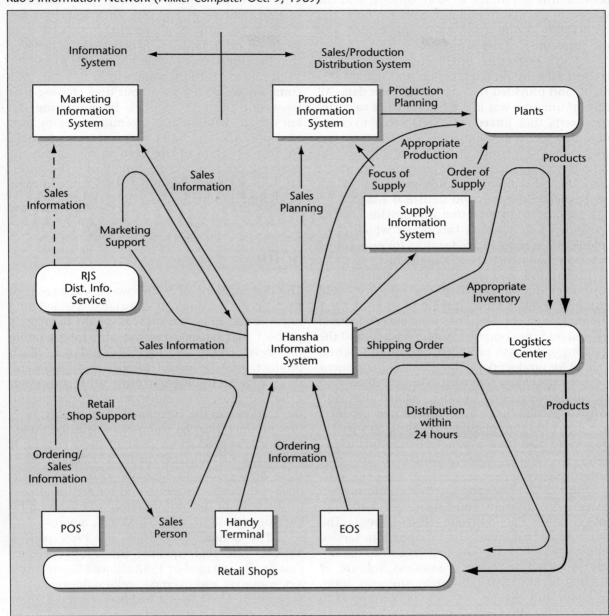

customer buying trends, shelf space planning and ways of improving the store's sales, profitability and customer service. The owner of one such store commented: 'A Kao sales person comes to see us two or three times a week, and we chat about many topics. To me, he is both a good friend and a good consultant . . . I can see Kao's philosophy, the market trend and the progress of R&D holistically through this person.' According to Dr Maruta, the RJSs embodied Kao's principle of the information advantage: their purpose was to provide this advantage to store owners, and the success of the RJSs in building up the volume and profitability of the stores was ample evidence of the correctness of the principle.

Kao's Marketing Intelligence System (MIS) tracked sales by product, region and market segment, and provided raw market research data. All this information was first sifted for clues to customer needs, then linked with R&D 'seeds' to create new products. New approaches to marketing were sought by applying artificial intelligence to various topics, including advertising and media planning, sales promotion, new product development, market research and statistical analysis.

Additional information was provided by the Consumer Life Research Laboratory which operated ECHO, a sophisticated system for responding to telephone queries about Kao products. In order to understand and respond immediately to a customer's question, each phone operator could instantly access a video dispaly of each of Kao's 500 plus products. Enquiries were also coded and entered into the computer system on-line, and the resulting data base provided one of the richest sources for product development or enhancement ideas. By providing Kao with 'a direct window on the consumer's mind,' ECHO enabled the company to 'predict the performance of new products and fine tune formulations, labelling and packaging.' Kao also used a panel of monitor households to track how products fitted into consumers' lives.

In 1989, Kao separated its information systems organization and established a distinct entity called Kao Software Development. The aim was to penetrate the information service industry which, according to Japan Information, was projected to reach a business volume of ¥12,000 billion ($80 billion) by the year 2000. In 1989, the market was ¥3,000 billion ($20 billion). One IBM sales engineer forecast, 'by 2000, Kao will have become one of our major competitors, because they know how to develop information technology, and how to combine it with real organization systems.'

In 1989 Kao's competitors, including Lion and Procter & Gamble, united to set up Planet Logistics, a system comparable to Kao's VAN. Through it, they aimed to achieve the same information richness as Kao. But Dr Maruta was not worried by this development. Irrespective of whatever information they collected, he believed that the competitors would not be able to add the value and use it in the same way as Kao did: 'As a company we do not spend our time chasing after what our rivals do. Rather, by mustering our knowledge, wisdom and ingenuity to study how to supply the consumer with superior products, we free ourselves of the need to care about the moves of our competitors. Imitation is the sincerest form of flattery, but unless they can add value to all that information, it will be of little use.'

Sofina

The development of Sofina was a microcosm of Kao's *modus operandi*. It illustrated the learning organization in action since it sought to create a product that satisfied the five principles guiding the development of any new offering: 'Each product must be useful to society. It must use innovative technology. It must offer consumers value. We must be confident we really understand the market and the consumers. And, finally, each new product must be compatible with the trade.' Until a new product satisfied all these criteria, it would not be launched on the market. At every stage during Sofina's creation, ideas were developed, criticized, discussed and refined or altered in the light of new information and learning by everyone involved, from Dr Maruta down.

The Sofina story began in 1965 with a 'vision.' The high quality, innovative product that finally emerged in 1982 allowed Kao to enter a new market and overtake well-established competitors. By 1990, Sofina had become the highest selling brand of cosmetics in Japan for most items except lipsticks.

The Vision

The vision, according to Mr Daimaru (the first director of Sofina marketing), was simple: to help customers avoid the appearance of wrinkles on their skin for as long as possible. From this vision an equally simple question arose. 'What makes wrinkles appear?' Finding the answer was the spring that set the Kao organization into motion.

Kao's competence until then had been in household and toiletry personal care products. However, Kao had long supplied raw materials for the leading cosmetics manufacturers in Japan, and had a technological competence in fats and soap that could, by cross pollination, be adapted to research on the human skin. Accordingly, the efforts of Kao's R&D laboratories were directed towards skin research, and the results used in the company's existing businesses such as Nivea or Azea, then sold in joint venture with Beiersdorf. From these successes came the idea for growth that steered the development of Sofina.

The Growth Idea

The idea was to produce a new, high quality cosmetic that gave real vlaue at a reasonable price. During the 1960s, there was a strong perception in the Japanese cosmetics industry that the more expensive the product, the better it was. This view was challenged by Dr Maruta, whose travels had taught him that good skin care products sold in the United States or Europe were not as outrageously expensive. Yet in Japan, even with companies like Kao supplying high quality raw materials at a low price, the end product was still beyond the reach of ordinary women at ¥10–20,000.

As a supplier of raw materials, Dr Maruta was aware of how well these products performed. He also knew that though cosmetics' prices were rising sharply, little was being spent on improving the products themselves, and that customers were paying for an expensive image. Was this fair, or good for the customer? Kao, he knew, had the capacity to supply high quality raw materials at low cost, and a basic research capability. Intensive research to develop new toiletry goods had led to the discovery of a technology for modifying the surface of powders, which could be applied to the

development of cosmetics. Why not use these assets to develop a new, high quality, reasonably priced product, in keeping with Kao's principles?

To enter the new market would mean a heavy investment in research and marketing, with no guarantee that their product would be accepted. However, it was decided to go ahead; the product would be innovative and, against the emotional appeal of the existing competition in terms of packaging and image, its positioning would embody Kao's scientific approach.

This concept guided the learning process as Sofina was developed. It was found that the integration of Kao's unique liquid crystal emulsification technology and other newly developed materials proved effective in maintaining a 'healthy and beautiful skin.' This led Kao to emphasize skin care, as opposed to the industry's previous focus on make-up only. All the research results from Kao's skin diagnosis and dermatological testing were poured into the new product and, as Dr Tsutsumi of the Tokyo Research Laboratory recalled, in pursuing problems connected with the product, new solutions emerged. For example, skin irritation caused by the new chemical was solved by developing MAP, a low irritant, and PSL, a moisturiser. By 1980, most of the basic research work had been done. Six cosmetics suitable for the six basic skin types had been developed, though all under the Sofina name.

During this stage, Kao's intelligence collectors were sent out to explore and map the new market environment. Information on products, pricing, positioning, the competition and above all, the customers, was analyzed and digested by the Sofina marketing and R&D teams, and by Kao's top management. Again and again Dr Maruta asked the same two questions: How would the new product be received? Was it what customers wanted?

The Growth Process

Test marketing began in September 1980, in the Shizuoka prefecture, and was scheduled to last for a year. Shizuoka was chosen because it represented three percent of the national market and an average social mix; neither too rich nor too poor, neither too rural nor too urban. Its media isolation meant that television advertisements could be targeted to the local population, and no one outside would question why the product was not available elsewhere. The local paper also gave good coverage. In keeping with Kao's rule that 'the concept of a new product is that of its advertising,' the Sofina advertisements were reasoned and scientific, selling a function rather than an image.

Sofina was distributed directly to the retail stores through the Sofina Cosmetics Company, established to distinguish Sofina from Kao's conventional detergent business and avoid image blurring. No mention was made of Kao. Sofina's managers found, however, that retailers did not accept Sofina immediately, but put it on the waiting list for display along with other new cosmetics. The result was that by October 1980, Kao had only succeeded in finding 200 points of sale, against an object of 600. Then, as the real parentage of Sofia leaked out, the attitude among retailers changed, and the Sofina stand was given the best position in the store. This evidence of Kao's credibility, together with the company's growing confidence in the quality and price of the product, led to a change of strategy. The 30-strong sales force was instructed to put the Kao name first and, by November, 600 outlets had been found.

Sofina's subsequent development was guided by feedback from the market. Direct distribution enabled Kao to retain control of the business and catch customer responses to the product at first hand. To Mr Masashi Kuga, Director of Kao's Marketing Research Department, such information 'has clear added value, and helps in critical decision making.' During the repeated test marketing of Sofina, Kao's own market research service, formed in 1973 to ensure a high quality response from the market with the least possible distortion, measured the efficacy of sampling and helped decide on the final marketing mix. This activity was usually supported by 'concept testing, focus group discussions, plus product acceptance research.' Mr Daimaru visited the test market twice or three times each month and talked to consumers directly. Dr Maruta did the same.

Every piece of information and all results were shared by the Sofina team, R&D, Kao's top management, corporate marketing and sales managers. Discussions on Sofina's progress were attended by all of these managers, everyone contributing ideas about headline copy or other issues on an equal basis. Wives and friends were given samples and their reactions were fed back to the team.

From the reactions of customers and stores, Kao learned that carrying real information in the advertisements about the quality of the product had been well received, despite differing from the normal emphasis on fancy packaging. This they could never have known from their detergent business. Another finding was the importance of giving a full explanation of the product with samples, and of a skin analysis before recommending the most suitable product rather than trying to push the brand indiscriminately. They also learned the value of listening to the opinion of the store manager's wife who, they discovered, often had the real managing power, particularly for cosmetics products.

Decisions were implemented immediately. For example, the decision to improve the design for the sample package was taken at 3.30 P.M., and by 6.30 P.M. the same day the engineer in the factory had begun re-designing the shape of the bottle.

The results of this test marketing, available to the whole company, confirmed the decision to go ahead with Sofina. Kao was satisfied that the product would be accepted nationally, though it might take some time. A national launch was planned for the next year. Even at this stage, however, Mr Maruta was still asking whether consumers and retail store owners really liked Sofina.

The Learning Extended

Sofina finally went on nationwide sale in October 1982. However, the flow of learning and intelligence gathering continued via the hansha and MIS. Kao, the hansha, the retailers and Sofina's customers formed a chain, along which that was a free, two-way flow of information. The learning was then extended to develop other products, resulting in production of the complete Sofina range of beauty care. In 1990, the range covered the whole market, from basic skin care to make-up cosmetics and perfumes.

In fact, the product did not achieve real success until after 1983. Dr Tsutsumi dated it from the introduction of the foundation cream which, he recalled, also faced teething problems. The test result from the panel was not good; it was too different from existing products and was sticky on application. Kao, however, knowing it was a superior product that lasted longer, preserved and used their previous experience to convert the stickiness into a strength: the product was repositioned as 'the longest lasting foundation that does not disappear with sweat.'

In the early 1980s, while market growth was only two to three percent, sales of Sofina products increased at the rate of 30 percent every year. In 1990, sales amounted to ¥55 billion, and Kao held 15.6 percent of the cosmetic market behind Shiseido and Kanebo, though taken individually, Sofina brands topped every product category except lipsticks.

Within Japan, Sofina was sold through 12,700 outlets. According to Mr Nakanishi, director of the Cosmetics Division, the marketing emphasis was by that time being redirected from heavy advertising of the product to counselling at the point of sale. Kao was building up a force of beauty counsellors to educate the public on the benefits of Sofina products. A Sofina store in Tokyo was also helping to develop hair care and cosmetics products. A Sofina newspaper had been created which salesmen received by fax, along with the preveious month's sales and inventory figures.

Knowledge gathered by the beauty advisers working in the Sofina shops was exploited for the development of the next set of products. Thus, Sofina 'ultra-violet' care, which incorporated skin lotion, uv care and foundation in one, was positioned to appeal to busy women and advertised as 'one step less.' The Sofina cosmetics beauty care consultation system offered advice by phone, at retail shops or by other means to consumers who made enquiries. From their ques-

tions, clues were sought to guide new product development.

A staff of Field Companions visited the retail stores to get direct feedback on sales. Every outlet was visited once a month, when the monitors discussed Kao products with store staff, advised on design displays and even helped clean up. Dr Maruta himself maintained an active interest. Mr Kuroyanagi described how Dr Maruta recently 'came down to our floor' to report that while visiting a certain town, he had 'found a store selling Sofina products, and a certain shade sample was missing from the stand.' He asked that the store be checked and the missing samples supplied as soon as possible.

Despite Sofina's success, Kao was still not satisfied. 'To be really successful, developing the right image is important. We've lagged behind on this, and we must improve.'

As the Sofina example showed, in its domestic base Kao was an effective and confident company, renowned for its ability to produce high quality, technologically advanced products at relatively low cost. Not surprising then, that since the 1960s it had turned its thoughts to becoming an important player on the larger world stage. But could the learning organization operate effectively outside Japan? Could Kao transfer its learning capability into a very different environment such as the US or Europe, where it would lack the twin foundations of infrastructure and human resource? Or would internationalization demand major adjustments to its way of operating?

Kao International

When the first cake of soap was produced in 1890, the name 'Kao' was stamped in both Chinese characters and Roman letters in preparation for the international market. A century later, the company was active in 50 countries but, except for the small neighbouring markets of South East Asia, had not achieved a real breakthrough. Despite all its investments, commitment and efforts over 25 years, Kao remained only 'potentially' a significant global competitor. In 1988, only 10 percent of its total sales was derived from overseas business, and 70 percent of this international volume was earned in SE Asia. As a result, internationalization was viewed by the company as its next key strategic challenge. Dr Maruta made his ambitions clear; 'Procter and Gamble, Unilever and L'Oréal are our competitors. We cannot avoid fighting in the 1990s.' The challenge was to make those words a reality.

The Strategic Infrastructure

Kao's globalization was based not on a company-wide strategy, but on the product division system. Each product division developed its own strategy for international expansion and remained responsible for its world-wide results. Consequently, the company's business portfolio and strategic infrastructure varied widely from market to market.

South East Asia   As Exhibit 7 illustrates, Kao had been building a platform for production and marketing throughout South East Asia since 1964, when it created its first overseas subsidiary in Thailand. By 1990 this small initial base had been expanded, mainly through joint ventures, and the company had made steady progress in these markets. The joint ventures in Hong Kong and Singapore sold only Kao's consumer products, while the others both manufactured and marketed them.

One of Kao's biggest international battles was for control of the Asian detergent, soap and shampoo markets, against rivals like P&G and Unilever. In the Taiwanese detergent market, where Unilever was the long established leader with 50 percent market share, Kao's vanguard product was the biological detergent, *Attack*. Launched in 1988, Attack increased Kao's market share from 17 percent to 22 percent. Subsequently, Kao decided on local production, both to continue serving the local market and for export to Hong Kong and Singapore. Its domestic rival, Lion (stationary at 17 percent) shortly followed suit. In Hong Kong, Kao was the market leader with 30 percent share and in Singapore, where Colgate-Palmolive led with 30 percent, had increased its share from five percent

to 10 percent. Unilever, P&G and Colgate-Palmolive had responded to Kao's moves by putting in more human resources, and consolidating their local bases.

In Indonesia, where Unilever's historic links again made it strong, Kao, Colgate-Palmolive and P&G competed for the second position. In the Philippines, Kao had started local production of shampoo and liquid soap in 1989, while in Thailand it had doubled its local facilities in order to meet increasing demand. To demonstrate its commitment to the Asian market where it was becoming a major player, Kao had established its Asian headquarters in Singapore. In that market, Kao's disposable diaper Merry had a 20 percent share, while its Merit shampoo was the market leader.

North America

Step 1 – Joint venture   In 1976, Kao had embarked on two joint ventures with Colgate-Palmolive Company, first to market hair care products in the US, and later to develop new oral hygiene products for Japan. The potential for synergy seemed enormous; Colgate-Palmolive was to provide the marketing expertise and distribution infrastructure, Kao would contribute the technical expertise to produce a high quality product for the top end of the United States market.

In 1977 there was a considerable exchange of personnel and technology, and a new shampoo was specially developed by Kao for the United States consumer. Despite the fact that tests in three major United States cities, using Colgate-Palmolive's state-of-the-art market research methods, showed poor market share potential, the product launch went ahead. The forecasts turned out to be correct, and the product was dropped after 10 months due to Colgate-Palmolive's reluctance to continue. A Kao manager explained the failure thus:

> First, the product was not targeted to the proper consumer group. High-price, high-end products were not appropriate for a novice and as yet unsophisticated producer like us. Second, the United States side believed in the result of the market research too seriously and

EXHIBIT 7
The History of Kao's Internationalization

	Company	Year	Capital	Main Products
ASIA				
Taiwan	Taiwan Kao Co. Ltd	1964	90	detergent, soap
Thailand	Kao Industrila Co. Ltd	1964	70	hair care products
Singapore	Kao Private Ltd	1965	100	sales of soap, shampoo, detergents
Hong Kong	Kao Ltd	1970	100	sales of soap, shampoo, detergents
Malaysia	Kao Ptc. Ltd	1973	45	hair care products
Philippines	Pilippinas Kao Inc.	1977	70	fats and oils
Indonesia	P.T. PoleKao	1977	74	surfactants
Philippines	Kao Inc.	1979	70	hair care products
Indonesia	P.T. Dino Indonesia Industrial Ltd	1985	50	hair care products
Malaysia	Fatty Chemical Sdn. Bdn.	1988	70	alcohol
Singapore	Kao South-East Asia Headquarters	1988		
Philippines	Kao Co. Philippines Laboratory			
NORTH AMERICA				
Mexico	Qumi-Kao S.A. de C.V.	1975	20	fatty amines
	Bitumex	1979	49	asphal
Canada	Kao-Didak Ltd	1983	89	floppy disk
USA	Kao Corporation of Americal (KCOA)	1986	100	sales of household goods
	High Point Chemical	1987	100 (KCOA)	ingredients
	Kao Infosystems Company	1988	100 (KCOA)	duplication of software
	The Andrew Jergens	1988	100 (KCOA)	hair care products
USA	KCOA Los Angeles Laboratories			
EUROPE				
W. Germany	Kao Corporation GmbH	1986	100 (KCG)	sales of household goods
	Kao Perfekta GmbH	1986	80 (KCG)	toners for copier
	Guhl Ikebana GmbH	1986	50 (KCG)	hair care products
Spain	Kao Corporation S.A.	1987	100	surfactants
W. Germany	Goldwell AG	1989	100	cosmetics
France	Kao Co. S.A. Paris Laboratories			
Spain	Kao Co. S.A. Barcelona Laboratories			
W. Germany	Kao Co. GmbH Berlin Laboratories			

did not attempt a second try . . . Third, it is essentially very difficult to penetrate a market like the shampoo market. Our partner expected too much short-term success. Fourth, the way the two firms decided on strategy was totally different. We constantly adjust our strategy flexibly. They never start without a concrete and fixed strategy. We could not wait for them.

The alliance was dissolved in 1985. However, Kao had learned some valuable lessons about United States marketing methods, Western lifestyles and, most of all, about the limitations of using joint ventures as a means of breaking into the United States market.

Step 2 – Acquisition In 1988, Kao had made three acquisitions. In May, it bought the Andrew Jergens Company, a Cincinnati soap, body lotion and shampoo maker, for $350 million. To acquire Jergens' extensive marketing know-how and established distribution channels, Kao beat off 70 other bidders, including Beiersdorf and Colgate-Palmolive, and paid 40 percent more than the expected price. Since then, Kao has invested heavily in the company, building a new multi-million dollar research centre and doubling Jergens' research team to over 50. Cincinnati was the home town of P&G, who have since seen Jergens market Kao's bath preparations in the United States.

High Point Chemical Corporation of America, an industrial goods producer, was also acquired in 1988. As Kao's United States chemical manufacturing arm, it had since begun 'an aggressive expansion of its manufacturing facilities and increased its market position.' The third acquisition, Info Systems (Sentinel) produced application products in the field of information technology.

In Canada, Kao owned 87 percent of Kao-Didak, a floppy disk manufacturer it bought out in 1986. A new plant, built in 1987, started producing 3.5 inch and 5.25 inch diskettes, resulting in record sales of $10 million that same year. Kao viewed floppy disks as the spearhead of its thrust into the United States market. As Mr Kuroyanagi explained: 'This product penetrates the US market easily. Our superior technology makes it possible to meet strict requirements for both quantity and quality. Our experience in producing specific chemicals for the floppy disk gives us a great competitive edge.' In what represented a dramatic move for a Japanese company, Kao relocated its world-wide head office for the floppy disk business to the United States, partly because of Kao's comparatively strong position there (second behind Sony) but also because it was by far the biggest market in the world. The United States headquarters was given complete strategic freedom to develop the business globally. Under the direction of this office a plant was built in Spain.

Europe Within Europe, Kao had built a limited presence in Germany, Spain and France. In Germany, it had established a research laboratory, and through its 1979 joint venture with Beiersdorf to develop and market hair care products, gained a good knowledge of the German market. The strategic position of this business was strengthened in 1989 by the acquisition of a controlling interest in Goldwell AG, one of Germany's leading suppliers of hair and skin care products to beauty salons. From studying Goldwell's network of beauty salons across Europe, Kao expected to expand its knowledge in order to be able to develop and market new products in Europe.

Kao's French subsidiary, created in January 1990, marketed floppy disks, skin toner and the Sofina range of cosmetics. The research laboratory established in Paris that same year was given the leading role in developing perfumes to meet Kao's world-wide requirements.

Kao's vanguard product in Europe was Sofina, which was positioned as a high quality, medium priced product. Any Japanese connection had been removed to avoid giving the brand a cheap image. While Sofina was produced and packaged in Japan, extreme care was taken to ensure that it shared a uniform global positioning and image in all the national markets in Europe. It was only advertised in magazines like Vogue, and sales points were carefully selected; for example in France, Sofina was sold only in he prestigious Paris department store, Galeries Lafayette.

Organizational Capability

Organizationally, Kao's international operations were driven primarily along the product division axis. Each subsidiary had a staff in charge of each product who reported to the product's head office, either directly or through a regional product manager. For example, the manager in charge of Sofina in Spain reported to the French office where the regional manager responsible for Sofina was located, and he in turn reported to the Director of the Divisional HQ in Japan. Each subsidiary was managed by Japanese expatriate managers, since Kao's only foreign resource was provided by its acquired companies. Thus, the German companies remained under the management of its original directors. However, some progress was made towards localization; in Kao Spain (250 employees) there were 'only six to ten Japanese, not necessarily in management.' Kao's nine overseas R&D laboratories were each strongly connected to both the product headquarters and laboratories in Japan through frequent meetings and information exchange.

Mr Takayama saw several areas that needed to be strengthened before Kao could become an effective global compeitior. Kao, he believed 'was a medium-sized company grown large.' It lacked international experience, had fewer human resource assets, especially in top management and, compared with competitors like P&G and Unilever, had far less accumulated international knowledge and experience of Western markets and consumers. 'These two companies know how to run a business in the West and have well established market research techniques, whereas the Westernization of the Japanese lifestyle has only occurred in the last 20 years,' he explained. 'There are wide differences between East and West in, for example, bathing habits, that the company has been slow to comprehend.'

Kao attempted to redress these problems through stronger involvement by headquarters' managers in supporting the company's foreign operations. Mr Kuroyanagi provided an insight into Kao's approach to managing its overseas units. He described how, after visiting a foreign subsidiary where he felt change was necessary, he asked a senior colleague in Japan to carry out a specific review. The two summarized their findings, and then met with other top management members for further consultation. As a result, his colleague was temporarily located in the foreign company to lead certain projects. A team was formed in Japan to harmonize with locals, and sent to work in the subsidiary. Similarly, when investigating the reason for the company's slow penetration of the shampoo market in Thailand, despite offering a technologically superior product, headquarters' managers found that the product positioning, pricing and packaging policies developed for the Japanese market were unsuitable for Thailand. Since the subsidiary could not adapt these policies to meet local requirements, a headquarters' marketing specialist was brought in, together with a representative from Dentsu – Kao's advertising agent in Japan – to identify the source of the problem and make the necessary changes in the marketing mix.

Part of Mr Kuroyanagi's role was to act as a 'liaison officer' between Kao and its subsidiaries. Kao appointed such managers at headquarters to liaise with all the newly acquired companies in Europe and Asia; their task was to interpret corporate strategies to other companies outside Japan and ensure that 'We never make the same mistake twice.' He described himself as 'the eyes and ears of top management, looking round overseas moves, competitors' activities and behaviours and summarizing them.' He was also there to 'help the local management abroad understand correctly Kao as a corporation, and give hints about how to overcome the cultural gap and linguistic difficulties, how to become open, aggressive and innovative.'

Kao's 1990 global strategy was to develop 'local operations sensitive to each region's characteristics and needs.' As Mr Takayama explained, these would be able 'to provide each country with goods tailored to its local climate and customs, products which perfectly meet the needs of its consumers.' To this end, the goals of the company's research centres in Los Angeles, Berlin, Paris and Santiago de Compostela in Spain, had been redefined as: 'to analyze local market needs and characteristics and integrate them into the product development process,' and a small market research unit had been created in Thailand to support local marketing of Sofina. Over time, Kao hoped, headquarters' functions would be dispersed to SE Asia, the US and Europe, leaving to the Tokyo headquarters the role of supporting regionally based, locally managed operations by giving 'strategic assistance.' There were no plans to turn Jergens or other acquired companies into duplicate Kaos; as described by Dr Maruta 'We will work alongside them rather than tell them which way to go.'

The lack of overseas experience among Kao's managers was tackled via a new ¥9 billion training facility built at Kasumigaura. The 16 hectare campus, offering golf, tennis and other entertainment opportunities was expected to enjoy a constant population of 200, with 10 days' training becoming the norm for all managers. To help Kao managers develop a broader and more international outlook, training sessions devoted considerable attention to the cultural and historical heritages of different countries. A number of younger managers were sent to Europe and the United States, spending the first year learning languages and the second either at a business school, or at Kao's local company offices.

'If you look at our recent international activity,' said Mr Kuroyanagi, 'we have prepared our stage. We have made our acquisitions . . . the basis for globalization in Europe, North America and South East Asia has been facilitated . . . We now need some play on that stage.' Kao's top management was confident that the company's R&D power, 'vitality and open, innovative and aggressive culture' would ultimately prevail. The key constraints, inevitably, were people. 'We do not have enough talented people to direct these plays on the stage.' Kao could not and did not wish to staff its overseas operations with Japanese nationals, but finding, training and keeping suitable local personnel was a major challenge.

Kao expected the industry to develop like many others until 'there were only three or four companies operating on a global scale. We would like to be one of these.' Getting there looked like taking some time, but Kao was in no rush. The perspective, Dr Maruta continually stressed, was very long term, and the company would move at its own pace:

> We should not think about the quick and easy way, for that can lead to bad handling of our products. We must take the long term view . . . and spiral our activity towards the goal . . . We will not, and need not hurry our penetration of foreign markets. We need to avoid having unbalanced growth. The harmony among people, products and world-wide operations is the most important philosophy to keep in mind . . . only in 15 years will it be clear how we have succeeded.

Case 7: Carl Zeiss Jena: Managing Catastrophe

By Manfred F.R. Kets de Vries and Marc A. Cannizzo[1]

Dr Jörg Dierolf was the first West German executive to take up full-time responsibilities at Carl Zeiss Jena, a firm located in the former Communist German Democratic Republic (GDR). He was charged with a daunting task: supervising the restructuring of this world-famous manufacturer of precision optical instruments which, after 45 years of socialist management, stood on the brink of financial ruin. The company had no 'professional' management (in a free market sense), no reliable accounting systems, and no marketing competence. Two-thirds of its staff – 17,000 people in all – would have to be laid off. This would certainly be among the most challenging – and exciting – jobs in his whole career.

Now, soon after his arrival in May 1991, he sat on the terrace of the company's guesthouse, peering through his Zeiss binoculars at the wooded hills surrounding Jena, and pondered the job that awaited him.

Company History[2]

The Carl Zeiss company had an illustrious, and turbulent, history in the course of which its name became synonymous with quality. The firm was founded in 1846 by Carl Zeiss, a skilled mechanic and entrepreneur who produced microscopes in the small university town of Jena (50 kilometers from Weimar, in the state of Thuringen). His most important customer was the natural sciences faculty of the Friedrich Schiller University in Jena. In the mid 1860s, Zeiss made the acquaintance of an assistant professor of physics, Ernst Abbe, beginning a collaboration that would last over 20 years. Their first major breakthrough came in 1866 when Abbe calculated the mathematical theory upon which modern microscopy operates. This enabled Zeiss craftsmen to move beyond the trial-and-error process of lens adjustment and to achieve quality levels with greater efficiency. At about the same time a division of labor was introduced into the manufacturing process, which had until then involved the production of each microscope, from start to finish, by a single craftsman.

In 1884, Zeiss and Abbe entered into partnership with Otto Schott, a developer and manufacturer of special optical glass. The Schott name has been associated with that of Zeiss ever since.

From humble beginnings, the Zeiss company grew in size and reputation. The quality of its instruments was attested to in letters from such eminent scientists as Robert Koch (discoverer of the tuberculosis bacterium), Schaudinn (discoverer of the cause of syphilis) and, in this century, Albert Einstein. In 1887, following the death of Zeiss, Abbe bought out his partner's share of the company from the heirs and placed this, together with his own holding (as well as his stake in Schott), into a foundation named after Carl Zeiss. The foundation's statutes set out the company's aims (the further advancement of the precision mechanical and optical industry) and its policy with regard to the social welfare of its workers. Its provisions for redundancy pay and pension

[1] Source: © 1992 by INSEAD, Fountainebleau, France. This case was written by Marc A. Cannizzo, Research Associate, under the supervision of Manfred F.R. Kets de Vries, Professor at INSEAD. It is intended to be used as a basis for class discussion rather than to illustrate either effective or ineffective handling of an administrative situation. Financial support from the INSEAD Alumni Fund Case Programme is gratefully acknowledged. Reprinted with permission of INSEAD.

[2] A detailed historical account of the company in Jena until 1945, and in Oberkochen thereafter, is found in Armin Hermann's book *Nur der Name war geblieben: die abenteuerliche Geschichte der Firma Carl Zeiss* (Stuttgart: Deutsche Verlags-Anstalt, 1989). See also Exhibit 1 of this case.

benefits were enlightened for the times; and the introduction of a 12–day annual leave for all workers was previously unheard-of. The profits of the company were to be divided into thirds: one for commercial reinvestment, one for distribution to employees, and the remainder for scientific research. The third portion cemented the lasting and mutually beneficial relationship between Carl Zeiss and the Friedrich Schiller University.

With the publication of the Statute of the Carl Zeiss Foundation in 1896, Abbe earned himself a place in history not only as an accomplished scientist, but also as a social visionary. To this day, his picture hangs alongside that of Carl Zeiss in the company's reception hall.

By the turn of the twentieth century, the firm had extended its product range to include telescopes, camera lenses and binoculars; surveying equipment followed a few years later. The First World War and its aftermath subjected the firm to a boom-and-bust cycle (wartime expansion followed by drastic cuts). The company also weathered successive waves of political change – from monarchy to republic and from Fascism to Communism. In 1933, the firm attempted to deflect the worst effects of Hitler's Nazification of German enterprises by stressing technical competence over political orientation. There were individual displays of courage when certain directors tried to shield Jewish employees from persecution. As an important supplier to the military establishment (gun sights, binoculars, aerial photography equipment), the company was not without influence and was able to adopt a policy of pragmatism and compromise rather than blind ideological adherence.

With the collapse of Nazi Germany, Zeiss came under the control of the American army, which occupied Thuringen for a brief period in April 1945. Before turning over the region to the Soviets, as dictated by the Yalta accords, the Americans evacuated 84 key Zeiss personnel, along with blueprints and as much production equipment as they could lay their hands on, in an operation lasting just 48 hours. The evacuees were taken to the US zone of occupation, living first in Heidenheim-an-der-Brenz, and later in the village of Oberkochen, near Stuttgart. Here they set about re-establishing the firm, though without the benefit of the blueprints and equipment. The latter, it was believed, had been shipped on to the United States.

Meanwhile, the remaining Zeiss employees in Jena strove to re-activate what was left of the company, and had actually achieved small-scale production when, in October 1945, Stalin ordered the complete dismantling of German industrial plant and its transportation east as war reparations. At Zeiss, anything that could be unscrewed or unbolted was removed, along with 274 *Zeissianer* [3] who were conscripted to work in the Soviet Union for five years. Like their colleagues in Oberkochen, the few survivors in Jena had to re-launch the company from scratch.

In 1948, Carl Zeiss Jena was nationalized by the authorities and became a 'peoples-own enterprise' (Volkseigener Betrieb, VEB). At this point it was clear that the separation of Zeiss Jena and Zeiss Oberkochen would be anything but temporary. The personal contacts that had been maintained between the two locations since 1945 ended under political pressure and the onset of the Cold War.

Subsequent decades saw the development of a sometimes bitter rivalry, as Jena and Oberkochen litigated over exclusive rights to the commercially precious Carl Zeiss brand name. Jena claimed to be the legitimate continuation of the original company and regarded Oberkochen as a mere offshoot with no authority to act independently. Oberkochen maintained that the Soviet expropriation of the company in Jena had prevented that firm from upholding the principles of the Carl Zeiss Foundation in the GDR and that the original company continued to survive only in West Germany. To buttress their position, the Oberkochener had taken the precaution of obtaining the consent of a West German court to transfer the seat of the Foundation from Jena to Heidenheim-an-der-Brenz, in Baden-Wurttemberg.

By 1971, the two sides had grown weary of litigation and came to a global accord governing

---

[3] As Zeiss employees were called.

EXHIBIT 1
Key Dates in the History of
Carl Zeiss

1846	Carl Zeiss company founded in Jena (Thüringen)
1866	Ernst Abbe teams up with Carl Zeiss
1889	Carl Zeiss Foundation organized by Abbe
1945	US Army temporarily occupies Jena; evacuates key Zeiss personnel
1946	Zeiss Oberkochen established (US zone of occupation) Zeiss Jena is confiscated/dismantled by Soviet occupation forces
1948	Zeiss Jena is converted into a VEB (people's-own enterprise) under the Communists
1949	Carl Zeiss Foundation is legally transferred to Heidenheim (West Germany); however, a foundation of the same name, recognized by East German government, continues to exist in Jena.
1965	VEB Carl Zeiss Jena becomes the center of an industrial combine (Kombinat)
1971	London Agreement reached between Zeiss Oberkochen and Zeiss Jena governing the use of trademarks
1989 November	Opening of the Berlin Wall and the 'inner-German' border
1990 May	Bibelried Declaration between Zeiss Oberkochen and Zeiss Jena foresees reunification under one Foundation
June	VEB Carl Zeiss Jena is converted into Carl Zeiss JENA GmbH and comes under the control of the Treuhandanstalt
July	German economic and monetary union goes into effect
September	London Agreement amended to allow Jena to carry the Zeiss name; however, the name is modified to Jenoptik Carl Zeiss JENA GmbH
October	Unification Day: the German Democratic Republic ceases to exist and the eastern part of Germany joins the Federal Republic of Germany
1991 June	Agreement reached to separate Jenoptik Carl Zeiss JENA GmbH into Jenoptik GmbH (100 percent owned by the State of Thüringen) and Carl Zeiss Jena GmbH (51 percent owned by Carl Zeiss Oberkochen, 49 percent by Jenoptik GmbH)
October	Jenoptik GmbH and Carl Zeiss Jena GmbH are entered in the Jena commercial registry as seperate legal entities

the use of the Zeiss name. Under the London Agreement (named after the venue for negotiations), Oberkochen was given exclusive rights in the USA, West Germany, and several other European countries, while Jena was granted the Comecon area (former East Bloc). A third important category (including Great Britain and Scandinavia) came under a 'coexistence' arrangement, whereby both companies could use the Carl Zeiss name, provided they used distinguishable logos.[4]

---

[4] Jena retained the traditional lens-shaped logo, while Oberkochen used a white square.

Zeiss Jena under the Communist Regime

In a society officially dedicated to socialist principles and scientific achievement, Carl Zeiss Jena was something of a favorite child of the Communist regime. It became the flagship enterprise of the GDR, and served as a showcase for technological advance under socialism. Although the social reformism of Abbe was played down (officially, he was seen as trying to put a human face on capitalism), the commitment to technical quality was one tradition the regime wanted to see continued. The company soon became an important supplier to the Soviet space industry and military establishment.

To accentuate its importance, the company was placed at the center of an industrial combine (Kombinat) which integrated, both vertically and horizontally, the optical and mechanical precision instruments sectors of the economy. The Kombinat was conceived by GDR economic planners in the 1960s as communism's answer to the multinational enterprises that had developed in the West. Based on the principle that 'bigger is better', the Kombinat sought to reap economies of scale as well as to ensure the reliability of supplies (the 'command' economy was notoriously inefficient in this respect). Subcontracting was unknown; the company produced almost everything it needed, including its own screws. One Zeiss manager later described this as 'industrial incest'.

In 1985, as part of an Eastern Bloc strategy to establish technological independence from the West, Zeiss was directed by the government to spearhead a research and production effort into integrated circuits, as these were difficult to obtain in Western markets due to CoCom[5] restrictions. The project absorbed vast resources (one estimate put the figure at several billion US dollars) and resulted in a one-megabyte chip which was still a decade behind its Western equivalent. The project diverted much capital that the state could have made available for investments in Zeiss's core businesses, and thus contributed indirectly to the steady deterioration of the company's production facilities.

There were other costs associated with working in a Communist system: scientists did not enjoy free access to Western scientific literature, and permission to travel to the West (for sales or scientific meetings) was granted only to politically 'reliable' employees.

As a Kombinat, Zeiss had an employment peak of 70,000 and managed production plants in nearly a dozen East German locations. The company dominated its home region, employing nearly 30,000 in and around Jena, which had a population of 100,000. Every other family was dependent on Zeiss in one way or another: the company owned 60 percent of the town's residential housing. It maintained an orchestra and a football team. Like other enterprises in the GDR, it offered extensive (and free) health care facilities to its employees, and operated vacation homes, including seaside resorts. A *Zeissianer* could literally spend all his working and leisure hours in the company of colleagues. As one West German executive (who joined the company in 1991) put it, Zeiss offered its employees everything except a funeral service.

Under the socialist system, overstaffing and underemployment became a way of life at Zeiss, as indeed at most East German companies. The authorities would direct school-leavers to their places of employment according to the State Plan.[6] In this way, the 'right to work', which was enshrined in the GDR constitution, could be upheld; moreover, the absence of visible unemployment could be used as a propaganda weapon against the capitalist West.

---

[5] Coordinating Committee of Multilateral Export Controls, set up by 15 Western nations in Paris in 1949 with the purpose of preventing high-technology exports (of military value) from reaching the Soviet Bloc.
[6] One employee recalled a doggerel from past decades 'Wer nichts kann, und wer nichts weiss, der geht zu Zeiss' ('He who can do nothing, and knows nothing, goes to Zeiss').

The End of the Communist Order

The Communist 'command' economy, which had shown signs of erosion for many years, began to disintegrate with the opening of the GDR's borders in November 1989. Within months the system of state-directed subsidies, prescribed prices, rigid production schedules and pre-determined 'revenue surpluses' (known as 'profits' in the West) would be a thing of the past as companies found themselves thrust into a market economy.

The most palpable end to the old order at Zeiss came with the departure of its general manager, Wolfgang Biermann, in December 1989. Biermann had taken over the leadership of Zeiss in 1975 when the company was suffering from a lack of direction. Appointed by the Central Committee of the Socialist Unity Party (*Sozialistische Einheitspartei Deutschland*, SED, as the East German communist party was called), Biermann, a party stalwart – he himself became a full member of the Central Committee in 1976 – had a mandate to get the company moving again. With his powerful political backing, he pursued this goal with great zeal. According to subordinates, Biermann was addicted to work, coming to his office on the eleventh floor of the old Zeiss headquarters at dawn and often staying until after midnight. Every decision, every detail, required his approval. He was described as ruthless and was once quoted in the press as follows: 'I put a rope around the necks of my managers and pull it tight; and sometimes I ease up.' In what one executive referred to as a 'Stalinist tradition', Biermann promoted people and then enjoyed chopping them down again. Every month he would hold a meeting, open to all employees, at which he would call on his senior managers to account for their activities. In the course of these sessions they were harangued, vilified and held up to public scorn for alleged misdeeds at work (such as mismanagement, or using company property for personal use) and at home (perhaps late rental payments, or overdrawn bank accounts). The rank-and-file workers, with whom Biermann claimed to have a good relationship, took considerable pleasure in these proceedings.

In his 14 years at the top, Biermann made a lasting impression on Zeiss employees at all levels of the company. Feelings about him were certainly strong, if ambivalent. Managers acknowledged that the old boss was very effective at getting things done, even if they were achieved through 'management by fear'. Over a year after Biermann's departure one *Zeissianer*, a chauffeur, commented (perhaps a touch wistfully) that the former head had 'brought order' to the company.

In the mid 1980s it was clear to some Zeiss managers that the company, along with the entire GDR economy, was slowly being run into the ground. Soviet President Gorbachev and his policy of perestroika (or 'restructuring') gave them hope that Zeiss's rigid management regime could itself be reorganized, with more responsibility delegated downwards. Dr Klaus-Dieter Gattnar, the deputy general manager (and eventual successor to Biermann), recalls that the book *In Search of Excellence* (by Thomas J. Peters and Robert H. Waterman; New York: Harper & Row, 1982) came into their possession during this period. With Biermann's permission, translations were prepared for the management team. They were excited by the new ideas and hoped to introduce some of them to Zeiss. Biermann shared in the enthusiasm, but only so far as to say (as paraphrased by Gattnar), 'That's how we already do it, just like in the book'. Any hopes for change were dashed.

By November 1989, with the old system crumbling, Biermann grew more and more withdrawn and left the running of day-to-day affairs to his subordinates. 'The man was no longer capable of managing', recalls Gattnar. 'He was sick, scared.' Gattnar and his colleagues had already been discussing contingency plans among themselves, at first without the knowledge of Biermann ('That was sheer counter-revolution', Gattnar joked). But eventually they approached the boss for a frank discussion: 'It was good that we did so . . . Without this discussion we would not have had any real legitimacy to carry on what we were doing.'

Even before the GDR border opened (9 November 1989), Gattnar appointed a commission to examine what Zeiss would have to do to adapt to a market economy. Another important issue was the possible effect of the introduction of the Deutschemark (D-Mark, or DM) into the GDR (which at the time was quite unimaginable). A third question concerned property rights: how could Zeiss reverse the expropriation of 1948 and rejoin the Carl Zeiss Foundation?

A Chaotic Interregnum Begins

Biermann's high political profile under the SED regime forced him to leave Zeiss in December 1989, whereupon Gattnar, as next in line, took charge of the company. The new acting general manager was in his mid-50s and had been with Carl Zeiss Jena for 35 years, starting as a junior technician and gradually working his way up the ladder. For the 16 months following his new appointment, he tried to steer the company away from the brink of collapse. It was a period during which the pendulum, as he put it, 'swung from autocracy to near-anarchy'. He described his first tasks

> The first problem was to convert the firm from what had been until that point a one-man show. This company was fatally oriented around one person . . . The desk in my office was full of paper . . . I needed seven hours a day on average to get through it all. I didn't need the company . . . The first step was to move many decisions from my desk to the divisions, to other desks, where they belonged . . . I struggled with this for half a year because it was not so easy to decentralize such a centralized organization without running the risk that it would cease functioning.

At the same time, the *Kombinate* had to be prevented from breaking up. With political authority threatening to collapse, and workers and managers experiencing their first euphoric taste of freedom, there was a temptation on the part of a number of enterprises to declare their independence and to manage their own affairs. In the

case of Pentacon, a camera producer in Dresden, Gattnar signed off, but not without first warning the plant manager of the odds against commercial survival. In the end, Pentacon was the first company in the Zeiss *Kombinate* to suffer dissolution.

Gattnar dealt with the other plant managers by sending them 'out into the world' in search of commercial partnerships. He gave them complete freedom of action and was severely criticized for this by other members of his management team. But he was convinced that his managers would soon wake up to reality and return to the fold. In this he was proved correct:

> No one broke away. While the other Kombinate fell apart, ours did not. They [the managers] quickly realized that they could be strong only if they stayed together, that individual plants would be hard-pressed to survive on their own.

In a time of political and social upheaval, with political demonstrations against the still-governing SED almost a daily occurrence,[7] the task of keeping the company operational proved difficult:

> In November and December 1989, we lost 300 million [Ostmark[8] in sales] . . . because, for example, in a plant of 4500 workers, 700 to 800 did not show up for work on any given day. They simply drove over to the Federal Republic [West Germany, on visits] . . . The conditions were so unstable.

In addition to absenteeism, there was a steady loss of qualified workers who went west in search of higher-paid jobs. At first, many went on their own initiative; later, there was active solicitation of Zeiss workers by West German firms who sent recruitment agents to Jena. The Zeiss management felt powerless to prevent such departures.

With Communist authority in the country discredited, there began a wave of worker

---

[7] Self-proclaimed 'reformist' elements of the SED continued to govern the country in the hope of preserving the communist system in the upcoming election (planned for March 1990).

[8] The GDR currency, which was replaced by the West German D-Mark in mid 1990. Its effective (black market) rate to the DM was approximately 6:1.

demands for a full disclosure of company affairs, the correction of individual wage discrepancies and a multitude of other grievances that had been suppressed under the old regime.

One day, a throng of employees from different Zeiss factories turned up at the gates of the Göschwitz facility (outside Jena) where sensitive research and production of defense- and space-related equipment took place. Dr Reinhold, the head of the U-works (as the facility was called), responded swiftly by opening the doors and allowing the 'visitors' to walk about and convince themselves that there were no 'dark' secrets. Afterwards, he organized a press conference and gave the media tours of the plant.

Perhaps the most difficult social issue at Zeiss – and indeed in the country at large – was the popular demand for the removal of all who had collaborated clandestinely with the authorities in the past. At the top of the list were the secret informants of the Ministry of State Security (known as the Stasi). Identifying such individuals was difficult, and suspicions abounded. Membership of the SED alone was not decisive, as perhaps a quarter of the employees had been party members, and many of these had joined for reasons other than ideology (for example, to advance their careers). The higher an individual ranked in the corporate hierarchy, the greater were the reasons for suspecting him of undercover Stasi activity. Though Gattnar was never accused of any personal wrong-doing, his post as deputy general manager under the old system made his current position a tenuous one. He had risen under Biermann and was regarded as a product of the same system. When he was confirmed as general manager by the Ministry of Mechanical Engineering, in February 1990, his employment contracts were limited to four to six months.

Groups of workers, or their representatives, demanding the removal of department heads whom they considered unfit to manage frequently approached Gattnar. Gattnar resisted, demanding proof of professional incompetence before acting. It wasn't sufficient, he said, for someone merely to label a superior a 'Stalin'.

In cases where the pressure for removal was too great, senior managers were transferred to other parts of the company. Thus, one plant manager was moved to the Zeiss retail outlet of *Industrieläden* (industrial shops); another, relieved of his duties in Jena, turned up at Zeiss's sales office in Czechoslovakia.

Gattnar justified this practice of transferring managers as a way of keeping technical expertise within the company. He was convinced that Zeiss could not afford to lose such people, with their decades-long experience, even if they were unpopular or tainted politically. With mild sarcasm Gattnar suggested, 'I could have sacked half the plant managers, just to show that I was doing something'.

In some cases, there were practical arguments in favor of keeping politically 'undesirable' individuals: because blueprints and technical documentation were frequently not updated, or neglected altogether, employees who carried detailed knowledge of plant layouts and operations in their heads were considered indispensable.

Critics pointed to Gattnar's actions as evidence that the old boy network (referred to as *Seilschaften*, or rope-teams, in the mountaineering sense) was alive and well. One manager at Zeiss who had not been a party member said, 'Gattnar is a good technician, highly intelligent, but he never could free himself of the Seilschaften'. The same manager likened senior management to a group of soldiers who 'all eat out of the same goulash pot [*Gulaschkanone*]'. Moreover, in his opinion, Gattnar had been a yes-man under Biermann and any criticisms he now made of the old boss were self-serving: 'It takes no skill to trip a person who is already in the process of falling down the stairs'. Commenting on the 'revolution' of November 1989, he felt it had gone too quietly and had 'stopped at the factory gates'. There were some lock-outs of plant managers by workers, but in general the same managers stayed on and continued to run their factories into the new year.

During the first half of 1990 the mood in Jena reflected that of the country in general: optimism tinged with uncertainty. The first free national elections in March confirmed that the days of the GDR as a separate country were numbered.[9] The symbols of Communist domination had long since vanished; the most visible of these being the red star which had crowned Zeiss's 15–storey administrative headquarters. The in-house newspaper, previously produced by 'resident' SED party functionaries, was now in the hands of a press/public relations team who answered to management. *Der Scheinwerfer* ('The Spotlight'), as it was called, was eventually relaunched under the more elegant name of *Prisma*.

Zeiss management spoke with confidence of the company's ability to adapt to the market economy. However, most people equated a 'market economy' at this point with the luxuries they had seen personally, for the first time, on their trips over the border. They believed that soon they, too, would participate in that prosperity. If any staff cutbacks were envisaged at this time, they were expected to be modest and strictly necessary. There was strong popular belief in Zeiss as a company dedicated not only to quality products, but to its people as well. It would look after its own as it always had. If any enterprise in East Germany was suited to join the free market this was it.

Initial Reorganization Plans

With the inauguration of German economic and monetary union on 1 July 1990 (the day on which the D-Mark replaced the *Ostmark* as legal tender), the government privatization agency known as the *Treuhandanstalt* (or Treuhand) took formal control of Zeiss Jena. The first task was to convert the 'people's own enterprises' (VEBs) into limited liability companies (*Gesellschaft mit beschränkter Haftung*, GmbH) under West German company law. At the same time, the decision was taken to disband the *Kombinat*; thus, companies which had been independent entities all along (and never integral to Zeiss), such as the microchip producer Hochvakuum Dresden, were spun off

with their fates to be determined separately by the Treuhand. This process, accomplished swiftly, reduced the Zeiss enterprise from 70,000 to around 27,000 employees, concentrated in and around Jena.

In addition to these moves, the company was to be reorganized into product divisions (*Geschäftsbereiche*). For years, the company's structure had been based on pure production facilities; research, development and distribution had been centralized. This structure had evolved under the 'command' economy, where production took priority over all other activities in fulfilling the quotas dictated by the State Plan. In the early years of the GDR, before centralization of R&D, it had not been uncommon for research staff at Zeiss to be enlisted in packing instruments into shipping crates at the end of each month to meet production deadlines.

The aim of the present reorganization was to bring product development, marketing (or what was understood as such) and accounting back under one roof along with production so that design, process, control and customer feedback could be integrated for each product. Basic research and pre-assembly (machining) departments as well as some purchasing activities were to remain centralized if they served all, or several, product divisions.

The *Geschäftsbereich* model was in fact similar to that introduced at Zeiss Oberkochen several years earlier, and its adoption in Jena was probably influenced by the direct contacts which were made between the two companies after the opening of the border.

Zeiss Oberkochen had followed the dramatic political events in East Germany at the end of 1989 with great interest. At the behest of the CEO Dr Skoludek, Jena was contacted for permission to lay a wreath at the Ernst Abbe memorial on 20 January, Abbe's birthday. The ribbon read simply 'Friends and Admirers from Oberkochen'. The West Germans felt that historical imperative would surely bring the separated company together again. To illustrate the personal links between Jena and Oberkochen, one executive recalled how, in the mid-1970s, one could wander through the Oberkochen workshops and hear the

---

[9] The majority voted in favor of parties advocating political reunification with West Germany.

dialect of Thüringen spoken by the (now grown up) children of the first generation of workers evacuated there from the East.

With German unification in the offing, there was no longer a rationale for two Zeiss companies. Both sides agreed that the two would have to come together, and announced this in a communiqué in May (the Bibelried Declaration). But the main question was, on what terms? The legal differences remained. As Dr Gattnar put it, Jena held that 'Abbe had two legitimate children', while Oberkochen continued to maintain that the second child (meaning Jena) was at best a 'half-breed'. The family struggle over the Abbe inheritance was again at the top of the agenda.

Eastern Markets Collapse

In the spring of 1990, Jena still enjoyed full order books from customers in the former Eastern Bloc (their export markets lay almost entirely in the East), and saw itself negotiating as an equal partner with Oberkochen. After the middle of the year, when the D-Mark had replaced the *Ostmark*, the situation began to look more precarious. Although the West German government agreed to guarantee the conversion of Soviet rouble export proceeds at the previous East German rate of 4:1 until the end of 1990, all future sales would have to be priced, and paid for, in hard D-Mark. The scarcity of foreign exchange, combined with the imposition of budgetary austerity in the Soviet Union and other countries of the former Eastern Bloc forced a virtual drying up of orders from the East.

The collapse of Zeiss's Eastern markets came as a heavy blow to the company, for they had reckoned, in the worst case, with a 25 percent decline in exports. In fact, the new order flow reflected an export volume at five percent of its former magnitude. Gattnar called this a 'great error' of judgment on his part.

The second half of 1990 brought home a number of hard truths to the company. In August, a team of West German consultants, engaged by Jena upon the recommendation of the Treuhand,

proposed that the analytical instruments business (used for analysing the chemical properties of substances) be closed down for lack of competitive potential. The company balked at their conclusion: Zeiss had long experience in this area and was in the process of rolling out new products for the autumn trade fair in Leipzig. On the other hand, the consultants believed that the following areas could achieve competitiveness on the world market: microscopes, surveying instruments, optical medical instruments, dimensional engineering metrology, and photogrammetry.[10] The company's scientific aerial camera (produced in the high-tech Göschwitz facility, also known as the U-works) already enjoyed a good market share in the West.

In microscopes, for example, Zeiss enjoyed a strong brand name, offered good technical advice, and had a good price–performance relationship; on the negative side, there was insufficient customer-oriented servicing, long delivery times (roughly three months), and inferior product design. The electronic elements were also considered to be outdated. Thus it was recommended that Zeiss should refocus on its traditional core competence, namely optics and precision mechanics. Jena, unlike its Western counterpart, was not represented at the top (most profitable) segment of the market, access to which was judged to be prohibitively costly. But it was recommended that the company concentrate on extending its market coverage in the middle and low segments. Recommended staffing for microscopes was set at 700, an employment cut of 50 percent.

In June, Dr Gattnar had spoken of having to trim 5000 jobs at the company. The collapse of Zeiss's Eastern markets meant that this figure would have to be revised upward. In September, the number of jobs to be eliminated was publicly revealed to be 10,000. At this point, employees began to grow restless at the apparent indecision

---

[10] Metrology involves high precision measuring instruments for quality control; they were accurate to 0.1 μm (micomillimeter); photogrammetry is a technique for producing photographs with 'true' (undistorted dimensions, typically used in architecture and map-making).

of the government and the Treuhand concerning the company's future.

Political Tensions Grow in Jena

On 6 September, thousands of Zeissianer took to the streets under banners proclaiming 'Jena fights for the inheritance of Ernst Abbe'. Their objective was to re-enter the Carl Zeiss Foundation in order to secure the financial benefits defined by the statutes. It was common knowledge that the VEB Zeiss had not created reserves from which to fund pensions, but had simply paid these out of current revenues. The dire financial situation of the company now meant that employees would have to take matters into their own hands. A second demonstration followed on the 11th, during which all roads leading into Jena were blocked by protesters. Direct action paid off: on 14 September, in the last weeks of its existence, the GDR parliament (*Volkskammer*) passed a resolution returning 20 percent of Zeiss Jena to the (Jena-based) Carl Zeiss Foundation (from which it had originally been expropriated). This was a partial, but not insignificant, reversal of the expropriation that had taken place 32 years earlier. It also strengthened symbolically (and perhaps legally) Jena's claim to be a 'legitimate' child of the Abbe legacy.

This victory did not change the increasingly gloomy commercial outlook for the company. To make matters worse, there appeared to be a change in Oberkochen's attitude toward Jena. At Bibelried, Oberkochen had offered marketing assistance and know-how to Jena, but had been careful not to pledge any financial support. In September, this spirit of cooperation was still present, as reflected in an agreement allowing Jena to continue to use the Carl Zeiss Jena name throughout the soon-to-be enlarged Federal Republic of Germany (the disappearance of the GDR would otherwise have left Jena at the mercy of Oberkochen, under the terms of the London Agreement). The company therefore added 'Jenoptik' to its name and became Jenoptik Carl Zeiss JENA GmbH. By the end of the year, how-

ever, Dr Gattnar noticed a hardening of Oberkochen's position. There was now talk of preserving no more than 5000 jobs in the East. 'They [the Oberkochener] noticed that we had become weak in the knees because of our exports to the East . . . Things [discussions] became one-sided . . . which led to a widespread feeling here [in Jena] that we were being annexed.'

The East German *Zeissianer* became deeply distrustful of Oberkochen's motives They suspected that Jena was to become, at best, an 'extended workbench' of the western firm, if not a mere sales outlet (serving as a bridgehead to the East); that Jena had to be eliminated as a competitor to Oberkochen, given the half dozen product lines (microscopes, optical/medical, surveying, binoculars, planetaria, and optical systems/components) which overlapped between the two companies; and that even the team of western consultants who continued to be engaged by Jena were acting as agents for the West Germans.

Added to this was the feeling that the Treuhand displayed little interest in dealing with Jena itself, but preferred to listen to the proposals coming out of Oberkochen concerning Jena's future. The Treuhand was in fact planning to appoint three Oberkochener to the Supervisory Board[11] of Jena; the conspiratorially-minded (and the press) took further note of the fact that the CEO of the western Zeiss had been a schoolmate of the Treuhand president.

While Oberkochen was causing him enough trouble, Gattnar encountered a climate of real hostility in Jena. The latest plans to cut staff even further sent shock waves throughout the company. 'We [the management] were considered to be completely inept,' recalls Gattnar. He had faced numerous worker assemblies in the autumn of 1989, but the meetings now were different: 'One felt a real wave of hatred' running through the crowd, he said. With more and more lay-offs

---

[11] Under German corporate law, the Supervisory Board (*Aufsichtsrat*) is a non-executive board which oversees the activities of the company's executive management (*Vorstand*).

planned, the rank-and-file were asking what right the men 'at the top' (many of them holdovers from the previous regime) had to stay on. The situation, in Gattnar's view, had become highly politicized and essentially uncontrollable.

Recognizing that Jena was fast becoming a social powder-keg (another mass demonstration in the streets of Jena took place on 13 February 1991), the State of Thüringen stepped in at this point to support the maintenance of at least 10,000 jobs at Zeiss. As trustee of the Jena-based Carl Zeiss Foundation, the state turned to the Treuhand in March 1991 and agreed to have the remaining 80 percent of Zeiss Jena transferred to the Foundation. The Treuhand remained very much involved in working out the future of Zeiss, however, not least because Thüringen could not afford to bankroll the rescue alone, but had to rely on the financial resources of the federal government. Thüringen and the Treuhand did have a common aim: to try to secure as many jobs as possible at Zeiss by extracting employment guarantees from private investors (in this case, Zeiss Oberkochen).

Government authorities also took a more active stance in underwriting 'make-work' programs (so-called Arbeitsbeschaffungsmaßnahmen, or ABMs). In mid-1991, roughly 1000 people were employed in ABMs, typically clearing out Zeiss buildings for demolition or renovation. In addition, the company made unused administration buildings available to government-sponsored staff retraining programs (for eventual employment in the services sector). Courses began in April with an initial capacity for 700 participants. To develop its own sales competence, Zeiss initiated a technical marketing program that was attended by 110 people. All in all, these efforts were considered insufficient, given that the number of *Zeissianer* on 'short hours-zero' (*Kurzbeit-Null*)[12] – which stood at 10,000 in April – was still rising.

Gattnar's Position Grows Precarious

Dr Gattnar was becoming increasingly isolated. He later recalled not being invited to public meetings in Jena at which union leaders and politicians of various stripes would address the workers. It was customary for the Zeiss chief to be given an opportunity to explain management's side. Now political slogans threatened to displace dialogue. At one meeting, which Gattnar did not attend, a state minister spoke of seeking the removal of the entire Zeiss management. Gattnar felt that this undermined his authority, perhaps fatally.

The issue of management staffing below the executive board[13] still had to be settled. In October 1990, employee representatives at Zeiss had insisted (with, it was suspected, the backing of Oberkochen) that a personnel commission be established to supervise the filling of the top two layers of management in the company on an open-application basis. This time Gattnar relented, though the body that was formed had no decision-making power. In Gattnar's opinion, the Commission turned out to be a 'flop', making ineffectual recommendations concerning staffing. He felt that competent people with leadership potential, but with compromised political pasts, would not apply for management positions given the poisoned atmosphere. Few recommendations were acted upon.

Finally, there was the question of reorganization into product divisions. The *Geschäftsbereiche*, conceived during the first half of 1990, had spent most of the year on the drawing board undergoing constant changes, and were supposed to be implemented at the beginning of 1991 with a three-month conversion period to iron out wrinkles. Collapsing the various production sites into consolidated divisions proved to be no easy task, however, and the deadline was again shifted, this time to the middle of 1991.

Half of the men who were to run these divi-

---

[12] This was a euphemism for completely idled workers who still drew wages.

[13] The executive management (or *Vorstand*).

sions had been plant managers prior to 1990, and had experienced at least one year of decentralized decision-making. The exercise of such managerial freedom had produced mixed results: the closing of poorly priced deals could hardly be avoided, given that the company was living from hand to mouth. Pricing strategy was still an unknown science, accurate product costing unavailable, and old habits, such as dumping products on Western markets at heavily discounted prices, would die hard. There was the case of one manager who purchased automobiles for his department, displaying priorities that raised not a few eyebrows. Another was leasing unused commercial land within his domain, on a long-term basis, to third parties.

Part of this behavior could be explained by the entrepreneurial flair of Gattnar himself ('You have to permit some chaos to encourage creativity'). The boss led by example: in order to convert receivables from the Soviet Union into cash, he negotiated the delivery of a decommissioned Soviet submarine, to be towed to a scrapyard and sold. The deal was torpedoed for want of the necessary export license.

To defuse the explosive social situation that prevailed in Jena and in other parts of eastern Germany at the beginning of 1991, the federal government agreed to postpone layoffs from June until the end of that year. Now the hardest task – emotionally – lay before management: selecting the 10,000 employees who would remain out of the 27,000. The exercise unleashed endless discussions among the division heads in those cases where cutbacks affected several divisions in the reorganization. The task was further complicated by the fact that each factory had its own union that looked after the interests of its own workers. To add to the confusion, personnel records were incomplete or poorly maintained. Gattnar spent much of his time presiding over turf disputes: 'The managers could not solve it themselves'.

It was agreed with the unions that for each of the 10,000 posts, several employees with the necessary professional qualifications would be identified. Final selection would, however, take into account 'social' factors so as to protect single

parents and other economically vulnerable members of society. Some Zeiss managers admitted that from a purely business point of view this was not an optimal solution.

This selection process was begun under a cloak of secrecy, and no one would be officially notified until the autumn when the first 'blue letters' (dismissal notices) went out. Employees on 'short hours-zero', numbering 13,000 by May 1991, suspected that they would be among the casualties, but everyone had to adopt a wait-and-see attitude. One employee observed that the uncertainty was exacerbated by inadequate access to internal information, especially for those who remained at home even though measures had been taken to keep everyone informed: apart from newspapers, regular meetings were held and these were well-attended, as they helped relieve the strong feeling of isolation of the unemployed. Drinking problems were becoming evident on the housing estate of Lobeda, just outside Jena, where thousands of Zeiss families lived close together in long rows of similar apartment blocks.

The absence of informative internal communications turned the company into a breeding ground for rumors. Gattnar acknowledged that management had failed to pay enough attention to this issue and that one of his biggest mistakes was not finding a spokesman of adequate stature who could keep the employees informed. The general manager himself performed well in front of the troops but there was only so much time he could devote to this activity.

At this point, Gattnar was thoroughly discouraged and ready to throw in the towel. 'Not once,' he observed, 'did we have the peace necessary to manage a business . . . We were always rushing from one crisis to another'. Now, attacked on all sides, he was hard-pressed to find a good reason why he was doing all this.

After 35 years in the company, however, he suspected he knew. He recalled walking through the workshops and being approached by colleagues, some weeping, saying 'You know, we built this plant up together . . . why do I have to go?' And yet, on one other occasion, a colleague of many years came up to him and said, 'If I have to be laid off, then I would prefer it to be done by a *Wessi*[14] and not someone from here.'

A Restructuring Agreement is Reached

This last wish was answered when, after 18 months of negotiations, an agreement was reached between the Treuhand, Carl Zeiss Oberkochen and the State of Thüringen to restructure the company in Jena with the help of Western management. The plan envisaged physically dividing the enterprise (people, land, buildings, machinery and all) into two parts: one, with 2800 employees, embracing Zeiss's core product lines, would become a 51 percent subsidiary of Oberkochen – the other 49 percent to be held indirectly by Thüringen (see Exhibits 2 and 3). It would continue to carry the Zeiss name (Carl Zeiss Jena GmbH) and work towards full status as a member of the West German Carl Zeiss Foundation.[15] The other part, renamed Jenoptik GmbH (100 percent owned by the State of Thüringen) would initially take responsibility for 7200 people, but planned to retain only 1700 as its own work force, developing advanced opto-electronic products at the main research facility in Göschwitz (the former U-works, where the military and space-related contracts had been carried out under the old regime). The other 5500 people, many of whom were holders of technical degrees, would be made available to outside companies seeking to invest in the Jena region. In addition, Jenoptik held much of the former Zeiss Kombinat's commercial properties (770,000 square meters), far more than it needed for its own use; these could be sold or leased to investors, joint venture partners or as part of other commercial agreements.

The restructuring package, totaling DM 3.6 billion (US$ 2 billion[16]), was funded by the Treuhand and the State of Thuringen. The proceeds were to cover the company's old debts (nearly DM 1 billion) as well as the costs of staff redundancies (DM 600 million was earmarked for this purpose). The remainder would go into recapitalization, modernization of plant and equipment, and to cover losses that would be incurred during the coming several years.

The 'Return' of Zeiss Oberkochen

After a separation of nearly half a century, Zeiss Oberkochen would return to Jena. The Oberkochener had come a long way since 1946. They had started up after the war on their own, against great odds, and attributed their survival to technical know-how, tradition and perseverance. In 1989, the company generated sales (consolidated) of DM 2.3 billion (US$ 1.3 billion) and employed 14,000 people. The post-war road had been rocky: at the beginning of the 1970s, the company stood on the brink of financial disaster when its subsidiary, Zeiss Ikon, succumbed to the competitive pressures of Japanese camera producers. After attempting to keep the subsidiary afloat, management finally recognized that it was no longer viable, and withdrew entirely from the amateur camera field, taking substantial write-offs in the process. As a result of this experience, according to one senior manager in Oberkochen, the company learned other lessons:

> We also had to reduce our excessive reliance on bank debt . . . [because] the bankers at this time were trying to bring their influence to bear . . . In four or five years, a 'self-cleansing' took place, a strength from within the company . . . something our finance head at the time called the 'miracle at Zeiss.'

---

[14] A popular term for West Germans; East Germans were called Ossis.

[15] The Foundation in Heidenheim was eventually registered in Jena as well; the existing entity in Jena was thereupon renamed the Ernst Abbe Foundation and now holds various non-profit making institutions, such as the Jena optics museum and an optical school.

[16] The DM/US$ rate on 30 June 1991 was 1.79.

EXHIBIT 2
Carl Zeiss Ownership
Structure

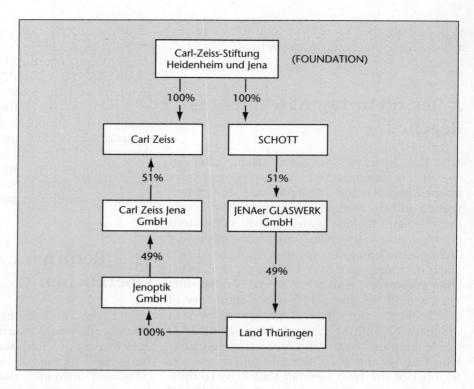

Zeiss executives were conscious of the company's legacy and they spoke respectfully of the founders, the idealism, and the enduring values enshrined in the statutes of the Carl Zeiss Foundation. Entering the company's reception area in Oberkochen, visitors encountered the familiar portraits of Carl Zeiss and Ernst Abbe, their expressions visionary, reflective, determined, and yet benevolent. Four times a year, an executive conducted a one-day introductory seminar on the company's history and current activities for new employees and apprentices. The sense of loyalty was fierce. Even retired *Zeissianer* continued to play a role in the company's life, taking visitors on tours of the production facilities.

One executive observed that there was a great deal of motivation to be derived from working for a foundation, as this offered a 'third way' between working for the State (here he had Zeiss Jena in mind) and working for outside shareholders. The financial limitations imposed by not having access to equity markets were a necessary price to be paid.

Zeiss Oberkochen was still dominated by technicians with an 'obsession with quality' as one executive put it. But over time a marketing culture had to establish itself given the strong competitive pressures in the international optics/precision mechanics field (fully 50 percent of the company's turnover came from abroad):

I'll give you an example: when a colleague of mine, responsible for advertising, attended a planning session for a new product brochure, he asked his counterparts on the product side: 'What is the target market? What are the particular attributes of the product? How do we reach our target market?' . . . [and got the response] 'Don't ask so many dumb questions, just write the brochure'. That was typical 20 years ago!

The prospect of corporate reunion with Jena caused considerable excitement in Oberkochen, but emotion had to be tempered by commercial realism. 'If anything could be done, then it would involve at most 3000 staff [in Jena] . . . Anything more is an illusion', according to Manfred Berger, head of Oberkochen's marketing services. The

EXHIBIT 3
The new Carl Zeiss Jena Gmbh

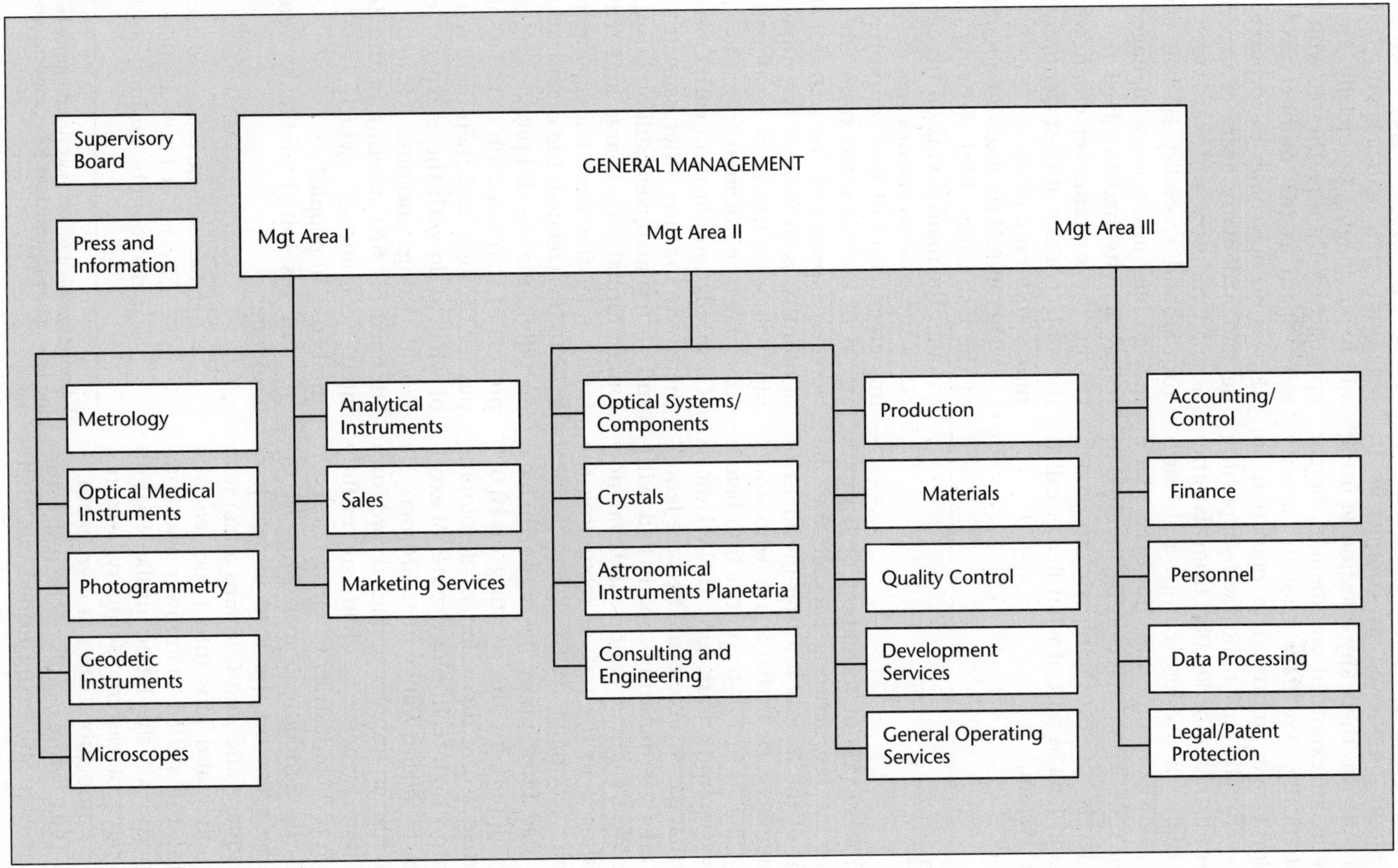

western executives were sensitive to the charge that they might be viewed as conquerors in Jena. 'At no time was there any question of using Jena merely as an extended workbench', Berger stated emphatically, 'We have enough capacity here; we don't need more'. The operation in Jena would eventually have to be a self-supporting unit and not distract Oberkochen from its other on-going activities in western Europe and North America. There was recognition, however, that a good deal of time would have to be invested at numerous levels of the company to coach counterparts in Jena as part of what Berger called a 'godfather' system.

Jenoptik

Critical to the successful formation of Jenoptik GmbH under the restructuring package was the commitment of the former minister-president of Baden-Wurttemberg, Dr Lothar Späth, who would take over as CEO, at first of the entire firm before restructuring (Jenoptik Carl Zeiss JENA GmbH) and then of that part which would become Jenoptik GmbH, after restructuring. Späth had withdrawn from West German politics and was now dedicating himself to the task of rebuilding the East German economy. With keen political instinct, he had burst upon the scene in Jena, proclaiming support for the securing of 10,000 jobs, and broadcasting his vision of developing the region into a high-technology center of excellence (similar to Silicon Valley in California). He brought with him an impressive track record from his home state, where he had successfully attracted high-tech industries to what had been a predominantly agricultural area. Most of his time would be spent on the road in search of investors (Germans and non-Germans alike) who would put money and jobs into Jena; Jenoptik would provide the skilled manpower and commercial property, for the latter, unlike that in many other parts of eastern Germany, was not encumbered by ambiguous titles of ownership.

By May 1991, while details of the restructuring agreement were still being ironed out, there

was an urgent need to get things moving again in Jena under new management. The company was still hemorrhaging financially. The Treuhand had approached Dr Jörg Dierolf who had agreed to assist Späth as his 'number two'. Dierolf, aged 55, was no newcomer to corporate restructuring; he had had many years of experience in West German industry and was widely regarded as a 'turn-around' specialist. He had seen big companies go bust under inept management: his most recent activity had involved the winding-up of Co-op, the supermarket chain which had been the subject of one of West Germany's largest bankruptcy and fraud cases.

Dierolf had no illusions about the intricacies of the task before him. Arriving in Jena, he ran through the main points on his agenda: the spin-off of the core businesses was only one item, but implementation of this would have to await the arrival of the managers from Oberkochen. They were not expected on the scene for another couple of months, even though executive offices on the ninth floor of the Zeiss headquarters had been redecorated many months earlier in expectation of a speedy reunification with Oberkochen.[17] But there were so many other issues to tackle: Gattnar and his top men were still on board, although no longer formally in charge and with an unclear future role; the next management layer would have to be screened; the organization of the product divisions was still progressing too slowly; the process of staff selection (and lay-offs) had to be pushed through; and then there was the question of what to do with those expensive consultants. Would things become clearer once Dierolf attended his first meeting of the Zeiss 'management committee' which, he understood, numbered 40 people?

But his initial problems were even more mundane:

> When I arrived, no office had been prepared for me . . . I came at 11:00; at 10:30, someone had vacated a room by pushing out the occupants

---

[17] Ironically, these offices had stood empty because no one in the Jena management had felt confident enough to occupy them.

and seating them in the ante room, and I ended up in a little cubicle . . . Then they told me that the secretary they had planned for me didn't want to work for a *Wessi* . . . Eventually, I became acquainted with two [local] people . . . and on the way to lunch I explained to them my hardship and then that afternoon I walked around and mentioned how sad it was, how handicapped I was, just to test the reactions of the people. And next morning Frau Löbel came by, saying 'He [Dierolfl] comes all the way from the West to help us; we can't abandon him.' After a brief chat with her, I said 'Frau Löbel, you're on; let's get on with the job' . . . So we started as a two-person team in that cubicle . . .

Jörg Dierolf knew that he could not stay in his small office at Jena as it would have sent a signal to all that he could be outmaneuvered (*ausgetrickst*) by the old *Seilschaften* (to be 'put in their pipe and smoked' as he put it). So he turned to his secretary for advice (she 'knew the conditions here inside out') and learned of the empty executive offices on the ninth floor of the Zeiss headquarters. 'I asked for the key . . . and so I set myself up on the ninth floor. This sent, of course, a clear signal to all, as no one had dared to move in, and now this freshly arrived *Wessi* was sitting there.'

Gradually, Dierolf built up his personal staff, which was mostly locally recruited, and located them on the ninth floor. As a result, the eleventh floor, 'the so called "Biermann floor"', where the former Zeiss chief had presided, lost its importance and 'everyone knew that here [on the ninth floor] was a group which really called the tune'.

Having established himself, Dierolf asked to see an organization chart:

The chart I was given was the most 'adventurous' I have ever seen in my entire career . . . It looked like a chess board with lots of boxes containing names and abbreviations, and the boxes were so linked to one another that one could not determine who was responsible for what and to whom . . . an ideal system to avoid responsibility. Dr Gattnar had signed it off just before my arrival and without my consent . . . There were certainly games being played . . .

Dierolf had agreed with Späth and the Treuhand that he would be the undisputed number two man in the company. Gattnar had attempted to include his fellow managing directors as equally-ranked, with himself recognized, 'through signals which during 40 years came to be understood very well here', as de facto general manager reporting to Späth. 'Luckily, I had anticipated this and ensured that not only the personnel department but also financial control would report to me'.

There followed a conference with the existing 'management committee', which numbered 40 people in all. This, Dierolf's 'first and last' meeting of its size, allowed him to become acquainted with the incumbent top managers. The group was soon trimmed following implementation – finally of the divisional structure that had been discussed for so long. It was clear that there was no longer any meaningful role for Gattnar and his top men, including the head of finance, whom Dierolf described as a 'pleasant . . . and decent person . . . He wouldn't hurt a fly' but who nevertheless 'belonged to the nomenklatura here, as they call it, and had no [longer any] charisma . . . it was gone. Running a company requires 50 percent charisma'.

On the first level of direct reports (plant managers), some men were retained to head the new divisions, others were replaced by more junior people. According to Dierolf:

It has been my experience that it always pays off if you take people from the second level down and give them the chance to make a career jump they would not get anywhere else, than if you depend on people who have already made a career in the past . . . You can't expect a manager who has had a top position here to turn around and say that everything he has done in the past is now placed in doubt and that he is now ready to move in a new direction . . .

Selection of the first management layer took a week; Dierolf was aware that by moving quickly he ran the risk of making a poor staffing decision in individual cases, but he did have some advice from the management consultants who remained engaged at the company.

Dierolf in turn gave full responsibility to his newly appointed (or reconfirmed) division heads to select their own subordinates without interference on his part. He also introduced an open-door policy which he called 'management by walking in', something he himself had first encountered in the United States:

> I believe in the philosophy where you trust your colleagues [in this case, direct reports] as equals, that you select and surround yourself with top people so that you have the feeling that they could just as well be in your position with just a few more years of experience.

Since the company was in need of all the western managerial resources it could get its hands on, Späth and Dierolf made use of the external consultants in a novel way: they invited them to take on line responsibilities ('You've analyzed this company for a whole year . . . [but] you rarely have the chance to gather line experience . . .'). In this way, the local managers would benefit from working directly with the consultants. Moreover, the consultants would not stay on forever. In Dierolf's view, 'If I brought in a [permanent] *Wessi* manager, then the *Ossis* wouldn't have a chance [to advance]; they would see the *Wessi* staying in place until retirement'.

Arrival of the Oberkochener

In July 1991 the management team from Oberkochen arrived in Jena, led by Michael Hiller, who acted as speaker *primus inter pares*. Hiller was in his late 40s, had worked at Zeiss for 13 years and was considered one of the best executives at the firm. Before Zeiss, he had worked in management consulting, which included a four-year stint in Brazil as a general manager.

Hiller was drawn to his current assignment by the unique personal and historical challenge it presented. 'This is no administrator's job', he pointed out, 'otherwise, Oberkochen could have sent a *Beamte* [literally, civil servant] out here'.

Oberkochen was beginning to understand that Jena would be no ordinary subsidiary, but that a considerable degree of local discretion would be necessary to achieve a self-supporting operation that could fulfill the social and financial commitments of the Carl Zeiss Foundation.

Hiller came to Jena with few preconceptions and professed a willingness to listen and learn from the locals. Apart from certain staff positions (legal, finance/accounting), the divisional business units at Zeiss Jena were all filled by locals, in some cases by men who had been drawn from the third and even fourth management levels. The division heads themselves were screened according to technical competence, political acceptability and managerial/leadership qualities or potential. Failure on any one point could mean rejection. There were some close (borderline) cases that made decisions difficult, but Hiller was generally satisfied with the process.

Further down, inside each division, discretion was left to the division heads to select their own subordinates (in an approach similar to that employed at Jenoptik). Here, technical competence, political acceptability and 'social vulnerability' were the guiding criteria for selection.

Hiller rejected characterizing eastern Germany as a developing country – the skill levels of the East Germans were so high – but he did acknowledge that pragmatism was necessary to get things done in such an unstructured environment. 'The people here', he observed, 'are good problem-solvers' in a day-to-day tactical sense. They would need coaching to develop longer-term, strategic thinking, something that lay outside their previous experience.

Hiller recalled that his chief problems since coming to Jena had been logistical in nature: for example, the technical norms and standards encountered had been quite unfamiliar to him. Also, the collapse of the socialist system had caused suppliers to the firm to vanish, almost overnight. Much improvisation and reliance on the good local contacts of his staff proved crucial in getting things moving again.

Zeiss and Jenoptik Divide the Assets

Soon after the team from Oberkochen arrived in Jena, the task of physically splitting up Jenoptik Carl Zeiss Jena GmbH had to be tackled. This was an enormously complex affair that would dominate the attention of senior managers for the next several months. It included separating, idling or transferring employees, an exercise which was complicated by the fact that the labor union councils, whose cooperation was important, were still organized along production plant, rather than divisional, lines. Equipment had to be moved from one site to another or, if this proved impossible (as in the case of high-precision machines), agreements drawn up to provide for subcontracting between Zeiss and Jenoptik. Entire buildings had to be renovated, torn down, or built from scratch.

There existed the natural temptation at both companies to recruit the best-qualified staff to their own side. While most employees could be associated with a specific product area, insiders acknowledge that there was some competition for extraordinarily talented people, but this was more the exception than the rule.

Dierolf likened the division of assets to a 'divorce proceeding' where objectivity was difficult to achieve, even if the parties acted with the best intentions: 'It leads to unavoidable frictions, because there are unavoidable opposing interests, and since we humans are not noble and good by nature, this leads to personal frictions, which can go quite deep at times . . .'

Conflicts were resolved through direct contact and at times tough negotiations between the seniors on both sides.

Local staff who worked in close proximity to western managers at this time was exposed to eye-opening doses of reality. One local staff member at Jenoptik explained that he had gradually realized, during the summer of 1991, just how inflated his perception of the true value of Zeiss Jena as a going concern had been. So much of the physical plant was simply not worth renovating; instead,

tearing down and building anew was often the only rational action. Hiller served that it was difficult for local employees to accept the economic reasoning that underlay such decisions. As one employee remarked, 'How do you explain to the people here that the company is worth only one D-mark [the symbolic purchase price Oberkochen paid to the Treuhand]?'

With Späth on the road soliciting investors[18] and Dierolf negotiating the joint venture and cooperation agreements as well as supervising the Zeiss-Jenoptik split, only limited attention could be devoted to the operating side of the business. One frustrated manager at Jenoptik observed that 'Meetings are preoccupied with the present problems, rather than future strategic activities; how do we divide the assets? How do we cut costs? Who else do we have to dismiss?'

Since Zeiss Jena and Jenoptik were not due to separate legally until October, they continued to run common accounts and losses were covered from a central fund. In anticipation of the separation, there was incentive to do as little as possible 'because one would ask, "Who initiated a particular contract?" 'To whom are revenues to be booked?" "Who paid for the materials, the labor?"'

The morale in Jena, particularly at Jenoptik, during the third quarter of 1991 was described as 'bad' and communications even worse than before. There was still great disappointment over the course of events during the previous year. One employee at Jenoptik observed:

> Until mid-1990, the enthusiasm was great that 'we are preserving Zeiss in Jena'. In my opinion, that mood changed radically because of unfortunate public relations, perhaps consciously, by Carl Zeiss Oberkochen . . . [Some Jena people wanted to] organize competitively against Oberkochen. This attitude was widespread, but now it has turned to one of resignation.

There was also some frustration over the frequent

---

[18] He was achieving considerable success: by the end of 1991, he had negotiated with 50 firms the outplacement (or 'sale' as one employee put it) of nearly 3000 of the 5000 'reserve' labor force.

absence, however understandable, of Lothar Späth: 'Gattnar had his open assemblies every four to eight weeks . . . Späth used to attend protest meetings. Now he communicates through the press and television'.

The in-house magazine *Prisma* was discontinued in June pending the establishment of separate Zeiss Jena and Jenoptik publications. The public/press relations people, who were normally in charge of preparing *Prisma*, were not sure what was going on but believed that a summer issue was being prepared by the external management consultants and would contain important information concerning the company's future. The two new magazines were launched toward the end of the year.

To the visitor, Jena presented an outwardly calm face during the summer of 1991, but this was in reality a particularly stressful time for Zeiss employees in view of the lay-offs expected to be announced in September. An employee noted that the despair continued to be greatest among those who sat at home on 'short hours-zero'. The suspense was finally broken with dispatch of some 14,000 'blue letters', announcing lay-offs effective on 31 December.

> Many people did not believe until the very end that they were on the [dismissal] list . . . They denied it until the very end . . . The shock was visible when they got the news in black and white and were told that this was their last day.

Reinhold, in charge of Jenoptik's research center in Göschwitz, had the unenviable task of addressing a letter of dismissal to his own wife, who worked in the same facility, as well as to one of his two secretaries; leading by example was the only credible thing he could do.

The formal launching of Zeiss Jena and Jenoptik as separate legal entities took place on 1 October 1991.

Referring to the future of Zeiss Jena, Hiller expected that the subsidiary would eventually develop an identity of its own. To support this, he cited plans by which Jena would become the sole center for Zeiss planetary (the equivalent division in Oberkochen would discontinue its operation); moreover, Jena would continue its R&D activities and develop products locally (in coordination with Oberkochen) and would be allowed to retain the old Zeiss Jena trademark (the lens) on its own products (Oberkochen's square-shaped logo, on the other hand, would be used in all advertising).

If the survivors were celebrating the retention of their jobs, then they did so privately. One woman at Zeiss (relocated to new offices on the edge of Jena) spoke nostalgically of the 31 years she had spent working in the old administrative headquarters in the middle of town: 'But,' she said, gesturing to her colleagues, 'we should be happy that we have work'. Meanwhile, in the old headquarters, now occupied by Jenoptik, a man with over 20 years' service at Zeiss paused to reflect on the loss of the distinguished corporate name. Like the woman, however, he could only say, 'At least we have work'.

Case 8: Encyclopaedia Britannica

By Jeffrey Rayport and Thomas Gerace[1]

I didn't realize it at the time, but my best childhood birthday present was not the 'Mace Brown autograph' baseball glove or the slightly used J.C. Higgins bicycle or even the Red Ryder air rifle. It was an imposing set of 25 blue-bound books purchased on the installment plan from a door-to-door salesman and proudly placed in a bookcase with glass doors, lock and key. Mom and Dad impressed on me that the shiny new *Britannica Junior Encyclopaedia* represented such a major family investment that the books really belonged to all three of us children.

In 1944, it was a significant financial sacrifice for the family of a steelworker that lived from paycheck to paycheck. I don't know what the *Britannica* cost them back then, but today's deluxe edition of the 'adult' encyclopaedia starts at a cool $1,499. Our first family television set was still six years in the future and the Pennsylvania winters were harsh, so there was ample opportunity for me to spend hours poring through those wonderful books.

(Kelly, 1995)

The *Encyclopaedia Britannica* – the oldest English language encyclopaedia, having published 15 editions over the course of more than 225 years – seemed unsinkable in 1990. In the 1980s, Britannica sales grew at an average of 8.1 percent per year and reached a record high of $627 million for the year ended September 30, 1989 (*S & P Creditwire* 1995). In 1990, the company sold 117,000 copies at $1,300 each. The company had been profitable in 19 of the previous 20 years. In the next three years, however, Britannica saw its sales erode with the explosion of CD-ROM-based encyclopaedias. CD-ROM was the technology of storing computer files on compact disks (CDs); a single CD could hold 650 megabytes of information, or more than 465 high density floppy disks. The vast storage space allowed CD-ROM publishers to include graphics, sound, and video, which typically formed larger files than simple text. CD-ROM encyclopaedias were cheap to manufacture and often preferred by institutions, for they required far less shelf space than a set of encyclopaedias.

In 1992 and 1993, the company lost $4.6 million and $15 million, respectively. By 1994, the company's encyclopaedia sales volume had fallen 53.5 percent from its 1990 level, to 51,000 copies. With revenues tumbling to $453.7 million in 1994, the company found itself without money for development of new technologies (Kelly 1995).

In April 1995, Britannica released a statement that read, in part

> Technology and the Information Age have radically transformed our landscape and will require our company to make a significant transition from our historical past. To continue to grow and develop our business, we must reinvest. We need capital and are confident we can secure it. Our goal is to preserve *Encyclopaedia Britannica* as an institution and to continue to develop new products and explore alternative sales channels.

One month later, *The New York Times* reported that Britannica management was seeking

[1] Source: Research Associate Thomas A. Gerace prepared this case under the supervision of Professor Jeffrey F. Rayport as the basis for class discussion rather than to illustrate either effective or ineffective handling of an administrative situation. Copyright © 1995 by the President and Fellows of Harvard College. To order copies, call (617) 495–6117 or write the Publishing Division, Harvard Business School, Boston, MA, 02163. No part of this publication may be reproduced, stored in a retrieval system, used in a spreadsheet, or transmitted in any form or by any means – electronic, mechanical, photocopying, recording, or otherwise – without the permission of Harvard Business School.

a buyer (Landler 1995). Industry analysts believed that the owner, the William Benton Foundation, hoped to raise $400–$500 million on the sale. The Benton Foundation published Britannica to raise revenues for the University of Chicago. Potential buyers included publishers such as Viacom's Simon & Schuster and K-III Communications, controlled by Kohlberg, Kravis, and Roberts, the leveraged buyout firm, and technology companies such as Microsoft (ibid.).

The Paper Age[2]

If history is in the telling, few sources have enjoyed more power over history than *Encyclopaedia Britannica*. For more than two centuries, Britannica noted, recorded, classified, and published the collective knowledge of the human race – at least, those dwelling in the industrialized world. With more than 4000 contributors – one-third of whom were not English speakers – submitting works in some 54 languages in its latest edition (McDowell 1995), the *Encyclopaedia Britannica* enjoyed an enviable position among reference works. Thus, when Truman Capote's death was mentioned in *Britannica*, but the Union Carbide disaster in Bhopal, India, that same year, was not, *Newsweek* mentioned the omission; when an entry under 'dogs' questioned the validity of studies using canines in biomedical research, hundreds of scientists protested (*Chicago Sun-Times* 1992). It might have shocked the three men who began Britannica to know what an important work their encyclopaedia would become.

In 1768, printers Andrew Bell and Colin Macfarquhar, and printer and antiquary William Smellie, founded *The Encyclopaedia Britannica: A Dictionary of Arts and Sciences* in Edinburgh, Scotland. The first edition, published in three volumes (2,659 pages and 160 copperplates), were sold for £12 in 1771. The novelty of Britannica lay in mixing long essays on important subjects with short, dictionary-like entries for technical terms and other subjects. *The Daily Mail* reported, 'The first Britannica described Japan as "a small island off the coast of California" and devoted only five lines to China. It had a simple one-line entry for Woman – "female of man (*The Daily Mail* 1995)."'

The second edition, 10 volumes and 8,595 pages, was released in parts between 1777 and 1784. The new version added biographical articles and included history with the various geographical articles. In turn, the third edition, published between 1788 and 1797, was 18 volumes (14,579 pages). During the writing of this edition, founder Macfarquhar died; Andrew Bell purchased his share of Britannica from his heirs.

The fourth edition (20 volumes containing 16,033 pages) was reflected in the quite similar fifth and sixth editions. In contrast, the Supplement to the fourth, fifth, and sixth editions, appearing in six volumes between 1815 and 1824, reshaped the content of the entire encyclopaedia. Instead of compiling digests from independent publications, nearly all of the encyclopaedia entries were original, signed contributions, and many authors were distinguished British and French scholars. During the publication of this supplement, Britannica was sold to the publisher Archibald Constable, who went bankrupt in the great financial crash of 1826.[3] Edinburgh publisher Adam Black, founder and chairman of A&C Black Publishers, bought Britannica and produced its seventh edition (21 volumes, 17,101 pages and 506 plates) between 1830 and 1842. Black added an extra volume: a general index for the other 21 volumes. This feature was retained in subsequent versions.

The eighth edition was similar to its predecessor, while the ninth (24 volumes, including an index, published between 1875 and 1889) achieved a certain fame for its progressive stance on a number of the scientific and religious controversies of the times.

---

[2] The history of the Encyclopaedia Britannica is drawn from the history contained in the publication's fifteenth edition, Encyclopaedia Britannica, *The New Encyclopedia Britannica* (Chicago, Il: 1994), 15th edition, Vol. 4, pp. 487–8.

[3] The crash combined with the heavy spending habits of Sir Walter Scott, a writer for Constable, to cause his firm's collapse. Constable died one year later. John Carey, 'Myth Maker,' *The Sunday Times*, (February 26, 1995), Section: Features.

In 1901 American publishers Horace E. Hooper and Walter M. Jackson purchased Britannica from A&C Black and published the tenth edition, an 11–volume update to the ninth. The eleventh edition differed significantly from previous ones, as editors chose to divide lengthy articles into more specific ones, creating 40,000 articles (the ninth edition had 17,000) in 29 volumes. Britannica would remain in American hands throughout the century.

In 1920, Sears, Roebuck & Company purchased Britannica and began selling an inexpensive version of the encyclopaedia through mail order. That same year the company began door-to-door sales, following the trend set by Avon, Fuller Brush and, from its start in 1917, *World Book Encyclopaedia*. Britannica continued using the door-to-door sales method through 1995, giving salespeople a commission on each sale.[4]

In the year that followed, the company released three volumes to supplement the eleventh edition, and named the combined eleventh edition (29 volumes) and supplements (three volumes) the twelfth edition. The addition of another three volumes created the thirteenth. Sears found the mail order venture too costly and sold Britannica in 1923. For five years (1923–1928) the widow of the former editor and publisher of the *Encyclopaedia Britannica*, Horace Hooper, and William Cox owned the encyclopaedia. Sears bought it back in 1928.

In the fourteenth edition – 24 volumes including a complete atlas – 'space was found for many new articles on scientific and other subjects by cutting down the ample style and learned detail in the 11th edition . . . More than 3,500 authors of all nationalities contributed articles (Encyclopaedia Britannica 1994).' In 1932, Elkan Harrison Powell, a vice president of Sears Roebuck, became president of Britannica. Powell developed the direct-sales methods that grew the company's market in the years following the Depression. The new management also implemented a system of continuous revision, updating and reprinting the encyclopaedia each year rather than releasing massive revisions on an irregular schedule.

In 1941, William Benton, vice president of the University of Chicago and a former advertising executive, convinced Sears, Roebuck, and Company to give the *Encyclopaedia Britannica* to the University. When University trustees refused the gift, because of the financial risks the encyclopaedia might pose, Benton supplied $100,000 in working capital, became majority stockholder, and named himself chairman of the board. Mr. Benton passed ownership of Britannica to the William Benton Foundation when he died in 1973. Profits from the encyclopaedia were to be donated to the University of Chicago.

In 1961, Britannica acquired *Compton's Pictured Encyclopaedia* from F.E. Compton & Company. Compton's was founded by Frank E. Compton in 1922, as a general reference book for young people. Compton's was the first encyclopaedia to use drawings and photographs on the same page as text. In 1968, 'pictured' was removed from the title. None the less, Compton's continued its graphical tradition, with editions in the late 1980s containing more than 22,500 photographs and nearly 2,000 maps.[5] When Compton's joined Britannica, Compton's was positioned as a less expensive, student's encyclopaedia. In February 1993, a set of Compton's sold for $599, compared to $1200 for Britannica.

In 1964, William Benton paid $14 million for the G&C Merriam Company, which owned *Webster's Dictionary*. Three years later, the company began perhaps its largest editorial effort in history, the creation of the fifteenth edition of the *Encyclopaedia Britannica*. Under the leadership of Benton and Charles E. Swanson, president of Britannica from 1967 to 1985, the encyclopaedia was divided into three parts: the *Micropoedia* for ready reference articles of no more than 750 words, the *Macropoedia* for in depth knowledge, and the *Propoedia*, a 10-subject outline of the entire world of knowledge. The fifteenth edition noted, 'The editorial creation of the work cost $32 million,

---

[4] Direct sale information was provided by the Direct Sales Association in Washington D.C. on August 11, 1995.

[5] Information on *Compton's* history is taken from 'Encyclopaedia Brittannica,' *The New Encyclopaedia Britannica* (Chicago, Il: 1994), 15th edition, Vol. 2, pp. 507.

exclusive of printing costs, representing the largest single private investment in publishing history up to this time.'[6] The edition was released in a 30-volume set, the 10-volume *Micropoedia*, the 19-volume *Macropoedia*, and a one-volume *Propoedia*.

Benton – and the Benton Foundation that took on ownership of Britannica after his death in 1973 – and the University of Chicago worked closely on Britannica. Chicago's president, Robert M.Hutchins, was named chairman of the board of editors. The University lent its name and resources to the publication in exchange for royalties of three percent (totaling approximately $80 million between 1943 and 1995).[7]

In the early 1980s, Britannica began leasing space from booksellers nationwide to promote sales. Typically the company would place a Britannica employee and several sets of encyclopaedias in each store, paying a flat rate plus a percentage of sales for the space. When entering a new bookstore, Britannica would often buy the store's mailing list to use for direct mailings.[8]

In 1985, the company completed a $24 million revision of the fifteenth edition. The most notable change was the addition of a two-volume index to the entire edition, consisting of 1,700 pages and almost 410,000 entries. The index was designed to eliminate confusion that resulted from having the separate *Micropoedia* and *Macropoedia* sections. The company also expanded the *Micropoedia* by two volumes – moving almost all the encyclopaedia's biographies there and allowing some articles to run longer than the previous 750-word limit – and condensed the *Macropoedia*. The new fifteenth edition comprised 32 volumes,

for a total of 32,165 pages or 44 million words. The new set cost consumers $1,249 to $6,000, depending on the binding, which ranged from a durable cotton to leather (McDowell 1995).

Going Global with Coproduction

Since 1964, the *Encyclopaedia Britannica* had become, in fact, much more than the oldest English-language encyclopaedia. In that year, Britannica first appeared in Portuguese, publishing the *Encyclopaedia Barsa*. Using a modern arrangement known as coproduction – where two or more publishing companies joined forces to produce an encyclopaedia written by one in the language of the other(s) – Britannica expanded its reach around the globe.

The French version was announced in 1968. One year later, Britannica joined Tokyo Broadcasting Corporation (TBS)[9] and Toppan Printing Company to publish *Buritanika Kokusai Dai Hyakka Jiten* (Britannica International Encyclopaedia). The company published a children's version in Italian, *Il Modulo*, in 1973, *Encyclopaedia Barsa* for Spain in 1985, and four years later *Encyclopaedia Hispanica* for Latin America.

In 1980, the company teamed with China's Encyclopaedia Publishing House to begin development of the *Concise Encyclopaedia Britannica*, an eight-volume, eight-million character set largely based on the *Micropoedia* section of the fifteenth edition. In September that year, Vice-Premier Deng Xiaoping welcomed a delegation from Britannica to celebrate the publishing of the first Chinese edition.

Entering China was not without risk. In January, 1987, the vice chairman of Britannica's board of editors, Frank B. Gibney (1987) reflected on the company's experience there. One of the greatest concerns on entering the China, he noted, was insuring the integrity of the writing:

---

[6] Ibid.

[7] Edwin McDowell, Encyclopedia Britannica's Stock to go to the University of Chicago, *The New York Times* (October 2, 1980), p. A1. McDowell explains, 'The law requires that regular foundations have no more than 50 percent of their net worth in any one company and that they spend at least five percent of their net worth every year. So-called supporting foundations do not have to payout five percent; the exact amount has to be worked out with the Internal Revenue Service.'

[8] Information taken from an interview with a Cambridge, Massachusetts bookseller, August 11, 1995.

[9] Not to be confused with the Japanese Broadcasting Company, NHK.

Most of our political differences finally centered around some of the 24 articles on China (out of the total of 71,000) which Chinese editors prepared themselves, subject to our review. True to standard Marxist hyperbole, communist armies were forever 'smashing' their 'traitorous' or 'counter-revolutionary' enemies; Mao Tse-tung's 'correct line' was constantly triumphing over 'right opportunist' or 'left adventurist' wrongs within the party. After discussions, our colleagues agreed to a 'no adjective' policy.

After reaching agreement on the content, the company had to contend with potential obstruction to publishing the work by more conservative members of the Communist party:

> Only once was there any danger that the project might be stopped. In 1983, a short but intensive campaign by party hard-liners against 'spiritual pollution' took aim at the influence of Western ideas among Chinese intellectuals. A showdown took place in Peking and the naysayers lost – but it was a close call.

> Beyond doubt, the venture owed its survival to the steady support of Deng and leaders who gave top priority to modernization. Visiting Deng in late 1985, we were told flatly: 'The encyclopaedia is a key step in our modernization . . .. We need this and more books like it to educate our people. We will continue in this effort.' (ibid.)

Britannica survived these potential pitfalls and published the first Chinese version of the Encyclopaedia in late 1986. Within a few months, the first printing of 50,000 copies was sold out, despite the 156 yuan price tag, which represented more than the monthly salary of many of the company's editors in Beijing.

Britannica announced a Taiwanese version in 1988–1989, and launched its Turkish edition over four years, between 1986 and 1990; a Korean edition was published between 1992 and 1994.

Britannica Italiana – an advanced version of the encyclopaedia in Italian – was being developed in 1995, as was the company's Hungarian version. Meanwhile, the company had announced a copublication agreement with Progress Publishers of the then Soviet Union to publish a Russian-language version of the 12-volume *Micropoedia*. The Russian edition was slated to contain 'local editorial material having particular relevance to the Union of Soviet Socialist Republics . . . To ensure that no arbitrary changes or additions are made that would be inaccurate or contrary to Britannica standards of objectivity, there will be an editorial review board appointed by Britannica, with Progress Publishers' collaboration.' (*PR Newswire* 1990) The Russian Britannica was hailed as evidence of Mikhail Gorbachev's glasnost; it would be the first international encyclopaedia published in the Soviet Union since 1917.

Britannica's international expansion was not, however, without its pitfalls. By the mid-1990s, the company found it necessary to seek legal protection for the intellectual property it published around the world. For example, to protect its six-year investment in the Chinese edition, Britannica was forced to take immediate action. The Tan Ching Book Company of Taipei in the Republic of China (Taiwan), had copied the Chinese-language *Concise Encyclopaedia Britannica* (Rudd 1989). Encyclopaedia Britannica reported that approximately 10,000 sets of the pirated version had been sold. The pirated editions were sold for as little as $135 per set, compared to Britannica's price in that region of $492. In 1988, officials of the company were sentenced to jail for copyright violation, but the sentence was overturned a year later. Moreover, Britannica lost its civil case when, on May 26, 1989, a Taipei District Court judge ruled, 'Encyclopaedia Britannica does not possess a Republic of China copyright on the books because Taiwanese–American trade agreements were broken along with diplomatic relations in 1978 (ibid.).'

The Tan Ching Book Company publisher continued to publish its pirated version during a prolonged court battle and even had the gall to warn consumers to 'watch out for the fakes that have lately appeared in the market' in their advertising (Eckhouse and Viviano 1991). In Taiwan's Supreme Court, Britannica won its case. Tu Chieh-hsiang and Chang Chia-hsien of the Tan Ching Book Company were convicted and sentenced to 14 and 12 months in jail, respectively. Britannica was awarded $803,000 in damages (*San Francisco Chronicle* 1991).

The Digital Age

As Britannica expanded around the world and into different languages, the company also launched into new electronic channels. The company hoped to leverage its vast database to enter the electronic research and education markets. Throughout the l980s, Britannica used a combination of licensing agreements and acquisitions to build its electronic presence.

In August, 1981, the company licensed its fifteenth edition content to Mead Data Central, for inclusion on Mead's Lexis-Nexis information retrieval service. This marked Britannica's first venture into electronic publishing. The company was clearly concerned with the impact of this license on its print publishing business. As *Business Week* (1981) reported, 'To protect the markets for its printed volumes, however, the publisher will not offer the electronic version to any schools, libraries, or individuals that are subscribers to the Mead Corp. subsidiary's retrieval services.'

Britannica also launched a program to attract young people to its products. In November, 1983, the Encyclopaedia Britannica Educational Corporation introduced 12 educational software programs for use with Apple computers. The software was designed to help school children with vocabulary, reading, and word-processing. Vocabulary exercises ranged from the most basic to more advanced levels, and included SAT-preparation exercises for older students (*Byte* 1993). Each program cost between $25 and $50; different combinations could be purchased for between $43 and $115.

The company announced the acquisition of DesignWare and Edu-Ware, subsidiaries of Management Sciences of America, Inc., in February, 1985. Britannica reported that the new companies, which specialized in design and development of entertainment and educational software, would form a new division, Britannica Learning

Corp. At the time of purchase, DesignWare had 14 titles available for the Apple II, IBM, Atari, and Commodore computers; Edu-Ware had 30 titles for the Apple II and IBM computers.

Stanley D. Frank, president of the new division and executive vice president of Encyclopaedia Britannica Inc., commented that the new division's mission was consistent with the company's long involvement in education, and that he was extremely optimistic about the software publishing field.

> Industry forecasts indicate that this business has been growing at about 30 percent per year and is expected to increase at this same rate or higher during the next five years, as the installed base of computers continues to grow, creating greater need for quality software. All forecasts show that the software industry growth will exceed that of the hardware or microcomputer industry itself. (*Business Wire* 1985)

One week after the christening of Britannica Learning Corp., the company embarked on a reorganization, which included expanding its Compton's Encyclopaedia operation. Encyclopaedia Britannica, Inc. president, Charles E. Swanson, announced that Compton's, previously part of Encyclopaedia Britannica (USA), would become its own division. Patricia A. Wier, formerly Britannica's vice president for planning, development, and control, was named president of the new Compton's Learning Co. Compton's would become the company's fifth division, alongside Encyclopaedia Britannica USA, Encyclopaedia Britannica International, the Britannica Learning Corp., and Merriam Webster Inc.

Britannica also purchased American Learning Corporation in 1985. American Learning, which operated 82 centers that provided specialized learning instruction using audio-visual equipment, had operating profits of $522,000 on revenues of $6.8 million in 1984. Within one year, Britannica sold 22 percent of the company in a public offering (with an initial public offering price of $10 per share) to raise revenues to build new centers. The company then repurchased two percent of the company on the open market 11 months later at $5 per share (*Chicago Tribune* 1986). In mid-1987, American Learning's 104 centers introduced new software for the Apple II, designed to help with specific reading comprehension skills (Henry 1987). American Learning was renamed Britannica Learning Centers in January 1989. Plagued by poor management, the Britannica Learning Centers proved unable to make a profit; Britannica sold them to the Sylvan Learning Corporation in 1992 after Britannica Learning Centers' share price fell to $1.

Focusing instead on its consumer software line, Britannica Learning Corp. acquired Blue Chip Software, a 15–person software company concentrating on the development of business skills, in January 1986. The Blue Chip's most popular title, Millionaire, taught would-be investors to buy and sell stocks, trade on margin, and invest in options. Millionaire, which retailed for $50, sold more than 100,000 copies (Akst 1986). Britannica intended to take over manufacturing for Blue Chip, reducing the company's workforce to five full-time personnel.

Six months later, the company announced the acquisition of the Encyclopaedia Britannica Educational Corporation (EBEC). Encyclopaedia Britannica, Inc. planned to purchase a 75 percent stake in EBEC from William Benton's children (Storch 1986; *Business Wire* 1986). Despite the similarity in name, Encyclopaedia Britannica Inc. and EBEC had been separately owned and operated since owner William Benton's death, when the Encyclopaedia Britannica, Inc., became property of the Benton Foundation, while EBEC remained in family hands. The Educational Corporation was a supplier of films and educational materials to elementary and secondary schools; it also had a contract to distribute the Encyclopaedia Britannica to schools and libraries.

In August 1988, Britannica announced that it would partner with Educational Systems Corp. (ESC) to build an electronic version of Compton's Encyclopaedia. The ESC system, which had an installed base of 450 proprietary systems and an additional 200 systems on order, cost schools approximately $100,000. The companies planned to build a networkable CD-ROM, designed for sale to elementary and secondary schools (Phelps 1988).

Data Integrity

While technology certainly made publishing the massive Encyclopaedia Britannica easier, the company learned a difficult lesson in August 1986, when editors discovered a saboteur had altered computer files. In a memorandum to editorial staff, editor-in-chief Tom Goetz announced, 'evidence of deliberate sabotage in the EB computer files,' most notably the changing of references to 'Jesus Christ' to 'Allah' and the insertion of the names of some Britannica executives as historical figures in other articles. A disgruntled former editor had made the changes, using a password that had not been changed since he had been laid-off. While the company's 44-million-word 1987 update was safe, employees had to check at least some of the 1988 edition for alterations (Warren 1986).

CD-ROM

In its September 11, 1982 issue, *The Economist* explored the land of electronic publishing in its article, 'Electronic Libraries, Pocket-sized Britannicas?' The article discussed the efforts of a University of Colorado team that was trying to design read-only memory (ROM) chips that could contain an entire book. The Economist concluded that the industry-standard 64 K ROMs (that held 64,000 bits of information) were not sufficiently advanced technology for the project. An electronic book would cost more than $300; an electronic Britannica would cost hundreds of times that.

The Economist projected that the 1 megabit (1,024,000 bit) ROMs then under development would not deliver sufficient memory for the task. The journal also stated that the 4 megabit ROMs were five or six years in the future. What *The Economist* could not project was the introduction of compact disk technology or the advent of the CD-ROM. While magnetic and optical storage media seemed expensive and slow in 1982, the CD provided a massive (650 megabit), and increasingly quick alternative in the late 1980s and early 1990s.

In 1985, however, Groliers' Encyclopaedia announced that it had developed a CD-ROM encyclopaedia for DOS computers. Groliers, a subsidiary of the multi-billion dollar Hatchette publishing and multimedia group, published the *Encyclopaedia Americana* and *The New Book of Knowledge*. The suggested retail price of the software in 1985 was only $199, but the hardware required to run it totaled approximately $10,000 and was thus not suitable for the commercial market (Kaul 1992). In 1992, Groliers introduced a multimedia version of the software for Windows and Macintosh computers for $395. The product was selling for $99.95 in August, 1995 (please see Exhibit 1 for a comparison of popular CD-ROM titles).

In March, 1989, Encyclopaedia Britannica, Inc. and ESC announced *Compton's Multimedia Encyclopaedia* (CMME). The networkable CD-ROM allowed multiple users to access the 5000 articles and 12,000 images available in the *Multi-media Encyclopaedia*. While the addition of color, animation, and sound might have been the most apparent change from the print version, the greatest innovation was the CD's organization and search capabilities. Students could enter a topic and receive a list of related articles. Users could browse through related images and then select background on a specific one, follow a timeline and read selected stories, or select a region of a spinning globe and read about geography. The product even included the 65,000 entries found in *Webster's Intermediate Dictionary*, which allowed students to look up words they didn't recognize in Compton's text. *Compton's Multimedia Encyclopaedia* was available for purchase by schools and libraries for the 1989–1990 school year for $750.

Stanley Frank, executive vice president of Britannica Inc., described it as 'a groundbreaking innovation in electronic publishing . . . We have combined the strengths that long have been a part of Compton's Encyclopaedia with state-of-the-art features in electronic publishing to produce a truly unique learning resource (*PR Newswire* 1989).'

EXHIBIT 1
A Comparison of CD ROM Encyclopedias available in 1995

	Encyclopaedia Britannica	World Book	Compton's Multimedia Encyclopedia	Encarta	New Grolier Multimedia Encyclopedia
Retail Price	$995	$395	$79.95	$89.95	$89.95
Text	44 million words	10 million words 17,000 articles	9 million words 33,700 articles	9 million words 26,000 articles	10 million words 33,000 articles
Graphics	*	3,000 photos	7,000 photos	5,600 photos	4,000 photos
Maps	*	256 maps	global atlas	800	15 animated maps
Sound	*	*	100 clips	8 hours	40 minutes
Video and animation	*	*	15 videos 30 animations	9.5 videos 29 animations	6 videos 53 animations

Sources: Information for World Book, Compton's Encarta, and Grolier's is compiled from Mike Langberg, 'Print Encyclopedias In Quandry; Keeping Afloat as CD-ROM Versions Invade,' *San Jose Mercury News* (July 3, 1994) p. D5, and Harry Wessel, 'Encyclopedias for Computers Add More Facts, Fun; Here's What You Need to Know About the Brand-New Versions of the Three Major CD-ROM Multimedia Encyclopedias,' *Orlando Sentinel* (November 7, 1994), p. D1. Information for Britannica is taken from Heather Green, 'Britannica Online: Old Firm in New Era,' *Bloomberg Business News* (June 27, 1995).

In February 1990, Britannica announced that it had selected Radio Shack's Tandy computer line as the exclusive platform on which to market the consumer version of CMME. Like the latest institutional version of the software, the consumer version contained the complete text of the 26–volume print version of Compton's, 15,000 photographs, 60 minutes of sound (including Martin Luther King, Jr.'s 'I have a dream' speech, recordings of Bach's music, and animal sounds), 5800 maps, charts, and graphs, a search and retrieval system, and the complete *Webster's Intermediate Dictionary*, all on a single CD (*The Washington Post* 1989; *United Press International* 1990). The Tandy 2500XL with monitor cost $3,600. The retail version of Compton's cost $850, which executive vice President Stanley Frank noted was 'only slightly higher than what is paid for the print volumes (*Video Marketing News* 1990).'

Two months after the start of its commercial trial, Britannica had acquired Del Mar software, a text retrieval software developer that had co-developed *Compton's Multimedia Encyclopaedia*. Britannica had licensed Del Mar's SmarTrieve product, used to formulate searches from plain-text inquiries, as the foundation of Compton's Multimedia search system.

As the success of Microsoft's Windows operating system became more apparent, Britannica began developing compatible software. In April 1991, the company announced an MS Windows version of the CMME. The new software added the capability of having multiple windows open simultaneously and superimposing geographical information about a region on top of its map (*Education Computer News* 1991).

Six months later, Britannica announced a second edition of *Compton's Multimedia*. The new version had 25 percent new content – primarily current events information – and improved graphics, search capability, and animation. *Information Today*, however, reported 'One of the main drawbacks of Compton's is that the product seems to discourage printing. In order to print a section of text, the user must copy it to the clipboard and then paste it into the Notebook. The information can then be printed.' (Rosen 1992) The company also lowered its retail (normally $995) and institu-

tional (normally $895) pricing by $100, and offered upgrades on its 1.0 edition for $150.

With the new release, Britannica Software also announced the Family Choice CD-ROM, featuring 15 popular titles – Algebra 1, First Semester and Algebra 1, Second Semester, The Berenstain Bears Junior, Jigsaw, The Berenstain Bears Learn About Counting, Body Transparent, Designasaurus, Grammar Examiner, Jigsaw! The Ultimate Electronic Puzzle, Just the FAX, Math Maze, Millionaire 11, Revolution '76, States and Traits, Super Spellicopter, and The Fiction Advisor all for a retail price of $199 (*CD-ROM Professional* 1991).

In February, 1992, Stanley Frank, president of Britannica Software, announced the company had changed its name to Compton's New Media. The company also announced that it was preparing a CD-I version of *Compton's Multimedia*. CD-I was a proprietary system developed by Philips Interactive Media for the home market. Compton's New Media stated that the CD-I development was consistent with its desire to develop products for a variety of platforms. CD-I, however, failed to compete with the existing electronic games and home computer CD ROM equipment.

In the summer of 1992, Compton's New Media moved its headquarters from San Francisco to a 45,000-square-foot facility in Carlsbad, California, near Palomar Airport. This new facility – twice the size of the old one – was to house the rapidly expanding Compton's staff. General manager Norman Bastin said Compton's New Media's payroll included 85 employees, but would double over the next year. The company was confident that the CD-ROM encyclopaedia market was poised to explode, as a multimedia personal computer and the *Compton's Multimedia Encyclopaedia* could be purchased for as little as $1,700. CD-ROM sales in general were $482.2 million in 1990, and were expected to grow beyond $2.65 billion by the 1995 (Kaul 1992).

In August, 1992, Britannica unveiled a new electronic index to the *Encyclopaedia Britannica*. The index allowed users to create a relevance-ranked list of encyclopaedia articles electronically, but, notably, the company did not provide users electronic access to the contents of *Britannica*. Included with the index was an electronic version of *Merriam-Webster's Ninth New Collegiate Dictionary* (*IDP Report* 1992). The index, which used SmartTrieve's full-text retrieval system and had been three years in development, retailed for $299.

Early in 1993, Microsoft announced the first edition of its own CD ROM encyclopaedia, *Encarta*. Based on *Funk & Wagnalls New Encyclopaedia*, *Encarta* offered users advanced multimedia and search capabilities. Reviews and surveys in 1993 indicated that while some users preferred Groliers' text, the Microsoft product took better advantage of the new format than the competition (Salpeter 1993; Banet 1993). (Please see Exhibit 2 for selected sales figures for print and CD ROM encyclopaedias).

Missing the Boat

While the first copies of Microsoft's *Encarta* hit the shelves, Britannica began to re-evaluate its CD-ROM flagship. On March 1,1993, Encyclopaedia

Britannica president and chief financial officer Peter Norton sent a memo to employees informing them that, 'from time to time EB has received expressions of interest [in Compton's New Media].' Norton informed his organization that the company had asked the Chicago office of investment bankers Lazard Freres & Co. to do a 'more in-depth assessment of the marketplace (Hilts 1993).' In an article alluding to the potential sale of Compton's, *Publishers Weekly* noted:

> According to industry talk, all print reference products have been suffering since the rise of electronic publishing. Compton's Learning Division was one of the pioneers in the area, and was viewed as one of the more successful publishers, with *Compton's Multimedia Encyclopaedia* (on CD-ROM). Just one year ago, Compton's New Media announced an innovative joint program with R.R. Donnelley, offering publishers a complete package of production, marketing, and distribution of multimedia titles (ibid.).

On June 29, 1993, Encyclopaedia Britannica, Inc. announced the retirement of its chairman and

EXHIBIT 2
Selected Sales Statistics for Print and CD ROM Publishing

		1990	1991	1992	1993	1994
All books	units	2,144,300,000	2,181,000,000	2,192,300,000	2,221,900,000	2,274,400,000
	dollars	$15,437,600,000	$16,918,500,000	$16,918,500,000	$17,993,700,000	$18,791,000,000
Subscription Reference Books[1]	units	1,100,000	1,100,000	1,100,000	1,200,000	1,200,000
	dollars	$540,500,000	$552,400,000	$572,300,000	$602,000,000	$641,300,000
CD ROM	units	*	*	*	2,951,612	7,726,271
	dollars	*	*	*	$89,328,836	$290,647,731
CD ROM Reference	units	*	*	*	1,180,645	3,090,508
	dollars	*	*	*	$35,731,534	$116,259,092

Sources: Information on print material publishing was provided by the Association of American Publishers (dollar sales) and the Association of American Booksellers (unit sales). Information on CD ROM sales was provided by the Software Publishers Association. Information on CD ROM reference sales is estimated by case writers based on CD ROM sales statistics and information indicated that reference materials comprise 40% of all CD ROM sales.
[1] Subscription Reference Books is a category containing and consisting primarily of print Encyclopedia sales.

chief executive, Robert P. Gwinn, and the appointment of his successor, Peter Norton. Gwinn had led Britannica since 1973. One month later, Norton agreed to sell Compton's New Media to the Tribune Company, a $2.1 billion media conglomerate, with six daily newspapers (including The Chicago Tribune), seven TV stations, and the on-line service called Chicago On-line. With $28 million in revenues, Compton's fetched $57 million for Britannica.

That same month, the Encyclopaedia Britannica Educational Corp. announced that it had developed a multimedia CD-ROM for geography called *Geopedia*. *Geopedia* contained 1200 geography articles, more than 3000 pictures, 55 games and learning activities, 1,000 completely new maps, and 15 minutes of full-motion video (*Education Technology News* 1993).

Then, in August, Britannica announced that it had created the Britannica Instant Research System, a CD-ROM set containing the entire text of the *Encyclopaedia Britannica* in searchable format. The company would not, however, sell the two-CD set (Britannica was too large to fit on a single CD), to the commercial market. The *Chicago Tribune* reported:

> Britannica intends to sell the searchable book only to publishing companies and other businesses that do substantial amounts of fact-checking. The current plan is to license the CD-ROM version to firms that will pay $2,100 a year for three years for the right to run the discs on two workstations.

> 'This is a powerful, adult-level research and retrieval tool to be used in the kind of intensive research applications demanded by publishers, news organizations and business and government agencies,' associate publisher of Encyclopaedia Britannica Karen Barch said (*Chicago Tribune* 1993).

System installation for users was expensive and difficult. Users had to load the two CD system onto a one gigabit hard drive before using it. One gigabit drives cost approximately $1,100 (*Online Newsletter* 1994).

In Fall 1994, Britannica announced that it would begin the electronic distribution of the *Encyclopaedia Britannica* to universities and some public libraries over the Internet. Already on-line were *Compton's Interactive Encyclopaedia* – offered through Prodigy and America On-line – and *Gorilla's Academic American* – on America On-line and CompuServe. Britannica was considering a number of pricing models, including a subscription price and reference-by-reference (i.e. fee-per-inquiry) pricing. Joseph Esposito, who had been the head of Merriam Webster and was then president of Encyclopaedia Britannica North America, commented, 'We're doing it ourselves because you just can't make money licensing your content. It's rather unfortunate that so many of the content providers have put themselves in a position where they're held hostage to the on-line services.' (*Publishers Weekly* 1994)

In the fall of 1994, Britannica announced it had developed a CD-ROM of the *Encyclopaedia Britannica* for the consumer market. The CD was priced at $895, compared to the $100 for Groliers or Compton's, and, while it had a robust search engine, it did not include multimedia. In December, 1995, the company offered the CD at a promotional price of $495.[10] The single-disc Britannica CD contained a dictionary, a thesaurus, and the 65,000 articles and 44 million words of the traditional Britannica.

According to Esposito, 'Most people buy the CD ROM and print versions together, making up fully 40 percent of our sales. Virtually no one is buying CD-ROM without the print version' (*Interactive Content* 1995). Britannica management believed that CD-ROM was an 'interim technology.' No one, however, seemed to know just how long the 'interim' might last (ibid.).

In July 1995, Britannica announced that it was offering free trial access to Britannica On-line – its Internet site – to Time Warner's Pathfinders[11] subscribers. Pathfinder was a advertising-based, free service offered by Time Warner on the Internet's World Wide Web[12] and included content

---

[10] Promotional price recorded by casewriters at the Harvard Coop, Cambridge, Massachusetts.

[11] www.pathfinder.com

[12] For more information about the Internet's Worldwide Web, please see *The Internet*, HBS Note #9-794-073 by Thomas A. Gerace and Gregory S. Smirin.

from *Time, Sports Illustrated, People, Money, Entertainment Weekly* and *Fortune*. The site also featured information from Warner Brothers and HBO (*The San Diego Union-Tribune* 1995).

Charting the Future

For 227 years, the *Encyclopaedia Britannica* was the flagship of general reference books. Famous for its authors – Benjamin Franklin on electricity, Sir Walter Scott on chivalry, George Bernard Shaw on socialism, Leon Trotsky on Lenin, T.E. Lawrence on guerrilla warfare, and Orville Wright on Wilbur Wright (Simson 1992) – as it was for breadth and depth of material, Britannica was an English language institution. In the early 1990s, however, searchable CD-ROMs – featuring graphics, sound, and video – began to replace these more expensive print ancestors.

In April 1995, Encyclopaedia Britannica revealed that the company had not shown a profit since 1990, and attributed its poor financial performance to its conservative multimedia strategy (*Reuters European Business Report* 1995). On May 16, 1995, the front page of *The New York Times* carried an article entitled, 'Slow-to-Adapt Encyclopaedia Britannica Is for Sale.'

On June 29, 1995, president and CEO Peter Norton announced his retirement after 10 years in the position. Norton was replaced by Joseph Esposito, who had been president of Encyclopaedia Britannica North America. In that position, Esposito had overseen product development, sales, and marketing of all Britannica products in the United States and Canada (*Business Wire* 1995).

Faced with declining revenues and market share, Esposito recognized that the company had to meet the challenges of a future dominated by multimedia alone. Suitors included Microsoft, publishing giant Times-Mirror Co., Hachette Filipacchi Magazines in France, and Germany's Bertelsmann A.G. Potential investors seemed to find the $400 million price tag and the additional tens of millions required to make the company profitable a high price to pay for the Britannica database and brand (Borden 1995).

References

Akst, D. (1986) Britannica Aquires Blue Chip Software, *Los Angeles Times*, Business, January 7, p. 5A.

Banet, B. (1993) CD-ROM Encyclopaedias: Multimedia Approach to Electronic References; Evaluation compares Compton's, New Media's, Compton's Interactive Encyclopaedia, Grolier Electronic Publishing's New Grolier Multimedia Encyclopaedia, Microsoft Encarta, and World Book Inc.'s Information Finder; includes related articles on pricing and Encyclopaedia Britannica's Britannica Fact-checking system on CD-ROM; Software Review, *The Seybold Report on Desktop Publishing*, October 4, p. 3.

Borden, J. (1995) Thumbing Through the Books at Britannica: Microsoft, Others Take a Look, But Price is High, *Crain's Chicago Business*, June 19.

Business Week (1981) Encyclopaedia Britannica, Inc., August 31, p. 74E.

Business Wire (1985) Ency-Britannica Forms New Business Unit, Acquires Computer Software Firms, February 20.

Business Wire (1986) Encyclo-Britannica Announces Acquisition, August 20.

Business Wire (1995) Joseph J. Esposito Appointed President and Chief Executive Officer of Encyclopaedia Britannica, June 29.

Byte (1993) Encyclopaedia Britannica Software, November, p. 662.

CD-ROM Professional (1991) Two new versions of Compton's Encyclopaedia, educational software disc now available from Britannica Software, November, p. 114.

Chicago Sun-Times (1992) Britannica Entry Needs Revision, Editorials, January 27, p. 13.

Chicago Tribune (1986) A Subsidiary of Britannica to go Public, June 12, p. 5.

Chicago Tribune (1993) Britannica is on CD, But We Can't Have One, August 8, p. 7.

The Daily Mail (1995) We're Bound to Bounce Back, says the Boss of Britannica, April 6, p. 29.

Eckhouse, J. and Viviano, F. (1991) Laws Don't Worry Product Counterfeiters, *San Francisco Chronicle*, February 12, p. A1.

The Economist (1982) Electronic Libraries, Pocket-sized Britannicas? September 11, p. 85.

Education Computer News (1991) Britannica Introduces Windows Format for Compton's, April 16, Section 8.

Education Technology News (1993) Britannica Introduces Geopedia, July 6.

Encyclopaedia Britannica (1994) *The New Encyclopaedia Britannica*, 15th edn, vol. 4, p. 488. Chicago, Il.

Gibney, F.B. (1987) Britannica is Becoming a Chinese Best-seller, *Los Angeles Times*, January 18, Part 5, p. 1.

Henry, T. (1987) Reading Skills Soar with Britannica Reading Course, *United Press International*, July 4.

Hilts, P. (1993) Compton's Multimedia Group is Up for Sale; Compton's Learning Co. and Compton's New Media Inc. being offered for sale by Encyclopaedia Britannica Inc., *Publishers Weekly*, March 1, p. 10.

IDP Report (1992) Encyclopaedia Britannica Provides CD-ROM Index for Printed Version, June 26.

Interactive Content (1995) New Media Strategies Elude Britannica; Encyclopaedia Britannica's Losses are Largely Due to its Conservative Media Strategy, April, p. 5.

Kaul, C. (1992) This Encyclopaedia Explodes with Sound, *Los Angeles Times*, April 4, p. D6.

Kelly, T. (1995) Lost in Cyberspace: The Encyclopaedia Britannica, *San Francisco Examiner*, June 17, p. A15.

Landler, M. (1995) Slow-to-Adapt Encyclopaedia Britannica is for Sale, *The New York Times*, May 16, p. D1.

McDowell, E. (1995) Encyclopaedia Britannica Revised, *The New York Times*, March 25, p. C13.

Online Newsletter (1994) Britannica Launches its First Electronic Encyclopaedias, April.

Phelps, C. (1988) ESC Teams with Britannica, *San Diego Business Journal*, August 22, p. 14.

PR Newswire (1989) Britannica, Education Systems Corp. Unveil Compton's Revolutionary New Multimedia Encyclopaedia, March 30.

PR Newswire (1990) Plans Are Announced for Unprecedented Russian-Language Britannica: First International Encyclopaedia in the USSR since 1917, December 18.

Publishers Weekly (1994) Encyclopaedia Britannica Goes Online; Encyclopaedia Britannica Inc. Plans Electronic Distrinution to Public Libraries by Way of Internet, *Publishers Weekly*, February 14, p. 14.

Reuters European Business Report (1995) Encyclopaedia Britannica Reveals Financial Woes, April 5.

Rosen, L. (1992) Compton's Learning Co's Compton's Multimedia Encyclopaedia Database, *Information Today*, June, p. 25.

Rudd, D.C. (1989) Britannica Battling Taiwan Book Pirate, *Chicago Tribune*, June 4, p. 1.

Salpeter, J. (1993) The Multimedia Encyclopaedias Face Off; Software Review; Compton's Multimedia Encyclopedia, Microsoft Encarta: Evaluation, *Online*, September, p. 110.

The San Diego Union-Tribune (1995) Britannica Now An Internet Open Book, July 11, p. 4.

San Francisco Chronicle (1991) Taiwanese Publisher Imprisoned for Pirating Encyclopaedia, February 12, p. A1.

Simson, M. (1992) Viking Mines Britannica, *Publishers Weekly*, June 1, p. 20.

S & P Creditwire (1995) Encyclopaedia Britannica's CP Rated 'A-1' by S & P, January 5.

Storch, C. (1986) Britannica Now Has 75% of EBEC, *Chicago Tribune*, August 21, p. 3.

United Press International (1990) Britannica Chooses Tandy Computers for its Software, February 29.

Video Marketing News (1990) Britannica Takes CD-ROM into the Classroom; Encyclopaedia Britannica Inc.'s Visual-Based Version of the Encyclopaedia, November 12, p. 5.

Warren, J. (1986) Word is Out: Sabotage at Britannica, *Chicago Tribune*, September 5, p. 1.

The Washington Post (1989) Britannica Introduces CD set: Sight, Sound of 26 Volumes Ave on 1 Disc, September 20, p. F7.

Case 9: Southwest Airlines: Expanding Beyond the Southwest

By Don Parks and Ivan Noer[1]

The cover page of Southwest Airlines' 1990 annual report stated simply:

> In 1990, we made a profit.
> (Herbert D. Kelleher, Chairman, President, and CEO in Southwest Airlines Annual Report 1990)

Southwest and United Airlines were the only major carriers that reported an operating profit in 1990. While the airline industry had just experienced its worst performance in the era of deregulation, Southwest was flying high providing low-fare, short-haul routes between city pairs. As a niche carrier, Southwest experienced steady growth during the last twenty years. 'When we first began to fly outside Texas I got a letter from a congressman,' recalls Kelleher. 'He wrote: "Herbie, you're going to destroy Southwest Airlines, flying outside Texas." I wrote back, "Congressman, Man, not God, ordained the boundaries of the State of Texas."' (*Forbes* 1991)

Company History

The year was 1971. From a sketch on a napkin, America's low-fare, short-trip airline was born, flying three Boeing 737 jets to three Texas cities: Houston, Dallas, and San Antonio. Five years earlier, Kelleher and a group of investors put up $560,000 to found Southwest (*Business Week* 1989). The company's business philosophy was

clear: Offer low-fare seats, every flight, every day. As soon as Southwest started flying, the fare wars started in earnest. In a heated war with Braniff, Southwest gave away leather ice buckets and fifths of liquor on its flights in order to keep its planes full (*Financial World* 1989). Even if the competition the company experienced initially was the fiercest anyone had experienced in the airline industry, Southwest captured a lot of local fans and sympathy.

Southwest's big break came in 1974, when all other airlines serving Dallas's Love Field moved to the then new Dallas-Fort Worth (DFW) Intercontinental airport. This move was required by a contract signed in 1968, before the birth of Southwest. Thus, the company was not obligated to move to DFW. Court battles with both the board of the DFW airport, as well as other airlines, followed. However, Southwest won the court battles before the US Supreme Court, giving the company a monopoly at Love Field (ibid.). Love Field was attractive because of its location close to downtown Dallas, and thus was more convenient for business travelers than DFW.

Ironically, Southwest was forced into the commuter role because of regulations. This was based on the Love Field section of the 'Wright amendment' to the International Air Transportation Competition Act of 1978, which stated that no common carrier could provide scheduled passenger air transportation for compensation between Love Field and one or more points outside Texas and its four contiguous states. By limiting Love Field flights to Texas and its four contiguous states – New Mexico, Arkansas, Louisiana, and Oklahoma – the amendment attempted to limit the ability of Southwest to compete with existing airlines. However,

[1] This case was prepared by Don M. Parks, Southwestern University, and Ivan Noer, University of Wyoming. The case was originally published in Annual Advances in Business Cases 1993 by the Society for Case Research. Copyright © 1993 by Don M. Parks. Reprinted by permission of Don M. Parks.

EXHIBIT 1
Fleet Size

	1986	1987	1988	1989	1990
Number of aircaft	63	75	85	94	106

Source: *1990 Annual Report.*

EXHIBIT 2
Available Seat-Miles

	1986	1987	1988	1989	1990
Available seat miles (in millions)	63	75	85	94	106

Source: Estimated from graph in *1990 Annual Report.*

Southwest took advantage of the limitation, catering to business travelers looking for shuttle service to places like Oklahoma City and Albuquerque (Southwest Airlines Form 10K Report).

In order to expand beyond its five-state market on flights to and from Love Field, Southwest had to find a way to change the Wright amendment or work within it. Southwest chose to adhere to the letter of the law, if not the intent. On flights that originated at Love Field and had destinations outside the five-state area, the plane had to land at another airport where passengers changed planes and continued their flight to final destinations. Only Love Field operations were restricted by the amendment.

Southwest's traffic reports showed that routes like Harlingen–Houston and Midland–Dallas were among the 200 largest US travel markets, and the company's experience was that air travel tended to double in any city within 12 months after it began its service with more frequent flights and low fares. In addition, Southwest was the first carrier to introduce lower fares for weekend and evening travelers (*Financial World* 1989).

Kelleher's biggest mistake so far was his 1984 purchase of Muse Air. This was taken as a defensive move against Continental, which had expressed interest in buying Muse Air. The company was founded by Lamar Muse, Kelleher's predecessor as CEO, who had earlier left Southwest in

a dispute with its board. Muse Air flew Southwest's same routes from Love Field and also provided long-haul flights to Florida and to California from Houston. Muse Air offered food and assigned seating, perks Southwest did not. Soon after the acquisition, Southwest was losing heavily. Kelleher bought the failing Muse Air for $68 million and preserved its full-service product, renaming it TranStar. The first year Southwest operated the airline it made $2 million, compared with the $22 million Muse had lost the previous year. In 1987, Continental went at Muse Air with more frequent service and cheaper fares. Kelleher cut his losses and closed the airline. The Muse debacle reaffirmed Kelleher's determination to stick to his no-frills niche (ibid.). Skeptics warned that the TranStar mistake illustrates Southwest's limits (*Newsweek* 1988).

In contrast to what many critics predicted back in 1971, Southwest was a success. As of 1991, Southwest was the seventh-largest major airline in the United States, based on originating passengers. It ranked tenth based on passenger traffic (revenue passenger-miles) (*Wall Street Journal* 1991).

The company grew from three aircraft in 1971 to 13 aircraft in 1979. As of 1991, Southwest flew 124 Boeing 737s, the youngest pure jet fleet in the country. Exhibit 1 shows the growth in Southwest's fleet size. The company flies over 20 million customers a year to 32 cities (34 airports) in 14 states in the West, Southwest, and Midwest

(Southwest Airlines Annual Report 1991). Exhibit 2 shows recent growth in available seat-miles.

Southwest had the lowest cost structure in the industry, mainly due to the company's ability to maintain its original concept: Offer a low-fare, high-frequency, no-frills carrier (Southwest Airlines Annual Report 1990).

The airline industry recently experienced one of its worst recessions ever, but Southwest went through the storm almost intact and with its ambitions undiminished.

Southwest had little choice but to expand outside its original regional service area because little room existed to expand in Texas, where it served ten airports, or in adjoining states (*New York Times* 1991). In July 1991, Southwest raised the number of cities it served in California to seven, about a 30 percent increase in service (ibid.). In August 1991, Southwest entered the St. Louis-Kansas City market with six daily trips between the two cities, charging an unrestricted fare approximately one-third the cost of the least costly fare previously offered (*Aviation Week and Space Technology* 1991a). Entering these new markets put Southwest up against other major carriers which had a strong foothold in the California market. In addition to its 124 aircraft in operation, it had 50 aircraft on order and options on 68 more (Southwest Airlines Annual Report 1990). Exhibit 3 shows future delivery positions and options for aircraft.

Company Management

Nothing in Kelleher's background pointed to airlines. The son of a Campbell Soup Company manager, he grew up in Haddon Heights, New Jersey, and graduated from Wesleyan University in Connecticut and New York University law school. In 1961, he started a law firm in San Antonio. Five years later Kelleher was one of the group of investors who founded Southwest. His stake was $20,000. During Southwest's early years, Kelleher acted only as general counsel and director. In 1978, he was named chairman, and in 1981, he took over as CEO.

After becoming CEO, Kelleher immediately became the airline's most visible property. Within the organization, many of its 9,000 employees simply called their CEO 'Uncle Herbie.' He starred in most of Southwest's TV commercials and also recorded a rap video, called 'The Southwest Shuffle,' which was shown to new employees. Kelleher's image as being a little scatterbrained often resulted in people underestimating him, thinking he was completely crazy (*Business Week* 1989). However, considering what he has done with Southwest, the man has been nothing to laugh about. Some critics argue that Kelleher may one day trip himself up. 'He holds power very tightly,' says one former senior executive. 'Only Kelleher makes major decisions' (ibid.: 55). This centralized decision making made people ask how the airline can succeed without him. The airline may be too dependent on one man (*Business Month* 1990).

Southwest's management was streamlined over the past decade, so that as of 1992, only four or five officials reported directly to Kelleher, compared to more than 13 earlier. Major reasons given for this include accommodation of growth, freeing Kelleher to look at long-term developments and to maintain good employee relations (*Aviation Week and Space Technology* 1991b).

Type	Seats	1990	1991	1992	1993	1994	1995	1996	1997	1998	1999
737-200	122	46	—	—	—	—	—	—	—	—	—
737-300	137	50	3	6	6	3	—	—	—	—	—
737-500	122	10	8	7	7	10	10	10	16	16	16

Source: *1990 Annual Report.*

EXHIBIT 3
Future Delivery Positions

EXHIBIT 4
Executive Officers

Name	Position	Age	Officer Since
Herbert Kelleher	Chairman of the Board, President and CEO	59	1967
Coleen Barrett	Executive Vice President – Customers, Corporate Secretary	46	1978
Gary Barron	Executive Vice President, Chief Operations Officer	46	1978
John Denison	Executive Vice President – Corporate Services	46	1986
Gary Kelly	Vice President – Finance, Chief Financial Officer	35	1986
James Parket	Vice President – General Counsel	44	1986
Ronnie Ricks	Vice President – Governmental Affairs	41	1986
Donald Valentine	Vice President – Marketing	42	1984
James Wimberly	Vice President – Ground Operations	38	1985

Source: *Form 10-K Report.*

Exhibit 4 presents a list of Southwest's executive officers, their positions, and their ages.

Southwest's operation was so closely a reflection of Kelleher and his outgoing personal style that some observers believe that succession might be, in the long run, the airline's most obvious problem. One observer said:

> Replacing Herb will be an impossibility, and when he leaves or retires, Southwest may face its most serious problem. Maintaining Southwest's type of operation was based on Kelleher's personal relations and ability to relate to people. I'm not sure anyone else could even come close to doing it (ibid.: 77).

Other analysts argue that Kelleher developed one of the best management teams in the industry. 'The management team is young and aggressive and consists of people who could take over and run the airline' (ibid.). Kelleher maintained the company's seat-of-the-pants, hands-off management style when he took command as chairman in 1978. Kelleher abhorred permanent committees because they 'take on a life of their own.' Instead, to tackle specific problems he set up *ad hoc* committees, whose members included employees, right down to ticket agents and flight attendants (*Financial World* 1989).

In an industry marked by labor-management battles, Kelleher maintained good relations with a virtually all-union work force. A no-layoff policy and a profit-sharing plan – employees owned 13 percent of the airline – encouraged workers to be committed to the company's long-term future. Southwest had the lowest employee turnover rate in the industry (Southwest Airlines Annual Report 1990). Kelleher's motivational style yielded results. Each Southwest dispatcher routes about 90 planes a day, three times more than the average dispatcher at United. Pilots and flight attendants spent more hours in the air than the industry average. Mechanics help baggage handlers when they fall behind (*US News and World Report*). Southwest counted on high productivity and extreme loyalty from its 9000 workers. When oil prices skyrocketed in the fall of 1990, employees bought the airline $135,000 worth of jet fuel through payroll deductions (Southwest Airlines Annual Report 1990). Strong morale and per mile pay make Southwest's pilots among the hardest working – and most handsomely rewarded – in the industry. Working like race-car pit crews, its ground personnel turn aircraft around in as little as 8. 5 minutes (*Newsweek* 1988).

Competition

Airlines were divided into three major categories: major airlines, national airlines, and regional airlines (Standard and Poor's Industry Surveys June

	1986	1987	1988	1989	1990
Load factor		58.3%	58.9%	57.7%	62.7% 60.7%

Source: *1990 Annual Report.*

EXHIBIT 5
Load Factor

1991). From a geographical viewpoint, Southwest was a regional airline with a strong foothold in Texas and its neighboring states during the 1970s and most of the 1980s. However, its recent route expansions clearly made the company, geographically speaking, an airline with national route coverage. By definition, however, Southwest was a major airline (having more than $1 billion in annual revenue). In 1990, the industry experienced the most turbulent business conditions since airline deregulation in 1978. At year-end 1990, Southwest and United were the only major airlines in the United States to report an operating profit. '[Southwest] is the only airline that appears to make money at the moment,' one industry analyst said during the summer of 1991 (*New York Times* 1991). As can be seen in Exhibit 5, Southwest's load factor in 1990 did not decline significantly in spite of the industry collapse.

Southwest generally skirted head-to-head competition with the industry giants on coast-to-coast flights. It focused instead on a network of flights that averaged just under one hour apiece, usually between smaller US cities. Although Southwest continuously expanded its route network, it did not change its basic operating philosophy when it went into interstate service against much larger and longer established competitors. It continued to compete on the basis of its low-fare, high-frequency, short-haul, no-frills operation (*Aviation Week and Space Technology* 1991b). The competition in the airline industry was expected to remain fierce in the near future (ibid. 1991c). The summer of 1991 was marked by heavy price wars among major competitors. Southwest reintroduced a discount fare it offered in the fall of 1990, in which purchasers of full-price tickets could buy a second passage on the same flight for $20 ('Take Along Fare') (*Wall Street Journal* 1991b). In 1991, plans were made for building a high-speed rail network linking Houston, Dallas-Fort Worth, and San Antonio. Although no action had been taken, Southwest's management certainly would not like to see high-speed trains take customers away on the company's intrastate routes in Texas (*Business Week* 1991).

Southwest recently battled its chief rival, America West, head on in the Las Vegas and Phoenix markets (*Forbes* 1988). America West had a slew of financial woes and found it increasingly difficult to match Southwest's $53 average ticket price (*Wall Street Journal* 1991c). One of the few airlines born since deregulation that was still flying, America West's prospects were hazy. Heavy leverage and aggressive expansion in the late 1980s made for a weak balance sheet. With the second-lowest labor costs among the major airlines, the Phoenix-based carrier would seem to have had a major cost advantage. 'The bad news is they competed with Southwest, which had even lower labor costs,' one industry analyst said (ibid.). 'Southwest could charge low prices because it provided no-frills service and had among the lowest costs in the industry. This was not the case for America West, which, compared to Southwest, offered a wider range of services, such as in-flight meals. Several ticket-discount offers by America West during late 1990 and early 1991 raised quick cash but served to aggravate the carrier's money woes. America West was forced to renegotiate with its banks in 1991 because it was in violation of certain loan covenants. In the summer of 1991, America West became the third major carrier in bankruptcy, and Edward Beauvais, the company's CEO at that time, said it would be necessary for the carrier to restructure its route network (*Aviation Week and Space Technology* 1991d).

Strategy

Since 1971, Southwest developed its industry niche and (contrary to many airlines) stuck to it. The concept was to offer frequent, no-frills, low-fare service in short-haul markets using a point-to-point system rather than a hub-and-spoke system. That meant about 10 daily flights between two cities, with no in-flight meals (Southwest served only drinks and snacks), and a single class of open seating. Southwest was not listed on a computer reservation system, so travelers or travel agents had to call Southwest's own ticket agents to get on a flight (*Financial World* 1989). Southwest had a frequent flier program that was based on number of trips, not mileage (Southwest Airlines Annual Report 1990). Recent industry service ratings gave Southwest high scores, especially with regard to on-time reliability (*Denver Post* 1991). The company had one of the best overall customer service records and had been given very high ratings on the overall customer satisfaction index (Consumer Reports 1991).

'We emphasize cost control, a sound market, and growth at a reasonable rate, and that makes the finance official's job easy,' Gary Kelly, financial vice president, said (*Aviation Week and Space Technology* 1991b). Southwest was able to keep costs down mainly because it was a no-frills carrier offering limited service. Southwest had the lowest cost structure in the industry, with expenses at 5.8 cents per available seat-mile, compared with an industry average of 7.5 cents (1989 numbers) (*Financial World* 1989). Exhibit 6 shows Southwest's activity cost chain based on operating expenses per available seat-mile. Operating the same type of plane (Boeing 737) on every route helped to keep maintenance costs at a minimum (Southwest Airlines Annual Report 1990). Boarding passes were reusable plastic cards, and, to save boarding time, there was no assigned seating. To save investment in labor and equipment, Southwest did not even transfer baggage to other carriers. That was the passengers' responsibility (*Forbes* 1991). Furthermore, having the lowest costs in the industry allowed Southwest to charge low prices. Its entry into the St. Louis–Kansas City market provided a good example: Southwest offered a 21-day advance purchase fare of $29 one way, and an unrestricted fare of $59 one way. Prior to Southwest's entry into the market, the lowest unrestricted coach fare available on the route was $156 one way, offered by Air Midwest (*Aviation Week and Space Technology* 1991a).

Kelleher's zaniness permeated Southwest, especially in promotional campaigns. In 1988, for the opening of Sea World in San Antonio, Kelleher had one of the 737s painted to look like a killer whale (*Time* 1988). On a flight to Austin in the winter of 1988, flight attendants were dressed as reindeer and elves, and the pilot sang Christmas carols over the loudspeaker system while gently rocking the plane (*Business Week* 1989). On-board antics have ranged from the zany to the mildly outrageous. 'As soon as y'all set both cheeks on your seats, we can get this 'ol bird

	1990	1989	Change (%)
Salaries, wages, and benefits	2.07	1.95	6.2
Profit sharing and employee savings plans	.11	.08	37.5
Fuel and oil	1.47	1.14	28.9
Maintenance materials and repairs	.51	.51	—
Agency commissions	.44	.42	4.8
Aircraft rentals	.16	.15	6.7
Landing fees and other rentals	.37	.35	5.7
Depreciation	.48	.49	−2.0
Other	1.12	1.11	0.9

Source: *1990 Annual Report.*

EXHIBIT 6
Operating Expenses per Available Seat-Mile (in cents)

moving' was one quoted cockpit announcement (*Forbes* 1991). Such examples illustrate what Kelleher meant when he said flying Southwest was supposed to be fun.

Kelleher acknowledged that Southwest had not added a great many routes to its schedule since 1981, when he became CEO. 'But we attack a city with a lot of flights, which is another form of aggression in the airline industry,' he explained. 'We won't go in with just one or two flights. We will go in with 10 or 12. That eats up a lot of airplanes and capacity, so you cannot open a lot of cities. You hit them with everything you've got in one or two places instead of trying to fight them everywhere' (ibid.: 49).

Southwest's low-fare, high-frequency, point-to-point service was received very well in the western markets, including New Mexico, Arizona, Nevada, and California. As of early 1991, the company had 48 percent of its system capacity, as expressed in available seat-miles (ASMs), in this geographic region (Southwest Airlines Annual Report 1990). This region contained 11 cities, including El Paso, and was the focus of Southwest's expansion activities during the late 1980s. Service was initiated in Oakland in 1989 and in Burbank and Reno in 1990. Despite fierce competition in these markets, Southwest was successful with its formula of low fares and frequent flights. During 1990, Southwest acquired more gate facilities at Oakland, nearly doubling the capacity for future Oakland flight operations. In 1991, Phoenix ranked third in Southwest's system in terms of originating customer boardings. The new Terminal Four facility in Phoenix could become the

largest in terms of daily departures. Las Vegas ranked fourth in terms of originating customers. Company management felt this region should continue to provide expansion opportunities in the future (ibid.). 'The Heartland' was Southwest's most mature region. From its original 'Texas Triangle' – San Antonio, Dallas, and Houston – Southwest became a dominant force in short-haul, point-to-point travel to the destinations it serves. As of early 1991, the company captured a 60 percent share of the intrastate Texas market. Growth opportunities in this region consist primarily of additional frequencies in existing markets (ibid.). Exhibit 7 shows the cities served by Southwest, after opening its new service from Sacramento, California (June 1991).

In mid-1991, Southwest started to look west. It raised the number of cities it served in California to seven. It was flying in California since 1982 but only began concentrating on the lucrative north-south market almost 10 years later. Even if some analysts argued that Southwest was the leading carrier in certain key California markets (the load factor in the California market for Southwest was as high as 61.6 percent during the summer of 1991; 55 percent was the breakeven point), the company faced heavy competition from United Airlines, which dominated the key Los Angeles-San Francisco run. Furthermore, the California market was seen as having too much capacity (*New York Times* 1991). 'We are very well equipped to fight a war [against the majors in the California market],' Kelleher said, citing the company's strong balance sheet (ibid.). At the end of the first quarter of 1991, Southwest's debt-to-capital ratio

EXHIBIT 7
Cities Served by Southwest

Albuquerque	Detroit	Lubbock	Reno/Tahoe
Amarillo	El Paso	Midland	Rio Grande Valley
Austin	Houston	Nashville	Sacramento
Birmingham	Indianapolis	New Orleans	St. Louis
Burbank	Kansas City	Oakland	San Antonio
Chicago (Midway)	Las Vegas	Oklahoma City	San Diego
Corpus Christi	Little Rock	Ontario	San Francisco
Dallas (Love)	Los Angeles	Phoenix	Tusla

Source: *New York Times*, June 16, 1991.

EXHIBIT 8
Selected Consolidated Financial Data (in thousands of dollars except per share amounts)

	1991	1990	1989	1988	1987	1986
Operating revenues:						
Passenger	$1,267,897	$1,144,421	$ 973,568	$ 828,343	$ 751,649	$ 742,287
Freight	26,428	22,196	18,771	14,433	13,428	13,621
Other	19,280	20,142	22,713	17,658	13,251	12,882
Total operating revenues	1,313,605	1,186,759	1,015,052	860,434	778,328	768,790
Operating expenses	1,250,669	1,104,880	917,426	774,454	747,881	679,827
Operating income	62,936	81,879	97,626	85,980	30,447	88,963
Other expenses (income), net	19,096	7,126	(13,356)	620	1,374	23,517
Income before income taxes	43,840	74,753	110,982	85,360	29,073	65,446
Provision for income taxes	16,921	27,670	39,424	27,408	8,918	15,411
Net income	$ 26,919	$ 47,083	$ 71,558	$ 57,952	$ 20,155	$ 50,035
Net income per common and common equivalent share	$.63	$1.10	$1,58	$1.23	$.42	$1.03
Cash dividend per common share	$.1000	$.0967	$.0933	$.0883	$.0867	$.0867
Total assets	$1,837,291	$1,471,138	$1,415,096	$1,308,389	$1,042,640	$1,061,419
Long-term debt	$ 627,016	$ 326,956	$ 354,147	$ 369,541	$ 251,130	$ 339,069
Stockholders' equity	$ 628,521	$ 604,851	$ 587,316	$ 567,375	$ 514,278	$ 511,850
	Consolidated Financial Ratios (%)					
Return on average total assets	1.6	3.3	5.2	5.1	1.9	4.8
Return on average stoclholder's equity	4.4	7.9	12.4	10.8	4.0	10.3
Debt as a percentage of invested capital	49.5	35.1	37.6	39.4	32.8	39.8
	Consolidated Operating Statistics					
Revenue passengers carried	22,669,942	19,830,941	17,958,263	14,876,582	13,503,242	13,637,515
Revenue passenger-miles (RPMs)	11,296,183	9,958,940	9,281,992	7,676,257	7,789,376	7,388,401
Available seat-miles (ASMs)	18,491,003	16,411,115	14,796,732	13,309,044	13,331,055	12,574,484
Load factor	61.1%	60.7%	62.7%	57.7%	58.4%	58.8%
Average length of passenger haul	498	502	517	516	577	542
Trips flown	382,752	338,108	304,673	274,859	270,559	262,082
Average passenger fare	$55.93	$57.71	$54.21	$55.68	$55.66	$54.43
Passenger revenue yield per RPM	11.22¢	11.46¢	10.49¢	10.79¢	9.65¢	10.05¢
Operating revenue yield per ASM	7.10¢	7.23¢	6.86¢	6.47¢	5.84¢	6.11¢
Operating expenses per ASM	6.76¢	6.73¢	6.20¢	5.82¢	5.61¢	5.41¢
Fuel cost per gallon (average)	65.69¢	77.89¢	59.46¢	51.37¢	54.31¢	51.42¢
Number of employees at year end	9,778	8,620	7,760	6,467	5,765	5,819
Size of fleet at year end	124	106	94	85	75	79

Source: *1991 Annual Report.*

was 32 percent, compared with 45 percent for American and 36 percent for Delta. United's ratio was a lean 30 percent at the end of 1990 (ibid.).

Another new entry by Southwest during the summer of 1991 was the St. Louis-Kansas City market. Southwest entered this market offering a 21-day advance purchase fare of $29 one way. Kelleher said that such low fares were not promotional. 'These are the fares that will be there,' according to Kelleher (ibid.). Even if the low prices were likely to help fill the company's planes, the traffic between St. Louis and Kansas City had declined during recent years. Kelleher argued that this sharp decline could be attributed to the high fares charged on the routes, and not to an economic decline involving the two cities. Kelleher said that Southwest was prepared to expand its service in the market as traffic warranted. He anticipated that the company would be able to double the number of flights offered on the St. Louis–Kansas City route within a year (*Aviation Week and Space Technology* 1991a).

Finances

In 1990, Southwest's consolidated net income was $47.1 million ($1.10 per share) compared to the record of $71.6 million ($1.58 per share) in 1989, a decrease of 34.2 percent. Passenger revenues, which accounted for 96.4 percent of total revenues, increased by 17.5 percent in 1990 to an all-time high of $1144.4 million. Part of this increase resulted from fare increases implemented during 1990 and a larger percentage of higher-yielding (per mile) short-haul traffic in 1990 as compared to 1989. Despite a weakening general economy and slower domestic traffic growth, Southwest achieved above-average traffic growth and load factors during 1990. Operating expenses increased 20.4 percent in 1990 to $1104.9 million from $917.4 million in 1989 (Southwest Airlines Annual Report 1990). (Refer to Exhibit 8 for more financial information.)

The collapse in industry profits in 1990 had a major impact on all US airlines. Among the majors, only Southwest and United made a profit.

Although this result was seen as positive from Southwest's point of view, the turbulent industry conditions did affect Southwest's financial performance in a negative direction. Two consecutive quarters of losses (fourth quarter of 1990 and first quarter of 1991) showed that Southwest was affected by the unfavorable economic conditions. However, Southwest's profits were not impacted to the degree of most other major carriers, because traffic on Southwest's short-haul routes did not decline as much as it did on international routes. The financial condition of Southwest's competitors provides uncertainties. How this could impact Southwest was not predicted. For example, the reduction of service by other carriers in Southwest's markets might or might not prove beneficial for Southwest through additional traffic growth (ibid.; Second Quarter Report 1991).

Therefore, a number of strategic issues faced Southwest Airlines. Some industry observers wondered whether Southwest should acquire one or more of its ailing competitors, initiate a hub-and-spoke system, or begin to use computer reservation systems. Herb and Southwest still had their work cut out for them.

References

Aviation Week and Space Technology (1991a) Southwest's New Route Moves May Affect Airline Merger, July 29, p. 20.

Aviation Week and Space Technology (1991b) Southwest's Success, Growth Tied to Maintaining Original Concept, May 27, pp. 75–7.

Aviation Week and Space Technology (1991c) Airline Industry Forecasts for '91 See the Strong Gaining and the Weak Losing, March 18, p. 85.

Aviation Week and Space Technology (1991d) America West Declares Bankruptcy, Begins Route Restructuring, July 8.

Business Month (1990) A Busy Boss Can Never Fly Solo, August, pp. 22–3.

Business Week (1991) Capital Wrapup, October 21, p. 45.

Business Week (1989) Southwest Airlines: Flying High with 'Uncle Herb', *Business Week*, July 3, pp. 53–5.

Consumer Reports (1991) The Best (and Worst) Airlines, July, p. 468.

Denver Post (1991) Southwest Takes Honors for On-time Performance, September 6.

Financial World (1989) The Love Line, March 21, pp. 2–28.

Forbes (1991) Hit 'em Hardest with the Mostest, September 16, p. 48.

Forbes (1988) Risk Taken, November 14, p. 108.

Newsweek (1988) Southwest's Friendly Skies, May 30, p. 49.

New York Times (1991) Southwest Air's Push West, June 16.

Time (1988) Swim the Friendly Skies, June 6, p. 59.

US News and World Report (1988) Proud to Serve, March 7, p. 55.

Wall Street Journal (1991a) 20 Years Ago They Said We'd Never Go Far, advertising supplement, June 17.

Wall Street Journal (1991b) Southwest Airlines, June 18.

Wall Street Journal (1991c) Flight Plans: How the Airlines Stack Up, June 17.

Case 10: Canon: Competing on Capabilities

By Sumantra Ghoshal and Mary Ackenhusen[1]

In 1961, following the runaway success of the company's model 914 office copier, Joseph C. Wilson, President of Xerox Corporation, was reported to have said, 'I keep asking myself, when am I going to wake up? Things just aren't this good in life.' Indeed, the following decade turned out to be better than anything Wilson could have dreamed. Between 1960 and 1970, Xerox increased its sales 40 percent per year from $40 million to $1.7 billion and raised its after-tax profits from $2.6 million to $187.7 million. In 1970, with 93 percent market share world-wide and a brand name that was synonymous with copying, Xerox appeared as invincible in its industry as any company ever could.

When Canon, 'the camera company from Japan,' jumped into the business in the late 1960s, most observers were sceptical. Less than a tenth the size of Xerox, Canon had no direct sales or service organization to reach the corporate market for copiers, nor did it have a process technology to by-pass the 500 patents that guarded Xerox's Plain Paper Copier (PPC) process. Reacting to the spate of recent entries in the business including Canon, Arthur D. Little predicted in 1969 that no company would be able to challenge Xerox's monopoly in PPCs in the 1970s because its patents presented an insurmountable barrier.

Yet, over the next two decades, Canon rewrote the rule book on how copiers were supposed to be produced and sold as it built up $5 billion in revenues in the business, emerging as the second largest global player in terms of sales

and surpassing Xerox in the number of units sold. According to the Canon Handbook, the company's formula for success as displayed initially in the copier business is 'synergistic management of the total technological capabilities of the company, combining the full measure of Canon's know how in fine optics, precision mechanics, electronics and fine chemicals.' Canon continues to grow and diversify using this strategy. Its vision, as described in 1991 by Ryuzaburo Kaku, President of the company, is 'to become a premier global company of the size of IBM combined with Matsushita.'

Industry Background

The photocopying machine has often been compared with the typewriter as one of the few triggers that have fundamentally changed the ways of office work. But, while a mechanical Memograph machine for copying had been introduced by the AB Dick company of Chicago as far back as 1887, it was only in the second half of this century that the copier market exploded with Xerox's commercialization of the 'electrophotography' process invented by Chester Carlson.

Xerox

Carlson's invention used an electrostatic process to transfer images from one sheet of paper to another. Licensed to Xerox in 1948, this invention led to two different photocopying technologies. The Coated Paper Copying (CPC) technology transferred the reflection of an image from the original directly to specialized zinc-oxide coated paper, while the Plain Paper Copying (PPC)

[1] Source: This case was written by Mary Ackenhusen, Research Associate, under the supervision of Sumantra Ghoshal, Associate Professor at INSEAD. It is intended to be used as a basis of class discussion rather than to illustrate either effective or ineffective handling of an administrative situation. Reprinted with the permission of INSEAD. Copyright © 1992 INSEAD, Fontainebleau, France.

technology transferred the image indirectly to ordinary paper through a rotating drum coated with charged particles. While dry or liquid toner could be used to develop the image, the dry toner was generally preferable in both technologies. A large number of companies entered the CPC market in the 1950s and 1960s based on technology licensed from Xerox or RCA (to whom Xerox had earlier licensed this technology). However, PPC remained a Xerox monopoly since the company had refused to license any technology remotely connected to the PPC process and had protected the technology with over 500 patents.

Because of the need for specialized coated paper, the cost per copy was higher for CPC. Also, this process could produce only one copy at a time, and the copies tended to fade when exposed to heat to light. PPC, on the other hand, produced copies at a lower operating cost that were also indistinguishable from the original. The PPC machines were much more expensive, however, and were much larger in size. Therefore, they required a central location in the user's office. The smaller and less expensive CPC machines, in contrast, could be placed on individual desks. Over time, the cost and quality advantages of PPC, together with its ability to make multiple copies at high speed, made it the dominant technology and, with it, Xerox's model of centralized copying, the industry norm.

This business concept of centralized copying required a set of capabilities that Xerox developed and which, in turn, served as its major strengths and as key barriers to entry to the business. Given the advantages of volume and speed, all large companies found centralized copying highly attractive and they became the key customers for photocopying machines. In order to support this corporate customer base, Xerox's product designs and upgrades emphasized economies of higher volume copying. To market the product effectively to these customers, Xerox also built up an extensive direct sales and service organization of over 12,000 sales representatives and 15,000 service people. Forty percent of the sales reps' time was spent 'hand holding' to prevent even minor

dissatisfaction. Service reps, dressed in suits and carrying their tools in briefcases, performed preventative maintenance and prided themselves on reducing the average time between breakdowns and repair to a few hours.

Further, with the high cost of each machine and the fast rate of model introductions, Xerox developed a strategy of leasing rather than selling machines to customers. Various options were available, but typically the customers paid a monthly charge on the number of copies made. The charge covered not only machine costs but also those of the paper and toner that Xerox supplied and the service visits. This lease strategy, together with the carefully cultivated service image, served as key safeguards from competition, as they tied the customers into Xerox and significantly raised their switching costs.

Unlike some other American corporations, Xerox had an international orientation right from the beginning. Even before it had a successful commercial copier, Xerox built up an international presence through joint ventures which allowed the company to minimize its capital investment abroad. In 1956, it ventured with the Rank Organisation Ltd. in the UK to form Rank Xerox. In 1962, Rank Xerox became a 50 percent partner with Fuji Photo to form Fuji Xerox which sold copiers in Japan. Through these joint ventures, Xerox built up sales and service capabilities in these key markets similar to those it had in the United States. There were some 5000 sales people in Europe, 3000 in Japan and over 7000 and 3000 service reps, respectively. Xerox also built limited design capabilities in both the joint ventures for local market customization, which developed into significant research establishments in their own rights in later years.

Simultaneously, Xerox maintained high levels of investment in both technology and manufacturing to support its growing market. It continued to spend over $100 million a year in R&D, exceeding the total revenues from the copier business that any of its competitors were earning in the early 70s, and also invested heavily in large-size plants not only in the US but also in the UK and Japan.

Competition in the 1970s

Xerox's PPC patents began to expire in the 1970s, heralding a storm of new entrants. In 1970, IBM offered the first PPC copier not sold by Xerox, which resulted in Xerox suing IBM for patent infringement and violation of trade secrets. Canon marketed a PPC copier the same year through the development of an independent PPC technology which they licensed selectively to others. By 1973, competition had expanded to include players from the office equipment industry (IBM, SCM, Litton, Pitney Bowes), the electronics industry (Toshiba, Sharp), the reprographics industry (Ricoh, Mita, Copyer, 3M, AB Dick, Addressograph/Multigraph), the photographic equipment industry (Canon, Kodak, Minolta, Konishiroku) and the suppliers of copy paper (Nashua, Dennison, Saxon).

By the 1980s many of these new entrants, including IBM, had lost large amounts of money and exited the business. A few of the newcomers managed to achieve a high level of success, however, and copiers became a major business for them. Specifically, copiers were generating 40 percent of Canon's revenues by 1990.

Canon

Canon was founded in 1933 with the ambition to produce a sophisticated 35mm camera to rival that of Germany's world-class Leica model. In only two years' time, it had emerged as Japan's leading producer of high-class cameras. During the war, Canon utilized its optics expertise to produce an X-ray machine which was adopted by the Japanese military. After the war, Canon was able to successfully market its high-end camera, and by the mid-1950s it was the largest camera manufacturer in Japan. Building from its optics technology, Canon then expanded its product line to include a mid-range camera, an 8mm video camera, television lenses and micrographic equipment. It also began developing markets for its products outside of Japan, mainly in the US and Canada.

Diversification was always very important to Canon in order to further its growth, and a new products R&D section was established in 1962 to explore the fields of copy machines, auto-focusing cameras, strobe-integrated cameras, home VCRs and electronic calculators. A separate, special operating unit was also established to introduce new non-camera products resulting from the diversification effort.

The first product to be targeted was the electronic calculator. This product was challenging because it required Canon engineers to develop new expertise in microelectronics in order to incorporate thousands of transistors and diodes in a compact, desk model machine. Tekeshi Mitarai, President of Canon at that time, was against developing the product because it was seen to be too difficult and risky. Nevertheless, a dedicated group of engineers believed in the challenge and developed the calculator in secrecy. Over a year later, top management gave their support to the project. In 1964, the result of the development effort was introduced as the Canola 130, the world's first 10-key numeric pad calculator. With this product line, Canon dominated the Japanese electronic calculator market in the 1960s.

Not every diversification effort was a success, however. In 1956, Canon began development of the synchroreader, a device for writing and reading with a sheet of paper coated with magnetic material. When introduced in 1959, the product received high praise for its technology. But, because the design was not patented, another firm introduced a similar product at half the price. There was no market for the high priced and incredibly heavy Canon product. Ultimately, the firm was forced to disassemble the finished inventories and sell off the usable parts in the 'once-used' components market.

Move into Copiers

Canon began research into copier technology in 1959, and, in 1962, it formed a research group dedicated to developing a plain paper copier (PPC) technology. The only known PPC process was protected by hundreds of Xerox patents, but

EXHIBIT 1

Canon, Inc.: Ten-Year Financial Summary (in ¥ millions)

	1990	1989	1988	1987	1986	1985	1984	1983	1982	1981
Net sales:										
Domestic	508,747	413,854	348,462	290,382	274,174	272,966	240,656	198,577	168,178	144,898
Overseas	1,219,201	937,063	757,548	686,329	615,043	682,814	589,732	458,748	12,322	326,364
Total Sales	1,727,948	1,350,917	1,106,010	976,711	889,217	955,780	830,383	657,325	580,500	471,262
Percentage to previous year	127.9	122.1	113.2	109.8	93.0	115.1	126.3	113.2	123.2	112.5
Net income	61,408	38,293	37,100	13,244	10,728	37,056	35,029	28,420	22,358	16,216
Percentage to sales	3.6	2.8	3.4	1.4	1.2	3.9	4.2	4.3	3.9	3.4
Advertising expense	72,234	54,394	41,509	38,280	37,362	50,080	1,318	41,902	37,532	23,555
Research and development	86,008	75,566	65,522	57,085	55,330	49,461	38,256	28,526	23,554	14,491
Depreciation	78,351	64,861	57,627	57,153	55,391	47,440	39,995	30,744	27,865	22,732
Capital expenditure	137,298	107,290	83,069	63,497	81,273	917,863	7,594	53,411	46,208	54,532
Long-term debt	262,886	277,556	206,083	222,784	166,722	134,366	99,490	60,636	53,210	39,301
Stockholders' equity	617,566	550,841	416,465	371,198	336,456	333,148	304,310	264,629	235,026	168,735
Total assets	1,827,945	1,636,380	1,299,843	1,133,881	1,009,504	1,001,044	916,651	731,642	606,101	505,169
Per share data:										
Net income:										
Common and common equivalent share	78.29	50.16	51.27	19.65	16.67	53.38	53.63	46.31	41.17	34.04
Assuming full dilution	78.12	49.31	51.26	19.64	16.67	53.25	53.37	45.02	38.89	33.35
Cash dividends declared	12.50	11.93	11.36	9.09	11.36	11.36	9.88	9.43	8.23	7.84
Stock price:										
High	1,940	2,040	1,536	1,282	1,109	1,364	1,336	1,294	934	1,248
Low	1,220	1,236	823	620	791	800	830	755	417	513
Average number of common and common equivalent shares in thousands	788,765	780,546	747,059	747,053	746,108	727,257	675,153	645,473	564,349	515,593
Number of employees	54,381	44,401	40,740	37,521	35,498	34,129	30,302	27,266	25,607	24,300
Average exchange rate ($1 =)	143	129	127	143	167	235	239	238	248	222

Year	Cameras	Copiers	Other Business Machines	Optical & Other Products	Total
1981	201,635	175,389	52,798	40,222	470,044
1982	224,619	242,161	67,815	45,905	580,500
1983	219,443	291,805	97,412	48,665	657,325
1984	226,645	349,986	180,661	73,096	830,388
1985	197,284	410,840	271,190	76,466	955,780
1986	159,106	368,558	290,630	70,923	889,217
1987	177,729	393,581	342,895	62,506	976,711
1988	159,151	436,924	434,634	75,301	1,106,010
1989	177,597	533,115	547,170	93,035	1,350,917
1990	250,494	686,077	676,095	115,282	1,727,948

EXHIBIT 2
Sales by Product (in ¥ millions)

Canon felt that only this technology promised sufficient quality, speed, economy and ease of maintenance to successfully capture a large portion of the market. Therefore, corporate management challenged the researchers to develop a new PPC process which would not violate the Xerox patents.

In the meantime, the company entered the copier business by licensing the 'inferior' CPC technology in 1965 from RCA. Canon decided not to put the name of the company on this product and marketed it under the brand name Confax 1000 in Japan only. Three years later, Canon licensed a liquid toner technology from an Australian company and combined this with the RCA technology to introduce the CanAll Series. To sell the copier in Japan, Canon formed a separate company, International Image Industry. The copier was sold as an OEM to Scott Paper in the US who sold it under its own brand name.

Canon's research aiming at developing a PPC technical alternative to xerography paid off with the announcement of the 'New Process' (NP) in 1968. This successful research effort not only produced an alternative process but also taught Canon the importance of patent law: how not to violate patents and how to protect new technology. The NP process was soon protected by close to 500 patents.

The first machine with the NP technology, the NP1100, was introduced in Japan in 1970. It was the first copier sold by Canon to carry the Canon brand name. It produced 10 copies per minute and utilized dry toner. As was the standard in the Japanese market, the copier line was sold outright to customers from the beginning. After two years of experience in the domestic market, Canon entered the overseas market, except North America, with this machine.

The second generation of the NP system was introduced in Japan in 1972 as the NPL7. It was a marked improvement because it eliminated a complex fusing technology, simplified developing and cleaning, and made toner supply easier through a new system developed to use liquid toner. Compared with the Xerox equivalent, it was more economical, more compact, more reliable and still had the same or better quality of copies.

With the NP system, Canon began a sideline which was to become quite profitable: licensing. The first generation NP system was licensed to AM, and Canon also provided it with machines on an OEM basis. The second generation was again licensed to AM as well as to Saxon, Ricoh, and Copyer. Canon accumulated an estimated $32 million in license fees between 1975 and 1982.

Canon continued its product introductions with a stream of state-of-the-art technological innovations throughout the seventies. In 1973 it added color to the NP system; in 1975, it added laser beam printing technology. Its first entry into high volume copiers took place in 1978 with a model which was targeted at the Xerox 9200. The NP200 was introduced in 1979 and went on to win a gold medal at the Leipzig Fair for being the most economical and productive copier available. By 1982, copiers had surpassed cameras as the company's largest revenue generate (see Exhibits 1 and 2 for Canon's financials and sales by product line).

The Personal Copier

In the late 1970s, top management began searching for a new market for the PPC copier. They had recently experienced a huge success with the introduction of the AE-1 camera in 1976 and wanted a similar success in copiers. The AE-1 was a very compact single-lens reflex camera, the first camera that used a microprocessor to control electronically functions of exposure, film rewind, and strobe. The product had been developed through a focused, cross-functional project team effort which had resulted in a substantial reduction in the number of components, as well as in automated assembly and the use of unitized parts. Because of these improvements, the AE-1 enjoyed a 20 percent cost advantage over competitive models in the same class.

After studying the distribution of offices in Japan by size (see Exhibit 3), Canon decided to focus on a latent segment the Xerox had ignored. This was the segment comprising small offices (segment E) who could benefit from the functionality offered by photocopiers but did not require the high speed machines available in the market. Canon management believed that a low volume 'value for money' machine could generate a large demand in this segment. From this analysis emerged the business concept of a 'personal side desk' machine which could not only create a new market in small offices but potentially also induce decentralization of the copy function in large offices. Over time, the machine might even create demand for a personal copier for home use. This would be a copier that up to now no one had thought possible. Canon felt that, to be successful in this market, the product had to cost half the price of a conventional copier (target price $1,000), be maintenance free, and provide 10 times more reliability.

Top management took their 'dream' to the engineers, who, after careful consideration, took on the challenge. The machine would build off their previous expertise in microelectronics but would go much further in terms of material, functional component, design and production engineering technologies. The team's slogan was 'Let's make the AE-1 of copiers!,' expressing the necessity of know-how transfer between the camera and copier divisions as well as their desire for a similar type of success. The effort was led by the director of the Reprographic Production Development Center. His cross-functional team of 200 was the second largest ever assembled at Canon (the largest had been that of the AE-1 camera).

During the development effort, a major issue arose concerning the paper size that the new copier would accept. Canon Sales (the sales organization for Japan) wanted the machine to use a larger-than-letter-size paper which accounted for 60 percent of the Japanese market. This size was not necessary for sales outside of Japan and would add 20–30 percent to the machine's cost as well as make the copier more difficult to service. After much debate world-wide, the decision was made to forgo the ability to utilize the larger paper size in the interest of better serving the global market.

EXHIBIT 3
Office Size Distribution, Japan 1979

Source: Yamanouchi, Teruo, Breakthrough: The Development of the Canon Personal Copier, *Long Range Planning*, Vol. 22, October 1989, p. 4.

Copier Market Segment	Number of Office Workers	Number of Offices	Working Population
A	300+	200,000	9,300,000
B	100–299	30,000	4,800,000
C	30–99	170,000	8,300,000
D	5–29	1,820,000	15,400,000
E	1–4	4,110,000	8,700,000

Three years later the concept was a reality. The new PC (personal copier) employed a new-cartridge based technology which allowed the user to replace the photoreceptive drum, charging device toner assembly and cleaner with a cartridge every 2000 copies, thus eliminating the need to maintain the copier regularly. This enabled Canon engineers to meet the cost and reliability targets. The revolutionary product was the smallest, lightest copier ever sold, and created a large market which had previously not existed. Large offices adjusted their copying strategies to include decentralized copying, and many small offices and even homes could now afford a personal copier. Again, Canon's patent knowledge was utilized to protect this research, and the cartridge technology was not licensed to other manufacturers. Canon has maintained its leadership in personal copiers into the 1990s.

Building Capabilities

Canon is admired for its technical innovations, marketing expertise, and low-cost quality manufacturing. These are the result of a long-term strategy to becoming a premier company. Canon has frequently acquired outside expertise so that it could better focus internal investments on skills of strategic importance. This approach of extensive outsourcing and focused internal development has required consistent direction from top management and the patience to allow the company to become well grounded in one skill area before tasking the organization with the next objective.

Technology

Canon's many innovative products, which enabled the company to grow quickly in the seventies and eighties are in large part the result of a carefully orchestrated use of technology and the capacity for managing rapid technological change. Attesting to its prolific output of original research is the fact that Canon has been among the leaders in number of patents issued worldwide throughout the eighties.

These successes have been achieved in an organization that has firmly pursued a strategy of decentralized R&D. Most of Canon's R&D personnel are employed by the product divisions where 80–90 percent of the company's patentable inventions originate. Each product division has its own development center which is tasked with short- to medium-term product design and improvement of production systems. Most product development is performed by cross-functional teams. The work of the development groups is coordinated by an R&D headquarters group.

The Corporate Technical Planning and Operation center is responsible for long-term strategic R&D planning. Canon also has a main research center which supports state-of-the-art research in optics, electronics, new materials and information technology. There are three other corporate research centers which apply this state-of-the-art research to product development.

Canon acknowledges that it has neither the resources nor the time to develop all necessary technologies and has therefore often traded or bought specific technologies from a variety of external partners. Furthermore, it has used joint ventures and technology transfers as a strategic tool for mitigating foreign trade tensions in Europe and the United States. For example, Canon had two purposes in mind when it made an equity participation in CPF Deutsch, an office equipment marketing firm in Germany. Primarily, it believed that this move would help develop the German market for its copiers; but it did not go unnoticed among top management that CPF owned Tetras, a copier maker who at that time was pressing dumping charges against Japanese copier makers. Canon also used Burroughs as an OEM for office automation equipment in order to acquire Burroughs software and know-how and participate in joint development agreements with Eastman Kodak and Texas Instruments. Exhibit 4 provides a list of the company's major joint ventures.

Canon also recognizes that its continued market success depends on its ability to exploit new research into marketable products quickly.

EXHIBIT 4
Canon's Major
International Joint
Ventures

Category	Partner	Description
Office Equipment	Eastman Kodak (US)	Distributes Kodak medical equipment in Japan; exports copiers to Kodak
	CPF Germany	Equity participation in CPF which markets Canon copiers
	Olivetti (Italy) Lotte (Korea)	Joint venture for manufacture of copier
Computers	Hewlett-Packard (US)	Receives OEM mini-computer from HP; supplies laser printer to HP
	Apple Computer (US)	Distributes Apple computers in Japan; supplies laser printer to Apple
	Next, Inc. (US)	Equity participation; Canon has marketing rights for Asia
Semiconductors	National Semiconductor (US)	Joint development of MPU & software for Canon office equipment
	Intel (US)	Joint development of LSI for Canon copier, manufactured by Intel
Telecommunications	Siemens (Germany)	Development of ISDN interface for Canon facsimile; Siemens supplies Canon with digital PBX
	DHL (US)	Equity participation; Canon supplies terminals to DHL
Camera	Kinsei Seimitsu (Korea)	Canon licenses technology on 35mm Camera
Other	ECD (US)	Equity participation because Canon values its research on amorphous materials

It has worked hard to reduce the new product introduction cycle through a cross-functional pro-gramme called TS 1/2 whose purpose is to cut development time by 50 percent on a continuous basis. The main thrust of this programme is the classification of development projects by total time required and the critical human resources needed so that these two parameters can be opti-mized for each product depending on its impor-tance for Canon's corporate strategy. This allows product teams to be formed around several classi-fications of product development priorities of which 'best sellers' will receive the most empha-sis. These are the products aimed at new markets or segments with large potential demands. Other classifications include products necessary to catch up with competitive offerings, product refinements intended to enhance customer satisfaction, and long-run marathon products which will take considerable time to develop. In all development classifications, Canon emphasizes three factors to reduce time to market: the fostering of engineering ability, efficient technical support systems, and careful reviews of product development at all stages.

Canon is also working to divert its traditional product focus into more of a market focus. To this end, Canon R&D personnel participate in international product strategy meetings, carry out consumer research, join in marketing activities, and attend meetings in the field at both domestic and foreign sales subsidiaries.

Marketing

Canon's effective marketing is the result of step-by-step, calculated introduction strategies. Normally, the product is first introduced and perfected in the home market before being sold internationally. Canon has learned how to capture learning from the Japanese market quickly so that the time span between introduction in Japan and abroad is as short as a few months. Furthermore, the company will not simultaneously launch a new product through a new distribution channel – its strategy is to minimize risk by introducing a new product through known channels first. New channels will only be created, if necessary, after the product has proven to be successful.

The launch of the NP copier exemplifies this strategy. Canon initially sold these copiers in Japan by direct sales through its Business Machines Sales organization, which had been set up in 1968 to sell the calculator product line. This sales organization was merged with the camera sales organization in 1971 to form Canon Sales. By 1972, after three years of experience in producing the NP product line, the company entered into a new distribution channel, that of dealers, to supplement direct selling.

The NP copier line was not marketed in the US until 1974, after production and distribution were running smoothly in Japan. The US distribution system was similar to that used in Japan, with seven sales subsidiaries for direct selling and a network of independent dealers.

By the late 1970s, Canon had built up a strong dealer network in the US which supported both sales and service of the copiers. The dealer channel was responsible for rapid growth in copier sales, and, by the early 1980s, Canon copiers were sold almost exclusively through this channel. Canon enthusiastically supported the dealers with attractive sales incentive programs, management training and social outings. Dealers were certified to sell copiers only after completing a course in service training. The company felt that a close relationship with its dealers was a vital asset that allowed it to understand and react to customer's needs and problems in a timely manner. At the same time, Canon also maintained a direct selling mechanism through wholly owned sales subsidiaries in Japan, the US and Europe in order to target large customers and government accounts.

The introduction of its low-end personal copier in 1983 was similarly planned to minimize risk. Initially, Canon's NP dealers in Japan were not interested in the product due to its low maintenance needs and inability to utilize large paper sizes. Thus, PCs were distributed through the firm's office supply stores who were already selling its personal calculators. After seeing the success of the PC, the NP dealers began to carry the copier.

In the US, the PC was initially sold only through existing dealers and direct sales channels due to limited availability of the product. Later, it was sold through competitors' dealers and office supply stores, and, eventually, the distribution channels were extended to include mass merchandisers. Canon already had considerable experience in mass merchandising from its camera business.

Advertising has always been an integral part of Canon's marketing strategy. President Kaku believes that Canon must have a corporate brand name which is outstanding to succeed in its diversification effort. 'Customers must prefer products because they bear the name Canon,' he says. As described by the company's finance director, 'If a brand name is unknown, and there is no advertising, you have to sell it cheap. It's not our policy to buy share with a low price. We establish our brand with advertising at a reasonably high price.'

Therefore, when the NP-200 was introduced in 1980, 10 percent of the selling price was spent on advertising; for the launch of the personal copier, advertising expenditure was estimated to be 20 percent of the selling price. Canon has also sponsored various sporting events including World Cup football, the Williams motor racing team, and the ice dancers Torvill and Dean. The company expects its current expansion into the home automation market to be greatly enhanced by the brand image it has built in office equipment (see Exhibit 1 for Canon's advertising expenditures through 1990).

Manufacturing

Canon's goal in manufacturing is to produce the best quality at the lowest cost with the best delivery. To drive down costs, a key philosophy of the production system is to organize the manufacture of each product so that the minimum amount of time, energy and resources are required. Canon therefore places strong emphasis on tight inventory management through a stable production planning process, careful material planning, close supplier relationships, and adherence to the kanban system of inventory movement. Additionally, a formal waste elimination program saved Canon 177 billion yen between 1976 and 1985. Overall, Canon accomplished a 30 percent increase in productivity per year from 1976 to 1982 and over 10 percent thereafter through automation and innovative process improvements.

The workforce is held in high regard at Canon. A philosophy of 'stop and fix it' empowers any worker to stop the production line if he or she is not able to perform a task properly or observes a quality problem. Workers are responsible for their own machine maintenance governed by rules which stress prevention. Targets for quality and production and other critical data are presented to the workers with on-line feedback. Most workers also participate in voluntary 'small group activity' for problems solving. The result of these systems is a workforce that feels individually responsible for the success of the products it manufactures.

Canon sponsors a highly regarded suggestion program for its workers in order to directly involve those most familiar with the work processes in improving the business. The program was originally initiated in 1952 with only limited success, but in the early 1980s participation soared with more than seventy suggestions per employee per year. All suggestions are reviewed by a hierarchy of committees with monetary prizes awarded monthly and yearly depending on the importance of the suggestion. The quality and effectiveness of the process are demonstrated by a 90 percent implementation rate of the suggestions offered and corporate savings of $202 million in 1985 (against a total expenditure of $2 million in running the program, over 90 percent of it in prize money).

Canon chooses to backward integrate only on parts with unique technologies. For other components, the company prefers to develop long-term relationships with its suppliers and it retains two sources for most parts. In 1990, over 80 percent of Canon's copiers were assembled from purchased parts, with only the drums and toner being manufactured in-house. The company also maintains its own in-house capability for doing pilot production of all parts so as to understand better the technology and the vendors' costs.

Another key to Canon's high quality and low cost is the attention given to parts commonality between models. Between some adjacent copier models, the commonality is as high as 60 percent.

Copier manufacture was primarily located in Toride, Japan, in the early years but then spread to Germany, California and Virginia in the US, France, Italy and Korea. In order to mitigate trade and investment friction, Canon is working to increase the local content of parts as it expands globally. In Europe it exceeds the EC standard by five percent. It is also adding R&D capability to some of its overseas operations. Mr Kaku emphasizes the importance of friendly trading partners:

> Friction cannot be erased by merely transferring our manufacturing facilities overseas. The earnings after tax must be reinvested in the country; we must transfer our technology to the country. This is the only way our overseas expansion will be welcomed.

Leveraging Expertise

Canon places critical importance on continued growth through diversification into new product fields. Mr Kaku observed,

> Whenever Canon introduced a new product, profits surged forward. Whenever innovation lagged, on the other hand, so did the earnings . . . In order to survive in the coming era of extreme competition, Canon must possess at least a dozen proprietary state-of-the-art technologies that will enable it to develop unique products.

While an avid supporter of diversification, Mr Kaku was cautious.

> In order to ensure the enduring survival of Canon, we have to continue diversifying in order to adapt to environmental changes. However, we must be wise in choosing ways toward diversification. In other words, we must minimize the risks. Entering a new business which requires either a technology unrelated to Canon's current expertise or a different marketing channel than Canon currently uses incurs a 50 percent risk. If Canon attempts to enter a new business which requires both a new technology and a new marketing channel which are unfamiliar to Canon, the risk entailed in such ventures would be 100 percent. There are two prerequisites that have to be satisfied before launching such new ventures. First, our operation must be debt-free; second, we will have to secure the personnel capable of competently undertaking such ventures. I feel we shall have to wait until the twenty-first century before we are ready.

Combining Capabilities

Through its R&D strategy, Canon has worked to build up specialized expertise in several areas and then link them to offer innovative, state-of-the-art products. Through the fifties and sixties, Canon focused on products related to its main business and expertise, cameras. This prompted the introduction of the 8mm movie camera and the Canon range of mid-market cameras. There was minimal risk because the optics technology was the same and the marketing outlet, camera shops, remained the same.

Entrance into the calculator market pushed Canon into developing expertise in the field of microelectronics, which it later innovatively combined with its optics capability to introduce one of its most successful products, the personal copier. From copiers, Canon utilized the replaceable cartridge system to introduce a successful desktop laser printer.

In the early seventies, Canon entered the business of marketing micro-chip semiconductor production equipment. In 1980, the company entered into the development and manufacture of unique proprietary ICs in order to strengthen further its expertise in electronics technology. This development effort was expanded in the late eighties to focus on opto-electronic ICs. According to Mr Kaku:

> We are now seriously committed to R&D in ICs because our vision for the future foresees the arrival of the opto-electronic era. When the time arrives for the opto-electronic IC to replace the current ultra-LSI, we intend to go into making large-scale computers. Presently we cannot compete with the IBMs and NECs using the ultra-LSIs. When the era of the opto-electronic IC arrives, the technology of designing the computer will be radically transformed; that will be our chance for making entry into the field of the large-scale computer.

Creative Destruction

In 1975 Canon produced the first laser printer. Over the next 15 years, laser printers evolved as a highly successful product line under the Canon brand name. The company also provides the 'engine' as an OEM to Hewlett Packard and other laser printer manufacturers which when added to its own brand sales supports a total of 84 percent of world-wide demand.

The biggest threat to the laser printer industry is substitution by the newly developed bubble jet printer. With a new technology which squirts out thin streams of ink under heat, a high-quality silent printer can be produced at half the price of the laser printer. The technology was invented accidentally in the Canon research labs. It keys on a print head which has up to 400 fine nozzles per inch, each with its own heater to warm the ink until it shoots out tiny ink droplets. This invention utilizes Canon's competencies in fine chemicals for producing the ink and its expertise in semiconductors, materials, and electronics for manufacturing the print heads. Canon is moving full steam forward to develop the bubble jet technology, even though it might destroy a business that the company dominates. The new product is even more closely tied to the company's core capabilities, and management believes that successful development of this business will help broaden further its expertise in semiconductors.

Challenge of the 1990s

Canon sees the office automation business as its key growth opportunity for the nineties. It already has a well-established brand name in home and office automation products through its offerings of copiers, facsimiles, electronic typewriters, laser printers, word processing equipment and personal computers. The next challenge for the company is to link these discrete products into a multifunctional system which will perform the tasks of a copier, facsimile, printer, and scanner and interface with a computer so that all the functions can be performed from one keyboard. In 1988, with this target, Canon introduced a personal computer which incorporated a PC, a fax, a telephone and a word processor. Canon has also introduced a color laser copier which hooks up to a computer to serve as a color printer. A series of additional integrated OA offerings are scheduled for introduction in 1992, and the company expects these

products to serve as its growth engine in the first half of the 1990s.

Managing the Process

Undergirding this impressive history of continously building new corporate capabilities and of exploiting those capabilities to create a fountain of innovative new products lies a rather unique management process. Canon has institutionalized corporate entrepreneurship through its highly autonomous and market focused business unit structure. A set of powerful functional committees provide the bridge between the entrepreneurial business units and the company's core capabilities in technology, manufacturing and marketing. Finally, an extraordinarily high level of corporate ambition drives this innovation engine, which is fuelled by the creativity of its people and by top management's continuous striving for ever higher levels of performance.

Driving Entrepreneurship: The Business Units

Mr Kaku had promoted the concept of the entrepreneurial business unit from his earliest days with Canon, but it was not until the company had suffered significant losses in 1975 that his voice was heard. His plan was implemented shortly before he became president of the company.

Mr Kaku believed that Canon's diversification strategy could only succeed if the business units were empowered to act on their own, free of central controls. Therefore, two independent operating units were formed in 1978, one for cameras and one for office equipment, to be managed as business units. Optical Instruments, the third business unit, had always been separate. Since that time, an additional three business units have been spun off. The original three business units were then given clear profitability targets, as well as highly ambitious growth objectives, and were allowed the freedom to devise their own ways to achieve these goals. One immediate result of this decentralization was the recognition that Canon's past practice of mixing production of different products in the same manufacturing facility would no longer work. Manufacturing was reorganized so that no plant produced more than one type of product.

Mr Kaku describes the head of each unit as a surrogate of the CEO empowered to make quick decisions. This allows him, as president of Canon, to devote himself exclusively to his main task of creating and implementing the long-term corporate strategy. In explaining the benefits of the system, he said:

> Previously, the president was in exclusive charge of all decision making; his subordinates had to form a queue to await their turn in presenting their problems to him. This kind of system hinders the development of the young managers' potential for decision-making.
>
> Furthermore, take the case of the desktop calculator. Whereas, I can devote only about two hours each day on problems concerning the calculator, the CEO of Casio Calculator could devote 24 hours to the calculator . . . In the fiercely competitive market, we lost out because our then CEO was slow in coping with the problem.

In contrast to the Western philosophy of stand-alone SBUs encompassing all functions including engineering, sales, marketing and production, Canon has chosen to separate its product divisions from its sales and marketing arm. This separation allows for a clear focus on the challenges that Canon faces in selling products on a global scale. Through a five-year plan initiated in 1977, Seiichi Takigawa, the president of Canon Sales (the sales organization for Japan), stressed the need to 'make sales a science.' After proving the profitability of this approach, Canon Sales took on the responsibility for world-wide marketing, sales and service. In 1981, Canon Sales was listed on the Tokyo stock exchange, reaffirming its independence.

Canon also allows its overseas subsidiaries free rein, though it holds the majority of stock. The philosophy is to create the maximum operational leeway for each subsidiary to act on its own initiative. Kaku describes the philosophy through an analogy:

> Canon's system of managing subsidiaries is similar to the policy of the Tokugawa government, which established secure hegemony over the warlords, who were granted autonomy in their territory. I am 'shogun' [head of the Tokugawa regime] and the subsidiaries' presidents are the 'daimyo' [warlords]. The difference between Canon and the Tokugawa government is that the latter was a zero-sum society: its policy was repressive. On the other hand, Canon's objective is to enhance the prosperity of all subsidiaries through efficient mutual collaboration.

Canon has also promoted the growth of intrapreneurial ventures within the company by spinning these ventures off as wholly owned subsidiaries. The first venture to be spun off was Canon Components, which produced electronic components and devices, in 1984.

Building Integration: Functional Committees

As Canon continues to grow and diversify, it becomes increasingly difficult but also ever more important to link its product divisions in order to realize the benefits possible only in a large multi-product corporation. The basis of Canon's integration is a three dimensional management approach in which the first dimension is the independent business unit, the second a network of functional committees, and the third the regional companies focused on geographic markets (see Exhibit 5).

Kaku feels there are four basic requirements for the success of a diversified business.

1. a level of competence in research and development;

2. quality, low-cost manufacturing technology;

3. superior marketing strength;

4. an outstanding corporate identity, culture and brand name.

Therefore, he has established separate functional committees to address the first three requirements

EXHIBIT 5
Canon Organization Chart

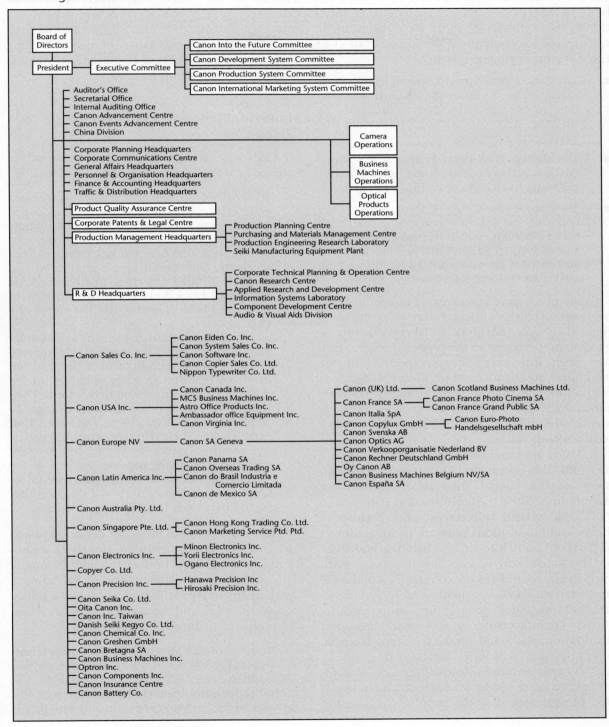

of development, production and marketing, while the fourth task has been kept as a direct responsibility of corporate management. The three functional committees, in turn, have been made responsible for company-wide administration of three key management systems:

■ The Canon Development System (CDS) whose objectives are to foster the research and creation of new products and technologies by studying and continuously improving the development process.

■ The Canon Production System (CPS) whose goal is to achieve optimum quality by minimizing waste in all areas of manufacturing.

■ The Canon Marketing System (CMS), later renamed the Canon International Marketing System (CIMS), which is tasked to expand and strengthen Canon's independent domestic and overseas sales networks by building a high quality service and sales force.

Separate office have been created at headquarters for each of these critical committees, and over time their role has broadened to encompass general improvement of the processes used to support their functions. The chairpersons of the committee are members of Canon's management committee, which gives them the ability to ensure consistency and communicate process improvements throughout the multiproduct, multinational corporation.

Using information technology to integrate its world-wide operations, Canon began development of the Global Information system for Harmonious Growth Administration (GINGA) in 1987. The system will consist of a high-speed digital communications network to interconnect all parts of Canon into a global database and allow for the timely flow of information among managers in any location of the company's world-wide organization. GINGA is planned to include separate but integrated systems for computer integrated manufacturing, global marketing and distribution, R&D and product design, financial reporting, and personnel database tracking, as well as some advances in intelligent office automation. As described by Mr Kaku, the main objective of this system is to supplement Canon's efficient vertical communications structure with a lateral one that will facilitate direct information exchange among managers across businesses, countries, and functions on all operational matters concerning the company. The system is being developed at a total cost of 20 billion yen and it is targeted for completion in 1992.

Managing Renewal: Challenges and Change

Mr Kaku was very forthright about some of the management weaknesses of Canon prior to 1975:

> In short, our skill in management – the software of our enterprise – was weak. Management policy must be guided by a soundly created software on management; if the software is weak, the firm will lack clearly defined ideals and objectives. In the beginning we had a clearly defined objective, to overtake West Germany's Leica. Since then our management policy has been changing like the colors of a chameleon.
>
> In the past our management would order employees to reach the peak of Mount Fuji, and then before the vanguard of climbers had barely started climbing, they would be ordered to climb Mount Tsukuba far to the north. Then the order would again be suddenly changed to climb Mount Yatsugatake to the west. After experiencing these kind of shifts in policy, the smarter employees would opt to take things easy by taking naps on the bank of the river Tamagawa. As a result, vitality would be sapped from our work force – a situation that should have been forestalled by all means.

Mr Kaku's first action as President of Canon was to start the firm on the path to global leadership through establishing the first 'premier company plan,' a six-year plan designed to make Canon a top company in Japan. The plan outlined a policy for diversification and required consistently recurring profits exceeding 10 percent on sales.

> The aim of any Japanese corporation is ensuring its perpetual survival. Unlike the venture businesses and US corporations, our greatest objective is not to maximize short-term profits. Our vital objective is to continually earn profits

on a stable basis for ensuring survival. To implement this goal, we must diversify.

By the time the original six-year plan expired in 1981, Canon had become a highly respected company in Japan. The plan was then renewed through 1986 and then again into the 1990s. The challenge was to become a premier global company, defined as having recurring profits exceeding 15 percent of sales. R&D spending was gradually increased from 6 percent of sales in 1980 to 9 percent in 1985 as a prerequisite for global excellence. As described by Mr Kaku:

> By implementing our first plan for becoming a premier company we have succeeded in attaining the allegorical top of Mount Fuji. Our next objective is the Everest. With a firm determination, we could have climbed Fuji wearing sandals. However, sandals are highly inappropriate for climbing Everest; it may cause our death.

According to Mr Kaku, such ambitions also require a company to build up the ability to absorb temporary reversals without panic; ambition without stability makes the corporate ship lose its way. To illustrate, he described the situation at Canon during the time the yen depreciated from 236 to the dollar in 1985 to 168 to the dollar in 1986. With 74 percent of Canon's Japanese production going to export markets, this sudden change caused earnings to fall to 4.6 billion yen, one tenth of the previous year. Some board members at Canon sought drastic action such as a major restructuring of the company and cutting the R&D budget. Mr Kaku had successfully argued the opposite:

> What I did was calm them down. If a person gets lost in climbing a high mountain, he must avoid excessive use of his energy, otherwise his predicament will deepen . . . Our ongoing strategy for becoming the premier company remains the best, even under this crisis; there is no need to panic. Even if we have to forgo dividends for two or three times, we shall surely overcome this crisis.

While celebrating the company's past successes, Mr Kaku also constantly reminds his colleagues that no organizational form or process holds the eternal truth. The need to change with a changing world is inevitable. For example, despite being the creator of the product division-marketing company split, he was considering rejoining these two in the nineties:

> In the future, our major efforts in marketing must be concentrated on clearly defining and differentiating the markets of the respective products and creating appropriate marketing systems for them. In order to make this feasible, we may have to recombine our sales subsidiaries with the parent company and restructure their functions to fully meet the market's needs.

While constantly aware of the need to change, Kaku also recognizes the difficulties managers face in changing the very approaches and strategies that have led to past successes:

> In order for a company to survive forever, the company must have the courage to be able to deny at one point what it has been doing in the past; the biological concept of 'ecdysis' – casting off the skin to emerge to new form. But it is difficult for human beings to deny and destruct what they have been building up. But if they cannot do that, it is certain that the firm can not survive forever. Speaking about myself, it is difficult to deny what I've done in the past. So when such time comes that I have to deny the past, I inevitably would have to step down.

Case 11: Shell Sells Billiton: Stabilis Fortuna Merendis?

by Bob de Wit and Richard Renner [1]

Finalizing the transaction took more than a year due to complex South African regulations on capital export, but it was more than worth it according to Gencor-chairman Brian Gilbertson. As of 1995 the South African mining company Gencor has taken over Billiton, the mineral resources subsidiary of the Royal Dutch Shell Group of Companies, for US$ 1.144 billion. Gilbertson is confident that this acquisition is a once-in-a-lifetime deal, catapulting the new parent company into the top five mining companies in the world. The question is, however, whether Gencor's ambitions will come. Will Billiton enable Gencor to be a major force in the mining industry, or will the opposite happen – will the new acquired Billiton again reveal itself as the huge loss maker it has been for the large majority of 25 years it has been a Shell subsidiary. The losses didn't hurt Shell too much since Billiton accounted for only two percent of total revenues, but for Gencor continued losses by Billiton could bring the company in jeopardy. Will Gencor be a world leader in mining or virtually bankrupt within ten years? Can Gencor do better than Shell, one of the world's best-led companies? Gilbertson is confident, and even Shell's President Mr Herkströter admits at a shareholder meeting that the new parent might bring Billiton back into the black figures: 'Maybe Gencor can do something Shell could not.'

Royal Dutch/Shell

The Royal Dutch/Shell Group of Companies originates from an alliance in 1907 between the Dutch NV Koninklijke Nederlandsche Petroleum Maatschappij (Royal Dutch Petroleum Company) and the British Shell Transport and Trading Company Ltd. The parent companies of the group, Royal Dutch (60 percent) and Shell Transport (40 percent), primarily act as intermediaries for group investments, and jointly own three *holding companies*: Shell Petroleum NV, The Shell Petroleum Company Ltd., and Shell Petroleum Inc. The first two holdings jointly hold all or part of the operating companies, directly or indirectly. The responsibilities of the holdings are primarily to control and finance activities by:

- formulating investment policies;

- evaluating the group companies' investment programs;

- deciding on capital expenses;

- evaluating investment performances;

- controlling overall shareholder value.

The Group operates on a world-wide basis in oil, natural gas, and chemicals. Each *operating company* concentrates on one or several of the following activities: exploration, exploitation, production, transport, and marketing and sales. The operating companies are accountable for their results, and for building up and maintaining activities. They may consult the group service companies or, through them, other group companies. The *service companies* bridge the group companies' activities by means of advice and attuning objectives or financial means. They also connect

[1] Source: This case was written as a basis for class discussion rather than to illustrate effective or ineffetive handling of an administrative situation. This case was compiled from publicly available sources. Copyright 1998 by Bob de Wit.

the operating companies' investment plans and the holdings. In addition, service companies carry out all activities that are most efficiently executed centrally.

Strategic Planning at Shell

Shell is well known for continuously striving to look beyond horizons. Their explicit strategic plans are well implemented and controlled, and have been rewarded by sustained high performances in the international oil industry. Shell invests pro-actively and creatively in the demanding and rapidly changing oil industry, and allocates significant resources for promising new activities on the basis of a long-term vision. The 'Shell Group Planning System,' the annual strategic planning cycle, is famous for using scenarios to formulate operating companies' visions since the 1970s. Although the strategic planning process pays attention to financial consequences of the new plans, it is not focused on detailed financial analyses. According to Shell an overly narrow focus on financial details distracts management attention from innovative strategic thinking.

Only after the strategic planning process and developing or adjusting a vision, do operating companies present investment proposals. In this phase detailed financial analyses are made in order to evaluate investment proposals on criteria of feasibility and minimum rates of return. The coordination and planning of operating companies' activities are primarily being carried out and supported by the service companies. Board members of the service companies that are also board members of a holding company are appointed in the Committee of Managing Directors (CMD). The CMD develops general objectives and long-term plans, while each CMD member has particular responsibilities. The mining activities were also assigned to one of the members.

The second management echelon consists of Coordinators for sectors, functions, or regions. The Coordinator Metals was also Managing Director of Billiton, with a primary responsibility to formulate a policy plan for the metals sector. The final version of the policy plan was evaluated by the 'Metals Panel,' consisting of a number of CMD-members and coordinators of the Royal Dutch/Shell Group of Companies.

Shell's Diversifications in the 1970s

At the end of the 1960s the major oil companies showed a strong urge to diversify into remote activities like hotels and office furniture, and more or less related activities such as coal and metals. Shell was no exception. It started diversifications into coal and metal. It was believed that diversifications would guarantee long-term sustainable growth.

In the short term the future of the oil and gas industry looked bright and shiny, but Shell worried about some long-term issues such as increasing power of the OPEC-countries and the finite world oil and gas reserves. It was also generally agreed that the strong growth rates of the oil industry could not continue. Another motive was Shell's very strong financial and economic position at the end of the 1960s, and the high financial reserves. Shell wanted to employ its reserves in a useful way. It decided to search for new opportunities and to spread interests and investments.

Prior to the decision to enter the world of non-ferrous metals and ore, Royal Dutch/Shell had studied several possible diversifications for two years. The Dutch top manager who led the study and was also the driving force behind acquiring Billiton, Mr Swart, was a man with a clear background in oil. He studied chemical technology at the Technical University of Delft, the Netherlands, and started his career in Shell's Amsterdam laboratory. Then he became involved in designing and putting refineries into operation in several countries. In 1965 he became Managing Director of Shell Curacao and a Director of Shell Venezuela. Half a year before acquiring Billiton Mr Swart was appointed as a Group Managing Director of Royal Dutch/Shell.

Potential diversifications had to meet two important criteria. Compared with the traditional activities the magnitude of the new activities had to be considerable, both in terms of potential turnover and required capital investments, and the new activities had to be related to the traditional ones. Mr Swart said in 1985, looking back on the decision to enter the metals:

> It was important to find a new activity that would give enough room to manoeuvre. The point is, the oil industry is colossal, in which Shell plays a very big role. There is no related branch big enough for Shell. At this moment Shell need not be very big in metals, but in 10 or 15 years it may be the time for Shell that it wants to be and also needs to be that big. By then Shell has invested in that branch for 25 years, not only money, also people.
>
> (Shell Venster 1985)

At that moment Shell's diversification policy into activities of considerable magnitude had already been abandoned.

In 1984 the head of Shell's Non-Traditional Business, Mr Van der Toorn, explained Shell's diversification philosophy (Shell Venster 1984):

> . . . . One thing Shell still knows for sure, is that we will one day run out of oil. At that moment Shell wants to substantially participate in new and profitable industries with growth potential. This is a matter of doing, growing into it, learning the profession. And learning takes time. A new activity must be treated with the highest respect. It may be new for Shell, but not for others. . . . Oil companies face a high financial turnover, and are inclined to think in comparable amounts of money. This we don't do. It is important that we search for opportunities in industries that closely relate to the Group's strengths. We do this by selectively investing in a limited number of new activities. We should not think that with our deep pockets and Shell management we will easily perform the job. On the contrary, we participate on a limited scale and at arm's length in joint ventures that operate independently. The management of these activities are in the hands of highly respected people in that branch. . . . Large capital investments and huge turnovers are not the sole criteria any more in our striving to diversify. We put more emphasis on a gradual development of projects that contain synergies with the extraordinary knowledge and experience within the Group on energy needs in most countries in the world, and in the many markets for oil and chemical products. Another difference with

former times is that we do not need to take hasty decisions. We have and take our time to learn new things, by trial and error. While learning, we decide whether we want to continue.

The rationale behind entering the metals business had been formulated as follows:

1   Metals are – like oil, gas and chemical products – raw materials for a wide range of companies and industries.

2   The metals industry explores, exploits, processes, recycles, and sells non-ferrous metals, industrial minerals, and related products, which are exactly the same activities Shell employs in oil, gas and chemicals.

3   Shell strives for more intensive use of its geological know-how, drilling, and technological knowledge, in other fields than oil and gas.

Shell already noticed important differences between the oil industry and the metal industry, but also the many and obvious similarities. Both industries employ geological and geophysical methods; both process the raw materials to products before they are ready to use; all products must be mass-shipped by especially constructed ships; marketing and sales of both industries often focus on the same clients; both industries require high capital investments; and both industries require excellent relations with governments of host countries and diplomacy skills.

Shell Buys Billiton

After deciding to enter the world of metals, Shell started to develop some projects on an individual basis, such as exploiting magnesium reservoirs in the northern region of the Netherlands, Groningen. Shell was also interested in the bauxite/aluminium activities of Holland Aluminium, a joint venture between the Dutch steel company Hoogovens and Billiton. Shell became convinced, however, that an acquisition would be better and quicker than growing activities from scratch. The target firm should be internationally active in exploration and processing, and with a head office in Western Europe.

Billiton was the preferred target. It had been active in mining, metallurgy and non-ferrous activities on a world-wide basis. On July 13, 1970, Shell bought Billiton for 423 million Dutch guilders. According to Shell and Billiton, the acquisition was to the benefit of both firms. First, because of the significant size of Billiton, Shell entered the metal industry quickly. This would be an excellent basis for rapidly forming a fourth leg within the Shell Group, the other legs being oil, gas, and chemicals. Without this major acquisition it could have taken some 40 years to develop a mining leg. Shell did not have that patience. Second, the strong diversification of Billiton allowed Shell to quickly become an important producer of a variety of non-ferrous metals, particularly tin. Third, the vertically integrated structure of Billiton was a big advantage to Shell. In one strike Shell bought competencies in exploration, exploitation, processing, marketing, sales, and research of ore and metals. Last but not least, both companies are Dutch (Shell 60 percent, Billiton 100 percent), which make cultural and language problems unlikely, and the head offices of Shell and Billiton were coincidentally both located in The Hague, the Netherlands.

Although love came from both sides, the newly weds had to get used to each other. Company cultures appeared to differ on crucial points. For example, oil companies tend to focus on projects where investments are huge and aided by technological initiatives, a policy that was maintained while investing in aluminium activities. Many years later Billiton's Managing Director Mr Slechte admitted that, in retrospect, the big investments into aluminium should not have been made, and that a significant part of Billiton's losses could be blamed on the laborious cooperation between Shell and Billiton. He said: 'Billiton's mining philosophy did not come about as expected. They just looked up at the new Shell people. They thought: if they say so, who are we to argue to the contrary. Unjustified, because the Billiton people possessed the professional knowledge on metals (Het Financieele Dagblad 1989).'

Shell's assumption of clear and important similarities between their and Billiton's activities led to another disappointment. In reality the differences appeared to dominate the similarities. Fundamental and unbridgeable differences showed up in applied technologies, competition, markets, and characteristics and applications of the products. Differences appeared even at fundamental levels. For example, a distinction between upstream (exploration and exploitation) and downstream (processing, refining, transport, marketing and sales) activities, useful and accepted in the oil industry, was also introduced at Billiton. A mistake, because the characteristics of upstream and downstream oil activities were not applicable to the metal industry. Only a few dozen major oil firms perform significant upstream activities, in metals many hundreds. The downstream oil sector generates well-defined products for well-defined markets (e.g. car fuels), while there are thousands of applications of metals for very diverse markets.

The Non-ferrous Metal Industry

The metal industry can be divided into the basic metal and metal processing industries. The most important basic metals are iron and steel, industries with strong (supra-national) government involvement. All other metals are categorized into the non-ferrous industry, and are exploited by multinational firms such as Billiton. The non-ferrous metal industry had an asset base of around US$ 100 billion (1990 figure), which is significantly smaller than the oil industry.

Aluminium is the world's most important non-ferrous metal. In terms of tonnes produced, aluminium comes third behind only iron and steel. Since 1886, when an electrolytic process to make aluminium was developed, the aluminium industry has grown to the most widely applied non-ferrous metal. Other important non-ferrous metals are copper, zinc, lead, nickel, tin, gold, silver, magnesium, titanium, and tungsten. The non-ferrous metal industry operates world-wide, and can be subdivided into exploration, mining, metallurgy, metal processing, and sales. Vertically integrated firms that cover all activities from exploration to sales, like the integrated oil companies, have only emerged in aluminium. The non-ferrous metal deposits are scattered around the globe, and per metal there are typically only few deposits. The buyers are primarily located in the industrial areas of North America, Europe, and Japan.

Metals are raw materials for other industries. Demand and supply of huge quantities of goods meet at transparent markets. Ores and most metals (except for the very rare ones) are commodities, just like sugar and coffee. Prices are set by forces of demand and supply at a certain moment, and can fluctuate quite dramatically – and so can the profits. On the waves of economic cycles the five dominant buyers of metals – construction, capital goods, durable consumer goods, packaging and transportation – change consumption of metals, which influences market prices.

After World War II the western countries, primarily the United States, were accountable for the large majority of world demand in metals. During this era the turnover of metals showed impetuous growth rates. There was also a big need for investments into mining and metal processing industries. The 1970s showed, however, an unexpected declining growth in demand of metals. The first significant decline took place in 1973 during the first oil crisis. The second decline coincided with the second oil crisis in 1979, at the brink of the international debt crisis.

Despite the crises the total capacity expanded at the same velocity as in the post-World war period. Consequently huge overcapacity and unbalanced world metal markets characterized most of the 1980s. There was so much overcapacity on world markets that even when demand picked up the prices remained low. Economic growth at the end of the 1980s made a change, albeit for a short time. Overcapacity disappeared, prices were on the increase, and the metals industry became profitable again. Until 1989, when the world economy deteriorated, prices for metals dropped, and losses returned. The subsequent years showed further worsening: demand continues to be low while supply grew. Improvement of the situation, market growth and a better balance of demand and supply, depended primarily on industrial production in western

countries. Unfortunately, the timing of market improvements is hard to predict.

Structural Changes in the Non-ferrous Metal Industry

From early days mining has been concentrated in developing economies. For them mining is an important source of income and foreign currencies. Mines are also exploited for social (employment) or political purposes, so that in many cases profitability was not first and foremost. Governments of developing economies showed growing interest in mining, and increasingly participated in upstream activities in their respective countries. In some cases governments controlled all national upstream activities, and invested in new mining capacity. They also set up national metal processing to export processed products with higher added value, which again increased government influences in the metal industry.

The profitability of the metal industry is affected by both cyclical and structural factors. Fluctuating demand and prices are inherent of commodity goods such as most metals. The increasing influence of governments of developing countries was structural, and had a profound effect on the metals industry. The previously balanced industry chain of mining, melting, processing, and marketing was distorted and became fragmented and disintegrated.

The Aluminium Industry

Crucial factors in the aluminium industry are huge economies of scale, high capital intensity, a need for cheap electricity, closely held technology, and internationalization. Six major international integrated firms originally dominated the aluminium industry for many years, from bauxite mining (the primary aluminium ore) to processing aluminium. The vertical and horizontal integration strategies of the international companies reflect their striving for market control, by securing supply (upstream) and developing applications (downstream).

Limited competition and the inelastic price

of aluminium characterized the period of market dominance by the 'big six.' The large integrated companies formed *de facto a cartel* and kept prices high and stable. High stable prices combined with rising demand gave favorable prospects for the aluminium industry, which led to an incredible investment boom in the 1970s.

Soon expectations appeared to be much too rosy. The aluminium industry ended up in a depression, and except for a short period at the end of the 1980s the crisis continued until the 1990s. The collapse of aluminium demand was primarily related to shrinking world-wide industrial activity in the early 1980s. However, a simultaneous aggressive pricing policy of the aluminium cartel simultaneously led to the substitution of plastics for aluminium, particularly in construction, packaging, and transportation, which again reduced the rate of growth in demand. In addition, prices of electricity increased significantly as a direct result of the two oil crises in 1973 and 1979.

The impact of lower demand was aggravated by permanent oversupply of aluminium, because of the large investments in the 1970s. Since many investments came from governments, there was another effect: control of the big six companies on the aluminium market dropped radically. This was most clearly reflected in their inability to withhold quotation of aluminium prices on the London Metal Exchange in 1978 and the Commodity Exchange in New York in 1983. Until then, aluminium prices were set by the big six (producer pricing), while currently the markets dominate prices (market pricing). Fluctuations of aluminium prices have become as common as fluctuations of other commodities' prices (Holloway 1988).

The changing structure of the aluminium industry and a deteriorating profitability stimulated competition between the big aluminium multinationals, which stopped solidarity between these companies in 1983. Alcan, one of the big six, started a 'free rider' strategy by discontinuing world producer prices first, in order to benefit from its position as a low-cost producer.

The Oil Companies in the Non-ferrous Metal Industry

Between the Second World War and the end of the 1960s the major oil companies faced more than two decades of stable growth. Demand for oil products increased, and the international oil companies became enormous firms, in terms of size, number of activities and financial wealth. The 1970s ended the stability of the world energy markets. Oil demand dropped when prices rose, and governments as well as consumers realized that oil and gas reserves were finite.

These considerations made oil companies searching for new future routes for long term survival. A popular answer among oil companies was a rapid diversification of their business portfolios, preferably into industries that suggested relatedness. One very important condition for success was synergy: the presence of factors that increase performance by combining activities. Many oil companies spotted mining and the metal industry. They assumed major similarities between the oil industry and the metal industry: international dispersion, extensive projects and long lead times, economic and political risks, the application of joint ventures, governmental involvement, and international trade and transport (Billiton Brief 1982).

Consequently mining and metal companies became targets for most of the major oil companies. The metal sector was regarded as a potentially enduring and stable source of income, once mines and installations had come on stream. In addition, the future prospects for metals were favorable at the time. The Club of Rome predicted prosperity for basic industries, expecting rising world demand and increasing prices, while oil demand would drop according to expectations. Metal companies shared these expectations, oil companies assumed the expectations, and soon the newly entered oil companies invested huge amounts of money – to metal industry standards. For oil companies the investments were not particularly big. Compared with the metal industry, turnover, net results, and investment capital of the oil industry are much larger.

But predicting is difficult, especially about the future. Just when production capacity in the metal industry was extended two world economic recessions, aggravated by two oil shocks, dropped back the demand of metals. Prices collapsed and the metal industry became loss making. Many oil companies withdrew from the metal industry and sold off their interests. Royal Dutch/Shell was the only major oil company with significant metal activities in 1995. In 1989, Shell took over a share in a copper and zinc mine (Les Mines Selbaie) from Exxon, that was actively withdrawing from the industry (The Financial Times 1989), except from minor activities such as a copper mine in Chile. Eventually Shell also decided to concentrate on its 'core activities.'

Billiton: Stabilis Fortuna Merendis

In 1860 a group of Dutch entrepreneurs obtained a concession to mine tin on the Indonesian island Billiton, currently called Belitung. For many years the actual mining was left to the Chinese. The Billiton Company provided credit and bought up the tin. Gradually Billiton became more actively involved in the mining process, and took over all mining activities at the beginning of the twentieth century. Billiton was very profitable, paid high dividends of often over 100 percent to their shareholders, who felt very lucky. Billiton adopted a heraldic motto: 'stabilis fortuna merendis,' meaning 'fortune constantly favors the deserving.'

In anticipation of possible termination of the tin-concession Billiton started to expand outside of Indonesia in 1927. In the Dutch town Arnhem it established the tin-smelter Hollandsche Metallurgische Bedrijven (Dutch Metallurgical Companies), started to exploit a tin mine in Africa, and built the world's largest tin smelter in Texas City (USA). After having been active for 75 years in only exploitation of tin ore and production of tin, the company extended activities in 1935 by bauxite mining (aluminium ore) on Bintang, Indonesia and in 1939 also in Surinam,

another Dutch colony. The new mining activity, mining bauxite and producing alumina, developed into Billiton's most important activity.

After the Second World War Billiton started new activities primarily in the Netherlands. It acquired interests in the synthetic resin producer Adriaan Honig and the Dutch biggest chemical pigments factory Haagen. A first step toward vertical integration in tin was set by establishing the Eerste Nederlandse Witmetaalfabriek (First Dutch White Metal Factory), to produce solder. In Indonesia Billiton resumed tin-activities, using new equipment and methods. In 1958 the newly established 'Republik Indonesia' did not continue the tin-concession, and nationalized all bauxite mining.

Bauxite/Alumina/Aluminium

Billiton was forced to an active reorientation, and it decided on the most obvious: aluminium. From the mid-1950s bauxite from Surinam became Billiton's mainstay. Demand for bauxite showed large growth rates, due to an increasing number of aluminium applications, the Korea Crisis and the American weapon industry. However, Billiton faced competition from the six major integrated multinationals, Alcan, Alcoa, Kaiser, Reynolds, Pechiney, and Alusuisse. It decided to also vertically integrate by expanding into producing the intermediate product alumina and the end product aluminium.

A lack of know-how and financial resources forced Billiton to cooperate with the big six and some other companies. At the end of the 1960s Billiton had formed joint ventures with the Dutch steel company Hoogovens and other companies, for example in Australia, to extract bauxite, with Alcoa in Surinam to produce alumina, and with Hoogovens to melt aluminium at Aldel in Delfzijl, the Netherlands.

Metallurgy

At the beginning of the 1960s Billiton started to expand the metallurgical division by specializing in refining, processing, and selling non-ferrous metals. For example, in 1968 Billiton took a 50 percent share in the Kempensche Zink Maatschappij (Kempen Zinc Company), and invested heavily in extensions and renovations. Billiton's main objective was to produce basic metals, primarily aluminium, tin, lead, and zinc, then processing the output to intermediate products, and get a good position at the buyer's markets.

Industrial and Construction Activities

Billiton not only started to diversify into related activities, but also into industrial and construction activities. It acquired several small and medium-sized production plants of synthetics, plastic tubes, synthetic resins, and pigments in the Netherlands, the United Kingdom, and other countries, as well as construction, building and building materials firms such as De Vries Robbé in 1969. The basic idea was to create a full-integrated industry chain, to secure a stable demand and enable contracting turnkey projects. In 1969 Billiton also participated in an offshore oil and gas consortium ('Consortium Noordwinning') with a concession for exploration on the Dutch Continental shelf.

At the end of the 1960s Billiton was active in over 80 participations. All activities were divided into three divisions: mining, metallurgy, and industry. Billiton's image in the Dutch financial world was close to that of a trader in unassorted goods. In most of the firm's industries Billiton was only a medium-sized company at best. Although financial results had been prosperous, financial institutions had major doubts whether the company would ever be able to escape from its mediocre status. Billiton could not afford investing into all bauxite, alumina, aluminium, zinc, and synthetics activities. In this position Billiton entered 1970, the year of revolutionary changes.

Billiton's Take-over by Royal Dutch/Shell

Shell took the initiative. It approached Billiton's management board, which was astonished by Shell's advances. Shell said that it only considered a friendly take-over, it would withdraw their offer in case Billiton rejected their approach. Billiton accepted the take-over bid, after announcing that it would also have survived independently, on the basis of two arguments[2]:

1   *Shell's financial strength and technological capabilities* would consolidate Billiton's position and strengthen economies of scale. Billiton realized quite well that its intended further growth would require major financial resources and upgraded technological capabilities. Both would become problematic. In addition, as a result of increasing scale economies in the metal industry the political risks and the consequences of a major mining project failure were getting too big to be carried by a firm of Billiton's size.

2   *Shell guaranteed independence and a key position within the Group*. It was agreed that Billiton would become the core firm for all mining and processing of ores and non-ferrous metals. Billiton would remain relatively independent as a separate division within the Royal Dutch/Shell Group. Billiton was promised to participate in all important decisions.

Additional arguments of less importance were the projection of a stronger competitive position *vis-à-vis* the big six multinationals in aluminium; a stronger basis for R&D expenses; positive effects of mutual activities; increased political strength, especially important in developing economies; and entrance to Shell's world-wide contacts in business and finance.

Billiton's Organization After the Take-over

Soon after the take-over the 'Coordination Committee for Mining and Metals' was established, on which were seated Mr Swart, who actually initiated the acquisition and became member of Billiton's non-executive board, and Mr Nauta as Billiton's CEO. This committee aimed at integrating Billiton and the other Shell companies, and

---

[2] Sources: (1) Shell Petroleum N.V. (1970), Bericht aan de aandeelhouders van Billiton en Singkep Tin (Announcement to the shareholders of Billiton and Singkep Tin), The Hague, (2) a mutual press release of 27 May 1970: Shell doet bod op Billiton (Shell makes a bid for Billiton), and (3) a mutual statement of the management boards of Shell and Billiton, including explanation, July–September 1970.

would establish tasks, targets and organization form for Shell's new metal division.

Billiton became relatively independent, a sort of multinational within a multinational. The organizational structure became similar to Shell's: a small number of holdings that control the many operating companies, and a service company Billiton International Metals BV (BIM). Most active companies in the metal industry worked under the Billiton umbrella, only few used their own names, the Shell name, or the name of one of the joint ventures.

The Service Company provided for advisors to operating companies in exploration, production, transport, processing, marketing, some applications of metals, and management of large metal projects. Additionally the Service Company connected the Billiton operating companies, evaluated economic developments, plans, and investments, and helped to adjust all elements.

Comparable with the situation at Royal Dutch/Shell the management board of each Billiton operating company was held responsible for the results and the long term plans of its activities. Support was provided by the Service Company and through this unit by other Shell companies. In practice, the Service Company fulfilled the classic central head office role for the first 15 years after the take-over. In 1985 Billiton was approximately halfway between decentralization, Shell's business philosophy, and centralization, the common practice in the metal industry. Only then was Shell's matrix organization implemented.

Billiton's Strategic Planning

Before 1970 Billiton's head office focused on financial and administrative support of the operating companies. A deliberate development of activities, supporting planning work, and project evaluations were non-existent. After 1970 this changed drastically. The first years were focused on adjusting the Billiton organization to Shell's, but then medium-term and long-term business plans had to be developed, the management board had to formulate and advise Shell about the future development policy. Decisions had to

be taken and a future direction had to be set on the basis of recent information and prognoses. Because of the very long lead times of projects, decisions had to be taken that had visible effects after only 10 years. Billiton was handicapped because it had little experience in this field. It had to learn a lot, and above all, Billiton had to prove its targets, knowledge, and policy, to itself and to Shell.

At Shell's Group level the Metals Panel, a coordination committee metals, had been established. In this committee future directions were set for Billiton's operating companies and other companies in the metal division. The service company Billiton International Metals (BIM) was responsible for realizing and monitoring Shell's corporate planning for the metal division, applying Shell's scenario's of possible economic, social, and political developments on a world scale. On the basis of these scenario's corporate and division plans were being worked out, and adapted by Billiton for specific metal issues. Then medium term plans were prepared per metal and per operating company, while the management boards of the operating companies were closely involved in formulating the medium-term plans. The plans had to be approved by BIM, which also had a major role in the annual investment appraisals.

The conventional lines of communication at Billiton were directed vertically through the heads of divisions. Also from Shell came the system of personal unions in various executive functions. In 1984 Billiton's CEO Mr Van der Graaf was also vice-chairman of BIM, member of the Metals Panel, chairman of Billiton Nederland's non-executive board, member of the non-executive board of NV Billiton Surinam, and member of non-executive boards of several other operating companies.

Billiton's Human Resources Management After the Take-over

In the world of metals a well-known saying is: 'One can only talk metals after at least 20 years' work.' For this reason most metal companies focus on one or only a few metals. However, Billiton's goal was, obliged by Shell, to become a geographical dispersed multi-metal group of companies with downstream and upstream activities.

A second deviation from conventional metal-wisdom after the take-over was Billiton's job-rotation. In the metals business it takes a long time before someone really feels settled in a particular branch, and so job rotation is an exception. Someone starts in alumina and typically stays there. He becomes experienced and an authority in the field. Billiton deviated from this after 1970 because it emphasized the advantages over the disadvantages of job rotation, that is, broad experience and general knowledge follow from diverse functions in a variety of fields.

The Billiton employees were also restricted in achieving more experience in metal because of a large inflow of Shell people during Billiton's fast growth period. The pool of Billiton employees was not sufficient to fill higher management positions, and so many new managers and specialists came from Shell. These people did not bring in specific knowledge and experience in metals, and often returned to oil, gas, or chemicals after a number of years.

The involvement of Billiton employees in new joint ventures was also limited. Although Billiton deliberately formed joint ventures to learn from the new activities in non-ferrous metal, few Billiton people got that chance.

One Bed, Two Dreams: Six Phases Between Take-over and Disposal

Shell's goal to quickly develop a fourth major division Mining & Metallurgy, came from its past experience of a slowly growing chemicals division. In 1970, after more than 40 years, the chemicals division still only counted for one eighth of Shell's turnover. It was the intention to develop the new Mining and Metallurgy division at high speed. Billiton would set up new projects, form joint ventures with several partners, and take over companies, in order to quickly become a diversified and substantial division. Shell gave Billiton 25 years to reach that goal, because by then it expected a severe downturn of oil activities. Mr Swart said: 'In 1990–1995 Shell should ask the question whether it has reached its goal of having a strong position in the metal industry, because then the oil industry has just sunk.' (Shell Venster 1985)

The new metal division had to grow until it counted for at least 10 percent of Shell's turnover. This meant that Billiton had to become a firm with an asset base of US$ 12 billion. In the context of the total metal industry turnover this was an extremely ambitious goal, and obviously unrealistic according to some Billiton managers. They were, however, outvoted by Shell managers.

Phase I (1970–1976): Restructuring and Autonomous Growth

Compared to its later size, Billiton's activities in the metal industry were of limited volume, with mining of only bauxite and tin. When Shell took over Billiton, it had the following stakes in the mining industry:

- Bauxite mines and long-term tolling contracts for aluminium production in Surinam;

- Participations in tin mines and tin smelters in Indonesia, Africa, and South East Asia;

- Holland Aluminium (50 percent, aluminium smelting);

- Hollandsche Metallurgische Industrie Billiton (tin and lead smelting);

- Kawecki-Billiton (50 percent, 'speciality metal products');

- The Kempensche Zinkmaatschappij (50 percent, zinc smelting);

- H.J. Enthoven & Sons (lead smelting);

- Billiton Enthoven Metals Ltd (BEM);

- H.J. van der Rijn (wholesale in non-ferrous intermediate products) (Olie 1973).

Billiton's metal activities counted for approximately 60 percent of total turnover in 1970. Pressured by the new parent Royal Dutch/Shell the hotchpotch of unrelated subsidiaries was brought back drastically. Billiton's extension to an integrated construction company was stopped, building and building materials firms were sold (such as De Vries Robbé of 4000 employees), as well as synthetics, plastics, and chemicals. Within a few years Billiton's activities were fully focused on mining, metallurgy, and trade of non-ferrous metals.

After this period of restructuring Billiton was ready for rapid expansion. The first plans were made to become a medium-sized company in the 1980s. It included expansion of existing sectors, the development of an extensive worldwide exploration program to find ores and develop mines, and participation in many joint ventures. On the field of research new ideas were developed on ore processing and production of metals. The speed of these changes was fast, although not as fast as projected by Shell in its previous plans.

Based on changes in the previous two years in oil, chemicals and metals, Shell decided in 1972 that the development of mining and metals should be limited to autonomous growth. Two Billiton top managers, Mr Nauta and Mr Van Saarloos, disapproved of this decision and left the company, because their new position offered insufficient challenges for the future. Consequently Billiton's management board counted only one man with a Billiton history, Mr Van der Graaf. The two other members of Billiton's top management originated from Shell, one level below there was a significant influx of Shell people with applicable skills – e.g. in finance, planning, and processing.

Billiton could not count on massive support from Shell for major investments to expand activities, and so it grew at a relatively slow pace. Billiton used the time to study further opportunities and developments, including expansion into aluminium and (for Billiton) new metals such as copper and nickel. This led to an impressive number of plans and proposals, on the basis of which Billiton expanded massively in a later stage. Much attention was paid to research, in terms of money and human capital.

Billiton also strived for expansion of market-

ing and sales activities that were bundled in a separate company. It aimed at building international trade activities on the fields of ores, non-ferrous metals, and intermediate products, and bought existing companies in Western Europe. The originally missing link of a marketing and sales organization was considered essential to successfully integrate vertically in the industry chain of metals, and should be connected.

Despite seven years of only 'autonomous growth', Billiton was expanding quite quickly:

1972 – take-over of Stokvis (wholesale of metals);

– obtaining a majority share of the German Denkhaus GmbH (wholesale of stainless steel and non-ferrous intermediate products);

1973 – building a new electrolytic zinc smelter for replacement of the obsolete thermic process (250 million Dutch Guilder investment);

1974 – participation in the Canadian Nanisivik zinc mine;

1975 – take-over of M.L. Polak & Zoon (one of Europe's biggest trade and processing companies in non-ferrous and ferroscrap);

– take-over of International Metals & Ores Ltd. (trade of raw metals) and its subsidiary Metal Scrap and By-products (scrap);

– participation in exploiting the Cuajone copper mine in Peru;

1977 – take-over of British Lead Mills (lead melting);

– take-over of Neo Metal BV and Alcu Metal BV (lead and copper melting).

Much of the growth came from acquisitions, and gave Billiton introductions into new fields in the world of metals. Billiton became a world-wide dispersed firm that covered the whole spectrum of non-ferrous metals. After the period of restructuring from 1970–1972, the total number of employees increased between 1973 to 1979 from 4100 to almost 6000, while turnover took off from £45 to £600 million a year (Shell Venster 1979). See Exhibit 1.

EXHIBIT 1
Billiton's turnover 1970–79
(in £million)

Source: Shell annual reports.

	1970	1971	1972	1973	1974	1975	1976	1977	1978	1979
Turnover	45	123	142	159	253	223	482	597	613	770

EXHIBIT 2
Billiton's investments
1970–86 (in £million)

Source: F. Hendriks (1987),
*Shell: Energie, Metalen,
Bosbouw en Zaaizaad* (Shell:
Energy, Metals, Forestry,
Sowing seeds), Utrecht: Jan
van Arkel, pp 286–287.

	1970	1971	1972	1973	1974	1975	1976	1977
Investments	7	24	25	37	26	35	20	70

	1978	1979	1980	1981	1982	1983	1984	1985	1986
Investments	63	34	126	316	504	310	176	66	55

Phase II (1977–1984): Extensive Investments

Billiton started to invest heavily around 1977. Billions of dollars were spent in research, exploration, and promising new projects, even while the metal industry was in a deep crisis. The relatively small Billiton developed in 10 years to one of the world's 20 biggest non-ferrous metal firms. The total invested capital grew from US$ 135 million to almost US$ 900 million. Ten years of diversification into metals had been satisfying for Shell.

The center of gravity was Billiton's aluminium-strategy, formulated in the mid-1970s. Shell aimed at making Billiton one of the world's biggest six or seven aluminium companies. In the first instance Billiton focused on mining, but in 1975 the strategy changed to also include smelting and refining. Vertical integration was necessary to get control over all aluminium activities, from bauxite and alumina to the production of aluminium. It invested in major joint ventures in Brazil, Australia, and Ireland, with a total amount of US$ 2.3 billion. The Surinam operations were expanded (bauxite and alumina), and in Guinea (Boké) it participated in a bauxite mine.

Billiton's investments between 1970 and 1986 show one small peak (1977–1978) and one big peak (1980–1984) both related to expansion into the aluminium industry (see Exhibit 2).

Aluminium was the spearhead because it was by far the biggest non-ferrous metal. Without a strong position in aluminium Billiton would never be big enough to substantially contribute to Shell's Group-results. For the same reason Billiton simultaneously focused on nickel, copper, zinc, lead, and tin, the most important non-ferrous metals after aluminium.

Mining and processing of nickel was a true growth area. According to Billiton's projections demand for nickel would rise dramatically in the future, because it would become more and more applied in advanced technical equipment. Billiton invested in nickel mining projects in Australia (Windarra), and Colombia (Cerro Matoso). Billiton also participated in a deep sea mining consortium, to harvest nickel holding manganese nodules – potato look-alikes.

Billiton paid much attention to other companies' activities to evaluate possible participations in developing new findings. More and more projects were brought under Billiton's attention when it became better known. Billiton invested in traditional metals such as copper, lead, zinc, tin, magnesium salt, and tungsten, and new and special metals for more advanced applications or with high melting points. The company foresaw prosperous times for these specialties in the long run, and invested in a titanium plant in Deeside (UK) and a magnesia plant in Veendam (the Netherlands).

Recycling of metals was another opportunity for Billiton. It was expected that the major ore deposits would be worked-out, and since small deposits would be more expensive to exploit, recycling of metals would become more important in the future. Billiton undertook a serious attempt to make recycling a success, both technically and commercially.

Growth was still an important drive ten years after the take-over, shortly before the second investment wave of 1980–1984. The head of planning at BIM Mr Tausk said (Shell Venster 1979):

> Billiton is clearly developing into a big mining and metal company, active in all places where raw materials and other resources, such as energy, are available. Where Billiton will end is hard to predict. This depends on many things, like the world economy, Shell's cash position, and Billiton's own performances. Assuming that Billiton is on the right track, one can expect that Billiton will be four times the current size in ten years. A good perspective for Billiton, but also for the Royal Dutch/Shell Group that expected much in 1970. And quite rightly.

After 1980 the non-ferrous metal industry fell into a depression. The industry was plagued by overcapacity, weak demand, and severe price drops. This led to world-wide and extensive losses, cost reduction programs, and eventually closures of mines and plants. Only in 1987, when the prices of metals rose, did Billiton become profitable again. Exactly during this period Billiton put many new projects into operation, which

appeared much harder than projected. In addition, longer lead times and technical problems raised initial costs seriously. Also, many of Billiton's new metals entered poor markets, which led to disappointments on the income side (The Shell Review 1990) (see Exhibit 3).

Billiton's diversification policy had been questioned and discussed more than once. Billiton argued that broad diversification would spread risks, that it would become less dependent on a cyclical decline of one metal. During several periods some of Billiton's activities were indeed remarkably profitable, improving overall results, but after 1980 prices for all non-ferrous metals were so poor that no metal could compensate losses in others.

In mining and processing, project preparations typically take three or four years before production, which brings along huge risks. Since demand and prices of mining products can be quite capricious, the profitability of investment in mining and processing are hard to project. Even taking this adverse characteristic of metal markets into consideration, Billiton's performance in investment failures was striking. Time after time 'me-too' projects were being developed, Billiton analysed markets and followed trends. This behavior of adaptation and imitation made Billiton a sure participant in projects at the brink of overcapacity and spoilt markets (Hendriks 1987). One example was the magnesia-project in Veendam, the Netherlands. This 420 million guilders project, jointly developed by Billiton (60 percent) and the Noordelijke Ontwikkelings Maatschappij (Northern Development Company, 40 percent), included extracting and processing of magnesium

	1980	1981	1982	1983	1984	1985	1986
Turnover	720	617	641	733	995	961	772
Profits	23	−39	−95	−91	−62	−187	−44

	1987	1988	1989	1990	1991	1992
Turnover	862	1185	1662	1361	1287	1260
Profits	15	109	168	97	8	−41

EXHIBIT 3
Billiton's turnover and profits of 1980–1992 (in £million)

Source: Shell annual reports.

containing salts to magnesia, which would be used to produce heat-resistant materials for applications in ovens in the steel industry. The moment the project became operational, in 1982, demand and prices of magnesium were very low, so that it took a lot of effort to get the product into the market (Shell Venster 1983). Billiton was not the only troubled firm; competitors faced comparable problems, some even closed or idled plants waiting for better times.

Despite the crisis of the metal industry, Shell invested more money in Billiton in a few years after 1980 than in the whole previous decade since the take-over. In 1981 Billiton invested £316 million, in 1982 £504 million, in 1983 £310 million, and in 1984 £176 million. Billiton was convinced that the new investments would prepare the company to benefit from the next economic recovery. Although it became a bit more careful to start new projects, Billiton still embraced good opportunities, and the exploration activities, the company's future, continued. Such investments while facing shrinking turnover and record losses would probably have killed an independent metal company.

Most spectacular investments had been decided upon at the end of the 1970s, when an overwhelming number of new plans and projects were being made. After five years and the immense amount of almost £ 1.5 billion of investments, Billiton had become internationally active in many ores and metals, and vertically integrated with activities upstream as well as downstream, with an international marketing and sales network. Shell knew that Billiton's investments did not pay off as projected, but it preferred long-term growth over short-term gains. It understood very well that exploration, development, and research were expensive although necessary for getting a strong position in the long term.

A large number of new projects were being developed in cooperation with others, a common practice in the metals industry. This is partly explained by the large sums of required capital for exploration, mining, and processing activities, and partly by market risks as a consequence of fluctuating prices of metals. Other cooperative agreements are based on combining a mining firm that supplies the ore and a smelter for the next processing phase. In a number of cases Billiton deliberately started joint ventures in potentially profitable segments in the metal industry to learn and get experience. In most joint projects, however, Billiton took only the role of financier, while the partner also brought in management. For example, in 1985 only some 30 Billiton people were employed at one of Billiton's joint ventures.

Phase III (1982–1985): Consolidation

Slowly Billiton came to the conclusion that the market situation would deteriorate, and changed course. New activities were postponed, only running projects beyond the point of no return could proceed. In 1983 approximately 100 out of 430 employees of BIM, Billiton's service company that acted as a parent, were relocated. These were mainly people that generated new projects. The exploration program was reduced. From sheer necessity Billiton had to consolidate. Its ambition to become one of the world's leading upstream aluminium firms was put on hold. Although projects in Ireland, Australia, and Brazil had brought Billiton a firm basis of raw materials bauxite and alumina, its melting capacity was far from those of the big six.

In 1982 Billiton decided to stop its deep-sea mining project. It considered stopping exploitation of a nickel mine in Australia, but since Billiton had just opened a new nickel mine and melting plant in Colombia (Cerro Matuso), this was postponed. Billiton did not consider withdrawing from the nickel industry, although the most optimistic scenario expected overcapacity until 1992. Competition would be high the coming years, but Billiton was hoping to have ensured a strong position in nickel through its recent and modern installations and plants.

This was Billiton's main argument: market developments were the prime cause of its problems and Billiton was hoping that the economy would pick up soon. Despite huge overcapacities in several market segments Billiton would benefit from the recent and modern installations and plants. The only question left was the timing of recovery (Billiton Brief 1983).

Billiton said it changed its policy independently from the parent company, Shell. It projected problems, however, if no action was taken (Het Financieele Dagblad 1982). It was clear that in the context of huge recent investments and poor metal markets new investments were not likely to be financed by Shell. It was decided to concentrate on successfully bringing projects into operation and efficiently exploiting running installations and plants. Billiton's top manager Mr Van der Graaf said in 1983:

> Our policy is now to finish projects and bring into operation. New investments will only be available for current and proven companies. We feel something is structurally changing in the West, as a result of which future developments are less predictable than before. We have to be careful with new expansion plans, because mistakes will never be compensated. (Shell Venster 1983)

The new 'challenge' was to exploit Billiton's expertise it had built up in former years. Billiton was convinced that there would always be a market for a quality product at the right price, even during recessions. It focused on reductions of production costs, and selectively stimulating research to find new and cheaper production methods. Cost reductions would guarantee future profitability, since Billiton could not influence market prices, and no dramatic price improvements were expected. Billiton was still optimistic about its future. Under conditions of a cooperative economic situation Billiton would be profitable in 1985 or 1986, when expenses and income would meet. This appeared to be wishful thinking. Overcapacity was the rule, no signs of economic improvement could be observed. Only in 1987 did restructuring of the metal industry and improved prices for metals lead to changes.

In 1984 consolidation, cost cutting, and disposal of unprofitable and marginally profitable activities had replaced Billiton's investment policy. In that year it took provisions to close or sell off cash-demanding activities with poor prospects. Billiton wanted to generate a positive cash flow. It was about time it became financially independent from the parent, by all possible means: cost cutting, ceasing unprofitable activities, limiting working capital, reducing overhead costs and head office expenses, reducing exploration and research. By improving existing activities future investments would become possible again. Billiton started to think about its strengths and weaknesses, in order to be better prepared for further developments after the consolidation phase. Billiton wanted to face the future with a clear picture of its capabilities and positions.

Phase IV (1985–1991): Further Consolidation and a New Strategy

Things had to change. In 1985/1986 Shell's corporate top management changed Billiton's management positions. Member of Shell's corporate Board of Management Mr Van Engelshoven was appointed chairman of the Supervisory Board, while Mr Slechte became Coordinator Metals after Mr Van der Graaf's retirement in 1986. Their assignment was to bring Billiton back into black figures, if necessary in a reduced shape. The primary aluminium activities, however, had to be maintained.

Mr Slechte seriously considered an alternative option for Billiton: splitting up and sell in parts. The future prospects were still bad, and other oil companies had begun selling off their metal activities, a trend that continued for some years. For most oil companies the diversifications into metal had turned out to be a disaster. Another option that Mr Slechte had considered was again investing extensively. Eventually it was decided that simply improving existing activities would be the best way. Even if Shell would decide to sell Billiton, the firm had to be in shape anyway. Mr Slechte considered his task at Billiton essentially as fulfilling a management function. Appointing an 'outsider' was, according to Mr Slechte, not a problem. Management fundamentals are identical in all industries, and other members of the management-team compensated a possible shortage of detailed and metal-related knowledge.

One of Mr Slechte's first activities was to formulate a new strategy for the metal industry. Within a few months most managers were involved in drawing up 'business reviews', in which factors that influenced activities were identified. The operating companies, divisions, and staff analyzed themselves (environmental analyses, SWOTs), and formulated alternative strategies for their businesses. A total of 32 analyses were presented to the Executive Committee of BIM. The results of the reviews formed the basis for the new Billiton strategy, which should enable Billiton to survive, and eventually grow in the coming years. Billiton's new 'mission' was to provide a positive contribution to the Royal Dutch/Shell Group. No later than 1988 would Billiton be back in the black, but in order to achieve this Billiton had to break even under most unfavorable conditions.

The 'dog eat dog' scenario (survival of the fittest) reflected these conditions: each attempt to balance demand and supply were being nullified by new and cheaper or more efficient existing production capacity. The 'cheaper' producers captured the 'expensive' producers' places that had to close the gates because of low prices and high costs. In this scenario overcapacity did not change, and further reduced prices in a continuous spiral of cause and effect. The 'Dog Eat Dog' scenario actually described the existing situation since 1980, and Billiton did not foresee any changes in the near future.

In order to get Billiton out of the red soon, Billiton started to focus on those elements it could control: the costs. The biggest losses came from the aluminium activities. Billiton was still convinced that its future would be in aluminium, because it was well positioned with some good and modern facilities. None the less costs could be cut. The same approach was taken for other projects. Everything possible was done to improve cost structures. One problem Billiton faced in its quest was that in most major joint ventures it was not in the lead.

Apart from cost cutting exercises, many loss-making or marginally profitable activities were stopped or sold. In France and England production of solder was terminated, in England a tita-nium plant was sold, in Thailand and Indonesia tin-dredging firms were closed, in Canada a tungsten and molybdenum mine were closed, while a major participation in a big zinc and lead mine was sold. In the Netherlands Metrec, a Dutch metal processing firm, was closed. Preparations were made to sell or reduce some other activities, such as tin and lead smelter HMIB in Arnhem, the Netherlands. The head office in Leidschendam was further reduced until only 125 employees were left. In 1983 Billiton counted world-wide 5800 employees, and in 1986 only 4600.

In the 'good old days' of expansion BIM was primarily responsible for deciding on investments in new projects and activities. In the consolidation phase responsibilities returned to the operating companies that were closer to the subsequent markets. They knew better how to survive in their branch, and how to prosper in the future. The policy and organizational changes required cultural conversions, for which an action plan was being drawn up. This 'ABC' plan (Attitude, Behavior, Communication) clearly dissociated from Billiton's old hierarchical structure. BIM had to become less bureaucratic and truly act as an adviser and service company. BIM was made clear that its *raison d'être* was related to a demand for its services and the value for the operating companies. BIM's formal hierarchical pyramid was being replaced by a Shell-style matrix organization.

A matrix consisting of a regional organization plus functional divisions, along the lines followed elsewhere in Shell, replaced the product-oriented organization. Mines had to be exploited with lower costs, the downstream sector had to advance the added value of products by means of product differentiation, improved technologies, and more marketing. Research had to become more supporting to operating companies, and focused on improving products and raising efficiencies, to increase its added value.

Billiton's dependency on aluminium activities had to be reduced, since it was reasoned that Shell's dictated returns were not feasible in the aluminium industry. The gold industry promised better returns; consequently Billiton invested in a better gold mine portfolio. In 1989 gold mining counted for five percent of Billiton's total turnover. Bauxite, alumina, and aluminium still stood for 70 percent of turnover, and nickel, lead, silver, and zinc combined, the remaining 25 percent. In 1992 Billiton had gold mines in Chile, Australia, Ghana, and Indonesia.

For the first time since 1980 Billiton returned to black figures in 1987. A modest profit of £15 million (two percent ROI) was improved in 1988: £109 million (13 percent ROI). The objective to quickly return to profitability was reached. Mr Slechte indicated that the higher prices of metals were the primary reason for the financial improvements, and that the real proof of a structural change for the better would be given in a new recession.

Phase V (1991–1992): Back to Core Business

The economic situation deteriorated in the early 1990s, and Billiton again faced overcapacity and plummeting prices of metals. In 1991 the prices collapsed when eastern European countries and former Soviet republics raised their exports of metals. In 1992 Billiton was back in the red.

Considering its relatively strong position in mining and exploration, specifically the Group's 'overall competence', Billiton decided to expand mining activities up to the point that they would account for 80 percent of all investments. Also strong were marketing and trading, which increasingly contributed to Billiton's results. Billiton's marketing and trading had built up strong long-term relations with clients, which secured a firm future basis. Continuation of policy was decided with regards to bauxite, alumina and aluminium. Only exceptionally promising projects would be studied, on the basis of strict criteria, active searching for new opportunities would not be allowed.

Really problematic was the situation in the downstream sector. The performances were disappointing, and most of the activities were making losses. It appeared to be extremely difficult to find the synergies Billiton had been looking for so long, and to develop successful higher value-added products. The downstream activities were

Billiton's only loss-maker in 1991, in 1992 they were the principal loss-maker.

At the end of 1991, Billiton's last profitable year, Shell emphasized that the metal sector would not be sold. It would not follow other oil companies' routes. Shell was focused on the long term. Billiton had been developed to a diversified metal company, and was an excellent platform for further development. As long as Billiton generated profits that were consistent with the other Group sectors, Shell saw no reason to discontinue metal activities. It felt at ease with metals in its business portfolio.

On 1 July 1992 Mr Herkströter became the new CEO of the Royal Dutch/Shell Group, and asked whether the company would expand familiar businesses or diversify, he replied:

> The best results will be achieved in businesses we understand. For the time being I won't consider diversifying. Usually diversifications originate from the urge of a well-filled wallet. Well, if you think of being able to diversify with only money, you will fail. If you have nothing to offer but money, a certain expertise which makes you do things better than others, don't even start. (Shell Venster 1992)

According to Mr Herkströter saying 'no' is not Shell's best side, and neither is giving up things: 'You keep what you get', is the common consent.

In 1992 Billiton went back into the red, concluded that its metal processing was not sufficient, and announced withdrawal from the loss-making downstream sector. Within a few years Billiton would dispose of all downstream activities, and since the center of gravity of processing was located in the Netherlands, the company would withdraw the majority of its home country activities within a few years.

Phase VI (1993): Shell Decides to Sell Billiton

On May 11, 1993, Royal Dutch/Shell announced Gencor's interest in most of Billiton's metal activities, and stressed the fact that it was Gencor who took the initiative. Gencor is a South African mining company, and was primarily interested in Billiton's mining and aluminium activities in Surinam, Australia, Brazil, Chile, Canada, Colombia, Ghana, Indonesia, Ireland, and South Africa, and its marketing and trading activities (Billiton Marketing & Trading, BMT). BMT operated in 22 subsidiaries in the United Kingdom, Germany, France, the Netherlands, and Japan. The acquisition would make Gencor an international mining firm. Shell would withdraw from the metal market altogether, a move that would 'fit into its strategy to concentrate on its core activities oil and gas'. Shell would be last in the line of multinational oil firms to leave the metal industry.

The metal sector had remained a small part of the Royal Dutch/Shell Group of Companies; in 1992 it represented only approximately two percent of its US$ 80 billion turnover, and 3.5 percent of the Group's investments of over US$ 60 billion. In 23 years Billiton had become an international firm, but the main ambition to represent approximately 20 percent of the Group's turnover was not achieved by a long shot. Billiton had not become the group's cash cow. On the contrary, according to Shell the metal industry appeared to be much less profitable than expected, and also much less than the oil industry, and highly cyclical.

Shell did not expect quick improvements in the metal sector situation, because of a number of structural changes. Consumption of metals had been reduced because of replacement by other basic materials, a more economic use of metals, new technologies, and environmental consciousness. The explosive growth that had been projected in the 1970s had never been realized. For example, the world-wide demand of aluminium rose between 1950 and 1974 by 780 percent, and on this basis it had invested in mining and metals, but between 1974 and 1990 demand had only increased by 26 percent. Although Shell is well known for looking beyond horizons, it had not been able to 'read' the future of metals.

Within Billiton people did not react negatively to the idea of transferring to Gencor. Billiton's way of thinking would possibly correspond more with Gencor's than with Shell's, whose dominant direction was clearly oil and gas. In addition, Gencor would continue Billiton as a 'going concern', including its name, and as a core for a new international mining company. It said it would not change the management of the Billiton companies. Gencor expressed its confidence in a successful take-over, because of Billiton's low production costs in mining and aluminium, and high quality management. Moreover, the phrase in Gencor's mission statement: '. . . real long-term growth and an internationally leading position in mining and metals' sounded very familiar, while the consequence of the possible 'merger' was music to Billiton's ears: Gencor/Billiton would become one of the world's top five mining companies.

It was remarkable, though, that Gencor was expanding at the moment the metal industry was in a recession. Apart from the planned acquisition of Billiton, it was constructing the largest aluminium smelter in the Western world. Aluminium prices were dropping dramatically, and aluminium smelters were shut down. Historically low prices were listed for zinc, copper, lead, and nickel, companies stopped production and processing of these metals. Gencor's investment policy seemed to be contrary to Shell's, that always decided to invest at times the metal industry was doing quite well.

Billiton's downstream activities that had been decided to be sold or terminated, and did not enjoy Gencor's interest, were now close to dead. In 1993 the following mid/downstream activities were disposed of:

- Tiofine (titaniumdioxide), sold with big loss;

- H.J. Enthoven, British Lead Mills, and Le Plomb Français (lead in England and France), sold to Quenxco;

- Kawecki-Billiton Metaalindustrie (aluminium), sold to Roba Holding BV;

- Rijnvis (wholesale of metals), partly sold and partly terminated as at 31 December 1993;

- Billiton Precursors (very pure organometal compounds), sold to Air Products;

- Billiton Refractories, sold to J.M. Huber;

- HMIB tin and lead smelting (closed);

- Billiton Zinc, sold to a Belgium company;

- Budel zinc smelter, sold to Pesiminco.

Gencor's Core is Ore

In the mid-1980s Gencor was known among investors as a bureaucratic conglomerate that performed badly. In 1986 Derk Keys was appointed by institutional investors as the new CEO. After five and a half years Derk Keys left a highly successful entrepreneurial and decentralized group, and became Minister of Economic Affairs. Investors were happy; Gencor's rating had improved substantially.

In 1993 Gencor decided to focus only on mining activities. The decision created a mass of new energy among management, and became an enormous success. The stock value of the new focused mining firm quickly rose higher than the former conglomerate's. Gencor invested almost a billion US Dollars in the Columbus stainless steel project and started building one of the world's biggest aluminium smelters, Alusaf.

Gencor's activities were almost entirely concentrated in South Africa. It had to internationalize to compete with other, international, mining companies. Billiton was an exceptional opportunity, said Gencor, and not expensive, although a lot of money – US$ 1,144 billion. To get the cash Gencor sold its North Sea oil interests and a number of stakes in foreign companies, for US$ 335 million. This was in line with Gencor's vision: 'world class ore is our core'. It sold non-core businesses to get mining and metal activities.

The acquisition of Billiton was a bet on the aluminium industry, for this was Billiton' center of gravity. The new Gencor would be the world's seventh aluminium firm in terms of size. Since Gencor was relatively inexperienced in aluminium, it decided to change little at Billiton. Apart from aluminium, Gencor was interested in:

- Billiton's well filled portfolio of 'first class properties', and low production costs;

- entrance through Billiton into joint projects with Aluminium Company of America, Reynold Metals, Alcan, and others;

- 'excellent Billiton management';

- Billiton's international marketing and trading organization to sell Gencor's metals and minerals;

- Billiton's bauxite and alumina projects for supplying raw materials to the Alusaf smelter;

- Billiton's Cerro Matuso mine in Colombia for supplying ferrous nickel to Gencor's stainless Steel plant in South Africa.

The new Gencor would generate 24 percent of turnover in aluminium and related metals, 18 percent chrome, manganese and stainless steel, 16 percent titanium minerals, 12 percent gold, 10 percent platina group metals, 10 percent coal, and 2 percent nickel. In all activities except nickel Gencor would be a world top-10 firm.

At the time Gencor was working on acquiring Billiton, Gencor was also actively involved in three other strategically important agreements. Gencor's coal company Trans-Natal Coal was combined with Rand Mines, also leading to a world top position. Gencor sold its stakes in four high cost marginal gold mines to Randgold, specialized in marginal gold mines. This last act is particularly interesting, because it reflected Gencor's opinion that gold, once South Africa's pillar, was history for an investor.

How Much Luck Can One Expect?

Gencor approached Shell at the moment that aluminium prices had plummeted because of Russian exports, to a historical pit of US$ 1185 per ton. This situation had improved at the moment of the take-over. But what would happen after, analysts wondered. Moreover, Gencor had arrived at a huge debt situation, which had reduced its flexibility to survive harsh times. Without a wealthy and nice parent company like Royal Dutch/Shell, Gencor/Billiton would not survive a major recession. Are there really synergies? Why would Gencor be a better parent company than one of the world's best-run companies, Shell? Will Gencor be a prosperous world leader in mining; does it deserve fortune, *stabilis fortuna merendis*? Or is Gencor close to bankruptcy, and should Billiton adopt a new, and more appropriate motto, *nemo dat quod non habet* – nobody gives what he doesn't have?

References

Billiton Brief (1983) Marktomstandigheden zijn de voornaamste oorzaak van onze problemen (Market situations are the main cause of our problems), November.

Billiton Brief (1982) De diversificatie van olie-maatschappijen in de mijnbouw (Diversification of oil companies in mining), December.

The Financial Times (1989) How Billiton climbed out of the pit, 4 September.

Het Financieele Dagblad (1989) Billiton wacht op zeven vette jaren (Billiton is waiting for seven fat years), 4 March.

Het Financieele Dagblad (1982) Noodgedwongen con-solidatie bij Billiton (Forced consolidation at Billiton), 27 December.

Hendriks, F. (1987), *Shell: Engergie, Metalen, Bosbouw en Zaaizaad* (Shell: Engergy, Metals, Forestry, Sowing Seeds), Utrecht: Jan van Arkel.

Holloway, S.K. (1988), *The Aluminum Multinationals and the Bauxite Cartel*, London: Macmillan.

Olie (1973) Billiton is meer dan tin alleen (Billiton is more than only tin), August.

The Shell Review (1990), Metals: the non-ferrous metals industry, July.

Shell Venster (1992), Interview with Herkströter, August.

Shell Venster (1985) Overneming Billiton 't best bewaarde geheim (Acquisition of Billiton the best kept secret), October.

Shell Venster (1984) Activiteiten non-traditional business. Van der Toorn: Eens zal de olie op zijn (Activities non-traditional business. Van der Toorn: One day we will run out of oil), September.

Shell Venster (1983) Billiton moet op adem komen (Billiton has to take a breath after a stormy growth period), May.

Shell Venster (1979), De Toekomst van Billiton (The Future of Billiton), April.

De Volkskrant (1993) Met Billiton vertrekt een oud-koloniaal naar Zuid-Afrika (The once colonial Billiton moves to South Africa), 15 May.

Case 12: Corporate Strategy at Grand Metropolitan

By David Sadtler and Andrew Campbell[1]

Allen Sheppard had become chief executive officer (CEO) of Grand Metropolitan (GrandMet) in 1986 and had added the chairmanship of the company in 1987. Since the company's founding in 1947, GrandMet had also been headed by two other chairmen – Maxwell Joseph and Stanley Grinstead – and each change in leadership had been accompanied by a significant shift in corporate strategy. Sheppard now faced a decision about whom should be given the opportunity to leave his mark on the company by succeeding him as the next CEO.

Two very capable senior GrandMet managers were the most obvious candidates for the job. Ian Martin, the chief operating officer (COO), had worked closely with Sheppard since he joined the company in the 1970s. He had successfully turned around and rejuvenated a number of GrandMet businesses, most notably Pillsbury, a US acquisition. George Bull, CEO of GrandMet's food operations, had a strong marketing background and had successfully built up International Distillers and Vintners (IDV), GrandMet's most profitable division. Sheppard realized that whatever choice he made would have an important influence on the company's future corporate strategy. Therefore, he needed to think through the alternative candidates and the directions in which they would take the company. His decision would help to define a new era in GrandMet's history.

The corporation Sheppard would be turning over to his successor had grown dramatically since its inception and, as of 1993, was among the top 15 United Kingdom public companies in market capitalization. Its past financial performance had been relatively strong (see Exhibits 1, 2 and 3) and its spread of operations was quite broad (see Exhibit 4). GrandMet's growth had been effected both through internal development and by way of an extremely active program of acquisition (the major acquisitions in its corporate life are summarized in Exhibit 6). It would be a challenge for any successor to improve on this impressive track record.

The Early Years

The business from which GrandMet emerged was founded by Max Joseph. Born in 1910, he became an estate agent and learned the property business prior to World War II. His business prospered. 'Before he reached 30 he already owned a Rolls Royce and a house on Hampstead Heath.'

After war service, Max Joseph began purchasing hotels: the first was the Mandeville in 1947 and then the Washington in 1950. The next major purchase was the Mount Royal at Marble Arch, which was by far the biggest thus far. London hotels were followed by the acquisition of hotels in Monte Carlo, Paris, New York City, Madrid, and Amsterdam.

As the company grew, better financial control was required. Stanley Grinstead was hired in 1960 as chief accountant, followed by Ernest Sharp, to help strengthen financial and managerial control. This triumvirate ran GrandMet during the 1960s. Despite increasingly complex operations, the group remained unbureaucratic. Joseph was said to 'panic' whenever there were more than six people at a meeting. He never

[1] Source: This case was written by David Sadtler and Andrew Campbell, of Ashridge Management Centre, as the basis for class discussion, rather than to illustrate either effective or ineffective handling of an administrative situation. Used with permission.

EXHIBIT 1
Grand Metropolitan Group: Adjusted Figures Balance Sheet 1983–1992 (in £ millions)

	1983	1984	1985	1986	1987	1988	1989	1990	1991	1992
Fixed assets										
Intangible assets – brands	0.0	0.0	70.2	119.3	608.0	588.3	2,652	2,317	2,464	2,492
Tangible assets	2,100.9	2,291.0	2,654.3	2,625.7	2,725.2	3,279.4	3,839	3,756	2,764	2,638
Investments	131.2	139.2	133.3	129.8	177.2	206.1	144	214	851	713
	2,242.1	2,430.2	2,857.8	2,874.8	3,510.4	4,073.8	6,635	6,287	6,079	5,843
Current assets										
Stocks	604.7	683.8	653.7	646.3	733.7	761.1	1,269	1,349	1,286	1,381
Debtors	618.5	693.4	731.0	731.4	827.5	873.5	1,451	1,541	1,561	1,830
Cash	51.3	106.9	143.4	88.0	113.4	137.8	215	243	261	309
Creditors										
Borrowings	(995.2)	(1,067.9)	(1,162.8)	(1,020.8)	(1,471.6)	(889.1)	(3,856)	(3,131)	(2,860)	(2,750)
Creditors	(869.2)	(986.9)	(1,063.3)	(1,084.4)	(1,269.6)	(1,463.9)	(2,547)	(2,534)	(2,304)	(2,265)
Provisions	(46.3)	(81.5)	(91.1)	(43.9)	(70.4)	(55.1)	(325)	(328)	(569)	(561)
	1,605.9	1,778.0	2,068.7	2,191.4	2,373.4	3,438.1	2,842	3,427	3,454	3,787
Summarised balance sheet										
Fixed assets	2,242.1	2,430.2	2,857.8	2,874.8	3,510.4	4,073.8	6,635	6,287	6,079	5,843
Other assets (excluding cash)	307.7	308.8	230.3	249.4	221.2	115.6	(152)	28	(26)	385
Net borrowings	2,549.8	2,739.0	3,088.1	3,124.2	3,731.6	4,189.4	6,483	6,315	6,053	6,228
	(943.9)	(961.0)	(1,019.4)	(932.8)	(1,358.2)	(751.3)	(3,641)	(2,888)	(2,599)	(2,441)
Net assets	1,605.9	1,778.0	2,068.7	2,191.4	2,373.4	3,438.1	2,842	3,427	3,454	3,787
Capital and reserves	1,566.4	1,744.1	2,035.2	2,164.8	2,345.1	3,406.7	2,810	3,401	3,422	3,759
Minorities	39.5	33.9	33.5	26.6	28.3	31.4	32	26	32	28
	1,605.9	1,778.0	2,068.7	2,191.4	2,373.4	3,438.1	2,842	3,427	3,454	3,787
Gearing	58.8%	54.0%	49.3%	42.6%	57.2%	21.9%	128.1%	84.3%	75.2%	64.5%

EXHIBIT 2

Grand Metropolitan Group: Adjusted Figures Profit and Loss Account 1983–1992 (in £ millions)

	1983	1984	1985	1986	1987	1988	1989	1990	1991	1992
Turnover	4,468.8	5,075.0	5,589.5	5,291.3	5,705.5	6,028.8	9,298	9,394	8,748	7,913
Operating profit	396.3	438.1	445.1	453.3	554.4	582.1	914	1,021	1,027	949
Associates profits	10.7	5.8	8.1	7.0	7.9	11.5	18	23	10	16
	407.0	443.9	453.2	460.3	562.3	593.6	932	1,044	1,037	965
Net exceptional items	(19.2)	(36.1)	(40.7)	0	0	0	0	0	0	0
Disposal of fixed assets	10.2	22.6	4.7	8.7	15.4	100.0	68	54	32	13
Sale or termination of business				(67.0)	(31.5)	305.0	502	112	(450)	41
Interest	(111.8)	(109.6)	(105.9)	(101.3)	(120.2)	(93.0)	(280)	(239)	(171)	(94)
Profit before taxation	286.2	320.89	311.3	300.7	426.0	905.6	1,222	971	448	925
Taxation	(83.3)	(85.6)	(64.4)	(61.1)	(90.0)	(250.8)	(337)	(305)	(223)	(295)
Profit after taxation	202.9	235.2	246.9	239.6	336.0	654.8	885	666	225	630
Minorities & pref. dividends	(5.0)	(4.0)	(4.7)	(2.8)	(2.8)	(8.3)	(8)	(6)	(7)	(6)
Profit attributable	197.9	231.2	242.2	236.8	333.2	646.5	877	660	218	624
Extraordinary items	1.6	(20.2)	29.9	0	0	0	0	0	0	0
Profit for year	199.5	211.0	272.1	236.8	333.2	646.5	877	660	218	624
Ordinary dividends	(58.0)	(67.1)	(79.2)	(87.5)	(103.1)	(129.1)	(167)	(198)	(218)	(246)
Transferred to reserves	141.5	143.9	192.9	149.3	230.1	517.4	710	462	(0)	378
Attributable profits/dividends	3.4	3.4	3.1	2.7	3.2	5.0	5.3	3.3	1.0	2.5

Note: Figures have been adjusted for FRS 3 going back to 1986. However, figures for 1983–1985 have not been adjusted.

EXHIBIT 3
Grand Metropolitan Group: Financial Performance by Segment (in £ millions)

	1983	1984	1985	1986	1987	1988	1989	1990	1991	1992
Turnover										
Food	737	778	778	750	825	1,253	2,872	3,506	3,026	2,647
Drinks	1,511	1,551	1,698	1,721	2,410	2,581	2,784	3,000	2,425	2,858
Retailing						1,671	2,040	2,531	2,051	1,540
UK Consumer Services	1,055	1,175	1,234	1,212	1,049					
US Consumer Products	864	1,235	1,502	1,270	635					
Hotels	301	336	378	338	333					
Discontinued					454	523	1,602	357	1,246	868
Total	4,468	5,075	5,590	5,291	5,706	6,028	9,298	9,394	8,748	7,913
Trading Profit										
Food	31	16	28	39	44	84	245	309	300	186
Drinks	177	206	228	244	323	316	389	473	454	505
Retailing						179	230	278	236	211
UK Consumer Services	74	67	75	83	79					
US Consumer Products	98	122	84	91	68					
Hotels	27	32	38	30	38					
Discontinued					20	75	103	22	81	47
Total	407	443	453	487	572	654	967	1,082	1,071	949

Discontinued:	1987	1988	1989	1990	1991	1992
	Liggett	Hotels	Hotels	Betting	Brewing	Express dairy
	Contract services	US soft drinks	Betting	Other	Tenanted pubs	B. King's distribution
	Diversified Products	Children's World	Other		Liquid milk &	
	Quality Care	Diversified			chilled products	
	Children's World	Products			UK drinks wholesaling	
		Quality Care			Off-licences	
		Contract services			Service restaurants	

himself had an office at GrandMet and ran the company and his other investments from an outside office nearby.

Joseph's basic theme was to purchase 'trading property assets.' The idea was that the cash flow of the properties acquired should be sufficient to cover the cost of the debt taken on to acquire them. Good management would increase the cash flow, and the value of the assets would rise because of inflation and the increasing demand for hotels. Joseph was buying assets that he believed would increase in value with debts he could service out of the cash flow. Joseph's skill in raising money and the strong asset base of the company enabled the process of acquiring good assets to continue apace. As one manager com-

mented: 'Joseph had a tremendous reputation in the city and a talent at closing deals.' The company then went public in 1961, as Mount Royal, Ltd. In 1962 its name was changed to Grand Metropolitan Hotels.

In the mid- to late 1960s nonhotel acquisitions began. There were two criteria: (1) companies whose businesses were related to hotels (drinks, food, catering, pubs); and (2) asset-intensive businesses, in which the 'trading property asset' concept could be continued and extended. The major acquisitions of this period began with Levy and Franks (1966), which included Chef & Brewer pub-restaurants, as well as off-license stores. After several catering businesses, Express Dairy was purchased in 1969 for £32 million.

Express provided one quarter of all milk products door-to-door in Britain, and also owned restaurants, hotels, and food stores. Joseph made an offer for the business within 48 hours of hearing it was available. Many of Express's depots were in valuable city-center locations.

A move into a less-related business came in the early 1970s with the acquisition of Mecca, the bingo halls, dance halls, and casino group. It also contained food, drink, and leisure operations and was property intensive.

> With the exception of Express, all of the acquisitions to date had been on friendly terms. Max Joseph generally invited the former owners or top management to join the GrandMet board; examples included Frank Berni from Berni Inns and Eric Morley from Mecca. The result was a growth of the main board to 18. Many of the businesses continued to run much as they had prior to acquisition with little interference from the center short of sorting out major problems as and when they arose. It is probably fair to say that neither Joseph nor Grinstead showed much inclination to become deeply involved in day to day operations.
>
> (Williamson and Rix 1988)

These acquisitions arose opportunistically and were executed very quickly, owing to the lack of bureaucracy. Complex analytical evaluation models were eschewed. Joseph only wanted to know that existing cash flow would 'wash the face' of the cost of borrowing, and that the operations were something they could manage. Then he would go ahead if he liked the 'feel' of the business and the price looked attractive.

The same thinking was extended to the acquisition of the brewer, Truman, Hanbury, Buxton (THB). Also in the right sector and asset intensive, the acquisition of Truman turned out to be a difficult task; but after nine months, GrandMet's offer of £48 million was accepted. As with Express, Joseph noted that breweries were often on valuable city-center sites.

The true significance of this acquisition became apparent when the possibility of the acquisition of Watney Mann, as a 'follow-on' to THB, was presented to Joseph. This was a much larger brewery and constituted a very bold step for

GrandMet: three separate offers were made and five different letters were sent to each of Watney's 30,000 shareholders. When it was finally concluded at a cost of £435 million, it was the largest acquisition in the United Kingdom to date. It also included IDV, a wine and spirits operation, which GrandMet attempted to sell off after the acquisition. In the event, that divestiture failed and GrandMet was left with an uncomfortably high level of debt.

The Pressure of the 1970s

At about this time (1973), economic conditions in Britain deteriorated. This was the period of the three-day week, the secondary banking crisis, and a subsequent collapse in the property market. GrandMet had taken on large debts to acquire Watney Mann and, with the failure of the disposal of IDV, was now coming under significant financial pressure. In 1974 the company announced the first fall in trading profit in its history.

The priority at this stage for GrandMet was therefore to generate sufficient trading profits to service its borrowings and to survive until the value of the property portfolio was again sufficient to underpin more investment. To this end, Max Joseph recruited Allen Sheppard from British Leyland to address the operating profitability of Watney Mann. At the same time, IDV was separated out from Watney Mann and set up as a separate business unit under Anthony Tennant, a former Truman director.

Sheppard and Tennant each set about building the strength of their respective operations and recruiting good managers to help them. Sheppard went about his task by dramatically cutting costs and head count at the breweries while at the same time revitalizing regional brands. Profit and cash flow increased dramatically, and significant capital was released from the business. Similarly, at IDV, Tennant set about strengthening the position of the individual brands and promoting them effectively. Major rationalization was not pursued.

Both business strategies worked, and by the end of the 1970s, GrandMet was once more in a

EXHIBIT 4
GrandMet's Principal Group Companies

	Country of incorporation	Country of operation	Percentage of equity owned	Business description
Food				
ALPO Petfoods, Inc.	US	US	100%	Manufacture and marketing of dog food, cat food, and dog treats
Brossard Surgelés SA	France	France	100%	Manufacture and marketing of frozen bakery products
Conservas Chistu, SA	Spain	Spain	100%	Manufacture and marketing of fresh and shelf-stable vegetables
The Häagen-Dazs Company, Inc.†	US	US, Japan, Canada, Europe	100%	Manufacture and distribution of superpremium ice cream and frozen desserts
The Pillsbury Company†	US	US	100%	Manufacture, marketing, and distribution of bakery products, frozen and shelf-stable vegetables and frozen pizza
Pillsbury Canada Ltd	Canada	Canada	100%	Manufacture, marketing, and distribution of vegetables, dough, and pizza snacks
Pillsbury GmbH†	Germany	Germany	100%	Manufacture and marketing of ready meals, canned soups, frozen gateaux, and savoury products
Pilstral SA†	France	Europe	100%	Manufacture of baked goods and coordination of the Green Giant vegetable business across Europe
Drinks				
AED SA	Spain	Spain	100%	Importation, distribution, and marketing of wines and spirits
R&A Bailey & Company	Ireland	Ireland – exporting worldwide	100%	Production, distribution, marketing, and exporting of cream liqueur
Carillon Importers Ltd.	US	US	100%	Importation, distribution, and marketing of wines, spirits, and other adult beverages
Cinzano SpA†	Italy	Worldwide	100%	Production, distribution, and marketing of vermouth; local distribution of wines and spirits

Company	Location		Ownership	Business
Croft & Ca Lda.	Portugal	Portugal – exporting worldwide	100%	Production, distribution, marketing, and exporting of port wine
Croft-Jerez SA	Spain	Spain – exporting worldwide	100%	Production, distribution, marketing, and exporting of sherry
Gilbey Canada Inc.†	Canada	Canada	100%	Production, distribution, marketing, and wholesaling of wines and spirits
Heublein Inc.†	US	Worldwide	100%	Production, importing, and marketing of wines and spirits
International Distillers and Vintners Ltd.†	England	Worldwide	100%	Production, distribution, marketing, exporting, and importing of wines, spirits, and other adult beverages
Justerini & Brooks Ltd.	England	U.K. – exporting worldwide	100%	Distillation, marketing, and export of Scotch whiskey
S&E&A Metaxa SA†	Greece	Greece	100%	Production, distribution, and marketing of spirits
Sovedi France SA	France	France	100%	Importation, distribution, and marketing of wines and spirits
The Paddington Corp.	U.S.	U.S.	100%	Importation, distribution, and marketing of wines and spirits
Branded Retailing and Pubs				
Burger King Corporation†	U.S.	U.S., Canada, Europe	100%	Fast-food retailing
Grand Metropolitan Estates Ltd.†	England	U.K.	100%	Management of the group's property activity
Inntrepreneur Estates Ltd.	England	U.K.	50%	Property investment company
The Chef & Brewer Group Ltd.	England	U.K.	100%	Management of pubs
Pearle Inc.†	U.S.	U.S., Netherlands	100%	Retailing of eye-care products and services
Corporate				
Grand Metropolitan Finance PLC	England	U.K.	100%	Financing company for the group

†Carries on the business described in the countries listed in conjunction with its subsidiaries and other group companies.

strong financial position – its earnings had increased and its balance sheet was immeasurably stronger, owing in large measure to the revitalization of the property market and its attendant effects on the assets in GrandMet's balance sheet.

During this period, GrandMet's financial affairs and the demands for control from the center were becoming ever greater. Accordingly, in 1975 the first full-time financial director was appointed, and steps were taken to increase formal controls. Peter Cawdron, Group Strategic Development Director, explained

> GrandMet very nearly went under during the 1970s. It was touch and go on a number of occasions. Falling profits made it hard to service debt and falling asset values meant that the company was in danger of breaking its bank covenants. Then suddenly it all changed. Near the end of the 1970s, cash flow started to improve, asset values rose, and from having a perilous balance sheet GrandMet became one of the companies with strong asset backing

US Diversification

One of the legacies of the period of financial pressure and subsequent consolidation was a belief on the part of Joseph, Grinstead, and Sharp that they did not want in future to be so dependent on the UK economy, the collapse of which in the early 1970s had almost cost them the company. They were thus receptive to propositions to invest abroad.

The first such opportunity arose when it became apparent that IDV's United States distributor, The Paddington Corporation, could be acquired. This would involve acquisition of Paddington's parent, the Liggett Group, which was also one of the major cigarette manufacturers in the United States and possessed a number of other related businesses (soft drinks, bottling, fitness products, and Alpo dog food). While the logic of purchasing the US distributor for the group's largest branded spirits product (J&B Scotch) was clear to all, Max Jospeh was dubious about the deal, since it was not heavily property related

and, being in the United States and in a number of unfamiliar businesses, represented a significant managerial stretch for GrandMet. Despite his opposition, however, Stanley Grinstead, who had now taken over as chairman, championed the acquisition and completed it in 1981 for $450 million.

Shortly thereafter the possibility of purchasing Intercontinental Hotels from financially pressed Pan Am arose. This was a more familiar business for GrandMet, and Joseph, Grinstead, and Sharp had little difficulty in making up their minds. The deal was done in one week for $500 million. None the less, the Intercontinental Hotel acquisition represented a significant departure from GrandMet's previous approach to buying trading property assets, whether in hotels or elsewhere. Few of the hotels were owned; most were operated under managment contracts. Thus there was little real asset backing to the large sum paid for Intercontinental.

Shortly thereafter, Joseph died. Grinstead set out to make his mark on GrandMet via a programmed search for acquisitions in 'US branded services.' Grinstead believed that GrandMet needed a broader base of businesses. He predicted that service businesses would grow faster than manufacturing businesses and felt that the United States would provide a suitable balance to GrandMet's UK operations. These acquisitions included Children's World (a childcare operation), Quality Care (a home health-care company), and Pearle Optical (the largest US optician chain). Pearle was acquired for $386 million, a nineteen times exit multiple. At this stage, financial analysts began to ask questions about the wisdom of the strategy and the extent of the financial gamble GrandMet was taking with such far-flung acquisitions. (*Management Today* 1987).

Operating Improvements

At the time of the US diversification program, major operational improvements were being effected in the existing portfolio. Allen Sheppard had assembled a team around him that included

Clive Strowger (from British Leyland), Ian Martin (from ITT), and David Tagg, who subsequently became responsible for GrandMet's management development programs. Together this team aggressively attacked the problems of the brewing business, separating it from the pub-retailing business. The brewery's workforce was cut by 50 percent (a reduction of 5000), and £82 million of capital had been released by 1986. Significant changes were undertaken in the marketing of regional brands and in the management of the pub estates (which were segmented into different 'brands' and market segments).

At the same time, the restaurant operations (especially Berni Inns) were further segmented and rationalized, and excess sites were disposed of. Similarly, Express Foods had been ailing and was assigned to Sheppard. He installed Clive Strowger in Express, and within two to three years, performance had increased dramatically. Again, rationalization was the key, as peripheral businesses were disposed of, costs were cut, and marketing improved.

Thus the Sheppard team, which was now responsible for UK brewing and food operations, continued to apply its formula to all of the businesses in its portfolio: it rationalized costs, disposed of peripheral businesses, improved marketing, and took steps to build a system of delegation and empowerment of operating managers. The goal was to institutionalize the search for superior performance and continuous improvement.

The management philosophy created by Sheppard was attractive to a certain kind of highly energetic, often impatient manager who is prepared to become closely involved in operational details. One ex-GrandMet manager, now chief operating officer of another major company, and with wide experience of three other companies, stated, 'I don't believe in going back. But Sheppard is the one manager I would willingly work for again.' The philosophy was frequently referred to as 'restless management' because of Sheppard's habit of jumping up and pacing around during meetings. It was also known as 'the light grip on the throat' referring to Sheppard's insistence on performance improvement and belief in decentralization.

The building of IDV, which went through its sharpest internal growth phase in the early 1980s, produced what eventually became GrandMet's largest profit contributor. During this period, IDV introduced 55 new products and boasted 32 percent of the new products of the seven biggest drinks companies. 'No new branded spirit in recent years has been more successful than Bailey's Irish Cream, introduced by GrandMet a decade ago and now the world's No. 1 liqueur (*Fortune* 1991).'

Anthony Tennant managed IDV with a style very different from Allen Sheppard's. His strategy was built on four planks:

1   own the distributors and get close to the customer;

2   commit to the development of new products;

3   maintain a heavy marketing spend; and

4   form alliances to aid geographic expansion.

Tennant, first head of GrandMet's IDV and then as CEO of Guinness is the prime architect of the industry's new strategy. His strategic *coup de main* at GrandMet was persuading RJR Nabisco's boss Ross Johnson to sell him Heublein Inc. in 1987 for $1.2 billion, a stiff price at the time but a steal in retrospect. Heublein gave IDV 13 percent of the American spirits market and full ownership of the world's leading vodka brand, Smirnoff, enhancing a portfolio that already included top brands such as J&B Scotch and Gilbey's gin.

(ibid.)

Grinstead described the GrandMet approach in the 1986 annual report as follows (see also Exhibit 5):

The group has a varied portfolio of companies but at the same time ensures that each company is a substantial competitor in its own market place. It has developed through operational experience and market research, a remarkable knowledge of the hotel, leisure, food, property, retailing and alcoholic beverage markets in the United Kingdom and the United States in particular . . . The group has built

EXHIBIT 5
GrandMet's Portfolio,
1985

United Kingdom	United States	International
Brewing	Consumer products	Hotels
Watneys	Dog food	Intercontinental hotels
Consumer services	Soft drinks	Wine and spirits
Retailing (pubs and	Tobacco	
bookmakers)	Fitness products	
Gaming (casinos)	Preschool nurseries	
Contract services	Food (cheese)	
(catering and private	Home nursing	
hospitals)	Opticians	

brands in many markets which are of immense value and which are continuously maintained and strengthened by skilful marketing. In addition it has an enviable record of success in new brand introduction. The breadth of the Group's activities provides an exceptional opportunity for the training of management. The range and variety of its international markets allows the development of a cadre of senior management which compares very favourably with those of the other United Kingdom or United States corporations . . . These are some of the important ways in which Grand Metropolitan adds value to the planning and activity of its component companies.

(Grand Metropolitan Annual Report, 1986).

By 1986, however, despite significant improvement in UK operations and the sale of the cigarette operations of the Liggett Group, performance was proving disappointing. Although there were no financial pressures, the former high annual rate of growth in earnings per share had declined until growth disappeared in 1986. One observer noted that

Grinstead turned the company in a new direction without, however, putting in place all the controls necessary to ensure the strategy's success. Management was still highly decentralized; problems within subsidiaries were allowed to go too far before head office reacted. And despite the reorientation toward drinks and leisure, GrandMet still lacked sufficient focus.

(*Financial Weekly* 1988)

By 1986, the City had lost confidence in GrandMet and the shares were downrated accordingly. It was widely suggested that GrandMet (see Exhibit 5) lacked coherence. Eventually bid rumors began to circulate, and one or two predators (e.g. Alan Bond in Australia) assembled share stakes. Shortly thereafter (1987) Stanley Grinstead stepped down and Allen Sheppard took over as chairman. The heat was still on, however, and Sheppard was quoted as saying, 'If I'm not careful, some nineteen-year-old will come along and break me up.'

Portfolio Restructuring

Under Sheppard, two of GrandMet's three largest acquisitions were completed. First, Heublein, a project begun under Grinstead, was bought from Nabisco for £855 million, driven by the desire to control key brands like Smirnoff. Consistent with the style of the Joseph regime, this project was completed in four days and in the process doubled IDV's spirit sales.

The other major project was the acquisition in 1989 of Pillsbury for $5.7 billion. This was a bitter fight and one that involved protracted legal disputes and other classic American bid defense tactics. Pillsbury provided GrandMet with the keystone for a global food business, building on the smaller operations of Express, Alpo, and smaller regional businesses like Peter's Savoury Products. It also offered major rationalization possibilities.

The GrandMet team moved quickly into Pillsbury's Minneapolis headquarters after the deal. Led by Ian Martin, head of US operations for GrandMet, the team removed about one-third of the company's managers. Some 1,500 staff were fired before the year was out. An interview at the time described GrandMet's intentions to 'revive Pillsbury's food business by trimming its excessive costs, rebuilding its famous but underexploited brands and developing new food products and markets.' Ian Martin was quoted as saying, that 'We've introduced more pace, momentum, and a hard edge to management.' All major aspects of the operation were subject to intense scrutiny: 'We're up to our armpits, studying issues such as production, distribution and quality. The real competitive edge is quality. If we get that right, the other things will follow.' (*Financial Times* 1989). Martin summarized the approach in another interview: 'The three basics are cut costs, build brands and develop new products – in that order. That sounds like a cliche, like Onward Christian Soldiers, but it's true.' (*Fortune* 1991)

The City initially was concerned about the size of the Pillsbury deal and the $750 million provision for restructuring costs. However, since interest cover for the group was high, there was little concern about debt pressure. Much of the concern was focused on GrandMet's ability to turn around Burger King, Pillsbury's fast food subsidiary, which was locked into a fierce war with McDonald's.

In parallel with these two major acquisition initiatives, the Sheppard team initiated what subsequently became referred to as 'Operation Declutter.' All businesses that did not offer the promise of strong branding, dominant share position, and international scope (see section entitled 'Vision 2000' below), were divested. Operation De-clutter and the focus on food, drinks, and retailing was built on the idea that global leadership in a few businesses is better than a less powerful presence in many. At the same time, Sheppard, noted, 'we considered and rejected the idea of becoming a single-cell business. This route would provide maximum focus; it would also

expose us to a fair degree of risk – all our eggs would be in one basket.'[2]

Sheppard's decisions in the betting shop business are illustrative of this strategy. Shortly after he became chairman, GrandMet bought William Hill to add to its Mecca operations and so became the largest and most profitable company in the UK industry. The strategy was to use the strength of the management in this sector to enter the US market and so become an international leader. However, shortly after entering the US market, Sheppard decided that the US venture was too risky and would lower GrandMet's reputation in the US market. He then sold the entire operation, showing a substantial profit.

In the chairman's statement in the 1987 report and accounts, Sheppard stated, that 'The major business portfolio restructuring of the past three years has been completed and we are now in a position to develop rapidly in our chosen business areas.' The disposal program undertaken as part of Operation De-clutter had been a wide-ranging one, and that program has continued to this day. The principal acquisitions and disposals of the past five years are summarized in Exhibit 6.

Management Team

When Sheppard took over, he moved quickly to assemble his team of proven operating managers around him as a top team for the group. Strowger became finance director, while remaining responsible for food operations. Ian Martin took over GrandMet's American operations, and David Tagg became personnel director.

Anthony Tennant was recruited to become the chief executive of Guinness, following the scandal that ousted Ernest Saunders. Tennant was succeeded at IDV by George Bull, and the division continued with the same strategy and with a large degree of autonomy from the center 'IDV is another world with a different style of

---

[2] Allen Sheppard's speech of December 10, 1992, at the strategic planning conference in London.

EXHIBIT 6
GrandMet's Strategic Acquisitions and Disposals Since 1987

ACQUISITIONS

	Food	**Price**
1988	Kaysens (frozen gateaux)	£21.5m
1988	Peter's Savoury Products (meat and pastry products)	£75m
1989	The Pillsbury Company (Green Giant, Pillsbury, Häagen-Dazs etc.)	£5,800m
1990	Belin Surgelés (French frozen cake company)	(not disclosed)
1990	Jus-rol (frozen pastry)	£46.5m
1991	Aunt Nellie's (glass jar-packed vegetables)	(not disclosed)
1991	Bistrial (French cake manufacturer)	(not disclosed)
1991	Jurgen Langbein (German soup company)	(not disclosed)
1992	McGlynn's Bakeries (US frozen bakery products)	(not disclosed)
1992	Knack & Back (refrigerated dough)	(not disclosed)

	Drinks	
1989	Sileno (Portuguese wine and spirit distribution)	(not disclosed)
1989	Metaxa (International brand; Greek/German distribution)	(not disclosed)
1989	Mont La Salle Vineyards (Californian wines and brandy)	(not disclosed)
1990	Anglo Española de Distribución SA (Spanish distributor)	(not disclosed)
1991	R & J Emmet pic (Irish liqueur)	£33m
1991	New Zealand Wines & Spirits	(not disclosed)
1992	Cinzano (vermouth and sparkling wines)	(not disclosed)

	Retailing	
1988	Vision Express (US) (eyecare)	£40m
1988	Eye + Tech (US) (eyecare)	£32m
1989	Eyelab (US) (eyecare)	(not disclosed)
1989	Burger King (see Pillsbury)	(see above)
1989	UB Restaurants (fast food restaurants)	£180m
1991	Inntrepreneur Estates formed (50/50 owned with Courage/Foster's Brewing Group)	(not disclosed)

DISPOSALS

	Company	**Reason**	**Price**
1988	Soft Drink Bottling Plants	No brand control	£705m/£400m
1988	Inter-Continental Hotels	Level of investment required to obtain additional hotels to provide adequate long term returns to shareholders too high	£2bn/£1.2bn net
1989	London Clubs (casinos)	After hotels were sold did not fit strategy	£128m
1989	S&A Restaurants	To comply with US licensing laws	£434m/£263m
1989	Van de Kamps (seafood)	No international branding potential	£140m/£89m
1989	Bumble Bee (seafood)	No international branding potential	£269m/£171m
1989	William Hill and Mecca retail betting interests	No international potential	£750m
1990	Wimpy table service restaurants	Not appropriate for conversion to Burger King	(not disclosed)
1990	158 Berni Restaurants	Upgrading business portfolio	£120m

Continued

1991	GrandMet Brewing	No international potential. Key brands not owned (£55m to be repaid after four years)	£316m
1991	Pizzaland/Pastificio/Perfect Pizza	No international branding potential	(not disclosed)
1991	Wienerwald (German restaurant chain)	No international potential	(not disclosed)
1991	The Dominic Group (liquor retailers)	No international potential	£49.5m
1992	Express Dairy/Eden Vale	Commodity oriented, nonstrategic	£359m
1992	Express Ireland	Commodity oriented, nonstrategic	(not disclosed)
1992	BKDS (Burger King Distribution Services)	Noncore to Burger King strategy	(not disclosed)
1992	Eatfresh	No international potential	(not disclosed)
1992	Express foods	Commodity oriented, nonstrategic	£96m

management and jealous of its autonomy,' commented one manager. 'Recently GrandMet has begun to have more influence on IDV, putting pressure on us to improve operations, lower costs, and take some rationalization decisions we have been avoiding.'

Sheppard also resolved to build a strong and active board of directors. He recruited Richard Giordano of BOC, Frank Pizzitola of Lazards, John Harvey-Jones of ICI, Colin Marshall of British Airways, and David Simon of BP. The GrandMet board is an active and vigorous forum for debate and corporate governance. 'Little time is spent on formalities. The agenda is divided into formal and action items and the formal part generally takes about 30 seconds,' says Sheppard. 'Then we discuss, not so much results to date as what actions we are taking to improve the results in the forecast period. Our discussions are very much to do with real live issues and action points rather than just reporting. We all feel quite passionately about the company and we've got ten people on the Board, all of whom regard themselves as chief executive.' (*Director* 1992) Exhibit 7 summarizes the backgrounds of GrandMet's current directors.

Sheppard's new team made many other changes in management. Tagg changed nearly all the personnel directors, Strowger changed some of the finance directors, and in America Ian Martin changed whole layers of management. Sheppard was determined to stamp his restless management philosophy on the group as quickly as possible.

A key part of the central philosophy at GrandMet is the development and empowerment of operating managers. The personnel function, under David Tagg, carries wide-ranging responsibility in this regard. Williamson and Rix describe it thus:

> GrandMet possesses a strong central personnel function which is designed to spot potential problems before they show up in reported financial results. It is there also to attract good management to train them, to understand their skills, so as to accumulate a critical mass of knowledge within the group, and a pool of proven managers who can be transferred into a subsidiary when problems arise or market developments necessitate unfamiliar shifts in strategy or organization.
>
> (Williamson and Rix 1988)

Another key capability lies in the corporate acquisition team under Peter Cawdron, group strategy development manager and a former Warburgs banker:

> Acquisitions are the result of a formal planning and review system underscored by the company's vision of the future. The corporate head office in London's Hanover Square initiates and assesses all major acquisitions and also undertakes studies on behalf of operating units in collaboration with them. . . . GrandMet's acquisition strategy is an attacking one. It identifies what it wants, chooses its target, and goes for it. Consider the Pillsbury deal. Having decided to become a global food player and realized the need for rapid entry into the US

market, GrandMet proceeded by screening every respectably sized food company in the United States, evaluating the respective businesses and their managements. All the major US food companies were then assessed by charting them along two axes, desirability and do-ability, to determine which company appeared the best fit. Pillsbury stood out well above the others.

(McNiel 1991)

Vision 2000

Early in the Sheppard regime, it became clear that a formalized statement of the business goals for the group was needed, both for internal and external consumption. Sheppard therefore assigned this job to Peter Cawdron, who undertook the task with the help of outside consultants and a wide-ranging programme of input from senior executives and board members; the project took 12 to 15 months to complete. In the resulting document, entitled *Vision 2000*, Sheppard articulated a corporate statement of GrandMet's mission as follows:

> Grand Metropolitan is respected internationally for its management, enterprise and growth record. It is a dynamic and innovative company dedicated to success.
>
> GrandMet specializes in highly branded consumer businesses where its marketing and operational skills ensure it is a leading contender in every market in which it operates. The nature of these businesses – in food, drinks and retailing – is complementary, which adds to the value of the group as a whole.
>
> Its style is about winning – never satisfied and always innovative. GrandMet strives to be a good employer and a good neighbour, and a contributor to the wealth and well-being of all the communities and environments in which it operates.

Sheppard underlined the importance he placed in the vision statement:

> The investment of time and resource in the process of developing a Corporate Vision and long-term strategy for Grand Metropolitan has

proved to be a major motivator and integrating force throughout the Group. It has challenged the energy of our managers to strive towards their highest aspirations. It has positioned us to exploit strategic opportunities much more quickly and efficiently in the future. Finally, but not least, it has caused us to build and enhance the strategic capability of the Corporate Centre. The whole process, together with our successful management philosophy, has given stimulus and credibility to Grand Metropolitan's ability to continue to add value to all its businesses in the years to come.

(Sheppard 1989)

A close look suggests that the centre of GrandMet has three influences:

- It creates a tough and challenging culture in which top management expects and demands superior operating performance and cost leadership. This often involves introducing radical culture change and shaking up management.

- It nurtures talent. GrandMet pays a great deal of attention to motivating people and moving them around so that they can make an impact on more than one business within the group. The careers of the top 150 executives in the company are periodically reviewed by the board. Sheppard himself is said to be expert not only at motivating individuals but at being sure they are in the right place to make the most of their particular abilities. He underlines his commitment both to management development and to business growth by encouraging risk taking. A failure is not a career-ender, and playing it safe is not acceptable.

- It strives simultaneously for operating improvements and enhanced branding. 'Many companies are good at brand management and developing new products. Others are good at cost management and operating control. At GrandMet we are good at both in being able to release cash from operations and have the marketing skill to invest it wisely in brands,' explained Allen Sheppard.[3]

---

[3] Speech to Strategic Management Society, October 1992.

EXHIBIT 7
GrandMet's Board of
Directors

Sir Allen Sheppard, *Chairman and Group Chief Executive*
Joined GrandMet as a director in 1975 after 18 years in the motor industry. He became group chief executive of GrandMet in 1986 and chairman in 1987. He is chairman of The Prince's Youth Business Trust and deputy chairman of Business in the Community. He is also chairman of London First and London Forum and a nonexecutive deputy chairman of Meyer International. Age 59.

Richard V. Giordano KBE (USA), *Deputy Chairman*
Chief executive of the BOC Group from 1979 to 1992 and chairman from 1985 to 1992. He is a nonexecutive director of the BOC Group, Reuters Holdings, The RTZ Corp, and Georgia Pacific Corp in the United States. Appointed nonexecutive director of GrandMet in 1984 and deputy chairman in 1991. Age 58.

Ian A. Martin, *Group Managing Director and Chief Operating Officer*
Became chairman and chief executive of Warney Mann & Truman Brewers in 1982 having joined the company in 1979. He was appointed to the board of GrandMet in 1985 and group managing director and chief operating officer in 1991. He is chairman of International Distillers & Vintners, GrandMet Inc, and the North American Advisory Committee. He is also a nonexecutive director of St. Paul Companies Inc and Granada Group. Age 57.

George J. Bull, *Chairman and Chief Executive, Food Sector*
Joined International Distillers & Vintners in 1962, prior to its acquisition by GrandMet and became chief executive in 1984. He was appointed to the board of GrandMet in 1985. He was appointed chairman and chief executive of the food sector and chairman of The Pillsbury Company in July 1992. He is also chairman of the Far East Business Development Advisory Committee. Age 56.

John B. McGrath, *Chief Executive, Drinks Sector*
Joined Warney Mann & Truman Brewers as group director in 1985 and appointed managing director in 1986. He was appointed managing director and chief operating officer of International Distillers & Vintners in 1991. He was appointed to the board of GrandMet in June 1992 and also became chief executive of the drinks sector. He was a prime mover in the creation of the Portman Group. Age 54.

David P. Nash, *Group Finance Director*
Joined the GrandMet board in December 1989, having previously held various positions in Imperial Chemical Industries and Cadbury Schweppes. He is chairman of GrandMet finance and other group finance and holding companies and is responsible for group information technology systems. He is chairman of the Eastern European Advisory Committee. Age 52.

David E. Tagg, *Chief Executive, Property and UK Retailing and Group Services Director*
Joined Warney Mann & Truman Brewers as personnel director in 1980. He was appointed to the board at GrandMet in 1988. He is responsible for GrandMet

EXHIBIT 7 –
Continued
GrandMet's Board of
Directors

Estates and is chairman of The Chef & Brewer Group and also responsible for the group personnel, legal, and company secretarial functions. He is chairman of the European Advisory Committee, GrandMet Community Services, and of the Group Pension Funds. He is a nonexecutive director of Storehouse. Age 52.

Sir John Harvey-Jones MBE
Was chairman of Imperial Chemical Industries from 1982 to 1987, having joined that company in 1956 from the Royal Navy. He is nonexecutive chairman of *The Economist* newspaper and nonexecutive deputy chairman of Guinness Peat Aviation Limited. Appointed a nonexecutive director of GrandMet in 1983 and deputy chairman from 1987 to 1991. Age 68.

Professor Dr Gertrud Höhler (Germany), *Management Consultant, Höhler Consultants*
Founded Berlin-based Höhler Consultants in 1985. Her clients include the majority of the 50 largest companies in Germany. She serves on advisory councils for the German Federal Defence Ministry and the German Federal Ministry for Research & Technology. She has been professor of general literary studies and German studies at the University of Paderborn since 1972. Appointed a nonexecutive director of GrandMet in November 1992. Age 51.

Sir Colin Marshall, *Deputy Chairman and Chief Executive, British Airways*
Joined British Airways as chief executive in 1983 and became deputy chairman in 1989 having previously held positions in Sears, Avis, and Hertz. He is currently a nonexecutive director of The Midland Bank, IBM, U.K. Holdings, and HSBC Holdings. Appointed a nonexecutive director of GrandMet in 1988. Age 59.

David A. G. Simon CBE, *Group Chief Executive and Deputy Chairman, The British Petroleum Company*
Joined BP in 1961 and in 1982 became chief executive BP Oil International – BP's worldwide oil refining and marketing group. In 1986, he was appointed a managing director, BP Group, joining the group main board with responsibility for finance and Europe. He is currently chairman of BP Exploration, BP Oil, and BP Chemicals. Appointed a nonexecutive director of GrandMet in 1989. Age 53.

In a 1990 interview in *The Times*, Sheppard expanded on his philosophy:

> We have checks and balances in the corporate governing sense, but we don't believe in safety nets for our management. We don't have one-and-a-half people doing each person's job. What one has to do is have absolutely excellent people and encourage them to take authority to do their own thing, like a small business. My job is to ride that anarchy, working within a strategic plan, rather like a herd of horses. I have to somehow capture all that movement; that is what management is all about.

> (*The Times* 1990)

The Future

As Allen Sheppard re-examined GrandMet's choices for the future, he noted a number of important companies as his principal corporate strategy competitors:

- In spirits, GrandMet is the largest in case sales; two of the other three global operators, Allied Lyons and Guinness, are British; the fourth, Seagram, is Canadian; all are now emulating the generic strategy developed by Tennant of reducing costs, building global brands, controlling distribution, and cranking out new products.

- In the food sector, GrandMet reckons it is eighth in the world 'league table,' the sector is dominated by three true giants, Philip Morris, the largest consumer products company in the world, Unilever, and Nestlé; all are financially strong and intensely acquisitive.

- The retailing sector is more fragmented; GrandMet faces rivals in each segment (e.g. McDonald's) and more broadly spread rivals such as Pepsico (drinks, snacks, and fast food) and Whitbread (beer and restaurants).

Given this situation, Sheppard had to pick a successor who could set out the best strategic direction for the future. Therefore, he had to find an answer to two questions: in which direction should GrandMet's corporate strategy be developed, and who is the right person to accomplish this task?

References

Director (1992) Gripping Yarns, August.

Financial Times (1989) Squeezing the Doughboy, 3 July.

Financial Weekly (1988) Tough Team at GrandMet, January 21.

Fortune (1991) Profits Soar for Global Brands, November 4.

Management Today (1987) Glasnost at GrandMet, October.

McNiel, R. (1991) Acquisitions – the GrandMet Approach, *FT Mergers and Acquisitions International*, February.

Sheppard, A. (1989) Statement – The development of a long-term strategy for Grand Metropolitan, April.

The Times (1990) The Working Class Hero who Turned His Back on the Party, December 22.

Williamson, P. and Rix, B. (1988) Grand Metropolitan PLC(A), 9–788–01, London Business School.

Case 13: KLM and the Alcazar Alliance

By Ron Meyer, Bob de Wit and Howard Kwok [1]

As chairman of KLM Royal Dutch Airlines, Pieter Bouw had just taken the difficult decision to abandon the alliance talks with Austrian Airlines, SAS Scandinavian Airlines System and Swissair. The intensive negotiations between the four airlines, code-named Alcazar after a four-towered Moorish fortress, had begun in late 1992 and had progressed quite successfully throughout the spring and summer of 1993. The four carriers had agreed to merge their operations, to become the largest airline in Europe, ahead of the Big Three, Air France, British Airways and Lufthansa. Alcazar's size, it was argued, would give the new company the scale economies, route network and market power needed to survive the upcoming shake-out. As the European airline industry consolidated under the pressures of deregulation and increased US and Asian competition, it was believed that only four or five European carriers would still be around by the end of the century, and the Alcazar partners were convinced that by intensive cooperation they could be the best in this surviving group.

However, the talks were extremely complex. As Paul Mueller, head of Swissair's External Relations group, put it: 'We are looking at doing something that has never been done before in Europe by considering a multi-crossborder joint-venture.' The negotiations did not only involve the four companies, but also their two US partners, 49 labor unions, two work councils, six national governments, and the European Community and US

antitrust authorities – each with their own agenda. This gave rise to many areas for disagreement, such as equity split, valuation of partners' input, location of the headquarters, distribution of management positions, importance of national hub airports and choice of US partner. Yet, by the fall of 1993, all issues had been resolved, with the exception of the US partner selection. KLM stood by its choice of Northwest Airlines, in which it held a 20 percent stake, while Austrian, SAS and Swissair preferred the much larger and stronger Delta Airlines, in which Swissair held a five percent stake. The inability of the Alcazar partners to bridge this gap eventually led to the collapse of the talks on November 21, 1993.

This left Bouw in the position of having to reconsider KLM's future strategy. The European airline industry had not yet consolidated and the number of realized strategic alliances was still small. Bouw wondered whether the talk of a shake-out had been exaggerated, maybe inspired by the uncertainties created by industry recession and deregulation? In that case, KLM was well positioned to be successful without a European partner. Since he became chairman in 1991, he had pushed through tough cost cutting measures and had worked hard on improving KLM's service quality. This had resulted in modest profits over 1993, compared with heavy losses over 1992.

However, the shake-out might have just been postponed. Jan Carlzon, ex-CEO of SAS might have been right when he explained that industry restructuring by means of mergers, acquisitions and alliances is sometimes stuck for a while, but then can suddenly happen quickly. He called this the ketchup bottle effect: 'You shake and shake the bottle and nothing seems to happen until it all comes pouring out at once.' In that case, Bouw would want to use the existing window of opportunity to reach the necessary critical

[1] Source: This case was written as a basis for class discussion rather than to illustrate effective or ineffective handling of an administrative situation. This case was compiled from publicly available sources and supplemented by information kindly provided by KLM. The authors would like to thank Mattias Engberg, Henri Mesters, George Pemberton, Waley Salami and Louis Vos for their valuable input. Copyright 1996 by Ron Meyer and Bob de Wit.

mass, before he had his back to the wall. The question was whether increased size should be sought through alliances, mergers or acquisitions, and which partners were available and viable. And in the back of his mind he wondered whether the Alcazar partners might eventually reunite, once it had become more obvious whether Delta or Northwest was the better ally. One thing was clear to him, KLM's future was 'up in the air.'

Regulation in the Airline Industry

Traditionally, the airline industry has been heavily regulated by governments around the world. National authorities have controlled entry into the industry by granting or refusing permission for airlines to be established and by determining the routes that they have been allowed to fly. Moreover, flight frequencies and seating capacities have been strictly regulated, along with the type of service provided (scheduled or charter). Governments have usually also attempted to control price levels, often intervening to prevent price competition among airlines.

While common protectionist reasoning is partially to blame for this state of affairs, the sheltering of national airlines also has an important emotional origin. Most countries have traditionally had one airline – the flag carrier – that literally carries the national flag to foreign countries. Airlines have been the symbol of their nations' qualities and much patriotic pride is derived from seeing these ambassadors in foreign skies. The flag carriers have fulfilled the same role as national Olympic teams, enhancing a country's self-esteem by competing abroad. As a consequence, governments have not only been willing to protect their national champion, but more often than not they have also been the owner of the airline. This dual role as regulator and owner has usually not been a stimulus for deregulation and competition.

On international routes this high level of regulation has necessitated the negotiation of bilateral aviation service agreements between the governments concerned before the national airlines can begin their cross-border services. In such aviation service agreements the different kinds of air traffic rights assigned to each party must be determined (see Exhibit 1), as well as details in terms of routes, capacities, frequencies and sometimes even the type of aircraft that may be employed. Before an agreement can be

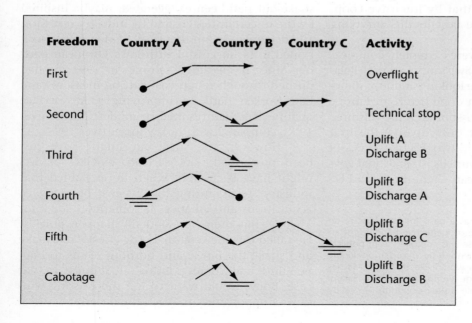

Freedom	Country A	Country B	Country C	Activity
First				Overflight
Second				Technical stop
Third				Uplift A Discharge B
Fourth				Uplift B Discharge A
Fifth				Uplift B Discharge C
Cabotage				Uplift B Discharge B

EXHIBIT 1
The Five Freedoms and Cabotage

Adapted from: McKern, R.B. (1990) *Evolving Strategies in the International Airline Industry*, Stanford GSB.

reached, many issues in the areas of national economic interests, flag carrier interests and even national security must first be hammered out. Both bargaining parties must also keep in mind how their bilateral agreement will influence their recurrent negotiations with other countries. This political complexity makes the entire process of securing an aviation service agreement difficult, uncertain and time-consuming.

Beside bilateral agreements, international airline relations are also governed by the International Air Transport Association (IATA), to which most airlines in the world belong. As an international industry association, IATA has as objective to promote the interests of its members, the airlines. This objective has been pursued by setting standards, providing members with industry data and by regulating international airline prices. Until the 1970s, the latter task, of setting international airfares, worked very well. Although IATA rate negotiations could be complicated, due to the fact that all airlines and governments involved needed to approve the suggested airline prices, all parties accepted the need to regulate in the first place. This shared understanding, that a uniform set of international airline rates was necessary, ultimately ensured that a common ground could be found. However, once the American government decided to deregulate its domestic market in 1978, the seed for future disagreement had been sown.

Deregulation in the United States

In October 1978, the US domestic market, the largest air transport market in the world, was deregulated by the passing of President Carter's Airline Deregulation Act. From that moment on, domestic services within the US have operated free from all the traditional forms of regulation. Pricing, routes, capacity – everything has been fully liberalized.

The impact on US airlines has been enormous. Initially, small carriers rapidly expanded their networks and new rivals entered the market. As the competitive intensity sharply increased, prices were slashed and collectively the airlines made record losses. Adaptation to the new reality resulted in numerous mergers and acquisitions, and a fundamental change in the way airlines did business. The carriers struggled back to profitability by differentiating their product through such novelties as frequent-flyer plans and sophisticated computer reservation systems (CRSs), as well as refining the hub-and-spoke system to establish more efficient routes. The hub-and-spoke system allowed airlines to serve less profitable, lower volume routes using smaller aircraft feeding into the central hub. The larger, more expensive aircraft were then used to maximum capacity on a limited number of high volume routes out of the hub. Delta Airlines, for example, built up a powerful hub at Atlanta, fed by numerous short-haul routes. In contrast, the now defunct Pan-Am failed to establish a hub, attempting to rely instead on its dominance of the international routes.

In the process of consolidation, many airlines did not survive. Others emerged far stronger, and have progressively used their strength to compete more successfully in the domestic as well as international markets. Deregulation has also spawned a group of innovative new entrants, such as Southwest and ValuJet. Furthermore, the US now has the lowest commercial airfares in the world. These results of deregulation were not lost on legislators in other countries. Between 1986 and 1988 the Canadian domestic market was largely liberalized, while the regulatory controls were lifted in the Australian domestic market in October 1990. The UK domestic market has not yet been totally deregulated, although the regulations have gradually been rolled back.

Deregulation in Europe

In 1986, the European Court of Justice ruled that the Competition Articles of the Treaty of Rome also applied to air transportation services within the European Community (EC). In effect this meant that the airline industry was required to compete freely across European borders just like other industries. This left the governments in the European Community split on how intra-EC competition should be advanced. On the one side, the Netherlands and the UK favored a rapid move towards a more liberal environment. The other EC governments, however, were concerned about the damaging side-effects of sudden deregulation and preferred a slower paced change of the old restrictive practices.

The compromise was a program of gradual liberalization. The first two phases, referred to as the First and Second Packages, were implemented in 1987 and 1990. Entry into intra-EC markets was made a little easier, with multiple designations of airlines allowed in the denser markets, and considerable freedom granted to airlines to serve thinner routes with small aircraft. Capacity restrictions were to be eased and pricing was to be more liberally regulated. Finally, there were the first moves towards greater competition through the granting of fifth freedom traffic rights.

The third and biggest step, the Third Package, was adopted in July 1990 and took effect on January 1st 1993. Two important regulatory powers were adopted by the EC. European regulators were empowered to act against overpricing and predatory pricing, while also having the authority to control state subsidies to airlines. More importantly, however, three major areas of liberalization were pushed through:

1   *Air fares.* Airlines now have the freedom to set fares without government interference. However, as the European Commission is proposing to introduce Value-Added Tax (VAT) on intra-EC flights and to abolish in-flight duty free sales, this will not necessarily result in lower prices.

2   *Market access.* No member state will be able to limit capacity to any extent on the basis of nationality, although a member state will be reserved the right of appeal. This means that airlines will ultimately (after a four-year transition period, ending January 1 1997) be able to operate on routes not involving a stop or start in their home country (cabotage).

3   *Licensing of air carriers.* Airlines will be required to satisfy common European financial, technical and safety standards annually. Any air carrier meeting these EC standards will be entitled to a license.

Deregulation on Trans-Atlantic Routes

An open skies agreement was signed between the Netherlands and the US in September, 1992. The agreement allows Dutch airlines to fly into any city in the US. In return, the US airlines are also allowed to fly into any city in the Netherlands. The agreement provides for the deregulation of pricing, capacity, routing flexibility, and fifth freedom

EXHIBIT 2
World Scheduled Passenger Traffic Forecast for 1993–1995 (in billion passenger-kilometers)

Region of Airline Registration	Actual			Estimated		Forecast					
	1981	1991	% Annual Growth	1992	%	1993	%	1994	%	1995	%
Africa	32.5	39.1	1.9	44.0	12.5	46.6	5.9	49.5	6.2	52.7	6.5
Asia/Pacific	176.6	359.3	7.4	407.1	13.3	445.2	9.3	491.5	10.4	543.8	10.6
Europe	384.6	552.2	3.7	548.8	−0.6	564.4	2.8	589.5	4.4	617.5	4.7
Middle East	30.6	45.4	4.0	53.1	17.0	56.7	6.9	60.4	6.5	64.5	6.8
North America	431.5	759.8	5.8	808.6	6.4	857.6	6.1	914.4	6.6	978.8	7.0
Latin America/ Caribbean	61.1	87.5	3.7	90.7	3.6	69.0	5.9	102.8	7.1	110.9	7.9
World	1116.9	1843.3	5.1	1957.2	6.7	2066.5	5.9	2208.1	6.9	2368.2	7.3

Source: International Civil Aviation Organization (ICAO), 1992

EXHIBIT 3
The Development of High
Speed Trains

Source: Airbus Industries,
quoted in *The Economist*, June
12, 1993

To improve public transportation in Europe, the EC asked the European Community of Railways in December 1989 to prepare a broad plan for a European high-speed rail network to be realized by the year 2000. The plan focuses on 14 corridors to be developed in the coming years: It is the intention that eventually there will be a high-speed train network covering all of Europe. The expansion of these high-speed trains is a significant potential threat to the airline industry in Europe. Most train stations in Europe are located in the city center so that the passengers can save a significant amount of time in commuting to and from the airports. The figure below gives the current traveling mode trade-off. If high-speed trains become operational the train-airplane transition point, currently at 625 kilometers, would shift much further to the right, endangering medium-haul routes.

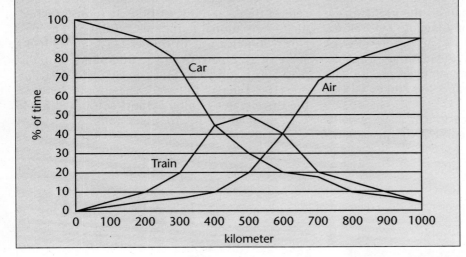

operations. Such an open skies agreement was the first of its kind between a European country and the US. Both governments cited the agreement as an example of promoting free competition.

This agreement was followed by US anti-trust immunity for KLM Royal Dutch Airlines and Northwest Airlines, the US airline in which KLM had acquired a $400 million stake in 1989. The immunity, the first of its kind granted by the US Justice Department, effectively gave both airlines permission to collaborate on pricing, code-sharing and any other aspect without fear of anti-trust prosecution. This was a major coup for KLM and Northwest, since the agreement faced fierce opposition and lobbying by the major US carriers.

At the same time, British Airways was seeking US approval for the acquisition of a $750 million stake in loss-making USAir. One fundamental difference between the BA-USAir deal and KLM–Northwest alliance was the lack of open skies agreement between the UK and the US. While both governments were interested in an open skies agreement, the US demand that more slots at Heathrow should be available to US airlines remained a stumbling block.

Competition in the Airline Industry

From 1970 through 1989, the collective international airline industry registered reasonable profits. Especially after the economic recession in the early 1980s, the industry flourished as it rode the wave of sustained international economic growth, increasing international trade and a booming tourism sector. In 1989, however, the industry took a dramatic turn for the worse. Just as airlines had pumped profits into new planes, thereby significantly increasing seating capacity, several national economies started to falter and passenger growth flattened out. The Gulf War also negatively impacted international travel, in particular international tourism. The result was that between 1990 and 1992 the combined airlines lost $11.5 billion on their international scheduled services, which is more than all the profits made in the previous 74 years combined. In 1992 alone, the industry lost $4.8 billion. According to IATA chairman, Pierre Jeanniot, 'the main, inescapable, reason for these losses has been overcapacity. The result has been extended and sometimes vicious fares wars' (IATA 1993).

Although IATA forecasts a healthy growth in passenger traffic in the coming years (see Exhi-

bit 2), the proportion of business travel is expected to decline. Airplane manufacturer Airbus predicts that by early in the 21st century only one fifth of the passengers will be making a business trip. Businesses have been under pressure to cut traveling expenses, which has not only lead to price sensitive buying behavior, but also to a switch to alternatives such as video-conferencing, electronic mail and high-speed trains (see Exhibit 3).

In terms of the total scheduled traffic, North America is the largest air transport market in the world (see Exhibit 4). It accounted for 36.5 percent of the total traffic in 1992. In terms of scheduled international traffic (see Exhibit 5), Europe – North America was in the lead. The route had a share of 22.2 percent of the international traffic. Asia–North America (13.4 percent) and Asia–Europe (10.4 percent) followed. These routes between the three major economic blocs accounted for 46 percent of all the international traffic.

EXHIBIT 4

Major Traffic Flows Between Regions in 1992 (Percent of IATA Total Scheduled Traffic – RPKS)

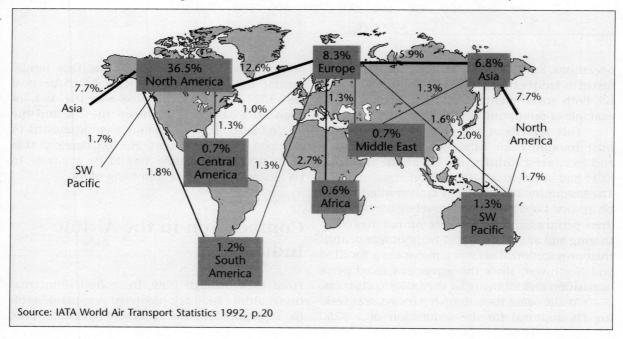

Source: IATA World Air Transport Statistics 1992, p.20

EXHIBIT 5

Major Traffic Flows Between Regions in 1992 (Percent of IATA Scheduled International Traffic – RPKS)

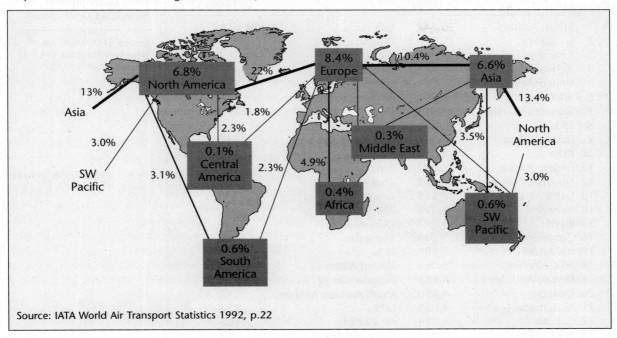

Source: IATA World Air Transport Statistics 1992, p.22

Competitors in the Airline Market

When judging by the number of international passengers, six of the top 10 airlines in 1992 were European, namely British Airways, Lufthansa, Air France, Alitalia, SAS Scandinavian Airlines System, and KLM Royal Dutch Airlines. Two US companies (American Airlines and United Airlines) and two Asian companies (Singapore Airlines and Japan Airlines) shared the remaining four spots (see Exhibit 6). In the top 10 of international cargo airlines Lufthansa occupied first place, followed by Federal Express and Air France. In the US domestic market, Delta had the lead, followed by American, United, Northwest, and Continental.

What this overview illustrates, is that the international airline industry is still relatively fragmented. Some international routes might be cozy duopolies, but the broader picture shows a high level of fragmentation, without a high level

of differentiation. This has prompted many industry analysts and participants to forecast that concentration is imminent. At the same time, however, liberalization has accommodated the entry of a large number of new competitors. These new entrants, particularly plentiful in the US, often focus on charter flights and shuttle services on high density routes. It does not look as if the established carriers have the ability to halt these intrusions into their backyard, which prompts other analysts to forecast a further fragmentation of the industry (*The Economist* 1996).

Industry Structure and Competitive Dynamics

Competition in the airline industry is heavily influenced by airlines' ability to fully utilize their capacity. Much like hotels, amusement parks and telecommunication services, most of the operating expenses of an airline vary only with the amount of capacity available, not with the level of usage. The major costs, such as aircraft depre-

	Airline	Passengers (×1000)	Airline	Freight Tonnage (×1000)
1	British Airways	20,247	Lufthansa	669
2	Lufthansa	15,156	Federal Express	659
3	American Airlines	12,827	Air France	507
4	Air France	11,813	Korean Air Lines	431
5	United Airlines	9,684	Japan Airlines	411
6	Alitalia	8,731	Singapore Airlines	387
7	Singapore Airlines	8,512	British Airways	377
8	SAS	8,482	KLM	375
9	Japan Airlines	8,336	Cathay Pacific	342
10	KLM	8,250	Northwest Airlines	305
11	Cathay Pacific	8,082	Swissair	216
12	Northwest Airlines	7,638	Thai Airways	215
13	Delta Air Lines	7,595	American Airlines	214
14	Swissair	6,715	Alitalia	207
15	Iberia	5,777	Qantas	189
16	Continental	5,200	Malaysian	181
17	Malaysian	5,081	El Al	176
18	Thai Airways	5,065	United Airlines	171
19	Korean Air Lines	4,881	Nippon Cargo	136
20	Qantas	4,850	Saudi Arabian Airlines	132
21	Air Canada	4,053	UPS	112
22	Gulf Air	3,924	Air Canada	102
23	Aer Lingus	3,717	Delta Airlines	99
24	Saudi Arabian	3,602	Varig	97
25	Sabena	3,142	Gulf Air	93
26	Aeroflot	3,089	SAS	92
27	Garuda Indonesia	2,672	Continental	92
28	TWA	2,640	Iberia	85
29	Mexicana	2,634	Garuda Indonesia	84
30	Austrian Airlines	2,596	Sabena	77

EXHIBIT 6

IATA Member's Rankings 1992 (International Scheduled Operations)

Source: IATA World Air Transport Statistics 1992, p. 34–35.

ciation, fuel, wages and landing charges, are independent of the number of passengers on board. This puts considerable pressure on an airline to keep up occupancy, without sacrificing the price paid per passenger. This challenge can be expressed in the following formula:

$$(\text{Yield} \times \text{Load factor}) - \text{Unit cost} = \text{Unit operating income}$$

Yield is defined as the revenues received per occupied seat per kilometer (revenues/RPK, revenue passenger kilometer). Thus, yield indicates the price level at which the capacity has been sold. The load factor is a measure of the amount of capacity sold, in other words, the occupancy rate. It is defined as the portion of total capacity (available seat kilometers, ASKs) that has been paid for (RPKs/ASKs). The unit costs are the operating expenses per available seat kilometer (expenses/ASK).

The more efficient an airline is in terms of its expenses per available seat kilometer, the lower is the load factor needed to stay out of the red. This break-even load factor is an important measure of an airline's competitiveness:

$$\text{Unit cost}/\text{Yield} = \text{Break-even load factor}$$

Competition in the industry, naturally, focuses on these three variables. Airlines either try to realize a very low unit cost, a high load factor or a high yield – and, more often than not, a combination of these three. Almost all of the major airlines use the hub-and-spoke system in their traffic networks, in order to increase the load factor. Smaller aircraft are used in most feeder lines and large capacity aircraft, such as the Airbus 310 and the Boeing 747, are used on trunk lines.

For the hub-and-spoke system to fully utilize its advantages, the coordination of flight schedules is very important. If the connecting flights can take off soon after the feeder flights' arrivals, the total traveling time can be reduced to a minimum. The short traveling time can be a very powerful selling point, necessary to compete with direct flights of other airlines. As a consequence, there are certain periods during the day when there is a very high frequency of arriving and departing flights, while it can be slow at other moments.

Due to this scheduling importance, there often is very strong competition for take-off and landing time slots at major international airports, especially if they are highly congested. However, competition for these time slots does not take place not on a level playing field. The national champion will often claim historic rights to certain take-off and landing times. Furthermore, the local air transport regulatory authorities, that usually ration the scarce time slots, tend to favor the flag carrier over foreigners and upstarts.

Another avenue for raising load factors has been the use of computer reservation systems (CRSs). CRSs have huge databases that allow travel agents hooked up to the computer network to obtain on-line information about flight schedules, seat availability and prices, and to make reservations for their clients. Travel agents can also employ their CRS for car and hotel reservations. Of course, the airline owning the CRS can determine the information provided and products sold via this channel and will use this power to promote its own services. This trend was started in the US in the late 1970s, where there are now three major systems (Apollo, Worldspan and Sabre). Airlines that were either too late in enticing travel agents to make use of their system, or where unable to invest the millions needed to build a CRS, joined existing systems, as co-hosts,

paying a fee per reservation to the system owner. In Europe and Asia, airlines were also daunted by the price tag attached to building a CRS of their own. However, the prospect of letting American competitors in the back door by adopting their CRSs was even more threatening. This eventually lead to an Asian (Abacus) and two European (Galileo and Amadeus) CRS consortia.

An added benefit of computer reservation systems is that they not only use, but also produce, much information. Current and historic data can be analyzed to recognize trends, segments and price sensitivities, that can be used to determine the capacity needed for certain flights, the marketing required and the prices that can be asked. Particularly on the last point, airlines have developed yield management programs, that change fares and offer discounts in a way that optimizes the yield/load-factor trade-off.

Frequent Flyer Programs (FFPs) are another tool for enhancing both load factor and yield. In such a loyalty program, a seasoned traveler can accumulate points based on the miles/kilometers flown with the airline or one of the FPP associates (hotel, car rental or other airline). The points can be traded in for a class upgrade (economy – business – first class), an extra baggage allowance or complimentary air tickets. The first frequent flyer programs were started by US airlines, but now most major airlines offer such programs. FFPs mainly offer protection against price shopping, particularly by business travelers.

On the cost side, efforts throughout the past years have focused on trying to reduce flight crew, ground services, and aircraft maintenance expenses (see Exhibit 7). As wages are the largest cost item (normally between a quarter and a third of all costs), many airlines have reduced their number of employees or at least have frozen hirings. Streamlining working practices is a norm for many airlines. Some airlines, particularly in the US, have also tried to lower wages, either by striking a deal with labor unions, or by circumventing unions altogether. Maintenance and ground service costs have often been reduced by outsourcing these activities to competitors or specialized third parties, especially at non-hub airports. The other two cost components, fuel and aircraft purchas-

Crew	15%	Ground services	* Hub	10%
Fuel	15%		* Other end	10%
Maintenance	12%	Sales	* Own organization	10%
Aircraft	8%		* Commission	10%
Catering	5%			

EXHIBIT 7
Average Cost Structure in the Airline Industry (% of total)

Source: C. Barton, L. Bradshaw, R. Brunschwiler and T. Bull-Larsen, 'Is there a future for Europe's airlines?,' *McKinsey Quarterly*, no. 4, 1994, pp. 29–40.

ing, offered some room for scale advantages, but not much, given the negotiation power of the suppliers.

Globalization and Alliances

The airline industry has a long history of cooperative arrangements. However, until the late 1980s most of these collaborative agreements were limited in scope, focusing on operational matters, such as shared airplane purchasing and maintenance, or on running a route jointly. In an internationally fragmented market, with government-endorsed duopolies on most routes, there was little pressure to go further than such arms-length arrangements.

As deregulation started to gain momentum, however, many of the major airlines became convinced that globalization of the industry would be just a matter of time. Having a world-wide route network was judged to offer a potentially significant competitive advantage. A global airline would be able to serve passengers from origin to destination without ever turning them over to a competitor. This service would be appreciated by the customer, which would be reflected in the yield, while simultaneously increasing the network-wide load factor. The increased world-wide size of such a global carrier would also lead to scale economies in purchasing, maintenance, ground organization and marketing.

Since the late 1980s several major airlines have begun to lay the groundwork for a global airline. As organic growth by itself is too slow, and the outright acquisition of foreign airlines is forbidden or politically too delicate, alliances have become the favored method for building a global network. Often these alliances have been sealed by the purchase of a small equity stake by one company in the other, or by the exchange of minority holdings. For instance, British Airways has purchased a stake in USAir, Qantas (Australia), and in two small European regional airlines. Another example is Swissair, which has formed the European Quality Alliance with Austrian Airlines, Finnair and SAS Scandinavian Airlines System, while simultaneously joining forces with Delta Airlines and Singapore International Airlines. The complexity of this world-wide match-making scene, where the 'marriages' of the future are currently being proceeded by flirting, dating and engagements, is illustrated in Exhibit 8. Few of the current 'couples' have taken their 'eternal vows' yet, so the possibilities for new romances still abound. However, the threat that the best catches will quickly settle down with their current partners, leaving the 'wall-flowers' partnerless 'old maids', is quite real. This explains the anxiety with which formerly staunch bachelors are now scanning marriage opportunities.

KLM Royal Dutch Airlines

Koninklijke Luchtvaart Maatschappij NV, known in English as KLM Royal Dutch Airlines, was incorporated on October 7, 1919. It is the oldest scheduled airline in the world. The airline started its first scheduled flight between Amsterdam and London in 1920 and established the world's first intercontinental service, with its Amsterdam–Jakarta route in 1927. Since then it has built up a route network with more than 150 destinations on six continents (see Exhibit 9).

EXHIBIT 8
Cooperative Agreements and Equity Stakes (end 1992)

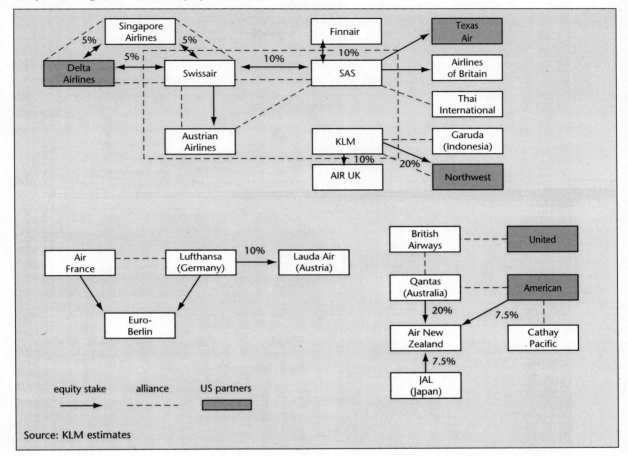

Source: KLM estimates

Throughout much of the company's history, the government of the Netherlands has been the majority shareholder. However, by the mid-1980s the government began reducing its ownership, so that by 1992 they held only 38 percent of the shares, although they still continued to appoint the majority of the Supervisory Board.

KLM's fortunes throughout the 1980s had more or less mirrored the trends in the industry at large (see Exhibit 10). The company grew steadily and its net income was maintained at a satisfactory level. However, the malaise in the airline industry that started in 1989 also heavily influenced KLM. The company tallied up losses of over a billion guilders within a three-year period.

In its 1992/93 annual report, KLM outlined the three policy 'cornerstones' on which it intended to build its response to the changes in the airline industry:

1   Enhancing customer preference;

2   Achieving competitive cost levels; and

3   Strengthening market position.

In order to enhance customer preference, KLM would be focusing on improving the quality of its services in different market segments. The company also indicated that it intended to offer a wider range of products so that there would be more choices available for different customers.

EXHIBIT 9

KLM Route Map 1994

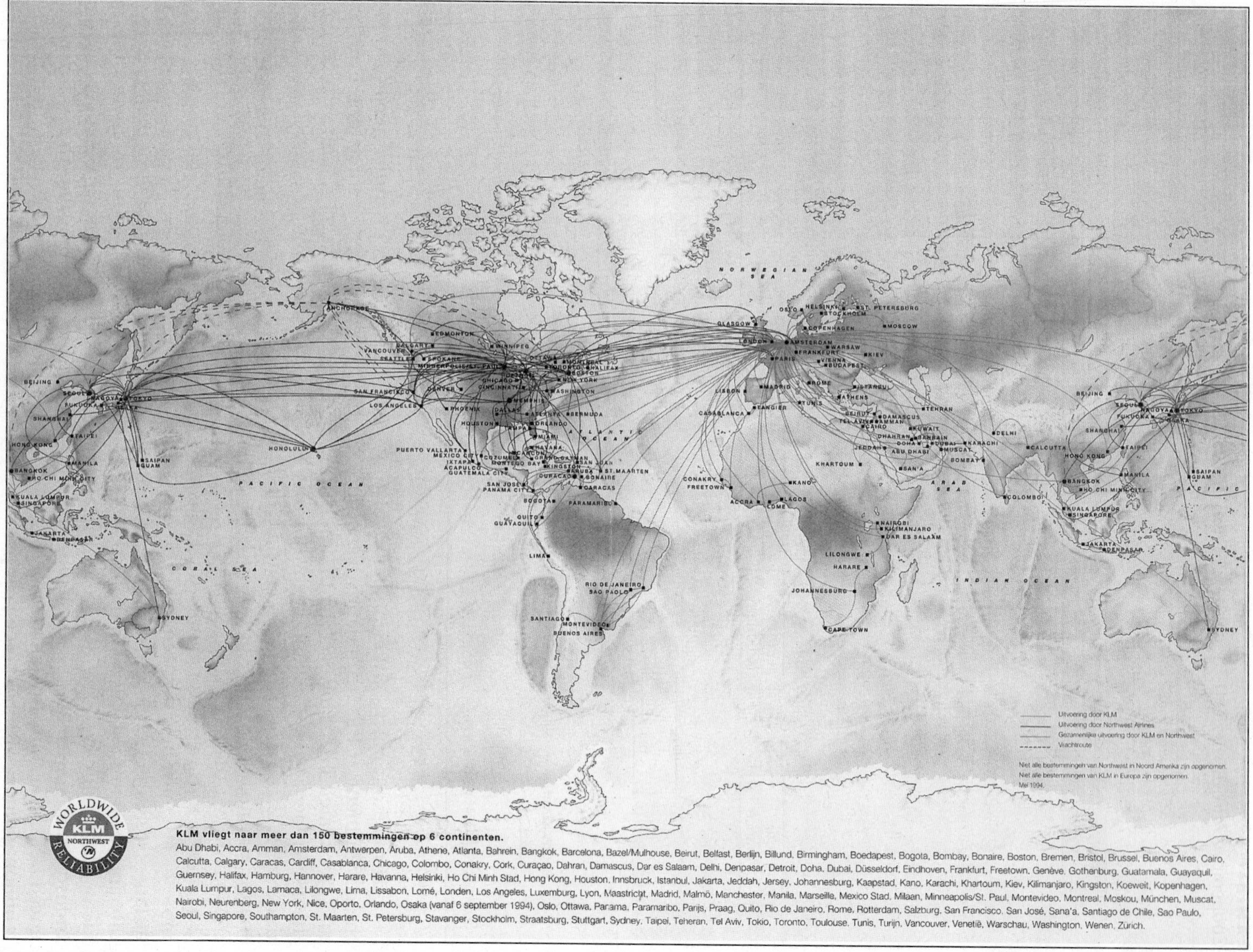
WORLDWIDE RELIABILITY
KLM
NORTHWEST
PACIFIC OCEAN
ATLANTIC OCEAN
INDIAN OCEAN
NORWEGIAN SEA
ARAB SEA
CORAL SEA
Uitvoering door KLM
Uitvoering door Northwest Airlines
Gezamenlijke uitvoering door KLM en Northwest
Vrachtroute
Niet alle bestemmingen van Northwest in Noord Amerika zijn opgenomen.
Niet alle bestemmingen van KLM in Europa zijn opgenomen.
Mei 1994.
KLM vliegt naar meer dan 150 bestemmingen op 6 continenten.
Abu Dhabi, Accra, Amman, Amsterdam, Antwerpen, Aruba, Athene, Atlanta, Bahrein, Bangkok, Barcelona, Bazel/Mulhouse, Beirut, Belfast, Berlijn, Billund, Birmingham, Boedapest, Bogota, Bombay, Bonaire, Boston, Bremen, Bristol, Brussel, Buenos Aires, Cairo, Calcutta, Calgary, Caracas, Cardiff, Casablanca, Chicago, Colombo, Conakry, Cork, Curaçao, Dahran, Damascus, Dar es Salaam, Delhi, Denpasar, Detroit, Doha, Dubai, Düsseldorf, Eindhoven, Frankfurt, Freetown, Genève, Gothenburg, Guatamala, Guayaquil, Guernsey, Halifax, Hamburg, Hannover, Harare, Havanna, Helsinki, Ho Chi Minh Stad, Hong Kong, Houston, Innsbruck, Istanbul, Jakarta, Jeddah, Jersey, Johannesburg, Kaapstad, Kano, Karachi, Khartoum, Kiev, Kilimanjaro, Kingston, Koeweit, Kopenhagen, Kuala Lumpur, Lagos, Larnaca, Lilongwe, Lima, Lissabon, Lomé, Londen, Los Angeles, Luxemburg, Lyon, Maastricht, Madrid, Malmö, Manchester, Manila, Marseille, Mexico Stad, Milaan, Minneapolis/St. Paul, Montevideo, Montreal, Moskou, München, Muscat, Nairobi, Neurenberg, New York, Nice, Oporto, Orlando, Osaka (vanaf 6 september 1994), Oslo, Ottawa, Panama, Paramaribo, Parijs, Praag, Quito, Rio de Janeiro, Rome, Rotterdam, Salzburg, San Francisco, San José, Sana'a, Santiago de Chile, Sao Paulo, Seoul, Singapore, Southampton, St. Maarten, St. Petersburg, Stavanger, Stockholm, Straatsburg, Stuttgart, Sydney, Taipei, Teheran, Tel Aviv, Tokio, Toronto, Toulouse, Tunis, Turijn, Vancouver, Venetië, Warschau, Washington, Wenen, Zürich.

EXHIBIT 10
Selected KLM Operating Statistics (in million Guilders)

	1992/93	1991/92	1990/91	1989/90	1988/89	1987/88	1986/87	1985/86	1984/85	1983/84
Finance										
Operating Revenue	8222	7913	6555	6460	5971	5580	5376	5854	5657	5030
Operating Expenses	8126	7497	6840	6150	5581	5278	5076	5586	5377	4920
Net Income	(562)	125	(630)	340	374	314	301	312	290	103
Traffic										
Number of Passengers (000)	9497	8222	7484	7168	6880	6632	5655	5413	5334	5016
Cargo/Mail (million KG)	422	385	371	356	343	404	360	323	358	311
Load Factor (%)	69.4	70.5	71.0	71.4	70.8	70.2	66.7	67.3	70.0	65.4
Break-Even Load Factor (%)	71.2	67.1	76.9	68.9	66.5	65.8	62.4	64.1	66.3	64.4
Personnel	21.163	25.596	26.080	25.195	23.599	22.257	21.235	20.262	19.193	18.265

Source: KLM Annual Report 1992/93.

Furthermore, the 'Kick-Plus' quality-improvement program would be implemented to increase on-time departures, improve customer satisfaction and reduce baggage losses.

The second plank of its strategy would be to continue the turnaround program 'Competitive Cost Levels,' that was introduced in early 1991 to bring down unit cost. In the 1992/93 fiscal year, this program had resulted in a productivity increase of 24 percent and drop in the unit cost of nine percent. In KLM's view greater economies of scale would also contribute to a more competitive cost level and therefore the carrier continued to pursue the rapid expansion of its route network.

The completion of the 'wave system' at its Amsterdam Schiphol Airport home base was seen as a major contributor to the strengthening of its market position. The purpose of the wave system is to optimize and expand connections between flights to and from Schiphol by rescheduling the aircraft movements into waves. KLM believed that it could capture a larger share of the market for passengers with Schiphol as departure or arrival point through the convenience of this system. Of course, KLM also profited from travelers' preference for Schiphol over other hubs. The airport's high popularity among, in particular, business travelers and the airport's continual program of upgrading, were much to the benefit of KLM.

KLM's Alliances

KLM is no stranger to alliances. It had been a partner in the KSSU (KLM, SAS, Swissair, UTA) technical alliance for nearly two decades. The four airlines coordinated the purchase and maintenance of aircraft (SAS and Swissair), engines (KLM), and landing gear (UTA), to reduce training, inventory and overhead costs. The alliance fell apart in 1990 as their fleet compositions and future needs became too divergent – leaving SAS and Swissair to carry on with Finnair and Austrian in the European Quality Alliance.

Currently, KLM's most dominant alliance is with Northwest Airlines on the North Atlantic route (see Exhibit 11). In the early 1980s, KLM tried to negotiate a transatlantic treaty with Air Atlanta and Florida Express, but these attempts were unsuc-

EXHIBIT 11
KLM's cooperation with
other airlines (as of January
1993)

Sources: KLM Annual Report
1992/93 and *Airline Business*,
July 1994.

Partner	Equity	Started	Details
Martinair	29.8%	1964	Charter company
ALM Antillean	40%	1981	Amsterdam – Netherlands Antilles; codesharing and marketing agreement
Air UK	14.9%	1987	Amsterdam – UK; codesharing and FPP
Northwest	20%	1989	Europe – North America; all aspects
Cyprus Airways	0%	1991	Amsterdam – Larnaca; codesharing
Transavia	80%	1991	Charter company; FPP
Nippon Cargo	0%	—	Amsterdam–Tokyo; joint venture

cessful. In 1989, however, KLM was able to secure a deal with Northwest, the fourth largest carrier in the US. This alliance was solidified by a $400 million capital injection by KLM into the struggling American airline, giving KLM a 20 percent stake. The KLM–Northwest alliance involves a comprehensive marketing agreement in the passenger services of the two airlines, including joint flights and frequent flyer program. Furthermore, there is cooperation on ground handling, sales, catering, information services, maintenance, and purchasing. Although both KLM and Northwest were still keeping their own identities, it seems that the two are becoming increasingly intertwined.

In the European regional market KLM has an alliance with Air UK, Cyprus Airways and Transavia, a Dutch charter company. Air UK has recently grown to become the second largest airline at Schiphol, partially due to its flight schedule being tightly coordinated with KLM's. In an attempt to duplicate this success, KLM acquired a 35 percent stake in Air Littoral, a French regional carrier, in 1991. However, due to competitive and regulatory pressures, the partnership never came to full bloom, and in November 1992 KLM sold its stake. KLM continued to search for suitable regional partners within Europe, particularly in Germany, but ultimately concluded that any partnership would probably meet the same fate as its 'affair' with Air Littoral.

KLM has also been searching for a larger European partner, to achieve the 'critical mass' it believes is necessary to survive the coming industry shake-out. The company's first step was in 1990, when it teamed up with British Airways in a bid to acquire 20 percent each of the Belgian flag carrier, Sabena. After considerable effort the purchase fell through due to political wrangling – the European Commission was worried about a powerful BA–KLM–Sabena bloc, while Sabena's position changed under a new chairman. Informal approaches were also made to the members of the European Quality Alliance – SAS, Austrian Airlines, Finnair and Swissair – but these were not answered with equal interest. British Airways and KLM were back at the bargaining table in late 1991, this time to discuss a possible merger. The plan was for the two airlines to set up an Anglo-Dutch holding company that would combine their services, marketing, and maintenance. If it would have been concluded, the merged companies would have become the largest airline in Europe, with a market value of more than $3.9 billion. Together with KLM's stake in Northwest, the new cross-border giant would have been a major player in most of the markets around the world. However, the negotiations collapsed in March 1992. Valuation difficulties and the assignment of seats on the Management Board were mentioned as major issues. BA's insistence on a 80:20 split of shares and the leading role in the new company were unacceptable to KLM. Furthermore, it was not at all clear whether KLM and BA would be able to share each other's aviation service agreements, in particular the open skies agreement that KLM and the Dutch government were working on with the US authorities.

The Alcazar Negotiations

After the failed negotiations with British Airways, KLM re-initiated the contacts with the members of the European Quality Alliance – SAS, Swissair

EXHIBIT 12
Intra-European and
Trans-Atlantic
Marketshares

Source: KLM documents.

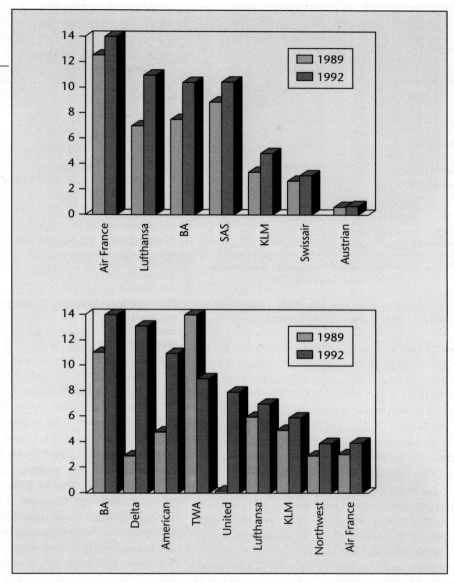

and Austrian Airlines (Finnair had withdrawn in late 1991). The first informal meeting between the CEOs of the four was held in December 1992. On February 26, 1993, the four announced that they were ready to launch detailed talks on the feasibility of setting up a 'global airline system', in order to become the fourth force in Europe, larger than the Big Three, Air France, British Airways, and Lufthansa. The four European airlines said that they planned to examine how a possible part-

nership, code-named Alcazar after a four-towered Moorish fortress, could be structured and how long it might take to get off the ground. The objectives of these talks were:

1   to form a 'customer-driven global route net-work;'

2   to achieve 'greater efficiency and lower cost levels at the four airlines;'

	Austrian	**KLM**	**SAS**	**Swissair**
Finance (× $1000)				
Operating revenue	780,812	3,939,800	3,901,000	3,477,700
Operating expenses	828,417	3,714,500	3,564,000	3,600,200
Net income	(73)	(241,500)	(192,000)	14,857
Traffic				
Passengers	2,596,048	8,250,111	14,489,308	7,433,265
Load factor	57.1	69.5	63.1	60.3
Freight tons	31,712	374,852	111,184	230,299
Load factor	50.3	69.6	58.5	61.7
Fleet	30	63	132	60
Personnel	4,441	25,907	18,813	20,882

EXHIBIT 13
Selected Operating Statistics of Alcazar Partners in 1992

Source: IATA World Air Transport Statistics 1992

3   to strengthen the 'joint market position of the partners based on various European hubs.'

The cooperation among the four airlines would create the largest airline in Europe, with a 20 percent share of the passengers carried by West European airlines (see Exhibit 12). The consolidated annual sales would be approximately $15 billion, based on a fleet of 300 aircraft carrying about 32 million passengers a year to more than 200 destinations. The group would employ about 70,000 people. The joint force would be able to compete with the giants of the industry. In addition, the link-ups provided ways of tapping into a wider network than the airlines could find on their own. And the potential in cost savings could also be very substantial.

Alcazar was presented as an ideal team. Although Austrian Airlines is smaller, KLM, SAS and Swissair are roughly the same size (see Exhibit 13), making overbearance by one of the partners unlikely. Furthermore, the four have close similarities in their strategy, structure and culture. All four have a small domestic market, that is unable to support a strong international airline, making them outward looking. Furthermore, their quality positioning, cost structure and human resource policy are comparable. The potential for a deal was present.

The Other Corner Towers of the Fortress

Swissair is the flag carrier of Switzerland, although the company is not owned by the national government. Its main hub is Zurich's Kloten airport, while the airport in Geneva also handles quite a bit of Swissair traffic. Swissair is perceived in the market as a premium airline par excellence. The airline targets international business travelers, thereby achieving one of the highest levels of first class and full fare paying passengers in Europe, despite the fact that its prices are also one of the highest. The high fares are at least partially due to the company's high operating costs. Especially the generous wages paid to its unionized employees contributed to this high cost structure.

Besides Swissair's participation in the European Quality Alliance, the company also has two important intercontinental partners, Delta Airlines and Singapore Airlines. This Global Excellence Alliance was sealed in 1989 and involves coordination between the partners in the areas of marketing (e.g. codesharing, common FFP, advertising), fares, timetables, ground organization (e.g. through check-in, common passenger handling and transfer services), and aircraft procurement. Delta, the third largest carrier in the US (see Exhibit 14), is a very strong partner, with the same quality image as Swissair. Although Delta and Swissair compete on a number of routes, their networks are almost fully complementary. Singapore International Airlines (SIA), widely known for its excellent customer service and operating efficiency, fits very well with Swissair and Delta. It is one of the largest and strongest carriers in the Asian market, with an extensive route network that, together with those of Delta and Swissair, covers the world. All three partners have taken a five percent stake in each other to cement the alliance, although it is rumored that Delta has been primarily motivated by the fear of a take-over.

Despite these alliances, it is questioned whether in the long run Swissair will have the critical mass needed to survive. More disconcerting to the company in the short run, however, is Switzerland's increasingly insular position as non-member of the European Community. Swissair is worried that being outside the deregulated European market might result in a very disadvantageous competitive position. If in future the Swiss government would have to renegotiate aviation service agreements with officials at the European Community level, instead of with national authorities, this would put the Swiss in a very poor negotiation position. Especially the prospect that its EC-competitors would be allowed to engage in cabotage, while Swissair would be denied this free-

dom, frightened the company. It was widely believed that Swissair, somehow, needed to become an inside player within the EC.

SAS, on the other hand, already has a foothold in the European Community, by means of its hub in Copenhagen, Denmark. As a unique example of international aviation cooperation, the airline has been jointly owned by a consortium of the national airlines and governments of Denmark, Norway, and Sweden since 1946. In 1981, after Jan Carlzon became the President and CEO of SAS, the airline started a complete reorganization, to ward off a financial crash landing. Carlzon repositioned the company as the businessman's airline, focusing on high quality services to frequent business travelers in Europe. Part of Carlzon's strategy has been to view air transport as just one element in a door-to-door travel concept. SAS has developed into a comprehensive travel services group providing flights, food, hotels, credit cards, and package tours.

Since 1987, SAS has signed cooperation agreements with seven airlines outside Europe. The list includes Air New Zealand, Qantas, and Thai International in Asia Pacific, Continental Airlines in the US, and Varig in South America. The collaboration with Continental involves joint marketing and FFP on connections via New York to Continental's American destinations. In

	Continental		Delta		Northwest	
Finance (× $1000)						
Operating revenue	5,403,313		11,579,156		7,963,785	
Operating expenses	5,559,331		12,401,273		8,272,589	
Net income	(299,429)		(564,826)		(308,804)	
Traffic (× $1000)	Int'l	Total	Int'l	Total	Int'l	Total
Passengers	5,200	38,358	7,595	83,117	7,638	43,541
Load factor	64.8	63.5	62.7	61.3	69.5	65.4
Freight tons	92	234	99	449	305	477
Load factor	46.3	48.2	49.1	51.2	57.4	55.6
Fleet		328		554		372
Personnel		35,804		79,157		45,766

EXHIBIT 14
Selected Operating Statistics of US Partners of Alcazar Airlines in 1992

Source: IATA World Air Transport Statistics 1992

Europe, SAS has pushed hard to intensify cooperation with its partners in the European Quality Alliance, since its establishment in 1990. The company's partnering enthusiasm can be explained by Carlzon's often stated belief that at most five European airlines would be around in the year 2000 – Air France, BA, Lufthansa, and clusterings of the smaller airlines. Carlzon did not want to undergo consolidation, but to initiate it.

The junior partner in the Alcazar talks was Austrian Airlines. As can be seen in Exhibit 11, Austrian is a relatively small airline, but with a good hub in Vienna and an interesting network, particularly to Central and Eastern Europe. To compensate for its small network, the airline has established cooperative agreements with more than 10 airlines. The partners are all European, with the exception of All Nippon Airlines in Asia. Austrian is fully aware that its size makes an independent future almost impossible. It has long standing relations with Swissair, although relations with the third German-speaking airline, Lufthansa, are also quite friendly.

Initiating the Partnership Talks

Championed by the Presidents of the four partners, the talks progressed quickly. As the negotiations grew increasingly complex and technical, a total of 16 joint working groups were formed to consider the financial, legal and technical details of the cooperation. The committees worked on topics such as the creation of a multi-hub traffic system based around Amsterdam, Copenhagen, Zurich, and Vienna, integration of the fleets and future aircraft purchasing policies, the merging of frequent flier programs, rationalizing of structures and cutting of costs, labor and government relations, and valuation of the new entity. From the outset, it was clear that a number of obstacles would need to be cleared.

First, the partners would have to obtain the agreement of the European Community's competition directorate. They needed to convince the regulatory authorities that the proposed partnership would benefit passengers and would not impede competition. It would be important to avoid the suggestion that the cooperation was a

guise to protect the oligopolistic advantages of the past.

Second, the Alcazar partners, despite their six original nationalities, would have to preserve the air traffic rights, that each derives from bilateral national agreements. Normally, aviation service agreements are signed between two governments and only benefit the airlines of the two countries involved in the arrangement. However, if a multi-hub traffic system is created without one clear national identity, the question is whether it can make use of the bilateral ASAs enjoyed by its pre-merger parts. The alternative is that it would have to renegotiate ASAs with each individual country covered by its network, which is an almost impossible task.

The third hurdle was that the partners would have to bridge four company cultures and six national cultures. Each of the airlines would be bringing in a different government, a different legal system and different business practices into the negotiations. In addition, there would be 49 labor unions and two work councils that would need to be dealt with, making the negotiations even more complicated.

The Elusive Memorandum of Understanding

In order to avoid trench warfare with the unions, all four parties agreed to address their legitimate concerns at an early stage. These negotiations went smoothly in the Netherlands, while minor resistance was faced in Scandinavia and Switzerland. In Austria, however, the unions feared that as the smallest partner Austrian Airlines would suffer a disproportionate number of job losses. By assuring the unions that the intended alliance would be genuinely multi-hubbed, and that growth would be sought for all hubs, an accord was finally reached.

In May 1993, the joint working groups concluded that a merger would be the best approach to cooperation. The proposal would result in KLM, SAS, and Swissair each holding 30 percent of the new airline and Austrian Airlines holding 10 percent. The new airline would initially retain the four individual brands, but a common identity was seen as a distinct future option. The legal structure would consist of the four parent companies setting up a joint daughter company. Management of the four airlines would be delegated to the daughter, while the four holding companies would still retain the air traffic rights. At informal discussions early in 1993 this concept received positive feedback from the US regulatory authorities, and it was expected that other countries would follow the American lead.

A memorandum of understanding was expected to be signed during the summer of 1993, so a final agreement could be concluded by January 1 1994. However, a number of complex issues would still need to be worked out. Although a 30:30:30:10 split was proposed, the relative financial share of the airlines was still an issue to be settled. There was fear in Switzerland that the proposed 30 percent share of Swissair in the alliance would undervalue the actual worth of the airline.

The location of the new company's headquarters was also a divisive issue, because of the strategic and national implication of the ultimate decision. While all partners were interested in housing the headquarters, Amsterdam seemed the front runner because of its strategic position, the expansion potential at Schiphol airport and the advantages the partners would gain from the open skies agreement between the Netherlands and the US. However, SAS was likely to make a strong pitch for Copenhagen, which it had developed successfully into its main international hub.

Another issue was SAS's significant non-airline holdings. While Carlzon was still a staunch believer in door-to-door travel services, the other partners preferred that the new company would only be involved in passenger and cargo air transportation services. Last but not least, the four were also divided on the selection of a US partner. Three of the four airlines had forged links with American carriers and it was understood that only one transatlantic partnership could be maintained.

Counter Currents

In the same month, the Swiss government had for the first time indicated unease about Swissair losing its independence and had ordered the airline to put forward alternative plans. A Swiss newspaper claimed the alliance would result in the suppression of the Swissair name, the loss of 10,000 Swissair jobs, and the transplantation of important decision-making to Amsterdam. At the same time, similar opposition had already broken out in Austria, where Lufthansa was understood to be discussing an alternative commercial partnership agreement with Austrian Airlines.

In September, in the middle of intense negotiations on Alcazar, Swissair published its consolidated interim results. They revealed a loss of SFR 65 million ($46.1 million), putting more pressure on Swissair to relax on the issue of equity valuation. At the same time, Mr Jan Carlzon resigned his position as chief executive of SAS, a position he had held since 1981, in order to concentrate on Alcazar. 'I have told the board that if Alcazar does not succeed, I will not remain in this position,' he said. There were rumors that Carlzon's resignation was because of the continuous poor performance of SAS. Apart from the position as chief executive of SAS, Mr Jan Reinas, Carlzon's temporary successor, also took over as Chief Operating Officer from Mr Kjell Fredheim, a key Carlzon lieutenant, who was transferred to head corporate development. Mr Steffen Harpoeth had already quit as Deputy President, effectively completing the removal of Carlzon's team from the top management of SAS.

In October, Lufthansa signed a wide-ranging commercial partnership with United Airlines, the largest US international airline. The Lufthansa-United alliance was primarily designed to increase the two airlines' world-wide revenues, but the two airlines expected it to provide cost cutting opportunities as well. According to analysts, the deal would lead to intensified competition on international routes, especially across the North Atlantic. In addition, Mr Jurgen Weber, Lufthansa's Chairman hoped the deal would help swing Austrian Airlines to cooperate with Lufthansa, rather than join the Alcazar merger.

In early November, KLM announced its better than expected 20 percent increase in net profit for the second quarter of its 1993/94 fiscal year. According to KLM's chairman, Mr Pieter Bouw, the airline's program of lowering costs and improving service to passengers meant that KLM was less dependent on the Alcazar alliance than it had been. 'What we want to avoid, and what we have avoided, is that partnership is KLM's only strategy for survival,' he said.

Moving Toward Agreement

In August, the airlines agreed to shelve the US partner issue in the interest of reaching early agreement on other important issues. By late October, the four airlines had found common ground on almost all vexing questions, including the valuation of assets, the headquarters' location and the joint management structure. The four airlines agreed to a complex formula to compensate Swissair in recognition of its net asset value being greater than its 30 percent share in Alcazar. Amsterdam was selected as the new headquarters and Swissair's President, Otto Loepfe, would be the first CEO.

The US partner was the last significant issue threatening the Alcazar talks, although the US partner played only a minor role in the overall benefits of the alliance. The KLM-Northwest connection appeared to be the most promising, because the Netherlands and the US have an open skies agreement. Also, KLM has a 20 percent equity stake in Northwest. However, in early 1993 Northwest had still been balancing on the brink of 'Chapter 11,' and although its finances had improved, it remained a risk in the eyes of the other Alcazar partners. Swissair also felt strongly about being associated with Delta's quality image and its more attractive domestic network. Moreover, the ties between the two were just beginning to bear fruit. Austrian Airlines and SAS also favored Delta. The issue was felt to be so important that none of the four airlines wished to proceed with the Alcazar project without knowing and being comfortable with the selection. At last, the four decided to resolve the issue of selecting a US partner before signing a memorandum of understanding.

In early November, talks were held in Stockholm to resolve the choice of a US partner. Although rumors of a collapse were dismissed by the airlines involved, failure to achieve the breakthrough increased worries that the Alcazar project might fail. At this point, the Alcazar partners decided to go back to US Transportation Department to test whether KLM's open-skies agreement with the US would be extended to the whole of Alcazar. However, the political climate in the US had changed dramatically. The four company holding structure, initially accepted by the US regulators, was now being questioned by the Clinton administration. In order to get the Alcazar concept accepted, the companies were asked to first give up their current links with US partners, then negotiate the Alcazar structure, and only reestablish an American partnership afterwards. Immunity from antitrust persecution would not be guaranteed up front.

On November 21 1993, the four airlines in the Alcazar talks said in a joint statement that they had decided to abandon their seven-month old negotiations because of 'fundamentally different views' on a US partnership.

KLM's Future Flight Path

Failure of the talks had left the four airlines with the dilemma of how to secure their long-term future in the increasingly competitive and consolidating airline industry. Austrian Airlines had already held talks with Lufthansa and had not ruled out an alliance with Swissair. SAS had restructured its top management and intended to pursue its cost cutting drive in order to return to profit. Swissair had already made clear that it needed an EC partner, which now probably would be one of the Big Three, Air France, British Airways, or Lufthansa.

KLM, finally, also still needed to do something to enhance its prospects of surviving the twentieth century. KLM's CEO, Bouw, was relieved that the short-term pressure to merge had become less intense. The airline industry was recovering from its slump and overcapacity was beginning to ease, resulting in more black than red numbers among the carriers. Moreover, KLM's cost cutting program and quality improvements had placed the company in a better position to deal with the competitive consequences of airline deregulation and globalization than two years ago. However, while these developments provided some breathing space, they did not take away the necessity of scale enlargement. Consolidation of the industry had been 'delayed,' but not 'canceled.' Bouw, therefore, gathered with his senior staff to set a course for the future. The question was whether its future included Northwest and possibly other strategic allies.

References

The Economist (1996) Bandits at Nine O'clock, February 17.
IATA (1993) IATA Annual Report.

Case 14: The Salim Group

By Hellmut Schütte, Lizabeth Froman and Marc Canizzo [1]

Liem Sioe Liong has been remarkably industrious. After leaving his native province of Fukien in China in 1937 and starting with nothing in Indonesia, he built an empire which had a US$8 billion in turnover in 1990. Luck was also on his side. When he began supplying peanut oil and staples to the Indonesian army during the fight for independence in the 1950s, Liem forged a bond with the chief supply officer of the Diponegoro division, Lieutenant Suharto, who later rose through the army ranks to become president of Indonesia. This early friendship helped Liem to prosper during a period when then President Sukarno was promoting businesses run by the indigenous population at the expense of those run by the Overseas Chinese living in the country.

As in many Southeast Asian countries, the ethnic Chinese who migrated to Indonesia have become an economically powerful minority, representing less than five percent of the population but controlling over 40 percent of the country's wealth. Their success has been attributed to growth in the Asian economies, the immigrant status of the Chinese which motivated them to succeed in their new country and the social values and organization of the Chinese culture.

By making aggressive use of his contacts and his negotiating skills, Liem has built a network of businesses that dwarfs other Indonesian groups and is, in fact, the largest Overseas Chinese conglomerate. Liem's Indonesian businesses today represent five percent of the country's GDP. In 1990, 40 percent of Group sales and 25 percent of Group assets were located outside Indonesia. Liem, now 75 years old, is handing the reins of the Salim Group over to the youngest of his three sons, Anthony Salim (Salim is the Indonesian name of Liem).

Anthony's mission is to focus the company's businesses and strengthen the Group's competitive position. Like his father, he has been described as a 'clever, gutsy operator . . . loyal to friends and . . . outwardly unassuming.' The elder Liem is 'famous for driving a hard bargain,' but his son is reputed to be even tougher. In addition, Anthony is more internationally minded and more committed to the art of professional management.

Background on the Indonesian Political System

At the end of the Second World War, Indonesia declared its independence from the Dutch. Over the 20 years of President Sukarno's leadership, Indonesia was united as a country but suffered economic decline. President Sukarno replaced the elected House of Representatives with an appointed Assembly that zealously pursued domestic politics and waged foreign policy feuds with the Netherlands and Malaysia at the expense of the country's economic prosperity.

Following what was claimed by the government to have been a communist-led coup attempt in 1965, Major-General Suharto assumed executive power in March 1966 and has served as Indonesia's president ever since. A new political order was established based on a constitutional

[1] Source: This case was written by Lizabeth Froman and Marc Canizzo, under the supervision of Hellmut Schütte, Affiliate Professor at INSEAD. It is intended to be used as a basis for class discussion rather than to illustrate either effective or ineffective handling of an administrative situation. Comments from Philippe Lasserre, Professor at INSEAD, are gratefully acknowledged. Reprinted with the permission of INSEAD-EAC. Copyright © 1992 INSEAD-EAC, Fontainebleau, France.

republic. Two political parties remain – the Indonesian Democratic Party (PDI) and the Islamic United Development Party (PPP). A third political group, Golkar, is dominated by the military and has won substantial majorities in elections to the House of Representatives since 1971.

Indonesia has been politically stable since 1968. Tensions still arise, however, due to some Muslim integrist circles and the discontented intelligentsia. The antipathy toward the economically prosperous Chinese minority has also caused violent outbreaks. Because of his long reign, Suharto has created a succession problem. In order to unite the various factions in the country, the president of Indonesia needs three qualifications: he needs to be from an operating unit of the military, from the central island of Java, and a Muslim. For many years, no one was properly groomed for the position.

Demands for political reform continue. Suharto has come under increasing criticism for allowing the Overseas Chinese to dominate the business scene and for the growing gap in income distribution in the country. He recently announced plans to encourage businesses to sell 20 percent of their equity to employees or to cooperatives.

Indonesia has achieved economic stability through a series of five-year plans setting specific sectoral growth targets. The first five-year plan (1969–1974) focused on agricultural production and infrastructure. Further plans set goals to increase social welfare benefits and generate adequate employment opportunities, primarily with private sector investment. Indonesia is the fifth most populous country in the world with 180 million people, 40 percent of whom are under the age of 15. To achieve the latest plan's goal, five percent real growth is essential. This growth is expected to come from the manufacturing sector. Local manufacturing has been encouraged through tariffs and quantity restrictions, looser monetary policies and the free convertibility of the rupiah, which has led to a boom in foreign investment. However, high interest rates and the current credit crunch in Indonesia are obstacles to the attainment of the government's goal.

The Liem Investors

The Liem investors are the shareholders of most of Liem's businesses. They include Liem himself; Djuhar Sutano, a friend from Liem's Fukien province in China; Sudwikatmono, President Suharto's foster brother; Ibrahim Risjad, said to have close ties to the military; and Anthony Salim, Liem's son. In 1990, the Liem investors took four of the top six spots in the list of Indonesia's highest personal taxpayers. Government officials and other Suharto relatives figure prominently among the other investors in Liem's companies. Liem is but one of a number of beneficiaries of the Suharto regime's practice of granting monopoly rights to insiders. The government has shielded Liem from losses through substantial equity infusions and, by allowing Liem in many cases to own the competition too, through artificial competition. Liem has enjoyed privileged access to capital and preferential buying arrangements for his goods.

Organization of the Group

The Salim Group is made up of over 350 companies of varying sizes that are operationally separate. About 100 are centrally administered, while the rest are more passive investments. As Anthony admits, 'The formation of the Salim Group was by accident, not design. [Our growth] was driven by opportunities available to us. The new Group leader is looking to divest smaller holdings and to take greater control of key businesses. The Group currently employs 135,000 people.'

Liem influences operations in his disparate companies through resource allocation, particularly that of intangible resources such as information and connections. Cohesion among business units is accomplished in part through the small numbers of managers rotated around different companies in the Salim Group, whose loyalty is therefore to Liem and not to the individual businesses. This level of trust allows subsidiaries' operations to be decentralized while cash flow is allocated centrally. A small group of Executive Directors oversees the strategy of all the affiliates. Equity not held by the Liem family is placed in

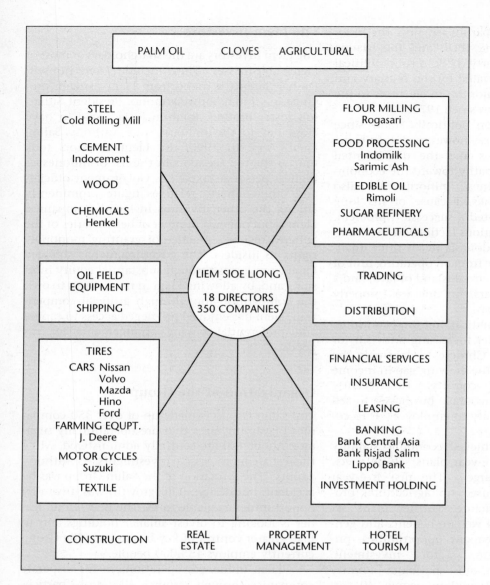

EXHIBIT 1
Liem Holdings

friendly hands (either with trusted individuals or with management). Entrepreneurship is strongly encouraged and is rewarded in managers and younger family members, as demonstrated by the many start-up businesses run by the top team (see Exhibit 1).

Liem's Development

Commodity monopolies Through the sixties Liem concentrated on businesses in cloves, coffee, rubber and soybeans. In 1969 Liem gained access to new capital through his relations with Bulog, Indonesia's logistics agency for commodities. Bulog had been run by Suharto and was later managed by Bustanil Arifin, who is related to Suharto by marriage. The monopoly arranged for Liem's Bogasari Flour Mill (BFM) provided the capital to fuel the growth of his holdings in the seventies. BFM contributes 20 percent of its profits to political and charitable organizations run by Suharto-related shareholders.

Government support In the 1970s, Indonesia encouraged import substitution industries by guaranteeing sustainable profits through price fixing. Liem built strong concerns in cement, steel, assembly and distribution of foreign cars, and banking. Forestry products, chemicals and agribusiness were opportunistically expanded. Real estate became a prime focus in Indonesia and in the 'Golden Triangle' of the Riau Islands, Singapore and Malaysian Johor.

Government support of Liem's investments is best exemplified by the history of Indocement, one of the star performers on the Jakarta Stock Exchange JSE) and a credit deemed worthy of European bond investors. By 1980 Liem owned five cement companies and was being encouraged to expand capacity through above-market government pricing. By 1985 Liem could boast of the largest production complex in the world. However, the recession in the early eighties in Indonesia, prompted by the fall in oil prices, led to cutbacks in government infrastructure spending. Liem was losing a lot of money and was granted a government supported restructuring. His five companies were merged into Indocement Tunggal Prakarsa with the government taking a 35 percent stake for US$325 million. Expensive US dollar loans were refinanced with rupiah credits issued by state owned banks. Two years later, profit requirements were waived so that Indocement could once again list its shares on the JSE. In 1990, Indocement earned 47 percent gross profit margins.

A similar story of consortia, artificial competition, government buying arrangements and equity injections can be found in the steel industry.

Cross ownership Through cross ownership arrangements with other Indonesian-Chinese tycoons, Liem has been able to control his markets and his competition. Such shareholding agreements include Liem's friends Ciputra and his Metropolitan Group in properties, Eka Cipta Wijaya and his Sinar Mas Group in chemicals and agribusinesses, and Robert Kuok in commodities trading.

Liem's first attempt in banking came in the early 1950s with Bank Windu Kentjana. This was not a success, despite strong links with the military. In the late 1950s Liem purchased the Bank Central Asia (BCA) in Indonesia, which languished for 15 years. In 1975 Liem brought in Mochtar Riady, owner of the most successful private bank in Indonesia, Panin Bank, to aid the ailing BCA. The merged group flourished. Riady was recently bought out, his Lippo Bank being a formidable competitor. BCA is owned 32 percent by two of Suharto's children. Liem still holds 15 percent of Lippo.

International growth In the 1980s, Liem established offshore holding companies and aggressively grew his investments outside Indonesia. Primarily through the First Pacific Group in Hong Kong (discussed in the next section), Liem controls banking and property in Hong Kong, real estate development in Singapore, drug stores in the Philippines, a US Savings and Loan, a Dutch trading house and an Australian communications firm. Liem uses the banking division of First Pacific to tap new sources of capital – it arranged private financing for Indocement – and to scout out and review international acquisitions.

The company has also turned its attention to Vietnam, where it has engaged in commercial real estate and coal mining. The latter project is a US$27 million venture embarked upon with two other Indonesian industrial groups (Astra, Gemala) and entails a long-term commitment (30 years).

Joint ventures with foreign partners Building on his skill in finding solid business partners and investors, Liem established a number of joint ventures with foreign partners. In Indonesia, the Group is discussing a US$240 million chemical production facility with Amoco Chemical and already has a joint venture with Henkel from Germany. More recently, the group entered into partnership with Dow Chemical to produce polystyrene resin. Liem is teaming up with Japanese companies in a wide range of industries. Working with Japan's largest general contractor, Taisei Corp., Liem is developing an industrial park. He is expanding the range of cars marketed for Mazda Motor Co. and Nissan Motor Co. Bank LTCB-Central Asia was set up with the Long-Term Credit Bank of Japan and Nikko Securities Indonesia, and joint ventures are being negotiated in the softdrink industry with Yakult Honsha Co. and in wire harnesses with Sumitomo Electric Industries Ltd. First Pacific is expanding its telecommunications business through agreements with British Telecom.

Ever open to new opportunities and an extended geographic reach, the Group entered into a partnership with a Swedish firm (SKW Trostberg) to buy an East German company producing agrochemicals. This acquisition comes in addition to the outright purchase of a fatty alcohols company in the former East Germany, which cost the Group $40 million.

The First Pacific Group

First Pacific Group, located in Hong Kong, was founded in 1982 and is listed on the Hong Kong, Dutch and US stock exchanges. The Liem investors retain 65 percent ownership and tight management control. First Pacific is run by Manuel Pangilinan, a Filipino educated in the US. While he was with American Express, he became the trusted advisor of Liem and Anthony and was asked to start up a vehicle for international expansion. The company's stated goal is the 'increase of shareholder value' (1990), which has largely been accomplished through opportunistic acquisitions. Performance is measured by growth of per share earnings and net asset value. The current business divisions are Marketing and Distribution (Trading); Banking; Real Estate; and Telecommunications. Each division manages its own portfolio of businesses (see Exhibit 2).

The 1990s are stretching the limits of the group's capital. Despite grumblings from First Pacific's treasury staff about the need to digest the current businesses, all divisions are looking at new growth opportunities. These opportunities are analysed within First Pacific's merchant bank. First Pacific has been kept relatively cash tight for its expansion plans, which require direct investment (and some control) from Indonesia.

The Group's Activities

Trading In 1983 First Pacific acquired the ailing Dutch trading company Hagemeyer with roots in Indochina. The company now operates in 21 countries, represents thousands of branded consumer products and generates US$1.4 billion in sales. Hagemeyer is increasing its international presence through acquisitions of specialty products companies in Europe, North America and Asia.

In June 1991, First Pacific proposed a merger between Hagemeyer and Internatio-Mueller NV in the Netherlands after First Pacific announced in May that it had already amassed 43.2 percent of the shares of the underperforming conglomerate; this investment amounted to about US$100 million. The proposal was rejected in August with Internatio pledging to focus on two main businesses – engineering and wholesaling of pharmaceuticals. Discussions continue and First Pacific has been offered representation on Internatio's board. This year, Hagemeyer is also completing the acquisition of a German trading company which it is financing through the private placement of new shares worth Guilders 60 million.

Banking First Pacific launched its banking division with: (1) the purchase of Hong Nin Bank, a small Hong Kong-based retail bank; (2) a new brokerage unit, First Pacific Securities; and (3) the acquisition of Hibernia Bank, the twelfth largest bank in California. In 1998 the poorly performing securities unit was divested, as was Hibernia Bank. Proceeds were used expand the Hong Kong retail banking network through the acquisition of Far East Bank. First Pacific has continued in US banking with United Savings Bank, a savings and loan catering to Chinese clients in the San Francisco area. All current banking operations world-wide (outside Indonesia) have been consolidated under First Pacific Bancshares, a separately listed company on the Hong Kong Stock

EXHIBIT 2
The First Pacific Group
Structure

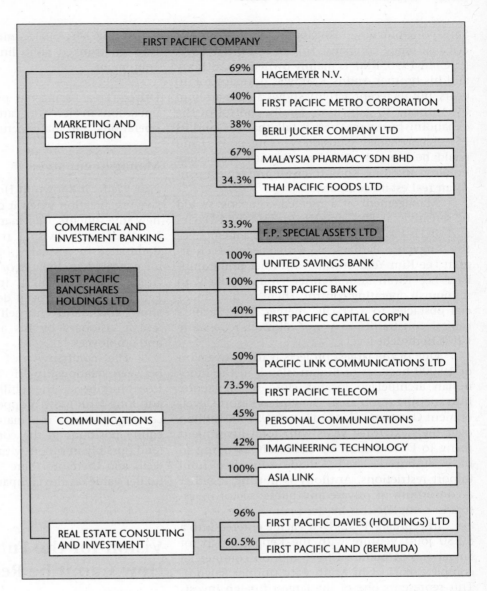

Exchange and Hong Kong's sixth largest banking group.

There is no clear commitment to this sector despite its usefulness as a source of new capital. Stock analysts predict the sale of the division, but new opportunities for growth are constantly examined. First Pacific made a bid for the Hong Kong branch of the scandal-shaken BCCI in the summer of 1991. Instead, the Lippo Group made the final bid but withdrew at the beginning of 1992.

Real estate First Pacific Davies, purchased in 1985 from founder and chairman David Davies, is one of Hong Kong's leading real estate agencies involved in property brokerage, valuations and project management. The group has associations with major real estate agencies in the UK, the US and Australia. David Davies is a long-standing and very well respected Hong Kong real estate expert, having previously served as CEO of Hong Kong Land, a Jardine company.

Another Liem offshore company, KMP Pty of

Singapore, purchased Singapore's largest commercial real estate company, United Industrial Corp. (UIC) in 1990. KMP is mainly owned by Anthony and his brother Andre. KMP was dormant for 10 years, but its recent activity shows a clear attempt by Anthony to gain more family control of the expanding business. There is talk that UIC and its 75-percent-owned subsidiary Singapore Land could be merged with First Pacific's real estate holdings in Hong Kong to create the largest pan-Asian real estate company.

Management of a merged company would be sensitive, as FP Davies is run by David Davies and UIC is run by Leong Chee Whye, a member of the Singapore Parliament, with executive chairman Lee Kim Yew, brother of former prime minister Lee Kwan Yew. Neither group is likely to relinquish operating control. There are also financial obstacles to a FP-UIC merger; First Pacific's capital constraints may not allow it to assume UIC's high debt level.

One of the largest projects is the conversion of 19,000 hectares of Bintan island, in the Indonesian archipelago located close to Singapore, into a leisure resort area. The Bintan Resort Development Company plans to invest US$600 million over the next three years with total investment rising to US$3 billion by 1998. UIC is trying to have Bintan declared a trade zone free from import restrictions. Anthony is putting together a consortium of private and public sector investors to complete this master plan.

In February 1992, First Pacific entered into a 50/50 joint venture with the Keppel group (of Singapore) to build a US$75 million commercial complex in Ho Chi Minh City (former Saigon). This represents one of the largest foreign investments in Vietnam to date.

Telecommunications First Pacific agreed in August to buy the 50 percent of Pacific Link Communications currently owned by a Luxembourg affiliate of US-based Millicom Inc for US$150 million. This is expected to increase FP's earnings tenfold. Private minority investors (from Indonesia) will provide a portion of the capital.

The company has also found a very profitable niche in the mobile phone market and is expanding its telecommunications division through trunked radio lines and distribution of equipment.

Other First Pacific has purchased and divested operations in New York catering, Hong Kong retail operations, and manufacturing plants.

Management style

First Pacific is known in Hong Kong as an aggressive organization when it comes to opportunistic new investments. Top management includes the heads of each division (two Europeans) but is dominated by a small group of Filipino bankers all educated in the US or Britain and recruited from Western financial institutions by Manny Pangilinan. FP has been described as a one man show, and Manny himself as a financial genius and a visionary by his admiring management and employees.

The company tries to strike a balance between relationship-driven transactions (either from Indonesia, the Philippines or elsewhere) and long-term growth opportunities such as telecommunications. Top managers have important equity positions in the companies they manage (and possibly in others within the Salim Group as well) and therefore share 'the increase of shareholder value' as the company's goal.

Vision for the Future: How Can it be Realized?

Anthony Salim is working toward building a Pan-Asian company by: (1) streamlining the Group's holdings; (2) consolidating the family's control at the expense of the other Liem investors, and (3) strengthening his companies' balance sheets. Anthony is perceived as a very capable manager and negotiator who could work comfortably anywhere in the world. He is trying to gain international credibility by professionalizing management and using new, non-Indonesian holding groups as acquisition and growth vehicles. He has purchased reputable and traditional companies such as Hagemeyer, Hibernia and Shanghai Land, and the Group has engaged top-name advisors – Price Waterhouse, Jardine Fleming, Citibank and Goldman Sachs, among others – despite having some of these firms' capabilities in-house.

Through opportunistic expansion, the Salim Group has successfully established itself as an Asian company, not just an Indonesian one. It has moved into Europe and North America with centralised decision making but decentralised operations management. It is well positioned to become Indonesia's first truly multinational company.

Case 15: The Champagne Industry in 1993

By Karel Cool, James Howe and James Henderson[1]

The present crisis is touching all within the interprofession, growers and houses alike, and difficult decisions are being made together on both sides. The world economic difficulties are worse than in 1974 and although the consumer has no dissatisfaction with champagne, today there is no 'ambiance de fête'. The success formula is missing.

(Jean-Charles Ducellier, president of the Union de Maisons de Champagne, March 1993.)

Champagne is one of France's most prestigious products. More than mere sparkling wine, it is a drink associated with luxury, celebration and good times. The booming world economy in the 1980s was one such good time, especially for the highly profitable champagne industry. Unfortunately for Champagne's growers and producers, the 'champenois,' the party did not last into the 1990s. In an industry that had for so long only known success, the hangover was particularly painful.

By March 1993, the situation in Champagne had reached crisis. Despite tumbling prices, sales remained flat. Mushrooming stocks were draining the industry of cash. Large and small firms alike began to shed staff. The March 1993 negotiations between the grape growers and the champagne makers would be crucial to the industry. Would the industry be capable of sorting itself out or would the crisis take on even bigger dimensions?

[1] Source: Copyright © 1994 INSEAD-CEDEP, Fontainebleau, France. Revised 1997. This case was written by Karel Cool, Professor at INSEAD and CEDEP, James Howe, MBA 1993 and James Henderson, PhD student. It is to be used as a basis for class discussion rather than to illustrate either effective or ineffective handling of an administrative situation.

History of the Champagne Industry

Grapes had been grown in the chalky soils of the Champagne region, east of Paris, for several millennia. However, it was not until the seventeenth century that local producers, including Dom Perignon and his Benedictine monks, developed a reliable method for the production of sparkling wine: 'la méthode champenoise.' The drink was an instant success even if its consumption was limited to European aristocracy.

The first champagne house, Ruinart, was founded in 1729 under royal permission. Soon, others followed. By 1845 annual shipments had reached 6.5 million bottles a year. New markets were found among the wealthy of Russia, the United States and Australia. By the turn of the century, sales had climbed to 30 million bottles. Exhibits 1 and 2 give data on sales volumes.

From its earliest days, the production of champagne was divided between two different groups: the 'récoltants' who grew the grapes, and the 'négociants' who fabricated and sold the champagne. The growers formed an association to represent their collective interests (the Syndicat Général des Vignerons de Champagne) in 1882, and the producers a similar association (the Syndicat du Commerce des Vins de Champagne) in 1904. In 1911, the two groups organized their first joint meeting to discuss an issue, which would continue to dominate their future meetings: pricing. However, little success was made in establishing formal price regulation. The following 25 years would see the development of laws defining the production methods of champagne ('appellation d'origine controlée').

The industry's first ever crisis occurred in the

EXHIBIT 1
World sales of champagne
(bottles million)

Source: CIVC

Year	France	Export	Total	Year	France	Export	Total
1861			11.0	1974	75.6	29.9	105.5
1870			17.0	1975	94.0	28.2	122.2
1900			30.0	1976	105.6	37.9	143.5
1945	18.0	3.8	21.8	1977	124.6	45.7	170.3
1946	12.1	12.8	24.9	1978	131.9	54.1	186.0
1948	19.5	9.9	29.3	1979	128.4	55.8	184.2
1950	19.6	13.2	32.8	1980	121.4	55.0	176.4
1952	18.7	11.9	30.6	1981	109.4	49.6	159.0
1954	22.2	10.8	33.0	1982	102.6	43.9	146.5
1956	31.3	13.0	44.3	1983	109.9	49.6	159.5
1958	27.6	13.1	40.7	1984	125.3	62.8	188.1
1960	35.4	13.9	49.3	1985	122.6	72.8	195.4
1962	42.5	15.4	57.9	1986	129.5	75.4	204.9
1964	52.1	18.2	70.3	1987	136.4	81.5	217.9
1966	64.9	22.0	86.9	1988	147.3	90.0	237.3
1968	60.0	26.5	86.5	1989	154.6	94.3	248.9
1970	71.2	31.1	102.3	1990	147.6	84.8	232.4
1972	83.4	39.7	123.1	1991	138.8	75.6	214.4
1973	80.5	44.2	124.7	1992	140.8	73.4	214.2

1920s. Sales of champagne had peaked at 39 million bottles in 1910, but fell back to 12 million bottles in 1921. Export markets, particularly the United States, continued to decline strongly in the 1930s. In the same period, the Champagne region produced bumper harvests. In 1934, the harvest was equivalent to 102 million bottles, compared to sales of 27 million bottles. Stocks

	Million Bottles					**Price**		
	1988	1989	1990	1991	1992	1990	1991	1992
UK	20.65	22.79	21.29	14.02	14.66	69.8	74.5	67.3
Germany	12.31	12.95	14.24	14.05	13.61	71.5	78.2	73.8
US	14.51	13.67	11.67	10.19	10	81.7	90.2	86.6
Italy	8.43	9.11	9.63	9.04	8.12	88.1	98.1	94.8
Switzerland	8.56	9.32	8.6	6.31	6.43	75.9	81.5	76.2
Belgium	5.45	5.87	5.89	5.24	5.77	69.5	72.0	67.2
Netherlands	1.59	1.99	1.65	1.7	1.46	70.1	75.4	71.2
Spain	0.89	0.95	0.98	0.91	1.02	88.2	95.7	93.7
Japan	0.77	1.29	1.51	1.43	1.02	110.6	110.3	104.4
Australia	1.37	1.59	1.23	0.83	0.88	87.9	91.3	84.7
Others	15.47	14.79	8.1	11.89	10.47			
Total	90.0	94.3	84.8	75.6	73.4			

EXHIBIT 2
Export markets: volumes (million bottles) and Ex-cellar prices (FF)

Source: CIVC.

reached 150 million bottles in 1934, over five years' supply. The price of grapes crashed to FF 1.3 a kilo (the equivalent of FF 4.3 in 1993). Despite attempts to lower the surplus through sales of cheap table wine, there was still more stock than the market could absorb.

The growers were starving and showed their anger by rioting in the streets of Reims, the capital of the Champagne region. The government and professional bodies took action: a decree of 28th September 1935 limited the yield per hectare of vineyard and specified production quantities. The surplus began to reduce.

During the occupation of France by Germany, a professional body was created to represent both growers and producers: the 'Comité, Interprofessionel du Vin de Champagne (CIVC).' The organization was given the task of negotiating with the occupying forces. The committee chose to adopt a wider role, however. It attempted to stabilize the relationship between growers and houses and acted as a center of information and research on the industry. Pricing agreements were established in 1959. Growers committed to selling a fixed percentage of their output to the champagne houses at prices set by the CIVC for periods of up to six years. The agreements were the beginning of a new period of prosperity and stability.

This stability was shaken in 1971 when Moët & Chandon, then controlling 25 percent of the

market, merged with the cognac firm Hennessy and later took over the House of Dior. The era of the multinational 'luxury goods' company had arrived in Champagne. Other houses rushed to acquire perfume or similar luxury good producers. Moët-Hennessy itself embarked on a series of acquisitions of established champagne houses, such as Mercier and Ruinart. Reflecting on the wave of changes in the industry, Christian Bizot, President of Bollinger observed in L'expansion April 18 1991: 'We are moving towards a Champagne of two speeds. On one side the Finance-Industrialists, for whom champagne is an investment like any other. On the other the family houses with vineyards, concerned about the image of the wine.'

However, the industry weathered the ownership changes and even held together during the economic downturn of the 1970s when drastic measures were taken: grape prices at FF 19.5 a kilo and maximum yields at 7,500 kg/ha. Industry observers gave a lot of credit to the industry association, CIVC, and the way in which the industry had managed itself: 'Industry associations are the only way for agricultural sectors to succeed. The CIVC is an obvious and envied proof. But success is never definitively achieved. It only continues so long as it is managed with a spirit of compromise and fairness' (Yves Bonnet, Government Commissioner).

Structure of the Champagne Industry

Organization

By 1993, there were 15,000 registered grape growers (*récoltants*) who together controlled 87 percent of the vineyards. Of these, 10,500 were member-owners of one of the 145 cooperatives through which they had access to champagne production. Around 8000 of the growers had less than one hectare of land. The growers were key to champagne's 'culture of the vine': more than in any other wine region, small plots were given individual care (e.g. immediate attention after storms). Some of the champagne houses which owned considerable areas of land trusted the management of their vineyards to a large number of independent (but salaried) growers, in order to achieve the required intensity of care.

The cooperatives processed 40 percent of Champagne's grapes, but directly sold only eight percent of their bottles. Thirty-eight made and commercialized their own wine. The majority of their output was commercialized through the growers or houses. The cooperatives were considered to be the prime movers of Champagne's cheapest wines ('the premier prix').

Some of the growers had themselves integrated into the production of champagne: the *récoltants-manipulants* (grower-producers). In 1950 there had been only 1450 with 2.5 million bottles of production. By 1992 they numbered

EXHIBIT 3
Shipments of the producers, cooperatives and growers (million bottles and % of total)

	France			Exports			Total			Overall total
	Producers	Coops	Growers	Producers	Coops	Growers	Producers	Coops	Growers	
1984	68.5	11.1	45.7	59.8	1.5	1.5	128.3	12.6	47.2	188.1
1985	65.8	9.3	47.6	68.7	2.2	1.9	134.5	11.5	49.5	195.5
1986	67.2	9.7	52.6	70.6	2.6	2.2	137.8	12.3	54.8	204.9
1987	72.3	11.5	52.6	75.5	3.5	2.5	147.8	15.0	55.1	217.9
1988	78.0	12.0	57.3	83.3	4.0	2.6	161.3	16.0	59.9	237.2
1989	80.7	12.4	61.5	86.7	4.1	3.5	167.4	16.5	65.0	248.9
1990	74.8	11.9	60.8	78.4	3.0	3.4	153.2	14.9	64.2	232.3
1991	70.6	9.8	58.4	70.2	2.7	2.7	140.8	12.5	61.1	214.4
1992	77.4	12.9	50.4	67.5	3.4	2.5	144.9	16.3	52.9	214.1

	France			Exports			Total			Overall total
	Producers	Coops	Growers	Producers	Coops	Growers	Producers	Coops	Growers	
1984	0.36	0.06	0.24	0.32	0.01	0.01	0.68	0.07	0.25	188.1
1985	0.34	0.05	0.24	0.35	0.01	0.01	0.69	0.06	0.25	195.5
1986	0.33	0.05	0.26	0.34	0.01	0.01	0.67	0.06	0.27	204.9
1987	0.33	0.05	0.24	0.35	0.02	0.01	0.68	0.07	0.25	217.9
1988	0.33	0.05	0.24	0.35	0.02	0.01	0.67	0.07	0.25	237.2
1989	0.32	0.05	0.25	0.35	0.02	0.01	0.67	0.07	0.26	248.9
1990	0.32	0.05	0.26	0.34	0.01	0.01	0.66	0.06	0.28	232.3
1991	0.33	0.05	0.27	0.33	0.01	0.01	0.66	0.06	0.28	214.4
1992	0.36	0.06	0.24	0.32	0.02	0.01	0.68	0.08	0.25	214.1

Source: SGV

EXHIBIT 4
Champagne sales of the major houses, 1991

	Employees	Sales (FF m)	% export	% in supermarkets	Sales (Bottles m)	% export
*LVMH**	—	5245	—	—	40.7	68.8%
Moët & Chandon	1541	2298	68.6%	50.0%	19.3	80.6%
Veuve Clicquot	na	619	81.4%	45.0%	7.4	85.0%
Canard Duchene	698	176	11.1%	81.0%	2.2	12.0%
Henriot	na	48	20.6%	very low	0.6	30.9%
Pommery	400	550	70.0%	30.0%	6.4	74.6%
Mercier	—	—	—	—	3.7	20.6%
Ruinart	—	—	—	—	1.3	20.0%
Marne & Champagne	433	1398	94.8%	67.6%	16.3	42.7%
Marne & Champagne	173	736	19.3%	92.7%	9.0	36.1%
Lanson	230	559	40.0%	47.0%	5.6	60.1%
Besserat de Bellefon	30	103	35.5%	very low	1.7	19.9%
*Seagram**	392	1280	43.0%	41.0%	11.5	58.8%
GH Mumm & Cie	—	—	—	—	7.6	58.3%
Perrier-Joët	—	—	—	—	2.6	65.0%
Heidsieck Monopole	—	—	—	—	1.3	50.0%
Laurent Perrier	—	1000	—	—	9.7	47.4%
Laurent Perrier	180	610	61.0%	22.0%	6.1	61.5%
Castellane	98	350	20.0%	50.0%	3.1	22.1%
Others	—	—	—	—	0.5	—
*Remy Cointreau**	337	632	65.0%	50.0%	6.5	70.0%
Piper-Heidsieck	—	—	—	—	2.7	66.4%
Krug	—	—	—	—	0.2	67.5%
Vranken	75	380	30.0%	66.0%	4.6	28.9%
Jacquart	98	365	20.0%	35.0%	4.0	15.2%
Tattinger	242	328	61.0%	24.3%	3.4	57.0%
Duval-Leroy	73	290	25.0%	60.0%	4.4	28.8%
Union Auboise	41	260	10.5%	80.0%	—	—
Roederer	150	255	65.5%	very low	2.4	64.5%
GH Martel & Cie	38	198	10.0%	90.0%	—	—
Bollinger	127	142	78.0%	4.5%	—	—
Bricout	49	129	22.0%	very low	—	—
Boizel	23	122	30.0%	70.0%	—	—
Deutz	100	117	40.0%	very low	—	—
De Cazanove	37	108	40.0%	70.0%	—	—
Pannier	35	107	14.0%	40.0%	—	—
De Venoge	57	106	40.0%	30.0%	—	—
Pol Roger	60	100	60.0%	very low	—	—
CVC de Chouilly	28	99	40.0%	65.0%	—	—

Source: LSA and Impact International.
* Total champagne sales — excluding other interests.

about 4500 representing 25 percent of total production (52.9 million bottles). The average sized vineyard was 2.5 hectares; only 80 produced more than 50,000 bottles per annum.

The 'négociants' or champagne houses numbered 261, up from 247 in 1988, and produced 145 million bottles of champagne in 1992. Twenty-eight were in the special club of high quality champagnes, 'the grandes marques.' The houses commercialized nearly 1200 different brands. In the post-war period, champagne production had concentrated among a smaller number of houses. In 1953, the 10 largest houses held 46 percent of champagne production. By 1993, this had increased to 52 percent (*Harpers* 'Champagne 1994'). The eight largest houses controlled over 80 percent of Champagne's sales in value. A number of multinational liquor groups either directly controlled or held stakes in most of the top ten houses. Exhibit 3 gives the breakdown of sales between the growers, cooperatives and producers. See Exhibit 4 for the market shares of the major players in 1992.

The 'Comité Interprofessionel du Vin de Champagne (CIVC)' was champagne's controlling body and consisted of six representative grape growers and six champagne houses. The main task of the CIVC was to organize the working relationship and agreements between the growers and producers. In addition, the organization coordinated training, research and information within the industry. The 1941 treaty, which founded the CIVC, specified four sanctions which the body could impose: fines, the withdrawal of professional licenses, confiscation of production and closure of production facilities.

One of the recent services of the CIVC was the provision of pricing information on all contracts between growers and producers through the French on-line information system, 'Minitel' (by dialing '3616 CIVC'). Contracts typically specified a commitment by a grower to supply a certain percentage of its crop to the houses at a price set or suggested by the CIVC. Before 1989, the price was set at approximately 34 percent to 36 percent of the average price of a bottle of house champagne during the previous season. The houses contracted to buy a certain percentage of their grape needs from the growers as a whole at the CIVC set price. The percentages varied between houses. After 1989 the CIVC issued 'indicative prices,' which were almost universally used as a reference in individual contracts. The actual price paid to a grower would be scaled by grape quality. Grapes could range from an 80 percent 'quality rating' (the lowest level) which would receive 80 percent of the reference price to a high of 100 percent 'quality rating.' The quality rating was a function of the area in the Champagne region where the grapes had been grown.

Major Champagne Makers

Louis Vuitton Moët-Hennessy LVMH's origins date back to the 1743. By 1993, it had transformed itself into the world's largest luxury goods group. Its champagne brands included Moët & Chandon, Veuve Clicquot, Pommery, Mercier, Canard-Duchene, and Ruinart. The Moët & Chandon brand was by far the world's most popular champagne, accounting for nearly 40 percent of all champagne export sales by volume and a higher percentage by value. Champagne and wines accounted for 24 percent of the FF 21.7 billion group sales in 1992. Cognac and spirits (Hennessy and Thomas Hine) represented 26 percent of sales, leather goods and luggage ('Louis Vuitton,' 'Loewe International' and 'The French Company') a further 22 percent, and perfumes ('Christian Dior,' 'Lacroix' and 'Givenchy') 25 percent. LVMH was also highly diversified internationally. Since the late eighties, LVMH has had a cross holding in Guinness to 24 percent.

The chairman of LVMH, Bernard Arnault, had brought a shock wave to the company and industry after his appointment in 1989. Arnault was credited with an Anglo-Saxon profit-oriented business style, gained during his three years in property development in the United States.[2] His

---

[2] On returning to France in 1983, he bought the bankrupt Willot textile empire from the French Government to acquire the Christian Dior fashion brand (Dior perfume was owned by Moët-Hennessey). Arnault promptly fired more than 8000 employees, including most of the headquarters staff.

vision for the future of LVMH was to dominate the luxury goods markets in which it was present and to exploit synergies in research (LVMH had a combined research center for problems in vine biotechnology, leather and other relevant interests), creativity (for instance Lacroix commissioned the development of new perfumes to Dior), sales network (sales force and distribution activities were to be rationalized), advertising (luxury goods need to be supported by large promotional budgets; LVMH's size would lead to greater negotiating power with the media).

Marne et Champagne   Founded in 1933, Marne et Champagne sold over 16 million bottles of champagne in 1992. The house, which sold the Marne et Champagne and Lanson brands, was the leader in budget champagnes and the most aggressive price cutter in the industry. Marne et Champagne had lead the way into 'Buyers Own Bottle' production, producing cheap champagne for retailers under a total of more than 300 brands. The company processed 22 million bottles of champagne in 1992, buying from more than 3000 growers.

Seagram   The Canadian wine and spirits group owned the champagne houses Mumm, Perrier-Joët and Heidsieck Monopole, and was in third place in the world rankings. Mumm, aimed at the upper middle segment, was Champagne's second most popular brand in 1992. Perrier-Joët was Seagram's mid-priced champagne and was growing more rapidly than the other two brands. Heidsieck Monopole was described as a 'fighting brand' but had not increased sales in three years. Paul Coureau, assistant general director was quoted in *Marketing*, May 1991, as saying: 'We want to grow in Champagne, but not at any price. If the financial situation deteriorates, we'll find opportunities.'

Laurent-Perrier   Laurent-Perrier was the most successful champagne producer of the post war period, rising from bankruptcy in 1938 to fourth in the world ranks with sales of nearly 10 million bottles of all its brands in 1992. In 1993, Grand Metropolitan acquired 21 percent of its stock.

Their involvement would bring improved distribution in markets where Laurent-Perrier was under-represented. However, Bernard de Nonancourt, the 73-year-old charismatic chairman, wanted the company to remain family controlled and managed. The company had recently moved into other wine investments (Bordeaux and Burgundy) but remained very much focused on champagne.

Rémy-Cointreau   Rémy owned the brands Krug (premium champagne), Charles Heidsieck (up market) and Piper Heidsieck (mass market) and was in fifth place in the world champagne rankings. The French headquartered drinks company derived 43 percent of its sales from cognac, 11 percent from champagne and 46 percent from other wines and spirits in 1992. Of turnover, 58 percent was in Europe, 12 percent in the US and 27 percent in the Far East. Rémy was heavily indebted after its purchase of Piper in October 1988 and needed cash flow to pay heavy interest charges. The company owned only four percent of its grape supplies and in January 1991 had signed a supply contract with Jacquart. The house had been quietly shedding its workforce since 1992.

Champagne Jacquart   Thirty growers in the Reims area wishing to have their own champagne production facilities formed Champagne Jacquart in 1962. In 1993, Jacquart was by far the largest cooperative, selling over 4 million bottles of champagne under its own brands. The house processed over 10 million bottles from 8000 growers and competed across the full range of champagne wines. Around a third of all sales were through mass-market outlets and 20 percent of the company's sales was made in export markets. Jacquart was completely self-sufficient in its grape needs and was unique among the cooperatives in having a stock market listing. In 1991, Jacquart signed a supply and distribution contract with Rémy Cointreau. Rémy benefited by increasing its provision of grapes, and Jacquart obtained international distribution.

EXHIBIT 5
Profitability of Champagne
Houses

Source: Banque de France
Survey of 70 Champagne
Houses

		1988	1989	1990	1991	1992
Gross operating margins	Industry	20.8%	23.6%	23.7%	21.9%	12.5%
	Small	11.1%	13.1%	18.2%	17.7%	5.8%
	Medium	15.4%	19.3%	22.7%	17.0%	9.1%
	Large	22.6%	25.3%	24.2%	23.2%	13.5%
Change in turnover	Industry	9.0%	12.9%	7.6%	−1.1%	−9.2%
	Small	18.2%	4.6%	18.2%	−5.6%	−3.6%
	Medium	12.1%	18.1%	10.7%	−1.2%	−6.6%
	Large	9.0%	12.2%	6.5%	−0.8%	−10.0%

EXHIBIT 6
The Economics of Champagne Production

	Champagne Growers			Champagne Houses		
	1990	1991	1992	1990	1991	1992
Variable Costs per Bottle (FF)						
Grape Growing	3.41	3.50	3.75	3.41	3.50	3.75
Price of Grapes				36.00	33.75	28.80
Cost of Grapes	3.41	3.50	3.75	31.33*	29.06*	25.20*
Pressing	0.61	0.68	0.77	0.61	0.68	0.77
Bottling	3.27	3.40	3.47	3.27	3.40	3.47
After Bottling	3.15	3.43	3.82	3.15	3.43	3.82
Total Variable Costs	10.43	11.01	11.80	38.36	36.57	33.26
Total Fixed Costs (FF 000)						
Grape Growing	2,563.064	2,467.355	2,709.859	428.141	452.677	454.403
Pressing	63.973	75.107	81.264	104.797	123.516	123.876
Bottling	38.384	41.750	41.004	62.878	68.661	62.505
After Bottling	499.305	567.939	608.682	817.938	934.002	927.855
Overhead						
Total Fixed Costs	3,369.699	3,375.218	3,686.680	3,425.972	3,741.875	4,177.731
Financial Charges (FF 000)	227.132	259.878	321.365	828.507	952.948	1,238.923

Source: Banque de France, SGV and case writers' estimate from various sources.
*weighted average.

Profitability

The profitability of the champagne houses in 1992 was at an all time low. Gross operating margins were only 12.5 percent for the industry as a whole, but varied greatly by size of company. In 1992, the Banque de France surveyed 50 champagne houses of three sizes: small (less than FF 50 million in sales), medium (between FF 50 million and FF 200 million sales) and large (greater than FF 200 million in sales). The results are shown in Exhibit 5.

Year	Price	% change	Year	Price	% change
1960	3.05	—	1977	7.98	%11.1
1961	3.04	−%0.5	1978	9.41	%17.9
1962	3.25	%7.1	1979	51.56	%22.8
1963	3.25	−%0.1	*1980	23.50	%103.3
1964	3.25	%0.0	**1981	20.00	−%14.9
1965	3.35	%3.1	1982	19.03	−%4.8
1966	4.00	%19.4	1983	15.53	−%18.4
1967	4.30	%7.5	1984	18.07	%16.4
1968	4.59	%6.7	1985	23.03	%27.4
1969	4.99	%8.7	1986	22.19	−%3.6
1970	4.88	−%2.2	1987	21.77	−%1.9
1971	5.42	%11.1	1988	22.80	%4.7
1972	6.65	%22.7	1989	27.00	%18.4
1973	8.37	%25.9	***1990	32.00	%18.5
1974	8.45	%1.0	***1991	30.00	−%6.3
1975	6.10	−%27.8	***1992	24.00	−%20.0
1976	7.18	%17.7			

* Including FFr 10 supplement for bad harvest.
** Including FFr 3 supplement for bad harvest.
*** Indicative CIVC price only.

EXHIBIT 7
Price of champagne grapes (nominal FF/kg)

Source: CIVC

	1–3 ha	3–5 ha	>5 ha	Average
Seeds and pesticide	8182	8998	7370	8363
Other agrochemicals	8282	8277	7836	8204
Materials	2206	2212	2430	2247
Maintenance	2104	1246	1297	1630
Salaries (harvest)	22,433	22,247	22,783	22,418
Total variable costs	*43,207*	*42,980*	*41,176*	*42,862*
Salaries (permanent)	16,598	27,728	45,839	25,984
Maintenance of vineyard	10,363	11,462	10,001	10,733
Depreciation (vines)	14,493	13,053	11,144	13,353
Depreciation (plantation)	3493	3545	3248	3472
Other fixed costs	501	829	743	669
Total fixed costs	*45,448*	*56,617*	*70,975*	*54,211*
Social security	36,377	25,516	19,048	29,140
Cost of production	*125,032*	*125,113*	*131,739*	*126,213*
Land rental	17,743	32,722	39,951	26,235
Total costs	*142,775*	*157,835*	*164,690*	*152,448*
Cost per kilo of harvest	11.93	13.27	13.87	12.78
Average yield (Kg/ha)	11,969	11,892	11,877	11,933
Estimated assets				42.500
Number sampled	266	145	69	480

Not included: financial and administrative charges and grower's income.

EXHIBIT 8
The costs of grape production in 1992 (FF/ha)

Source: Syndicat des Vignerons. Analyse de Groupe.

EXHIBIT 9
Stocks in the champagne industry

Source: CIVC.

As of mid year	Growers		Producers		Total	
	Bottles (m)	stocks/ sales	Bottles (m)	stocks/ sales	Bottles (m)	stocks/ sales
1962	52		148		200	
1963	52		153		205	
1964	66		169		235	
1965	79		183		262	
1966	73		188		261	
1967	77		185		262	
1968	92		194		286	
1969	95		199		294	
1970	91	3.4	191	2.5	282	2.8
1971	110	3.4	234	2.8	344	3.0
1972	110	3.2	227	2.6	337	2.7
1973	115	3.3	240	2.7	355	2.8
1974	146	4.4	284	3.9	430	4.1
1975	178	4.4	306	3.8	484	4.0
1976	180	3.8	300	2.8	480	3.1
1977	238	4.4	330	2.8	568	3.3
1978	252	4.2	323	2.5	575	3.0
1979	183	2.9	270	2.2	453	2.4
1980	215	3.5	289	2.5	504	2.8
1981	188	3.4	261	2.5	449	2.8
1982	168	3.2	224	2.3	392	2.6
1983	248	4.5	288	2.8	536	3.3
1984	348	5.8	315	2.5	663	3.5
1985	348	5.3	320	2.4	668	3.4
1986	279	4.5	344	2.5	623	3.1
1987	295	4.3	381	2.8	676	3.3
1988	312	4.3	410	2.6	722	3.1
1989	289	3.7	403	2.4	692	2.8
1990	305	3.6	420	2.5	725	2.9
1991	333	4.3	463	3.4	796	3.7
1992	359	5.2	504	3.5	863	4.1

Note: the stock includes the bottles in second fermentation, wine in blocage, and champagne bottles ready for sale.

The Economics of Champagne Production

The Appendix gives a brief description of the production process of champagne. Exhibit 6 provides an estimated breakdown of the production economics of the grower-producers (including cooperatives) and houses.

Raw materials

With three pressings, exactly 1.2 kg of grapes was required per bottle of champagne. The contracted price in 1992 was FF 24 per kilo, but had been as high as FF 32 per kilo in 1990. In that same year, grapes in the spot market had traded at close to FF 60 per kilo. See Exhibit 7 for the evolution of the grape prices and Exhibit 8 for the production cost of grapes.

By percentage of firms					
Age of stock	1988	1989	1990	1991	1992
Less than 2 years	22.9	19.1	13.9	11.1	20.2
From 2–3 years	42.7	42.6	33.3	18.5	19.0
From 3–4 years	21.3	20.6	25.0	28.4	15.2
More than 4 years	13.1	17.7	27.8	42.0	45.6
Total	100.0	100.0	100.0	100.0	100.0
Average age	3 yrs, 2 mths	3 yrs, 1 mth	3 yrs, 4 mths	4 yrs, 1 mth	4 yrs, 2 mths

EXHIBIT 10
Average age of stock held

Source: Banque de France

	1988	1989	1990	1991	1992
Interest charges/Value added	13.1%	14.1%	15.5%	16.4%	23.5%
Debt/Turnover	78.0%	73.7%	76.6%	86.5%	104.5%
Average cost of debt	9.1%	9.8%	10.4%	8.6%	9.5%
Short term debt/All debt	33.1%	24.0%	24.1%	31.3%	33.0%
Sales/Capital Employed	.75	.81	.79	.73	.61
Productive assets/sales	.34	.33	.34	.33	.40

EXHIBIT 11
Financial Figures
Champagne Houses

Source: Banque de France.

Finance charges

Interest charges cost the champagne houses around FF 1.2 billion in 1992. This was especially significant for the 'grandes marques' that kept older stocks. Regulations required that champagne be aged a total of 12 months, but many houses chose to age their wine at least three years (the minimum required for a 'grande marque'). Discussions in 1992 had been held to increase the minimum aging time to 15 months from the 12 months already set. However, no change was made. The exact level of stock was determined by the allowed harvest size, the quantity of grapes required to produce a litre of wine, and demand. The champagne houses had 504 million bottles in stock in 1992, or about 3.5 years of sales. The cooperatives held around 359 million bottles (including the reserve wine held in casks), or over five years of sales. See Exhibits 9 and 10 for additional data on the level of stocks.

Generally, banks offered lower interest rates on up to a quarter of the value of the stock and would finance another quarter at higher short-term rates. The houses financed the remainder of the stock from their own funds (Revve Francaise de comptabilite 1993). Increased stocks caused working capital requirements to rise by 6.8 percent in 1992 to a level equal to 590 days of sales. Interest payments accounted for 23.5 percent of value added in 1992, up from 15.5 percent in 1990 (see Exhibit 11). This was equivalent to 12.3 percent of industry turnover, more than double the average finance charges for the wine and spirits sector as a whole (5.4 percent of sales).

Salaries

Salaries were the largest operating expense of the champagne houses, accounting for 42 percent of added value in 1992. At an average salary of FF 223,000 per year, champagne workers were the highest paid in the wine business where the average was only FF 143,000. Although the number of

EXHIBIT 12
Sales and ex-cellar prices of the producers, cooperatives and growers

	Bottles (m)			Sales (FFm)			Price per Bottle			Totals		
	Houses	Coops	Growers	Houses	Coops	Growers	Houses	Coops	Growers	Bottles (m)	Sales (FFm)	Price
1986	137.8	12.5	54.6	8316.4	533.6	2249.9	60.3	42.7	41.2	204.9	11099.9	54.2
1987	147.8	14.7	55.3	8758.6	632.1	2239.4	59.3	43.0	42.1	217.8	11720.2	53.8
1988	161.4	15.8	60.1	9895.0	732.2	2622.2	61.3	45.8	43.6	237.3	13240.4	55.8
1989	167.4	16.3	65.2	11323.8	865.7	3000.4	67.6	53.3	46.0	248.9	15189.8	61.0
1990	153.2	14.9	64.2	11349.4	913.0	3274.4	74.1	61.1	51.0	232.4	15536.9	66.9
1991	140.8	12.5	61.1	11211.2	797.1	3358.7	79.6	63.5	55.0	214.4	15366.9	71.7
1992	144.9	16.3	52.9	10072.5	879.4	2964.4	69.5	53.9	56.0	214.2	13916.3	65.0

Average ex-cellar price of
a bottle of Champagne
(producer and coops only)

Year	Price	Year	Price
1960	8.38	1977	21.02
1961	8.68	1978	23.28
1962	9.01	1979	28.79
1963	9.34	1980	34.35
1964	9.51	1981	42.48
1965	9.62	1982	49.84
1966	10.20	1983	51.05
1967	11.26	1984	48.55
1968	11.56	1985	54.33
1969	12.27	1986	58.86
1970	13.09	1987	57.81
1971	13.84	1988	59.93
1972	15.83	1989	66.34
1973	19.08	1990	72.97
1974	21.67	1991	78.31
1975	18.80	1992	69.00
1976	19.36		

Source: CIVC, SGV.

employees was reduced in 1992 by 0.8 percent, salary costs continued to increase.

Pricing

Champagne commanded a premium price to most sparkling wines. The 'grandes marques' were careful to maintain a prestige image through pricing, positioning their product as a luxury good. The lower quality 'premier prix' champagnes were priced to compete with sparkling wine. Exhibit 12 shows the volume and price levels of the various types of champagne. See also Exhibit 2 for export prices.

EXHIBIT 13
Sparkling Wine
Consumption

	Champagne (m bottles)	Champagne (% total)	Sparkling Wine	Total (m bottles)
Germany	15.2	3%	491.1	506.3
US	10.9	5%	206.2	217.0
Italy	6.0	6%	103.6	109.6
UK	14.7	35%	27.2	41.9
Belgium	6.3	27%	17.0	23.2
Switzerland	7.3	40%	10.9	18.2

EXHIBIT 13
Sparkling Wine
Consumption

EXHIBIT 14
Sparkling wine from Spain, Germany and France (m bottles)

	Cava sparkling wine			German sekt			French 'Vin Mousseux'		
	Total	Spain	Export	Total	Germany	Export	Total	France	Export
1985	111.5	82.7	28.8	281.7	268.9	12.8			
1986	115.3	84.3	31.0	308.8	294.7	14.1			
1987	129.7	89.0	40.7	338.3	323.1	15.2			
1988	138.9	91.7	47.2	357.1	341.6	15.5			
1989	142.0	93.9	48.1	376.4	353.4	23.0	112.9	73.5	39.4
1990	139.7	92.5	47.2	423.8	400.6	23.2	115.8	77.8	38.0
1991	132.7	87.9	44.8	438.1	419.4	18.7	114.7	76.6	38.1
1992	130.6	85.2	45.4	452.3	434.1	18.2	126.6	85.6	41.0

Source: Burson Marsteller, Madrid; Verband Deutscher Sektkellereien.

The Challenge from Sparkling Wines and 'Petits Champagnes'

World-wide sales of sparkling wine had grown consistently over the last four decades, rising from a consumption of around 100 million bottles a year in the l950s (a third of which was champagne) to 560 million bottles in 1970 and 1.8 billion bottles in 1992 (an eighth of which was champagne). In France, high quality sparkling wine was up by 20 percent in 1992. Demand for home produced 'Sekt' in Germany continued 10 years of uninterrupted growth, even if export demand fell slightly from its peak in 1989 of 23 million bottles. Sparkling wine in the UK was in decline by seven percent in 1992, dominated by the fall in champagne sales. Demand for sparkling wine in the US increased two percent, largely to

the benefit of local producers, while imports fell. Exhibit 13 shows the importance of sparkling wine consumption in various countries. See also Exhibit 14.

Of particular concern to the 'champenois' were the Spanish produced Cava sparkling wines that had vastly improved their quality during the 1980s and achieved considerable success in the North American and European markets. Cava exports to the US grew from 11 million bottles in 1985 to 33 million in 1992 (around 17 percent of the sparkling wine market). In 1992 total world exports of Cava wines were around 45 million bottles, from a production of 130 million bottles.

The Spanish wine makers benefited from low costs and unrestricted vine planting.[3] The two

---

[3] Only around 25,000 ha of the 156,000 ha Catalonian district of Penedès was under vineyards in 1993.

EXHIBIT 15
Comparative Test Results for Champagne and Sparkling Wine

The French consumer magazine '50 Million de Consommateurs' conducted comparative 'blind' tests with French sparkling wine experts (50) and 'connaisseurs' (50) to evaluate:

1.) whether the experts and amateurs had a different judgement on the overall quality of sparkling wines, and

2.) whether champagne came out ahead of other sparkling wines. The wines were scored on 24 criteria (e.g. taste, colour, persistence of bubble, acid level). The table below provides an overall evaluation score of each wine as well as a comparable retail (FF) in 1991.

Champagne	Expert	Amateur	FF/bottle	Sparkling wine	Expert	Amateur	FF/bottle
Canard Duchene	12.9	11.2	100	*Saumur*			
Barancourt	12.6	10.2	98	Saumur	10.4	7.8	21.0
Jacquart	12.4	10.4	105	Gratien-Meyer	9.3	9.4	45.0
Dorgeval	12.1	12.3	77	Ackermann	9.0	9.0	28.0
Leclerc Briant	11.9	9.9	120	Cadre Noir	7.3	8.3	34.0
Perrier Jouet	11.9	10.5	140				
Laurent Perrier	11.7	11.0	98	*Alsace*			
Moet-Chandon	11.6	9.9	135	Dopff & Irion	12.7	9.1	48.0
Lanson	11.4	11.0	109	Kuentz-Bas	10.3	9.7	48.0
Rothschild	11.4	11.7	96	Laugel	9.9	9.9	38.0
Taittinger	11.1	11.3	120	Wolfberger	9.4	10.5	36.0
P. Larson	11.0	11.7	73				
Veuve Clicquot	11.0	11.0	133	*Limoux*			
Gimonnet	10.6	9.1	129	Aimery	9.1	8.6	24.0
Mercier	10.4	11.3	86				
Mumm	10.4	10.2	134	*Bourgogne*			
Veuve Emile	10.3	11.2	78	Charmelieu	9.1	10.1	35.0
Pommery	10.1	10.2	121	A. Delorm	8.1	9.1	47.0
Delafon	10.0	9.6	73				
J. Vesselle	10.0	10.5	135	*Vouvray*			
Lafitte	10.0	9.4	91	G. Huet	9.0	11.0	45.0
Feuillate	9.9	12.3	102	Vouvray	8.6	9.3	52.0
Duval Leroy	9.7	10.5	97				
Piper Heidsieck	9.4	9.7	115	*Spain*			
De Castellane	8.3	9.4	102	Freixenet	9.7	8.6	36.0
F. Delacour	7.4	9.4	88	Courdoniu	8.0	9.3	31.0

Source: 50 Million de Consommateurs, January 1992, #246.

largest Cava producers, Codorniu and Freixenet sold over 100 million bottles in 1990, a far larger production than the largest of Champagne's houses. In the previous decade several producers had made determined efforts to emulate champagne's level of quality, but at low retail prices.

Pedro Bonet, marketing director of Freixenet explained his firm's focus: 'Maintaining a top price-quality relationship has been a key to our success.'

The French champagne houses themselves commenced production of sparkling wine at the beginning of the 1970s. Moët & Chandon was the first house to do so, acquiring a vineyard in California in 1976. Eight other champagne houses (Mumm, Roederer, Taittinger, Piper-Heidsieck, Deutz, Pommery, Bollinger and Laurent-Perrier) were to follow. Michel Villedey, president of Bollinger, explained the move into US production in 1989 in *Business Week*, December 11: 'We're only a few years away from maximum output [in France] and we don't want to just go to sleep.' The US was not the only center to receive the attentions of the 'grandes marques'; they also expanded production into Australia, Latin America and Spain. The quality and size of vineyards and the potential for reducing costs attracted Moët, which saw its foreign production moving toward 50 percent in 1989. Grape prices in Spain were less than 10 percent of those in France. The champagne houses promoted their new world production as a prestige product. Labelling and bottles similar to the domestically produced wine were used. Although at pains to avoid the use of the word 'champagne' on their sparkling wine, they adopted French sounding brands, such as Moët's Californian 'Domaine Chandon.'[4] Bottles of 'grandes marques' sparkling wine typically sold for half to two thirds the price of the imported product. Domaine Chandon sold 4.2 million bottles and Mumm Napa 1.4 million bottles in 1992.[5] Several commentators thought that the grandes marques were responsible for promoting a switch to sparkling wines. Gary Heck, chairman of US sparkling wine producer Korbel, commented: 'The French have legitimized US-made champagne.'

Elsewhere, the 'grandes marques' were battling against the champagnes of the cooperatives and cheap own-brands in supermarkets. These wines were considerably cheaper than the 'grandes marques' but the quality of the grower and coop-produced champagnes was high in relation to their price. The director-general of Mumm, Philippe Pascal, commented after tastings by his

company's experts in 1993: 'I was surprised by their level of quality. Four of the bottles were good even in comparison to Mumm and Moët & Chandon. Three years ago this would not have been possible.' Exhibit 15 also describes the results of a similar tasting among amateurs and professionals.

Some of Champagne's most traditional houses launched secondary, lower quality brands known as 'petits champagnes.' Taittinger re-introduced a brand called 'Irroy' in 1992, a product which the company had first sold in the 1860's but had left without promotion for many years. Irroy retailed at 25 percent less than the flagship Taittinger brand. The re-launch was judged so successful that Taittinger developed a new cheap champagne, 'Saint-Evremond.' Philippe Court, chief executive of Taittinger explained: 'There have always been secondary champagnes, just as there are second or third pressings of Bordeaux. The secondary brands come out at certain times and then disappear. We decided that the time was right to bring them out again' (*Financial Times*, June 10 1993). Others saw the petits champagne as a new permanent feature of the champagne market. Observed Michel de Nonancourt, Financial Director of Laurent-Perrier: 'Through these marques we are battling against the premier prix champagnes found in the supermarkets. We do not intend these new entrants to gain a permanent hold in the market.'[6]

The champenois were also determined to protect the name of their product from other uses. In some parts of the world, notably in the US and Australia, 'champagne' can be used as a generic description of sparkling wine.[7] In the EU the name was far more protected. The producers recently obtained a prohibition on the labeling 'méthode champenoise' within the EU. In 1993 the UK courts banned the sale of a sparkling alcoholic drink, called 'elderflower champagne,' made from flowers grown in the South of England, upholding the CIVC's case that the name

---

[4] In Spain Moët produced 'Chandon' in Germany, Argentina and Australia the house produced 'M. Chandon.'

[5] They were still small compared to the US market leader Gallo Winery, which sold 65 million bottles.

[6] In interview, June 22nd 1994.

[7] To classify as 'champagne' in Australia, the wine needed only to be fermented in the bottle and be aged at least six months.

'champagne' belonged exclusively to its members and the French region.

The battle to protect champagne's name has not been restricted to drinks. When Yves Saint Laurent launched a new perfume in 1993 called 'Champagne,' it was immediately met with legal action by the houses, which succeeded in forcing the name to be removed in France. However, YSL had one of the most successful perfume launches of all time. For a perfume to be profitable in its first year was extremely rare, but 'Champagne' achieved just that, with 1993 revenues of $39 million against marketing expenses of $17 million.

Crisis in the Early 1990s – The Bubble Burst

In 1989, champagne achieved record sales of 249 million bottles. In the same year the collective agreements held in September between growers and producers collapsed. The grape growers saw an opportunity to capture more of the large retail margins for themselves by producing more of their own champagne. Given the strictly limited area of vineyards, they would need to keep more of the grape production for themselves. Others saw the opportunity to capture higher prices by selling later into the spot market. In negotiations over the collective agreement, the growers reduced the proportion of the crop they were prepared to sell to the champagne houses who were only able to buy 83 percent of their predicted sales. No deal was struck and, for the first time in over 40 years, pricing was left to the free market.

The rush to provide champagne was made with little regard to quality. Most of the new production was made by producers with little experience and was aged the legal minimum of one year. Lower quality seemed to matter little in a market where demand was consistently above supply.

The negotiations in September 1990 were little short of chaotic. Few of the industry's players had any real experience of negotiating with one another. Individual contracts posed a bureaucratic nightmare to many of the firms. Laurent-Perrier, for instance, found itself negotiating over a two-week period with 1,200 individual growers. In these circumstances, it was not surprising that grape prices began to soar from around FF 27 per kilo in 1989 to around FF 60 per kilo in 1990 in a few contracts (The reference price was FF 32 per kilo). Rather than capitalize on these high prices, many growers continued with their plans to commence champagne production. The producers of the grandes marques reacted to the increased costs by raising the prices of their champagne by around 20 percent in 1990. The price rises were introduced at the point the world economy was slipping into recession and the start of military tensions in the Gulf. Consequently, champagne consumption fell for the first time in nearly a decade, by seven percent. Simultaneously, grape prices fell to FF 30 per kilo in 1991.

Despite signs that demand would continue to fall, and the growing presence of cheap champagne on the markets, the grandes marques further raised prices by around 10 percent in 1991. Most saw this as the only way to maintain profitability and champagne's prestige position. Claude Taittinger of Champagne Taittinger was quoted in 1991 as saying: 'We must settle for increasing our prices, our quality and our image, rather than our quantity,' (*International Management* 1991), but warned that champagne producers must be careful not to exceed a price where customers would begin substituting: 'Just as countries turned to alternative energy sources, people will turn to alternative sparkling wine.' Bernard de la Giraudière, Laurent-Perrier's joint managing director looked back on the events of 1991 (in the *Wall Street Journal* December 30 1992): 'Consumers simply refused to accept repeated price increases.' Demand for champagne continued to fall.

In January 1991 the French food and beverage company, BSN-Danone, decided to exit the champagne business, selling its Pommery and Lanson businesses to LVMH for FF 3.1 billion (39 times 1990 earnings). LVMH promptly sold the Lanson brand to Allied Lyons and Marne et Champagne for FF 1.6b but kept the 500 acres of

EXHIBIT 16
Price of Vine Growing Land
in Champagne

Average per hectare in thousand French Francs	Planted		Unplanted	
	1991	1992	1991	1992
Cote d'Epernay	1500	2000	950	1000
Cote de Blancs	2000	2500	1000	1250
Grande Valley de la Marne	1250	1800	800	1400
Region de Cogny Sazanne	1000	1100	800	1100
Grande Montagne	1000	1250	600	900
Petite Montagne Sect. Ouest	700	800	400	400
Vallee de la Vesle	550	700	500	600
Nogent L'Abbesse	550	700	500	600
Vitry le Francois	700	850	1100	1200
Vallee de la Marne	1100	1200	500	650
– Close to Epernay	1200	1300	800	900
– Close to Dormans	1000	1100	450	550
Vallee de L'Ardre	600	800	300	400

EXHIBIT 17
Wine in 'blocage' (reserve
stock) in million bottles

	Total	Growers	Houses
1986	21.1*	13.7*	7.4*
1987	—	—	—
1988	—	—	—
1989	—	—	—
1990	—	—	—
1991	—	—	—
1992	67.1	39.2	27.9

*released in 1988.

acquired vineyards to increase its grape provision (see Exhibit 16 for prices of champagne vineyards).

The collapse of the collective agreements and the ballooning stocks provided an opportunity to firms wishing to buy finished champagne. In the regulated market before 1989, each house was served with a quantity of grapes according to its sales the previous year. After 1989 there were no such restrictions. The glut of champagne triggered the prominence of 'champagne speculators', most notably the Belgian Vranken. Hervé Augustin, managing director of Champagne de Castellane commented: 'The stock is spoiling the whole position. When it is in surplus, there is always some company who will upset the equilibrium by offering at too low a price. Stock regulates the market, and prices are going down day by day.'

In 1992, the CIVC attempted to limit the supply of grapes and champagne but achieved only limited success. In previous harvests, 4000 kilos of grapes were pressed to produce the 'cuvée' (premium wine) of 2050 litres. Pressed a second and third time, the grapes yielded another 410 litres and 205 litres, respectively. This led to a ratio of 150 kg of grapes for each 100 litres of wine. In 1992, the third pressing of grapes[8] at harvest time

---

[8] See the appendix for the production process of champagne.

was suspended. This increased the amount of grapes to 160 kg required to produce 100 litres of wine.

Furthermore the CIVC negotiated the re-introduction of a 'blocage' or reserve stock of champagne, last used in the bumper crops of 1982, 1983 and 1986. Only 9,000 kilos of grapes per hectare would be fully processed into bottles. The rest (67 million bottles equivalent of wine) would be held in tanks at the champagne houses, cooperatives and growers but financed entirely by the growers until officially released (See Exhibit 17 for the amount of wine in reserve stocks). Typically, blocage was released within four years. For example, the 1986 blocage was released in 1988.

Lower sales and higher costs, particularly interest payments, forced the houses into redundancy programs. Mumm and Piper Heidsieck laid off 12–15 percent of their workforce in 1992. Moët & Chandon fired 245 staff. Furthermore, LVMH's Director General Bernard Arnault called in the management consulting firm McKinsey and warned his managers to cut overheads, before he 'got McKinsey to do it for them.' In December 1992, in the *Wall Street Journal* Jean-Claude Rouzaud, Head of Louis Roederer observed: 'Most champagne makers are operating at a loss. If things continue like this for much longer, a lot of houses will be in serious trouble.'

The grandes marques, including Moët and Taittinger, attempted to stimulate demand in the Christmas period with advertising campaigns. The promotions were judged to have had little effect; the houses cut prices even further.[9] Noted Phillipe Court of Taittinger: 'Taittinger has reduced prices along with the other houses. We might not like it, but we had no choice.'

Despite the promotional efforts, champagne sales only reached 214 million bottles in 1992, equal to the previous year's sales. In early 1993, Moët & Chandon announced 'temporary' price decreases of 10 percent in France, Germany and Switzerland, but also five percent price increases in the UK, Spain and Italy, in order to 'correct for recent currency movements.'

Some industry observers thought that champagne's problems could be traced to a shift in consumer lifestyles. Says Phillipe Pascal, Mumm's managing director: 'People have fundamentally changed their behavior. It is cocooning, it is family values. I want a nice home for my children, and I spend less time in fancy bars and clubs. We really are in a watershed period' (*Wall Street Journal*, December 30 1992). Jean-Claude Damay, a consultant to the champagne industry believed that the marketing of champagne had confused this changing group of customers: 'The consumer has deduced that champagne is a superfluous product, which one can do without. We have entered an era where the "price-quality" ratio comes first.'[10]

March 1993: A Crisis Meeting

In March 1993, an extraordinary meeting of the CIVC was convened, with formal consent of the French Ministry of Agriculture, to address the champagne crisis. Six champagne houses and six growers were part of the consultative committee. The main topic under discussion was the surplus and whether a three-year plan could be put into place before the harvest 'for the good of the whole champagne trade.' Stocks were at record levels: about 900 million bottles.[11]

Experts judged that the crop of 1993 could well be 'gigantic' (some thought that a 430 million bottle crop was possible (*Harpers* March 25 1993)).

[9] Average price cuts in 1992 were 12.1 percent and sales were down 9.2 percent. The Banque de France estimated that value added by the industry was a third less in 1992 than in 1991.

[10] 'Le défi du champagne: conjuger fête et crise', 1993.

[11] The growers were: Marc Brugnon, president of the Syndicat General des Vignerons, Daniel Berat, grower at Belval-sous-Chatillon, Roger Closquinet, grower at Vinay, Phillipe Feneuil, Grower at Chamery, Yves Jolly, Grower at Ville-sur-Arce and Jean Mary Tarlant, grower at Oeuilly. Representing the négotiants were: Jean-Michel Ducellier, president de l'Union des Maisons de Champagne and chairman of Ayala champagne, Yves Bénard of Moët & Chandon, Francois-Xavier Mora of Lanson, Philippe Pascal of G H Mumm, Jean-Claude Rouzaud of Roederer and Claude Taittinger of Taittinger.

The champagne houses were open in their anxiety about the rising level of stock: 'To accumulate stocks, even if not in bottles (the blocage), has the consequence of slowing the end of the crisis,' claimed Jean-Claude Rouzaud of Roederer. Rouzaud further reminded members of the growers' association that the champagne houses had FF 10 billion of debt in 1993, equivalent to one entire year's revenue for the industry.

The following issues were on the agenda of the March meeting:

1   The price that would be paid for grapes (the 'reference price' in 1992, set at the beginning of the harvest as a 'general guide to pricing' was FF 24 per kilo).

2   The percentage of the growers' production which they would contract to sell to the champagne houses (in 1992 it had been 53.2 percent). All such agreements were made directly between the growers and houses.

3   The maximum allowable yield of grapes ('rendement') per hectare (the limit was 11,900 kilos per hectare in 1992). The limit was negotiated with the French government agency responsible for the certification ('Institut nationale des appelations d'origines') of the various wines in France. Yields above this level could not be used to make champagne. They were either made into non-appelation wines or pressed and stored to mix with the next year's harvest in case of a poor growing season.

4   The use of reserve stocks ('blocage') of wine (in 1992 all grapes over 9000 kg per hectare, up to the maximum of 11,900 kg per hectare could be stored – a measure which resulted in the equivalent of about 67 million bottles being blocked).

5   Use of the second and third pressing of grapes. In 1992 the third pressing had been suspended and the second pressing had been limited to 500 litres of juice from each 4000 kg of grapes). This reduced the yield of the 1992 harvest by 4.5 percent or 9.6 million litres of wine. 160 kg of grapes was therefore required for each 100 litres of wine in 1992.

On March 8, representatives of both sides of the industry met in the town hall of Epernay. Outside, a crowd of young grape growers had gathered to shout at the authorities, 'for the second time in 40 years,' according to a local police commissioner. One displayed a large pile of grapes with the message 'For sale! Unsold!' Could an agreement be worked out that would satisfy the champagne houses and growers alike? Would stability return to the relationship or was a deepening of the crisis inevitable?

Appendix: The production of champagne

The Champagne region provides an ideal environment on which to grow the various grape varieties required for the wine. In addition to the excellent drainage and mineral supply of the chalk soils, the climate is very mild (average temperatures of 10c are above the 9c minimum required to ripen grapes). Chalk soils have provided another bonus to the local evolution of the industry. The ease with which the area can be excavated has led to the construction of over 250 km of storage caves – in which is currently stored nearly 1 billion bottles of champagne.

The timeline for the production of champagne is shown in the simplified picture given below. After the harvest, the grapes are pressed into juice and, after filtering, into wine. There are three varieties of grapes: Chardonnay (white), Pinot noir and Meunier (both black grapes). The wines are blended according to the desired flavor of the champagne. The precise mixture is a carefully guarded secret of each champagne house. In 1992, 4,000 kilos of grapes were pressed to produce the 'cuvée' (or premium wine) of 2,050 litres. Pressed a second time, the grapes yielded an additional amount of juice ('premiere taille') of 410 litres. The grapes could be pressed a third time to produce the 'deuxieme taille' of 205 litres. The three-step pressing of the 4000 kilos of grapes produced a total of 2666 litres of wine (150 kg of grapes for each 100 litres of wine).

Following the first fermentation of the wine in casks, which lasted only a few weeks, the wine

EXHIBIT 18
Timeline for Champagne
Production

Source: CIVC.

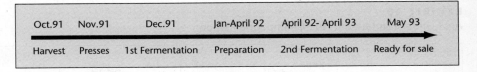

Oct.91	Nov.91	Dec.91	Jan-April 92	April 92- April 93	May 93
Harvest	Presses	1st Fermentation	Preparation	2nd Fermentation	Ready for sale

EXHIBIT 19
Yield of Grapes per Hectare
1940–1992

Period	Yield (kilos per hectare)	Period	Yield (kilos per hectare)
1940–1949	3,760	1980–1984	9,559
1950–1959	4,990	1985–1989	10,262
1960–1969	7,580	1990	11,960
1970–1974	9,111	1991	11,200
1975–1979	7,689	1992	11,900

was bottled with a small dose of natural yeast and sugar, leading to secondary fermentation in the bottle and the characteristic bubbles. A minimum storage time of one year was required before the champagne could be prepared for sale. During this period a sediment developed in the bottle, which was removed by a process called 'dégorgement'. The bottles were turned slowly and raised over a period of eight days for mechanical operations or several weeks for manual operations until the sediment gathered in the neck of the bottle. The top of the bottle was then frozen, and the cork and 'ice plug' (containing the sediment) removed. Each bottle was then topped up with additional champagne, containing an amount of sugar dependent on the desired sweetness of the champagne (brut, sec or demi-sec). After re-corking and labeling the champagne was ready for sale.

Although the yearly production of champagne is governed by nature, improved methods of viniculture and resistant grape varieties have steadily increased the yield of grapes per hectare (see Exhibit 19).

The laws of 'appelation' limited the maximum harvest to 11,900 kg per hectare in 1992. Annually, each wine region in France, negotiated with the French government agency responsible for the origin certification ('appelation contrôlée') to set the amount of kilos of grapes per hectare

that would be accepted as 'appelation' from the region. Any grapes over this limit were either pressed and stored until the following year to mix with the new harvest, were destroyed or were made into non-appelation wine.

The area under plantation in the Champagne region had been consistently on the increase since the 1920s (see Exhibit 20). The maximum area of land available for legal grape production in the champagne region was 35,000 hectares. From planting, a new vineyard required three seasons until it produced grapes of usable quality and six years until it produced a normal yield. Vines had a usable lifetime of 30 years.

Given the limited amount of land, the bargaining about the share of the harvest had been quite intense. The following gives the percentage of the harvest that the houses had purchased in each year since 1988:

Year	% bought*
1988	51.3
1989	50.7
1990	47.7
1991	50.1
1992	53.2

*Includes purchases of wine ('vins clairs')

EXHIBIT 20
Area Under Plantation in the Champagne Region

year	ha	year	ha	year	ha	year	ha	growers	houses
1832	20,000	1900	14,209	1939	7,909	1987	25,646	22,710	3,511
1869	16,500	1910	13,400	1941	8,556	1988	26,221	22,685	3,536
1877	16,401	1920	5,900	1950	10,450	1989	27,088	23,596	3,492
1882	16,500	1922	5000	1960	11,870	1990	27,542	23,600	3,942
1886	14,311	1930	8,360	1970	18,050	1991	27,943	23,611	4,332
1890	14,299	1933	8,490	1980	23,900	1992	28,515	24,420	4,095
1895	15,466	1935	8,986	1986	25,427	1993	30,919*		

Source: CIVC.
*estimate.

References

Revue Française de Compatabilité (1993) Les Stocks de Champagne: Un Mal Nécessaire, February.
International Management (1991) Champagne's Bubble Bursts, May.

Case 16: The National Bicycle Industrial Company: Implementing a Strategy of Mass-customization

By Suresh Kotha and Andrew Fried[1]

A group of senior managers, including the Managing Director of the National Bicycle Industrial Co. (NBIC), a subsidiary of Japanese industrial giant Matsushita, were reflecting upon the success of their firm over the last few years. NBIC is a leading manufacturer of bicycles. In 1987, the firm introduced the most innovative and revolutionary production system the Japanese bicycle industry had ever seen. The system, named the *Panasonic Order System* (POS), employed state-of-the-art techniques in bicycle production to manufacture 'custom-made' bicycles. Using robots, computers, and skilled workers, the system blends human skills and advanced manufacturing automation to allow potential customers to custom-order bicycles. When ordering a custom-made bicycle, customers can choose from about eight million possible variations based on model type, color, frame sizes, and other features. Using this system the firm delivers a high-quality 'crafted' bicycle within two weeks of the customer's order.

With the introduction of POS the firm gained national and international attention and became the envy of the industry. In 1992, General Motors Corporation, the world's largest manufacturing firm, sent a team of executives to study the firm's 'mass-customization' strategy and its implementation through the POS.[2]

Despite the firm's growing recognition, the senior management group was considering changes in the firm's mass-customization strategy. To explore what changes were required by senior management, and the questions they might raise, this case looks at the Japanese bicycle industry, NBIC's strategy and position within that industry, and the nature of issues facing the company during mid-1993.

The Japanese Bicycle Industry

The Japanese bicycle industry's history dates from the Meiji restoration period, which began around 1868. It was during this period that European-styled bicycles were first introduced into Japan. During the Meiji restoration, Japan's governing body and its government began modeling the Japanese political system after Western governments. The State, to end its isolation from the rest of world, encouraged foreigners to visit Japan.

As foreigners arrived in Japan, they brought with them their bicycles. When these bicycles needed repairs, they sought the assistance of hunting gun repair shops, established during the earlier Tokugawa period. These small shops, in and around cities like Tokyo and Osaka, began to fix bicycles. Skills acquired with pipes and screws to produce guns during the Tokugawa period enabled shop owners to apply their talents to service and repair bicycles. Over time these small repair shops began to produce bicycles modeled after European bicycles. The first domestic bicycle frame was manufactured in 1889, exactly 29 years after the invention of the bicycle by Pierre Michaux in France. Slowly, this gave rise to the Japanese bicycle industry (JETO 1990).

---

[1] Source: This case was prepared by Assistant Professor Suresh Kotha of the Stern School of Business, NYU while visiting at IUJ and research assistant Andrew Fried of IUJ, as the basis for class discussion rather than to illustrate either effective or ineffective handling of an administrative situationn. Some field research was provided in the early stages of the project by Ken Zekavat. Copyright © 1993 Suresh Kotha.

[2] The term 'mass-customization' was first coined by Stanley M. Davis in *Future Perfect* (Reading, Mass.: Addison-Wesley, 1987).

EXHIBIT 1
Bicycle demand in Japan
1982–1992 (units, 000s)

Source: Japan Bicycle
Manufacturer's Association.

Year	Production	Shipment (1)	Export (2)	Import (3)	Total Demand (1−2+3)
1982	6,532	6,624	674	13	5,963
1983	7,039	6,996	864	6	6,138
1984	6,810	6,839	856	28	6,011
1985	6,785	6,808	888	40	5,960
1986	6,583	6,638	682	158	6,114
1987	7,379	7,742	416	580	7,636
1988	7,509	7,624	325	900	8,119
1989	7,792	7,881	200	857	8,538
1990	7,969	8,033	226	667	8,474
1991	7,448	7,416	203	940	8,153

EXHIBIT 2
Bicycle production by type
(000s units)

Source: Japan Bicycle
Promotion Institute.

	1984	1985	1986	1987	1988	1989	1990	1991
Roasters	57	42	37	38	35	38	35	27
Light cycles	916	1017	1339	2296	2893	3486	3694	3511
Sports cycles	1465	1304	999	883	761	562	501	405
Juvenile cycles	756	795	726	770	772	770	788	747
Children*	566	565	542	546	555	520	527	477
Mini cycles	2871	2753	2687	2570	2192	2065	1822	1426
Others**	181	308	254	275	301	350	602	855

* Geared towards preschool children with 12"–16" wheels. The standard size bicycle had wheels which were 26 or 27 inches.
** Includes adults tricycles, motorcross bikes, mountain bikes, high-risers, heavy weight load-carrying bicycles, track racing bikes, bicycles for acrobatics, etc.

Bicycle demand in Japan grew rapidly in the early 1970s due to the robust growth in the economy and the resulting strong consumer demand. Several environmental changes including the growth of suburban residential areas and the building of large shopping areas in the periphery of cities contributed to an increase in bicycle demand. The bicycles were mainly for commuting to railway stations and shopping areas and back. Additionally, the introduction of the small or 'miniwheel' that coincided with the popularity of the 'miniskirt trend' vastly improved women's appeal for bicycles[3]. Women became an important market segment and the industry introduced a greater variety of colors and models to appeal to this segment. The growing demand resulted in bicycle standardization and the adoption of mass production systems by Japanese manufacturers.

The 1973 'oil shock' had a chilling effect on Japan, and bicycle production dropped over 18 percent to 7.6 million. The industry hoped that demand for bicycles would develop (in lieu of automobile purchases) under a 1973 energy savings plan, but this trend didn't develop and bicycle demand plateaued around 7 million units. Exhibit 1 shows the production, shipment,

[3]In the past, Japanese bicycle manufacturers produced bicycles originally designed around European models. The lower average height of Japanese women made it difficult for them to use such bicycles. The miniwheel's small wheel diameter, lower saddle mount and U-type frames made it very appealing to women.

exports and imports of bicycles in Japan for a 10-year period starting from 1982. The domestic production and shipment of bicycles has remained somewhat stable throughout the late 1980s and early 1990s. Exports of Japanese bicycles have gradually declined as the Japanese yen has increased in strength and imports into Japan from neighboring Taiwan and China have grown steadily during this period. Exhibit 2 shows bicycle production for the different segments in Japan.

Manufacturers and Assemblers

Bicycle producers in Japan are subdivided by the industry into two groups: manufacturers and assemblers. The distinction between these two types lies mainly in (a) the degree of backward vertical integration achieved by the firms that belong to each group, and (b) the level of final product assembly carried out before shipment by firms in each group. For example, the manufacturers produce their own bicycle frames and forks, the two critical structural components of the bicycle, and purchase the remaining components from parts suppliers. Also, the bicycles pro-

duced by this group were appropriately 70 pecent assembled at the time of shipment to wholesalers. The assemblers purchase all their components from outside parts suppliers and only assemble the bicycles as their name denotes. Historically, manufacturers accounted for most bicycles produced. Starting in the 1980s, the shipment of bicycles between the manufacturers and assemblers was evenly spilt with each accounting for approximately 50 percent of the industry.

In 1992, the Japanese bicycle industry consisted of over 80 bicycle manufacturers and hundreds of parts suppliers. The top five manufacturing firms were Bridgestone, National, Miyata, Maruishi, and Nichibei Fuji. Bridgestone Cycle Co. was the industry leader with 18 percent of the domestic market. Bridgestone was followed by NBIC and Miyata, with nine percent and eight percent of the market respectively. The top five assemblers were Yokota, Deki, Hodaka, Saimoto and Wani. Yokota lead the group of assemblers with nine percent of the market. Deki and Hodaka were next with eight percent and seven percent of the market respectively. Together the top five members of each group

EXHIBIT 3
Market shares of major bicycle producers

Source: Cycle Press, No. 76, February, 1993.

Companies	1992 Production (units, 000)	Market Share	1993 Production (Est.)
Top five manufacturers			
Bridgestone	1400	18%	1450
National	700	9%	700
Miyata	640	8%	610
Maruishi	310	4%	310
Nichibei Fuji	200	3%	200
	3250	43%	3270
Top five assemblers			
Yokota	710	9%	750
Deki	630	8%	700
Hodaka	530	7%	570
Saimoto	400	5%	400
Wani	290	4%	290
	2560	34%	2710

accounted for over 75 percent of bicycles produced in Japan (See Exhibit 3).

Parts Suppliers

In 1992, there were approximately 327 firms that produced individual parts and related items. Compared to bicycle producers, parts supplier firms were in the business of producing standardized parts in large volume and were more automated than complete bicycle producers.

In 1992, Shimano was the largest supplier of bicycle parts commanding a dominant market share. The other major parts suppliers were Araya, Sakae, and Cat Eye. Unlike the Japanese automobile industry, where exclusive suppliers are the norm, bicycle parts suppliers sold components to multiple firms. The growing supply of bicycle parts from Southeast Asian countries made it very difficult for Japanese suppliers to compete in labor-intensive segments of the industry such as bicycle chains, pedals and wheels. To remain competitive some suppliers began moving their production facilities to South East Asian countries where labor costs were lower than in Japan. Others entered into joint ventures with parts suppliers from Taiwan and China.

Distribution

Bicycles in Japan were distributed through wholesalers, retailers, supermarkets, and department stores.[4] There were approximately 1,600 wholesalers and about 38,000 retailers in 1990. While many wholesalers were subsidiaries of the large manufacturers such as Bridgestone, NBIC and others, retail outlets for the most part were small 'mom and pop stores.' Approximately 60 percent of bicycles sold were transferred from wholesalers to retailers and the remaining were distributed through supermarkets and department stores located throughout Japan. In the past large company owned wholesalers dominated the distribution of bicycles. Recently, large supermarket chains and household superstores or 'home centers' have started to sell bicycles. According to industry experts, the growing number of such outlets was one important reason for the steady rise in imported bicycles (see Exhibit 4).

Company Background

NBIC was Japan's second largest manufacturer of bicycles in 1992 with sales reaching about ¥20 billion. The firm marketed bicycles under three different brand names, Panasonic, National and Hikari. NBIC targeted each brand at a unique market segment, and together the three brands covered the wide spectrum of bicycles sold in Japan. They ranged from high quality, high price sports and fashion bicycles (Panasonic) to bicycles that were used primarily for transportation from home to the nearest train station or supermarket and back (Hikari). National and Hikari brands together constituted the bulk of NBIC's production and sales. Panasonic, the company's more expensive line, accounted for a little less than 20 percent of total production in 1992.

NBIC began to manufacture and sell bicycles in 1952. At first growth in sales was slow, but picked up rapidly within a few years after the firm's inception. Between 1952 and 1965, the firm produced almost a million bicycles. In 1965, due to ever increasing demand the firm completed the construction of a new factory in Kashihara city on the outskirts of Osaka, and moved its operations to this factory (see Appendix A for a brief outline of the company history). At Kashihara city the firm had two factories located next to each other. NBIC's management called them the mass production factory and custom-factory. The custom-factory, initially conceptualized as a pilot plant, was built in 1987.

In 1992 according to published estimates, the firm produced a combined total of 700,000 bicycles in these two factories. Over 90 percent of these were produced in the mass production factory and shipped to Matsushita's sales subsidiaries. High-end Panasonic bicycles were produced

---

[4] According to industry reports, labeling firms as either wholesalers or retailers was problematic, because a majority of them operated jointly as wholesale and retail ventures.

EXHIBIT 4
The Japanese bicycle distribution system – 1992.

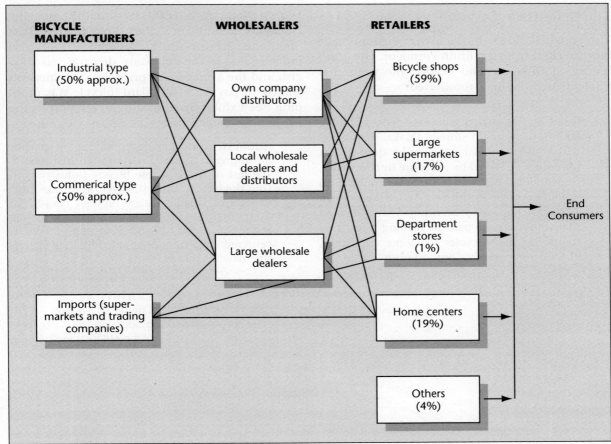

in the custom-factory and shipped to dealers to be delivered to individual customers. While most line workers worked at the mass production factory, a few of NBIC's best skilled workers produced bicycles at the custom-factory. Operating on a single-shift basis throughout the year, they produced a small fraction of the firm's production at this factory.

In early 1993, the firm employed 470 people with a little over 66 percent classified as direct or line workers, and the rest as indirect workers. A little over 50 percent of indirect workers were in the production engineering and design departments of the firm. The line workers belonged to the company union and actively participated in 'quality circle' programs. Workers met once a month, as part of these programs, to discuss quality and safety issues. Additionally, management periodically tested line workers and ranked them according to their skill level. The highest skilled workers were given the opportunity to work at the custom-factory where wages were higher.

NBIC 'sold' its bicycles to 10 sales companies. These sales companies distributed bicycles to approximately 9000 retailers located throughout Japan that were part of the Matsushita group. Regular monthly meetings were held between management at NBIC and the sales companies to discuss sales trends and manufacturing concerns.

Mass-customization Strategy

The Genesis

The original idea for making custom-made bicycles came from the firm's President. The firm's Managing Director, who headed the team that implemented the idea, recollected:

> It all started when our President visited a famous department store in Osaka. He noticed that women could custom order dresses that were then delivered by the store in two weeks. He wondered if it was possible for National to produce bicycles in this way. When we were on a trip to the US, he mentioned this idea. At that time we were used to making a few specially designed bicycles for some customers, like Olympic racers, but offering a custom-made bicycle to everyone was a different matter altogether.

Within a few days after their return, the Managing Director began giving serious thought to the idea mentioned by the firm's President. The bicycle industry was in the doldrums, demand was sluggish and the average unit price the customer was willing to pay for a 'standard' bicycle was dropping (see Exhibit 5). According to a report in the *Far East Economic Review* (December 7 1989):

> Although some Japanese component makers are riding high on the mountain bike boom, the rest of the Japanese bicycle industry is in the doldrums. The stronger yen has hurt exports of Japanese-made bicycles because of their higher cost overseas. Today, bicycle assembly for the US and European markets is centered in Taiwan, dominated by such aggressive new makers as Giant, Merida, and Fairy.

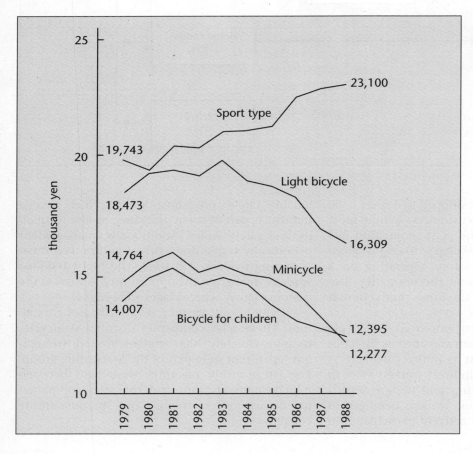

EXHIBIT 5
Change in average production value per complete bicycle unit (yen)

Though the average price of a sporting bicycle was increasing, this segment was not growing as anticipated by many large producers. It was under these conditions that the managing director with other senior managers at NBIC decided to change the firm's strategy by trying something bold. According to one senior manager:

> We were manufacturing bicycles in lot sizes greater than 50 in our factory. Now we were challenged by our President to produce bicycles in lot sizes of one. More importantly, the orders received were to be completed and delivered within two weeks. We not only had to convince ourselves that this was possible, but we had to convince our design people, our manufacturing people and line workers that this was a *good* and *feasible* idea.

Initially, not everyone at NBIC was unanimous in their support for this revolutionary idea. Some senior members at NBIC felt that it would require a large investment and also entailed a tremendous risk for the firm. They asked: What if NBIC failed in this attempt? Some also argued that the market for the sports bicycle in Japan was shrinking, though admittedly at a slower pace when compared to other segments (see Exhibit 2). Further, some industry analysts outside the firm said that such a strategy would be impossible to develop and implement. As one senior manager speaking for his colleagues recollected:

> We also had our own doubts during those early days, though we never mentioned this to our president or workers because we were committed to at least trying to see if this project would work. However, in our mind we gave it a 50 percent chance of success.

According to the Managing Director, the firm had only a few broad objectives when it started on the road to customization. First, the firm wanted to double the amount of high value-added products the firm sold by accommodating the *individual* needs of the customer. Second, NBIC wanted to devise a 'system' of production and delivery that clearly differentiated its high-end Panasonic brand from competitor products, and also meet the growing need for variety in the marketplace. During the late 1980s, as the demand for bicycles plateaued, there was increasing competition among the manufacturers. To gain market share, firms introduced many new model types. For example, NBIC offered over 250 different models types during 1987, and within each model type customers had a choice of color and other options. Management changed about 80 percent of models yearly. Similarly, not to be out done, the industry's largest producer offered over 300 models during the same period.

Within a few weeks of its inception, the Managing Director assembled a project team that consisted of senior members of his management team, a designer, a few process engineers and some highly skilled, experienced line workers. Discussing the implementation of the project he fondly recalls:

> We worked long hours. We proposed and debated many new ideas for days. We started with a few people, but as the project began to progress, more people were added. Within a few weeks we established a pilot plant in a large empty warehouse next to the factory. Still, numerous issues had to addressed and solved, but as time went on we were convinced that the project was doable. We knew we had the capability, because many of us had spent most of our professional lives making bicycles.

Motivated by the relentless effort of their leader, the team successfully tackled one concern after another to complete the project in a mere four months. By July 1987, the team converted the pilot plant to one that was fully operational and running. It was seven months since the firm's President visited the department store in Osaka.

The firm in June 1987 unveiled its strategy to Japan's bicycle industry to the dismay and surprise of its major competitors. The new system they had devised was aptly named the *Panasonic Ordering System*.

The Panasonic Ordering System (POS)

The Order Process

A customer ready to order a high-end bicycle walked into a Panasonic bicycle dealer equipped for POS and the dealer, using a unique measuring and gauging machine, noted the exact physical measurements of the customer including the size of the frame, the length of seat post, the position of the handle bar, and the extension of the handle bar stem. The customer was allowed to select the model type, the color scheme, and other features for their bicycle. Details on the number of models, colors and options that were available are provided in Exhibit 6. When completed, the dealer immediately sent this information to the control room of the custom-made factory via facsimile transmission.

Once the facsimile order form was received in the master control room of the custom factory, the receiving attendant immediately entered the information into the firm's host computer to register and control the customer's order specifications. The host computer then assigned each order a unique bar code label. This label, which

traveled with the evolving bicycle, instructed and controlled each stage of manufacturing operation. At various stages in the process, line workers accessed the customer's unique requirement using the bar code label and a scanner. This information, displayed on a CRT terminal at each station, was fed directly to the computer controlled machines that were part of a local area computer network. Using such information, workers at each station performed the required sequence of operations assisted by machines. Exhibit 7 provides an overview of the entire manufacturing process used by NBIC, and Exhibit 8 provides an illustration of the POS factory layout.

The Manufacturing Process

At the heart of the POS lay the design and manufacturing capabilities of NBIC. Almost all the machines used in the manufacturing process were developed and built exclusively for use in the custom-factory. A significant portion of this development work was carried out by the firm's own design and process engineers with assistance from the parent company's engineering staff. While the computer hardware used in POS was purchased from outside vendors, much of the software employed to control and monitor the

	Type	No. of Models
Bicycles	Road	10
	Triathlon	5
	Time Trial	3
	ATB	2
	Track	1
Frame	Road & Triathlon	4
	Time Trial	—
	ATB	—
	Track	1
	Frame Color	Pattern
	1 Color	15
	2 Colors	40
	3 Colors	15

EXHIBIT 6
POS system selection of models available (Japan)

Source: NBIC Company Records.

EXHIBIT 7
The production process at the custom-factory

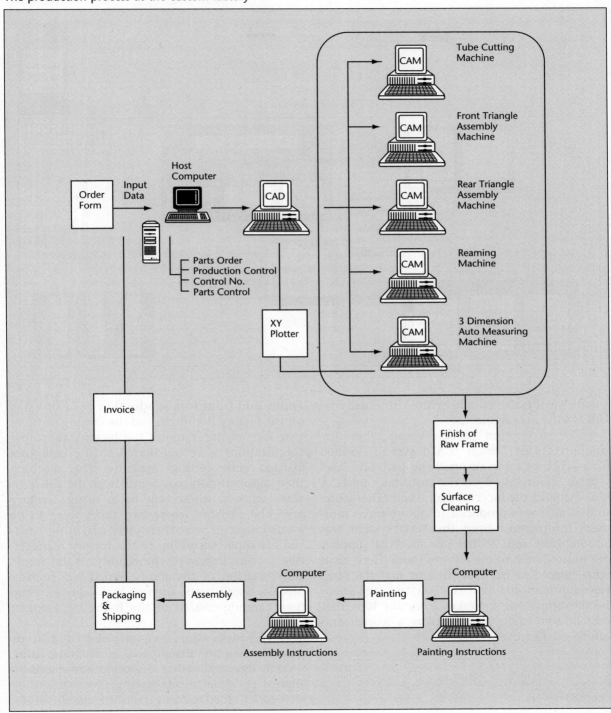

EXHIBIT 8
Layout of the POS/PICS factory

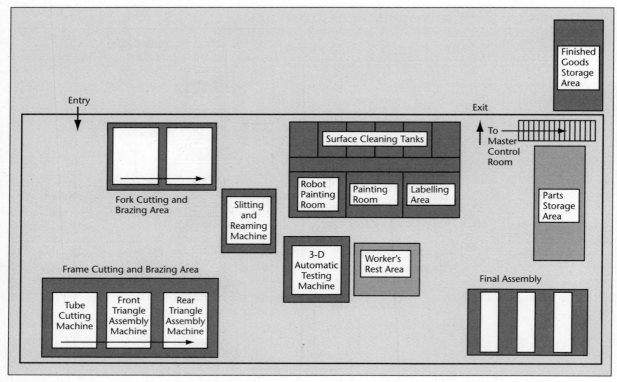

system was developed and written internally by NBIC's software engineers.

The production process began when the Computer-Aided Design (CAD) system, located in the control room scanned the bar code label to access information on the customer's order. A 'blue print' of the bicycle's frame and other structural details was produced in about three minutes.[5] Information from the CAD system was automatically sent to the raw material supplies area located next to the control room. Here small lights, placed in front of the raw material bins, were automatically lit based on the customer's specifications. The materials from the bins that were lit were then picked up by a worker and sent to the factory.

---

[5]According to the factory manager, prior to the introduction of the CAD system this process took the company draftsmen about 180 minutes.

Frame and front fork production   The first step on the factory floor involved the cutting of tubes that formed the frame of the bicycle. Customer specifications were transferred to the computer assisted 'tube cutting' machine. This machine then automatically sized and held the tubes in place while a worker cut them using a rotary saw. The surfaces where two tubes were to be welded together were then 'arch' cut, using a special machine. According to the factory manager, this process improved the rigidity of the frame and precision of the joints during the brazing process. Small parts, such as brake guides, were then carefully brazed to the frame by a skilled worker.

The tubes were then carried to the 'front triangle assembly' machine. This machine, using special jigs and other features, automatically aligned and held the tubes together, while they were *tack* welded to form the front triangle of the frame. The joints of the frame were then *brazed* by automatic brazing machines. Following this process, a worker using the 'rear fork assembly machine' *tack* welded the chain stay hanger section, the seat stay and the seat lug section. These were then brazed to the frame. These processes brought together the front and rear triangle sections to complete the bicycle frame. According to NBIC's process engineers, the automated machines used in brazing process incorporated optical sensors capable of detecting temperature differences to +/− one percent. Such precision was required to ensure metal integrity, and to prevent the warping of the tubes during the process.

The final step involved the use of a 'slitting and reaming' machine. In this process the seat lug, attached earlier, was slit and the inside of the seat tube reamed. This process ensured that the seat pillar could be adjusted smoothly and fixed firmly. The time taken to cut, braze and assemble the frame was about 25 minutes.

The tubes that formed the front fork of the bicycle were cut and assembled using processes similar to that of the frame.

Quality check The completed frame and fork were then placed on a three-dimensional automatic measuring machine, designed by the firm's parent company engineers. This machine checked the actual measurements of the assembled frame and fork against the customer's original specification stored in the host computer's memory banks. Small variations, if any, were detected and displayed on a CRT terminal or plotted using the attached plotter. This process was completed in less than 60 seconds.

Painting Both completed frame and front fork were then moved by overhead conveyors to the surface cleaning area and immersed in special solutions. This process prevented the early rusting of the frame and improved the ability of the subsequent paint to adhere more uniformly to the surfaces. The cleaning process took about 10 to 15 minutes to complete. The bicycle frame and front fork were then transferred to a 'preliminary' painting room to be automatically

painted by a robot. Again, the robot received its instructions from the factory's host computer via the bar code label. According to the factory manager, NBIC was the first bicycle manufacturer to introduce a robot in the painting process for bicycles.

Following this, two skilled workers completed the 'final' by painting the 'hard-to-reach' areas using electrostatic spray guns. Finishing touches and customer's 'special' painting instructions were completed by the workers.

Labeling and engraving process This process involved printing or engraving the customer's name on the bicycle frame or handle bar stem. A skilled worker, using a silk screen process, printed the customer's name and transferred it on to the frame. Or alternatively, a name engraving machine engraved the name of the customer on the handle stem. With the completion of this process, the frame was ready for the final assembly process.

Final assembly and shipping The final assembly involved the mating of the completed frame and fork with the appropriate wheels, chain, gears, brakes, tires and other components that constitute a complete bicycle. During this process the 'derailleur' adjustment and the 'rotation' adjustment of the bearing section were completed. Also, the seat pillar and seat lug section were checked and adjusted according to customer specifications. Each bicycle was fully assembled and tested by a single skilled craftsman. The assembly process was performed in any one of the three main assembly stations and took about 30 minutes. The completed bicycle was then boxed and sent to a holding area, outside the factory, to be picked up for delivery. They were generally shipped the same day.

The entire manufacturing and assembly time required to complete a single customer order was approximately 150 minutes. In 1989, the factory employing 18 workers (15 workers were employed in 1987) had the capability to make about 60 custom-order bicycles daily. It received orders for approximately 12,000 bicycles, an increase of 20 percent over the previous two years. A significant

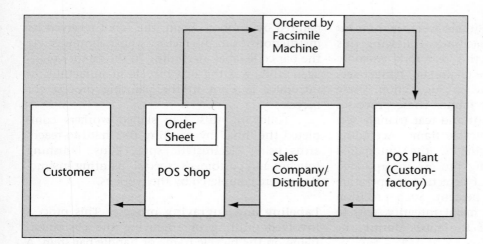

EXHIBIT 9
NBIC's Distribution System

portion of these orders where from customers in Japan.

A year after the introduction of the POS, the company unveiled a new system named Panasonic Individual Customer System (PICS). The purpose of PICS was to offer custom-made bicycles to customers in overseas markets, especially in countries like Australia, the US and Germany. PICS used the same customized manufacturing technology as the POS, but offered customers the choice of much larger frame sizes more suitable to western customers. The time taken from order to delivery was increased from two weeks to three weeks under PICS.

Marketing and Distribution

According to General Manager of Sales at NBIC, customer service, 'appropriate' pricing, and extensive communication were all an integral part in NBIC's mass-customization strategy. Domestic customers were guaranteed a delivery time of two weeks, not a day more but also not a day less. He pointed out that: 'We could have made the time shorter, but we want people to feel excited about waiting for something special.' According to a manager at the factory, custom-made Panasonic bicycles were priced only about 20 to 30 percent higher (depending on the particular model and features selected) when compared to a 'comparable' bicycle produced at the mass production factory.

Under the POS, it was the factory that was given the responsibility to communicate directly with customers. Shortly after the factory received the customer's order, a personalized computer generated drawing of the bicycle was mailed with a note thanking the customer for choosing the POS. This was followed up with a second personal note, three months later, inquiring about the customer's satisfaction with his or her bicycle. Finally, a 'bicycle birthday card' was sent commemorating the first anniversary of the bicycle.

According to the General Manager in-charge of sales, dealership selection played an important role in pursuing their strategy. In early 1993, only about 15 percent of 9,000 domestic dealerships were part of the POS (see Exhibit 9). They explained the reasons for this:

> We cannot afford to make mistakes. Mistakes can be very costly. It is important that customers don't lose confidence in our system. We have to be very careful in selecting knowledgeable and committed dealers so that they send us the correct information. We can't tolerate mistakes at any stage.

Response to POS

Competitors Imitate NBIC

NBIC's strategy of offering a truly custom-made bicycle surprised all its major competitors. Within months, the two other leading manufacturers of bicycles scrambled to develop and implement their version of mass customization. In a year, both offered their own 'unique' versions of mass customization. But, they were unable to duplicate all aspects of NBIC's strategy as noted by a senior manager at Bridgestone in early 1993:

> The trouble with this segment is that it is too small, perhaps 10,000 or more. It costs a lot of money to advertise for such a small segment. Since NBIC was the first firm to introduce this idea, they have established a strong image in the customer's mind. When you mention customization, the consumer only thinks of Panasonic. Also, National's parent company Matsushita is famous for its marketing savvy, and it is difficult for us to match them. We as a company have not paid much attention to this segment. I expect we will in the future, because we too want to be known for our innovativeness.

According to a knowledgeable source in the industry, NBIC was the only company to have successfully mastered the art of mass customization, and that competitors were unable to offer the same degree of variety NBIC offered. Unlike NBIC, leading competitors simply increased the inventory of frames types and model sizes they carried to accommodate the variety demand by its customers. According to the Managing Director:

> One of our competitive advantages is that we are located in Osaka close to all the major parts suppliers. Frequency and reliability of parts delivery from our suppliers has helped us 'truly' custom build bicycles. There is little need to hold large inventories of finished frames and other parts unlike others outside the Kansai region.

Extensive Media Coverage

Soon after the announcement of the POS, journalists following this industry began expounding on its revolutionary nature. These Japanese stories were soon picked by foreign journalists who write about Japanese manufacturing practices. Within a span of two years, NBIC was featured in *Fortune*, the *New York Times*, and *Washington Post*. One leading American television network, ABC, featured the firm in its regular prime-time *World News Tonight* program hosted by its chief anchor person Peter Jennings. The German Public Television network produced a documentary for European audiences. Additionally, NBIC receives many requests from other manufacturing firms for information about its new system. Within a few years of the introduction of POS, *Fortune* magazine (Moffat 1990) noted that:

> The concept has so intrigued executives and engineers that they have been flocking from as far away as Italy to this factory in Kokubu, in western Japan, to study it. Big Japanese manufacturers of consumer goods are also taking note, hoping to improve their own production system. . . . [NBIC] built these one-of-a kind models by replacing mass production with flexible manufacturing. The method is being employed all over Japan to shrink small-lot production jobs to lots of one.

While NBIC's customized bicycles manufactured under the POS system only accounted for two percent of total production, the effect of worldwide attention had a dramatic effect on the company's high-end segment.

Company's Sales Increase

Before the introduction of POS, NBIC's market share was languishing behind its two major competitors in the high end segment. Within, a few years of the introduction POS and PICS, the firm's total high-end (Panasonic) market share position improved dramatically. For the first time in its history, NBIC become the industry's second largest manufacturer of high-end bicycles (see Exhibit 10 and Exhibit 11).

Reflecting on the events of the last few years, members of the senior management at NBIC glowed with pride about the achievements of their firm. Despite the repeated attempts by competitors to offer customized bicycles, the 'Panasonic' name was increasingly viewed as the only 'truly' mass customized bicycle in Japan. The firm was now viewed as the leader and innovator in the

EXHIBIT 10
Production by Top Four Manufacturers (units, 000s)

Estimates published by *Cycle Press*, 1993.

Companies	1987	1992	1993 (Estimate)
Bridgestone	1,330	1,400	1,450
National	754	700	700
Miyata	620	640	610
Maruishi	379	310	310

EXHIBIT 11
NBIC 'Panasonic' Brand Growth 1986–1992

	1986	1987	1992	Future Target
Units (% of total production)	4%	7%	18%	—
Revenues (% of total sales)	10%	13%	27%	50%

industry. Still, this was not the time to rest on past laurels, there were some major concerns facing NBIC and the industry in 1993.

Outlook for the Future

Total company sales in 1992 grew marginally by 1.2 percent, but exports of NBIC's Panasonic bicycles were down by over 50 percent. This significant decrease in exports was the result of many factors including: the aggressive export strategies of firms in Taiwan, China and other neighboring countries; the continued strengthening of the Japanese yen against the US dollar; the softening of the demand for bicycles in Europe and the United States; and the increased competition in overseas markets. The news on the domestic front was not very encouraging either. The sales of domestic bicycles had been stagnant for some time. Forecasts for 1993 indicated only modest overall growth. According to an industry source, the Japanese industry was steadily undergoing structural change. The assemblers were beginning to exploit the growing supply of less expensive bicycle parts from overseas, to the dismay of major manufacturers. According to early industry predictions for 1993, Yokota's share of the market was expected to grow even larger in 1993. And Deki, the second largest assembler, was expected to match NBIC in the production of bicycles (see Exhibit 3).

Role of Customization at NBIC

In early 1993, given the domestic and international situation, senior managers were pondering the future role of mass customization at NBIC. The lessons and the manufacturing skills the firm had acquired in the custom factory were readily transferable to the mass production factory. Skilled workers from the custom factory were regularly used for training line workers in the larger mass production factory. Over the last few years, the mass production factory was undergoing slow, but significant changes. Lot sizes employed in production were steadily decreasing. Over the last few years lot sizes were reduced from 50 to a mere 20 in 1993.

Senior management were now examining the feasibility of turning the mass production factory into a custom-shop. The goal was to increase the revenues contributed by high-end segment to 50 percent of total sales within the next five years. More importantly, its likely impact on the firm's overall strategy was unclear. Some managers were under the view that the size of this custom segment should not be nurtured to grow beyond the current size. The firm should maintain it as a small high-value niche market to maintain customer interest and high prices. Others argued for a strategy to increase the size of this segment.

Appendix A The History of National Bicycle

1918	■ Matsushita Electric (Parent Company) was founded.
1952	■ Commencement of bicycle manufacturing and sales.
1956	■ Began manufacturing and selling racing bicycles.
1960	■ National Bicycle Factory established in Sakai city.
1965	■ Production of National bicycle reached one million units.
	■ National Bicycle completed new factory in Kashihara city.
1967	■ Japanese National bicycle racing team adopts bicycles for World Championships.
1971	■ Commencement of export of Panasonic bicycles to the United States.
1972	■ Japanese Olympic bicycle team adopts Panasonic bicycles for the Munich Olympics.
	■ Production total reaches 3 million.
1973	■ National Bicycle installed new automated assembly line.
1974	■ Gojyo National Bicycle Parts Co. was established (wheel assembly factory).
1979	■ Commencement of export to Europe, Canada, and Australia.
	■ Formation of the Panasonic Racing Team in the United States.
1980	■ Seven millionth bicycle produced.
1983	■ Eight millionth bicycle produced.
1985	■ Nine millionth bicycle produced.
1986	■ Adoption of 'Panasonic' brand name for top-class racing bicycles in Japan.
1987	■ Unique 'Panasonic Order System' initiated starting on June 1st – receives acclaim from both inside and outside the industry.
	■ Ten millionth bicycle produced.
1988	■ First orders received February 1st for 'PICS' 3-week delivery order system for United States customers.

Source: NBIC Company Records.

References

JETO (Japan External Trade Organization) (1990) Your Market in Japan – High Grade Bicycle and Wear, Report.

Moffat, S. (1990) Japan's Personalized Production, *Fortune*, October 22, p. 132.

Case 17: Teléfonos de México

By Robert E. Hoskisson, Jennifer Alexander, Tom Blackley, Linda Chen, Dru Ubben, John Economou, Sewardi Luis, and Richard Martinez[1]

On September 18, 1989, the president of Mexico, Carlos Salinas de Gortari, announced the privatization of TELMEX. The atmosphere throughout the offices of TELMEX had been electrified that day. Although privatization of Mexico's state-owned telephone services monopoly was intended to radically improve service for Mexican citizens, it also meant drastic changes in both the firm's structure and daily operations.

Following the privatization announcement, the government pledged to continue to maintain oversight of telecommunications within the country. This was to ensure that a smooth transition took place while transforming the company from public to private. Then, in December 1990, the Mexican government sold its controlling interest in TELMEX to a consortium of Mexican investors led by the Groupo Carso and two foreign telephone companies: France Télécom and Southwestern Bell International Holdings (headquartered in San Antonio, Texas). Under this agreement, the government granted TELMEX the power to be the exclusive provider of long-distance service through the end of 1996. Thereafter, competition would be allowed, and TELMEX was required to connect competing networks with its local networks at mutually acceptable rates, to be approved by government officials as well.

Since Salinas's announcement, TELMEX has expanded revenues at the rate of 18 percent per year, compared to the annual 6 percent expansion in the public sector in the early 1990s (see the financial statements given in Exhibits 1 through 5). Furthermore, phone lines had increased from 5 lines per 100 people to 8.7. TELMEX also replaced 80 percent of its obsolete exchanges with digital exchanges, and developed new microwave, optical fiber, and satellite systems.

Although the TELMEX executive committee was aware of the effort already expended to achieve these results, they knew that TELMEX could – and must – continue to improve its service and operations if it wanted to remain the dominant long-distance telephone service provider in the Mexican market. An analysis of the financial statements of the company was all it would take to convince the executive committee members that long-distance service was, thus far, the most profitable aspect of the telephone business. However, given that current regulations in the Mexican telecommunications industry will allow for open competition in the long-distance market at the end of 1996, some analysts expect that TELMEX is likely to lose much of its market share to foreign competitors.

Against a backdrop of rapidly changing technology, a volatile and competitive global telecommunications industry, an unstable domestic economy and currency, and ambiguous customer demands, the executive committee faced a formidable challenge as it considered critical strategic decisions.

The Age of Privatization

Mexico was one of the first of the developing countries to privatize its telecommunications industry in the late 1980s. Prompted by the deregulation of AT&T, the global stock offering by

---

[1] Source: From *Strategic Management: Competitiveness and Globalization* by Leonard J. Hitt *et al.* © 1996 West Publishing. Used by permission of South-Western College Publishing, a division of International Thomson Publishing, Inc., Cincinnati, Ohio, 45227.

EXHIBIT 1

Financial data highlights

Source: Teléfonos de México, 1993, AnnualReport

	1993	1992	1991	1990
Consolidated*				
Revenues	24,602	22,363	19,675	16,248
Total expenses	14,320	12,657	11,085	10,383
Operating income	10,282	9,706	8,590	5,865
Net income	9,003	8,614	8,446	4,751
Total assets	52,902	47,031	45,233	40,831
Long-term liabilities	5,906	5,992	6,389	8,025
Net annual investment	7,087	7,914	7,303	7,751
Communities	18,281	15,738	12,869	10,221
Access lines in service (in thousands)	7,621	6,754	6,025	5,355
Kms. of LD circuits in service†	82,491	83,106	69,720	59,999
Domestic LD calls†	1,402,852	1,261,934	1,084,689	965,603
International LD calls†	387,462	351,258	257,749	211,786
Total liabilities total assets (%)	30.0	28.9	35.0	42.6
Data Per Share				
Earnings per share (N$)	0.85	0.81	0.80	0.45
Book value (N$)	3.49	3.15	2.77	2.21
Market value at year-end (N$)	10.450	8.775	7.150	2.030
Dividend per share (N$)	0.250†	0.150	0.075	0.025
Number of outstanding shares (in millions)	10,603	10,603	10,603	10,603

Note: Figures in million new pesos, unless otherwise indicated.
*The financial information for 1990 through 1993 has been updated according to the third reexpression document to Bulletin B-10 and, accordingly, it is stated in pesos with a purchasing power as of December 31, 1993.
†Proposed as of year-end 1993.

British Telecom, and the lifting of the protected monopoly status of Japan's NTT in the mid-1980s, a wave of privatization surged in developing countries in Asia and Latin America. However, many of the more developed nations, for instance, Germany, had not privatized their phone companies by 1993 due to political opposition

The economic arguments in favor of private enterprises are compelling. Additional financial, technical, and managerial resources (desperately needed in most emerging economies) could be provided by private telecommunications firms. Furthermore, as a result of increased competitive pressures in the industry, lower costs are expected. Private operators of telecommunications networks have been expected to restructure the work-force, introduce new technologies, and purchase components in larger volumes. Commercially minded firms could also increase their responsiveness toward customers and work to expand coverage of telecommunications services.

Because TELMEX is such a large part of the Mexican economy (upon privatization, TELMEX shares represented about one-third of the value of shares in the Mexican stock market), the executive committee understood that TELMEX's privatization strategy would serve as an example to the rest of the world. Even though partial privatization had taken place in many countries, completely open telecommunications markets existed only in a few countries such as Canada and the United States.

The TELMEX executive committee knew

EXHIBIT 2
Operating results

Source: Teléfonos de México,
1993, *Annual Report.*

Year ended as of December 31	1993		1992	
	Millions of N$	% of Operating Revenues	Millions of N$	% of Operating Revenues
Operating Revenues				
Long-distance service				
International	4,850	19.7	4,746	21.2
Domestic	8,295	33.7	7,773	34.8
Local service	10,529	42.8	9,102	40.7
Other	928	3.8	742	3.3
Total revenues	24,602	100.0	22,363	100.0
Expenses				
Salaries and related costs	5,784	23.5	5,307	23.8
Depreciation	2,909	11.8	2,374	10.6
Other operating and maintenance	3,488	14.2	3,003	13.4
Telephone service tax	2,139	8.7	1,973	8.8
Total expenses	14,320	58.2	12,657	56.6
Operating Income	10,282	41.8	9,706	43.4

that some countries in Latin America had faced competition from newly licensed specialized service operators. Cellular networks, in particular, had grown quickly in Mexico, Venezuela, Argentina, and Chile. New service players, like Argentina's IMPSAT and Mexico's IUSACELL, the largest wireless cellular operator in the country, were taking their specialized service experience on the road and winning licenses in international markets. In late 1993, IUSACELL, allied with Bell Canada, led a consortium that garnered a coveted cellular operation concession in Ecuador. This move served as a signal of the increased competition that was to come. These same non-basic service providers were also shaping up as potential competitors in the basic services market as the monopolies of privatized carriers expired.

The Telecommunications Industry Trends

Telecommunications systems consist of three components: customer equipment, such as tele-

phones and private branch exchanges (PBXs, see Glossary); transmission equipment, such as the cables connecting individual phones to the local exchange and lines connecting one exchange to another; and the exchanges themselves, where telephone calls are completed by linking one telephone to another.

Recent changes in technology have affected all three of these components. Product lines have broadened customer equipment from the old rotary telephone to items such as pushbutton telephones, fax machines, answering machines, and networked computers. The medium for transporting calls has been upgraded from copper wires to fiber optic cables. Fiber optics has enabled more information to be transmitted with greater reliability than ever before. In addition, alternative methods of transmission, such as microwave and satellite systems, have also become available.

Originally, human operators acted as the exchanges that connected telephone calls. Operators were replaced by electromechanical switches, which were in turn replaced by electronic exchanges. The most recent innovation was digital exchanges. Each stage of advancement in

EXHIBIT 3
Consolidated statements
of income*

Source: Teléfonos de México,
1993, AnnualReport

	1993	1992
Operating Revenues		
Long-distance service		
International	4,849,817	4,745,91
Domestic	8,294,563	7,772,517
Local service	10,528,765	9,102,152
Other	928,415	742,519
	24,601,560	22,363,098
Operating Expenses		
Salaries and related costs	5,783,780	5,307,171
Depreciation	2,908,681	2,373,735
Maintenance and other expenses	3,488,182	3,002,856
Telephone service tax	2,139,048	1,973,440
	14,319,691	12,657,202
Operating Income	10,281,869	9,705,896
Integral cost of financing		
Interest income	(1,434,560)	(1,543,859)
Interest expense	929,959	1,009,213
Exchange (gain) loss	(32,578)	64,270
Monetary effect	(28,062)	(251,402)
	(565,241)	(721,778)
Income before income tax and employee profit sharing	10,847,110	10,427,674
Provisions for:		
Income tax	1,197,716	1,199,049
Employee profit sharing	646,301	614,670
	1,844,017	1,813,718
Net Income	9,003,093	8,613,955

*Thousands of Mexican new pesos with purchasing power at December 31, 1993.

exchange technology resulted in increased quality, reliability, versatility, and cost effectiveness.

The growing interdependence between the technologies for communication and computing has been another trend affecting the telephone industry. Business users required an integrated solution for their computing and communications needs in order to more freely input, transmit, and process messages of all kinds (e.g. voice, text, data, images) within a dispersed but interconnected computer system. In this context, then, 'telecommunications' refers to systems that can handle this full range of message types. Telephone companies around the world have been struggling – and in some cases, failing – to satisfy these emerging needs.

As a result of this changing environment, telecommunications companies (private and state owned) in industrialized nations have invested heavily in converting to digital systems that are increasingly linked by fiber optic cables. In developing countries, on the other hand, the main dilemma has been to decide whether to extend basic service to a wider segment of the population or to offer more modern systems for existing business customers. TELMEX faces important decisions regarding these industry trends.

	1993	1992
Operating Activities		
Net income	9,003,093	8,613,955
Add: items not requiring the use of resources:		
Depreciation	2,908,681	2,373,735
Amortization	77,869	77,858
Changes in operating assets and liabilities:		
(Increase) decrease in:		
Accounts due from subscribers	(1,254,900)	(703,588)
Other accounts receivable	15,277	201,646
Prepaid expenses	(9,005)	(28,462)
Trust fund contribution	301,477	179,237
(Decrease) increase in:		
Employee pensions and seniority premiums		
Reserve	1,209,307	1,212,203
Contributions to trust fund	(890,505)	(981,938)
Payments to employees	(439,027)	(418,086)
Monetary effect of reserve	(76,444)	(139,261)
Accounts payable and accrued liabilities	(207,243)	696,661
Taxes payable	424,961	(673,022)
Deferred credits	83,945	20,245
Resources provided by operating activities	11,147,406	10,431,183
Financing Activities		
New loans	1,870,542	1,808,579
Repayment of loans	(1,083,101)	(2,497,033)
Reduction in purchasing power of debt	(651,112)	(164,062)
Application of advances on sale of receivables	(901,311)	(1,093,081)
(Decrease) increase in capital stock and		
premium on sale of shares	(76,721)	1,450
Cash dividends paid	(1,644,865)	(902,043)
Incorporation of Instituto Tecnologico de		
Teléfonos de Mexico, S.C.		(648)
Resources used in financing activities	(2,486,568)	(2,846,838)
Investing Activities		
Investment in telephone plant	(8,356,371)	(7,961,053)
Reduction in telephone plant inventories	1,269,844	47,245
Resources used in investing activities	(7,068,527)	(7,913,808)
Net increase (decrease) in cash and short-term		
investments	1,574,311	(329,463)
Cash and short-term investments at BOY	3,981,245	4,310,708
Cash and short-term investments at EOY	5,555,556	3,981,245

*Thousands of Mexican new pesos with purchasing power at December 31, 1993.

EXHIBIT 4
Consolidated statements of changes in financial position*

Source: Teléfonos de México, 1993, *Annual Report*.

EXHIBIT 5
Consolidated balance
sheets*

Source: Teléfonos de México,
1993, AnnualReport

	1993	1992
Assets		
Currents assets:		
Cash and short-term investments	5,555,556	3,981,245
Accounts receivable:		
Subscribers	4,389,184	3,134,284
Interconnecting carriers	234,245	226,311
Advances to suppliers	286,908	229,641
Other	738,419	818,847
	5,648,756	4,409,083
Prepaid expenses	609,001	659,899
Trust contribution	236,278	537,725
Total current assets	12,049,591	9,587,952
Property, plant and equipment, net	36,189,632	34,200,627
Inventories, primarily for use in construction of the telephone plant	1,141,280	2,619,989
Other assets	3,521,308	622,913
Total assets	52,901,811	47,031,481
Liabilities and Stockholders' Equity		
Current liabilities:		
Current proportion of long-term debt	1,161,906	999,259
Accounts payable and accrued liabilities	1,889,529	2,096,722
Taxes payable	848,339	423,378
Total current liabilities	3,399,774	3,519,409
Long-term debt	5,905,719	5,991,940
Reserve for employee pensions and seniority premiums	3,845,811	1,066,216
Deferred credits	2,201,395	3,108,761
Total liabilities	15,852,699	13,596,326
Stockholders' equity:		
Capital stock:		
Historical	1,056,580	1,057,561
Restatement increment	15,557,484	15,557,263
	16,614,064	16,614,824
Premium on sale of shares	2,848,620	2,849,416
Retained earnings:		
Unappropriated earnings of prior years	24,789,899	17,895,625
Net income for the year	9,003,093	8,613,955
	33,792,992	26,509,580
Deficit from restatement of stockholders' equity	(16,206,564)	(12,538,665)
Total stockholders' equity	37,049,112	33,435,155
Total liabilities and stockholders' equity	52,901,811	47,031,481

*Thousands of Mexican new pesos with purchasing power at December 31, 1993.

Mexico: political and economic issues

H. Carlos D., director of marketing at TELMEX, had prepared a report (see Exhibit 9) for the executive committee detailing the state of the economy at the time of Salinas' privatization announcement. His analysis indicated that Mexico's political unrest and economic instability contributed to high inflation, declining savings and investment, capital flight, and excessive foreign and domestic debt. Mexico's era of privatization was undertaken as a method of economic reform.

As a result of Mexico's privatization program, during the last few years the state had sold much of the telephone, automotive, pharmaceutical and secondary petrochemical sectors, the state-owned steel industry, and other manufacturing interests. According to the Bank of Mexico, the number of *parastatals* (government-owned enterprises) had declined from 1,155 in 1982 to less than 200 in 1994 (Kamm 1994).

In addition, by December 1987, the government had entered into the Economic Solidarity Pact and the Pact for Economic Growth and Stability agreements with representatives of business and labor. These agreements were aimed at stabilizing the economy through restrictive fiscal and monetary policies and at 'opening up' the economy in accordance with World Bank stipulations related to loans to Mexico. The pacts had far reaching effects, including a reduction in inflation from 159 percent in 1987 to 19 percent in 1989, decreasing external debt as a percentage of GDP from 75.8 percent in 1987 to 35.7 percent in 1991, and a decrease in interest rates on the 28-day cetes (government treasury bonds) from 77.3 percent in 1986 to 13.6 percent in 1992. Additional trade barriers were removed by decreasing the maximum tariff rate from 100 to 10 percent in 1987, and the introduction of NAFTA eliminated most tariffs for US and Canadian goods and services in 1993. Furthermore, state control over the foreign exchange market was eliminated (although the Bank of Mexico had authority to devalue the peso in order to hedge against straying economic conditions) (Teléfonos de México 1993).

The Prelude to the 1994 Peso Devaluation

Mexico was plagued by much social unrest and economic uncertainty in 1994. Despite the hopes of Mexican businesses and foreign investors as a result of the implementation of NAFTA, the Mexican economy was not as stable as it seemed. Even as the December 1994 presidential election approached, the ruling political party in Mexico (the PRI) was under pressure to institute reforms that would open the country's political system to competing political parties. There had been allegations of political favoritism and abuses in the traditional one-party system for decades. Furthermore, rebels from the state of Chiapas in southern Mexico battled government troops and threatened terrorism in Mexico City.

By the time President Zedillo was inaugurated, Mexico's foreign reserves had been depleted from $30 billion in March to about $12 billion on December 1, 1994. On December 20, the government decided to alleviate this problem by devaluing the peso in order to gain foreign monies from increased exports. This action collapsed investor confidence in Mexico's 'free market' economy, resulting in the loss of half of the remaining foreign reserves in one day. On December 22, in order to combat-lost confidence, Mexico went to a free-floating currency exchange system (Barthy 1994; Solis and Torres 1995).

In February 1995, the Mexican economy had rebounded to some degree, due in part to the successful negotiation of a $20 billion loan guarantee from the United States. However, on February 15, Grupo Sidek, a Mexican conglomerate, defaulted on commercial payment papers. This situation caused greater uncertainty in the Mexican economy and the peso fell to a value of six pesos to the dollar, a 45 percent devaluation. After $50 billion in further loan guarantees from the United States and other financial institutions were secured, the peso recovered to a devalued rate of 35 percent during the spring of 1995 (Carroll 1995).

The Effects of the Mexican Economy on TELMEX

TELMEX's revenues and earnings are affected greatly by fluctuations in Mexico's monetary exchange rate. Exchange gains or losses included in the cost of financing are calculated by translating monetary assets and liabilities denominated in foreign currencies at the rates of exchange at the end of each month. Approximately 20 percent of TELMEX's revenues are derived from international long-distance charges (see Exhibit 2), which are stated in US dollars. Additionally, about 80 percent of TELMEX's debt is in US dollars. Thus, the recent devaluation of the peso had caused long-distance revenues to decrease in worth by half, and TELMEX expected constant-peso rates and settlement rates paid by US long-distance carriers to decline further throughout 1995 (TELMEX 1993).

The economic and political crisis of Mexico had also caused TELMEX's stock to suffer. The price of TELMEX ADRs (American Depository Receipts) on the NYSE on February 24, 1995, was $28; a substantial decline from its 52-week high of $70 (Wall Street Journal 1995). The effect of Teléfonos de México's decrease in value on the Mexican economy was substantial because the drop in TELMEX's price carried worries over into the currency markets (TELMEX comprises one-third of the Mexican Bolsa), thereby causing the peso to fall further (Carroll 1995).

The worries surrounding Mexican economic and political instability have caused applications for concessions of ownership of Mexican assets to decrease. However, in a development affecting TELMEX's potential competitors, government officials, in mid-April 1995, decided against charging a licensing fee for new entrants to the phone market. At a recent cabinet meeting. 'Participants decided a fee would be counterproductive, reasoning that the current phone system is so far below world standards that it is a drag on the whole economy' (ibid.).

The 1990 Concession Agreement

TELMEX operated under Mexican communications regulations and a license agreement referred to as a 'Concession,' granted by the Mexican Ministry of Communications and Transportation. The redefinition of the concession in 1990 was focused on providing the phone company with sufficient funds to accelerate line expansion, since limited access to telephone service, not cost, is the customer's primary complaint. Some key points and guidelines set under the Concession were as follows:

- The government had the right to take over the management of the company in cases of imminent danger to internal security or the national economy, and the company may not sell or transfer any of its assets without the government's right of first refusal.

- Establishment of a price cap system in order that the company would have the ability to increase local service rates to meet its costs and to reduce long-distance rates in anticipation of competition at the end of 1996.

- Excise taxes of 72 percent on local service charges have been replaced with a value-added tax (VAT) of 10 percent.

- Specific targets for service expansion and improvement, including overall installations

EXHIBIT 6
Consortium Divisions

Partner	Consortium Ownership	Equity	Voting
Grupo Carso	51.0%	10.4%	26.0%
France Télécom	24.5%	5.0%	12.5%
Southwestern Bell	24.5%	10.1%	12.5%
Total	100.0%	20.5%	51.0%

EXHIBIT 7
Consortium government

Partner	Board of Directors	Executive Committee	Advisory Group
SWBIH	3	1	25
FT	3	1	25
SWBIH/FT roving	1		
Grupo Carso	12	2	3–4
TELMEX (CEO)		1	
Total	19	5	~55

(12 percent annual line increase), public phones, installation and repair delays.

n   Long-distance telephone competition would commence in December 1996 (Lexus/Nexus 1991).

The Concession would remain in force until the year 2026, at which time it may be renewed for another 15 years. However, upon early or unnatural termination of the Concession, the telecommunications assets of TELMEX revert to the government free of charge. Therefore, any assets developed by others (foreign companies) risk being relinquished to the government upon termination of the Concession agreement. Even with all of these preparation clauses written into the Concession, as mentioned earlier, TELMEX faced strong challenges as the Mexican long-distance market opened up to foreign competition at the end of 1996.

The Consortium

In December 1990, the government of Mexico sold all of its TELMEX shares to a consortium of owners (see Exhibit 6). The consortium ownership was divided such that Mexican-conglomerate Grupo Carso owned 51 percent while France Télécom (FT) and Southwestern Bell International Holdings (SWBIH) each held 24.5 percent. This ownership consortium presented the winning bid of $1.758 billion.

All three entities in the consortium were active partners in TELMEX. Grupo Carso (GC) was a diversified conglomerate with proven busi-

ness acumen. GC provided the majority Mexican ownership required for the sale of TELMEX,[2] and also represented the expertise in the consortium with regards to the Mexican political, cultural, and socioeconomic environment (Atterbury 1991). GC assumed responsibility for 'financial and real estate matters; legal and government relations; human resources and labor relations; and general management of day-to-day operations'.[3]

France Télécom has an international reputation for information systems development and deployment of digital technology. In addition, FT has 'modernized the entire country of France, bringing it from 4 million access lines in 1971 to over 28 million [at the end of 1990]' (Atterbury 1991). France Télécom's responsibilities included expansion and modernization of the network, international long distance, and expansion of the public telephone network. Southwestern Bell was included in order to take advantage of its expertise in efficient operations. Southwestern Bell's capacity comprised operations and service quality, to include the substitution of digital equipment for analog equipment, outside plant rehabilitation, operator services, marketing, wireless services, and directory/printing services.[3]

TELMEX operations were governed by a board of directors, executive committee, and advisory group composed as illustrated in Exhibit 7 (Atterbury 1991: D1). The advisory group has a support role for the executive committee to which it reports. Its primary function is to improve

---

[2] Fifty-one percent of TELMEX is required by the government to be owned by Mexican nationals.

[3] Speaker's notes of presentation by John Atterbury, page 2.

EXHIBIT 8
Number of Lines in
Service (thousands)

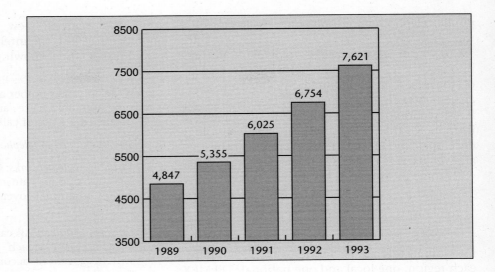

operations through investigating alternative strategies.

TELMEX's Primary Operations and Improvements

TELMEX's primary emphasis in 1993 was improving quality of service, increasing the number of lines in service (see Exhibit 8), and upgrading outside plant facilities (physical plant assets that are not located within buildings). To these ends, in 1993 TELMEX replaced 925,369 lines in exchanges, converting them to digital technology. In addition, 867,228 new lines were added (a 12.8 percent increase over 1992). In Mexico City, TELMEX replaced one central office each week, such that by the end of 1995, Mexico City's phone system was 100 percent digital. In 1993, its network was 65 percent digital, compared to 52 percent in 1992. This upgrading resulted in an overall penetration rate of 8.7 lines per 100 inhabitants. The following subsections describe the primary operations and additional improvements by TELMEX.

Long Distance

To increase the capacity and reliability of the long-distance network in 1993, 8,701 kilometers of fiber optic network were installed, resulting in a 64 percent increase in the 13,500-km network. These efforts were augmented by the beginning of construction on the submarine cable Columbus II, which was a fiber optic cable between Europe and America, which promised to improve telecommunications between the continents.

Included in the modernization of the long-distance network was the addition of digital operator positions in 39 traffic centers across Mexico. A total of 1,420 positions were created, which increased the capacity and the quality of service offered by operators of domestic and international long distance.

The opening of Mexican markets in numerous industries presented an increased load of international long distance as multinational companies increased their presence. As a result of the expansion of TELMEX's network and increased economic activity in 1993, a total of 1.4 billion domestic long-distance calls were handled, representing an increase of 11.2 percent over 1992. International long-distance calls reached 387.5 million, an increase of 10.3 percent. (See Exhibits 1 through 3 for the changes in the company's revenues from 1992 to 1993.)

Public Telephones

This lucrative market was attacked by TELMEX aggressively in 1993. During that year, 51,431 public telephones were put into service and the total grew to 177,995, a 122 percent increase since 1990. This increased access to two public telephones per 1,000 inhabitants, which was ahead of the schedule as required by the Concession agreements. In addition, TELMEX installed the latest technology in its public phones. The firm introduced the chip debit card, a technology developed by Alcatel (France) among others. It allowed users to purchase phone usage in advance with some measure of security.

Telcel

Mexico's cellular concessions have been divided into nine regions. There were two licenses for each region, one local and one national. TELMEX had the national concession, which it serves through its Telcel cellular unit. TELMEX offered cellular telephone services through its subsidiary, Radio Movil Dipsa, under the trademark Telcel. At the end of 1993, Telcel offered its services to 195,409 users, a 43 percent increase over 1992. Telcel's coverage included 218 cities in Mexico as well as 1,220 rural communities. In addition, Telcel offered domestic and international roaming service with 1,200 cities in the United States and 36 cities in Latin America and the Caribbean.

New and Potential Services

The commercial offering of integrated digital network (see Glossary) services expanded from 1992 to 1993 with 218,635 total connections, up 39.3 percent. Large users were linked through fiber optic digital local networks, satellite networks, and private circuits. Meanwhile, the first steps were being taken to create specialized groups to handle middle-sized and small users. In addition, TELMEX opened 19 new commercial information centers to serve customers by telephone, allowing the public to contact their business office about their telephone bills as well as to set up service for new lines. Furthermore, in 1994, TELMEX partnered with GTE Airfone to offer telephone services in domestic and international aircraft flying over Mexico.

Overall, TELMEX has an aggressive R&D pro-gram in developing new services. One of the ongoing projects is the intelligent network, which would provide the following features:

- *Advanced 800 service*: Provides selective access by telephone number and/or geographic area, programmable date and time service, and detailed statistics of calls received.

- *Service charged to telephone cards*.

- *Virtual private networks*: Offers the customer the facilities of a private network with domestic and international coverage, using the switched public network.

- *Universal number*: All calls from the customers of a user will reach the most convenient switching center, according to the origin of the call.

- *Personal number*: Allows the subscriber to receive his/her domestic and international calls on the telephone and at the date and hour he/she decides.

Furthermore, TELMEX was planning to implement a system called Videotex. This will allow data banks to be accessed for texts and images, including sources such as telephone directories, libraries, electronic newspapers, and banking services in the home. TELMEX was also expanding videoconferencing services both with regard to delivery of service to the public and in the training of personnel.

Administrative/Operational Improvements

Among the administrative/operational improvements and advances pursued by TELMEX was the creation of a network administration center, application of the synchronous digital hierarchy framework, and the creation of a technical institute for training its employees.

A network administration center (NAC) is the central control point from which a communications network is controlled and optimized. A communication network is a living entity because links are constantly in transition. Some links fail, while others are brought down for maintenance. This requires constant monitoring and optimization to ensure quality and reliable service as well as efficient utilization. TELMEX's equipment and systems that performed network administration (elements in the switching and transmission plant) were upgraded to facilitate greater network quality and coordination.

The application of an Integrated Services Digital Network (ISDN – see Glossary) framework increases the speed and expands the capabilities of transmission routes. In addition, an Intelligent Network (see Glossary) integrates an intelligent administrative system, such as TELMEX's NAC, which eases the input/output flow of information at any point in the route, without having to multiplex and demultiplex (see Glossary). These improvements make the network management and information handling more reliable.

Training is a vital part of TELMEX's ability to remain competitive. Created in 1991, the Technologies Institute of Teléfonos de México (Inttelmex) offers approximately 25,000 courses, with more than 200,000 participants. In 1992–1993, 70 training programs were developed in new technologies. This has significantly increased the development of core competencies within TELMEX.

TELMEX's Suppliers

Prior to privatization, TELMEX depended on two primary suppliers, Teleindustria Ericsson and Alcatel-Indetel, to meet its switching equipment needs. Teleindustria Ericsson, a Swedish company's local subsidiary, and Alcatel-Indetel, a subsidiary of a French company, had developed good relations with TELMEX because of their long-standing presence in the Mexican market. Both companies, however, had suffered to some extent since the privatization of TELMEX. In responding to customer demands and competitive pressure, TELMEX had increased demand on its suppliers by setting three priorities: price, quality, and delivery time.

Ericsson had been slow to adapt to the changes and especially slow in realizing that customer service was an essential component of qual-

ity. As a result, increased competition had reduced its market share and, in some cases, forced Ericsson out of select markets. Alcatel, on the other hand, had adjusted by restructuring its company to increase productivity and reduce costs. Consequently, Alcatel-Indetel not only remained competitive in the Mexican market, but also realized that many of its Mexican manufactured products could compete in global markets. (Southwestern Bell International Holdings 1995).

AT&T, a major new supplier in Mexico, has been the only new vendor to penetrate Mexico's switching market, joining Ericsson and Alcatel. In 1991, after several previous rejections, AT&T was chosen to become TELMEX's third switching supplier due to its successful and speedy installation record with one of TELMEX's subsidiaries. Also, in mid-1994, AT&T signed an agreement with TELMEX to jointly provide value-added service to Mexican subscribers. The network will utilize AT&T equipment combined with the existing TELMEX infrastructure. AT&T's close relationship with TELMEX in the long-distance market (and now the value-added market) made it an unlikely candidate to be a supplier of equipment to any of TELMEX's future competitors in the long-distance market. This close relationship between the two partly accounts for market analysts' expectations that AT&T would match up perfectly with TELMEX, to the detriment of TELMEX's potential competitors, such as Grupo Alfa (ibid.).

Relative newcomers to Mexico, such as NEC, Siemens, Northern Telecom, and Philips' Telecomunicaciones y Sistemas Profesionales, have chosen to compete in niche markets due to the dominance of Ericsson and Alcatel, as well as their inability to obtain contracts with TELMEX.

TELMEX'S Competition

TELMEX's executive committee also concerned itself with the many companies vying for a chance to oppose TELMEX. Despite the uncertainty about Mexico's political and economic future, foreign telecommunications carriers have been flocking to Mexico, with US carriers Bell Atlantic and

MCI leading the pack. The next wave of alliances was already under way. Indeed, the stage was being set for long-distance and international service competition that would last well into the twenty-first century. Wildcard entrants included Telefónica de España, Latin America's most pervasive foreign carrier. None the less, the Mexican market appeared to be shaping up as the exclusive breeding ground for US telecommunications operators and their strong local partners. MCI, for instance, had created an alliance with Mexico's largest bank, and Sprint and Bell Atlantic both had partnerships with the cellular powerhouse Grupo IUSACELL (ibid.).

Government Action

To create an environment of competitiveness for the future, the Mexican government enacted legislation to 'level the competitive playing field'. Although TELMEX lobbied the government aggressively in order to establish barriers for the potential entrants in its industry, several new rules announced in late June 1994 disappointed the long-distance (LD) monopolist. The new rules state that there are no limits to the number of long-distance companies that could enter the industry in 1997 and that TELMEX had to connect 60 of its switches – significantly higher than the 10 switches originally requested by TELMEX to the long-distance carriers. TELMEX also had to increase the availability of all its switches by January 1, 2001, and allow customers to sign up for a single LD carrier as opposed to specifying a carrier on each call. Finally, TELMEX would charge its competitors for handling the local portion of the long-distance calls based on its actual costs, without benefiting any LD carrier over another.

The relative uncertainty regarding new entrant rules for the long-distance industry had not seemed to deter potential entrants. As of December 1994, 40 Concession applications from companies and joint ventures had been accepted by the Mexican Communications and Transportation Secretariat (Secretaria de Comunicaciones y Transporte).

AT&T and Grupo Alfa

The announcement of an AT&T–Grupo Alfa joint venture on November 10, 1994, was a big blow to TELMEX and a major surprise to the analysts who thought that AT&T, the world's largest provider of global telecommunications services, would have great (and exclusive) synergies with TELMEX. Grupo Alfa, a conglomerate in high-growth industries such as food and petrochemicals, owned 51 percent and AT&T will own 49 percent of the $1 billion joint venture. The venture targeted mainly corporate customers for local and long-distance voice and data transmission services. These services were likely to be extended to residential subscribers, along with offerings of cellular phone services. Although it did not have any expertise in the communication industry, Grupo Alfa offered a deep knowledge of the Mexican market and contact with the Garza's of Monterey, one of Mexico's oldest and wealthiest families, which would help AT&T in lobbying the Mexican government to provide more predictable and favorable regulations.

Analysts regarded the AT&T–Grupo Alfa joint venture as a major setback for TELMEX. News reports commented on TELMEX's missed opportunity to participate in a project that would span the Americas:

> One thing is clear AT&T regards TELMEX as an inferior business partner compared to Alfa – even though Alfa has no telecommunications experience. (Keller and Torres 1994)

The analyst's concerns were mirrored by the actions of public investors. The day after the joint venture announcement, TELMEX's stock price declined by about 10 percent whereas Grupo Alfa's increased by 6.5 percent.

MCI and Grupo Financier Banamex-Accival

MCI, the sixth largest global telecommunications service provider, has engaged in a joint venture with Mexican Grupo Financier Banamex-Accival announced on January 26, 1994. The $1 billion investment was split 45 percent MCI, 55 percent

Banamex. Plans entailed linking the customers of Mexico City, Guadalajara, and Monterey, three of Mexico's largest cities, with fiber optic cables. This system would deliver advanced business requirements, voice, data, and video services.

As the largest financial group in Mexico, Banamex could provide MCI with a huge potential customer base from its 110,000 large business customers and two million retail banking clients. Furthermore, MCI could utilize Banamex's satellite and private microwave network to allow electronic funds transfers and use of automatic teller machines.

Bell Atlantic Corporation and Grupo IUSACELL

On December 2, 1993, Bell Atlantic completed a purchase of an initial 23 percent ownership stake in IUSACELL. This was increased to 42 percent, a total $992 million, on August 9, 1994. IUSACELL has the cellular concessions covering several regions of central Mexico. IUSACELL was considered tiny, compared to TELMEX, which had a national cellular concession through its Telcel subsidiary. However, with the investment of Bell Atlantic, IUSACELL, could expand into local and long-distance services, in addition to its cellular service.

Sprint Corporation and TELMEX: An Opportunity

Sprint Corporation and IUSACELL were in negotiations for some time concerning an alliance to tap Mexico's LD market. Sprint, one of the three largest long-distance service providers in the United States, may have been a perfect match for IUSACELL, which offers advanced technology and services in the cellular industry. The negotiations were broken off, however, when Bell Atlantic invested so heavily in IUSACELL. Regulations require that Mexican interests have at least a 51 percent stake in the telecommunications partnership. As it stood, Bell Atlantic, an American company, already owned 49 percent.

The failure of the Sprint-IUSACELL alliance appears to have provided an opportunity for TEL-MEX to join with Sprint. In addition to protecting its market share in Mexico, a partnership with Sprint might provide TELMEX with access to other global markets, such as Europe, Brazil, Venezuela, and most of Central America, in which Sprint already has operations. In fact, a nonequity strategic alliance between Sprint and TELMEX was announced on December 14, 1994.

Motorola Corp., Grupo Protexa, and Baja Cellular Mexicana

Motorola Corp., Grupo Protexa, and Baja Cellular Mexicana represent a recently formed alliance that is searching for a fourth partner (long-distance carrier) to round out the consortium. Motorola, recognizing the potential for growth in northern Mexico especially, has penetrated the market by developing a consortium with two North-Mexican cellular phone providers. This consortium linked up to extend service to all of the regions bordering the United States. The proximity of the United States could make it easy for the group to provide a US-Mexico long-distance service. The long-term plan of this consortium was to provide cellular and long-distance service to compete directly with TELMEX.

Motorola maintained expertise in cellular transmission technology and hardware. In May 1995, it secretly purchased the license to operate in North Central Mexico. Baja Cellular controls two cellular regions, one in Baja California and another along Mexico's Northwest region. Motorola purchased 42 percent of Baja Cellular for a reported $100 million. Proceeds from the deal will be used to modernize Baja's cellular operations. Grupo Protexa, which controls two cellular regions covering central and northeastern Mexico, announed a $1.5 billion deal with Motorola to develop these franchises. Furthermore, Grupo Protexa and Sprint Corp. have recently failed in negotiations to develop long-distance service in Mexico, losing the chance to fill the fourth seat in the consortium. Upon filling this fourth seat, the consortium will likely become a formidable competitor. In the words of Baja Cellular co-founder Jose Manuel Villalvazo, this deal is:

EXHIBIT 9
Background Data

- Mexico is the 13th largest economy, yet ranks 83rd in lines per capita.
- Mexico covers 760,000 square miles.
- In telecommunications, Mexico has a promising future in data services. Having more engineers per capita than the United States makes Mexico an excellent resource for less expensive, sophisticated data services and data entry.
- TELMEX plans to spend some $8 billion through 1995 expanding and upgrading its network. By 2000, it expects to have 35 million phones wired in an all-digital network, up from 12 million.
- Since gaining certification as TELMEX's third supplier, AT&T has won a $150 million three-year contract to connect 54 Mexican cities and towns with more than 8,300 miles of fiber-optic cable and switching equipment.
- TELMEX does not offer discounts for 800-lines.
- In Mexico, 9 of every 100 inhabitants have a telephone; there are currently 7,621,000 lines.
- The cellular telephone is one of the most successful areas in telecommunications. It is already a market without barriers. The most important regions that use this service are Mexico City, Guadalajara, Monterey, and Tijuana, having about 500,000 to 650,000 subscribers.
- One of the markets that represents the biggest telecommunications segment is the private network for banks, stock markets, and large corporations such as the following: Bancomer-Canadian Equipment NEC – controls 150 stations; Banamex – its network reaches 260 cities, including 10 outside of Mexico; Pemex – acounts for a network with unions of microwaves via satellite.
- Seventy percent of the calls from Mexico to the United States are made through AT&T and the same percentage from the United States to Mexico is also made through AT&T.

the first step toward something much more broad . . . we are missing a fourth seat, and that is the operator of a long-distance service.
(*Wall Street Journal* 1994)

GTE Corp., Grupo Financier Bancomer, and Valores Industriales

On September 8, 1994, GTE Corp. agreed to form an alliance with two major Mexican companies to explore entering the Mexican local and long-distance phone market in 1997. Grupo Financier Bancomer is the second largest financial group in Mexico. Valores Industriales is the holding company for both Fomento Mexicano, a Mexican brewer, and the largest Coca-Cola franchise in Mexico. Although detailed information concern-

ing the venture is not yet at hand, analysts suggest it will involve an investment of hundreds of millions of dollars. Projected ownership of the joint venture would be Mexican partners 51 percent and GTE 49 percent. While this venture enjoys significant technical and political clout, the partners do not appear to be moving as aggressively as others. Thus, they are considered a dark horse in the telecommunications race.

Challenges Ahead

The major questions facing the TELMEX executive committee were numerous. Should TELMEX seek out additional alliance partners besides

EXHIBIT 10
Glossary

Access line	A telephone line reaching from a telephone company's central office to a business or residence.
Central office	Switching facilities owned and operated by the local service provider.
Consortium	Collective equity body owning TELMEX, consisting primarily of SWBIH, FT, and GC.
Integrated digital network	Same as ISDN.
Intelligent network	Network consisting of three blocks: (1) intelligent processors that go beyond the digital switch, (2) common channel signaling, and (3) digital end-to-end connectivity.
ISDN	Integrated services digital network; provides end-to-end digital connection with standard user interfaces.
Multiplexer/Demultiplexer	Hardware that consolidates multiple lines into one, then at the other end reverses the process. This is done to maximize utilization of resources.
Private branch exchange (PBX)	Stored program-controlled customer-premises equipment that performs switching functions.

Sprint? If so, what for? What areas of the Mexican telecommunications market can TELMEX hope to dominate after 1996, and how should it prepare for this? Where should TELMEX concentrate its investments in the meantime? How can the company balance its Concession responsibilities with the need to prepare for heavy competition, especially in long distance? What type of corporate strategy should TELMEX pursue? Should the company attempt to compete in its various segments on cost, differentiation, or otherwise? How might TELMEX diversify some of its risk? What sources of capital remain for TELMEX to utilize, especially since the devaluation of the peso, as it attempts to hold market share in the future?

References

Atterbury, J. (1991) Analyst questions re TELMEX bid, D3, January 1.

Barthy, R.L. (1994) Mexico: Suffering the Conventional Widsom, *Wall Street Journal*, October 5, A18.

Carroll, A.B. (1995) Mexico Rejects Phone Market Entry Fees, *Wall Street Journal*, April 12, A11.

Kamm, T. (1994) Learning Lessons from Privatization inLatin America, *Business Forum*, Winter/Spring, pp. 25–7.

Keller, J.J. and Torres, C. (1994) AT&T Corp. and Grupo Alfa Plan Venture, *Wall Street Journal*, November 10, A3.

Lexus/Nexus (1991) *Mexico Service*, May 17.

Solis, D. and Torres, C. (1995) Mexico's Move to Quash Chiapas Rebels Carries a Big Risk to Zedillo, *Wall Street Journal*, February 13, A10.

Southwestern Bell International Holdings (1995) Internal Study.

Teléfonos de México (1993) *Annual Report*, pp. 56–60.

TELMEX (1993) *Annual Report*, p. 17.

Wall Street Journal (1994) Motorola to Purchase 42% of Mexican Cellular Firm, June 23, A11.

Wall Street Journal (1995) Stock Tables, February 24, C5.

Case 18: Cartier: A Legend of Luxury

By Sumantra Ghoshal, François-Xavier Huard and Charlotte Butler[1]

The Birth and Growth of a Legend

In 1817, a man named Pierre Cartier returned from the Napoleonic Wars and opened a shop in the Marais, Paris's artisan quarter, where he sculpted powder horns and decorative motifs for firearms. His son, Louis-François (1819–1904) adapted to the more peaceful and prosperous times of the Restoration by becoming first the apprentice and later, in 1847, the successor of Monsieur Picard, a 'maker of fine jewellery, novelty fashion and costume jewellery.' In 1859, Louis-François opened a shop on the Boulevard des Italiens, flanked by the favorite cafés of the smart set. He soon attracted the attention and patronage of the Princess Eugénie, cousin of Napoléon III and soon to become Empress of France.

Alfred Cartier took over from his father, Louis-François, in 1874. In the turbulent decade following the collapse of the Second Empire and the revolt of the Communards, the company survived by selling the jewels of La Barucci, a famous courtesan of the time, in London. Like his ancestors, Alfred adapted to changing times and the whims of a new set of customers, the wealthy bourgeois, adding objets d'art, clocks, snuff boxes and fob watches to his range of wares. His son, Louis, became his associate in 1898.

[1] Source: This case was written by François-Xavier Huard and Charlotte Butler, Research Associates, under the supervision of Sumantra Ghoshal, Associate Professor at INSEAD. It is intended to be used as a basis for class discussion rather than to illustrate either effective or ineffective handling of an administrative situation. Financial support from the INSEAD Alumni Fund European Case Programme is gratefully acknowledged. Reprinted with the permission of INSEAD. Copyright © 1990 INSEAD-CEDEP, Fontainebleau, France. Revised 1992.

Louis Cartier

> Cartier . . . the subtle magician who breaks the moon into pieces and captures it in threads of gold.
>
> (Jean Cocteau)

Louis brought to the firm his 'creativity, his commercial genius and an extraordinary dynamism.' Full of curiosity, passionately interested in artistic and technical innovation, Louis introduced platinum into jewellery settings, making them lighter and easier to wear, and showed a distinctive flair for design. His was the inspiration for new items such as the watch with a geometric hull, designed for his friend, the Brazilian pilot Santos Dumont. Jewellery designer Jeanne Toussaint (1887–1978) added her creativity to that of Louis. The result was the famous animal collection, including the beast that was to become Cartier's best-known international trade-mark, the fabulous jewelled panther.

Cartier moved to the Place Vendôme, home of the greatest names in jewellery, but Louis had no intention of allowing Cartier to become just another jewellery firm. The clockmaker, Jaeger and Lalique, the goldsmith and luxury glass manufacturer, both worked for him. At the 1925 World Fair, it was clear that rather than cling to the company of traditional jewellers, Louis preferred to mix with people from other creative fields, such as the couturiers Lanvin and Louis' father-in-law, Worth.

With his brothers, Louis opened shops in London (1902) and New York (1908), while at the Court of St. Petersburg he established Cartier as a rival to Fabergé. Cartier ruled over the crowned heads of Europe, 'the jeweller of kings and the King of jewellers.' Royal warrants came from Edward VII of England (Louis created 27 diadems for his coronation), Alphonse XII of Spain and Charles of Portugal.

In the early decades of the 20th century, Cartier reached its apogee. There was not a monarch, business tycoon or film star who was not a client. Louis even conquered the literary world, designing the swords carried by authors such as Mauriac, Duhamel, Maurois and Jules Romains for their enrollment as members of the Académie Française. And it was Jean Cocteau who, in 1922, inspired Louis to create his famous ring composed of three interlocking circles, a magical symbol in Indian legend.

But Louis' descendants were to live through less glorious times. The Second World War engulfed many of the clients who had been the mainstay of the great jewellery houses and, after four generations of entrepreneurial, successful Cartiers, the firm seemed to lose its sense of direction. The New York store was sold, amid some dispute and discord within the family.

In 1964, a man came knocking at the door of the legendary jewellers. He was a manufacturer of mass-produced cigarette lighters, an inventive spirit who had applied all the latest technical refinements to the development of a new product. To mark the event, he wanted to decorate this new product with silver and christen it with one of the great names of the jewellery establishment. Rejected by other jewellers, he made his way to Cartier.

Robert Hocq

Robert Hocq was the head of Silver Match. A self-educated man, his dreams were forged among the machines in his workshop. Trailing behind the great names of Dupont and Dunhill, Silver Match had adopted the 'copied from America' style of the new consumer society, furnishing disposable lighters to the mass market. Positioned in the middle range, the Silver Match lighters were sold through tobacco shops.

Robert Hocq had defined the market he was aiming for – the gap between his current products and the 'super luxury' of Dunhill and Dupont. All that his lighters needed was 'a little something' that would elevate them to the realm of 'authentic' luxury goods. And in a world of plastic and cheap imitations, he needed the guarantee that only a name associated with true luxury could provide. Whether prompted by the need for money or the memory of past innovations, in 1968 Cartier agreed to grant Hocq a temporary license.

The lighter's original design, a simple column in the Greek architectural style encircled by a ring, was slowly elaborated. Two radical innovations were incorporated. First, its oval shape was a direct descendant of Louis Cartier's favorite form, then quite unknown in the world of lighters. Second, Robert Hocq introduced the use of butane gas. The sale of gas cartridges would be a lucrative sideline even though, for the moment, clients were more accustomed to using liquid fuel.

To commercialize the new products, Le Briquet Cartier S.A. was established. The lighters were to be sold through the same outlets as Silver Match, a network of retailers. By 1968, the deal had been finalized and Robert Hocq turned to the task of finding the right person to sell his Cartier lighter.

Alain Perrin

The candidate who entered Robert Hocq's office, did so in response to an advertisement he had seen in the paper. The meeting began at six o'clock in the evening, and ended at midnight over an empty bottle of whisky. Alain Perrin often exhausted those around him whether at home, at the 12 schools he attended or during the long nights of his student days. He had arm-wrestled with Johnny Halliday, dined with the Beatles and in short, led the Parisian life of insouciance of the 60s generation. Born into a family of scientists, he dreamt only of a business career. While at the Ecole des Cadres he imported Shetland sweaters for his friends. Cutting school to race all over trading sweaters for farmers' old furniture, he earned the nickname 'King Pullover.'

After the death of his father in 1965, Alain Perrin directed his ebullient energy towards more serious objectives. He returned to school to finish his studies and then began work in a paper recycling company. Bored by this, he started his own company dealing in antiques. One shop led to another, and finally to three.

In May 1969, he was still only 26.

On the road, a suitcase of the new Cartier lighters in his hand, Perrin visited those existing Silver Match clients who seemed best suited to the new product's image; wholesalers and fine tobacco stores or civettes. The ligher was an immediate success. The civettes gave it star billing; to be able to handle a Cartier product was tantamount to selling real jewellery. In competing with traditional jewellers, this gave them a long-sought legitimacy.

All profits were reinvested by Hocq in order to acquire the permanent and exclusive right to the Cartier name. His relations with Cartier grew ever closer.

Hocq's activities were not confined to lighters. Two days after Cartier acquired a 70-carat diamond in a New York sale, Richard Burton bought it for 14.5 million francs as a gift for Liz Taylor. Cartier's profit on the deal was minimal but the publicity surrounding the sale was invaluable. Orchestrated by Hocq, the event was a media coup for Cartier.

In 1971, backed by a group of financiers, Robert Hocq bought the jewellery business and the Paris and London shops from the Cartier family. In 1976, he bought back the New York store. Alain Dominique Perrin became General Manager of the lighter division.

Must Lighters

In 1972, the trademark 'Les Must de Cartier' was born.

When the lighters were first launched in December 1969, Robert Hocq was discussing the project with a colleague. Tapping a magazine advertisement, Hocq asked him 'Cartier . . . what exactly does Cartier mean to you.' In English, the man answered: 'Cartier is a must, Sir.' At the time, the reply baffled Hocq, but several years later, he remembered the incident.

> Modern man has a need to let the world know that he has succeeded. To do this, he needs to be able to buy symbols of social prestige. True luxury objects produced by the great jewellers cannot give him the recognition he yearns for, since they are exclusively one-of-a-kind.

Must lighters are the materialization of social status.

In 1974, following the example of Dupont, Cartier pens joined the lighters in shop windows. Whereas the lighter was, by its very nature, connected with tobacco shops, pens opened up new distribution channels. In 1975, the addition of leather goods opened up yet another.

With the Cartier pen-lighter duo, stores were no longer selling an object but a prestige concept. At the same time, Cartier was anxious to expand distribution of its jewellery. However, although lighters and pens could hold their own amidst displays of necklaces and rings in neighborhood jewellery stores, Cartier jewels were simply not meant to be surrounded by the ordinary and anonymous.

Exclusive Cartier boutiques were created. In them, under the slogan 'Les Must de Cartier' and set against the rich bordeaux red chosen for the line, Cartier jewels were diplayed to advantage. Later on, leathers, lighters and pens too were shown against this same distinctive setting. Strict guidelines defined the product mix, decoration and service which each distributor had to provide. Cartier then began sending inspectors round to monitor discreetly that these conditions were being respected.

The Must line was not to everyone's taste. The very select Comité Colbert excluded Cartier from its membership and shortly afterwards Cartier withdrew from the Syndicat de Haute Joaillerie, the organization of fine jewellers which represented the most prestigious houses of the Place Vendôme. For a time, relations between 'that cowboy Perrin' and the other jewellers were strained.

In 1973, Cartier founded a new company under the emblem 'Les Must de Cartier,' to be kept entirely separate from its jewellery interests. Alain Perrin became its President. Concerned that too much of the jewellery business was concentrated in the Paris area (65 percent of sales), he convinced Robert Hocq that the concept and products should be exported.

> I needed to move from the state of an elegantly sleepy retailer to that of a young, contempor-

ary, international concern, capable of creating products for a world-wide market, and not just Paris, London or New York.

Once a year, Alain Perrin travelled round the world. In 10 to 12 stops from the Middle East to Australia, from Hong Kong to the United States, he picked up orders and sold the universality of the Must concept.

Must Watches

Buying back the New York store in 1976 led to a new activity.

As a jeweller, Cartier made a solid gold watch: the Tank. Its reputation (which went back to Louis Cartier) had inspired innumerable imitations. The American market in particular was infested by a plague of watches in plated brass, copies of the Tank. For 500 or 1000 francs, an imitation of the real thing (costing 10,000 to 15,000 francs) could be bought. Even the New York store, long out of the control of the Cartier family, was selling this type of imitation.

To end these shoddy practices, Alain Dominique Perrin fought fire with fire. He brought out a vermeil watch, based on an original model. This meant that for only 2000 francs more than the price of a cheap imitation, people could buy themselves a real Cartier watch, a true descendant of the masterpieces created by Louis Cartier in solid gold and brilliants.

The extension of the luxury Must line into watches allowed Cartier to surpass Dupont. From then on, Cartier's line of lighters, pens, leathers and watches were always displayed quite separately. Retailers had to reserve 'a space within a space' for them in their stores and the style of presenting the goods had to be in keeping with (and directly inspired by) the Must boutiques.

Perfume

The idea of launching a perfume, planned for 1981, presented a dilemma.

On the one hand, the very nature of the product contradicted Cartier's expressed wish to limit itself to 'lasting products which clients covet

and to which they become attached.' Cartier had originally resolved only to produce objects that were 'never thrown out.'

On the other hand, perfume was inevitable. Historically, it had been the first diversification channel for every luxury brand, and constituted the most obvious path in the public mind.

A further problem was how to launch the perfume – and hence follow in the footsteps of most other luxury brands – without breaking another of Cartier's golden rules: 'Avoid what is already being done.'

Cartier's product managers came up with the idea of a 'case/refill.' The case was conceived as an object in the Cartier tradition, lasting forever and never going out of fashion – an expensive product priced well above the competition – while the refill, in utilitarian plastic, would be priced well below the competition for the same quantity of perfume. The bevelled shape of the refill would ensure that it could not stand upright or be used without the case. Sale of the perfume to a client without a case would be forbidden.

The idea seemed simple yet seductive. Opposition came from market specialists, who did not believe that it would work. Previous similar attempts, albeit limited, had failed.

But Cartier's marketing team felt that the Cartier cachet would overcome any reservations in the perfume market, and that the very novelty of the case, 'a totally new gift idea,' would open up a whole new area of marketing. Perrin decided to go ahead with the launch. It was an immediate success.

At a later date, having legitimized its entry into the perfume market, Cartier brought out its perfume in a classic bottle – with a leather pouch. It was presented as a 'travel' version.

> In the luxury market, it's the survival of the fittest. You have to have the largest market share and be the most creative. Then you can do as you like with the market.

Transition

In 1979, Robert Hocq was run over and killed by a car while crossing the Place Vendôme. His daughter Nathalie became head of the group until 1981, when she moved to the United States. At that time, the Must collection represented a turnover of 250 million francs. The same year, Must and Cartier Joaillier merged, regrouping under the name Cartier International. Alain Dominique Perrin became President of the Board of Directors.

In 1983, Cartier was acquired by the Richemont group, a 3.3 billion Swiss francs tobacco and luxury goods conglomerate of South African origin.

The Forces of Creativity

On becoming President of the company following the Richemont takeover in 1983, Alain Perrin announced to *Business Week*, 'By 1990 we'll show a turnover of 300 million dollars.' The actual turnover in 1990 reached US$950 million, representing an average annual growth rate of 27 percent per year over 10 years (see Exhibit 1). Consolidated sales, including other brands acquired or under licence, amounted to US$1.350 billion. A 1990 McKinsey study evaluated the world luxury market at US$50 billion in retail sales, thus giving the Cartier brand four percent of sales – the largest for any single brand – in a highly fragmented market.

In jewellery, representing 25 percent of its turnover, Cartier is one of the world leaders after the US firm Winston. It is number one in the sale of luxury watches (40 percent of the market and 550,000 annual sales), and deluxe leather goods (10 percent of turnover) with 1.6 million articles sold in 1989 (see Exhibit 2).

According to Alain Perrin, creativity is the engine that has powered Cartier to this spectacular success. For him, it is the soul, the very essence of the group. Under Perrin, the lifeblood of the company is derived from the friction between a series of dualities. Thus, creation at Cartier is yesterday's memory, juxtaposed with today's insights into the environment. Perrin loves to cultivate such disequilibrium because 'It forces us to move forwards.'

> One of the best sources of profit is creativity. Creativity is what? It is doing something your competitors do not do. Or doing it first. Or doing it stronger or better. Everything that is creative contains a plus on something . . . and creativity is the backbone of Cartier.

Product Development

The design for every new Cartier product is discussed and prepared according to a very precise

EXHIBIT 1
Cartier: Rate of Growth, 1985–90

Source: *Le Figaro*, December 10, 1990

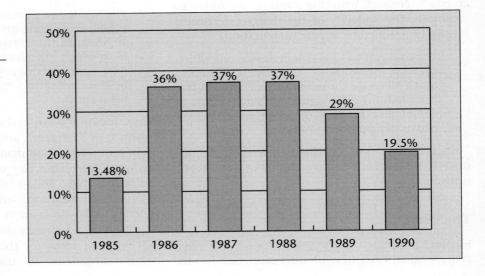

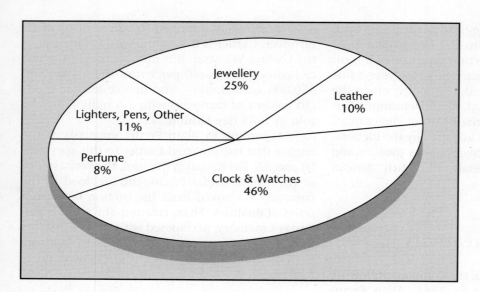

EXHIBIT 2
Cartier: Sales by Product

process involving all the 200 people working at Cartier International. The launch of a product takes two to three years. A 'product plan' three years ahead of the launch describes the evolution of the line: one major launch per year and spin-offs from each major project.

Nothing is launched until Perrin is convinced Cartier can 'do it right.' 'I'd rather lose one year than introduce a half-baked concept.'

Once the designs have been selected, the Drafting department elaborates models and prototypes 'while stressing quality and keeping in constant contact with the creator.' In order to reproduce the audacity of the designs, technical creativity is added to artistic imagination.

> The oval pen was a real brain teaser, one which the best specialists in the business refused to touch when we consulted them. It took us two years to bring out the product, since we had to design and produce our own cartridge. We patent designs every year.

Such creativity rests on this paradox: 'Each product is an exceptional creation, but we invent nothing.'

The Old . . .

Cartier's past is where the search for present creativity begins. Each new product launched has its ancestor among the collections of chalk and pastel drawings made by Louis Cartier and represents 'the spirit of creation and the style of Cartier, adapted to our time and to the trends we are setting for the future.'

At the turn of the century, a piece of Cartier jewellery destined for the mistress of a client was accidently delivered to his wife. To avoid a repetition of this error, Cartier began to keep exhaustive records on clients, the models they chose and the gems used. These records became Cartier's archives.

> The first lesson a product manager has to learn is how to navigate his or her way through our archives. In this treasure trove, we search for ideas which will fall onto fertile ground, germinate, ripen and one day, when the time is right, be launched onto a market which is not quite ready for it.

While looking at an archive photograph of the governor of Marrakesh and at the massive watch that Louis Cartier had made for him, Alain Perrin predicted that 'One day we'll have to launch a watch like that.' Today, 'the Pasha watch is one of our star products, and has brought large watches back into fashion.'

Perrin had already delved into the archive's rich seam of ideas for the Must line. When he became President, its use became systematic.

Consequently, the company began to develop lines whose names – Santos, Panthère, Pasha, Cougar – owed nothing to the American culture of the sixties and seventies that dominated elsewhere.

. . . And the New

Cartier's business is to be a trend-setter not a follower; 'to influence people in their behavior, in their choice, in their taste . . . Other companies follow customers; but customers follow Cartier.' To do this, 'We spend a lot of time and money on surveying the market and the competition . . . on getting the information that will lead us to understand and make decent forecasts on trends.'

Perrin has files on each of his major competitors going back 20 years. 'I know more about them than they do about themselves.' He even has 'people making window checks on competitors' products all over the world, all the year round.'

> Starting from concrete information on competition, on distribution, on consumption, on people's choices, on political trends, on fashion, all these ingredients at the end give us the quality of information that we need to be able to create a product which we know will be fashionable, and have an influence on the culture of the year 2000.

Image

For Perrin, brand image is the basis of an effective marketing strategy. 'Luxury, for the client and the manufacturer alike, means communicating around a brand in the same way that jewellery communicates around a gem.' But promotion should be based on the name and image of the company rather than the product.

> Our brand name was built very slowly, and it's set in concrete. We survive economic, political and regional conflicts without disturbance. Crises seem to stimulate the market for high value added products. In recent years we have even witnessed a growing demand for rela-

tively old Cartier jewels. This is unhoped-for support for our image.

Perrin is proud of Cartier's pioneering marketing methods. 'We were the first to use heavy marketing, the first to communicate in the way we do, the first to use heavy public relations to create events around culture, promote artists, and probably the first to succeed in controlling our distribution as we did.' He enjoys manipulating the opposite marketing poles of secrecy and publicity.

Secrecy . . .

Through secrecy about past events affecting the company, Cartier is able to protect its legend.

> One of our strengths is our ability to maintain a certain mystery about the economic entity which is the company. We bring magic and dreams to consumers who don't want to see their favorite brands discussed in the media, and lacking any sense of the romantic.

According to Perrin, breaching this secrecy could bring the luxury industry crashing down. Thus, he regards going public as a sure way to perdition. 'Waging public battles on the floor of the stock exchange is a serious error for the luxury goods sector. It kills the magic. My craft is to make money with magic.' Luxury businesses who go public 'risk losing their soul. A luxury business has nothing to gain from seeing its name indiscriminately positioned in alphabetical order in the daily quotations listing.'

. . . And Publicity

But then again, 'Cartier is a name which lives in the news.' The luxury goods sector is an important consumer of publicity. Cartier's public relations department has a team of 20 people, and each new product launch is accompanied by astounding creative pageantry, courtesy of a company called Delirium.

Undoubtedly, Perrin himself is Cartier's best communication tool. A high profile figure, he is photographed everywhere; beside Elton John on his French tour, at the launch of the 'restos du coeur' (soup kitchens set up by the French comedian, the late Coluche), on the slopes of a fashionable ski resort, at a Red Cross benefit or attending a conference at HEC (a leading French business school).

Another powerful weapon is Cartier's universal implantation.

'I remember,' notes a competitor, 'finding myself in a tiny airport deep in the heart of Venezuela. The very first thing I saw as I got off the plane and entered the makeshift building was a Cartier watch.'

Cartier files all the magazine photos or articles which mention its name, or that of one of its products. Its picture gallery includes the tennis player Jimmy Connors, Dynasty star Linda Evans, French film star Jean-Paul Belmondo, Pakistan's ex-Prime Minister Benazir Bhutto, and also 'rogues' such as Libya's President Ghadafi, the ex-gangster Mesrine, giving his companion a Cartier necklace just hours before being shot down by the police. The sale of the Duchess of Windsor's jewels 'among which ours were prominent' also served Cartier well.

Another famous picture shows Perrin perched on the top of a steam-roller, the day in 1981 when he destroyed 4000 counterfeit Cartier watches. The defense of the Cartier name against counterfeiters costs the company nearly US$3.5 million a year.

Cartier has created its own highly effective communication and marketing weapon: the use of sponsorship and culture.

By marrying Cartier with contemporary art we seduced the anti-luxury and anti-uniform population. We also seduced the media which, since 1981, had been cool towards the luxury goods industry. By positioning the firm in the future rather than in the past, we at last managed to reach a younger clientèle.

Most famous is the Cartier Foundation for Contemporary Art, a cultural center established just outside Paris in response to a 1983 market survey which found that young people were interested in contemporary art, and that 70 percent of those attending exhibitions were less than 25 years old. A meeting place, as well as an exhibition and seminar center, the Foundation hosts young artists from across the world and offers them financial support. Exhibitions have included a retrospective dedicated to the 'Solex,' the little moped symbolizing a whole generation of young Frenchmen and women, and another on the cars of Enzo Ferrari.

Sponsorship is an impressive form of communication. It unites Cartier's employees around an adventure which attracts both the media and the public across the world. Patronage costs Cartier 30 to 40 million francs a year. But it earns us media coverage worth 200 to 250 million francs.

Marketing

Perhaps Perrin's trickiest balancing act has been to maintain Cartier's image as an elite purveyor of expensive luxuries while thriving in the mass markets of watches, wallets and pens.

Exclusivity . . .

At the fusion of Cartier Joaillers and Les Must in 1981, demarcation lines were established to keep the Must line clearly separate. In the company's London office in Bond Street, 'Must people worked upstairs, Cartier people downstairs.' To compensate for the Must 'wide distribution' image and to keep the Cartier name close to its roots, the 'high jewellery' business was relaunched. By developing a line of 'signed' jewels with extremely limited editions, Cartier strengthened its presence in the US$50,000–$100,000 market segment (the top of the jewellery market goes above US$100,000).

One of Cartier's principles is never to test any of its products commercially. 'Our products, whether we are talking about a piece of fine jewellery or a Must pen, must be exclusive. There has to be a "certain something" that makes them stand out, something that goes against the norms. We do "anti-marketing".'

. . . And Volume Sales

> With the Must line I was perfectly conscious that by producing thousands of watches or pens instead of one-of-a-kind objects, I was running the risk of affecting the image of our company. If it is true that men and women wish to call attention to themselves by having a Cartier lighter or pen or sunglasses, it is also true that they wish to be recognized as part of an exclusive milieu and not as just anyone.

Quality must never be sacrificed. 'The same care must be exercised over each of the 300 operations necessary to the making of a lighter as in the 1400 hours it took to make the Odin necklace (US$600,000). Industrial quality has to stand comparison with the traditional, painstaking care of the individual craftsman. Cartier's workshop has 67 craftsmen, setters, polishers and jewellers, 'three times more than most leading jewellers.'

Cartier's success in watchmaking illustrates the manipulation of these contradictions. Cartier's adversary was Rolex, whose massive sporty wrist-watches in steel and gold had set the trend. Alain Perrin felt that a watch of equal quality, but with more creative lines and more style could become an effective rival to the Swiss brand. Through his efforts, a large clientèle was now familiar with luxury products. Their appetites whetted, they were demanding more . . .

However, he also believed that the Must line would not be strong enough to compete against Rolex. The Must concept, used and reused since 1972, risked becoming stale through repetition.

Perrin decided that henceforth, Cartier would develop its exclusive collections under a generic name taken from Cartier's history. 'I was going to put products inspired by the exclusive designs of Louis Cartier within the reach of thousands of people.'

On October 20, 1978 20 Mystère jets brought Cartier's guests to Paris's Le Bourget airport from the four corners of the world. Among them were Jacky Ickx, Ursula Andress and Santos Dumont's grandson. They were to be present at the launch of the 'Santos Dumont,' a wrist-watch with a shape inspired by the famous aviator's watch. The first watch to have screws on its body, it was 'immediately copied by the competition.' In 1981, it was followed by another success, the first moonphase Pasha watch.

In 1990, Cartier overtook Rolex as the world leader in luxury time-pieces.

Distribution

> We had to get Cartier out of the temple . . . We had to shake Cartier out of its retailer's lethargy in order to make it a profitable luxury goods company, distributing internationally.

'Leaving The Temple'

Cartier's journey into the light had begun when Perrin set off round the tobacconists with his suitcase full of lighters. The move signalled Cartier's move away from the discreet salons of the jewellers and its entry into the wider world of the gift shop.

By December 1989, 33 percent of Cartier's revenues (15 percent of volume) came from its network of 135 stores. The rest came from concessions. Cartier used its profits gradually to purchase all the distributors controlling its 7500 name-brand points of sale. This takeover was complete by 1990.

In Japan, Cartier entered the market early in 1971 by renting the usual corner spaces in hotels and department stores. By 1989, Cartier had bought an entire building, cancelled the contract with its importer and in its place established a joint venture (Cartier controlling 51 percent of the shares) to manage the 16 Japanese points of sale.

> It's the only way to consolidate our margins and control our brand name. The retail margin accumulated with the gross margin is what makes us profitable. But more importantly, it's the assurance that the name will be represented as it ought to be, whether it's in Melbourne, Madrid or Paris.

Logistics

In the mid 1980s, Cartier was confronted by an almost total blockage of its logistics system. 'We were no longer able to guarantee supplies, but at the same time we were troubled by an increase in intermediary inventory. Our network took some hard knocks.' Cartier responded by reinforcing the coordination between sales and production and introducing a sophisticated computer system. This system was designed around 13 months' sales projections and was piloted from Freiburg in Switzerland by Cartier's General Agent (Switzerland is a duty-free zone where products can be circulated quickly with the minimum of customs formalities). Freiburg, Cartier's central supplier, manages all plant deliveries and covers sub-contractors supplying all 22 sales affiliates. It then centralizes the statistics needed to update sales and manufacturing plans.

Freiburg also controls the customer service file. 'We have to be able to repair all our models, including those we no longer produce. After-sales service is assured indefinitely. It's a valuable contact with clients and it makes them return to our stores.' Product maintenance costs Cartier seven million dollars each year, and represents 240,000 repairs.

Strategy

Focus . . .

Cartier is one of the very rare luxury houses that will not allow any licensing of its name (with the exception of the development of a brand of cigarettes, a decision imposed by the holding company which also owns Rothmans). Perrin will never develop a new line simply because there is a market for it. Except for scarves, he has not ventured into the fashion businesses. 'There is no Cartier make-up, clothes, shoes or ties, and as long as I am here there never will be.'

> Cartier could do what the other luxury houses do: a little bit of everything. We haven't wanted that, since every name has strict limits. Our business is gems, jewellery, watch making, lighters, pens.

. . . And Diversification

On the other hand, 'We have developed all of our traditional products. Now, Cartier is condemned to external growth.' Acquisitions will prevent the Cartier name becoming over-exposed and besides, 'If there is something that can add to the group, it is better to buy it than to leave it to your competitors.'

EXHIBIT 3
Cartier: Sales by Brands

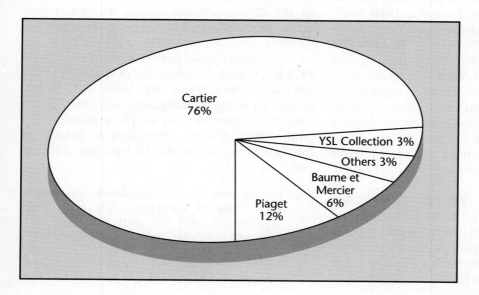

Every acquisition is designed 'to consolidate our leadership in the luxury industry.' Thus, in 1988, Cartier bought the two Swiss watch-makers, Baume & Mercier (70,000 watches per year in a market segment close to that of the Must line) and Piaget (17,000 watches in an exclusive market 'more than Rolls Royce, maybe Lagonda'). They were, says Perrin, 'sleeping beauties.' He has separated the two 'for their own good. I don't want them to talk to each other any more.' Cartier also acquired the distinguished jewellers Aldebert (80 million FF in annual sales), which has seven stores in Paris, Cannes and Monte Carlo.

Since 1989, Cartier has held a six percent share in Yves Saint Laurent, the high fashion firm for which it had produced a line of jewellery. A contract with Ferrari allows Cartier to go beyond the defined limits of luxury goods, as it did years ago with cigarette lighters (see Exhibit 3).

> We wanted to introduce our expertise, our distribution, our know-how into the male and female accessory businesses. The deals also set a kind of barrier at the bottom of the pyramid . . . With Ferrari and Yves St. Laurent we have got the market share we could not have got with the Cartier name.

> We will go no further in diversification, which has remained relatively restrained.

Management

> If you decentralize creativity too much it is no longer creativity, it's a mess . . . the information must come from the satellites, from the subsidiary or from the markets, but the final decision must come from one man.

Absolutism . . .

Under Perrin, absolutism lives on in France: 'In a company with a strong name, a strong personality, the President must be in charge.'

Perrin is the ultimate arbiter of what is produced by the firm. It is he who decides which products will be launched, he who examines, refuses or approves each of the 1200 designs submitted to him by the marketing department, he who pulls apart each product before its launch. 'I am,' he says, 'that kind of man. I want to participate very much in the creativity, in the production, in the quality. I am an active executive.'

But all these choices are, he maintains, 'the choices of any good manager . . . anybody could be Alain Perrin at the head of Cartier.'

> At Cartier, we are a management team. I can disappear tomorrow morning . . . My management people are very able to go on . . . The team is built around Cartier, not around me . . . It took twenty years, but there is no recipe . . . It is by finding the people to match . . . It is the quality of these people which guarantees our growth.

Observers note a sense of shared excitement among a workforce embarked on 'the adventure of Cartier.' 'Everyone sees him, and he enters anyone's office at any time. Ask anyone here and you'll get the impression that they know him personally. They'll tell you, "his greatest assets are his attentiveness to others and his great generosity".'

Such a direct relationship can cause difficulties. It is an area where Perrin's balancing act has occasionally failed. When Perrin took over the management of Cartier, he was assisted by an executive committee composed of the 15 managers responsible for different areas of the company. However, Cartier's expansion rendered this system increasingly difficult, whereupon Perrin appointed a General Manager. Unsurprisingly, Perrin's direct, impulsive and omnipresent management style had trouble accommodating this new structure and so he modified it, transforming the General Manager into a Vice President. Three General Managers were then appointed to run the operational functions of Marketing, Finance and Operations (coordinating the sales affiliates from Freiburg).

Perrin also has a group of close advisers, 'people who have been with me for a long while, between about six and 12 years.' They help him with his top management tasks of creation, communication and production and have been selected because 'I found in them all the qualities that I don't think I could find in myself. So let's say I am looking for complementary colleagues.' He also uses them as 'a task force to check and control what is being completed and achieved on the operational side.'

Any occasional conflicts between the normal line organization and his advisory group, Perrin sees as another source of creative energy.

'A company without conflict is a company without life . . . If you take it the positive way, a conflict must end up with something creative. So I believe in conflicts.' His role is to 'be the referee' of this 'calculated chaos,' so that it does not result in paralysis.

'If you know how to manage conflict, it ends up being very constructive.'

. . . And Autonomy

At the same time, Perrin insists that 'a company is not only a money machine' but 'a mosaic of men and women . . . a place where people live together . . . And the relationships that you have to create inside a company are human relationships, they give everyone the opportunity to express themselves.' One of Cartier's great successes has been 'in motivating people . . . And you cannot motivate the 4600 people working for Cartier if you don't give them the absolute conviction that a soul exists . . .'

At Cartier, this soul is composed of 'the partners plus the management,' and before taking any final decision, the top man 'must take the time and go round the world if necessary, and listen to the partners.'

At Cartier, it is 'natural for many, many people around me in this company to come up with a new concept . . . They can always try, they know they can try . . . The art of management is to put the ideas of others together. Creativity is something you manage exactly like an industry.'

Perrin believes that 'everybody has within himself a fantastic power of creation and of interpretation.' The modern executive is 'one who knows how to use what is inside the brain of the people, not only what he knows, not only his techniques, but his power of creation.'

'The secret of Cartier' says Perrin, 'is that we try to extract something from everybody, and give everybody the chance to participate in the creation.' And by this, he means not just the product, but 'the way you decorate a new office, the way you organize a new factory, a new distribution network . . . I like to have creative meetings, and this is the way we work.'

You must allow people the freedom to express themselves. I very often say in meetings, and we all do the same, express yourself. If you say something stupid, don't worry, we will let you know. But I prefer people to say ten stupid things, because the eleventh one will be the idea.

A New Temple

In 1990, Cartier International was installed in its new offices on the rue François ler in Paris. Housed in one of the city's grandest former private residences, Cartier is within striking distance of the large foreign luxury shops on the avenue Montaigne, and demonstrably a long way from the old-style jewellers of the Place Vendôme. All its stores will eventually be transformed along the same lines as this new corporate headquarters.

A considerable investment program will see the renovation of the boutiques. There will be room for leisurely browsing, as well as intimate alcoves in which to personalize private sales. Luminous window displays in green, ivory and mushroom tones will be reduced in size and show only a few items. The centerpiece will be a column decorated in gold leaf, against which some of Cartier's most exclusive jewels will be thrown into sharp relief.

The next generation of acolytes in the Cartier temple is also being assured. Recruitment is based on student placements. Every year, a hundred students work in the company, vying to fill 20 positions. In 1990, Cartier created a sales school, Sup de Luxe, which will train salespeople from the stores as well as distributors of Cartier products.

Perrin prefers managers who have 'experienced the terrain.' 'The manager who is only a technocrat and who has never gone out into the field, talked to a client or gone to a factory and talked to the workers, worked with them, understood how to transform a piece of steel into a watch . . . understood what the process of production is really like, as well as distribution . . . is somebody who is less complete.'

When you hire four guys D-day, and after two years look at them, one has been everywhere and knows everybody, and this is the one you are going to promote right away . . . One day, the fact that he has learnt so much from all kinds of horizons will help him have a broader view and have this famous intuition, the power to make a decision . . . The others are already stuck in one direction, doing what they do best.

Global Strategy

The expansion of Cartier outside France began in the 1970s, with the export of the Must concept. By 1991, Cartier was present in 123 countries with 145 boutiques and a network of 10,000 concessions.

Cartier spread early to Hong Kong (1969) and Japan (1971). At the time, few believed there could be a market for Cartier's products in the Far East.

To fight off the competition in Hong Kong, Cartier played its cultural card and launched the 'Cartier Master Series' in 1988. The first year was 'an unbelievable success.' By 1990, Hong Kong had five boutiques and 114 retailers and was one of Cartier's three regular international launching pads, along with Paris and New York.

And yet, Perrin is clear that Cartier will never stray too far from its heartland. 'We must be strong at home. America represents 20 percent, of which the greater part is the United States, and Asia 25 percent.' Since 1983, Cartier has gradually pulled back from the Middle East market (only three percent in 1990, which left the company less exposed to the effects of the Gulf War) (see Exhibit 4).

Our European penetration is a voluntary strategy. Europe is the origin of luxury. It is a product of our culture. I believe that the market most loyal to the artistic professions is the one that has conceived them. I will always ensure that Europe never represents less than 50 percent. Most of the major names have chosen the opposite strategy and Asia claims between 60 percent and 80 percent of their revenues. But who can guarantee that there won't be a reversal in the Asian market?

In the early 1990s, Cartier looks to expand into Eastern Europe. Openings are planned in Budapest, Warsaw, Prague and Moscow. The Cartier name is already known in Hungary. At the turn of the century, Louis Cartier directed the company from a palace in Budapest, where he lived for six months of the year while pursuing an affair with the beautiful Hungarian woman who became his second wife.

Meanwhile, Cartier is strengthening its position in the American market. A consumer research firm was commissioned for study to identify areas with the most highly paid populations. Shops will be opening in San Diego, San Jose, Phoenix . . . 'We're going to places where money flows like ice in the sun . . .'

Integrated Manufacturing

Perrin sees the integration of its industrial facilities as Cartier's next major strategic challenge. The process will be led from Saint Imier in Switzerland, the headquarters of Cartier's industrial arm, CTL (Luxury Technology Company).

With the exception of a few smaller outfits and its jewellery workshop, Cartier has hitherto lacked the means to manufacture its other products. Some of them, such as glasses frames (introduced in 1983 and manufactured by Essilor) and perfumes, are subcontracted to major industrial companies. For the rest, Cartier depends on networks of small local craftsmen who have traditionally supplied the fashion and luxury goods industry. Paris is rich in such craftsmen, who are

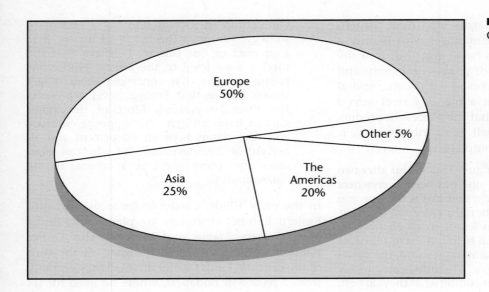

EXHIBIT 4
Cartier: Sales by Region

Europe
50%

Other 5%

Asia
25%

The
Americas
20%

closely tied to the greatest names in jewels. Cartier's leather goods are produced in France, Italy and Spain. Nothing comes from the Far East.

In 1988, Cartier completely integrated its cigarette lighter and pen production by opening a plant in Freiburg (100 employees) and another in Franconville (200 employees).

Next, 'We decided that the artisan watch manufacturing in Switzerland should be integrated, as this activity accounts for more than 40 percent of sales.' Relations with the watchmakers, to whom Cartier subcontracted 80 percent of its watch-making business, had been strained. 'Respect for deadlines among some of our sub-contractors had deteriorated drastically. The big companies are fighting to dominate a network of manufacturers who are themselves struggling to keep up with the expansion of the business.'

In 1989, Cartier invested in a 50 percent shareholding in Cristallor, the watch-case manufacturing affiliate of Ebel (a very exclusive Swiss manufacturer and a long-time Cartier sub-contractor). With Piaget and Baume & Mercier, Cartier also acquired two manufacturing companies, Prodor and Complications. Further additions have resulted in an industrial armoury which Perrin

hopes will make Cartier invincible first in watches, and then in jewellery. Since October 1991, the majority of watches made by the company have been assembled at the plant in Saint Imier. As a result, Cartier has reversed the proportion of watches it sub-contracts.

In the future, Cartier will be able to manufacture 75 percent of its production, the remaining 25 percent will give the company flexibility. 'This push towards integration allows us to consolidate our margins and our quality, and affirms our leadership.'

By a twist of fate, Piaget and Rolex face each other on opposite sides of the street in Geneva. Alain Perrin likes to feel the vibrations from his closest rival so nearby. 'In 1991,' he predicted, 'the battle will really start.'

The future of the luxury industry, considers Perrin, will be 'in the hands of two or three or four groups, no more.' The names that will dominate? 'Cartier of course, as number one. Chanel. Vuitton. Dior. Yves St. Laurent. Dunhill. Hermes . . .'

Cartier is planning a three-pronged strategy: to reinforce its presence where it is already strong, to expand in Eastern Europe and, in anticipation of 1993 and the end of duty-free shopping, to open shops in every European airport. These will become 'centers of luxury products, at the expense of alcohol, tobacco and perfume.'

But even as he describes the changes to prepare for the future, Perrin is equally emphatic about the inherent continuity and timelessness of the company.

There is no significant change in the spirit of Cartier between 1847 and 1990, and there will be none by 2000 or 3000 . . . Cartier has been the companion of all the success stories of the world for 150 years. As long as the world is the world, that success story will never cease.

Case 19: Saatchi & Saatchi WorldWide: Globalization and Diversification

By Ron Meyer[1]

Robert Louis-Dreyfus, chief executive of Saatchi & Saatchi Worldwide (Saatchi), was faced with what business journalists would euphemistically call a challenge. His company had run up considerable losses in 1989 and 1990, largely due to preferred dividends and extraordinary items, but had been able to remain marginally profitable on regular (pretax) operations. In the first six months of 1991, however, even this turned into a £4 million loss, and the outlook for the near future was dim. According to the *Wall Street Journal* there appeared to be no signs of recovery in the key advertising markets for the rest of 1991, or even through 1992 (*Wall Street Journal* 1991). Furthermore, while Louis-Dreyfus had done much to improve the company's equity position, mostly be selling off peripheral businesses, Saatchi was still burdened by a heavy debt load. It was clear that Louis-Dreyfus had to act quickly to ensure the short-term survival of his financially troubled company. However, he also had to set out a clear strategy to improve the firm's long-term prospects.

Louis-Dreyfus had been hired as chief executive officer (CEO) in January of 1990 at the moment that Saatchi had been balancing on the brink of financial insolvency, due to its empire-building acquisition spree. He undertook a full financial and strategic review that concluded that the board's decision to concentrate on the communication business (advertising, direct marketing, public relations, media services, and so on) and to turn away from the concept of a full-range services company was correct. The case for selling a broad package of services to multinationals, from advertising to computer expertise and management consulting, could make sense, but the bottom-line results indicated that the company had overpaid when buying these businesses. By mid-1991, Louis-Dreyfus had disposed of 10 out of 12 of the consulting businesses (for a total net extraordinary costs in 1989 and 1990 of £99 million) and had pushed through a recapitalization plan, which provided some short-term breathing space.

Long-term survival, however, would have to come from turning around the company's core advertising business. In the past many philosophical and heated debates about 'globalization' had occurred in the office of Maurice Saatchi, one of the two founding brothers. Now Louis-Dreyfus had to decide whether the company's vision to offer 'global' advertising services was to remain the company's central strategy for the future or whether there were other alternatives open.

The Triumphant Early Years (1970–1986)

The Saatchi brothers founded their company in the Soho district, London's ad agency heartland, in 1970. Charles Saatchi, described as one of the most eccentric and reclusive businessmen since Howard Hughes, was barely 27 years old at the time, and brother Maurice was 24.

[1] Source: This case was written by Ron J.H. Meyer, with the assistance of Nancy Peterson and Kathleen Pinnette, as a basis for class discussion rather than to illustrate effective or ineffective handling of an administrative situation. This case was compiled from publicly available sources and supplemented by information kindly provided by Saatchi & Saatchi. Copyright © 1994 by Ron Meyer, Rotterdam School of Management, Erasmus University.

The agency soon built up a reputation for simple, provocative ads. The 1971 print ad promoting contraception, for example, showed a pregnant man and asked, 'Would you be more careful if it was you who got pregnant?' The agency came to prominence in 1979 with the advertising campaign that helped the Conservatives oust the Labour Party in Britain and put Margaret Thatcher in office. 'Labour Isn't Working,' said one poster depicting a long line of unemployed people.

They were an unlikely pair to conquer Madison Avenue, but in the 1980s, the Iraqi brothers focused their attention on just that. Maurice and Charles were ignored or laughed at when they announced that they someday would rule over the world's largest advertising agency. By 1988, after a long spree of acquisitions, their concern employed 16,600 people in 58 countries, and had client billings of $13.5 billion, giving it control of five percent of the world-wide advertising market, according to *Advertising Age*. The company's biggest international accounts included British Airways, Proctor & Gamble, Sara Lee, Johnson & Johnson, and Toyota. Saatchi's competitors were no longer laughing.

The brothers had set themselves on their spectacular growth course by acquiring other advertising companies. The largest coup was the $400 million buyout in 1986 of Ted Bates agency, based in New York. This triumph allowed Saatchi to take the title of the world's biggest ad business. In the meantime the Saatchi's had also set their sights on the consulting business, announcing that Saatchi would become the largest consultancy too. The purchase of 12 consultancy firms, including big companies like Hay Management, proved they were serious.

The Saatchi's were eminently successful, or so it would seem when looking at the numbers. *Money Observer* reported (January 1989) only 37 UK companies had succeeded in raising their dividends by more than 10 percent a year over the previous decade. Saatchi was the leader of the pack, achieving a compound average of over 20 percent, due to record-breaking new business gains of four percent of the UK advertising market. Exhibit 1 outlines Saatchi's growth and major acquisitions between 1970 and 1988.

The Seeds of Destruction (1986–1988)

While the financial highlights up to 1988 looked quite impressive (see also Exhibits 2 and 3), Saatchi's appetite for acquisitions was accompanied by some symptoms of indigestion. Following the purchase of Bates in 1986, a string of client account losses and staff departures plagued the company. Especially in the United States, Saatchi lost several accounts due to the fact that client companies did not want to deal with the same ad agency as their competitors had. Large consumer product companies, such as Proctor & Gamble and Colgate-Palmolive, were concerned about confidentiality and conflicts of interest because their merged ad agency now also carried a competitor's account, so they withdrew hundreds of millions of dollars worth of business.

One of the important staff departures was that of Marten Sorrell, Saatchi's top financial executive[2] His expertise was sorely missed, when, soon after his departure, Saatchi bought out Ted Bates for what many view as an exorbitant price. Besides his financial expertise Sorrell had also played cheerleader to investors at Saatchi. After his departure, no one replaced him as an intermediary between management and the shareholders. This reinforced the perception that the brothers were interested in other things besides Saatchi and shareholder value.

Another problem was that some of Saatchi's acquisitions, like Hay, had completed their earn-out periods. Some executives feared that those companies no longer had the incentive to keep the profit increases going as strongly. Poorly handled earn-out deals encouraged the selling shareholders to milk the business, because that's the way they get the maximum earn-out.

Then in 1987 the brothers undauntedly attempted to bid for two British banks, Midland and Hill Samuel. This backfired on them miser-

---

[2] Mr. Sorrell, a brilliant empire builder, went on to make the WPP Group the biggest global ad company (see Exhibit 7) by buying J. Walter Thompson and Ogilvy & Mather, thus overtaking Saatchi's lead position.

EXHIBIT 1
Eighteen Years of
Uninterrupted Growth

Date	Pretax profits (£ millions)	Noteworthy events
1970		Saatchi & Saatchi formed.
1975	0.4	Merger with Compton Partners to construct publicly quoted company.
1979	2.4	Saatchi & Saatchi becomes largest UK agency.
1981	3.6	Second agency network started by acquisition of Dorland Advg. Saatchi becomes largest European agency group.
1982	5.5	Saatchi becomes a worldwide agency network by the acquisition of Compton Communications in the United States.
1983	11.2	US stock exchange listing obtained.
1984	20.0	Enters consulting market with acquisition of Hay Group.
1985	40.4	Forms marketing services by acquisition of Rowland (PR), Siegal & Gale (design), and Howard Marlboro (sales promotion).
1986	70.1	Major expansion in advertising with acquisition of Dancer Fitzgerald Sample, Backer & Spielvogel, and Ted Bates Worldwide. Saatchi become world's largest agency group.
1987	124.1	Paris listing obtained. Acquisition of Litigation Sciences and Peterson & Company. Merged nineteen units into two global networks: Saatchi & Saatchi Advertising Worldwide, ranking No. 2, and Backer Spielvogel Bates Worldwide, ranking No. 3.
1988	138.0	Formation of Zenith centralized media buying. Acquisition of Gartner information systems consultancy. Becomes world's tenth largest consulting firm. Tokyo listing obtained.

ably and signalled shareholders to their apparent lack of focus. For the first time shareholders of the publicly owned company and others openly began to question the brothers' strategy for the business. Had the company's vast growth, by means of aggressive acquisitions, truly added value to the companies purchased? Or was Saatchi, as some critics claimed, an example of 'dyssynergy?'

As problems started to mount, Saatchi's share price showed a significant drop (see Exhibit 4), which presented the company with further difficulties. The key to Saatchi's growth in the 1980s was its high stock price, a weak dollar, and a policy of buying companies on an instalment plan. Saatchi's strong price-earnings ratio, which topped 27 times, allowed it to raise capital in London for a downpayment on acquisitions followed by performance-based payments typically over three to five years. The declining dollar helped to make the American acquisitions relatively cheap. However, when the share price fell, the company could no longer raise money.

The Unravelling Giant (1989–1991)

By early 1989 it had become clear to Saatchi's directors that the company's financial results would take a turn for the worse. After 18 years of nonstop growth, Saatchi's operating profit in the first half of 1989 was set to decline by approximately 40 percent compared with the first half of 1988. Publicly Saatchi bravely stated that 'we see this as a pause for breath in our growth,' and claimed that there was no deep or secret reason for the weak financial results. It was merely a case of advertising suffering because some US clients were worried about the 'new' Bush administration and the budget deficit. Ad spending postponed from the first half to the second half that year had caused the damage. However, by mid-June of 1989 Saatchi had seen itself forced to put its consultancy division up for sale.

Saatchi had collected a mishmash of 12 consulting companies offering advice ranging from employee compensation and jury selection to real estate strategies and computer systems. Victor E. Millar, head of Saatchi Consulting, was given the assignment to dispose of all of these companies as quickly as possible.

The pressure to sell was high, as the company was strapped for cash. All the profits for the year would be used for dividends; therefore a sale would provide breathing space. Selling proved more difficult though as buyers were interested in bits and pieces, due to the wide variety of services Saatchi owned. Also, the urgency of the sale, from Saatchi's perspective, encouraged lower bids. The company was at first wary to sell these businesses at such a tremendous loss. Hesitation only worked against Saatchi, and when it finally completed its divestments, it sold the businesses for about £100 million after initially expecting between £250 and £350 million.

The company that had been unable to pay preferred dividends in October 1990 confirmed that it would be unable to pay dividends on its ordinary shares in early 1991. Huge fiscal year net losses were triggered by massive writedowns on its disposal of the consulting businesses for 1990. The company said the write-downs, amounting to £76.9 million, reflected a hardnosed

EXHIBIT 2
Saatchi's Revenue and Pretax Profits, 1978–1988

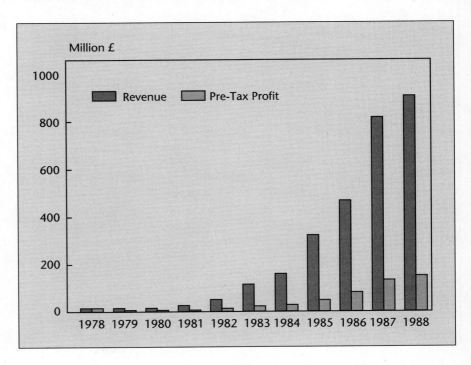

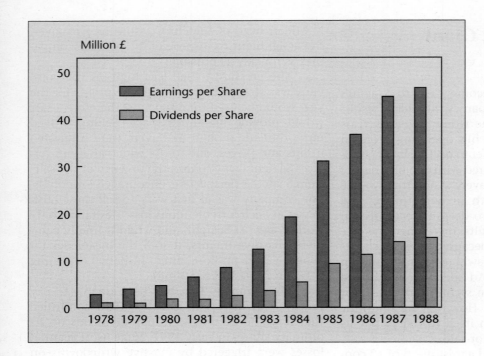

EXHIBIT 3
Saatchi's Earnings and
Dividends per Share,
1978–1988

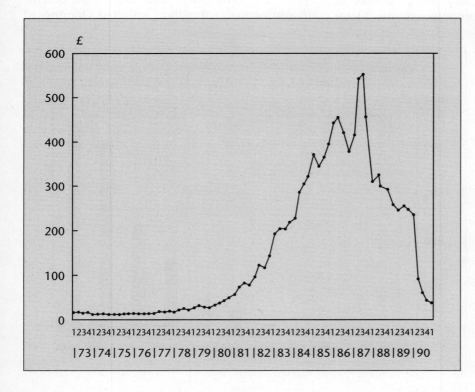

EXHIBIT 4
Saatchi's Long-Term Share
Price, 1973–1990

decision by Saatchi to take its lumps in 1990 (see Exhibit 5).

In January 1991 Saatchi unveiled a major recapitalization plan to save itself from insolvency. At the time analysts believed it was unlikely the troubled company would be able to redeem the original shares in 1993. The plan was revised in February to allow the troubled advertising company to survive intact but proposed handing over control to its preferred shareholders.

The plan, which was approved in March 1991, gave Saatchi's Europreference holders 65 percent of the company, and handed the two largest holders, ESL and London-based St. James's Place Capital, a seat apiece on the board. Both also provided additional capital to the company by underwriting a sizable chunk of a new £55 million rights offering. With the consultancy businesses divested and the balance sheet strengthened, Saatchi was now prepared to move forward in its strategy of focusing on its communications businesses.

Saatchi's 'Total Communication Services' Strategy

The Saatchi brothers relinquished responsibility as joint chief executives on January 1, 1990, handing the position over to the French-born advertising executive, Robert Louis-Dreyfus. Maurice and Charles remained on the board, and Maurice also stayed on as chairman. The new chairman's role was to focus on client relationships and broader strategy, while that of the chief executive was to concentrate on operational management and to assume profit responsibility toward the board. The choice of Louis-Dreyfus fell in line with Saatchi's announced plan to sell consulting and concentrate on communication services (see Exhibit 6).

Louis-Dreyfus announced his strategy to expand Saatchi's share of the advertising pie, primarily through internal growth as opposed to

EXHIBIT 5
Consolidated Profit and Loss Account
(in £ millions)

	1990	1989	1988
Turnover	4,353.6	4,364.1	3,796.1
Revenue (gross profit)	808.1	973.5	862.2
Profit ordinary activities before exceptional items and tax	35.8	61.3	116.4
Exceptional items	(0.2)	(39.5)	21.6
Profit ordinary activities before tax	35.6	21.8	138.0
Taxation on profit on ordinary activities	(23.1)	(37.2)	(50.4)
Profit (Loss) on ordinary activities	12.5	(15.4)	87.6
Minority interests	(5.3)	(2.9)	(3.7)
Preference dividends	(28.5)	(18.2)	(8.8)
Extraordinary items	(76.9)	(22.0)	
Profit attributable to ordinary shareholders	(98.2)	(58.5)	75.1
Ordinary dividends	(14.2)	(25.1)	
Retained profit (loss)	(98.2)	(72.7)	50.0
Profit (Loss) per ordinary share (in pence)	(15.3)	(23.1)	48.1

EXHIBIT 6
Saatchi's Directors in 1990

Saatchi, Maurice, BSc Econ, 44, chairman. Worked on new business develop-ment at Haymarket Publishing from 1968 to 1970, when he formed Saatchi & Saatchi. Chairman of Saatchi since 1985. Trustee of the Victoria and Albert Museum and governor of the London School of Economics.

Louis-Dreyfus, Robert, MBA, 44, chief executive. In 1982 appointed COO of IMS, the leading pharmaceutical market research company; in 1984 CEO. Negotiated sale of IMS to Dun & Bradstreet in 1988. Joined Saatchi as chief executive in January 1990.

Levitt, Theodore, PhD, 66, Non-executive director. Currently emeritus profes-sor of business administration at Harvard. Appointed in March 1991.

Mellor, Simon, BSc, 36, director. Joined Saatchi in 1976. Director of corporate communications since November 1990.

Russell, Thomas, PhD, 59, Non-executive director. Elected director of IMS in 1984 and chairman in 1987.

Saatchi, Charles, 47, director. Co-founder.

Scott, Charles, FCA, finance director, CFO of IMS from 1986 until he joined Saatchi in January of 1990.

Sinclair, Jeremy, 44, deputy chairman. Founding member of Saatchi.

EXHIBIT 7
Top Ten Advertising Organizations in 1990

Rank	Organization	Gross Income ($ millions)	% Growth (over 1989–90)
1.	WPP Group	2,712.0	12.9
2.	Saatchi & Saatchi	1,729.3	9.7
3.	Interpublic Group	1,649.8	10.4
4.	Omnicom Group	1,335.5	13.4
5.	Dentsu	1,254.8	(0.6)
6.	Young & Rubicam	1,073.6	16.0
7.	Eurocom Group	748.5	58.5
8.	Hakuhodo	586.3	0.1
9.	Grey Advertising	583.3	19.1
10.	Foote, Cone & Belding Communications	563.2	5.9

Saatchi's traditional method of acquisitions. When he took over at Saatchi, the major interna-tional agencies controlled about 18 percent of total ad revenue world-wide, with Saatchi's share about 25 percent of that (see Exhibits 7 and 8). In the next 10 years, Louis-Dreyfus predicted, the major agencies' share of total ad revenue would double, and 'I would like to increase our share of the sector to a third from 25 percent (*Business*

Week 1990).' Louis-Dreyfus intended to achieve such spectacular internal growth by implement-ing a two-pronged strategy, namely, by offering 'one stop shopping' and 'global communications services.'

Saatchi had learned from its past experience in consulting that cross-reference of clients between service companies has its limits, but believed that this was not a problem for the

EXHIBIT 8
Top Ten US-Based
Consolidated Agencies in
1990

Rank	Agency	Gross Income ($ millions)	% Growth (over 1989–90)
1.	Young & Rubicam	1,001.4	15.7
2.	Saatchi & Saatchi Advertising Worldwide	825.7	11.5
3.	Ogilvy & Mather Worldwide	775.3	10.8
4.	McCann-Erikson Worldwide	744.7	11.3
5.	BBDO Worldwide	723.8	10.2
6.	Backer Spielvogel Bates Worldwide	715.6	8.0
7.	J. Walter Thompson	690.7	10.3
8.	Lintas Worldwide	676.5	10.4
9.	DDB Needam Worldwide	625.2	16.2
10.	Grey Advertising	583.3	19.1

EXHIBIT 9
Saatchi's Communication
Activities

Activity	Company	Clients
Advertising	**Saatchi & Saatchi Advertising Worldwide** No. 2 International Advertising Agency 135 offices in 32 countries	General Mills, Sara Lee, Proctor & Gamble, J&J, Hewlett Packard, Toyota
	Backer Spielvogel Bates Worldwide No. 6 International Advertising Agency 159 offices in 46 countries	Philip Morris, Hyundai, King Fisher, Rover, BAT Industries, Mars
	Independent Agencies Campbell, Mithun, Esty No. 16 Advertising Agency in US 7 offices in US and Canada	Chrysler, Kroger, ConAgra, Texaco, 3M
	KHBB: No. 17 Advertising Agency in UK **AC&R**: No. 38 Advertising Agency in US **Hall Harrison Cowley**: UK regional network	
Direct Marketing	**Kobs & Draft Worldwide** No. 6 International Direct Marketing Agency 21 offices in 18 countries	Chase Manhattan, IBM, Mars, Rover
Public Relations	**Roland Worldwide** No. 6 International Public Relations Company 29 offices in 19 countries	Du Pont, J&J, Mars, P&G, Sandoz
Media Services	**Zenith Media Worldwide** Established 1988, offices in London, Paris, Madrid, Barcelona, and Milan	Allied Lyons, Amstrad, Philip Morris
Other	**Howard Marlboro Group** – In-store marketing **HP:ICM** – Face-to-face communications **Siegal & Gale** – Corporate identity and design **National Research Group** – Market research **Yankelovich Clancy Shulman** – Market research	

EXHIBIT 10
An Example of Transnational Advertising

PAN-EUROPEAN ADVERTISING FOR PROCTOR & GAMBLE

Proctor & Gamble (P&G) is Saatchi's number one client, with operations in 130 countries. About 70 percent of P&G's business is done in world brands, of which Pampers is one of the most famous. It was introduced to the US market in 1968 as the first disposable diaper in the world. Expansion followed in the mid-1970s, first in Europe and followed by the Middle East and Asia. Today it is brand leader in 14 European markets and has recently been launched in Poland and Yugoslavia, with Hungary to follow soon. But today's success was not always the case.

In the early eighties Pampers had not kept up with technical developments, and by the mid-eighties had found itself squeezed by low-cost competitors moving up-market, leading to lower prices and sagging profitability. In 1985 the company relaunched with an upgraded product in all European markets. Millions of dollars were invested in new production lines. All countries shared the same objectives: rebuild share and maintain profitability in the face of higher product costs.

However, while the objectives were the same, the marketing executions differed in each country. Since there was no agreed learning on 'what really worked,' each country did what it judged best for its market. Advertising, media, promotional activity were done on an individual market basis. There were 10 different TV campaigns produced across Europe. The results of the launches were disappointing across Europe, as the exceptional product performance did not match the higher prices and unexpected product issues surfaced. The problem became worse when each country tried to fix it their own way. R&D, agencies, and the plant had several requests from each country to address.

As Pampers reached its lowest point at the end of 1985, the company realized it needed to fundamentally reorganize in order to survive. The right balance needed to be found between global, European, and local marketing. The most significant issues identified were lowering manufacturing costs by striving for economies of scale, searching for innovative product initiatives with pan-European application, and sharing worldwide and European ideas in areas such as product, packaging, advertising, and direct marketing. In 1986 the European diaper business was reorganized into a pan-European operation to reap transnational synergies. Two new senior positions were created at P&G, namely, a divisional manager with volume and profit responsibility for the total diaper business across Europe, and a European marketing manager.

Saatchi decided to reorganize its team to mirror the P&G structure. Together the companies worked on 'keeping it simple and back to basics.' The basics for the advertising development came out of the previous experience gleaned from 10 different pieces of advertising. The pan-European approach meant that Saatchi has given P&G much less advertising (through standardization), but of much higher quality (by transferring learning effects across borders). Since 1987 the formula has been an undeniable success, as the following Euro volume growth figures show:

Index vs. previous year

1986	100
1987	110
1988	132
1989	127
1990	127

closely related communications activities. Saatchi's managers believed that a client buying Saatchi's advertising services would also be willing to let the Saatchi Group take care of its other communication needs such as direct marketing, public relations, and market research. Having the total range of communications services, it was felt, would maximize the opportunities for cross-reference and might attract new clients preferring 'one-stop shopping.' Louis-Dreyfus therefore agreed that Saatchi should keep all its communication service companies (see Exhibit 9) and should hold regular meetings at the national level to determine cross-referral opportunities.

While there were opportunities for synergy, there was also the threat of conflicting client accounts among the company's ad agencies. Saatchi therefore decided to create two distinct and separate advertising agency networks, which were seen to be in direct competition with one another, thus ensuring client confidentiality.

Saatchi's Global Marketing Approach

The second, long-standing aspect of Saatchi's strategy, besides being a total communications services company, was to build up the company's capability for launching 'global' advertising campaigns. Maurice and Charles had been early converts to the idea of global marketing, championed by Theodore Levitt of Harvard Business School. The idea basically holds that cultures are becoming so similar that products can be marketed the same way everywhere. Louis-Dreyfus supported the global advertising notion, but with more caution than the Saatchi brothers. He agreed that Saatchi was right to expand into different markets to serve multinational clients, but added, 'Creativity isn't the same everywhere. You can't apply the same principles in England, France and America.'[3]

---

[3] Graham Thomas, vice chairman of Saatchi, in a memorandum to the authors dated April 8, 1993.

While warning against excessive 'globalization,' Louis-Dreyfus by no means abandoned his belief in the basic premises. He and Maurice recruited Theodore Levitt to the company board in March in 1990 and reiterated that global marketing is an evolutionary process. Thus, Saatchi will be at the forefront of implementing this strategy for clients who compete transnationally, but will also rededicate itself to those clients currently operating only in local environments. A listing of Saatchi's Western European clients, multinational versus local, is set forth in Exhibit 11. Multinational clients are those operating in more than one country, but needn't necessarily be pursuing transnational standardization, although they could potentially in the future.

To be able to offer multinational clients global advertising campaigns, Saatchi has arranged its advertising business within a regional and worldwide matrix (see Exhibit 12). On the one hand the company is organized geographically, with agencies in each country of operation and coordination between neighboring countries achieved by means of regional management boards. On the other hand Saatchi is also organized by client, whereby world-wide account directors (WADs) and regional account directors (RADs) are responsible for representing multinational client needs across all agencies. WADs and RADs are currently running the 12 biggest international accounts.

Saatchi's Future

In May 1990 Saatchi's shares rose slightly following the news that Louis-Dreyfus had dismissed Roy Warman and Terry Bannister, two senior managers at Saatchi. The dismissals were interpreted by the markets as a sign that Louis-Dreyfus had won strategic control of the company from the Saatchi brothers, and that he now had the authority to get to grips with its financial problems.

A year later, as the share price continued to drop, Louis-Dreyfus had implemented the recapitalization plan that strengthened the Saatchi balance sheet and divested its consulting business

Country	MNC Clients	Local Clients	Total 1990 ($ m)
Austria	15	20	65
Belgium	24	11	15
France	53	30	275
Germany	42	35	238
Ireland	17	15	23
Italy	26	20	286
Netherlands	37	20	73
Spain	25	31	131
United Kingdom	60	41	745

EXHIBIT 11
Primary West European Clients

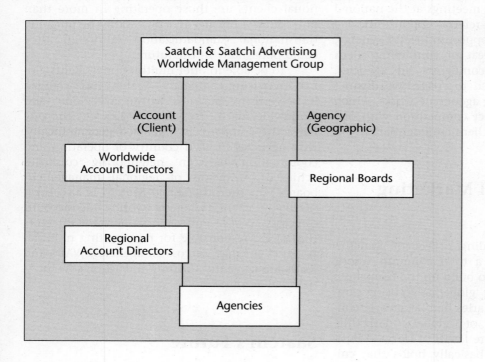

EXHIBIT 12
Organizational Diagram of Saatchi's Advertising Business

for a loss. The company had its strategy of total communications service and global advertising on track. However, the operating margins were still under great pressure and would continue to fall during 1991. Furthermore, world advertising expenditure was expected to decline in 1991 (see Exhibit 13).

Meanwhile, Maurice Saatchi, chairman,

rededicated the company to the principles of creativity that had built it in the first place and offered a new definition of great advertising. 'It means creative work that is so simple and direct that it strikes a chord in humans everywhere,' he said. But the question on Louis-Dreyfus's mind was whether this was enough to get Saatchi out of the red.

EXHIBIT 13
Estimated World Advertising Expenditure (annual % change)

	1991 vs. 1990		1992 vs. 1991		1993 vs. 1992		1994 vs. 1993	
	Current Prices	Constant Prices	Current Prices	Constant Prices	Current Prices	Constant Prices	Current Prices	Constant Prices
Major Media*								
North America	−1.8	−5.9	1.4	−2.2	3.2	−0.8	3.3	−0.7
Europe	3.4	−2.0	8.0	2.4	8.3	2.2	8.8	2.1
Asia/Pacific	6.0	1.7	8.1	3.9	8.3	3.6	8.5	3.8
Latin America	11.8	n/a	14.6	n/a	18.0	n/a	18.6	n/a
ROW	9.6	n/a	9.9	n/a	11.4	n/a	12.3	n/a
Subtotal**	2.0	−2.9	5.5	0.7	6.6	1.3	7.0	1.4
Direct Mail								
North America	4.7	0.6	5.1	1.2	5.1	1.0	5.0	0.9
Europe	4.0	−1.4	5.0	−0.6	7.0	0.8	8.0	1.4
Other Media***								
US	5.0	0.7	5.0	1.3	5.0	1.0	5.0	1.0
Japan	4.3	1.1	5.6	2.7	5.7	2.2	5.7	2.2
Total	2.7	−2.0	5.4	0.9	6.3	1.3	6.7	1.4

*TV, print, radio, cinema and outdoor.
**Constant prices exclude Latin America and the rest of the world.
***Includes point-of-sale, sales promotion expenditure.

References

Wall Street Journal (1991) Saatchi Posts First Half Loss, September 6.
Business Week (1990) Saatchi's New Chief Sees Slow Turnaround, with a Return to Earnings Stride in 1994, March 22.

Case 20(A): Cap Gemini Sogeti: Building a Transnational Organization

By Tom Elfring[1]

As the hundreds of group managers of Cap Gemini Sogeti (CGS) poured into the conference building in Prague on this nice summer day, June 25, 1992, the company's executive chairman, Serge Kampf, wondered what their ideas would be regarding the transformation of the organization. After all, he had not only called these managers together to present his own vision of what the future organizational form might look like, but also to get their input and to arrive at decisions that would be widely supported throughout the company. Kampf realized that restructuring the organization would be a difficult task, but he also knew that to continue the company's success it was imperative that CGS and the large number of recently acquired firms be moulded into a coherent transnational company.

Although reorganizations are always difficult, CGS had quite a few factors making the task more easy. CGS was a growing firm in a growing industry – world-wide CGS held the fourth place in the 'big league' of information technology service companies, while in Europe CGS was by far number one. Internally, Kampf could also count on widespread support for his efforts to build CGS into a global company. During the four day Marrakesh Rencontre in June 1990, the 550 attending group managers had opted overwhelmingly for a strategy of globaliza-

tion, with the intent of belonging to the top three information technology services corporations world-wide. This bottom-up decision had created a shared vision of the company's future and willingness throughout the organization to change.

However, Kampf and CGS were also faced with some daunting challenges. First, competition within the information technology services industry had grown increasingly intense since 1990 and the firm's net income had suffered as a consequence. Second, after the Marrakesh Rencontre, CGS had acquired a large number of companies that needed to be merged into the CGS organization. Finally, building an effective transnational organization would probably mean that the company's well-known strict decentralization policy would need to be adapted, either marginally or radically. Any further move away from the high level of local autonomy, however, would probably meet with some anxiety, if not resistance.

To Serge Kampf it was clear that the group managers' bold Marrakesh decision for a global push was a vote 'for a dream or a nightmare.' Since June 1990 he had brought together many of the building blocks for the envisioned global company, but now at this Prague Rencontre it was up to group managers to help realize the dream. The building blocks needed to be brought together to form an effective transnational company. Of course, the question was, how? What type of organizational setup and systems would suit the demands of a knowledge-intensive service firm operating on an international scale? To this pressing question the group managers – and Serge Kampf – needed to find an answer.

[1] Source: © 1994 by Tom Elfring. This case was prepared by Tom Elfring, Rotterdam School of Management, Erasmus University, with the assistance of Saskia van Rijn. This case is intended for classroom discussion, not to illustrate the effective or ineffective handling of a managerial situation. Unless mentioned otherwise, all information was obtained with the kind assistance of Cap Gemini Sogeti. The author would like to thank Ron Meyer for his useful comments. Used with permission of the author.

The Company's History

The growth of Cap Gemini Sogeti had been built on its ability to 'make computer systems work' and meet the requirements of the client. The Cap Gemini Sogeti Group's official birthdate was January 1, 1975. In that year Gemini Computer System merged with the Cap/Sogeti Group. The latter group was the result of a merger between Cap, a computer services firm, and Sogeti, a business management and information-processing company. At that time Cap had 780 employees, Gemini employed about 320 people, and Sogeti was the smallest, with 250 workers on the payroll. Cap Gemini Sogeti started out with European subsidiaries in Great Britain, The Netherlands, Switzerland, and Germany, but most of its business was conducted in France. This new Cap Gemini Sogeti Group had a good start in life through powerful (French) government patronage and the national management tradition of contracting out services instead of performing these tasks themselves.

Cap Gemini Sogeti (CGS) grew from small autonomous groups of programmers-for-hire scattered around France, with a common policy of tight financial control and a thoroughly professional reputation. During the 1980s, CGS acquired a large number of mostly smaller firms in Europe and some in the United States. They improved their position in the market for professional information technology services, such as information technology (IT) consulting, customized software, and education and training. Their expansion in the 1980s was centered on these services, and CGS achieved an average annual growth rate of about 30 percent, of which roughly two-thirds was due to internal growth. The remaining one-third had been the result of friendly acquisitions and alliances. This seemed to be the only way to provide global coverage some of the clients required.

An important acquisition was that of Sesa (Société d'Études des Systèmes d'Automation) in 1987. It could be seen as a turning point, because Sesa was a distinguished French software house with a broader corporate culture than the narrowly based CGS, with its origins in 'body shopping,' hiring out computer specialists on a daily basis to work on customers' contracts. In the late eighties, CGS concentrated on the integration of the Sesa team and on consolidating and streamlining its organization, thereby improving its profitability.

CGS's Current Position

Cap Gemini Sogeti is now Europe's number one computer services and consulting company and one of the industry's leaders world-wide. Located in 15 European countries and the United States, the group specializes in software services, its goal being to assist its clients in drawing the greatest possible benefit from information technologies. Ever since its creation in 1975, the group has upheld a strong development policy, multiplying its revenues, profits, and size. In 1992, however, CGS incurred the first losses in its history. The net group loss of $14.9 million is partly due to $60 million worth of restructuring (see Exhibits 1 and 2.)

Cap Gemini has always had a certain gloss and sparkle (even by French standards). It is proud, elitist, almost arrogant and has a single-minded devotion to developing methods and tools for writing better, more accurate software. In France, especially in government circles, software skills are equated directly with pure intellectual effort and are much prized, which has resulted in substantial government backing and patronage. Much of Cap Gemini's success was said to be due to its simple management strategy; it concentrated on what it does best (professional software engineering) and wasted little time arguing about whether it should be selling computer hardware, applications packages, or administrative services, all of which have diluted the effort of many other software houses. It articulated this philosophy to its employees continuously.

Michel Berty, general secretary of Cap Gemini Sogeti, described his satisfaction with people with well-developed minds. Two-thirds of

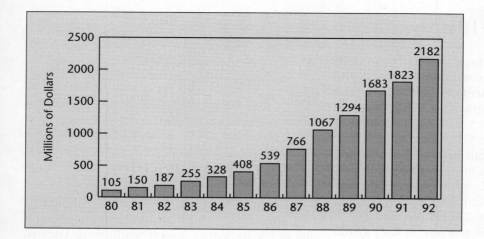

EXHIBIT 1
CGS Revenue, 1980–1992

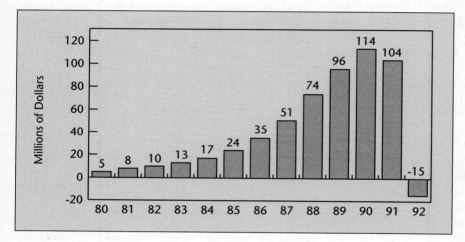

EXHIBIT 2
CGS Net Income, 1980–1992

Soget's employees have an advanced engineering degree. 'They are good,' he says. 'They have learned to work and to reason. Human qualities are also essential but are not always so well developed.'

One of Cap Gemini's formulas for success has been an inviolate decentralization policy that stipulates that when any of its branches – 250 in 1989 – reaches 150 staff, it splits in two, and a new manager is appointed to head the new branch. Eric Lutaud, a member of the corporate development team at Cap Gemini Sogeti, explains: 'We are so decentralized that at any point in time we have several people doing things that are not kosher.'

This highly decentralized style of organization, however, was subject to very strong financial controls. Cap Gemini believed local operations had to be in the hands of locally hired managers to be successful. 'To keep in touch with fast-moving IT markets, we work in terms of bottom-up, not top-down.' Unlike most European firms, Cap Gemini tied compensation to performance.

Besides the responsibility for innovations at the local level, CGS also had a more traditional and centralized unit to look to for innovations. In 1984 Cap Gemini Sogeti created Cap Gemini Innovation, specializing in applied research. Its principal missions included staying on the leading edge of new technologies, experimenting with and validating technical advances in the profession, and transferring skills among the teams taking part in group projects. This research and

EXHIBIT 3
A Comprehensive Range of Services

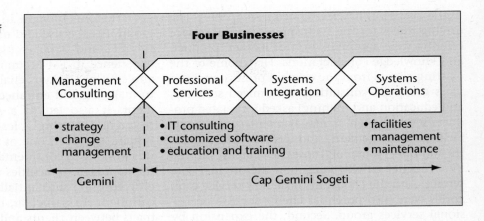

Four Businesses

Management Consulting	Professional Services	Systems Integration	Systems Operations
• strategy • change management	• IT consulting • customized software • education and training		• facilities management • maintenance

Gemini ←→ Cap Gemini Sogeti →

EXHIBIT 4
Information Technology Services by CGS

Facilities Management:	taking over all or part of a client's IT resources (hardware, software, and staff) and running this operation for a given time period and with commitment to results.
Systems Integration:	providing a client with a complete IT solution integrating hardware and software, with a commitment to respect established costs and delivery times.
IT Consultancy:	involves analyzing an IT problem and developing solutions; designing, planning, and organizing information systems: implementing solutions either by developing customized software, or by adapting already-existing applications.
Management Consulting:	helping and assisting firms to transform their business by integrating disciplines such as strategy, operations, and information technology.

development policy was carried out jointly at four research centers in France, Belgium, and The Netherlands, bringing together researchers and technicians from more than 10 countries. The sums invested in this activity have grown steadily since 1985, at which time they represented $20 million; at the end of 1991, the figure had climbed to $109 million.

Traditionally Cap Gemini Sogeti's business was the provision of general technical backup for customers' data-processing departments. But the most profitable and fastest-growing part of the business results from companies wanting Cap Gemini Sogeti to design and set up a specific

project. For this you need staff with in-depth knowledge of the customer's sector (see Exhibits 3 and 4.)

From One to Four Related Businesses

The number of different types of services related to IT has grown tremendously in the past decades. The move from a very focused firm to one with a more complete service offering was rather gradual in the 1980s but has accelerated in the 1990s. The driving forces for the swift move to a full-service offering were a combination of market, product, and knowledge considerations. First, some of the existing clients from the original professional services group (IT consulting, customized software, and education and training) asked for related products/services such as management consultancy, facilities management, and systems integration. In addition, some of those new areas showed much higher growth rates than the original core service. And the clients in those new service categories were also potential clients for the professional services group. Second, the expansion by acquisitions and alliances had also been partly knowledge driven. The degree to which targeted firms were able to fill in the gaps in the CGS skills portfolio was a serious consideration. The takeover of Hoskyns was valuable in terms of its competencies in facilities management. Hoskyn's speciality is outsourcing, or running a customer's entire data-processing department, a business that was growing at 25 percent a year, nearly twice as fast as other computer services. Its other main lines of business were IT consultancy and systems integration. The development of the market for facilities management was more advanced in the UK than in continental Europe. CGS used the Hoskyns competencies to expand its firm's operations in continental Europe.

Facilities Management

Contemporary corporations expect their information systems to keep pace with competitiveness. That is the function of their IT departments, which must be able to accommodate growing technological complexity, be easily adaptable, make practical use of their experts' time and stay fully in control of quality and costs. In its response to each of these criteria, facilities management (FM) has proven its effectiveness as a powerful resource for helping companies implement their strategies and achieve their objectives, while allowing them to concentrate on their own business. The acquisition of Hoskyns marked the commitment of Cap Gemini to move into that market in a serious way.

Hoskyns brought to the Cap Gemini Sogeti group its expertise and market-leader position in the UK, and 3500 employees. The 25 years of experience in FM accumulated by the managers and staff of Hoskyns enabled Cap Gemini Sogeti to make a grand entrance into facilities management. It also led to a second strategic breakthrough: achieving a leading position in Great Britain. However, one of the UK managers, who was working in continental Europe, remarked that the approach to facilities management in the UK differed quite substantially from practice on the continent. In particular, the content of the contracts between clients and service-provider varied because they were based on disparate approaches. For example, the UK manager generally wanted to stay in control of the operations, while in the Scandinavian countries joint ventures with equal shares are often established to regulate facilities management contracts, and in The Netherlands quite a number of partnerships with minority shares are to be found.

CGS strengthened its position in the facilities management market and in the Scandinavian market simultaneously by an $88.3 million friendly bid for Programator, its Scandinavian competitor, in February 1992. In joining forces with Programator, Cap Gemini Sogeti confirmed its stated goal of becoming the number one computer services company and market leader in northern Europe. In acquiring Programator, which generated 40 percent of its turnover from facilities management, CGS mainly targeted the FM market in Scandinavia and thus pursued its FM development strategy. As a result of this operation, Cap Programator was the uncontested professional services leader in this region, unequalled in terms of number of locations, and able to handle all types of IT projects at both local and international levels. The acquisition of Programator should have enabled CGS to generate a turnover of more than $500 million in northern Europe in 1992.

Consultancy

When more and more of CGS's customers asked for collaboration on problems of major technology projects linked to their specific activity, Sogeti created a consulting group that was structurally and professionally independent of Cap Gemini Sogeti. Gemini Consulting was created by bringing together three leading consultancy firms: the MAC Group, United Research, and Gamma International. United Research, MAC Group and Sogeti are betting that the increased speed of corporate decision making will mean that a linked network of consultants will succeed where individual firms cannot. 'In the past,' says Scott Parker, co-managing director of MAC, 'companies hired one consulting firm to plan their strategy, then engaged another to help implement it. Today, the markets are moving too fast for that. If your product life cycle is two years, you can't use up one year studying the issue. So MAC, which specializes in strategy; United Research, which helps organizations manage change; and Sogeti, whose units design IT systems, will pool their specialities to take a project from strategic planning through implementation.'

A business analyst was, however, a bit skeptical about the related diversification of CGS into other services. 'In particular, inclusion of consultancy in their integrated service offering looks nice in theory but might be difficult to implement. I hope they've learned from the problems encountered by Saatchi and Saatchi and also by Arthur Andersen in offering consultancy services as part of the package.'

In 1992 Gemini Consulting took a controlling interest in Gruber, Titze and Partner (GTP), Germany's third largest management consultancy firm. The skills of Gemini and GTP were complementary, and the combined operation (340 consultants in Germany) would boost Gemini's presence in Germany and become its largest subsidiary in Europe.

Gemini Consulting was legally, organizationally, and culturally separate from Cap Gemini Sogeti. The major reason was that the culture, the organization, and the internal management procedure at Gemini Consulting are integral to and inseparable from the firm's ability to deliver the results its partner-clients expect. And these were quite different from the Cap Gemini Sogeti way of doing business.

Systems Integration

Systems integration involves submitting all-in-one bids to deliver working packages of hardware and software that, for instance, will automate a factory or computerize a billing process. The customers' primary focus is no longer on choosing what equipment to buy but on maximizing the contribution of IT to the enterprise's success and well-being. Systems Integration submits all-in-one bids to deliver working packages of hardware and software.

In the SI process, the integrator often selects technology, builds interfaces, and provides integration, installation, operation, training, and technology refreshment. Systems Integrators develop, implement, and manage for their customers all the technologies used to provide information as a strategic corporate asset. While they work in close partnership with their customers to address business needs, the customers ultimately control their business and the direction it is going in. The value of systems integrators and systems managers is their technical resources and in-depth understanding of their customers' markets. Cap Gemini Sogeti argued that they could be trusted more, as they were free from the pressure to peddle their own merchandise (see Exhibit 5.)

The four related businesses CGS did serve represented about 38 percent of the total market of IT services. However, there was still a huge part of the total IT services market in which CGS wasn't involved, like tax audit consulting, packaged software (systems products, applications products), turnkey systems and hardware sales, and processing and network services.

Increasingly, customers of IT-service firms, such as CGS, require that the service suppliers have prior knowledge about the industry from which the customer stems. An understanding of the particular industrial context is beneficial for the customer because no time is wasted by the supplier in investigating the industrial setting and introducing IT applications. As a result the service suppliers can judge relatively quickly and accurately what it takes to satisfy customers' demands. By showing in-depth knowledge of the clients' industrial context, service suppliers can

EXHIBIT 5
Market for IT Services 1990

The 'Big League' in IT Services		1990 European Revenues, $ Millions		
	$ Millions		Country	Revenue
1 EDS (excluding GM revenue)	2,788	1 Cap Gemini Sogeti	France	1,464
2 IBM (about 3.3% of the total revenue)	2,280	2 Finsiel	Italy	875
3 Computer Sciences Corp (3/31/91)	1,738	3 EDS + SD Scicon	USA	300†
4 Cap Gemini Sogeti	1,683	4 IBM	USA	700
5 Anderson Consulting (about 75% of total)	1,420	5 Sema Group	France	559
		6 O.I.S (Olivetti)	Italy	667
		7 Sligos	France	532
Next ones are far below:		8 GSI	France	375
Finsiel (Italy)	875	9 Volmac	Holland	347
Sema Group (France)	667	10 CGI	France	325
CSK (Japan)	618	11 Axime	France	325
Olivetti (Italy)	559	12 Programator	Sweden	298
Sligos (France)	532	13 Logica	UK	253
SD-Scicon (UK)	412	14 CISI	France	250

† = estimated revenue in Europe.

more convincingly argue that they can indeed offer state-of-the-art IT solutions. In a number of cases the competitive context and demanding clients in a particular country forced the local Cap Gemini unit to find innovative solutions. These innovative solutions, being developed in one country, can be applied by other CGS units working in other countries.

One aspect of organizational capabilities concerns the creation of optimum conditions for pooling application expertise generated from completed projects. It becomes important as a skill for full-service suppliers, and CGS had developed some capabilities for the upgrading of organizational memory. The solutions implemented were aided by IT-based tools such as electronic bulletin boards and extensive electronic mail facilities (including voice mail). In addition, it appeared that these formal aspects of routines were complemented by the reliance on informal networks of professionals who cooperated in previous project-teams.

Information could also be acquired at competence centers, which provided line managers with skills related to a given technique or applica-

tion. Development of project routines helped to structure project management. Organizing for cross-market opportunities was based on knowledge of the industry represented in reference databases developed by CGS that offered descriptions and information on activities.

Reconfiguration of the Competitive Context

Cap Gemini Sogeti's strategies were partly a response to the changes in the European competitive context. The acquisitions and alliances were necessary to gain market share and remain one of the top players in a fast-concentrating market. An industry analyst concluded that the industry had entered a Darwinian phase: those who failed to get stronger would be absorbed. One element of growth strategies is to increase geographical coverage. The need to be present in more countries was closely related to the internationalization of the business community and in particular to the fact that a rising number of clients throughout

Europe wanted IT-system developers to create systems that worked across national boundaries.

The setup of the international support division was motivated by the need to offer solutions to multinational clients. This unit combines the commercial and technical support functions required by the operational groups. These ranged from providing assistance in technical developments, such as quality assurance and research and development (R&D) programs, to marketing developments. The latter focused on initiating and coordinating international projects and, if necessary, dealing with the top management of client companies.

The move from one to four related businesses can be seen as a result of the changes in the way business was done. Spotting business opportunities for each other became increasingly important. CGS was beaten in its home market by competitor Arthur Andersen when they were given a systems-integration contract for the Paris Stock Exchange after Andersen consulted for the French treasury ministry. Cooperation with the newly formed Gemini Consultants, however, had been similarly beneficial. A United Research (one of the partners in Gemini Consulting) contract with Mobil Oil Corporation in the United States led to a contract for CGS to work on Mobil's European distribution network. CGS's new service offering matched the cross-marketing capabilities of competitors such as the large accountancy/consultancy firms.

A different but related aspect in these cross-marketing efforts was CGS's ability to achieve boardroom access. Cooperation with Gemini Consulting provided a direct link to the top management of client companies. That is important because, as a result of growing complexity and uncertainty, IT management had become an essential corporate function affecting large parts of the organization. Decisions concerning investments in information technology were very often made at the middle-management level, in particular by managers of the IT departments. Increasingly, however, because of the growing corporate importance and complexity of IT investments, it had become a concern of top management.

Besides the growing competition from the large accountancy conglomerates, the IT services market was also attractive for the large computer manufacturers. They were expanding their service activities to compensate for declining profit margins on hardware. CGS had a strong selling point in its objectivity and independence from the computer equipment vendors. The strategies of IBM could have a substantial influence on CGS performance, since about 60 percent of its clients were IBM users. Its relationship with the struggling US giant was a mixture of competition and collaboration.

EXHIBIT 6
CGS's Major Acquisitions and Alliances

Company (country, main business)	Year	Type
Sesa (France, software house)	1987	Takeover
SCS (Germany, computer services)	1990	Takeover
Hoskyns (United Kingdom, facilities management)	1990	Takeover
Daimler-Benz (Germany, industrial group)	1991	Alliance
Debis Systemhaus (Germany, software services)	1991	Merger
Programator (Sweden, facilities management)	1991	Takeover
MAC Group (US, management consultancy)	1991	Alliance
United Research (US, management consultancy)	1991	Alliance
Volmac (Netherlands, software house)	1992	Alliance
GTP (Germany, management consultancy)	1992	Takeover

Probably the most serious competitive threat came from Electronic Data Systems (EDS), the IT services firm owned by General Motors. EDS was boosting its European sales and trying to expand its non-GM business. Just as with CGS, EDS had been trying to grow in Europe as fast as possible. For example, SD-Scicon, one of the main European IT services firms in the 1980s, sold its German subsidiary (Scientific Control Systems, SCS) to CGS. To counter that move and the takeover of Hoskyns, EDS reacted in 1991 by buying, after a serious takeover fight, the UK part of SD-Scicon (see Exhibit 6.)

The Marrakesh Rencontre

At the Marrakesh meeting in June 1990, it was decided that the hallmarks of the group were to be a comprehensive service and a well-run organization staffed by highly motivated men and women.

These managers were presented with a choice between three different strategies: staying local but adding some new related services; expanding geographical coverage with the existing focus of service provision; or expanding the service offering in combination with achieving global presence. Each of these strategies was discussed intensively with regard to content and implications. When the results of the poll were announced, it became clear that the managers had opted overwhelmingly for the third strategy, global presence.

The Current Organizational Structure

The director of the newly formed Cap Volmac in the Benelux remarked that internal coordination and cooperation in the world-wide operations of Cap Gemini Sogeti should improve quickly, because only then can CGS really profit from the trend of increasing client demand for IT services – showing that they can indeed offer the promised solutions.

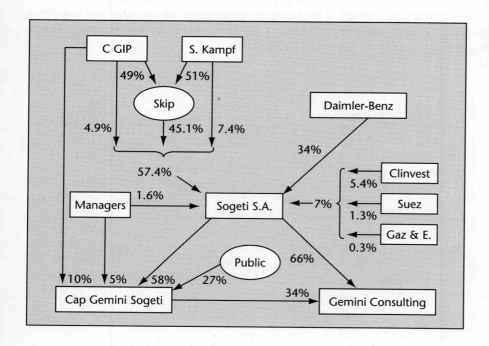

EXHIBIT 7
Capital Structure after Alliance with Daimler-Benz

CGS's alliance with Daimler-Benz in 1991 was a direct result of the decisions taken in the Marrakesh meeting and represented a response to the changes in competitive context as sketched above. CGS obtained financing of $585 million through this alliance, concluded after a year of negotiations in July 1991. It gave Germany's largest industrial group 34 percent of Sogeti, the holding company that owns 58 percent of Cap Gemini Sogeti (see Exhibit 7.) Daimler-Benz also has the option of taking full control of Sogeti and Cap Gemini in February 1995. However, Serge Kampf, who controls Sogeti through another holding company, SKIP, has the option of buying back the 34 percent Daimler-Benz stake starting in 1994, before the German group can exercise its option.

In addition, CGS set up a joint venture with Debis Systemhaus, Daimler's software arm. In the joint venture, Sogeti's German activities and Daimler's informatics operations were brought together. Debis was a newcomer to the computer industry, it being established in 1990 as a 100 percent subsidiary of Daimler-Benz providing services internally as well as working with outside companies. The Systemhaus had a staff of 3600 people with revenue of over $400 million. The largest percentage of its business was in IT services, and it covered a wide range of services, from software packages to full-system implementation, and from consultancy and training to computer center, network, and telecommunications management.

One of the challenges for Cap Gemini Sogeti was to integrate the acquisitions and alliances of local companies and the local CGS units. The establishment of a new Cap Gemini Benelux, to be named Cap Volmac, an alliance of existing CGS units and Volmac was representative for challenges encountered by CGS in increasing geographical coverage. In February 1992, the alliance and shares exchange between CGS and Volmac, the leading Dutch IT services firm in which CGS already had a small stake, was made public. This move was in line with the attempts of CGS to increase its European market coverage and met the demand from multinational clients to handle IT services contracts spanning several countries. For CGS the strong market position of Volmac in facilities management, one of the new lines of business with above-average growth rates, was particularly attractive. CGS and Volmac would pool their activities in the new firm in the Benelux region. Sixty percent of Cap Volmac would be owned by a new holding group. The other 40 percent would be divided between Volmac's existing public shareholders, institutional investors and the World Software Group, which was Volmac's holding company. The new holding group would in turn be roughly two-thirds owned by CGS and one-third by the World Software Group. The new Cap Volmac had around 4,000 staff and annual sales of slightly under $500 million.

The Prague Rencontre

The main issues to be discussed by the participants of the Prague Rencontre on June 25, 1992, were the following:

> How can the existing organizations (such as Hoskyns, Programator, Volmac, and Debis) be integrated and 'welded' more cohesively into the group, as changes in demand increase?
>
> What should the organizational structure look like?
>
> How can expertise of acquired companies be retained when experts can leave so easily?
>
> How can a common company culture be created?
>
> How can cross-selling be made a success?
>
> What role can Gemini play in the restructuring?

With respect to these issues and the necessary changes, Serge Kampf remarked that important CGS values such as cooperation, teamwork, and manager mobility should be respected, and he emphasized that 'even though we want to rebuild a new house together, we cannot destroy the foundations of the old one.' What such a house should look like was the question he hoped the Prague Rencontre delegates would be able to resolve.

Case 20(B): Cap Gemini Sogeti: Building a Transnational Organization

By Ron Meyer, Hervé Amoussou and Tom Elfring[1]

On January 10, 1995, Serge Kampf, chief executive officer of Cap Gemini Sogeti (CGS) and chairman of Sogeti, met with 35 executives of CGS and Gemini Consulting to rethink their joint future. Two and a half years had passed since the Prague Rencontre at which CGS had plotted a course towards becoming a transnational organization (see Case 20(A)). The goals agreed upon in Prague had been ambitious. A reorganization program called Genesis had been adopted, with the intent of meshing together the divers companies that CGS had acquired, or had formed an alliance with, between 1990 and 1992. As a consequence of Genesis, the reborn CGS had come to share the same working procedures and services throughout the entire firm. Much had also been done to create a common culture and shared ambition among the 25,000 employees spread across 16 countries on two continents. This extensive change process had been guided by Gemini Consulting, specialists in 'Business Transformation™'.

Yet, despite the enormous efforts put into building a lean and mean organization, profits were still nowhere near the pre-integration level of 1991 (see Exhibit 1). Of course, CGS was facing a number of very strong international competitors, such as EDS, IBM and Andersen Consulting. However, many analysts were wondering whether CGS had bitten off more than it

could chew. Merging five large information technology service firms (Hoskyns, UK; Debis, Germany; Programator, Sweden; Volmac, The Netherlands; CGS, France) into a coherent transnational group was a Herculean task. The result, Kampf had predicted in 1990, would be 'a dream or a nightmare.' While the current reality was still somewhere in between, it was paramountly clear to Kampf and the assembled managers that a powerful impulse was needed for CGS to gain a strong competitive edge and for profitability to rebound.

For Gemini Consulting more or less the same was true. Gemini was the result of an alliance between the MAC Group (USA), United Research (USA) and Gamma International/Sogeti (France), formed in 1991. The next year GTP (Germany) was acquired, bringing to four the number of organizations that needed to be integrated into a coherent group. Much like CGS, Gemini was also confronted with a pack of strong international competitors, not intent on giving Gemini the luxury of sorting out its internal reorganization at its ease. Not surprisingly, Gemini's marketshare and profitability were also under pressure.

As Kampf and the upper echelons of CGS and Gemini Consulting started on their two-day meeting, they were determined that it should result in some breakthrough initiatives. The question was whether these initiatives should be sought in the existing strategic direction of the companies or whether a bold redirection was needed. Could a strong competitive position be obtained by 'debugging' and extending the current strategy or would the companies have to rewrite their strategic program?

[1] Source: This case was prepared by Ron J.H. Meyer, in collaboration with Hervé Amoussou and Tom Elfring. The case is intended for classroom discussion, not to illustrate the effective or ineffective handling of a managerial situation. Unless mentioned otherwise, all information was obtained with the kind assistance of Cap Gemini. Copyright 1997 by Ron Meyer, Rotterdam School of Management, Erasmus University.

EXHIBIT 1
CGS Financial Results 1989–1994

(in millions of French francs)	1989	1990	1991	1992	1993	1994
CONSOLIDATED REVENUE	7,055	9,172	10,028	11,884	11,028	10,176
NET INCOME (LOSS) before amortization of goodwill	586	682	629	20	(330)	4
NET INCOME (LOSS)	525	623	560	(72)	(429)	(94)
DIVIDENDS DISTRIBUTED	152	196	262	—	—	—
NET MARGIN (%)	7.4	6.8	5.6	(0.6)	(3.9)	(0.9)
NUMBER OF SHARES*	25,251,046	27,939,313	37,472,775	41,964,338	42,431,755	53,068,478
EARNINGS PER SHARE, (FF) before amortization of goodwill	23	24	18	0	(8)	0
EARNINGS PER SHARE (FF)	21	22	15	(2)	(10)	(2)
AVERAGE HEADCOUNT** for the period	12,974	16,489	17,971	21,675	20,900	19,001
TOTAL NUMBER OF EMPLOYEES as of December 31	13,540	18,919	16,892	21,374	20,559	19,823
PROFESSIONAL STAFF	11,426	15,542	14,012	17,932	17,061	16,717

* Adjusted for share splits and bonus share issues
** In 1992 and 1993 49% of the headcount of Cap Debis was included

The Prague Rencontre

The Prague Rencontre (June 24–27, 1992) was attended by 670 managers from all five parts of the company: Cap Gemini America, Cap Gemini Europe, Cap Sesa (the French entity), Hoskyns (the British entity) and Cap Gemini International Support. The first speech, by Robert Sywolski, chairman of Cap Gemini America, emphasized global change. He first spoke of his Czech origin and then showed a video tape that demonstrated how fast the world had changed during the last three years. Images of the Gulf War, the fall of the Berlin wall, the putsch against Gorbachev, the German reunification, the outburst of rage in Yugoslavia and the release of Nelson Mandela plunged the whole assembly into a maelstrom of emotions about change. He described all these events as macro changes and explained that with the disintegration of the Soviet Union, business was winning over politics.

Then came Geoff Unwin, chairman of Hoskyns, who focused on changes in the data processing service sector. He stressed that powerful actors from the automotive industry, telecommunications, computer hardware, banking and auditing were entering the industry. He added that 40 percent of the world's software was already being produced in India. The third member of the management team to speak was Christer Ugander, chairman of Cap Gemini Europe, who presented a set of figures that demonstrated how profoundly CGS had changed between the Marrakech (1990) and the Prague Rencontre (see Exhibit 2).

Finally, Serge Kampf introduced *GENESIS*

	Marrakech, May 1990	Prague, June 1992
Number of Employees	14000	25000
Percentage in France	43	23
Percentage in the USA	24	10
Managers at the Meeting	550	670
Potential Market for Service	$57 billion	$87 billion
World Market Share	2.1%	3.2%
European Market Share	6.5%	8%
Employees/Million Inhabitants	100 for F, NL, CH	300 for NL, S
	25–50 for N, CH, DK	100 for F, SF
		50–100 for UK, N

EXHIBIT 2
State of the Group
1990–92

('*CGS Entering a New Era of Success, Innovation and Service*'), the process that was going to create a new CGS. The first step in this process was going to be the introduction of a new organizational structure. Kampf had been working on a proposal for a new structure with Gemini consulting for over a year. They had considered four structural alternatives:

- *A region-based organization.* A structure along geographical lines was more or less the existing situation within CGS. However, this form held little scope for cross-border synergies and, therefore, was quickly rejected.

- *A sector-based organization.* As CGS's services need to be tailored to customer needs, it would be logical to bring together CGS units with similar clients into the same division. Such a structure along industry sector lines (bank industry servicing division, automotive industry servicing division, etc.) was rejected due to four reasons. First, the differences in European corporate law were judged to be too large. Second, the differences between the US and Europe made cross-Atlantic integration particularly tricky. Third, some sectors, like the defense industry, absolutely required a regional organization. And last, but not least, the transformation from a pure regional to a pure sector-based form was judged to be too difficult.

- *A matrix organization.* This organizational form would be half way between the existing regional form and the industry sector organization. However, it was feared that conflicts between sector and region management would inhibit cooperation.

- *A dual organization.* In this structure the regions would remain dominant, but each would also receive the responsibility for coordinating world-wide efforts within a certain sector.

Kampf proposed that the latter organizational structure be chosen. He sketched an organizational chart consisting of seven regions, to be called Strategic Business Areas (SBAs): the US, the UK, the Nordic countries, the Benelux, Germany, the Paris region, and a southern region made up of the French provinces, Spain, Italy, Switzerland and Austria. Each SBA would be split into approximately 7 'divisions', of approximately 3500 exployees each (see Exhibits 3 and 4).

Redrawing organizational charts was not enough, Kampf knew. Therefore, the second and third day of the Prague meeting were spent on discussing how to really transform the organization. The organizational structure was further hammered out, with an emphasis on improving service to clients and creating transnational sales and production teams. Importantly, while striving for cross-border integration and consistency, it was made clear that reducing

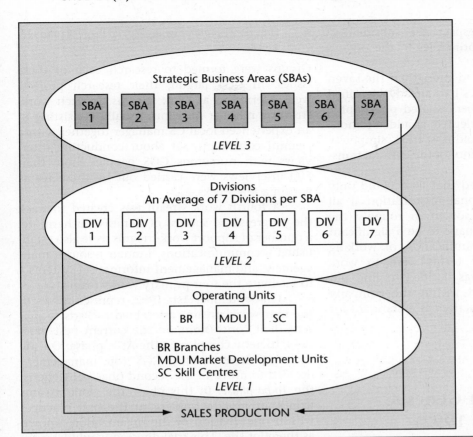

EXHIBIT 3
Cap Gemini Sogeti
Structure

EXHIBIT 4
Cap Gemini Sogeti's
Management Team

Executive Chairman: Serge Kampf		Group Vice Presidents
Central Functions	Development	Eric Lutaud
President: Michel Jalabert	Finance	Vincent Grimond
	Image & Communications	Jacques Collin
	Quality & Innovation	Wolfgang Schönfeld
	Human Resources	Adolfo Cefis
Regions President: Geoff Unwin, assisted by Jean-Paul Figer	Sectors President: Jacques Arnould assisted by Philippe Gluntz	
SBA 1 United States	Gas & Oil	Michel Berty/Robert J. Sywolski
SBA 2 United Kingdom	Financial Services	Tony Fisher/Tony Robinson
SBA 3 Nordic Countries	Utilities	Anders Skarin/Christer Ugander
SBA 4 The Benelux	Distribution	Chris van Breugel/Bernd Brix
SBA 5 Germany	Industry	Karl Heinz Achinger
SBA 6 Ile de France	Telecommunications	Alexandre Haeffner/Henri Sturtz
SBA 7 French Provinces, Spain, Italy, Switzerland, Austria	Space, Air Traffic Control, Railways	Alexandre Haeffner/Gennaro de Stasio

reporting levels and respect for subsidiarity[2] should also be guiding principles in the organizational design.

It was also decided to strengthen the seven corporate values that CGS had already identified as central to their members' shared philosophy. An eighth value, client-oriented, as added to honesty, solidarity, liberty, boldness, trust, simplicity and fun, to signal the essence of the cultural transformation.

Finally, it was agreed that CGS could only function as a transnational organization if all parts of the company worked in roughly the same way. There would have to be a significant amount of cross-border unification of working methods if cross-border teams were to work together. Therefore, it was decided to find out where excellence existed within the company and to use these best practices as a standard for the entire company.

The Initiation of Genesis (June–December 1992)

Following the Prague Rencontre, Michel Jalabert, CGS's former-president of Central Functions, was named General Manager of the Genesis Project and Francis Behr became Deputy General Manager. They set out to quickly execute the first phase of the Genesis Project, codenamed the *As-is phase*. The objective of this phase was to collect best practices throughout the company, that could serve as the basis for unification. At Prague, Kampf had identified the three major areas where unification should be pursued:

- *What do we sell?* The service offering portfolio.

- *How do we sell?* The sales process.

---

[2] CGS borrowed this concept from the European Community. It is the principle that only issues of supranational importance should be dealt with at the EC level. All other issues, and the associated powers, should be devolved to the national governments.

- *How do we produce what we sell?* Project management.

Groups were formed to research each of these issues. In CGS jargon, their research projects were referred to as work streams. In each workstream a number of teams, usually consisting of an experienced local CS manager together with a Gemini consultant, set about conducting interviews with numerous CGS people. More than 500 interviews were carried out by these teams within a few weeks.

A fourth work stream was created to track the progress and success of Genesis. Futhermore, a number of support work streams were also established – communications, human resource management and management information systems – to facilitate the four primary workstreams.

On September 1st, 1992, representatives of the four work streams assembled in Paris to present their conclusions on the current best practices, thereby completing the As-is phase. On the basis of these results, CGS top management decided to move to the second phase of Genesis, the *To-be phase*. In this phase the work streams would attempt to implement the best practices within one division of the organization, known as the pilot site. This trial division would later act as a model for the transformation of the entire organization.

In order to keep all employees informed of progress, it was also decided to establish a newspaper, edited by the communications work stream, and to develop a dictionary of new terms in the company. Furthermore, e-mail and a hot line were made available for questions.

The Service Offering Portfolio Work Stream

While almost every project for a client is unique, it was believed that an explicit overview of the types of service offerings available within CGS was important. An explicit portfolio would provide the terminology for CGS people to communicate with one another. Moreover, a portfolio overview could be used to communicate a clear message of CGS's abilities to clients.

The analysis of 300 interviews with CGS marketing executives provided an outline of the portfolio (see Exhibit 5). All services were first divided into five groups of IT businesses, referred to as business lines: Consulting, Project Services, Information Systems Management, Education & Training, and Software Products. Each business line was subsequently divided into sets of related services, referred to as service lines. Concrete service offers to clients combine elements from the service lines and tailor them to the particular client needs.

The Sales Process Work Stream

In the As-is phase, more than 500 sales people had been interviewed and over 1000 business proposals had been analyzed. These revealed a number of common reasons for failure of a business proposal: costs were often incorrectly evaluated, clients had not been contacted when they were ready to decide and the company's image had not been supportive enough. The research also revealed some critical success factors in the sales process: it was necessary to understand the client's needs, to establish contacts at the appropriate level in the client's organization, to propose high quality solutions and to realize that CGS was selling to groups of people, not to individuals.

Especially this latter point had not yet been fully recognized. Increasingly clients had come to understand that IT investments were of strategic importance. Consequently, the buying decision had become a long process involving a lot of specialists and decision makers. This insight led to the development of a new commercial approach,

EXHIBIT 5
CGS's Service Offering Portfolio

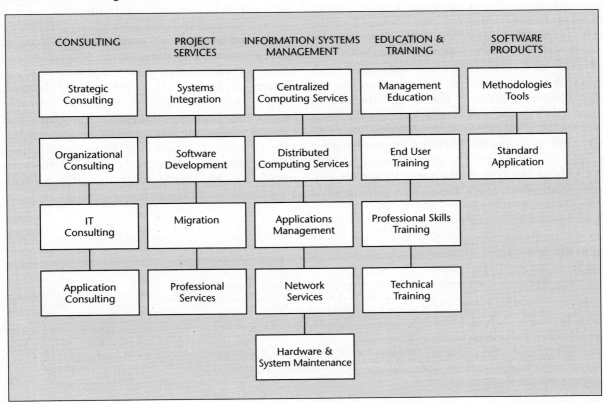

called Team Buying/Team Selling (TB/TS). In this approach a selling team is formed to match the buying team of the prospective client. TB/TS was tested in SBA 4 (Benelux), where projects for NATO and the Dutch ministries of Justice and Finance were acquired.

The sales process work stream also outlined a seven stage process for the acquisition and development of client accounts (see Exhibit 6), also called the sales funnel. A detailed 'How To' guide was written describing each stage, including a list of actions and outputs.

The Project Management Work Stream

Each national entity had its own project management methodology to ensure service quality, like LOGIC in Scandinavia, PRISM in the UK, SDM in the Netherlands and EXPERT in France. It was recognized by all that international customers and cross-border projects would require a common methodology. Therefore, the project management work stream designed a new system, PERFORM, integrating the best elements of the various national approaches into an international, open, and efficient tool. 'Built on CGS's 20 years of experience in methodologies, PERFORM is a modular system that can integrate foreign systems. This is a major advantage since some clients, like the armed forces, have their own systems,' explains Reinhard Degen, the manager later in charge of PERFORM implementation in SBA 5 (Germany). The greatest asset of PERFORM is its ability to fit the large, long-term projects that often characterize the international

clients. PERFORM includes other features such as profitability tools and commercial support techniques, and complies with the ISO 9000 quality norm.

Sweden was selected as pilot site and the methodology was tested on 16 projects. By December 1992, more than 350 project leaders and engineers had attended PERFORM courses. According to the head of SBA (The Nordics), Anders Skarin, 'integration of PERFORM in our systems takes place smoothly. Our quality system, like the accounting procedures, is part of our ordinary work.'

The Extension of Genesis (1993–1994)

The To-be phase had been successful, but overall 1992 had been a terrible year. Competition had so badly mauled CGS that it was in the red at the end of the fiscal year and had to lay off 600 employees for the first time in its 25 year history. It was under these circumstances that the top 80 managers of CGS met each other at the Béhoust castle in France on January 21, 1993. Michel Jalabert, head of the Genesis project, stated the intention of meeting: 'Last year, our partners and friends of Gemini Consulting helped us to develop the Service Offering Portfolio, the Team Buying/Team Selling process and so on. Now the initiative is ours.' CGS was ready to launch the full-scale transformation of the entire company.

EXHIBIT 6
The Seven Stages of Sale Process

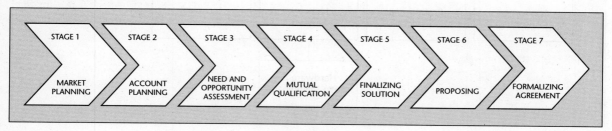

The first step was to identify 81 Managers of Change (MOC), whose responsibility it would be to help people within their region to transform their working habits and to use the new tools, like PERFORM and the sales funnel. Fourteen MOC came from SBA 7 (Southern Europe), 12 each from SBA 4 (Benelux) and SBA 1 (US), 10 from both SBA 6 (Paris) and SBA 5 (Germany), eight from SBA 3 (Nordics) and SBA 2 (UK), and seven people from the Central Functions. The Managers of Change attended a two-week training program in February 1993 at the Béhoust castle, where they learnt about the new methods and how they could be implemented in the regions. The MOC from each region also established the current state of Genesis in each SBA – the Base Line – as a reference point to direct and measure change.

The second step taken by CGS top management was to outline seven Axis of Development, that would help to restore CGS's profitability. The axis of development were:

- *Service Offering*. To extend group-wide high growth and high profitability service offers.

- *Sales*. To become a partner of the client thanks to TB/TS.

- *Project Management*. To increase quality management of the projects.

- *Structure*. To promote transnational behavior.

- *Sectors*. To foster growth in each selected sector.

- *Communication*. To strengthen brand image.

- *Benchmarking*. To monitor performance after change implementation.

In each region seven so-called Champions were selected, each with the task of coordinating one of the axis of development in their SBA. Together the Managers of Change and Champions in each region worked to produce a development plan for their SBA, called the Business Case. This plan took the Base Line document as a starting point and detailed how the Axis of Development could be implemented in the region. By April 1993 these plans had been completed and each of the Group Vice Presidents in charge of an SBA knew the specific actions that had to be taken in his organization.

Realizing Change

In September 1993, for the first time in the history of CGS, Kampf delegated the bulk of the company's operational activities. Geoff Unwin became Chief Operating Officer (COO), while Kampf, as Chief Executive Officer, remained responsible for image and communication, corporate development and shareholder relations. Pierre Hessler, formerly general manager Operations for IBM Europe, was named Deputy General Manager of CGS, second to Geoff Unwin.

Surveys indicated that an overwhelming number of managers endorsed Genesis, but Hessler still wondered about 'morale of the troops.' He organized a round of informal interviews in France, Sweden, Switzerland and the United States that revealed underlying skepticism. Francis Behr therefore organized a second round of formal interviews, with the topics: Knowledge of the group's strategy, labor environment, communication, and perception of Genesis. The outcome of these interviews was worrying. While managers throughout the group where satisfied with the level of written communication, some were confused about CGS's strategy. Moreover, Genesis was widely perceived as a marketing tool. As for morale, job satisfaction and anxiety were both widespread.

Hessler decided to accelerate the change process by launching Genesis 2. The new program aimed to foster the effects of Genesis by putting emphasis on human resource management and communication. A monthly distinction, the Profitable Growth Award, was introduced to congratulate the employees whose contribution to growth and profit had been outstanding. He also launched the company's first international advertising campaign, to improve the company's image and morale. The advertising slogan 'Total Respect. That's what Business needs today' was chosen for this campaign.

It was clear, however, that pushing through real changes would be a long and arduous task. As Michel Jalabert put it, 'Five years will not be superfluous to transform a group of more than 20,000 employees across two continents.'

The New Challenge

While five years might be needed to transform CGS, it was doubtful whether CGS's competitors and shareholders were willing to give the company that much time. As Serge Kampf met with the 35 top executives of CGS and Gemini Consulting on January 10th, 1995, to discuss the future strategy of the two companies, all participants felt the intense pressure to improve performance. In 1994 their combined European market share had fallen from 9 percent to 8.2 percent, according to Dataquest, while EDS and Andersen Consulting had been able to increase their slice of the market. The company's financial performance had not been very much better (see Exhibit 1).

As a consequence, shareholders were becoming restless, seeking prompt and decisive action. One shareholder was of particular importance to CGS and Gemini, namely Daimler-Benz. Through its computer services subsidiary, Debis, Daimler-Benz had a 34 percent stake in the Sogeti holding company (see Exhibit 7 in Case 20(A)). Kampf had not exercised his right to buy back these shares in 1994 through another holding company, SKIP. Under these circumstances Daimler-Benz now had the option of buying a controlling stake of the Sogeti holding before January 1st, 1996. It did not seem as if Daimler-Benz was particularly interested in tying up even more capital in Sogeti, especially given Daimler's stretched financial resources after years of large-scale diversification. However, Daimler-Benz did feel that its 34 percent stake, that had cost it $585 million in 1991, brought it almost no influence in the management of the company. Given the worrying state of affairs at CGS, influence was something that Daimler-Benz definitely did wish to obtain.

As Kampf and the assembled managers discussed these pressures, a number of key questions continually surfaced. How could CGS and Gemini accelerate their integration processes? How could both companies use their internal diversity as an advantage instead of experience it as a disadvantage? How could CGS and Gemini add value to each other in search of a competitive edge? And what stance should the company take *vis-à-vis* Daimler-Benz? Before the meeting was over, these questions would have to be answered.

Case 21: Burroughs Wellcome and AZT

By Ram Subramanian[1]

As the bell sounded to signify the opening of the New York Stock Exchange, it was soon drowned out by another noise. Five men, chained to a balcony inside the Exchange, were blowing a horn to draw attention to a banner that they held. The banner read: 'Sell Wellcome' (Chase 1989).

One April morning, four young men, nattily attired in business suits, audaciously walked into Burroughs Wellcome's headquarters in North Carolina. They ejected the occupant of an executive office, sealed the doors tight, and chained themselves to a radiator. Meanwhile one of their cohorts called the press to describe the break-in (Crossen 1989).

Were these international terrorists attacking harmless establishments to seek release of their prisoner brothers? No, they were Acquired Immune Deficiency Syndrome (AIDS) activists protesting what they described as unfair pricing tactics employed by Burroughs Wellcome for the AIDS drug, azidothymidine, or AZT.

The Pharmaceutical Industry[2]

The major domestic players in the pharmaceutical industry (Standard Industrial Classification two-digit code 28) include: Merck, Abbott Labs, American Home Products, Eli Lilly, Johnson & Johnson, Bristol-Myers Squibb, Schering-Plough, and Burroughs Wellcome. The primary competition from outside the United States includes Glaxo Holdings, Hoechst, and Ciba-Geigy. The industry is very competitive, with no single company holding a dominant market share position. In 1989, the top four firms accounted for nearly 25 percent of industry sales.

After an unsuccessful attempt at unrelated diversification during the 1970s and early 1980s, pharmaceutical companies embarked on a strategy to build market share (within the industry) by investing heavily in research and development. Currently in 1991, the industry spends around 15 percent of sales on R&D, one of the highest among major US industries. Industry experts believed that R&D spending was essential for effective product differentiation and consequently for improved economic performance. Past history also indicated that being the first to introduce new drugs resulted in increased profits.

The industry's marketing expenses are about 20 percent of sales. The expenses are mainly for recruiting and training salespeople who visit physicians and hospitals to provide information about their company's products. Other marketing expenses include advertising in scientific journals and direct mailing costs.

The industry exhibited annual revenue growth of about eight percent during 1975–1985. Its Return on Equity (ROE) has consistently been higher than other industries during the 1980s.

Several threats, however, have emerged for the US pharmaceutical industry in recent times. A number of foreign companies, apart from marketing their products with increased vigor in the United States, have formed a large number of joint

[1] Source: This case was prepared by Professor Ram Subramanian of the F.E. Seidman School of Business at Grand Valley State University. The author wishes to thank Kathy Bartlett of Burroughs Wellcome Company for her helpful comments. Research assistance was provided by Cindy Hietala and Ron Villenueva. Every effort has been made to present the facts of the case objectively from available public data as well as company documents furnished to the author. This case was presented at the 1991 North American Case Research Association Meeting. All rights are reserved to the author and North American Case Research Association. Copyright © 1991 by Ram Subramanian. This case was edited by T.L. Wheelen and J.D. Hunger for their book. Reprinted with permission.

[2] Adapted from Zahra *et al.* (1991).

ventures with US companies to strengthen their competitive position. The government has undertaken several steps to reduce the time span of patent protection, presumably to open up the competition. Finally, the increasing popularity of generic drugs also poses a significant threat for the industry.

Historical Background to the Development of AZT

AIDS is caused by a virus called human immunodeficiency virus (HIV). Actually a retrovirus, HIV has a unique capability that makes it very insidious. A retrovirus is a ribonucleic acid (RNA) virus that has a special enzyme. Ordinarily RNA viruses cannot replicate because they do not have deoxyribonucleic acid (DNA). But with the help of its special enzyme, a retrovirus is able to build DNA from its RNA. Sometimes these DNA copies become integrated into the host cells. Because they are similar, the host cell has no way of knowing that these are, in fact, 'infected' DNAs manufactured by the retrovirus. Therefore these foreign DNAs also become part of the host cells and cause the disease when they multiply.

In 1964, a Michigan Cancer Foundation researcher first synthesized a compound called azidothymidine (AZT) as a possible cure for cancer. When tests showed that the compound was not effective as a cancer cure, the research was abandoned and the compound forgotten.

Burroughs Wellcome, a subsidiary of UK-based Wellcome PLC, has always encouraged its scientists to find cures for obscure diseases. In 1981, the company resynthesized AZT in its quest for a compound that would be effective against bacterial infection (Burroughs and Wellcome 1991). Meanwhile, one of its chemists, Janet Rideout, was studying the chemical structure of the HIV virus. The intention was to find a cure for the disease by studying the chemical structure of the disease-causing agent. She found that AZT was similar in structure to the enzyme that the retrovirus needed to replicate inside the host cell.

Because AZT was toxic, she felt that it would effectively neutralize the retrovirus and prevent it from multiplying inside the host cell. When Burroughs Wellcome was actively looking for a cure for AIDS, Rideout suggested AZT.

By late 1984, Burroughs had determined that AZT was effective against some cat and mouse retroviruses. Because the company then did not have the facilities for testing AZT on live HIV, it sought the help of the National Cancer Institute (NCI). Sam Broder, a senior researcher at the institute, took an active part in the testing process.

The tests conducted by the NCI and others proved that AZT was effective against the HIV. Nineteen AIDS-affected patients were given the drug and while two dropped out of the program, 15 showed improvement in their immune system and also noticeably gained weight (O'Reilly 1990). The media and the medical community enthusiastically received public reports of these early results. In some ways, this enthusiasm sowed the seeds for Burroughs Wellcome's subsequent troubles with the drug.

Drug companies have to go through a lengthy period of field testing a drug before seeking approval from the Federal Drug Administration (FDA). After the initial tests by the NCI indicated the potency of the drug, the company established a program of wide-scale field testing. As the news of the drug's efficacy spread across the country, multitudes of AIDS patients begged the company to use them for the testing. The company then faced an ethical dilemma.

Drug companies test drugs in one of two ways. One, called the placebo trial, tests a drug by using two groups of people. The first group is given the drug while the second group is given a placebo (a harmless pill). In the second method of historical trials, the drug is given to every patient and the health changes of these patients are compared with untreated patients.

Because of problems associated with intervening variables in historical trials, the scientific community generally prefers placebo trials. This preference and the fact that the compound tested may turn out to be harmful prompted Burroughs Wellcome to use placebo trials (Burroughs and Wellcome 1991). A lot of negative publicity resulted from this decision. AIDS activists saw this decision as stemming from greed – greed, because the company wanted to use the faster placebo trials instead of historical trials. Also, the company had to give placebos to half the group tested, knowing full well that these patients were likely to die, while those given AZT were likely to live.

The company elected to proceed with large-scale testing using the placebo method. After the drug was tested almost the whole of 1986, the FDA approved it in March 1987. Before putting it on the market, the company thought long and hard about the drug's price. Finally, in mid 1987 the company marketed AZT under the brand name 'Retrovir' with a price that effectively cost an AIDS patient $10,000 for a year's supply of the drug.

The company had not bargained for the backlash on its pricing policy. Through various media, AIDS activists voiced their protests and sought the help of the federal government. The principal AIDS activist group was Act-Up (Aids Coalition to Unleash Power), largely comprising homosexual middle-class professionals (Crossen 1989).

Using sophisticated confrontational techniques and a grassroots approach to activism, Act-Up has considerable influence. In response to the strident protests of AIDS patients, led by Act-Up, Burroughs Wellcome lowered the price of AZT in December 1987 by 20 percent so that the annual cost to a patient was now $8,000. The company claimed that the price reduction was due to production efficiencies. The price was cut an additional 20 percent (to $6,400 per patient per year) in September 1989 because the drug was shown to benefit a substantially larger group of patients – thereby increasing its market.

Activists' Reasons for the Protests

AZT does not cure AIDS. However, it prolongs the victim's life by slowing the effect of the HIV virus (Millsand and Masure 1990). Scientists calculated that with the help of AZT an AIDS victim's life could be prolonged by as much as five years. When AZT was introduced commercially by Burroughs Wellcome in early 1987, it was one of the most expensive drugs ever. Typically, consumers of pharmaceuticals are not price sensitive because the cost of medication is covered by health insurance. However, in 1987, with Medicaid not yet authorized to cover the treatment of the disease, most AIDS patients did not have insurance that would cover treatment for AIDS.

The company's pricing policy outraged AIDS activists who soon banded together to voice their protests publicly. There was an underlying sense of urgency in the protesters' action. The federal government had funded a $20 million program to provide AIDS patients with AZT. The program was due to expire in October 1989, leaving the 7000 patients in the program to deal with the problem of raising funds in addition to dealing with their illness. Even the subsequent cuts in prices that reduced the price of the drug from $10,000 to $6400 for a year's supply did not mollify AIDS activists. The activists based their protest on two factors that surrounded the introduction of AZT.

One factor fuelling the indignation of AIDS activists was that Burroughs Wellcome was reaping the profits of a drug that it did not develop. A chemical that was originally developed as a cancer cure by a Michigan Cancer Foundation researcher was resurrected by the company based on published reports in 1974 by a West German scientist, W. Ostertag, who demonstrated that AZT was effective in blocking the reproduction of certain kinds of retroviruses (Chase 1989). Subsequent research by Burroughs Wellcome researchers confirmed Ostertag's findings, and they developed AZT as a drug that was effective against AIDS. Protesters claimed that the company saved millions of dollars because much of the basic research had already been done for them by others. AIDS activists argued that since the drug did not cost nearly as much to develop as drugs normally do, the company's prices for the drug indicated its greed and its propensity to exploit ill people. Burroughs Wellcome did not reveal details about AZT costs and profit margins. However, analysts familiar with the drug industry believe that the company makes 70 percent to 80 percent gross profit on AZT, which, although high, is in line with average industry profit margins (ibid.). These high margins, argue those in the drug industry, are necessary to offset losses from hundreds of drugs that never see the light of day.

The second reason for the protests was that agencies such as the National Cancer Institute did much of the testing – a significant part of product development costs in the drug industry. Normally, a drug company pays for the testing of its products and adds these costs to the drug's development cost. Protesters argued that the company saved millions of dollars because NCI did much of the expensive hospital testing. The drug's prices did not reflect these savings.

Company's Point of View

Burroughs Wellcome is owned by the London-based Wellcome PLC. Ironically, the company that received a lot of negative publicity over its pricing policy for AZT is the largest charity in the United Kingdom, in 1989 distributing $55 million to fund medical libraries and research (Burroughs and Wellcome 1991). Long known for concentrating its resources on finding cures for obscure diseases and providing an excellent atmosphere for scientific research, the company was totally unprepared for the wave of negative publicity that surrounded AZT. In recent interviews the company explained its rationale behind the pricing of AZT, which was meant to pacify the protesters and diffuse the situation.

According to company officials, even though Burroughs Wellcome did not create the chemical AZT, it spent more than six years and a lot of money (the company did not reveal actual figures) taking an abandoned compound and making it a potent drug to treat AIDS. The company performed years of expensive animal testing and also gave away the drug free to 5000 people at a cost of $10 million as part of an Investigational New Drug (IND) program prior to obtaining FDA approval to market the drug (Burroughs and Wellcome 1990). To put the company involvement with the drug in perspective, a top executive of Burroughs Wellcome noted that, whereas a project of this size would have taken up only 20 percent of Merck's (the industry leader) time, it took 100 percent of Burroughs Wellcome's time.

Once the drug was approved by the FDA, the company had to spend more than $80 million in designing the production process for the compound (Haigher 1987). A drug normally takes a decade from conception to commercial development, so a company usually has a lot of time to design the production process to make the drug at the lowest possible cost. But, in the case of AZT, because things began moving very quickly after the initial tests, the company had less than six months to perfect the production process. A key ingredient, thymidine, was hard to come by because world-wide demand for the compound, obtained as a side product from the DNA in salmon and herring sperms, was very low. Burroughs Wellcome had to locate companies with the appropriate technology to manufacture large quantities of both natural and synthetic thymidine. These sources, consequently, proved to be very expensive. The high price of AZT was justified, in part, by the expensive manufacturing costs incurred by the seven-month process of converting the raw material into the finished compound (ibid.). The company claimed that when the production process was streamlined in late 1987, the savings were passed on to the users.

The second reason for the high price of AZT, from the company's point of view, was the uncertainty about the market for the drug. When the drug was initially approved in 1987, the FDA permitted the use of the drug only for terminally ill patients – an estimated 50,000 people. This small market, coupled with the fear that a better drug to combat AIDS could come along at any time (as several companies were working on AIDS drugs), prompted the company to price AZT at $10,000 for a year's supply. The company has pointed out that when the FDA subsequently approved the sale of the drug to all people who showed AIDS symptoms, the company cut prices in response to the expanded market. Also, recent medical evidence indicates that AZT is effective even at half

EXHIBIT 1
Selected 1989–1990
Financial Data for Firms in
Drug Industry

Source: *Business Week* (April
13, 1990).

Company	Sales in Billions of Dollars	Profits in Millions of Dollars	ROE as a Percentage
Burroughs Wellcome	$2.40	$332.8	23.9%
Bristol-Meyers Squibb	9.19	747.0	14.7
Johnson & Johnson	9.76	1,082.0	27.5
Merck	6.55	1,495.4	44.8
Eli Lilly	4.18	939.5	25.0
American Home Products	6.75	1,102.2	55.9

the normal dosage – reducing the per patient annual cost to around $3000.

Did Burroughs Wellcome profit significantly from AZT? Estimated sales of AZT were $200 million in 1989 and $290 million in 1990 – between eight percent and 12 percent of Wellcome PLC's world-wide sales (Gorman 1989; Burroughs Wellcome 1991). Its return on equity (ROE), at 23.9 percent in 1990, was among the lowest in the drug industry (primarily because it generally pursues the research and development of arcane, rather than useful, drugs), with industry leader in sales Merck showing a 44 percent ROE and American Home Products (the maker of Anacin) 56 percent (O'Reilly 1990). To provide a financial incentive to spur drug manufacture, the US federal government invoked the Orphan Drug Act in 1985 permitting Burroughs Wellcome to manufacture AZT on an exclusive basis for a period of seven years commencing from 1987. Exhibit 1 shows selected financial data for an illustrative list of companies.

Government's Role

As the protests against the pricing of AZT continued unabated, Congress, at first highly supportive of the company, called company executives to Washington to respond to charges of price gouging. A House Subcommittee on Health and the Environment conducted a hearing on the drug's pricing policy. Senator Edward Kennedy's office even researched the possibility of nationalizing the drug in an effort to control its prices. Partly in response to these investigations, the company slashed the drug's prices on two occasions. But company officials have always maintained that changing market conditions, not governmental interference, led to a reduction in AZT's price.

References

Burroughs Wellcome (1991) Retrovir Milestones, Company Press Release, April.

Burroughs Wellcome (1990) The Development of Retrovir, Company Press Release, June.

Chase, M. (1989) Burroughs Wellcome Reaps Profits, Outrage from its AIDS Drug, *Wall Street Journal*, September 15, pp. AI, 5.

Crossen, C. (1989) AIDS Activist Group Harasses and Provokes to Make its Point, *Wall Street Journal*, December 7, pp. AI, 9.

Gorman, C. (1989) How Much Reprieve from AIDS? *Time*, October 2, pp. 81–2.

Haigler, T.E. (1987) Testimony Before the House Committee on Energy and Commerce, March 10.

Mills, J. and Masur, H. (1990) AIDS-Related Infections, *Scientific American*, August, pp. 50–7.

O'Reilly, B. (1990) The Inside Story of the AIDS Drug, *Fortune*, November 5, pp. 112–29.

Zahra, S.A. *et al.* (1991) Merck: Strategy Making in America's Most Admired Corporation, in Pearce, J.A. and Robinson, R.B., *Strategic Management*, Richard D. Irwin, Homewood, Ill.

Case 22: The Body Shop International – the Most Honest Cosmetic Company in the World

By Andrew Campbell[1]

Every year the cynics wait for The Body Shop to trip over its ideologically pure feet and every year they are disappointed. Although imitators have inevitably arisen, Body Shop benefits from being clearly identified as the leader of the pack in the growing market for toiletries and cosmetics aimed at the environmentally oriented, health conscious consumer.

The Body Shop 'originates, produces and sells naturally based skin and hair products and related items through its own shops and through franchised outlets.' The business has grown rapidly since it opened its first shop in Brighton in 1976, and in 1990 it had a turnover of £84.5m and 457 outlets in the UK and overseas. In the seven years since its flotation the company has increased both turnover and profits by a factor of nine, and has been described as 'the share that defies gravity.' This is despite the onset of a recession in retailing. Financial performance for the last five years is detailed in Exhibit 1. Although it is not one of the largest retail operators, The Body Shop has been particularly influential because of its phenomenal success, its strong underlying philosophy and the press coverage it has received.

Much of the press coverage has centered around managing director Anita Roddick, a charismatic, outspoken and determined figure who has a simple formula to explain the secret of her legendary success: 'I look at what the cosmetics trade is doing and walk in the opposite direction.'

The extent of this success is such that she claims that The Body Shop is Britain's most international store. 'We produce over 300 products sold in well over 300 shops from the Arctic Circle to Adelaide, covering 31 countries and 13 languages, without once diluting our image.' Actually by February 1990 The Body Shop was operating with 457 shops, 139 in Britain and 318 in 37 other countries. A further 25 UK outlets and 180 overseas were due to open in the following 12 months, including a shop in Japan in October 1990. Preliminary research has been conducted into the feasibility of opening in Moscow.

Anita Roddick has won many accolades from the business community, including the Business Enterprise Award for company of the year, and Business Woman of the Year. In her acceptance speeches she savages corporate approaches to business and in particular traditional ways of doing business in the retail and cosmetics sectors:

> Retailing itself has taught me nothing. I see tired executives in tired systems. These huge corporations are dying of boredom caused by the inertia of giantism. All these big retailing companies seem to be led by accountants and they seem to have become just versions of the post office or the department of motor vehicles.
>
> Retailing at the moment is a combination of war and sport in designer uniforms, with its obsession with corporate raiding, acquisitions of acres, strategies, niche markets, specialization and empire building, where their only sense of adventure is in their profit and loss sheet. We have never once been seduced into believing we are anything more than simply traders.

Her belief is that the essential difference between The Body Shop and other retailers is explained in the words of Niemann Marcus: 'Profit is not the objective of my business. It is

[1] Source: Ashridge Strategic Management Centre, © 1991, revised February 1992. Reprinted by permission of the author.

EXHIBIT 1
The Body Shop's Financial
Performance 1986–1990
(in £'000)

	1990†	1989†	1989‡	1987*	1986*
Turnover UK & Eire	56,901	41,412	54,754	21,255	13,560
Turnover Overseas	27,579	13,997	18,253	7,221	3,834
Turnover – Total	84,480	55,409	73,007	28,476	17,394
Pre-tax profit	14,508	11,232	15,243	5,998	3,451
Earnings per share	10.0p	7.4p	10.2p	4.65p	2.58p
Number of outlets UK	139	112	112	89	77
Number of outlets overseas	318	255	255	186	155

	Group Turnover			Group Trading Profits		
	1990†	1989†	1989‡	1990†	1989†	1989‡
United Kingdom & Eire	56,901	41,412	54,754	13,486	9,745	13,015
Other EEC countries	6,962	4,136	5,445	1,566	904	1,254
Rest of Europe	3,910	2,717	3,966	996	932	1,270
USA	5,839	874	874	(1,941)	(1,632)	(1,820)
Rest of North America	5,860	3,194	4,244	1,481	887	1,082
Australasia	3,544	2,119	2,454	915	326	422
Asia	1,464	957	1,270	389	222	324
	84,480	55,409	73,007	16,892	11,384	15,547

* = Year ended September 30
† = Year ended February 28
‡ = 17 months ended February 28

providing a product and a service.' So how does she do it?

It is so easy. First, know your differences and exploit them, then know your customers and educate them, then talk about the image of your company as well as the products, and finally be daring, be first and be different.

One of the rules of any successful company is to find out what your original features are and shout them out from the rooftops. We have found that when you take care of your customers really well, and make them the focal point, never once forgetting that your first line of customers are your own staff, profitability flows from that.

The Body Shop has an extraordinary effect on people who come into contact with it. 'It arouses enthusiasm, commitment and loyalty more often found in a political movement than a corporation,' says journalist Bo Burlingham.

'Customers light up when asked about it, and start pitching its products like missionaries selling Bibles.' John Richards, director of retail research at Country NatWest Securities, comments: 'I've never seen anything like it. The nearest comparison would be something like flower power in the 1960s.'

The Body Shop Story

Anita Roddick was one of four children of Italian immigrants and helped in the family cafe at the Sussex seaside resort of Littlehampton, which is still the base for her retailing empire. She has fond memories of the cafe, a popular meeting place for local children. 'We had the first juke box in the town after the war, the first knickerbocker glories and the first Pepsi-Colas. I didn't know it then but

I was receiving subliminal training for business life; I was at the center of that magical area where buyer and seller come together.'

At an early age she decided that she wanted to see the world and went to work for the International Labour Office of the United Nations in Paris. It was while travelling internationally for the UN that the seeds of her future calling were sown. Visiting such exotic spots as Polynesia, Mauritius and the New Hebrides, she observed the simple but effective way remote communities lived.

'I just lived as they did and watched how they groomed themselves without any cosmetic aids. Their skin was wonderful and their hair was beautifully clean.' She watched the Polynesians scoop up untreated cocoa butter and apply it to their skin with remarkable results. She also observed Sri Lankans using pineapple juice as a skin cleanser, and later discovered that natural enzymes in it help remove dead cells.

Today, Anita spends about two months every year travelling the world picking up tips for natural ingredients to go into Body Shop products. 'Women in other societies know that these well tried and tested ways work and do not need a scientist or advertising agency to sell them.' When Anita gets back from a trip abroad she will regale managers with tales of her adventures. Walls in warehouses and factories are hung with words and images and displays of Third World art.

When she returned from her travels, Anita married and opened a restaurant with her husband Gordon. He too got the wanderlust and set off on a horse back ride from South America to New York that was to take him two years. She did not feel that she could cope with the restaurant on her own and decided to open a shop instead, selling skin and hair products made from the natural recipes gleaned on her travels.

'You cannot call this shop The Body Shop'

Starting with a bank loan of £4000, Anita Roddick opened the first Body Shop in Brighton in 1976 with a blaze of publicity. She was jammed between two funeral parlors who wrote her a letter saying, 'You cannot call this shop the Body Shop,' because the coffins would pass twice a day and they were expecting some cute photographer from *She* magazine to take that happy snap shot of the week. Her response was straightforward, as she recalls:

I have always been petrified of headmasters and solicitors, but I think that the two most talented things that I have ever done in my life were to ignore those letters and then to use that to promote the company. So what I did was quite simple, and I think it should be standard practice for any young company setting up: the anonymous phone call! I rang up the local Evening Argus in Brighton and said to them, 'Do you know what is going on in Kensington Gardens? This poor woman on her own, with a new baby, whose husband is trekking across South America on a horse, is being intimidated by two Mafia undertakers. Her little shop is called THE BODY SHOP . . .' – I mean, I had written the story over the phone and we got our first free editorial. We have never ever paid for an advert since.

Many of the features which made The Body Shop different came about because of lack of funds in those early stages. The company could only afford 20 products to begin with, which was not enough to fill the shop. So making each product in five different sizes gave a wider range straight away. There are now over 300 products, but they can still be bought in five different sizes – customers like to be able to try the small sizes first. The Body Shop still uses the cheapest bottles, referred to in the early days by the Press as 'urine sample bottles,' and they can still be brought back for refills (a system originally introduced because they were in short supply, but now symbolic of the company's policy of recycling). Similarly symbolic are carrier bags which carry the question: 'Why aren't telephone bills, gas bills, electricity bills, rate demands, income tax forms, public notices, circulars, newspapers, printed on recycled paper? This is a recycled paper bag. The Body Shop introduces changes for the better.'

The success of The Body Shop grew out of

Roddick's almost naive belief in herself and the value of sheer hard work. 'We worked hard, therefore we survived,' she says. 'We didn't have any understanding of the commercial methods taught by business colleges. In fact I would suggest that anyone with an ounce of individuality should not go to a business school . . . because you are structured by academics who measure you in the science of business. They use a business language that is predictable, and where going out and doing is not part of the course.'

The Body Shop expanded rapidly under the franchise system which developed a strong camaraderie through the help given to each franchise in setting up and through allowing everyone to do their own labeling. There are currently around 5000 applicants wanting to take up a Body Shop franchise, and it takes three years to succeed. 'Unless you're absolutely obsessed you don't get a look in.'

Applicants undergo strict vetting, including an offbeat questionnaire with unlikely questions such as: 'How would you like to die? What is your favorite flower? Who is your heroine in history or poetry?' Roddick believes that basic business skills can be provided by the company but the right attitude and values cannot. 'We have the back-up to teach almost anyone to run a Body Shop,' she says. 'What we can't control is the soul.'

The Body Shop has managed to achieve a remarkable level of uniformity within their now global network of shops. 'They are all the same – and they all work. I think it is interesting that we are not seen as an English company but as a cross-cultural one, with a product range with international ingredients.'

Operations

In the early days bottles were filled, labeled and capped by hand and each order picked and filled individually. The process is now fully automated. There is a manufacturing department with a staff of seven covering manufacturing, quality control, product development and customer complaints.

Twenty-five percent of manufacturing is done in-house, the rest by contract manufacturers. The range grows by 80–90 percent each year. In 1990 construction is due to be completed on new manufacturing and blow-moulding facilities as well as a research and development and office building in Littlehampton.

Each supplier to The Body Shop is required to sign a declaration guaranteeing none of the ingredients used has been tested on animals during the previous five years. To show its complete opposition to cruelty in the name of beauty, in 1989 The Body Shop resigned from the Cosmetic Toiletry and Perfume Association amid accusations that the trade body lacked the necessary passion and imagination to eliminate animal testing quickly enough.

Franchise System

At the start of the company, Anita and Gordon Roddick could not afford to open new shops themselves even though business was booming, so they developed the concept of 'self-financing.' If someone else would put up the money to open a new shop, the Roddicks would help with their expertise in running the operation, help re-fit the shop, and grant a license to use the company name and sell the products. The company now has a franchise manager who provides a consultancy service and organizes the relocation of older shops to prime sites.

The franchise system also operates overseas, with a head franchisee for a country or group of countries who is granted exclusive rights to use The Body Shop trademark and to distribute its products. Those who operate their own shops successfully are given the right to sub-franchise within their area, and have responsibility for training sub-franchisees.

As in the UK, shop designs and graphics are strictly enforced and franchisees have to stock 85 percent Body Shop products. Unlike the UK, however, no annual operating fees are charged to overseas franchisees and products are sold subject to an overseas distribution discount.

Scandinavia was the first overseas area in which The Body Shop became popular, followed by Canada which became the first overseas operation to manufacture products itself. Samples are still sent to the UK for quality control before each batch is bottled, and the 'heart ingredients' are provided by Body Shop International and blended in the UK. Other ingredients are approved by the UK before manufacture in Canada.

The Body Shop Philosophy

In essence Anita Roddick promotes an ethical code of behavior for the global citizen – and that includes multinational companies. She believes in the empowerment of people, through jobs, work, honest earning. 'Our idea of success is the number of people we have employed, how we have educated them and raised their human consciousness, and whether we have enthused them with a breathless enthusiasm. Our solution to third world poverty is trade not aid.'

The philosophy is explained to the customer as follows:

- The Body Shop continues to trade today on the same principles that have held firm since its beginning in 1976.

- We use vegetable rather than animal ingredients in our products.

- We do not test our ingredients or final products on animals.

- We respect our environment: we offer a refill service in our shops, all our products are biodegradable, we recycle waste and use recycled paper wherever possible, we use biodegradable carrier bags.

- We use naturally based, close-to-source ingredients as much as we can.

- We offer a range of sizes and keep packaging to a minimum: our customers pay for the product, not elaborate packaging or for more than they need (and this helps keep the prices down too).

The philosophy is put into practice on many levels, some more visible than the others:

- Our products reflect our philosophy.

- They are formulated with care and respect:
  - respect for other cultures;
  - respect for the past;
  - respect for the natural world;
  - respect for the customer.

- The Body Shop joined forces with Greenpeace over a two year period in a campaign to 'Save the Whale' and in the UK we are involved with the Friends of the Earth during 1987–88, in a campaign to raise public awareness of the dangers of acid rain and other environmental hazards, and to encourage others to take positive action to protect their environment, such as recycling household and workplace waste.'

Roddick and her employees have real enthusiasm for the company and its products. She says

I see business as a renaissance concept, where the human spirit comes into play. How do you ennoble the spirit when you are selling moisture cream? Let me tell you, the spirit soars when you are making products that are life serving, that make people feel better. I can even feel great about a moisture cream because of that.

There are some very visible manifestations of the company's philosophy in the way the company operates. For example, each employee at the Littlehampton head office has two wastepaper baskets, one for recyclable and one for non-recyclable waste. The company even runs training courses on recycling.

Commitment by top management to such values is vital. 'The people who make the policy decisions . . . must lead with integrity, commitment and passion, otherwise a cynicism pervades the whole place,' says Roddick. 'Corporate culture is the more important part of a growing company like The Body Shop – it is the values, the rituals, the goals, the hero's characteristic of a company's style.'

The Responsibility of Profits

After The Body Shop was launched on the Unlisted Securities Market and the shops were all proving profitable. Roddick set up an environmental and communities department to translate

EXHIBIT 2
The Toiletries Industry

THE TOILETRIES INDUSTRY

The market for haircare products is complex and fragmented. In the UK in 1988 the total size of the skincare market alone was over £138 million. Although nearly 50 percent of the market for skincare creams and lotions is accounted for by the top 5 companies, a large number of small companies makes up the remaining 56 percent.

The shampoo market is also highly fragmented with the top 10–11 brands accounting for half the market and the other 80–90 competing for the rest. The conditioner market is becoming more and more competitive with many brands competing for a small market share. The top companies in the UK in terms of market share in both shampoos and conditioners are Elida Gibbs, Beecham, Alberto Culver, Johnson & Johnson and Revlon. The fastest growing brand is Timotei, which has a share of just under 10 percent and caters to two growing trends, that for 'natural' products and that for a shampoo designed for frequent use without damaging the hair.

There is a wide spectrum of products, with new products or reformulations continually being introduced as companies seek to create or imitate new fashion fads. This means that advertising is used extensively, with the premium brands being advertised in upmarket women's glossy magazines. Television advertising is also used for both hair and skincare products, often aimed at educating the consumer about a new type of product. The proliferation of new products has also lead to a blurring of product categories, e.g. moisturing cleanser, conditioning shampoo.

The industry can be segmented by a number of different criteria, such as price range (premium, middle and budget); target market age group; function (health and hygiene, beauty products), and so on. Growth is mainly in upmarket product ranges and consumers are primarily women, although sectors which have shown high growth recently are products for men and own label products, with Boots now taking 6–7 percent of the market for cleansers, moisturisers and astringents. After Boots, the most important in the own label sector are Marks & Spencer, Sainsbury's, Yves Rocher and Superdrug. Safeway and Woolworths also have their own skincare ranges. In terms of distribution, supermarkets now account for about 30 percent of the total hair care market; there is a growing tendency to view such products as shampoo, hairspray and conditioners as 'grocery' items, and they are increasingly sold in larger or 'family size' packs. Another area where there has been growth recently is in anti-ageing products. Women (including younger women) are taking an increasing interest in the health of their skin and the adverse affects of wind, sun and polluted air.

Own label products are also a threat to established brands in the soap market, such as Imperial Leather, Lux and Shield. Sales of soap reached a peak in 1986 and the market is now thought to be declining, with products such as bath oil or foam overtaking soap for the first time in 1987. The two main trends in the soap market in recent years have been 'fruity' soaps, first made popular by The Body Shop but imitated by others; pure, fragrance-free brands such as Simple and Pears; and liquid soap, which now accounts for around 5 percent of the total market.

The Body Shop dominates the UK market for natural make-up mainly because most manufacturers of 'natural' cosmetics, such as Creightons, have not entered the color cosmetics market. Health-oriented manufacturers of toiletries and makeup include Innoxa, whose slogan is 'pure and beautiful' and which is the only makeup recognized by the British Medical Association.

As a result of the recent growth in environmental awareness throughout Europe, numerous small players have been active in the 'green' cosmetics market. However, only Yves Rocher is a significant competitor for The Body Shop. Monsieur Rocher's passion is 'plants and natural beauty' and this is explained in the Green Book of Beauty, a mail order catalogue for toiletries and makeup. Mail order constitutes the heart of this company's activities and it has in addition more than 1,200 Beauty Centres world-wide.

her beliefs and concerns into practical projects. Each franchised outlet is required to take on a community project in its area, 'which is there to give the young women in the organization additional status and helps them realize that everyone has the ability to change the world for the better.' All projects are taken on within working hours, and franchisees choose what they want to do. There is no coercion.

This determination to use private profit for public good is now reaching out to some of the remotest parts of the third world, where one of the latest projects is setting up a paper making plant in a Tibetan refugee camp. The paper is processed from pineapple and banana leaves and will be used for wrapping Body Shop products.

In Southern India, The Body Shop has set up a boys' town for destitute youngsters. The boys are taught rural craft and to make Christmas cards, and the money from the sales is put into trust funds. When the youngsters leave at the age of 16 they have the means to purchase a herd of sheep or a horse and cart, giving them a vital start. So far over 3000 jobs have been created and the scheme has made about £100,000 profit, and supplies The Body Shop with soap bags and wooden foot massagers.

The whole process is seen to be self-perpetuating with ingredients obtained from the Third World, providing work and sustenance for under-privileged societies, making products that are sold to the more fortunate, the profits of which are ploughed back into an educational program which aims to make people more aware of the critical social issues of our time.

The plight of the inhabitants of the Amazon rain forest has been the subject of a world-wide campaign by the company, which has raised £250,000 for their defense. It has mobilized employees for petition drives and fund-raising campaigns, carried out through the shops and in company time. It has produced window displays, t-shirts, brochures and videotapes to educate people about the issues, and has even printed appeals on the side of its delivery trucks.

The Body Shop was the first company in Britain to use Jojoba oil in cosmetics. Jojoba is obtained from a desert plant and is a substitute for sperm whale oil. Apart from helping protect whales, there are other powerful reasons for using oil from the desert plant. Jojoba can be grown on some of the poorest land in the world, which is totally unsuitable for conventional crops, and in regions where people are living in abject poverty.

This approach isn't restricted to far away places. Chris Elphick of Community Learning Initiatives suggested that perhaps Roddick might care to go and practise some of her philosophies in Easterhouse, an area just to the east of Glasgow which has 56 percent male unemployment and frequent deaths from solvent abuse. Her response was predictable. Within eight months she had won over all the local councillors, opened a soap factory called Soapworks and dedicated 25 percent of all profits to the local community. When asked about unions, she told them: 'You only need unions when management are bastards. We will talk to you one to one if there is a problem.' Employees are treated with respect and made to feel that their roles are important. Soapworks is involved in the community and has funded the building of a playground for local children. In the first full trading year Soapworks produced over four million bars of soap and expected to produce more than 15 million bars in 1990. A bath-salt filling line has been added, and the workforce now stands at 85.

The commitment to 'profits with principles' is also evident in initiatives for employees, such as the £1 million invested in 1989 in building and equipping a workplace nursery for head office staff.

Journalist Bo Burlingham claims that the campaigning approach is part of a carefully researched and executed business strategy. Roddick wants causes that will generate excitement and enthusiasm in the shops, and says:

> You educate people by their passions, especially young people. You find ways to grab their imagination. They're doing what I'm doing. They're learning. Three years ago I didn't know anything about the rain forest. Five years ago I didn't know anything about the ozone layer. It's a process of learning to be a global citizen. And it produces a sense of passion you won't find in a department store.

No Advertising

An important aspect of The Body Shop's product philosophy is that, in keeping with its claim to be the most honest cosmetics company, it does not call its products 'beauty' products, nor does it use idealized images of women to sell them. Roddick explains:

> The cosmetics industry is bizarre because it's run by men who create needs that don't exist, making women feel incredibly dissatisfied with their bodies. They have this extraordinary belief that all women want is hope and promise. They have this absolute obsession with not telling the truth, which is bizarre because some of the products they make are actually good. But to me it's dishonest to make claims that a cream that is basically oil and water is going to take grief and stress and 50 years of living in the sun off your face. It's bullshit to consistently endorse its main product line which is garbage, waste and packaging.

Salespeople in The Body Shop are expected to be able to answer questions, but are trained not to be forceful.

The Body Shop does not advertise and its point of sale materials concentrate on giving information about the ingredients in the product, and educating the customer about its use. In fact, the information sheets about the products were first introduced because the products in the early days sometimes looked unappetising: 'We thought we had to explain them because they looked so bizarre. I mean, there were little black things floating in some of them. We had to say these were not worms.' Containers have clear, factual explanations of what is inside and what it is good for. On the shelves are notecards with stories about the products or their ingredients. There are stacks of pamphlets with such titles as *Animal Testing and Cosmetics* and *What is Natural?* There is a huge reference book called *The Product Information Manual* with background on everything Body Shop sells.

The level of information The Body Shop offers provides a powerful source of competitive advantage. It differentiates the company from its competitors, and it creates obstacles for would-be copycats. Customers feel they *know* its values and business practices, and the effect is to create a loyalty that goes beyond branding. 'I've just taken what every good teacher knows,' says Roddick. 'You try to make your classroom an enthralling place . . . I'm doing the same thing. There is education in the shops. There are anecdotes right on the products, and anecdotes adhere.'

Although the company does not advertise directly, good public relations is fundamental to their marketing strategy. Roddick quickly learned the same lesson as Marks & Spencer – that product advertising is unnecessary when a company has built up a strong and continuing public image. Says journalist Michel Syrett:

> Roddick courts publicity. She makes herself deliberately available to the press and is a constant source of good copy. 'The press like us,' she commented at the CBI last year. 'I'm always available and I'm loudmouthed and quotable.' Her views on healthcare, environmental issues and the soullessness of big business are not manufactured and are entirely consistent with the aims and philosophy on which The Body Shop has been founded.

The money that would normally be spent on marketing is largely invested in the company's employees. 'It takes more or less the same approach that it uses with customers, attacking cynicism with information,' says Bo Burlingham. 'It deluges employees with newsletters, videos, brochures, posters and training programs, to convince them that while profits may be boring, business does not have to be.'

There is a training center in London which anyone in the company can attend free of charge. Courses are almost entirely devoted to instruction in the nature and uses of the products, and are so popular that the school cannot keep up with demand.

The company newsletter reads almost like an underground newsletter. Burlingham again: 'More space is devoted to campaigns to save the rain forest and ban ozone-depleting chemicals than the opening of a new branch. Sprinkled throughout are quotes, bits of poetry, environmental facts and anthropological anecdotes.'

The Move into Color Cosmetics

It might appear to the casual observer that a move into color cosmetics (makeup as opposed to skin and haircare products) would be inconsistent with this philosophy and approach. After all, the mainstream color cosmetics industry is characterized by glossy advertising showing the customer an idealized image of the woman she could become if only she would use this or that eyeshadow or lipstick.

But Anita Roddick had the answer to any criticism there might be. She commissioned academic research on the psychology of makeup from Dr. Jean Ann Graham in the United States to prove that women derive psychological support from painting their faces. The range was launched in collaboration with Barbara Daly, a well-known makeup expert who had designed the Princess of Wales' makeup on her wedding day. The packaging was minimal and the design stylishly simple. Products were coded to guide customers as to which colors go together, and again information leaflets were available, as well as a video showing how to apply makeup using both a young and an older woman as models. The range has proved successful with customers and in 1989 represented around 10–15 percent of Body Shop's turnover, a steadily increasing proportion.

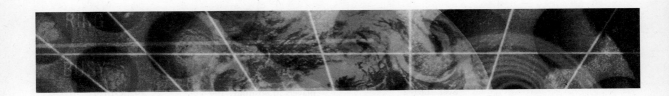

Combined Index: Strategy – process, content, context

Aaker, D.A. 335
Abegglen, J.C. and Stalk,
    G. 322, 840
Abell, D. 334, 812
Abrahamson, E. xix
accountability see corporate
    accountability
Ackerman, R.W. and Bauer,
    R.A. 831
Ackoff, R.L. 153, 230, 830–1
acquisitions and mergers
    424–5, 449–50
  and culture 465–7
  foreign 784
  game 109–10, 453–4, 457–8
  at Grand Metropolitan
    1085–6
  history of 454–7
  phenomenon of 451–3
  pitfalls 451
  and predictable overpayment
    467–8
  at Shell 1060–73
  and synergy 457–67
  valuations 452
action
  and intention 201
  occurrence of 203
  organizational 693–5
  organizational output 192
    goals: constraints defining
      acceptable performance
      193
    organizational learning
      and change 194
    problem-directed search
      194
    programs and repertoires
      193
    sequential attention to
      goals 193
    standard operating
      procedures 193
    uncertainty
      avoidance 193–4
  pattern of 150
  as politics 201
  rational choice 189
    consequences 189
    goals and objectives 189
    options 189

adaptation/advantage 332–3
  creating sustainable
    competitive advantage
    338–9
  developing tangible/
    intangible resources
    335–8
  positioning in industries,
    markets, businesses 333–5
Aineias the Tactician 25
airline industry
  regulation 1092–3
    deregulation in Europe
      1093–4
    deregulation on trans-
      Atlantic routes 1094–5
    deregulation in the USA
      1093
    see also KLM royal Dutch
      Airlines; Northwest
      Airlines: Republic Airlines;
      Scandinavian Airlines
      System (SAS); Southwest
      Airlines; Stantret Airlines;
      Virgin
Albach, H. 838
Albert, M. 580
Aldrich, H.E. 132, 593
Alexander the Great 27
Alkhafaji, A.F. 809
Allaire, Y. and Firsirotu, M. 229
alliances see international
  strategic alliances
Allison, G.T. 165, 232, 239, 660
Alpha Corporation 277
Anderson, J.R. 76
Andrews, K.R. 70, 72, 84, 152
anergy 470
Anheuser-Busch 459
Anslinger, P.L. and Copeland,
  T.E. 414
Ansoff, H.I. 220, 231
Ansoff, I. and Stewart, R. 830
Argyris, C. 239, 241, 704
Arrow, K.J. 707
Arthur, D. Little matrix 415
Arthur, W.B. xx, 239, 600
  et al 390
Astley, W.G. and Van der Ven,
  A.H. 594
AT&T 463

Avon 339–41
Axelrod, R. 583

Baden-Fuller, C.W.E
  and Pitt, M. 146
  and Stopford, J.M. 73, 594,
    599, 600
Badracco, J.L. 555
Bailey, A. and Johnson, G. xxii
Bain, J. 386
bamboo network see network
  strategy, overseas Chinese
Barnard, C.I. 129, 830
Barnes, L.B. 540
Barney, J.B. 332, 336, 337, 343,
    392, 661
barriers to entry 386–7
Bartlett, C.A. and Ghoshal,
  S. 722, 724, 727, 733, 812
Bassiry, G.R. and Denkmejian,
  H. 848
Bate, P. 242
Baum, J.A.C. and Singh,
  J.V. 593, 661
Baysinger, B.D. and Hoskisson,
  R.E. 814
Bazerman, M.H. 77
Behling, O. and Eckel, N.L. 2
Bennis, w. and Nanus, B. 658,
    880
Berle, A. and Means, G. 808,
    824, 830, 849, 850
Bertolus, J. and Morin, F. 848
Best, M.H. 511, 581
bicycle industry
  Japan 1141–3
    distribution 1144, 1145
    manufacturers/
      assemblers 1143–4
    parts suppliers 1144
    see also National Bicycle
      Industrial Co (NBIC)
Bierce, A. 71
Billiton
  bauxite/alumina/aluminium
    1060
  bought by Shell 1056–7,
    1061
  decision to sell 1070–2
  human resources
    management 1062–3

industrial/construction
activities 1061
metallurgy 1060–1
organization after take-
over 1061–2
stabilis fortuna merendis
1060
strategic planning 1062
take-over/disposal 1063
back to core business 1070
consolidation 1067–8
extensive investments
1065–7
further consolidation/new
strategy 1068–70
restructuring/autonomous
growth 1063–4
Blair, M. 810
Bleeke, J. and Ernst, D. 555
Bleicher, K. 848
boards see management boards
Body Shop International
1224–5
financial performance 1225
move into color cosmetics
1232
name of 1226–7
operations 122
franchise system 1227–8
philosophy 1228
no advertising 1231
responsibility of
profits 1228, 1230
story of 1225–6
and toiletries industry 1229
Boeker, W. 321
Boss, R.W. 540
Boston Consulting Group
(BCG) 369, 433, 452
matrix 415
bounded rationality 71, 77,
539
Bourgeois, L.J. and Brodwin,
D.R. 242, 321, 659, 667,
812
brand positioning 335
Bucholz, R.A. 810
bulk-production 643–4
Bungay, S. and Goold, M. 229
Buono, A.F. and Nichols,
L.T. 809
bureaucratic organization 536
bureaucratic politics 185, 186
characteristics 197–8
dominant inference pattern/
general propositions 201
action and intention
201
chiefs and Indians 202
foreign policy 202
sideways/upwards isssues
202
where you stand depends
on where you sit 202
organizing concepts
action as politics 201
action-channels 200

interests, stakes, power 200
parochial priorities,
perceptions and
issues 199–200
players in positions 199
problem and problems 200
streams of outcomes 201
policy as political
outcome 198
Burgelman, R.A. 159, 232
Burroughs Wellcome 1219
AZT
activist's reasons for
protests 1221–2
background 1220–1
company's point of
view 1222–3
government's role 1223
see also pharmaceutical
industry
business
defined 334–5
globalization of 727
business process reengineering
239
business strategy 9, 10, 23–4,
73, 86, 508
adaptation and advantage
332–3
creating sustainable
competitive advantage
338–9, 343, 383–95
developing tangible/
intangible resources
335–8, 343, 383–95
positioning in industries,
markets, business 333–5,
342, 367–82
international perspective
406–7
mobility barriers 407
resource mobility 407–8
paradox of markets and
resources 329–30
inside-out-perspective
331–2, 341–3, 358–67
outside-in-perspective
330–1, 341, 343, 344–58
business units see strategic
business unit (SBU)
buyer needs 348–9
Buzzell, R.D. and Gale,
B.T. 331, 342, 515, 599

Calder, B. 660
Calori, R. 502
and De Woot, Ph. 64, 318
et al 231, 321, 322
Campbell, A.
et al 413, 425, 501
and Goold, M. 420, 425
and Yeung, S. 809, 812, 819
Campbell Taggart 459
Canon 1038, 1040
building capabilities 1044
manufacturing 1047–8
marketing 1046–7

technology 1044–6
financial summary 1041
industry background 1038
competition in the
1970s 1039
Xerox 1038–9
joint ventures 1045
leveraging expertise 1048
challenge of the 1990s
1049
combining capabilities
1048
creative destruction
1048–9
managing the process 1049
business units 1049–50
challenges and change
1052–3
functional committees
1050, 1052
move into copiers 1040,
1042–3
office size distribution 1043
organization chart 1051
personal copier 1043–4
sales by product 1042
Cao Xueqin 57–8
Cap Gemini Sogeti (CGS) 1200
acquisitions.mergers 1207
at Marrakesh 1208
current position 1201–3
extension of Genesis
1216–17
financial results 1211
financial summaries 1202
from one to four related
businesses 1203–4
consultancy 1204–5
facilities management
1204
systems integration
1205–6
history 1201
information technology
services 1203
initiation of Genesis 1214
project management
work stream 1216
sales process work
stream-16 1215–16
service offering portfolio
work stream 1214–15
management team 1213
new challenge 1218
organizational structure
1208–9
Prague Rencontre 1209,
1211–12, 1214
realizing change 1217
reconfiguration of
competitive context
1206–8
rethinking in 1210
services 1203
state of the Group 1212
structure 1213
dual organization 1212

matrix organization 1212
region-based 1212
sector-based 1212
capabilities 332, 337–8, 343,
    358, 364–5
    building 1044
        manufacturing 1047–8
        marketing 1046–7
        technology 1044–6
    classification 396–8
    customer linking 403, 406
        close communication/joint
            problem solving 404
        coordinating activities
            404–5
    defined 337
    developing in market-driven
        organizations 405
    gaps 710
    inside-out 397–8
    market sensing 400–1, 406
        accessible memory 403
        mutually informed
            interpretations 402
        open-minded inquiry
            401–2
        synergistic information
            distribution 402
    organizational 788, 992–4
    outside-in 397–8
    predator 366–7
    spanning 397–8
    role of 398–9
capabilities-based competition
    becoming 361–3
        do not delegate leadership
            of transformation
            363–4
        make progress visible/bring
            measurement/rewards
            into alignment 363
        organize around chosen
            capability/have
            necessary skills 363
        shift strategic framework to
            achieve aggressive
            goals 363
    dimensions 360
        acuity 361
        agility 361
        consistency 361
        innovativeness 361
        speed 361
    future of 367
    and logic of growth 366–7
    principles 358–61
    processes 360
Carl Zeiss Jena 995
    arrival of Oberkochener
        1012
    chaotic interregnum 1000–2
    collapse of Eastern markets
        1003–4
    end of Communist order
        999–1000
    Gattnar's position grows
        precarious 1005–7

history 995–7
initial reorganization
    plans 1002–3
Jenoptik 1010–12
ownership structure 1008
political tensions in 1004–5
restructuring agreement
    1007
return of Zeiss Oberkochen
    1007–8, 1010
under Communist regime
    998
Zeiss/Jenoptik divide assets
    1013–14
Carmax 596–8
Carroll, A.B. 810
Cartier
    birth/growth of legend 1173
        Alain Perrin 1174–5
        Louis Cartier 1173–4
        Must lighters 1175–6
        Must watches 1176
        perfume 1176
        Robert Hocq 1174
        transition 1176–7
    distribution 1181
    forces of creativity 1177
    global strategy 1185
    image 1179
        publicity 1179–80
        secrecy 1179
    integrated
        manufacturing 1185–7
    logistics 1182
    management
        absolutism 1183–4
        autonomy 1184
    marketing 1180
        exclusivity 1180
        volume sales 1181
    new temple 1184–5
    product development
        1177–8
        new 1179
        old 1178–9
    rate of growth 1177
    sales
        by brands 1182
        by products 1178
        by region 1186
    strategy
        diversification 1182–3
        focus 1182
cash flows
    cost side 767
        exchange rate
            advantages 768
        factor costs 767
        scale advantages 768
    manufacturing system 768
    marketing system 769
    price side 768
        structure of markets 768–9
        value of distribution/brand
            presence 769
        value of product family
            769

vs cost structure 766–7
Caves, R.E.
    et al 377
    and Porter, M.E. 383, 387
CEO *see* chief executive officer
    (CEO)
Ceteco 162–4
Chaffee, E.E. 692
Chakravarthy, B.S. and
    Lorange, P. 153, 161,
    164–5, 231
champagne industry 1120
    challenge from sparkling
        wines/petits champagne
        1132–5
    costs 1128
    crisis 1135–7
    crisis meeting 1137–8
    economics of production
        1127, 1129
        finance charges 1130
        pricing 1131
        raw materials 1129
        salaries 1130–1
    export markets 1122
    history of 1120–2
    price 1128
    production 1138–9
    sales of major houses 1124
    shipments 1123
    stocks 1129
    structure
        major makers 1125–6
        organization 1123, 1125
        profitability 1126
    world sales 1121
Champagne Jacquart 1126
Chandler, A.D. 513, 563, 581,
    659
change forces 317
    can be rolled back 302
        renewal path 304–5, 310
        resistance path 303, 310
    cannot be rolled back 305
        restructuring path 306–7
        revitalization path 305–6,
            310
    difficult to identify 314
        bottom-up experimenting
            314–16
        focused reengineering 314
    identified 311
        cascading implementation
            312–13
        corporate alignment
            311–12
    see also change path;
        strategic change
change management 297
change path 250
    campaign 307–10
    choosing 297
    creating proactive
        breakpoints/turning
        points 311
        change forces can be
            identified 311–14

change forces difficult to
identify 314–16
identifying reactive paths
301–2
change forces can be rolled
back 302–5
change forces cannot be
rolled back 305–7
mapping out change arena
98–301
proactive 317
reactive 316–17
see also change forces;
strategic change
chaos
and boundaries around
instability 675
creation of order 679
create resource slack 681–2
design use of power
679–80
encourage self-organizing
groups 680
expose business to
challenging situations
681
improve group learning
skills 681
new perspectives on
meaning of control
679
present ambiguous
challenges 681
provoke multiple
cultures 680–1
as fundamental property of
nonlinear feedback
systems 677–9
and process of spontaneous
self-organization 675–7
unstable where long-term
future is unknowable
673–4
Charkham, J. 807
Charreaux, G. and Pitol-Belin,
J. 848
Chase, M. 1219
Chatterjee, S. 418
Chen, C.C. and Meindl, J.R. 660
Chesbrough, H.W. and Teece,
D.J. 519
chief executive officer (CEO)
as architect of organization
purpose 671–3
constraints on 688–90
duality with chairman in the
West 847–8
as organization leader
669–70
as personal leader 671
roles 688–9
and use of crescive approach
690–1
Child, J. 132, 658
Christensen, C.R. 129
et al 84, 658, 666
Citibank 277

clan organization 319, 320,
536–7
Clark, S. 861
Clarkson, M.B.E. 809
Clausewitz, K. von 23
Coase, R.H. 535
Cochran, Ph. L. and Wartick,
S.L. 813
cognition 75
limitations
information processing
capacity 76
information sensing ability
76–7
information storage
capacity 77
nature of 76
problems
cognitive bias 77
cognitive rigidities 77–8
cognitive maps 72, 78, 85, 239,
696
and objective knowledge 78
as socially constructed 78–9
as subjective 78
cognitive psychology 125–6
collaboration
between firm and
environment 513–18
between markets and
hierarchies 518–19
building secure defenses
528–30
collegiality 530
as competition 522–3,
525–6, 532
deciding on 'home' country
530
discrete organization 509–10
embedded organization
511–12
establishing specifc
performance requirements
529
and learning 531–2
limiting transparency 528–9
limiting unintended
transfers 529–30
proceeding with care 532
reasons for 526–8
technology-sharing 529
Collins, J.C. and Porras, J.I. 17,
809, 812, 813
Collis, D.L. and Montgomery,
C.A. 332
Columbia-TriStar 465
communication, global 749
company-wide quality control
(CWQC) 263, 267, 268
competences 332, 337–8
attitude 337
capability 337
knowledge 337
competition 30, 344, 509
airline industry 1095–6
globalization and alliances
1100

market 1097
structure/dynamics
1097–1100
atomistic 510
and bulk-production 644
business units vs corporate
competencies 628–9
as collaboration 522–3,
525–6, 532
homogeneous/perfectly
mobile resources
entry mobility barriers
386–7
first-mover advantages 386
sustained competitive
advantage 385–6
and knowledge-based
operations 644–6
market share vs opportunity
share 627–8
single-stage vs multistage
636–8
industry foresight/
intellectual leadership
638
market position/market
share 639
migration paths 638–9
speed vs perseverance
629–31
stand-alone vs integrated
systems 629
structured vs unstructured
631–6
today vs tomorrow 626–7
zero-sum 510
competitive advantage 34, 37,
40, 329–30, 385, 773
building 769–70
defending domestic
dominance 770–1
local responsiveness 771–2
loose bricks 770
context for 773–4
critical markets 772
disadvantages 774–6
environmental models 383
generic strategies 350
cost leadership 351–2
differentiation 352–3
focus 353–4
pursuit of multiple 355–6
stuck in the middle 354–5
sustainability 356–8
and industry change 777–8
and innovation 774–7
national cluster 778
buyers, channels, suppliers
778–9
domestic buyers who are
internation/
multinational 780
improve national
environment 780
locating within nation 780
related industries 779–80
roots of 437–9

superior
  position 37–9
  resources 37
  skills 37
  where/how to compete 781
    choosing industries/
      strategies 781–2
    diversification 782–4
    locating regional
      headquarters 784
    role of alliances 784–5
    selective foreign
      acquistions 784
  see also sustained
    competitive advantage
competitive benchmarking 531
competitive diamond 775
  elements of 776
  home base 783
competitive process, and
  strategic center 557–8
competitive strategy
  and competitive
    position 344
  five-forces framework 345–8,
    383
  and industry attractiveness
    344
  and market share 384–2
competitive structure, global
  751
competitiors, multinational
  756
complexity 24
  characteristics 42–5
    wicked problems 45–50
  disorganized 43
  interaction matrix 41–2
conceptual mapping 85, 120–2
  and ambiguity 125–6
  creation and maintenance
    122–5
  imposing order on chaos
    125–6
  maintaining order by
    dynamic conservatism
    127–8
  stability and change 126–7
  what to do when maps are
    weak
    dialectical process 130
    goal setting 129
    muddling through 129
    negative thinking 129
conceptual models 185
  bureaucratic politics 185,
    186, 197–8
  dominant inference
    pattern/general
    propositions 201–2
  organizing concepts
    199–201
  policy as political outcome
    198
  concluding remarks 202–4
  organizational process 185,
    190–1

dominant inference
  pattern/general
    propositions 195–7
  organizing concepts 192–5
  policy as organizational
    output 191–2
rational policy 185, 186,
  187–8
  dominant inference
    pattern/general
    propositions 189–90
  organizing concepts 188–9
  policy as national
    choice 188
Conner, K.R. 63
content see business strategy;
  corporate strategy;
    network strategy;
    strategy content
context see industry context;
  international context;
    organizationl context;
    strategy context
Contractor, F.J. and Lorange,
  P. 511, 579
convergence/upheaval patterns
  see organizational
    evolution
cooperation see corporate
  cooperation
coordination see corporate
  coordination; strategic
    coordination
Cordiner, R. 849, 850
core competence perspective
  364–5, 415–16, 424, 483
  and core products 442–3
  defined 437–9
  how not to think of 439–40
  identifying/losing 440–2
  redeploying to exploit 448–9
  strategic architecture 446–7
  tyranny of SBU 443–5
    bounded innovation 446
    imprisoned resources
      445–6
    underinvestment 445
core products 442–3
Corning Glass 755–6
corporate accountability 852–5,
  871
  enforcement 855–6
  broader regulatory
    framework 856–8
  ownership patterns 859–60
  societal pressures 858–9
  structure/functioning of
    boards 860–6
corporate center 425, 468–9,
  484–5, 500
  added value mechanisms
    485–6
  development of strategies
    479–84
  financial control 491–6
  parenting advantage
    statement 482

reasons for parenting
  opportunities 481
  strategic control 496–500
  strategic style 487–91
  styles 485–7
  as successful 474–9
  tensions 485
  value-creation insights
    474–5
    bounded thinking of
      managers 476
    clear focus 478
    development of new
      products 476
    distinctive parenting 475,
      477–8
    heartland criteria 475,
      478–9
    linking national/global
      network 475
    overheads 475–6
    raising skills 475
    sharpening strategic
      thinking 476–7
  value-destroying
    influences 469, 472–3
    beating the odds paradox
      474
    beating the specialists
      paradox 474
    central function/services
      471
    as common 472–4
    corporate development
      471–2
    enlightened self-interest
      paradox 473
    linkage influence 470–1
    10 percent vs 100 percent
      paradox 473
    stand-alone influence
      469–70
corporate competencies 628–9
corporate composition 417
  relatedness
    opportunities for resource
      leveraging 418
    opportunities for strategy
      alignment 419
  tests
    attractiveness 418
    better-off 418
    cost-of-entry 418
corporate cooperation, as
  competition 523–4
corporate coordiantion 413,
  417, 419, 425
  control mechanisms 420
  cooperation mechanisms
    420
  international perspective,
    costs of 503
corporate democracy, and
  stakeholder analysis 836–7
corporate excellence 826–7
corporate governance 807,
  813, 818–19

accountability 852–5
  enforcement 855–66
composite lifespace 866
  multinational, global,
    hybrid 866–7
  national comparisons 869
  negotiating boundaries
    868–9
convergence of systems 850
  Germany 851–2
  Japan 850–1
  USA 851
defined 854
dualistic 838
flaws in Japan 845
  board members appointed
    by president 846
  boards too large 846
  ineffective statutory
    auditors 846–7
  limited monitoring power
    of chairman of the
    board 845–6
  ritualized general meeting
    of shareholders 845
flaws in the West 847
  CEO/chairman duality
    847–8
  lack of neutrality of outside
    directors 848
  multiple directorships 848
functions
  conformance 814
  forming 813–14
  performance 814
Japan-US comparison of
  stakeholder relations
    842–4
key implications of different
  approaches 839–40
and management boards
  870–3
monistic 838
pluralistic concept 838,
  849
  applicability 849–50
relationship between firm/
  main bank 840–2
and stakeholder values 810
corporate mission 811–12, 819,
  874–5
  Ashridge model 876
  definition 875
    behaviour standards 878
    purpose 876–7
    strategy 877–8
    values 878–9
  emotional bond 879–80
  and mission statement 812
  planning 882–3
  roles
    direction 812
    legitimization 812
    motivation 812
  sense of 880–1
  and strategic intent 881–2
  and vision 880–1

corporate responsiveness 413,
  415
corporate restructuring 827–8
corporate strategy 10–11, 86,
  89
  composition and
    coordination 416–17
  corporate center
    coordination 425, 484–500
    role 425, 468–84
  international
    perspective 501
    cost of coordination 503
    functioning of capital/
      labor markets 501–2
    leveraging of relational
      resources and strategy
      alignment 502–3
    preference for control
      503–4
  issues
    corporate composition
      417–19
    corporate coordination
      419–20
  mergers and acquisitions
    424–5, 449–68
  paradox of responsiveness
    and synergy 412–13
    core competence
      perspective 415–16, 424,
      436–49
    portfolio perspective
      413–15, 423–4,
      426–36
creativity 100–1
  at Cartier 1177
  conditions for 101–2
  as disruptive and
    constructive 102
crescive approach 667, 683,
  688
  CEO constraints
    freedom to plan 689
    limitation of power 689
    monitoring of
      opportunities/threats
      688–9
    strategies produced by
      groups not individuals
      690
    tight control systems
      hinder planning
      process 689–90
critical markets 772
Crossen, C. 1219
culture
  and acquisitions 465–7
  constraints 24
  defined 59
  dimensions 60–3
    individualism/collectivism
      59, 144, 579–80
    international perspective
      144–5, 579–80
    long-term vs short-term 60,
      230–1, 322, 652

masculinity/femininity 59
power distance 59, 145
uncertainty avoidance
  59–60, 144, 193,
  712–13
and leadership 288–9
multiple 680–1
and organizations 230
theory of 58–9
Cummings, S. 23
  and Davies, J. 812
customers 330
  multinational 756, 758
  shift in competitive focus
    763
Cyert, R.M. and March,
  J.G. 299

Daimler-Benz 814–16
D'Aveni, R. 240
David, F.R. 812
David, P.A. xx, 390
Day, D.L. 242
Day, G.S. 330, 335, 343, 395
De Bono, E. 74
De Geus, A. 216, 224
decisions 29, 86, 967
  bureaucratic politics model
    166
  management process 796–7,
    982–3
    centralization 797, 799
    formalization 797
    socialization 797
  organizational process model
    166
  pattern of 150
  rational actor model 165
deliberate strategy 151
Demb, A. and Neubauer, F.F.
  813, 818–19
Deming cycle 266
Deming, W.E. 266, 267
Deshpandé, R. and Webster, Jr.
  F.E. 400
Dewey, J. 125
Dickson, P.R. 395
Dierickx, I. and Cool, K. 336
Dill, w. 831
d'Iribarne, P. 54
discrete organization 509–10,
  518–19, 522
distribution
  at Cartier 1181
  and cash flows 769
  global 749
  multinational 758
diversification 177, 541
  at Cartier 1182–3
  at Grand Metropolitan 1081
  processes 178–9
    building a 'comfort' factor
      for risk taking 178
    consciously preparing to
      move opportunistically
      178
    developing new ethos 178

generating genuine, top-level psychological commitment 178
and relatedness 418
at Shell 1055–6
step-by-step approach 177–8
vertical/horizontal 417
Dixit, A.K. and Nalebuff, B.J. 145
Donaldson, T.
  and Davies, J.H. 814
  and Preston, L.E. 809
Doscher, M. and Stewart, R. 830
Dosi, G. and Kogut, B. 723
Douglas, S.P. and Wind, Y. 727, 731
Dretske, F. 337
Driscoll, J.W. 540
Drucker, P. 839
Dunning, J. 727
Durand, T. 337
Dutton, J.E. 80
Dyer, J.H. and Ouchi, W.G. 581
dynamic conservatism 127–8

Eccles, M. 195
economic strategy 89
economies of scale 535, 722
  in standardization 746–7
Eden, C. 72
effective strategic planning
  content 209
    data, numbers, facts 209–10
    financial analysis 210
    generic strategies 211
    short-term focus 210
  corporate culture 215–16
  entrenched interests 214–15
  management commitment 212–14
  obstacles 205–7
    avoiding 212–16
    content of plans 209–11
    monitoring/reward processes 211–12
    planning processes 207–9
  processes
    formal presentations 208
    massive paperwork 208–9
    no decisions 209
    numerous observers 208
    process counts 209
    regularly scheduled reviews 208
    restricted discussion 209
    strict time limits on reviews 208
    uniform procedures 207–8
  staff control 214
  see also strategic planning
Eisenhardt, K.M. 807
embedded organization 511–12, 520
emergent strategy 151
Emery, F.E. and Trist, E.L. 43

employees 228, 320–1, 448–9, 583, 838–9
enactment, strategic management in see organization/s, enactment process
Encyclopaedia Britannica 1015–16
  on CD-Rom 1021–4
  charting the future 1026
  data integrity 1021
  and digital age 1020–1
  going global with coproduction 1018–20
  missing the boat 1024–6
  and the paper age 1016–18
end-product markets 436
entrepreneurs 543, 1049–50
environment
  adaptability 591–2
  enacted 133–4
  interpretive perspective 134–5
    implications 135
  models of 383
  negotiated 193
  objective 131–2
  perceived 132–3
environmental connectedness 43–5
Epaminondas of Thebes 27
Epstein, E.M. 810
equilibrium strategies
  configurations
    feasible strategy set 107
    information flows 107
    payoffs 107–8
    players 108
evaluation strategy 40
  challenge of 33–4
  criteria 91–3
  principles 34
    advantage 34, 37–9
    consistency 34, 35
    consonance 34, 36–7
    feasibility 34, 39–40
Evans, J.S. 159

Falsey, T.A. 812
Fayol, H. 54, 668
federations
  coordinated 790–1
  decentralized 789–90
feedback systems 674
  defined 677
  and increasing returns 649–50
  loops 678
  negative/damping 677–8
  nonlinear 675–6, 678
financial control 425
  key features
    budgets 450, 492
    business autonomy 493
    multiple, separate profit centres 491–2
    planning process 492–3

short term criteria 493–4
  tight control style 494–5
Fink, S.L.et al 127
Finkelstein, S. 659
first mover advantages 386
First Pacific Group 1116
  activities
    banking 1116–18
    management style 18
    telecommunications 18
    trading 1116
fitness-set theory 622–3
five forces model (Porter) 345–8, 383
five frictions (of inertia)
  action disconnects 708–9
    capabilities gaps 710
    collective action problems 710
    embedded routines 709–10
    leadership inaction 709
  distorted perception 703
    grooved thinking 704
    hubris and denial 703–4
    myopia 703
  dulled motivation 704
    cannibalization costs 705
    cross subsidy comforts 705
    direct costs of change 704–5
    failed creative response 705
    inadequate strategic vision 706–7
    reactive mind-set 706
    speed and complexity 706
  political deadlocks 707
    department politics 707
    incommensuarable beliefs 707–8
    vested values 708
forecasting, evolutionary processes 603–5
Forrester, J. 289
frame-breaking change 285
  reasons
    industry discontinuities 281
    pent-up need for change 284
    pockets of resistance 283
    product internal company dynamics 282
    product life-cycle 281–2
    risky and uncertain venture 284
    synergy 283
  scope 282
    altered power and status 282
    new executives 283
    reformed mission and core values 282
    reorganization 282–3
    revised interaction patterns 283
Fredrickson, J.W.et al 321

Freeman, R.E. 833
  and Gilbert, Jr., D.R. 812,
    818
  and Liedtka, J. 818
  and Reed, D.L. 814, 817
Friedman, M. 808
Frito-Lay 304–5, 459
Frontinus 27
functional strategy 508

game theory 84–5
  equlibrium strategies 106–8,
    119
  history of 103–4
  key concepts 104–6
  normal/matrix form 104–5
  strategic principles 108, 119
    foresight 108–12
    know yourself as well as
      others 112–15
    one-time or repeated
      interactions 115–17
    unification of minds
      117–18
games 198
  bargaining 200
  pace of 201
  rules of 201
General Radio 275–6
generative thinking 84, 93–102
  mental activity elements
    80–1
generic strategies
  and being stuck in the
    middle 354–5
  cost leadership 350, 351–2
  differentiation 352, 352–3
  fallacy of 615–16
  focus 350, 353–4
  notion of 350
  pursuit of more than one
    355–6
  sustainability of 356–8
Gerlach, M. 512, 579
Gersick, C.J.G. 239
Getler, W. 854
Ghemawat, P. 159, 239
Gilbert, X. and Lorange, P. 227
Ginsberg, A. and Bucholz,
  A. 297
global business 753
  vs global competition 765–6
  cost structure vs cash flow
    766–7
global competition 753
  business characteristics
    755–6
  cash flows 767
    cost side 767–8
    managerial system 768
    marketing system 769
    price side 768–9
  integration of activities 754
  integration-responsiveness
    grid 756
    change factors 761–5
    example of 759–61

pressures for coordination
  756–7
pressures for local
  responsiveness 758–9
local responsiveness 755
strategic coordination 754
strategic intent 769
  building layers of
    competitive advantage
    769–72
  critical markets 772
  vs global business 765–6
  cost structure vs cash flow
    766–7
global convergence 720,
  721–2, 730–3
global strategy, at Cartier 1184
globalization 719–20, 724,
  733–4, 741–2
  of businesses 727
  of companies 726–7
  conditions for
    standardization 747
    communication/
      distribution
      infrastructure 749
    global market segments
      747–8
    potential synergies 748–9
  and cultural differences 738
  of economies 727
  implementation of
    standardization 749
    external constraints
      749–51
    internal constraints 751–2
  as international
    integration 725–6
  as international scope 725
  as international similarity
    725, 731–2
  and marketing 739–41
  philosophy 744
    economies of scale 746–7
    homogenization of world's
      wants 744–5
    low price/acceptable
      quality 745–6
  and scarcity 737–8
  and standardization 736–7
  strategy options 752–3
  and technology 734–6
  traditional perspective on
    international strategy
    742–4
goals 87, 193, 363, 536–7
Godet, M. 154
Gomes-Casseres, B. 512
Goold, M. and Lansdell, S.
  415
government
  demands by host 758–9
  global restrictions 750
  impact of 762–3
  role of 652–3
Govindarajan, V. 419
Grand Metropolitan 1074

acquisitions/disposals
  1085–6
board of directors 1088
early years 1074, 1077–8
financial figures 1075–7
future of 1089–90
management team 1084,
  1086–7
operating improvements
  1081–3
portfolio restructuring
  1083–4
pressure of the 1970s 1078,
  1081
principal group companies
  1079–80
US diversification 1081
vision 2000 1087, 1089
Grant, R.M. 338
Greenleaf, R. 292
Greiner, L.E. 239
Grencor 1072
  and Shell 1072–3
growth-share matrix 428
  categories 428–30
    cash cows 429
    dogs 429
    question marks 429
    stars 428
  in practice 433–6
  quantified 431–2
  strategy of 430–1
Guthrie, J. and Turnbull, S. 810

Hall, W.K. 616
Hambrick, D.C. 389
  and Mason, P.A. 321, 659
Hamel, G. 74, 146, 240, 555,
  594
  et al 510, 522
  and Prahalad, C.K. 412, 594,
    600, 812, 881, 882
Hamermesh, R. et al 372, 373
Hammer, M. 239, 248, 249
  and Champy, J. 239, 248
Hampden-Turner, C. xxiii, 63
  and Trompenaars, A. 653,
    712
  and Trompenaars, F. 64, 228,
    579
Hannan, M.T. and Freeman,
  J. 394, 593, 599–600, 658
Harley-Davidson 308–10
Harrigan, K.R. 516, 549
Hart, O.D. 807
Hart, S.L. 162
Haspeslagh, P. 414
Hawley, A. 621
Hawley's formulation 620–1
Hax, A.C. 23, 812
  and Majluf, N.S. 161
Hayashi, K. 227
headquarters see corporate
  center
Hedberg, B.L. et al. 160
Hedley, B. 414, 415, 423
Hedlund, G. 724

Henderson, B.D. 414, 423
Henry, K. 146
heterarchical organization 724
Hicks, J. 642–3
hierarchies 511, 535, 536–6
  collaborative arrangements
    518–19
  flat 644–5
Hofer, C. and Schendel, D. 383,
  415
Hoffman, W.M. 812
Hofstede, G. 24, 63, 144, 145,
  228, 229, 230, 231, 321,
  503, 579, 712
Hogarth, R.M. 72, 146
Holderness, C. and Sheehan,
  D. 861
Honda Motors 364–5, 366,
  893, 895–6
  activities 895
  assembly line 906–7
  competition and the
    individual 900–1
  designing automobiles
    904–6
  financial performance 897
  global context 896
  growth 895
  innovative strategic thinking
    896–7
    reforms 898–9
    right first time/build in
      quality 897–8
  as Japanese firm 901–3
  leaders 898
  organizational process 900–1
  organizational structure 901
  product strategy 903–4
  production planning 907–8
  production planning/
    product marketing as
    coherent 908
  reconciling dichotomies at
    899–900
  relationships with
    components makers
    908–9
  significant milestones 894
  strategic challenges 909–10
Hrebiniak, L.G. and Joyce,
  W.F. 594
Huff, A.S. 137
Hurst, D.K. et al 74

Ikea 728–30
Imai, M. 241, 248–9
imperfectly imitable resources
  389–90
  and causal ambiguity 391–2
  and social complexity 392
  and unique historical
    condtion 390
implementation see strategy
  implementation
improvement 266
incentives see monitoring/
  reward systems

increasing returns 601, 640–1
bulk production 643–4
knowledge-based
  operations 643–4
  capitalization 646–8
  competition 644–6
managerial questions 649
  feedbacks in market
    649–50
  sufficient resources 650
  what comes next 650
  which ecologies 650
operating systems 642–3
and perfect competition
  641–2
reasons
  customer groove-in 643
  network effects 643
  up-front costs 643
and service industries 648–9
incrementalist approach 151,
  154–5, 154–7, 165, 227,
  275
and explicit plans 158–60
and formal plans 160–2
and innovation 155
and muddling through 157,
  165, 174
and subproblems 156
and wicked problems 155–7
see also logical incrementalism; strategic planning
industry 610, 616–17
change 777–8
competing recipes 615
competition today vs
  tomorrow 626–7
  business units vs corporate
    competencies 628–9
  market share vs
    opportunity share 627–8
  single-stage vs multistage
    competition 636–9
  speed vs perseverance
    629–31
  stand-alone vs integrated
    systems 629
  structured vs unstructed
    arenas 631–6
competition in traditional
  616
and competitive advantage
  350–8
creation 593–4, 599
defined 333–4
and the future 624–6
market share 612
  and profitability 613–15
maturity and success 611–12
positioning within 335
prenatal 624
receipes 596
role in determining
  profitability 610–11
rules 594, 595
structural analysis 345,
  634–5

buyer needs 348–9
five-forces framework
  345–8
supply/demand balance
  349–50
and supply side similarity
  333
industry context
increasing returns 600–1,
  640–50
international perspective
  651
  locus of control 651–2
  network of relationships
    653
  role of government 652–3
  time orientation 652
malleability of 591–2
paradox of compliance/
  choice 591–2
industry creation 593–4,
  599, 610–17
industry evolution 592–3,
  598–9, 601–10
population ecology
  599–600, 617–23
proactive creation 600,
  624–40
rules/recipes 595–6
industry evolution 592–3,
  598–9, 601–2
basic concepts 602
changes in industry
  boundaries 609
consolidation 608
  concentration/mobility
    barriers 608
  exit barriers/consolidation
    608
  long-run profit potential
    609
framework for forecasting
  603–5
  processes 605
  relationships 605–8
influence of firms on
  structure 609–10
product life cycle 602–3
  criticism 603
inertia 702
five frictions 702–3
  action disconnects 708–10
  distorted perception 703–4
  dulled motivation 704–5
  failed creative response
    705–7
  political deadlocks 707–8
key 710–11
information technology
  983–6, 1203
innovation 155, 220–1, 239–40
bounded 446
new rules 774
  establish norms on
    regulations/product
    standards 776
  establish outstanding

competitiors as motivators 777
seek out buyers with difficult needs 775
sell to most sophisticated buyers/channels 775
source from most advanced/international home-based suppliers 776
treat employees as permanent 776
true costs of stability 777
vs kaizen 270–4
inside-out perspective 329–30, 331–2, 333, 341–2, 343
capabilities 397
integrated network model 796
integrated systems 629, 1185–7
integration-responsiveness grid 756
example 759–61
global strategic coordination access to raw materials/ energy 757
cost reduction 757
investment intensity 756–7
multinational competitors 756
multinational customers 756
technology intensity 757
universal needs 757
local responsiveness customer needs 758
distribution channels 758
host government demands 758–9
market structure 758
substitutes/need to adapt 758
mapping 761
affect on functions within a business 765
changes in underlying industry economics 761–2
changing rules of the game 764
firms learn 764
impact of governments 762–3
shifts in competitive focus of customers 763
intended strategy 151
international diversity 720, 722–4, 731
fragmentation 720
integration 720
linkages 720
scope 725
similarity 725, 731
international context dimensions and subjects 724–5
companies, businesses, economies 726–7, 733

global integration 732–3, 773–85
international scope, similarity, integration 725–6, 731–2, 753–72
transnational organizations 733, 785–97
international perspective 797–8, 797–9
level of nationalism 798
preference for central decision-making 799
size of country 798–9
paradox of globalization/ localization 719–20
global convergence 721–2, 730–1, 733–41
international diversity 722–4, 731, 741–53
international perspective business-level strategy 406–7
mobility barriers 407
resource mobility 407–8
corporate level strategy 501
cost of cordination 503
functioning of capital/ labor markets 501–2
leveraging of relational resources/strategy alignment 502–3
preference for control 503–4
development of 18–19
game/subgame 198
industry context 651
locus of control 651–2
network of relationships 653
role of government 652–3
time orientation 652
international context 797–8
level of nationalism 798
preference for central decision-making 799
size of country 798–9
network strategy 578–9
level of individualism 579–80
market for corporate control 582
type of career paths 582–3
type of institutional environment 581–2
organization context 711–12
locus of control 712
prevalence of mechanistic organizations 713
uncertainty avoidance 712–13
strategic change 318–19
strategic thinking 142–3
level of individualism 144–5
level of uncertainty avoidance 144

position of science 143–4
position of strategists 145
strategy formation 226–7
level of professionalization 227
time orientation 322
international strategic alliances 543–4
functions 544
managerial implications 552
objectives 544–5
leaning 546–7
leaping 550–1
learning 545–6
leveraging 548–9
linking 549
locking out 551–2
structures 544
international structural stages model 786–7
failure of 787–8
investment at Billiton 1065–7
multinational 756–7
Isenberg, D.J. 77
Itami, H. 336, 338

Janis, I. 704
Jarillo, J.C. 511, 523
Jaworski, B. and Kohli, A.K. 330, 405
Jelinek, M. 161, 220
Jensen, M.C. and Meckling, W.H. 807
Johanson, J. and Mattson, L.G. 534, 562–3
Johnson, G. 154, 166, 232, 658, 660, 667–8
and Scholes, K. 77
Jones, T.M. 809
Juran, J.M. 266–7

Kagono, T. et al 227, 229, 230, 231, 242, 318, 319, 321, 322, 579
kaizen 261–2
essence of 262–3
implications for 265–8
and management 263–5
and suggestion system 269–70
and TQC 268–9
vs innovation 270–4
Kakabadse, A. et al 711
kamban 263
Kanter, R.M. 232, 319, 519, 578
Kao Corporation 976
decision process in 982–3
history of internationaliz-ation 991
information network 985
and information technology 983–6
Kao International 989–90
layout of offices 984
learning organization 976–8

managing information in 980–2
organizational capability 992–4
organizational structure 981
paperweight organization 978, 980
review of operations 979
Sofina 986
    growth idea 987
    growth process 987–8
    learning extended 988–9
    vision 986–7
strategic infrastructure 990
    North America 990–2
    South East Asia 990
Kao, J. 74, 146, 575
Kaplan, S. 414
Kawasaki, S. and MacMillan, J. 542
Kay, J.A. 333, 519, 727
Keasey, K. *et al* 813
keiretsu 838
    and main bank 840–2
Kelley, R.E. 658
Ketchen, D.J. *et al* 6
Kets de Vries, M.F.R. 660
Kleisthenes 26
Klemm, M. *et al* 812
KLM Royal Dutch Airlines 1091–2, 1100–1, 1103
    Alcazar negotiations 1104–6
    alliances 1103–4
    cooperative agreements/ equity stakes 1101, 1104
    counter currents 1109–10
    elusive memorandum of understanding 1108–9
    future flight path 1110–11
    initiating partnership talks 1108
    moving toward agreement 1110
    operating statistics 1103
    other negotiations 1106–8
    route map 1102
Knagg's law 156
knowledge 338
    defined 337
knowledge-based operations 643–4
    strategy 646–8
    and technology 644–6
Kodak 663–5
Kogut, B. 321, 727
Kohli, A.K. and Jaworski, B. 400
Kotter, J.P. 321, 659
    and Heskett, J.L. 849
Krueger, W. 318
Krugman, P.R. 727
Kuhn, T.S. 74

Langley, A. 72, 77, 156
Langtry, B. 810
lateral thinking 74
Laurent, A. 54

Laurent-Perrier 1126
Lawrence, P.R. and Lorsch, J.W. 300, 413
leadership *see* organizational leadership
learning 218, 681
    adaptive/generative 286–7
    and collaboration 531–2
    continuous 241–2
    extension of 988–9
    and international strategic alliances 545–6
    nature of 285–6
    problem-oriented 4
    tools-oriented 4–5
learning organization 241–2, 249–50, 976–8
    decision process 982–3
    developing 296
    information technology 983–6
    leadership in 287–96
    managing information 980–2
    paperweight organization 978, 980
Leavy, B. and Wilson, D. 661
Lenz, R.T. and Lyles, M. 77, 156
Leonard-Barton, D. 332, 661
Lessem, R. and Neubauer, F.F. 64, 228, 579–80, 581, 582, 653, 712
Levins's fitness-set theory 622–3
Levitt, T. 725, 727, 730–1, 741, 874
Lewin, K. 297
Lieberman, M.B. and Montgomery, D.B. 386
lifespace
    composite 866
        multinational, global, hybrid 866–7
        national comparisons 869
        negotiating boundaries 868–9
    corporate 853
Lindblom, C.E. 129
Lippman, S. and Rumelt, R. 391
little dying 126–7
    organizational response to crisis
        acknowledgment 127
        adaptation and change 127
        defensive retreat 127
        shock 127
    personal response to terminal illness
        acceptance 127
        anger 127
        bargaining 127
        denial/isolation 127
        depression/grief 127
local management 752
local responsiveness 755

and competitive advantage 771–2
localization 719–20
Lockheed Martin 459–60
Lodge, G.C. 854, 871
logic 74
logical incrementalism 165, 173, 183, 693, 695
    critical strategic issues 175–6
        incremental logic 176–7
        precipitating events 176
    emergent strategy 184
    formal systems
        planning 173–4
        as managed 183–4
    power-behaviour 174
    strategic change 174–5
    strategic subsystems 177
        diversification 177–9
        divestiture 179
        government-extenal relations 180–1
        major reorganization 179–80
    see also incrementalist approach
Long, W.F. and Ravenscraft, D.J. 414
Loral Corporation 459–60
Lorange, P. 164–5, 219, 231
    and Vancil, R.F. 153, 165
Lorenzoni, G. and Baden-Fuller, C. 524, 534
Lotka-Volterra models 621–2
Louis Vuitton Moët-Hennessy 1125–6
Lowerdahl, B.R. 336

McCaskey, M.B. xix, 72, 74, 77, 85, 241
Macchiavelli, N. 23
McCoy, C.S. 812
McGrew, A.G. *et al* 727
McMillan, J. 145
MacMillan, K. and Farmer, D. 534, 535
Mahoney, J.T. 516
    and Pandian, J.R. xxii
Maidique, M.A. 242
Makridakis, S. 153, 231
management *see* strategic management
management boards
    in perspective 870–3
    and responsibility 872–3
    structure/function 862–3
        committees/number of meetings 865–6
        labor participation 864–5
        membership: executive/ non-executive 864
        tiers 863–4
managers 62
    defined 52
    initiative 662–3
    role of strategic 138–9
March, J.G.

and Olsen, J.P. 129
and Simon, H.A. 72, 238
Margolis, H. 704
market share/profitability
    relationship
    better to be small or stuck in
        the middle 373–5
    cause and effect 375–8
    and competitive strategy
        381–2
    dissecting 370–2
    importance 378
        heavy vs light investment
            intensity 380
        R&D and marketing vs
            manufacturing 378–80
    reasons for 369–70
    and return on investment
        (ROI) 368–9
    and small-share businesses
        372–3
market structure 758
    and cash flows 768–9
market-driven organizations
    330, 405
market/s 511, 535
    collaborative arrangements
        518–9
    defined 334
    and demand side similarity
        334
    and market segment 334
    opportunities 330
    orientation 395–6, 406
    position 335, 368, 639
    sequential entry 110–12
    share 627–8, 639
marketing 395
    brand name 920–1
    at Canon 1046–7
    at Cartier 1180–1
    and cash flows 769
    distribution 919–20
    and globalization 739–41
    international 747, 750
    and market-share/
        profitability relationship
        378–80
    at NBIC 1152
    pricing 919
    product positioning 919
    at Saatchi & Saatchi 1197
    and strategic center 563–4
    strategy
        continued growth 923–4
        ensuring success 924–5
        product introduction
            922-3
Marne et Champagne 1126
Marshall, A. 641–2, 643
Maruyama, M. 230
Marx, T. 166
Mason, R.O. and Mitroff, I.I.
    xxiii, 24, 63, 73, 129, 156
mechanistic organizations 228,
    319–20, 713
median effort game 117–18

Meindl, J.R. et al 660
mental models
    skills
        balancing inquiry and
            advocacy 294
        distinguishing espoused
            theory from theory in
            use 294
        recognizing/defusing
            defensive routines 294
        seeing leaps of abstraction
            294
Mercedes-Benz 81–3
Merck 520–2
mergers see acquisitions and
    mergers
Mexico
    political/economic
        issues 1162
        effects of economy on
            Telmex 1163
        prelude to peso
            devaluation 1162
        privatization in 1156–8
        telecommunications
            industry trends in 1158–9
Meyer, A.D. 240, 310
    et al 240, 297
military strategy 23
    ancient approaches to
        learning of 27–8
    ancient theorists 25–6
    origins of 25
    and the strategoi 26–7
Mill, J.S. 857
Miller, D. 238
    et al 651
    and Friesen, P.H. 240, 662
Miller, L. 292
Milner, H. 727
Mintzberg, H.A. xxii, 39, 63,
    154, 161, 162, 165, 166,
    227, 228, 232, 238, 289,
    319, 330, 419, 666, 691,
    813, 871
    and Waters, J.A. 150–1
    and Westley, F. 243, 244
mission see corporate mission
Mitroff, I. 291
Model T Ford 736–7
Modigliani, F. and Miller, M. 453
Mohn, R. 855
monitoring/reward
    processes 211, 363, 448,
        466–7
    executive problems 823
    limited accountability
        211–12
    random progress reviews 211
Montaigne, M. de 51
Morgan, G. 146
Morgan Motor Company
    246–8
Morgenthau, H. 187–8
Morison, E. 127
MTV Networks 20–2
multibusiness strategy 508

multifocal organization 761
multinational corporations
    (MNCs) 785
    administrative heritage
        788–9
    building organizational
        capability 788
    centralized hub 791–2
    coordinated federation
        790–1
    decentralized federation
        789–90
    and failure of structural
        matrix 787–8
    and structural fit 785–7
    see also transnational
        organization
Murphy, T. 868

Nabisco 304–5
Nanus, B. 659
Narver, J.C. and Slater, S.F. 400
Nash equilibrium 106–7
Nash, T. 848
National Bicycle Industrial Co
    (NBIC) 1141
    background 1144–5
    history of 1155
    mass-customization strategy
        1146–7
    outlook for the future 1154
    Panasonic ordering system
        (POS) 1148
    manufacturing process
        1148–52
    response to POS
        competitors imitate 1152–3
        extensive media coverage
            1153
        sales increase 1153–4
    role of customization 1154
national cluster 778
    buyers, channels, suppliers
        778–9
    improving competitive
        environment 780
    locating within the nation
        780
    related industries 779
    serving home base buyers
        who are international/
        multinational 780
    where/how to compete 781
        choosing industries/
            strategies 781–2
        diversification 782–4
        locating regional
            headquarters 784
        role of alliances 784–5
        selective foreign
            acquisitions 784
Nayyar, P.R. 418
NBIC see National Bicycle
    Industrial Co (NBIC)
NCR 463
Nelson, R.R. and Winter,
    S.G. 338, 593, 661

network strategy 10, 11, 533–5
  boundaries/relationships
    513
  firm and environment
    13–18
  markets and hierarchies
    518–19
  created and sustained
    539–41
  as economically efficient
    537–9
  efficiency/effectiveness
    539–40, 542
  implications of 541–3
  international perspective
    523, 543–52, 578–9, 653
  level of individualism
    579–80
  market for corporate
    control 582
  type of career paths 582–3
  type of institutional
    environment 581–2
  as mode of organization
    535–7
  oversees Chinese 566–8
    business and culture 574–5
    family business in
      operation 570–4
    family/personal
      relationships 575–6
    operational generalizations
      576–8
    rise of Chinese business
      568–70
  paradox of competition/
    cooperation 508–9
  discrete organization
    509–10, 522–3, 525–32
  embedded organization
    511–12, 523, 524,
    533–43, 553–66
  socio-economic 524, 566–83
non-ferrous metal industry
    1057–8
  and the aluminium industry
    1058–9
  and the oil companies
    1059–60
  structural changes in 1058
non-rational thinking 71
  and emotions 71–2
  and intuition 72
  and routine/habit 72
  see also rational thinking
Nonaka, I. 160, 232, 242, 319,
    338
  and Johansson, J.K. 229
Noorderhaven, N.G. 74, 145
Northwest Airlines 464–5

objectives 681
  long-term 29–30, 31
  setting 489–90
  shareholder vs management
    823–6

Ohmae, K. 84, 227, 228, 721,
    732
Oldelft 963
  acceptance of strategic
    planning 971–4
  financial summary 974–5
  history 963–4
    advent of strategic
      thinking 965–6
    frist attempts at strategic
      planning 967–8
    impending crisis 966–7
    introduction of strategic
      decision-making 967
    years of holding course
      964–5
  organization chart 972
  product age guide 973
  strategic planning cycle 968
    corporate scrums 970
    plans/options 969–70
    post-scrum booklets 970
    situation analyses 968–9
operating strategy 462–3
opportunity share 627–8
organization context
  international perspective
    711–12
  locus of control 712
  prevalence of mechanistic
    713
  uncertainty avoidance
    712–13
organization/s
  business level 31
  and change 238–42
  characteristics
    continuous adaptation 242
    continuous improvement
      241
    continuous learning
      241–2, 249–50, 285–96
  cooperation 509
  corporate level 31
  disintegration of 678
  enactment process 139
    creation of context 140
    encouraging multiple
      realities 140–1
    managerial analysis 140
    and reality 141–2
    testing and experimenting
      141
  and environment 131–4
  externally-oriented 330
  functional level 31
  inertia in 239
  interpretive perspective
    134–5
    implications 135–9
  ossification of 678
  position of employees in
    320–1
  prevalence of mechanistic
    319–20
  response to crisis 127
  stability in 238–9

stratified model 228
successful 330
organizational
  action 693–5
  capabilities 788
  efficiency/effectiveness
    539–40
  inheritance 661–2
  malleability 668
  plasticity 668
organizational boundaries
  changes in 609
  firm/environment
    horizontal integration 515
    scale 513, 515–16
    scope 513, 516
    vertical integration 515,
      516–18
  markets/hierarchies 518–19
organizational configuration
  models 790–1
organizational context
  incrementalism 667–8,
    691–701
  inertia and transformation
    668, 701–11
  inheritance/initiative 661–3
  international context
    711–13
  paradox of control/chaos
    657–8
    organizational dynamics
      659–61, 666–8, 673–82
    organizational leadership
      658–9, 666, 667, 668–73
    planning/implementation
      667, 682–91
organizational evolution 249,
    284–5
  convergence/upheaval 275,
    278–9
  consequences 280–1
  examples 275–8
  fine-tuning 279
  incremental adjustment to
    environmental shifts
    279–80
  frame-breaking change
    281–2, 284
  reasons for all at once
    283–4
  scope 282–3
organizational leadership 348,
    658–9, 666
  central 488–9
  in chaos 657, 666–7
  in control 657, 667
  and creative tension 288
  crescive approach 667
  developing 296
  inaction 709
  intellectual 638
  and learning 287
  new roles 288–9
    as designer 289–90
    as steward 292
    as teacher 290–2

new skills 292–3
building shared vision 293
surfacing/testing mental
    models 293–4
systems thinking 294–6
personal 90
role of 275
sustaining 443
theories of 53–6
thinkers and doers 667
organizational process 185, 203
at Honda 900–1
dominant inference pattern/
    general propositions
    195–6
administrative feasibility
    196–7
limited flexibility/
    incremental change 196
organizational action 196
government behaviour 190
coordination 190–1
learning and change 191
responsiveness 190
organizing concepts
action as organizational
    output 192–4
central coordination and
    control 194–5
decisions of government
    leaders 195
factored problems/
    fractionated power 192
organizational actors 192
parochial priorities,
    perceptions, issues 192
policy as organizational
    output 191–2
organizational purpose 12–13,
    819
corporate governance
    813–14, 852–73
corporate mission and vision
    811–13, 819, 874–83
international perspective
    818–19, 838–52
paradox of profitability/
    responsibility 805–6
shareholder value 807–8,
    811, 817, 820–9
stakeholder values 808–11,
    817–18, 829–37
organizational relationships
categories
    economic forces 515
    political/legal forces 515
    sociocultural forces 515
    technological forces 515
firm/environment
    direct horizontal
        (competitive) 513
    downstream vertical
        (buyer) 513
    indirect horizontal
        (industry outsider) 514
    upstream vertical (supplier)
        513

organizational structure
at Cap Gemini Sogeti
    1212–13
at Honda 901
Ouchi, W.G. 318, 319, 320, 536
outside-in perspective 329–31,
    333, 341, 342, 343
capabilities 397
and positioning within
    market or industry 335
overseas Chinese
bamboo network 566–8
business and culture 574–5
family business in operation
    570
    Charoen Pokpand Group
        571–2
    Salim Group 572–4
generalizations
    centralized control/
        informal transactions
        576–7
    informal management
        style 577–8
    low profile 576
    network enterprises not
        unitary companies 577
    power of family/personal
        relationships 575–6
rise of business by 568–70

Panasonic ordering system
(POS)
manufacturing process
    148–50
    final assembly/shipping
        1151–2
    frame/front production
        1150–1
    labeling/engraved process
        1151
    marketing/distribution
        1152
    painting 1151
    quality check 1151
order process 1148
paperweight organization 978,
    980
paradigm 78–9, 697–8
dissonance with 698
integrated model of process
    698–9
and strategic drift 699
parent company see corporate
    center
Parkhe, A. 550
Parkinson, J.E. 814
Parkinson's laws 272
Pascal, B. 51
Pascale, R.T. and Athos, A.G.
    318, 320, 322, 579
Patel, P. and Pavitt, K. 725
path dependency 601
Pearce, J.A. 812
Penrose, E.T. 336, 383
Pericles 26
Peters, T.J. 371

and Waterman, R.H. 700,
    812, 826
Petrauskas, H.O. 868
Pettigrew, A.M. 7, 232, 239,
    660
and Whipp, R. 6
Pfeffer, J. 660, 661
pharmaceutical industry
    1219–20
see also Burroughs Wellcome
Philip of Macedon 27
Philips Electronics NV 420–3,
    771–2
Phillips, L. et al 374
Piercy, N.F. and Morgan,
    N.A. 812
PIMS see Profit Impact of
    Market Strategy
Pinchot, G. 159
Piore, M. and Sabel, C.F. 511,
    580
planners 222–3
as analysts 224
as catalysts 225
left-hand/right-hand 225–6
as strategy finders 224
see also strategic planning
plans
as tools to communicate and
    control 224
see also incrementalist
    approach; strategic
    planning
Plutarch 27
Polanyi, M. 338
policies 87
Pondy, L.R. 72
et al 239
Poole, M.S. and Van de Ven,
    A.H. 17
population ecology 599–600,
    617
and adaptation perspective
    617–18
adaptation/selection
    processes 600
external constraints 619
internal constraints 618–19
Levin's fitness-set theory
    622–3
and organization/
    environment relations
    619–20
    Hawley's formulation
        620–1
    Lotka-Volterra models
        621–2
and selection process 617
Porac, J.F. et al 334
Porter, M.E. 218, 331, 335, 339,
    341, 373, 383, 387, 390,
    412, 417, 458, 502, 510,
    513, 515, 522, 533, 595,
    598–9, 611, 702, 726, 732,
    839, 840
portfolio perspective 413–15,
    423–4, 426

concept 426–7
  growth-share matrix
    428–30
  matrix quantified 431
  strategy 430–1
  practice 433
  sound portfolio, unsoundly
    managed 433–4
  unbalanced 434–6
  restructuring at Grand
    Metropolitan 1083–4
positional advantage 37–8, 39
  types 38
    policies 38–9
    size and scale 38
    trade names 39
positioning approach see
    outside-in perspective
positive-sum game 512
Powell, W.W. 511
  and DiMaggio, P.J. xix
Prahalad, C.K.
  and Bettis, R.A. 418
  and Doz, Y. 413, 595, 727,
    731–2
  and Hamel, G. 332, 337,
    415, 424, 558
Preece, S. 523
Prime Computer 276–7
problem-solving 13–14, 69, 404
  creativity in 73–5
  as a dilemma 16–17
  and generative thinking
    73–5
  logic in 74
  as a paradox 17–18
  as a puzzle 16
  and rational thinking 70–3
  as a trade-off 17
  see also strategic problems
Procter & Gamble 304–5
product development, at
    Cartier 1177–9
product life cycle 602–3
  criticism 603
  predictions 606–7
product positioning 335, 634
product strategy
  assembly line 906–7
  coherence of planning/
    marketing 908
  designing automobiles
    904–6
  guiding technology
    development 903–4
  planning 907–8
  relationships with
    components makers
    908–9
production quantity
  game 113–15
Profit Impact of Market Strategy
  (PIMS) 342, 369, 370–2,
    374, 376, 378
profitability 805–6
  shareholder value
    perspective 807–8, 811

stakeholder values
    perspective 808–11
purpose see organizational
    purpose

quality control (QC) circles 96,
    263, 265–8
  and kaizen 268–9
Quinn, J.B. 159, 161, 165, 232,
    300, 519, 659, 693
Quinn, R.E. 17
  and Cameron, K.S. 17

Ramanuja, V. and Varadarajan,
    P. 418
Rappaport, A. 807, 817, 852
Rathenau, W. 849, 850
rational policy 185, 186
  characteristics of 187–8
  dominant inference pattern/
    general propositions
    189–90
  and foreign affairs 187–8
  organizing concepts
    action as rational choice
    189
    national actor 188–9
    problem 189
    static selection 189
  policy as national
    choice 188
rational thinking 70–3, 83–4,
    86–93
  defined 74
  mental activity elements
    80
  see also non-rational
    thinking
Ravenscraft, D.J. and Scherer,
    F.M. 424
reality 85
  in enacted world 141–2
realized strategy 151
reasoning
  elements
    conceiving 79
    diagnosing 79
    identifying 79
    realizing 79
  nature of 79
Rechner, P.L. and Dalton, D.R.
    847
Redding, S.G. 143, 566
reengineering 248, 250–1
  essence of 254–5
  focused 314
  in Ford and MBL 251–3
  principles 256
    build control into process
    259
    capture information once
    and at source 260
    link parallel activities
    instead of integrating
    results 258–9
    organize around outcomes
    not tasks 256

put decision point where
    work is performed 259
subsume information-
    processing work into real
    work that produces
    information 258
treat geographically
    dispersed resources as
    though centralized 258
users as performers of
    process 256–7
think big 260–1
regulatory environment
  broad 856
    enforcement 857–8
    scope 856
    sources 857
    strictness 856–7
  ownership patterns 859
    private, shareholding
    860–2
    public or governmental
    859–60
  societal pressures 858–9
Reich, R. 727
  and Mankin, E. 555
Reid, P. 308
Rémy-Cointreau 1126
Republic Airlines 464–5
reputation models 115–17
resource
  allocation 489–90
  leveraging 412, 414, 418
resource-based approach
    335–6, 342–3, 383–4, 701,
    711
  human resources 338
  identification 338
  key concepts
    competitive advantage 385
    firm resources 384–5
    sustained competitive
    advantage 385
  relational vs competences
    366–7
  sustained competitive
    advantage 387–8
    framework 393–4
    imperfectoy imitable
    resources resources
    389–92
    rare resources 388–9
    sustitutability 392–3
    valuable resources 388
  tangible vs intangible 336,
    338
responsibility 805–6
  shareholder value
    perspective 807–8, 811
  stakeholders value
    perspective 808–11
Reve, T. 513
reward processes see
    monitoring/reward
    processes
risk 542–3
Rittel, H. 43, 45, 73

and Webber, M. 63, 156
Ruigrok, W. and Van Tulder, R. 726
Rumelt, R.P. 23, 166, 332, 418, 658, 668

Saatchi & Saatchi 1188
  advertising agents 1194–5
  directors 1194
  financial summaries 1191–3
  future 1197–8
  global marketing 1197
  growth 1190
  and Proctor & Gamble 1196
  seeds of destruction 1189–90
  total communication services strategy 1193–4, 1195, 1197
  triumphant early years 1188–9
  unravelling the giant 1191, 1193
Salim Group 1112
  development
    commodity monopolies 1114
    cross ownership 1115
    government support 1115
    international growth 1115
    joint ventures 1115–16
  and First Pacific Group 1116–18
  Indonesian political system 1112–13
  investors 1113
  organization 1113–14
  vision for the future 1118-19
Sanchez, R. *et al* 332
SBU *see* strategic business unit (SBU)
Scandinavian Airlines System (SAS) 305–6
Schein, E.H. 61, 288
Schelling, T. 187–8
Scherer, F.M. 335
Schneider, S.C. 144, 227, 229, 230
Schoemaker, P.J.H. xxii
  and Russo, J.E. 72, 77
Schon, D.A. 128
Schumpeter, J.A. 240
Schwenk, C.R. xxiii, 72, 76, 78, 146
scope, economies of 412
Seagram 1126
self-organization 675–6
  amplifying issues/building political support 676
  breaking symmetries 676
  changing frame of reference 677
  critical point/unpredictable outcomes 676–7
  detecting/selecting small disturbances 676
  and groups 680
Selznick, P. and Forrester, J. 289

Senge, P.M. 73, 241, 249–50, 321, 659, 813
service industries, and increasing returns 648–9
share/profitability relationship *see* market share/profitability relationship
shareholder value 806, 807–8, 811, 817, 820
  Anglo-American 838
  development of 820–3
  endorsement of 822
  excellence and restructuring 826–8
  Japanese 838
  Japanese corporations
    board members appointed by president 846
    boards are too large 846
    ineffective statutory auditors 846–7
    limited monitoring power of chairman of the board 845–6
    ritualized general meeting 845
  management vs shareholder objectives 823
    compensation 824
    labor market for corporate executives 824–5
    ownership position 823–4
    threat of takeover 824
  problems of rewarding executives 823
  rationale for 828–9
shareholders 414, 452
Sheehan, N. 704
Shell Group 289–90, 1054–5
  buys Billiton 1056–7, 1061
  diversifications in the 1970s 1055–6
  and Grencor 1072–3
  strategic planning at 1055
  take-over/disposal 1063
    back to core business 1070
    consolidation 1067–8
    decides to sell Billiton 1070–2
    extensive investments 1065–7
    further consolidation/new strategy 1068–70
    restructuring/autonomous growth 1063–4
Shrivastava, P. and Grant, J. 162
Simon, H.A. 71, 72, 73, 132, 145
  and March, J.G. 145
Sims, H.P. and Lorenzi, P. 660
Sirower, M. 424
Skinner, B.F. 704
SMH (Swatch and Omega brands) *see* Swatch
Smircich, L. and Stubbart, C. xix, 74, 78, 85, 660

Smith, A. 52
Solomon, R.C. 809
Sony 465, 636–8
Sorensen, T. 191
Southwest Airlines 1028
  available seat-miles 1029
  company management 1030–1
  competition 1031–2
  executive officers 1031
  financial data 1035, 1036
  fleet size 1029
  future delivery positions 1030
  history 1028–30
  strategy 1033–4, 1036
Spencer, A. 814
Spender, J.C. xix, 594, 596
Stacey, R.D. 154, 160, 241, 319, 666
stakeholder values 806, 808–11, 817–18, 871
  analysis and corporate democracy 836–7
  classical grid 834–5
  and corporate governance 810
  defined 832
  development of 829–32
  Japan-US comparison 842
    Chrysler 843–4
    legal restrictions on banks 844
    roles of German 'Hausbank' 844
    Toyo Kogyo 843
  and prescriptive propositions 832–3
  primary 810
  real world grid 835
  secondary 810
  and strategy formulation 833
  use of 833–4
stakeholders 32
Stalk, G. 287
  et al 332, 337, 341–2
stand-alone systems 629
standardization 742
  conditions 747
    availability of international communication/distribution 749
    existence of global market segments 747–8
    synergies associated with global 748–9
  economies of scale 746
    flexible factory automation 746–7
    primarily product driven 747
    production costs/total cost 747
  external constraints 749–50
    government/trade restrictions 750

interdependencies with
resource markets 750–1
nature of competitive
structure 751
nature of marketing
infrastructure 750
global 743
homogenization of world's
wants 744
growth of intracountry
segmentation price
sensitivity 745
lack of evidence of 744
implementation 743–4
internal constraints 751
existing international
operations 751–2
local management
motivation/
attitudes 752
low price/acceptable quality
745
overpriced/underpriced in
different countries 746
price positioning 745–6
price sensitivity 745
pattern 743
Stantret 948
Stantret Airlines
Air Link-Up project 949
background 948–9
business plan 952
expanding staff 956, 958
financial aspects 958
founding of 950–1
market for air transport 951,
953
mounting crisis 961–2
new issues/pressures 958–60
side ventures 956
Sleptsov's management style
955-6
Sleptsov's negotiation
methods 953–4
structure/members of staff
957
Starbuck, W.H. 141
Steiner, G.A. 160, 219, 231
and Schollhammer, H. 227
stockholder see stakeholder
values
Stone, C. 809
Stopford, J.M. 786
strategic architecture 446–7
strategic business unit (SBU)
439, 628–9, 1049–50
defined 821
tyranny
bounded innovation 446
imprisoned resources 445–6
underinvestment 445
tyranny of 443–5
strategic center 552–3
agenda
brand power and other
support 559
partner selection 561–2

sharing business idea
558–9
trust and reciprocity 560–1
role 553–4
borrowing-developing-
lending new ideas 556–7
developing competencies
of partners 555–6
perceptions of competitive
process 557–8
subcontracting to
outsourcing 555, 565
simultaneous structuring/
strategizing 562–3
learning races 564–5
marketing/information
sharing 563–4
strategic challenge, at
Honda 909–10
strategic change 7, 8, 696
boom-and-bust 240–1
continuous 238, 240–2,
248–9, 261–74
and creative destruction 240
discontinuous 249, 275–85
and inertia 239
international perspective
318–9
mechanistic organizations
319–20
position of employees
320–1
role of top management
321–2
time orientation 322
issues
magnitude of change 242,
243–4
amplitude 244–5
scope 244
pace of change 242, 245
tempo 245
timing 246
and lock-in factors 239
paradox of revolution/
evolution 237–8
continuous change 238,
240–2
discontinuous change
238–40
punctuated equilibrium view
239
and reengineering 248,
250–61
and stability 238–9
strong/weak forces of 250,
297–322
see also change forces;
change path
strategic choice 89–90, 132,
347
strategic control 425
key features 500
business autonomy 497
decentralization 496
extensive planning process
496–7

resource allocation/long-
term investment 497–8
tight strategic/financial
controls 499
strategic coordination
global 754
and global competition 767
strategic drift 699
strategic management 131
adaptive approach 691–2
at Cartier 1183–4
cultural constraints 51
defined 52
in enacted world 133–4, 139
creation of context 140
encouraging multiple
realities 140–1
managerial analysis 140
and reality 141–2
testing and experimenting
141
explanatory models 696
integrated model of process
98–9
nature of paradigm 697–8
notion of strategic drift 699
in France 54
from Shakespeare to
Taylor 52
in Germany 53
in Holland 54–5
idiosyncrasies of American
theories 60–1
stress on individual 61–2
stress on managers rather
than workers 62
stress on market process 61
international perspective
228
interpretive perspective
134–5, 692
adapting to environment
135–7
rethinking constraints,
threats, opportunities
137–8
role of strategic managers
138–9
in Japan 53
linear model 691
normative implications
700–1
and objective environment
131–2
overseas Chinese 55–6
and perceived environment
132–3
process
formulation/
implementation 695–6
organizational action
693–5
rational view 692–3
role of top 321–2
and theory of culture in
58–60, 62–3
transfer to poor countries 56

Russia and China 57–8
strategic planning 151, 152,
    164–5, 217–18, 425, 487,
    635
  acceptance of 971–4
  advantages
    coordination 153
    direction 152
    formalization/
      differentiation of tasks
      153
    long-term thinking/
      commitment 153
    optimization 153
    programming 152–3
  contingency 154
  and culture 230
  effective 204–5
    avoiding the obstacles
      212–16
    obstacles to 205–12
  explicit 157–6
    commitment vs flexibility
      159
    coordination vs autonomy
      159
    direction vs latitude 159
    optimization vs learning
      159–60
  fallacies 219–20
    detachment 220–1
    formalization 222
    prediction 220
  first attempts 967–8
  and forecasts 153–4
  formal 158, 160–1, 218, 222,
    226, 227–9
    decision-making 181
    differentiated vs integrated
      tasks 161–2
    informal vs formal process
      161
    in practice 181–2
    process 181
    special studies 182
    total posture planning
      182–3
  future of 166
  future scenarios 154
  implementation 682–3
    collaborative 685–6
    commander 684
    crescive 687–91
    cultural 686–7
    organizational
      change 684–5
  importance of 229
  incremantalist approach,
    and unpredictability 157
  ineffective 166, 204–16
  and intentional strategies
    152
  key features 491
    extensive planning process
      487–8
    flexible controls 490

resource allocation/
  objective setting 489–90
strong central leadership
  488–9
pitfalls 219
process 167
  budgeting 168, 172
  incentives/staffing 169
  monitoring, control,
    learning 168–9, 172
  objective setting 168,
    169–71
  strategic programming
    168, 171–2
as strategic programming
  225
successful 968
  corporate scrums 970
  plans/options 696–70
  post-scrum booklets 970
  situation analyses 968–9
see also effective strategic
  planning; incrementalist
  approach
strategic principles 108
  foresight 108–9
    credible/noncredible
      signals 109–10
    sequential market entry
      110–12
  know yourself as well as
    others 112–13
    production quantity game
      113–15
  munification of minds to
    promote cooperation
    117–18
  one-time and repeated
    interactions 115
    reputation 115–17
strategic problems 69
  as complex 42–3
  interaction matrix 41
  nature of 41–2
  as simple 43
  solutions 200
  tame 43, 73
  wicked 45–7, 73
    characteristics 47–8
    implications for policy
      making 48–50
    quest for new methods 50
  see also problem-solving
strategic programming 217,
  223
  codification 223
  conversion 223
  elaboration 223
strategic thinking 7, 8, 217,
  218, 965–6
  art of 100–1
  cognition 75
    nature of 76–9
  cognitive maps 85, 131–42
  conceptual mapping 85,
    120–30

and determining the critical
  issue 96–100
game theory 84–5, 103–19
as innovative 896–9
international perspective
  142–3
  individualism 144–5
  position of science 143–4
  position of strategists 145
  uncertainty avoidance 144
object of 95–6
out of the box 74, 75
paradox of logic and
  creativity 69–70
  generative thinking 73–5,
    84, 93–102
  rational thinking 70–3,
    83–4, 86–93
reasoning 75
  nature of 79–81
strategist
  capabilities-approach 332
  competence-based approach
    332
  constraints
    reality 101
    resources 101
    ripeness 101
  as creative 93–4, 100–1
  inside-out approach 331–2
  and insight 93
  international perspective
    145
  as inventors 155
  mind of 93–5
  as natural/instinctive 94
  as organizational developers
    155
  outside-in approach 330–1
  and positioning 335
  rules of the game 331
  and samurai concept 895
strategy
  and analysis 95–6
  ancient approaches to
    learning about 27–8
  at Cartier 1182–3
  complexity 41–2
    characteristics of 42–50
  debates 13–14
    paradoxes 16–18
    perspectives 15–16
    tensions 14–15
  deducing from behavior 88–9
  defined 25–6, 28, 86–7, 132,
    697–8
  determining the critical
    issue 96–100
  dimensions 5–7, 28–9
    coherent, unifying,
      integrative pattern of
      decisions 29
    content 8–11
    context 11–12
    differentiating managerial
      tasks at corporate,

business and functional
levels 31–2
economic/non-economic
contribution of firm to
stakeholders 32
firm's competitive domain
30
long-term objectives 29–30
process 7–8
SWOT 30–1
evaluation 33, 40, 91–3
challenges 33–4
principles 34–40
formulation 89
cases 695–6
corporate competence/
resources 89, 90
market opportunity 89, 90
obligations to society 89–90
organizational action view
of 693–5
personal values/aspirations
89, 90
rational view of 692–3
identification of issues 4–5
international perspective
18–19
cases 19–22
nature of 3–4
organizational purpose 12–13
origin of 25
practical lessons from
strategoi 26–7
readings 22–4
reasons for not articulating
88
successful 246
summary statements of 87–8
as unified concept 32
strategy content 6
levels 8–9
business 9, 10
corporate 10–11
functional 9
network 10, 11
see also business strategy;
corporate strategy;
network strategy
strategy context 6
determinist 11
industry 12
international 12
organizational 12
voluntarist 11
see also industry context;
international context;
organizational context
strategy formation 7, 8
decision-making 165–6,
185–204
external control 230
internal control 229
international perspective
226–7
level of professionalization
227–9

paradox of deliberateness
and emergentness 150–2
incrementalism
perspective 154–7, 165,
173–84
planning perspective
152–4, 164–5, 167–72
plans and planning 157–8
explicit 158–60
formal 160–2
future of 166, 217–32
ineffective 166, 204–216
time orientation 230–1
strategy implementation 90–1,
683, 702
cases 695–6
collaborative approach 683,
685–6
commander approach 683,
684
crescive approach 683, 688
CEO use of 690–1
reasons for rise of 688–90
cultural approach 683,
686–7
organizational action view
of 693–5
organizational change
approach 683, 684–5
strategy process 5
analysis-formulation-
implementation 7–8
as comprehensive 7, 8
as linear and rational 7
see also strategic change;
strategic thinking;
strategy formation
Strebel, P.J. 240, 250
structural fit 785–7
subcontracting practices 542
and risk 542–3
and strategic center 555, 565
Sun Tzu 23
supply/demand balance 349–50
sustained competitive
advantage 338–9, 343,
350, 383, 385
firm resources 387–8
framework 393–4
imperfectly imitable
resources 389–92
rare resources 388–9
substitability 392–3
valuable resources 388
resource homogeneity and
mobility 385–6
see also competitive
advantage
Suzuki, S. and Wright,
R.W. 840
Swatch 81–3, 912
financial data 926
future of 925–6
market introduction 922–3
continued growth 923–4
ensuring success 924–5

product/process technology
918
construction 918–19
marketing 919–20
production 919
sales 925
structural change 912–16
subsidiaries 927–6
team 921–2
turnaround at ETA 916–18
SWOT (strengths, weaknesses,
opportunities, threats)
analysis 30–1, 73–4
and business environment
330, 333, 384
and collaboration 531
and formulation of strategy
89
in strategic management
132, 137–8
Sykes, A. 807
synergy 450, 452
achieving 460
and the acquisition game
457–8
competitive challenge
458–9
examples 459–60
cornerstones 460–1
operating strategy 462–3
power and culture 465–7
strategic vision 461–2
systems integration 463–5
defined 451
and global standardization
748–9
limitation 456
occurrence of 412–13
and overpayment 468
through coordination 413
visualization of 453
systems integration 463–5
systems thinking 294–5
skills
avoiding symptomatic
solutions 295
distinguishing detail
complexity from
dynamic complexity 295
focusing on areas of high
leverage 295
moving beyond blame 295
seeing interrelationships,
not things; Process, not
snapshots 295

Tannenbaum, R. 126
Taylor, F.W. 52, 53, 54, 221
technology 644–6
multinational 757
strategy 646
discounting 646
linking and leveraging 647
networking 646–7
psychological positioning
647–8
Teck Hua Ho and Weigelt, K. 84

Teece, D.J. 581, 583
  et al 332
telecommunications, industry
  trends 1158–9
Telmex 1156
  challenges 1170–1
  competition 1167–8
    AT&T/Grup Alfa 1168
    Bell Atlantic Corp/Grup
      IUSACELL 1169
    government action 1168
    GTE Corp, Grup Financier
      Bancomer, Valores
      Industrials 1170
    MCI/Grupo Financiero
      Banamex-Accival 1168–9
    Motorola Corp, Grupo
      Protexa, Baja Cellular
      Mexicana 1169–70
    Sprint Corp 1169
  concession agreement 1163–
    4
  consortium 1164
  effects of Mexican economy
    on 1163
  primary operations/
    improvements 1165
    administrative/operational
      1166–7
    long distance 1165
    new/potential services 1166
    public telephones 1165–6
    Telcel 1166
  and privatization 1156–8
  suppliers 1167
tensions
  assumptions 14–15
  strategy paradoxes 16, 17–18
    dilemma 16–17
    puzzle 16
    trade-off 17
thinking *see* lateral thinking;
  strategic thinking; systems
  thinking
Thompson, A. and Strickland,
  A.J. 231
Thompson, J.D. 238
Thorelli, H.B. 511, 534
Thurow, L. 581
Tichy, N. and Devanna, M. 659
Tolstoy, L.N. 57
total quality control
  (TQC) 263, 267, 268–9
transaction costs 535–6
  and opportunism 540
  and trust 539–41
transnational organization 724,
  733
  challenge of 792–3
  characteristics 793–4
  distributed,
    interdependent
    capabilities 794–5
  flexible integrative process
    796–7
  multidimensional
    perspective 794

see also multinational
  corporations (MNCs)
Treynor, J.L. 828
Tricker, R.I. 813
Trompenaars, A. 230
Tushman, M.L. *et al* 240, 249,
  662
Tversky, A. and Kahneman, D.
  77

value chain 458
vertical integration 417
  advantages
    avoidance of contracting
      costs 516
    economics of scale 516
    exploitation of dissipation-
      sensitive knowledge 517
    exploitation of non-
      marketable capabilities
      517
    implementing system-wide
      changes 517
    increased bargaining power
      517
    operational coordination
      516
  disadvantages
    dulled incentives 517
    high capital investment
      517
    high governance costs 517
    reduced exposure to
      external know-how 518
    reduced flexibility 517
Virgin 930–1
  in the 1980's 936–7
  and airline industry 937–9,
    943
  from rock market to stock
    market 939–40
  group line-up 942
  key dates 932–3
  and Oldfield's Tubular Bells
    935–6
  portrait of Branson
    family/early life 944–5
    hero of the world 946–7
    hippy entrepreneur 945–6
    the real Richard Branson
      947
  sale of record company 940–1
  as voice of youth 931, 933–5
virtual corporation 519
vision 288, 681, 813, 986–7
  and mission 880–1
  skills
    blending extrinsic/intrinsic
      vision 293
    communicating/asking for
      support 293
    distinguishing positive
      from negative visions
      293
    encouraging personal
      vision 293

  visioning as ongoing
    process 293
  strategic 461–2
Von Winterfeldt, D. and
  Edwards, W. 72

Wack, P. 154
Wartick, S.L. and Wood,
  D.J. 810
Waterman, R.H. *et al* 243
Webster, F. 330, 395
Weick, K.E. 78, 80, 134, 137,
  146, 660
  and Bougnon, M.G. 74
Weidenbaum, M. and Hughes,
  S. 229, 512, 524
Wernerfelt, B. 336
Wheelen, T. and Hunger, D. 231
Whitley, R. 63
Whitman, D. 872
Whittington, R. xxii
wicked problems 73
  characteristics
    ambiguity 47
    complicatedness 47
    conflict 47–8
    interconnectedness 47
    societal constraints 48
    uncertainty 47
  criteria
    adversarial 50
    integrative 50
    managerial mind
      supporting 50
    participative 50
  implications for policy
    making 48–50
  and incrementalism 155–7
  properties
    abilities to formulate
      problem 45
    explanatory characteristics
      46
    finality 46
    level of analysis 46
    relationship between
      problem and solution 46
    replicability 47
    reproducibility 47
    testability 46
    tractability 46
Wildavsky, A. 154
Williamson, O.E. 61, 511, 535,
  536, 540, 580
Wilson, D.C. 594
Woo, C.Y.Y. and Cooper, A.C.
  372, 373
Worthy, J. and Neuschel,
  R. 854

Xenophon 26

Yoshimori, M. 814
zaibatsu 840
Zand, D. 540
zero defects (ZD) 263
zero-sum game 510, 536, 542